RISK
MANAGEMENT
AND
INSURANCE

McGraw-Hill Insurance Series

RISK
MANAGEMENT
AND
INSURANCE

FIFTH EDITION

C. Arthur Williams, Jr.

Professor of Economics and Insurance
University of Minnesota

Richard M. Heins

Professor of Business
University of Wisconsin-Madison

McGRAW-HILL BOOK COMPANY

New York St. Louis San Francisco Auckland Bogotá
Hamburg Johannesburg London Madrid Mexico Montreal New Delhi
Panama Paris São Paulo Singapore Sydney Tokyo Toronto

To Roberta and Ruth

This book was set in Times Roman by Better Graphics.
The editors were John R. Meyer and Joseph F. Murphy;
the cover was designed by Infield, D'Astolfo Associates;
the production supervisor was Joe Campanella.
Halliday Lithograph Corporation was printer and binder.

RISK MANAGEMENT AND INSURANCE

2 3 4 5 6 7 8 9 0 HALHAL 8 9 8 7 6 5

ISBN 0-07-070561-5

Library of Congress Cataloging in Publication Data

Williams, C. Arthur (Chester Arthur), date
    Risk management and insurance.

    (McGraw-Hill insurance series)
    Includes bibliographies and indexes.
    1. Risk management. 2. Insurance, Business.
3. Insurance. I. Heins, Richard M. II. Title.
III. Series.
HG8051.W5 1985   368   84-12217
ISBN 0-07-070561-5

CONTENTS

PREFACE

Like the first four editions of *Risk Management and Insurance*, this fifth edition is designed primarily for introductory one-semester or one-quarter courses in risk management and insurance. The contents and structure of this text are based on the twin beliefs that (1) the study of insurance, a major tool of risk management, should be preceded by an understanding of the procedures and concepts of risk management itself and (2) most students will take only one course in this area and, therefore, this course should cover both risk management and insurance. For students interested in risk management or insurance as a career, this balanced treatment of both subjects also provides a comprehensive introduction to the field, which can be followed by more intensive studies of particular parts and case courses. The authors are pleased to count among the readers of earlier editions many persons already either professionally engaged as risk managers or holding a wide variety of positions in the insurance industry.

The text is divided into four parts. Part 1 acquaints the student with risk—its nature and its effects—and discusses the purposes and scope of risk management. Part 2, which deals with business (defined broadly to include nonprofit and public organizations) risk management, describes the risk management function in business, how a business can identify and measure its loss exposures, the loss exposures of a typical firm, the major tools of risk management, how to select among these tools, how to analyze insurance contracts, some leading policies, and insurers and their operations. Part 3 covers the unique aspects of family risk management. Part 4 deals with government regulation of insurers.

Significant changes from the third edition include the following:

1 The text has been updated to reflect the many important developments in risk management and insurance since the fourth edition was published. For example, this fifth edition includes discussions of retroactive liability insurance, the 1984 standard workers' compensation and employers' liability policy, the Social Security amendments of 1983, the effect on pension plans of the Tax Equity and Financial Responsibility Act of 1982, the development of 401(k) plans and the expansion of flexible benefits plans, universal life insurance and flexible premium variable life insurance,

residual disability income insurance, changes in federal estate taxes and gift taxes because of the Economic Recovery Tax Act of 1981, and the response of insurers through horizontal or vertical integration to the rapidly changing financial services marketplace.

2 Chapter 1 starts with a short discussion of why the study of risk management and insurance is important to the reader.

3 The section on captive insurers in Chapter 11 has been expanded.

4 A new section entitled "The Capital Asset Pricing Model, Portfolio Theory, and the Worry Factor" has been added to Chapter 13. This section emphasizes the importance of considering the interrelationships among the various pure risk exposures and the speculative risk exposures.

5 Chapters 18 and 19 on property and liability insurance have been almost completely revised. Chapter 18 now covers basic property insurance protection, theft and employee dishonesty insurance, boiler and marine insurance, glass insurance, and marine insurance. In Chapter 19 we discuss liability insurance, some package contracts that combine property and liability insurance, and some miscellaneous contracts.

6 The case used in Chapter 33 to illustrate life insurance programming has been changed from a one wage-earner family to a two wage-earner family.

7 Two learning aids have been added to each chapter. In addition to the review questions included in previous editions, each chapter now begins with a set of learning objectives and ends with some key concepts.

8 Some less important details have been omitted in order to make the text more readable. Many sentences have been shortened or rewritten in order to clarify the presentation.

Because this text covers the entire field of risk management and insurance in depth, some teachers may prefer to omit certain chapters to emphasize the others or to meet time constraints. They may also wish to rearrange the chapters. For example, a teacher who wishes to emphasize business risk management could omit Part 3 on family risk management and assign only selected pages in Chapters 15 through 29, which deal primarily with insurance. A teacher who wishes to emphasize insurance could assign only selected pages in Chapters 1 through 13, which provide a background in risk management. Chapter 14 continues the Chapter 13 discussion on quantitative approaches to selecting the proper tools for those teachers who prefer additional in-depth coverage on this topic. Most teachers will probably prefer to omit it. Teachers who prefer to cover family risk management before business risk management can rearrange chapters to accomplish this purpose. An *Instructor's Guide*, containing sample text assignments, is available from the publisher.

Although Professor Heins's contributions to the first two editions were substantial, Professor Williams was solely responsible for this fifth revision and the two previous editions.

The authors are indebted to many persons who contributed directly or indirectly to the completion of this edition and the four previous editions. We again express our appreciation to the persons named in the prefaces to the first four editions. For this fifth edition, specific mention should also be made of five persons who reviewed the fourth edition and made some highly constructive comments: Robert Camp, Ft. Hays State University; Joseph S. Gerber, University of Arizona; George L. Head, Insurance Institute of America; H. Wayne Snider, Temple University; and Les Strickler, Oregon State University. Although we have not accepted all their comments, we did find each of their reviews extremely helpful. Professor Bob Hedges of Temple University has sent us, over the years, numerous insightful critiques on various sections of the text. His critiques of the fourth edition were especially detailed and valuable. Helpful comments have also been received from Professors Andrew Whitman and Dongsae Cho and from several graduate assistants at the University of Minnesota. These individuals have shared with Professor Williams the pleasant task of teaching an introductory course in which earlier editions of this text have been used. Most of the manuscript has been typed by Suzanne Cook and Pam Sutherland, who somehow managed to convert illegible handwriting into clean copy. The dedication reflects our continuing thanks for the support we have received from our wives. Any errors, of course, are the responsibility of the authors.

As we stated in the third and fourth editions, the late Professor Ralph Blanchard of Columbia University once remarked that writing a text is like staging a Broadway play. It is almost impossible to predict how the audience will react. We have again tried to produce a revision that is better than its predecessors. The reader must be the final judge.

C. Arthur Williams, Jr.

Richard M. Heins

PART ONE

INTRODUCTION TO RISK
AND RISK MANAGEMENT

Risk exists whenever the future is unknown. Because the adverse effects of risk have plagued mankind since the beginning of time, individuals, groups, and societies have developed various methods for managing risk. Since no one knows the future exactly, everyone is a risk manager not by choice, but by sheer necessity.

The purpose of this text is to examine carefully one important class of risks. Restricting the detailed analysis to this limited class permits the discussion to focus sharply on certain concepts, many of which will also be applicable to other types of risks. Once certain fundamental ideas have been presented, the text will explain in some detail the need for, and the application of, various tools of risk management, first by a business firm (defined broadly to include public and nonprofit organizations) and second by a family (defined to include one or more individuals).

Part 1 of the text introduces the reader to the general subject of risk and risk management. After defining risk and analyzing its adverse effects, this part introduces the reader to the risk management process and the objectives of risk management.

1

RISK AND RISK MANAGEMENT

LEARNING OBJECTIVES

After you have completed this chapter, you should be able to:

1 Summarize why the study of risk management is important.
2 Explain why risk is not the same concept as the chance of loss or uncertainty.
3 Distinguish between pure risks and speculative risks.
4 Explain the economic costs of pure risks.
5 Describe briefly the five basic steps in risk management.
6 Translate the possible contributions of risk management into risk management objectives.

INTRODUCTION

People have always sought ways to deal with the uncertainties of life. This book will examine how businesses (and other organizations—public and private) and families (including single persons) might effectively manage a major class of exposures to loss through a process called risk management.

This introductory chapter first explains briefly why the study of risk management is important. It then defines and analyzes the concepts of probability, risk, uncertainty, and reaction to risk; describes various ways in which risks can be classified; shows how risk imposes significant economic losses upon organizations, individuals, and societies; outlines the five steps in the risk management process; explains how effective risk management contributes to the welfare of businesses, families, and society; and discusses the objectives of risk management.

WHY THE STUDY OF RISK MANAGEMENT IS IMPORTANT

Risk management is the identification, measurement, and treatment of exposures to potential accidental losses. Examples of some recent major accidental losses to businesses that were managed with varying degrees of success are the property damage, liability suits, deaths, and disabilities incurred as a result of the MGM Grand Hotel fire, the collapse of a skywalk in the Kansas City Hyatt Regency Hotel, and the crash of an American Airlines DC-10 after takeoff at Chicago-O'Hare International Airport. An example of a major "accidental" loss that is less sudden is the liability and workers' compensation claims currently being made for asbestosis against asbestos manufacturers, insulation installers, and others arising out of exposure to this substance over a period of many years. Most accidental losses are not this dramatic, but many lesser incidents each day threaten the survival of some businesses, cause their earnings to dip below acceptable levels, interrupt their operations, or slow their growth. All businesses face the threat of losses that may never occur. Worry about these possibilities does more than make life less pleasant; it may stop a business from engaging in certain activities and otherwise alter how it conducts its operations. Proper risk management enables a business to handle its exposures to accidental losses in the most economic, effective way.

Risk management also enables a business to handle better its ordinary business risks. Freed of concern about the accidental losses noted above, a business can pursue more aggressively and intelligently its regular activities. In addition, the quality of its decisions on such matters as new construction, introducing a new product, or extending its operations into a foreign country is improved by considering how this construction or activity would affect its exposures to accidental losses if it decided to move ahead.

These contributions of risk management to the survival and profitability of a business will be explored in more detail later in this chapter. Although the discussion to this point has been limited to a business, risk management can be practiced successfully by other organizations such as nonprofit hospitals, educational institutions, and local governments, and by families, including single persons.

In a sense risk management is not an option. We need merely to exist to face some of the exposures that will be discussed in this text. If we simply ignore these exposures, we will have selected a risk management approach by default that almost certainly will not be the best approach. By managing these exposures properly we should be able to achieve more acceptable results at minimum cost.

Organizations of all sorts have recognized the increasing importance of sound risk management. As life has become more complicated, more interrelated, and more uncertain, new loss exposures have been created and the severity of many old exposures increased. In most large firms and many smaller ones top management has assigned primary responsibility for risk management to a specialized department. Employee benefit plan management, even though it may be administered solely or partly by the personnel department, is a risk management function to the extent it deals with Social Security benefits, pensions, medical expense benefits, death benefits, disability benefits, and similar payments.

Risk managers handle loss exposures by controlling them (for example, through the installation of automatic sprinklers and the rehabilitation of injured workers) and by financing the losses that still occur despite their control efforts. Losses can be financed by transferring them to someone else such as an insurer or by retaining them within the organization or family unit.

Insurance is a key tool of risk management. Used in the correct way, insurance produces important benefits for both the organization or family unit and for society. Both private and public insurance play vital roles in risk management and in the economic, social, and political life of our nation. In 1983 the private insurance business generated premiums in excess of $300 billion, controlled assets valued at close to $1 trillion, and employed almost 2 million persons. The Social Security system collected taxes that exceeded all the corporate income taxes combined and for many persons exceeded their personal income tax.

Why is the study of risk management important? Up to this point we have discussed briefly the importance of this management function to organizations, families, and society. How would you personally benefit from studying risk management? First, more persons become risk managers at some stage in their professional careers than ever expected to do so. We must all manage the exposures we face in our personal lives. Second, even if you do not become a professional risk manager, your activities will affect your organization's risk manager. You will in turn be affected by his or her activities. Third, risk management and insurance touch our lives in other highly significant ways through the organizations and families they save or stabilize through loss indemnification, the accidents they either prevent or reduce in severity, the long-term projects in which they invest, and the security they provide by reducing the uncertainty in our lives. Finally, the importance of the insurance business to all of us is demonstrated by the fact that the United States Supreme Court over 70 years ago labelled the private insurance business "a business affected with a public interest," thus subjecting it to much closer government regulation than most businesses. As a citizen, you should share that greater concern.

PROBABILITY AND PROBABILITY DISTRIBUTIONS DEFINED

The discussion now turns to some concepts that are important in risk management—probability and probability distributions. The probability associated with a certain outcome is the relative likelihood that that outcome will occur. Probability varies between 0 and 1. If the probability is 0, that outcome *will not* occur. If the probability is 1, that outcome *will* occur. The closer the probability is to 1, the more likely it will occur.

A probability distribution shows for each possible outcome its probability of occurrence. Illustrations are the two probability distributions shown in Figure 1.1. Each of these two distributions shows the possible total dollar losses from fires that a business might experience during the coming year together with the probability that each of these total dollar losses will occur.

The possible outcomes and probabilities plotted in Figure 1.1. are as follows:

Distribution A	
Losses	Probability
$ 0	.10
20,000	.15
40,000	.20
60,000	.20
80,000	.20
100,000	.10
120,000	.05

Distribution B	
Losses	Probability
$ 50,000	.05
60,000	.90
70,000	.05

Because one and only one of the outcomes in a probability distribution can occur within the period for which the distribution is constructed, the sum of the probabilities must equal 1. The reader can check the two distributions in Figure 1.1 to see that this is true.

RISK DEFINED

Textbook writers and other authors have defined risk in various ways.[1] No one definition is "correct." This text defines risk as *the variation in the outcomes that could occur over a specified period in a given situation*. If only one outcome is possible, the variation and hence the risk is 0. If many outcomes are possible, the risk is not 0. The greater the variation, the greater the risk.

How this risk might be measured more precisely will be discussed in Chapter 4. The most commonly used statistical yardstick measures the extent to which the possible outcomes differ from the outcome that would be expected to occur on the average in

[1] For example, risk has been defined as (1) the subject of insurance, whether a person or a thing, (2) chance of loss, or (3) uncertainty concerning the outcome. For a more complete discussion see p. 4 of the first edition of this text and part 1, "The Meaning and Measurement of Risk," in J. D. Hammond (ed.), *Essays in the Theory of Risk and Insurance* (Glenview, Ill.: Scott, Foresman and Company, 1968). Although the authors of this text continue to distinguish among chance of loss, risk, and uncertainty, they have altered their definitions slightly from the first edition.

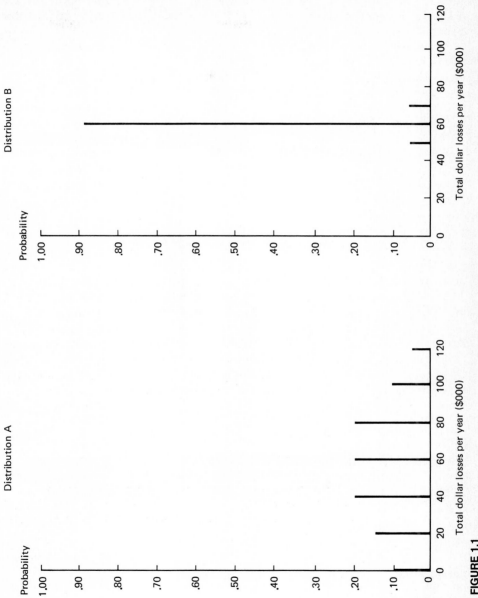

FIGURE 1.1
Two hypothetical probability distributions of total dollar losses per year.

7

the long run. The degree of risk is inversely related to the ability to predict which outcome will actually occur. If the risk is 0, the future is perfectly predictable. If the risk in a given situation can be reduced, the future becomes more predictable and more manageable.

Under distribution A, plotted in Figure 1.1, the outcomes can vary widely. Distribution B, on the other hand, is characterized by fewer possible outcomes, one of which is highly likely to occur. The variation in the possible outcomes, i.e., the risk, is high for distribution A and low for distribution B. Under distribution A it is difficult to predict next year's actual outcome; under distribution B one can predict with confidence a narrower range within which the actual outcome will fall.

Risk, therefore, is a characteristic of the entire probability distribution, whereas there is a separate probability for each outcome. In a two-outcome situation for which the probability of one outcome is 1 and the probability of the second outcome is 0, the risk is 0 because the actual outcome is known. Clearly, risk and probability, as defined in this text, are different concepts.

OBJECTIVE AND SUBJECTIVE ASPECTS: STATE OF THE WORLD AND STATE OF THE MIND

Both probability and risk have their objective and subjective interpretations. The objective probability distribution and its associated risk is the distribution that actually exists—it is a state of world. The subjective probability distribution is what the risk manager believes to be true—it is an estimate, a state of the mind. The true state of the world often differs from a person's assessment of that state. Because people act on the basis of what they believe to be true, it is important to recognize this distinction. To the extent that their estimates are incorrect, people base their decisions on false premises. Consequently risk managers must constantly strive to improve their estimates. Even with perfect estimates of probability and risk, decision making in a risky situation is a difficult task.

Probability

The objective probability of a certain outcome is the proportion of times that outcome would occur, assuming an infinite number of observations and no change in underlying conditions. Objective probability is the same for all persons in a given situation. Under certain special circumstances this probability can be determined by a priori reasoning. A number of equally likely outcomes must exist, some of which represent the particular outcome whose probability is being determined. For example, the probability of obtaining a head when a "fair" coin is tossed is ½ because (1) there are two equally likely outcomes—a head and a tail[2]—and (2) one of these outcomes is a head. The probability of drawing a king from a deck of cards is $\frac{1}{13}$ because (1) there are 52 equally likely outcomes and (2) four of these outcomes are kings. The probability of drawing a king of hearts is $\frac{1}{52}$, a king of hearts or a king of spades $\frac{1}{26}$, and any card in the suit of hearts ¼. The probability of obtaining an ace when a die is thrown is ⅙.

---

[2] It is assumed that the coin will not remain standing on its edge.

In the much more common situations where a priori reasoning is not possible, objective probabilities must be estimated. These estimates are based upon statistical evidence or judgment. Even where a priori reasoning is possible, many persons do not know how to calculate these probabilities. Instead they must estimate these objective probabilities in some other way. These estimates may vary widely among persons, depending upon the information they have, their ability to analyze this information, their biases, and so on. For example, the objective probability that a certain loss will occur may be $\frac{1}{50}$, but one person may estimate this probability to be $\frac{1}{100}$, while another estimates it to be $\frac{1}{20}$. Because these estimates may differ among persons facing the same objective probability, they are called "subjective" estimates.

In many situations where a priori reasoning is not possible, statistical evidence may be available, at least to some persons, that will shed some light on the objective probabilities. For example, one cannot determine a priori the probability that a light bulb coming off a production line will be defective, that the number of phone calls a day through a specified exchange will exceed 100, or that a person aged thirty-five will die in the coming year. In cases such as these, if we assume that the underlying conditions do not change, the probability can be estimated by computing the proportion of times the outcome in question occurs in a long series of repeated observations. For example, the statistician can compute the proportion of defective light bulbs among a large number of tested bulbs, the proportion of days over a long period of time in which the number of phone calls at the exchange exceeded 100, and the proportion of deaths in a large group of people, all of whom were aged thirty-five at the beginning of the year. Probability can be measured in this way because, according to the law of large numbers, which may be proved mathematically or demonstrated empirically, as the number of independent observations increases, the proportion of times a certain outcome occurs tends to approach the underlying probability. If the underlying conditions are changing, statistical evidence is sometimes available that would indicate the trends, cycles, or seasonal fluctuations that should be taken into account. However, not everyone has the same amount or kind of information available, and those who have the same information may not interpret it in the same way. For example, if the probability of a certain loss has increased steadily during the past five years, will the probability next year reflect a continuance or a correction of this trend?

Up to this point attention has been limited to situations in which the event is repeatable. Otherwise one cannot speak about the proportion of outcomes in the long run. Probability, however, can also be interpreted as a degree of belief. Under this interpretation, it is reasonable to apply the concept to unique events. For example, one can talk about the probability that a certain candidate will be elected president, that a specific product will be a success, or that a particular person will die. In these cases objective probabilities do not exist, but it may still be useful to make decisions as if they did. Some statisticians believe that this concept of subjective probability has little value and may, in fact, be misleading.

In summary, objective probability is the proportion of times a particular outcome would occur in the long run assuming that underlying conditions remain unchanged. In some special circumstances this probability can be calculated exactly through a priori reasoning. In all other instances, subjective probability estimates must be used. One way to estimate the underlying objective probability is to observe the proportion of times that a particular outcome has occurred in the past under basically the same conditions. The closer the experience approximates a long-run situation, the more reliance one can place in this indicated probability. If experience of this sort is not available or is unreliable, probability estimates must be based on other factors, some of which are extremely subjective. In events that are not repeatable, it may be useful to state subjective probabilities as degrees of belief, but there is no underlying objective probability.

Risk

Risk has been defined as the variation in the possible outcomes that exists in a given situation. As was true for probability, a distinction can be made between objective risk—the variation that exists in nature and is the same for all persons facing the same situation; and subjective risk—each person's estimate of the objective risk. In order to measure the variation that exists in nature, one would have to know the underlying probability distribution and how to assess the variation inherent in that distribution. For example, a gambler skilled in probability theory may be able to calculate precisely the probability of each hand that might be dealt in a game of cards. In other words, the gambler has an exact picture of the underlying probability distribution. Nevertheless, he or she still does not know what cards will be dealt; there are many possible outcomes. The variation in the results can be measured by using one or more commonly accepted yardsticks, to be described in Chapter 4, which will enable the gambler to compare the objective risk in one situation with the objective risk in another.

In most situations, however, one does not know the objective risk inherent in the situation. Instead this risk must be estimated. For example, if one must rely upon subjective probability distributions instead of objective probability distributions, one must clearly rely upon subjective estimates of risk. The variation in the estimated probability distribution might be calculated in the same manner as the risk in an objective probability distribution. Even if one knows the underlying probability distribution, one may not know how to calculate the variation in the potential outcomes, and thus one forms a subjective estimate of the risk. The estimated variation may be greater or less than the true variation.

UNCERTAINTY DEFINED

Uncertainty is the doubt a person has concerning his or her ability to predict which of the many possible outcomes will occur. Uncertainty is a person's conscious awareness of the risk in a given situation. It depends upon the person's estimated risk—what that person believes to be the state of the world—and the confidence he or she has in this belief. A person may be extremely uncertain about the future in a situation where in reality the risk is small; on the other hand, this person may have great confidence in his or her ability to predict the future when in fact the future is highly uncertain. Unlike probability and risk, uncertainty cannot be measured by any commonly accepted yardstick.

REACTION TO RISK DEFINED

A person's reaction to risk is the way in which he or she behaves or responds in an uncertain situation. One factor affecting this reaction is the person's uncertainty. Other things being equal, one would expect the person to react more strongly, either positively or negatively, the greater this person's uncertainty. Other factors that may be of equal or greater importance are the magnitude of the potential gains or losses involved and the effect of these gains or losses upon the person's economic status. For example, one may react more strongly to a situation where the uncertainty is the same but the potential gains and losses are ± $10,000 instead of ± $10. A person may also react differently if he or she is wealthy instead of poor. A wealthy person may be more uncertain than a poor person about the future, but the wealthy person may fear the future less because of his or her greater ability to withstand adversity.

Even if all these conditions (uncertainty, potential gains and losses, and economic status) are the same, however, people may react differently because their personalities, as determined by their heredity and their environment, vary. Indeed, the same person may have a different affinity for or aversion to risk at different ages and in different situations.

Individuals making decisions under risk should be aware of the effect of their own risk attitudes upon their decisions. Upon closer inspection they may decide to alter these attitudes. If they are making decisions on behalf of a family or a business, they should examine the extent to which they should adopt the attitude of others (for example, their spouse's, their family's, their immediate superior's, their department's, or their firm's). Persons delegating these decisions to someone else should also study that person's attitude toward risk and how it affects the decisions he or she makes. In some instances it may be appropriate to specify the attitude that should be assumed in making decisions.

Factors Affecting Risk Attitudes

Many researchers have investigated the demographic characteristics, personality traits, and environmental conditions that determine a person's reaction to risk.[3] These investigations have contributed substantially to the understanding of how persons behave in situations involving risk. They suggest that such behavior is extremely complex, depending upon a host of factors and varying over time. They also indicate that a person may react differently to financial risks than to physical and social risks.

Investigations that have attempted to describe a person's reaction to risk in terms of one demographic or personality trait have generally yielded contradictory results. For example, some studies suggest that women tend to be more averse to risk than men; others suggest no difference in risk aversion between men and women. Similar contradictory evidence exists concerning the effects of age, of intelligence, and of education.

[3] For a collection of articles on risk-taking behavior, see part II in J. D. Hammond, op. cit. See also Mark R. Greene, *Risk Aversion, Insurance and the Future* (Bloomington: Graduate School of Business, Indiana University, 1971), and Paul J. H. Schoemaker, *Experiments on Decisions under Risk: The Expected Utility Hypothesis* (Boston: Kluwer-Nijhoff Publishing, 1980).

One extremely interesting and important finding is that individuals tend to be more willing to accept risk after they participate in a group facing the same risk than they would have previously as individuals. Consequently group (for example, committee) decisions tend to be riskier than the average decision made by the members of the group prior to their group experience. The most popular explanation of this risky shift is that individuals view themselves as being at least as willing as their peers to accept risks. Recent experiments, however, suggest that groups do not always behave in this way. Indeed, under certain circumstances the group decision may be more cautious than the average of the individual decisions.[4]

PERVASIVENESS OF RISK

Most human activities involve some risk and uncertainty. This pervasiveness of risk can be illustrated by the following examples, which could be multiplied almost without limit. Placing a new product on the market or purchasing a new plant may prove to have been an unwise business decision; a gambler may lose on a particular bet; increasing use of technology may affect the social structure of our population in some unpredictable and unfortunate ways; because of a new statute or court decision, certain persons may unexpectedly become guilty of violating the law; a hopeful suitor may receive a negative response to a proposal; certain forms of exercise may damage a middle-aged heart; and the unfriendly actions of one nation may cause another to respond with overwhelming force.

The potential losses in a situation involving risk can be classified according to whether their effects are economic, social, political, psychological, physical, or legal. Of course, the same loss can have economic and social effects or involve some other combination of effects. Since it is impossible to handle all these aspects of risk in this book, the text deals primarily with the economic effects. On the other hand, most of the general discussion on the principles and tools of risk management would also be of value in handling the other aspects of risk. Furthermore, the economic effects of risk can seldom be completely isolated, and in discussing the handling of economic risks, it is necessary to pay some attention to the associated noneconomic effects.

PURE AND SPECULATIVE RISKS

Situations involving risk may be classified as pure or speculative.[5] A *pure risk* exists when there is a chance of loss but no chance of gain. For example, the owner of an automobile faces the risk associated with a potential collision loss. If a collision

---

[4] For a comprehensive analysis of this subject, see Russell D. Clark, III, "Risk Taking in Groups: A Social Psychological Analysis," *Journal of Risk and Insurance,* vol. XLI, no. 1 (March, 1974), pp. 75–92.

[5] A. H. Mowbray, R. H. Blanchard, and C. A. Williams, Jr., *Insurance* (6th ed., New York: McGraw-Hill Book Company, 1969), pp. 6–8. Two other classifications discussed in earlier editions of this text distinguish between (1) static and dynamic risks and (2) fundamental and particular risks. For the static-dynamic classification see Allan H. Willett, *The Economic Theory of Risk and Insurance* (New York: Columbia University Press, 1901, and Philadelphia: University of Pennsylvania Press, 1951), pp. 14–23. For the fundamental-particular classification see C. A. Kulp and J. W. Hall, *Casualty Insurance* (4th ed., New York: The Ronald Press Company, 1958), pp. 3–7.

occurs, the owner will suffer a financial loss. If there is no collision, the owner does not gain. The owner's position remains unchanged. A speculative risk exists when there is a chance of gain as well as a chance of loss. For instance, expansion of an existing plant involves a chance of loss and a chance of gain. Pure risks are always distasteful, but speculative risks possess some attractive features.

Pure risks also differ from speculative risks in that they generally are repeatable under essentially the same conditions and thus are more amenable to the law of large numbers, already described in the section ''Probability'' under ''Risk Defined.'' This means that one can more successfully predict the proportion of units that will be lost if they are exposed to a pure risk than if they are subject to a speculative risk. One notable exception to this statement is the speculative risks associated with games of chance, which are highly amenable to this law.

Finally, in a situation involving a speculative risk, society may benefit even though the individual is hurt. For example, the introduction of a socially beneficial product may cause a firm manufacturing the product it replaces to go bankrupt.[6] In a pure-risk situation society almost always suffers if any individual experiences a loss. A possible exception occurs when property is misplaced; ignoring moral issues, society may gain if the property is worth more to the finder than to the loser.

Figure 1.1 depicted two pure-risk situations: In each situation the only possible outcomes are no loss or various total dollar losses during the coming year. Because there are no gains, the risk in such situations can be redefined as the variation in the possible *losses* (not outcomes). It is generally measured by the extent to which the possible losses may differ from the loss expected on the average in the long run.

Several experiments suggest that individuals may react differently in pure-risk and speculative-risk situations.[7] For example, in one experiment most subjects were unwilling to participate in a speculative venture that presented a possible gain of $100 and a possible loss of $4,900 unless the probability of winning was at least .99; i.e., the probability of losing was .01 or less. On the other hand, most subjects were unwilling to pay a fee of $100 to avoid a loss of $5,000 in a situation where the only two possible outcomes were either the $5,000 loss or no loss—unless the probability of loss was .10 or more. For lower probabilities of loss they preferred to retain the risk associated with a possible gain of $100 (the premium saving) or a net loss of $4,900 (the $5,000 loss less the premium saving). One possible explanation for this difference in risk attitudes is that in the speculative-risk situation the subjects had to take action to assume the risk. In the pure-risk situation the subjects had to take action to rid themselves of the risk. Another possible explanation is that in the pure-risk situation the subjects did not fully appreciate the risk they were retaining.

Both pure and speculative risks commonly exist at the same time. For example, the ownership of a building exposes the owner to both pure risks (for example, accidental damage to the property) and speculative risks (for example, rise or fall in property

---

[6] Wagers always result in some winners and some losers. Other speculative-risk situations may result in all winners or all losers.

[7] Hammond, op. cit., pp. 122–134. For some additional pure-risk experiments see Schoemaker, op. cit., especially chaps. 5 and 7.

values caused by general economic conditions). The distinction, however, is still important because special techniques exist for handling pure risks.

TYPES OF RISK HANDLED BY RISK MANAGERS

Although many of the concepts and tools to be presented in this text are applicable to all types of risk, the discussion focuses on the types of risks that are typically handled by "risk managers" in a business.

The risk manager is concerned with *most but not all pure risks*. He or she is not typically concerned with speculative risks except to the extent that the creation of speculative risks forces the risk manager to face certain pure risks; for example, the acquisition of a new plant creates a potential fire loss. The risk associated with potential losses to the firm's own product as a result of faulty processing by employees illustrates a pure risk for which a risk manager's firm typically looks to other departments for correction.

Chapter 12 will indicate that insurers for the most part have restricted their coverages to an expanding, but still restricted, list of pure risks. Perhaps the best way to describe the risks handled by risk managers is to say that they include all insurable and quasi-insurable risks. It is, however, much more simple and, with a few exceptions, as correct to say that the risk manager is concerned with pure risks. This text will follow this common practice. Because other managers in a business work primarily with speculative risks, were it not for the risk manager pure risks would receive inadequate attention. Yet their impact on an organization or a family is highly significant.

Dynamic changes in technology and social forces are constantly creating new types of pure risks. The hijacking of a jumbo jet, the kidnapping of a key executive, a suit against a board of directors, a nuclear explosion, and pollution liability are potential losses that did not exist or were much less likely prior to 1950.

As we will explain in more detail later in this text, the potential economic losses that are the risk manager's concern can be categorized as follows: (1) property losses caused when property of the firm or family is damaged or destroyed or disappears, (2) liability to others because of damage to their property or persons, and (3) personnel losses caused usually by the death, poor health, retirement, or unemployment of employees, owners, or family members.

ECONOMIC COSTS OF RISK

Life without any risk or the uncertainty that it creates would be difficult and not entirely pleasant. We take pleasure in anticipating gains that may never be realized and even more pleasure in realizing unexpected gains. Life is more interesting, and the human race more alert and imaginative, because of risk and uncertainty. As Friedrich Nietzsche said, "A heart full of courage and cheerfulness needs a little danger from time to time or the world gets unbearable."[8]

[8] R. Flesch, *The Book of Unusual Quotations* (New York: Harper & Row, Publishers, Inc., 1957), p. 55.

Still, we do not enjoy being concerned about losses even if they never occur, and to suffer unexpected losses is clearly painful. Life is insecure, and the human race is more frustrated, worried, and afraid because of this insecurity. Only these negative aspects are present in pure-risk situations, because there are no *gain* possibilities.

The economic costs of uncertainty have been discussed by many writers. A. H. Willett, in his discussion of the economics of insurance, refers to the costs of uncertainty arising out of (1) the unexpected losses that do occur and (2) the uncertainty itself even if there are no losses.[9]

Costs of Unexpected Losses

Each day some businesses and families suffer losses in pure-risk situations. For example, a fire destroys a warehouse; an explosion causes a store to shut its doors until the damage is repaired; a customer injured by a defective product sues the manufacturer; the key executive of a business is killed in an automobile accident; a family member is disabled or becomes unemployed. Some of these losses are minor. Others have disastrous effects.

The costs of these unexpected losses to the individual economic unit, the firm or family, and in many instances to society (e.g., through production losses and higher prices, decreased taxes, increased welfare payments, and social unrest) are clear to most people, but the most important costs associated with uncertainty itself are less often appreciated.

Costs of Uncertainty Itself

The *first* cost of uncertainty itself is the physical and mental strain caused by fear and worry. As noted above, persons differ in their estimates of the probability distribution, their assessment of the risks involved, their uncertainty, and their reaction to risks. For some persons a gambling instinct, the pleasure of making small bets, or some other psychological drive may make risk bearing attractive. However, most people, if fully informed about their exposures to pure risk, worry. The intensity of this worry depends upon the factors already listed as determining their reaction to risk.

The *second* cost of uncertainty is a distortion in the use of resources (land, labor, capital, technical knowledge) causing inefficiencies, oversupply of some goods and services and undersupply of others, prices that are too high for some goods and services and too low for others, and higher average prices. The basic reasoning is that ideally the last unit of each resource should be committed to that use for which its productivity would be the highest. Because this "marginal productivity" (the output made possible by the last resource unit) tends to decrease as the resources committed to a given use increase, resources are used optimally when the marginal productivity of each use is the same. Otherwise total output could be increased by transferring a resource unit from the use with the lowest marginal productivity to one with a higher

---

[9] Allan H. Willett, *The Economic Theory of Risk and Insurance* (New York: Columbia University Press, 1901, and Philadelphia: University of Pennsylvania Press, 1951), pp. 24–31.

marginal productivity. Pure risks distort this allocation because persons facing such risks tend to worry. They expect higher returns from the more risky uses of their resources. Consequently, too many resources tend to flow into "safe" uses, too few resources into "risky" uses. Indeed, no resources may be committed to very risky uses. In real life, the effects of pure risks are even more complicated because individuals act on the basis of *estimated* risks, which may not correspond with the *true* risks, and an individual's response to uncertainty is not always as rational as the above discussion would suggest.

For an individual firm or family, the uncertainty and fear generated by pure risks may cause the entity to avoid or limit certain activities that, if it were not for the pure risks involved, would be judged highly desirable. For example, a business may decide not to build a new plant because of potential fire and windstorm losses even though in all other respects building this plant seems like an excellent idea. Plans for marketing a new product or service may be abandoned because of potential product liability suits. A second effect of uncertainty on individual firms is a shortening of planning horizons. Short-run planning may dominate long-range planning even though what is best in the short run (for example, renting instead of owning a fleet of trucks) may not be best in the long run. A third problem is that in order to have liquid funds available to meet potential losses, firms or families may "hoard" resources in liquid or quasi-liquid form instead of using them, say, to purchase more efficient machinery or to provide more educational opportunities for employees or family members. Finally, others may react negatively to the entity's pure risks. Investors may be reluctant to join a firm as partners or stockholders, banks may limit or charge more for loans, suppliers may be unwilling to wait for payment of their bills, and employees may question their prospects with a firm whose future is uncertain.

Within an industry, the existence of uncertainty may produce a less than optimum allocation of resources among individual firms. Within society, this uncertainty may cause "safe" industries to be overdeveloped and "risky" industries to be under-developed. Indeed, society may have to forgo the products of a very risky industry. For example, would the airline industry have attained its present status if individual airlines had to bear physical damage losses to their jumbo jets? Uncertainty may in fact cause some resources to be withheld from any industry. The net effect of these distortions is that productivity overall is lower than it should be, thus raising the general price level. Furthermore, prices tend to be too high for the products and services of hazardous industries and too low for the safe products and services. Incorrect estimates of the risks involved and irrational reactions to risk may produce further distortions.

In summary, the costs of uncertainty, in addition to the costs of the losses that do occur, are generally (1) a reduction in well-being because of fear and worry and (2) less than optimum production, price levels, and price structures. Because pure risks present no offsetting benefits, businesses and families have strong reasons to manage these risks successfully.

THE FIVE STEPS IN THE RISK MANAGEMENT PROCESS

Risk management is the identification, measurement, and treatment of property, liability, and personnel pure-risk exposures. The process includes five steps:

1 The loss exposures of the business or family must be identified. Risk identification is the first and perhaps the most difficult function that the risk manager or administrator must perform. Failure to identify all the exposures of the firm or family means that the risk manager will have no opportunity to deal with these unknown exposures intelligently.

2 After risk identification, the next important step is the proper measurement of the losses associated with these exposures. This measurement includes a determination of *(a)* the probability or chance that the losses will occur, *(b)* the impact the losses would have upon the financial affairs of the firm or family, should they occur, and *(c)* the ability to predict the losses that will actually occur during the budget period. The measurement process is important because it indicates the exposures that are most serious and consequently most in need of urgent attention. It also yields information needed in step 3.

3 Once the exposure has been identified and measured, the various tools of risk management should be considered and a decision made with respect to the best combination of tools to be used in attacking the problem. These tools include primarily *(a)* avoiding the risk, *(b)* reducing the chance that the loss will occur or reducing its magnitude if it does occur, *(c)* transferring the risk to some other party, and *(d)* retaining or bearing the risk internally. The third alternative includes, but is not limited to, the purchase of insurance. In selecting the proper tool the risk manager must establish the costs and other consequences of using each tool or combination of tools. He or she must also consider the present financial position of the firm or family, its overall policy with reference to risk management, and its specific objectives.

4 After deciding among the alternative tools of risk treatment, the risk manager must implement the decisions made. If insurance is to be purchased, for example, establishing proper coverage, obtaining reasonable rates, and selecting the insurer are part of the implementation process.

5 The results of the decisions made and implemented in the first four steps must be monitored to evaluate the wisdom of those decisions and to determine whether changing conditions suggest different solutions.

This process will be discussed in greater detail in subsequent chapters.

As is true of management in general, risk management may be described as both an art and a science. Risk managers must still rely heavily upon nonquantitative techniques that depend upon deduction and intuitive judgments. Yet certain broad principles of risk management have been developed. Furthermore, during the past two decades, quantitative techniques have become more commonplace and more sophisticated. These principles and some of the current developments in scientific risk management will be presented at various points in this text. In time these guides to risk management will be improved and new ones will be created, but sound judgment will continue to play an important role.

POSSIBLE CONTRIBUTIONS OF RISK MANAGEMENT

Because risk management, as defined in this text, is concerned with pure risks, it may be regarded by some as the true "dismal science." Pure risks can only hurt a firm or family, and the purpose of risk management is to minimize the hurt at minimum cost. Upon closer investigation, however, one discovers that the possible contributions of risk management to businesses, families, and society are highly significant.

To a Business

The possible contributions of risk management to a business can be divided into five major categories. The contributions that the risk manager will make in a particular case depend upon the objectives set for this function (see the next section) and the extent to which these objectives are achieved.

First, risk management may make the difference between survival and failure. Some losses, such as large liability suits or the destruction of a firm's manufacturing facilities, may so cripple a firm that without proper advance preparation for such events the firm must close its doors. Even if risk management did not contribute to the economic health of businesses in any other way, this one benefit would make it a critical function of business management.

Second, because profits can be improved by reducing expenses as well as increasing income, risk management can contribute *directly* to business profits (or, in the case of nonprofit organizations or public agencies, to operating efficiency). For example, risk management may lower expenses through preventing or reducing accidental losses as the result of certain low-cost measures, through transferring potentially serious losses to others at the lowest transfer fee possible, through electing to take a chance on small losses unless the transfer fee is a bargain, and through preparing the firm to meet most economically those losses that it has decided to retain.

Third, risk management can contribute *indirectly* to business profits in at least six ways.

1 If a business has successfully managed its pure risks, the peace of mind and confidence this engenders permits its managers to investigate and assume attractive speculative risks that they might otherwise seek to avoid. For example, if a firm had to worry about windstorm damage to its plants and industrial injuries to its employees, it might elect to limit itself to its present markets. Freed of this worry, it might expand to new markets.

2 By alerting general managers to the pure-risk aspects of speculative ventures, risk management improves the quality of the decisions regarding such ventures. For example, a firm that was deciding whether to lease or purchase a building might reach the wrong decision if it ignored the differing economic impacts of accidental physical damage to the building.[10]

3 Once a decision is made to assume a speculative venture, proper handling of the

---

[10] The technique suggested for making decisions such as this is capital budgeting. Pure risks are generally ignored in the literature on capital budgeting, but they should not be ignored in practice. For a typical discussion of capital budgeting, see L. D. Schall and C. W. Haley, *Introduction to Financial Management* (3d ed., New York: McGraw-Hill Book Company, 1983), chaps. 7 and 8. For a brief discussion of how pure risks might be incorporated in capital budgeting decisions, see Chap. 14 of this text.

Chapter 13 also emphasizes that in determining the worry and anxiety created by pure risks the risk manager should consider the interrelationship between the uncertainties generated by the pure-loss exposures and those generated by the speculative-loss exposures.

pure-risk aspects permits the business to handle the speculative risk more wisely and more efficiently. For example, a business may develop its product lines more aggressively if it knows that it is adequately protected against suits by persons who may be harmed accidentally by defective products.

4 Risk management can reduce the fluctuations in annual profits and cash flows. Keeping these fluctuations within bounds aids planning and is a desirable goal in itself. Investors regard more favorably a stable earnings record than an unstable one.

5 Through advance preparations, risk management can in many cases make it possible to continue operations following a loss, thus retaining customers or suppliers who might otherwise turn to competitors.

6 Creditors, customers, and suppliers, all of whom contribute to company profits, prefer to do business with a firm that has sound protection against pure risks. Employees also prefer to work for such firms.

Fourth, the peace of mind made possible by sound management of pure risks may itself be a valuable noneconomic asset because it improves the physical and mental health of the management and owners.

Fifth, because the risk management plan may also help others, such as employees, who would be affected by losses to the firm, risk management can also help satisfy the firm's sense of social responsibility or desire for a good public image.

To a Family

Risk management can provide families with the same five major classes of benefits. For example, by protecting the family against catastrophic losses, risk management may enable a family to continue a lifestyle that might otherwise be severely threatened or disrupted. Indeed the continued existence of the family unit might be at stake. Second, sound risk management may enable the family to reduce its expenditures for insurance without reducing its protection. Because a family cannot deduct insurance premiums from its taxable income, a dollar reduction in insurance premiums may be worth more than an additional dollar of income.[11] Third, if a family has adequate protection against the death or poor health of the breadwinner, damage to or disappearance of their property, or a liability suit, they may be willing to assume greater risks in equity investments or career commitments. They may also find that it is easier to secure a mortgage or personal loan. Fourth, family members are relieved of some physical and mental strain. Fifth, families may also gain some satisfaction from a risk management program that helps others as well as themselves or that improves their image.

To Society

To the extent that individual businesses and families benefit from risk management, so does the society of which they are members. Society also benefits from the more

---

[11] In Benjamin Franklin's day there were no income taxes. Consequently his advice on thrift needs updating. Today a penny saved may be better than a penny earned.

efficient use risk management permits of business and family resources and from the reduction in social costs associated with business and family financial reverses.

OBJECTIVES OF RISK MANAGEMENT

The possible objectives of risk management can be derived from the possible contributions of risk management. Implicit in the preceding discussion are the possible objectives of (1) mere survival, (2) peace of mind, (3) lower risk management costs and thus higher profits, (4) fairly stable earnings, (5) little or no interruption of operations, (6) continued growth, and (7) satisfaction of the firm's sense of social responsibility or desire for a good image.[12]

To this list could be added (8) satisfaction of externally imposed obligations. Illustrations of such obligations are safety regulations imposed by the Occupational Safety and Health Act to be described in Chapter 10, employee benefit plan arrangements prescribed by a collective bargaining agreement, and insurance requirements imposed by a secured creditor.

In a particular case, a firm or family may not be interested in some of these objectives. Among the objectives in which they are interested they may place a higher value on attaining some objectives than others. Conflicts among the objectives may force the firm or family either to abandon or to scale down the level of some of those objectives.

To illustrate, a firm may be interested in mere survival—not stable earnings, continuity of operations, or growth. Another firm may want survival and fairly stable earnings but may not seek continuous operations. Some firms and families establish a social responsibility—public image objective; others do not.

A firm or family may be interested in continuous operations or growth but may place much less emphasis on attaining these objectives than on mere survival and economy. Peace of mind may be an objective but may not be nearly as important as low risk management costs. The desire for a good image may be present but may not be a strong consideration.

A firm that is initially interested in growth and continuous operations may, after being informed of the cost of achieving these objectives, abandon them or settle for a lower growth objective and continuation of only part of their operations. A firm or family with a strong desire for peace of mind may reevaluate its position if this is necessary to keep the cost within an acceptable level. External obligations may require certain reports and actions that cause the entity to spend more on risk management programs than its other objectives would dictate or to adjust these other objectives. Similarly, the social responsibility objective may suggest some actions not supported, at least in the short run, by the other objectives, thus forcing a reevaluation of the relative importance of these objectives.

Part of the task of risk management, therefore, is to determine the optimum mix of objectives. To determine this mix, the risk manager may have to examine the feasi-

---

[12] This listing of objectives was first suggested in Robert I. Mehr and Bob A. Hedges, *Risk Management: Concepts and Applications* (Homewood, Ill.: Richard D. Irwin, Inc., 1974), chaps. 1 and 2.

bility and desirability of numerous mixes. Chapters 13 and 14 on how to select the proper tools of risk management for a given situation will examine this procedure more carefully.

Some additional insights into setting objectives for a business organization are provided in two writings summarized briefly below. Although these writings suggest different frameworks, they supplement, rather than contradict, one another and the preceding discussion.

Post- and Pre-Loss Risk Management Objectives Consistent with General Objectives

Professors Robert Mehr and Bob Hedges were the first to emphasize in a text that the risk management objectives of a business must be consistent with the firm's general objectives.[13] These general objectives are (1) profits (or in the case of nonprofit organizations and public agencies, efficient delivery of services), (2) good citizenship, and (3) satisfaction of the personal tastes and preferences of those in charge. The risk management objectives they consider to be consistent with these general objectives can be divided into (1) objectives to be achieved after a loss has occurred and (2) objectives to be achieved prior to the occurrence of any loss. The possible post-loss objectives are (1) survival, (2) continuity of operations, (3) earnings stability, (4) growth, and (5) good citizenship and a favorable public image. The possible pre-loss objectives are (1) economy, (2) the avoidance of stress and anxiety, or, in their terms, "a quiet night's sleep," and (3) good citizenship and a favorable public image. Mehr and Hedges stress that the conflict among these goals forces consideration of their interaction.

Risk Management Objectives Consistent with Corporate Goals, Corporate Environment, and Specific Corporate Attributes

According to Dr. Darwin Close, risk management objectives are a function of (1) corporate goals, (2) the corporate environment, and (3) attributes peculiar to a particular oganization.[14] Risk management policy, he explains, should reflect the basic corporate goals of survival and profits adjusted to any specific emphasis on growth or stability. A stability objective, he argues, suggests a conservative approach to risk management; a firm emphasizing growth (pre-loss) might take more chances because it needs capital for expansion. The environment (clients, competitors, suppliers, and government) may be stable or shifting and homogeneous or heterogeneous. Businesses operating in a stable-homogeneous condition can adopt objectives that are complete, specific, all-encompassing, and not subject to frequent review and evaluation. Specific company attributes that affect risk management objectives are (1) the company development and history, (2) the personalities and experience of present management, (3) the nature and amount of company assets, and (4) the nature of company operations.

---

[13] Ibid.

[14] Darwin B. Close, "Developing a Risk Management Policy Statement," *Risk Management*, vol. XXIII, no. II (November, 1976), pp. 6–8.

SOME KEY CONCEPTS

Risk   Variation in the potential losses. Risk is related inversely to our ability to predict what will happen.

Probability or chance of a loss   The relative likelihood that the loss will occur. Probability varies between 0 (the loss will not occur) and 1 (the loss will occur).

Probability distribution   A listing of all the possible outcomes that might occur and the probability of each possible outcome. The sum of these probabilities must equal 1.

Uncertainty   The doubt in our minds concerning whether we can predict the future.

Reaction to risk   How we behave in a situation where the future is unknown.

Pure risk exposure   An exposure in which the only possible outcomes are losses or no loss. A gain is not possible.

Costs of uncertainty itself   The costs to businesses, families, and society that arise out of concern about potential losses even if they never occur.

Risk management   The identification, measurement, and treatment of pure risk exposures.

Risk management objectives   The post-loss and pre-loss objectives that a business or family wishes to achieve through risk management.

REVIEW QUESTIONS

1 Distinguish among chance of loss, risk, uncertainty, and reaction to risk.

2 Each of two business firms owns 50 automobiles. One firm is very much concerned about collision losses sustained by its automobiles; the other is not. How do you explain this difference?

3 A risk manager estimates that the probability that her employer's home-office building will be seriously damaged during the next year is $\frac{1}{50}$.

   a Is $\frac{1}{50}$ an objective or subjective probability?

   b Is her uncertainty $\frac{1}{50}$?

4 Distinguish among pure risks and speculative risks. Give two illustrations of each type.

5 How would you define the class of risks typically handled by risk managers?

6 What two major types of economic costs are caused by uncertainty? Illustrate each type.

7 Is all uncertainty undesirable? Illustrate your answer.

8 Describe briefly the five steps in the risk management process.

9 How can risk management increase a business's or an individual's "profitability"?

10 Besides increasing "profits," what contributions can risk management make to a firm or family?

11 What are the possible objectives of risk management?

12 What is meant by the proper "mix" of risk management objectives?

SUGGESTIONS FOR ADDITIONAL READING

Ahearn, J. L., and S. T. Pritchett: *Risk and Insurance* (5th ed., St. Paul: West Publishing Company, 1984), chap. 1.

Carter, R. L., and N. A. Doherty (eds.): *Handbook of Risk Management* (London: Kluwer-Harrop Handbooks, 1974), pt. 1.

Greene, M. R., and O. N. Serbein: *Risk Management: Text and Cases* (2d ed., Reston, Va.: Reston Publishing Company, Inc., 1983), chap. 2.

_____, and P. Swadener: *Insurance Insights* (Cincinnati: South-Western Publishing Company, Inc., 1974), pt. 1.

Hammond, J. D. (ed.): *Essays in the Theory of Risk and Insurance* (Glenview, Ill.: Scott, Foresman and Company, 1968).

Hardy, C. O.: *Risk and Risk-Bearing* (Chicago: The University of Chicago Press, 1923).

Knight, Frank: *Risk, Uncertainty and Profit* (London: London School of Economics and Political Science, 1933).

Kulp, C. A., and J. W. Hall: *Casualty Insurance* (4th ed., New York: The Ronald Press Company, 1968), chap. 1.

Lalley, Edward P., *Corporate Uncertainty & Risk Management* (New York: Risk Management Society Publishing, Inc., 1982), chap. 1.

MacDonald, D. L.: *Corporate Risk Control* (New York: The Ronald Press Company, 1966), chap. 1.

Mehr, R. I., and B. A. Hedges: *Risk Management: Concepts and Applications* (Homewood, Ill.: Richard D. Irwin, Inc., 1974), chap. 1.

————, and ————: *Risk Management in the Business Enterprise* (Homewood, Ill.: Richard D. Irwin, Inc., 1963), chap. 1.

Mowbray, A. H., R. H. Blanchard, and C. A. Williams, Jr.: *Insurance* (6th ed., New York: McGraw-Hill Book Company, 1969), chap. 1.

Pfeffer, Irving: *Insurance and Economic Theory* (Homewood, Ill.: Richard D. Irwin, Inc., 1956).

————, and D. R. Klock: *Perspectives on Insurance* (Englewood Cliffs, N.J.: Prentice-Hall, Inc., 1974), chap. 14.

Schoemaker, Paul J. H., *Experiments on Decisions Under Risk: The Expected Utility Hypothesis* (Boston: Kluwer-Nijhoff Publishing, 1980).

Willett, A. H.: *The Economic Theory of Risk and Insurance* (Philadelphia: The University of Pennsylvania Press, 1951).

Williams, C. A., Jr., G. L. Head, R. C. Horn, and G. W. Glendenning: *Principles of Risk Management and Insurance* (Malvern, Pa.: American Institute for Property and Liability Underwriters, 1981), vol. 1, chap. 1.

PART **TWO**

BUSINESS RISK MANAGEMENT

Part 2 deals with the risk management problems facing a business firm, defined broadly to include public agencies and nonprofit institutions such as churches, colleges, and hospitals. Much of the discussion is equally applicable to family risk management, which is the subject of Part 3.

Our plan in this section is as follows: (1) We explore the nature of the risk management function in business and its relationship to other management functions; (2) we identify and measure the major potential property, liability, and personnel losses facing a typical business firm; (3) we describe and evaluate the tools that can be used to handle these exposures; (4) we suggest some approaches to selecting the proper tools; (5) we present a framework for analyzing insurance contracts; and (6) we apply this framework to some important examples. Next (7) we discuss some supplementary insurance decisions, such as the choice of an insurer, a producer, and a pricing method and how to prepare for dealing with loss adjusters. Finally (8) we indicate the special aspects of foreign exposures and their treatment.

Relatively few readers will be charged directly with the risk management function in a firm, but many will be asked to evaluate the risk manager's work and make risk management policy decisions. Others will be involved in activities that affect or are affected by the work of the risk manager. Furthermore, as we noted above, many of the concepts important in business risk management are equally applicable to family risk management, a direct responsibility of at least one member of each family.

A. The Business Risk Manager's Function and Relationship to Other Business Management Functions

CHAPTER 2

THE RISK MANAGEMENT FUNCTION IN BUSINESS

LEARNING OBJECTIVES

After you have completed this chapter you should be able to:

1 Explain why risk management is a management function.
2 Describe the major responsibilities of current risk managers, their titles and reporting levels, and how their departments are organized.
3 Explain how policy statements, records, and reports contribute to the performance of the risk management function.
4 Tell how a risk manager should be evaluated.
5 Summarize the relationship between risk management and other management functions.

INTRODUCTION

The management of a business, large or small, is a complex task involving a variety of management functions. One of these functions is risk management. The risk management process and its contributions to the profits and stability of a business were discussed in the preceding chapter. The current chapter explains why risk management is properly considered a management function, to what degree risk management is a responsibility of all levels of management, what duties and organizational structure are associated with the risk management function, and how this function is related to other business management functions.

A MANAGEMENT FUNCTION

Risk management involves the application of general management concepts to a specialized area. One of the most famous early French authorities in the general management area, Henri Fayol, defined management as follows:

> To manage is to forecast and plan, to organize, to command, to coordinate and to control. To foresee and plan means examining the future and drawing up the plan of action. To organize means building up the dual structure, material and human, of the undertaking. To command means maintaining activity among the personnel. To coordinate means binding together, unifying and harmonizing all activity and effort. To control means seeing that everything occurs in conformity with established rule and expressed command.[1]

Risk management requires the drawing up of plans, the organizing of material and individuals for the undertaking, the maintaining of activity among personnel for the objectives involved, the binding together and unifying of all the activities and efforts, and finally the controlling of this activity and seeing that everything occurs in conformity with established rules and objectives.

Fayol also suggested that all activities to which industrial undertakings give rise can be divided into six basic functions:

1 Technical activities (production, manufacture, adaptation)
2 Commercial activities (buying, selling, exchange)
3 Financial activities (search for an optimum use of capital)
4 Security activities (protection of property and persons)
5 Accounting activities (stock taking, financial statements, costs, statistics)
6 Managerial activities (planning, organization, command, coordination, control)[2]

Thus at an early date Fayol identified risk management (i.e., the security function) as one of the prime functions of management, even though at that time the security function was much more limited in its scope than it is today. According to Fayol,

> The object of this [security activity] is to safeguard property and persons against theft, fire and flood, to ward off strikes and felonies and broadly all social disturbances or natural disturbances liable to endanger the progress and even the life of the business. It is the master's eye, the watch-dog of the one-man business, the police or the army in the case of the State. *It is, generally speaking, all measures conferring security upon the undertaking and requisite peace of mind upon the personnel.*[3] [Emphasis added by the authors.]

Except for the last sentence, Fayol appears to be emphasizing the loss-control aspects of the modern risk management function; the security function would be more broadly conceived today.

---

[1] Reprinted with permission from Henri Fayol, *General and Industrial Management* (New York: Pitman Publishing Corporation, 1949), pp. 5–6. This book is an English translation of a work originally published in French in 1916.
[2] Ibid., pp. 3–6.
[3] Ibid., p. 4.

SECURITY FUNCTION A RESPONSIBILITY OF ALL DEPARTMENTS AT ALL LEVELS

Fayol's six management functions must be carried on at all levels of activity, in all departments. The relative importance of each function varies, of course, according to the department involved and the level of activity. For example, the security function must be performed by departments other than the risk management department at all levels.[4] The importance of the security function tends to be greater for the manager of each of these departments than for the persons working for the manager. Similarly, the risk management department must perform the other five management functions, not just the security function. The higher the position in the risk management department, the more important the other five management functions tend to become.

RISK MANAGEMENT RESPONSIBILITY OF OFFICERS AND DIRECTORS TO OWNERS

The officers and directors of a business have a legal responsibility to the stockholders or owners of a business for the proper management of pure risks. Several recent court decisions emphasize that directors and officers may be held legally responsible for breach of these duties. From these decisions it appears that the failure to effect proper insurance coverage, to pay premiums when due, to keep coverage in force and to otherwise carry out the security function may well be the basis for personal liability suits against the officers or directors of a business. The legal standard of performance, as announced by several courts, is that officers and directors must exercise the care that an ordinary prudent person would exercise under similar circumstances.[5]

MODERN MANAGEMENT'S APPROACH TO PURE RISK AND THE SECURITY FUNCTION

Like other management functions, the security function is handled differently in large, medium, and small firms. However, firms of all sizes are paying more attention to this important function and, as will be indicated below, size is not the only factor determining the sophistication of the risk management activity.

The Large Firm

Although it is impossible to center *all* pure-risk or security decisions in a single department or functional division, large firms have found it desirable to develop individuals or departments with specialized technical skills and to assign them specific pure-risk responsibilities.

---

[4] How the other departments in a business perform or relate to the security function is discussed in more detail later in this chapter.

[5] Gaylord A. Jentz, ''Are Corporate Directors Liable to the Corporation for Failure to Insure the Corporate Assets?'' unpublished paper, University of Wisconsin, 1957.

The Scope of the Risk Manager's Duties   In 1980 the Risk and Insurance Management Society, in cooperation with *Time* magazine, studied the present status and future role of risk management. Questionnaires were mailed to 2,897 United States RIMS members.[6] About 49 percent responded before the cutoff date. Most respondents worked for large organizations. Over half worked for businesses generating annual sales revenues of $250 million or more, the median sales revenue being $400 million. About 32 percent of the respondents' organizations were manufacturing concerns.

Almost 60 percent of the respondents were full-time risk managers with no additional duties. All respondents managed property and liability exposures, but only about 24 percent of the full-time risk managers (32 percent of the others) also had some responsibility for employee benefits. Because this text treats risk management as the identification, measurement, and treatment of potential property, liability, and personnel losses, the reader may be surprised to find that so many RIMS members are not involved in employee benefit plans. The reason is that personnel risk management is considered such a highly specialized topic and so closely related to personnel management that this phase of risk management is often assigned exclusively to specialists in the personnel department or shared by the risk management and personnel management departments. When the responsibility is shared, risk managers and related financial personnel are more likely than personnel departments to select the insurer and negotiate concerning the insurance or to administer the financial aspects of a program under which the employer retains the risk exposure. Such programs are called retention (or, to use a more popular term, self-insurance) programs. Personnel departments are more likely to take the lead in collective bargaining, establishing the eligibility requirements and benefits, and administering the daily operations. Three recent changes may increase the role of the risk management department. First, more recent types of employee benefit plans providing such benefits as homeowners' insurance, automobile insurance, and prepaid legal expenses are more closely related to traditional risk management concerns. Second, variable or cafeteria plans, explained in Chapter 22, are becoming more popular. Under these plans each employee selects his or her own benefit package within certain constraints. The individual negotiations required to implement these plans are more likely to require the skills of the risk management department. A third change is the increasing likelihood that property and liability exposures will be created or intensified by the employee benefit program. For example, a drug counseling program may create a liability exposure.[7]

A 1977 RIMS survey revealed more information on the responsibilities and authorities of risk managers.[8] Only 1 percent of the full-time risk managers in that survey said they were essentially insurance buyers with little authority even to select the

---

[6] *The Present Status and Future Role of Risk Management: A Survey of U.S. Risk Managers,* conducted by the Risk and Insurance Management Society, Inc., and *Time* magazine, April, 1981.

[7] T. B. Morehart and J. J. O'Connell, "The Risk Manager's Role in Employee Benefits Administration," *Risk Management,* vol. XXIV, no. 10 (October, 1977), pp. 42–46.

[8] *The Risk and Insurance Manager Position: A Study of Responsibilities and Compensation,* conducted for the Risk and Insurance Management Society, Inc. (Princeton: Sibson and Company, Inc., January, 1978). For more details on this survey see the fourth edition of this text.

TABLE 2.1
COMMON AREAS OF RESPONSIBILITY FOR FULL-TIME RISK MANAGERS

Risk determination and evaluation (identifying potential loss exposures and the size of the potential loss)

Risk financing (determining deductible levels and policy limits, whether to insure or retain the exposure, and placing insurance coverage)

Loss prevention engineering (designing mechanical systems and procedures to prevent or minimize loss or property from perils such as fire, explosion, or windstorm)

Security (administering security personnel and/or advising on security procedures to prevent or minimize loss or property from human perils such as crime, vandalism, or riot)

Safety administration (designing and/or administering systems and procedures to prevent or minimize loss from employee injuries and diseases, including review of compliance with government regulations)

Claims handling administration (liaison with insurer on all claims or administration of self-insured claims handling facilities)

Employee benefit plan design and/or administration

Administration of risk management unit program:
  Insurance accounting (premium allocation, loss statistics, and other recordkeeping functions)
  Unit budgeting
  Management of unit personnel (if more than two in the unit)

Source: The Risk and Insurance Manager Position: A Study of Responsibilities and Compensation, conducted for the Risk Management Society, Inc. (Princeton: Sibson and Company, Inc., January, 1978), p. 16.

insurer. Most had some responsibility for all the areas listed in Table 2.1 except for employee benefit plan design or administration.

Over 80 percent of the risk managers reported full authority for (1) risk determination and evaluation, (2) handling property and liability claims, and (3) administering the risk management unit. Over 80 percent reported full or shared authority for the following additional areas: (4) risk financing, (5) handling workers' compensation claims, and (6) handling product liability claims. Authority for loss prevention engineering, security, and safety administration was most likely to be advisory only or shared. Among those who had some responsibility for employee benefit plans, their authority was seldom full.

In the 1980 survey about 48 percent of all respondents claimed complete authority in the final selection of insurers; another 35 percent had partial authority. Only 39 percent had complete authority in the final selection of agents and brokers, but another 42 percent claimed partial authority.

In 1975, Professor John O'Connell conducted a more detailed survey of RIMS members.[9] His findings were similar to those of the 1977 survey, but the depth of his survey and his methodology permitted some additional observations about the differ-

[9] John J. O'Connell, *Variables Related to Differences in the Risk Management Function among Large Organizations,* unpublished doctoral dissertation, Ohio State University, 1975. The findings are summarized in articles appearing in *Risk Management* in December, 1975, and January, February, March, and April, 1976.

ences in risk management practices among different types of organizations. A major conclusion was that

> . . . the size of the organization surveyed did not seem to be a major determinant of risk management activity. . . . Some small organizations had more sophisticated risk manage- ment programs than did large firms. . . . A better indicator of risk management was the degree of risk that a firm faced. . . . Even though organizational size may determine some minimum level of work for a risk management department, the actual activities and the diversity of the function in any given firm are probably more related to the work environment than to any other variable.[10]

Firms facing the greatest risks because of their work environment tend to implement more comprehensive risk management programs.

Title and Qualifications of the Risk Manager   The administration of the risk management program is usually assigned to a top financial officer of the firm.

Almost two-thirds of the respondents in the 1980 RIMS survey had the title of manager; the next most popular title was director. About 10 percent were vice presidents and 4 percent were treasurers. Unlike previous surveys, more respondents reported titles including the word "risk" than "insurance." About 38 percent reported directly to a vice president, 18 percent to a treasurer, and 8 percent to the president.

About 86 percent of the respondents had attended college; about 23 percent had some postgraduate education. About 16 percent had completed the Associate in Risk Management program of the Insurance Institute of America; about 12 percent had earned the Chartered Property and Casualty Underwriter designation of the American Institute of Property and Liability Underwriters.

Size and Organization of the Department   The risk management department usually has a small staff. Of all the respondents in the 1980 RIMS survey, about 70 percent supervised a staff of five or fewer persons. The median number was 2.8.

"Seeking the proper risk management organization, like many other things, is similar to Ponce de Leon's search for the mythical fountain of youth. It does not exist. Instead it is an ever changing product of its environment."[11] Small staffs of one or two typically included the risk manager, an assistant, and a secretary; or the risk manager, a property and liability specialist, and an employee benefits specialist. Larger staffs may include, in addition to the risk manager and a secretary, a property and liability insurance manager, a loss control manager, and an employee benefits manager. The property and liability risk manager may have a staff of specialists in various lines of insurance. The employee benefits specialists may have subordinates specializing in pensions, death benefits, disability income benefits, medical expense benefits, and unemployment benefits. The loss-control manager may supervise specialists in control-

---

[10] John J. O'Connell, "Study Indicates Continuing Risk Management Movement," *Risk Management,* vol. XXIII, no. 4 (April, 1976), pp. 54–56. For more details on the "work environment," see Chap. 3 of this text.

[11] Russell A. Drake, Jr., "Factors Impacting on the Risk Management Function," *Risk Management,* vol. XXIV, no. 10 (October, 1977), p. 11.

ling fire and related losses, crime losses, industrial injury and diseases, and liability losses. Still larger staffs may include subspecialities in each of these areas.

Large diversified firms must decide whether to have a centralized or decentralized operation. Under a centralized operation the risk manager would supervise a staff operating for the most part out of the home office. Under a decentralized operation each subsidiary, division, branch, or plant would have a risk manager, each of whom would report to the corporate risk manager. Under a centralized operation the same philosophy and objectives are more likely to pervade all risk management decisions. The staff is likely to be smaller, more experienced, and better able to handle unusual problems. Centralization also makes possible some savings through quantity discounts and the use of blanket policies described in Chapter 17. On the other hand, having a risk management department at each subsidiary may provide more informed, prompt, personal attention to the problems arising at that level. The more geographically dispersed and the greater the diversity in the firm's operations, the stronger the case for decentralization. A common approach is a centralized operation except that loss control and foreign operations are handled by local people.[12] About 92 percent of the 1980 RIMS survey respondents considered their risk management function to be centralized; about 27 percent expected their function to become more centralized by 1985.

Policy Statements   Many businesses have policy statements promulgated by top management which define for their organization the risk management objectives and the duties and responsibilities of the risk manager. An example of such a statement is provided in Table 2.2. Professors Darwin Close and John O'Connell have identified five advantages of such a policy statement to an organization:[13]

1 Establishes explicitly the general goals and objectives of the risk management function within the organization
2 Defines the duties of the risk management department and its authorities and responsibilities
3 Coordinates risk treatment on a reasonably standardized basis among the various subdivisions of the organization
4 Establishes and improves communication channels and management information systems
5 Provides for program continuity and facilitates transition during times of department personnel changes

Such a policy statement aids the risk manager as follows:

1 Provides a framework within which to assess the risk manager's responsibility for uninsured or uncovered losses
2 Emphasizes the importance of the risk management function by alerting top

---

[12] M. R. Greene and O. N. Serbein, *Risk Management: Text and Cases* (2d ed., Reston, Va.: Reston Publishing Co., Inc., 1983) pp. 8–11. See also Chap. 31 of this text.
[13] D. B. Close and J. J. O'Connell, "A Guide to Formulation of Risk Management Policy Statements," *CPCU Annals* (September, 1976), pp. 195–200.

TABLE 2.2
GENERAL MILLS, INC., RISK MANAGEMENT POLICY STATEMENT

Activities of the Risk Management Department are influenced by the Company's general insurance philosophy which can be summarized as follows:

1 Eliminate or reduce as far as practicable the conditions and practices which cause insurable losses.
2 When risk cannot be eliminated or reduced to workable levels
   a Purchase commercial insurance that will provide idemnity for catastrophic losses,
   b Either insure or assume, whichever judgment indicates to be in the Company's best interest, those risks not considered to be of major importance individually to the operating or financial position of the Company.

But, in any event, to retain whatever portion of the risk for General Mills' account that premium reductions make economically attractive.

The Risk Management Department's responsibility for implementing this policy includes:

1 Assisting divisions and subsidiaries to design and operate fire control and loss prevention programs.
2 Reviewing new construction and facility alteration plans to assure risk control features and insurance acceptability.
3 Developing insurance coverage policies and programs and keeping them up to date to assure their effectiveness.
4 Negotiating and placing (or otherwise approving) all insurance contracts and bonds to assure conformity with established programs.
5 Reviewing foreign insurance programs.
6 Approving insurance provisions of leases and contracts prior to execution.
7 Reporting and adjusting all insurance claims.
8 Serving in an advisory capacity to the Corporate Accounting Department and subsidiaries to determine insurable values.
9 Administering and operating GMI's subsidiary insurance companies, Gold Medal Insurance Co., and Medallion Insurance Company Limited.

In carrying out these responsibilities, the Risk Management Department requires the cooperation of people throughout the subsidiaries, divisions, and departments for information, risk identification and analysis, and coordinated implementation.

---

management to the magnitude of the potential losses and the complexity of risk management decisions

3 Establishes the position of the risk management department at some specific point on the organization chart and specifies what rights and responsibilities the risk management department possesses in its dealings with other departments

Close and O'Connell also list six desirable characteristics of policy statements:

1 Explicitly states the objectives and plans of both the organization as a whole and the risk management department. As stated in Chapter 1, risk management policy should be a function of (1) corporate goals, (2) the corporate environment, and (3) specific company attributes.
2 Consistent internally and with other policy statements.
3 Flexible enough to be adaptable to change and to provide some discretionary

power for the risk manager. Too much flexibility, of course, is also to be avoided, because the statement would then provide little or no guidance.

4 Limited to goals and objectives. The procedures or steps to be taken to attain these goals and objectives should be left to the risk management department. To go further may prevent the manager from taking effective action and destroy his or her initiative.

5 Written. Preparing a written document forces a more careful policy statement and enables the statement to meet the needs of both the organization and the risk manager stated above. On the other hand, a written policy must be reviewed and updated periodically and at times may be interpreted too literally.

6 Communicated to all affected persons. This communication should take place while the policy is being formulated and after it goes into effect.

Different policy statements may be developed by different levels of management. For example, the risk manager commonly develops a more detailed policy statement that implements top management's general policy statement.

Only 41 percent of the 1980 RIMS survey respondents reported having a written risk management policy but over 74 percent expected one by 1985. Among those with written policies, over 53 percent had received Board of Directors' approval. Almost one-third of the other 46 percent expected such approval in the next five years.

Records and Reports[14] Risk managers in large firms keep records of various sorts. Among the most important are lists of insurance contracts, including their expiration dates, valuation records showing the value and location of all property in which the firm has a financial interest, personnel records on the firm's employees, comprehensive analyses of the different types of losses faced by the firm (see Chapter 3), and data on past losses. Loss data are useful in determining potential future loss frequency and severity (see Chapters 3 and 4), selecting the proper tool of risk management (see Chapters 13 and 14), obtaining the lowest possible prices from insurers (see Chapter 28), and designing loss-control programs (see Chapter 10).

Many risk managers have compiled manuals that contain the firm's policy statement, present in summary form the total risk management program (the major provisions of insurance contracts purchased, public insurance programs such as a state workers' compensation fund in which the business is a participant, loss-control programs, a brief description of federal and state acts affecting the risk management program, and the employee benefit program), and describe the obligations of the risk management department and other divisions under this program. Such manuals are useful as a reference and educational device. Their preparation also forces a comprehensive review of the total program and emphasizes departmental interrelationships. These interrelationships necessitate many reports among the various departments dealing with risk management. For example, if the firm plans to purchase a new plant,

[14] Based largely on papers by James Cristy and C. H. Austin in *The Growing Job of Risk Management,* AMA Management Report no. 70 (New York: American Management Association, 1962), and on Douglas I. Craven, *Guidelines for Developing an Insurance Manual* (New York: Risk and Insurance Management Society, 1975).

ideally the risk manager should be informed and involved in the decision. About 38 percent of the 1980 RIMS survey respondents had risk management manuals; another 34 percent expected to develop such manuals by 1985.

The Medium- or Small-Sized Business Firm

Whereas the principles of risk management are the same regardless of the size of the business, many important differences exist in the application of these principles to risk management problems in business firms of different sizes. In a small sole proprietorship, where the owner may operate the business, the decisions in the insurance and pure-risk areas must be made and implemented by this one person. In this situation, division of labor is not possible. Small sole proprietors must to the best of their ability perform all the functions of business management, including accounting, finance, and marketing. Usually they must rely upon outside advisers or experts to give them the technical information necessary for the conduct of their business affairs. In the risk management area they will often rely upon local insurance agents and brokers, their bankers, or their public accountants to identify the pure risks they face and to suggest how they should be handled. In addition, their attorneys often will give them information that will be helpful in dealing with the various legal exposures they may encounter.

As businesses increase in size, more division of labor develops among the specific affairs of the firm, including the risk management function. Small- and medium-sized firms, however, are at best likely to have a part-time risk manager on their staff. As noted earlier, however, some small firms operating in a dynamic, heterogeneous environment tend to have sophisticated risk management programs.

Evaluation of Performance

Because risk managers make decisions under uncertainty, much of their performance is difficult to evaluate in the short run. For example, suppose a risk manager decides not to purchase collision insurance on a low-valued automobile that is damaged in an accident the next day. The risk manager and superiors will regret the fact that the firm must bear this loss itself, but the decision may have been the correct one. If the risk manager were to make the same decision year after year, the premium savings might well exceed the collision losses. One way, therefore, to judge the performance of risk managers is to compare average results over a long period of time. Another is to determine whether they successfully avoid disruptions in cash flows or profits that go beyond the tolerances of their firms. In the short run the best procedure may be to evaluate how they perform the five steps in the risk management process. Is their performance consistent with the objectives stated in the firm's risk management policy statement? Are they rational in their decision making? Are they well informed on matters relating to risk management? Do they communicate satisfactorily with other managers? How well do they manage their own staffs and their operations? How have they performed compared with risk managers in other firms? These evaluations are best made as part of a periodic independent audit of the risk management function in the firm.[15]

The Future

The risk management function continues to grow in importance and complexity. One reason is that top management is becoming more cost conscious and more aware of how sound risk management helps to minimize expenses. Risk management has also shared in the increasing attention paid to such areas as cash flows, capital budgeting, employee benefit plans, social responsibility, and social insurance programs. Other reasons for the rise of risk management are several that create new exposures or expand or complicate existing ones. Examples are inflation, technological developments, social forces such as rising crime rates and claim consciousness, mergers and other acquisitions that concentrate more property and activities under one ownership, and legislation such as the Consumer Product Safety Act and the Occupational Safety and Health Act, which are described in Chapters 7 and 10, respectively. According to a 1973 *Fortune* survey about 86 percent of the Top 500 industrial corporations and 58 percent of the Second 500 already have foreign operations.[16] These foreign operations complicate the task of the risk manager; they also make that task more interesting. For example, as will be explained in Chapter 31, the risk environment may be substantially different, distance may create communication problems, local laws may limit the insurance arrangements that can be made, and foreign exchange problems may cause difficulties.

As the risk manager's responsibility has become more important, so has risk management education. The Risk and Insurance Management Society, the leading association of risk managers, currently includes over 3,800 member companies in about 77 chapters throughout the United States and Canada. Corporate members include 90 percent of the top *Fortune* 1,300 companies. The Society publishes a journal entitled *Risk Management,* conducts numerous conferences and seminars, engages in legislative activities, and sponsors with the Insurance Institute of America a program in risk management leading to a special designation. Until 1975 the Society was known as the American Society of Insurance Management. Both the membership and the activities of the Society have increased dramatically in recent years.

The American Management Association also has a separate insurance and employee benefits division that holds conferences on many subjects relating to the risk management function. This section has also published a series of bulletins dealing with insurance and risk management.

---

[15] "AMFAC Executive Recommends Five-Year Risk Manager Audit," *Journal of Commerce* (May 3, 1974), p. 2. See also Russell B. Gallagher, *Auditing the Corporate Insurance Function,* AMA Research Study 68 (New York: American Management Association, 1964), and Darwin B. Close, "Evaluating the Risk Management Fuction," *Risk Management* vol. XXIV, no. 6 (June, 1977), pp. 21–28.

[16] *How Major Industrial Corporations View Property/Liability Insurance,* (New York: Market Research Department, *Fortune,* 1973), p. 27.

At least one magazine[17] and six looseleaf risk management periodicals[18] deal with matters of direct concern to risk managers.

THE RELATIONSHIP OF RISK MANAGEMENT
TO OTHER FUNCTIONS

The discussion now turns to specific relationships between risk management and six other management functions: (1) accounting, (2) finance, (3) marketing, (4) production, (5) engineering and maintenance, and (6) personnel. These relationships are important because these departments perform part of the total risk management function and may create exposures of which the risk manager should be aware.

Accounting Department

The accounting department performs many important risk management activities. Through various internal auditing controls the accounting department attempts to reduce the opportunities for employee fraud. Illustrations of this loss-control technique include comparison of invoices with purchase orders, checking disbursements for proper authorizations, and comparison of cash receipts with postings to customer accounts. Through asset accounts the accounting department identifies and measures property loss exposures. Through valuation accounts such as the allowance for bad debts, the department recognizes the probable cost of retaining certain loss exposures. By allocating risk management costs among the various departments of the firm, the accounting department helps the risk manager monitor the performance of the risk management program and isolate problem areas. Decisions on the amount of loss a firm may safely retain must be based in part on an analysis of the financial statements prepared by the accounting department. The accounting department is less likely than the others to create special loss exposures. However, computers and other expensive equipment used by accountants may create important property loss exposures. The firm may be sued because of faulty information supplied by the accounting department, which misleads investors or creditors.

Finance Department

The finance department makes many determinations affecting risk management. First, the risk manager normally reports to a financial vice president. For this reason risk management is sometimes considered a part of financial management. Even where this view prevails, however, the special characteristics of risk management are usually

---

[17] *Business Insurance,* weekly.
[18] *Insurance Buyer's Guide* (Chicago: Cudahy Publishing Co., periodically); *John Liner Letter* (Wellesley, Mass.: Shelby Publishing Company, monthly); *Practical Risk Management* (San Francisco: Warren, McVeigh, Griffin, and Huntington, monthly); *Rimco Risk Report* (Dallas: Rimco Risk Management Inc., monthly); *Risk Management Manual* (Santa Monica: Merrit Company, bimonthly); *Risk Management Reports* (Darien, Conn.: Risk Planning Group, bimonthly). Similar publications are available in specialized areas such as municipal risk management.

recognized. Second, it is the finance department, using accounting information, that analyzes the effect of disruptions in profits and cash flow. The levels beyond which such disruptions would interfere with the firm's goals are critical benchmarks for the risk manager and the risk management program. Third, in determining whether the firm should purchase some expensive equipment or a new building, the financial manager considers (or should consider) the pure loss exposures created by these actions. Fourth, if the firm borrows money using property as collateral, the lender will usually insist that its interest in the property be protected by insurance. The finance department must arrange for this protection as part of the negotiation or proposal. This fourth example might also be considered to be a way in which the finance department creates special loss exposures. Otherwise, the finance department resembles the accounting department in this respect.

Marketing Department

The marketing department's principal involvement is the creation of loss exposures, identification of these exposures, and loss-control efforts designed to minimize their effects. In marketing the product or service, the marketing department may use defective packaging that leads to liability claims. It may overstate the advantages or uses of the product or fail to state certain dangers associated with some uses. Through a so-called hold-harmless agreement with other businesses (manufacturers, wholesalers, or distributors) the marketing department, in its eagerness to sell, may accept some legal responsibilities that it would otherwise not have to bear. (The reader will note that from the point of view of the other party, a loss exposure has been handled via a noninsurance transfer.) In transporting the product to customers, the marketing department exposes the firm to some important losses, a typical example being the exposure to loading and unloading accidents. The marketing department may also handle purchasing activities, in which case it may also assume under contracts some liability exposures the firm would not otherwise have. Marketing departments should be aware of the loss exposures they are creating and should keep the risk management department informed. By using more care in the selling or distribution of the product or service, they may reduce the probability of a loss or potential severity without diminishing marketing effectiveness. Finally, in pricing the goods or services sold, a function usually assigned to the marketing department, this department should recognize risk management costs. Recognizing these costs gives the firm a true picture of the contribution each product makes to the firm's profits, and the areas where loss control efforts are most badly needed.

Production Department

The production department is in a somewhat similar position. In designing and manufacturing the product or service, this department typically exposes its employees to frequent and often serious injuries. The product it manufactures or the service it provides may cause property damage or bodily injury to others, who may then seek legal redress. The department should identify and evaluate the dangers associated with both the product or service, and the process by which they are created. Safer production lines, more careful design, and tighter controls illustrate loss control efforts associated with the production department.

Engineering and Maintenance Department

The department (or departments) responsible for plant design, physical maintenance, and housekeeping performs functions that are critical in reducing the frequency and severity of losses.

Personnel Department

The personnel department has many risk management responsibilities. The clearest example is the design, installation, and administration of employee benefit programs. Although some firms give the risk manager full responsibility for employee benefit programs, most firms give the personnel department full or shared responsibility for these plans. As stated earlier, where risk managers and the personnel department share responsibility for these plans the personnel department usually negotiates the benefits with a union, establishes the eligibility requirements and benefits, and administers the daily operations. The risk manager selects the insurer and negotiates the coverage or manages the financial aspects of a retention program.

As the department commonly assigned responsibility for selection and training of personnel, the personnel department also plays an important role in controlling job-related injuries and diseases. In many cases this department is assigned direct responsibility for employee safety and industrial hygiene. In other cases it shares this responsibility with the engineering or risk management department. The personnel department also seeks ways to minimize absenteeism and unemployment. Some of these activities also create loss exposures. For example, the design and administration of a pension plan, if improperly handled, can result in successful suits against the firm by aggrieved employees.

Need for Two-Way Communications among Risk Manager and Others

These myriad relationships between the risk manager and other managers show why there must be continuous, systematic two-way communications between them and why risk management in its broad sense is performed throughout the firm. This text is concerned with the risk management function no matter where that function is performed. Future chapters, therefore, are organized according to the steps in the risk management process, not by what department or division performs the step.

Outside Services and Consultants

The risk management department must also relate to outsiders who (1) help perform the risk management function or (2) create additional exposures through services provided other departments.

The smaller and less sophisticated the risk management department, the more heavily the firm will tend to rely upon insurers, insurance agents, or brokers (see Chapter 26) to handle the risk management function. Even larger, sophisticated departments may find these services extremely useful. Among the many services the risk manager might be able to obtain from these insurers, agents, or brokers are (1) the identification and measurement of loss exposures, (2) suggestions on how to handle these exposures, (3) obtaining insurance, when that is considered the proper approach, from the best insurer under the best policy and the best pricing method, (4) loss-control services, (5) claims adjustment services, (6) assistance in meeting legal requirements (such as the filing of proof of financial responsibility under a compulsory automobile insurance or workers' compensation law), and (7) management services (such as administering a retention program).[19] Many insurers, agents, and brokers have developed risk management departments or subsidiaries that specialize in risk management services.

In addition to insurers, agents, and brokers, a number of other organizations sell general or, more often, specialized risk management services.[20] Some risk management consultants are prepared to assume all the duties of risk manager for a firm with no such "in-house" capability. They also conduct special projects for businesses that have their own risk manager, including performance audits of the risk management department. Other consultants concentrate on the financial, control, and claims administration of retention programs. Still others specialize in controlling industrial injuries and meeting OSHA requirements, analyzing loss experience and estimating probable future experience, appraising property, controlling crime losses, establishing and maintaining accounting records, and providing legal advice on the exposures created by certain activities.

Outsiders have the advantage of being more objective, being better able to concentrate on a particular problem, and having wider experience based on work with many firms. On the other hand, internal management is still responsible for the actions taken. Insiders should know the distinctive aspects of the firm better than outsiders, and the use of outsiders *may* increase risk management costs.

The risk manager must also be concerned with outside services performed for other divisions of the firm, because the use of these services may create additional risks for the firm. For example, the use of independent contract labor or independent contract hauling, the renting of property, or the use of rented equipment including data-processing machines may result in substantial liability. Here, again, it is important that the risk manager obtain the services of the legal department or of outside legal representatives to examine the nature of such contracts in order to see that the interests of the firm are properly protected, either by insurance or by hold-harmless clauses in these arrangements.

---

[19] C. A. Williams, Jr., G. L. Head, and G. W. Glendenning, *Principles of Risk Management and Insurance,* vol. 1 (Malvern, Pa.: American Institute for Property and Liability Underwriters, 1979), pp 52–55.
[20] Robert I. Mehr and Bob A. Hedges, *Risk Management: Concepts and Applications* (Homewood, Ill.: Richard D. Irwin, Inc., 1974), pp. 220–223, and 248.

SOME KEY CONCEPTS

Security function One of the six basic management functions listed by Henri Fayol in 1916. Risk management is the modern version of the security function.

Risk management policy statement A statement of (1) the risk management objectives of a business and (2) the authority and responsibility of the risk manager.

REVIEW QUESTIONS

1 "Even if risk management is defined in the narrow sense to mean the management of pure risks only, this function is not confined to one department of the firm." Comment on this statement.
2 Smith is a member of the board of directors of a medium-sized corporation, whose stock is publicly traded. What personal interest does Smith have in the proposal of the risk manager?
3 Is the risk management department usually responsible for employee benefit plans? Explain.
4 List the common areas of responsibility of full-time risk managers.
5 For what areas do most full-time risk managers have full authority? For what areas is their authority commonly shared with others?
6 According to the O'Connell study, what characteristic of a firm most determines the degree of sophistication of its risk management program?
7 **a** What are the advantages of a risk management policy statement to the business? To the risk manager?
  b Prepare a checklist for evaluating a risk management policy statement.
8 What types of records do risk managers usually keep? Why?
9 In what respects does the risk management function in the small- or medium-sized firm differ from the same function in a large corporation?
10 The ABC Corporation wishes to evaluate the performance of its risk manager who has held that position for two years. What would you recommend?
11 The accounting department serves risk management in two ways: (1) It provides information that the risk manager needs in order to perform his or her function, and (2) it applies some of the tools of risk management itself. Cite one illustration of each of these two services.
12 The chief financial officer of a business has reason to be interested in the activities of the risk manager and vice versa. Support this statement with illustrations.
13 The marketing division of the firm may create many risks about which the risk manager should be informed. Cite some examples of these risks.
14 In many firms the personnel department is almost as deeply involved in risk management as is the risk management department. Explain this statement.
15 The production department is actively concerned with the application of one tool of risk management. What is this tool?
16 What outside services might the risk manager use in his or her work?
17 Why should the risk manager be concerned about outside services used by other divisions in the firm?

SUGGESTIONS FOR ADDITIONAL READING

Baglini, N. A.: *Risk Management in American Multinational and International Corporations* (New York: Risk Studies Foundation, 1976).

————: *Global Risk Management* (New York: Risk Management Society Publishing, Inc., 1983).

Carter, R. L., and N. A. Doherty (eds.): *Handbook of Risk Management* (London: Kluwer-Harrop Handbooks, 1974), pt. 3.

Fayol, Henri: *General and Industrial Management* (New York: Pitman Publishing Corporation, 1949).

Flippo, Edwin B.: *Principles of Personnel Management* (5th ed., New York: McGraw-Hill Book Company, 1984).

Greene, M. R., and O. N. Serbein: *Risk Management: Text and Cases* (2d ed., Reston, Va.: Reston Publishing Co., Inc., 1983).

How Major Industrial Corporations View Property/Liability Insurance (New York: Market Research Department, *Fortune,* 1973).

Mayer, R. R.: *Production and Operations Management* (4th ed., New York: McGraw-Hill Book Company, 1981).

Mehr, R. I., and B. A. Hedges: *Risk Management: Concepts and Applications* (Homewood, Ill.: Richard D. Irwin, Inc., 1974), chap. 2.

Meigs, W. B., and R. F. Meigs: *Accounting: The Basis for Business Decisions* (6th ed., New York: McGraw-Hill Book Company, 1984).

Schall, L. D., and C. W. Haley: *Introduction to Financial Management* (3d ed., New York: McGraw-Hill Book Company, 1983).

Stanton, William J.: *Fundamentals of Marketing* (7th ed., New York: McGraw-Hill Book Company, 1984).

The Risk and Insurance Manager Position: A Study of Responsibilities and Compensation, conducted for the Risk and Insurance Management Society, Inc. (Princeton: Sibson and Company, Inc., January, 1978).

Williams, C. A., Jr., G. L. Head, R. C. Horn, and G. W. Glendenning: *Principles of Risk Management,* (2d ed., Malvern, Pa.: American Institute for Property and Liability Underwriters, 1981), vol. 1, chap. 1.

Wyatt, J. W., and M. B. Wyatt: *Business Law* (6th ed., New York: McGraw-Hill Book Company, 1979).

B. Risk Identification and Measurement Fundamentals and Applications

CHAPTER 3

RISK IDENTIFICATION AND MEASUREMENT FUNDAMENTALS

LEARNING OBJECTIVES:

After you have completed this chapter, you should be able to:

1 Interpret or develop a checklist of loss exposures.
2 Apply the financial statement or other methods to determine an organization's major exposures to loss.
3 Explain why a risk manager needs to measure these loss exposures, what two dimensions must be measured, and why each of these two dimensions should be measured.
4 Describe briefly some of the more common ways used in practice to measure loss frequency and loss severity.

INTRODUCTION

The first step in business risk management is to identify the various types of potential losses confronting the firm; the second step is to measure these potential losses with respect to such matters as their likelihood of occurrence and their probable severity. This chapter and the next chapter discuss certain approaches and yardsticks that might be used to identify and measure exposures to loss; Chapters 5 through 9 will identify and analyze the property, liability, and personnel loss exposures of a typical business.

RISK IDENTIFICATION

Risk identification is the process by which a business *systematically* and *continuously* identifies property, liability, and personnel exposures as soon as or before they emerge. Unless the risk manager identifies all the potential losses confronting the firm, he or she will not have any opportunity to determine the best way to handle the undiscovered risks. The business will unconsciously retain these risks, and this may not be the best or even a good thing to do. To identify all the potential losses the risk manager needs first a checklist of all the losses that could occur to any business. Second, he or she needs a systematic approach to discover which of the potential losses included in the checklist are faced by his or her business. The risk manager may personally conduct this two-step procedure or may rely upon the services of an insurance agent, broker, or consultant.

Checklist of Potential Losses

Checklists of potential losses are published by (1) individual insurers, (2) insurance publishing houses, (3) the Insurance and Employee Benefits Division of the American Management Association, and (4) the Risk and Insurance Management Society.

Section Three of the American Management Association's *Risk Analysis Guide to Insurance and Employee Benefits,* by A. E. Pfaffle and Sal Nicosia, provides a checklist of (1) possible assets and (2) possible exposures to loss.[1] This "Assets-Exposure Analysis" checklist is reproduced in Appendix A. The possible assets are divided into two major categories: physical assets and intangible assets, with numerous subcategories. The possible exposures to loss are classified as (1) direct exposures, (2) indirect or consequential exposures, and (3) third-party liabilities. According to the classification system used in this text, these three categories are (1) direct property exposures, (2) indirect property exposures and net income exposures, and (3) liability exposures. Personnel exposures are not included in the AMA list, which is designed primarily for the analysis of property and liability exposures.

Section Two of this guide is a "Risk Analysis Questionnaire" which contains a list of questions designed (1) to remind the risk manager of possible loss exposures, (2) to gather information that will describe in what way and to what extent the particular business is exposed to that potential loss, and (3) to summarize the existing insurance program including premiums paid and losses incurred. For example, here are some sample (paraphrased) questions:

If a building is leased from someone else, does the lease make the firm responsible for repair or restoration of damage not resulting from its own negligence?

Are company-owned vehicles furnished to directors, executives, or employees for business and personal use? If so, to what extent?

Are there any key service facilities or warehouses whose function must continue even though the structures and equipment may be damaged?

Indicate the maximum amount of money, checks, and securities that may be on hand in any one office during and outside business hours.

Indicate premiums and losses during the past four years for any excess workers' compensation insurance policies carried.

---

[1] A. E. Pfaffle and Sal Nicosia, *Risk Analysis Guide to Insurance and Employee Benefits* (New York: Amacom, 1977).

Part of this questionnaire asks the risk manager questions that summarize the eligibility requirements, benefits, and financial experience of employee benefit plans. Most checklists published by insurers and insurance publishing houses are part of a similar risk questionnaire that serves a broader purpose than merely providing a checklist of potential losses.

The Risk and Insurance Management Society has published *Fact-Finding Questionnaire for Risk Managers,* written by Bernard J. Daenzer, which may also prove highly useful to many risk managers.[2]

Instead of using published checklists, the risk manager may wish to develop one of his or her own. This is a time-consuming task, but developing a checklist enables the risk manager to add potential losses that are not included in the published checklists. *Some* published checklists are limited to insurable risks (sometimes readily insurable and sometimes insurable by a single insurer). Risk management requires a wider horizon. By using published checklists as a starting point, however, the risk manager should be able to avoid omitting any of the more common types of losses. A second reason for constructing one's own checklist is that the questions can be arranged in a manner that is most meaningful to the risk manager. Published questionnaires tend to organize the questions on potential losses into sections dictated by the types of insurance available, such as fire insurance, automobile insurance, and crime insurance. One alternative consumer-oriented classification system is the following:

A Property losses
  1 Direct losses associated with the need to replace or repair damaged or missing property
  2 Indirect losses, such as the need to demolish the remainder of a building suffering a severe direct loss
  3 Net income losses, such as the interruption of business because of a direct loss causing a building to be untenantable
B Liability losses arising out of damage to or destruction of others' property or personal injuries to others
C Personnel losses
  1 Losses to the firm itself as a result of the death, disability, or old age of employees, customers, or owners
  2 Losses to the families of personnel or to the personnel themselves as a result of their death, disability, old age, or unemployment

In Chapters 5 through 9 the major property, liability, and personnel exposures of a business will be analyzed according to this outline. This analysis can be the basis either for creating a new checklist or for better understanding some published checklist.

A risk manager who decides to construct his or her own checklist will need more than a good imagination. Existing checklists provide a good starting point. The risk manager should also study the losses already incurred by his or her firm and the losses

---

[2] Bernard John Daenzer, *Fact-Finding Questionnaire for Risk Managers* (New York: Risk and Insurance Management Society, 1978).

reported by such publications as *Business Insurance* and *Risk Management*. Attending chapter or national meetings of risk managers and informal meetings with other risk managers should also generate some ideas.[3]

Application of Checklist

The second step in risk identification is to use the checklist developed in step 1 to discover and describe the types of losses faced by a particular business. In some instances the person applying the checklist is so familiar with the property, operations, and personnel of the business that he or she can identify its risks by taking each item in the checklist and reflecting on the ways in which the business is exposed to that potential loss. However, because most businesses are complex, diversified, dynamic operations, a more systematic method of exploring all facets of the specific firm is highly desirable. Six methods that have been suggested are (1) the risk analysis questionnaire, (2) the financial-statement method, (3) the flow-chart method, (4) on-site inspections, (5) planned interactions with other departments, (6) statistical records of past losses, and (7) analysis of the environment.

Before each of these methods is explored, three points should be emphasized. First, the risk manager should not rely upon any one method. Timely information from other departments, for example, may reveal an exposure the financial-statement method would miss. Each method supplements the other. Second, risk identification is a continuing process. The exposures may change from day to day. Third, applying the checklist of potential losses to the firm's exposures may suggest some gaps in the checklist itself that should be corrected.

The Risk Analysis Questionnaire   The risk analysis questionnaire does more than provide a checklist of potential losses. It directs the risk manager to secure in a systematic fashion specific information concerning the firm's properties and operations. To secure this information the risk manager will consider all the sources of information used in the other five methods. The difference is that the questions in the questionnaire direct the inquiry.

The Financial-Statement Method   A second systematic procedure for determining which of the potential losses in the checklist apply to a particular firm and in what way is the financial-statement method proposed by A. H. Criddle.[4] By analyzing the

---

[3] Some analysts use insurance *policy* checklists to determine potential losses. The most useful policy checklists are those that group policies according to the types of exposures to which they apply (for example, banks, families, or department stores). If the person reading the list knows the types of losses covered under each contract, he or she is alerted to the most important types of risks faced by businesses of this sort. This, however, is an awkward, inefficient way to identify the relevant potential losses. Furthermore, it identifies, at best, only all insurable risks. On the other hand, these checklists provide an extremely useful listing of the insurance contracts to be considered in selecting the proper tool. See, for example, R. C. McCormick, *Coverages Applicable* (Indianapolis: The Rough Notes Company, revised periodically).

[4] A. Hawthorne Criddle, "A Theory of Risk Discovery," *National Insurance Buyer*, vol. VI, no. 1 (January, 1959), pp. 8, 14–18, 31, 35, 39. The concept was more fully developed in A. H. Criddle, "The Use of Financial Statements in Corporate Risk Analysis," *Identifying and Controlling the Risks of Accidental Loss*, AMA Report no. 73 (New York: American Management Association, 1962).

balance sheet, operating statements, and supporting records, Criddle maintains, the risk manager can identify all the *existing* property, liability, and personnel exposures of the firm. By coupling these statements with financial forecasts and budgets, the risk manager can discover *future* exposures. This follows because every business transaction ultimately involves either money or property.

Under this method each account title is studied in depth to determine what potential losses it creates. The results of the study are reported under the account titles. Criddle argues that this approach is reliable, objective, based upon readily available data, presentable in clear, concise terms, and applicable by either risk managers or professional consultants. Moreover it translates risk identification into financial terminology that is more familiar, and consequently should be more acceptable, to other managers in the firm and to outsiders such as accountants and bankers. Finally, in addition to aiding in risk identification, financial statements are useful in risk measurement and determining the best way to handle the exposure.

Criddle recognizes that the risk manager must supplement the financial records with other sources of information such as an inspection of the premises or legal documents. His thesis is that analyzing the financial statements will suggest these additional steps.

The following analysis illustrates in abbreviated fashion how one account title, coupled with some appreciation of the various losses that could occur, can help to identify potential losses:

Account title	Specific property, Personnel, or activity	Potential loss	Peril

Inventory	Raw materials:
	  In suppliers' hands
	  In transit to warehouses in
	    suppliers' trucks
	  Warehouse
	  In transit to manufacturing
	    plant in firm's own trucks
	  Manufacturing plant
		Property losses
		  Direct
		  Indirect
		  Net income
			Fire, windstorm, explosion, other physical perils Vandalism, risk, burglary, other human perils

	Finished goods:
	  Manufacturing plant
	  In transit to warehouse
	    Firm's own trucks
	    Common carrier
	  Warehouse
	  In transit to retailers
	    Firm's own trucks
	    Common carrier
	  In independent retailers'
	    hands
		Liability losses arising out of trucks, premises, products, injuries to employees	Negligence Breach of warranty Injuries to employees (workers' compensation) Automobile accidents (no fault)

		Personnel losses to firm/family	Death, poor health, unemployment, retirement

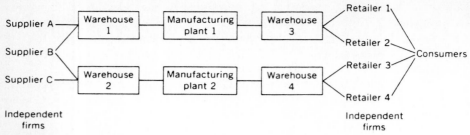

FIGURE 3.1
Flow chart—total operations. (The marketing, accounting, and other supporting managerial functions are not shown explicitly in this diagram, but their presence should be recognized.)

The Flow-Chart Method   A third systematic procedure for identifying the potential losses facing a particular firm is the flow-chart approach.[5] First, a flow chart or series of flow charts is constructed, which shows all the operations of the firm, starting with raw materials, electricity, and other inputs at suppliers' locations and ending with finished products in the hands of customers. For example, Figure 3.1 shows the major operations of a hypothetical firm. Figure 3.2 is a more detailed picture of one part of those operations. More detailed pictures can and should be prepared. Second, the checklist of potential property, liability, and personnel losses is applied to each property and operation shown in the flow chart to determine which losses the firm faces. For example, Figure 3.1 suggests, among others, the following potential losses:

Property losses:
Replacement or repair of trucks, manufacturing plant, machinery, raw materials, goods in process, or finished goods, subject to physical and human perils on the manufacturing premises or in transit
Shutdown or slowdown of manufacturing operations because of direct property losses
Liability losses:
Liability for bodily injury or property damage to customers because of defective products, to visitors because of defects in the premises, and to others because of negligent operation of the firm's trucks
Legal responsibility under (1) the workers' compensation law for bodily injuries to employees and (2) automobile no-fault laws
Personnel losses:
Losses to firm because of death or disability of key employees
Losses to families of employees because of death, poor health, retirement, or unemployment of employees

[5] A. J. Ingley, "Problems of Risk Analysis," *The Growing Job of Risk Management*, AMA Management Report no. 70 (New York: American Management Association, 1962), pp. 137–138. After describing how a flow chart can be used to identify risks, Ingley, an experienced risk manager, states that the "question is not simply what *could* happen but how often and to what extent. You also want to know what effect it would have on your company's health." This is the task of risk measurement.

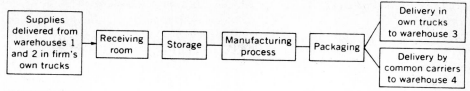

FIGURE 3.2
Flow chart—manufacturing plant 1.

On-Site Inspections   On-site inspections are a must for the risk manager. By observing firsthand the firm's facilities and the operations conducted thereon the risk manager can learn much about the exposures faced by the firm.

Interactions with Other Departments   A fifth way to identify the losses facing a business is through systematic and continuous interactions with other departments in the business. Included among these interactions are (1) extended visits with managers and employees of other departments during which the risk manager attempts to obtain a complete understanding of their activities and the potential losses created by these activites, and (2) oral or written reports from other departments on their own initiative or in response to a regular reporting system that keeps the risk manager informed of all relevant developments. These departments are constantly creating or becoming aware of exposures that might otherwise escape the risk manager's attention. Indeed the risk manager's success in risk identification is heavily dependent upon the cooperation he or she secures from other departments.

Unfortunately risk managers often hear about new exposures long after they are created. For example, one risk manager was surprised to learn from his morning newspaper that his employer had purchased an expensive river barge two weeks earlier. As a result, for two weeks the firm was exposed to some serious property, liability, and personnel losses that were ignored in its risk management planning. Moreover, if these losses had been explicitly considered, the firm might have decided not to buy the barge.

Statistical Records of Losses   A sixth approach that will probably suggest fewer exposures than the others but which may identify some exposures not otherwise discovered is to consult statistical records of losses or near losses that may be repeated in the future.

Analysis of the Environment   Professor John O'Connell has recommended a careful analysis of the external environment as well as internal exposures as an approach to identifying the exposures of a particular firm.[6] Following a structure suggested by Dr. William Dill, Dr. O'Connell identifies four components of the

---

[6] John J. O'Connell, ''Systematic Risk Identification,''*Risk Management*, vol. XXIII, no. 3 (March, 1976), pp. 34–36.

''relevant'' environment: (1) customers, (2) suppliers, (3) competitors, and (4) regulators.[7] In analyzing each component, important considerations are the nature of the relationships, their heterogeneity, and their stability. For example, is the product distributed directly to one group of buyers or indirectly, through wholesalers and retailers, to many persons? Are the customers families, businesses, or government agencies? Are there single or multiple suppliers of important services? What contractual arrangements have been made with suppliers? Does competition with others require speedy advertising campaigns and possibly encourage improper product claims? What special obligations are imposed by outsiders such as government regulators, consumers, and unions? How rapidly are these relationships changing?

Use of Outsiders to Identify Loss Exposures

A risk manager may rely on insurance agents or brokers or risk management consultants to do the detailed work of risk identification.[8] Some advantages (objectivity, ability to concentrate on the assigned task, and broad experience) and disadvantages (risk manager still responsible, risk manager better informed about distinctive aspects of the firm and possibly higher costs) were listed in Chapter 2. The reason that costs may or may not be higher is that agents and brokers may be paid for this service through the commissions they receive whether they render this service or not. Risk management consultants, on the other hand, charge a fee for their services. Furthermore, an increasing number of agents and brokers receive a fee in addition to or in place of a commission.[9]

Relying completely on outsiders, however, for risk identification may have some other important disadvantages. First, although many agents and brokers have demonstrated far more imagination than most risk managers in uncovering exposures to loss, some limit their analyses to insurable risks. This observation is less applicable to risk management consultants who tend to be less insurance-oriented. Furthermore, the number of agents and brokers who are risk management oriented is increasing. Second, because of the time and the energy that must be expended in preparing a comprehensive survey, particularly for a large firm, many insurance agents and brokers who depend upon commissions paid by an insurer will be understandably reluctant to undertake this task unless they have a reasonable chance of providing at least part of the insurance suggested by the survey. Until the risk manager has had an opportunity to do some informed thinking about potential losses and the ways in which they might be handled, he or she may not be prepared to limit the firm's access to insurers in any way. As noted above, however, like risk management consultants, many agents and brokers will now provide this service for a fee without any commitment regarding the placement of insurance.

A more satisfactory approach, where it is possible, is for the risk manager to prepare

---

[7] For the relationship between this environment and risk management objectives, see the Close and O'Connell reference in Chap. 2, fn. 13.

[8] See Chap. 26 for a discussion of insurance agents, brokers, and consultants.

[9] See Chaps. 26 and 27.

his or her own analysis first and to check this analysis with an outsider survey solicited after the risk manager is better acquainted with the firm's needs and the possible solutions to loss-exposure problems. Preparation of an independent survey is time-consuming, difficult work, but there is no better way to capitalize on the risk manager's intimate knowledge of his or her firm's property, operations, and management philosophy. The preparation of a survey will also give the risk manager a much better appreciation of the potential losses facing the firm than any survey by an outsider can give; he or she will be much better able to notice changes in potential losses and should be able to make more intelligent decisions with respect to possible solutions.

The Best Method

No single method or procedure of risk identification is free of weaknesses or can be called foolproof. The strategy of management must be to employ that method or combination of methods that best fits the situation at hand. The choice is a function of (1) the nature of the business, (2) the size of the business, and (3) the availability of in-house expertise. For example, published checklists and outsiders are used more frequently by smaller firms that cannot afford to have the task done by specialists in their own management structure. Larger firms with a more sophisticated risk management department may show more originality in identification procedures.

RISK MEASUREMENT

After the risk manager has identified the various types of potential losses faced by his or her firm, these exposures must be measured in order (1) to determine their relative importance and (2) to obtain information that will help the risk manager to decide upon the most desirable combination of risk management tools.

Dimensions to Be Measured

Information is needed concerning two dimensions of each exposure: (1) the loss frequency or the number of losses that will occur and (2) the severity of those losses. For each of these two dimensions it would be desirable to know at least the value in an average budget period and the variation in the values from one budget period to the next. The total impact of these losses if they should be retained, not only their dollar value, should be included in the analysis.

The next chapter will investigate how probability distributions might be used to measure these potential losses; the present chapter tells why we need information on each of these dimensions and describes one approach to measuring loss frequency and loss severity.

Why We Need Each Dimension

Both loss-frequency and loss-severity data are needed to evaluate the relative importance of an exposure to potential loss. Contrary to the views of most persons, however, the importance of an exposure to loss depends mostly upon the potential loss severity, not the potential frequency. A potential loss with catastrophic possibilities, although infrequent, is far more serious than one expected to produce frequent small losses and no large losses. On the other hand, loss frequency cannot be ignored. If two exposures are characterized by the same loss severity, the exposure whose frequency is greater should be ranked more important. An exposure with a certain potential loss severity may be ranked above a loss with a slightly higher severity because the frequency of the first loss is much greater than that of the second. There is no formula for ranking the losses in order of importance, and different persons may develop different rankings. The rational approach, however, is to place more emphasis on loss severity.

An example may clarify the point. The chance of a automobile collision loss may be greater than the chance of being sued as a result of the collision, but the potential severity of the liability loss is so much greater than the damage to the owned automobile that there should be no hesitation in ranking the liability loss over the property loss.

A particular type of loss may also be subdivided into two or more kinds of losses depending upon whether the loss exceeds a specified dollar amount. For example, consider the collison loss cited in the preceding paragraph. This loss may be subdivided into two kinds of losses: (1) collision losses of $100 (or some other figure) or less and (2) losses over $100. Losses in the second category are the more important, although they are less frequent. Another illustration would be the losses associated with relatively small medical expenses as contrasted with extremely large bills. Such a breakdown by size of loss shows clearly the desirability of assigning more weight to loss severity than to loss frequency.

In determining loss severity the risk manager must be careful to include all the types of losses that might occur as a result of a given event as well as their ultimate financial impact upon the firm. Often, while the less important types of losses are obvious to the risk manager, the more important types are much more difficult to identify. Chapters 5 and 6 will discuss, for example, the recognition and measurement of direct, indirect, and net income property losses. The potential direct property losses are rather generally appreciated in advance of any loss, but the potential indirect and net income losses (such as the interruption of business while the property is being repaired) that may result from the same event are commonly ignored until the loss occurs. This same event may also cause liability and personnel losses.[10]

The ultimate financial impact of the loss is even more likely to be ignored in evaluating the dollar value of any loss. Relatively small losses, if retained, cause only minor problems because the firm can meet these losses fairly easily out of liquid assets. Somewhat larger losses may cause liquidity problems which in turn may make it more difficult or more costly for the firm to borrow funds required for various purposes. Finally, very large losses may have serious adverse effects upon the firm's financial planning, and their dollar impact may be much greater than it would be for a firm that

---

[10] This recognition of all the losses associated with a given event has been termed the *loss unit concept.* See R. I. Mehr and Bob A. Hedges, *Risk Management in the Business Entrprise* (Homewood, Ill.: Richard D. Irwin, Inc., 1963), pp. 187–189. Recognizing that more than one unit may be involved in the same occurrence has been called the *catastrophe area concept.* See R. I. Mehr and B. A. Hedges, *Risk Management: Concepts and Applications* (Homewood, Ill.: Richard D. Irwin, Inc., 1974), pp. 213 and 242.

could more easily absorb these losses. Ultimately the loss could be the ruin of the business as a going concern.

To illustrate, a fire could destroy a building and its contents valued at $300,000; the ensuing shutdown of the firm for six months might cause another $360,000 loss. This $660,000 loss might force the firm to shut its doors, an action that would result in an ultimate loss of the difference between the going-concern value of the business, say $2,400,000, and the value for which the remaining assets could be sold, say $1,500,000, causing a $900,000 loss.

Loss severity also depends upon the *number of units* involved in the loss. For example, if a firm has three adjacent warehouses, one fire may cause considerable damage at all three warehouses.

Finally, in estimating loss severity, it is important to recognize the timing of any losses as well as their total dollar amount. For example, a loss of $5,000 a year for 20 years is not as severe as an immediate loss of $100,000 because of (1) the time value of money, which can be recognized by discounting future dollar losses at some assumed interest rate, and (2) the ability of the firm to spread the cash outlay over a longer period.

Loss-frequency and loss-severity data do more than identify the important losses. They are also extremely useful in determining the best way or ways to handle an exposure to loss. For example, the average loss frequency times the average loss severity equals the total dollar losses expected in an average year. These average losses can be compared with the premium the firm would have to pay an insurer for complete or partial protection. The variation (or estimated risk) in the loss freqency and loss severity sheds light on the predictability of the losses and how serious the losses might be in a bad year. These thoughts are developed further in Chapters 13 and 14, which deal with the selection of the proper risk management tools.

Loss-Frequency Measures

One measure of loss frequency is the probability that a single unit will suffer one type of loss from a single peril. For example, there is the probability that one building will be damaged because of a fire, or the probability that one product will produce a liability suit because of its negligent manufacture. Richard Prouty, the risk manager of a large business, suggested about 25 years ago that instead of using numerical estimates, the risk manager might express this type of probability as (1) "almost nil" (meaning in the opinion of the risk manager the event will not happen), (2) "slight" (meaning that, though possible, the event has not happened to the present time and is unlikely to occur in the future), (3) "moderate" (meaning that it has happened once in a while and can be expected to occur sometime in the future), or (4) "definite" (meaning that it has happened regularly and can be expected to occur regularly in the future).[11] Though not as precise as the probabilities discussed in the next chapter, these

---

[11] Richard Prouty, *Industrial Insurance: A Formal Approach to Risk Analysis and Evaluation* (Washington, D.C.: Machinery and Allied Products Institute, January 19, 1960). For comments on this approach see Robert Rennie, "The Measurement of Risk," *Journal of Insurance,* vol. XXVIII, no. 1 (March, 1961), pp. 87–91. A. E. Pfaffle and S. N. Nicosia suggest the same four categories in Pfaffle and Nicosia, op. cit., p. 9.

measures have the advantage that, given time to think about the exposures and study past experience, most risk managers can provide the necessary estimates. Making these estimates also encourages a more careful systematic approach to risk management.

Instead of estimating the probability that a single unit will suffer one type of loss from a single peril during the coming year, the risk manager can, in the same way, estimate the probability that the unit will suffer that type of loss from many perils, say windstorm and explosion as well as fire. This probability *will* be higher because of the additional possible causes of loss; the probability *category* may or may not be higher, depending upon the magnitude of the increase. Another example is the probability that a single unit will suffer simultaneously more than one type of loss (for example, physical damage to a building, loss of the use of that building, and liability for bodily injuries or property damage to others) from the single peril. This probability will be lower because more than one type of loss would have to result from a single occurrence; the probability *category* may or may not be lower. Still another example is the probability that *at least* one of several units, say five buildings, will suffer the same type of loss from the same single peril. This probability will be higher than the probability that any specific unit would suffer such a loss because there are several units that may have a fire. The probability category *may* be higher. On the other hand, the probability that all of those units will suffer the same type of loss from the single peril will be lower and *may* move into a lower category. Given all the combinations of units, types of losses, and perils that are possible, the number of probabilities that could be estimated is extremely large. Not all these probabilities are worth the time and effort involved in estimating a probability category. Once the risk manager has determined what probabilities are most useful in decision making, however, if more precise information is not available, he or she can use Prouty's four categories or some similar approach.

Loss-Severity Measures

Two measures commonly used to measure loss severity are the maximum *possible* loss to one unit per occurrence and the maximum *probable* loss to one unit per occurrence.[12] For the moment, we will concentrate on occurrences causing only one type of loss. The maximum possible loss is the worst loss that could *possibly* happen; the maximum probable loss is the worst loss that is *likely* to happen. The maximum probable loss, therefore, is usually less than the maximum possible loss. A worse loss could occur but the chance of its occurrence is less than some percentage selected by the risk manager, such as once every 40 years. Because different risk managers may select different percentages, they may disagree on the value of the maximum probable loss even though they estimate the probability distribution to be the same. Of these two measures, the maximum probable loss is the most difficult to estimate but also the most useful.

In a recent article, Alan Friedlander suggested four measures of physical damage losses due to fire per building per occurrence.[13] The (1) "normal loss expectancy" is

[12] See Prouty, op. cit., and Pfaffle and Nicosia, op. cit., p. 9.
[13] Alan W. Friedlander, "Assessing Fire Loss Potentials," *Risk Management,* vol. XXIV, no. 10 (October, 1977), pp. 26–34.

the dollar loss expected from a single fire when both private and public protection systems are operative. The (2) "probable maximum loss" is the dollar loss expected from a single fire when a critical part of the protection system such as an automatic sprinkler is out of service or ineffective. The (3) "maximum forseeable loss" is the dollar loss expected when none of the private protection systems are functioning. The fire in this case would probably burn until stopped by a fire wall, until it burns all its fuel, or until the public fire department, summoned by an outsider, arrives. The (4) "maximum possible loss" is the dollar loss expected from a fire when all private and public protection systems are inoperative or ineffective. Generally, the probability of occurrence declines as we move from the normal loss expectancy to the maximum possible loss. The four values depend upon innumerable factors such as construction, occupancy, private protection, and public protection.

As explained previously, however, a single occurrence may involve more than one type of loss. In estimating the maximum possible loss and the maximum probable loss the risk manager, ideally, would consider all types of losses that might result from a given peril. Fire loss potentials, for example, would include the possibly of net income losses, liability suits, and injuries to the firm's employees. The risk manager should also recognize that, though the probability may be low, more than one unit may be involved in a single occurrence, thus causing the loss potential to increase. The probability is high, for example, that a building and its contents will be damaged in the same occurrence.

Finally, in a series of articles directed to risk managers, Professors David Cummins and Leonard Freifelder have emphasized the importance of the maximum probable yearly *aggregate* dollar loss—either from a single peril or from several perils. The maximum probable yearly aggregate loss is the largest total loss amount that an exposure unit or group of exposure units is likely to suffer during a one-year (or other budget) period.[14] Like the maximum probable loss, this amount depends upon a probability level selected by the risk manager, but unlike the maximum probable loss, this measure does not refer just to the severity of a single occurrence. Instead it depends upon the number of occurrences as well as their severity. In the language of the next chapter, it depends upon the probability distribution of the total dollar losses per year, not upon the probability distribution of the dollar losses per occurrence. Like the maximum probable loss per occurrence, the losses can include all types of losses from the perils and exposure units included in the analysis.

SOME KEY CONCEPTS

Risk identification   The process of identifying the exposures to potential property, liability, or personnel losses.

Checklist   A listing of all the loss exposures that might possibly exist.

Financial statement method   The use of financial statements, together with a checklist, to identify the exposures of a particular business.

---

[14] J. D. Cummins and L. R. Freifelder, "Statistical Analysis in Risk Management: Types of Probability Distributions—Part I," *Risk Management*, vol. XXV, no. 9 (September, 1978), p. 59. The presentation is continued in the October, November, December, and January, 1979 issues.

Flow-chart method The use of flow charts, together with a checklist, to identify the exposures of a particular business.

Risk measurement The process of determining the likelihood of a loss from an exposure and its probable severity.

Moderate probability The likelihood of a loss if this loss has happened once in a while in the past and can be expected to occur some time in the future.

Maximum probable loss The worst loss that is likely to occur because of a single event.

Maximum probable yearly aggregate loss The largest aggregate dollar loss that is likely to occur during the year. This aggregate loss depends upon the number of occurrences per year as well as their severity.

REVIEW QUESTIONS

1 "In a sense the most vital task in the performance of the risk management function is the establishment of a careful and systematic method of risk identification."
   a Why is risk identification so important?
   b Explain briefly the two steps in risk identification.
2 Prepare a brief checklist of exposures to loss.
3 How can a risk manager use financial statements to determine which of the potential losses in a checklist apply to his or her firm?
4 What other sources can a risk manager use to determine the potential losses faced by his or her firm?
5 A business firm relies upon a local insurace broker to identify the risks faced by the firm. What are the possible advantages and disadvantages of this approach?
6 **a** For what reasons should a risk manager measure loss exposures?
   b What dimensions should be measured?
7 "Potential losses should be ordered in importance according to their loss severity." To what extent is this statement true? false?
8 In determining loss severity it is important to recognize (a) all types of losses, (b) their ultimate impact, (c) the number of units affected, and (d) their timing. Explain.
9 **a** Instead of using precise probability estimates Prouty suggested four probability categories. Explain.
   b The probability of loss may differ according to the number of units, the types of loss, and the perils involved in the loss. Explain.
10 The risk manager of a firm maintains that the dollar value of the maximum probable loss to a building as a result of a steam-boiler explosion is $200,000, while his assistant estimates it to be $150,000. Both agree that the maximum possible loss is the complete destruction of the building.
   a Why do their estimates of the dollar value of the maximum probable loss differ?
   b Why might the maximum possible loss exceed their estimate?
11 Explain how Friedlander would assess fire loss potentials.
12 Compare maximum probable loss and maximum probable yearly aggregate dollar loss.

SUGGESTIONS FOR ADDITIONAL READING

Carter, R. L., and N. A. Doherty (eds.): *Handbook of Risk Management* (London: Kluwer-Harrop Handbooks, 1974), pt. 4.

Daenzer, Bernard J.: *Fact-Finding Questionnaire for Risk Managers* (New York: Risk and Insurance Management Society, Inc., 1978).

Greene, Mark R., and Oscar N. Serbein: *Risk Management: Text and Cases (2d ed., Reston, Va.: Reston Publishing Company, 1983), chap. 3.*

MacDonald, Donald L.: *Corporate Risk Control* (New York: The Ronald Press Company, 1966), chaps. 3 and 4.

Mehr, R. I., and B. A. Hedges: *Risk Management: Concepts and Applications* (Homewood, Ill.: Richard D. Irwin, Inc., 1974), chaps. 7 and 8.

————, and ————: *Risk Management in the Business Enterprise* (Homewood, Ill.; Richard D. Irwin, Inc., 1963), chap. 6.

Pfaffle, A. E., and Sal Nicosia: *Risk Analysis Guide to Insurance and Employee Benefits* (New York: Amacom, 1977).

Prouty, Richard: *Industrial Insurance: A Formal Approach to Risk Analysis and Evaluation* (Washington, D.C.: Machinery and Allied Products Institute, January 19, 1960).

CHAPTER 4

RISK MEASUREMENT AND PROBABILITY DISTRIBUTIONS

LEARNING OBJECTIVES

After you have completed this chapter, you should be able to:

1 Distinguish between temporal probability of loss and spatial probability of loss.

2 Use some elementary rules of probability to determine the probabilities of such outcomes as a fire and an automobile accident the same year or neither a fire nor an automobile accident the same year.

3 Calculate, given a probability distribution of total dollar losses per year (or other budget period), the probability of no losses, the probability that the losses will exceed a specfied amount, the expected losses, and the risk.

4 Explain how probability distributions can be constructed from historical data or theoretical distributions.

5 Describe how you might construct the probability distribution of the total dollar losses per year, given the distributions of *(a)* the number of occurrences per year and *(b)* the dollar losses per occurrence.

INTRODUCTION

A more sophisticated way to measure potential losses than the approaches discussed in the preceding chapter involves probability distributions of the sort presented in Chapter 1. Unfortunately, this method is more difficult to explain and the data needed to construct the required probability distributions are commonly not available. Nevertheless, probability distributions make possible more comprehensive risk measurements than the techniques discussed earlier; also, they are becoming a more common tool of modern management, and data sources are improving. Furthermore, probability distributions improve one's understanding of the more popular risk measurements and are extremely useful in determining which risk management devices would be best in a given situation.

Before turning to probability distributions this chapter explains several interpretations and elementary rules of probability that should also prove useful to a risk manager. The discussion of probability distributions deals with three different ways of measuring loss experience: (1) total dollar losses per year (or some other budget period, such as a month or a calendar quarter), (2) the number of occurrences per year, and (3) the dollar losses per occurrence. The discussion will indicate (1) the useful information that can be derived from these distributions and (2) how these distributions can be constructed. Appendixes B, C, and D present some additional material on probability distributions and their uses.

TWO INTERPRETATIONS OF PROBABILITY

When a risk manager states that the probability is 1/10 that a particular warehouse will be damaged by fire during the coming year (or some other budget period), he or she is indicating the relative likelihood that this loss will occur.[1] As noted in Chapter 1, probability varies between 0 and 1, 0 indicating that there will be no loss and 1 that the loss will occur. Two interpretations of this 1/10 are possible:

1 During the coming year 1/10 of the presumably very large number of warehouses in the world independently (see below under Compound or Joint Outcomes) exposed to the same loss under the same conditions will be damaged by fire. This interpretation follows from the law of large numbers explained in Chapter 1.

In the relatively unusual case where one firm has itself a very large number of such warehouses independently exposed to loss, the firm can expect about 1/10 of its warehouses to be damaged by fire.

2 If the same warehouse is exposed to fire losses under the same conditions over a very long period of time, fire damage will occur in about 1/10 of the years of exposure.

Both interpretations are useful to risk managers. In estimating the probability that the warehouse noted above would suffer a fire loss, the risk manager should study the losses experienced by a large number of similar warehouses in the recent past. If about 1/10 of these warehouses were damaged by fire, the risk manager has some statistical foundation for the estimate of 1/10. The risk manager should also study the loss experience of the particular warehouse since it was constructed, but this experience is probably too limited to be useful. Estimates based on such reviews of past experience

---

[1] For the present we will ignore the fact that the warehouse may be damaged by fire more than once during the coming year. A more exact statement is that the probability is 10 percent that the particular warehouse will be damaged by fire *at least once* during the coming year. Later in this chapter, in discussing the Poisson distribution, we will deal with this problem.

must usually be tempered by the realization that (1) "similar" warehouses are almost never exactly the same (for example, they may differ as to location, some construction features, and housekeeping), and (2) conditions may change quickly over time. Nevertheless, the review of past experience provides some basis for an informed estimate of the probability of loss. This point is discussed further in the sections on probability distributions.

The second interpretation is extremely useful in determining what to do about the exposure. Most firms do not have enough similar exposures to predict with some confidence in the short run (under the first interpretation) what fraction of their exposures will suffer a loss. On the other hand, as will be explained in Chapter 13, it is useful to consider what fraction of years in the long run the firm will experience such a loss.

The example used in the preceding discussion illustrates one type of probability statement—the probability that a particular exposure unit will suffer a loss of any size because of a specific peril. Among the many other possibilities are probability statements that:

1 A loss will result from two or more perils.
2 A loss between,say, $5,000 and $10,000 will occur.
3 Two or more units, say, warehouses, will experience losses during the coming year.
4 A property loss exceeding, say, $50,000 and a liability loss exceeding the same amount will occur the same year.
5 At least one of several units, say, automobiles owned by the firm, will be damaged during the coming year.

These more complex probability statements will be clarified in the discussion that follows of some important rules of probability and probability distributions.

SOME RULES OF PROBABILITY

Some important rules of probability apply to (1) mutually exclusive outcomes and (2) compound or joint outcomes.[2]

Mutually Exclusive Outcomes

Two outcomes are mutually exclusive if they cannot occur together. For example, a warehouse cannot both burn and not burn; total dollar losses arising out of liability suits cannot at the same time be more than one of the following—zero, $1,000, $10,000, $50,000, or $100,000. Under one important (objective) probability theorem, the probability that the actual outcome will be any one of a set of two or more mutually exclusive outcomes is equal to the sum of the probabilities of the separate outcomes. In the liability loss example cited above, the probability that the loss will be either

---

[2] In estimating probabilities individuals sometimes use estimates that violate these rules.

$10,000 or $50,000 is equal to the probability that the loss will be $10,000 plus the probability that the loss will be $50,000. For example, if the probability of a $10,000 loss is $\frac{1}{10}$ and the probability of a $50,000 loss $\frac{1}{20}$, the probability of either a $10,000 or a $50,000 loss is $\frac{1}{10} + \frac{1}{20} = \frac{3}{20}$.

The sum of the probabilities of all possible mutually exclusive events must be 1, because one of these events is certain to occur. For example, the probability that the warehouse will either burn or not burn is 1. Consequently if the probability that the warehouse will burn is $\frac{1}{10}$, the probability that it will not burn is $1 - \frac{1}{10} = \frac{9}{10}$. In the liability example, if a person wants to know the probability that the firm will experience some loss, various amounts being possible, the probability that there will be no loss can be subtracted from 1.

Compound or Joint Outcomes

A compound or joint outcome is the occurrence of two or more separate events during the same period. Examples are fires at both warehouse A and warehouse B, a property loss and a liability loss arising out of the same accident, or industrial injuries to two or more workers.

The method for determining the probability of a compound outcome depends upon whether the separate outcomes are independent. Two outcomes are independent of one another if the occurrence of one outcome does not affect the probability that the other will occur. For example, the probability that a warehouse in New York City will burn is not affected by a fire loss to a warehouse in California. Consequently the two outcomes are independent. On the other hand the probability that a particular warehouse will burn is increased if an adjacent warehouse is already burning. Consequently a loss to one of these buildings is not independent of a loss to the other.

If two or more outcomes are independent, the (objective) probability of a compound event is the product of the probabilities of the independent events. For example, if the probability that the warehouse in New York City will burn is $\frac{1}{20}$ and the probability that the warehouse in California will burn is $\frac{1}{40}$, the probability that both will burn is $(\frac{1}{20})(\frac{1}{40}) = \frac{1}{800}$, making it an unlikely outcome. This compound probability theorem can be combined with the theorem on mutually exclusive outcomes to calculate the probability of the other three possible compound outcomes, as follows:

> Loss in New York, not in California: $(\frac{1}{20})(1 - \frac{1}{40}) = \frac{39}{800}$
> No loss in New York, loss in California: $(1 - \frac{1}{20})(\frac{1}{40}) = \frac{19}{800}$
> No loss in either location: $(1 - \frac{1}{20})(1 - \frac{1}{40}) = \frac{741}{800}$

The sum of the probabilities for the four mutually exclusive compound events should and does equal 1.

If the separate outcomes are not independent, the calculation of compound probabilities is more complicated. For example, if there are two separate outcomes, A and B, the probability that both outcomes will occur is determined by multiplying the probability of A by the probability (called the *conditional probability*) of B, given that

A has occurred.[3] The same result can be obtained by multiplying the probability of B times the conditional probability of A, given that B has occurred.

For example, if the probability of a fire loss for each of two warehouses, A and B, is $\frac{1}{40}$, the probability that both warehouses will burn, assuming independence, is $(\frac{1}{40})(\frac{1}{40}) = \frac{1}{1600}$. However, if the conditional probability of a fire loss to either warehouse increases to $\frac{1}{3}$ if the other warehouse catches on fire, the probability that both A and B will burn is $(\frac{1}{40})(\frac{1}{3}) = \frac{1}{120}$. In addition to fires at both locations, three other outcomes are possible with the following probabilities:

> Loss to warehouse A, not B: $(\frac{1}{40})(1 - \frac{1}{3}) = \frac{2}{120}$
> Loss to warehouse B, not A: $(\frac{1}{40})(1 - \frac{1}{3}) = \frac{2}{120}$
> Loss to neither A nor B: $1 - \frac{1}{120} - \frac{2}{120} - \frac{2}{120} = \frac{115}{120}$

The value for the final outcome is calculated on the assumption that the probabilities of the four outcomes must sum to 1.

Note that compared with the situation involving independent outcomes, two probabilities are higher—the probability that both warehouses will burn and the probability that neither warehouse will burn. As the degree of dependence increases, these two probabilities approach the probability that one warehouse will respectively burn or not burn.

Alternative Outcomes

Some probability statements tell the chance that at least one of two or more outcomes will occur within a given time. Such probability statements have already been mentioned in connection with mutually exclusive outcomes. If the outcomes *are* mutually exclusive, the probability that at least one of the alternative outcomes will occur is the sum of the probabilities that these alternative outcomes will occur.

If the outcomes *are not* mutually exclusive, the calculation is more complex. Only the probability that at least one of two outcomes will occur will be considered here. This probability is the sum of the probabilities of the two separate outcomes less the probability that they both occur. To illustrate, consider the case of warehouses A and B presented in the preceding section on compound outcomes. The probability that either A or B will burn, assuming independence, is $\frac{1}{40} + \frac{1}{40} - (\frac{1}{40})(\frac{1}{40}) = \frac{79}{1600}$. This probability can also be calculated by summing the probabilities for the three possible joint outcomes in which either A or B suffer a loss:

> A and B: $(\frac{1}{40})(\frac{1}{40}) = \frac{1}{1600}$
> A, not B: $(\frac{1}{40})(1 - \frac{1}{40}) = \frac{39}{1600}$
> B, not A: $(\frac{1}{40})(1 - \frac{1}{40}) = \frac{39}{1600}$

---

[3] If there are three separate outcomes—A, B, and C—the probability that A, B, and C will occur is equal to the probability of A times the probability of B given that A has occurred times the probability of C, given that both A and B have occurred. The order in which A, B, and C are to occur can be changed without altering the result. For compound outcomes involving four or more separate outcomes, this approach is simply extended.

For the situation in which independence was *not assumed,* the probability that either warehouse will burn is $\frac{1}{40} + \frac{1}{40} - \frac{1}{120} = \frac{5}{120}$. Alternatively, summing the probabilities for the three possible joint outcomes involving a loss at A or B yields $\frac{1}{120} + \frac{2}{120} + \frac{2}{120} = \frac{5}{120}$.

In this instance where there are only two exposures to loss, it would be mechanically easier to calculate the alternative probability by subtracting from 1 the probability that no loss will occur. If there were three or more exposures, however, and we were interested in the probability that at least one of two specific warehouses would burn, the basic formula is easier to use. For example, assume three warehouses—A, B, and C—each with a $\frac{1}{40}$ chance of burning. The probability that either A or B will burn, assuming independence, is still:

Probability of A burning		Probability of B burning		Probability of A and B burning	
$\frac{1}{40}$	$+$	$\frac{1}{40}$	$-$	$\frac{1}{1600}$	$= \frac{79}{1600}$

Similarly the probability that either A or C will burn is $\frac{79}{1600}$.

PROBABILITY DISTRIBUTIONS

A probability distribution, shows for each possible outcome, its probability of occurrence. Because the outcomes are mutually exclusive, these probabilities sum to 1. Three useful probability distributions show as possible outcomes (1) the total dollar losses per year (or other budget period), (2) the number of occurrences per year, and (3) the dollar losses per occurrence. Each total dollar loss, of course, can be obtained by multiplying the number of occurrences that year by the average dollar loss per occurrence. To illustrate these three types of probability distributions we will consider (1) the total dollar direct property (not including net income, liability, or personnel) losses a firm might experience because of collisions involving its fleet of automobiles, (2) the number of collisions per year, and (3) the total dollar property losses per collision.

This illustration deals with one type of loss (direct property) to all units exposed to the loss (the fleet of cars) from one cause (collision). As indicated in Chapter 3, probabilities and, hence, probability distributions, can be constructed for numerous combinations of (1) types of losses, (2) units exposed, and (3) causes of loss. Examples are: property losses to shipments from theft, liability losses arising out of a given product from negligence or breach of contract, workers' compensation benefits to all workers with job-related injuries or diseases, death benefits to employees injured on or off the job, and, the most comprehensive example possible, all types of losses to all exposure units from all accidental causes. In practice, fortunately, the risk manager does not have to consider every possible combination. Usually he or she will study and handle separately the three major types of losses (property including net income,[4]

---

[4] Net income losses are often handled separately but since these losses usually accompany direct or indirect property losses it would seem wise to consider all property losses jointly as well as separately.

liability, and personnel), all units of a given class (all buildings, contents, shipments, employees, products of a given type, cars, etc.), and a few major perils (such as fire, explosion, negligence, or death) or all accidental causes except those specifically excluded. The risk manager must remember, of course, that a business may suffer losses of various sorts during the same year, and that the cumulative effect of these losses will be far greater than if they occurred in different years.

In determining the possible losses to be included in the probability distribution of total dollar losses per ocurrence, the risk manager should recall the points made in Chapter 3. The risk manager should include all the types of losses that might occur as a result of a given event, consider the ultimate financial impact of each loss, remember that more than one unit may be affected by a single occurrence, and use discounted values for losses that will be spread over an extended period of time. In addition, the risk manager should recognize a complication that has been ignored up to this point—namely, that some exposure units may suffer more than one loss per budget period. For example, each automobile may be involved in more than one collision per year.

Finally, for many risk management decisions, taxes are such an important factor that the risk manager should also construct probability distributions of the total *after-tax* dollar losses and the *after-tax* dollar losses per occurrence. The only difference from the pre-tax distributions would be that after-tax values would be substituted for the pre-tax dollar losses. For a further discussion of taxes, see Chapters 11 and 13.

TOTAL DOLLAR LOSSES PER YEAR

The probability distribution of the total dollar losses per year shows each of the total dollar losses that the business may experience in the coming year and the probability that each of these totals might occur. For example, assume that (1) a business has a fleet of five cars, each of which is valued at $10,000, (2) each car may be involved in more than one collision a year, and (3) the physical damage may be partial or total. Also assume prompt replacement of any car that goes out of service, thus reducing net income losses to a minimal level. A hypothetical probability distribution that might apply in this situation is shown in Table 4.1.[5] In real life, the number of outcomes in a similar situation would be considerably larger, but, in order to emphasize the principles involved, the hypothetical distribution has been intentionally oversimplified. Although it is conceivable that all five cars (or even more considering replacements) will be totally destroyed, the illustration assumes that $20,000 is the worst total loss that will occur.

---

[5] The probabilities in the table may look too precise and complex for an explanatory table but this table must be consistent with the probability distributions of the number of occurrences and the dollar losses per occurrence presented later. For example, the probability of no occurrences, which can be calculated exactly given the average number of occurrences per year, is .6065. The probability of no dollar losses per year should also be .6065. Perfect consistency, however, has not been the objective. The dollar losses per year, for example, could assume many more values than those shown in Table 4.1 given the four possible losses per occurrence stated on page 76. See Appendix D for more details.

TABLE 4.1
HYPOTHETICAL PROBABILITY
DISTRIBUTION OF TOTAL DOLLAR
PROPERTY LOSSES PER YEAR TO A
FLEET OF FIVE CARS

Dollar losses per year	Probability
$ 0	.606
500	.273
1,000	.100
2,000	.015
5,000	.003
10,000	.002
20,000	.001
	1.000

TABLE 4.2
PROBABILITY THAT TOTAL
DOLLAR LOSSES IN THE TABLE
4.1 DISTRIBUTION WILL EQUAL
OR EXCEED CERTAIN
SPECIFIED VALUES

Specified value	Probability
$ 500	.394
1,000	.121
2,000	.021
5,000	.006
10,000	.003
20,000	.001

Useful Measurements

If the risk manager can estimate accurately the probability distribution of the total dollar losses per year, he or she can obtain useful information concerning (1) the probability that the business will incur some dollar loss, (2) the probability that "severe" losses will occur, (3) the average loss per year, and (4) the risk or variation in the possible results. These measurements will be illustrated using the probability distribution in Table 4.1.

Given this distribution, the probability that the business will suffer no dollar loss is almost .61. Because the business must suffer either no loss or some loss, the sum of the probabilities of no loss and of some loss must equal 1.0. Consequently, the probability of some loss is equal to about $1.0 - .61$, or .39. An alternative way to determine the probability of some loss is to sum the probabilities for each of the possible total dollar losses; i.e., $.273 + .100 + .015 + .003 + .002 + .001$, or .394.

The potential severity of the total dollar losses can be measured by stating the probability that the total losses will exceed various values. For example, the risk manager may be interested in the probability that the dollar losses will equal or exceed $5,000. These probabilities can be calculated for each of the values in which the risk manager is interested and for all higher values. For example, the probability that the dollar losses will equal or exceed $5,000 is equal to $.003 + .002 + .001$, or .006. Table 4.2 shows the probability that the dollar losses will equal or exceed each of the values in Table 4.1.

Another extremely useful measure that reflects both loss frequency and loss severity is the expected total dollar loss or the average annual dollar loss in the long run. Because the probabilities in Table 4.1 represent the proportion of times each dollar loss is expected to occur in the long run, the expected loss can be obtained by summing the products formed by multiplying each possible outcome by the probability of its occurrence; i.e., $\$0(.606) + \$500(.273) + \$1,000(.100) + \$2,000(.015) +$

$5,000(.003) + $10,000(.002) + $20,000(.001), or $321. This measure indicates the average annual dollar loss the business will sustain in the long run if it retains this exposure.[6]

Three possible uses of this table would be to determine (1) the probability that the dollar losses would equal or exceed the insurance premium that might be required to purchase complete financial protection, (2) the probability that the dollar losses, if retained, could cause serious financial problems, and (3) the maximum possible and probable annual total (yearly aggregate) losses. For the first use, both the losses and the premium should be converted to an after-tax basis because, as will be explained in Chapter 11, the tax consequences of, say, a $1,000 loss may not be the same as the tax consequences of a $1,000 premium. Assume for the moment that the losses in Table 4.1 are after-tax losses and that the after-tax premium for complete protection is $600. According to Table 4.2, the probability that the after-tax total dollar losses will equal or exceed this $600 premium is 12 percent. (To equal or exceed $600, the total dollar losses would have to be $1,000 or higher.) To illustrate the second use, assume that a loss of $18,000 or more would be considered a serious financial loss. (The seriousness of each loss also depends upon its after-tax value.) The probability of a loss of $18,000 or more is 0.1 percent. As for the third use, the maximum possible annual total loss is $20,000. If the risk manager considers unlikely any losses that have less than a 0.2 percent chance of occurring, the maximum probable annual total loss (the largest loss that is likely to occur) is $10,000. Raising this probability criterion to, say, less than 0.5 percent reduces the maximum probable annual total loss to $5,000.[7]

Two probability distributions may have the same expected loss but may differ greatly with respect to risk or the variation in the possible results. For example, an expected value of $321 may be produced by the distribution in Table 4.1 or by a $321 loss every year. Considerable risk is present in the first instance, but there is no risk when one knows what will happen each year. The greater the variation in the possible results, the greater the risk. If the risk is small, the annual losses are fairly predictable and the business may be well advised to treat these losses as an operating expense. If the risk is large and some of the unpredictable losses could be serious, it may be wise to shift these potential losses to someone else.

Up to this point, no yardstick has been suggested for measuring risk, but its relationship to the variation in the probability distribution has been noted. Statisticians measure this variation in several ways. One of the most popular yardsticks for measuring the dispersion around the expected value is the standard deviation. The standard deviation is obtained by subtracting the average value from each possible value of the variable, squaring the difference, multiplying each squared difference by

[6] Two other measures that may be of interest to the risk manager are the mode and the median. The mode is the most likely single outcome; the median is the "middle" outcome—the outcome for which there is a 50 percent chance that it will be exceeded. In Table 4.1 both the mode and the median are zero. In more symmetrical distributions such as those shown in Figure 1.1, the mode and the median are much closer to the mean. If the distribution is perfectly symmetrical and peaked in the middle, the three measures have the same value.

[7] If the probability criterion were less than 0.6 percent, the maximum probable loss would still be $5,000.

the probability that the variable will assume the value involved, summing the resulting products, and taking the square root of the sum. For the distribution in Table 4.1, the calculation is as follows:

(1) Value	(2) Value—average	(3) (Value—average)^2	(4) Probability	(5) (3) × (4)
$ 0	$ 0—321	$(-\$321)^2$	.606	62,443
500	500—321	$(179)^2$	.273	8,747
1,000	1,000—321	$(679)^2$	.100	46,104
2,000	2,000—321	$(1,679)^2$	.015	42,286
5,000	5,000—321	$(4,679)^2$	.003	65,679
10,000	10,000—321	$(9,679)^2$	.002	187,366
20,000	20,000—321	$(19,679)^2$	.001	387,263
				799,888

The standard deviation is $\sqrt{799,888}$ or about $894.

When there is much doubt about what will happen because there are many outcomes with some reasonable chance of occurrence, the standard deviation will be large; when there is little doubt about what will happen because one of a few possible outcomes is almost certain to occur, the standard deviation will be small. These observations suggest that the standard deviation of the probability distribution could serve as a measure of the risk associated with that distribution. However, statisticians have also suggested that for many purposes the coefficient of variation described next is a better measure of dispersion.

The coefficient of variation is calculated by dividing the standard deviation by the expected value. In other words, the standard deviation is expressed as a percentage of the average value in the long run. Because a standard deviation of $20 is much more significant if the expected loss is $10, say, than if it is $2,000, the coefficient of variation has more appeal as a measure of economic risk than the standard deviation. Many writers, however, prefer to relate the standard deviation to the maximum amount exposed, their reasoning being that a standard deviation of $20 is much more important if the maximum amount that can be lost is $100, say, instead of $10,000. Although, as explained below, the coefficient of variation is the more useful measure, the best procedure is to relate the standard deviation to both of these bases and to others that may be of interest in a particular problem. For the distribution in Table 4.1 the risk relative to the expected value is $894/$321 or 2.8. The risk relative to the maximum exposure is $894/$20,000 or .04. The coefficient of variation is the more useful measure because the expected value often serves also as the predicted value and the coefficient of variation indicates the relative error in the prediction.

These measures of risk, unlike the probability of loss, have no simple interpretation; they are bounded by 0 and infinity, not by 0 and 1. However, by comparing any of these measures for two or more distributions, one can determine the relative degrees of risk inherent in those distributions.

The standard deviation itself, however, does yield some additional information. First, if the probability distribution can be estimated by a so-called normal distribution, to be described shortly, the standard deviation can be used to determine the probability that the outcomes will fall between two specified values. This application is discussed later in this chapter.

Second, if one knows the mean and the standard deviation but nothing else about the distribution, one can still estimate with confidence the *maximum* probability that the outcomes will deviate from the average value by a specified amount or more. According to the Chebyshev Inequality, the probability that the outcomes will fall k or more standard deviations from the mean is $1/_k{}^2$ or less. To illustrate, in Table 4.1 the mean is $321 and the standard deviation $894. If one had no further information concerning the probability distribution, one could still state that the probability is 25 percent (½ squared) or less that the losses will be larger or smaller than $321 by at least 2($894) = $1,788. The actual distribution indicates a much lower percentage than 25 percent (0.6 percent) that the outcomes will be less than $321 − $1,788 (an impossibility) or more than $321 + $1,788 = $2109.

Third, assuming the same underlying conditions, both the expected value and the standard deviation increase as the number of units exposed to loss increases. For example, if in Table 4.1 the firm had 20 cars instead of 5, the expected value would be higher and the standard deviation larger. However, whereas the mean would be 4 times as large, the standard deviation would increase only according to the square root of the increase. Instead of being 4 times as large it would be $\sqrt{4}$ or 2 times as large. If the firm had 500 cars, the mean would be 100 times as large, the standard deviation $\sqrt{100}$ or 10 times as large. Consequently the risk relative to either the mean or the maximum possible loss, which would increase the same number of times as the mean, would decrease. More specifically, increasing the number of cars to 20 would reduce the risk to $\sqrt{¼}$ or ½ of its 5-car value. Consequently increasing the number of exposure units, other conditions affecting each unit remaining the same, reduces the risk but less than proportionately. A law of diminishing returns operates, under which the number of units must be increased by substantially larger and larger amounts to achieve a corresponding relative reduction in risk. For example, increasing the number of cars from 5 to 20 reduced the risk to ½ of its 5-car value. To reduce the risk again to ½ of this 20-car value would require 20 (2^2) or 80 cars. Furthermore, because the risk with 20 cars would be smaller than the risk with 5 cars, the absolute change in risk resulting from the movement from 20 cars to 80 cars would be much smaller than in moving from 5 cars to 20 cars. These relationships between risk and the number of exposure units are extremely important concepts to risk management.

How to Construct a Probability Distribution

To construct a probability distribution one can use (1) historical data, or (2) theoretical probability distributions.

Historical Data By observing the number of times the various potential dollar losses have occurred over a long period of time under essentially the same conditions, one can estimate the probability of each possible outcome. This estimate would be the proportion of times each outcome has occurred in the past. But seldom does one have extensive enough experience to construct a reliable probability distribution in this fashion. Changes are occurring constantly in the risk environment that shorten the relevant experience period. Past losses can be adjusted to reflect some of these changes such as higher repair costs, higher workers' compensation benefits, or an increase in the number of exposure units. For example, assume that fire losses five years ago totalled $10,000. Repair costs today are 50 percent higher than they were then. During the budget period, repair costs are expected to be 10 percent higher than they are today. The adjusted losses would be $(1.5)(1.1)$10,000 or $16,500. Other changes for which no acceptable adjustments may be possible include changes in the quality of the construction, in environmental hazards, or in safety programs.

If, say, only the experience during the past five years is relevant, the risk manager would have only five observations on annual experience. Five observations do not provide enough information to sketch a probability distribution unless the five observations are approximately the same and there is good reason to believe that the risk or variation in the possible results is extremely small. By using monthly instead of annual observations, the risk manager would have 60 observations instead of five, but the variation in monthly data is likely to be greater than the variation in annual data. In any event, few businesses are likely to experience anything approaching the full range of their possible losses in five years. Consequently, except in a few situations (eg., a business making many shipments, all of approximately the same value, or a business with many employees exposed to industrial injuries), a business cannot rely upon its own historical data to construct a probability distribution of total dollar losses per year, per month, or during some other period of time.

Trade associations, private insurers, and government agencies may be able to provide supplementary information, but (1) data from these sources are commonly limited to average losses—not frequency distributions—and (2) the data combine the loss experience of many firms that may differ from a particular firm in many significant ways.

At best the risk manager can generalize on the basis of a sample of information. The estimated distribution of losses, which is necessarily subjective, will be influenced by the information at the risk manager's disposal, by whether he or she tends to be an optimist or a pessimist, and by other factors.

Theoretical Distributions   Instead of relying on data of his or her own or on those provided by others, the risk manager may be able to supplement this information with some probability distributions based on theoretical considerations. Statisticians have used this approach to develop useful estimates of the probability distributions in other fields. For example, the most important theoretical probability distribution is the normal distribution. The nature of this distribution is indicated by the bell-shaped curves in Figure 4.1. The exact location and shape of this curve is determined by a formula described in most introductory statistics texts. The curve is a function of only two variables—the expected value and the standard deviation. The peak of the curve always occurs at the expected value. As is demonstrated in Figure 4.1, the smaller the standard deviation, the more clustered the outcomes will be around the expected value.

The normal distribution has been used with considerable success to describe the

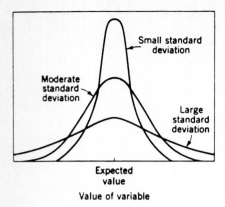

FIGURE 4.1
Normal probability distributions.

probability distributions of errors in measuring a line, the neck sizes of college males, the annual message use of telephone subscribers, and the acidity of liquid dyes. Various statistical methods can be used to determine the adaptability or ''goodness of fit'' to available data.

The normal distribution is a particularly attractive probability distribution because it is relatively simple to determine the probability that the variable will fall within a certain range of values.[8] For example, the probability is 68.27 percent that the variable will fall within the range bounded by the expected value plus or minus 1 standard deviation; 95.45 percent that the variable will fall within the plus or minus 2 standard deviation range; and 99.73 percent that the variable will fall within the plus or minus 3 standard deviation range. With the aid of tables of the area under the normal curve found in almost all introductory statistics texts, one can make similar computations for other multiples of the standard deviation. For example, the probability is 98.76 percent that the variable will fall within the plus or minus 2.5 standard deviation range about the expected value. Because the distribution is symmetrical with respect to the expected value, the probability that the variable will fall between the expected value and the expected value plus 2.5 standard deviations is one-half of 98.76 percent, or 49.38 percent. The probability that the variable will exceed the expected value plus 2.5 standard deviations is 50 percent minus 49.38 percent, or .62 percent. The probability that the variable will exceed the expected value plus 1 standard deviation is 50 percent less one-half of 68.27 percent, or 15.86 percent.

Even if one were correct in assuming that the probability distribution of total losses was normal, the distribution that the risk manager would construct would still be an estimate because he or she would have to estimate the expected value and the standard deviation. It is much easier to estimate these two parameters, however, than to estimate

---

[8] The reader may have observed that the vertical axis in Figure 4.1 has not been labeled. That axis does not represent the probability that the event will occur. Unlike the distributions in Figure 1.1, which were discrete distributions dealing with a limited number of outcomes, the normal distribution is continuous, covering *all* values from $+ \infty$ to $- \infty$. The area under this curve is the probability measure. The total area under the curve is 1, and the area encompassed by any range of values and the curve is the probability that some value in that range will occur.

the entire probability distribution. Even a small sample of data may provide reasonably reliable estimates. In addition, the risk manager can supplement his or her own experience with the experience of others—insurers, trade associations, statistical agencies, and other firms. If, for example, a trade association reports that similar firms suffer annual losses of $500 per year and the risk manager's own data indicate a $300 loss, he or she may want to estimate the average loss as some weighted average of these two figures. The more confidence the risk manager has in his or her own data, the heavier the weight he or she will assign to the $300. Some of the supplementary sources that the risk manager might wish to consult will be cited in Chapters 5 through 9, which deal with property, liability, and personnel losses.

In determining the average loss, the risk manager should consider (1) the variability in the annual losses used to estimate the average annual loss and (2) any trends in the annual losses. If, for example, the annual losses have been steadily increasing each year, the average annual loss over the period may not be the best estimate to use. In any event, before the average loss is calculated, the loss experience should be adjusted in the manner described earlier under "Historical Data" to reflect some of the changes in underlying conditions.

Unfortunately, estimating a few parameters is not the only problem. It is clear that the normal distribution would not provide a suitable approximation to the distribution in Table 4.1, which is not an unlikely distribution for a business with a few exposure units. If the business had many more cars exposed to loss, it is true that the most likely outcome would be losses of some amount and the curve would be more nearly bell-shaped. Research has indicated, however, that the normal distribution is not in most instances a satisfactory approximation. Other theoretical probability distributions are being investigated, but much work remains to be done. Fortunately much more is known now about the theoretical probability distributions of (1) the number of occurrences per year and (2) the dollar losses per occurrence. As Appendix D indicates, given these two distributions it is possible to construct a probability distribution of the total dollar losses per year.

NUMBER OF OCCURRENCES PER YEAR

As indicated above, researchers have been much more successful in their studies of the probability distribution of the number of occurrences per year, although much remains to be done in this area. If each occurrence produces the same dollar loss, the distribution of the number of occurrences per year can be transformed into a distribution of the total dollar losses per year by multiplying each possible number of occurrences by the uniform loss per occurrence. If the dollar loss per occurrence varies within a small range, the distribution of the total dollar losses per year can be approximated by multiplying each possible number of occurrences by the average dollar losses per occurrence. If the dollar losses per occurrence vary widely, one needs the probability distributions of the dollar losses per occurrence and the number of occurrences per year to develop information about the total dollar losses per year. However, even if information concerning the losses per occurrence is lacking, the risk manager will improve his or her understanding of the risk situation if he or she knows the probability distribution of the number of occurrences per year.

The Poisson Distribution

One theoretical probability distribution that has proved particularly useful in estimating the probability that a business will suffer a specified number of occurrences during the next year is the Poisson distribution. According to this distribution, the probability that there will be r occurrences is

$$\frac{m^r e^{-m}}{r!}$$

where m is the mean or expected value, e is always 2.71828 . . . , and $r!$, called factorial r, is equal to $r(r-1)(r-2) \ldots 1$. The standard deviation of this distribution, according to statistical theory and verified empirically, is $\sqrt{m}$. The Poisson distribution has the great advantage that to use it the risk manager must estimate only the average number of occurrences.

To illustrate the application of this formula, assume that the fleet of five cars whose probability distribution of total losses per year was presented in Table 4.1 has been experiencing about one collision every two years. The mean therefore is ½ or .5. The probability distribution is as follows.

Number of collisions	*Probability*		
0	$\dfrac{(.5)^0 e^{-.5}}{0!}$	$= \dfrac{(1)(.6065)}{1}$	$= .6065$
1	$\dfrac{(.5)^1 e^{-.5}}{1!}$	$= \dfrac{(.5)(.6065)}{1}$	$= .3033$
2	$\dfrac{(.5)^2 e^{-.5}}{2!}$	$= \dfrac{(.25)(.6065)}{2 \times 1}$	$= .0758$
3	$\dfrac{(.5)^3 e^{-.5}}{3!}$	$= \dfrac{(.125)(.6065)}{3 \times 2 \times 1}$	$= .0126$

.9982

1.0

The Poisson distribution assumes there is no limit to the possible number of collisions. The illustration, however, was not continued beyond three collisions in the probability calculations because the probability of any larger number of collisions is extremely small.

In this example, the mean or expected number of collisions per year in the long run is .5. The standard deviation is $\sqrt{.5} = .707$. The probability of no collisions is almost .61. The probability of more than three collisions is $1 - .9982 = .0018$. The probability of more than one collision is $1 - .6065 - .3033 = .0902$.

The Poisson distribution works well when (1) there are at least 50 units exposed independently to loss and (2) the probability that any particular unit will suffer a loss is the same for all units and less than $\frac{1}{10}$. These conditions can be satisfied in two ways. First, the business can have at least 50 persons, properties, or activities, each of which can suffer at most one occurrence per year, the probability being less then $\frac{1}{10}$ that any particular unit will have an occurrence. Such low probabilities are common in risk management problems. In this instance the number of occurrences is limited to the number of exposure units, whereas the Poisson distribution assumes no limit. However, the Poisson distribution probabilities for occurrences in excess of the number of exposure units will be so small that they can be ignored.

Second, the number of persons, properties, or activities may be less than 50, but each unit can have more than one occurrence during the exposure period. Each day, hour, minute, or other subperiod is considered a separate independent exposure, thus greatly increasing the number of units exposed to loss. For each of these units the probability of an occurrence is very small (much less than $\frac{1}{10}$). Such multiple-occurrence possibilities are also common in risk management problems.

In other words, if each unit can have at most one occurrence per year, the number of persons, properties, or activities should be at least 50 if the risk manager wants to use the Poisson distribution. If each unit can have more than one occurrence a year, the Poisson distribution can be used with a smaller number of exposure units.

The firm whose fleet of cars has been used to illustrate the probability distribution of collision losses in this chapter has only five cars, but each of these cars can sustain numerous collisions during the year. Consequently each day, say, might be considered a separate exposure during which the probability of a collision involving each car is extremely small. The Poisson distribution, therefore, provides a reasonable estimate of the underlying probability distribution.

The probability of an occurrence should be the same for each exposure unit if the Poisson distribution is to be used. If the probability is not the same for each unit, the negative binomial distribution, whose characteristics will not be discussed in this text, may be more appropriate. Another complication is that the units may not be independently exposed to loss. For example, a fleet of cars may be housed every night in the same garage. Except for the discussion earlier in this chapter of compound probabilities when the outcomes are dependent, this situation will not be discussed further. In most situations, if the dependence is only occasional, a qualitative adjustment will suffice.

Appendix B describes two additional theoretical distributions of the number of occurrences per year. Appendix C shows how to calculate the number of exposure units required to predict the number of occurrences in the future with a specified degree of accuracy.

DOLLAR LOSSES PER OCCURRENCE

Researchers have also had some success describing the probability distribution of the dollar losses per occurrence. This distribution would state the probabilities that the dollar losses in an occurrence would assume various values. For example, for the fleet of five cars that has served as an illustration throughout this chapter, assume the possible losses per collision to be $500, $1,000, $5,000, and $10,000 with probabilities respectively of .900, .080, .018, and .002. The expected value is $640. The log-normal curve, which will not be explained here except to state that it is a normal distribution applied to the logarithms of the losses instead of to the losses themselves, appears to describe adequately the distribution of the losses per occurrence for many types of losses.[9] With a distribution of this sort one can calculate, among other things, the probability that the dollar losses per occurrence would exceed some specified amount.

COMPONENT DISTRIBUTIONS AND THE PROBABILITY DISTRIBUTION OF TOTAL DOLLAR LOSSES PER YEAR

Because the total loss in a year is the product of the number of occurrences per year and the average loss per occurrence, one can make some statements about the total dollar loss per year if one has probability distributions for the number of occurrences and for the losses per occurrence. For example, the expected total dollar loss per year is equal to the expected number of occurrences times the expected dollar loss per occurrence. For the fleet of five cars, the expected number of occurrences is ½, the expected dollar loss per occurrence $640, and the expected total dollar loss $321. In this case the three values were derived independently. However, if the risk manager knew only the expected number of occurrences and expected dollar loss per occurrence, he or she could calculate the expected total dollar loss as the product of the two known values or (½)($640) = $320. (The $1 difference from $321 can be explained by rounding errors and approximations used by the authors in constructing the total annual loss distribution.) Indeed, as Appendix D illustrates, given the probability distributions of the number of occurrences and of the dollar loss per occurrence, it would be possible to estimate the entire probability distribution of the total dollar losses per year.[10]

---

[9] The gamma distribution has also proved useful in this regard.

[10] The standard deviation of the total dollar losses per year can also be calculated as follows:

$$\begin{matrix}\text{Standard} \\ \text{deviation} \\ \text{of total} \\ \text{dollar} \\ \text{losses}\end{matrix} = \sqrt{\left(\begin{matrix}\text{Standard} \\ \text{deviation} \\ \text{of number} \\ \text{of ocurrences}\end{matrix}\right)^2 \left(\begin{matrix}\text{Expected} \\ \text{dollar} \\ \text{loss per} \\ \text{occurrence}\end{matrix}\right)^2 + \left(\begin{matrix}\text{Standard} \\ \text{deviation} \\ \text{of dollar} \\ \text{loss per} \\ \text{occurrence}\end{matrix}\right)^2 \left(\begin{matrix}\text{Expected} \\ \text{number} \\ \text{of} \\ \text{occurrences}\end{matrix}\right)}$$

All of the values required to calculate this standard deviation have been presented earlier in this text-except the standard deviation of the dollar loss per occurrence. This value, calculated according to the procedure shown on pages 68–69, is $739. According to this formula, therefore, the standard deviation of the total dollar losses in this case is

$$\sqrt{(\sqrt{.5})^2 \ (\$640)^2 \ + \ (\$739)^2 \ (.5)} = \sqrt{.5 \ (409,600) \ + \ (546,121) \ (.5)} = \$691.$$

The difference between $691 and the $894 calculated on page 69 is explained by the approximations used by the authors in constructing the probability distributions of (1) the total annual dollar losses and (2) the dollar losses per occurrence. See footnote 5.

SOME KEY CONCEPTS

Spatial probability of loss   The proportion of similar units exposed to loss over a given time period that will experience a loss, given a very large number of units exposed.

Temporal probability of loss   The proportion of similar times during which a unit is exposed to a loss that the loss will occur, given a very large number of times exposed.

Expected loss   The average loss in the long run. The expected loss is the mean of the probability distribution of losses, not the mode.

Coefficient of variation   The standard deviation divided by the mean or the expected value. A measure of the dispersion, scattering, or variation of the outcomes in a probability distribution. The larger the coefficient of variation, the less predictable is the future outcome.

Theoretical probability distributions   Probability distributions for which a formula has been developed based on some assumptions about the behavior of the variable. Useful distributions in risk management are the Poisson Distribution, the Normal Distribution, the log-normal distribution, and others.

Probability distribution of total dollar losses per year   A listing of all the total dollar losses that might occur in a year and the probabilities of each possible total dollar amount. The two component probability distributions that determine this probability distribution are the probability distributions of (1) the number of occurrences and (2) the dollar loss per occurrence.

REVIEW QUESTIONS[11]

1 Probability may be interpreted using either a space or time dimension. Explain this statement.
2 The probability that a firm will experience a fire is $\frac{1}{10}$. The probability that it will suffer a theft loss is also $\frac{1}{10}$. If independence is assumed, calculate the probability that the firm will have:
  a Both a fire loss and a theft loss ($\frac{1}{100}$)
  b Neither a fire loss nor a theft loss ($\frac{81}{100}$)
  c A fire loss or a theft loss, but not both ($\frac{18}{100}$)
3 A firm manufactures three different types of products. The probability that the firm will be sued for a defective product of type A is $\frac{1}{100}$, type B $\frac{1}{50}$, and type C $\frac{1}{10}$. Assuming independence, what is the probability that the firm:
  a Will not be sued for any defective products? (43,659/50,000)
  b Will be sued for defective products of all three types? (1/50,000)
  c Will be sued for a defective product of either type B or type C? (59/500)
4 Given the following probability distribution for a business of total property losses per year:

Loss value	Probability
$ 0	.800
500	.150
1,000	.030
5,000	.010
10,000	.007
25,000	.002
50,000	.001
	1.000

[11] Items in parentheses are answers.

a What is the probability that the business will suffer some dollar loss in the next year? (.200)
b What is the probability that the business will suffer losses totaling $5,000 or more? (.020)
c What is the expected total dollar loss? ($325)
d If the standard deviation is $2,200, how would you measure the risk? (7 or .04)
e If the expected number of occurrences is .5, what is the average loss size? ($650)
f What is (1) the maximum possible loss and (2) the maximum probable loss (assuming a less than 1 percent probability criterion)? ($50,000 and $10,000)

5 a How can the risk manager estimate the probability distribution of total dollar losses per year?
b If a theoretical probability distribution is discovered that adequately describes the general shape of the probability distribution of total dollar losses, does this mean that the risk manager will have an accurate picture of the probability distribution of total dollar losses?

6 A business has 40 retail outlets scattered throughout the United States. The risk manager does not know the probability distribution of total annual dollar losses to contents at all locations but estimates the average value per year to be $50,000 and the standard deviation to be $10,000.
a What is the *maximum* probability that the actual theft losses next year will *exceed* $70,000? Hint: Assume the distribution is symmetrical and remember the Chebyshev Inequality. (Between 12 and 13 percent)
b If the risk manager can assume that the probability distribution is *normal,* what is the probability that the losses next year will *exceed* $70,000? (Between 2 and 3 percent)

7 If the firm in question 6 should increase its retail outlets to 160, each of which has the same quality of exposure to loss as the original 40:
a What would be the new value of:
(1) The mean? ($200,000)
(2) The standard deviation? ($20,000)
b How would the risk change?
c What is the *maximum* probability that the losses would be less than $160,000 or more than $240,000? (25 percent)
d How would you answer part c if you could assume *normality?* (Between 4 and 5 percent)

8 The Beacon Corporation has 500 employees. Industrial injuries during the past 15 years averaged about 5 a year. An employee can be injured more than once a year.
a Explain how you would calculate the probability that next year industrial injuries will total 10 or more. The actual calculation need not be performed.
b How would your calculation be affected if you discovered that although industrial injuries averaged 5 a year, there were no losses during each of the first five years, 5 losses during each of the second five years, and 10 losses during each of the last five years?

9 What theoretical probability distribution describes the distribution of the dollar losses per occurrence for many types of losses?

SUGGESTIONS FOR ADDITIONAL READING

Carter, R. L., and N. A. Doherty (eds.): *Handbook of Risk Management* (London: Kluwer-Harrop Handbooks, 1974), pt. 2.
Cummins, J. D., and L. R. Freifelder: "Statistical Analysis in Risk Management," an eight-part series appearing in the September, 1978, through April, 1979, issues of *Risk Management.*
Denenberg, H. S., et al.: *Risk and Insurance* (2d ed., Englewood Cliffs, N.J.: Prentice-Hall, Inc., 1974), chap. 2.

Financial Applications for Risk Management Decisions (San Rafael, Calif.: Fireman's Fund Insurance Company and Risk Services Group, Inc., 1983), chaps. 1–4.

Greene, Mark R.: *Decision Analysis for Risk Management—A Primer on Quantitative Methods* (New York: The Risk and Insurance Management Society, 1977).

————, and J. S. Trieschmann: *Risk and Insurance* (6th ed., Cincinnati: South-Western Publishing Company, Inc., 1984), chap. 4.

————, and Oscar N. Serbein: *Risk Management: Text and Cases* (2d ed., Reston, Va.: Reston Publishing Company, 1983), chap. 3.

Mehr, R. I., and B. A. Hedges: *Risk Management in the Business Enterprise* (Homewood, Ill.: Richard D. Irwin, Inc., 1963), appendix to chap. 4.

Neter, J., W. Wasserman, and G. A. Whitmore: *Applied Statistics* (2d ed., Boston: Allyn and Bacon, Inc. 1982).

Williams, C. A., Jr., G. L. Head, R. C. Horn, and G. W. Glendenning: *Principles of Risk Management and Insurance* (2d ed., Malvern, Pa.: American Institute for Property and Liability Underwriters, Inc., 1981), vol. 1, chaps. 4 and 5.

CHAPTER 5

PROPERTY LOSS EXPOSURES

LEARNING OBJECTIVES

After you have completed this chapter, you should be able to:

1 Describe the types of property that are exposed to loss.
2 Explain why one does not have to be a sole owner to suffer a property loss.
3 Distinguish between direct property losses and indirect property losses.
4 Determine the amount of the loss that could be sustained if some property was taken, damaged, or destroyed.

INTRODUCTION

The discussion now turns to the major types of property, liability, and personnel losses faced by a business. This chapter deals with direct and indirect property losses; Chapters 6 through 9 deal with net income losses (another type of property loss) and the other two major loss categories. We will consider the kinds of direct and indirect property losses that might occur, their causes, how they might be valued, and some illustrative loss-frequency and severity data.

TYPES OF PROPERTY LOSSES

Property losses can be classified in at least four ways, according to (1) the class of property affected, (2) the cause of the loss, (3) whether the loss is direct or indirect, and (4) the nature of the firm's interest in the property.

Property Class

Property may be divided into two broad classes: (1) real estate or land and its appurtenant structures or attachments and (2) personal property or property that is movable and not attached to land. Personal property is also commonly divided into two subclasses: (1) personal property in use and (2) personal property for sale.

Real estate is illustrated by vacant land, an office building, a manufacturing plant, a warehouse, a garage, or some other structure. Personal property includes such items as machinery, patterns and dies, furniture and fixtures, raw materials, goods in process, finished goods, merchandise for sale, supplies, and money and securities. Except for the finished goods and the merchandise for sale, these examples illustrate personal property in use.

Cause of the Loss

The possible causes of property losses that should be of concern to a risk manager are too numerous to list. It is instructive, however, to consider various ways in which these causes or perils have been classified and to discuss briefly some of the more important perils.

Classifications   One classification divides the causes of property losses into three classes: (1) physical, (2) social, and (3) economic.[1] Physical perils include such natural forces as fires, windstorms, and explosions that damage or destroy property. Social perils are (a) deviations from expected individual conduct such as theft, vandalism, embezzlement, or negligence, or (b) aberrations in group behavior such as strikes or riots. Economic perils, the least common of the three, may be due to external or internal forces. For example, a debtor may be unable to pay off an account receivable because of an economic recession or a contractor may not complete a project on schedule because of a management error. Two or more of these perils may be involved in one loss. For example, a negligent act by an employee may lead to an explosion; an economic recession and a windstorm may together so severely cripple a debtor's department store that the debtor cannot pay the amount owed a wholesaler; strikers may set fire to a plant.

A second classification, closely related to the first, classifies perils as (1) physical, (2) human, or (3) economic. The only difference is that human perils include social perils and those economic perils, such as management errors, that are internal to the firm. Risk managers are concerned for the most part with physical and human perils.

Some Selected Perils   The perils most commonly associated with property losses are fire, smoke, explosion, windstorm, hail, collision, water damage, glass breakage from any cause, riot, vandalism, theft, employee dishonesty, and failure of a person to meet an expressed obligation for any reason. Four of these perils—fire, explosion, windstorm, and theft—are described briefly below to indicate the type of information

[1] Adapted from Charles O. Hardy, *Risk and Risk Bearing* (Chicago: The University of Chicago Press, 1923), pp. 2–3.

about a peril that should prove useful in identifying and measuring loss exposures and how to control them.

Fire results from combustion.[2] Oxygen, or an oxygen-bearing compound, unites with some other chemical element or compound to produce perceptible heat. For a fire to occur, therefore, oxygen, a substance capable of union with oxygen, and some means of raising the temperature of the substance to an ignition point must be present. The oxygen generally comes from the air but some oxygen-bearing compounds such as cotton release enough oxygen under heat or pressure to permit combustion. Usually heat is applied from some external source but spontaneous combustion can result from a buildup of heat within the substances involved. Combustibility depends upon (1) the adequacy of the oxygen supply, (2) the ratio of exposed surface to mass, (3) the time the substance is subjected to heat, and (4) the degree of atmospheric humidity. Evaporating moisture dissipates much of the heat, but moisture, being a good conductor, may also permit deeper penetration. The vulnerability of property to heat depends in part on its combustibility, but fire can also ruin property that is not combustible; e.g., by melting or by distorting its shape.

An explosion "is any release of energy with violence sufficient to injure or damage."[3] Four categories of explosions are (1) molecular disintegrations (explosions of TNT, for example), (2) rapid combustion (most explosions of dust, vapors, and gases in air), (3) nuclear fission, and (4) nonreactive releases of energy such as the "exploding" of a flywheel rotating at high speed, or a boiler explosion. Explosibility of a substance depends upon (1) the concentration of substances in the air (explosion is possible only within a range of explosible densities), (2) particle size (generally the smaller the particle the greater the explosibility), (3) heat (a substance is explosible only if its temperature exceeds its ignition point), (4) pressure (the greater the pressure, the more oxygen available for combustibility), and (5) miscellaneous factors such as the time the substance is exposed to heat and water vapor present in the air. The trigger force can be a flame, a shock, or a spark. The destructiveness of a reactive-type explosion is the rate of speed at which the reaction progresses which in turn depends upon the natural susceptibility to disintegration or oxidation and the factors of explosibility listed above. Dust explosions can cause serious secondary blasts if they jar dust that has accumulated on girders, shelves, and other surfaces. The destructiveness of energy-escape explosions depends mainly on the quantity of explosive force within a boiler or other equipment. Secondary explosions may result from the sudden contact of steam and cool air.

Windstorm losses to buildings depend upon the force or velocity of the wind and the quality of the building materials and workmanship.[4] Although less violent windstorms may and do cause extensive damage, tornadoes and hurricanes are particularly serious events. A tornado, which may cause winds as high as 450 miles an hour, cuts a narrow swath as a rule. Buildings in its path tend to explode or collapse because of the

[2] This discussion of the fire, explosion, and theft perils is basically a brief summary of chaps. 10 and 14 of Donald L. MacDonald, *Corporate Risk Control* (New York: The Ronald Press Co., 1966).
[3] Ibid., p. 172.
[4] See P. I. Thomas and P. B. Reed, *Adjustment of Property Losses*, 4th ed. (New York: McGraw-Hill Book Company, Inc., 1977), pp. 178–179. This book also discusses several other perils and their effects.

vacuum-like effect caused by the swirling winds. A hurricane has a much wider path of 50 to 100 miles or more with an eye or calm area in the middle. Hurricanes may last for several days and often travel over a very long distance. For example, a hurricane may enter the Florida Coast, move northward, and exit through New England. Wind velocities may reach 100 to 150 miles an hour with a strong suction effect near the center. Flying debris may add to the property damage caused by tornadoes and hurricanes. Buildings with light frame walls or lightly framed roofs are particularly susceptible to the high winds accompanying hurricanes or the fringe of a tornado.

Crime or theft losses may be caused by outsiders or insiders. Outsiders may be classified according to (1) the nature of the crime or (2) whether they are professionals or amateurs. Outside crimes include: burglary, the forcible entry to or exit from the premises for the purpose of stealing; robbery, the taking of property from a person by force or threat of force; shoplifting, and similar crimes abetted by the victim's inattentiveness, distraction, or brief absence; forgery; and the passing of counterfeit checks. Career thieves support themselves by stealing. They include (1) professionals who proceed only after carefully assessing the situation including the risks involved, and (2) ordinary thieves who tend to be more impulsive and less careful. Amateur thieves do not support themselves principally by stealing. They may have an emergency need, a costly addiction, a thirst for thrills, or a mental disorder. They tend to perform like ordinary thieves.

Employee dishonesty usually results in embezzlement, which is the taking of property in the custody of a person not its owner for the benefit of that person. Employees, however, may also take property belonging to an employer that is not "property" in the custody of that person. Three categories of dishonest employees have been identified: (1) mature thieves who accept a job with the intention of stealing, (2) employees with financial emergencies who usually can justify in their own mind their decision to steal from their employers, and (3) pilferers who steal on a small scale for a variety of reasons such as modest increases in their income (or, by stealing nonmonetary items such as hams and typewriters, decreases in their expenses), social pressures, getting even, or excitement. Employees with financial pressures and pilferers may include even the most trusted employees. Indeed, pilferers may include *most* employees if taking a company pencil, paper clip, notepad, or similar small item is included.

Direct or Indirect Loss

Property losses are (1) direct or (2) indirect. Property suffers a *direct* loss when the property itself is directly damaged or destroyed or disappears because of contact with a physical or social peril. To illustrate, a building is destroyed by fire, interior walls are defaced by vandals, an automobile is damaged in a collision, or money and securities are stolen from a safe.

Property suffers an *indirect* loss when its value is lessened as a result of direct damage to some other property. This concept is best explained through some examples. First, property such as meat, wine, computers, medicines, or ancient manuscripts may be damaged if their environment is altered because of direct damage to property that affects that environment, such as temperature and humidity controls, an air conditioner, a heater, or an electric power plant.

Second, some property consists of two or more components. If some, but not all, of these components suffer a direct property loss, the remaining components may be lessened in value because the damaged components cannot be replaced. The classic example is a pair of earrings, one of which is lost. Other examples are (1) machines that cannot operate because certain parts are damaged or (2) clothing that consists of two or more parts, one part of which is destroyed.

Third, if a building is severely damaged, even though it is not completely destroyed it may have to be completely rebuilt. The loss of that part of the building that was not damaged but has to be torn down to permit rebuilding is an indirect loss. The loss is (1) the cost of tearing down the undamaged part and (2) the value of the undamaged part.

A related indirect loss arises out of building codes that require replacement of a building (or part of a building such as a roof) not meeting the present code, if the undesirable building (or part thereof) is damaged to the extent of, say, 50 percent or more. For example, a frame building may have to be replaced with a brick building if the frame building is damaged more than 50 percent. The indirect loss is (1) the cost of tearing down the undamaged part, (2) the value of the undamaged part, and (3) the difference between the value of the building required by the ordinance and the value of the original building.

Interests in Property

Property has a much broader meaning than mere physical or tangible assets. According to legal definitions, *property* refers to a bundle of rights that may flow from or be part of the tangible physical assets, but which independently possess certain economic values.[5] These rights assume many forms that can be obtained in various ways. In order to identify and measure the property losses to which his or her business is exposed, the risk manager should be aware of the different kinds of interests that may exist and how they might be valued. The exposures that result from these interests may be property, including net income, or liability exposures. Only the direct and indirect property loss exposures are considered below.

Owners   The clearest property interest is sole ownership. An ownership interest may result from a purchase, a foreclosure on a mortgage or a conditional sales contract, a gift, or from some other event. If the property suffers a direct or indirect loss, the owner bears the amount of that loss. If a business owns only part of the property, it bears only part of the loss.

---

[5] The following definition is illustrative: "The word is also commonly used to denote anything which is the subject of ownership, corporeal or incorporeal, tangible or intangible, visible or invisible, real or personal; everything that has an exchangeable value or which goes to make up wealth or estate. It extends to every species of valuable right and interest, and includes real and personal property, easements, franchises and incorporeal hereditaments." *Samat* v. *Farmers' & Merchants' National Bank of Baltimore*, 247 Fed. 669, 671 (4th Cir. 1917).

Secured Creditors   A secured creditor has an interest in property pledged as security for the loan, because the creditor's ability to collect from the debtor is diminished if the property is damaged or destroyed. The potential loss is the unpaid balance of the loan.

Examples of secured creditors are mortgagees for the amount of the mortgage, builders under a mechanics' lien for the value of work performed on the property, transportation companies or warehouse companies for their transportation or storage charges, and, under a conditional sales contract, vendors for the unpaid balance of the purchase price.

In each of the above examples, multiple property interests exist. For example, the mortgagee has an interest equal to the amount of the mortgage; the mortgagor has an ownership interest equal to the value of the property. The vendor, who retains title to the property merely as security, has an interest equal to the unpaid balance of the purchase price; like the mortgagor, the vendee has an ownership interest equal to the property value.

Vendors or Vendees   The losses faced by vendors and vendees under conditional sales contracts have been described above. In other sales situations the party who holds title at the time the property is damaged or lost is the one responsible for the loss.

In transactions where the terms of sale are not clear as to when title passes, the courts have relied upon the method of billing and shipment as an expression of intent. All states except Louisiana have enacted the Uniform Commercial Code, which clarifies some of these questions. In general, the rules are as follows: *(a)* Goods shipped f.o.b. point of shipment places title in the buyer when goods are delivered to the common carrier, since the buyer is paying the costs of freight and the common carrier therefore is the buyer's agent. *(b)* Goods shipped f.o.b. point of destination transfers title to the buyer when goods are received from the common carrier, since the common carrier is the agent for purposes of shipment of the seller. *(c)* Goods shipped f.a.s. (or free alongside) passes the title to the goods when they are delivered intact alongside the conveyancing equipment, and therefore loss or damage during the course of shipment must normally fall upon the buyer. *(d)* Goods shipped c.o.d. (or collect on delivery) normally does not affect the passing of title. Such a provision in the bill of lading merely indicates that the shipper is retaining the right of possession in the goods until payment is made. Title passes to the buyer if he or she is to pay tranportation charges at the time the goods are received by the carrier, but the seller reserves a lien on the property until payment has been made. *(e)* Goods shipped c.i.f. (or cost, insurance, freight) normally passes title at the time the goods are delivered to the common carrier at the point of shipment, and the insurance documents and title papers are given to the common carrier at that time.

Tenants   Tenants generally do not have any property-loss exposures in their status as tenants, but three exceptions deserve notice. First, under common law, a tenant is responsible for damage to the premises caused by the tenant's negligence. The law of negligence is discussed in Chapter 7. Second, some leases require that the tenant return the property to the landlord in as good a condition as it was received, wear and tear excepted. Such a provision makes the tenant responsible for accidental losses to the property as well as losses caused by the tenant's negligence. On the other hand, under some leases the tenant escapes liability for either accidental losses or losses caused by his or her negligence.

Third, the tenant may make some improvements to the real estate from which he or she expects to obtain some benefit. If these improvements are by law, contract, or custom removable by the tenant when the lease expires, the tenant has an ownership interest. If these improvements are not removable and, as explained above, the tenant is negligent or responsible under the lease for damage to the building, the improvements become part of the potential building loss. If the improvements are irremovable and the lease may be canceled if the building is severely damaged, the tenant suffers a net income loss that will be explained in Chapter 6.

Bailees A bailee is a person who has possession of personal property belonging to others. The bailee can be a laundry, a warehouse, a garage, or some other business that cleans, repairs, processes, stores, or otherwise works on property belonging to others. As will be observed in Chapter 7, in the section ''Bailee Liability Exposures,'' the obligation of the bailee for damage to the property is normally dependent upon the nature of the bailment. In general, however, a bailee is responsible for damage to the bailed property only if he or she is negligent.

Representative of Owner Sometimes because of an agreement made prior to the loss or because of a desire to maintain customer goodwill, bailees assume responsibility for accidental losses to customers' property even though they are not negligent. A bailee who follows this practice has an interest in the property as representative or agent of the owner.

Other Interests Some other interests that may give rise to property loss exposures will be described briefly to indicate the wide variety that exists.

Businesses granted easements may develop an interest in the property to which they are attached. An easement is a right granted by the owner to another to use his or her real property. Examples are the right to drive or walk through the grantor's building or to use the building for certain storage purposes. The right is acquired by either express or implied grants. An easement can also be obtained (by what the law calls ''prescription'') by using the property over a long period of time. Depending upon the deed, the easement rights may be binding only upon the immediate parties or may pass to the successors of both parties.

Licenses may also create such interests. A license is a personal privilege given by the owner to another to use his or her real property for some specific purpose such as placing on it an advertising sign. Normally licenses are revocable at the will of the owner of the property, but in some cases the licensee spends considerable money improving his or her license and the privilege is not easily revoked. Although a licensee cannot be as certain that his or her right will continue as a business granted an easement, the licensee will nevertheless suffer a loss if the property is damaged.

A final interest that more commonly affects families than businesses is a life estate.

A life estate gives a tenant full use of certain land and buildings during his or her lifetime. Upon the tenant's death, interest in the property passes to a remainderman, who becomes the owner of the property. Both the life tenant and the remainderman will suffer a loss if the property is damaged or destroyed. The life tenant will lose the use of the property for the rest of his or her life; the remainderman loses the ownership interest he or she will eventually acquire.

VALUATION OF POTENTIAL PROPERTY LOSSES

Once the risk manager has identified the various property losses faced by the firm, he or she must value those exposures.

The following discussion approaches the loss-valuation problem primarily from the point of view of an owner concerned about direct property losses.

Methods of Valuing an Owner's Direct Property Loss Exposure

Whether the property be real estate or personal property, several basic measures of value are recognized by appraisers and others working professionally in this field. It is important to note that each method of property-loss valuation has certain advantages and disadvantages, depending on the purpose or emphasis of the valuation. For example, an appraisal of property for credit purposes may be quite different from a similar appraisal for risk management purposes. For risk managers the preferred methods are the last two of the eight methods described below plus, for personal property, the market value.

Original Cost   Original cost is simply the amount of money paid for the property at its acquisition by the business firm. For evaluating potential losses, however, original cost has many weaknesses. First, the value is completely dependent upon the price level and bargaining position of the business firm at the time of acquisition. Second, original cost takes no account of the physical depreciation or wear and tear that has occurred during the period of use since acquisition. Original cost also ignores what may have occurred because of technological, fashion, or other changes.

Original Cost Less Accounting Depreciation   Accountants traditionally have valued plant and equipment at original cost less depreciation, depreciation being the amount of the original cost that has been charged as an expense against the income earned since the acquisition of the property. Original cost less depreciation is not a useful measure because of the deficiencies of the original cost measure and because accounting depreciation may have little or no relationship to engineering or physical depreciation. Recent continued high inflation has caused accountants to add alternative valuation methods.

Market Value   In the case of real estate, the market value established by obtaining offers to purchase may be of value to the risk manager. The difficulty with this approach, however, is that market value is closely linked to the supply-and-demand function for real estate of the particular kind involved (what a willing seller or buyer will accept or pay for a particular piece of property) and the lot value, which usually is not destroyed by most contingent events. Market value is also somewhat difficult to establish, since each building is unique, and completely duplicate facilities seldom exist for most forms of real estate. Finally, the market value may be higher than the direct property loss because it may include some payments for the right to use the property immediately. In other words, it may measure the direct loss plus the net income loss.

Personal property that is readily obtainable in established markets may be valued according to current purchase or invoice prices from these market sources. A typewriter can be valued quite easily by obtaining the purchase price of similar typewriters either in the new or used market and thereby determining the cost of such property in the market. On the other hand, in certain situations market value may be too low. A new car, one week old, may have a lower market value than its true value.

Tax-Appraised Value   The value placed upon property, both real or personal, for tax purposes has been suggested by some as a way of establishing potential loss to property interests; but these values have many deficiencies. For example, some states and localities set the tax value at less than their estimate of the true value. Tax values may also be closer to the true value on new properties than on old properties.

The Economic or Use Value   Still another way of valuing property loss is by measuring the present value of the income it produces. For example, if a property produces a net income of $50,000 at the end of each year for three years, the present value of this income stream is the sum of the present values of each of the three $50,000 incomes. The present value of each $50,000 is the lump-sum equivalent value at the present time. A sum of $50,000 payable one year from now is worth less than $50,000 right now because of the ability to earn some interest on the lump-sum equivalent during the year and because of some uncertainty concerning the receipt of the $50,000 at the end of the year. If the person appraising the property assumes a 10 percent discount, each dollar payable at the end of the year is worth $1/1.10 or about $0.91 at the present time. In other words, $0.91 accumulated at 10 percent for one year will yield $1 at the end of the year. The present lump-sum equivalent of $50,000 payable at the end of one year is about $50,000 (0.91) or $45,500. The same procedure is followed with the other incomes except that the discount must be applied more than once. The $50,000 payable at the end of the second year, for example, must be discounted first to the end of the first year and then to the present. This second discounting process yields [$50,000 (0.91)] (0.91) = $45,500 (0.91), or about $41,400. The $50,000 payable at the end of the third year has a lump-sum equivalent of $41,400 (0.91), or about $37,700. The approximate present value of the three incomes, therefore, is $45,500 + $41,400 + $37,700 = $124,600. In practice this computation can be performed much more simply. Tables are available in college algebra and mathematics of finance textbooks and handbooks which show the present value of $1 payable at the end (or the beginning) of each year for n years. For example, if the interest rate is 10 percent, the present value of $1 payable at the end of each year for three years is $2.4868. The present value of $50,000 payable at the end of each year for three years is, therefore, $50,000 (2.4868), or $124,340, which is close to the approximate answer developed earlier.

As the number of periodic payments increases, the present value gets closer and closer to the periodic payment divided by the assumed interest rate. Consequently, the present value of a long series of payments of $50,000, assuming 10 percent interest, can be closely approximated as $50,000/0.10, or $500,000. Since a long series of payments is usually assumed in appraising buildings and some other long-term property, this much more simple formula can be used in such cases.

This capitalization procedure is often used when the property is rented or peculiarly designed and the income and profit position of the firm would be directly affected by its destruction. The major disadvantage associated with using this approach to determine direct losses is that, like the market value, this economic value also reflects net income losses, which should be measured separately. Furthermore, the value may be greatly affected by the location of a building and the skill of the management. And finally, the valuation estimates of the future incomes and the discount rates are very subjective.

Reproduction Value   Reproduction cost is the cost of reproducing or replacing the existing property exactly at current prices. This measure may produce an unrealistic value. For example, the materials or design used to construct a building now twenty years old may be outdated. To reproduce a computer that is ten years old may cost more than buying a more effective, modern computer.

Replacement Cost New   Replacement cost new is the cost of replacing the property with new property that is not exactly the same but meets current reasonable specifications. For example, a risk manager may determine what it would cost to replace a building by another that is equivalent in terms of space or volume at the same or another location but of reasonable, current design. The basic problem here is that the business firm would be getting a new building for an old one. On the other hand, the argument can be made that so long as the old building stands it can be used in its present design and construction. As soon as it is destroyed, however, additional unplanned costs will be imposed on the business firm and, therefore, should be considered in any risk manager's appraisal of potential loss. The fact that a roof is 10 years old does not in any way diminish the cost of replacing it with a new roof; therefore, the cost of the new roof should be considered the potential loss. Similarly, the cost of replacing some personal property, such as a machine, may be preferred as the estimate of the potential loss because the present property is performing its function adequately and new property is the only possible replacement. Perhaps the most important argument in favor of this method, however, is that most losses are partial and the cost of repairs is not reduced by physical depreciation.

Replacement Cost New Less Physical Depreciation and Obsolescence   In many property-loss valuations risk managers subtract from replacement cost new an allowance for physical depreciation, economic obsolescence, or both. Their reasoning is that the business will gain if a property is replaced with new property. No loss will have occurred. The older the property, the more risk managers argue that this is true. The firm should recognize, however, that a loss will force it into a replacement decision that would normally not be made at that time and that replacement will require additional financing. The risk manager should determine what position the firm wishes to take on this matter. In recent years, the trend in property-loss valuations has been away from this method and more toward using the replacement cost new method.

As will be explained in Chapter 17, property insurers commonly use this concept to measure the loss. They call this measure the actual cash value. Replacement cost insurance, however, is also available.

One difficulty associated with this measure is the task of measuring physical depreciation and economic obsolescence. Physical depreciation is the result of age and wear and tear. Economic obsolescence is illustrated by a change in fashion or the development of new, more efficient machinery. Property differs in the extent to which its value is affected by these two factors.

In valuing the cost of replacing personal property on either this basis or the basis of replacement cost new, one must be careful to include all the costs (e.g., transporting, installing, and ticketing costs) that would be incurred in obtaining the replacement. The risk manager should also recognize that the same property has different replacement costs as it moves through the channels of distribution—from the manufacturer to the wholesaler to the retailer to the ultimate consumer. Finally, in assessing either real or personal property losses one should include the expenses associated with cleaning up the debris following an accident.

In estimating building replacement cost, risk managers can use appraisal information services that periodically publish construction price indexes for various types of buildings in localities throughout the country.

Methods of Valuing Other Interests

As noted above, an owner may also suffer indirect property losses. A loss to property damaged because its environment is altered is valued the same way as direct losses. Similarly, if a building is severely damaged, making it necessary to tear down what remains, the value of the remaining section is determined the same way as a direct loss. If one pair of a matched set or an essential part of a machine is destroyed and cannot be replaced, the decline in value of the remaining parts may vary from almost zero to their complete value depending upon their relationship to the destroyed part.

Representatives of owners, tenants, bailees, and vendors or vendees, depending upon who holds the title, can estimate their potential losses in the same way as owners. In some instances, the cost of replacement without any deduction for depreciation is the proper measure. For example, under a lease the tenant may be required to replace the damaged or destroyed property with new parts or a new building. Secured creditors face the loss of the unpaid balance of the secured debt.

PROPERTY-LOSS FREQUENCY AND SEVERITY DATA

As noted in Chapter 4, most firms will not generate enough experience of their own from which the risk manager can estimate the probable loss frequency and severity.

Some external sources of accident data that may prove useful to the risk manager are *Insurance Facts,* an annual publication of the Insurance Information Institute[6] and *Uniform Crime Reports,* an annual publication of the Federal Bureau of Investigation.[7] For example, *Insurance Facts* contains information on fires, tornadoes, earthquakes, and automobile collisions.

Statistical exhibits filed by insurers with state insurance departments sometimes contain loss-frequency and severity data. The risk manager can obtain these data where they are available. Some insurers develop such data for internal use but the public seldom has access to such information. Public agencies such as the state department of motor vehicles may also gather data of interest to risk managers.

SOME KEY CONCEPTS

Property loss exposure   Exposure to loss from the damage, destruction, or taking of property.
Peril   The cause of a loss. Examples are fire, windstorms, water leakage, and vandalism.
Direct property loss   A loss that occurs because property that is damaged, destroyed, or taken by a specified peril must be repaired or replaced.
Indirect property loss   A loss that occurs because some property is adversely affected by the fact that some other property is damaged, destroyed, or taken by a specified peril. For example, food in a refrigerator spoils when fire destroys a transformer.
Property interest   The rights that a business possesses in a piece of property; for example, as an owner, representative of the owner, or a secured creditor.
Replacement cost new   The cost of replacing or repairing the property damaged, destroyed, or taken without any deduction for physical depreciation or economic obsolescence.
Replacement cost new less depreciation and economic obsolescence   The cost of replacing or repairing the property damaged, destroyed, or taken less a deduction for physical (not accounting) depreciation and economic obsolescence.

REVIEW QUESTIONS

1 The text classifies property losses in four ways. Name and explain briefly these four ways.
2 How does a direct property loss differ from an indirect loss?
3 Cite three illustrations of indirect property losses.
4 Cite four illustrations of interests in property other than sole ownership.
5 Two or more firms may have a property interest in the same real estate. Use three examples to illustrate the truth of this statement.
6 A firm purchases goods f.o.b. point of destination. At what point does the title pass to the firm? What other terms of shipment are possible and what is their effect upon the passing of title?
7 Twenty years ago a firm purchased a building, which was then five years old, for $200,000. The price was generally considered a bargain. The firm's current balance sheet states that the building is worth $200,000 less depreciation of $120,000. From these data can you tell what the direct loss would be if the building were totally destroyed by fire? If not, why not?
8 According to one construction index, the cost of building the structure described in question

---

[6] *Insurance Facts* (New York: Insurance Information Institute, annual).
[7] *Uniform Crime Reports* (Washington, D.C.: Federal Bureau of Investigation, annual).

7 has increased 50 percent over the past 2 years. The risk manager decides, therefore, to value the building at $300,000. Comment on this valuation.

9 How would you value the direct property loss sustained by each of the following if a building were destroyed by fire?

a The owner

b A bank that holds a mortgage on the property

c A tenant

10 Cite some sources of information concerning the frequency of property losses of various types.

SUGGESTIONS FOR ADDITIONAL READING

Beckman, G. M., W. F. Berdal, and D. G. Brainard: *Law for Business and Management* (New York: McGraw-Hill Book Company, 1975), part IV.

Insurance Facts (New York: Insurance Information Institute, annual).

Keeton, R. E. *Basic Text on Insurance Law* (St. Paul, Minn.: West Publishing Company, 1971), chaps. 3 and 4.

Mehr, R. I., and B. A. Hedges: *Risk Management: Concepts and Applications* (Homewood, Ill.: Richard D. Irwin, Inc., 1974), chap. 7.

———— and ————: *Risk Management in the Business Enterprise* (Homewood, Ill.: Richard D. Irwin, Inc., 1963), chaps. 6, 8, and 9.

Rodda, W. H., J. S. Trieschmann, E. A. Wiening, and B. A. Hedges: *Commercial Property Risk Management and Insurance,* vols. I and II (2d ed., Malvern, Pa.: American Institute for Property and Liability Underwriters, 1983), chap. 1.

Smith, Michael L.: *Selection of Deductibles in Property and Liability Insurance,* unpublished doctoral dissertation, The University of Minnesota, 1974, chap. 5.

Thomas, P. I.: *How to Estimate Building Losses and Construction Costs* (4th ed., Englewood Cliffs, N.J.: Prentice-Hall, Inc., 1983).

————, and P. B. Reed: *Adjustment of Property Losses* (4th ed., New York: McGraw-Hill Book Company, 1977), chaps. 14, 16, and 17.

CHAPTER 6

NET INCOME LOSS EXPOSURES

LEARNING OBJECTIVES

After you have completed this chapter, you should be able to:

1 Define a net income loss.
2 Distinguish between a net income loss caused by a decrease in revenues and one caused by an increase in expenses.
3 Identify and measure the net income loss exposures of a business.
4 Distinguish between a rent loss and a rental value loss.
5 Distinguish between a business interruption loss and an extra expense loss.

INTRODUCTION

The direct and indirect property losses discussed in Chapter 5 are often not the only losses that occur when property is damaged, destroyed, or taken. Until that property is replaced or restored to its former condition, the business may suffer a reduction in its net income (revenues less expenses) because it loses the use of that property—in whole or in part. As a result, either (1) revenues are decreased or (2) expenses are increased.

Although in many instances the net income loss will far exceed the direct and indirect property losses, businesses tend to be less aware of net income exposures than direct and indirect property exposures. Risk managers also find it more difficult to measure the loss potential of net income exposures because of the many variables involved. This chapter describes the leading net income exposures and their loss potential.

DECREASES IN REVENUES

The major ways in which revenues may be decreased as a result of an accidental loss to property include (1) a loss of rent, (2) an interruption in the firm's operations, (3) an interruption in the operations of important suppliers or customers, (4) loss of profits on finished goods, and (5) smaller net collections on accounts receivable.

Loss of Rent

If a building is accidentally damaged or destroyed, and the tenant is not responsible for the payment of rent during the period the property is untenantable, the landlord loses the rent, less any noncontinuing expenses, for the time necessary to restore the structure to a tenantable condition.

The responsibility of the tenant in case the property becomes untenantable is usually specified in the lease. Typically the landlord is responsible for the loss of rent, but this is not always true. If the lease is silent, common law holds the tenant responsible, but most states have statutes that excuse the tenant from the rental payments. (If the tenant *is* responsible, the landlord's risk manager may still prefer to include this exposure in the risk analysis but recognize that it has been handled through a noninsurance transfer. See Chapter 11.)

Interruption in Operations

Because assets are damaged or taken, a business or other organization may have to suspend or reduce its operations. For example, a department store may have to close its doors or part of the store until the assets are repaired or replaced. Assets that, if damaged or taken, might cause such a shutdown include the store premises, furniture and fixtures, or merchandise for sale. A manufacturer may have to cease or reduce production until it replaces assets such as the plant, machinery, patterns and dies, raw material inventories, or goods in process. As these examples imply, it is customary to measure the loss to a mercantile or service business in terms of the reduction in sales. The loss to a manufacturing firm depends upon the reduction in production—not sales. The loss a manufacturer might suffer because of a loss to its finished goods is considered below.

The loss caused by such a business interruption would be (1) the net profit the business would have earned if there had been no interruption plus (2) the expenses that continue despite the interruption. Illustrative of such continuing expenses are the payroll of certain key employees, services performed by others under contract, interest expense, depreciation and taxes on undamaged property, and some portion of advertising and insurance expenses.

The period of the shutdown or reduction in operations will vary according to what assets are damaged or taken and the nature of the direct or indirect loss. Sometimes partial damage to a vital asset can cause the firm to shut down for an extended period. To this period must be added the time required after operations are resumed to achieve normal sales or production volume.

The net profit loss will depend upon the state of the economy as well as circumstances peculiar to the industry and the individual firm. Trend, cyclical, and seasonal factors should be considered in estimating the loss. The estimate of continuing expenses will be influenced by similar considerations.

Pro forma income statements for various shutdown periods provide a useful framework for estimating these losses.

Contingent Business Interruption

Some businesses depend so much upon receiving raw materials, power, or merchandise from a single supplier that interruption of that supplier's operations will, in turn, interrupt the firm's production or sales. Similarly, a business may be so dependent upon sales to a single customer that if that customer's operations, and consequently its purchases from the business, are slowed by damage to or taking of its assets, the business will also suffer a business interruption loss. This loss, called a *contingent business interruption loss,* depends upon how much the firm depends upon a single supplier or customer, the susceptibility of those suppliers and customers to interruption losses, and the likely restoration period.

Loss of Profits on Finished Goods

As mentioned above, a manufacturer's operations are assumed to be interrupted when the production process, not its sales, are interrupted. Yet, if finished goods are destroyed or taken, the manufacturer will lose the profits it would have made if it had been able to sell these goods. Consequently a manufacturer should also consider among its net income exposures the possibility that it will lose the profits on its finished goods.

The profits that merchants (as contrasted with manufacturers) may lose because of damage to or taking of merchandise they have for sale are included in the business interruption loss. Indeed, because that merchandise may be turned over more than once during the shutdown period, the net profit that is part of the business interruption loss may exceed the profit loss on the merchandise that was actually damaged or taken. Sometimes, however, the potential loss is measured better by the loss of profit on the merchandise on hand for sale. For example, the merchandise may be irreplaceable. Sometimes it is replaceable but the selling season will be over before the merchandise can be replaced. Finally, if the merchandise hs been sold but not delivered, the loss is the selling price including profits.

Smaller Net Collections on Accounts Receivable

If a firm's accounts receivable records are damaged or taken, it may encounter much greater difficulties than usual in collecting from customers. The larger the number of customers and the smaller the average account, the greater these difficulties are likely to be. The records can sometimes be reconstructed from other documents, but the reconstruction costs reduce the net collections.

If the firm suffers a substantial property loss, even if the accounts receivable records remain intact, some customers may reason that with so many other problems the firm will not be paying as much attention to its collections. Consequently they may delay or skip some payments.

INCREASES IN EXPENSES

Expenses may be increased because of an accidental loss in a variety of ways including (1) rental value losses, (2) extra expenses incurred to keep the business operating, (3) cancellation of a valuable lease, and (4) the loss of use by a tenant of irremovable improvements and betterments.

Rental Value Losses

If a business that owns a building cannot occupy the structure because of accidental physical damage, the owner loses the rental value of the building for the time it takes to make repairs. The rental value can be measured by the cost of equivalent premises elsewhere less noncontinuing expenses.

If a business is a tenant instead of an owner, the loss depends upon whether the lease or the common law requires the tenant to pay the contract even if it cannot occupy the premises because of physical damage. If the tenant need not pay the rent, it loses only the amount by which the rental value of equivalent premises exceeds the discontinued contract rent and noncontinuing expenses times the number of months necessary to restore the premises. If the tenant *must* pay the rent, the monthly loss is the rental value of equivalent premises.

If the business operations are interrupted until the building is repaired, it is customary to assume that the rental value exposure is included in the business interruption exposure. If the business must or wishes to continue operations at another location, regardless of the extra expense, the rental value exposure becomes part of the broader extra expense exposure described next.

Extra Expenses

Newspaper publishers, dairies, dry cleaners, banks, and other businesses that believe they must continue operating to preserve their relationships with customers could suffer irreparable damage if damage to or taking of their assets interrupted these operations. If their customers are forced to turn to their competitors for temporary service, they may lose a large portion of these customers forever. Consequently these firms would probably incur extra expenses to continue as near normal operations as possible.

To estimate the extra expenses that might be incurred in such a situation, the risk manager, in conjunction with others in the firm, should develop a plan that will be followed after an accident to continue operations. The plan serves two purposes. First, the plan itself will permit the firm to proceed more expeditiously following the accident than if there were no pre-loss planning. Second, the plan provides a reasoned estimate of the extra expenses that will be incurred to continue operations.[1]

The extra expenses might include such items as the cost of moving to and from temporary quarters; the extra rent for those quarters; the rental of temporary equipment; higher prices for rush orders of raw materials, supplies, or merchandise; additional transportation charges; and higher labor costs. Generally these extra expenses are higher the first 30 or 60 days following a loss than subsequently.

In addition to those firms that believe they must maintain their operations to keep their customers, certain businesses such as a public utility are required to maintain continuous service. Sometimes a firm has both an extra expense and a business interruption exposure. For example, a diversified firm may render services or manufacture products, some of which cannot and others of which can be discontinued. Another firm may be willing to interrupt its operations in the short run but prefer to operate with alternate facilities at extra expense in case of an extended shutdown.

In addition to incurring extra expenses to continue operations, the firm may incur some extra costs to expedite repairs, thus shortening the period operations are either shut down or continued elsewhere.

Cancellation of Lease

Many leases provide that if the building is damaged by at least, say, 50 percent, the lease is canceled either automatically or at the option of either party. The tenant suffers if the property is worth more than the rent it pays or if it has paid a bonus or advance rental payment that is not refundable.

Rental Value Higher than Rent Sometimes a long-term lease on a building calls for a contract rent that is less than the rental value of equivalent premises elsewhere. Such a lease is valuable to the tenant. If the lease provides for cancellation automatically or at the option of the landlord and such a loss does occur, the landlord would probably ask for a higher contract rent equal to the building's rental value. The tenant, therefore, faces a potential loss equal to the present value for the remainder of the lease of the difference between the rental value and the contract rent. The shorter the time remaining under the lease, the smaller this present value. If in addition to having the lease canceled, the business must move to new quarters, the rent difference is only part of the loss. The firm will also incur the cost of moving to a new location and the additional costs, if any, of operating at the new location.

The calculation of the present value of the difference between the rental value and the rent is illustrated in the following example. A business has a lease under which it pays $2,500 a month to rent space whose current rental value is $3,500. The unexpired term of the lease is four years or 48 months. The firm estimates that the rental value will remain $3,500 for the remainder of the lease period. If the lease is canceled, the

---

[1] Edward W. Siver, "Measuring Risk to Protect Income: Developing a Catastrophe Plan," *Risk Management* (April, 1973), pp. 32–33.

firm will lose the difference between $3,500 and $2,500, or $1,000, paid at the beginning of each month for 48 months. The present value or lump-sum equivalent value of this loss is the amount that, invested at a certain rate of interest, would permit monthly withdrawals of $1,000 for 48 months. The appropriate interest rate is the after-tax return the business could earn on a safe, liquid investment during those 48 months. A 6 percent rate of return will be assumed in this example. The present value of the stream of monthly differences is the sum of the present value of each monthly payment calculated as follows:

$$\frac{\$1,000}{(1 + {}^{0.06}/_{12})^n}$$

where $1,000 is the value of the monthly difference, ${}^{0.06}/_{12}$ is the 6 percent interest rate converted to a monthly basis, and n is the number of months from the present when the rent would be paid. The calculation would be as follows:

Month	Difference	Discount factor	Present value of difference
1	$1,000	1.005^0	$1,000
2	1,000	1.005^{-1}	995
3	1,000	1.005^{-2}	990
. . .	. . .	. . .	. . .
46	1,000	1.005^{-45}	799
47	1,000	1.005^{-46}	795
48	1,000	1.005^{-47}	791
			$42,793

If the difference is constant, as it is in this example, the present value of the stream of differences can be calculated by multiplying the difference by the present value of $1 a year for the remainder of the lease period. As noted in Chapter 5, the present value of $1 paid periodically for selected periods and interest rates is tabled in most college algebra and mathematics of finance textbooks and handbooks. For this example the present value of $1 paid at the beginning of each month for 48 months, assuming 6 percent interest compounded monthly, is $42.793. The present value of $1,000 paid at the beginning of each month is $1,000 (42.793) = $42,793.

This $42,793 leasehold interest will decline as the unexpired term of the lease shortens. For unexpired terms of 36, 24, and 12 months, for example, the leasehold interest will be respectively $33,035, $22,676, and $11,677.

Present-value calculations are extremely important in risk management. The concept was introduced briefly in Chapter 5 and will reappear many times in this text.

Because leases tend to be written for shorter periods now than in the past, this type of loss receives less attention today than it did formerly. Rapid inflation, on the other hand, makes this loss more likely and more severe.

Bonuses or Advance Rental Payments   If the firm has paid a bonus to secure a lease or has paid the last month's rent in advance and neither payment is refunded in case the lease is canceled, the firm faces an additional leasehold interest loss. Each of these two types of loss will be illustrated below. To simplify the presentation, annual rental payments will be assumed instead of monthly payments.[2]

To illustrate the bonus loss, assume that a firm paid a bonus of $15,000 to secure a 10-year lease. If the lease is canceled with four years remaining, what is the firm's loss because of the bonus payment? Two calculations are necessary. First, the $15,000 is prorated over the 10-year lease period by asking what additional rent paid annually for 10 years would have a present value of $15,000. The present value of $1 paid at the beginning of each year for 10 years, assuming 6 percent compounded annually, is $7.8017. Therefore, the additional annual rent that would have a present value of $15,000 is $15,000/7.8017 or $1,920. The second calculation is the present value of $1,920 paid at the beginning of each year for the four years remaining in the lease. Because the present value of $1 paid at the beginning of each year for four years is $3.6730, the leasehold interest loss because of the bonus is $1,920 (3.6730) or $7,052.

The calculation of the advance rental payment loss is much easier. Assume an advance payment of $30,000 for the last year of the lease with four years remaining when the lease is canceled. The loss is technically (1) the present value of the annual interest foregone on the $30,000 deposit ($1,800 at 6 percent paid at the end of each of the next three years) plus (2) the present value of the $30,000 which if not paid in advance would have been paid three years from now. The calculation is as follows:

$$\frac{\$1,800}{1.06^1} + \frac{\$1,800}{1.06^2} + \frac{\$1,800}{1.06^3} + \frac{\$30,000}{1.06^3}$$
$$= \$1,698 + \$1,602 + \$1,511 + \$25,188$$
$$= \$30,000$$

In other words no calculation is necessary. The loss is the advance rental payment. That payment, if invested now, would yield $1,800 interest at the end of the next three years plus $30,000 at the end of the third year.

Irremovable Improvements and Betterments

Sometimes a tenant makes improvements to a rented building that cannot be removed when the tenant leaves the building. A firm makes this investment because it believes the improvements will have use value while it occupies the premises. What loss does the tenant sustain if these irremovable improvements are damaged or destroyed?

If the lease requires the landlord to repair the improvements, the tenant loses only

---

[2] For an analysis of the more complicated situation in which the firm has paid a bonus or advance rent and the rental value is higher than the rent, see p. 100 of the fourth edition of this text.

the use of the improvements while the repairs are being made. This loss becomes part of the broader business interruption loss.[3]

If the tenant is responsible under the lease for accidental damage to any part of the building, including the improvements, the cost of repairing damage to the improvements becomes part of a large responsibility described in Chapter 5. The loss of use of the improvements while repairs are being made would be part of the business interruption loss.

What will the firm lose if the lease does not specifically cover the restoration of improvements? If the tenant intends to replace the improvements, it should recognize a potential property loss equal to the cost of replacing the improvements with no deduction for depreciation. The loss of use of the improvements during the repair period would be part of the business interruption loss. If the tenant would not restore the improvements, the loss could be calculated as if the original cost of the improvements was a bonus paid at the time of the improvements. In practice it is customary to use a more simple pro rata approach. To illustrate, if improvements costing $15,000 were made at the beginning of a 10-year lease and destroyed at the end of six years, it is assumed that 40 percent of $15,000 or $6,000 has been lost. This pro rata approach ignores the fact that the improvements may not decline uniformly in value over the lease period, the time value of money, and the effects of inflation.

If the tenant's lease is canceled because of the accidental loss, as explained in the discussion of leasehold interest, the pro rata method described in the preceding paragraph can be used to calculate the loss. It makes no difference in this case whether the improvements were actually damaged by the accident.

SOME KEY CONCEPTS

Net income loss   A decrease in revenues or an increase in expenses that occurs because one loses the use of property that is damaged, destroyed, or taken.

Rent loss   The loss of contract rent that occurs when a tenant is excused from paying rent when a building that is damaged or destroyed is rendered untenantable. Also the loss of the contract rent the tenant may be required to pay even though he or she cannot occupy the building.

Business interruption loss   The profits that are lost and the expenses that continue when a business has to suspend or reduce its operations because assets are damaged, destroyed, or taken.

Rental value loss   The loss of the cost of equivalent premises if an owner-occupant or a tenant cannot occupy a building that was damaged, destroyed, or taken less any contract rent that may be discontinued.

Extra expense loss   The extra amount a business spends to continue at least part of its operations if damage to or taking of its assets would otherwise interrupt its operations.

Leasehold interest loss   The loss to a tenant, in case a building is damaged, of a valuable lease under which the rental value exceeds the rent.

---

[3] An alternative approach would list the cost of repairing the improvements as a potential property loss that had been transferred to the landlord.

Improvements and betterments   Improvements made by a tenant to a building that cannot be removed if the tenant leaves the building.

REVIEW QUESTIONS*

1 How do net income losses differ from indirect property losses?

2 A building whose rental value is $24,000 a year is rented for $18,000 a year under a lease that has five years to run. The lease excuses the tenant from paying the rent if an accident renders the property untenantable. If the physical damage to the building exceeds 50 percent, the lease is automatically canceled.

If a fire causes enough damage to the building to render it untenantable for six months but not enough to cancel the lease:

a What net income loss will the landlord suffer?

b What net income loss will the tenant suffer?

3 Assume the same facts as in question 2 except the fire is serious enough to cause the property to be untenantable for nine months and to cause automatic cancellation of the lease. At 6 percent interest the present value of $1 paid at the beginning of each year for five years is $4.4651.

a What net income loss will the landlord suffer?

b What net income loss will the tenant suffer? ($26,791)

4 A windstorm damages a manufacturing plant and a warehouse in which finished goods are stored until sold.

a What net income loss does the business suffer because of the damage to the manufacturing plant?

b What net income loss does the business suffer because of the damage to the warehouse?

5 A department store has been operating at a slight loss during the past year. Does it have any business interruption exposure?

6 Under what conditions would a contingent business interruption exposure exist?

7 Explain why a firm with a few large customers is less likely than a firm with many small customers to have difficulty collecting on its accounts receivable if its records are destroyed by vandals.

8 a Why might a business consider itself to have an extra expense exposure instead of a business interruption exposure?

b Might both exposures exist?

9 Five years ago a business paid a bonus of $20,000 to secure a 10-year lease. If the lease is canceled, what will be the leasehold interest loss because of the bonus? Assuming 6 percent interest, the present value of $1 paid at the beginning of each year for five years is $4.4651; for 10 years $7.8017. ($11,148)

10 Five years ago a tenant spent $20,000 on irremovable improvements that it expected to use under a 10-year lease. If these improvements are destroyed and not replaced, what loss does the tenant suffer? ($10,000 if prorated)

SUGGESTIONS FOR ADDITIONAL READING

Mehr, R. I., and B. A. Hedges: *Risk Management: Concepts and Applications* (Homewood, Ill.: Richard D. Irwin, Inc., 1974), chap. 8.

* Items in parentheses are answers.

———— and ————: *Risk Management in the Business Enterprise* (Homewood, Ill.: Richard D. Irwin, Inc., 1963), chap. 9.

Rodda, W. H., J. S. Trieschmann, E. A. Wiening, and B. A. Hedges: *Commercial Property Risk Management and Insurance,* vols. I and II (2d ed., Malvern, Pa.: American Institute for Property and Liability Underwriters, 1983), chap. 1

Thomas, P. I., and P. B. Reed: *Adjustment of Property Losses* (4th ed., New York: McGraw-Hill Book Company, 1977), chaps. 25 and 26.

CHAPTER 7

LIABILITY LOSS EXPOSURES: I

LEARNING OBJECTIVES

After you have completed this chapter, you should be able to:

1 Explain the four points a plaintiff must make to win an action based on negligence.
2 List and distinguish among the defenses available to the defendant.
3 Describe how damages are evaluated in a civil action.
4 Explain why a business owner or manager must be concerned about the negligent acts of others.
5 Summarize the major categories of sources of liability.
6 Distinguish the care the owner of real property owes to an invitee from that he or she owes to a trespasser or a licensee.
7 Explain the various legal bases on which a product liability action may be based.
8 Describe how the liability of a common carrier for damage to goods of others in its possession differs from the liability of ordinary bailees.
9 List some conditions under which the members of a Board of Directors may be held personally responsible for losses to stockholders and others.
10 Explain the special liability problems faced by professionals.

INTRODUCTION

In addition to the property loss exposures described in Chapters 5 and 6, a business faces the possibility that it will be held legally liable for property damage or personal injuries suffered by others. In his treatise on the common law, the noted jurist Oliver Wendell Holmes, Jr., discusses the early history of legal liability.[1] After examining various writings on ancient civilizations, Justice Holmes concludes that the early forms of legal redress were in fact grounded in the passion for obtaining vengeance. For example, in Jewish law as reported in a well-known passage in the Bible, revenge is taken against the thing causing the loss:

> If an ox gore a man or woman, that they die: then the ox shall be surely stoned and his flesh shall not be eaten; but the owner of the ox shall be quit. But if the ox were wont to push with his horn in time past and it had been testified to his owner, and he had not kept him in, but that he had killed a man or woman; the ox shall be stoned and his owner shall also be put to death.[2]

Similarly, the Greeks made provisions in their law for satisfaction of revenge when an intentional harm or injury had occurred. Plato wrote that slaves who had killed other men had to be given to relatives of the deceased. When an oxcart ran over a man, the oxen had to be surrendered to the injured party or to his or her relatives. These early legal concepts have gradually changed over the years to meet the needs of a more advanced, complex civilization. The fact that our modern law has extended legal responsibility to cover the consequences of unintentional or accidental acts or omissions greatly expands the liability exposures of firms and families.[3]

After defining legal liability and discussing its kinds and types, this chapter examines in some detail the concept of tort liability, which is the major concern of the risk manager. The chapter explores the components of a successful tort action and discusses the magnitude of the losses that could occur as a result of that action. The

---

[1] Oliver Wendell Holmes, Jr., *The Common Law* (Boston: Little, Brown and Company, 1923), pp. 1–38.

[2] Exod. 21:28–29. This early Jewish law was a forerunner of the principles of *scienter*, relating to liability for keeping dangerous animals, found in our modern law. If the animal is known to be dangerous because of past acts, liability of the possessor or keeper is clearly established for the consequences of the animal's acts.

[3] For a convenient summary of actual cases that illustrate the legal concepts presented in this text, especially Chaps. 7 and 8, the reader is referred to *Insurance Casebook* (Englewood, N.J.: The Underwriter Printing and Publishing Company, annual). For example, some descriptive titles from chap. 12 of the 1979 edition on "Negligence" are as follows:

> Action against architects for negligence
> Hospital not liable for injuries to escapee patient
> Landowner not responsible for drowning deaths of children
> Comparative negligence in shooting incident
> Dog owner liable for injury
> Liability to invitee or trespasser
> Good Samaritan rule applied
> Employer, not manufacturer, could have caused the accident
> Exploding soda bottle
> Carrier not liable for assault on passenger
> Duty of construction company in building home
> Use of doctrine of *res ipsa loquitur*
> Passenger talking to driver at time of collision not guilty of contributory negligence
> Cause of action lay in negligence, not in assault and battery
> No recovery for patron who fell off stool
> User of spa assumed risk of unsafe condition
> Hamster is "product" for strict products liability purposes

discussion then turns to some specific liability exposures and problems, including bailee exposures and those that involve premises, business operations, and professional services.

The special exposures associated with employee injuries and motor vehicle accidents will be described in Chapter 8.

SOME PRINCIPLES OF LEGAL LIABILITY

The term *liability* is used in various ways in our present language. In general usage, the term has become synonymous with "responsibility" and involves the concept of penalty when a responsibility may not have been met. A person may be generally obligated to another, because of moral or other reasons, to do or not to do something; the law, however, does not recognize moral responsibility alone as legally enforceable. *Legal* liability has been defined as "that liability which courts recognize and enforce as between parties litigant."[4] Thus the term "legal liability" is narrower than moral obligation, since the courts and the law determine legal liability.

Various Kinds and Types of Legal Liability

An individual or a business firm may be held legally responsible in various ways. The two major classes of general legal liability are (1) civil liability and (2) criminal liability. Civil liability is distinguished from criminal liability by the nature and form of the action as well as by the penalties imposed. In a criminal action, the actual legal procedure is begun by the law-enforcement officer on behalf of society or the state. For example, the district attorney or attorney general of either the federal or state government normally initiates the criminal action against the individual or business firm. Criminal liability must be clearly established by statute or administrative rule, whereas in civil liability, the statutes, administrative rules, and prior court decisions announce the rights of the parties as opposed to each other.

A civil liability action is brought normally by one party against another party for the wrongs alleged. Penalties consist of indemnity for the loss or punitive damages imposed by the courts, restitution of the property or loss, injunctive relief precluding future conduct or action, and other remedies, including possession of the property or an accounting of the property entrusted. These civil actions are brought by the litigants at their own expense (except that the court costs may be imposed on the losing party). In criminal liability cases, when it is clearly shown that the defendant is unable to hire counsel, the state will provide such counsel at its own expense.

While avoidance of criminal liability is important as far as business or individual conduct is concerned, generally the risk manager's activities are confined to meeting the civil liability exposures, leaving these other problems to legal counsel and the conscience of those involved.

The concept of civil liability may be further classified into the varying kinds of sources of legal actions that may be brought to establish civil liability. For example, in

---

[4] *Abbott v. Aetna Cas. & Sur. Co.*, 42 F. Supp. 793, 806 (D. Md. 1942).

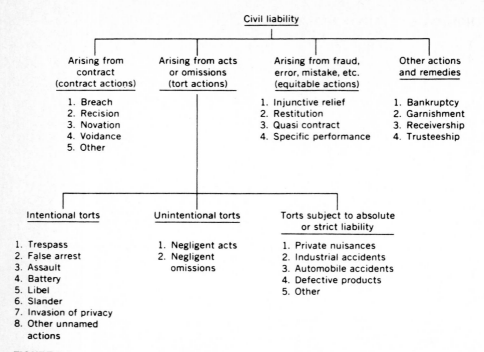

FIGURE 7.1
Civil liability analysis. [Equitable actions are actions or suits seeking equal and impartial justice, based on the spirit of fairness, justness, and right, as distinguished from the common law, which may not have afforded an adequate remedy. See *Black's Law Dictionary* (4th ed., St. Paul, Minn.: West Publishing Company, 1951), p. 632.]

Figure 7.1 the sources of civil liability are classified into (1) those arising from contract or similar agreements, (2) those arising from acts or omissions, which are called "torts," (3) those arising from fraud, error, mistake, etc., referred to generally as equitable actions, and (4) some actions and remedies that do not fall in the first three categories. Actions based on contracts and tort actions seek money awards. Equitable actions seek some other remedy such as the performance of specific contracts.

In order to bring a civil action it is not necessary that the type of action be named as such but merely that the theory of recovery be established for deciding the rights of the parties. For example, breach of contract may in fact be accomplished by the commission of a tort. The plaintiff's attorney may decide to bring the action in contract law to recover damages suffered by the breach rather than to bring the action in tort law because of problems in establishing proof. It may be more difficult to show actual negligent conduct and the legal duty of the defendant than to show nonperformance of the contract obligation. It is important to note that the figure does not attempt to catalog all the various types of actions that may be brought and their specific remedies. It merely reflects generally on the more important theories of recovery that may be espoused in a legal civil liability action.

HOW CIVIL LEGAL LIABILITIES ARE ESTABLISHED

Various writings state that the law protects only those persons who can afford it. Although the statement is, of course, an oversimplification of the actual administration of the law, it makes an important point. Anglo-American jurisprudence is built upon the principles of advocacy and trial by combat; that is, the parties present their cases before the bar, outlining all the facts of the case as well as the law involved. The magistrate or judge must make the final determination from the written and oral presentations made to the court. This process of law requires that the litigant must either in his or her own behalf or with a professionally skilled attorney present the case as forcefully and as accurately as possible. This process of administration has proved effective over the years in that justice and fair play generally have prevailed. On the other hand, the law does not profess to give justice specifically but to give each party the opportunity to have his or her "day in court." Having that day in court may be dependent upon the financial ability of the individual to obtain proper legal counsel.

Another important point is that the rights of a party are not protected in a civil case unless that party takes the initiative to assert them. In other words, the law does not protect those who sleep on their rights. Most states have what are referred to as statutes of limitations, which impose time requirements upon the bringing of a legal action against another in a civil liability case. Failure to bring the legal action within the period of limitations will bar forever the injured party's right to recovery.

In addition to the statutes of limitations, other important provisions of the law must be met; for example, all the statutes relating to legal process must be complied with as well as statutes governing rules of evidence and methods of obtaining evidence. Generally speaking, the plaintiff in a civil liability case must carry the burden of proof by "the preponderance of the evidence." Some jurisdictions in negligence actions shift these burdens of proof during the course of the trial; such action depends upon the facts of the case and the legal principles involved. For example, under the doctrine of *res ipsa loquitur* the burden of proof may shift to the defendant. The term *res ipsa loquitur* means "the thing speaks for itself," namely, for the fact that the plaintiff was injured under circumstances clearly establishing the possible negligence of the defendant. For example, an engineering company was held responsible when a ceiling it had installed fell, causing bodily injury to a person below. The court argued that ceilings do not ordinarily fall unless someone was negligent, and that the defendant was solely responsible for the installation. Hence, the jury could conclude that the contractor was negligent unless he could prove otherwise.

The entire process of litigation is very technical and normally requires the skill and services of a competent attorney. It has been said that "he who attempts to litigate his own case has a fool for a client."

HOW AWARDS ARE DETERMINED

Historically, the role of the judge (or judges) in litigation is not only to supervise the conduct of the trial by ruling upon proper procedures and admissibility of evidence, but also to hold the opposing attorneys, as officers of the court, directly accountable for their conduct to the court as well as to their clients. The judge may impose serious penalties for improper conduct or procedure engaged in by either opposing counsel. In the absence of a jury trial (usually optional with either the defendant or plaintiff in most civil cases in most jurisdictions) the court performs the function of "trier of fact" as well as determiner and interpreter of the law involved. The jury role is traditionally limited to finding the facts of a case upon instructions from the judge as to the law.

The nature and extent of the damages sustained by the plaintiff may be an issue of fact determined by the jury (or the judge, if no jury), or it may be an issue of law determined by the judge. Evidence as to the exact amount and nature of damage suffered by the plaintiff is introduced and the kind of evidence admitted and the use of evidence is ruled upon by the judge as a matter of law. The use of demonstrative evidence, such as colored slides showing especially gruesome, bloody scenes of the plaintiff's injuries may be excluded from the trial on the ground that they shock the conscience of the court as to what is fair and reasonable in the conduct of a trial.

Damages may be special, general, or punitive. Special damages are the tangible losses incurred by the plaintiff such as the loss of earnings, medical bills, property repair costs, and legal fees. General damages may be allowed for losses that are not directly measurable, such as pain and suffering. Punitive damages may be allowed where the conduct of the defendant is grossly negligent, reckless, and done without regard to life or property. Punitive damages are being awarded more frequently than in the past.[5]

Jury awards, once determined, may be reduced by the court where they are held to be "unreasonable" for the injury sustained.

A recent case in Minnesota shows how large these awards may be. A mother and her two-year-old son suffered brain damage in a January 1, 1973 automobile accident.[6] In October, 1974, the son was awarded $1.5 million as follows:

$ 7,306 Medical expenses before the trial
   994,008 Future medical expenses
   250,000 Future wage losses
   250,000 Physical and mental suffering

The mother's award of $210,000 included the following:

$ 10,696 Medical expenses before the trial
    85,000 Future wage losses
   125,000 Physical and mental suffering

Chapter 9 explains how future wage losses can be calculated. The allowance for physical and mental suffering is highly subjective.

---

[5] A few states prohibit any award for punitive damages, but some observers claim that in these states the same objective is achieved through increasing the award for special and general damages. For a comprehensive analysis of the concept of punitive damages and whether they are or should be insurable, see John D. Long, "Should Punitive Damages Be Insured?" *Journal of Risk and Insurance,* vol. XLIV, no. 1 (March, 1977), pp. 1–17.

[6] "Accident Victims Win $1.7 Million Judgment," *The Minneapolis Star,* Sept. 25, 1974, p. 15a.

According to *Personal Injury Valuation Handbooks,*[7] the first $1 million award was made in 1962. Hundreds of such awards have been made since that time.

THE CONCEPT OF TORT LIABILITY

The word "tort" is derived from the Latin *tortus* meaning twisted. Tortious conduct is indeed twisted or crooked. In general common use in the English language, the word "tort" means wrong. Legally speaking, however, a *tort* is a civil wrong other than breach of a contract for which the court will provide a remedy in the form of an action for money damages.[8] On the other hand, Prosser indicates that there is no satisfactory definition for the word "tort" and that it might be better to define a tort action by enumerating the things that it is not. Prosser says that a tort is not a crime; it is not a breach of contract; it is not necessarily concerned with property rights or problems of government. Tort occupies a large residual field of other types of legal actions. In this sense, tort is a sort of a legal garbage can to hold what cannot be put elsewhere in the law.

Basically there are three kinds of torts: (1) intentional torts, involving conduct that may be by intention or design (but not necessarily with the intention that the resulting consequences should occur), (2) unintentional torts, involving the failure to act or acting not as a reasonably prudent person would have acted under similar circumstances, and (3) wrongs for which a business may be held absolutely or strictly responsible. Intent or fault is not an issue under absolute or strict liability.

The first two kinds of torts are examined in some detail in this chapter. Except for the comments made in connection with private nuisances and product liability, discussion of the third category is deferred until the next chapter.

Intentional Torts

The intentional-tort field includes the type of conduct that can be identified as premeditated or planned but whose consequences are not necessarily anticipated.[9] Various specific kinds of intentional torts have been recognized by the courts. They include the following:

Trespass   Trespass consists of the entry of a person or a thing upon land in the possession of another without permission. This action is designed to protect the exclusive possession of land and its physical status or condition. The trespasser is

---

[7] *Personal Injury Valuation Handbooks* (Cleveland: Jury Verdict Research, Inc., updated monthly). This source gives for verdicts classified in various ways (for example, by type of injury or by source such as product liability and malpractice) the probable verdict, the median verdict, the middle 50 percent range, the average verdict, and the verdict range. It aso presents numerous examples of recent awards.

[8] W. L. Prosser, *Handbook of the Law of Torts* (4th ed., St. Paul, Minn.: West Publishing Company, 1971), p. 3.

[9] For a more detailed discussion of intentional torts and tort law in general intended for nonlawyers see Ronald A. Anderson, *The Insurer's Tort Law* (Ocean City, N.J.: The Littoral Development Company, 1971).

responsible for damages caused by this act. Generally, there are punitive damages and, in many states, a special statutory penalty.

Conversion   Conversion is the wrongful disposition and detention of personal property belonging to another. Conversion usually results from the failure of a person who had legal possession of personal property to return it as agreed. The penalties are essentially the same as for trespassing.

Assault   A person is assaulted when that person becomes apprehensive that he or she will be touched without consenting to this contact. Generally speaking, mere words, however violent, are not sufficient to amount to an assault. In order to have the essentials of an assault, there must be a clear and present danger evident to the plaintiff, and the apparent ability by the defendant to execute the threatened act. Damages may be awarded for physical illness resulting from the apprehension and, when present, for humiliation.

Battery   Battery is an unpermitted and unprivileged contact with another. An assault becomes a battery when contact is made. The gist of the action for battery is not the hostile intent to execute the touching but rather the absence of consent of the innocent party. Recovery is allowed for physical and mental harm.

False Imprisonment   False imprisonment or arrest is the illegal and unlawful confinement of another within boundaries fixed by the defendant without legal justification and with the intention that the act or breach of duty shall result in such confinement. The restraint may be by means of physical barriers or by threat of force, either or both of which intimidate the plaintiff into compliance with the orders. The restraint upon the plaintiff's freedom may also be imposed by the assertion of legal authority that the defendant contends he or she possesses. Damages may be awarded for mere interference with the plaintiff's freedom of motion plus, if present, physical harm, loss of time, damage to reputation, and humiliation.

Libel and Slander (Defamation of Character)   Libel and slander are tort actions that involve the invasion of the interest, reputation, and good name of a person by communicating to others information that diminishes the esteem in which the plaintiff was held, or excites adverse feelings or opinions against the plaintiff. Defamation is usually made up of the twin torts of libel and slander, the first being written, the other, oral. The courts have held that an allegation of insanity, an assertion that a woman has been raped, or other language that holds the plaintiff up to hatred, contempt, or ridicule or would cause the plaintiff to be shunned or avoided is a proper action for defamation. The courts similarly have held that to allege that the plaintiff has attempted suicide, refused to pay just debts, is immoral or unchaste, is a coward, a drunkard, a hypocrite, a liar, or a crook, or to make any other oppressive, insulting, or dishonorable accusation is defamation. Ridiculing and making fun of the plaintiff have also been held to be defamatory in nature. In the case of libel and slander, truth is a defense, and the failure to prove the falsity of the charge would defeat the action. Though true, however, the facts may not support completely the charge, expressed or implied, by the accuser.

Normally, proof of special damages is required; mere hurt feelings are not sufficient. On the other hand, the courts very early have established certain specific exceptions to the showing of special damages; these include the allegation that the plaintiff has committed specific crimes or possesses a loathsome disease, holding the plaintiff up to ridicule in his or her business, trade, profession, or office, and possibly the allegation that the plaintiff is given to unchastity.

In suits involving defamation of character, the courts have held that certain forms of privileged communications will not invoke liability under the tort of defamation. Absolute immunity from defamation suits has been granted, for example, to judges and members of grand or petit juries, members of the legislature, and certain executive officers of government in the discharge of their duties. Qualified or conditional privilege is extended to other interests in society, such as publishers or newspapers and magazines and commercial credit agencies. Newspaper accounts must be limited to the facts, and suits of defamation may not be brought if the facts are fairly and honestly presented, without any intent to do injury to the person's character. Commercial credit agencies investigating a person's character or financial reputation must have some specific objective in regard to a business or commercial interest and must make their inquiries honestly and carefully.

Other Intentional Torts   In addition to the above intentional torts, many others have been recognized by the courts under varying circumstances. For example, invasion of privacy, malicious and unlawful prosecution, interference with family relations, and interference with contractual relations are some of the other intentional torts.

An Unintentional Tort: Negligence

Most of the cases brought for personal injury or property damage involve the unintentional tort of negligence. The dividing line between an intentional tort and an unintentional tort is made in terms of the conduct of the defendant. The attorney bringing the case for the plaintiff must choose the theory of recovery that he or she is best able to prove. For example, one case involved a salesman who attempted to demonstrate a fly spray by spraying the product profusely around a grocery store. The wife of the grocer, who was allergic to this particular product, developed a very serious personal injury as a result of inhalation of the fumes. The plaintiff's attorney in this case could have brought the action on a theory of negligence, namely, that the salesman did not act as a reasonably prudent person would have acted in failing to discover whether or not any possible injuries might result to the people who inhale such fumes. In the particular case, however, the action was brought on a battery charge, namely, that the spraying of the fly spray was intentional, and that the touching of the plaintiff by this product was a battery committed on the grocer's wife, causing her great bodily harm.

Ingredients for a Cause of Action   An action for negligence requires the following ingredients for a cause of action:

1 Legal duty to act or not act. Legal duty implies that the plaintiff can show that the defendant should have used a legal duty of care in acting or failing to act in the manner involved. A legal duty of care is the normal basis of proving or showing existence of negligence. The duty varies depending upon the situation and the parties involved.

2 The breach of legal duty. Similarly the plaintiff must prove that the defendant clearly breached the legal duty to act or not to act as a reasonably prudent person would have done under similar circumstances. The definition of a ''prudent person'' also varies depending upon the circumstances.

3 Proximate cause between the breach of duty and the injury suffered. The plaintiff must show that the breach of legal duty by the defendant was the *proximate or closest cause* in producing the injury to the plaintiff. Showing that the defendant's negligence truly caused the plaintiff's injuries is, of course, a very troublesome area in law. The facts are often very complex and involve other possible intervening forces. For example, in one case, the plaintiff was severely injured in an automobile accident, and his wife was uninjured. An ambulance was called to the scene of the accident and the plaintiff and his uninjured wife were placed in the ambulance. While returning to the hospital the ambulance was struck by another car, and the wife subsequently died of injuries sustained. The question of proximate cause raised in the trial was whether the injury caused by the first driver to the husband was the causal negligence resulting in the injury to the wife in the second accident. Had the accident not occurred in the first place, the ambulance ride would not have been necessary. On the other hand, the ambulance driver's negligence or the negligence of the other third party hitting the ambulance might be a separate intervening negligence factor which would cut off the liability of the first accident driver.

The doctrine of proximate cause draws a circle around the scope of responsibility of the negligent offender and attempts to cut off those liabilities for which he or she should not be held responsible. For example, the courts inquire as to whether or not the defendant could have foreseen the consequences of that act when he or she engaged in it, whether the defendant created an unreasonable chance of harm to others, and whether the injuries were within the foreseeable consequences of the negligent acts. In addition, the plaintiff's exposure must be in the *zone of risk,* namely, sufficiently close to the actual commission of the negligence in the first place, in order to make it foreseeable; there must be no separate intervening cause; and the physical forces unleashed by the defendant must bear some relationship to the ultimate injury that the plaintiff suffers.

4 Damages sustained. In the showing of damages in a negligence action, the plaintiff may allege actual bodily injury or damage to property. In addition, the courts are allowing recovery for mental suffering and pain or emotional distress caused by the alleged shock imposed as a result of the defendant's conduct. In a case involving the invasion of the right of privacy (which happens to be an intentional tort) the court allowed recovery to a mother who was making delivery of her child when the doctor allowed a nonmedical person in the delivery room to watch the actual birth. The mother sustained humiliation and mental suffering as a result of such conduct, and the court allowed recovery for her mental distress. Another court case allowed recovery to a woman who was almost hit by an oncoming vehicle. The mental anxiety resulting from such a near miss produced shock and mental injury to the plaintiff for which the court allowed recovery.

Defenses

The defendant may be able to show that he or she was not negligent and thus not responsible for the damages sustained by the plaintiff. However, even if the defendant is negligent, he or she may be able to assert additional defenses such as those described below.

Assumption of Risk   The defense of assumption of risk enables the defendant to show that the plaintiff consented to the clear and present danger of the possible negligent conduct of the defendant and failed clearly to establish his or her objections to such conduct. The assumption of risk defense is often used in host-guest cases in the operation of vehicles where the driver's conduct is sufficiently bad and is known to the plaintiff guest. The driver in defense may allege that the guest in the vehicle did not leave the vehicle or clearly establish his or her objections to the negligent driving.

Contributory Negligence   Another defense, contributory negligence of the plaintiff, may remove any claims against the defendant for alleged negligent conduct. The contributory negligence defense is usually asserted in those states where it is allowed on the theory that both parties were at fault and that neither should recover from the other. Intersectional automobile accidents commonly illustrate a situation where both parties are at fault. Under a strict interpretation of the contributory negligence doctrine, neither party should collect because of the liability of the other.

Numerous statutes have been enacted in the United States to overcome the much-discussed evils of the contributory negligence doctrine. For example, the Federal Employers' Liability Act, the Merchant Marine Act, and the State Railway Labor Acts all provide that the contributory negligence of an injured worker shall not bar recovery but that the worker's damages shall be reduced in proportion to his or her negligence. About forty states, plus several Canadian provinces, have adopted similar comparative negligence rules by statute or court decision. For example, in Minnesota and Wisconsin, which have partial comparative negligence statutes, if the plaintiff's negligence is less than the defendant's negligence, money is granted for 100 percent of the plaintiff's injuries, less his or her own percentage of negligence. In Mississippi, which has a complete comparative negligence statute, each party receives 100 percent of his or her damages diminished by his or her own percentage of negligence. The following example illustrates the difference between these two statutes:

			Recovery	
	Damages	**Percentage of negligence**	**Wisconsin and Minnesota**	**Mississippi**
A	$10,000	25	$7,500	$7,500 ⎫ net of
B	5,000	75	0	1,250 ⎭ $6,250 to A

Another offsetting doctrine to the contributory negligence defense is that of *last clear chance*. Many states contend that this theory indicates the proper way to mitigate the evils of the contributory negligence defense. Under this doctrine, if the plaintiff can clearly show that his or her negligence had been spent and that the defendant had a last clear chance to avoid the injury, then recovery will be granted. One such case involved the negligent conduct of an elevator operator in leaving the gate open. The plaintiff negligently walked into the open elevator shaft and grabbed a protruding cable. The elevator operator heard the screams of the plaintiff (who had spent his negligence) and proceeded to drop the car, further injuring the plaintiff. In this situation, because the elevator operator had a last clear chance to avoid the injury and failed to do so, the plaintiff recovered.

Even in contributory negligence states claims are usually settled out of court on a more liberal basis than the legal doctrine would suggest. For example, assume that the plaintiff prevails only about half the time in cases with certain characteristics. An insurance adjustor representing the defendant may in such cases settle the claim for about half of what it would be worth.[10] In the language of Chapter 4, the insurance adjustor would settle the claim for its expected value. Courts in contributory negligence states also sometimes appear to ignore a small degree of negligence on the part of the plaintiff.

Charitable and Governmental Immunity Defenses   In the development of the common law concept of liability, the courts at various times have granted immunity to certain activities and institutions. Among others, immunity has been granted to charitable institutions and the government itself. These concepts of immunity, however, have been undergoing rapid change, and many states have virtually lifted the immunity.

In the case of charitable institutions, the theory of immunity from liability is based upon the concept that a charitable institution is a trust and that the property of a charity cannot be used to pay judgments. This concept would permit hospitals, nursing homes, and other charitable activities to be conducted without fear of legal liability for their negligence.

The common law rule of nonliability has given way, however, to a more modern concept that the charitable institution is liable (1) to persons receiving benefit from its

---

[10] Corydon T. Johns, *An Introduction to Liability Claims Adjusting* (3d ed., Cincinnati: The National Underwriter Co., 1982), chap. 15, especially pp. 547–556.

activities for injury caused by the negligence in the selection of employees, and (2) to anyone else for injury caused by negligent acts or omissions of its employees.

Governmental immunity is based upon the concept that the king can do no wrong. The courts have held generally that immunity applies to governmental activities related to the functions of governing. These would include legislative activities and such other administrative duties as the conduct of education, law enforcement, and fire protection. On the other hand, governmental immunity has been removed for those functions referred to as *proprietary*. These would include the operation of municipal light and power plants, maintenance of streets, and the operation of parks and playgrounds. Here again the tendency has been continually to narrow the area of immunity, and more and more decisions have been rendered holding municipalities and other branches of government liable for the negligent conduct of their employees and for negligence in general. Over two-thirds of the states have passed statutes that erase at least part of the immunity for the state and local governments against liability for governmental functions. Most of these statutes waive governmental immunity except with respect to certain specified functions. A few remove immunity only with respect to certain areas such as the operation of government vehicles. Many of these laws limit the amount of the lawsuits that may be brought. The federal government has waived immunity under the Federal Tort Claims Act.

The Imputed Liability of Others: Vicarious Liability

Various doctrines in the law hold people responsible for the negligent conduct of others. Several examples of this imputed or vicarious liability are presented below.

Liability Arising Out of Activities of Agents or Employers   The most frequent examples of one person being held responsible for the acts of another arises under the doctrine that one person, called the "principal," is held responsible for the tortious acts of an agent while such agent is acting on behalf of the principal. For a business this doctrine means that the employer is responsible for the tortious acts of employees or other agents while they are acting on behalf of the business. Whether the second party is an agent is often an issue to be decided by the jury. The decision depends upon the degree of control the principal has over this second party. The injured party can sue the employee or other agent, the employer, or both. Employers such as IBM or General Motors generally make far better targets for plaintiffs than do employees. Having paid a claim on behalf of an employee, the employer can try to recover from the employee, but this would be unpleasant, costly, and probably unproductive.

Liability Arising from Activities of Independent Contractors, Joint Venturers, or Joint Tort-Feasors   One of the more troublesome areas of liability law relates to the contingent liability of a firm or individual for the negligence of persons or firms hired as independent contractors. Initially, the law adopted the general rule that the employer was not liable for the tortious conduct of an independent contractor, whereas the employer would assume liability for the activities of his or her own employees. The basic reason for the nonliability rule was that an employer was deemed to have no right of control over the manner in which the work is to be done, it being regarded as the contractor's own responsibility; i.e., the latter is the proper party to be charged with the responsibility of preventing the loss.

Opposed to this reasoning is the argument that the employer is the person primarily benefiting from the work; the employer selects the contractor and is obligated to pick someone who is financially responsible for the consequences of his or her acts. If the contractor has been unwisely chosen, then the employer should be held responsible.

The general rule of nonliability of the employer has been whittled away by court decisions to the point where one can say that little still remains. In the first place, some courts have held the employer liable for failure to select a competent contractor. Second, the employer is usually held responsible for his or her own negligence in connection with the work to be done. So far as the employer gives directions, furnishes equipment, retains any control whatever, he or she is held responsible. The employer must interfere with and stop any unnecessarily dangerous practices, as well as inspect the work after it is completed to see that it is safe. Furthermore, certain duties are held to be ''nondelegable''; that is, the employer must take certain safety measures, such as fencing off operations that may cause an unreasonable chance of harm to others.

Beyond these exceptions, the courts have also recognized imputed liability for independent contractors where the operation to be performed is ''inherently dangerous.'' In these cases, such as blasting, clearing land by fire, tearing down walls and chimneys, the courts have held that a high probability of loss is created, and the employer is held to be strictly liable for injuries or damage suffered by third persons caused by the independent contractor's activities.

In many commercial and personal activities several persons or firms are apt to engage in a joint undertaking. Here again the law recognizes the right of a third party to bring an action for recovery of damages caused by any or all of the joint venturers. Each or all may be sued for the total damages suffered, and in that sense the negligence of one is imputed to the other.

Assumption or Elimination of Liability by Contract Businesses commonly assume under a contract liability for losses to others for which they would not be liable except for the contract. For example, under a lease a tenant may assume what otherwise would be the landlord's responsibility for injuries to third parties arising out of defects in the premises. Under a sales order a manufacturer may assume what would otherwise be the responsibility of the wholesaler or the retailer for injuries to persons using the product. Other examples will be presented in Chapters 10 and 11 under ''Transfer.''

Statutory Liability The legislatures of several states have seen fit to impose statutory liability for certain acts of others. Three of the most notable of these laws are described below:

1 Dram shop laws. About one-third of the states have dram shop laws that hold a tavern or place of business where liquor is dispensed liable not only for all resulting injuries that an intoxicant may receive, but also for injuries he or she may inflict upon others. Another one-third of the states have dram shop laws that make the dispenser liable only for injuries to third parties.

2 Parent liability for torts of children. The common law rule historically has been that parents are not liable for the tortious conduct of their children. Some legislatures, however, have enacted laws that change this common law rule. For example, the law may hold the parent liable for damages up to a specified amount. In general, however, parents are still not liable for the negligent acts of their children.

3 Liability of those who keep animals. Under the common law, keepers of animals of dangerous species, such as lions or tigers, which are known (or can be reasonably supposed) to have dangerous propensities are liable for the damage that such animals may cause, regardless of the care and safety used in maintaining them. On the other hand, with respect to domesticated animals, such as dogs, cats, and other household pets, the court requires that the plaintiff, in alleging the possible negligence or liability of the owner, prove that the owner knew or should have known (the law refers to this as "scienter") of the dangerous propensities of the animal. Until a few years ago owners were generally not considered to have such knowledge until after the animal had bitten someone. Consequently, this interpretation was called the "first-bite doctrine." Today in most states the owner or keeper of domesticated pets may be held responsible for the first bite. The keeper is liable if he or she knew or should have known the pet to have vicious propensities even if the pet had never attacked anyone. Some states have statutes that place a still heavier responsibility upon dog owners by abolishing the scienter rule with respect to these pets. Some court decisions appear to go this far.

Other examples of imputed liability will be discussed in Chapter 8 in the section dealing with automobile liability.

SPECIFIC LIABILITY EXPOSURES AND PROBLEMS

A business faces liability arising out of its property and its activities. These sources of liability can be categorized as follows:[11]

1 Ownership, use, or possession of premises
2 Activities that are considered to be a public or private nuisance
3 Sale, manufacture and distribution of products or services,
4 Property of others in the care, custody or control of the business
5 Fiduciary relationships such as the management of employee benefit plan assets or service on the firm's Board of Directors
6 Professional activities
7 Vehicles—usually automobiles, but may include aircraft, watercraft, and other vehicles
8 Employees who may suffer a job-related injury or disease
9 All property and activities not listed under any other category

[11] The authors are indebted to Bob A. Hedges of Temple University for suggesting a similar categorization.

In the following discussion and in Chapter 8 the liability loss exposures created by each of these sources, except the catchall category, will be discussed in the order in which they have been listed above. The discussion is meant to be informative, but not exhaustive.

Liability Arising from Ownership, Use, and Possession of Land

Some serious liability exposures may be associated with the ownership, use, and possession of land. The life tenant, for example, has a certain duty to preserve and protect the property from future loss, which might entail liability to the remaindermen for waste. In the excavation of land, the adjoining property owners are entitled to lateral support and are privileged to use drainage established by the natural terrain. Any interruption of either of these two rights may invoke liability. The following discussion, however, will deal more exclusively with the liability exposures of a property owner or possessor to visitors on his or her property.

The legal liability of a landowner to individual visitors upon his or her property depends on the status that they occupy at the time of the visitation. The law has placed visitors to land into three classifications:

1 *Trespassers:* "A trespasser may be defined as one who unauthorizedly goes upon the private premises of another without invitation or inducement, express or implied, but purely for his own purposes or convenience and where no mutuality of interest exists between him and the owner or occupant."[12]

2 *Licensees:* "A licensee is defined as one who stands in no contractual relationship to the owner or occupier of the premises, but is permitted or tolerated thereon, expressly or impliedly, or inferentially, merely for his own interest, convenience or pleasure, or for that of a third person."[13] A licensee differs from a trespasser in that he or she is permitted to go onto the land with the possessor's consent; however, the licensee is there for his or her own purpose and not for any benefit or business advantage to the possessor.

3 *Invitees:* "The invitee, also called a business visitor—is a person invited, expressly or impliedly, to come onto the land of the possessor for the business advantage of the possessor."[14]

Liability to Trespassers   The owner of the land is normally not bound to anticipate the presence of a trespasser, for the law assumes that the owner has the right to enjoy the safe and peaceful possession of his or her land without interference. A trespasser thus enters land without specific permission, express or implied, and must assume the unsafe conditions of the premises as they exist. The owner of the land is under no duty to provide the intruder with a safe place on which to trespass, and the

---

[12] See *Keesecker* v. *G. M. McKelvey Co.,* 141 Ohio St. 162, 47 NE. 2d 211 (1943.)
[13] Ibid.
[14] *Restatement of Torts* (St. Paul, Minn.: The American Law Institute, 1934), sec. 332. "A business visitor is a person who is invited or permitted to enter or remain on the land in possession of another for the purpose directly or indirectly connected with the business dealings between them."

general rule is that there is no liability to an undiscovered trespasser who is injured because of the unsafe premises. Responsibility is increased slightly with regard to known trespassers, since the lawful possessor has a duty not to use the property as a trap or to alter it in any way so as to create a hidden peril to the unwary, known trespasser. The owner of the land or lawful possessor must refrain from doing anything intentionally to injure the uninvited visitor, and in some jurisdictions the owner must use reasonable care for the trespasser's safety. [15]

A very notable exception in the law relating to trespassers is found in the *attractive nuisance doctrine,* which imposes a special duty of care upon a person maintaining an artificial condition on land that attracts children. Generally speaking, trespassing children occupy the same position before the law as trespassing adults; but, because children lack as much judgment, many jurisdictions have placed special legal responsibility for injuries to such trespassing children where the injuries result from conditions of land that are highly dangerous to them. Under the attractive nuisance doctrine, children enjoy the status and protection of invitees, and in some cases the landowner has been held absolutely liable even though they were trespassers.

Section 339 of the *Restatement of Torts* defines the doctrine of attractive nuisance as follows:

> *(a)* The place where the condition is maintained is one upon which the possessor knows or should know that such children are likely to trespass, and *(b)* the condition is one of which the possessor knows or should know and which he realizes or should realize as involvng an unreasonable risk of death or serious bodily harm to such children, and *(c)* the children because of their youth do not discover the condition or realize the risk involved in intermeddling in it or in coming within the area made dangerous by it, and *(d)* the utility to the possessor of maintaining the condition is slight in comparison to the risk of young children involved therein.

The courts have found in addition that some enticement or entrapment should be present in most of the circumstances in order to encourage children to enter on the land. The condition normally must be artificial; that is, not a natural cliff or a tree or natural vegetation. The child must be below an age of reason, which in some jurisdictions is as high as sixteen years. Generally speaking, the age of seven to nine is the highest age at which an individual is still considered a child not possessing sufficient intelligence or awareness to appreciate his or her peril.

The following have been held in various cases to be attractive nuisances and have been classified by the courts as such, finding liability to the children for injuries sustained: artificial bodies of water, swimming pools, sewers, electric power lines, construction work of all kinds, gasoline, oil tanks, ladders, cyclone fences, chemical refuse, ash hoists, dumps, railroad turntables, parked cars, junk yards, lumber piles, lawn mowers, unsteady mailboxes, snow piles, muddy basement floors, parking lots with merry-go-rounds, and others.

---

[15] See *Frederick* v. *Philadelphia Rapid Transit Co.,* 337 Pa. 136, 10 Atl. 2d 576 (1940). "When the owner-operator is on guard as to the presence of a trespasser, the latter immediately acquires the right to proper protection under the circumstances."

Liability to Licensees   The common law holds that the possessor of land does not owe a licensee any duty to make the premises safe for his or her reception. On the other hand, the licensee is entitled to the same obligations as are owed to a discovered trespasser; that is, the landowner must use reasonable care for the licensee's protection to avoid injuring him or her by any active negligence and must provide warning of known concealed dangerous conditions. While the licensee is required to accept the premises as the possessor uses them, he or she is entitled to know the dangers that the possessor knows. In one interesting case, *Shock* v. *Ringling Bros., etc., Combined Shows,* 5 Wash. 2d 419, 105 P.2d 838 (1940), children were injured while watching the circus unload at the railroad yard. The court held that there was no mutuality of interest as between the children and the circus company, and that the children were licensees permitted on the property as spectators. Typical licensees include police and firefighters who enter upon the premises under license given by law. On the other hand, letter carriers, garbage collectors, and meter readers have been held to be invitees. Generally speaking, a visitor to a restaurant or a lunchroom is in the position of an invitee, but in the particular case of *Sheridan* v. *Ravn,* 91 Cal. App. 2d 112, 204 P.2d, 644 (1944), a customer went behind the counter and by so doing ceased to be an invitee. Since he was not where he belonged, the court held that the proprietor owed him no duty other than that of warning him of known defects in the premises and refraining from any willful injury. In another case, a customer who had visited a store and purchased certain articles, decided on her way out to go back and use the telephone. She went to a hallway, reached out to turn on the light, and fell down a stairway. The court held that a person visiting a store for transacting business is normally an invitee, and the store owner must use reasonable care to see that the premises are in a reasonably safe condition. On the other hand, in this case the customer was held to be a licensee, since the business which she was to perform at the time of the injury was not of any benefit to the defendant.[16]

Liability to Invitees   An invitee is a visitor to the premises for the benefit of the owner or occupier of the premises as well as of himself or herself. The common law generally imposes a duty of reasonable care to make the premises safe for anyone accepting an invitation to do business thereon—a duty to inspect and to warn of dangers. The typical cases in this area of law have involved business visitors who engaged in specific transactions with the owner or occupier of the premises. The court held in a food-market case that a business invitation includes also the use of the parking lot, since parking is a part of the business transaction. Therefore the premises include not only the building but also any other property used in the business venture.[17]

In some states, safe place statutes have reinforced the duties of care required of landowners or possessors of land open to the public. A safe place statute makes the owner of the propety absolutely liable for injuries caused by frequenters or business visitors to his or her property where the injury is due to some unsafe condition. In bringing an action under the statute, the plaintiff does not have to show specific

[16] *Westbrock* v. *Colby Inc.*, 315 Ill. App. 494 (1942).
[17] See *Tschumy* v. *Brooks Mkt.*, 60 Cal. App. 2d 158, 140 P. 431 (1943).

negligence with reference to the care or maintenance of the premises, but merely to show that the injury was caused by a defect.

Liability Arising from Maintaining Public or Private Nuisance

A business may be sued for maintaining either a public or private nuisance in relation to the use and enjoyment of its premises. These nuisance actions require that the claimant show substantial harm as the result of some activity and indicate that the value gained by the user of the land is much less in proportion to the harm or risk that it creates. Public nuisance actions normally involve possible criminal liability for interference with the rights of the community at large. They may involve, for example, the construction of an unsafe roadway or the performance of business transactions corrupting the morals of the community.

Private nuisances, on the other hand, may be the cause of a civil action. They include such highly dangerous activities as blasting, storing explosives, drilling oil wells, or laying pipelines. They may also involve such things as keeping vicious animals, shooting fireworks in the streets, ringing bells or blowing whistles, or making disturbances that may invade the quiet and solitude of others. An unpleasant odor, a whiff of smoke, or an increased fire hazard due to the presence of certain types of buildings may also be the basis of suit. Private nuisances that threaten the safety of others may expose the firm to *absolute liability* or liability without fault. In such cases the business will be held responsible for any losses suffered by others as a result of these activities even if it exercised the utmost care in the conduct of those activities. Two other examples of absolute liability—workers' compensation and automobile compensation—are discussed in Chapter 8.

Legislation such as the Clean Air Act of 1966, the Water Pollution Control Act of 1972, and the Noise Control Act of 1972 regulate the manner in which businesses dispose of their wastes and regulate noise emission levels; violations of these regulations may expose the firm to civil suits as well as the penalties prescribed in the law.

Liability Arising from the Sale, Manufacture, and Distribution of Products or Services

Special liability problems exist for businesses in relation to the manufacture, sale, or distribution of goods and services. Legal problems arise out of the sales contract itself, involving promises and obligations concerning the performance of the products or services sold. In addition, the product or service itself may be defective or manufactured and designed in a negligent manner so as to produce serious harm to those using it. Tied to the product itself may be the necessary services of delivery, installation, and maintenance, which may be negligently performed.

1 Breach of warranty actions arising from sales contract. Breach of warranty actions arising from the sales of goods or services may be based upon either express or implied warranties. An *express* warranty has been defined as "an affirmation of fact or a promise by the seller relating to the goods which may serve as an inducement for the buyer to purchase the goods." If the purchaser relies upon the statement of the seller and the product does not meet these expressed guarantees or promises, then liability for the purchase price and the property damages resulting from the breach may be established by a suit based on breach of express warranty. It is important therefore in the sale of products that the retailer or seller does not make statements that go beyond the normal performance to induce the purchase.

In addition to the express warranty actions, the common law has established certain *implied* warranties attached to most sales contracts, the breach of which may give rise to liability. They are: *(a)* implied warranty of title, *(b)* implied warranty of fitness for a particular purpose, and *(c)* implied warranty that the goods are of merchantable quality.

In the sale of goods the seller makes the implied warranty that he or she has title to the goods and may convey them free and clear of other claims in the absence of any expressed reservations. If it subsequently develops that the seller does not have this title, then he or she is liable to subsequent buyers for the purchase price and any other damage suffered as a result of breach of this warranty.

Where goods are purchased by description or catalog number, the buyer may specify that the article ordered must be used to fit or fufill a particular purpose. Where the buyer specifically indicates to the seller that the article must be suitable for a particular purpose as a condition of purchase, and where the buyer relies on the skill and judgment of the seller concerning the capacity of the goods to fulfill this purpose, then failure of the product to perform accordingly may also result in legal liability. For example, if a particular type of furnace is installed to heat your home properly and you rely on the installer's skill and judgment concerning the size and type of furnace required, then failure of the product to heat your home may involve the seller in a liability resulting from breach of the implied warranty of fitness.

The third warranty of merchantability governs situations involving food or other products that must maintain a certain minimum quality. Goods are said to be merchantable when they are free from hidden defects and are fit for the use for which they are ordinarily intended. For example, during the 1950s Cutter Laboratories manufactured a polio vaccine that subsequently caused patients who had been vaccinated to contract the disease. Suits followed, and even though the manufacturer offered evidence to show it used great care and skill in manufacturing the vaccine, the court allowed recovery for breach of warranty of fitness.

2 Liability arising out of negligence. In addition to breach of warranty actions, many product or service liability suits are based on the tort of negligence.[18] If liability is to be successfully proved, it must rest upon the fact that the defendant either created the condition or refrained from removing it, and that creation or nonremoval was the result of the defendant's carelessness. For example, actions have been successfully brought under this theory against manufacturers of canned tuna and soft drinks which contained deleterious substances.

3 Under certain circumstances, courts have held manufacturers responsible for injuries arising out of defective products without regard to negligence. Only the defect need be proved by the plaintiff. This finding of *strict liability,* as it is called, raises

---

[18] *MacPherson* v. *Buick Motor Co.*, 217 N.Y. 282, 111 N.E. 1050 (1916).

serious problems for the defendant manufacturer since it cannot defend itself by showing that it used proper and reasonable care.[19] Such findings have become more common in recent years and have been applied to a wide variety of products.

In October, 1972, Congress passed the Consumer Product Safety Act, which (1) increased the responsibility of sellers to buyers *before* they are injured and (2) made it much more likely in many cases that injured consumers will be able to collect damages from sellers.[20] The act requires the Consumer Product Safety Commission to develop product safety standards for consumer products that in its judgment have unreasonably large injury potential. These standards may deal with the performance, composition, content, design, construction, finishing, or packaging of the product. If the commission determines that no feasible product safety standard can be developed for a certain product, it can ban further distribution of the product.

Every manufacturer of a product that is made subject to safety standards must certify that the product complies with the relevant standard. Any manufacturer, distributor, or retailer who determines that a product is not up to standard or that it contains a potentially dangerous defect must report this fact to the commission. After a hearing the commission may require the business (1) to give public notice of the defect and (2) to repair, replace, or refund the purchase price, the choice being left to the business.

Private injury litigation should be influenced in at least two ways. First, violation of a safety standard will probably be held to be negligence per se in many cases. Second, the data accumulated by the commission on the causes of accidents and the results of product tests will probably be used in such litigation.

Product liability exposures have, as a result of inflation and judicial trends, become increasingly important in recent years. Businesses are more likely to be held responsible for losses to the users of their products or services, and the awards are likely to be much higher. In a recent case that attracted much attention, a Florida boy was paralyzed in a high school football game. In 1975, a jury found that the helmet he was wearing was not designed properly, and awarded a $5,200,000 judgment against the manufacturer. Before this award could be appealed, a settlement was reached under which the plaintiff will receive monthly payments that could still total more than $3 million.[21] This award included special, general, and punitive damages as explained on page 108. Product liability losses include in addition the costs of investigating the case and defending the business in court. Sales may also be adversely affected and in many cases the product must be recalled. The effect of these trends has been to make it difficult for some firms to secure any insurance to protect themselves against this

---

[19] The terms "strict liability" and "absolute liability" are commonly used interchangeably. The distinction made here is that although neither type of liability considers whether the business is at fault, the strict liability doctrine does consider whether the product was defective. Absolute liability would make the business responsible even if the product were not defective.

[20] J. R. Patton, Jr., and Bowes Butler, "The Consumer Product Safety Act: Its Impact on Manufacturers and on the Relationship between Seller and Consumer," *The Business Lawyer* (April, 1973), pp. 725–740.

[21] For other illustrations of multimillion dollar product liability awards, see "Why Everybody is Suing Everybody," *U.S. News and World Report* (December 4, 1978), p. 53. The largest award was $128 million against the Ford Motor Company, reduced by a judge to $7 million, for defects in a Ford Pinto.

exposure, and to increase substantially the premiums for this insurance. Some businesses have closed their doors because of the cost of product liability insurance or the fear that uninsured claims would destroy them financially.

About half the states have enacted legislation that restricts in some way the rights of consumers in a product liability claim.[22] The actions are divided into five groups: (1) imposing a statute of limitations from either the date the product was introduced or the date of the accident, (2) allowing as a defense the fact that the product met the "state of the art" at the time it was manufactured, (3) elimination or restriction of claims based on a failure to warn the consumer, (4) allowing a defense that a product met government standards, and (5) allowing a defense that a product was altered after it left the manufacturer.

Legislation has also been proposed at the federal level, but Congress has not yet enacted any changes. A proposal made by the Commerce Department a few years ago to encourage uniform state laws shows what might happen eventually. This proposal sets forth the basic standard of responsibility to which product sellers will be held. For example, the standard for manufacturers would be strict liability for defects in construction, but not for defects in design, defects caused by a failure to warn, or defects arising out of faulty maintenance, for which the injured party would have varying burdens of proof. Liability for a product defect would extend through the product's "useful safe life," which is the time the product would normally be likely to perform or be stored in a safe manner. In claims involving harm caused more than ten years after the date of delivery to a purchaser, there would be a rebuttable presumption that the product was used beyond its useful safe life. A product would be deemed safe if it met the state of knowledge reasonably available at the time of its manufacture. Retailers and distributors would be liable only for their own negligence, unless the injured party would be unable to bring a claim against the manufacturer because he or she were unavailable or out of business. Claims would have to be brought within three years after the injured party knew or should have known about the injury. Pain and suffering awards in nonserious cases would be limited to $25,000. Punitive damages could be awarded only if the claimant showed by clear and convincing evidence that the harm resulted from the seller's reckless disregard for the safety of product users.

Bailee Liability Exposures

In many commercial and noncommercial activities, personal property is surrendered to another for a temporary period of time. The person taking possession may perform some service pertaining to the property, borrow it for his or her own use, or keep it for the owner's benefit, after which time the property must be returned to the owner or lawful possessor. These transactions where possession of personal property is vested in one person and eventual lawful right of possession vests in another are called *bailments*. The owner or original possessor of the goods is called the *bailor*; the person receiving possession for the temporary period of time is called the *bailee*. In order to have a bailment relation, three distinguishing characteristics must normally be present

[22] *Business Insurance* publishes periodically a score card on state product liability legislation.

in the contractual relationship: (1) The title to the property or the ultimate right to possess it must be retained by the bailor; (2) the possession and temporary control of the property must be surrendered to the bailee; and (3) ultimate possession of the property must revert to the bailor unless he or she orders the transfer to some other designated person.

Important liability questions arise concerning the rights and duties of the bailee for any possible claims that the bailor may make for damages while the property was in the custody and care of the bailee. In establishing the legal duty of care to be exercised by the bailee, the law has classified bailments into three general categories: (1) bailments for the benefit of the bailor (where property is left with the bailee without any compensation for care and safekeeping); (2) bailments for the benefit of the bailee (in which case the bailee often borrows or uses the property involved for a period of time, usually without compensation to the rightful owner); and (3) bailments for the mutual benefit of the bailor and bailee (where both parties benefit from the bailment, which may involve the repair, carriage, storage, or safekeeping of the property). Each party to the last-mentioned transaction receives some benefit; the bailor receives the service rendered by the bailee, for which he or she usually pays a fee to the bailee.

In establishing these three classes of bailment relationships, the courts clearly recognize different degrees of care required of the bailee. In a transaction for the exclusive benefit of the bailor, the bailee is required to exercise only slight care. In transactions for the exclusive benefit of the bailee, extraordinary care is essential. In other words, the law looks behind the purpose of the transaction and demands that the degree of care vary according to the respective benefits conferred on the parties involved. In a bailment for the mutual benefit of the parties, the law normally demands ordinary care on the part of the bailee, in other words, the degree of care that average individuals or companies would usually exercise over their own property.

In addition, the courts recognize that the amount of care expected of the bailee varies with the nature and substance of the bailment. For example, the degree of ordinary care normally required to protect a very valuable negotiable security would be much greater than the amount of care required to protect an ordinary piece of paper; the higher the value of the article bailed, the higher the standards of protection. Where property is bailed for mutual benefit, the bailor is usually held liable for any defect in the property rented or bailed about which he or she may or should have known. The bailor is ordinarily responsible for any damage suffered by the bailee as the result of such defects unless the bailor notifies the bailee prior to the injury or damage.

Under some circumstances, either the bailee or bailor may change the degree of care required by a written statement in the contract itself. For example, the parking ticket issued to a person parking a vehicle in a commercial parking lot may state, as one of the terms of the bailment relationship of the automobile, that the owner of the lot is not responsible for loss by theft of personal property inside the vehicle unless the property is placed in the possession of the parking attendant. Such restrictions upon liability are normally recognized by the law, provided that the agreement meets all the tests of a valid legal contract, including the presence of adequate consideration. In addition, many courts have held that a bailee, regardless of the nature of the bailment, may be held absolutely liable for misdelivery of the goods or property bailed. Consequently, the bailee must make certain that repossession is granted only to the rightful party, namely the bailor, or to someone the bailor may select.

One of the more common commercial relationships involving bailment is the transport of goods by common carrier.[23] The common carrier in receiving the goods performs the acts of a bailee and assumes certain duties of care with reference to the handling of such goods. The written contract for carriage, called a *bill of lading*,[24] sets forth the terms and conditions of the bailment. The amount of care required of the common carrier, however, greatly exceeds that of ordinary care by statute. Under the various bills of lading acts, for motortruck carriers[25] as well as railroads and aircraft, the common carrier is liable for all loss of goods with the following exceptions: (1) an act of God; (2) action of an enemy alien; (3) exercise of public authority; (4) any inherent defects in the nature of the goods themselves; or (5) any negligence or fault of the shipper, including misaddressing the package or mislabeling the merchandise. Thus the common carrier becomes virtually an insurer of goods, unless the loss or damage falls within the exceptions thus stated. Acts of God normally are those acts of nature that are neither preventable nor controllable by the common carrier, and about which it has no reasonable warning or opportunity to avoid damage. In a flood that occurred several years ago in the Missouri River Valley, a federal court held that the damage to goods located in flooded railway cars was caused 40 percent by an act of God and 60 percent by the negligence of the railway companies in failing to place the boxcars on higher ground. Litigation established the percentage of responsibility of the common carriers' liability policies in paying the damage for the freight loss.

Many other commercial transactions involve bailments. Automobile repair agencies exercise physical control over automobiles being worked upon and have a duty to use ordinary care in the protection of such property. In one case, a garage tow truck, operated by an employee of the garage, was pulling a vehicle that was being steered and braked by an employee of the customer; the automobile subsequently collided with a pole. The court held that the automobile was not in the actual physical control of the garage but in the control of the customer and that no liability existed for the garage under the bailment law. Questions arise as to the actual surrendering of control of the property to the bailee, and the bailee's responsibilities arise only where such actual physical control has been surrendered.

---

[23] *Common carriers* are carriers engaged in the transprt of goods for the public according to regular time schedules, defined routes, and for established rates. It has long been a general rule of law that the common carrier is responsible for the safe delivery of goods. This was further established by statute with the passage of the Interstate Commerce Act of 1887 and subsequent amendments of 1915 and 1935 regulating interstate carrier operations. Each state likewise passed statutes regulating intrastate operation. *Contract carriers* haul under a specific contract; *private carriers* carry their own goods in their own equipment.

[24] A bill of lading is a written document given by the carrier to the shipper that acknowledges receipt of the goods by the carrier and sets forth the contract for carrying the property. If the bill of lading limits the liability of the carrier to a maximum amount in the event of loss or damage, it is called a "released bill of lading."

[25] Under the Motor Carrier Liability Act of 1935, as amended, interstate trucking operations must provide adequate "security for the protection of the public." The Interstate Commerce Commission under this section specifies that each trucker provide certain minimum insurance protection for loss or damage to the contents of any one vehicle and for aggregate losses or damages at any one time and place. Self-insurance may be permitted if the financial stability of the carrier warrants the permission.

Some interesting cases have developed in regard to the parking of cars in parking lots. Where the business establishment provides an attendant to park the vehicle for the customer, courts have held that a bailment has occurred and that care arising from a mutual benefit bailment must be exercised. On the other hand, where the business establishment merely provides space for the customer to park his or her own car, the courts have held that a lease arrangement exists that does not impose the same kinds of duties of care as would be imposed in the usual bailment situation. The same would hold true with reference to restaurants and nightclubs where facilities are provided for checking of coats and other personal articles. If facilities are merely provided with no attendant in charge, usually no bailment is found. However, where the attendant actually gives a receipt for the goods checked, the bailment relationship is established, and all the duties of care and the liabilities for misdelivery arise.

Liability Arising from Fiduciary Relationships

Fiduciary relationships have become a more important source of liability in recent years. Two important examples are (1) the responsibility of members of a board of directors to manage the assets of a corporation in the best interests of the stockholders and (2) the responsibility of employee benefit plan managers or administrators to the plan participants.

According to the *Corporate Director's Guidebook*[26] published by the American Bar Association, directors who do not act in good faith will be subject to personal liability for their actions. Examples are conflict of interest transactions or transactions imposing unfairness upon minority shareholders. A director must also not use inside information to favor himself or herself. He or she may not knowingly or recklessly participate in the distribution of misleading information by the corporation. Federal securities laws impose certain liabilities upon directors even though they act in good faith. For example, if a regulation statement used to distribute securities contains untrue statements, directors will be subject to suits by purchasers of the securities. To defend themselves, directors must demonstrate that they made a reasonable investigation of the statements made. In addition to their potential liability as a member of the board as a whole, directors may expose themselves to personal liability as members of the audit committee, the executive committee, or other board committees.

The Employee Retirement Income Security Act (ERISA) of 1974 greatly increased the responsibility of persons who manage pension plan assets and of other employee benefit plan fiduciaries. The major features of ERISA will be described in Chapter 22. Under ERISA any person (including company officers) who exercises any discretionary authority or control over the management or administration of the plan is considered to be a fiduciary. A fiduciary is required to take certain actions and is prohibited from taking certain other actions. In general a fiduciary must be an honest, prudent person who always acts in the best interests of the plan participants and their

---

[26] *Corporate Directors Guidebook* (Chicago: Section of Corporation, Banking, and Business Law, American Bar Association, 1976), pp. 27–30.

beneficiaries. Failure to meet this standard may expose the fiduciary to civil actions, fines, and other penalties.

Professional Liability Exposures

Special liability problems confront persons who engage in professional pursuits or perform services requiring special care and skill. Courts have defined the term *profession* as follows: "The word implies professed attainment in special knowledge as distinguished from mere skill. A practical dealing with affairs as distinguished from mere study or investigation, and an application of such knowledge to uses for others as a vocation, as distinguished from its pursuit for its own purposes."[27] In surveying the common law, however, one finds that although lawyers, doctors, dentists, accountants, architects, and other occupations involving advanced training and licensing are clearly professionals, some courts have added such unexpected groups as operators of pool halls and operators of school buses. On the other hand, one court excluded management consultants. One trend is clear, however; more occupations are qualifying for professional status, at least insofar as professional liability is concerned.

The rise of professionalism in the United States has produced interesting developments in civil law. The individual practitioner has discovered, sometimes after painful and expensive litigation, that his or her conduct is not measured by the common law tests of quality used in the ordinary relationships among individuals.[28] On the contrary, the law has recognized that the professional calling imposes responsibilities far above those of persons engaged in less skilled or less intellectual pursuits.

The Malpractice Problem Facing the Professions The necessity and desirability of imposing fairly rigid controls over professional conduct is certainly not denied by the patients or clients and least of all by the professions themselves. Professional status, as we have indicated, is dependent upon the quality and sophistication of the services rendered by all practicing members. It is for that very reason that the individual professions have not looked only to legal censure to preserve the quality and stature of their services, but have imposed strict and rigid rules of self-control and self-policing as a matter of self-preservation. Actions to bring about disbarment, loss of certification or license, and finally expulsion from the organized profession are usually brought in the name of the professional organizations against the violating individual. Codes of professional ethics, which carefully summarize the moral responsibilities of the individual members, are promulgated and enforced by most professional groups. State practice and licensing laws are usually sponsored by the individual profession.

A problem arises for the professional practitioner, however, when the control and regulation takes the form of litigation by the client or patient concerning the particular standards and qualities of the individual's conduct. It is in these situations and with this

[27] James A. Ballentine, *Law Dictionary* (Rochester, N.Y.: Lawyers' Cooperative Publishing Company, 1948), p. 1028.

[28] In cases involving ordinary negligence, the usual test applied is whether or not the defendant acted as an ordinarily reasonable, prudent person would have acted. See *Restatement of Torts*, supra, note 18, at sec. 283.

type of legal control that the professional faces the severe test that may bring about complete failure and economic ruin.

The malpractice or liability action strikes at the very heart of the practitioner's greatest and most cherished asset, his or her professional reputation. The bad publicity arising from such a suit, even in situations where the defendant is entirely innocent and the eventual outcome is entirely favorable, may spell complete ruin of a professional career that took a lifetime to build.

Loss of reputation and professional standing are not the only consequences of malpractice litigation. Final judgment may be rendered against the practitioner for tremendous sums for the injury caused by careless, unexpected, unpredictable, or unintentional blunders. The loss in terms of trial time in testifying in the defense of one's actions, the legal and court costs that are usually assessed to the loser, to say nothing of the emotional and physical strain of enduring the whole ordeal, are some of the other losses suffered as a consequence of litigation.

Several factors make the malpractice problem extremely difficult to meet and solve. First of all, the common law regulations of standards of conduct are not easily identified and defined. The legal test of performance is vague and impossible of accurate interpretation in any given set of facts outside the courtroom walls. Second, the rapid advance in the technology of professions makes the practitioner extremely vulnerable to suit because of failure to possess knowledge of the advancements or changes in the field and to exercise skill and care in its application. Also, this rapid change in the underlying technical knowledge of the professions makes older legal requirements of performance outmoded and obsolete. As an example, a doctor using penicillin for the first time could not be sure that he or she would be absolved from prosecution for experimentation if the drug produced unfavorable results in the patient. On the other hand, the doctor could be prosecuted for lack of skill and care if he or she failed to use the drug when the conditions called for its use according to the technical information common to the profession at the time. Just as technology changes, so does the law. Today the legal standard would probably absolve the user of this drug, whereas 30 years ago the doctor might have been prosecuted for experimentation.

The Current Impact of the Malpractice Problem   Greater numbers of malpractice claims and suits are being brought every year, larger verdicts are being awarded, and education and technology are constantly raising the standards of performance expected of the practitioners. Legal rights, which have existed for a long period of time, are currently being exercised with greater intensity by injured plaintiffs and their legal counsel. Premiums for malpractice liability insurance have risen dramatically. Because of underwriting losses, many insurers have discontinued writing malpractice insurance or changed the terms under which they will write this insurance. As they did for product liability, some states have changed the legal system applicable to medical malpractice liability by limiting attorneys' fees, shortening the statute of limitations, placing a ceiling on awards, and encouraging or requiring nonbinding or binding arbitration.

This upsurge in professional liability claims and suits has been explained in several ways. One explanation is that a general weakening of the nonprofessional ties between the professional servant and the patient or client has taken place. The country doctor, considered not only a professional servant, but also a close personal friend by patients, has been gradually replaced by specialists residing in metropolitan centers. Patients today travel many miles from their social circles for medical care and attention. Consequently, they do not usually hesitate to sue the stranger for malpractice, whereas no thought of suit would arise from similar misconduct of the honored and respected country doctor. One leading medical malpractice insurer recently reported that, on the average, they receive one claim per year per fourteen doctors insured. Comparable statements can be made about the legal, accounting, and pharmaceutical professions. Another reason that has been advanced for the increased frequency of suits has been the general "claims consciousness" of the public as a whole.

SOME KEY CONCEPTS

Tort   A civil wrong other than a breach of contract.

Negligence   The most important nonintentional tort affecting risk management. Failure to do or not to do what a prudent person would have done in the same situation.

Comparative negligence   A defense for the defendant which reduces the award to the plaintiff by the percent of his or her contributory negligence.

Damages   The compensation that the plaintiff may recover in the courts for losses sustained. Consists of damages for personal injuries and property damage as well as punitive damages.

Vicarious liability   Liability for the negligent acts of others.

Contractual liability   Liability assumed under some contract such as a lease that would not be present except for the contract.

Licensee   A person on the premises with the consent of the owner. A licensee is owed more care than a trespasser, but less than an invitee.

Breach of implied warranty   A common cause of action in a product liability suit. The implied warranty may be that the seller had the necessary title, the product was suitable for the purpose it was sold, or that the product was of merchantable quality.

Strict liability   A legal doctrine under which a manufacturer is held responsible for injuries arising out of defective products, regardless of whether or not the manufacturer was negligent.

Bailee liability   The liability of a bailee for damage to property of others in his or her care, custody, or control.

Malpractice liability   The liabilty of a professional for errors or omissions in the pursuit of his or her profession.

REVIEW QUESTIONS

1 Distinguish between criminal and civil liability.

2 **a** What are the various kinds or sources of legal actions that may be brought to establish civil liability?

   b Is it possible for more than one source of legal action to exist in the same situation?

3 "Law does not protect those who sleep on their rights." What does this statement mean?

4 **a** What is an intentional tort?

   b Cite some examples of intentional torts.

5 Comment on the legal liability status of the following:

    a A person whose dog bites a neighbor

    b A newspaper columnist who accuses a government official of being a liar

    c A member of congress who, on the floor of the House of Representatives, calls a newspaper columnist a liar

    d A department store that by mistake causes someone to be arrested

6 In order to make out a cause of action for negligence, what must the plaintiff demonstrate?

7 a In what way can the burden of proof be shifted from the plaintiff to the defendant?

    b Why would this be an important shift?

8 The plaintiff in a particular case was totally and permanently disabled in a boating accident. At the time of the accident he was thirty years of age and was earning $30,000 a year. His boat was completely destroyed in the accident. What factors will be considered in determining how much the defendant will have to pay this plaintiff?

9 What defenses might be asserted by the defendant in a case involving negligence?

10 In a particular case, it is agreed that both the plaintiff and the defendant were negligent. The plaintiff was responsible for 25 percent of the negligence involved and the defendant for 75 percent. The plaintiff suffered losses of $60,000 in the accident, while the defendant's losses were $30,000.

    a How would this case probably be settled in a contributory negligence state? in a comparative negligence state?

    b Comment on the fairness of these various settlements.

11 John Smith is a partner in a construction firm. Comment on John's liability for negligent actions by each of the following parties:

    a John's partner

    b An employee of the partnership

    c An employee of another construction firm participating with John's firm in a joint venture

    d A plumber hired to install some new pipes in the partnership's home-office building

12 What is the responsibility of the owner of a manufacturing plant for injuries to each of the following persons:

    a A curious adult who enters the premises despite signs forbidding him to enter

    b A mail carrier

    c A salesperson

    d A customer

13 Children receive a favored position under the attractive nuisance doctrine.

    a What is the attractive nuisance doctrine?

    b Cite several examples of items that some courts have considered to be attractive nuisances.

14 What types of legal actions might be brought to establish legal liability in each of the following cases?

    a The casing on a power mower broke and injured the person mowing the lawn.

    b A man became ill as a result of some impurities contained in a seasoning purchased by his wife.

    c Some soft-drink bottles that a retailer had placed near a radiator exploded, causing serious injuries to some customers.

    d A customer requested a refrigerator with a true freezer compartment. The store sold her instead a refrigerator with a section which, though colder than the rest of the refrigerator, was not a true freezer. The customer became ill as a result of eating some food that would have been kept fresh in a true freezer but was not preserved in her refrigerator.

    e The steering wheel of a car suddenly failed to work, and an accident resulted.

15 Many retailers believe that they do not have to be concerned about product liability because this is the manufacturers' responsibility. Do you agree?

16 The strict liability doctrine has become more common in product liability cases. What does this mean?

17 Comment on the liability of each of the following:

  a A laundry for customers' goods

  b A parking lot for cars stored on the premises

  c A firm for a hired car

  d A tenant for the building occupied

18 The liability of a trucking firm or a railroad as a common carrier continues for 48 hours beginning at 7 A.M. after written notice of arrival has been sent or given to the consignee. After that time, the legal responsibility of the carrier is that of a warehouse only. Why is this information important to the consignee?

19 Green has just been appointed to the board of directors of a publicly held corporation. Has she any exposure to personal liability in this capacity?

20 What special problems are associated with professional liability?

SUGGESTIONS FOR ADDITIONAL READING

Anderson, Ronald A.: *The Insurer's Tort Law* (2d ed., Ocean City, N.J.: The Littoral Development Co., 1971).

Corpus Juris Secundum (New York: The American Law Book Co., and St. Paul, Minn.: West Publishing Company, 1948).

Donaldson, James H.: *Casualty Claims Practice* (4th ed., Homewood, Ill.: Richard D. Irwin, Inc., 1984).

Holmes, Oliver Wendell, Jr.: *The Common Law* (Boston: Little, Brown and Company, 1923).

Kulp, C. A., and J. W. Hall: Casualty Insurance (4th ed., New York: The Ronald Press Company, 1968), chap. 5.

Malecki, D. S. (ed.): *Professional Liability: Impact in the Eighties* (Malvern, Pa.: Society of Chartered Property and Casualty Underwriters, 1983).

Malecki, D. S., J. H. Donaldson, and R. C. Horn: *Commercial Liability Risk Management and Insurance,* vols. I and II (Malvern, Pa.: American Institute for Property and Liability Underwriters, 1978).

Mehr, R. I., and B. A. Hedges: *Risk Management: Concepts and Applications* (Homewood, Ill. Richard D. Irwin, Inc., 1974), chaps. 9–10.

Personal Injury Valuation Handbooks (Cleveland: Jury Verdict Research, Inc., updated monthly).

Prosser, W. L.: *Handbook of the Law of Torts* (4th ed., St. Paul, Minn.: West Publishing Company, 1971).

CHAPTER 8

LIABILITY LOSS EXPOSURES: II

LEARNING OBJECTIVES

After you have completed this chapter, you should be able to:

1 Distinguish workers' compensation from employers' liability.
2 Describe briefly the employments and the accidents and diseases covered under workers' compensation.
3 Explain the benefits provided under a typical state workers' compensation program.
4 Summarize the different types of security arrangements found under state workers' compensation laws.
5 List the special statutes and court doctrines affecting the finding of negligence in automobile accident cases.
6 Describe the nature and purpose of financial responsibility laws and unsatisfied judgment funds.
7 State the major arguments for and against automobile compensation or no-fault laws.
8 List the key ways in which state automobile no-fault laws are likely to differ from one another.
9 Explain how the no-fault concept might be extended to product liability and professional liability claims.

INTRODUCTION

This chapter continues the discussion of liability loss exposures started in Chapter 7. Two important exposures will be considered: the liability of a business to its employees for job-related injuries or diseases and its liability for bodily injuries or property damage sustained as the result of a motor vehicle accident. In both cases the law of negligence has been superseded at least in part by "no-fault" statutes. Under a no-fault statute the injured party receives a benefit regardless of who was responsible for the accident. Brief mention will also be made of other areas to which no-fault concepts may be applied in the future.

EMPLOYERS' LIABILITY AND WORKERS' COMPENSATION

An employment relationship creates many uncertainties for both employers and employees. For example, under common law, an employee may be held personally responsible for damage caused by negligent performance on the job. In addition, the employee may suffer physical pain and financial loss because of a work accident.

The employer, on the other hand, must comply with numerous federal and state laws that govern such relationships, such as the Fair Labor Standards Act, state unemployment compensation laws, the Social Security Act, and the Occupational Safety and Health Act. Violation of these laws may impose civil as well as criminal liability. In addition, employers must meet their legal obligations under workers' compensation statutes and common law or statutory concepts of employers' liability. These latter obligations will be emphasized in the following discussion.

Common Law Liability for Employers

Prior to 1837, an employee seldom, if ever, sued an employer because of an industrial injury. In that year, in a famous English case, *Priestley* v. *Fowler,* the judge, Lord Abinger, made it clear that an employee would find it more difficult to collect from the employer under the law of negligence than would a complete stranger.[1] This inferior position of the employee reflected in part the laissez faire attitude of the industrial revolution. The employee, like the stranger, was forced to prove negligence on the part of the employer, had to share the recovery with his or her legal counsel, and often was forced to wait many years for recovery because of crowded court calendars and difficulties of proof. The employee, like the stranger, lost the right to recover if he or she was guilty of contributory negligence. Actions also expired upon the employee's death. Verdicts often bore little relationship to the merits of the employee's case. The employee's plight was worse than that of the stranger, however, because fellow employees were often unwilling to testify for fear of losing their jobs. In addition, the courts allowed the employer to plead certain special defenses to these actions that were quite effective in defeating the worker's claim. These defenses were (1) the fellow-servant rule (if the injury was caused by the negligence of a fellow servant, then the employer was relieved from liability. Since many industrial processes involved cooperative work, many injuries fell within this category) and (2) assumption of risk (in the

---

[1] This case involved a butcher's helper and a boy employee who were delivering meat. The wagon was overloaded by the butcher's helper and fell over on the boy, causing injury. See *Priestley* v. *Fowler,* 3 M. & W. 1, 150 Eng. Rep. 1030 (Ex. 1837).

absence of statutory rules or provisions in the employment contract, the employer was not liable for injury caused by unsafe conditions of work if the worker knew of such conditions and voluntarily entered or continued in the employment).

Nevertheless, courts slowly began to recognize a special duty owed to the "servant" by the "master," distinct from those owed to the general public. While they held that the master was not an insurer of a servant's safety, they maintained that the master owed a duty to provide working conditions that were reasonably safe, considering the nature of the employment, or to warn the servant of unsafe conditions that the servant might not discover by the exercise of due care. This duty was gradually extended to include inspection, maintenance, and repair of the premises within the master's control and of the tools that the worker used. If an injury was due to the employer's violation of these duties, the employee could bring action for recovery of damages sustained. In addition, the courts began to chip away at the employer's defenses. For example, the employer could not plead the fellow-servant rule if the negligent employee was a supervisor or one with whom the injured employee normally had little contact. Some courts substituted a comparative negligence doctrine for contributory negligence.

By the early 1900s, employers' liability statutes had been enacted in most jurisdictions. The federal government had enacted the Federal Employers' Liability Act, applying to interstate railroad employees, and the Jones Act, applying to merchant seamen. These laws, like the courts, tended to modify and limit the employer's use of the fellow servant, assumption of risk, and contributory negligence defenses. Specific safety statutes were enacted to prescribe minimum safety appliances and working conditions, making it easier for the worker to show negligence of the employer by violation of the law. However, the basic defects of a system dependent upon negligence claims remained, and the early 1900s were years of social agitation and reform. As a result, workers' (formerly workmen's) compensation laws were enacted that completely changed, for most employers and employees, the concepts of employer responsibility for injuries "arising out of and in the course of employment." Under workers' compensation a covered employer became absolutely responsible for the economic losses suffered by his or her employees because of job-related injuries and diseases. Who was at fault did not affect this responsibility. On the other hand, the employee gave up the right to sue the employer because of such losses. Workers' compensation became the exclusive remedy of the employee against the employer. Employers' liability, however, remains the legal redress for (1) employees not covered under the workers' compensation law, (2) those disabled by a possibly job-related disease not covered under the law, and (3) those permitted by law before or after an accident to elect not to come under workers' compensation.[2] In addition, some workers' compensation laws permit employees to sue fellow employees who are responsible for their injuries, and employers may elect to assume such claims. In a few

[2] Some states permit an employee to elect *before* an accident not to be covered under workers' compensation; however, few employees elect to do so. Such an election *may* be permitted *after* an accident if the employer willfully injured the employee, the employee was an illegally employed minor, or the employee was injured in a different state that does not provide automatic coverage. See R. I. Mehr and B. A. Hedges, *Risk Management: Concepts and Applications* (Homewood, Ill: Richard D. Irwin, Inc., 1974), pp. 298–302.

instances, spouses of injured employees have been permitted to sue the employer for loss of consortium. In some other cases, the injured employee may sue a third party such as a railroad, which through a hold-harmless agreement is able to transfer its common law liability to the employer. Finally, during the past few years the concept that workers' compensation is the exclusive remedy of the employee against the employer has been subjected to a new challenge through the "dual capacity" theory. For example, assume that a worker is injured on the job while using a machine that is manufactured by the employer. Under the dual capacity theory the employer is involved in this accident in two capacities: (1) as the employer and (2) as the manufacturer of the machine. The employee may be entitled either to claim workers' compensation benefits or to sue the employer in his or her capacity as the manufacturer of the defective product.

Workers' Compensation

Workers' compensation introduced the following revolutionary changes:

1 As stated above, the concept of negligence and fault on the part of the worker or the employer was abandoned as the basis of financial responsibility. Rather, all accidents or injuries related to "industrial causation" or arising out of the employment were to be compensated. The cost of injuries was determined to be a cost of manufacture and therefore passed on to the consumer through higher prices. In other words a no-fault concept was adopted.

2 The benefit amounts were scheduled by statute rather than awarded by juries. The injured worker was to be compensated only for economic losses, not for pain and suffering.

3 Administration was in most cases given to an administrative agency of the state, which had authority to make rules and regulations concerning interpretations of the law, subject to judicial review.

Workers' compensation laws were enacted as early as 1902, but it was not until 1911 that Wisconsin passed the first law to become effective that was not later declared unconstitutional. Nine other states acted later that year. By 1920, all but six states and the District of Columbia had passed such legislation. In addition, the federal government, in 1908, enacted a law covering civilian federal employees. In 1948, Mississippi became the last state to adopt the workers' compensation approach to industrial injuries and diseases.

National Commission on State Workers' Compensation Laws   Because of its dissatisfaction with the performance of state workers' compensation laws, in 1970 Congress established as part of the Occupational Safety and Health Act a national commission to evaluate state workers' compensation laws. In its July, 1972, report, the National Commission on State Workers' Compensation Laws supported the basic concept of workers' compensation, but emphasized what it considered serious deficiencies in existing programs. The Commission recommended many standards for an effective program, 19 of which it deemed essential. The Commission urged all states to meet these standards by July 1, 1975. It recommended that Congress check the degree of compliance as of that date and, if necessary, with no further delay, act to guarantee compliance with these recommendations. Congress has not acted on the Commission report but, until a few years ago, it seriously considered bills that would establish federal standards which, if not satisfied within a state by a specified date, would apply to occupational injuries and diseases in that state. The effect of the Commission report, however, has been considerable. Although no state has yet satisfied all the Commission recommendations, and 13 satisfy 10 or less standards, state workers' compensation programs are much closer to meeting these recommendations today than in 1972. Also, many states have adopted several important Commission recommendations not included among the 19 essential recommendations.

In compliance with another Commission recommendation, an Interdepartmental Policy Group including the Secretaries of Labor, Commerce, and Health, Education, and Welfare, plus the Federal Insurance Administrator, was appointed to encourage and assist the states in administering workers' compensation, and to examine certain areas more closely. In 1974, an Interdepartmental Task Force was formed to conduct further research. In 1977, the Policy Group, using the Task Force's findings, recommended that the states be granted more time to meet the National Commission's essential recommendations, but that they be encouraged to go beyond the nineteen essential recommendations. The Policy group modified some of the Commission's recommendations and added some of their own. The Policy Group reports have also stimulated program changes at the state level. Although the state laws vary considerably, the following early 1984 summary of the employments covered, injuries and diseases covered, benefits, and funding requirements will indicate the basic approach.[3]

Employments Covered Workers' compensation laws cover all employments that are not specifically excluded. The most commonly excluded employments are domestic service, casual work, and agricultural employment.[4] Railroad workers engaged in interstate commerce are excluded under all state laws because they are covered under the Federal Employers' Liability Act. About one-fourth of the states exclude employers with less than a certain number of employees. Until recently, many states permitted employers to determine whether they would bring their employees under the law. However, if they elected not to be covered, they lost the assumption of risk, fellow-servant, and contributory negligence defenses in any employers' liability suits. Only three such elective laws remain.

Accidents and Diseases Covered All laws cover injuries "arising out of and in the course of employment." They also cover occupational diseases. The laws are fairly uniform in language but have been interpreted differently as to what injuries "arise out

[3] For current detailed information on these laws, see *Analysis of Workers' Compensation Laws,* prepared annually by the Chamber of Commerce of the United States. The Employment Standards Administration Office of Workers' Compensation Programs of the United States Department of Labor also periodically prepares detailed summary charts.
[4] Self-employed persons are not generally covered, but some states permit voluntary coverage of sole proprietors and working partners.

of and in the course of employment.'' The principal question is whether the injury is job related. Otherwise, the only two defenses available to the employer are that the injury was intentionally inflicted or that, subject to certain exceptions, the employee was intoxicated at the time of the injury. Examples of some troublesome claims are back injuries which may have been caused by some nonwork activity, heart attacks on the job, injuries suffered during a coffee break, or on the way to work, and injuries resulting from horseplay. Determining what diseases, as opposed to injuries, should be attributed to the worker's occupation has proved to be especially difficult.

Benefits   The laws provide four types of benefits: (1) medical benefits, (2) disability income benefits, (3) death benefits, and (4) rehabilitation benefits. All jurisdictions will pay all the injured worker's medical expenses incurred as a result of a job-related injury or disease.

The disability benefits are related to the worker's wage at the time he or she was disabled. Most of the disability claims involve temporary total disability, for which a typical benefit is two-thirds of the weekly wage, but in no case more than a specified maximum amount per week nor less then a specified minimum, beginning with the fourth or eighth day of disability and continuing until the claimant has recovered or until a stated period, such as 360 weeks, has expired. If the disability lasts longer than, say, two or three weeks, the worker is also compensated retroactively for the waiting period. For example, if the fraction is two-thirds and the maximum weekly benefit is $300, a worker with a $330 weekly wage would receive a weekly benefit of $220. A worker with a weekly wage of $450 or more would receive $300. The maximum weekly benefit is usually less than the state average weekly wage. All but nine states adjust the maximum annually as the state average weekly wage increases. Eight states pay higher benefits when the worker has dependents.

Weekly permanent total disability benefits are determined in the same way as temporary total disability benefits, except that in some states the maximum or minimum weekly benefit is different. In most, but not all, states these weekly benefits are continued for the lifetime of the worker. In about 13 states permanent total disability benefits awarded previously are adjusted annually to maintain the disabled worker's standard of living or purchasing power. Usually the annual adjustment cannot exceed a stated percent, such as 6 percent.

Permanent partial disability benefits usually include two components. During the medical healing period the worker typically receives a temporary total disability benefit. Following this period the worker receives weekly two-thirds of any reduction in earnings, subject to a specified maximum and specified minimum, unless the impairment responsible for the disability is ''scheduled.'' If the permanent partial disability involves the loss of an arm, the loss of a foot, the loss of sight, or some other scheduled impairment, the worker receives a lump sum equal usually to a weekly benefit, determined the same way as weekly temporary total disability benefits, times a specified number of weeks. The number of weeks varies with the nature of the impairment, not the effect the injury may have on the worker's actual earnings. Other disability benefits are based on the actual wage loss; scheduled permanent partial disability benefits are based generally upon the presumed or average expected wage loss. One argument in favor of this approach is that it removes the disincentive for disabled workers to return to employment. States vary greatly in the number of weeks they specify for a given impairment. States also differ dramatically in the way they rank the severity of different injuries.

In 1979 Florida became the first state to base permanent partial disability benefits in part on the actual wage loss. Florida pays an impairment benefit of $50 for each percentage of impairment for injuries rated 1 percent to 50 percent and $100 for each additional percentage of impairment for injuries rated 50 percent to 100 percent. The pure wage loss benefit is a weekly payment equal to 95 percent of the difference between 85 percent of the worker's pre-disability earnings and the worker's earning after reaching maximum medical improvement. The weekly wage loss benefit, however, cannot exceed two-thirds of the worker's prior earnings. In 1983 Louisiana adopted a similar approach.

In 1983 Minnesota made the permanent partial disability benefit depend upon whether the employer either made a bona fide job offer to the worker or convinced some other employer to make such an offer. If the employee receives such an offer, the benefit will be a lump sum tied to the impairment but not the wage. If the employee does not receive such an offer, the benefit is weekly compensation tied to the worker's wage payable for a number of weeks that varies with the nature of the impairment. This economic recovery compensation is larger than the special impairment award.

The death benefits include a limited funeral expense benefit and an income for dependents, which is usually expressed as a percentage of the deceased worker's weekly wage, subject to a specified minimum and a specified maximum. A widow with children may receive a higher percentage, say 66⅔ percent, than a widow without children, who receives, say, 50 percent. In slightly over one-half the states, widows receive benefits until they die or remarry, but the remainder limit the benefits to some specified number of weeks. In about nine states, death benefits awarded previously are adjusted annually to reflect increases in the cost of living or the state average weekly wage.

Five jurisdictions operate their own rehabilitation centers. About two-thirds of the jurisdictions provide some maintenance benefits for persons undergoing rehabilitation. Many disabled workers receive benefits under a federal-state vocational rehabilitation program, which serves persons with all types of occupational and nonoccupational disabilities.

Second-Injury Fund Another measure designed to help handicapped workers is a second-injury fund, found in all states. This fund is designed to encourage the employment of handicapped workers by transferring to the fund, which is administered by the state, all responsibility for the extra workers' compensation benefits, if any, associated with the handicap. For example, if a worker with one eye loses the sight of his or her other eye, the worker is compensated for blindness. The employer is responsible only for the benefit payable in case the worker had lost one eye; the second-injury fund pays the difference. A second approach limits the employer's responsibility to the first 52 or 104 weeks of disability payments plus a portion of the medical expenses. Some states have broad funds covering most prior handicaps, but most states limit their fund either to a few serious handicaps—generally the loss of a hand, arm, foot, leg, or eye—or to second injuries that, combined with the previous handicap, produce permanent total disability. Many methods are used to finance these funds, the most common being special payments in death cases where there are no dependents to receive compensation benefits or assessments expressed as a percentage of the insurance premium paid, or, in the case of self-insurers, the premium that would have been paid if they had not been self-insured. Four states finance their funds in whole or in part from general revenues.

Security Arrangements   In addition to prescribing the benefits to be paid, legislators have been concerned, from the beginning of workers' compensation legislation, about the ability of employers to make these payments when the occasion arises. The table given below shows the present situation with respect to the funding of benefits. Although workers' compensation is clearly social legislation, most states have not established state funds. The heavy reliance on private insurers can be explained by the fact that when workers' compensation was introduced, private insurers were already experienced writers of employers' liability insurance and workers' collective insurance (a form of health insurance); the British had adopted this approach; "government in business" was opposed by many; and competition among insurers was considered necessary to stimulate the loss-prevention and reduction activities which at that time were so sorely needed. The principal counterarguments in favor of state funds were that workers' compensation insurance, being social insurance, should be written by nonprofit public insurers; private insurers were unwilling to insure all employers needing protection; public insurers should be able to operate with lower expense loadings; and competitive state funds provide a yardstick for measuring the performance of private insurers.

Funding medium	Number of states
Monopolistic state fund	4
Monopolistic state fund or self-insurance	2
State fund, private insurer, or self-insurance	13
Private insurer or self-insurance	30
Private insurer	1
Insurance not required*	1
Total (including the District of Columbia)	51

*Technically not required but in practice private insurance or approved self-insurance is required.

Increasing Cost of Workers' Compensation   During the 1970s, the cost to employers of workers' compensation rose dramatically. In 1972, the cost of workers' compensation insurance and self-insurance was 1.13 percent of payroll; in 1980, the cost was almost 2 percent.[6] Workers' compensation rates have increased in several

[6] Daniel N. Price, "Workers' Compensation: Coverage, Benefits, and Costs, 1980," *Social Security Bulletin*, vol. XLIV, no. 5 (May, 1983), pp. 18–19.

states in one year by more than 30 percent. For some industries and for some employers within an industry the increase in those states has been even greater. The result has been intense employer concern and the establishment in several states of commissions charged with reviewing the law and its administration.

Several factors have been suggested as reasons for the increase. First, benefit liberalizations encouraged by the National Commission raised the cost. Second, inflation has increased the cost of medical care, administrative costs, and through higher wages, disability and death dollar benefits. Other charges are that state administrative agencies have become more liberal in their interpretation of the law, and that workers have been encouraged to file claims and malinger because of higher benefits, high tax rates on earned income (workers' compensation benefits are not taxable), and high unemployment rates.

Whatever the reasons, workers' compensation has become one of the most important areas of concern for risk managers. For many businesses it is the most costly property and liability exposure in an average year.

Frequency and Severity Data

For comparative industry information on work-injury frequency and severity rates, the reader can consult reports by the Bureau of Labor Statistics of the U.S. Department of Labor on the annual survey of occupational injuries and sicknesses. These reports provide information for all employees covered under the Occupational Safety and Health Act.

During 1982, per 100 full-time workers there were 7.7 recordable cases of job-related injury or sickness (all deaths and diseases and all injuries resulting in loss of consciousness, restriction of work or motion, transfer to another job, or medical treatment other than first aid), 3.5 of which were fatalities or disabilities causing lost workdays.[7] The lost workdays were 58.7 per 100 full-time workers, almost 17 per lost workday case. Because the survey reports only the days lost in the year in which the case is diagnosed and recognized as work-related, the average days lost per case may exceed 17 days. The loss experience varied among industries as follows:

Industry	Per 100 full-time workers		
	Recordable cases	Lost workday cases	Lost workdays
Contract construction	14.6	6.0	115.7
Agriculture, forestry, and fishing	11.8	5.9	86.0
Mining	10.5	5.4	137.3
Manufacturing	10.2	4.4	75.0
Transportation and public utilites	8.5	4.9	96.7
Wholesale and retail trade	7.2	3.1	45.5
Services	4.9	2.3	35.8
Finance, insurance, and real estate	2.0	.9	13.2

[7] *Occupational Injuries and Illnesses for* 1982 (Washington, D.C.: U.S. Department of Labor, Bureau of Labor Statistics, 1984).

The incidence rates also vary by size of the firm. Rates are lowest for firms employing less than 20 workers (3.5 per 100 full-time workers) or at least 2,500 workers (5.5 per 100 full-time workers). Firms employing between 50 and 500 workers had the highest rates.

MOTOR VEHICLE ACCIDENT LIABILITY

One of the most complicated and most widespread areas of potential liability in business (or family) activity surrounds the use of automobiles and other motor vehicles. This is true in part because of the large number of accidents involving these vehicles, the wide variety of circumstances surrounding these accidents, and the speed with which they occur. Businesses (and families) are usually aware that the ownership, maintenance, or use of a motor vehicle creates a serious liability exposure, but they often do not appreciate the complexity or magnitude of this exposure. The discussion here will deal with (1) the special factors affecting the finding of negligence and liability in automobile accidents, (2) the frequency and severity of automobile accidents, (3) the financial responsibility requirements states have imposed upon drivers to protect innocent victims of their negligent acts, and (4) automobile compensation or no-fault laws.

The Finding of Negligence and Liability

Despite the large number of states with no-fault laws, the law of negligence continues to play an important role in automobile liability. Not all states have no-fault laws, and none of the present no-fault laws have completely abolished the application of tort liability. The finding of negligence relating to the use of vehicles normally depends upon a jury's decision as to certain questions of fact: (1) Did the defendant fail to have the vehicle under proper control? (2) Did the defendant fail to exercise proper lookout? (3) Did the defendant operate the vehicle at an excessive speed? An affirmative answer to any one of the three above questions will result in finding the defendant negligent. The owner of a vehicle, however, cannot be concerned only about his or her own driving habits and ability to meet the above negligence tests. Liability may also exist under certain conditions in the use of the owned automobile when it is operated by someone other than the owner.

The *law of agency* may impute the negligent conduct of the operator to the owner when the operator is acting as an agent of the owner. For example, if A asked B to go to the grocery store and purchase some articles, A could be sued if A's agent, B, operates A's vehicle negligently.

Some states have enacted *vicarious liability* statutes that make the owner liable for personal injuries or property damage caused by the negligence of any person operating the automobile with the owner's permission. The operator need not be the owner's agent; indeed the operator may be driving the car strictly for his or her own benefit with the reluctant permission of the owner.

Questions often arise concerning the responsibility of the owner of the family car for the tortious driving of his or her children. Although these questions are of much greater concern to families than to businesses, they sometimes affect businesses. Many states have recognized liability of parents for their children's driving through court decisions by what is referred to as the *family car doctrine*. Since the parent is responsible for the provision of food, clothing, shelter, and transportation for the family, the use of the car by any member of the family for these purposes has been held to make the parent legally responsible. In addition, many states have made the signer of the license application for a minor responsible for the operation of all vehicles by the minor, not only the vehicle owned by the parent.

Another variation of the agency problem relates to liability arising from nonowned automobiles. For example, in an important court decision in California, *Malloy* v. *Fong,* 37 Ca. 2d 356, 232 P.2d 241 (1951), a church was held liable for the negligent operation of a vehicle by a volunteer who had agreed to transport children to a public playground for a church function. In the particular case, the child, who was riding on the outside of the vehicle, was involved in an accident. As a result, the suit was brought against both the driver of the car and the church for this tortious conduct. Since the operator of the vehicle did not have any assets and did not carry insurance, the ultimate loss fell upon the church organization, which had to pay the judgment for $41,500 for such conduct. It is important to note that many vehicles are used in behalf of commercial establishments or individuals without their specific knowledge but with their general authorization. Under these conditions, this authorization may impose serious and important legal exposures upon the authorizing agency or individual.

Joint venture situations arise where two or more parties use the vehicle in a particular pursuit for a common objective, such as a business trip or some other commercial activity. When injury is sustained by a third party as a result of this type of activity, the third party may sue any member of the joint venture even though no one of the joint venturers may be operating the vehicle; the negligence of the operator is imputed to all the other members of the joint venture. The courts in most states have circumscribed this theory of recovery and have limited it only to those situations where a business or commercial purpose is in fact involved. Mere social relationships ordinarily do not impute negligence under the joint venture theory.

Joint control usually arises where the operator of the vehicle and the guest jointly look for road signs or in some other way control the vehicle together. When the vehicle is under such joint control, the negligence of one may be imputed to the other in a suit by a third party.

In order to avoid a suit brought by a guest who may be injured in an automobile as the result of the driver's negligent operation, many states have enacted *guest* statutes. These statutes will exempt the owner or the operator of the vehicle from liability to a guest in the vehicle unless the conduct of the driver is viewed as willful, wanton, and grossly negligent or is proved to be done with an intent to do bodily injury to the guest. The purpose of these statutes is to preclude hitchhikers and other social guests from suing the owner of the vehicle and thereby taking advantage of what otherwise might be friendly conduct. Still other states have not enacted guest statutes, but require that drivers with guests in their vehicles only exercise that degree of skill and care that they would normally exercise in their own behalf. If they normally drive recklessly, hosts have no liability to their guests if the hosts' reckless driving causes the guests to be injured.

Recognizing that there is a need for immediate medical attention at the time and scene of an automobile accident, many states have enacted what is referred to as the Good Samaritan law. In the absence of such a statute, physicians and surgeons could be held personally liable for any malpractice that might result from their voluntarily assisting or aiding injured persons on a public highway. As a result, members of the medical profession have avoided becoming involved in accidents because of potential personal liability. The Good Samaritan law encourages a physician to render aid at the time and scene of the accident by barring all tort liability claims arising from these activities.

Frequency and Severity Data

According to the National Safety Council there were approximately 29 million motor vehicle accidents in 1982, which resulted in about 46,000 deaths and almost 5.0 million injuries.[8] The total economic loss from these traffic accidents has been placed at almost $60 billion. In 1972, the estimated loss was about $29 billion, less than half the 1982 total.

Motor vehicle accident costs are determined by the number of accidents and their average severity. As the number of vehicles registered multiplied at an amazing rate (about 102 million passenger cars registered in 1973, compared with about 62 million in 1960), the number of automobile accidents increased significantly. In 1974, however, the number declined as maximum speed limits were reduced and other steps were taken to combat the oil crisis. Inflation, however, caused the average cost per accident to rise substantially. Since 1974 the number of automobile accidents has remained about the same.

Unlike accident frequency, accident severity has increased. Average payments for automobile bodily injury liability insurance claims increased from $1,926 in 1972 to $5,041 in 1982, an increase of 162 percent. Over the same period, property damage liability insurance claims increased by 170 percent, from $355 to $958. Also, during this same period, the Consumer Price Index increased by only 131 percent. Wages, however, have risen more than the price index. So have medical care and automobile repair costs, particularly the cost of repairing damaged cars. Finally, juries have also become notably more liberal in determining awards.

National Safety Council data show that in 1982, although drivers under the age of 30 were only about 34 percent of all drivers, they were about 50 percent of the drivers involved in accidents. On the other hand, drivers aged 65 or more were over 9 percent of all drivers, but only about 6 percent of the accident drivers.

Probability estimates of the likelihood of having an automobile accident depend upon much more than the age of the driver. Insurance data suggest such factors as the territory in which the car is garaged, the type of vehicle (a private passenger car, a commercial vehicle such as a truck, or a public vehicle such as a bus or taxi), the purpose for which the vehicle is used (for example, business or pleasure), the sex and marital status of the driver, whether the driver had driver training, the academic performance of the driver, and the driver's motor vehicle violation and accident record. The use of some of these factors such as age, sex, and marital status in setting

---

[8] *Insurance Facts, 1983–84 edition,* (New York: Insurance Information Institute, 1983), pp. 69, 75.

insurance rates has been prohibited in some states and questioned in others on one or more of the following grounds: a causal relationship does not exist; there is a wide variation in the loss potential of those sharing the same age, sex, or marital status; because age, sex, or marital status is not within the control of the insured, using those factors does not provide any loss control incentives; and it is socially undesirable to differentiate rates according to these factors.

Financial Responsibility Requirements

In too many cases automobile accident victims have not been compensated for their losses, despite the fact that under the law of negligence they have a legal right to recover their losses. The reason is that the negligent drivers have been financially irresponsible. Uninsured-motorists coverage, to be described in Chapter 19, was a private response to this problem. State legislatures have also responded through (1) financial responsibility laws, (2) compulsory automobile liability insurance, and (3) unsatisfied judgment funds.

Financial Responsibility Laws Financial responsibility laws, the original and still a common approach, encourage, but do not require, all drivers to be financially responsible. These laws vary somewhat in details, but the following description of a typical law indicates the basic approach. First, if a person is convicted of certain offenses such as drunken driving, reckless driving, or speeding, that person must prove that he or she would be financially responsible for motor vehicle losses he or she may cause in the next three years up to, say, $15,000 for bodily injuries incurred by one person and $30,000 per accident, and up to $10,000 per accident for property damage. The proof usually takes the form of an automobile liability insurance contract,[9] but cash, certain securities, and surety bonds are also acceptable. Failure to meet this requirement will cause the operator to lose his or her driver's license and the owner to lose his or her registration.

Second, on ocurrence of an accident involving bodily injury or a stated minimum of property damage, the license of the operator and the registration of any car are suspended unless, or until, evidence of financial responsibility is filed with state authorities covering, up to the limits stated earlier, any damage for which a judgment might later be incurred. Mere involvement in the accident is sufficient to trigger the requirement; the driver need not be the guilty party, the one exception being that in some obvious cases, such as a legally parked car being hit by a negligent driver, the innocent driver may be excused. The proof may take the form of an insurance contract, cash, or a surety bond. If such proof is not forthcoming, the requirement is generally terminated only by exoneration of blame for the accident; release by or agreement with the injured party; or lapse of a year without suit being filed.

In some states motorists involved in accidents must also furnish proof of future financial responsibility, for, say, three years. In practically all states with these laws, if a judgment is returned against an uninsured motorist, he or she must satisfy that

---

[9] Under contracts used as proof the insurer is obligated to pay any damages, even though the insured may have violated the contract. However, the insured must reimburse the insurer for any payments it would not have made except for this special obligation under the financial responsibility law.

judgment up to the limits of the financial responsibility law or his or her license and registration will be suspended until the judgment is satisfied up to those limits and proof of financial responsibility for, say, the next three years is provided.

Financial responsibility laws have been praised for their voluntary approach and the absence of extensive enforcement machinery. They have been criticized because they are only partially effective. Many motor traffic victims go uncompensated. Some financially irresponsible drivers regain their licenses after one year because the victim, realizing that the defendant has no assets, decides not to file a suit.

Uninsured-motorists coverage, described in Chapter 19, is the insurer's answer to this objection. All but a few of the states with financial responsibility laws require that insurers include uninsured-motorists coverage in all automobile liability insurance contracts. Most of these states permit the insured to reject this coverage, but he or she must specifically do so. In addition to providing a source of payment for the innocent victim, this coverage strengthens the operation of the financial responsibility law because one year is much less likely to elapse without a suit being filed. Those who object to this approach argue principally that the insured motorists pay the cost of accidents caused by uninsured motorists.

Compulsory Automobile Liability Insurance   Automobile compensation or no-fault laws go beyond financial responsibility laws in that they require owners and drivers to purchase insurance that will pay the no-fault benefits and a large portion of the residual liability claims. These laws are explained later in this chapter. Compulsory automobile liability insurance, however, predates no-fault insurance and affects some owners and drivers in about twelve states that do not have no-fault laws.

For many years most owners of public vehicles such as taxicabs and buses have been required to provide evidence of minimum financial responsibility. Similarly interstate motor common carriers have been required to have insurance or some other evidence that they will be able to pay claims occasioned by bodily injuries to passengers or others or damage to cargo or other property. In a few states young drivers or registrants have been required to post proof of financial responsibility.

Compulsory automobile insurance was at one time a much-debated issue. Proponents stressed that it was the simplest, most effective way to guarantee that motor vehicle accident victims would be able to collect from negligent drivers. Opponents, on the other hand, argued that not all drivers would obey the law; enforcement of the law would be expensive and difficult; insurers would be forced to cover some drivers they would prefer to reject; people would become more claims conscious and courts more liberal when they knew the defendant was insured, and insurance premiums would be subject to political pressures. In the debate on no-fault laws these issues received little attention because of the larger questions involved.

Unsatisfied Judgments Funds and Assigned-Case Plans   In 1947 North Dakota supplemented its financial responsibility law with a state unsatisfied judgments fund.[10]

---

[10] For a comprehensive description and evaluation of these funds, see G. Victor Hallmann, *Unsatisfied Judgments Funds* (Homewood, Ill.: Richard D. Irwin, Inc., 1968).

Maryland, Michigan, New Jersey, and New York later established similar funds. The four funds differ somewhat in details, but basically if the innocent victim of a motor vehicle accident secures a judgment against a negligent motorist who is unable to pay the judgment, the victim can apply to the state unsatisfied judgments fund for payment up to the limits of the state's financial responsibility law. The state fund is supported by assessments on both insured and uninsured resident owners of vehicles, but only insured resident motorists and uninsured residents who do not own a car are eligible for benefits. Once the fund pays the judgment, it becomes subrogated to the insured's claim against the negligent driver. These funds thus serve essentially the same purpose as private uninsured-motorists coverage and were in fact the inspiration for that coverage.

No-fault laws and compulsory insurance have reduced the interest in unsatisfied judgments funds. However, although the five states mentioned above now have no-fault laws that require compulsory automobile liability insurance, they still have unsatisfied judgments funds. In other compulsory insurance or no-fault states a closely related pool of private insurers serves a similar purpose. Although insurance is compulsory, not everyone obeys the law. Also there is the possibility of a hit-and-run accident. Consequently no-fault laws typically establish an assigned-case plan to handle such clams. This plan is underwritten and managed by the automobile insurers operating in the state. It is supported by assessments on insurers and self-insurers. Private uninsured-motorists coverage against residual tort liability claims is also sometimes required.

Automobile Compensation or No-Fault Laws

Over half the population live in the 24 states plus the District of Columbia and Puerto Rico that have replaced the tort liability system in part with automobile compensation or no-fault benefits. Under these no-fault laws, automobile accident victims receive certain benefits regardless of who was at fault. The replacement of the tort system, however, has been far less complete than in workers' compensation.

Criticisms of Tort Liability System   The criticisms of the tort liability system applied to automobile accidents are reminiscent of those made earlier in this century with respect to employers' liability:[11]

1 Correct apportionment of blame is almost impossible. The outcome is too frequently determined by chance, the skill of the victim's lawyer, the composition of the jury, and other extraneous factors. Automobile accidents pose a special problem because the speed with which they occur makes it extremely difficult for witnesses to describe what happened. Drivers and victims are tempted to be dishonest in their

---

[11] For data supporting points 2, 3, and 4, see A. F. Conard et al., *Automobile Accident Costs and Payments: Studies in the Economics of Injury Reparation* (Ann Arbor: The University of Michigan Press, 1964), and "Economic Consequences of Automobile Accident Injuries," *Department of Transportation Automobile Insurance and Compensation Study* (Washington, D.C.: U.S. Government Printing Office, 1970).

description of the accident because of the ease with which this can be done and their economic interests.

2 Recovery is delayed for months or even years because of lengthy investigation periods, court congestion, and appeals.

3 Tort settlements are not net benefits. Instead, the victim usually incurs some collection expenses, such as lawyers' charges, lost wages, and transportation costs. In addition to the collection expenses borne by the victims, society must maintain an expensive court system.

4 Tort settlements are not related to the economic loss but, like the determination of blame, are affected by many other considerations. Persons with large economic losses tend to be undercompensated for these losses; persons with small economic losses receive more than their economic losses.

Other criticisms, not leveled against employers' liability, include the following:

5 Courts have become so prone to find negligence in automobile cases that, if current trends continue, few defendants will escape a finding of negligence on their part.

6 Because of the trend in court decisions and the existence of liability insurance, tort law is much less effective than it was formerly as a method for placing the blame on careless drivers and encouraging them to drive more carefully.

7 Pain and suffering allowances, which are highly subjective, account for too large a proportion (over half, on the average) of the total settlements.

Criticisms such as these caused some persons to propose that the present negligence system be replaced by a motor vehicle compensation system similar to workers' compensation. Their arguments were persuasive in many states, but the counterarguments made by the defenders of the tort system have sometimes been more persuasive and even in no-fault states have influenced the characteristics of the compensation system. These arguments can be summarized as follows:

1 The tort liability system should not be expected to compensate all injured victims for all their economic losses. Only those who can prove negligence on the part of someone else are entitled to recover.

2 The difficulty of determining fault has been overestimated. In some instances there is no question concerning who was to blame.

3 Assessing blame is ethically sound and encourages safe driving. Insurance may reduce some of the financial implications, but the award or settlement may exceed the policy limits, persons with a bad driving record may have difficulty securing insurance, and rates usually vary with past driving performance. In any event the psychological impact of being found at fault should not be underestimated.

4 Although some cases are not settled for several months or years after the accident, most claims are settled within a reasonable period.

5 If a compensation plan completely replaced the tort liability system, disputes would still arise necessitating collection and administration cost. Witness workers' compensation where there are still numerous disputes over the extent and duration of the injured worker's disability and whether the injury did in fact arise out of and in the course of employment. The amount of court time spent on automobile cases is also less than commonly supposed.

6 Pain and suffering is a very real loss for which the victim should be compensated. Some victims suffer severe pain or disfigurements or dismemberments that alter drastically their personal relationships and activities, but have small economic losses. Some method of compensating these people for their intangible losses must be found.

The Columbia Plan   Proposals to abandon, at least in part, the tort system for handling automobile claims are not new, but it was not until the early seventies that any state enacted a no-fault law. Credit for the first carefully worked-out no-fault proposal is usually given to a Columbia University study team whose 1932 proposal became known as the Columbia plan. The Columbia plan, like workers' compensation, would have imposed upon the owners of motor vehicles absolute liability for personal injuries to occupants of their cars or to pedestrians, caused by the operation of the owners' motor vehicles. The amount of that liability was to be determined by a schedule similar to that used in workers' compensation, and the scheduled benefit was to be the exclusive remedy of the injured party. Insurers and lawyers were active opponents of the proposal.

Keeton-O'Connell Basic Protection Plan   The proposal that sparked the recent move toward automobile compensation plans was the basic-protection plan developed by Professor Robert Keeton, of the Harvard Law School, and Professor Jeffrey O'Connell, of the University of Illinois Law School.[12] In this plan, the product of years of research, the authors attempted to build upon earlier proposals. The basic features of the plan, as it was originally announced, can be summarized as follows:

1 Compulsory basic-protection insurance would compensate all persons injured in automobile accidents, regardless of fault. Pedestrians would collect from the insurer of the car that injured them. Occupants of a car would collect from the insurer of that car.

2 Compensation benefits would cover net economic losses only—primarily medical expenses and work loss (loss of earnings and the expenses of hiring someone else to provide services, normally household services, ordinarily provided by the injured party), not pain and suffering. Losses to property were not covered, but the plan could be and was later modified to provide this protection.

3 Net economic losses would be determined by subtracting from gross economic losses (a) 15 percent of any income loss to allow for tax savings and a reduction in work expenses, (b) any reimbursement from other sources such as private life and health insurance, and (c) a deductible equal to $100 or, if higher, 10 percent of the work loss. The deductible under (c) was omitted in later versions of the plan.

4 The maximum benefit would be $10,000 per person and $100,000 per accident, but if the accident claim exceeded $100,000, provision was made for recovery from an assigned-claims plan. Work-loss benefits would also be limited to $750 per month.

5 Benefits would not be paid in one lump sum but instead would usually be payable monthly as losses accrued.

6 If tort damages for pain and suffering would exceed $5,000 or if other tort

---

[12] R. E. Keeton and J. O'Connell, *Basic Protection for the Traffic Victim* (Boston: Little, Brown and Company, 1965).

damages would exceed $10,000, the injured victim could start a tort action. Any tort recovery, however, would be reduced by these amounts and by the no-fault benefits.

7 Private insurers would write the necessary insurance and an assigned-case plan would provide benefits when the vehicle was either uninsured or a hit-and-run car.

8 Residual liability insurance could be purchased to cover accidents in states not adopting the plan and tort actions in the home state made possible by 6.

Other Proposals   The Keeton-O'Connell plan generated several other proposals, a few of which we will summarize briefly.

In 1968 the American Insurance Association, a trade association of stock insurers, proposed a no-fault plan that would include property damage to automobiles as well as bodily injuries, place no limit on the maximum no-fault benefit per person, and with a few minor exceptions completely eliminate tort actions.

In 1969 Puerto Rico adopted a social-protection plan designed by J. B. Aponte and H. S. Denenberg. This tax-supported, government-administered program provides more limited no-fault benefits than Keeton and O'Connell proposed. Tort actions are possible for pain and suffering claims over $1,000 and for economic losses over $2,000.

In 1970 the American Mutual Insurance Alliance and the National Association of Independent Insurers proposed that all automobile owners be required to buy from private insurers at least $2,000 in medical benefits and $6,000 in wage-loss benefits that would be paid, regardless of fault, to all persons riding in the insured car or to pedestrians struck by that car. The injured party would thus receive benefits immediately but would retain the right to sue negligent parties responsible for his or her losses. The insurer would have subrogation rights to recover the no-fault benefits paid if the injured party later received a settlement or an award.

Federal Proposals   In 1971 the Secretary of Transportation recommended that Congress urge states to adopt no-fault automobile insurance legislation. This recommendation was based on an extensive two-year study of automobile insurance and the tort liability system. The same year, the DOT encouraged through a financial grant the development of a model no-fault bill by the National Conference of Commissioners on Uniform State Laws. In August 1972 the NCCUSL adopted the Uniform Motor Vehicle Accident Reparations Act. Unlike the other proposals, which established a dollar threshold for tort liability, UMVARA contained a verbal threshold related to the seriousness of the injury. Tort liability for bodily injuries would be abolished except in case of death, permanent significant loss of bodily function, permanent serious disability, or total disability lasting more than six months.

For a few years thereafter Congress seriously considered establishing minimum federal standards that, if not satisfied by the states within a few years, would be replaced by a federal no-fault program.

Summary of Key Features of No-Fault Proposals   From the preceding discussion it is apparent that all no-fault proposals share one common concept. Persons injured in an automobile accident, whether as occupants of an automobile or as a pedestrian, would receive certain benefits regardless of who was at fault. On the other hand, the proposals differ widely on the following key points:

1 Whether the program applies to property damage as well as bodily injury
2 The types of benefits paid on a no-fault basis and the dollar limits on those benefits
3 Whether other recoveries are deducted from the no-fault benefits
4 Under what conditions tort actions are permitted (Is the threshold a monetary or verbal threshold and how high is the threshold?)
5 Whether insurers possess subrogation rights with respect to no-fault benefits

The AIA proposal represents one extreme with unlimited (except for a $750 monthly maximum) no-fault benefits, no tort actions permitted, and no insurer subrogation rights. The AMIA-NAII plan, on the other hand, provided rather limited no-fault benefits, preserved all tort liability actions, and gave insurers subrogation rights. Both plans would deduct from the no-fault benefits only workers' compensation benefits and both applied only to bodily injuries.

Debate Issues   In debates on no-fault insurance those who are most critical of the tort liability system tend to favor complete no-fault plans. Those favoring partial no-fault proposals with no subrogation rights argue (1) that the change should be evolutionary or (2) that tort actions should be preserved for those with serious injuries. Partial no-fault plans with subrogation rights appeal to those who wish to preserve most of the tort system.

Key issues in these debates are how important and feasible it is to place the blame on the negligent driver, how much litigation would be reduced under the no-fault proposal, and whether payments should be made for pain and suffering.

Whether premiums will rise or fall has been one of the most debated issues. Factors favoring a premium increase under a no-fault plan are the increase in the number of persons receiving benefits and the higher benefits paid to persons with large economic losses. Factors favoring a decrease are the reduction or elimination of pain and suffering allowances and possible reductions in claim adjustment costs.[13]

State Laws   In 1970, Massachusetts became the first state to adopt no-fault legislation. Originally, property damage was not included but it was added in 1972 on an optional basis. No-fault benefits were limited to $2,000. Recoveries from other sources were not deducted; tort actions were permitted only if medical expenses exceeded $500, or if the injury caused death, dismemberment, permanent and serious disfigurement, loss of sight or hearing, or a fracture.

In early 1984, 24 states plus the District of Columbia and Puerto Rico, which includes about half of our nation's population, had some form of no-fault automobile insurance broadly defined. In 13 of these states plus the District of Columbia the

---

[13] No-fault laws should also change the relative costs among insureds. For example, because the no-fault insurer usually pays victims in the insured car, motorcycles are more expensive to insure. As a result motorcycles are excluded under many laws. Cars with strong bodies that are equipped with safety features should qualify their owners for low rates. The income of the insured may also become an important consideration.

prescribed first-party no-fault insurance is compulsory; lawsuits under the tort liability system are restricted; and residual liability insurance (covering the law suits that are permitted in the home state and elsewhere) is compulsory up to some specified limits.[14] Because of the variety of approaches used, no attempt will be made to describe each state law. The Michigan law, however, is of special interest because it imposes much more severe restrictions on lawsuits than the other state laws. This law covers on a no-fault basis unlimited reasonable medical and rehabilitation expenses; up to $1,000 funeral and burial expenses; and 85 percent of work loss up to $1,000 a month (adjusted for cost of living changes) for up to three years. These benefits are reduced only by benefits provided under any state or federal law, not other voluntary private insurance. Lawsuits are barred except in cases of death or serious injury, when economic losses exceed the no-fault benefits, or when the harm was intentionally caused.

Florida and Puerto Rico require first party no-fault insurance and place some restrictions on law-suits, but residual liability insurance is not compulsory.

The other ten no-fault states place no restrictions on law suits under the tort system. For that reason many observers do not consider these states to be no-fault states. In four of these ten states, no-fault insurance and liability insurance are compulsory, but the insured is always permitted to sue under the tort system.[15]

South Carolina and Texas differ from these three states only in that the first party no-fault insurance is optional.

In the four remaining states, insurance is not compulsory and no restriction is placed on lawsuits.[16] Most of these states require insurers to offer first-party no-fault benefits, but permit the insured to reject the coverage. Insurers often voluntarily offer such coverage in other states that have not passed no-fault statutes.

The District of Columbia enacted its no-fault law in 1983, the only jurisdiction to enact a no-fault law since 1976. In early 1979 Nevada repealed the no-fault law it had adopted in 1974. In early 1984 Pennsylvania replaced a no-fault bill that restricted law suits with one that does not. One common explanation for the slowing or plateauing of the no-fault movement is that premiums have risen more than was expected in no-fault states. The counterargument is that inflation caused premiums to rise substantially in both no-fault and fault states. Several comparisons of premium increases in no-fault states with those in fault states suggest that in some cases no-fault laws have increased costs.[17] No-fault laws tend to increase costs in states that do not restrict lawsuits or

---

[14] Colorado, Connecticut, Georgia, Hawaii, Kansas, Kentucky, Massachusetts, Michigan, Minnesota, New Jersey, New York, North Dakota, and Utah.

[15] Delaware, Maryland, Oregon, and Pennsylvania.

[16] Arkansas, New Hampshire, South Dakota, and Virginia.

[17] See, for example, U.S. Department of Transportation, *State No-Fault Automobile Insurance Experience, 1971–77* (Washington, D.C.: U.S. Government Printing Office, 1978) and "No-Fault Automobile Insurance: An Evaluative Survey," 30 *Rutgers Law Review* 909 (1977). For a compilation of studies of experience under the laws of Delaware, Florida, Massachusetts, and Michigan, see A. I. Widiss, R. R. Bovbjerg, D. F. Cavers, J. W. Little, R. S. Clark, G. E. Waterson, and T. C. Jones, *No-Fault Automobile Insurance in Action* (Dobbs Ferry, New York: Oceana Publications, Inc. 1977). For a summary of numerous recent surveys on the operation on no-fault laws see Jeffrey O'Connell, "Operation of No-Fault Auto Laws: A Survey of Surveys," 56 *Nebraska Law Review* (1977), reprinted in 650 *Insurance Law Journal* 152 (March, 1978), and J. O'Connell and J. Beck, "An Update of the Surveys on the Operations of No-Fault Auto Laws," *Insurance Law Journal* (March, 1979), pp. 129–143.

have low thresholds for a tort action. No-fault laws with high tort thresholds tend to reduce costs.

NO-FAULT LIABILITY FOR ALL KINDS OF ACCIDENTS?

With automobile no-fault insurance now a fact in so many states, and tort liability costs rising so dramatically, many persons have advocated the extension of the no-fault concept to other kinds of accidents. Product liability and malpractice cases are generally considered to be the most likely candidates for such an extension.

A leading, articulate spokesman for extending no-fault principles to other areas is Professor Jeffrey O'Connell, one of the coauthors of the Keeton-O'Connell basic-protection plan described earlier in this chapter.[18] Victims of product accidents or malpractice, he argues, are even worse off under the tort system than are automobile accident victims. Professor O'Connell recognized, however, that extending no-fault insurance to accidents arising from products or medical practice is much more difficult than compensating the smaller automobile accident losses on a no-fault basis. He cites two interrelated factors: (1) We do not know whether the extension would impose new and formidable burdens on anyone. For example, would holding ladder manufacturers responsible for all falls from ladders burden them unreasonably? (2) It would be necessary to identify sufficiently dangerous or otherwise distinctive activities such that it would be clear who should pay the loss. For example, is laying a cement patio so dangerous an activity that the contractor should be responsible for all falls on the patio? For these reasons Professor O'Connell believes some experimentation may be the only feasible and perhaps the most desirable way to proceed. He proposes an elective no-fault liability system under which manufacturers, doctors and others might be permitted under an enabling statute to select some or all of the accidents they typically create and agree to pay on a no-fault basis, in whole or in part, the lost earnings, medical expenses, property losses, and other tangible losses arising from those accidents. If they paid only part of the losses, some residual tort liability would remain. The stigma of fault would be removed or at least lessened. Legal services and expert witnesses would not be needed. No payments would be made for pain and suffering, and payments for economic losses would be reduced by other insurance covering the same loss. Each business, doctor, or other person would have to decide whether, on balance, it would be advantageous to elect the no-fault option. In time, he argues, society might want to impose compulsory no-fault liability on some of these activities.

In his more recent writings (1975 on), Professor O'Connell has argued that the no-fault approach "could be instituted without enabling legislation by contract between patients and health care providers, signed before treatment, or between consumers and product manufacturers or retailers, signed before purchase."[19]

---

[18] Jeffrey O'Connell, *Ending Insult to Injury* (Urbana: The University of Illinois Press, 1974). Professor O'Connell first made his proposal in an article entitled "Expanding No-Fault beyond Auto Insurance," 50 *Virginia Law Review* 749 (May, 1973).

[19] Jeffrey O'Connell, "An Alternative to Abandoning Tort Liability: Elective No-Fault Insurance for Many Kinds of Injuries," 60 *Minnesota Law Review* 3 (February, 1976), p. 529.

SOME KEY CONCEPTS

Workers' compensation   The program created by statute that makes the employer, regardless of fault, responsible for most job-related injuries and diseases.

Employers' liability   The common law or special statutory responsibility of employers for job-related injuries and diseases caused by their negligence but not covered under workers' compensation.

Second-injury fund   A state fund designed to encourage hiring of the handicapped by in principle transferring from the employer to the fund the costs of the extra workers' compensation benefits, if any, associated with the handicapped.

Financial responsibility law   A law that causes automobile operators (owners) to lose their license (registration) if they are convicted of certain offenses such as drunken driving and cannot post proof of financed responsibility (usually insurance), or if they are involved in an accident involving bodily injury or a stated minimum amount of property damage and cannot post proof of financial responsibility for that accident and perhaps future accidents.

Automobile compensation or no-fault law   A law that permits occupants of cars and pedestrians injured in an automobile accident to collect certain medical and income replacement benefits regardless of who was at fault. Under some laws, the occupant victims collect from the insurer of the car they were occupying; under other laws they collect first under their own automobile insurance policies if they are so insured.

REVIEW QUESTIONS

1 What defects in employers' liability led to the passage of workers' compensation statutes?

2 In what sense is workers' compensation a no-fault program?

3 Are all workers covered under workers' compensation? Explain your answer.

4 A worker earning $600 a week breaks her leg on the job. In a typical state what workers' compensation benefits will she receive if she cannot return to work for five weeks?

5 How do permanent partial disability workers' compensation benefits differ from permanent total disability benefits?

6 **a** What purpose is served by second-injury funds?

   b Compare the narrow and broad approaches to second-injury funds.

7 Workers' compensation provides an arena for testing the relative performance of public and private enterprises. Explain.

8 How has the National Commission on State Workers' Compensation influenced state workers' compensation programs?

9 Under what conditions may the owner of an automobile be held legally responsible for the negligent operation of that automobile by another driver?

10 In your state must a person have insurance to operate a vehicle? If not, what action has your state legislature taken to protect the public against uninsured motorists? Is your state typical?

11 Is automobile no-fault insurance a new idea? Explain.

12 Summarize the Keeton-O'Connell basic-protection plan in terms of the five key features of no-fault automobile insurance plans mentioned in the text.

13 If your state has a no-fault automobile insurance plan, describe it in terms of the five key features listed in the text.

14 Do you favor no-fault automobile insurance? Why or why not?

15 Summarize briefly the state no-fault automobile insurance plans that have been passed to date.

16 Workers' compensation completely replaced the tort system for covered workers; automobile compensation in its present form only partially replaces the tort system. Explain.

17 Should no-fault automobile insurance increase or decrease premiums? Explain.

18 Would you favor the extension of no-fault beyond automobile and workers' compensation? If so, why and to what areas?

SUGGESTIONS FOR ADDITIONAL READING

Automobile Insurance . . . For Whose Benefit?(New York: State of New York Insurance Department, 1970).

Barth, P. S., with H. A. Hunt: *Workers' Compensation and Work-Related Illnesses and Diseases* (Cambridge, Mass.: MIT Press, 1980).

Department of Transportation Automobile Insurance and Compensation Study (Washington, D.C.: U.S. Government Printing Office, 1970).

Department of Transportation, *State No-Fault Automobile Insurance Experience, 1971–1977* (Washington, D.C.: U.S. Government Printing Office, 1978).

Keeton, R. E., and J. O'Connell: *Basic Protection for the Traffic Victim* (Boston: Little, Brown and Company, 1965)

Kulp, G. A., and J.W. Hall: *Casualty Insurance* (4th ed., New York: The Ronald Press Company, 1968), chaps. 7, 8, 12, 13.

Malecki, D. S., J. H. Donaldson, and R. C. Horn: Commercial Liability Risk Management and Insurance, vols. I and II (Malvern, Pa.: American Institute for Property and Liability Underwriters, 1978).

National Commission on Product Safety, Final Report (Washington, D.C.: U.S. Government Printing Office, 1970).

National Commission on State Workmen's Compensation Laws (Washington, D.C.: U.S. Government Printing Office, 1973).

————: Compendium on Workmen's Compensation (Washington, D.C.: U.S. Government Printing Office, 1973).

————: *Supplemental Studies for the National Commission on State Workmen's Compensation Laws,* vols. I, II, and III. (Washington, D.C.: U.S. Government Printing Office, 1973).

O'Connell, Jeffrey: *Ending Insult to Injury* (Urbana; The University of Illinois Press, 1975).

Widiss, A I., R R. Bovbjerg, D. F. Cavers, J. W. Little, R. S. Clark, G. E. Waterson, and T. C. Jones: *No-Fault Automobile Insurance in Action* (Dobbs Ferry, New York: Oceana Publications, Inc., 1977).

Workers' Compensation: Is There a Better Way? A Report on the Need for Reform of State Workers' Compensation by the Policy Group of the Interdepartmental Workers' Compensation Task Force, January 19, 1977.

CHAPTER **9**

PERSONNEL LOSS EXPOSURES

LEARNING OBJECTIVES

After you have completed this chapter, you should be able to:

1 Explain why managers should be interested in the personnel loss exposures of their employees.
2 Calculate roughly for a given employee the earning power loss to his or her family if he or she were to die.
3 Calculate roughly the loss to the same employee's family under the needs approach.
4 Describe the losses to an employee and his or her family caused by poor health, unemployment, and superannuation.
5 Tell why a business might be concerned about key-person losses.
6 Explain the nature and importance of business discontinuation losses.

INTRODUCTION

The discussion now turns from potential property and liability losses to potential personnel losses—the financial losses that occur when one or more people (usually employees in whom the firm has some direct interest) die, reach an advanced age, become ill, or lose their jobs for some other reason.[1] Both the individual employees and the firm itself face these losses, and managers, including the risk manager, have

---

[1] It is more common to refer to these risks as personal risks, but the term "personal" has also been used to distinguish family risks from business risks. "Personnel" avoids this problem. Also, in a business these risks are often handled by the personnel department.

good reason to be interested in the losses to the employee as well as those to the firm. This chapter describes the nature and frequency of both types of losses to both employees and the firm.

LOSSES FACING INDIVIDUAL EMPLOYEES

The firm's employees obviously have reason to plan against the potential financial losses to themselves and their families associated with their death, superannuation, accidental injury or sickness, or unemployment. The risk manager of the firm is also interested in these potential losses to the individual employees for less obvious but very important reasons. Because of this interest, business risk management of personnel risks includes some family risk management.[2]

Reasons for the Interest of the Risk Manager

The risk manager is concerned with these potential financial losses to individual employees for the following reasons: (1) to attract and retain high-quality employees, (2) to raise employee morale and productivity, (3) to be prepared to negotiate with labor unions a reasonable employee benefit package, (4) to take advantage of certain tax advantages of employee benefit plans, (5) to improve the welfare of the employees, (6) to develop the image of a firm that cares about its employees, (7) to ensure compliance with federal and state laws regarding employee benefit plans, and (8) to prevent what many consider an unwarranted expansion of social insurance programs.[3]

Employer-Employee Relationships A business firm may be concerned about the potential financial losses to its personnel primarily because it wishes to improve relationships between the employer and the employee. It believes that its interest will attract high-grade new employees, increase employee loyalty to the firm, and reduce turnover and strikes. The firm may also believe that it will increase the productivity of its workers by freeing them from some of their worries and by replacing workers whose productivity has suffered through superannuation or disability. By tying the benefits of individual employees to the profitability of the firm, it may seek to motivate employees to enhance that productivity. Whether the firm will accomplish all these results is debatable, but the beliefs undoubtedly have some basis.

The firm may itself provide some of the necessary protection for the employees, in which case the firm must make the final decisions. Instead of actually providing the protection (or in addition to such protection), the firm may offer to advise the employee concerning his or her individual protection program. Although the responsibility for

---

[2] Business risk management of property and liability risks may also include some family risk management, but this is still the exception rather than the rule. For an explanation of the slower growth of employee benefit plans covering property and liability losses, see Chapter 22.

[3] Reasons why risk managers may prefer to avoid or limit their concern with these losses to employees are the costs involved, a possible negative effect on initiative and incentive, and possible misinterpretation of their motives as objectionable paternalism.

the final decision in this case rests with the employee, the risk manager must act as if he or she were choosing the form of protection.

Many firms are forced to take an interest in the personnel exposures of their employees because of collective bargaining demands or the threat of such demands. Prior to 1949, very few employee benefit plans were the result of collective bargaining. Unions were more interested in pressing for wage increases than for employee benefits. Some union leaders, in fact, mistrusted employer protection plans because they feared the plans would weaken the employees' loyalty to the union. The 1940s changed this climate because (1) wage controls during World War II directed attention to employee benefits as a valuable condition of employment; (2) prices leveled off in 1949, thus reducing the strength of union arguments for wage increases; (3) high income tax rates increased the attractiveness of employee benefits to employees (for reasons explained below and in Chapters 21 and 22) and decreased the real cost of these benefits to employers; and (4) two important court decisions in 1949 established without question the legal right of unions to bargain with employers insurance and pension benefits.[4]

Tax considerations play a major role in the establishment of employee benefit plans. As will be explained for specific benefits in Chapters 21 and 22, in many cases the annual payment the employer makes toward a benefit for the employee is not considered taxable income to the employee. Consequently for an employee in a 40-percent federal and state income tax bracket, a $300 employer contribution to an employee benefit plan is equivalent to a $500 salary increase. Compensation may also be improved through employee benefits making available life and health insurance protection that the executive could not purchase on his or her own at any cost or, in any event, only at a much higher cost.

Sense of Employer Responsibility   Employers may be interested in the welfare of their employees because they feel responsible for their well-being. The employer may take pride in an insurance and retirement program that is the best in the industry or may simply believe that it is his or her duty to provide a good program.

Public Relations   Some employers may have little sense of responsibility for the welfare of their employees, but they know that the general public may attribute some responsibility to the employer, and they recognize the value of good public relations.

Compliance with Government Regulations   The federal government and state governments have enacted several important laws, such as the Employee Retirement Income and Security Act of 1974, which impose certain requirements on employers with employee benefit plans. Failure to comply with these requirements may cause the employer to lose some tax advantages or to incur certain fines and other penalties.

---

[4] *Inland Steel Co. v. National Labor Relations Bd.,* 170 F.2d 247 (7th Cir. 1949) affirmed sub nom. *American Communications Ass'n v. Douds,* 339 U.S. 382 (1950) and *W. W. Cross & Co. v. National Labor Relations Bd.,* 174 F.2d 875 (1st Cir. 1949).

Threat of Extended Social Insurance Benefits   Many, perhaps most, businesses are opposed at present to the extension of social insurance programs much beyond the current level and types of protection because they fear that government intervention in any area of private enterprise is a forerunner of entry into their own industry. Many of these firms realize that the most effective way to prevent the extension of existing social insurance programs is to demonstrate that individuals are already adequately protected.

Nature and Importance of Losses to the Employees

Employees face a potential loss of earning power and unexpected expenses as the result of death, poor health, unemployment, or old age.

Death   The major loss faced by most families as a result of death is a loss of earning power. This loss to the family may be estimated by (1) forecasting the income after taxes that the individual would have received each year until his or her retirement but will not receive if he or she dies, (2) subtracting from each year's expected income the portion that would have been used to maintain the individual had he or she lived, and (3) discounting each of these differences to its present value. The last step is necessary because if money can be invested at a certain rate of interest, each dollar available at the present time is worth more than a dollar at some future date.

Applying this concept to a particular case may serve to clarify the preceding paragraph. Assume that a worker aged 30 earns a salary of $30,000 a year after taxes. Further assume that the individual's only income is this salary, that this salary will remain the same for the remainder of the person's working career, that the worker will retire after 35 more years of employment, that about one-fifth of the income, or $6,000, is needed for the worker's own maintenance costs, and that a reasonable after-tax interest rate would be 5 percent.[5] Under these assumptions, the estimate of the earning power loss that would be caused by death would be computed as shown in the table below. This estimate understates the actual loss to the family because (1) it assumes that no income is received until the end of each year, (2) it ignores the probable loss of valuable employee benefits (see Chapters 21 and 22), and (3) it also ignores the loss of household services provided by the worker.

If the annual income had been $60,000 and the maintenance cost $12,000, the estimated loss of earning power would have been twice $393,000, or almost $786,000.

---

[5] One rule of thumb developed by Citibank economists and insurance specialists is that, if a breadwinner dies, a family of four can maintain its standard of living with an after-tax income of 75 percent of its after-tax income before the breadwinner's death. This analysis suggests a maintenance cost reduction of 25 percent, not 20 percent. Citibank experts also claimed that a reduction of 40 percent would seriously lower the family's standard of living. See "Citibank Devises Simple Chart to Figure How Much Life Insurance Families Need," *The Wall Street Journal*, Dec. 6, 1976, p. 40. The chart mentioned in the headline shows how much private life insurance is needed to maintain the family's standard of living, given assumptions on gross earnings, spouse's age, investment earnings on insurance proceeds, and Social Security benefits. For example, Citibank estimated that in 1976 a family with $30,000 gross earnings and a spouse aged 35 would require private life insurance equal to 8 times the gross earnings.

Year	Income	Maintenance cost	Difference	Discount factor	Present value of loss*
1	$30,000	$6,000	$24,000	1.05^{-1}	$22,857
2	30,000	6,000	24,000	1.05^{-2}	21,769
3	30,000	6,000	24,000	1.05^{-3}	20,732
...	...	...	...	...	...
33	30,000	6,000	24,000	1.05^{-33}	4,797
34	30,000	6,000	24,000	1.05^{-34}	4,569
35	30,000	6,000	24,000	1.05^{-35}	4,351
					$393,000
					(approximately)

*If the difference is assumed to be constant, as it is in this case, the answer can be obtained by multiplying this difference by the present value of $1 a year for the remainder of the working career. For example, $24,000(16.3742) = $392,981. The present values of $1 for selected periods and interest rates are tabled in most college algebra and mathematics of finance textbooks and handbooks.

If the worker had been aged 60 with a $30,000 salary, only the first five present values would have to be summed, which would produce an earning power loss of only about $104,000.

Increasing the assumed interest rate would decrease the estimated loss. To illustrate, if in the first example the assumed interest rate were 8 percent instead of 5 percent, the estimate would be reduced from $393,000 to $279,200.

If, instead of remaining the same, the worker's income were assumed to increase during the remainder of his or her working career, the estimated loss would be increased. For example, if the worker's salary were assumed to increase at 4 percent a year, the estimated loss would be increased from $393,000 to about $682,000.

Because the estimates of future income, maintenance costs, and interest rates are crude at best and because the indicated loss at the younger ages will usually be far greater than the protection the person can afford to purchase, the dollar value obtained in this way is of limited practical value. However, the estimate is instructive because it emphasizes the magnitude of the earning power loss and demonstrates that this loss tends to diminish with age. As is demonstrated above, if an employee dies at a young age, the loss to his or her family will be greater than if he or she dies at a more advanced age.[6]

[6] Steady inflation plus normal salary progressions usually result in an increasing income over time. If this progress is rapid enough, the earning power may increase slightly with age at the younger ages because of the reduction in the sizable interest discounts applied to the larger later incomes. Eventually, however, this effect will disappear. For a set of tables expressing the "human life value" (discounted for interest and all factors other than mortality that might stop the person from working) as a multiple of gross earnings for selected occupations and ages based on average career expectations, see Alfred E. Hofflander, Jr., *Human Life Value Concepts,* unpublished doctoral dissertation, University of Pennsylvania, 1964. For example, given assumptions that seemed reasonable in the early 1960's, the multiple for an engineer, aged 25, is 36. For a comparison between the net loss of earning power as calculated in this text and the human life value discounted for all factors that might interfere with future earning power, see Juan B. Aponte and H. S. Denenberg, "A New Concept of the Economics of Life Value and Human Life Value," *Journal of Risk and Insurance,* vol. XXXV. no. 3 (September, 1968), pp. 337–356.

A more realistic way of determining the amount of protection that the individual's family should have against the loss of earning power is to assess the minimum needs of the family after death. If the family is to maintain the same standard of living after the breadwinner's death as before, the two approaches produce the same answers, but the needs approach is more realistic in that it recognizes that such a standard is impossibly high. Besides, minimum needs can be more accurately (though far from perfectly) estimated.

The needs approach generally recognizes the following types of income replacement needs:

1 A readjustment income close to the actual loss of income for a short period during which the family is expected to readjust their needs and desires to their new circumstances

2 A reduced but still substantial income following the readjustment period and continuing until children, if any, are self-sufficient (normally to age 18)

3 A further reduced but adequate lifetime income for the spouse beginning after the end of the dependency period

For example, the family of the individual whose earning loss was computed might develop the following needs:

1 $2,000 a month during a two-year readjustment period following his or her death

2 $1,600 a month during the next 13 years until the one child, now aged 3, attains age 18

3 $1,200 a month for the rest of the spouse's life beginning after the child reaches age 18

Chapter 33 shows how needs such as these can be translated into a lump sum; it also illustrates how the needs might be stated for a two-earner family.

The needs approach depends upon the individual's desires as much as (and perhaps more than) upon his or her needs. Consequently, two persons in approximately the same financial and family situation may develop a different needs pattern. The above needs, however, are generally recognized as the most important.

The second type of loss that a family suffers when the breadwinner dies is *additional expenses*. Funeral expenses, including the cost of the funeral itself, the cemetery lot, and the headstone, will affect all families and will probably run well in excess of $3,000. Probate costs and the fees of executors and administrators will be an additional cost, and for large estates these costs will be sizable. Finally, the federal estate tax and state inheritance and estate taxes may demand a sizable amount of cash. (Chapter 33 contains a brief summary of the major provisions of the federal estate tax.) For large estates, these taxes may make the loss caused by additional expenses far greater than the loss of earning power. If other assets in the estate must be sold at forced liquidation prices in order to provide the cash for these taxes, the additional expenses will be even greater. As a person ages, these unexpected expenses become more important relative to the loss of earning power.

For selected ages between ages 0 and 60, inclusive, Table 9.1 shows (1) the probability in 1978 that a person of a certain age would die within a year, and (2) the

TABLE 9.1
PROBABILITIES OF DEATH WITHIN A YEAR FOLLOWING
BIRTHDAY AND PRIOR TO AGE 65, 1978

	Probability of death			Probablity of death	
Age	Within a year	Prior to age 65	Age	Within a year	Prior to age 65
0	.0138	.24	35	.0016	.21
5	.0004	.23	40	.0024	.20
10	.0002	.23	45	.0039	.19
15	.0007	.23	50	.0062	.17
20	.0013	.22	55	.0091	.14
25	.0013	.22	60	.0149	.09
30	.0013	.21			

Source: Derived from *Vital Statistics of the United States, 1978, Volume II, Section 5, Life Tables* (Washington, D.C.: U.S. Department of Health and Human Services, Public Health Service, 1980), pp. 5–12.

probability that a person that age would die prior to attaining age 65. The probabilities are based upon the mortality rates reported for the entire United States population during 1978.

The probability of death within the next year is very small during the age span shown. The probability of death prior to age 65 is substantial. More than one out of five persons between ages 20 and 30 will die before reaching age 65. When this probability is considered together with the magnitude of the potential loss, the case for some active protection measures is clear.

The total population, of course, may be divided into subgroups with varying mortality rates. For example, the probabilities of death are lower for the white population than for the nonwhite population and for females than for males.

The leading causes of death are major cardiovascular-renal diseases and malignant neoplasms.

Poor Health Poor health, like death, may cause two types of losses: (1) loss of earning power through disability and (2) extra expenses.

If a person is totally and permanently disabled to the extent that he or she cannot work, the loss of earning power may be computed as it is in the case of premature death, but the disabled person's maintenance cost is not deducted except for any expenses involved in going to work or engaging in other activities that may be discontinued. The loss of earning power caused by this degree of permanent and total disability is therefore greater than the loss caused by death. For the example presented earlier, if the reduction in expenses is assumed to be negligible, the estimated earning-power loss would be over $491,000.

If the work-loss disability is temporary instead of permanent, the loss of earning power is computed in the same fashion, but the loss period is shorter. To illustrate: if the person whose situation was described earlier was prevented from working for 5

TABLE 9.2
DISABILITY DAYS PER PERSON PER YEAR, BY SEX AND AGE, UNITED STATES, 1981

Age	Restricted-Activity days		Bed-Disability days		Work-Loss days	
	Male	**Female**	**Male**	**Female**	**Male**	**Female**
All ages	17.3	20.7	5.8	7.9	4.6	5.3
Under 17 years	10.9	10.2	4.8	4.9	. . .	. . .
17–24 years	9.6	14.2	3.4	6.3	3.5	4.8
25–44 years	14.7	18.7	4.2	7.0	4.4	5.4
45–64 years	26.5	28.4	7.8	10.1	5.6	5.9
65 years and over	37.6	41.5	13.9	14.0	4.4	3.8

Source: National Center for Health Statistics, *Current Estimates from the Health Interview Survey: United States—1981,* U.S. Department of Health and Human Services, Public Health Service, series 10, no. 141 (October, 1982), p. 22.

years, the loss of earning power would be over $108,000. If the disability is such that the person can do some but not all of his or her work and, as a result, his or her wage is reduced, the analysis is the same, except that the reduction in wages is used instead of the total wage. For example, if the reduction in wages is 50 percent, the earning-power losses in the examples used to illustrate the total permanent work-loss disability and the total temporary work-loss disability would be one-half of the losses computed earlier.

Unexpected extra expenses accompanying an injury, a sickness, or an impairment take the form of hospital bills, surgical fees, charges for physicians' care (nonsurgical) in the hospital, at the doctor's office, or at the patient's home, dental bills, charges for nursing services, costs of artificial limbs and the like, and other medical expenses.

Estimating the probability that a person will suffer a "morbidity condition" and the extent to which that condition will be disabling is extremely difficult because (1) morbidity, unlike mortality, cannot be defined exactly,[7] (2) morbidity varies in seriousness as well as frequency, and (3) morbidity conditions are not reported on a regular basis to public authorities.

Because of the paucity of data on morbidity conditions, in 1956 Congress authorized a continuing National Health Survey to secure information about health conditions in the United States. Some recent data on the number of disability days per person derived from this survey of the civilian noninstitutionalized population are presented in Table 9.2 for various age and sex groups. Survey data do not reveal the probability of becoming disabled or the average number of days that elapse before a disabled person recovers. The average number of disability days depends upon the proportion of the population that is disabled during the year and the average length of their disabilities.

Insurance data reveal that out of 10,000 insured persons aged 27, 67 will be disabled for three months or longer within the next year. For groups of 10,000 aged 37,

---

[7] For example, two persons in exactly the same state of health may disagree as to whether they are ill or have an impairment. If they agree that they have a morbidity condition, they may disagree as to whether this condition is disabling.

47, and 57, the numbers who will be disabled in this way are 98, 168, and 311, respectively. The chance that a person in his or her twenties will suffer a disability lasting three months or more prior to age 65 is about ⅔.[8] The chance of a serious disability, therefore, is substantially greater than the chance of death, particularly at the younger ages.

According to the National Health Survey, on an average day in 1981 about 14 percent of the population had their activities limited to some degree by a chronic condition (defined as a condition that lasts at least three months). Almost 11 percent were limited in their major activity as a worker, homemaker, or student).

Chronic conditions accounted for about half of the restricted-activity days reported in Table 9.2. The remainder were caused by acute conditions—those lasting less than three months. Respiratory ailments alone accounted for more than one-fifth of these less-active days.[9] Injuries were responsible for only about 18 percent, work injuries for 5 percent. Sickness, obviously, is much more often the cause of disability than are injuries.[10]

Personal health care expenditures for medical care in 1982 were $287 billion or over $1,215 per capita, of which 47 percent was spent for hospital services, 22 percent for physicians' services, 8 percent for medicines and appliances, 7 percent for dentists' services, and 7 percent for all other medical care. Consumers of medical care paid about 32 percent of these expenses directly. Private health insurers paid 27 percent, and the government paid most of the remainder.[11]

National Health Survey data reveal that in 1981 hospital discharges per 100 persons were 14.2. The average stay was 7.4 days. The average person visited a physician almost five times. Females visited their doctors more often than males, and older persons were more frequent visitors than younger persons. Dental visits were less frequent, less than two per person.[12]

A most disturbing fact is the recent rapid rise in the cost of certain medical services. In 1983 the Consumer Price Index for all urban consumers was 304, the base year being 1967. The medical care price index was higher, at 366. The hospital room charge index was 643, the index for physicians' fees 362.

Unemployment Involuntary unemployment caused by economic factors—not mortality, morbidity, or superannuation—is another threat to a person's earning power. The potential loss can be computed in the manner described in the previous section, total unemployment being analogous to total disability, and partial unemployment to partial disability.

Unemployment may be classified as (1) aggregate unemployment affecting the

---

[8] Health Insurance Association of America, *1964 Commissioners Disability Table,* vol. III, p. 13.

[9] National Center for Health Statistics, *Current Estimates from the Health Interview Survey, United States—1981,* U.S. Department of Health and Human Services, Public Health Service, series 10, no. 141 October, 1982), pp. 13, 22, 24.

[10] Ibid., p. 20.

[11] R. M. Gibson, D. R. Waldo, and K. R. Levit, "National Health Expenditures, 1982," *Health Care Financing Review,* V, No. 1 (Fall, 1983), pp. 8, 12.

[12] *Estimates from the Health Interview Survey,* op. cit., pp. 25, 28, 30.

entire economy, (2) selective or structural unemployment affecting particular firms, industries, employee groups, or regions and (3) personal unemployment affecting workers individually. Other concepts are "disguised" unemployment—employment in a job that underutilizes a person's capacity; and "involuntary-voluntary" unemployment—voluntary unemployment because job seeking has become burdensome. Aggregate unemployment is caused by secular or cyclical factors acting upon most industries. Structural unemployment may result from seasonal fluctuations, technological changes, strikes, acts of God, changes in demand, and the like. Personal unemployment may occur because of difficulties in locating a job or in obtaining or holding a job for a variety of reasons.

During 1983, monthly unemployment rates for the civilian labor force ranged from 11.4 percent to 8.2 percent. Unemployment rates vary greatly over time. In 1933, about one-quarter of the labor force was unemployed in an average month. These data indicate the prevalence of unemployment on specified dates rather than the "probability" of unemployment.[13] The data also do not reveal the extent of partial unemployment, but it is known that many persons work less than 35 hours a week.

One measure of the magnitude of the unemployment loss is the duration of the unemployment. As one would expect, the average duration is related to the general state of the economy, but particular industries, areas, or persons can suffer substantial losses even when the economy is performing satisfactorily by most standards.

Unemployment data may also be analyzed by region, occupation, industry, race, age, sex, and other factors, but such analysis would be beyond the scope of this text.[14]

Superannuation   Even though many persons may not appreciate fully the seriousness of the potential financial losses associated with premature deaths, serious accidental injuries or sicknesses, and extended unemployment, the vast majority do fear these contingencies and recognize that some financial losses accompany them. Old age is much less often recognized as a source of financial problems.

At advanced ages, while a person's earning power usually stops or is considerably reduced, expenses continue. The person may prepare for this retirement period by saving and investing during his or her earning career, but (1) saving is neither painless nor automatic, and the amounts needed may be very great, and (2) the necessary amount is indefinite because it depends upon the length of the retirement period.

The probabilities that persons at selected ages will survive to age 65 are presented in Table 9.3. The table also indicates the average number of years that a person at each age will live beyond age 65. Consider the plight of a person now aged 35. The chances are about four out of five that this person will live beyond age 65, his or her probable retirement age. The average person age 35 will live 11 years beyond age 65. Therefore,

---

[13] Because unemployment is much less clearly a chance phenomenon than mortality or morbidity, the word "probability" is placed in quotes. The annual frequency of unemployment, which would provide a better estimate of the "probability," would be greater than the prevalence of unemployment, because the number unemployed during the year would exceed the number unemployed during the survey week in an average month.

[14] See the latest issue of the *Monthly Labor Review*.

TABLE 9.3
PROBABILITY OF SURVIVAL TO AGE 65 AND AVERAGE REMAINING
LIFETIME, 1978

Age	Probability of survival to age 65	Average remaining lifetime, years	Average remaining lifetime beyond age 65, years
0	.76	73.3	8.3
10	.77	64.6	9.6
20	.78	55.0	10.0
30	.79	45.7	10.7
35	.79	41.0	11.0
40	.80	36.4	11.4
45	.81	31.9	11.9
50	.83	27.6	12.6
55	.86	23.5	13.5
60	.91	19.7	14.7

Source: Derived from *Vital Statistics of the United States, 1978, Volume II, Section 5, Life Tables* (Washington, D.C.: U.S. Department of Health and Human Services, Public Health Service, 1980), pp. 5–12.

if the 35-year-old is willing to be considered average, he or she will have to accumulate a sum which, invested at a reasonable rate of return, will produce enough income to meet his or her expenses over a period of 11 years. If this person's expenses are $15,000 a year and a reasonable rate of return is 5 percent after taxes, the amount needed is about $124,600.

As the person grows older, however, the average number of years that he or she can expect to live beyond age 65 increases. If a person knew that he or she would live to be 100 years old and that his or her earning power would end completely at age 65, that person would have to accumulate over $245,600 by retirement age, assuming expenses of $15,000 a year and a 5 percent return after taxes on the balance of the accumulated sum. Few persons will live this long, but some will, and their identity is unknown.

Chapter 22 shows for selected situations what proportion of a worker's earnings prior to retirement would have to be continued for that worker to have the same standard of living the first year of retirement as during the last few years of employment.

Unlike the probabilities associated with the other perils, which have been declining over time, the probabilities associated with superannuation have been increasing. Much more attention is now being devoted to this peril than previously, partly because of the increasing proportion of aged persons in the total population. In 1920, 40 percent of the population was under 20 years of age, 54 percent was between 20 and 64, and 5 percent was aged 65 or more. In 1980, the corresponding percentages were 31 percent, 58 percent, and 11 percent. By the close of this century, because of declining birth rates during the sixties and the seventies the proportion of the population that is 65 years of age and over is expected to exceed 12 percent. By 2040 this proportion is expected to be 16–22 percent.

LOSSES FACING THE FIRM ITSELF

In addition to concern with potential losses to individual employees, the risk manager must deal with the potential losses to the firm itself as the result of the death or disability of an employee, a customer, or an owner. These losses may be classified as follows: (1) key-person losses, (2) credit losses, and (3) business-liquidation losses.

Key-Person Losses

Certain workers in a firm stand out because of their skill and knowledge or because they are an important source of business or of credit for the firm. The death or disability of these key persons may result in a serious loss to the firm by reducing sales, increasing costs, or restricting credit.

In some cases, the firm will suffer a reduction in its annual profit that it will never be able to recover. For example, assume that a key executive, aged 45, is expected to retire at age 65 and that this person's death or permanent and total disability would reduce the annual earnings of the firm by $100,000 a year. This executive's immediate economic death, therefore, could cost the firm the present value of $100,000 a year for the next 20 years. At a 5 percent rate of interest, the present value is almost $1,250,000. If, as assumed, the annual loss to the firm does not change over time, the potential loss to the firm will decrease each year. Under the conditions assumed, the potential losses to the firm 5, 10, 15, and 20 years hence are about $1,040,000, $770,000, $430,000, and zero. In another case, the firm may have made an investment in a project that will be abandoned because only the key person could have completed it. In still other cases, the services of the individual can be replaced at least in part, but the cost of replacement may be high, and the replacement may be delayed. Considerable judgment is involved in estimating the profits or investments that may be lost, the replacement costs, if any, and the delays that may occur and their impact.

Creditors of the firm (including banks, trade creditors, corporate bond purchasers, and the like) are also concerned about key persons because their death or disability may affect significantly the ability of the firm to repay its borrowings. Hence, if the risk manager does not take steps to protect the firm against this risk, the credit rating of the firm may suffer even if the key persons do not actually die or become disabled. As a result, credit and credit terms may be restricted.

The potential loss to the firm caused by the death or disability of key persons may also affect the attitude of other employees. They may wonder what effect the death or disability of some key workers would have on them personally, and their uncertainty will affect their attitude toward their work.

Credit Losses

Many firms extend credit to their customers. For example, financial institutions make loans to customers, and vendors of various types assume a creditor position as a result of the sale of securities, real estate, merchandise, and other types of property. It is important for the risk manager and the credit manager to recognize that the death, extended disability, or unemployment of a customer may either reduce the chance that the loan will be repaid or create a public relations problem if it is necessary to force repayment.

Business-Discontinuation Losses

Business-discontinuation losses are very likely to occur when a person with an ownership interest in a sole proprietorship, a partnership, or a *close* corporation dies or is disabled for a long period of time. Each of these forms of business organization is characterized by the fact that the owners are usually also active in the management of the firm. Hence their death or extended disability may have severe effects upon the future of the business enterprise.

Although some of the problems arising when an owner-manager dies are peculiar to each form of business organization, certain problems for the firm and for the heirs are common to all modes of organization. In order to avoid repetition, therefore, and to emphasize the applicability of these losses to all small businesses, the discussion that follows, unless otherwise noted, will apply to all three organizational forms.

The Nature of the Problem   When an owner-manager dies, his or her heirs will no longer receive that portion of the income from the business which was attributable to the owner's active participation and association with the firm. In a sole proprietorship, this portion is equal to a reasonable compensation for the personal services of the owner-manager, including recognition of his or her personal and nontransferable contribution to the goodwill of the firm. The loss for the heirs of partners and close corporation stockholders is the present value of the compensation of the deceased plus the deceased's share of his or her personal contribution to goodwill. Surviving partners and stockholders also suffer a loss equal to their share of the deceased's contribution to goodwill.

An alternative way of viewing these losses in the case of a partnership or close corporation is to regard the loss with respect to goodwill as a key-person loss to the firm, the loss being shared by the heirs and any surviving owners. The heirs of the deceased also suffer a loss equal to the present value of the deceased's salary.

These losses, however, are not the business-discontinuation losses to be discussed in this section. These losses, which would occur even when the business is continued, are in fact examples of losses of earning power and of key-employee losses discussed in earlier sections. Business-discontinuation losses, on the other hand, occur only if the firm goes out of business, and this is a very likely result for reasons to be developed in succeeding paragraphs. The remaining goodwill value may be completely lost because the assets may have to be sold piecemeal or at sacrifice prices.

The threat of discontinuation may affect the firm adversely even if it never comes to pass. The firm's credit rating may be reduced because its future is uncertain. Employee morale may suffer because their prospective earnings are dependent upon the continuance of the firm. In order (1) to avoid the death of the firm with attendant liquidation losses when an owner-manager dies, and (2) to improve the credit rating of the firm and employee morale even if such death does not occur, the risk manager should recognize these losses in his or her planning.

Similar arguments may be made in the case of permanent and total disability and superannuation, although discontinuation under these circumstances is not so probable. The partners or close corporation stockholders should note especially that they are likely to continue the salary of a disabled or aged co-owner even when he or she contributes no services.

Special Problems for Sole Proprietorships and Partnerships   Discontinuation of a sole proprietorship or a partnership is especially likely in case of death. In most states, the executor or administrator of the owner's estate must take immediate steps to liquidate the business assets unless the owner has expressly authorized the continuation of the business or unless all heirs are adults and they consent to the continuation of the business. Even if the executor or administrator is authorized to continue the business (1) until conditions for disposing of the business are more favorable, (2) as a long-term source of income for the family, or (3) until some heirs take over,[15] the return to the heirs is likely to be relatively low, and a shortage of working capital or other business problems may force the executor into a liquidation of the firm. A quick sale may also be necessary if a large portion of the personal estate plus the business estate[16] must be converted into cash in order to pay outstanding expenses, such as the costs of the owner's last illness, funeral expenses, taxes, and probate costs.[17] Even if some heirs take over, they may not succeed, and in the early years, at least, they will probably not be so successful as the deceased proprietor. Moreover, it might be necessary to liquidate some of the business assets in order to distribute equitable shares of the total estate to the other heirs.

Special Problems for Partnerships   In addition to these difficulties, the death of a partner poses a problem that is not present in the case of a sole proprietorship. Under the Uniform Partnership Act, which is in effect in about three-quarters of the states, if a partner dies, the partnership is dissolved, and the surviving partners must liquidate the business as soon as possible. The reason for this legislation is that each partner has the power to bind the partnership if he or she acts ostensibly in the interest of the partnership. Moreover, each partner has unlimited liability for the debts of the partnership. Consequently, the choice of one's partners is extremely important and is reserved for the partners themselves.

After a partner dies, the heirs may not want to continue as partners, or the surviving partners may not be willing to accept the heirs as partners. If the heirs and the surviving

---

[15] The executor or administrator remains personally liable to the heirs and the creditors unless they all consent to the continuance.

[16] The personal and business estates of a sole proprietor are not separated as are the estates of partners or stockholders in a close corporation. If the liquidation value of the business assets is less than business debts, the family estate will also shrink.

[17] It is estimated that on the average about one-third of the gross estate value is needed to meet these costs.

partners do continue the business, it may not be successful, and liquidation may be necessary at a later date. If the heirs intend to sell their interest to someone else, this person will have to be acceptable to the surviving partners before the business will be continued.

Special Problems for Close Corporations   The discontinuation problem in a close corporation is somewhat different and less obvious. Under this form of business organization, the owners hold stock in the corporation, and this stock is transferable to other persons. However, because the stock is closely held, it is not so marketable as the stock of public corporations. Under forced sale conditions, the heirs or surviving stockholders will probably suffer a sizable loss on the sale of the stock; a minority stockholder will suffer disproportionately.

Regardless of whether the deceased was a majority or minority stockholder, the best (although unsatisfactory) solution for the heirs and for the other stockholders may be to dispose of their stock in the business or to liquidate the business itself. The surviving stockholders, for example, will have to accept a successor to the deceased, who, if a majority stockholder, may run the business to their disadvantage or, if a minority stockholder, may constantly challenge the majority. The heirs of a majority stock-holder may not be capable of exercising their power to run the business, and in spite of their majority stockholdings, the effective management may fall into the hands of the minority. This contingency could be to their detriment. The heirs of a minority stockholder (especially when they are not willing or able to be active in the firm) are at the mercy of the majority. If the deceased stockholder shared the ownership with the survivor, the close working relationship that is necessary for a firm of this type may disappear. Even if no financial losses result in any of the above circumstances, life for the heirs and the survivors could be far from pleasant.

SOME KEY CONCEPTS

Personnel losses   Financial losses caused by the death, poor health, retirement, or unemployment of people, generally employees. Either the workers and their families or their employers may suffer such losses.

Earning power loss   The present value of a person's after-tax income less in the case of death the amount of that income the person would have spent on himself or herself if he or she had lived. A more complete definition would add the present value of employee benefits lost and the cost of replacing services the person would have rendered his or her family.

Needs approach   Determining the amount of the income loss to be replaced by stating the minimum needs of the survivors. Unlike the earning power loss approach, the needs approach assumes some reduction in the survivors' standard of living.

Key-person loss   The loss a business may suffer because of the death or disability of an employee with special skills, knowledge or relationships with others.

Business-discontinuation loss   The loss a sole proprietor, a partnership, or a close corporation may suffer because the death or disability of one of the owners causes the firm to go out of business.

REVIEW QUESTIONS

1 Business risk management of personnel risks includes some family risk management.
   a Explain this statement.
   b Why are business risk managers concerned about personnel losses to individual employees?

2 One employee, aged 30, earns $25,000 a year after taxes. Another employee, aged 62, earns $50,000.
   a How would you compute the loss of earning power if each of these employees were to die today?
   b For which employee would the loss of earning power be greater?

3 Distinguish between the human life value and the needs approach in determining the losses caused by death.

4 **a** What types of unexpected expenses are associated with death?
   b For what persons would these unexpected expenses be the major financial loss associated with death?

5 Compare the following probabilities:
   a That a person aged 25 will die before age 65
   b That a person aged 25 will reach age 65
   c That a person aged 25 will become disabled for a period of at least three months before reaching age 65

6 **a** How would you compute the loss of earning power if the two employees in question 2 became totally and permanently disabled today?
   b For which employee would the loss of earning power be greater?

7 Compare the importance of unexpected expenses associated with poor health with those associated with death.

8 **a** Published unemployment rates tend to underestimate the probability of becoming unemployed during the year. Why?
   b What are the different types of unemployment?

9 **a** What types of financial problems are associated with superannuation?
   b Why is society more concerned about these problems than it was in the past?

10 **a** What types of employees might be key persons in the business firm?
   b How would you compute the potential loss caused by the death or disability of a key employee?

11 Jones and Smith are equal active partners in a thriving business. If Jones should die tomorrow, what are the potential losses to:
   a Jones's heirs?
   b Smith?

12 The majority stockholder in a small manufacturing corporation believes that his heirs are immune from business-discontinuation losses because of their majority position. Do you agree?

SUGGESTIONS FOR ADDITIONAL READING

Gregg, D. W. and V. B. Lucas: *Life and Health Insurance Handbook* (3d ed., Homewood, Ill.: Richard D. Irwin,Inc., 1973), chaps. 1, 2, 42, 43, 45, 46, and 47.
Hofflander, Alfred E., Jr.: *Human Life Value Concepts,* unpublished doctoral dissertation, University of Pennsylvania, 1964.

Huebner, S. S., and K. Black: *Life Insurance* (10th ed., Englewood Cliffs, N.J.: Prentice-Hall, Inc., 1982), chaps. 2–4.

McGill, Dan M.: *Life Insurance* (rev. ed., Homeood, Ill.: Richard D. Irwin, Inc., 1967), chap. 1.

Mehr, R. I. and S. G.Gustavson: *Life Insurance: Theory and Practice* (3d. ed., Austin: Business Publications, Inc., 1984), chaps. 19 and 21.

National Center for Health Statistics, *Current Estimates from the Health Interview Survey*, U.S. Department of Health and Human Services, Public Health Service (issued periodically).

U.S. Department of Health and Human Services, Public Health Service: *Vital Statistics of the United States, 1978, Volume II, Section 5, Life Tables,* 1980.

Williams, Jr., C. A., J. G. Turnbull, and E. F. Cheit: *Economic and Social Security* (5th ed., New York: John Wiley & Sons, Inc., 1982), chaps. 2, 6, and 12.

White, E. H., and H. Chasman: *Business Insurance* (5th ed., Englewood Cliffs, N.J.: Prentice-Hall, Inc., 1980).

C. Tools of Risk Management: Their Nature and Selection

RISK CONTROL TOOLS: AVOIDANCE, LOSS CONTROL, SEPARATION, COMBINATION, AND SOME TRANSFERS

LEARNING OBJECTIVES

After you have completed this chapter, you should be able to:

1 Distinguish between risk control and risk financing tools.
2 Explain how a business might use the avoidance tool.
3 Distinguish between loss prevention and loss reduction programs.
4 Explain why accident and hazard records and analyses are a useful part of loss control.
5 Evaluate the benefits and costs of loss control.
6 Compare separation with combination.
7 Distinguish between transfers used as a risk control tool and those used as a risk financing tool.

INTRODUCTION

After the risk manager has identified and measured the risks facing the firm, he or she must decide how to handle them. There are two basic approaches.[1] First, the risk manager can use *risk control* measures to alter the exposures in such a way as (1) to reduce the firm's expected property, liability, and personnel losses, or (2) to make the annual loss experience more predictable. Risk control measures, which are the subject

---

[1] This twofold classification was first developed by Dr. George Head for the Insurance Institute of America program in Risk Management. See *Topical Outline, RM 54, Structure of the Risk Management Process, December 1973 Examination* (Malvern, Pa.: Insurance Institute of America, 1973), pp. 33–35.

of this chapter, include (1) avoidance, (2) loss control, (3) separation, (4) combination, and (5) some transfers.

Second, the risk manager can use *risk financing* measures to finance the losses that do occur. Funds may be required to repair or restore damaged property, to settle liability claims, or to replace the services of disabled or deceased employees or owners. In some instances, the firm will decide not to restore the damaged property or replace the disabled or deceased person. Nevertheless, it may also have suffered a financial loss through a reduction in its assets or its future earning power. The tools in this second category include (1) those transfers, including the purchase of insurance, that are not considered risk control devices and (2) retention, which includes "self-insurance." Risk financing methods will be discussed in Chapters 11 and 12.

Chapters 13 and 14 provide a framework for processing information about each of these methods in order that the risk manager might decide which set of tools would be best in a given situation. Except in the rare case where the firm can avoid the risk entirely, each of the tools of risk management can and commonly should be used with one or more other risk management tools. The risk manager should always *consider* the use of at least one risk control tool to see if it would be appropriate. Unless the exposure is eliminated, the risk manager *must* use at least one risk financing technique. He or she has no alternative.

In the discussion of each technique attention will be paid to its basic characteristics, considerations affecting its usage, and some observations on how it might be implemented and its performance evaluated.

AVOIDANCE

One way to control a particular pure risk is to avoid the property, person, or activity with which the exposure is associated by (1) refusing to assume it even momentarily or (2) abandoning an exposure assumed earlier. Most examples of risk avoidance fall in the first category. To illustrate, if a business does not want to be concerned about potential property losses to a building or to a fleet of cars, it can avoid these risks by never acquiring *any* interest in a building or fleet of cars. Similarly, contracting part of a manufacturing, contracting, or distribution task before the job is accepted may enable a business to avoid some but not all of the risks associated with that job.

A leading chemical firm once planned to conduct a series of experiments in a rural area containing one small town. While preparing for the experiments, the researchers discovered that the venture might possibly cause extensive property damage to the town. The risk manager was asked to purchase insurance against this possibility, but only a few insurers were willing to provide the protection, and the premiums for the insurance were much greater than the firm wished to pay. Finally the firm decided not to conduct the experiments.

A firm that marketed household goods considered entering the drug field. Shortly thereafter it was discovered that defective polio vaccine was responsible for some cases of poliomyelitis. As a result, the firm revised upward its evaluation of the probability of a product liability claim arising out of the manufacture of drugs and decided to defer any expansion plans.

Many firms have discovered that by lending their names to a softball team or by allowing a Cub Scout pack to meet on their premises, they would create additional sources of liability. Some of these firms have decided to avoid the risks involved by refusing all such requests.

A corporation planning an apartment complex decided not to include a swimming pool after it discovered an alarming increase in liability suits arising out of swimming pool accidents.

Avoidance through abandonment is much less common but it does occur. For example, if the chemical firm noted above had started to conduct its experiments before it discovered the potential damages involved, its decision not to continue would constitute an abandonment. Similarly, if the household products firm had already entered the drug field before the defective polio vaccine was discovered and subsequently decided to phase out this activity, it would be avoiding the risk through abandonment. Other examples would be the withdrawal by a firm of earlier sponsorship of a softball or bowling team, or the removal of a swimming pool from an apartment complex.

Avoidance through abandonment is to be distinguished from transfers of the property, person, or activity to someone else, a measure discussed later in this chapter. For example, the household products firm noted above might have sold its drug business to some other company. These transfers pass the risk to someone else; risk avoidance discontinues the source of the risk.

Avoidance, whether it be implemented by abandonment or by refusal to accept the risk, should also be distinguished from loss-control measures. Loss-control measures assume that the firm will retain the property, person, or activity creating the risk but that the firm will conduct its operations in the safest possible manner.

Considerations Affecting Use

Avoidance is a useful, fairly common approach to the handling of risk. By avoiding a risk exposure the firm knows that it will not experience the potential losses or uncertainties that exposure may generate. On the other hand, it also loses the benefits that may have been derived from that exposure. Systematic ways of determining whether avoidance or some other technique would be the best way to handle a risk will be discussed in Chapter 13, but some characteristics of avoidance should be noted here.

First, avoidance may be impossible. The more broadly the risk is defined, the more likely this is to be so. For example, the only way to avoid all liability exposures is to cease to exist.

Second, the potential benefits to be gained from employing certain persons, owning a piece of property, or engaging in some activity may so far outweigh the potential losses and uncertainties involved that the risk manager will give little consideration to avoiding the exposure. For example, most businesses would find it almost impossible to operate without owning or renting a fleet of cars. Consequently they consider avoidance to be an impractical approach.

Third, the more narrowly the avoided risk is defined, the more likely it becomes that avoiding that risk will create another risk. For example, a firm may avoid the risks associated with air shipments by substituting train and truck shipments. In the process, however, it has created some new risks.

Implementation and Evaluation

To implement a risk avoidance decision the risk manager must define all those properties, persons, or activities that create the exposure the firm wishes to avoid. With the support of top management the risk manager should recommend certain policies and procedures to be followed by other departments and employees. For example, if the objective is to avoid the risks associated with air shipments, all departments might be instructed to use train and truck shipments only.

Risk avoidance is successful only if there are no losses from the exposure the firm wishes to avoid. Indeed the method will not have been properly implemented if some prohibited activity took place but the firm was lucky and no loss occurred. To illustrate, if some air shipments are made in violation of the policy stated above, some correction is necessary even if the firm incurred no losses on those particular shipments. In addition the risk manager should of course reevaluate periodically the decision to use the avoidance technique.

LOSS CONTROL

Loss-control measures attack risk by lowering the chance that a loss will occur or by reducing its severity if it does occur. Loss control has the unique ability to prevent or reduce losses for both the individual firm and society while permitting the firm to commence or continue the activity creating the risk. Avoidance eliminates the risk, but to accomplish this objective the firm must avoid or discontinue the activity. The transfers described later in this chapter eliminate the loss for the firm transferring the risk, but someone else in society assumes the risk.

Loss-control measures may be classified in various ways: (1) according to whether they are loss-prevention or reduction measures, (2) according to the cause of the accidents they are designed to control, (3) according to the location of the conditions they are designed to change, and (4) according to their timing.

Loss-Prevention and Reduction Methods

Loss-prevention programs seek to reduce or eliminate the chance of loss. Loss-reduction programs seek to reduce the potential severity of the loss. Some loss-contol programs are both loss-prevention and loss-reduction programs.

The variety of *loss-prevention programs* is illustrated by the following examples: The chance of a fire loss can be reduced by fire-resistive construction, building in an area where there are few external dangers, and having many suppliers in order that a fire loss suffered by one supplier will not halt the firm's operations. The chance of a product liability suit can be reduced by tightening the quality-control limits, choosing distributors more carefully, and checking on statements made by salespersons or the advertising department that may lead to a suit based on an implied or express warranty. The chance of an industrial accident can be reduced by safety meetings, providing safety goggles, and checking the ventilation in the plant. Employers can reduce the chance that their workers will be unemployed by stabilizing the demand for their products and services through diversification, market research, and advertising and by producing for stock during slack seasons.

Loss-reduction programs can be subclassified as *minimization* or *salvage* programs. Both try to limit the amount of the loss, the distinction between the two being that minimization programs take effect in advance of the loss or while it is occurring, whereas salvage programs become effective after the loss is over. Automatic sprinklers, for example, are designed to minimize a fire loss by spraying water or some other substance upon a fire soon after it starts in order to confine the damage to a limited area. The restoration of the damaged property to the highest possible degree of usefulness would constitute a salvage operation. For example, one loss involved a few thousand mildewed, waterlogged shoes that might easily have been discarded as useless. Instead, the shoes were matched in pairs, treated with driers and buffing machines, and sold to a wholesaler. Raising a ship from the bottom of the ocean and restoring it to economic usefulness is another illustration of a salvage operation.

Other examples of loss-reduction programs include alternate facilities to reduce the net income losses arising out of direct losses to the original facilities, periodic physical examinations for employees, immediate first aid for persons injured on the premises, medical care and rehabilitation programs for injured workers, fire alarms, internal accounting controls, actions against persons responsible for losses suffered by the firm, and speed limits for motor vehicles.

Cause of the Accident

Loss-control techniques have also been classified traditionally as (1) engineering or (2) human relations approaches. Some measures, of course, deal with engineering and human problems simultaneously. A more recent suggestion classifies risk control techniques into 10 strategies for dealing with the release of destructive energy.

Engineering and Human Relations Approaches The person usually credited with the distinction between the engineering and human relations approaches is H. W. Heinrich, a pioneer in the human relations approach and many other safety concepts. According to Heinrich's "domino theory," a preventable accident is one of five factors in a sequence that results in an injury.[2]

1 Ancestry and social environment
2 Faults of person (inherited or acquired faults of person constitute proximate reasons for committing unsafe acts or for the existence of mechanical or physical hazards)

---

[2] H. W. Heinrich, *Industrial Accident Prevention* (4th ed., New York: McGraw-Hill Book Company, 1959), pp. 14–16. Heinrich states that 98 percent of industrial accidents resulting in injury are preventable. About one-half are practically preventable.

3 Unsafe act and/or mechanical or physical hazard
4 Accidents
5 Injury

In accident control, Heinrich argues, the bull's-eye of the target is the third step in the sequence.

The engineering approach emphasizes mechanical or physical causes of accidents such as defective wiring, improper disposal of waste products, poorly designed highway intersections or automobiles, and unguarded machinery. The consideration of engineering hazards is an essential part of any loss-control program but human failures are also extremely important. An examination of engineering hazards is supposed to be particularly pertinent to fire losses because tangible things, such as the construction of the building, the provisions for protection, the type of occupancy, and the external features, such as the quality of the surroundings, may contribute to fire hazard; even so, personnel failures have been blamed for over one-third of the losses by fire. In his study Heinrich claimed that unsafe acts of persons (operating or working at unsafe speed, using unsafe equipment or using any equipment unsafely, distracting or teasing workers, abusing equipment, making safety devices inoperative, etc.) are the major causes of 88 percent of the industrial accidents resulting in personal injuries to workers.[3]

The emphasis on human relations and consequently on the personal causes of risk became important during the thirties when the engineering approach, despite its dramatic achievements, was seen to be an inconclusive answer. According to Somers and Somers, just as the development of safety engineering around 1910 coincided with the development of scientific management by Frederick Taylor and others who argued that safety equals efficiency, so the development of the human relations approach to loss control, with its emphasis on safety education, safety contests, rest periods, and the like, coincided with the development of interest in the human relations field in industry.[4]

In more recent years, the emphasis on human relations has been expanded to include special attention to the psychological problems of the accident-prone individual. Some trucking firms, for example, use psychological tests of driver attitudes in selecting personnel and in trying to locate trouble spots. This development also coincides with the general awakening of interest in mental health.

This increased attention to human errors has been criticized on several grounds. First, it is argued, the effect of mechanical causes has been underestimated. For example, using unsafe equipment probably should not be considered solely a human error; it might be possible to make this equipment more nearly foolproof. Second, industry may devote so much of its resources to the more glamorous human relations preoccupations that engineering will be insufficiently considered. Third, blaming the

---

[3] Ibid., pp. 19–22. Note that personal faults, the second factor in Heinrich's sequence, are also responsible for engineering hazards.

[4] H. M. Somers and A. R. Somers, *Workmen's Compensation* (New York: John Wiley & Sons Inc., 1954), pp. 201–04.

worker for the industrial accident is not in accord with the principle of workers' compensation, which does not blame management or labor for industrial accidents.

Despite these criticisms Heinrich's "domino theory" is still relevant and popular. One modern expert, Dan Petersen, agrees with Heinrich's emphasis on the unsafe acts of persons. To Heinrich's accident sequence he has added a sixth factor, management fault, which sets the other five factors in motion. He also emphasizes that behind every accident lie not one, but many contributing factors, causes, and subcauses.[5]

Destructive Release of Energy   Dr. William Haddon, Jr., President of the Insurance Institute for Highway Safety, has suggested a more comprehensive way of classifying risk control techniques according to the cause of the accident.[6] According to Haddon accidents result from the transfer of energy in such ways and amounts and at such speeds that inanimate or animate structures are damaged. These accidents can be prevented either by controlling the energy involved or by changing the inanimate or animate structures it can damage. Haddon suggests 10 strategies, each of which attempts to suppress accident-producing conditions or enhance accident-retarding conditions. The 10 strategies with some illustrations are as follows:

1 *To prevent the creation of the hazard in the first place.* (Examples: prevent production of plutonium, thalidomide, LSD.)

2 *To reduce the amount of the hazard brought into being.* (Examples: reduce speed of vehicles, lead content of paint, mining of asbestos; make less beverage alcohol—a hazard itself and in its results, such as drunken driving.)

3 *To prevent the release of the hazard that already exists.* (Examples: pasteurizing milk, bolting or timbering mine roofs, impounding nuclear wastes.)

4 *To modify the rate or spatial distribution of release of the hazard from its source.* (Examples: brakes, shutoff valves, reactor control rods.)

5 *To separate, in time or space, the hazard and that which is to be protected.* (Examples: isolation of persons with communicable diseases; walkways over or around hazards; evacuation; the phasing of pedestrian and vehicular traffic, whether in a work area or on a city street; the banning of vehicles carrying explosives from areas where they and their cargoes are not needed.)

6 *To separate the hazard and that which is to be protected by interposition of a material barrier.* (Examples: surgeon's gloves, containment structures, childproof poison-container closures, vehicle air bags.)

7 *To modify relevant basic qualities of the hazard.* (Examples: altering pharmacological agents to reduce side effects, using breakaway roadside poles, making crib slat spacing too narrow to strangle a child.)

8 *To make what is to be protected more resistant to damage from the hazard.*

---

[5] Dan Petersen, *Techniques of Safety Management* (2d ed., New York: McGraw-Hill Book Company, 1978), pp. 13–20.

[6] William Haddon, Jr., "Strategies to Reduce Damage from Environmental Hazards,: *Status Report,* XV, no. 17 (Nov. 21, 1980). *Status Report* is published by the Insurance Institute for Highway Safety. Haddon first presented his energy release theory in William Haddon, Jr., M.D., "On Escape of Tigers: An Ecological Note," *Technology Review* (May, 1970), copyrighted by the Alumni Association of the Massachusetts Institute of Technology. This earlier version was summarized in the fourth edition of this text.

(Examples: immunization, making structures more fire- and earthquake-resistant, giving salt to workers under thermal stress, making motor vehicles more crash resistant.)

9 *To begin to counter the damage already done by the environmental hazard.* (Examples: rescuing the shipwrecked, reattaching severed limbs, extricating trapped miners.)

10 *To stabilize, repair, and rehabilitate the object of the damage.* (Examples: posttraumatic cosmetic surgery, physical rehabilitation for amputees and others with disabling injuries—including many thousands paralyzed annually by spinal cord damage sustained in motor vehicle crashes, rebuilding after fires and earthquakes.)

Haddon's analysis can be viewed as an extension of the third factor in Heinrich's accident sequence. However, unlike Heinrich, Haddon emphasizes the control of energy, a physical force, instead of human failings. Both analyses are worthy of study by risk managers.

Location

Risk control measures may also be classified according to the location of the condition they are designed to combat. For example, Dr. Haddon, the originator of the energy-release theory discussed above, has argued in another article that the likelihood and severity of losses from automobile accidents depend upon conditions within (1) people who use roadways, (2) vehicles, and (3) the general highway environment including such factors as road design and maintenance, law enforcement, and traffic density.[7] Two extensions of this concept are presented below.[8]

Loss	Locations
Fire damage to building	Person using a building, the building, and the surrounding community
Product liability	Product user or manufacturer, the product, and the legal environment

Timing

Another classification of risk control efforts groups the approaches according to their timing. One such classification asks whether the method is applied (1) before the

[7] William Haddon, Jr., "What We're Talking About," in C. W. Wixom (ed.), *Key Issues in Highway Loss Reduction* (Washington, D.C.: The Insurance Institute for Highway Safety, 1970), pp. 7–22. In this article Haddon also suggested a threefold classification according to timing: (1) precrash, (2) crash, and (3) postcrash. The two dimensions—location and timing—permit a ninefold classification of risk control techniques.

[8] Dr. George Head, "A Time/Place Framework for Accident Prevention and Control," *Topical Outline, RM 55, Risk Control, May, 1974 Examination* (Malvern, Pa.: Insurance Institute of America, 1974), pp. 92–95.

accident, (2) during the accident, or (3) after the accident. This classification has already been used as the criterion to distinguish between minimization (before and during) and salvage (after the accident). Loss-prevention measures by definition are all applied prior to the accident.

A second classification based on timing recognizes (1) the planning phase, (2) the safety-maintenance phase, and (3) the emergency-organization phase.[9] The planning phase includes those measures that precede the erection of a new building, the purchase of new machinery, or some other major change in the firm's operations requiring considerable advance planning. This is usually the most economical time to make any changes that seem desirable from the viewpoint of loss prevention or loss reduction. The fire walls, for example, may be thickened at small expense and without disturbing the utility of the building. Machines that are as foolproof as possible may be purchased nearly as cheaply as equipment that is no more productive but considerably less safe. The safety-maintenance phase includes all programs following the advance-planning stage, excluding the emergency phase. For the most part they consist of measures that check on the implementation and desirable modifications of the original decisions. To illustrate: The quality of the guard service and the alarm systems can be checked, as can the quality of the first-aid facilities and safety classes. The emergency phase includes those progams that become effective in an emergency—the fire-fighting facilities, emergency guards, and the like.

The Responsibility for Loss Control

The responsibility for loss control in industry is shared by (1) the government, (2) private organizations specializing in loss prevention and reduction, (3) unions, and (4) the individual firm. Within the individual firm, the responsibility is shared by all divisions in varying degrees. The role of the risk management department varies widely among companies.

Government The government is involved in loss control because (1) only the government can require all industries to provide information, meet certain standards, and stop undesirable practices, and (2) the government can provide certain services such as those of fire departments more economically and efficiently than can scattered private firms. The government exercises this responsibility through a variety of educational efforts (pamphlets, posters, and conferences); through statutes and codes regulating building construction, working conditions, safety equipment and safety clothing, maximum occupancy of rooms and elevators, sewage-disposal facilities, the operation of motor vehicles, and many other activities; by means of inspections designed to enforce the statutes and codes; by police and fire departments, rehabilitation programs, and the assembling and dissemination of statistical data related to loss prevention and reduction; and by the conduct and encouragement of research activities.

---

[9] W. T. Brightman Jr., "What the Underwriting Company Can Offer," *Insurance Costs and Controls: A Reappraisal,* AMA Management Report no. 19 (New York: American Management Association, 1958), pp. 36–37. Brightman was referring to fire loss prevention and reduction in his paper, but the classification is more generally applicable.

Private Organizations Specializing in Loss Control The private groups active in this area are too numerous to list, but a partial listing will indicate the range of activities. The National Safety Council is perhaps the most famous of these groups. The Council includes among its members individuals, business firms, schools, government departments, labor organizations, insurers, and others. It assembles and disseminates information concerning all types of accidents, cooperates with public officials in safety campaigns, encourages the establishment of local safety councils, and helps members to solve their own safety problems. Other examples are one division of the American Insurance Association, an organization of insurers, which publicizes the extent and causes of fire losses, investigates suspected cases of arson, grades municipalities according to the quality of their exposures to fire and their protection against fire loss, and suggests codes of various sorts; the Underwriters Laboratories, another insurance-sponsored organization, which tests equipment (television sets, electric wiring, safes, etc.) to determine whether it meets certain high safety standards; the National Fire Protection Association, which establishes numerous standards and codes, stimulates local prevention activities, and in numerous other ways tries to promote the service of fire prevention, educate the public, and encourage its members, including public officials, to adopt its suggestions; the Insurance Institute for Highway Safety, which provides financial assistance for other organizations engaged in traffic safety work and direct assistance in selected states; the National Automobile Theft Bureau, whose name indicates its concern; and the Jewelers' Security Alliance, a jewelers' trade association, which seeks ways to prevent theft, apprehend jewel thieves, and recover stolen property. Individual insurers maintain engineering departments that study the risks faced by their insureds, suggest ways in which these risks might be reduced, provide posters, films, pamphlets, and other educational materials, and conduct safety classes.

Unions Because unions are concerned with all matters affecting working conditions, they are active in loss control. Unions strongly support government regulations that would improve workplace safety; they belong to the National Safety Council and similar organizations, and they often demand new or more intensive loss control from employers.

The Firm The ultimate and major responsibility for loss control rests with the firm itself. This activity is properly regarded as a risk management function, but, as noted in Chapter 3, the risk management department of the firm may be only one of the divisions involved in this activity. Several years ago one risk manager stated that, no matter what the risk manager's supervisory responsibilities are with respect to loss control, the following should be minimum responsibilities:

1 To extend the loss-control concept to include all exposures
2 To become acquainted with and advise others about the insurance-cost implications of various safety and loss-control measures
3 To make sure that the company's insurance costs reflect the results of its safety and loss-control efforts

4 To see that good or bad safety and loss-control experience is brought to the attention of management, and that effective loss- or cost-reduction measures are made known throughout the organization[10]

This list is still relevant.

Loss-control specialists, regardless of where they are located, typically have staff authority, rather than line authority, with respect to loss control. Line authority implies a superior-subordinate relationship that permits one person to order another to do something. A supervisor, for example, has line authority over the worker he or she supervises. Staff specialists, on the other hand, cannot command line personnel to perform. To accomplish their objectives, they must usually rely upon persuasion and motivation of line managers or their subordinates. Staff specialists, including those charged with loss control, can exert this power because they are experts in their field, have certain status in the firm, and hope to have the support of the firm's top management in their work.

From the preceding discussion, and from the observation that risk management is to some degree a function of all levels of management, it is apparent that the loss-control specialist is responsible for only part of the loss-control function in the firm. Indeed, Petersen argues that, "Safety is and must be a line function."[11] Management, in consultation with the loss-control specialist, should set goals for the firm and assign responsibility for achieving these goals to line managers with the advice and assistance of staff specialists.

Just as risk managers may have other responsibilities, especially in small- and medium-size firms, so do loss-control specialists. For example, they may also be risk managers, personnel managers, or production managers. Small firms may depend upon outsiders such as firms specializing in loss control, insurance agencies or brokerage firms, or insurance companies. Even large firms may rely upon outsiders to provide advice and counsel in highly specialized areas or to render special services such as salvage operations, training classes, or the installation of certain safety equipment.

Loss and Hazard Analysis

The first step in loss control is to identify and analyze (1) the losses that have occurred, and (2) the hazards that caused those losses or might cause future losses. This step requires (1) a comprehensive reporting system, and (2) periodic inspections.

Loss Analysis   To obtain information on losses the loss-control specialist needs to develop (1) a network of informants, and (2) forms for reporting losses. The major informants are the line supervisors responsible for the operations where the accidents occur. They can provide many details about accidents, and by completing the forms

---

[10] T. V. Murphy, "A Company-wide Approach to Loss Prevention and Control," *Corporate Insurance: Management and Markets,* AMA Management Report no. 38 (New York: American Management Association, 1959), p. 41.

[11] Petersen, op. cit., p. 24.

they should become more aware of what causes accidents and of the importance of controlling them. On the other hand, these line supervisors are not safety specialists. They may not realize what information is needed for analysis, they may resent having to spend time completing the form, and their self-interest may cause them to provide incomplete or incorrect information. The forms therefore must be carefully designed. They must provide the information needed but be relatively easy to understand and to complete.

According to Heinrich, ideally one would study not only those accidents that caused injuries or property damage but also all those unplanned events that *might have* caused such losses. In other words, the "near-misses" as well as accidents causing losses would be reported and studied. In his investigation of industrial accidents, he found that out of 330 accidents of a similar type, 300 will produce no injury, 29 will produce minor injuries, and 1 will produce a major injury. Too often, he claims, safety engineers ignore, in their record-keeping and loss-control measures, accidents that do not cause injury. Moreover, they concentrate on those accidents that produce major injuries, but whether accidents result in injuries is largely a matter of chance.[12] Cost and the burden of reporting all such events have ruled against this approach in most cases. All firms, however, tend to take special notice of events that did not cause any loss but where it is clear they were extremely fortunate to escape a serious loss. At the other extreme, in studying injury losses, many firms look only at accidents that have caused injuries. They should also study property-damage-only accidents because the hazard that caused these accidents may cause injuries in the future. Of course, the property losses caused by such accidents are themselves worthy of investigation. In one study based on an analysis of over 90,000 accidents over a seven-year period at a steel company, on the average 500 property damage accidents occurred for every 100 minor bodily injury accidents.

Various philosophies exist on the structure of the report forms. For example, one form may be used for reporting all accidents, or different forms might be used for different types of accidents (for example, industrial accidents causing injuries and fire causing property damage). The forms also differ in the amount of detail they request concerning the accident and the persons and the property involved. The form may specify several possible causes of accidents among which the supervisor may choose, or the question about possible causes may be open-ended. The form may permit the supervisor to identify only one possible cause of the accident or it may require the naming of more than one possible cause. The form may or may not require the supervisor to suggest measures that might be taken to prevent a similar accident in the future.

The information on losses provided through these reports can be used to: (1) measure the performance of line managers, (2) determine which operations, if any, need to be corrected, (3) identify the hazards that have been responsible for the losses, and (4) provide information that can be used to motivate workers and managers to pay more attention to loss control.

---

[12] Heinrich, op. cit., pp. 32–33.

Most firms do not have sufficient accident experience to justify sophisticated statistical analysis, especially if that experience is segregated by division or department. For large firms, however, statistical measures may be feasible and desirable, especially in those lines characterized by higher loss frequencies.

Statistical records enable the loss specialist to compare the firm's loss experience with that of other firms in the same industry, and with the firm's loss experience in prior years. In addition, the specialist can analyze these records with respect to such accident characteristics as the peril; the nature of the accident; the nature and extent of the loss; the month, day, and hour of the accident; the supervisor or the worker involved; the operation affected; and the hazard or underlying cause of the accident— an unsafe condition or an unsafe act including the reason for the unsafe act. Accident records should summarize these characteristics for accidents during the most recent period, and also demonstrate how these characteristics have changed over time. If certain causes, times of day, supervisors, operations, or other characteristics appear frequently in the accident summary, or if frequency of appearance is changing, they are worthy of special attention. The loss-control specialist must remember, however, that some characteristics should normally appear more often. For example, some operations are more hazardous than others. Some perils occur more frequently than others. Primary attention should be focused on those characteristics that exceed their normal frequency.

Even though the accident records of small firms are more likely to be affected by chance fluctuations, they are still useful as an indicator of possible hazards. For example, if several accidents are reported that list defective ladders as at least one of the causes, the firm would be well advised to investigate their ladders and the conditions surrounding their use. Small firms, however, should be aware that they may be exposed to many hazards that, perhaps because of nothing more than chance fluctuations, have not yet caused an accident. They must rely more upon hazard analysis, which will be discussed shortly.

Hazard Analysis   Loss analysis should reveal hazards that need to be investigated more carefully. Hazard analysis, however, cannot be limited to the hazards that have caused accidents. Instead, it is necessary to investigate the possible existence of other hazards that have caused losses to the firm in earlier loss analysis periods or that the experience of other firms, insurers, or government organizations suggests should be investigated. Increasingly, loss-control specialists are made aware of new hazards which have not as yet caused a loss for anyone but which have been discovered through experimentation under controlled conditions. Hazards in new products such as newly developed pharmaceuticals have been uncovered in this way.

Hazards that have not caused losses also are discovered through inspections. Line supervisors are primarily responsible for these inspections, but loss-control specialists usually also become involved.

As an aid in making an inspection, the line supervisor or specialist often has a checklist that reminds the inspector of the many possible hazards and facilitates a comparison with existing conditions. The loss-control specialist usually is responsible for the design of these checklists and the forms used to report the results of the inspection. These inspection forms, like the accident reporting forms, vary greatly in the detail and nature of the information provided. For example, one form asks only for: (1) an evaluation of the general conditions regarding housekeeping, equipment, hand tools, and so on, and (2) recommendations for improving these conditions. A more comprehensive form asks for: (1) the unsafe conditions or acts noted, (2) whether each of these ''symptoms'' was discussed with the supervisor, (3) the causes found for each of these symptoms, and (4) suggestions as to future actions with respect to these causes.

One technique that has proved increasingly useful in analyzing the causes of accidents is *fault three analysis*.[13] This technique may be used in loss analysis to determine the causes of actual losses or in hazard analysis to determine the causes and effects in accident situations. It shows the multiple causes of accidents and whether all or only some of these causes must be present to precipitate an accident. It thus provides a basis for preventing such accidents.

Occupational Safety and Health Act

In late 1970, Congress passed the Occupational Safety and Health Act (OSHA), an extremely important piece of safety legislation.[14] Because of its importance and because it illustrates both public and private responsibilities for loss control, OSHA will be discussed here in some detail.

OSHA applies to private employers of one or more persons (but not the self-employed) engaged in a business affecting interstate commerce, except for some employers subject to special federal legislation such as the Federal Coal Mine and Safety Act. About three-fourths of the civilian labor force is thus affected. Federal government employees are covered under a separate federal program.

The major objective of the Occupational Safety and Health Act is to have the Secretary of Labor (1) establish safety and health standards, and (2) check compliance with these standards.

Voluminous standards have been developed. Many are ''consensus'' safety standards previously developed as voluntary guidelines for business by private associations such as the American National Standards Institute and the National Fire Protection Association. Some others came from federal regulations developed earlier for contractors and the maritime industries. Others are new standards proposed by the Secretary after consultation with an OSHA Standards Advisory Committee. Proposed new or revised standards must be published in the *Federal Register*. Interested parties have 30 days in which they can comment informally on the proposal. They also have 60 days after a standard is promulgated to challenge the standard before the U.S. Court of Appeals. An individual employer may apply for a temporary variance from a standard in order to have more time to comply. The employees of such an employer must be

---

[13] For an example, see R. I. Mehr and B. A. Hedges, *Risk Management: Concepts and Applications* (Homewood, Ill.: Richard D. Irwin, Inc., 1974), p. 433.

[14] The Consumer Product Safety Act, discussed in Chap. 7, is another highly significant piece of legislation with implications for risk management.

aware that the employer has applied for this variance and be allowed to appear at the hearing on the application.

Illustrative standards are the following:

All places of employment, passageways, storerooms, and service rooms shall be kept clean and orderly and in a sanitary condition.

Portable wood ladders longer than 20 feet shall not be supplied. (The standards on portable wood ladders alone fill more than 15 pages.)

In the absence of an infirmary, clinic, or hospital in near proximity to the workplace which is used for the treatment of all injured employees, a person or persons shall be adequately trained to render first aid.

To check compliance with these standards, federal inspectors have the right to enter without notice, but at reasonable times, any covered establishment. An employee can also request such an inspection by describing in writing what he or she considers to be a serious violation of some standard. The employer is not told the name of the complaining employee. During an inspection the employer and an employee representative may upon request accompany the inspector. As a result of a court decision in the late seventies, an employer can require the inspector to obtain a warrant for the search.

If an inspector discovers a violation that is more than *de minimis* (no direct or immediate relationship to job safety and health; e.g., no toilet partitions), the inspector is directed to issue a written citation describing the violation. This citation must be posted near the location of the violation. Within some reasonable time the employer must remove the hazard.

If death or serious physical harm could have resulted from the violation, the citation means a mandatory penalty up to $1,000. Less serious violations *may* mean a penalty up to the same amount. If the employer fails to correct the violation within the time stated in the citation, he or she *may* be penalized up to $1,000 for each day the violation continues. Penalties of $10,000 per violation may be levied for willful or repeated violations. If a willful violation results in the death of an employee, the employer is either fined $10,000 or imprisoned up to six months. These penalties are doubled if such a fatal willful violation is repeated.

An employer can appeal citations before a judge acting on behalf of the three-member Occupational Safety and Health Commission, which administers the safety-standards portion of the act. If one of the three commission members wants the entire commission to review the judge's decision, it is done. Commission orders may in turn be appealed to the U.S. Court of Appeals.

Employees must be notified of their rights under the law. They must also not be discharged or harassed because they exercise these rights.

In addition to meeting certain health and safety standards, employers of eight or more employees must maintain and make available to government representatives accurate records of work-related deaths, illnesses, injuries that cause the employee to miss work, and injuries without lost workdays that result in medical treatment beyond first aid, a diagnosis of occupational illness, loss of consciousness, restriction of work or motion, or transfer to another job.

An annual summary, which must be posted for the information of employees, shows the number of fatalities, the number of lost workday cases, the number of lost workdays, the number of nonfatal cases without lost workdays, and the number of cases involving transfer to another job or termination of employment.

In addition to accident records, the employer must keep records on the inspections and other safety activities in which he or she engages under the act. The employer may also be required to maintain records on employee exposure to certain potentially toxic materials or harmful physical agents.

States may assume responsibility for developing and enforcing occupational safety and health standards under plans approved by the Secretary of Labor. The state standards must be at least as effective as the counterpart federal standards. Many states have developed plans that have been accepted by the federal government.

The National Institute for Occupational Safety and Health, established within the Department of Health and Human Services, carries out certain research and educational functions assigned to that department. The Institute recommends new and improved standards. Because most of the consensus standards deal with injuries, the Institute is currently concentrating its attention on previously unrecognized occupational diseases such as angiosarcoma of the liver, which may result from exposure to vinyl chloride, used in the manufacture of plastics.

Determining Economic Feasibility

Although the prevention of all losses would be desirable, it is not always possible or economically feasible. The potential gains from any loss-control activity must be weighed against the costs involved. Unless the gains equal or exceed the costs, the firm would be better off not to engage in that activity. (Of course, if human suffering is involved, society may benefit greatly from expenditures that, from a selfish point of view, a firm would be ill-advised to make.) The firm, however, must be certain to consider all the gains (elimination or reduction of both the direct and indirect costs of accidents, reduction of uncertainty and the resulting worry prior to an accident, and improved public, customer, and employee relations) and all the costs of installing and maintaining the loss-control measures.

Costs of Accidents A discussion of the ''indirect'' costs associated with an accident, and their relationship to the direct or more obvious costs, would be incomplete without some mention to Heinrich's investigation of industrial accident costs. According to Heinrich, the cost of industrial accidents is usually stated only in terms of workers' compensation paid the injured employee for lost time and his or her medical expenses. The actual costs, however, are much greater because he found the ''incidental'' or ''hidden'' costs to be four times as great as the compensation benefits.[15]

If Heinrich's argument is accepted, the case for loss control, with or without insurance, is considerably strengthened. Some of the factors that Heinrich included among these hidden accident costs were as follows:

[15] Heinrich, op. cit., pp. 50–52.

1 Cost of lost time of injured employee

2 Cost of time lost by other employees who stop work to help the injured worker

3 Cost of time lost by supervisors or other executives preparing reports on the accident and training a replacement

4 Cost due to damage to the machine, tools, or other property, or to the spoilage of material

5 Cost to employer of continuing the wages of the injured employee in full, after his return, even though the services of the employee (who is not yet fully recovered) may for a time be worth only about half of their normal value

6 Cost that occurs in consequence of excitement or weakened morale due to the accident

Heinrich did not contend that his 4 to 1 proportion applied to every accident or to every plant. He also acknowledged that the ratio may vary in nationwide application.

Heinrich's major point—that the "indirect" costs are substantial—holds true, but many writers have challenged the 4 to 1 ratio. Grimaldi and Simonds, using the terms "insured" and "uninsured" to correspond to Heinrich's "direct" and "indirect," believe that: (1) the ratio of uninsured costs to insured costs in industrial accidents is probably less than 4 to 1 because some of the uninsured costs included by Heinrich are not valid, and (2) because there is no direct correlation between uninsured costs and insured costs, applying a single ratio to total direct costs to determine the indirect costs produces inaccurate results.

As an alternative to expressing uninsured costs as a single multiple of insured costs, Grimaldi and Simonds suggest the following formula for the ordinary run of accidents:[16]

Total cost = insurance cost
+ A × the number of lost-time cases
+ B × the number of doctor's cases (no lost time)
+ C × the number of first-aid only cases
+ D × the number of accidents causing no injuries but causing property damage in excess of a specified amount

where A, B, C, and D are the average uninsured costs for each category of cases, and the number of cases refers to the actual count of each type during the period under consideration.

Bird and Germain claim, however, that this revised concept has also proved to be an ineffective tool in safety motivation. Obtaining and updating the necessary information, they believe, is a difficult, time-consuming task. Allocating uninsured costs among departments poses technical problems and is even more likely to meet opposition than the allocation of insured costs. They suggest, instead, a ledger-costs concept, so-named because it involves only costs that appear on department ledgers.[17] Government agencies call it the "elements of production-accident cost" concept. This method

---

[16] R. H. Simonds and J. W. Grimaldi, *Safety Management* (3d ed.; Homewood, Ill.: Richard D. Irwin, Inc., 1975), p. 411.

[17] F. E. Bird and G. L. Germain, *Damage Control* (New York: American Management Association, 1966), p. 66.

of accident cost accounting does not include all accident costs, but it does add some accurate, noninsured costs that could be many times the insured costs. The factors considered in this accounting are the following:

1 Manpower:
    total workers' compensation benefits
    wages and medical costs paid during disability in addition to workers' compensation benefits
    time lost on day of injury and on subsequent days
    time spent on light work or reduced output
2 Machinery, material, equipment:
    cost of repairing damage, or cost of replacement
    lost production time

This method is applicable to all accidents, not only those that cause bodily injuries or that might have caused bodily injuries.

Despite their differences, Heinrich, Grimaldi and Simonds, and Bird and Germain all emphasize that accident costs tend to be underestimated.

Costs of Loss-Control Measures   The costs of installing and maintaining loss-control measures fall into three categories:

1 Capital expenditures and depreciation on special construction features such as fire walls, and equipment such as sprinklers and hose extinguishers
2 Expenses (salaries, fringe benefits, clothing, and training costs, for example) for guards, safety supervisors, firefighters, consultants, engineers, and others directly involved in safety work
3 Program expenses such as the cost of manuals and other training aids, employee time in training periods, extra packing and special cases, inspections, and preventive maintenance[18]

In determining the cost of any loss-control program, the risk manager must determine the most efficient way to conduct the program. For example, it may be possible to cut the number of guards, produce black-and-white movies instead of color films, or use less-elaborate safety manuals without reducing the effectiveness of the program. If the firm is insured, the risk manager should make certain that the firm is receiving all the services to which it is entitled. Some risk managers have found that they can save money in the long run by hiring a consulting loss-control engineering service to evaluate the recommendations made by the firm's insurers and to prepare the detailed plans and specifications for implementing these recommendations or modified recommendations.[19] If the firm is not insured, this consulting service may profitably supplement the firm's own staff.

[18] R. J. Ruppel, "Controlling the Cost of Loss Prevention," *Insurance Costs and Controls: A Reappraisal,* AMA Management Report no. 19 (New York: American Management Association, 1958), pp. 56–57.
[19] Frank H. Gage, "Special Engineering Services and Their Value," *Insurance Costs and Controls: A Reappraisal,* AMA Management Report no. 19 (New York: American Management Association, 1958), pp. 42–49.

Comparing Benefits and Costs In comparing the benefits of loss control with the costs, two problems arise. First, because the benefits are usually not certain, they must be multiplied by the probability that they will occur. Second, both the benefits and the costs may be spread over several years. Consequently, one should compare the *present value* of the *expected stream of benefits* with the *present value* of the *expected costs*. For an example of how this concept might be used to determine whether to install an automatic sprinkler in a building, see the discussion of capital budgeting applied to risk management in Chapter 14.

Evaluation

Loss-control measures can be evaluated by determining (1) whether accident costs were reduced by the imposition of these measures, and (2) whether the safety policies and procedures recommended by the risk manager are being observed. Changes in accident costs be measured by changes in insurance premiums, other dollar costs of accidents, loss frequencies, and loss severity. These changes should be analyzed in the aggregate, by department, and by type of exposure.

SEPARATION

Separation of the firm's exposures to loss instead of concentrating them at one location where they might all be involved in the same loss is the third risk control tool. For example, instead of placing its entire inventory in one warehouse a firm may elect to separate this exposure by placing equal parts of the inventory in ten widely separated warehouses. To the extent that this separation of exposures reduces the maximum probable loss to one event, it may be regarded as a form of loss reduction.[20] Emphasis is placed here, however, on the fact that through this separation the firm increases the number of independent exposure units under its control. Other things being equal, because of the law of large numbers, this increase reduces the risk, thus improving the firm's ability to predict what its loss experience will be.

COMBINATION

Combination or pooling, the fourth risk control tool, also makes loss experience more predictable by increasing the number of exposure units. The difference is that unlike separation, which spreads a specified number of exposure units, combination increases the number of exposure units under the control of the firm.

One way a firm can combine risks is to expand through internal growth. For example, a taxicab company may increase its fleet of automobiles. Combination also occurs when two firms merge or one acquires another. The new firm has more buildings, more automobiles, and more employees than either of the original companies.

Combination of pure risks is seldom the major reason why a firm expands its

---

[20] The probability of *some* loss actually increases. The probability that at least one of several units will suffer a loss is greater than the probability that any particular unit will suffer a loss.

operations, but this combination may be an important by-product of merger or growth. (An example of pooling with respect to speculative risks, which may be a *primary* objective of a merger or expansion, is the diversification of products by a business.) Insurers, on the other hand, combine pure risks purposefully; they insure a large number of persons in order to improve their ability to predict their losses.

A special case of combination, suggested by Dr. George Head, is duplication of an existing asset that is not used unless something happens to the original asset.[21] Spare parts or a duplicate machine illustrate the concept. Duplication reduces risk because it increases the number of exposure units. More importantly in this case, as a loss control device, duplication also reduces the probability of a net income loss because the duplicates may be available for use if the original asset cannot be used.

TRANSFER

Transfer, the final tool to be discussed in this chapter, may be accomplished in three ways. First, the property or activity responsible for the risk may be transferred to some other person or group of persons. For example, a firm that sells one of its buildings transfers the risks associated with ownership of the building to the new owner. A contractor who is concerned about possible increases in the cost of labor and materials needed for the electrical work on a job to which he or she is already committed can transfer the risk by hiring a subcontractor for this portion of the project. This type of transfer, which is closely related to avoidance through abandonment, is a risk control measure because it eliminates a potential loss that may strike the firm. It differs from avoidance through abandonment in that to transfer a risk the firm must pass it to someone else.

Second, the risk, but not the property or activity, may be transferred. For example, under a lease, the tenant may be able to shift to the landlord any responsibility the tenant may have for damage to the landlord's premises caused by the tenant's negligence. A manufacturer may be able to force a retailer to assume responsibility for any damage to products that occurs after the products leave the manufacturer's premises even if the manufacturer would otherwise be responsible. A business may be able to convince a customer to give up any rights the customer might have to sue the business for bodily injuries and property damage sustained because of defects in a product or a service. The contracts that implement such transfers are called exculpatory contracts. Because risk control transfers of this sort are easily confused with risk financing transfers, a brief comparison should be helpful.

In each of the examples presented above the *transferee excuses the transferor from responsibility for property or personal losses to the transferee.* The exposure itself is eliminated. Some risk control transfers limit but do not eliminate the exposure. For example, the transfer may limit, but not eliminate the transferor's dollar responsibility. Under a risk *financing* transfer *the transferor makes the transferee pay for losses that would otherwise have to be financed by the transferor.* For example, under a lease, a landlord may make a tenant pay for fire losses to rented premises even if the tenant is

---

[21] *Topical Outline, RM 54, Structure of the Risk Management Process, December, 1979, and May, 1980, Examinations* (Malvern, Pa.: Insurance Institute of America, 1979), p. 64.

not negligent. Under a purchase agreement, a retailer may obtain a promise from a manufacturer that the manufacturer will reimburse the retailer for any payments the retailer might have to make to others because of defects in the manufacturer's products. As part of a bailment relationship, a laundry may accept responsibility for damage to customers' property even if the business, except for the contract, would not be liable.

Risk control transfers can shift only property or personnel risks; risk financing transfers can, in addition, shift liability risks. A transferee cannot excuse a transferor from any liability the transferor may have to third parties because the rights of third parties are not reduced by this transfer. The transferee can, however, agree to finance any losses that may otherwise have to be financed by the transferor. Unless a risk control transfer is declared illegal, it offers complete protection for the transferor. The transferor is not responsible for losses suffered by the transferee. On the other hand, under a risk financing transfer, if the transferee fails for any reason to provide the promised funds following a loss, the transferor bears the loss. One agreement may produce a risk control transfer with respect to some potential losses and a risk financing transfer with respect to others. For example, a lease may excuse the tenant from responsibility for any damage to the premises and obligate the landlord to finance any liability the tenant may incur to others arising out of the premises.

A risk financing transfer creates a loss exposure for the transferee. The cancellation by the transferee of such an agreement can be viewed as a third example of a risk control transfer. By cancelling this agreement, the firm is no longer legally responsible for the losses it had earlier agreed to finance.

KEY CONCEPTS

Risk control tool   A technique designed to change the loss exposure itself, the objective being to reduce the frequency or severity of the potential losses or to make those losses more predictable.

Risk financing tool   A technique designed to provide money to deal with those losses that do occur.

Avoidance   Never having the exposure or abandoning an exposure that you acquired earlier.

Loss control   Changing the exposure to reduce the chance of loss (loss prevention) or the severity of the loss (loss reduction).

Domino theory   A theory of accident causation developed by H. W. Heinrich which states that an accident is the fourth of five factors in a sequence that results in an injury, the fifth factor.

Hazard   A condition that creates or increases the chance of a loss or its severity.

Accident costs   The total cost of accidents which includes those not insurable as well as those that are insurable. Large noninsurable costs provide a strong motivation for loss control.

Separation   Dividing the exposures to loss among two or more locations instead of concentrating them at one location.

Combination   Increasing the number of exposure units, thus reducing the risk.

REVIEW QUESTIONS

1 Distinguish between risk control and risk financing measures.
2 A risk manager argues that since avoidance always involves forgoing some activity, it is undesirable for a firm and for society.

      a How would you answer this?

      b Cite three situations in which avoidance might be desirable.

3 Distinguish avoidance through abandonment from transfers of the property, person, or activity.

4 Two safety engineers are engaged in a heated debate concerning the relative merits of the engineering and the human relations approaches to loss control.

      a What claims are probably being made by each engineer?

      b Which method is the better?

5 Classify each of the following loss-control measures according to (1) whether they are loss-prevention or reduction measures, (2) whether they illustrate the engineering or human relations approach, and (3) their timing:

      a Oily rags and paper are cleaned up each day.

      b Nonslip treads are placed on each stairway.

      c Brakes on motor vehicles are checked weekly.

      d Safety meetings are held monthly.

      e Machines are equipped with safety guards.

      f A private detective agency is equipped to respond quickly to a burglar alarm.

      g All key employees are required to take an annual physical examination.

      h A new product is manufactured during slack periods.

6 Would you classify Haddon's energy-release theory as a human relations or engineering approach? Explain your answer.

7 Safety in industry is the responsibility of many groups.

      a What contributions to safety within the individual firm are made by outside agencies?

      b Who within the firm is responsible for loss-prevention and reduction measures?

      c Do loss-control specialists have line or staff authority?

      d What role do line supervisors play in loss control?

8 Distinguish between loss analysis and hazard analysis.

9 Compare the Heinrich, Grimaldi-Simonds, and Bird-Germain approaches to measuring the total costs of accidents.

10 Describe briefly the responsibilities imposed upon employers by the Occupational Safety and Health Act.

11 Determining whether a particular loss-control measure is desirable is often a complex process.

      a What types of costs are involved in a loss-control program?

      b What is the fundamental principle upon which the decision should be made?

12 How would you evaluate the success of (1) avoidance and (2) loss-control measures?

13 Why are separation and combination classified as risk control measures?

14 Transfers may be risk control or risk financing measures. Explain.

SUGGESTIONS FOR ADDITIONAL READING

Accident Prevention Manual for Industrial Operations (8th ed., Chicago: National Safety Council, 1982).

Binford, C., C. Fleming, and Z. A. Proust: *Lost Control in the OSHA Era* (New York: McGraw-Hill Book Company, 1974).

Bird, F. E., and G. L. Germain: *Damage Control* (New York: American Management Association, 1966).

————, and R. G. Loftus: *Loss Control Management* (Loganville, Ga.: Institute Press, 1976).

Green, M. R., and O. N. Serbein: *Risk Management: Text and Cases* (2d ed., Reston, Va.: Reston Publishing Company, 1983), chap. 5.

Factory Mutual Engineering Division: *Handbook of Industrial Loss Prevention* (New York: McGraw-Hill Book Company, 1959).

Fire Protection Handbook (15th ed., Quincy, Mass.: National Fire Protection Association, 1981).

Heinrich, H. W.: *Industrial Accident Prevention* (4th ed., New York: McGraw-Hill Book Company, 1959).

Loss Prevention and Control, BNA Policy and Practice Series (Washington, D.C.: The Bureau of National Affairs, updated periodically).

MacDonald, Donald L.: *Corporate Risk Control* (New York: The Ronald Press Company, 1966), chaps. 10, 11, 14, 15, and 18, and pp. 228–231.

Mehr, R. I., and B. A. Hedges: *Risk Management: Concepts and Applications* (Homewood, Ill.: Richard D. Irwin, Inc., 1974), chaps. 4, 14, and 22.

Olishifski, Julian B.: *Fundamentals of Industrial Hygiene* (2d ed., Chicago: National Safety Council, 1978).

Petersen, Daniel C.: *Safety Management: A Human Approach* (Englewood Cliffs, N.J.: Aloray, Inc., 1975).

————: *Techniques of Safety Management* (2d ed., New York: McGraw-Hill Book Company, 1978).

————: *The OSHA Compliance Manual* (rev. ed., New York: McGraw-Hill Book Company, 1979).

Simonds, R. H., and J. W. Grimaldi: *Safety Management* (rev. ed., Homewood, Ill.: Richard D. Irwin, Inc., 1963).

———— and ————: *Safety Management* (3d ed., Homewood, Ill.: Richard D. Irwin, Inc., 1975).

Snider, H. W. (ed.): *Risk Management* (Homewood, Ill.: Richard D. Irwin, Inc., 1964), chap. 3.

Williams, C. A., Jr., G. L. Head, R. C. Horn, and G. W. Glendenning: *Principles of Risk Management and Insurance* (2d ed., Malvern, Pa.: American Institute for Property and Liability Underwriters, 1981), vol. 1, chap. 2.

CHAPTER 11

RISK FINANCING TOOLS: OTHER TRANSFERS AND RETENTION

LEARNING OBJECTIVES

After you have completed this chapter, you should be able to:

1 Describe how a business might be able to transfer risk through some noninsurance device.
2 Relate the strengths and weaknesses of noninsurance transfers.
3 Distinguish between planned and unplanned retention.
4 Explain in some detail the factors that *(a)* favor a decision to retain and *(b)* make retention less attractive.
5 Describe how a retention program might be funded.
6 Define a pure captive and explain why many businesses have elected to fund their retention program through this device.
7 Define *(a)* an association or group captive and *(b)* a profit center captive and explain why many businesses have found these captive insurers more attractive than pure captives.

INTRODUCTION

By changing the exposure itself, risk control measures, discussed in the last chapter, either reduce potential losses or make those losses more predictable. The risk financing tools to be explained in this chapter are ways of financing the losses that do occur. They include (1) transfers that are not risk control measures and (2) retention.

TRANSFERS

Chapter 10 indicated that transfers could be risk control measures or risk financing measures. Risk control transfers (1) shift the property or activity itself to someone else, (2) eliminate or reduce the transferor's responsibility for losses to the transferee, or (3) cancel obligations that the transferor has assumed for losses to others. Through risk financing transfers, the transferor seeks external funds that will pay for the losses that do occur.[1] Insurance, a risk financing transfer mechanism, is so important in the management of pure risks that the next chapter is devoted exclusively to that technique. This chapter deals with noninsurance risk financing transfers. These noninsurance transfers differ from insurance in that the transferees (1) are not legally insurers, and (2) usually do not accept enough exposure units for their losses to be fairly predictable.

Most noninsurance risk financing transfers are accomplished through provisions in contracts dealing primarily with other matters, but some are achieved through contracts designed specifically for this purpose. Many of these contractual arrangements transfer financial responsibility for direct property or net income losses; some deal with personnel losses; most transfer financial responsibility for liabilities to third parties. The transfers differ as to the extent of responsibility shifted. At one extreme, the transferor shifts only his or her financial responsibility (vicarious liability) for the negligent acts of the transferee. At the other extreme, the transferor is to be indemnified for the types of losses covered under the contract no matter who (the transferee, some third party, or an act of God) caused the loss.

Some Examples

A few examples will suffice to illustrate the nature of these contracts. Under one lease a landlord may be able to transfer to a tenant financial responsibility for damage to the property and bodily injuries to third parties that would in the absence of the lease be borne by the landlord. Under a second lease the tenant may instead be able to shift his or her potential losses to the landlord. Under a construction contract the owner may be able to shift to the contractor some or all of his or her responsibility for injuries to the public injured on the premises. A business shipping parcels by air, storing equipment in a warehouse, or sending its material to some other firm for further processing may through a special contract obligate the bailee to pay for losses in excess of its statutory or common law liability. A retailer may insist on a hold-harmless provision in his or her purchase contracts under which the manufacturer agrees to indemnify the retailer for any liability sustained because of defective products unless that defect was caused solely by the retailer's negligence.

A different kind of noninsurance transfer is a surety bond under which a person, called a ''surety,'' guarantees that another person, called a ''principal,'' will carry out some express obligation to some third person, called an ''obligee.'' Illustrative obligations are paying off a debt, supplying a certain quantity of products within a specified period, and constructing a factory by a stated date. If the principal does not fulfill his or

---

[1] Tort liability recoveries are excluded because they are so uncertain.

her obligation, the surety must either satisfy the obligation or pay some penalty stated in the bond. The surety can then try to recover his or her loss from the principal. In some instances the surety can claim cash or government securities that he or she required the principal to deposit as collateral at the time the bond was issued. Through the bond the obligee transfers the risk that the obligation will not be met to the surety. Even though the principal receives no protection, the principal obtains the bond because he or she wishes some advantage, such as a loan, a supply contract, or a construction contract, that the obligee will not grant without a bond.[2] Although there are some significant differences between an insurance contract and a surety bond that will be explained in the next chapter, the surety under most bonds is an insurer. The most common types of bonds written by insurers will be described in Chapter 12, under "Distinction between Insurance and Bonding," in Chapter 18 under "Surety Bonds," and in Chapter 32 under "Fidelity and Surety Bonds."

Limitations

Noninsurance transfers are useful and popular, but they have some important limitations of which the risk manager should be aware. First, the contract may transfer only part of the risk that the firm thought it had shifted to someone else. The risk manager should study the contract language carefully to determine its impact. Second, the language is often so complicated that it is extremely difficult to understand. Third, because the courts are reluctant to change statutory and common law, they tend to interpret transfer provisions narrowly if given an opportunity. Broad shifts of responsibility are sometimes declared invalid because they violate public policy or are grossly unfair to the transferee. Fourth because the contract provisions vary so widely, there are few precedents one can consult to determine how the courts will interpret a particular provision. Fifth, if the transferee is unable to pay the losses transferred, the transferor must pay the loss it thought it had shifted to someone else. Finally, the transferee, who now has the major incentive for loss control, may lack the expertise or authority for effective control.

Neutralization

Neutralization, which is closely related to transfer, is the process of balancing a chance of loss against a chance of gain. For example, a person who has bet that a certain team will win the World Series may neutralize the risk involved by also placing a bet on the opposing team. In other words, he or she transfers the risk to the person who accepts the second bet. A commercial example of neutralization is hedging by manufacturers who are concerned about changes in raw material prices or by exporters who would be

[2] When 100 percent collateral is required, the principal may question the need for a bond. The answer is that the surety is merely extending credit like a bank, and some collateral may be necessary. The obligee may prefer a bond because he or she receives also the benefit of the surety's investigation and avoids the task and risk of handling the collateral. The principal can often recover this collateral more rapidly from a surety, and the obligee may charge more for handling collateral than the bond premium. This is particularly true with respect to bonds required by courts in connection with litigation.

affected by changes in foreign exchange rates. Because there is no chance of gain associated with pure risks, neutralization is *not* a tool of pure-risk management.

RETENTION

The most common method of handling risk is retention by the firm itself. The source of the funds is the firm itself, including borrowed funds that the firm must repay.[3] This retention may be passive or active, unconscious or conscious, unplanned or planned.

The retention is *passive* or *unplanned* when the risk manager is not aware that the exposure exists and consequently does not attempt to handle it. By default, therefore, the firm has elected to retain the risk associated with that exposure. Few, if any, businesses have identified *all* their exposures to property, liability, and personnel losses. Consequently, some unplanned retention is commonplace and perhaps inevitable. For some firms, the task of risk identification has been so poorly performed that far too much risk is being passively retained. A related form of unplanned retention occurs when the risk manager has properly recognized the exposures but has underestimated the magnitude of the potential losses. Automobile liability exposures exemplify the type of potential loss that is often underestimated. In other cases, the risk manager, although aware of the risk, may continually postpone making a decision on how to handle it. To illustrate, a firm is often aware of the financial risks associated with the death of a key technician but fails to take any action designed to handle this risk.

The retention is *active* or *planned* when the risk manager considers other methods of handling the risk and consciously decides not to transfer the potential losses.

Unplanned retention may, by chance, be the best approach to a particular exposure, but it is never a rational way of handling the matter. Whether active or planned retention is rational or irrational depends upon the circumstances surrounding the decision to retain the risk. Sometimes risks are retained that most persons would agree should not be retained, whereas other risks are not retained when they should be. For example, some businesses retain the risk of being sued on account of a product liability exposure when a transfer of this risk is possible and highly desirable. Other firms transfer the risk associated with small losses when these losses could rather easily be retained.

Self-insurance is a special case of active or planned retention. It is distinguished from the other type of retention usually referred to as "noninsurance" in that the firm or family can predict fairly accurately the losses it will suffer during some period because it has a large number of independent, fairly homogeneous exposure units. Self-insurance is *not* insurance, because there is no transfer of the risk to an outsider. Self-insurers and insurers, however, share the ability, though in different degrees, to predict their future loss experience. Some writers would not consider a retention program to be self-insurance unless earmarked funds are accumulated in advance of any losses. Others discourage the use of the term because there is no transfer of the risk.

---

[3] Some authors consider borrowing to pay losses a separate technique because it transfers some risk to the lender.

Retention Only Possible Tool in Some Cases

In some cases retention is the only possible (or at least the only feasible) tool. The firm cannot prevent the loss, avoidance is impossible (or clearly undesirable), and no transfer possibilities (including insurance) exist. Consequently, the firm has no choice. It *must* retain the risk. For example, a firm with a plant located in a river valley may find that no other method of handling the flood risk is feasible. Abandonment and loss control would be too costly, and in this particular area flood insurance is not available. (For reasons why insurers do not accept all risks, see Chapter 12. For a description of the federal flood insurance program, see Chapter 34.)

In many more instances part, but not all, of the potential loss can be controlled or financed externally. For example, the firm may be able to purchase some flood insurance on a plant located in a different river valley, but the insurance contract may exclude certain events and the insurer may limit its responsibility to some fraction of the maximum possible losses. Sometimes insurance is not available unless the insured agrees to absorb the first part, say $50,000, of any loss. If these uninsured losses cannot be controlled or transferred elsewhere, the firm will be forced to retain them.

Factors to Be Considered when Retention Is Not the Only Possible Tool

In most cases retention is not the only possible tool. Usually the choice is between retention and insurance, with loss-control measures being employed in conjunction with either retention or insurance. The five major factors to be considered in making this choice are explained below. If the choice is between retention and some transfer device other than insurance, similar reasoning is involved.

Expenses If the risk manager purchased insurance, he or she would pay a premium which could be divided into two parts: (1) a loss allowance equal to the insurer's estimate of the insured's expected losses and (2) the loading the insurer adds to its loss allowance to cover its expenses and provide some margin for profit and contingencies. These expenses include the cost of acquiring business (mainly selling expenses), adjusting claims, rendering loss-control services, and performing general administrative tasks. By retaining the exposure, the business or family may be able to save part or all of this expense and profit loading.

The loading charged by the insurer varies among lines, among insurers, and among insureds. For instance, in many property and liability insurance lines, the average ratio is 30–40 percent of the premiums charged. Life and health insurance written in connection with employee benefit plans usually has an expense ratio under 10 percent. Different insurers charge different loadings because they do not all render the same services or operate with the same efficiency. Large insureds are commonly charged a lower-percentage loading than small insureds because in their pricing insurers usually recognize that their expenses do not increase proportionately with the size of the insured.[4]

---

[4] For more details, see Chap. 28, under "Modification Rating: Size-Discount Plans."

In analyzing these potential savings, risk managers must recognize that some of these expenses are incurred for services rendered to insureds, and that, if they choose not to purchase insurance, they must either forgo these services, provide these services themselves, or purchase them elsewhere. Loss adjustment and loss-control services provide the clearest illustration of this consumer benefit in property and liability insurance, but risk analysis services provided by the agent and the insurer must also be considered. If an employer self-insures a pension plan, he or she will probably have to engage a bank or trust company to invest the monies in the pension fund, and a consulting actuary to determine how much money should be placed in the fund each year. In most instances, the employer will save some, but not all, of the money that would be paid to an insurer to cover its loading; but in some instances the expenses would be higher. Insurers have the advantage that they can spread overhead costs over many insureds. They may also be able to service widespread operations more efficiently. Offsetting to some extent the loss of services provided by the insurer is the time and effort the risk manager would otherwise spend selecting the insurer, negotiating with the insurer the terms of the insurance contract and the price to be charged, and filing a proof of loss with the insurer.

Expected Losses and Risk If the business believes that its expected losses are less than those assumed by the insurer in calculating its premium, it may reason that in the long run it can save the difference between the two expected-loss estimates. Even if the two expected-loss estimates are the same, the business may be willing to gamble that in the short run its experience will be better than it will average in the long run.

An understanding of insurance pricing, such as that provided in Chapter 28, is important in evaluating the potential saving available from differences in expected loss estimates. Although small employers pay the same rate as other employers sharing a few major characteristics, large firms are rated under procedures that pay considerable attention to their unique characteristics or their individual loss experience. Consequently larger employers are less likely to have a valid reason for doubting the insurer's estimate.

The true expected loss, of course, may exceed the insurer's estimate. Furthermore, the expected loss is only part of the story. One must also remember that the loss experience in any single year may differ considerably from the expected loss. The risk or variation in the actual losses around the expected losses has been studied in Chapter 4. If the business faces possible losses next year that are larger than it is willing or able to retain, it may be willing to pay an insurer more than its expected-loss estimate simply to eliminate uncertainty in the short run. The extra amount it is willing to pay depends in part upon the severity of the potential losses and its ability to sustain these losses. It also depends upon the estimated risk or variation in the potential losses and the risk management objectives of the firm. For example, one would expect a firm emphasizing peace of mind and earnings stability to be concerned about variations that would not bother firms interested only in mere survival. Also, because firms with many exposure units can predict their losses more accurately than those with only a few units, one would expect, other things being equal, that these larger firms would be less concerned about risk.

Insureds who are willing to assume substantial risks but wish to be protected against losses exceeding a specified amount can combine insurance and retention through excess insurance or deductibles. Excess insurance and deductibles usually protect the insured against losses per unit or per occurrence in excess of some stated amount, but sometimes they cover excess total annual losses.[5]

A quasi-self-insurance arrangement that may be an attractive alternative to self-insurance for large insureds is to purchase insurance but to have the premium retrospectively rated. Under retrospective rating the premium paid for insurance depends upon the insured's loss experience during the period the insurance is in effect, but it cannot be less than a specified minimum premium nor more than a specified maximum premium. The insured must pay the insurer to service the program and for the protection afforded by the maximum premium, but in exchange the insured avoids servicing responsibilities and knows that his or her annual outlay cannot exceed the maximum premium. Many insured employee benefit plans, though not retrospectively rated, are priced in a similar way.

Opportunity Costs The opportunity costs involved in the timing of premium payments relative to alternative losses and expenses is another consideration. For example, even if the business reasons that the premium will be the same or less than the alternative losses and expenses, it might prefer to retain the risk if the time lag between the premium payment and the alternative loss and expense payments would permit it to earn an attractive rate of return on the declining balance of funds not yet spent for losses or expenses. To illustrate, assume that the premium is $115,000, payable at the beginning of the policy period. The expected alternative loss and expense payments are $40,000 payable immediately, $40,000 at the end of six months, and $40,000 payable at the end of eighteen months. These alternative payments total $120,000, but their present values, assuming that the firm can earn 12 percent annually on retained funds, are $40,000, $37,740, and $33,690, a total of $111,430. Thus, if instead of paying the $115,000 premium, the business pays its own losses and expenses, the return on the unpaid balance would produce a "profit" of about $3,570. High investment returns and large time lags before losses and expenses must be paid increase the importance of this cash flow consideration. The longer time lags associated with liability losses cause this factor to be a more important reason for retaining liability loss exposures than property loss exposures. As will be explained in Chapter 28, insurers now offer a variety of cash flow arrangements (such as paid-loss ratio and compensating balances plans) under which they agree to share with insureds the investment income they generate because of these time lags.

Quality of Services Some firms believe that many of the services provided by insurers can be better performed internally or by some servicing agency. For example, some risk managers argue that if the firm pays its own claims, it will pay them more promptly and more equitably. They believe that the firm's own staff will resist

---

[5] For more on excess insurance and deductibles, see the last section of Chap. 12, "Use of Insurance with Other Tools." See also Chap. 17 on "Deductibles."

unjustifiable claims that many insurers would pay. In addition, some managers are of the opinion that the firm gets more public relations value out of paying its own claims.

In response, insurers argue that because they lack experience, firms who settle their own claims tend to be less efficient and less effective. They also tend to be too lenient, especially with claims involving employees. This is particularly true if the firm has many small, widely dispersed locations and as a result must assign this responsibility on a part-time basis to someone at each location. The public relations value a firm obtains from settling its own claims may also be overestimated. In fact, dissatisfied claimants who may have been content to blame an insurer must now blame the business.

Supporters of retention reply that if these counterarguments are correct, an experienced independent servicing firm can be hired to adjust the losses under a retention program.

The relative quality of the loss-control and general-administration services under a retention program and an insured program is another bone of contention. Supporters of both retention and insurance claim superiority on this score. Insurers claim the advantage of experience gained by working with many firms over a long period of time; some can also claim the benefit of research staffs that are capable of studying specific problems. Yet the firm's own staff knows the firm better, can concentrate on the firm's problems, and may receive more cooperation from other employees than would an outsider. In certain lines, such as boiler and machinery insurance, the insurer does provide important, highly specialized inspection services; in other lines, the firm's employees may be the experts. With respect to some losses, such as dishonest acts by employees, the mere involvement of an insurer who is not so likely to be sympathetic with a dishonest employee may reduce the chance of loss.

One of the main advantages claimed for retention is that the firm itself is more highly motivated to control losses when it will bear these losses itself.

In pension plans a key consideration is the investment performance of the pension fund. Consequently the business will want to compare carefully the investment advice and services available from insurers and from banks and trust companies that might service a self-insured plan.

In recent years many insurers have "unbundled" their services. Consequently, if a firm decides to retain some property or liability exposure, it may be able to purchase from the insurer, say, its loss-control and claims- adjustment services. A firm with a self-insured pension plan may purchase administrative and investment services from an insurer.

Tax Considerations   The impact of taxes on a retention decision can be complicated. Only a few major points will be noted here. First, insurance premiums can be deducted as a business expense in calculating a firm's taxable income. Under a property or liability loss-retention program, however, the firm can deduct only actual losses. Because these losses may be spread irregularly over time, they may have less favorable consequences than regular premium deductions.

Second, if property losses are retained, the firm can deduct the decrease in the fair market value of the property, but this deduction is limited to the tax basis, usually the book value—original cost less accounting depreciation. For example, assume that a machine is completely destroyed. To replace this machine with a new machine will cost $40,000; to replace it with a machine in about the same condition would cost $30,000. The book value is the original cost of $25,000 less $15,000 accounting depreciation. The decrease in fair market value is $30,000 but the deduction is limited to $10,000.[6] If the property had been insured and the insurance payment exceeded the book value, the firm may recognize the gain in one of two ways. Regardless of whether it repairs or replaces the property, the firm can treat the gain as an "involuntary conversion" taxed immediately as a capital gain. Alternatively, if it repairs or replaces the property, it can deduct as depreciation expense in the coming years only the amount it could have deducted had there been no loss (plus a charge against any amount the firm may spend in addition to the insurance), thus increasing future income taxes. For example, suppose that in the earlier illustration the machine had been insured for $30,000. The firm could pay a capital gains tax on $30,000 less $10,000. Alternatively it could purchase the $30,000 machine but continue only the former annual depreciation charges until they accumulated to $25,000 − $15,000 or $10,000. If, instead, it purchased a $40,000 machine, it could increase its annual depreciation expense by a charge against the $40,000 cost less the $30,000 insurance payment.

Third, only amounts actually paid each year are deductible unless additional amounts are unequivocally payable in the future. To make current deductions for future payments, the firm must clearly establish that all the events have occurred which will determine its liability, and the amount it will have to pay can be determined with reasonable accuracy. Because of the time value of money, most firms prefer to take their tax deductions as soon as they can. This ruling affects principally liability losses including workers' compensation where the event may have occurred but the liability has not been established, or the amount to be paid is still to be determined.[7]

Employers who turn over funds to a bank or a trust company in connection with a self-insured employee benefit plan, usually a pension plan, can deduct these contributions at the time they are made. Furthermore, the return on the invested funds is not taxable income to the employer. Income tax considerations, therefore, do not favor an insured pension plan over a self-insured plan or vice versa.

Summary   In short, retention is favored by such factors as:

1 Lower expenses than the insurer's expense loading
2 Lower expected losses than the insurer's estimate

---

[6] The cost of repairing damaged property may be used as a measure of the decrease in its fair market value if the value of the property after it is repaired does not exceed the value of the property before occurrence of the damage. For more details on tax considerations, see Internal Revenue Service Publication 547, *Tax Information on Disasters, Casualty Losses, and Theft.*

[7] In practice, many firms deduct reserves established to cover estimated future costs of specific cases. Some also deduct reserves based on average costs including, in some instances, an estimate of losses on events that have occurred but have not yet been reported. To buttress their arguments they may obtain estimates from outside experts. The Internal Revenue Service has contested many such deductions. See David Warren, "Self-Insurance: An Overview," *Self-Insurance: A Risk Management Alternative* (Malvern, Pa.: Society of Chartered Property and Casualty Underwriters, March, 1978), and P. Bruce Wright, "To Deduct or Not to Deduct? That's the Self Insurer's Question," *Risk Management,* vol. XXX, no. 3 (March, 1983), pp. 12–15.

3 Many exposure units, which means the risk will be low and that the firm will be able to predict its losses with acceptable accuracy
4 Small maximum possible or probable losses
5 Financial ability to sustain maximum possible or probable losses in the short run
6 Risk management objectives that accept wide variations in annual losses
7 Expense and loss payments extending over a long period of time, resulting in large opportunity costs
8 Strong investment opportunities, resulting in large opportunity costs
9 Internal or noninsurer servicing advantages

Retention is made less attractive by such factors as:

1 Higher expenses than the insurer's expense loading
2 Higher expected losses than the insurer's estimate
3 Few exposure units, which means that the risk will be high and the firm will be unable to predict its losses with acceptable accuracy
4 Large maximum possible or probable losses
5 Financial inability to sustain maximum possible or probable losses in the short run
6 Risk management objectives that stress peace of mind and small variations in annual losses
7 Expense and loss payments extending over a short period of time, thus reducing the opportunity costs
8 Limited, low-return investment opportunities, resulting in low opportunity costs
9 Insurer servicing advantages

Taxes may also make property or liability risk retention less attractive but the effect of this factor deserves more detailed study than is appropriate for this text. The reader should compare this analysis with the factors affecting decisions under the worry method presented in Chapter 13.[8]

Funding Arrangements

Funding arrangements for retention plans range from no advance funding to captive insurers, including group or association captives.

No Advance Funding   Most decisions to retain property and liability losses do not involve any formal advance funding. The business simply bears the losses when they occur. This approach cuts administrative detail to a minimum; but if the losses fluctuate widely from year to year, the business may have to sell property on unfavorable terms in order to develop the cash required to meet the losses. Major losses are seldom financed through borrowing, partly because creditors consider retention of such large losses to be financial mismanagement. As a result they either refuse to grant such

[8] For a detailed examination of a retention-insurance decision, see J. S. Trieschmann and E. J. Leverett, Jr., "Self-Insurance of Workers' Compensation Losses," *Journal of Risk and Insurance*, vol. XLV, no. 4 (December, 1978), pp. 635–650.

credit or demand high interest rates. (Minor losses may be covered by borrowing, usually arranged in advance. The extra cost includes the charge for holding open the credit and the interest on any funds borrowed.) Another disadvantage of no advance funding is that the firm's operating statements are unduly influenced by chance results.

Liability or Earmarked Accounts Fluctuations in the operating statements can be avoided by creating a liability account or earmarking some portion of the surplus that will be credited each year with an amount equal to the expected losses and debited with the actual losses. Profits would be reduced each year by the expected loss amount. They would not be affected by the actual losses. This liability or earmarked surplus account, however, is a paper entry that does not provide any more liquidity. Furthermore, estimating the expected loss is not an easy task. Even if the estimate is accurate, unless the firm is large enough to be a self-insurer the actual losses in any year may differ significantly from the expected losses. Although never popular, this method has practically disappeared since the Financial Accounting Standards Board in its Statement No. 5 (FASB-5) prohibited its use in public financial statements.[9] The effect of this prohibition is that no certified public accountant can certify that a statement including such a liability was prepared in accordance with generally accepted accounting principles. The FASB argued, in effect, that this practice gave the appearance of greater stability and certainty than actually exists. The FASB does permit a liability to be recorded when, and not before, sufficient events have occurred to indicate that it is "highly probable" that a loss has occurred.[10]

Earmarked Asset Accounts A more conservative approach would, in addition to creating a liability or earmarked surplus account, establish a corresponding earmarked asset account consisting of assets that could be turned into cash with little difficulty. If losses exceeding those expected occur soon after the earmarked asset account is created, the liquidity problem will be only partially solved. The generally lower return on the liquid assets will be a deterring consideration in the formulation of such a fund. The FASB has also prohibited this practice in public statements.

Captive Insurers Many businesses have funded their property and liability risk retention program by organizing an insurer whose sole (or major) customer is the business itself.[11] Such insurers are "captive" insurers. One major attraction of this funding arrangement is that the captive insurer can purchase protection from reinsurers, who generally deal only with insurers. By nature and tradition reinsurers are more flexible in their approach to insurance. In addition, reinsurers are not subject to so many legal restrictions as are insurers servicing the general public. Consequently, reinsurers may be willing to sell coverages to the captive that its parent could not

[9] For an analysis of the arguments for and against this position, see R. J. Keintz and J. F. Lee, "Accounting for Future Losses: The Risk Management Problems," *Risk Management,* vol. XXII, no. 1 (January, 1975), pp. 6–14.

[10] For some interesting observations on this concept, see Mike Shannon, "Self-Insureds Keep Reserves under Tough Accounting Rule," *Business Insurance,* May 28, 1979, pp. 33 and 36.

[11] See Edward P. Lalley, *Self-Assumption, Self-Insurance, and the Captive Insurance Company Concept* (New York: Risk and Insurance Management Society, Inc., 1975), and *Self-Insurance: A Risk Management Alternative* (Malvern, Pa.: Society of Chartered Property and Casualty Underwriters, March, 1978).

obtain, at least without considerable effort, from insurers servicing the public directly. Reinsurers may also be willing to sell, at a lower cost, coverages that are available in the direct market. Until recently, a second major attraction was that premiums paid to the captive insurer could be deducted when determining the business's federal income tax. (The tax treatment of loss retained under other funding methods was described in the preceding section.) The firm still had to pay taxes on the captive insurer's profits but insurers are taxed under different rules that, among other things, permit a deduction of reserves established to cover (1) the estimated future cost of events that have already occurred, and (2) the portion of the premiums paid to cover losses that have not yet occurred. In late 1978, however, the U.S. Tax Court agreed with the Internal Revenue Service that premiums paid to a captive insurer were not a deductible item. In their view purchasing insurance from a captive is not purchasing insurance.[12] A third reason for forming a captive was to reduce fluctuations in the operating statements through regular premium deductions. Using reasoning similar to that of the Internal Revenue Service, however, FASB-5 has prohibited smoothing reported annual earnings through this device.

Possible disadvantages of captive insurers include the capital and personnel requirements to organize and operate a captive insurer, the special taxes that must be paid by insurers, and the legal obligation imposed in some states to participate in plans covering insureds who cannot secure insurance through normal channels and whose loss experience is typically less favorable to insurers.[13]

Captives typically purchase reinsurance to protect themselves against unusual losses. Sometimes, under a ''fronting'' arrangement, the parent firm buys insurance from an insurer which then purchases reinsurance from the parent's captive. The IRS treats both arrangements the same.

Currently the number of captives owned by United States corporations is estimated to be over 1,500. According to Conning and Company, in 1983 captive insurers accounted for over 10 percent of the total United States premium volume and one-third of the total funds devoted to retention programs.[14] Many of these captives, however, are not ''pure'' captives. Some are group or association captives owned by the members of the sponsoring group or association. Group or association captives usually closely resemble mutual insurers or reciprocal exchanges whose characteristics are described in Chapter 26. Unlike the ''pure'' captive, the group or association captive appears in concept to be a true insurer. Each member transfers its risk to the association captive; the members share the combined risks. If the group captive does not have sufficient assets to transfer losses, it can assess the group members.

An increasing number of captives with only one owner are not ''pure'' because they reinsure other insurers, or insure other firms as well as the exposures of the owner. From the viewpoint of these other insurers or firms, the captive is a true insurer. They transfer their risks to an insurer in whom they have no ownership interest. From the viewpoint of the owner, the nature of the arrangement is less clear. However, this

[12] "Tax Court Affirms IRS Veto of Captives in Carnation Co. Test Case," *Business Insurance,* Jan. 8, 1979, pp. 1 and 86.
[13] See Chap. 34.
[14] "26% of Property/Casualty Market Self-Funded: Study," *Business Insurance,* Jan. 30, 1984, pp. 3, 16.

captive's situation differs from that of the "pure" captive in that the parent of this captive is able to stablilize its experience through combination-increasing the number of independent exposure units insured. Nevertheless, from the viewpoint of the parent the arrangement is still technically not insurance because the parent does not transfer its risk to an outsider.

The reason many firms have involved others through a group or association captive or by insuring outsiders is a belief that involving others may make the parent's premiums tax-deductible. From the above discussion the argument seems stronger for the group or association captive than for the solely owned captive that sells to outsiders. The argument also is stronger the smaller the share of the firm in the combined exposures. For example, the argument will probably not be persuasive for the largest firm in a group or association arrangement under which that firm controls, say, 99 percent of the exposures in the pool. Where the line should be drawn is a highly subjective judgment.

Another reason many single-owner captives have insured others is that their owners believe they can increase their profits by entering the insurance business.

Over three-fourths of the captives are domiciled abroad, mostly in Bermuda. So-called offshore captives are attractive because (1) the foreign government is less restrictive in its regulation of insurance operations, including the types of coverages they write, (2) the insurer need not participate in the special plans noted above, and (3) there may be tax advantages, especially if the captive insures only foreign subsidiaries. The captive pays little or no tax to the host country and its earnings are not subject to United States income taxes until they are brought home. Colorado, Tennessee, Vermont, and Virginia have passed special laws designed to encourage the formation of domestic captives.

Employee Benefit Plans   Pension plans and other self-insured benefit plans are usually funded by periodic contributions made to a trustee such as a bank or trust company. Self-insured employee benefit plans are discussed in Chapters 21 and 22.

Group Self-Insurers   The opportunities for retention were enhanced by the Product Liability Risk Retention Act of 1981 and the passage in many states of legislation permitting group self-insurance as an alternative to the purchase of workers' compensation insurance. Under the Product Liability Risk Retention Act businesses are allowed to set up groups that will permit their members to retain their product liability risks without meeting the regulation of each state in which they will operate. These groups, however, must secure a charter as an insurer from one state and are thus technically insurers. These groups are expected to be chartered most commonly as captive insurers in one of the four states with special captive insurer laws.[15]

Group workers' compensation self-insurance statutes typically permit two or more firms with combined net worth exceeding a specified amount to form a joint self-insurance pool. Under an indemnity agreement each member agrees to be jointly and

---

[15] Until 1985 the groups can be chartered in Bermuda or the Cayman Islands, but they must meet the insurer capitalization requirements of some state.

The Act also permits businesses to purchase collectively product liability insurance on a group basis even though many states prohibit such group purchases.

severally responsible for all the claims and expenses incurred in any year in which the member belongs to the group. The members thus share the combined experience of the pool. Although these pools are insurers according to the definition suggested in this text, legally they are treated as self-insurers subject to special regulations. Group self-insurers commonly purchase excess insurance to cover pool losses in excess of some specified large amount.

Group self-insurance arrangements have also been developed in connection with employee benefit plans.

Retention Practices

The 1980 RIMS-TIME Survey used in Chapter 2 to illustrate the current status of the risk management function in business also sheds some light on current and planned retention practices.[16]

Complete retention of certain exposures (plus possibly excess insurance) was a common practice among the respondents and was expected to become more common. Listed below for four major types of domestic (United States) exposures are (1) the proportion who used "complete" retention for at least some of their exposures of each type and (2) the proportion who expected the use of retention to increase by 1985:

	Used "complete" retention	Expected increased usage
Property	68%	19%
Product liability	29	17
Liability other than product liability	40	24
Workers' compensation	52	29

Property exposures and workers' compensation exposures were retained by over half the respondents.

Except for workers' compensation exposures partial retention through deductibles in insurance contracts was an even more common practice than "complete" retention. Workers' compensation insurance at the time was not sold with a deductible. Listed below for each of the other three types of exposures are the proportions of those who used deductibles and who expected increased usage:

	Used deductibles	Expected increased usage
Property	84%	30%
Product liability	33	12
Liability other than product liability	49	20

[16] *The Present Status and Future Role of Risk Management*, conducted by the Risk and Insurance Management Society, Inc., and *Time* magazine, April, 1981, pp. 16–29.

Firms that employed full-time risk managers were more likely to use "complete" retention and deductibles than firms that assigned additional duties to the risk manager. Full-time risk managers were also more likely to expect this usage to increase during the next five years.

The respondents also were strongly interested in captives as a way of funding their retention agreements. Listed below for each of the four types of exposures are the proportions who used a captive insurer in 1980 and the proportions who expected increased usage by 1985. Firms with full-time risk managers were more likely to have captives.

	Used a captive	Expected increased usage
Property	11%	14%
Product liability	10	12
Liability other than product liability	13	15
Workers' compensation	10	12

Despite this interest in retention, however, respondents usually purchased insurance to cover part or all of some of their exposures of each type. About 96 percent purchased some form of property insurance, 65 percent product liability insurance, 86 percent other liability insurance, and 83 percent workers' compensation insurance.

At least half the respondents indicated that they used the following risk management–related services in their work:

Loss control	Computer-based information systems
Claims adjusting	Industrial hygiene
Property appraisal	Salvage and subrogation

Loss control and claims adjusting were reported by over 85 percent of the respondents. During the next few years the respondents expected insurers to be the most likely supplier of (1) claims adjustment services and (2) salvage and subrogation services with internal sources being the most likely source of (1) loss control services, (2) computer-based information systems, and (3) industrial hygiene services. Independent firms were expected to provide most property appraisals.

SOME KEY CONCEPTS

Noninsurance transfers   Devices other than insurance under which a business can transfer a potential loss to someone else. For example, the transfer may be accomplished through a provision in a lease.

Surety bonding   A noninsurance transfer under which a surety guarantees that a principal will carry out some expressed obligation to an obligee. If the principal fails to do so, the surety compensates the obligee in some way and then tries to recover its loss from the principal.

Retention   A risk financing tool under which the source of funds is the firm itself or borrowings it must repay.

Planned retention   Retention that results from a conscious decision. Active, not passive, retention.

Self-insurance   A special case of planned retention—not insurance. Exposures must be numerous enough for the loss experience to be fairly predictable.

Captive insurer   In its pure form, an insurer owned by a parent corporation which is also its only customer. One way of funding a retention program.

Association or group captive   A captive insurer owned by an association or group that insures only members of the association or group.

REVIEW QUESTIONS

1 Cite four illustrations of noninsurance risk financing transfers.

2 Noninsurance risk financing transfers have certain important limitations. Explain.

3 Distinguish between planned and unplanned retention.

4 A firm employs 1,000 workers. The risk manager of the firm believes that the firm should self-insure its workers' compensation obligation.

   a One reason the risk manager favors a self-insurance program is that she believes the firm can save the expense allowance included in the premium. Comment on this belief.

   b A second reason for favoring a self-insurance program is that her firm has had very few losses during the last three years, while, in her opinion, the workers' compensation insurance premium is designed for the average firm. Comment on this reasoning.

5 Would the opportunity cost consideration favor the retention of workers' compensation exposures more than the retention of property loss exposures? Explain.

6 A building with a fair market value of $100,000 and a book value of $40,000 is completely destroyed.

   a If the building is not insured, what amount is deductible from taxable income?

   b If the building was insured for $80,000, what is the tax situation?

7 List the factors that make retention (a) attractive and (b) not attractive.

8 What is the most common method of funding retention programs?

9 a What is a captive insurer?

   b Why have many businesses formed captive insurers?

   c What are the possible disadvantages of captive insurers?

   d Why do many captive insurers have several owners or sell insurance to outsiders?

10 Why are many captives "offshore" captives?

11 "Self-insurance is a special case of retention." Explain.

12 Separation and combination make retention more attractive. Explain.

SUGGESTIONS FOR ADDITIONAL READING

Goshay, Robert: *Corporate Self-Insurance and Risk Retention Plans* (Homewood, Ill.: Richard D. Irwin, Inc., 1964).

Greene, Mark, and Oscar Serbein: *Risk Management: Text and Cases* (2d ed., Reston, Va.: Reston Publishing Company, 1983), chaps. 6 and 7.

Lalley, E. P.: *Corporate Uncertainty and Risk Management* (New York: Risk Management Society Publishing, Inc., 1982).

MacDonald, Donald L.: *Corporate Risk Control* (New York: The Ronald Press Company, 1966), chap. 9.

Mehr, R. I., and B. A. Hedges: *Risk Management: Concepts and Applications* (Homewood, Ill.: Richard D. Irwin, Inc., 1974), chaps. 3 and 19.

Self-Insurance: A Risk Management Alternative (Malvern, Pa.: Society of Chartered Property and Casualty Underwriters, March, 1978).

Snider, H. W. (ed.): *Risk Management* (Homewood, Ill.: Richard D. Irwin, Inc., 1964), chaps. 4, 6, and 11.

Stephens, V. M., W. S. McIntyre, and J. P. Gibson: *Risk Financing: A Guide to Insurance Cash Flow Plans* (Dallas: International Risk Management Institute, Inc., 1983, and updated periodically).

Williams, N. A. (ed.): *Risk Retention: Alternate Funding Methods* (Malvern, Pa.: Society of Chartered Property and Casualty Underwriters, 1983).

CHAPTER 12

INSURANCE: A RISK FINANCING TOOL

LEARNING OBJECTIVES

After you have completed this chapter, you should be able to:

1 Explain how insurance differs from noninsurance transfers.
2 Distinguish among insurance, gambling, and bonding.
3 List the benefits and costs of insurance.
4 Explain why all risks are not insurable.
5 Explain why government insurers can insure some risks private insurers cannot.
6 Explain how insurance might be used with retention through deductibles and excess insurance.

INTRODUCTION

Insurance is not one of the basic tools of risk management, but it is easily the most important illustration of the transfer technique and the keystone of most risk management programs. This chapter defines insurance, compares insurance with gambling and with bonding, examines its benefits and costs, describes its limitations, traces its growth, and explains how it might be used with other tools.

INSURANCE DEFINED

Insurance can be defined from two points of view. First, insurance is the protection against financial loss provided by an insurer. Second, insurance is a device by means of which the risks of two or more persons or firms are combined through actual or promised contributions to a fund out of which claimants are paid. From the viewpoint of the insured, insurance is a transfer device. From the viewpoint of the insurer, insurance is a retention and combination device. The distinctive feature of insurance as a transfer device is that it involves some pooling of risks; i.e., the insurer combines the risks of many insureds. Through this combination the insurer improves its ability to predict its expected losses. Although most insurers collect in advance premiums that will be sufficient to pay all their expected losses, some rely at least in part on assessments levied on all insureds after losses occur.

INSURANCE NOT GAMBLING

The purchase of insurance is sometimes confused with gambling. Both acts do share one characteristic. Both the insured and the gambler may collect more dollars than they pay out, the outcome being determined by some chance event. However, through the purchase of insurance, the insured transfers an existing pure risk. A gambler creates a speculative risk.

DISTINCTION BETWEEN INSURANCE AND BONDING

From the viewpoint of the obligee, the protection provided by the surety bonds described under ''Transfer'' in Chapter 11 resembles insurance. Furthermore, corporate sureties are considered insurers under state laws, and most major property insurers have bonding departments. However, a typical property insurance contract differs from a typical surety bond in at least five major ways:

1 A surety bond has three parties to the contract—the principal, the obligee, and the surety. Two parties normally enter into an insurance contract—the insured and the insurer.

2 Under a surety bond, the principal usually obtains the bond and pays the premium, but the obligee receives the protection. (The principal, however, usually transfers the cost to the obligee by including the cost in the price of the services to be rendered.) An insured usually purchases an insurance contract to protect himself or herself.

3 A loss under a surety bond may be caused intentionally by the principal. An insurance loss should be accidental from the viewpoint of the insured.

4 Ideally, there would be no losses under a surety bond because the surety would not write the bond if there were any chance of loss and the surety would discover any potential losses in its investigation. An insurer expects some losses among the insured group. Ideally, a surety bond premium would not have to contain any expected-loss allowance. The premium would thus cover only the surety's investigation and other expenses and provide some margin for profit and contingencies. An insurance premium must provide for expected losses. In practice, sureties do incur some losses because their investigations are not completely effective, but losses are a much smaller proportion of surety bond premiums than of insurance premiums. Surety bond loss ratios also tend to fluctuate more widely over time because of lower loss frequencies and the sensitivity of much bond experience to economic cycles and natural catastrophes.

5 If a loss does occur, the surety can turn to the principal for reimbursement. An insurer does not have this right against an insured.

Not all property insurance contracts nor all surety bonds share the characteristics contained in the above list. Some surety bonds more closely resemble insurance than others. Nevertheless this distinction between typical property insurance contracts and surety bonds is valid and useful.

One type of surety bonding—fidelity bonding—differs so much from the other types that, instead of being included under surety bonding, it is usually considered a separate class. Fidelity bonding protects an employer against dishonest acts by his or her employees. Most fidelity bonds so closely resemble insurance that they are commonly called "dishonesty insurance." Originally fidelity bonds were written on the same basis as surety bonds. Some still are. Under these less common fidelity bonds, there are three parties to the contract—the employer, the employee, and the insurer or surety. The employee applies for the contract and pays the premium, but the employer has the protection. The insurer will investigate the employee carefully before writing the bond. Finally, although this right is not too valuable, the surety becomes a creditor of the employee if it makes any payment. One major difference between this fidelity bond and a surety bond is that the fidelity bond covers only the implied obligation of honesty, not ability. Surety bonds cover any nonexcluded failure to carry out the expressed obligation.

Most dishonesty insurance, however, is not written on this basis. An insurer protects the employer against losses caused by dishonest acts of his or her employee(s). The employer pays the premium. Although it is customary to require an application from each employee to provide underwriting information, the employee is not otherwise a party to the contract. The investigation of the employee's character is often at best perfunctory. Sometimes the insurer does not even have the employee's name. Losses are expected and recognized in the premium. The right to collect from the principal is no different from the right to collect from any thief. It is clear, therefore, that bonds written in this way more clearly resemble insurance than surety bonds.

BENEFITS AND COSTS OF INSURANCE

Insurance, like most institutions, presents society with both benefits and costs. The advantages will be discussed first.

Benefits

Indemnification The direct advantage of insurance is indemnification for those who suffer unexpected losses. These unfortunate businesses and families are restored or at least moved closer to their former economic position. The advantage to these individuals is obvious. Society also gains because these persons are restored to production, tax revenues are increased, and welfare payments are reduced.

Reduction of Uncertainty   The more significant but less obvious advantages of insurance arise from the fact that (1) it eliminates the insured's risk, uncertainty, and adverse reaction to risk and (2) it reduces the total risk, uncertainty, and adverse reaction to this risk in society. How it accomplishes this result is so important that it is worth repeating: prior to the purchase of insurance, each potential insured is subject to considerable risk, each knows that this risk exists (consequently his or her uncertainty is high), and each is worried about whether he or she will suffer any financial losses. Through the purchase of insurance, each insured transfers his or her risk to an insurer. The uncertainty is eliminated and he or she no longer is concerned about the financial loss.[1] The insurer is subject to some risk, but because it depends upon the experience of many insureds, the actual losses are likely to be close to the expected losses. The insurer, being aware of the law of large numbers, knows this. The insurer's uncertainty, therefore, is also small. Being a risk-bearer by profession, he or she should not be bothered much by the small risk that remains. Consequently, the risk, uncertainty, and adverse reaction to risk in society are reduced substantially through the purchase of insurance.

In practice, the uncertainty of the insurer, though smaller than that of its insureds, is not as small as the preceding discussion implies. The difficulty is that the insurer does not know the expected losses. It must estimate them. Consequently, in addition to having some small uncertainty about how close the actual losses will be to the expected losses, the insurer does not have complete confidence in its estimate of the expected losses. This estimate is important because it becomes the loss allowance in the premiums charged by the insurer. The estimate is typically obtained by observing what happened to a large number of exposure units in the past. The law of large numbers states that the larger the number of exposure units observed, the more likely it becomes that the actual losses during the experience period were close to the expected losses during that period. If the future is expected to repeat the past, the actual losses per exposure unit in the past can serve as a reasonable estimate of the expected losses per exposure unit in the future. Unfortunately, however, there are two problems. First, no matter how many exposure units are observed short of infinity, some small chance exists that the actual losses per exposure unit during the experience period differed substantially from the expected losses during that period. Second, and much more importantly, the future may not repeat the past. The world keeps changing. For example, the probable frequency and severity of fire damage losses, product liability claims, and medical expenses have changed dramatically in recent years. In this sense, therefore, insurers have much more uncertain operations than Las Vegas gambling casinos. The casinos can estimate their expected losses a priori and not worry about any significant changes. The probability of obtaining a head on the toss of a quarter is known a priori to be ½. It has been and always will be ½ unless the edges of the quarter

---

[1] The insured's uncertainty, of course, is not eliminated if the insured has any doubt concerning the insurer's ability to perform. Furthermore, if insurer reserves the right to levy an assessment or promises to return a dividend if the premiums exceed its needs, the insured assumes some risk concerning the dividend or an assessment. This risk should be small because it depends upon the combined experience of the insurer. Finally, if the premium depends upon the insured's own loss experience (see, for example, the experience and retrospective rating plans discussed in Chap. 28), some uncertainty remains.

wear out in such a way as to favor slightly one outcome over the other. Despite this additional uncertainty of insurers concerning their expected loss estimates (and thus their premiums), it remains true that the purchase of insurance reduces substantially the risk, uncertainty, and reaction to risk in society. Remember that before they purchased insurance, the insureds were also uncertain about their expected loss estimates as well as their actual losses relative to their expected losses.

Several benefits result from this reduction of risk for insureds and for society. First, by eliminating the insured's uncertainty with respect to the risk insured, insurance eliminates the physical and mental strain caused by the fear and worry associated with that risk.[2]

Second, because insurance reduces both individual and social risk and uncertainty, it also reduces in society, as well as within an industry and within a firm, inefficiencies in the utilization of existing capital and labor. The reduction of uncertainty will also encourage the accumulation of new capital because potential investors are less likely to hesitate, their planning periods are lengthened, credit is more generally extended, and fewer resources are hoarded. Insurance, therefore, results in more nearly optimum production, price levels, and price structures. The price structures are further improved by the fact that the insurer's estimate of the expected loss for each insured is generally superior to that of the individual unit. Peter F. Drucker, a noted management authority, has emphasized the importance of insurance in this regard as follows: "One of the greatest achievements of the mercantile age was the conversion of many of these physical risks into something that could be predicted and provided against. It is no exaggeration to say that without insurance an industrial economy could not function at all."[3]

Funds For Investment Insurers can make more funds available for investment than insureds who "save for a rainy day" not only because their risk is small but also because a constant inflow of new money makes it generally unnecessary for them to liquidate existing assets to pay claims. As indicated in Tables 12.1 and 12.2, in 1983 life insurers provided about 10.5 percent of the funds used in the United States money and capital markets and 14.1 percent of long-term funds raised in these markets. Property and liability insurers play a less important role than life insurers mainly because their contracts cover a shorter period and as a result they accumulate less premium dollars in advance of loss payments. Nevertheless, their contribution is considerable, particularly to investment funds. Self-insured private pension plans, which are insurance from the viewpoint of the covered employees, and which closely resemble insured pension plans in their objective and operation, also provide a substantial proportion of the funds for these markets. The same is true of public pension plans covering the employees of state and local governments. All these insurers combined provided 24.4 percent of the total funds and 33.3 percent of the investment funds. Not included in this total are government insurers, such as the Social

---

[2] According to the Capital Asset Pricing Method that is prominent in modern finance theory, the owners of a highly diversified portfolio of stocks face little or no uncertainties with respect to "nonsystematic risks" such as the pure risks that are commonly insured. For more details see the discussion of "The Capital Asset Pricing Model, Portfolio Theory, and the Worry Factor" in Chap. 13.

[3] Peter F. Drucker, *The New Society* (New York: Harper & Row Publishers, Incorporated, 1950), p. 57.

TABLE 12.1
SOURCES AND USES OF FUNDS (IN BILLIONS OF DOLLARS)

	1973		1983	
	Amount	**Percent**	**Amount**	**Percent**
Uses (funds raised):				
Investment funds	$127.2	59.4	$255.1	48.4
Short-term funds	71.4	33.3	96.5	18.3
U.S. government and agency securities privately held	15.5	7.2	175.6	33.3
Total uses	$214.1	100.0	$527.2	100.0
Sources (funds supplied):				
Insurers and pension funds:				
Life insurers	$ 15.9	7.4	$ 55.5	10.5
Property and liability insurers	5.8	2.7	9.9	1.9
Private self-insured pension plans	9.2	4.3	31.7	6.0
State and local government retirement funds	6.7	3.1	31.5	6.0
Total	$ 37.6	17.6	$128.6	24.4
Thrift institutions:				
Savings and loan associations	$ 26.5	12.4	$ 97.1	18.4
Mutual savings banks	4.7	2.2	15.8	3.0
Credit unions	3.6	1.7	9.2	1.7
Total	$ 34.8	16.3	$122.1	23.2
Investment companies (mutual funds)	$ 1.4	.7	$ 24.6	4.7
Commercial banks	78.3	36.6	140.0	26.6
Others	62.0	29.0	111.9	21.2
Total sources	$214.1	100.0	$527.2	100.1

Source: Derived from *Credit and Capital Markets 1979, Table 1* (New York: Bankers Trust Company, 1979) and *Credit and Capital Markets 1984, Table 1* (New York: Bankers Trust Company, 1984).

Security Administration, that operate social insurance programs and that are important buyers of United States government bonds.

At the close of 1982, life insurers controlled assets worth over $588 billion. At year-end, 1972, they owned less than half this amount. During 1982 life insurers increased their net assets by over $62 billion. New long-term investments alone totaled $110 billion. New investments far exceeded the net increase in assets mainly because they included short-term security purchases in which large amounts of money are reinvested every year, and reinvestment of funds made available by repayments on existing long-term investments (e.g., bond maturities and mortgage amortizations). Bonds and mortgages accounted for almost 70 percent of the assets, stocks for about 10 percent.[4]

[4] *1983 Life Insurance Fact Book* (Washington, D.C.: American Council of Life Insurance, 1983), pp. 67, 68.

TABLE 12.2
SOURCES AND USES OF INVESTMENT FUNDS (IN BILLIONS OF DOLLARS)

	1973		1983	
	Amount	Percent	Amount	Percent
Uses:				
Real estate mortgages	$ 79.9	62.8	$161.2	63.2
Corporate bonds	12.7	10.0	16.2	6.4
Corporate stocks	9.1	7.2	26.8	10.5
State and local government securities	15.3	12.0	46.3	18.1
Other uses	10.2	8.0	4.6	1.8
Total uses	$127.2	100.0	$255.1	100.0
Sources:				
Insurers and pension funds:				
Life insurers	$ 13.9	10.9	$ 36.0	14.1
Property and liability insurers	5.9	4.6	7.9	3.1
Private self-insured pension plans	7.7	6.0	23.1	9.1
State and local government retirement funds	7.3	5.7	18.0	7.1
Total	$ 34.8	27.4	$ 85.0	33.3
Thrift institutions:				
Savings and loan associations	$ 26.4	20.7	$ 77.5	30.4
Mutual savings banks	5.6	4.4	8.2	3.2
Credit unions	.5	.4	*	*
Total	$ 32.5	25.5	$ 85.7	33.6
Investment companies (mutual funds)	$ .2	.2	$ 39.6	15.5
Commercial banks	35.6	28.0	34.2	13.4
Others	24.1	18.9	10.6	4.2
Total sources	$127.2	100.0	$255.1	100.0

*Less than 0.05.
Source: Derived from *Credit and Capital Markets 1979, Table 2* (New York: Bankers Trust Company, 1979) and *Credit and Capital Markets 1984, Table 2* (New York: Bankers Trust Company 1984).

At year-end 1982, property and liability insurers had assets valued at $232 billion compared with $79 billion at year-end 1972. Because these insurers invest more heavily in common stocks than life insurers have, their asset values are more subject to market fluctuations.[5]

Loss Control   Although loss control is not an inherent part of the insurance concept, the insurance industry is a leader in loss control. Both individual insurers and trade associations are involved in various loss-control activities, some of which have been discussed under "The Responsibility for Loss Control" in Chapter 10. While

[5] More information on insurer investment portfolios is presented in Chap. 27.

recognizing the present contributions of insurers in this area, some observers believe that they should do much more.

Aid to Small Business Insurance encourages competition because without an insurance industry, small business would be a less effective competitor against big business. Big business may safely retain some of the risks that, if they resulted in loss, would destroy most small businesses. Without insurance, small business would involve more risks and would be a less attractive outlet for funds and energies.

Summary of Benefits In summary, insurance (1) indemnifies those who suffer unexpected losses, (2) eliminates the insured's physical and mental strain caused by fear and worry, (3) results in more nearly optimum production, price levels, and price structures, (4) releases funds for investment,[6] and (5) improves the competitive position of small business. In addition, the insurance industry in practice engages in some important loss-control activities.

Costs

Although the advantages arising out of the existence of an insurance industry are sizable, insurance is not without its costs.

Operating Expenses Insurers incur expenses such as loss control costs, loss-adjustment expenses, expenses involved in acquiring insureds, state premium taxes, and general administrative expenses. These expenses, plus a reasonable amount for profit and contingencies, must be covered by the premium charged. In real terms, workers and other resources that might have been committed to other uses are required by the insurance industry.[7] The following data illustrate the magnitude of these expenses, excluding the amounts for profits and contingencies. Life insurers in 1982 used about 16 percent of their total income to pay expenses, excluding taxes.[8] This percentage varies greatly among industrial, group, and ordinary insurance, between health insurance and life insurance, among insurers, and according to many other factors. In terms of premium income, these expenses were about 22 percent; but the income base is more representative in this case because the nonpremium income is sizable and, as is shown in Chapter 28, investment income is directly recognized in premium computations. Property and liability insurers use between 30 and 40 percent of their premium income to pay expenses, including loss-adjustment expenses but excluding federal income taxes. These percentages, like those in life insurance, vary greatly according to several factors, as well as among individual insurers. The higher

---

[6] An advantage of life insurance, which is not included in the above list because of its specialized nature, is the systematic savings plan provided by some types of life insurance. The advantages of this systematic saving for the individual are presented in Chap. 23. Society gains to the extent that additional funds are made available for investment.

[7] On the other hand, the insurance industry may be viewed as a creator of jobs within the industry.

[8] For more detailed information, see the latest edition of *Life Insurance Fact Book* (Washington, D.C.: American Council of Life Insurance, annual). Taxes were 2.3 percent of the total income.

expense ratio in this case largely represents differences in the nature of the protection sold. These differences are clarified in later chapters.[9]

Moral Hazard   A second cost of the insurance industry is the creation of moral hazards. A moral hazard is a condition that increases the chance that some person will intentionally (1) cause a loss or (2) increase its severity. Some unscrupulous persons can make, or believe that they can make, a profit by bringing about a loss. For example, arson, inspired by the possibility of an insurance recovery, is a major cause of fires. Others abuse the insurance protection by (1) making claims that are not warranted, thus spreading through the insurance system losses that they should bear themselves (e.g., claiming automobile liability when there is no negligence on the part of the defendant), (2) overutilizing the services (e.g., staying in a hospital beyond the period required for treatment), (3) charging excessive fees for services rendered insureds, as is done by some doctors and garages, and (4) granting larger awards in liability cases merely because the defendant is insured. Some of these abuses are fraudulent; others indicate a different (and indefensible) code of ethics where insurance is involved.

Morale Hazard   Another related cost is the creation of morale hazards. A morale hazard is a condition that causes persons to be less careful than they would otherwise be. Some persons do not consciously seek to bring about a loss, but the fact that they have insurance causes them to take more chances than they would if they had no insurance.

Opinions differ on the degree to which moral and morale hazards are created by insurance, but all agree that some persons are affected in each way and that morale hazards are more common than moral hazards.

Reduction of Costs   These costs created by the existence of an insurance industry are far outweighed by the sizable advantages described earlier. The proper course of action is to reduce these costs. Insurers are constantly trying to reduce their costs through innovations in such matters as administrative procedures and marketing methods. Selling insurance to groups of persons instead of to individuals is a prime example. The creation of moral hazard and morale hazard itself is offset, at least in part, by the loss-control activities of insurers. Moral hazard is specifically attacked through such measures as reporting services on suspicious fires, a systematic index of automobile personal-injury claims against all member insurers (which helps to reveal fraudulent claims), and close investigations of suicide claims. Morale hazard is most effectively handled by pointing out the direct relationship between premiums and losses and the sizable indirect losses and inconveniences that are not covered by insurance.[10]

---

[9] For more detailed information, see the latest edition of *Best's Aggregates and Averages* (Oldwick, N.J.: Alfred M. Best Company, Inc., annual).

[10] For example, see the discussion of the direct and indirect costs of industrial accidents in Chap. 10.

LIMITATIONS OF INSURANCE

Insurance is clearly a useful device for handling risk, but some risks cannot safely be handled by insurance. The following discussion refers principally to private insurance, but some references will be made to the greater potential scope of public insurance.

Limitation to Pure Risks

Insurance has been applied for the most part only to pure risks. With rare exceptions speculative risks have not been insured, either because the risks involved do not meet the characteristics specified in the following paragraphs or because there is no reason for applying insurance to the problem at hand.[11] For example, insuring against a speculative risk may involve a premium that would offset any advantages associated with the chance of gain. The best-known example of speculative-risk insurance permits purchasers of mutual fund shares to protect themselves against the shares being worth less than the purchase price a stated number of years later. This insurance has met with limited success up to this point, but recent market uncertainties may create more interest in the product. A second example is a life insurance policy issued by one insurer under which the face amount is adjusted upward as the Consumer Price Index increases.[12] Because insurance is not a static concept, it may be extended in the future to cover more speculative risks.[13]

Characteristics of an Ideally Insurable Risk

Among pure risks, the following conditions should be satisfied before the risk is *ideally* insurable:

1 A large number of independent units should be exposed to the risk and controlled by persons interested in insurance protection. This requirement follows from the law of large numbers, since an insurance operation is safe only when the insurer is able to predict fairly accurately its expected losses. Enough units must have been exposed in the past to provide some reasonable estimate of the expected losses in the past which, adjusted for changes in the loss environment, are used to estimate the losses expected per exposure unit in the future. Enough units must be insured in the future for future experience to approach the losses expected in the future.

A large number of insured units should be exposed to the risk because risk varies inversely with the square root of the number of units exposed. The units should be exposed independently, for otherwise what happens to one unit will determine what

---

[11] Legal obstacles may also exist.

[12] Mark Greene and Oscar Serbein, *Risk Management: Text and Cases* (2d ed., Reston, Va.: Reston Publishing Company, 1983), pp. 295–296. This life insurance contract differs from the variable life insurance and the cost of living endorsements described in Chapter 23 in that under those contracts the insurer does not assume the risk of consumer price increases.

[13] For a possible approach, see Orieon M. Spaid, "Insured Chronological Stabilization Plans," *National Insurance Buyer* (September, 1957), reprinted in H. Wayne Snider, *Readings in Property and Casualty Insurance* (Homewood, Ill.: Richard D. Irwin, Inc., 1959), pp. 47–52.

happens to other units and the effect will be the same as if there were many fewer units. If the insurer intends to write more than one type of insurance, the requirement of large numbers (but not of independence) can be relaxed for any one type of exposure. Although the insurer would prefer to be able to predict accurately its loss experience next year with respect to each type of exposure, it can operate safely as long as it can predict fairly well its composite loss experience. The law of large numbers works in the same way for this composite exposure as it does for each type of exposure. Hence the insurer need not have a large number of exposure units of just one type to satisfy the law of large numbers. It is sufficient if it has a large number of independent exposure units included among all its insureds. Indeed an insurer may for this reason consider a certain type of exposure to be insurable even if it expects to insure only one unit. On the other hand, the smaller the number of exposure units of a given type an insurer covers, the less able it will be to judge how well it is underwriting that type of exposure.

Ideally the exposure units insured should not be too heterogeneous. They should face about the same probability of an occurrence and the same potential loss severity. This condition holds whether the insurer intends to insure only one type of exposure or several different types. The greater the variation among exposure units in the probabilities of an occurrence and the magnitudes of the potential dollar losses, the more exposure units the insurer must have to achieve a certain degree of accuracy in predicting its future loss experience. For example, if an insurer insures 100 dwellings, 90 of which are worth $50,000 and 10 of which are worth $200,000, the relative variation in the potential losses will be greater than if the insurer insures 100 dwellings, all of which are worth $65,000, even though the total insured values are the same ($6.5 million) in each case. The problem would be even more evident if 99 of the dwellings were worth $10,000 and one were worth $5.51 million instead of 100 being worth $65,000 each. The loss of the $5.51 million dwelling would be equivalent to losing 551 $10,000 dwellings.

In order to make certain that the owners of a large number of units will be interested in insurance protection, two subrequirements must be satisfied. First, the potential loss must be serious enough in terms of its probability and its severity to cause many people to seek protection through insurance. On the other hand, the expected loss must not be so great that the size of the premium will discourage the purchase of insurance.

2 The loss should be definite or determinate in time, place, cause, and amount; otherwise, loss-adjustment problems are created. Another problem related to the next desirable characteristic is that the accumulation of loss experience becomes much more difficult when the loss is indefinite.

3 The expected loss over some reasonable operating period should be calculable. This condition is necessary if the premiums are to be set at the level necessary to produce with some certainty a reasonable, but not excessive, profit or operating margin for the insurer. Conditions 1 and 2 must exist before condition 3 can be satisfied, but in addition, the expected loss should either be fairly stable over time or otherwise be predictable.

4 The loss should be accidental from the viewpoint of the insured. From a business viewpoint, it is clearly unwise to insure a person against an intentional loss. It is also unwise to insure against losses that are certain to occur, such as wear and tear, or that are easily preventable.

Insurable Risks Not Always Ideal

Ideal insurable risks should meet all four requirements, but few risks (if any) currently insured by one or more insurers do possess all these characteristics. Most risks that are considered insurable, however, come close to being insurable risks either inherently or because certain safeguards have been introduced. Some risks whose insurability is questionable by these standards have nevertheless been insured because of the importance to the public of providing protection against a given peril, because of social pressures, because the risk is expected to become insurable in the future, or for some other reason. Insurers differ widely in their appraisal of many risks. Some insurers are anxious to insure risks that others flatly reject as uninsurable. Some insure risks to which only a few units are exposed because they seek predictability only for their total writings. The following illustrations may clarify these points.

The risk of a fire loss is an insurable risk. A large number of units owned by persons interested in insurance protection are exposed to fire; although many units may be adjacent to one another, independence can be achieved to a satisfactory degree for practical purposes by insuring only widely scattered units or by reinsuring adjacent units with other insurers; the loss is fairly definite in time, place, and amount; the expected loss is calculable; and the insured loss is accidental from the viewpoint of the insured since the insurance protection does not cover intentional losses.

The risk of death affects a large number of persons who are independently exposed for practical purposes and who are interested in insurance protection. The loss is definite in time and place, and since the amount payable is specified in the contract, it is definite in amount. The expected loss is calculable. If suicide is excluded, the loss is accidental from the viewpoint of the insured. Suicide is excluded during the early years of the contract but state law requires that suicide be covered after that time on the grounds that (1) society benefits from payments to the beneficiaries and (2) life insurance contracts are not likely to be purchased in contemplation of suicide one or two years later. This is an instance of a justifiable slight departure from ideal practice.

Another example is sickness insurance. Sickness is not definite in time and place, and some insurers question whether the sickness risk is insurable. On the other hand, insurance covering the costs of sickness is one of the most rapidly growing forms of insurance. At least three reasons can be advanced for this growth in spite of the questionable insurability. First, the sickness risk is one of the most important risks facing mankind, and if at all possible, protection should be made available. Second, the market is great, and if underwriting safeguards can be successfully introduced, sickness insurance can contribute a great deal to the growth of an insurer. Third, an insurer may be able to sell more life insurance because it also sells health insurance. Fourth, if private enterprise does not make sickness protection available, the government almost certainly will, and private insurers are opposed to government activity in areas that they believe they can service.

Aviation in its early days presented many risks that insurers hesitated to insure largely because they had no basis for determining the premium. But the infant aviation industry needed the protection, and insurance was written. Since loss experience has now been accumulated, the situation of aviation insurers has improved, although aviation insurance is still risky, particularly with respect to jumbo jets and hijacking. This example illustrates the writing of an uninsurable risk that was expected to become insurable. Many new kinds of insurance originate in the same way.

Institutional Constraints

Even though an insurer may decide that a particular type of exposure is commercially insurable, it may be unable to write that type of insurance because of several institutional constraints.

Regulatory Constraints   Most state laws prohibit the writing of life insurance by property and liability insurers and vice versa. This constraint, however, can be by-passed in various ways, for example, by writing the other type of insurance through a subsidiary.

Many state laws also list the kinds of insurance that can be written by any insurer. If the insurance under investigation is not on the list, it cannot be written. Many lists include "any line approved by the state insurance commissioner," in which case lines not specifically mentioned may be approved—but only after a process that may not be worth the effort. This limitation was more serious in the past.

State laws prescribe the minimum capital and surplus a domestic insurer must have to transact business (see Chapter 34). These minimum requirements vary with the kinds of insurance the insurer intends to write. Some requirements may be so high that an insurer will forgo writing a line it would otherwise prefer to include in its portfolio.

Another factor that may deter entry into a new line is how state insurance departments regulate rates for the field the insurer is about to enter. Certain lines sometimes require substantial red tape, making entrance into those lines much less attractive. The effect of regulation on the profitability of insurers in that line must also be considered.

Other Constraints   An insurer may wish to enter a certain line but may conclude that its present *personnel*—such as actuaries, underwriters, and claims adjusters—are not capable of writing and servicing this new line at a profit. Hiring new personnel may not be easy, and the reactions of existing personnel to new people, especially if they command higher salaries, may cause some serious problems.

Reinsurance facilities for the new line may also be needed. The interest of the insurer in writing the new exposure may be conditional on its ability to protect itself against catastrophe losses (which may occur even among exposures that for practical purposes are independent) and against substantial losses on single exposures.

Financing may also be a problem. To write more insurance at what the insurer considers an acceptable premium-to-net-worth ratio may require the insurer to seek more funds from its stockholders or to generate more surplus from internal operations.

Custom and tradition cannot be ignored. Most insurers hesitate to pioneer in areas that have not been successfully tested by other insurers. Despite the fact that the exposure under consideration appears to meet all the requirements established for a commercially insurable exposure, they may be understandably reluctant to enter a new area.

Risks Not Insurable by Private Insurers

Examples of pure risks that are generally considered to be uninsurable by private insurers through normal channels are those associated with flood losses to real estate (except under very special circumstances), bank insolvencies, and unemployment. The major problem associated with flood insurance is that the persons who would be interested in the protection would no doubt find the price too high. Furthermore, a single flood usually affects many persons. Because flood threatens many families and businesses, and because private insurance was not generally available, Congress passed the National Flood Insurance Act of 1968, under which the federal government provides subsidized protection.[14] Bank insolvencies are unpredictable and present catastrophic possibilities. The same is true of unemployment.[15] The expected loss is not calculable in the short run.

Risk Insurable by Government Insurers Only

Government insurers can insure risks that private insurers cannot because they can make the insurance compulsory. This compulsion enables them to spread the cost of the program over exposures of varying quality. It also enables them to vary premium rates over time as their needs dictate without fear of losing any insureds. It can even make up in this way losses suffered in the past. For these reasons government insurance is available to protect bank depositors against bank failures and to protect persons against unemployment. Further, instead of or in addition to raising premiums when this is necessary, the government can in many cases reduce the benefits by amending a law—an option not available to insurers bound by a legal contract. Through its taxing power, the government may also subsidize voluntary public or public-private programs of the sort described in Chapter 34. Even government insurers, however, would prefer the more stable operations made possible when the risk approximates the ideal insurable risk.

Insurable Risks Not Static

In conclusion, it should be noted that a risk that is generally uninsurable today may be considered insurable at some future date because of some change in the risk itself, because of improvements in the technical knowledge or other abilities of insurers, or because some more compelling reasons are introduced for insuring the risk.

Two recently introduced policies illustrate how the concept of an insurable risk is

[14] For more details see Chap. 34.

[15] Employers, however, self-insure supplementary unemployment benefits. See ''Supplementary Unemployment Compensation'' in Chap. 21. Also, some insurers have issued policies that continue an owner's mortgage payments if the owner dies, is disabled, or becomes unemployed.

continually being expanded. The first policy, sold to individual investors, guarantees these investors prompt and full payment of interest and principal on specified municipal bonds. (A related coverage, sold to the issuer of the municipal bond, guarantees the payment of interest and principal to the purchasers of bonds issued by the insured municipality. This coverage is more closely related to surety bonding.) Under the second policy, a home warranty program sold to real estate agents for distribution free to buyers of used homes, the insurer promises to pay the buyer during the first six months or year of home ownership the cost of repairing major structural defects and mechanical failures of heating, plumbing, and electrical systems. The real estate agent is responsible for seeing that prospective used homes are inspected and that sellers have made necessary repairs before the houses are listed for sale.

A third example illustrates how an expansion of the concept is sometimes regretted. In 1974, Lloyd's of London (see Chapter 26) marketed a computer leasing insurance policy under which Lloyd's promised to continue the payments to the lessor under a computer lease if the lessee terminated the lease prior to the nominal maturity date. Losses far exceeded expectations because IBM made some dramatic changes in their products that made many existing computers technologically obsolete. Many leases were cancelled with unexpectedly high losses for Lloyd's. The major problem was the failure to anticipate the rapid technological obsolescence of computers.[16]

A fourth example is back-dated liability insurance. In late 1980 the MGM Grand Hotel in Las Vegas had a serious fire. Eighty-four people died in the fire; more than 700 were injured. Suits were filed against MGM Grand Hotels, Inc., that far exceeded the limits of the corporation's liability insurance policies in effect at the time of the fire. Shortly after the fire, however, the corporation was able to secure additional protection against these law suits, plus others still to be filed as a result of the fire. The insurers reasoned that although some loss was almost certain, the amount of that loss was highly uncertain. In their opinion the premium that was paid was sufficient to cover the present value of the loss plus their expenses and a reasonable profit. Some observers argue that back-dated liability insurance is simply an extension of the practice whereby one insurer sometimes sells to another insurer the liabilities it has established for claims that are known but have not yet been settled. Others point out that in the insurer situation the cases are older and the final outcome more predictable. Some deny that this new coverage is insurance. Only a few insurers write this coverage.[17]

Retroactive liability insurance, a closely related product that preceded back-dated liability insurance, also provides back-dated coverage, but retroactive insurance does not cover losses that are known to have already occurred. Situations that may create a demand for retroactive liability insurance include (1) policies written with limits now considered inadequate to cover past events that may produce claims in the future and (2) the total lack of coverage of such events that now seems highly desirable. These

---

[16] Some observers believe that the concept of a computer leasing policy is still valid if the contract is more carefully drafted and insureds are more carefully underwritten. See C. W. Cipolla and S. E. Spilka, "What Went Wrong at Lloyd's?" *Best's Review,* vol. 80, no. 7 (November, 1979), pp. 22–26.

[17] "MGM Buys Back-Dated Cover," *Business Insurance,* Feb. 9, 1981, pp. 1, 22. "Back Dating: Issue Splits Risk Managers," *Business Insurance,* Apr. 20, 1981, pp. 1, 46.

TABLE 12.3
MAJOR INSURANCE OPERATIONS IN THE UNITED STATES: ESTIMATED ASSETS AND
PREMIUMS (IN BILLIONS)*

Operation	Assets			Premiums or taxes		
	1972	1982	Percent increase	1972	1982	Percent increase
Private insurers:						
Property and liability insurance	$ 79	$248	214	$38	$104	174
Life insurance	240	588	145	30	83	177
Health insurance†				27	94	248
Total	$319	$836	162	$95	$281	196
Public insurers:						
Old-Age, Survivors, Disability, and Health Insurance	$ 46	$ 57	24	$51	$196	284
Unemployment compensation funds	9	7	−22	5	16	220
Total	$ 56	$ 64	14	$56	$212	279

*Intentionally omitted are self-insured pension funds, the civil service retirement system, and state and local government retirement systems, because the employer does not transfer the risk. From the viewpoint of the employee, however, these operations are insurance. They have expanded rapidly.

†Health insurance is written, for the most part, by insurers also selling life insurance or property and liability insurance.

Source: Insurance Facts, 1983–84 Edition (New York: Insurance Information Institute, 1983), pp. 17, 18, 24. *1983 Life Insurance Fact Book* (Washington, D.C.: American Council of Life Insurance, 1983), pp. 56, 68. Data for life insurance premiums and assets do not include the relatively small operations of fraternals, mutual savings banks, and assessment associations. *Source Book of Health Insurance Data, 1982–83* (Washington, D.C.: Health Insurance Institute, 1983), pp. 26–27. The 1981 premium totals in this *Source Book* were adjusted upward by the 1981 to 1982 percentage increase in health insurance premiums reported for life insurers in the *1983 Life Insurance Fact Book.* Public insurer data from *Social Security Bulletins.*

two situations may arise, for example, because the legal climate has changed, increasing the potential loss; a merger or acquisition has occurred joining together two firms with different insurance coverages; or a risk manager simply decides that he or she made the wrong decision in the past. This type of insurance is much more commonly available than back-dated liability insurance but most insurers still do not write this coverage.[18]

GROWTH AND IMPORTANCE OF INSURANCE

The recent growth and importance of insurance as a method for handling risks can be indicated by the measures in Table 12.3 for the years 1972 and 1982. Because the figures speak for themselves, they are presented without further comment except to note that several less important operations have been omitted from the table. More

[18] Charles A. McAlear, "Retroactive Insurance: Turning Back the Clock for 300 Years," *Risk Management,* XXIX, No. 8 (August 1982), pp. 30–32. McAlear observes that ocean marine insurers wrote retroactive insurance when they started around 1613 (and still do) to insure vessels "lost or not lost" at the date the insurance commenced.

detailed information on the operations of particular types of insurers is given at other points throughout the text.

Another measure of the importance of the insurance business is the number of employees. In 1982, almost 2 million persons were employed by private insurers. Contrary to common belief, only about one-third were engaged directly in selling activities.

USE OF INSURANCE WITH OTHER TOOLS

Insurance may be applied as the sole method of handling a risk or in combination with some other method. Loss control may, of course, always be practiced in conjunction with insurance, but the advantages of, and possibilities for, combining insurance with retention require some explanation.

Deductibles and excess insurance are examples of insurance devices that make this useful combination possible. Deductibles make it possible for the insured to bear all or certain types of losses up to a specified amount, while the insurer assumes part or all of the losses in excess of this amount up to the policy limits. Normally the insured may choose one of several deductible amounts.

Regardless of the form of the deductible,[19] the obvious effect is a reduction in the premiums for a given amount of insurance protection. This is especially noticeable when the losses that are not insured because of the deductible are relatively quite numerous. Loss-adjustment expenses are also reduced for the insurer, and if the noninsured losses are small, the effect of excluding loss-adjustment expenses may even exceed the effect of excluding the losses themselves. These two reasons explain why deductibles are most frequently used when small losses are relatively more important than large losses and loss frequency is fairly high. Another reason why the premium may be reduced is that the insured must bear part of every loss and as a result has reason to be more careful.

An insured may choose a deductible because the maximum retained loss is small and may safely (and in the long run, economically) be met out of operating income or emergency funds. On the other hand, the insured may decide that he or she can safely self-insure losses up to a certain amount, even though that amount may be large, because it can be predicted with a fair degree of accuracy what his or her losses within the range up to the deductible are likely to be. In either case, the risks that cannot with safety be retained are transferred to the insurer. The premium savings may be used to pay the losses that have been retained, increase the amount of insurance protection against sizable losses, or both. Normally each dollar saved because of the deductible will purchase considerably more insurance protection against sizable losses than is lost against nonserious losses, because of the predominance of small losses and the relatively high loss-adjustment expenses associated with small losses.

Excess insurance is a form of deductible insurance; often the two terms are used interchangeably whenever the potential loss to be borne by the insured is sizable. Excess insurance, however, has acquired a more specialized meaning. The minimum amount borne by the insured under excess insurance is usually established by negotia-

---

[19] For a description of the forms available, see Chap. 17, under "Deductible Clauses."

tions between the insurer and the insured and commonly equals the maximum probable loss. The amount retained under deductible insurance is usually much smaller than the maximum probable loss. Moreover, instead of establishing the deductible amount through special negotiations, the insurer usually presents the insured with a choice of several specified deductible amounts. Another difference between deductible insurance and excess insurance is that under deductible insurance the insurer usually provides loss-control and claims-adjustment services for the entire loss, while under excess insurance the insured must arrange for outside services or provide them on his or her own. Consequently excess insurance is much less common than deductible insurance and is useful only to large businesses. The advantages of deductible insurance and excess insurance differ primarily in degree.

SOME KEY CONCEPTS

Insurance   A risk financing tool. A transfer under which the source of funds is an insurer. As an institution, insurance is a device that combines the risks of two or more insureds through actual or promised contributions to a fund out of which claimants are paid.

Insurable risk   A loss exposure that is insurable by a private or public insurer. Few, if any, such risks meet the requirements of an ideally insurable risk.

Moral hazard   A condition that increases the chance that some person will intentionally cause or increase the severity of a loss.

Morale hazard   A condition that causes persons to be less careful than they would otherwise be.

Deductible clause   A provision in an insurance contract that requires an insured to bear part of the potential losses covered under the contract, typically the first $100 or some other amount per occurrence. Through deductibles, insureds can combine insurance with retention.

REVIEW QUESTIONS

1 **a** Define insurance.
  b Which of the basic tools of risk management does it illustrate?
2 Distinguish between insurance, gambling, and bonding.
3 Insurance makes possible the substitution of certainty for uncertainty. To what extent is this statement true? false?
4 One of the advantages of an insurance institution is that it reduces the risk, the uncertainty, and the adverse reaction to risk in society. How does insurance attain these objectives?
5 What advantages do business firms, families, and society obtain from the fact that insurers indemnify insureds who suffer losses? from the fact that insurers reduce risk, uncertainty, and adverse reactions to risk?
6 Describe the role of insurers as financial intermediaries.
7 The existence of insurers also presents certain costs.
  a What is the nature of these costs?
  b How can these costs be reduced?
8 Insurance is almost exclusively concerned with pure risks. Why is this true? Will it always be true?
9 **a** What are the characteristics of an ideal insurable risk?
  b Do all risks covered by private insurers satisfy these characteristics? Use two types of insurance to illustrate your answer.

c Why might private insurers insure a risk whose characteristics differ considerably from those of an ideal insurable risk? Use two examples to illustrate your point.

d Why might government insurers be able to write certain risks that all or most private insurers would decline to write?

10 The risks that are considered insurable vary among insurers and over time. Comment on this statement.

11 Insurance is most useful when the chance of loss is high. Comment on this statement.

12 The deductible is an extremely useful insurance device.

a What forms may the deductible take?

b Under what conditions are deductibles useful?

c How does the deductible cut insurance premiums?

SUGGESTIONS FOR ADDITIONAL READING

Athearn, J. L., and S. T. Pritchett: *Risk and Insurance* (5th ed., St. Paul: West Publishing Co., 1984), chap. 3.

Berliner, Baruch: *Limits of Insurability of Risks* (Englewood Cliffs, N.J.: Prentice-Hall, Inc., 1982).

Bickelhaupt, D. L.: *General Insurance* (11th ed., Homewood, Ill.: Richard D. Irwin, Inc., 1983), chap. 2.

Crane, F. G.: *Insurance Principles and Practices* (2d ed., New York: John Wiley & Sons, Inc., 1984), chap. 1.

Denenberg, H. S., et al.: *Risk and Insurance* (2d ed., Englewood Cliffs, N.J.: Prentice-Hall, Inc., 1974), chap. 10.

Dorfman, M. S.: *Introduction to Insurance* (2d ed., Englewood Cliffs, N.J.: Prentice-Hall, Inc., 1982), chaps. 1 and 2.

Greene, M. R., and J. S. Trieschmann: *Risk and Insurance* (6th ed., Cincinnati: South-Western Publishing Company Incorporated, 1984), chap. 3.

Long, J. D.: *Ethics, Morality and Insurance* (Bloomington, Ind.: Bureau of Business Research, Indiana University Graduate School of Business, 1971).

Mehr, Robert I.: *Fundamentals of Insurance* (Homewood, Ill.: Richard D. Irwin, Inc., 1983), chap. 2.

————, and E. Cammack: *Principles of Insurance* (7th ed., Homewood, Ill.: Richard D. Irwin, Inc., 1980), chaps. 1 and 2.

————, and B. A. Hedges: *Risk Management: Concepts and Applications* (Homewood, Ill.: Richard D. Irwin, Inc., 1974), chap. 6.

Mowbray, A. H., R. H. Blanchard, and C. A. Williams, Jr.: *Insurance* (6th ed., New York: McGraw-Hill Book Company, 1969), chap. 5.

Pfeffer, Irving, and D. R. Klock: *Perspectives on Insurance* (Englewood Cliffs, N.J.: Prentice-Hall, Inc., 1974), parts I and IV.

Rejda, George E.: *Principles of Insurance* (Glenview, Ill.: Scott, Foresman and Company, 1982), chap. 2.

Riegel, Robert, J. Miller, and C. A. Williams, Jr.: *Insurance Principles and Practices: Property and Liability* (6th ed., Englewood Cliffs, N.J.: Prentice-Hall, Inc., 1976), chap. 2.

Vaughan, E. J.: *Fundamentals of Risk and Insurance* (3d ed., New York: John Wiley & Sons, Inc., 1982), chap. 2.

Willett, A. H.: *The Economic Theory of Risk and Insurance* (Philadelphia: The University of Pennsylvania Press, 1951).

Williams, Numan A.: *Insurance: An Introduction to Personal Risk Management* (Cincinnati: South-Western Publishing Co., 1983).

CHAPTER 13

SELECTING THE PROPER TOOLS: I

LEARNING OBJECTIVES

After you have completed this chapter, you should be able to:

1 Classify types of insurance in a given situation as essential, desirable, or available.
2 Use the insurance method to design a risk management program for a business.
3 Calculate the expected dollar loss, given a loss matrix.
4 Explain how you would use the worry method to select the proper tool, given a loss matrix.
5 Use the worry method to explain conditions that favor the purchase of insurance over retention and vice versa.
6 Explain what factors should affect the worry value.
7 Describe how the critical probability method might be used to decide between insurance and retention.

INTRODUCTION

Preceding chapters have described in some detail the nature, advantages, and limitations of the basic tools of risk management. Attention has also been paid to the factors to be considered in deciding whether to use each of these tools. In practice, because of the rapidly changing risk environment, the need for quick responses to immediate problems, and human and institutional limitations, risk managers often deal with one part of their total risk management program at a time. For example, they may concentrate their attention on industrial injuries or on losses to mail shipments. In making these decisions, they tend to follow the reasoning presented in the earlier discussions of the basic tools.

233

Periodically, however, risk managers should broaden their perspective and review at one time, on their own or with the aid of consultants or insurer representatives, their firm's total risk management program. In other areas of business management, the systems approach is forcing businesses to consider simultaneously more and more aspects of their operations; risk management should increasingly move in the same direction. One reason for a total review of risk management philosophy and procedures is the need to develop a statement of company policy that is consistent with the business's overall objectives and that recognizes the interrelationships among the various individual risk management areas and decisions. Without such a policy to guide individual decisions the risk manager may fail to recognize such interrelationships. For example, he or she may not realize that retaining the first $10,000 of losses per occurrence with respect to two or more types of losses (e.g., industrial accidents and physical damage losses to a fleet of cars) may expose the firm to more than a $10,000 loss per occurrence if a single occurrence involves these two or more types of losses. Without a policy statement the risk manager may also be inconsistent in his or her decision making over time or in the treatment of different risks. For example, a risk manager may without good reason use different standards to determine in January and in June what losses the firm should be willing to retain. The risk manager may also apply different standards to retention decisions involving potential automobile physical damage losses and building losses.

Periodic reviews of the total risk management program are desirable to revise the initial statement of company policy and to check compliance with the policy statement.

This chapter describes first how procedures and principles in common use might be employed to design a total risk management program. These principles should also prove useful when dealing with only part of a risk management program. Later the chapter will explain and illustrate some quantitative methods that are not as commonly used but could prove helpful in designing a total risk management program or parts of that program. The most useful of these quantitative methods plus the application of capital budgeting to risk management will be explained further in the next chapter.

AN INSURANCE METHOD

The first approach to total risk planning is a two-step procedure we will call the "insurance method." Insurance coverages serve as the focal point of the analysis. After the risk manager has identified and measured the potential losses, he or she first prepares a listing of the insurance coverages that would best cover these losses. The coverages in the list are divided into three groups primarily on the basis of the severity of the potential losses they cover. The risk manager then reviews the insurance contracts in each group to determine which of these losses might be more satisfactorily handled in other ways. Each of these two steps is explained in more detail below.

The Initial Listing

In step one, the risk manager must determine first what combination of insurance coverages would provide the best protection against the losses to which the business is exposed, on the assumption that the business would prefer to buy insurance whenever it is available. To make this determination the risk manager must understand insurance contracts and insurance pricing. The objective is to provide the most complete protection at minimum cost. Because some of the risks faced by the firm may not be insurable, the risk manager is alerted through this analysis to the fact that these risks will have to be handled by some tool other than insurance.

In addition to selecting the proper combination of coverages, the risk manager must select policy limits that provide as complete protection as possible. Generally, the policy limits in this initial listing should equal the maximum possible loss, but sometimes this loss may exceed the maximum coverage available. Losses in excess of the maximum amount available will have to be dealt with in some other way.

After the risk manager has determined the best combination of coverages and policy limits, he or she divides the insurance contracts in this combination into three groups: (1) essential coverages, (2) desirable coverages, and (3) available coverages.

The *essential* contracts include those that are compulsory because they are required by law (e.g., automobile liability insurance in some cases and workers' compensation insurance in most cases) or by contract (e.g., a group life insurance contract required under a union contract or property insurance required under a mortgage). The other insurance protection in this category is coverage against *high-severity* losses that could result in a financial catastrophe for the firm. Liability losses are an example of this type.

The *desirable* contracts provide protection against losses that could seriously impair the operations of the firm but probably would not put it out of business. Automobile physical damage insurance might be an example of this type.

The *available* contracts include all the types of protection that have not been included in the first two classes. These contracts protect against types of losses that would inconvenience the firm but would not seriously impair its operations unless several of them occurred within one year. Insurance against breakage of glass might be considered an available coverage.

Revised Listing

After the initial listing has been completed, the risk manager then reviews the contracts in each group to determine which of these losses might be more satisfactorily handled in other ways. For example, contracts that might be dropped from the essential category would include contracts covering:

1 Losses that can be transferred to someone other than an insurer at a smaller cost than the insurance premium

2 Losses that can be prevented or reduced to such an extent that they are no longer severe

3 Losses that happen so frequently that they are fairly predictable, thus making self-insurance an attractive alternative because of expense savings

In making these decisions, the risk manager can weigh the advantages and disadvantages of each tool presented in the three preceding chapters or can apply the quantitative approaches explained later in this chapter. Few, if any, contracts will be dropped from the essential category. Compulsory insurance must be purchased. Contracts covering potential catastrophic losses will be purchased unless they satisfy one of the three conditions stated above or the premium for the insurance seems unreasonably high relative to the frequency and severity of the exposure.

The discussion up to this point has been in terms of types of losses, but as we pointed out under "Risk Measurement" in Chapter 3, it may also be possible to divide any particular type of loss into two (or more) subtypes, depending upon the amount of the potential loss. For example, although the maximum possible loss of a given type is $1 million and the coverage against this loss is therefore an essential coverage, losses of $500 or less may be either so predictable or so unimportant that the risk manager would regard this type of insurance on the first $500 of loss as at best available insurance with only the excess being essential. The types of deductibles and excess insurance available from insurers would limit what could be done along these lines.

The risk manager then subjects the desirable coverages to the same type of analysis. The case for noninsurance methods is stronger with respect to these coverages because the consequences of not insuring are not so severe. Still, this insurance is desirable, and unless some other method of handling the loss is at least as attractive, insurance should be purchased. As in dealing with essential coverages, the risk manager may decide to buy the insurance with a deductible provision.

The available contracts rate the lowest priority. Some available contracts will be attractive to a particular risk manager because the insurer will perform certain services that the risk manager values highly. For example, although potential glass damage may be limited in its severity, the risk manager may believe that the rapid replacement service provided by the insurer justifies payment of the premium. Insurance against some relatively unimportant property losses may become attractive if the premium is, in the eyes of the risk manager, a bargain price. With respect to many of the available coverages, however, other risk management tools will appear more convenient, will cost less to apply, or will have some other relative net advantages.

This threefold classification does not tell the risk manager the point at which he or she should draw the line with respect to insurance purchases, particularly if the line must be drawn within one of the three classes, but it does suggest some priorities with respect to the use of funds available for insurance premiums. It also focuses attention on the consequences of not insuring. The essential and desirable insurance contracts that have not been eliminated in the second listing should be purchased unless the other demands for the premium dollars are clearly more important. What insurance these two classes will contain depends upon a host of factors, including the economic status of the firm, its risk management objectives, the nature of its exposures, its aversion to risk, and the accuracy of the measurements of its potential losses.

The risk manager must also decide what the business should do about those potential losses not included in the first listing because insurance was not available.

As a result of this analysis of the initial listing of insurance coverages and the uninsurable potential losses, the risk manager should produce a revised list that shows how each risk management tool should be used to handle each of the risks faced by the business. An *abbreviated* example of such a listing is presented below:

A Avoidance (not possible)
B Loss prevention and reduction
  1 Safety inspections of premises
  2 Annual physical examination for key employees
C Retention
  1 Losses up to $1,000 of any type
  2 Liability losses in excess of limits available from insurers
D Noninsurance transfers
  1 Hold-harmless agreement in lease of premises
E Insurance (with $1,000 deductible where available)
  1 First priority (essential)
    a Workers' compensation insurance
    b Liability insurance
    c Property insurance on building
  2 Second priority (desirable)
    a Automobile physical damage insurance
    b Disability insurance on key personnel
  3 Third priority (available)
    a Glass insurance
    b Leasehold insurance

Although this insurance method has been described as an approach to total risk planning, it can also be useful in dealing with part of the risk management program. For example, if a risk manager is deciding whether to buy a particular type of insurance, it would be helpful to classify the insurance as essential, desirable, or available.

Sample Applications

In Chapter 30, this conventional method is applied to a specific business situation. Chapters 32 and 33 apply the method to a specific family situation. Because family risk management is less complex, the first step in the two-step process is omitted in these two chapters.

QUANTITATIVE APPROACHES

Since the close of World War II, economists, psychologists, mathematicians, business people and others have paid increasing attention to the solution of business problems through quantitative methods. Linear programming, queuing theory, mathematical models, game theory, and statistical decision theory are a few illustrations of the quantitative approaches that have been introduced or greatly improved during the past four decades. Application of these modern techniques to insurance and particularly to risk management problems is of still more recent origin. Because these techniques are likely to be more widely applied in the future, it is important to consider at this point the possible use of these quantitative methods in selecting the "proper" tools of risk management. During the 1970s and 1980s risk managers have greatly increased their awareness of, interest in, and use of quantitative approaches. The application of these approaches, however, is more limited than one might expect because (1) the data necessary to apply them (except in a modified form) are commonly missing or inadequate, and (2) many practicing risk managers have not been trained in their use. These approaches have immediate value, however, in that (1) even with inadequate data they can be useful in making some important risk management decisions, and (2) they make explicit the assumptions and decision rules that are implicit in more conventional methods. By making these assumptions and the decision rules explicit, these quantitative approaches improve our understanding and application of the methods more commonly employed today.

The approach that will be developed most completely in this chapter can be summarized as follows:

1 Construct a loss matrix or table that presents the various losses or costs associated with *(a)* each possible decision and *(b)* each possible outcome.

2 Describe precisely the objective that the risk manager wishes to attain.

3 Design a decision-making rule that will attain this objective.

Specific examples will be used to explain the approach. This chapter will describe several possible objectives and decision-making rules in the context of a highly simplified example. The most useful of these decision rules will be discussed more fully in a more realistic setting in the next chapter.

The Loss Matrix

To illustrate the loss matrix concept, assume that a building owned by a business is exposed to loss by fire and that there will be either no loss or a total loss. Further assume that the risk manager must decide among three courses of action: (1) to retain the risk, (2) to retain the risk and introduce some safety measures that reduce the chance of a fire, or (3) to purchase insurance. Real life situations are, of course, far more complex. A risk manager must generally choose among many courses of action, and a building exposed to fire may suffer losses of various amounts.

The loss matrix in Table 13.1 shows, for each of the three possible decisions in this example, the *tangible* losses that the business will suffer under each of the two possible outcomes, *before* considering the effect of *income taxes*. These losses fall into two categories: (1) accidental losses that will be incurred only if there is a fire, and (2) costs that would be incurred whether or not there is a fire. The accidental losses in turn can be subdivided according to whether or not they would be insured under the insurance decision.

For this example, it is assumed that the insurance contract under consideration is a broad package contract protecting the business against most accidental losses, such as the cost of replacing the building, the loss of use of the building, debris removal costs, and liability to others. If the risk manager decides to retain the risk, and a fire occurs, the business will bear these losses, which are estimated to total $200,000.

If the business retains the risk and a fire occurs, it will also suffer some accidental

TABLE 13.1
BEFORE-TAX TANGIBLE LOSS MATRIX

Decision	Outcome			
	Fire		**No fire**	
1. Retain the risk	Insurable losses	$200,000		
	Noninsurable accidental losses	12,000		
		$212,000		$ 0
2. Retain the risk and introduce new safety measures	Insurable losses	$200,000		
	Noninsurable accidental losses	12,000		
	Cost of safety measures	6,000	Cost of safety measures	$ 6,000
		$218,000		$ 6,000
3. Purchase insurance	Insurance premium	$ 10,000	Insurance premium	$10,000

losses that would not be incurred if the business had purchased insurance. These extra losses are one type of "noninsurable accidental losses." The other type of noninsurable accidental losses is losses that are not insurable but occur whether the firm retains the risk or purchases insurance. Only the first type of noninsurable accidental losses is assumed to occur in this example and it is limited to the increased credit costs that lending institutions would be expected to impose if the firm's credit rating were damaged by retaining a $200,000 fire loss. These increased credit costs are estimated to be $12,000.

To simplify the presentation, in constructing this loss matrix no allowance was made for the fact that under a retention program some of the losses and costs would not be incurred immediately. This failure to recognize the opportunity cost of insurance (see page 203) favors the purchase of insurance. To correct this omission, the risk manager could use the expected present value of each of the losses and costs.

On the other hand, the table assumes that the risk manager places no value on the services, such as loss-control and loss-adjustment services, provided by the insurer. If the firm would incur some expenses to obtain these services internally or externally, these extra expenses should be added where appropriate.

If the risk manager retains the risk but no fire occurs, the firm will suffer no losses.

If the risk manager elects instead of retention alone to combine some new safety measures with retention, and a fire occurs, the effect on the insurable and noninsurable accidental losses depends upon the nature of these safety measures. In this example it is assumed that only the probability of a fire, not its severity, would be reduced. Consequently, the insurable and noninsurable accidental losses in the matrix are the same for this decision as for retention. However, the cost of the safety measures must also be recognized. For this example this cost is assumed to be $6,000 annually and no physical improvements are involved. (If a physical improvement were involved, the

TABLE 13.2
AFTER-TAX TANGIBLE LOSS MATRIX

Decision	Outcome			
	Fire		No fire	
1. Retain the risk	Insurable losses	$100,000		
	Noninsurable accidental			
	losses	6,000		
		$106,000		$ 0
2. Retain the risk	Insurable losses	$100,000		
and introduce new	Noninsurable accidental			
safety measures	losses	6,000	Cost of safety	
	Cost of safety measures	3,000	measures	$3,000
		$109,000		$3,000
3. Purchase insurance	Insurance premium	$ 5,000	Insurance	$5,000
			premium	

firm's real estate taxes might also be increased, and the physical improvement might be destroyed in a fire.)

If the safety measures are introduced and no fire occurs, the only loss is the cost of the safety measures.

If the risk manager purchases insurance and a fire occurs, a $10,000 premium is substituted for the sizable insurable losses. Normally some noninsurable accidental losses, such as inconvenience or the loss of use of some personal property, would remain. In this example, however, the only noninsurable accidental loss recognized under retention was increased credit costs that will not occur if the risk manager purchases insurance. Consequently, the only loss is the $10,000 insurance premium.

If insurance is purchased and no fire occurs, the loss is again the $10,000 insurance premium.

Up to this point the impact of income taxes has been ignored. Tax effects, however, are too important to omit. In this example it will be assumed that the business can deduct from its taxable income its insurance premiums, the cost of the safety measures, its insurable losses,[1] and its increased credit costs. If the tax rate is 50 percent, the deductible amounts should be multiplied by 0.50 and subtracted from the corresponding amounts in Table 13.1. To illustrate, for the retention-fire outcome, the $200,000 insurable loss is deductible. Consequently, the after-tax insurable loss is $200,000 − 0.50($200,000) or $100,000. The after-tax credit cost is $12,000 − 0.50($12,000) = $6,000. The total after-tax loss, therefore, is $106,000. Table 13.2 shows all the tax-adjusted entries.

Tangible losses, however, are not the only losses suffered by the firm. Because the

---

[1] Usually some but not all of the retained accidental losses can be deducted. For example, only the book value of a building destroyed by fire is deductible. See Chap. 11. The tax effect of insurance payments in excess of the book value should also be recognized.

business is uncertain about whether a fire will occur with resulting financial losses, its managers worry. This worry will be present whether or not a fire actually occurs. It is extremely difficult to assign a dollar value to the worry the managers will experience, but to ignore this cost would be misleading and could lead to some unwise decisions. The worry value is a highly subjective factor that depends upon the probability distribution (especially the severity of the possible losses and the risk), the risk manager's uncertainty about what will happen, the other risks faced by the firm,[2] and the firm's risk management objectives.

The risk management objectives should influence the worry factor because (1) they determine how much importance should be assigned to potential losses of various types and amounts, and (2) they reflect the risk attitudes of the business. To illustrate, a loss that would cause net earnings per share to drop 20 percent would be important if the firm's objective were to limit downside fluctuations to 10 percent, but would be of much less concern if the objective were mere survival. Similarly, if earnings stability were an objective, but the target were downside fluctuations of 30 percent or less, the 20 percent possibility would be less disturbing. A loss that would cause the firm to shut its doors for two months would bother a business that wants or needs to continue its operations more than it would a business desiring only stable earnings during the period of interruption. The strength of the desire for peace of mind, a "quiet night's sleep," or freedom from fear and worry reflects the business' attitudes toward risk. Other things being equal, some firms worry more than others about their ability to meet their post-loss objectives and the money value they would assign to this worry. A firm with a strong sense of social responsibility or a desire for a good public image may assign more importance to some potential losses than would be justified under the other post-loss objectives. It may also be more worried about the failure to achieve its objectives or the appearance of taking too many chances. Because its worry factor is higher, such a firm may lean toward more conservative decisions. The economy objective is implicit in the basic approach that seeks to minimize the average long-run cost. Once the cost of the tools selected is known, however, the firm may wish to reassess its other objectives, which might change the worry value. If the cost is too high, the post-loss objectives might become less ambitious or the desire for peace of mind or a good pre-loss image might be reduced. A post-loss growth objective may cause some potential losses to be rated more important than they otherwise would be, but a pre-loss growth objective may strengthen the desire for pre-loss economy. This would free more funds to finance pre-loss growth. Finally, externally imposed constraints can be viewed in most cases as dictating an extremely high worry value for all combinations of tools that do not satisfy the external constraint. For instance, to comply with a state statute, a small firm probably has to buy workers' compensation insurance; a firm that wants to get a mortgage on a building must purchase property insurance. In some cases, a firm might elect not to worry about meeting a particular external constraint, choosing instead to risk the consequences. For example, the penalty for noncompliance with a minor safety standard considered to have only

---

[2] The importance of considering all the risks faced by the firm is discussed later in this chapter in the section on "The Capital Asset Pricing Model, Portfolio Theory, and the Worry Factor."

nuisance value may be less than the extra cost of satisfying the constraint; however, such situations are unusual. Furthermore, ethical, social, and broader economic considerations may outweigh the more narrowly focused financial calculation.

For this example, the worry value for the retention decision is assumed to be $4,000. The potential tangible loss is $106,000, which causes the business some concern. Some clues on how to set the worry value in practice will be provided in this chapter and in Chapter 14. Because this worry value is the same regardless of whether or not a fire occurs, $4,000 must be added to both the retention-fire and the retention-no fire after-tax losses in Table 13.2. The total loss, including the worry value, is shown in Table 13.3.

For the decision to introduce new safety measures the worry cost is assumed to be somewhat less, say, $3,000. The reason is that although the potential loss is slightly higher, the safety program is expected to reduce substantially the chance of a fire, thus reducing slightly the risk manager's anxiety. Table 13.3 shows the necessary adjustment.

Finally, because the annual losses do not fluctuate if insurance is purchased, the worry value for the insurance decision is zero. Consequently the losses for the insurance decision are the same in Tables 13.2 and 13.3.

Objectives and Decision-Making Rules

It is impossible to consider each of the possible objectives that the risk manager might want to achieve in this case, but a few common objectives will suffice. The objectives will be divided into two major categories: (1) those objectives that assume the risk manager cannot estimate the probability of a fire loss, and (2) those objectives that assume the risk manager can estimate this probability.

TABLE 13.3
AFTER-TAX LOSS MATRIX

Decision	Outcome			
	Fire		No fire	
1. Retain the risk	Insurable losses	$100,000		
	Noninsurable accidental losses	6,000		
	Worry	4,000	Worry	$4,000
		$110,000		$4,000
2. Retain the risk and introduce new safety measures	Insurable losses	$100,000		
	Noninsurable accidental losses	6,000		
	Worry	3,000	Worry	$3,000
	Cost of safety measures	3,000	Cost of safety measures	3,000
		$112,000		$6,000
3. Purchase insurance	Insurance premium	$ 5,000	Insurance premium	$5,000

Probabilities Not Estimated   Two objectives will be considered under the first category.

Case 1. Minimize the maximum potential loss during the period (minimax). The risk manager with this objective wants to be protected against the worst possible loss, regardless of the outcome. In those cases where for each decision the loss is at least as high for one outcome (in this case a fire) as for any of the other outcomes, a common situation in risk management problems, the decision rule is simple. Select the decision which for that outcome produces the smallest loss. In Table 13.3, if there is a fire, the smallest loss, assuming a fire, is associated with the decision to buy insurance. Because this objective is unduly conservative in most instances and because insurance premiums are almost always a small fraction of the maximum insured loss, this decision rule would almost always lead to the purchase of insurance. (For a person favoring this objective the worry values should probably be higher than those assumed in this example, thus reinforcing the strong tendency to purchase insurance.)

Case 2. Minimize the minimum potential loss during the policy period (minimin). This risk manager wants the lowest possible loss, no matter what outcome occurs. if, as is true in the present example, the losses for each decision are at least as low for one outcome as for any of the other outcomes, the decision rule is easy. Assume that the most favorable outcome, in this case no fire, occurs, and select the decision producing the minimum loss for that outcome. This optimistic risk manager will almost never select insurance. (For a person favoring this objective the worry values would probably be less than those assumed in this example, thus raising the likelihood of a retention decision.)

Probabilities Estimated   The minimax and minimin objectives described above are of little value to risk managers. They will almost always lead the risk manager either to purchase insurance if the business is a "minimaxer," or not to purchase insurance if the firm is a "miniminer." They also ignore any information the risk manager may have concerning the probability distribution of the outcomes.

Assume that the risk manager estimates the chance of loss to be $3/100$ without any additional safety measures and $1/100$ with the proposed new safety efforts. Two objectives that make use of this additional information are considered below.

Case 3. Minimize the losses associated with the most probable outcome. Although not too useful, this objective deserves notice because some people may consider it reasonable. If the risk manager believes that a fire is more likely than no fire, he or she should buy insurance. If the risk manager believes the opposite, he or she should retain the risk. In most real life situations involving one exposure unit such a person would decide against insurance because in such cases the probability of most insurable losses is less than one-half. The consequences, however, could be drastic if the loss, though less likely, occurs.

Case 4. Minimize the expected (tangible and intangible) losses during the policy period. The risk manager who minimizes the expected loss will, in the long run, have the smallest average loss. "In the long run" can be interpreted in two ways. First, if the same situation is repeated many times, the average loss per year (or other budget period) will be minimized. Second, if the risk manager follows the same rule in making many decisions within a given year (or other budget period) the average loss per decision made will also be minimized.

To attain this objective, the risk manager must first compute the expected losses associated with each possible decision. The expected-loss figure for a given decision is the sum of the products formed by multiplying each possible loss associated with that decision by the probability that the loss will occur. The risk manager then selects the decision that yields the minimum expected losses.

In the present case, the expected losses for each decision are as follows:

1 Retain the risk.
$\frac{3}{100}(\$110,000) + \frac{97}{100}(\$4,000) = \$7,180$
2 Retain the risk and introduce some new safety measures.
$\frac{1}{100}(\$112,000) + \frac{99}{100}(\$6,000) = \$7,060$
3 Purchase insurance.
$\frac{3}{100}(\$5,000) + \frac{97}{100}(\$5,000) = \$5,000$

In this situation the risk manager should purchase insurance, because this decision should in the long run produce the lowest expected losses. The risk manager will be proved right, however, only if his or her estimates of the probability distribution and the worry value are correct.

If the risk manager lacks confidence in these estimates, he or she should determine how sensitive the decision is to changes in these estimates. For example, suppose that the risk manager has some question about the $\frac{3}{100}$ probability estimate but is fairly confident that the probability of a fire lies between $\frac{2}{100}$ and $\frac{4}{100}$. The expected losses should be recalculated assuming these two probability values. If the decision to purchase insurance is still preferred, as it is in this case (assuming no major reduction in the worry factor), the risk manager should be more confident that this is the proper course of action. If the preferred decision changes, the risk manager should recognize this sensitivity and reexamine the probability estimates. It is hoped that he or she can narrow these estimates to a range within which the preferred decision does not change. Otherwise, the method can only show the consequences of the various decisions over that range, which should better equip the risk manager to make the decision on some other basis.

The worry value can be reexamined in the same way. For example, assume that the risk manager prefers to specify a range of worry values for each decision instead of a single value. More specifically, assume that for the retention decision the risk manager specifies a range of $3,000 to $5,000. There is no need to test the effect of a $5,000 worry value because increasing the worry value above $4,000 will clearly make the insurance decision even more attractive. On the other hand, reducing the worry value below $4,000 would reduce the relative attractiveness of the insurance decision. To test whether a $3,000 worry value would change the decision, the risk manager should recalculate the expected loss for retention assuming a $3,000 worry value. The answer is $6,180. Because $6,180 exceeds $5,000, the expected loss for the insurance decision, insurance is still the preferred alternative. Indeed, the worry value would have to be less than $1,820 before retention would become preferable to insurance. The reason is that until the worry value drops below $1,820 the expected loss is less for insurance than for retention.

Specifying the worry value at the time the loss matrix is constructed is extremely difficult. Fortunately, at least two easier ways exist to quantify the worry value. Both require the risk manager to calculate first the expected after-tax *tangible* losses associated with each decision. Under the first of these two methods the risk manager need never specify exactly his or her worry value. Instead he or she has to state only whether the worry value exceeds a specified amount which depends upon the expected after-tax tangible loss calculations. The method is best explained through an example. Assume the facts presented in Table 13.3 except that the worry values have not been specified. Because worry is present for each decision no matter what outcome occurs, the expected loss for each decision can be restated as the expected after-tax tangible loss for that decision plus the worry value for that decision as follows:

1 Retain the risk.
$\frac{3}{100}(\$106,000)$ + worry, assuming retention
$3,180 + worry, assuming retention
2 Retain the risk and introduce new safety measures.
$\frac{1}{100}(\$109,000)$ + $\frac{99}{100}(\$3,000)$ + worry, assuming new safety measures
$4,060 + worry, assuming new safety measures
3 Purchase insurance.
$5,000

Note that, except for the worry value, the expected loss is less for retention than for insurance. This is not surprising because, as explained on page 201, the insurance premium is equal to the insurer's estimate of the insured's expected (insured) losses plus a loading to cover the insurer's expected expenses and profit. One reason the risk manager may be willing to pay more than the expected loss for insurance is to eliminate uncertainty and the resulting worry. Other reasons are presented on page 206.

Given the expected losses presented above for the three possible decisions the worry method decision rule can be rephrased as follows:

Purchase insurance if (1) worry assuming retention is greater than $5,000 − $3,180, or $1,820, and (2) worry assuming new safety measures is greater than $5,000 − $4,060, or $940.

If (1) is satisfied but not (2), retain the risk but introduce the new safety measures.
If (2) is satisfied but not (1), simply retain the risk.

If neither (1) nor (2) is satisfied, a new rule is required. Both retention and retention plus new safety measures are preferred over insurance. The risk manager must choose, therefore, between these two tools. He or she should retain the risk and introduce new safety measures if worry assuming retention less worry assuming new safety measures is greater than $4,060 − $3,180, or $880.

Phrasing the decision rule in this way requires the risk manager to state only whether the worry value or the difference between two worry values will exceed a specified amount. This task is much easier than assigning a specific value to each worry factor. The specific values assigned earlier in this case led to the purchase of insurance because

$$(1) \quad \$4,000 > \$1,820$$

and

$$(2) \quad \$3,000 > \$940$$

The worry value assuming retention could be as low as $1,820 without changing the decision. The worry factor, assuming new safety measures, could be as low as $940.

A second way in which the worry value can be quantified, given the expected tangible loss for each decision, is as follows. The worry value is the *maximum* amount the risk manager would be willing to pay in addition to the expected loss, ignoring the worry value, to eliminate the annual fluctuations in his or her loss experience. Such a value can be estimated by starting with $1 and increasing this amount until the risk manager believes the appropriate value has been reached. To illustrate, for the retention decision the expected loss, ignoring the worry value, is $3,180. If the business experienced a $3,180 loss each year, the expected loss would also be $3,180 but there would be no fluctuations, no uncertainty, and no worry. In this instance, however, the loss next year, ignoring the worry value, will be either $106,000 or $0. The risk manager has indicated, through the $4,000 worry value, that to achieve certainty he or she would be willing to pay as much as $4,000 in addition to the $3,180 tangible expected loss instead of facing a possible $106,000 or $0 loss. In other words, the risk manager finds no difference between accepting the certainty of losing $7,180 each year, and facing each year the possibility of losing either $106,000 or $0.

The Worry Method

Of the four decision rules presented above, the fourth is clearly the most rational. Because of the important role the worry value plays in this method of making risk management decisions, it will be called the worry method. Later in this chapter this worry method will be applied to a second highly simplified example. In the next chapter the worry method will be applied to a more complicated set of decisions and outcomes.

The Worry Method and Why a Person Might Purchase Insurance   The worry method provides a useful vehicle for explaining why, assuming insurance is not compulsory, a person might purchase insurance instead of retaining the risk.

As stated earlier, in establishing the premium it will charge a prospective insured, an insurer first calculates the losses it expects to experience on the average on insureds with the same amount and quality of exposure. To this expected-loss estimate the insurer adds a loading for its expenses, profit, and contingencies. (For more on insurance pricing, see Chapter 28.) Consequently, before a person will purchase insurance, he or she must be willing to pay an insurer more than the insurer believes that person's insurable losses will average per year in the long run. Why might people be willing to do this?

1 Because they worry about fluctuations in accidental losses. For example, if the worst outcome happens the first year, the firm may have no opportunity to average losses in the long run. The reader should review the earlier discussion on the many factors that determine the worry value.[3]

2 Because they may experience some uninsurable accidental losses as a result of retaining insurable accidental losses.

3 Because tax factors may favor the purchase of insurance.

4 Because they estimate their expected losses to be higher than does the insurer.

5 Because they value the services provided by the insurer, such as safety inspections and loss adjustments.

To illustrate, consider the simple case presented above in which the risk manager, using the worry method, decided to purchase insurance. Assume that the insurer, like the risk manager, estimates the chance of a fire to be $3/100$. According to the insurer, then, the expected insurable losses are $3/100$ ($200,000) or $6,000. If the insurer requires 40 percent of the premium to cover its expenses and profits, 60 percent is available for losses. The required premium, therefore, is $6,000/0.60 or $10,000. Why is the risk manager willing to pay $4,000 ($2,000 after taxes) more than the firm's expected losses for insurance in this case?

1 Because the risk manager's worry value is $4,000; i.e., because he or she is willing to pay $4,000 just to be rid of the fluctuations in his or her loss experience

2 Because the risk manager's expected accidental losses are increased by the expected value of the after-tax increased credit costs; i.e., by $3/100$ ($6,000) or $180

If, in addition, the firm had only been able to deduct part of the retained losses from its taxable income, the decision rule would have more strongly favored insurance.[4]

The insurance decision would also have been more strongly preferred if the risk manager had estimated the chance of a fire to be $5/100$ instead of $3/100$.[5]

Finally, if the risk manager expected to hire an independent agency to provide the safety inspections that the insurer would normally provide, or if he or she expected losses to rise because of the absence of these inspections, the decision in favor of insurance would be stronger.

Retention might have been preferred under one or more of the following conditions: a lower worry value, no uninsurable accidental losses, or a lower estimated chance of loss. Recognizing the opportunity cost of insurance would also make it less attractive.

---

[3] See also the discussion later in this chapter on "The Capital Asset Pricing Model, Portfolio Theory, and the Worry Factor."

[4] See Chap. 11.

[5] Query: For what probability of a fire would the risk manager be indifferent? Answer: Slightly less than $1/100$. If, on the other hand, the risk manager had estimated the chance of loss to be $2/100$, the rule would still favor insurance because of the two factors noted above.

The reader should compare this analysis with the listing on page 206 of the factors affecting a retention decision.

The Worry Method and No Probability Information The worry method was presented as a method to be used when the risk manager knows or can estimate the probability distribution. In an important class of decisions the worry method can be used when no such information is available but the risk manager is willing to accept the information that can be derived from the premium he or she is quoted for insurance. For example, assume that in the illustration used earlier in this chapter the risk manager had only the information presented in Table 13.1 plus the fact that the insurer typically uses 60 percent of its premiums to pay losses. From this information the risk manager could find that the insurer believed his or her expected insurable losses to be 0.60 ($10,000) = $6,000. The expense and profit loading is $4,000. The question then becomes: Is the risk manager willing to pay at least $2,000 more after taxes (assuming a 50 percent rate) than the after-tax expected losses of $3,000 to eliminate his or her worry? The answer will depend upon the risk manager's assessment of the impact of a $200,000 potential loss before taxes upon the firm and the risk attitudes of its management. If the answer is yes, insurance should be purchased. If the answer is no, the risk manager should ask whether his or her worry value is close enough to $2,000 that the noninsurable accidental losses and loss of insurer services associated with retention favor insurance. Considering the opportunity costs of purchasing insurance would increase the worry value required to favor an insurance decision.

One final example will illustrate the use of the worry method in an insurance decision and the importance of the worry factor. Assume that a business has $10,000 to spend on automobile insurance. With this $10,000, it can purchase either (1) complete physical damage insurance on its fleet of trucks or (2) automobile liability insurance. The insurer involved assumes that it will use 70 percent of its premiums to pay losses. According to this insurer, therefore, the firm's expected losses for either type of insurance are 0.70 ($10,000) = $7,000. There are, let us assume, only three possible decisions: (1) Retain. (2) Purchase physical damage insurance. (3) Purchase liability insurance. Because the expected losses are the same for physical damage insurance and liability insurance, the choice between them depends upon how the worry values for these two decisions compare. Because the potential liability losses are so much larger than the potential physical damage, most risk managers would probably be much more worried about the liability losses and would purchase liability insurance before physical damage insurance. Whether they would purchase liability insurance instead of retaining the liability risk would depend upon whether their worry value would exceed the after-tax loading of $3,000. For most businesses it probably would, even after considering the opportunity costs of insurance but ignoring possible uninsurable accidental losses and the loss-control and loss-adjustment services of insurers.

Risk Management Tools and the Worry Value In the case used in this chapter, worry values were established for one risk control tool, loss control, and two risk financing tools, retention and insurance. How would worry values be affected if some other major tools had been included in the analysis?

Because combination and separation reduce the risk inherent in the situation, they should reduce the worry. The less important the annual fluctuations in the loss experience become, the less the risk manager should worry. This helps to explain why a risk manager deciding whether to retain the risk or insure against losses on, say, 1,000 cars is more likely to retain the risk than a risk manager with one car.

Noninsurance transfers, like insurance, should reduce the worry value to zero unless the protection is incomplete or some concern exists over the ability of the transferee to pay if the occasion arises.

Whose Worry Value?   Up to this point in the discussion, it has been assumed that in applying the worry method the risk manager establishes a worry value consistent with top management's worry value. In order to make this assessment, the risk manager must be thoroughly acquainted with the firm's operations and the philosophy of its top managers. Top management typically gives the risk manager considerable leeway in establishing the worry value, but the risk manager must remember that he or she is managing the firm's affairs, not his or her own. A risk manager who disagrees with the attitudes of top management toward pure risks should attempt to persuade them to his or her point of view. Top management, in turn, should recognize that the risk manager needs to be aware of their risk preferences. They should also recognize that, in practice, the personal preferences of risk managers are bound to affect the decisions made. Consequently, top management should hire risk managers whose attitudes are consistent with their own.

In establishing worry values, risk managers may be tempted to consider the impact on their own jobs of various outcomes. For example, they may reason that if a fire occurs after they have recommended retention, they may lose their jobs. Consequently, they may recommend insurance in this situation even though they believe the firm would be well advised to retain the risk. Top management can encourage better decision making by judging risk managers on how they make decisions, not on short-run results.[6]

The Worry Method and the Insurance Method   The worry method is consistent with the insurance method in the sense that one would expect the worry value to be the highest for losses covered by insurance in the essential category and lowest for losses covered by insurance in the available category.

A Second Illustration   In order to give the reader more practice in applying the worry method, a second illustration is presented below. In this case, the risk manager faces four possible outcomes and four possible decisions. The after-tax tangible loss matrix is:

[6] See Chap. 2.

Decision	Amount Probability	$0 .900	$1,000 .070	$10,000 .029	$100,000 .001
		Loss Outcomes			
Retain		$0	$1,000	$10,000	$100,000
$10,000 insurance ($550 premium)		550	550	550	90,550
$100,000 insurance ($700 premium)		700	700	700	700
$100,000 insurance, $1,000 deductible ($550 premium)		550	1,550	1,550	1,550

If the firm retains the risk, it must bear whichever of the four losses occurs. If it purchases $10,000 insurance, it must pay an after-tax premium of $550 and, in addition, if the loss exceeds $10,000, bear the excess loss. If it purchases $100,000 insurance, it must pay an after-tax premium of $700, but its position is certain. If it purchases deductible insurance, it must pay an after-tax premium of $550 and, in addition, bear the first $1,000 of any loss.

The figures in this table assume that there are no uninsurable accidental losses as a result of retaining insurable accidental losses, that the amount the insurance would cover is the tax basis value if the loss is retained, and that the firm will incur no expenses administering any partial or complete retention program. The table also assumes that there are no opportunity costs in purchasing insurance.

If the risk manager wants to minimize the expected tangible dollar loss, he or she should first calculate the expected dollar loss for each decision using the above matrix. For each decision each of the four possible losses is multiplied by the probability of its occurrence and the four products summed. The results are as follows:

Retain .900($0) + .070($1,000) + .029($10,000) + .001($100,000) = $460

$10,000 insurance .900($550) + .070($550) + .029($550) + .001($90,550) = $640

$100,000 insurance .900($700) + .070($700) + .029($700) + .001($700) = $700

$100,000 insurance, .900($550) + .070($1,550) + .029($1,550) + .001($1,550) = $650
$1,000 deductible

Given the assumptions under which this table was constructed, it is not surprising that retention minimizes the expected tangible dollar loss. The reasoning is important enough to be repeated once more. As long as the insurer charges more than the risk manager's estimate of the expected loss covered by the insurance, retention will always produce a lower long-run average cost. The reason is that the insurer will include in its premium an estimate of the expected loss plus an expense and profit loading. Unless the insurer's estimated expected loss is substantially less than the risk manager's estimate, the premium will be higher than the risk manager's estimated expected loss.

If the assumptions under which the table was prepared were revised to include, for example, some administrative expenses under the complete or partial retention decisions, the expected tangible loss under those decisions would increase. Whether this addition would change the preferred decision would depend upon the amount added. To illustrate, to make complete insurance preferable to retention, the average expenses would have to be more than $700 − $460, or $240. Including the opportunity cost of insurance would, of course, operate in the opposite direction.

Even if these assumptions are unchanged, however, the firm may wish to purchase some insurance because it would otherwise worry about the fluctuations in its accidental losses. For each possible decision, the dollar value of the worry associated with that decision should be added to the expected tangible dollar loss for that decision. The worry value can be measured in the two ways described earlier. First, the worry value can be assigned a specific dollar amount. To obtain this amount, for each decision the risk manager should ask whether he or she would be willing to pay at least $1 over the expected tangible dollar loss to be certain that the loss would be this $1 plus the expected tangible loss, instead of the losses possible under that decision. If the answer is yes, the risk manager should repeat the question for $2, $3, and so on until the answer is no. The highest amount for which the answer is yes is the worry value. To illustrate, for complete retention how much more than $460 is the risk manager willing to pay to lose that amount plus $460 each year instead of possible losses of $0, $1,000, $10,000, or $100,000? Assume that the highest amount the risk manager is willing to pay for certainty is $400 plus the $460 expected tangible loss. Under the $10,000 insurance option, the risk manager worries less, but because of the $90,000 uninsured loss possibility, is still willing to pay as much as $200 plus the $640 expected tangible loss for certainty. Because the complete insurance option itself converts uncertainty into certainty, there is no worry value. Finally, under the $1,000 deductible option, the risk manager worries about a $1,000 loss, but this loss would not be serious. Assume the worry value for this decision is only $30. Given these worry values, the expected losses including the worry values are as follows:

Retain	$460 + $400 = $860
$10,000 insurance	$640 + $200 = $840
$100,000 insurance	$700 + $ 0 = $700
$100,000 insurance, $1,000 deductible	$650 + $ 30 = $680

The favored decision under this set of worry factors is deductible insurance.

Note that many different sets of worry values would lead to the same decision. For example, if the retention worry value were $300 instead of $400, the preferred decision would still be deductible insurance. This observation leads to the second approach to measuring the worry value, which involves a series of paired comparisons. First, determine how large the worry value under each decision has to be to prefer the option presenting the least uncertainty. In this case, buy complete insurance instead of

1 retention if the worry value assuming retention is greater than $700 − $460 = $240
2 $10,000 insurance if the worry value assuming $10,000 insurance is greater than $700 − $640 = $60
3 deductible insurance if the worry value assuming deductible insurance is greater than $700 − $650 = $50

To make these decisions, the risk manager need not assign a specific value to the worry factor. Instead it is enough to state only whether the worry value exceeds the specified amount. If the worry value for all three decisions is more than the specified amount, the preferred decision is complete insurance. If the worry value for one, but only one, of the decisions is greater than the specified amount (this is the situation assuming the worry factors developed in the preceding paragraph), that decision is preferred over complete insurance. If the worry value for more than one of the decisions is greater than the specified amount, the process must be repeated using those decisions only. For example, suppose that the worry value for complete retention is less than $240, and for deductible insurance less than $50. Because deductible insurance reduces uncertainty, the risk manager should ask whether the worry assuming retention less the worry assuming deductible insurance is more than the difference between the expected tangible dollar losses for these two decisions; i.e., $650 − $460 or $190. If so, buy deductible insurance. If not retain.

If the assumptions underlying the construction of the loss matrix are changed, the losses in the matrix and the critical worry values would, of course, also change.

The Capital Asset Pricing Model, Portfolio Theory, and the Worry Factor
According to the capital asset pricing model (CAPM), which plays an important role in modern finance theory, in a perfect capital market stockholders with widely diversified portfolios face little or no uncertainty with respect to the pure loss exposures of the businesses whose stock they own.[7] The total risk associated with each firm's stock can be divided into systematic risk and unsystematic risk. Systematic risk is caused by factors that affect all securities simultaneously, but in varying degrees. The systematic risk of a security is measured by β. If β equals, say, 2, on the average the rate of return

---

[7] For more details see David Mayers and Clifford W. Smith, Jr., "On the Corporate Demand for Insurance," *The Journal of Business*, LV, no. 2 (April, 1982), pp. 281–296. The following discussion relies heavily on the Mayers-Smith article. See also Richard L. Meyer and Fred B. Power, "The Investment Values of Corporate Insurance," *The Journal of Risk and Insurance*, L, no. 1 (March, 1983), pp. 151–156 and a forthcoming McGraw-Hill textbook by Neil Doherty entitled *Corporate Risk Management: A Financial Exposition.*

on that security will rise or fall twice as much as the entire market's rate of return. If β equals, say, 0.5, on the average the rate of return on that security will rise or fall only half as much as the market rate of return. Unsystematic risk is caused by factors such as marketing mistakes, explosions, or theft, which tend to be peculiar to a firm or industry.[8] A stockholder can reduce the unsystematic risk associated with his or her portfolio by including in the portfolio a large number of stocks, i.e., by relying on the law of large numbers. According to this model, therefore, the worry value of stockholders would be too small to explain why the corporations they own buy or should buy insurance.

Many persons have questioned the validity of CAPM,[9] but it continues to command considerable support among finance theorists. Although CAPM theorists downgrade the worry factor of stockholders with diversified portfolios, they have suggested other reasons why businesses might buy insurance.

Owners who have most of their money invested in a closely held business are not able to diversify the unsystematic risk associated with their business. Thus, they do worry about their loss exposures and have this additional reason to investigate the purchase of insurance.

The demand for insurance is also strong among individuals with respect to their personal lives. Because they cannot sell shares in their human capital, they cannot handle the associated unsystematic risk through diversification. Human capital can be reduced in value through death, disability, or a liability suit. Individuals may also have a good share of their wealth in a few assets such as a home, personal property, and a car instead of diversified securities. Consequently, they may worry enough about their uncertainties to justify the purchase of insurance. They may also value the services provided by insurers in settling liability claims.

To explain why large corporations with diffuse ownership buy insurance, CAPM theorists advance other reasons.[10] First and foremost, equityholders who can diversify their holdings are not the only claimholders in a corporation. Employees, managers, customers, and suppliers also have financial interests. Because of the limited liability of stockholders the firm can shift only part of its total risk to these owners. Consequently, if the firm purchases no insurance, the other parties may worry about what will happen to them in case a severe loss occurs. As a result, employees and managers may demand higher salaries, customers may demand lower prices for the firm's products or services, and suppliers may demand higher prices for their products or services. The firm may find it less expensive to provide more security for these persons through the purchase of insurance and thus reduce their demands.

Other reasons why such a business might buy insurance include transaction costs associated with bankruptcy that may justify paying the insurer's expense and profit loading to avoid this possibility, comparative advantages insurers may possess in

---

[8] Some pure risks may also involve some systematic risk. For example, fire and theft losses vary to some extent with the state of the economy. See Meyer and Power, op cit., pp. 154–155. See also Doherty, op. cit.

[9] See, for example, Bruce D. Fielitz, "Modern Portfolio Theory: Where Do We Stand?' *The Wall Street Transcript*, Oct. 30, 1978, p. 52, 299.

[10] Mayers and Smith, op. cit.

controlling losses or administering claims, demands imposed by bondholders, and tax advantages.[11]

Regardless of its validity, CAPM serves a useful purpose in that it reminds us that the total risk (systematic and unsystematic) associated with the rate of return on a portfolio of assets depends not only upon the risk associated with each of the component assets, but also upon how each of these individual risks is correlated with the others. To use a highly simplified example, suppose that a business faces only two risks—those associated with fire damage to its property and those associated with its business earnings. If these two risks are independent of one another, the total risk of the portfolio is greater than if the firm had only one of these risks. If the two risks are not independent and fires always tend to occur when business earnings are low (i.e., the two variables are perfectly negatively correlated), the portfolio risk is much greater than if the firm had only one of these risks. On the other hand, if fires always tend to occur when business earnings are high (i.e., perfect positive correlation exists), the total risk may be very small. The relationship among the risks in a portfolio is seldom this perfect, but any tendency for the risks to move together or in opposite directions (i.e., partial correlation exists) will produce a different total risk than if independence is assumed. The case for insuring versus retaining a particular pure risk may thus be weakened or strengthened when its effect on the total portfolio risk is considered.

To simplify the discussion, this complicating relationship among the risks included in a portfolio has been ignored elsewhere in this chapter and the next. However, risk managers and other persons involved in decisions involving risk should remember that ideally the organization should manage all pure and speculative risks simultaneously. Risk managers, therefore, should be part of the team involved in all decisions that involve any pure risks. For the present, however, pure risks are likely to be handled separately with risk managers being involved only in speculative risk decisions that clearly involve major pure risks. In their separate handling of pure risks, however, risk managers should investigate the interrelationships among these pure risks. Pure risk management objectives should also be developed as part of the total (pure and speculative) risk management objectives of the organization.[12]

The Critical Probability Method

The final quantitative approach to be discussed in this chapter is the critical probability method. Though not limited to a decision between retention and insurance, it is most

---

[11] Brian G. M. Main, ''Corporate Insurance Purchases and Taxes,'' *The Journal of Risk and Insurance,* L, no. 2 (June, 1983), pp. 197–223.

Like stockholders, bondholders can diversify their holdings but bonds often require that property mentioned in a bond indenture deed be insured against certain property losses. See Mayers and Smith, op. cit., and Doherty, op. cit.

[12] For a valuable exchange of views on this point see the following: J. David Cummins, ''Risk Management and the Theory of the Firm,'' *The Journal of Risk and Insurance,* XLIII, no. 4 (December, 1976), pp. 587–609, and Brian G. M. Main, ''Risk Management and the Theory of the Firm: Comment'' and J. David Cummins, ''Risk Management and the Theory of the Firm: Author's Reply,'' *The Journal of Risk and Insurance,* L, no. 1 (March, 1983), pp. 140–150. See also Dongsae Cho, ''Integrated Risk Management Decision-Making: A Workers' Compensation Loss Exposure Case Study,'' *The Journal of Risk and Insurance,* L, No. 2 (June, 1983), pp. 281–300.

easily explained in this context. To apply this method the risk manager must be willing to estimate the probability distribution of the losses that can be insured. The risk manager then specifies some chance he or she is willing to take that, if the risk is retained, the actual after-tax losses[13] will exceed the after-tax premium saved by not buying the insurance. If the probability that the losses will exceed the premium savings exceeds this critical probability, the proper decision is to buy insurance.

For example, assume that the after-tax insurance premium would be $8,000 and the critical probability is 10 percent. Listed below are several probability distributions that might apply in this instance.

	After-tax losses	Probability distribution			
		A	B	C	D
	$ 0	.50	.40	.20	.30
	1,000	.30	.35	.30	.30
After-tax	5,000	.14	.16	.30	.25
premium					
savings					
$8,000					
	10,000	.05	.03	.14	.12
	50,000	.01	.03	.04	.02
	100,000	.00	.03	.02	.01

According to the critical probability method in its purest form, the risk manager would retain the risk under distributions A and B and insure under distributions C and D. The probabilities that are matched against the 10 percent critical probability are 6 percent for A, 9 percent for B, 20 percent for C, and 15 percent for D.

One would expect the critical probability to vary inversely with the worry value the risk manager would establish for retention under the worry method. A worrier would be willing to take only a small chance that the losses would exceed the premium savings.

In its purest form, the critical probability method considers only the probability that the losses will exceed the premium savings. To make a decision solely on this basis ignores other information available from the probability distribution. For example, although probability distributions A and B both suggest retention under the 10 percent rule, there is much less exposure to severe losses under A than under B. The risk manager might wish to supplement the 10 percent rule with, say, a 5 percent rule for losses of $50,000 or more. Additional supplementary rules can be established for other critical values. With the 10 percent rule for losses of $8,000 or more and the 5 percent rule for losses of $50,000 or more, only distribution A would favor retention.

---

[13] Insurable losses plus the noninsurable accidental losses and expenses that would not be incurred if the firm purchased insurance.

SOME KEY CONCEPTS

Essential insurance   Insurance that is either compulsory or covers potential losses that would threaten the continued survival of the firm.

Desirable insurance   Insurance that covers potential losses that would be financially serious but would not threaten the firm's survival.

Available insurance   Insurance that covers potential losses that would not be financially serious.

Loss matrix   A listing of the dollar losses associated with each possible risk management tool and each possible outcome. For example, a decision to retain would produce a loss of $10,000 if a $10,000 loss occurs. A decision to purchase complete insurance would produce a "loss" of the insurance premium no matter what the outcome may be. The original loss matrix should be converted to an after-tax basis and extended to include the intangible costs (worry caused by short-run uncertainty) as well as the tangible dollar losses.

Expected tangible loss method   A method that directs the risk manager to select the tool that would produce the lowest average tangible dollar outlay in the long run.

The worry method   A variation of the expected tangible loss method that directs the risk manager to select the tool that would minimize the average tangible dollar outlay in the long run plus the value that the risk manager assigns to any worry caused by the short-run uncertainty, if any, that remains.

Critical probability method   A method that tells a risk manager to buy insurance instead of retaining the exposure if the probability that the losses will exceed the premium savings exceeds a critical probability selected by the risk manager. Persons with high worry values will normally set low critical probabilities.

REVIEW QUESTIONS*

1 Under the insurance method for selecting the best combination of risk management tools, what criteria determine whether an insurance contract covering a particular type of loss is "essential," "desirable," or "available"?

2 Should the risk manager automatically buy all essential and desirable coverages and reject all available coverages? Explain your answer.

3 Prepare an abbreviated revised listing showing how each risk management tool might be used by a hypothetical department store.

4 Assume that a business owns one truck valued at $30,000. The firm can insure this truck against any physical damage to the truck for $500. The before-tax tangible loss matrix, assuming only two possible outcomes—total destruction or no damage, no noninsurable accidental losses, and only two possible decisions—retention or insurance—is as follows:

	Outcome	
Decision	Destruction	No Damage
Retain the risk	$30,000	$ 0
Purchase insurance	500	500

*Items in parentheses are answers.

   a Construct an after-tax tangible loss matrix assuming a marginal tax bracket of 50 percent.

   b What decision would the risk manager make under the minimax and minimin objectives? How useful are those objectives?

   c Assume that the risk manager estimates the probability of total destruction of the truck to be $\frac{1}{100}$.

     (1) What decision would the risk manager make if he or she decided to minimize the loss associated with the most probable outcome?

     (2) Assume a worry value of $200 and construct an after-tax loss (both tangible and intangible) matrix. What decision would the risk manager make if he or she wanted to minimize the expected losses during the policy period?

     (3) What is the minimum worry value that would lead to an insurance decision under the worry method? ($100)

     (4) If the worry value is $200, what is the minimum estimate of the probability of loss that would lead to an insurance decision? ($\frac{1}{300}$)

5 Assume that the business with the truck in question 4 faces the prospect of a $300,000 liability suit because of the operation of the truck. The probability of the loss occurring is $\frac{1}{1000}$. The premium cost of complete liability protection is $500.

   a Construct an after-tax tangible loss matrix assuming only two possible outcomes, two possible decisions, and a 50 percent tax bracket.

   b What is the minimum worry value that would lead to an insurance decision? ($100)

   c Why might the actual worry value be much higher in this instance than in the question 4 case?

6 a What are noninsurable accidental losses?

   b How do these losses affect insurance-retention decisions?

7 Insurers charge premiums that cover their estimates of the insured's expected losses plus an expense and profit loading. If their estimate is correct, in the long run insureds could save money by retaining the risk. Why does anyone buy insurance?

8 a A business is concerned about insuring three different types of exposures. In all three cases the expected loss is $10,000. In the first instance the annual losses seldom depart more than $500 from the expected loss. In the second case the annual variation may be as much as $20,000, and in the third case as much as $50,000. Other things being equal, for which situation would you expect the worry value associated with retention to be the highest? Why?

   b How is the law of large numbers related to the worry value?

9 In question 4 assume that for a cost of $200 annually some loss-control measure would reduce the chance of loss to $\frac{1}{300}$. The insurer agrees to reduce its premium to $350 if this measure is introduced. The new before-tax tangible loss matrix is as follows:

	Outcome	
Decision	**Destruction**	**No Damage**
Retain the risk	$30,000	$ 0
Retain the risk, loss control	30,200	200
Purchase insurance	500	500
Purchase insurance, loss control	550	550

   a Construct an after-tax tangible loss matrix.

   b Construct an after-tax loss (tangible and intangible) matrix assuming a worry value of $200 when the chance of loss is $1/100$ and $150 when the chance of loss is $1/300$.

   c What decision should the risk manager make using the worry method?

   d Suppose insurance were not available to cover this risk. Should the firm introduce the loss-control measure?

10 Whose worry value should the risk manager use in making a risk management decision?

11 A workers' compensation insurer will protect a firm against industrial injuries to its 100 employees for a premium of $30,000. It will cover all losses in excess of $2,000 per accident for a premium of $20,000.

   a What is the insurer's probable estimate of the firm's expected losses if it retains the entire risk? (between $18,000 and $21,000)

   b What is the insurer's probable estimate of expected losses the firm will retain if it purchases the deductible policy? (between $6,000 and $7,000)

   c Explain how you would use the worry method reasoning to determine whether the firm should retain the risk, purchase complete insurance, or purchase insurance with a deductible.

12 The capital asset pricing model implies that stockholders with widely diversified portfolios face little or no uncertainty with respect to the pure loss exposures of the businesses whose stock they own. If so, why might the corporations they own still be interested in purchasing insurance?

13 **a** Explain the critical probability method.

   b What critical probabilities might be considered in addition to the probability that the losses will exceed the premium savings?

   c How is this method related to the worry method?

SUGGESTIONS FOR ADDITIONAL READING

Allen, T. C., and R. M. Duvall: *A Theoretical and Practical Approach to Risk Management* (New York: The American Society of Risk Management, Inc., 1971).

Bickelhaupt, D. L.: *General Insurance* (11th ed.: Homewood, Ill.: Richard D. Irwin, Inc., 1983), chap. 3.

Carter, R. L., and N. A. Doherty (eds.): *Handbook of Risk Management* (London: Kluwer-Harrop Handbooks, 1974), part 5.

Denenberg, H. S., et al.: *Risk and Insurance* (2d ed., Englewood Cliffs, N.J.: Prentice-Hall, Inc., 1974), chap. 4.

Doherty, Neil A.: *Corporate Risk Management: A Financial Exposition* (New York: McGraw-Hill Book Company, forthcoming)

Financial Applications for Risk Management Decisions (San Rafael, Ca.: Firemen's Fund Insurance Companies and Risk Sciences Group, Inc., 1983).

Gaunt, L. D., and M. E. McDonald: *Examining Employers' Financial Capacity to Self-Insure Under Workmen's Compensation* (Atlanta, Ga.: Georgia State University College of Business Administration, 1977).

Greene, M. R., and J. S. Trieschmann: *Risk and Insurance* (6th ed., Cincinnati: South-Western Publishing Company Incorporated, 1984), chap. 2.

————, and O. N. Serbein: *Risk Management: Text and Cases* (2d ed., Reston, Va.: Reston Publishing Company, 1983), chap. 3.

Hammond, J. D. (ed.): *Essays in the Theory of Risk and Insurance* (Glenview, Ill.: Scott, Foresman and Company, 1968).

Mehr, R. I., and E. Cammack: *Principles of Insurance* (7th ed., Homewood, Ill.: Richard D. Irwin, Inc., 1980), chap. 20.

————, and B. A. Hedges: *Risk Management: Concepts and Applications* (Homewood, Ill.: Richard D. Irwin, Inc., 1974), chaps. 1, 2, and 13.

Rowe, William O.: *An Anatomy of Risk* (New York: John Wiley & Sons, Inc., 1977).

Schlaifer, Robert: *Analysis of Decisions under Uncertainty* (New York: McGraw-Hill Book Company, 1969).

————: *Introduction to Statistics for Business Decisions* (New York: McGraw-Hill Book Company, 1961).

Stephens, V. M., W. S. McIntyre, and J. P. Gibson: *Risk Financing: A Guide to Insurance Cash Flow* (Dallas: International Risk Management Institute, 1983, updated periodically).

Williams, C. A., Jr., G. L. Head, R. C. Horn, and G. W. Glendenning: *Principles of Risk Management and Insurance* (2d ed., Malvern, Pa.: American Institute for Property and Liability Underwriters, 1981), vol. 1, chaps. 4 and 5.

CHAPTER **14**

SELECTING THE PROPER
TOOLS: II

LEARNING OBJECTIVES

After you have completed this chapter, you should be able to:

1 Use the worry method to select the proper tool in more complicated problems.
2 Relate risk management to capital budgeting and vice versa.

INTRODUCTION

Chapter 13 described a variety of ways in which a risk manager might select the best risk management techniques to use in a given situation. Two highly simplified examples were used to illustrate the application of the worry method—the most useful of the quantitative approaches presented in that discussion. In this chapter the worry method will be applied to a more complicated, though still simplified, example. This chapter will also explore how capital budgeting, an important financial management technique, can be related to risk management. *Those readers who prefer to do so can skip this chapter without affecting their understanding of the remainder of the text.*

THE WORRY METHOD REVISITED

Under the worry method the risk manager selects the decision that in the long run will produce the lowest average annual losses. Included in those losses is a charge for the worry that the business will experience because it is concerned about fluctuations in its losses from year to year. This value is highly subjective, but one would expect it to be

260

higher when the losses in any year could cause severe financial problems for the firm. The following application is designed to shed further light on this method.

The Fact Situation

A risk manager of a medium-sized business must decide how to handle the potential property losses the firm may suffer because it owns one building with its contents in a suburban location. Liability and personnel losses associated with the property losses are considered so unlikely that they will be ignored in the analysis.

The firm's balance sheet shows assets of $500,000, liabilities of $300,000, and capital and retained earnings of $200,000. According to its operating statement, last year its sales were $400,000, its expenses $350,000, and its net income before taxes $50,000.

The probability distribution of losses during the coming year varies depending upon whether an automatic sprinkler is installed. The two probability distributions are as follows:

| | Probability | |
Losses	Without sprinkler	With sprinkler
$ 0	.700	.700
500	.150	.150
1,000	.100	.100
10,000	.040	.040
50,000	.007	.009
100,000	.002	.001
200,000	.001	.000

The risk manager must decide among eight courses of action:

1 Retain the risk.
2 Retain the risk; install an automatic sprinkler.
3 Purchase $50,000 insurance.
4 Purchase $50,000 insurance; install an automatic sprinkler.
5 Purchase $200,000 insurance with a $1,000 deductible.
6 Purchase $200,000 insurance with a $1,000 deductible; install an automatic sprinkler.
7 Purchase $200,000 insurance.
8 Purchase $200,000 insurance; install an automatic sprinkler.

Listed below are some additional assumptions:

1 The automatic sprinkler will cost $9,000 to install and $100 annually to maintain. The annual depreciation on the sprinkler, assuming a 30-year life span, is $300.
2 The premiums for the three possible insurance policies are as follows:

Insurance amount	Without sprinkler	With sprinkler
$ 50,000	$1,620	$1,620
200,000 ($1,000 deductible)	1,650	1,350
200,000	1,990	1,690

These premiums were calculated on the assumption that the insurer used the same probability distributions of losses and that it uses about two-thirds of its premiums to pay losses.

3 If the building and contents loss is either $100,000 or $200,000, the sprinkler system, valued at $9,000, is also destroyed.

4 Noninsurable accidental losses are limited to:

$2,000 for a $50,000 uninsured building and contents loss
$4,000 for a $100,000 uninsured building and contents loss
$6,000 for a $150,000 uninsured building and contents loss
$8,000 for a $200,000 uninsured building and contents loss

5 If the decision is to retain the risk, the risk manager will pay an independent safety inspector $100 to provide services otherwise provided by the insurer.

6 The firm can deduct from its taxable income 80 percent of the insurable accidental losses other than the loss of the sprinkler system and all the noninsurable accidental losses, the sprinkler costs, the loss of the sprinkler system, and the insurance premiums. The tax bracket is 50 percent. Capital gains on insurance recoveries in excess of the tax basis of property damaged or destroyed can be ignored because they will easily be offset by capital losses carried over from former years.

7 The opportunity costs of purchasing insurance are ignored.

The possible decisions, the possible building and contents losses, and the possible total losses to the firm associated with each possible decision-building and contents loss combination are summarized in Table 14.1. Except when the sprinkler system is destroyed, each total loss box contains the following calculation:

(Insurable accidental losses) $[1 - (0.80) (0.50)]$
+ (Noninsurable accidental losses) $(1 - 0.50)$
+ Worry value
+ [Costs of applying the risk management method (insurance premium, automatic sprinkler costs, or safety inspection costs)] $(1 - 0.50)$

Total loss

If the sprinkler system is destroyed, a $9,000 loss less a 50 percent tax saving is added to the after-tax insurable accidental loss unless the remaining insurance is large enough to cover this loss.

TABLE 14.1

TOTAL LOSSES FOR EACH DECISION-BUILDING AND CONTENTS LOSS COMBINATION

	Building and contents loss						
Amount	$ 0	$ 500	$1,000	$10,000	$50,000	$100,000	$200,000
Probability:							
No sprinkler	.700	.150	100	.040	.007	.002	.001
Sprinkler	.700	.150	.100	.040	.009	.001	.000
Decision:							
1. Retain the risk	$ 0	$ 300	$ 600	$ 6,000	$30,000	$ 60,000	$120,000
	0	0	0	0	1,000	2,000	4,000
	1,000	1,000	1,000	1,000	1,000	1,000	1,000
	50	50	50	50	50	50	50
	$1,050	$1,350	$1,650	$ 7,050	$32,050	$ 63,050	$125,050
2. Retain the risk; install sprinkler	$ 0	$ 300	$ 600	$ 6,000	$30,000	$ 64,500	$124,500
	0	0	0	0	1,000	2,000	4,000
	500	500	500	500	500	500	500
	250	250	250	250	250	250	250
	$ 750	$1,050	$1,350	$ 6,750	$31,750	$ 67,250	$129,250
3. Purchase $50,000 insurance	$ 0	$ 0	$ 0	$ 0	$ 0	$ 30,000	$ 90,000
	0	0	0	0	0	1,000	3,000
	200	200	200	200	200	200	200
	810	810	810	810	810	810	810
	$1,010	$1,010	$1,010	$ 1,010	$ 1,010	$ 32,010	$ 94,010
4. Purchase $50,000 insurance; install sprinkler	$ 0	$ 0	$ 0	$ 0	$ 0	$ 34,500	$ 94,500
	0	0	0	0	0	1,000	3,000
	50	50	50	50	50	50	50
	1,010	1,010	1,010	1,010	1,010	1,010	1,010
	$1,060	$1,060	$1,060	$ 1,060	$ 1,060	$ 36,560	$ 98,560
5. Purchase $200,000 insurance, $1,000 deductible	$ 0	$ 300	$ 600	$ 600	$ 600	$ 600	$ 600
	0	0	0	0	0	0	0
	20	20	20	20	20	20	20
	825	825	825	825	825	825	825
	$ 845	$1,145	$1,445	$ 1,445	$ 1,445	$ 1,445	$ 1,445
6. Purchase $200,000 insurance $1,000 deductible; install sprinkler	$ 0	$ 300	$ 600	$ 600	$ 600	$ 600	$ 4,500
	0	0	0	0	0	0	0
	20	20	20	20	20	20	20
	875	875	875	875	875	875	875
	$ 895	$1,195	$1,495	$ 1,495	$ 1,495	$ 1,495	$ 5,395
7. Purchase $200,000 insurance	$ 0	$ 0	$ 0	$ 0	$ 0	$ 0	$ 0
	0	0	0	0	0	0	0
	0	0	0	0	0	0	0
	995	995	995	995	995	995	995
	$ 995	$ 995	$ 995	$ 995	$ 995	$ 995	$ 995
8. Purchase $200,000 insurance; install sprinkler	$ 0	$ 0	$ 0	$ 0	$ 0	$ 0	$ 4,500
	0	0	0	0	0	0	0
	0	0	0	0	0	0	0
	1,045	1,045	1,045	1,045	1,045	1,045	1,045
	$1,045	$1,045	$1,045	$ 1,045	$ 1,045	$ 1,045	$ 5,545

The Analysis

The expected losses under each of the eight decisions is as follows:

1 Retain	$1,860
2 Retain; sprinkler	1,440
3 $50,000 insurance	1,165
4 $50,000 insurance; sprinkler	1,096
5 $200,00 insurance, $1,000 deductible	980
6 $200,000 insurance, $1,000 deductible; sprinkler	1,030
7 $200,000 insurance	995
8 $200,000 insurance; sprinkler	1,045

The favored course of action is to purchase $200,000 insurance with a $1,000 deductible. A close second is a decision to purchase complete insurance. The deductible insurance decision is favored because the risk manager is not too worried about retaining losses of $1,000 or less but is quite concerned about large losses. The after-tax premium would be reduced $150 if an automatic sprinkler were installed, but this installation and subsequent maintenance would cost, after taxes, $200 a year.[1] The least favored decision is complete retention because of the large worry factor, the noninsurable accidental losses, and the higher probabilities of larger losses without a sprinkler.

As noted earlier, the worry value is highly subjective and difficult to quantify. Under the alternative approach discussed in Chapter 13, it is not necessary to specify exactly the worry value for each decision. The risk manager need only state whether the worry value exceeds or is less than a specified amount. For example, if the worry associated with each decision had not been valued in the loss table, the expected loss values would have been as follows:

1 Retain	$ 860 + W1
2 Retain; sprinkler	940 + W2
3 $50,000 insurance	965 + W3
4 $50,000 insurance; sprinkler	1,046 + W4
5 $200,000 insurance, $1,000 deductible	960 + W5
6 $200,000 insurance, $1,000 deductible; sprinkler	1,010 + W6
7 $200,000 insurance	995 + $0
8 $200,000 insurance; sprinkler	1,045 + $0

Decision 8 can be eliminated because its expected loss is more than Decision 7, the only other decision for which the worry value is 0. Decisions 3, 4, and 6 can also be eliminated because Decision 5 should be favored over these three alternatives unless W_5 is greater than W_3 + ($965 − $960), W_4 + ($1,046 − $960), or W_6 + ($1,010 − $960), which would seem unlikely. Consequently worry values need be compared only for decisions 7, 5, 1, and 2. Decision 7 should be preferred if

---

[1] If the risk manager looks beyond the current year, he or she may reason that because of inflation the premium savings may exceed the annual sprinkler costs in a few years.

$$W_5 > \$995 - \$960 = \$35$$
$$W_1 > \$995 - \$860 = \$135$$
and
$$W_2 > \$995 - \$940 = \$45$$

If, as Table 14.1 assumed, $W_5 < \$35$, $W_1 > \$135$, and $W_2 > \$45$, Decision 7 should be favored over Decisions 1 and 2 but not Decision 5. Decision 5, therefore, should be the preferred decision. To select the preferred approach, however, the risk manager does not have to state, as does Table 14.1, that W_5 is exactly $20, W_1 is exactly $1,000, and W_2 is exactly $500.

The other approach that may help to value the worry factor is to ask for each decision how much the risk manager would pay in addition to the expected loss, ignoring the worry factor, to eliminate the annual fluctuation in losses. For example, under Decision 1, what is the maximum amount the risk manager would be willing to pay in addition to the $860 expected tangible loss to experience $860 + W_1$ each year instead of annual losses varying from $50 to $124,050?

Although this case is more complicated than the one used to illustrate the worry method in Chapter 13, it is still far less complicated than real life situations. Preparing the loss table in more realistic cases can be a frustrating, demanding task. On the other hand, it is also highly instructive and rewarding. With experience the risk manager should begin to sense which features of the table are most important and which ones can be omitted. In more conventional approaches the risk manager generally simplifies the problem in this way, but risk managers are seldom so careful in determining what factors can be omitted and what relative importance should be attached to the remaining factors.

CAPITAL BUDGETING

Capital budgeting is the process financial managers use to decide whether to make long-term (more than one year) investments such as the purchase of a machine, the construction or purchase of a new building, or the leasing of a fleet of automobiles. Before exploring the relationship of risk management to capital budgeting, the essentials of the capital budgeting process will be explained briefly below using a highly simplified example.[2]

First, the cash flows associated with each investment under consideration must be determined. For example, assume that the business is considering the purchase of two buildings. Building A would cost $200,000, building B, $180,000. Both buildings would have a useful life of 20 years with no salvage value. The annual straight-line depreciation, therefore, would be $10,000 for building A, $9,000 for building B. The $200,000 cash investment in building A, it will be assumed, will generate annual *cash* revenues of $100,000 and annual *cash* expenses, excluding taxes, of $44,000. Taxes

---

[2] Capital budgeting is explained in most, if not all, financial management texts and many accounting texts. See, for example, L. D. Schall and C. W. Haley, *Introduction to Financial Management* (3d ed., New York: McGraw-Hill Book Company, 1983), chaps. 7 and 8.

depend upon accounting profits that recognize depreciation and other *noncash* expenses and some *noncash* revenues. To simplify the example, taxable income will be assumed to equal cash revenue minus cash expenses minus depreciation, which is the major noncash item. Assuming a tax rate of 50 percent, the tax expense is 0.50 ($100,000 − $44,000 − $10,000) or $23,000. Consequently the net *cash* inflow per year from building A would be $100,000 − $44,000 − $23,000, or $33,000. The $180,000 investment in building B would generate annual cash revenues of $94,000 and annual cash expenses, excluding taxes, of $39,000. The taxes would be 0.50 ($94,000 − $39,000 − $9,000), or $23,000. The net *cash* inflow would be $94,000 − $39,000 − $23,000, or $32,000.

Second, the financial manager must select some measure of profitability for determining whether either of these buildings is a good investment and, if both are acceptable and funds are limited, which is the better investment of the two. Two methods that can be used to make this selection are the internal rate of return and net present value. Usually these two methods lead to the same decisions.[3] Because they both take into account the time value of money, financial theorists prefer them over the accounting rate of return and payback period methods, which do not. In practice, however, the latter two methods are often preferred because of their simplicity.

Under the internal rate of return method, the financial manager calculates the discount rate that would equate the present value of the net cash inflow with the amount of the investment. For building A, what discount rate makes the present value of $33,000 payable at the end of each year[4] for 20 years equal $200,000? According to tables found in many financial handbooks and financial management texts, the present value of $1 received annually at the end of each year for 20 years is $6.259, assuming a 15 percent discount rate, and $5.929, assuming a 16 percent rate. If $33,000 is received annually instead of $1, the corresponding present values for these two interest rates are $33,000 (6.259) = $206,547 and $33,000 (5.929) = $195,657. Since $200,000 lies between these two values, the rate of return is between 15 and 16 percent. By linear interpolation the return is 15.6 percent.[5]

A more direct way to calculate this rate of return is to determine the present value of $1 that will produce a present value of $200,000 for the $33,000 paid annually at the end of each year for 20 years. For example, $200,000/$33,000 = $6.061, which lies between $6.259, the 15 percent return value, and $5.929, the 16 percent return value. The exact return can be determined by linear interpolation.

For building B the rate of return that equates the present value of a net cash inflow of $32,000 a year for 20 years with an initial investment of $180,000 is 17.0 percent.

If the rate of return on either of these investments is less than the cost of capital (the rate the firm must pay for the most desirable mix of funds for capital expenditures) or some other minimum return established by the firm, the investment is not worthwhile. If the rate of return is equal to or exceeds this minimum rate of return and adequate funds are available, the investment is acceptable. If the firm facing the building

[3] For exceptions, see Schall and Haley, op. cit., p. 229.
[4] A simplifying assumption.

[5] $15\% + \dfrac{\$206,547 - \$200,000}{\$206,547 - \$195,657}\% = 15.6\%$

decision demands at least a 12 percent return, both buildings A and B would satisfy this criterion. However, if only limited funds are available for long-term investments, making a choice necessary among acceptable proposals, the rates of return on the two competing proposals must be compared to determine which expenditures would be most profitable. Building B would be preferred because its rate of return (17.0 percent) exceeds that of building A (15.6 percent).

In determining which proposals would be most profitable one should also consider the risk or variation in the possible outcomes. If two proposals are expected to yield the same return, the one with the lower risk should be favored. If the returns and the risks differ, the financial manager must determine the extra return required from the proposal with the higher risk. For the present example it will be assumed that the risk, excluding pure risk, is the same for both buildings.

Under the net present value method, the financial manager calculates the present value of the net cash inflows, assuming the minimum acceptable rate of return. This present value is divided by the initial investment to determine a profitability index. The proposals are then ranked according to these indices. (If the index is less than unity, the proposal is clearly unacceptable.) For the two buildings being considered the profitability indices are as follows:

$$\text{Building A:} \quad \frac{\$33,000 \text{ (present value of \$1 received annually for 20 years, 12 percent discount rate)}}{\$200,000}$$

$$= \frac{\$33,000 \ (7.469)}{\$200,000} = 1.23$$

$$\text{Building B:} \quad \frac{\$32,000 \ (7.469)}{\$180,000} = 1.33$$

As is usually the case, the net present value method produces the same ranking as the internal rate of return method. Building B is preferred. If the risks on the two buildings had differed, a higher minimum rate of return could be used to calculate the net present value for the building with the higher risk.

Under the accounting rate of return method the after-tax *accounting* profit is divided by the average amount invested. With straight-line depreciation this average investment is half the initial investment. For these two buildings the accounting rates of return are as follows:

$$\text{Building A:} \quad \frac{\$100,000 - \$44,000 - \$10,000 \text{ depreciation} - \$23,000}{\$200,000/2}$$

$$= \frac{\$23,000}{\$100,000} = 23.0\%$$

$$\text{Building B:} \quad \frac{\$94,000 - \$39,000 - \$9,000 \text{ depreciation} - \$23,000}{\$180,000/2}$$

$$= \frac{\$23,000}{\$90,000} = 25.6\%$$

B is preferred because it yields a higher accounting rate of return (which is substantially higher than its more nearly theoretically correct internal rate of return). If the risks had differed, the building with the higher risk would not be preferred unless its rates of return exceeded that of the other building by some specified amount determined by the financial manager.

Finally, under the payback method the firm calculates how long it will take to recover its initial investment. The initial investment divided by the annual net cash inflow equals this time period. For the two buildings:

$$A: \frac{\$200,000}{\$ 33,000} = 6.1 \text{ years}$$

$$B: \frac{\$180,000}{\$ 32,000} = 5.6 \text{ years}$$

Building B would return the firm's investment in a shorter time. If the risks had differed, the building with the higher risk would have been expected to return the investment within a shorter period. The net cash inflows after the payback period is over are ignored in this analysis.

As stated earlier, the latter two methods often produce different rankings than the first two methods.

Throughout this discussion it has been assumed that the net cash inflow is the same each year. In practice this is often not the case. When the inflow differs over time, the mechanics are more complicated but the concept is the same. The four methods are also more likely to produce different rankings.

Relationship to Risk Management

Because most risk management decisions do not involve any long-term investment, capital budgeting has limited, though important, applicability to risk management. There are two occasions on which capital budgeting and risk management should be closely related.[6] First, when capital budgeting is used to decide among long-term investment opportunities, risk management considerations should *always* be included in the process. Furthermore, the decision on the long-term project should include an initial choice among risk management techniques. Second, some risk management techniques, such as the installation of an automatic sprinkler, involve a long-term investment that can be evaluated using standard capital budgeting techniques. In addition, in many risk management decisions, though there is no long-term investment, the timing of the cash outflows is important. That set of risk management tools is best which minimizes the present value of the cash outflows plus the worry value.

---

[6] For a more complete discussion of capital budgeting and risk management, see George L. Head, "A Capital Budgeting Approach to Risk Management Decisions," unpublished presentation at the August, 1974, annual meeting of the American Risk and Insurance Association. Dr. Head was the first to propose such an approach in *Topical Outline, RM 54, Structure on the Risk Management Process, December 1972 Examination* (Bryn Mawr, Pa.: Insurance Institute of America, 1972).

Although this approach is not capital budgeting, it is a close relative. All of these uses are explored below.

Decisions on Long-Term Projects A typical discussion of capital budgeting either ignores pure risks or assumes that the firm purchases insurance and includes the premium among the cash expenses. Ignoring pure risk *overstates* the internal rate of return, because accidental losses may occur and reduce the profitability of the proposed investment. Even if these losses do not occur, their expected value and worry about the annual fluctuation in the actual losses should be explicitly included in the analysis. This concept is explained further below. In addition to lowering the rate of return on all proposals, including these potential accidental losses in the analysis may change the priority rankings.

If the financial manager assumes that the firm will purchase insurance, and insurance is not the best risk management technique for one or more of the proposed investments, he or she is *understating* the internal rate of return that could be realized on that proposal. The financial manager may also be ranking the proposals incorrectly.

To illustrate the effect of pure-risk considerations, let us return to the capital budgeting decision between building A and building B. To emphasize the concept involved, the facts will be highly simplified. First, it will be assumed that only accidental property losses need to be considered. For building A the expected annual after-tax property losses are $2,000; for building B, $5,000. Building A is a fire-resistive structure with automatic sprinklers and other safety features. Building B is a frame structure with no sprinkler system.

Listed in Table 14.2 are the risk management techniques that can be applied to building A and building B together with, for each technique, (1) the expected after-tax cost of retained accidental losses,[7] (2) the value the risk manager assigns to the worry that the firm will experience because the actual retained losses will fluctuate around this expected value, and (3) the after-tax cost of applying the risk management technique. The worry values can be estimated by asking for each building-decision combination the maximum amount the risk manager would be willing to pay in addition to the expected after-tax cost of retained losses and the after-tax cost of applying the specified technique in order to eliminate the annual fluctuations in the firm's loss experience. To illustrate, for the building A-retention combination the expected after-tax cost of the retained losses is $2,000; it costs nothing to apply the technique. What is the maximum amount the risk manager is willing to pay to lose that amount plus $2,000 each year instead of losses that may vary from zero to the maximum possible loss? According to Table 14.2 this worry value is $1,500. The worry value is greatest for complete retention, much smaller when the worst possible loss is $1,000 under the deductible insurance, and zero when complete insurance eliminates the annual fluctuations. Installing a sprinkler in building B is assumed to reduce both the expected losses and the worry if the firm retains the risk. The worry

---

[7] Level costs each year have been assumed to simplify the explanation. In practice the expected accidental losses may decline as the building ages and its value declines. Inflation may counteract or more than offset this decline.

TABLE 14.2

	Building A			Building B		
Technique	Expected after-tax cost of retained losses	Worry value	After-tax cost of applying technique	Expected after-tax cost of retained losses	Worry value	After-tax cost of applying technique
1. Retention	$2,000	$1,500	—	$5,000	$5,000	—
2. Complete insurance	—	—	$2,500 premium	—	—	$6,500 premium
3. Insurance, $1,000 deductible	$400	$50	$1,900 premium	$700	$50	$5,400 premium
4. Retention plus sprinkler in building B	Not applicable			$4,000	$2,500	Installation cost $10,000, 20 year useful life, no salvage, annual maintenance cost $100.
5. Complete insurance plus sprinkler in building B	Not applicable			—	—	Installation cost $10,000, 20 year useful life, no salvage, annual maintenance cost $100. $5,200 premium
6. Insurance, $1,000 deductible plus sprinkler in building B	Not applicable			$700	$50	Installation cost $10,000, 20 year useful life, no salvage, annual maintenance cost $100. $4,000 premium

value is reduced because large losses become much less likely. Because the sprinkler system will have no effect on small losses, the expected after-tax cost of the retained losses and the worry value are the same for the two deductible insurance options—with and without a sprinkler. The premium for both complete and deductible insurance would be reduced by a sprinkler.

Because the preferred investment and risk management techniques are to be selected jointly, there are nine possible combinations to be considered under the capital budgeting process instead of two:

Building A, retention
Building A, complete insurance
Building A, deductible insurance

77

777777777777777777

Building B, retention
Building B, complete insurance
Building B, deductible insurance
Building B, retention and sprinkler
Building B, complete insurance and sprinkler
Building B, deductible insurance and sprinkler

For the first six combinations, the investment amount remains unchanged from the investment in the building, but the annual net cash inflows and the accounting profits are reduced by the expected loss, including the worry value, for each technique and building shown in Table 14.2.[8] For the sprinkler and retention-building B combination, the installation cost of the sprinkler, $10,000, is added to the building investment; the net cash inflow is reduced by $7,100, the expected loss shown for that combination in Table 14.2, less the $500 sprinkler depreciation item, or $6,600. The accounting profit is reduced by $7,100. For the sprinkler and complete insurance-building B

[8] The calculation is as follows:

Combination	Investment	Net cash inflow	Accounting profit
Building A, retention	$200,000	$33,000 − $ 3,500 = $29,500	$23,000 − $ 3,500 = $19,500
Building A, complete insurance	$200,000	$33,000 − $ 2,500 = $30,500	$23,000 − $ 2,500 = $20,500
Building A, deductible insurance	$200,000	$33,000 − $ 2,350 = $30,650	$23,000 − $ 2,350 = $20,650
Building B, retention	$180,000	$32,000 − $10,000 = $22,000	$23,000 − $10,000 = $13,000
Building B, complete insurance	$180,000	$32,000 − $ 6,500 = $25,500	$23,000 − $ 6,500 = $16,500
Building B, deductible insurance	$180,000	$32,000 − $ 6,150 = $25,850	$23,000 − $ 6,150 = $16,850
Building B, retention and sprinkler	$190,000	$32,000 − $ 6,600 = $25,400	$23,000 − $ 7,100 = $15,900
Building B, complete insurance and sprinkler	$190,000	$32,000 − $ 5,300 = $26,700	$23,000 − $ 5,800 = $17,200
Building B, deductible insurance and sprinkler	$190,000	$32,000 − $ 5,150 = $26,850	$23,000 − $ 5,650 = $17,350

combination, the $10,000 sprinkler installation cost is added to the building investment; the net cash inflow is reduced by $5,800 less the $500 depreciation item, or $5,300. The accounting profit is reduced by $5,800. For the sprinkler and deductible insurance-building B combination, the $10,000 sprinkler installation cost is added to the building investment; the net cash flow is reduced by $5,650 less the $500 depreciation, or $5,150. The accounting profit is $5,650.

For the nine possible combinations, the results under the four profitability measures are shown below.

	Building A			**Building B**					
Method	Reten-tion	Com-plete insur-ance	Deduc-tible insur-ance	Reten-tion	Com-plete insur-ance	Deduc-tible insur-ance	Sprin-kler, reten-tion	Sprin-kler, insur-ance	Sprin-kler, deduc-tible insur-ance
Internal rate of return	13.6%	14.2%	14.3%	10.6%	12.9%	13.2%	12.0%	12.8%	12.9%
Net present value (pro-fitability index)	1.10	1.14	1.14	.91	1.06	1.07	1.00	1.05	1.06
Accounting rate of return	19.5%	20.5%	20.6%	14.4%	18.3%	18.7%	16.7%	18.1%	18.3%
Payback period in years	6.8	6.6	6.5	8.2	7.1	7.0	7.4	7.1	7.1

Under all four profitability measures, building A with deductible insurance is the preferred investment. Complete retention would make building B a poor investment, because the internal rate of return would be less than the 12 percent minimum required. For building B, deductible insurance is the preferred risk management technique. The sprinkler-deductible insurance option is less attractive because the rate of return on the sprinkler installation (the $1,100 annual premium reduction less than $100 annual sprinkler maintenance cost of an investment of $10,000) is only 7.6 percent.

This capital budgeting procedure has the advantage that it will be familiar to financial managers, and it emphasizes the relationship between financial management and risk management.

Risk Management Decisions Most risk management decisions do not involve a separate investment such as the construction of a new plant, addition to an existing plant, purchase of a new machine, leasing of a fleet of automobiles, or expansion into a new product line. Instead the plant, machine, fleet, or product line already exists and the question is how to manage the pure risks associated with the property, people, and activities they encompass. The best decision a year or so ago may not be the best today because of changes in the financial structure of the firm, its management philosophy, insurance premiums, insurance coverages, effectiveness and cost of loss-control techniques, and numerous other factors.

In these situations, capital budgeting has more limited uses. Some risk management techniques, however, do involve long-term investments. Loss-control programs in particular often require expenditures that are expected to yield long-term benefits. Examples are expenditures for the installation of automobile sprinklers, safety guards on machinery, or fire doors. It is appropriate to judge the desirability of these long-term investments by the capital budgeting process.

Consider the sprinkler-installation possibility in the two-buildings example. Assume that the firm already owned building B, was retaining the risk, and was considering the installation of a sprinkler. For an initial investment of $10,000, over its useful life the sprinkler would generate an annual cash inflow of $1,000 through a reduction in the expected after-tax cost of retained losses, a $2,500 inflow through a reduction in the worry value, and a $100 outflow in after-tax maintenance costs. The annual net cash inflow, therefore, would be $3,400. The estimated internal rate of return on this investment is almost 34 percent. It is clear why the sprinkler-retention option in the earlier example was so much more attractive than retention alone.

Suppose the firm had already decided to purchase insurance. Would installing a sprinkler in addition be a good investment? The $10,000 investment would create a cash inflow of $1,300 through a reduction in the after-tax insurance premiums, and a $100 outflow in after-tax maintenance costs. The annual net cash inflow is $1,200, producing an internal rate of return of about 10.3 percent, which is below the minimum acceptable return.[9] This finding explains why complete insurance produced a slightly higher return in the preceding calculation than the sprinkler-insurance combination.

If none of the risk management tools involves a long-term investment, capital budgeting per se is not applicable because there is no investment on which to calculate an internal rate of return or a profitability index. However, it frequently happens that the timing of expenditures may vary substantially, making the cash flow concept relevant. For example, an insurance premium may have to be paid immediately, but if the insured retains the risk it may expect to incur some expenses immediately, pay no losses until at least six months later, and spread payments on all losses over a twelve-month period. In such a case, the present value of the cash outflow under the insurance decision, allowing some rate of return on invested assets, should be compared with the present value of the cash outflow under retention plus the worry value associated with retention. The risk manager should select the combination of tools that produces the smallest present value. The reader should compare this discussion with the discussion of opportunity costs on page 203.

---

[9] As noted in footnote 1, this reasoning ignores the effect of inflation. If the sprinkler continued to reduce the insurance premium by 20 percent over the 20-year period and premiums rose, the return could be much higher.

A CONCLUDING NOTE

These two chapters have discussed an insurance approach to selecting the proper tool and several quantitative approaches. Many other approaches exist or are being developed.[10] There is no best method, the choice depending primarily upon the data available and the abilities and interests of the risk manager. Quantitative methods, however, have increased in importance and should become more popular in the future.

Finally, humanitarian or corporate-image considerations have been ignored throughout this discussion, but they are extremely important. For example, a firm may decide to install safety guards on a machine to save lives or to project a favorable corporate image even though strictly (shortsighted?) financial considerations would not justify such an expenditure.

SOME KEY CONCEPTS

Capital budgeting A process used to determine whether to make long-term (more than one-year) investments.

Internal rate of return method A capital budgeting method under which the financial manager first calculates the discount rate that would equate the present value of the net cash inflow with the amount of the investment. If this discount rate is less than the firm's cost of capital or some other desired minimum return, the investment is not worthwhile. If the discount rate equals or exceeds this desired minimum return, the investment may be worthwhile but its internal rate of return must be compared with the corresponding returns on other possible investments.

REVIEW QUESTIONS

1 For the firm whose balance sheet and operating statement data are presented in Chapter 30, assume the following probability distribution of liability losses arising out of its premises and operations.

Potential loss	Probability
$ 0	.8500
1,000	.1200
10,000	.0250
50,000	.0045
500,000	.0005

---

[10] For a sample of these approaches, see the following articles: J. M. Cozzolino, "A Method for the Evaluation of Retained Risk" *Journal of Risk and Insurance*, vol. XLV, no. 3 (September, 1978), pp. 449–471; J. David Cummins, "Risk Management and the Theory of the Firm," *Journal of Risk and Insurance*, vol. XLIII, no. 4 (December, 1976), pp. 587–609; James V. Davis, "Determining a Firm's Loss-Retention Level," *Risk Management*, vol. XXV, no. 11 (November, 1978), pp. 48–49; Michael L. Smith, "Applying Risk-Return Analysis to Deductible Selection Problems: A Mathematical Approach," *Journal of Risk and Insurance*, vol. XLIII, no. 3 (September, 1976), pp. 377–392; Harris Schlesinger, "The Optimum Level of Deductibility in Insurance Contracts," *The Journal of Risk and Insurance*, vol. XLVIII, no. 3 (September, 1981), pp. 465–481; and Robert J. Eck, "An Economic Analysis of Insured Retention," *Risk Management*, vol. XXX, no. 5 (May, 1983), pp. 20–28. See also *Financial Applications for Risk Management Decisions* (San Rafael, Calif.: Fireman's Fund Insurance Companies and Risk Sciences Group, Inc., 1983) and Appendix E of this text on "The Expected Utility Approach to Selecting Risk Management Techniques."

Further assume that there are four possible insurance decisions:

Insurance amount		
Policy limit	**Deductible**	**Premium**
No insurance		$ 0
$ 10,000	$ 0	600
500,000	1,000	1,000
500,000	0	1,200

  a Prepare an after-tax tangible loss matrix.
  b Calculate the expected tangible losses under each of the four possible insurance decisions.
  c Instead of estimating exactly the worry value for each decision, show how you would compare these worry values to make your decision.
  d What decision would you prefer? Why?
2 How would the example presented in this chapter be affected if the sprinkler had produced instead the following probability distribution of losses and insurance premiums?

Losses	Probability
$ 0	.700
500	.150
1,000	.100
10,000	.050

Insurance	Premium
$ 50,000	$1,000
200,000	600
($1,000	
deductible)	
200,000	1,100

3 Capital budgeting has limited, though important, applicability to risk management. Explain.
4 How is the internal rate of return calculation used in capital budgeting affected by:
  a Ignoring pure risks?
  b Assuming all pure risks are insured?
5 How would the following changes in Table 14.2 after-tax costs affect the internal rate of return calculations for building B?
Complete insurance premium $6,000 instead of $6,500
Deductible insurance premium $5,000 instead of $5,400
Sprinkler installation cost $9,000 instead of $10,000
Complete insurance premium, assuming sprinkler, $4,500 instead of $5,200

SUGGESTIONS FOR ADDITIONAL READING

See the articles and books cited in footnotes of this chapter plus the readings suggested for Chapter 13.

D. Insurance Contracts and Their Uses

CHAPTER 15

SOME LEGAL ASPECTS
OF INSURANCE
CONTRACTS

LEARNING OBJECTIVES

After you have completed this chapter, you should be able to:

1 Explain why the legal definition of insurance is so important and how it varies among jurisdictions.
2 Describe the characteristics of an insurance contract that subject it to a special body of law.
3 List the four conditions that must be satisfied to make an insurance contract a valid contract.
4 Explain how an insured might lose his or her coverage because of concealment, a misrepresentation, or a breach of warranty.
5 Describe the importance to insureds of waiver and estoppel.
6 Tell the extent to which insurance contracts are standardized and the ways in which this standardization is accomplished.

INTRODUCTION

A risk manager has several reasons for understanding the fundamentals of insurance contracts—their construction and their interpretation. For example, in deciding whether to use insurance or some other tool, the risk manager should know what the insurer promises to do under its contract. Either at this decision level or later, it may be preferable to participate in the drafting of a tailor-made insurance contract instead of accepting the printed forms normally sold by the insurer. Even if the decision is to purchase one of the insurer's conventional products, the risk manager must have some basis for selecting among these various forms. Finally, after a contract is in effect, an insured should know his or her rights and responsibilities under the contract.

Except for Chapter 20, Chapters 15 through 25 deal with insurance contracts. After a discussion of some legal aspects of insurance contracts, two chapters are devoted to a framework for analyzing insurance contracts and concepts common to all contracts. The remaining seven chapters are devoted to some leading property, liability, and personnel insurance contracts, their major provisions, and their uses. Chapter 20 describes the social insurance programs that are an important part of a risk management program.

This chapter on some legal aspects of insurance first discusses what contracts the law considers to be insurance contracts and the reasons why this is important. Other topics include the unique characteristics of insurance contracts, the requirements for a valid insurance contract, some rules on the disclosure of information by the insured, the doctrines of waiver and estoppel, how mistakes in an insurance contract can be corrected, and the extent and nature of insurance contract standardization.

A LEGAL DEFINITION OF INSURANCE[1]

The significance of whether a particular contract is or is not *legally* insurance is not solely a question of semantics; it becomes important in a variety of ways. First of all, the fact that an insurance business is being transacted by a particular individual or firm raises the question of whether the firm is complying with state laws and regulations governing insurance.

Second, the question may be raised in a civil action whereby one party alleges certain rights that flow from insurance contracts. These actions may include suit to recover a promised benefit under the alleged policy, a return of premiums paid, or a money judgment for damages suffered by the claimant because of insurance coverages promised. The courts in these cases have tended to favor the theory that the claimant should recover from organizations holding themselves out as providing such benefits. What may be determined to be insurance in such civil actions, however, may not be held to be "doing a business of insurance" as related to state regulation.

Third, the issue may be raised in bankruptcy proceedings since the Bankruptcy Act excludes insurance corporations from the operation of the act. This exclusion has had the effect of shifting defunct insurers to an elaborate procedure and process of liquidation under state insurance laws and administration.

Finally, courts have been asked to rule on what is insurance in administering our tax laws. Insurance companies are entitled to special treatment regarding deductions for reserves, investment income, and accounting treatment of expenses. The United States Supreme Court has announced the general rule that the state's classification of a company will serve as a basis for making the decision for tax administration and

---

[1] The legal definition of insurance may differ considerably from the economic definition presented in Chap. 12 because, as will be apparent from the following discussion, it serves a different purpose. For a comprehensive study of legal definitions, see H. S. Denenberg, "The Legal Definition of Insurance," *Journal of Insurance*, vol. XXX, no. 3 (September, 1963), pp. 319–343.

treatment unless there has been a gross misuse of the name to hide the real purposes of the business enterprise.

Case law shows clearly that there is no single legal definition of insurance.[2] Certain tests that are often applied to the business or transaction in question are:

1 Is there a risk of economic loss to the beneficiary or insured
  a Independent of the contract itself?
  b Outside the control of either party?
  c That may be distributed among those who are subject to loss?
2 Is this risk assumed by the insurer or promisor?
3 Does the contract incorporate a plan to distribute the cost of the loss among a group exposed to risk?

Case law and commentary on the subject contain the following sometimes contradictory examples of what the courts have held to be or not to be insurance.[3] Transfers

Insurance	Not insurance
Indemnity for loss by theft	Lightning-rod salesman's guarantee
Indemnity for loss by death of cattle	Bicycle repair contract issued by a bicycle association
Contracts guaranteeing the performance of, or indemnifying against the nonperformance of, certain contracts	Agreement to protect employee from striking employees
Comprehensive guarantee of auto tires	Tire warranty promising indemnity against defects in the tire
Contracts for replacement of plate glass, if broken	Provision in lease making the lessor responsible for replacement of a chattel injured by fire
Newspaper promise to pay a stated amount to a person killed in an accident if at the time he had a copy of the newspaper on his person	Contract entitling members of groups to medical services free or at reduced rates

that are considered insurance in one state may not be considered insurance in another. Warranties are particularly troublesome. In general, when a manufacturer, contractor, or distributor promises to replace a product or redo work if the product or work proves defective, the warranty is not considered insurance. If the warranty covers only (or in addition) accidental losses, the warranty will probably be considered insurance. Warranties have also been considered insurance even when the promise to protect the buyer against defects in the product is made by an outsider, not the manufacturer, contractor, or distributor. For example, some insurers now sell warranty insurance on new cars.

[2] In certain states, such as Kentucky, the legislature has defined insurance. Courts sometimes cite these statutory definitions.
[3] See *American Jurisprudence* (Rochester, N.Y.: Lawyers' Cooperative Publishing Co., 1960), vol., XXIX, pp. 430–445.

CHARACTERISTICS OF INSURANCE CONTRACTS

When a person buys private insurance, he or she is entering into a contract with the insurer that entitles the person to certain advantages but also imposes certain responsibilities. Although the contract may be one of the most important to which the person will be a party during his or her lifetime, he or she may never read it unless and until a loss occurs.

Insurance contracts are subject to the same basic law that governs all types of contracts. On the other hand, one can be an expert in the general law of contracts and know very little about the application of this law to an insurance contract. Because insurance contracts have many characteristics not found in most other contracts, a special body of law has developed to handle the legal problems associated with insurance. The special nature of insurance contracts is best indicated by the following list of their prevailing characteristics:

Personal Contract

Insurance contracts are personal contracts. Although the subject of a property insurance contract, for example, is a piece of property, the insurance contract insures a person or persons, not the property. Suppose the insured is the owner. If the owner sells the property to someone else, the new owner is not insured under that contract unless the insurer agrees to an assignment of the contract to the new owner; the identity of the insured is an important factor in the insurer's decision to insure the property. On the other hand, an insurance contract may create rights for persons other than the insured such as a mortgagee under a standard mortgagee clause or the beneficiary under a life insurance contract. Life insurance contracts are personal contracts in the sense that the insurer is interested in the identity of the person purchasing the contract; but after the contract is used, it can be assigned to anyone without the consent of the insurer.

Unilateral Contract

Insurance contracts are commonly unilateral contracts. After the insured has paid the premium or premium installment and the contract has gone into effect, only the insurer can be forced to perform, because the insured has fulfilled his or her promise to pay the premium. On the other hand, if the insured does not pay the complete premium on the due date (as in the case of an assessable contract, an order placed on the phone, or a promise to pay the premium in installments) but promises to do so in the future, both parties have made promises to perform in the future, and the insurance contract is bilateral.

Conditional Contract

Insurance contracts are conditional contracts. Although only the insurer can be forced to perform after the contract is effective, the insurer can refuse to perform if the insured does not satisfy certain conditions contained in the contract. For example, the insurer need not pay a claim if the insured has increased the chance of loss in some manner prohibited under the contract or has failed to submit a proof of loss within a specified period.

Aleatory Contract

Insurance contracts are aleatory contracts; i.e., the obligation of at least one of the parties to perform is dependent upon chance. If the event insured against occurs, the insurer will probably pay the insured a sum of money much larger than the premium. If the event does not occur, the insurer will pay nothing.

Contract of Adhesion

Insurance contracts are usually contracts of adhesion. The insured seldom participates in the drafting of the contract although risk managers of large firms may occasionally do so and this practice is apparently becoming more common. Usually the insurer offers the insured a printed document on a take-it-or-leave-it basis. Courts frequently refer to this characteristic of insurance contracts when they interpret ambiguous provisions in favor of the insured.[4]

Contract *Uberrimae Fidei*

Insurance contracts are contracts of the utmost good faith. Both parties to the contract are bound to disclose all the facts relevant to the transaction. Neither party is to take advantage of the other's lack of information. The legal questions involving this characteristic usually center on the disclosure of information by the insured. These legal questions are important enough to merit the separate treatment given in the section "Disclosure of Information" later in this chapter.

Contract of Indemnity

Property and liability insurance contracts are, subject to certain exceptions, contracts of indemnity. The person insured under these contracts should not benefit financially from the happening of the event insured against. Life and frequently health insurance contracts are not contracts of indemnity. For an extended discussion of this important subject, see Chapter 17.

REQUIREMENTS FOR A VALID CONTRACT

According to the law of contracts, a contract must satisfy four conditions before it is legally enforceable. These four conditions and their special application to insurance are:

---

[4] This is true in spite of the fact that in some instances the state, not the insurer, drafts the contract. See the section on standardization in this chapter.

1 The contract must serve a legal purpose. It must not be contrary to public policy. An insurance contract, for example, cannot protect a person against damages awarded as a result of harm that person intentionally causes to the person or property of some other person.

2 One party must make a definite offer and a second party must accept the offer. If the person to whom the offer has been made refuses to accept the offer without some modifications, he or she is considered to have made a counteroffer, which must be accepted by the other person before the agreement is effective.

In property and liability insurance, technically the applicant makes an offer to the insurer, which accepts the offer, rejects it, or makes a counteroffer. The insurance agent usually has the power to accept the offer on behalf of the insurer he or she represents, and the contract is effective as soon as the agent agrees to bind the coverage.

In personnel insurance, prospective insureds complete a written application for insurance. Usually the applicant does not pay the premium at the time, and the application is considered an invitation to the insurer to make an offer. Not until the applicant has accepted the policy and paid or promised to pay the first premium has he or she accepted unconditionally a definite offer. Furthermore, the insurer sometimes conditions its offer upon the continued good health of the applicant until the date of delivery.

Even if the premium is paid with the application, the coverage is not immediately binding because the insurer's agent lacks the authority to make it so. Customarily, however, the agent issues a binding receipt that makes the coverage effective on (1) the date of application or (2) the date of the application or (if required) the medical examination, if later, provided that the prospective insured was acceptable on that date.[5] In this instance there has been an offer by the applicant and a conditional acceptance by the insurer. To illustrate the effect of the receipt, consider the following: A person applies for life insurance on February 10, pays the first premium with his application and obtains a binding receipt of the first type, and is killed in an automobile accident on February 12. If this person was insurable on February 10 according to the underwriting standards of the insurer, the coverage is effective even if the insurer does not receive the application from its agent until February 14.

Sometimes the insurer will reject the applicant's offer and make a counteroffer based on a different type of coverage or rate. Usually this counteroffer will delay the effective date until the insured accepts the counteroffer.

3 Each party to the contract must be required to make some consideration on behalf of the other party. The contract is not enforceable unless one party gives up a right, power, or privilege that he or she already has in exchange for an equivalent renouncement by the other. The contract is enforceable, however, even if one person promises to do much more than the other.[6] Under an insurance contract, the insured must pay or promise to pay a premium and meet certain conditions stipulated in the contract. The

---

[5] A few insurers issue life insurance binding receipts that provide temporary protection similar to that given by property and liability insurance binders.

[6] Contracts that require the government to pay a prominent person $1 a year in return for some valuable services illustrate this principle.

insurer must promise to make certain payments or provide certain services in case of loss.

4 The parties to the contract must be legally competent. Insane or intoxicated persons are not considered competent. Minors (persons under eighteen in some states and under twenty-one in others) may void a contract to which they are a party, except a contract for "necessities" (food, clothing, and shelter, for example), if they do so during their infancy. Only the minor has the option, however, and if he or she chooses not to void the contract, it is valid.

An insurer is competent if it meets certain statutory requirements described in Chapter 26. Insureds are generally considered to be competent unless they are insane or intoxicated. Insurance is not considered a necessity, but the rule with respect to minors has been modified in some states to permit infants to enter into legally enforceable life insurance contracts as early as age fourteen. The courts of a few states deny the rights of minors to void an insurance contract, on the ground that since the insurer has fulfilled its promise, the contract has been executed.

DISCLOSURE OF INFORMATION BY THE INSURED

An insurance contract, as was noted earlier, is a contract *uberrimae fidei*. Consequently, an insurer is entitled to rely upon information provided by the insured and to seek some relief if this information is incorrect. The doctrines that will be introduced by the insurer in any court case involving this issue will be the doctrines of concealment, misrepresentation, or breach of warranty. In the following discussion of these three doctrines, we shall assume first that there are no special statutes modifying the common law doctrines, and then describe the effect of the statutes upon these doctrines.

Concealment

Concealment is the failure to reveal certain facts known to the insured that are not such common information that the insurer should also know them. The common law doctrine of concealment is much more harsh with respect to ocean marine insurance than with respect to other kinds of insurance, because at the time ocean marine insurance law was being developed, the courts believed that insurers needed protection. Communications were very poor, and insurers were often asked to insure vessels thousands of miles away. In fact, the vessels were insured "lost or not lost," and some had already been sunk or damaged. Consequently an ocean marine insurer can successfully plead concealment if it can show that the fact concealed was material. A fact is considered to be material if previous cognizance of it would have caused the insurer to refuse the insured's proposal or make a counteroffer. The practices of other insurers in similar situations may be introduced as evidence and in some states become the standard to be applied.[7] The reasoning here is that if the insurer had not accepted the

---

[7] E. W. Patterson, *Essentials of Insurance Law* (2d ed., New York: McGraw-Hill Book Company, 1957), pp. 408–428 and 461.

offer, it would have had no obligation with respect to the loss. Note that the fact misrepresented need not have actually contributed to the loss that the insurer refused to pay. An insurer could claim that some information the insured concealed with respect to some cargo was material even if a loss to the cargo had nothing to do with the fact concealed.

The ocean marine insurer need not prove that the concealment was intentional; in fact it is sufficient for the insurer to show that the applicant should have had the information. Other types of insurers, however, must prove that the applicant *intentionally* concealed some facts that he or she knew to be material and that would not be apparent from an inspection of the exposure. This additional requirement reduces substantially the insurer's reliance upon the doctrine of concealment, because fraud is difficult to prove and failure to prove intent may result in a countersuit. The definition of materiality is the same as for ocean marine insurance. The following situation illustrates the application of this rule: Suppose that at the time a risk manager applied for fire insurance the building next door was on fire and that he or she did not report this fact to the insurer. This fire did not reach the insured building, but three weeks later a fire in the basement caused extensive damage. The insurer could probably successfully deny the insured's claim if it could prove that the risk manager knew about the fire next door and intentionally did not report the danger to the insurer. The materiality of the concealed fact would be evident. The fact that the claim that is being denied did not arise out of the unreported fire is inconsequential. On the other hand, if the risk manager did not know about the fire next door, the insurer would not be able to deny the claim successfully.

Misrepresentation

A *representation* is a statement made by the insured in applying for insurance, usually in response to a question by the insurer. The statement may express a fact or an opinion. Under common law an insurer can successfully plead misrepresentation of a *fact* if it can demonstrate that the factual information is (1) incorrect and (2) material. A fact is material if it meets the condition prescribed earlier. If an *opinion* is involved instead of a fact, the insurer must also show that the misrepresentation was intentional. The following cases illustrate these concepts: Assume that a property insurer includes in its application a question concerning the existence of other insurance and that the applicant answers the question incorrectly. To deny a claim successfully later, the insurer must prove that the incorrect answer affected its underwriting decision. The insurer need not prove that the insured intended to deceive. If an applicant for a life insurance contract responds affirmatively to a question asking whether his or her health is good, the answer is considered an opinion. To contest a claim successfully on the ground that this opinion is a misrepresentation, the insurer must prove that the answer was incorrect, material, and fraudulent.

Breach of Warranty

A warranty is a condition in an insurance contract. A representation achieves the status of a warranty if it becomes a condition of the insurer's promise. Courts are not likely to give it this status unless the contract clearly indicates that the insured's answer is a contract condition. A question may also arise as to whether the warranty is affirmative or promissory. An affirmative warranty states a condition that is supposed to exist on the date the statement is made; a promissory warranty states a condition that is to exist throughout part or all of the policy period. For example, an automobile insurance policy contains an affirmative warranty that states that no insurer has canceled an automobile insurance policy covering the insured during the past three years. A burglary policy contains a promissory warranty that states that during the policy period the burglar-alarm system described in the policy will be maintained in proper working order.

In order to void a contract on the ground that there has been a breach of warranty under common law, an insurer must simply prove that the condition has been breached. Unlike the situation with respect to misrepresentations, the insurer need not prove materiality of the condition. Furthermore, the courts are more likely to require more nearly literal compliance with a warranty than with a representation.

Statutory Modifications

The common law doctrines described above, particularly (but not limited to) the breach of warranty doctrine, were harshly applied during the eighteenth and early nineteenth centuries, and many insurers took advantage of insureds by denying claims on the basis of breaches that were clearly not material. As a result, many state legislatures have enacted statutes modifying the common law. These state statutes can be grouped into four classes:

1 Statutes declaring that all statements by the insured shall, in the absence of fraud, be deemed representations and not warranties. These statutes are limited for the most part to life and health insurance. All states in the case of life insurance, and most states in the case of health insurance, have statutes of this sort.

2 Statutes permitting the insured to recover unless the breach of warranty or, in some instances, the fact misrepresented either *(a)* increased the "risk" (meaning chance or severity of loss) or *(b)* materially affected the hazard assumed by the insurer. The type *(a)* statute seems to imply that the materiality will be determined by using the standard of a prudent insurer instead of the standard of the individual insurer in question. These "increase-the-risk" statutes, which are not "contribute-to-the-loss" statutes, are the most common modification of the case law affecting property and liability insurance.

3 Statutes permitting the insured to recover unless the breach of warranty or the fact misrepresented actually contributed to the loss. Common law requires only that the breach or the misrepresentation affect the insurer's decision to write the policy. Such a breach or misrepresentation may not have contributed in any way to a loss that occurs after the policy is in effect. Very few states have legislation that modifies the common law this radically.

4 One statute (New Hampshire) providing for a reduction in the amount paid under a fire insurance contract if the insured makes a nonfraudulent misrepresentation that does not contribute to the loss. The reduction depends upon the premium paid relative to the premium that would have been paid if the fact had not been misrepresented. As will be noted in Chapter 23, misstatements of age are handled this way in life insurance.

Among the variables to be considered are the type of insurance to which the statute applies, the type of insurer, the type of warranty (affirmative or promissory, for example), the type of hazard (physical or moral), the effect of fraud, and several others.

In practice, insurers should have little difficulty in proving the materiality of almost all statements by the insured that in current contracts are made conditions of the insurer's promise. As a result, despite academic and legal interest in the distinction between the doctrines of misrepresentation and breach of warranty, relatively few court decisions depend on this difference.[8]

The most important difference between personnel insurance and the other lines with respect to disclosure of information by the insured is the presence of an incontestable clause in personnel insurance contracts. In life insurance, these clauses vary somewhat among insurers, but their basic effect is to render the policy incontestable on the grounds of concealment or misrepresentation one or two years after the inception of the contract. This is true even if fraud (with a few rare exceptions) is involved. In health insurance, the same situation prevails after two or three years from the date of issue but, except for noncancelable and guaranteed renewable policies explained in Chapter 24, fraudulent misstatements usually still provide a basis for a contest.

Another relevant provision found in most personnel insurance contracts is the entire contract provision, which states that the policy, including the endorsements and attached papers, constitutes the entire contract. Because of this provision, an insurer wishing to void a policy or contest a claim on the basis of misstatements by the insured must refer to statements contained in a written application attached to the policy.

RIGHTS OF INSURED AT VARIANCE WITH POLICY PROVISIONS

In denying the right of the insurer to void a contract on the grounds that the insured violated some condition in the contract, concealed some information, or misrepresented some fact, the insured may cite the doctrines of (1) waiver and estoppel or (2) reasonable expectations.

Waiver and Estoppel

Legal scholars and some courts distinguish between waiver and estoppel as follows: A *waiver* is the voluntary relinquishment of a *known* right, whereas *estoppel* prevents a person from asserting a right because he or she has acted previously in such a way as to deny any interest in that right. A waiver usually involves a statement to the insured that he or she need not worry about compliance with some condition in the contract or

---

[8] The major effects of making a representation a warrranty are to make a deeper impression on the insured and to ease the job of the lawyer for the insurer. Courts are also prone to require closer compliance with a warranty.

disclosing certain information. Most courts appear to use the doctrines interchangeably. For example, it is common to read that the insurer waived this right and is, therefore, estopped from asserting this right at a later date. This practice will be followed in this text.

Whether the insured will be successful in claiming a waiver depends in part upon the time when the waiver was supposed to have occurred. The court decisions can be divided into three categories depending upon when the waiver supposedly took place:

1 Before the contract becomes effective. Waivers by the insurer during this period are likely to result in a valid contract because, the courts reason, the insured is in a vulnerable position since he or she has not received the contract. For example, if the insured has already breached a condition in the contract on the date it is issued and the insurer or its agent knows about this breach, the courts will usually hold that the insurer has waived the condition with respect to the breach.

2 After the contract is issued but before any loss. This period is the most difficult to discuss because of the tremendous variance in the court decisions. It is possible to state, however, that the insured is less likely to be successful in claiming a waiver during this period than in either of the other two. It is also possible to state that courts in reaching their decisions consider *(a)* the degree of ambiguity in the breached condition, *(b)* the authority of the insurance representative who is supposed to have been aware of the breach, *(c)* the kind of action that is supposed to have constituted a waiver, and *(d)* the seriousness of the breach.

3 After the loss. This third period offers the best opportunity for the insured to claim a waiver. Insurance adjusters must be careful not to require too much of the insured before they admit their liability; if they do, they may be held to have waived any breached conditions. Insurance adjusters, by first denying liability, have also been held on occasion to have waived post-loss requirements such as the submission of a proof of loss within a specified time.

Reasonable Expectations

As noted earlier, insurance contracts are usually contracts of adhesion. Courts, therefore, tend to interpret ambiguous provisions in favor of the insured. Two additional principles, however, explain many court decisions that are not adequately handled under the contract of adhesion or the waiver and estoppel doctrines.[9] Under the first principle, an insurer is not permitted an *unconscionable advantage* in an insurance transaction. Under the second, the objectively *reasonable expectations* of applicants and intended beneficiaries will be honored even if those expectations would have been negated by painstaking study of the policy provisions. Two important corollaries of this principle are that (1) policy language will be interpreted from the layman's point of view, not that of a sophisticated underwriter, and (2) even if the language is clearly understandable, the insurer must show that the insured's failure to read such language was unreasonable. Deviations from the reasonable expectations doctrine can be found,

[9] R. E. Keeton, *Basic Text on Insurance Law* (St. Paul, Minn.: West Publishing Company, 1971), chap. 6.

but according to one authority "insurance law appears to be moving in the direction the principle indicates."[10]

The reasonable expectations principle is illustrated by the following case. A man planning a round trip on a scheduled airline purchased an airplane trip policy that did not cover travel on other than scheduled airlines. On his return trip, his flight was canceled but the airline arranged for him and two others to charter a special flight with a firm operating under an air-taxi certificate. The plane crashed and the insured was killed. The insurer denied coverage on the ground that the insured was not at the time a passenger on a scheduled airline. The court, in a split decision, held the insurer liable. It argued that the contract was ambiguous and that "in this type of coverage, sold by a vending machine, the insured may reasonably expect coverage for the whole trip which he inserted in the policy, including reasonable substituted transportation necessitated by emergency."[11]

The reasonable expectation doctrine also explains the decisions in some cases in which the insurer delivered a policy that deviated significantly from the coverage for which the insured had applied or in which the insurer reduced the coverage in a renewal policy without informing the insured.

CORRECTION OF MISTAKES

Sometimes the insurance contract does not express the actual agreement between the insured and the insurer. If (1) an oral contract was made, (2) it was intended that this oral contract be reduced to writing, and (3) a mistake in incorporating the oral agreement in the written document was the result of a mutual mistake or a mistake on one side of which the other was aware, the aggrieved party may seek an equitable remedy of reformation of the contract; i.e., the aggrieved party may ask the court to reform the contract to represent the true agreement. Otherwise, the parole evidence rule applies, and testimony concerning oral agreements before or at the time of the written agreement cannot alter the written agreement.

Sometimes the mistake is an obvious one, such as writing an address 1856 Larpenter Avenue instead of 1856 Larpenteur Avenue, the first spelling being clearly incorrect. An example of a more troublesome error is the transposition (1865 for 1856) of the numbers in the address, because the two properties may not be equally attractive to the insurer.

STANDARDIZATION

Fortunately for the consumer, insurance contracts are highly standardized as a result of statutory or administrative directives, voluntary agreement, or customary practice. Otherwise choosing among the policies issued by thousands of insurers would be extremely difficult.

In most states the standard fire policy, which until recently was the foundation for

---

[10] Ibid., p. 357.
[11] *Steven* v. *Fidelity Cas. Co.*, 58 Col. 2d 862, 377 P.2d 284, 57 Col. Rptr. 172 (1962).

all fire insurance contracts, is prescribed word for word by statute.[12] All insurers, domestic or foreign, writing fire insurance on real property in those states had to use the prescribed policy.

The advantages of a statutory standard policy prescribed word for word are that (1) the insured need not consider differences in policy language when selecting an insurer, (2) all insureds are subject to the same treatment, (3) policy conflicts do not arise when two or more insurers are required to provide the necessary protection or become involved in the same loss, (4) court interpretations of the contract become more meaningful, (5) insureds and insurance agents save time and energy in contract analysis, and (6) loss experience can be pooled for rate-making purposes. On the other hand, (1) desirable changes may be delayed because these can be accomplished only by revising a statute, (2) a contract that survives the legislative process may not be the best one, (3) the policy designed to meet the needs of the average insured may not meet the needs of many insureds, and (4) the advantages of experimentation and competition are lost.

In some states use of a standard fire policy was made compulsory because of a directive from the state insurance department. The effect in practice was about the same as if there were a statutory policy.

The standard fire policy, however, is no longer part of every fire insurance policy on real estate. For example, states have permitted insurers to write the homeowner's and businessowner's policies described in Chapters 32 and 19 respectively without including a standard fire policy. This permission is consistent with the readability requirements now imposed upon insurance policies by separate state statutes or state insurance department directives. In 1985 the Insurance Services Office intends to replace the basic property protection contracts described in Chapter 18 with simplified commercial property forms that will not include the standard fire policy. The standard fire policy, therefore, is becoming a much less common feature of fire insurance. The provisions that appear in that policy, however, have been incorporated in more readable (and in some cases more liberal) fashion in the contracts that have replaced it.

A less restrictive statutory approach is the use of statutory standard provisions under which the state prescribes certain important provisions, but insurers can change the wording so long as the revised provision is at least as liberal as the statutory provision. This approach is best illustrated by life insurance and health insurance standard provisions. For example, all state laws prescribe clauses dealing with such matters as the period following the effective date within which any misstatements by the insured must be contested, the grace period following premium due dates within which premiums must be paid, and the minimum values to which the insured is entitled if he or she stops paying premiums. However, some important provisions, such as those describing the ways in which the insurers will pay out the proceeds, are not included among the standard provisions.[13] State laws also prohibit certain types of provisions.

---

[12] The fire insurance contract commonly includes this statutory policy plus at least one form that varies with the type of property insured. The forms are not prescribed by statute. Many forms may be standardized by agreement among insurers using the services of a rating bureau or by a state insurance department directive.

[13] State laws do require that the policy contain tables describing the options available.

For example, life insurers can only exclude certain causes of death, such as suicide, during the first two years or military service during wartime. A similar situation exists in health insurance, most states having adopted the 1950 Uniform Individual Accident and Sickness Policy Provisions Law, which prescribes 12 required provisions (covering such matters as the entire contract, the time limit on certain defenses, reinstatement, and claims notices and proofs of loss) and 11 optional provisions (such as those regarding a change of occupation, other insurance, and cancellation). In 1974, the National Association of Insurance Commissioners, whose recommendations have no legal effect but influence strongly the actions of individual states, adopted a model regulation that sets up minimum standards for individual health insurance policies.

In most states, insurance contracts must be approved by the state insurance department before they can be used. In the other states contracts can be used without prior approval but they are subject to subsequent disapproval.

Voluntary standardization is common in many property and liability insurance lines. To some extent, such as in workers' compensation insurance and automobile insurance, one of the original incentives for voluntary agreement was to make statutory or administrative action unnecessary. The voluntary products are generally known as "standard-provisions" contracts. All insurers using these contracts provide the same basic protection, but they have some flexibility with respect to the exact language and the arrangement of the provisions. These contract provisions are usually developed by rating bureaus,[14] which may also develop a common price for the product. In only one instance—workers' compensation—has this method produced complete standardization. In the past there was a high degree of standardization in automobile insurance, but increased competition in recent years has resulted in a more diversified set of products.

Other forces favoring standardization are the tendency of businesses to produce a product that is not too different from that of their competitors and a hesitancy to experiment with new phraseology that may expose them to new risks of interpretation. On the other hand, competition also favors some product differentiation, and insurance contracts are seldom completely standardized. The degree of standardization varies among lines, with workers' compensation insurance being the most highly standardized field and marine insurance the least standardized. Normally the insurance buyer can expect some product differentiation, but understanding of the contract issued by one insurer will have a high transfer value in understanding the contracts issued by other insurers.

SOME KEY CONCEPTS

Contract of adhesion   A contract drafted by one party to which the other party must adhere. Most insurance contracts are contracts of adhesion drafted by the insurer which causes courts to interpret ambiguous provisions in favor of the insured.

Contract *uberrimae fidei*   A contract of the utmost good faith. Both parties to the contract must disclose all the facts they have relevant to the transaction. Insurance contracts are contracts *uberrimae fidei*.

---

[14] See "Rating Bureaus" in Chap. 28.

Concealment   Failure by the insured to reveal certain facts he or she knows that are not such common information that the insurer should also know them. Except in ocean marine insurance an insurer must prove intent and materiality to deny a claim based on concealment. A concealment is material if the fact concealed would have caused the insurer either not to write the insurance or to write it under substantially different terms.

Misrepresentation   An incorrect answer by the insured in response to a specific question by the insurer. To deny a claim the insurer must prove only the materiality of a misrepresentation of a fact.

Breach of warranty   A breach of a contract condition which may include representations made by the insured that are incorporated into the contract. Under common law an insurer need not prove either intent or materiality to deny a claim on the basis of a breach of warranty. Statutes have modified this doctrine considerably.

Contribute-to-the-loss statute   A statute found in a few states that requires insurers claiming misrepresentation or breach of warranty to show that the fact misrepresented actually contributed to the claim the insurer refuses to pay.

Waiver and estoppel   Doctrines under which the insured may claim with varying degrees of success that some action by the insurer or its agent caused it to lose the right to deny the claim on the basis of some violation by the insured.

Standardized contracts   Contracts that are uniform at least in part as to content or both content and language. Insurance contracts are standardized to a large extent by law or voluntarily.

REVIEW QUESTIONS

1 A tire manufacturer offers to repair or replace any tire which for any reason fails to give trouble-free service for 18 months. Is this an insurance transaction?

2 Which characteristic of an insurance contract probably led to the following court decisions?
  a An ambiguous provision in the contract was interpreted in favor of the insured.
  b A contract covering the former owner of a building was held not to protect a new owner because the insurer had not consented to an assignment of the contract.
  c The insurer was held not responsible for a loss because the insured failed to submit a proof of loss within the proper time period.

3 An agent asks a risk manager to purchase a property insurance policy. The risk manager agrees, and the agent binds the coverage.
  a Who made the offer in this case?
  b When was the offer accepted? Why is the time important?
  c If the agent does not have the power to bind the coverage, when is the transaction completed?

4 A 16-year-old boy purchases an automobile insurance contract. At the end of the policy year, he demands the return of his insurance premium.
  a On what basis does he make this request?
  b Will he be successful?
  c What other insureds may be legally incompetent to purchase insurance?

5 An employee signed an application for individual life insurance on January 10. She did not pay any premium at that time. The underwriter at the home office of the insurer accepted the application on January 17 and mailed the contract to the agent that afternoon for delivery to the employee. When the agent called at the employee's home with the policy, he discovered that the employee had died. Is the insurer liable if the employee died on January 12? on January 18?

6 How would you answer question 5 if the employee paid the first premium with her application and received a binding receipt from the agent?

7 In its application for fire insurance, a firm failed to reveal that a disgruntled stockholder had threatened to set the building on fire if the president did not grant him an interview by the end of the week. The following week the building burned to the ground as the result of an accidental exposion.
   a Was the concealed fact material?
   b Can the insurer successfully deny liability in this instance?

8 An automobile insurer customarily asks an applicant whether any insurer has canceled his or her automobile insurance during the past three years. The new risk manager of a firm answers in the negative because he believes no cancellation has occurred; but actually a contract was canceled 18 months ago. The insurer issues the contract, and two months later there is a collision loss.
   a Was this misrepresentation material?
   b Can the insurer successfully deny liability?

9 **a** What is the nature of the statutory modifications of the common law doctrine of warranties?
   b How important is the warranty doctrine today?

10 **a** At the time an automobile insurance contract was being negotiated, the risk manager told the insurance agent that the firm's two automobiles were encumbered under a conditional sales agreement, but the agent did not note this fact in the application. Since this information is important to the insurer, it refused to pay a loss under the contract when it discovered the omission. Will the insurer be successful in its denial of the claim?
   b A risk manager informed her agent during the policy period that a building would be unoccupied beyond the period permitted under a fire insurance contract. The agent assured her that the period of nonoccupation would make no difference, but the insurer reacted differently following a loss. What is the probable outcome?

11 In his application for individual life insurance, an employee stated in reply to a direct question that he had not visited a doctor in the past three years. The employee's answer appears on a written application attached to the contract. Five years after purchasing the contract, the employee died, and the insurer discovered for the first time that the employee had visited a doctor several times in connection with a pain in his chest.
   a Will the statement made by the insured be considered a warranty?
   b Is the insurer liable for the face amount of the contract?

12 How does the incontestable clause in life insurance differ from the incontestable clause in health insurance?

13 In what ways has the doctrine of reasonable expectations benefited insureds?

14 Since automobile liability insurance is required or highly encouraged in all states, it has been suggested that each state legislature enact a statutory automobile liability insurance policy. What would be the advantages and disadvantages of such action?

15 Compare the type of standardization in:
   a Life insurance
   b Health insurance
   c Fire insurance
   d Automobile insurance

SUGGESTIONS FOR ADDITIONAL READING

Freedman, Warren: *Richards on the Law of Insurance* (4th ed., New York: Baker, Voorhis, & Company, Inc., 1952).

Greider, J. E., M. L. Crawford, and W. T. Beadles: *Law and the Life Insurance Contract* (5th ed., Homewood, Ill.: Richard D. Irwin, Inc., 1984).

Keeton, R. E.: *Basic Text on Insurance Law* (St. Paul, Minn.: West Publishing Company, 1971).

Lorimer, J. J., H. F. Perlet, F. G. Kempin, and F. R. Hodosh: *The Legal Environment of Insurance, vols. I and II* (2d ed., Malvern, Pa.: American Institute for Property and Liability Underwriters, 1981).

Patterson, Edwin W.: *Essentials of Insurance Law* (2d ed., New York: McGraw-Hill Book Company, 1957).

————, and W. F. Young, Jr.: *Cases and Materials on the Law of Insurance* (4th ed., Brooklyn: The Foundation Press, Inc., 1961).

Vance, W. R., and B. M. Anderson: *Handbook on the Law of Insurance* (5th ed., St. Paul, Minn.: West Publishing Company, 1951).

CONTRACT ANALYSIS: EVENTS COVERED

LEARNING OBJECTIVES

After you have completed this chapter, you should be able to:

1 Describe how an insurance contract is typically structured.
2 Explain why insurers include exclusions in insurance contracts.
3 Analyze an insurance contract to determine what events are covered, the seven basic questions being:
   a What perils are covered?
   b What property, sources of liability, or lines are covered?
   c What persons are insured against losses?
   d What losses are covered?
   e What time period is covered?
   f What locations are covered?
   g What special conditions that do not fit into any of the above six categories may limit the coverage?

INTRODUCTION

Analyzing an insurance contract can be a complex, difficult task. The sentences are sometimes arranged in seemingly random fashion; the language is often highly technical; and interpretation of the language may require references outside the contract to court decisions, statutes, custom, and negotiations with the insurer. Most risk managers must learn how to analyze insurance contracts in order to comprehend contracts drafted by insurers. The risk managers of some large businesses require this knowledge to participate in the drafting of tailor-made manuscript contracts.

This chapter describes first the structure of a typical insurance contract. The remainder of the chapter suggests a logical approach for determining what events are covered under the contract. The next chapter deals with the provisions affecting the amount the insured can recover if the loss is covered. The steps the insured must take following a loss and other post-loss provisions are covered in Chapter 29.

STRUCTURE OF THE CONTRACT

In some lines of insurance the terms "policy" and "contract" are used interchangeably because the contract consists only of the policy plus perhaps some riders or endorsements that extend, limit, or modify the policy. Automobile insurance contracts and life insurance contracts belong in this category. Other contracts consist of a basic policy plus a form that adapts the policy either (1) to a particular kind of insurance (for example, an inland transit policy plus a merchandise form produces a contract that protects a person shipping goods via common carriers against property losses in transit) or (2) to the needs and desires of particular insureds (for example, a special building form is added to the standard fire policy to provide coverage on buildings against all causes of loss not otherwise excluded. Endorsements that alter the basic contract (in this case the policy plus the form) may be attached.

The provisions in an insurance contract can be classified as (1) declarations, (2) insuring agreements, (3) exclusions, and (4) conditions. In many property and liability insurance contracts the provisions are grouped into these four categories and labeled accordingly, but in other lines the provisions must be rearranged to achieve this grouping.

Declarations

The declarations identify the insured; describe the property, activity, or life being insured; state the types of coverage purchased, the applicable policy limits, and the term of the coverage; and indicate the premium paid for each separate coverage purchased. The purpose of the declarations made by the insured is to give the insurer sufficient information to enable it, with information from other sources, to issue the desired contract at a proper price. These declarations are subject to the legal doctrines of concealment, misrepresentation, and breach of warranty discussed in Chapter 15 under "Disclosure of Information by the Insured." The insured should check his or her declarations to make certain that they are complete and correct and that the contract provides the coverages requested.

Insuring Agreements

The insuring agreements state what the insurer promises to do. The insuring agreements describe the characteristics of the events covered under the contract. A section of the insuring agreements may also define certain terms used in the contract.

Exclusions

The exclusions limit the coverage provided under the insuring agreements. They may exclude certain perils, property, sources of liability, persons, losses, locations, or time periods. The exclusions usually serve one or more of the following purposes:

1 To except losses that the insurer considers to be uninsurable because one or more of the characteristics of an ideally insurable risk outlined in Chapter 12 under "Limitations of Insurance" is seriously violated. For example, wars may affect many persons at the same time, thus violating the independent-exposure condition. Some losses occur so frequently that to include them would raise the premium to such unrealistically high levels that there would be insufficient demand for the contract to permit the law of large numbers to operate effectively. Other losses may be too indefinite as to cause, time, place, or amount, or the expected loss may be too difficult to determine in the short run. Intentionally caused losses are excluded not only because they violate the accidental-loss standard but also because public policy requires such an exclusion. Ordinary wear and tear losses are excluded because they are not accidental.

2 To reduce the morale hazard. For example, freezing of an automobile radiator is not covered under an automobile insurance contract because an insured can easily prevent this loss with antifreeze. This purpose is closely related to the reason for excluding wear and tear losses as not accidental.

3 To exclude losses that are traditionally covered under other contracts or that require some special underwriting or rating. For example, liability for injuries to employees is generally excluded under liability insurance covering the premises because this liability is usually covered under workers' compensation or employers' liability insurance, and because the extent of exposure is measured by payroll units, which may not be an appropriate measure of other liability exposures. Another example is business employee dishonesty insurance.

4 To lower the premium for protection against exposures that would be costly to include but which some persons do not have or do not consider important. For example, automobile liability exposures are usually excluded from general liability insurance. This exclusion permits insureds who have no automobile liability exposures to pay less for their general liability insurance.[1] This reason is most valid when many persons have the excluded exposure.

5 To produce a limited coverage that can be sold at an attractive rate. An insurer is more likely to seek this objective through a narrow insuring agreement. Limited health insurance contracts described in Chapter 24, under "Branches of Health Insurance," illustrate the point.

6 To exclude coverage the insurer is not prepared to service nor licensed to write such as boiler and machinery insurance, which emphasizes careful insurer inspections of the boiler and machinery. Another example is automobile insurance covering losses outside the United States and Canada.

---

[1] Sometimes insurers are able to provide reasonably priced insurance covering a group of exposures, each of which is held by only relatively few people. The package contract costs less than the sum of the separate parts because of the wider distribution of the exposures.

CHAPTER 16: CONTRACT ANALYSIS: EVENTS COVERED **297**

Some exclusions merely clarify what should be apparent from the insuring agreement. For example, the fire insurance policy excludes losses caused by riot unless fire ensues, in which case it covers the fire loss only. If this exclusion were omitted, the coverage would not be any greater, because a riot is not a fire, and fire and lightning are the only perils specified in the insuring agreement. Sometimes the exclusion is best explained by custom or tradition and disappears over time.

Conditions

The conditions define terms used in the other parts of the contract, prescribe certain conditions that must be satisfied before the insurer is liable, and may describe the basis for computing the premium. Most conditions describe the rights and obligations of the insured and the insurer following a loss.

A FRAMEWORK FOR ANALYSIS

In analyzing an insurance contract for the first time, one should first read quickly the entire contract to gain some understanding of the format and the content. During the second reading the analyst should slowly and carefully seek answers to the following questions from all portions of the contract.[2]

1 Under what circumstances would the insurer be responsible for the loss? What events are covered?
    a What perils are covered?
    b What property or source of liability, or whose life or health, is covered?
    c What persons are covered?
    d What losses are covered?
    e What locations are covered?
    f What time period is covered?
    g Are there any special conditions that do not fall into any of the other six categories that may suspend or terminate the coverage?
2 If the insurer is responsible for the loss, how much will it pay?
3 What steps must the insured take following a loss?

The remainder of this chapter will be devoted to the analysis of the event covered. The amount of recovery is the subject of the next chapter, and post-loss provisions are discussed in Chapter 29.

EVENTS COVERED

A particular event is covered only if it possesses characteristics that are covered under the seven-question analysis in the above outline. For example, if the peril, property, loss, time, and location are covered under a property insurance contract but the person

[2] This method of analysis is adapted from the method introduced in Robert Mehr and Emerson Cammack, *Principles of Insurance* (Homewood, Ill.: Richard D. Irwin, Inc., 1952), chaps. 7–11.

seeking payment is not, the insurer is not liable. Consequently a clear understanding of the information sought through each of the seven questions is extremely important.

Perils Covered

Relevant considerations in determining what perils are covered are (1) whether the contract is a named-periods or an all risks contract, (2) how the covered or excluded perils are defined, (3) the excluded perils, and (4) the chain-of-causation concept.

Named-Perils or All Risks Contracts   Named-perils contracts specify the perils covered. Loss by any perils not included in the list is not covered. The exclusions may except losses caused by the named peril on some occasions (e.g., a fire caused by war).

All risks contracts cover all perils not otherwise excluded. In other words, a named-perils contract lists the included perils; an all risks contract names the excluded perils. All risks contracts sometimes cover losses beyond one's wildest imagination because the insurer has not excluded the particular cause of loss. For example, insurers have paid claims because a police officer's horse licked paint off a car.

All risks contracts (1) generally provide broader coverage[3] than named-perils contracts, and (2) permit the insured to consider explicitly all the perils to which he or she might still be exposed if the contract is purchased. In some instances the all risks contract replaces two or more named-perils contracts that would require more effort to administer and that might provide overlapping coverage. On the other hand, the all risks contracts may cost more than the insured is willing to pay. Furthermore, the insured may not want or need protection against some of the perils, known or unknown, included in the all risks contract.

A life insurance contract and many of the newer property insurance contracts are all risks contracts. Fire insurance and theft insurance contracts illustrate the named-perils approach.

Perils Defined   A few contracts define the covered perils. For example, burglary is commonly defined as ''the felonious abstraction of insured property from within the premises by a person making felonious entry therein by actual force and violence, of which force and violence there are visible marks'' on the exterior of the premises. Sometimes the peril is defined in a statute. For example, most states have statutes that define a riot as (1) a violent or tumultuous act against the person or property of another by (2) three or more persons. The first part of this definition is important in distinguishing between a riot and an act of vandalism.

Most contracts leave the interpretation of the covered perils to the courts. Courts, for example, have defined the following: windstorm, explosion, accident, collision, and fires. Their interpretation of ''fire'' is particularly important because it adds so

---

[3] Sometimes with respect to particular losses named-perils coverage is more liberal. For example, automobile comprehensive insurance is all risks coverage but it excludes collisions, the most common cause of physical damage to automobiles. The comparison depends upon the exclusions and the provisions determining the amount of recovery.

much meaning to the statutory policy and because fires are experienced by so many insureds. According to the courts a fire has not occurred unless there has been a visible flame or glow. Scorching and consequent blackening, for example, may not have involved any fire. The courts have also held that the fire must be a "hostile" fire, not a "friendly" fire. A hostile fire is one that has escaped from its proper container. If an object is accidentally thrown into a furnace oven, the loss is not a fire loss because there has been no hostile fire. Some courts, however, also consider a fire raging out of control to be a hostile fire even if the fire remains in the proper container.[4]

The courts' interpretation of accident as a sudden, unexpected event is also important because some liability contracts cover accidents for which the named insured is legally responsible. Others are written on an "occurrence" rather than on an "accident" basis. Some courts have argued that an event is not an accident unless it is sudden. An occurrence, on the other hand, need not meet this requirement. Consequently the gradual pollution of a stream with industrial wastes *might* not be covered under an accident policy but would be covered under an occurrence policy unless specifically excluded. Some courts also argue that deliberate acts which have unintentional and unexpected results are not accidents, but they would be occurrences.

Excluded Perils   Whether the contract is written on a named-perils or an all risks basis, the exclusions in the contract pertaining to perils affect what perils are covered under the contract. Sometimes the courts add exclusions not mentioned in the contract. For example, fires are excluded under the fire contract if they are caused by war or are intentionally set by public authorities (except to prevent the spread of fire). The contract does not exclude fires set intentionally by the insured, but the courts have held that to cover them would be contrary to public policy. Automobile comprehensive insurance covers all perils except collision, wear and tear, mechanical or electrical breakdowns, freezing, war, and confiscation by duly constituted public authorities. Losses caused intentionally by the insured are excluded by the courts. Liability policies written on an occurrence basis specifically exclude losses caused intentionally by the insured. Life insurance contracts may exclude deaths caused by suicide the first two years the contract is in force.

Chain-of-Causation   Courts have also contributed to the interpretation of the covered perils through the proximate-cause or chain-of-causation doctrines. According to the proximate-cause doctrine, a policy covering a named peril covers not only losses caused directly by that peril but also losses caused by other perils set in motion by that named peril. To illustrate, a fire insurance contract covers not only hostile fire losses but also losses caused by smoke and water damage resulting from the fire. In fact a business can collect under its fire insurance policy for damage from smoke or water occasioned by a hostile fire next door even if there is no hostile fire on the insured premises.[5] A health insurer is held responsible under a contract covering accidental

---

[4] *L. L. Freeberg Pie Co. v. St. Paul Mutual Insurance Co.*, 10 CCH (Fire and Casualty) 255.

[5] The fire insurer may be able to recover its payment from the owner or tenant of the building next door if it can prove negligence on that person's part.

injuries not only for disability income losses or medical expenses caused by an accidental injury but also for losses caused by a disease contracted as a result of the accident.

Decisions on whether a specified peril is the proximate cause of some other peril depends upon how much space or time elapses between the two perils and whether there was some intervening cause. For example, the walls of a building left standing after a fire may collapse many days later and damage an adjoining building. To determine whether the fire was the proximate cause of the collapse of the wall, the court will consider the elapsed time and whether there were any strong winds in the meantime.

Insurers are in fact held responsible for many losses for which the named peril is not the proximate cause. For example, after a windstorm has damaged a property, a fire may ensue and cause smoke damage; the fire insurer must pay the fire and the smoke damage even though the windstorm is the proximate cause.

A more complete explanation than the proximate-cause doctrine is the chain-of-causation concept, which works as follows:

1 Construct a chronological chain of the perils involved. In the illustration cited above, this chain is as follows:

$$\text{Windstorm} \rightarrow \text{Fire} \rightarrow \text{Smoke}$$

2 Identify the peril (or perils) covered under the contract. In this illustration, this is fire.

3 The loss caused by all perils to the right of the specified perils are covered so long as they are a consequence of that specific peril and are not specifically excluded. In the illustration, this means that the policy covers the loss caused by fire and by smoke.[6]

Property, Sources of Liability, or Lives Covered

The *property* covered under a property insurance contract may be either real property or personal property. If it is personal property, it may consist of a specific item (e.g., a machine, an automobile, or a watch), a specific type of property (e.g., machinery, equipment, or jewelry), or simply all personal property or contents not specifically excluded. The latter approach (1) provides broader coverage, (2) enables the insured to check explicitly the property that is not covered, and (3) may include new types of property acquired while the contract is in force. On the other hand, for a given amount of insurance insurers usually charge higher premiums for this broad coverage than for more specific insurance.

If the contract covers a business building, the building item typically includes machinery used for the service of the building, such as plumbing, air-conditioning,

---

[6] A problem may arise when a peril that is specifically excluded interrupts the chain. For example, the fire insurance policy specifically excludes loss by theft. Suppose property is stolen as a result of the confusion surrounding the fire. Is the loss covered because the chain is fire → confusion → theft? A definite answer does not yet exist.

heating apparatus, and elevators. It also includes ovens, kilns, furnaces, and the like, under most conditions. Awnings, screens, storm doors, window shades, and the like, if owned by the building owner, are considered part of the building. Finally, personal property, such as janitors' supplies, fuel, and the like, that is used solely in the service of the building is covered under the building item. Commonly excluded under the building item are excavations, underground flues and drains, and foundations below the surface of the ground.

Contracts covering all personal property or contents commonly exclude automobiles, airplanes, animals, money, and securities. Contracts covering specific types of property may exclude specific subtypes of items (for example, a policy may cover a contractor's equipment but not his or her trucks).

Liability insurance may be written on a selective or a comprehensive basis. Selective liability insurance contracts cover named *sources of liability,* such as the ownership, maintenance, or use of premises; the manufacture or distribution of products or services; the practice of accounting; or the ownership, maintenance, or use of an owned automobile. These stated sources may be further limited through exclusions. For example, automobile liability insurance may exclude situations in which the automobile is used as a taxi or a bus.

Comprehensive liability insurance covers all sources of liability not specifically excluded. For example, a comprehensive general liability insurance policy covers all sources other than the ownership, maintenance, or use of an automobile or an airplane and some other specified sources. The advantages and disadvantages of comprehensive liability insurance, compared with selective liability insurance, are basically the same as those stated above in comparing broad personal property coverage with more specific coverage.

The *person whose life or health is insured* is named in a personnel insurance contract. Life insurance contracts usually insure one person; health insurance contracts commonly pay medical expenses occasioned by the poor health of the named insured or his or her family.

Persons Insured

Property insurance contracts may protect only the named insured against losses to property in which he or she has some financial interest. The insured may be a sole or part owner, a bailee with a liability interest in property in his or her care, custody, or control, or a secured creditor. Other persons whose property interests may be covered include such varied groups as the named insured's family, guests, legal representatives, secured creditors, customers, or employees. These other persons may be protected against losses to their own property or their liability to the named insured for damage to his or her property. They may be covered automatically or only at the option of the named insured.

Secured creditors, such as a bank mortgagee (or an automobile finance company), may receive special treatment under the contract. The usual procedure is to include in the owner's contract a standard mortgagee clause (or a standard loss-payable clause in automobile insurance) under which the insurer obligates itself to pay the mortgagee even if the owner violates the contract, so long as the breach was not within the control or knowledge of the mortgagee. Under these clauses, the insurer must also give the mortgagee separate notice of cancellation. The mortgagee can also sue the insurer in his or her own name. If the owner has violated the contract, the insurer has no obligation to the owner but must pay the mortgagee. In return for this payment the mortgagee must surrender to the insurer an equivalent amount of his or her claim against the owner. The insurer may, if it wishes, avoid sharing a claim against the owner by paying the mortgagee the total amount of the mortgage. If the insurer and the mortgagee share the claim, the mortgagee recovers his or her uninsured loss first if a foreclosure becomes necessary. If the owner has not violated the contract, the insurer usually makes the check payable jointly to the owner and the mortgagee. The mortgagee usually releases the money to the owner for repairs. The mortgagee could, however, claim this money and reduce the mortgage by an equivalent amount.

A property or liability insurance contract can be assigned by the named insured to some other party, such as a secured creditor, but the insurer must consent to the assignment. The insurer's consent is necessary because the hazard may be changed by the assignment. Life and health insurance contracts are assignable without the consent of the insurer, but the insurer is not bound to recognize the assignment until it has been filed with the insurer. In either case the assignee does not become a party to the contract and can collect only what the named insured would have collected except for the assignment. Following a loss an insured can assign any claim he or she may have against the insurer to some other person.

Liability insurance contracts, like property insurance contracts, may be limited to the named insured or extended to include other persons. Other possibilities are the insured's family, legal representatives, employees, friends permitted to drive his or her car, tenants who occupy a building he or she owns, and distributors who market a product he or she manufactures.

The beneficiaries of a life insurance contract are named in the contract. Health insurance contracts usually provide benefits for the person whose health is insured.

Losses Covered

Property insurance contracts cover direct losses, indirect losses, or net income losses. These three types of losses were defined in Chapters 5 and 6. Most property insurance contracts cover only direct losses unless they are endorsed to cover indirect or net income losses.

In addition to paying settlements or court or statutory awards to the claimant, liability insurance contracts provide certain supplementary services such as investigation of the claim; negotiation and, it is hoped, settlement with the claimant; defense of the suit, if this proves necessary; payment of premiums on bonds and of court costs that may be incurred in connection with the claim; and payment of expenses incurred by the insured in cooperating with the insurer. Some contracts include a medical payments section under which medical expenses incurred by certain persons are paid without regard to the insured's liability.

Health insurance contracts cover either a loss of income caused by the insured's disability or medical expenses. Contracts may limit the types of medical expenses covered. Life insurance contracts simply pay a specified amount upon the death of the insured.

Time Period Covered

The starting and expiration times of the coverage must be stated in the contract. So long as the peril commences before the expiration time, the entire loss resulting from that peril is covered.

Of particular interest are the hours at which the coverage begins and terminates (for example, noon or midnight) and the basis for determining the hour at the time of the loss (for example, (1) standard time or daylight saving time and (2) the time at the address of the named insured or the time at the place of loss). Sometimes the coverage does not begin until some event occurs, such as the departure of a ship or the award of a contract to a successful bidder.

The policy term for most property and liability insurance contracts is usually one year, but it may be some fraction of a year (for example, six months) or some multiple of a year (for example, three years). Some surety bonds run until canceled. Life and health insurance contracts may be written for a specified number of years or for the lifetime of the insured.

Cancellation   Insurance contracts may be canceled only by mutual agreement, based upon a new consideration, of the parties to the contract unless the contract contains a provision to the contrary. Most property and liability insurance contracts contain a cancellation provision that gives both the insured and the insurer the right to cancel the contract prior to the expiration date. Neither need give any reason for requesting the cancellation. If the insurer cancels the contract, the cancellation is effective a stated number of days after the insurer notifies the insured, and the insurer must return a pro rata portion of the premium to the insured. The required period of advance notice runs from midnight of the day on which notice is given. In many contracts ''notice'' means mailing of the notice, in which case the insured may receive less effective advance notice than the number of days stated in the contract.

If the insured cancels the contract, the cancellation is effective as soon as he or she notifies the insurer. The insurer must return a short-rate portion of the premium. The short-rate return is less than a pro rata return because the insurer is permitted to recognize that most of the expenses other than losses have already been incurred. For example, the short-rate return after 180 days on a one-year contract is 40 percent. The short-rate cancellation also discourages the purchase of insurance to cover only the more hazardous parts of the policy period.

Automobile liability insurance contracts covering the owners of private passenger automobiles usually prohibit the insurer from canceling the contract except for a few specified reasons, such as nonpayment of premiums or revocation of the insured's drivers' license or motor vehicle registration. Such a restricted cancellation provision is required by law in most states.[7] Most states also restrict the right of insurers to cancel homeowners' and other residence contracts. Some of these statutes pertain to contracts written for businesses as well as for families.

Life insurance contracts cannot be canceled by the insurer; the insured can stop paying premiums but cannot recover premiums already paid. Health insurance contracts include a wide variety of cancellation provisions.[8] At one extreme, which has become much less common, health insurance contracts permit the insurer to cancel the contract at any time after a stated number of days' notice. Noncancelable contracts, the other common extreme, require the insurer to continue the coverage until the insured attains some advanced age.

Locations Covered

Insurance contracts may be written (1) on a specified locations basis, or (2) as a floater or floating insurance, in which case they cover losses anywhere within a specified area that is not excluded. To illustrate, some contracts provide protection only if the loss occurs at one specified location; others cover all locations anywhere in the world that are not specifically excluded. Between these two extreme treatments of the locations covered there are numerous other possibilities. For example, policies may cover losses at any one of a number of specified locations, at specified locations plus any new locations acquired by the insured, or anywhere within the United States and Canada that is not specifically excluded. Sometimes the coverage is more restricted as to perils, property, persons, or other features at certain locations.

Special Conditions

After analyzing the six features of an insurance contract described above, the risk manager may find some conditions that do not fit easily into any of these six categories. For convenience they may be considered extra special conditions. For example, a fire insurance contract may suspend the coverage while there is any increase in the hazard within the knowledge or control of the insured, such as a change in occupancy from a retail store to paper manufacturing, without notification to the insurer. An automobile insurance contract normally covers anyone driving a covered car with the permission of the named insured; however, it does not cover any such person who uses the car while working in a business of selling, servicing, repairing, or parking automobiles. Instead of being considered a special condition, this automobile example might be considered to be a restriction on persons covered. Personal preference will dictate where to include it; the important point is not to omit this factor in the analysis.

---

[7] See Chaps. 18 and 19.
[8] For more details see Chap. 24.

SOME KEY CONCEPTS

Insuring-agreement The section of an insurance contract in which the insurer tells what events are covered, subject to the exclusions and conditions sections.

Named-perils coverage A contract that specifies the perils covered.

All risks coverage A contract that covers all perils not specifically excluded.

Chain-of-causation concept A legal doctrine that makes the insurer responsible for losses caused by perils covered under the contract and other perils that the covered perils may set in motion. For example, a fire policy covers fire, smoke, and water damage caused by a fire.

Standard mortgagee clause A provision in the insurance contract under which the insurer obligates itself to pay the mortgagee even if the owner breaches some contract condition so long as the breach was not within the control or knowledge of the mortgagee.

Floater A contract that covers all locations not specifically excluded.

Cancellation The termination of an insurance contract by an insurer or an insured prior to the end of the policy term. Insurance contracts give insurers and insureds varying cancellation rights.

REVIEW QUESTIONS

1 The provisions in an insurance contract can be classified as *(1)* declarations, *(2)* insuring agreements, *(3)* exclusions, and *(4)* conditions.

  a Describe briefly each of these sets of provisions.

  b Are contract provisions always grouped into these categories?

2 Do contract exclusions ever benefit the insured?

3 Summarize briefly the framework suggested in the text for analyzing insurance contracts with respect to events covered.

4 Would you prefer a named-perils or an all risks contract? Why?

5 An explosion in building A is followed by fire and smoke damage. Wind carries smoke from the fire into building B, causing further damage.

  a Are "explosions," "fire," "windstorm," and "smoke" defined in insurance contracts? If not, where are they defined?

  b What portion of the damage in building A would be covered under a fire insurance contract on building A?

  c What portion of the damage in building B would be covered under a fire insurance contract on building B?

6 Which of the following losses would be covered under a fire insurance contract?

  a Wallpaper turns brown as a result of the overheating of an oven.

  b A plastic container melts when placed on the filaments of an electric stove.

  c Some valuable heat-measuring equipment is lost when it falls into a kiln.

7 a Would you prefer comprehensive liability insurance or one covering only the manufacture and distribution of products and services? Why?

  b If a property insurance contract covers a department store but not its contents, what property is typically covered?

8 a The Smith Manufacturing Company owns a $100,000 building on which the First National Bank holds a $50,000 mortgage. The Smith Manufacturing Company has a $100,000 fire insurance contract covering the building. If the building is vacant for over four months (a

breach of a contract condition) when a fire occurs causing $60,000 damage, what is the responsibility of the insurer if the contract:
(1) Has been assigned to the First National Bank?
(2) Contains a standard mortgagee clause?
   b If the Smith Manufacturing Company had not breached a condition in the contract, how would the loss be settled if the contract contains a standard mortgagee clause?
 9 In analyzing a contract with respect to the losses covered, what questions would you ask if the contract is:
   a A property insurance contract?
   b A liability insurance contract?
   c A health insurance contract?
   d A life insurance contract?
10 Discuss the cancellation rights of insurers in:
   a Property and liability insurance
   b Life insurance
11 A property insurance contract covers contents located at three different addresses. Is this contract a floater?
12 In addition to those provisions dealing with events covered, what two other major sets of provisions remain to be analyzed?

SUGGESTIONS FOR ADDITIONAL READING

Denenberg, H. S., et al.: *Risk and Insurance* (2d ed., Englewood Cliffs, N.J.: Prentice-Hall, Inc., 1974), chap. 14.

Greene, M. R., and J. S. Trieschmann: *Risk and Insurance* (6th ed., Cincinnati: South-Western Publishing Company, Inc., 1984), chap. 9.

Mehr, Robert I.: *Fundamentals of Insurance* (Homewood, Ill.: Richard D. Irwin, Inc., 1983), chap. 6.

Mehr, R. I., and E. Cammack: *Principles of Insurance* (7th ed., Homewood, Ill.: Richard D. Irwin, Inc., 1980), chaps. 6–8.

Williams, C. A., Jr., G. L. Head, R. C. Horn, and G. W. Glendenning: *Principles of Risk Management*, vol. II (2nd ed., Malvern, Pa.: American Institute for Property and Liability Underwriters, 1981), chaps. 9, 10, and 14.

CHAPTER 17

CONTRACT ANALYSIS: AMOUNT OF RECOVERY

LEARNING OBJECTIVES

After you have completed this chapter, you should be able to:

1 Explain what four characteristics make most property and liability insurance contracts contracts of indemnity.
2 Explain why life insurance contracts are not contracts of indemnity.
3 Distinguish between specific property coverage and blanket coverage.
4 Describe the advantages and disadvantages of a reporting form.
5 Distinguish between separate-limits liability insurance and single-limit liability insurance.
6 Show with an example how the usual coinsurance clause in a property insurance contract works and explain the purpose of such a clause.
7 List and give examples of four ways in which deductibles can be classified.

INTRODUCTION

After the risk manager has determined what events are covered under the contract, he or she must determine how much the insurer will contribute toward the loss. The contract provisions affecting the amount of recovery include (1) those related to the concept of indemnity, (2) the policy limits, (3) coinsurance provisions, and (4) deductible clauses.

CONCEPT OF INDEMNITY

As noted in Chapter 15, under "Characteristics of Insurance Contracts," most property and liability insurance contracts are contracts of indemnity. Insureds will not benefit from events against which they have insured themselves. Life contracts are not contracts of indemnity; health insurance contracts are sometimes, but not always, contracts of indemnity.

Property and Liability Insurance

Four characteristics make property and liability insurance contracts contracts of indemnity: (1) the way in which they measure the loss, (2) the insurable interest requirement, (3) provisions dealing with duplicate insurance, and (4) subrogation rights. The purpose of these provisions is (1) to reduce any incentive the insured may have to cause the loss and (2) to distinguish an insurance contract from a gambling contract.

Measure of Loss   Property insurance contracts insuring against direct loss generally promise to pay no more than the actual cash value of the loss. Usually the actual cash value is interpreted to mean the cost of repair or replacement less an allowance for physical depreciation and economic obsolescence. Since this concept of actual cash value was used in Chapter 5 to measure the direct loss, it is clear that these contracts do not (if properly applied) result in overpayments to the insured. However, replacement cost insurance that does not reduce the payment by the amount of the physical depreciation or economic obsolescence has become much more common. The logic behind regarding the property loss as the cost of replacement new has been described in Chapter 5. To reduce the likelihood that insureds will benefit from a loss with this type of protection insurers usually require actual replacement of the property and a high percentage of insurance to the replacement cost new value. Some persons, however, still believe this insurance violates the concept of indemnity and most agree that it does in some cases.

More than 20 states require insurers to issue valued contracts on real estate under which the insurer must pay the face value of the contract if there is a total loss even if the face amount exceeds the actual loss.[1] Without these statutes the insurer would be required to pay only the amount of the loss. The insurer would keep the premium for the overinsurance but pay no extra benefits. The purpose of this legislation is to encourage insurers to reduce the likelihood of overinsurance by inspecting property before they insure it. Although insurers generally have elected to take a chance on overinsurance in these states, the effect of this legislation upon the principle of indemnity is probably slight. The reason is that in order for an overpayment to occur, there must be (1) a total loss and (2) overinsurance, both of which are infrequent events. Valued policies are also common in connection with insurance on rare articles because these articles are more easily and accurately valued before a loss than later.

---

[1] In a few states the statutes also apply to partial losses.

Finally, valued policies are a common feature of marine insurance, but the values are commonly based on invoice cost or some other objective measure and seldom violate the principle of indemnity.

Property insurance contracts covering net income losses usually limit recovery to the actual loss sustained and value the loss in the manner in which losses were measured in Chapter 6. Some valued policies also exist in this field, however, but the values are usually fixed at reasonable levels. Finally, liability insurance contracts provide the insured with defense services and promise to pay up to the contract limits whatever the court or statutes award the insured party or, more commonly, the negotiated settlement. Although the insurer may pay the plaintiff more than the insured would have been able to pay, the insured does not benefit from the insurer payment.[2]

Insurable Interest Property insurance contracts also promise to pay the insured no more than his or her insurable interest at the time of the loss. An insured possesses an insurable interest if he or she would lose financially if the loss occurred. The extent of the possible financial loss measures the amount of the insurable interest. A sole owner's insurable interest is measured by the possible loss to the insured property, whereas a part owner's insurable interest is limited to his or her share of the loss. A secured creditor such as a mortgagee has an insurable interest equal to the debt plus the cost to the creditor, if any, of the insurance protection. Other examples of insurable interests are the liability interest of a bailee in property in his or her care, custody, or control; the interest of a bailee or of some representative of the owner who acts as an agent for the owner; and the interest of persons holding judgments against the owner. Although the interest of a general creditor is considered to be too distant to justify an insurable interest, the creditor achieves an insurable interest when and if he or she obtains a judgment against the owner.

The insurable interest need not exist at the time the insurance is purchased. Bailees, for example, may purchase insurance on all the customers' property that they expect to come under their control within the next year. The interest must exist, however, at the time of the loss. Thus the principle of indemnity is preserved.

Avoidance of Duplicate Coverage Limiting the insured's recovery under the contract to his or her interest in the actual loss may not be enough, however, to make the insurance contract one of indemnity. The insured could still purchase several contracts and collect under each unless there were provisions preventing this duplicate coverage. Property and liability insurance contracts contain three types of provisions dealing with this problem.

The most common provision prorates the liability for the loss among the insurers involved. For example, if an insured who has purchased a $5,000 property insurance contract from insurer A, a $10,000 contract from insurer B, and a $15,000 contract from insurer C suffers a loss of $18,000, insurer A must pay $5/30 \times \$18,000$, or $3,000, insurer B, $6,000, and insurer C, $9,000.

---

[2] For example, the insurer promises to pay up to the contract limits, regardless of the bankruptcy or the insolvency of the insured.

Some contracts provide that the coverage is to be excess over other insurance covering the loss. For example, most automobile insurance contracts state that the insured is protected while driving automobiles he or she does not own but that the insured must exhaust first any protection obtained from the insurance on the nonowned automobile. Finally, other insurance is sometimes prohibited, and the purchase of other insurance would constitute a breach of warranty.

Subrogation   The principle of indemnity could still be violated if the insured could collect (1) from the insurer and (2) from some third party who might be responsible for the loss. Common law, however, states that after paying the insured, a property and liability insurer is subrogated to the insured's rights of recovery from anyone causing the loss. The insurer's right, however, is limited to the extent of its payment. Court precedents suggest that the insurer can recover only after the insured has been fully indemnified, but in practice the recovery is often prorated between the insured and the insurer. Sometimes the insurer recovers first.[3] To illustrate the first rule, if a $20,000 property, insured for $15,000, is totally destroyed by some tort-feasor, the insurer will pay the insured $15,000. If the insured and the insurer sue the feasor jointly and recover $18,000 net of costs, the insured will receive $5,000 and the insurer the remainder. Under the pro rata rule, the insured would receive one-fourth of the recovery or $4,500.

Although this right of the insurer is a common law right, property and liability insurance contracts contain subrogation clauses to remind insureds that this right exists and that any interference with this right may result in a denial of liability by the insurer. Sometimes the insurer will waive this right. For example, in a policy protecting a landlord, the insurer may agree to waive subrogation rights against a tenant.

In addition to preventing the insured from collecting twice, the subrogation principle increases the probability that tort-feasors will be punished for their misdoings.

Life Insurance

Unlike property and liability insurance contracts, most personnel insurance contracts are not contracts of indemnity. Insurers do attempt, however, to prevent insureds or their beneficiaries from gaining in economic terms from death or from accidental injury or sickness. To understand these statements, we must study with respect to personnel insurance the four principles that make the property or liability insurance contract a contract of indemnity. Because life insurance contracts differ from health insurance contracts in this respect, they will be discussed separately. Life insurance contracts are never contracts of indemnity. They contain none of the four types of provisions that usually make a property and liability contract a contract of indemnity.

---

[3] These three rules are analyzed in detail in R. E. Keeton, *Basic Text on Insurance Law* (St. Paul, Minn.: West Publishing Company, 1971), pp. 158–168. Professor Keeton notes that the rule may differ depending upon whether the insured shared part of the loss because the face amount of the insurance was less than the loss, a deductible applied to the loss, or there was a coinsurance penalty. A compromise solution is often reached.

Measure of Loss   Upon the happening of the event insured against, the insurer pays a stated number of dollars even if this sum exceeds the financial loss of the recipient. This procedure has been adopted because of the practical difficulties involved in measuring the financial losses caused by death. Insurers attempt to reduce the moral and morale hazards involved by requiring some reasonable relation between the value and the probable loss before they will issue a contract. Insureds also tend to purchase insurance amounts that are much less than their potential losses. Once the contract is issued, however, the insurer will pay the stated value regardless of the actual loss.

Insurable Interest   The applicant (sometimes by statute the beneficiary if the applicant is neither the insured nor the designated beneficiary) must have an insurable interest in the life of the insured person at the inception of the policy. This interest need not exist at the date of the loss. In other words, the situation is the reverse of that in property and liability insurance. Because the insurable interest need not exist at the time of the loss, it is possible for an applicant-beneficiary to benefit from the loss.

The insurable interest may, as in the case of property and liability insurance, arise out of some financial relationship, but it may also be based solely on *love and affection,* i.e., close blood relationships and marriage. If the person taking out the policy is the person whose life is being insured (and this is the usual situation), the irrebuttable presumption is that the beneficiary has an unlimited insurable interest in the insured's continued life and health.

Avoidance of Duplicate Insurance   Life insurance policies make no reference to other insurance covering the loss. The problems created by ignoring other contracts are attacked by requiring the insured to disclose other insurance contracts when applying for the insurance. Before a life insurer will issue a new contract, it will consider whether the existing contracts plus the new contract would pay more than the probable loss.

Subrogation   Life insurers do not possess subrogation rights, the theory being that because the value of a human life is unlimited, the insured's beneficiaries should be able to collect additional monies from persons who caused the insured's death.

Health Insurance

Health insurance contracts may provide (1) disability income insurance or (2) medical expense insurance. Disability income insurance contracts generally pay a stated amount per week or month while the insured person is disabled. Disability income contracts, like life insurance contracts, are generally not contracts of indemnity. The insurer pays a stated amount per week or month that may exceed the actual loss that period (but the number of payments depends upon how long the insured is actually disabled); the applicant must have an insurable interest only at the inception date; duplicate insurance is ignored; and the insurer has no subrogation rights. Like life insurers, disability income insurers try to avoid overinsurance at the time the contract is written.

Medical expense contracts are much more likely to be contracts of indemnity. Generally the insurer pays actual expenses incurred and an insurable interest must exist at the time of the loss. The contract may or may not contain a provision that stops the insured from collecting monies from two or more insurers for the same loss. Avoidance of duplicate recovery has become a much more common feature in the past two decades. Medical expense insurance issued as part of an employee benefit plan (see Chapter 21) usually contains a coordination of benefits provision that prevents double recoveries. A medical expense contract also may or may not include subrogation rights for the insurer, but these rights are becoming a more common feature of medical expense insurance.

CONTRACT LIMITS

Insurance contracts also contain contract limits that state the maximum amount the insurer will pay. These limits may reduce the recovery below the amount indicated by the provisions and concepts discussed above.

Property Insurance

Property insurance contract limits may be stated in a variety of ways. These limits may be classified according to (1) whether there is an explicit dollar limit, (2) whether the limits provide specific coverage or blanket coverage, (3) whether they are subject to special internal limits, (4) whether the limits differ depending upon the perils, persons, types of loss, or locations covered, and (5) whether the limits are responsive to changes in the values of the property covered.

Most contracts cover losses up to a stated number of dollars, but some contracts, illustrated by most automobile physical damage insurance, do not include a dollar limit. In these contracts the policy limit is in effect the maximum possible loss to the property.

If a single contract limit applies to many types of property at one location or property at two or more locations, this insurance is called *blanket* coverage. If different limits apply to narrowly defined types of property or to the same type of property at different locations, the insurance is called *divided* or *specific* coverage. For example, one limit may apply to a building, another to machinery, and still another to contents, or one limit may apply to contents at one location with a different limit applying to contents at another location. The effect is the same as if a separate contract had been written on each division of property, each having its own policy limit. A distinction might also be made between limits applying separately to a scheduled property item such as machine A and limits applying to a fairly specific type of property. The major attraction of blanket coverage over specific coverage is the flexibility it provides by making the face amount of insurance available to cover losses to any item covered under the contract. On the other hand, blanket insurance may cost more and be subject to more severe coinsurance (see below) and other restrictive provisions.

Another approach places a limit on a certain type of property but some subclass is subject to a lower *internal* limit. For example, one limit may apply to personal property but money losses may be limited to $100. This approach differs from the preceding case in that the internal limits are not separate, independent limits. In the above example a $100 recovery against a money loss is charged against the overall policy limit.

The limits may differ depending upon the peril causing the loss, the persons insured, the type of loss, and the location.

Most property insurance limits are fixed at the beginning of the policy period, but some limits vary according to actual or expected changes in the value of the property covered. For example, automobile physical damage insurance is seldom written with stated dollar limits. Instead the maximum payment under this insurance is the value of the car, which may vary during the policy period. Fixing dollar limits at the beginning of the period can cause problems when the value exposed fluctuates widely during the term of the policy.

To illustrate, take the case of insurance on the contents of mercantile or manufacturing premises where the stock fluctuates in quantity and value. The fixed-amount approach would make it necessary for the insured to carry continuously an amount of insurance equal to the maximum value of the stock and pay premiums for more insurance than he or she needs at other times, or to take less and run the chance of a loss exceeding the insurance, or continuously to watch the stock and the insurance and add or cancel insurance (at the higher short rates) to keep it in step with the stock. These alternatives entail excessive expense, risk, or labor, or all of them. Hence, *reporting forms* have been developed. These forms provide for a provisional amount of insurance, or a stated percentage of the total concurrent insurance, with maximum limits set for property in each location. Provisional values and a provisional premium are agreed upon. The insured makes monthly reports of values exposed to loss at each location. At the expiration of the contract term the values in excess of those covered by specific insurance are averaged, appropriate rates applied, and the premium adjusted by the insurer. The insured either pays an additional premium on coverage in excess of the provisional amounts or receives a refund on amounts by which the provisional amounts exceed the actual. The principal advantage of these forms is that the insured is never overinsured or underinsured. For a large insured with multiple locations, the price is also usually more attractive than for equivalent nonreporting insurance. The principal disadvantage is the effort involved in making the periodic reports. A different example of variable limits is a provision under which the policy limit increases at a stated percentage per month reflecting a specified assumed rate of increase in property values.

Most property insurance contracts provide for reinstatement of the policy limits to their original amount following a loss. A pro rata additional premium that covers the cost of the restored amount is sometimes payable.

Liability Insurance

Liability insurance contracts usually contain separate limits applicable to awards or settlements (1) for bodily injuries, and (2) for property damage. Until 1973 most bodily injury limits stated first, the maximum amount payable on account of the injuries sustained by one person, and second, the maximum amount payable per occurrence. For example, under a $25,000/$50,000 contract the insurer would pay no more than

$25,000 for claims arising out of injuries to one person. If two or more persons were injured in the occurrence, the insurer was not responsible for more than $50,000 of their combined claims, each individual claim being subject first to the per person limit. If two injured persons had claims of $40,000 and $20,000, respectively, the insurer would pay $25,000 plus $20,000, or $45,000. If three injured persons each had claims of $20,000, the insurer would pay $50,000. The property damage limit was usually a stated amount per occurrence. A major revision of an important group of liability insurance contracts in 1973 abolished the per person limit but maintained separate per occurrence limits for the bodily injury and property damage coverages.

Single-limit liability insurance contracts are becoming more common. A maximum amount is payable per occurrence, regardless of the number of persons involved and the mix of bodily injuries and property damage. Because of this flexibility, a $25,000 single-limit contract is more liberal than a policy with $10,000/$20,000 bodily injury limits and a $5,000 property damage limit or than a $20,000 bodily injury limit and a $5,000 property damage limit.

Most liability insurance contracts provide the same protection for each occurrence during the policy period, but sometimes aggregate limits state the insurer's maximum liability for all such events during the policy period.

The defense and investigation costs and other supplementary benefits are not subject to any limits (except for some internal limits on some items) and are provided in addition to the limits applicable to awards or settlements.

Medical payments coverage, often written in conjunction with liability insurance, is usually subject to a specified dollar limit per person. The medical expenses must also be incurred within a specified period of time following the accident. Sometimes there is also a limit per accident.

Workers' compensation policies do not place any dollar limit on compensation benefits other than those prescribed by statute.

Personnel Insurance

Life insurance contracts pay a stated amount upon death. This stated amount may increase or decrease during the lifetime of the insured. If death is caused by accidental means and the contract contains a multiple-indemnity rider, the insurer may pay some multiple—usually double—of the amount otherwise paid.

Health insurance contracts limit the amount paid in various ways. Disability income contracts usually state the amount paid per week or per month and the maximum number of weeks or months the benefit will be paid. Medical expense benefits of all types may be subject to a single amount or time limit, or separate limits may apply to each type of medical expense, such as hospital bills or doctors' fees. Internal limits may apply to such items as daily room-and-board charges and surgical fees. The limits may be doubled if the person is injured in certain specified types of accidents.

COINSURANCE

An important concept affecting the amount of recovery under many business property insurance contracts is coinsurance.

How It Works

The usual coinsurance clause states that if the insured fails to carry insurance equal to some specified percentage of the value of the property at the time of the loss, the insurer is responsible only for that portion of the loss that the amount of insurance bears to the amount required to escape any penalty. For example, assume that an insured six months ago purchased $100,000 of insurance on property with an actual cash value of $150,000. Assume further than the insurance contract contained an 80 percent coinsurance clause. If the property is worth $200,000 today, the amount the insurer would pay toward a loss today would be computed as follows:

$$\frac{\text{Amount of insurance}}{(\text{Coinsurance \%}) \left(\begin{array}{c} \text{value at} \\ \text{time of loss} \end{array}\right)} \times \text{ loss}$$

but not to exceed the loss or the amount of insurance, or

$$\frac{\$100,000}{0.80\,(\$200,000)} \times \text{ loss} = \text{⅝} \times \text{ loss}$$

If the loss were $80,000, the insurer would pay $50,000. If the loss were $170,000, the insurer would pay $100,000, the amount of insurance. The answer will always be the amount of insurance when the loss exceeds the required insurance. The answer will be the loss only when the amount of insurance exceeds the required insurance and equals or exceeds the value of the loss.

If the insured purchases insurance from two or more insurers, each of which issues a contract containing the same coinsurance clause, each insurer will follow the same procedure in determining its liability. For example, if the insured whose situation was analyzed in the preceding paragraph had also purchased $60,000 from some other insurer and the loss was $80,000, that insurer would pay ⅜ of $80,000, or $30,000. The insured would suffer no coinsurance penalty because the total amount of insurance would equal the amount required. If the total amount of insurance with all insurers exceeds the amount required, the liability of the insurer depends (usually) only upon a pro rata liability clause. For example, if the same insured carried $100,000 with the first insurer and $80,000 with the second, the first insurer would be responsible for ⅝ of the loss, or $44,444, and the second insurer for ⁴⁄₉, or $35,556.

Some property insurance contracts always contain a coinsurance clause. For example, blanket forms and reporting forms are available only if the insured accepts some coinsurance condition. In other instances the insured can elect to buy insurance on a "flat" (no coinsurance) or some coinsurance basis. The incentive for accepting a coinsurance clause is a reduced rate. For example, one fire insurance rating jurisdiction offers discounts from the flat rate on buildings as shown in the following table. The reasons for the different discounts will be explained shortly, but the reader should note the sizeable discounts available under certain circumstances. For example, according to this table, by having an 80 percent coinsurance clause included in a fire insurance contract, the owner of a fire-resistant building in a highly protected community can reduce the fire insurance rate by 70 percent.

	Coinsurance percent		
	50	80	90
Type of property and location	Discount percent		
Fire-resistant building			
Highly protected community	56	70	73
Poorly protected community	45	60	64
Frame building			
Highly protected community		10	15
Poorly protected community			

The Rationale

The purpose of coinsurance is to achieve indirectly large amounts of insurance relative to the value of the property. Because most property losses are small relative to the value exposed, the cost of providing insurance protection without any coinsurance on property of a specified value does not increase proportionately with the amount of insurance. For example, it does not cost twice as much to provide $80,000 of insurance on a $100,000 building as to provide $40,000 of protection. For the same reason, if all insureds with $100,000 buildings purchased $80,000 insurance contracts, the insurance premium rate (price per $100 of insurance) could be considerably less than if they all purchased $40,000 of protection. Consequently, it would be unfair to charge the same premium rate per $100 for $40,000 and $80,000 contracts. To state the matter more generally, the premium rate should depend upon the relation between the insurance and the value of the property.

One solution would be to prepare a table of graded rates that decrease as the ratio of insurance to value increases. Each property to be insured would have to be appraised and the ratio of the desired amount of insurance to the value calculated. The proper rate could then be obtained from the table. This solution has usually been rejected because the insurer would incur considerable expense in appraising each property presented for insurance. This solution would also be inadequate from the insurer's viewpoint if the property values fluctuated widely during the policy period.

An alternative solution is the coinsurance clause. Each of the coinsurance discounts should produce a rate corresponding to the graded rate for the corresponding percentage relation between the insurance and the property value. For example, the discount for an 80 percent coinsurance clause should be related to the graded rate for insurance equal to 80 percent of the property value. The coinsurance discounts should vary with the type of property and the grade of community protection, because smaller percentage losses are relatively more important with respect to high-grade properties in well-protected communities. The insureds who carry insurance equal to 80 percent or more of the value can select an 80 percent coinsurance clause, get the rate discount that will reduce the rate to the graded rate for 80 percent insurance to value, and yet avoid any coinsurance penalty. If a loss occurs, the insurer will pay the entire loss up to the insurance amount. Insureds who carry less insurance but elect the 80 percent clause will find that when a loss occurs, the insurer will assume that the insured has total insurance equal to 80 percent of the property value and determine its own liability on a pro rata basis. If, for example, the insurance amount is 40 percent of the property value, the insurer will pay only half the loss but in no case more than 40 percent of the property value. This coinsurance approach is less costly for the insurer to administer because it needs only to check carefully the value of the relatively few properties involved in a loss.

Difficulties in Application

Basing the coinsurance calculation on the value at the time of the loss can be troublesome for the insured because the insured may wonder whether he or she has purchased enough insurance to avoid a coinsurance penalty. This difficulty is especially evident with respect to personal property that fluctuates widely in value. One solution available to many insureds is an agreed amount endorsement, under which the insured and the insurer agree in advance upon the valuation for coinsurance purposes. Another solution with respect to personal property is the reporting form noted under "Policy Limits—Property Insurance" in this chapter, which is always written on a full-reporting (100 percent coinsurance) basis but in which the insurance always equals the amount exposed.

If a loss is small, the cost of appraising the entire property following a loss in order to determine its value for coinsurance purposes may exceed or almost equal the loss. Under a waiver of inventory clause, the insurer agrees to waive the requirement of a separate inventory if the loss is less than, say, 2 percent of the insurance amount. The coinsurance clause, however, still applies.[4]

DEDUCTIBLE CLAUSES

The purpose and general nature of deductible clauses have already been discussed in Chapter 12 under "Use of Insurance with Other Tools." Attention will be focused here on the different forms that deductibles can assume. The examples are taken primarily from property insurance and health insurance, where they are most common, but deductibles are also found in liability insurance contracts. Life insurance contracts do not contain deductible clauses; all losses are total.

The first way to classify deductibles is according to whether they apply to each item damaged, each person insured, each occurrence, accident, or illness, or the total losses in a stated period. Deductibles applicable to the total losses in a year are usually called

---

[4] An interesting variant of the typical coinsurance clause is used in burglary insurance covering merchandise, furniture, and fixtures. Under this clause the insurer states that it shall not be liable for a greater proportion of the loss on merchandise than the policy limit bears to the *lesser* of two values: (1) a coinsurance percentage times the actual cash value of the merchandise, or (2) a coinsurance limit. All policies contain coinsurance percentages and coinsurance limits. The coinsurance percentage varies by territory; it is higher in those territories where burglaries are more common. The coinsurance limit varies by trade group; it is higher for those trades with high-value, light-weight items. The coinsurance limit approximates the maximum probable burglary for each trade group, regardless of the value exposed.

"aggregate deductibles." Both the frequency and the severity of the losses determine whether an insured will have a claim in excess of an aggregate deductible.

Second, the deductible may be a specified amount, a percentage of the loss, a percentage of the face amount of insurance, or a waiting period before disability income losses are paid, or it may be determined in some other way. Expressing the deductible as a percentage of the loss differs from the other practices described above in that the deductible amount in dollars increases as the size of the loss increases. Sometimes a percentage deductible applies to losses after first subtracting a stated deductible amount; in other cases a percentage deductible is not permitted to exceed a stated dollar amount. Sometimes the deductible amount decreases as the loss size increases—for example, the insurer may agree to pay 125 percent of the losses in excess of $100 or more until the deductible amount is reduced to zero, after which the entire loss is paid. The result is a $100 deductible for losses of $100 or less, a $75 deductible for a $200 loss, a $25 deductible for a $400 loss, and no deductible for losses of $500 or more. A related concept in some disability income insurance contracts (mainly workers' compensation insurance) is a retroactive waiting period under which the waiting period is waived if the disability extends beyond a certain period. Still another type of deductible is a flat amount that decreases as the number of claim-free years increases.

Third, the deductible may apply to all losses covered under the contract or only to certain losses. For example, under an all risks contract the deductible may not apply to losses caused by fire and several other specified perils.

Fourth, the deductible may be a franchise, in which case the insurer pays all losses in excess of the franchise amount. For example, if the franchise is 3 percent of the amount of insurance, the insurer under a $10,000 contract would pay nothing on losses of less than $300 but would pay the total amount of larger losses. This approach is used primarily in marine insurance.

SOME KEY CONCEPTS

Contract of indemnity   A contract that will indemnify the insured for losses sustained but will not permit the insured to gain from the happening of the event insured against. Related concepts are measure of the loss, insurable interest, other insurance, and subrogation.

Divided or specific coverage   Property insurance that applies separate policy limits to narrowly defined types of property or to the same type of property at different locations.

Blanket coverage   Property insurance that applies a single policy limit to many types of property at one location or property at two or more locations. Blanket coverage permits property to be moved from one covered location to another without changing the amount of protection.

Reporting form   A property insurance form under which the policy limit is automatically adjusted to equal the value of the property covered.

Single-limit liability insurance   Liability insurance that imposes a single policy limit on all claims per occurrence, regardless of the mix of bodily injury and property damage and the number of claims.

Coinsurance clause   A clause that obligates the insurer to pay only the proportion of any loss that the amount of insurance purchased bears to the product of the coinsurance percentage and the value of the insured property at the time of the loss. An indirect way to achieve rate equity.

Deductible clause   A clause that requires the insured to retain part of the potential losses covered under an insurance contract, typically the first $100 or some other amount per occurrence.

REVIEW QUESTIONS*

1 Describe briefly the four sets of contract provisions affecting the amount of recovery.
2 **a** Are property and liability insurance contracts contracts of indemnity? Why or why not?
   b Are life and health insurance contracts contracts of indemnity? Why or why not?
3 Compare the concepts of insurable interest in *(a)* property insurance and *(b)* life insurance.
4 A $50,000 building, insured for $40,000, is totally destroyed by a fire caused by the negligent act of a neighbor. The insurer pays $40,000 and the insured and the insurer sue the tort-feasor jointly. If the recovery is $33,000 net of costs, how much will the insured recover? ($10,000 or, if prorated, $6,600.)
5 Under what conditions would a risk manager select each of the following?
   a Specific coverage
   b Blanket coverage
   c A reporting form
6 An insured suffers an insured loss during a policy period. How will the insured's recovery for this loss affect the policy limits applicable to future losses in:
   a Property insurance?
   b Liability insurance?
   c Health insurance?
7 From the viewpoint of the insured, which of the following liability limits is more liberal—a single limit of $50,000 or a $40,000 bodily injury limit and a $10,000 property damage limit? Why?
8 An insured purchases a three-year $90,000 fire insurance contract containing an 80 percent coinsurance clause on a building valued at $100,000. Two years later, when a $40,000 loss occurs, the building is valued at $150,000. How much will the insurer pay? ($30,000) How much would the insurer pay if the loss had been $130,000? ($90,000)
9 Why should an insured receive a larger coinsurance discount from the flat rate:
   a For an 80 percent coinsurance clause than for a 60 percent coinsurance clause?
   b If the insured has a fire-resistant building than if he or she has a frame building?
10 **a** Instead of using coinsurance clauses, fire insurers could have graded rates according to the percentage of insurance to value. Why was this approach rejected?
   b What problem arises under the coinsurance approach that would not arise under the graded-premium approach? What solutions are available?
11 Smith believes that the coinsurance clause will not be applicable to small losses his firm may incur because his contract contains a waiver of inventory clause. Is he correct?
12 Deductibles can be classified in at least four ways. Explain each of these four classifications.
13 **a** If an insurer agrees to pay 111 percent of losses in excess of $50, what deductible amount applies to a $350 loss? ($17)
   b If an insurance contract contains a $50 franchise clause, how much will the insurer contribute toward a $30 loss? ($0) a $75 loss? ($75).

* Items in parentheses are answers.

SUGGESTIONS FOR ADDITIONAL READING

Greene, M. R., and J. S. Trieschmann: *Risk and Insurance* (6th ed., Cincinnati: South-Western Publishing Company, Inc., 1984), chap. 9.

Horn, R. C.: *Subrogation and Insurance Theory and Practice* (Homewood, Ill.: Richard D. Irwin, Inc., 1964).

Keeton, R. E.: *Basic Text on Insurance Law* (St. Paul, Minn.: West Publishing Company, 1971), chap. 3.

Mehr, Robert I.: *Fundamentals of Insurance* (Homewood, Ill.: Richard D. Irwin, Inc., 1983), chap. 7.

Mehr, R. I., and E. Cammack: *Principles of Insurance* (7th ed., Homewood, Ill.: Richard D. Irwin, Inc., 1980), chap. 9.

Mowbray, A. H., R. H. Blanchard, and C. A. Williams, Jr.: *Insurance* (6th ed., New York: McGraw-Hill Book Company, 1969), chaps. 10 and 11.

Smith, Michael L.: *Selection of Deductibles in Property and Liability Insurance,* unpublished doctoral dissertation, The University of Minnesota, 1974.

Williams, C. A., Jr., G. L. Head, R. C. Horn, and G. W. Glendenning: *Principles of Risk Management and Insurance,* vol. II (2d ed., Malvern, Pa.: American Institute for Property and Liability Underwriters, Inc., 1981), chaps. 8, 11, 12, and 13.

CHAPTER 18

PROPERTY INSURANCE CONTRACTS

LEARNING OBJECTIVES

After you have completed this chapter, you should be able to:

1 Analyze the events covered and the amount the insurer must pay under the standard fire policy.

2 Define what property is covered under a general property form under the building item and under the two personal property items.

3 Describe the perils added by the extended coverage endorsement and the optional perils endorsement.

4 Describe how a business can secure all risk coverage on its buildings and its personal property.

5 Explain why a business might wish to purchase difference-in-conditions insurance.

6 Explain the principal features of rent insurance, business interruption insurance, and extra expense insurance.

7 Identify the various ways in which a business can insure against theft losses.

8 Distinguish between a blanket position bond and a commercial blanket bond.

9 Describe the most common surety bonds used by businesses.

10 Summarize the protection provided by a boiler and machinery insurance contract.

11 Explain the major features of cargo insurance.

12 List four important types of inland marine insurance business floaters.

INTRODUCTION

This chapter deals with property insurance. In Chapter 19 we will discuss liability insurance, some package contracts that combine property and liability insurance, and some miscellaneous contracts. This chapter describes the basic property protection provided by the fire insurance policy, some of its many forms and endorsements, theft insurance, dishonesty insurance or fidelity bonding, surety bonding, boiler and machinery insurance, glass insurance, inland marine insurance, and ocean marine insurance.

BASIC PROPERTY PROTECTION

The basic property insurance contract covering a building, its contents, or both is usually a standard fire insurance policy plus one or more forms and one or more endorsements.[1] The standard fire policy is the 1943 New York Standard Fire Policy explained below or some slightly modified version. Most states have statutes requiring the use of some standard policy to insure real property located in that state; others have state insurance department directives making the use of such a policy compulsory.

The general property form or some other descriptive form must be attached to the policy to complete the contract. Without the form the contract would not describe the property covered in sufficient detail to be operational. The form also gives the insurer the opportunity to modify the standard policy which (1) may be outdated because state legislatures seldom change the standard policy (e.g., the New York standard policy is a 1943 version) or (2) provides the same coverage for all insureds. Insurers may prefer to vary the coverage somewhat, depending upon the type of exposure or to vary the options that are available (e.g., some forms cover more perils than others).

The standard policy plus the descriptive form may be modified by one or more other forms or endorsements. These other forms may add, for example, business interruption insurance or extra expense insurance. Endorsements may increase or decrease the coverage. For example, they may add additional perils or exclude some parts of a covered building, such as the foundations. Some endorsements are so commonly used that they have been incorporated in one or more descriptive forms.

Unlike the standard fire policy, fire insurance forms and endorsements are not standardized by state law. Sometimes a state insurance department directive calls for standardization of the more popular forms and endorsements, but usually insurers are permitted to design their own contracts except for the statutory policy. Voluntarily, however, insurers tend to use the forms and endorsements developed by rating bureaus, some of which are described below.

To insure a building against direct and indirect property losses a business is most likely to purchase a standard fire policy plus (1) a general property form plus one or more endorsements that add more named perils or (2) a special building property form that provides all-risks coverage. Alternatively the business may purchase (1) above

---

[1] As indicated in Chapter 15, the Insurance Services Office is currently reviewing a set of simplified property insurance forms that may become effective by late 1985. In addition to being easier to read, these forms would make some important substantive changes in coverage.

plus separate difference in conditions insurance that provides all risks coverage except for those perils covered under (1). To insure personal property the choices are similar except that a special personal property form replaces the special building form under (2) above. A business will also typically purchase forms that will cover business interruption or extra expense losses.

Each of these kinds of insurance is discussed in varying detail below. The special multi-peril policy, a package policy that may be more appropriate for small and medium-size businesses, is discussed in Chapter 19.

Standard Fire Policy

Most of page 1 of the 1943 New York standard policy is a declarations section in which is printed such information as the insured's name and mailing address, the policy inception and expiration dates, the description and location of the property covered, the perils insured against, the amount of insurance applicable to each peril, and the code numbers of the forms and endorsements that are attached. The first page also contains a brief insuring agreement that states the insurer's basic promise. The second page is 165 numbered lines that describe such matters as perils not included, uninsurable and excepted property, cancellation, mortgagee interests and obligations, and requirements in case a loss occurs.

Perils The standard fire policy covers losses caused by fire, lightning, and removal from the premises endangered by fire. Not all fires are covered under the fire insurance contract, but the exclusions are few: (1) fires caused by "war," (2) fires intentionally set by public authorities (except to prevent the spread of fire), and (3) fires set intentionally by the insured. The policy does not specifically exclude fires set intentionally by the insured, but the courts have held that to cover them would be contrary to public policy.

Property The declarations section of the policy identifies briefly the insured property; the details are left for the descriptive form (to be described later). The policy also states that money, securities, bills, deeds, evidences of debt, and other numismatic property are never to be covered under the fire insurance contract. The reason for this exclusion is that the losses with respect to some of these properties, such as deeds, are difficult to value, while the losses of others, such as money, would be difficult to prove and could easily be exaggerated. Such losses are covered, however, under other contracts to be discussed in this chapter. Bullion and manuscripts are insured only if they are specifically mentioned in the form added to the policy.

Persons The policy covers the named insured or the named insured's legal representatives. Legal representatives could include a guardian, if any; the executor of the named insured's estate; a trustee in bankruptcy; an agent; or some similar party.

Losses The policy covers direct property losses, not indirect or net income losses. To avoid any doubt on this score, the policy specifically states that it does not cover

(1) any increased cost of repair or reconstruction by reason of any ordinance or law regulating construction or repair or (2) any loss resulting from interruption of business.

Location   The policy specifies that, with one exception, the property must be situated at the location named in the contract. The exception covers the enforced removal of the property from that location because it is endangered by fire. In this instance the coverage is continued for five days at the new location or locations in order to give the insured time to arrange new insurance. If two or more new locations are involved, the temporary insurance amount is allocated among the new locations according to the value at each location.

Time   The coverage commences at noon, standard time, at the location named in the contract, on a stated inception date to noon, standard time, on a stated expiration date. So long as the fire commences before the expiration time, the entire loss resulting from that fire is covered.

The policy term is usually one year or three years, but it may be some fraction of a year or some other multiple of a year. Both the insured and the insurer, however, have the right to cancel the contract prior to the expiration date. Neither need give any reason for requesting the cancellation. If the insurer cancels the contract, the cancellation is effective five days after the insurer notifies the insured, and the insurer must return a pro rata portion of the premium to the insured. If the insured cancels the contract, the cancellation is effective as soon as he or she notifies the insurer. The insurer must return a short-rate portion of the premium. Some states limit the insurer's right to cancel in the same manner as that described in Chapter 32 for homeowner's contracts.

Other Conditions Suspending or Terminating the Coverage   The policy describes two conditions that suspend the coverage while they exist. The first suspends coverage while there is an increase in the hazard within the knowledge or control of the insured. The courts, however, usually choose to ignore slight or temporary increases. An example of an increase that would suspend the policy would be a change in occupancy from a retail store to paper manufacturing without notification to the insurer. The policy would become effective again as soon as the original occupancy or an equally safe occupancy was restored. The second condition suspends the coverage after the property has been vacant or unoccupied for more than 60 consecutive days. A property is considered vacant if it contains no people or things; it is considered unoccupied if it contains no people. In order to break a spell of consecutive days of vacancy or unoccupancy, the insured must reoccupy the property and use it for the purpose for which it was intended; it is not enough to make a token return or to have a watchperson occupy the premises.

Other policy conditions that would enable the insurer to void the contract are failure of the insured to exercise due care to save the property during and after a loss or when neighboring property is endangered by fire, or an attempt by the insured in some way to defeat the subrogation rights of the insurer.

Amount of Recovery The insurer promises to pay the insured the actual cash value of the loss but never more than the cost of repair or replacement with material of like kind and quality. Usually the cash value is the cost of repair or replacement less physical depreciation, but it might be less if the property is obsolete; i.e., the obsolescence might reduce the actual cash value below the repair or replacement cost less physical depreciation. The actual cash value could exceed the repair or replacement cost less physical depreciation if the property had some additional market value because it was already in existence. The insurer, of course, will pay no more than the face value of the policy, which may be less than the actual cash value. Its obligation is also limited to the insurable interest of the insured. Finally, if the insured has other insurance, the insurer agrees to share the loss on a pro rata basis with the other insurers.

General Property Form

The general property form, which commonly completes a fire insurance contract covering direct or indirect property losses, contains nine sections dealing for the most part with perils, property, persons, locations, and the amount of recovery.

Perils Section VI extends the policy to cover additional perils. This extension is accomplished by including in the form itself two popular endorsements which become effective only if the declarations indicate that the insured has paid the required extra premiums. The first of these two endorsements is an *extended coverage endorsement* which adds the following perils: windstorm, hail, explosion, riot, riot attending a strike, civil commotion, aircraft, and vehicles. The coverage is limited by the ways in which the perils are defined or by exclusions. For example, windstorm damage does not include damage caused by rain, snow, sand or dust, whether driven by wind or not, unless the wind first damages directly the roof or walls of the building. Windstorm damage to metal smokestacks or, when outside of buildings, to trees, shrubs, or plants, awnings or canopies of fabric or slat construction, or radio or television antennas, is not covered. Smoke from agricultural smudging or industrial operations is excluded. Explosion does not include explosion by steam boilers, steam pipes, steam turbines, or steam engines if owned, leased, or operated by the insured. Riots are limited by the statutory definition noted in Chapter 16. Aircraft damage must result from the actual physical contact of the damaged property with the aircraft or from an object falling from an aircraft. Vehicles must also touch the damaged property for the loss to be covered. In addition, the vehicle cannot be owned or operated by the insured or any tenant of the described premises. The form does not cover vehicle damage to fences, driveways, or walls, or when outside of buildings, to trees, shrubs, or plants.

The *vandalism endorsement,* which becomes effective only if the insured also purchases the extended coverage endorsement, adds vandalism or malicious mischief, meaning only willful and malicious damage to or destruction of covered property.

Excluded under both endorsements are losses caused by nuclear reaction or nuclear radiation; war; or flood, surface water, waves, sewer or drain backup. Also excluded is water below the surface of the ground that exerts pressure on or flows, seeps, or leaks through foundations, basement floors or walls, driveways, or the like.

Property and Persons   This form can be used to insure (a) buildings, (b) personal property of the insured, and (c) personal property of others. How a building is defined is of special interest to insureds because: (1) the insured may require insurance only on the building or (2) the cost of insuring a building is less than the cost of insuring personal property having the same value. The building items include (a) attached additions and extensions, (b) fixtures, machinery, and equipment that is a permanent part of the building and is related to the service of the building, (c) yard fixtures, such as fences, and (d) personal property of the named insured used to maintain or service the building, such as fire-extinguishing apparatus, outdoor furniture, floor coverings, and appliances for refrigerating, ventilating, cooking, and laundering. Not included, however, is personal property located in apartments or rooms furnished by the named insured as a landlord.

As indicated in Chapter 6, a business should check to determine whether it is responsible for losses to telephone switching equipment, power transformers, or vending machines that are owned by others. If the business is responsible as a representative of the owner, care must be taken to have these items included in the coverage. If not, they should be excluded. The amount of insurance to be purchased is also affected because inclusion or exclusion determines the magnitude of the potential loss and the amount of insurance required to avoid a coinsurance penalty.

Personal property of the insured includes three kinds of property. First, business personal property owned by the named that is usual to the type of occupancy. Specifically included are bullion, manuscripts, furniture, fixtures, and supplies not otherwise covered under the policy (e.g., under the building item). Second, the named insured's interest in personal property owned by others to the extent that damage to that property would cause the named insured to lose the cost of services that he or she has provided with respect to that property (e.g., labor and material charges). Third, tenant's improvements and betterments which, by definition, is applicable only if the named insured is a tenant. Tenant's improvements and betterments is the tenant's use interest in fixtures, alterations, installations, or additions that: (1) are part of a building occupied but not owned by the named insured, (2) were made or acquired at the tenant's expense, exclusive of rent paid by the tenant, and (3) may not legally be removed by the tenant.

Personal property of others is personal property of others in the care, custody, or control of the named insured. Unlike the other two items, which protected the named insured's interest, this item covers the interests of others. The named insured may purchase this policy to avoid liability claims, as a goodwill gesture, or as part of an agreement for which the others pay a fee to the named insured.

Certain personal property is excluded under both of the personal property items: animals and pets; aircraft and watercraft (other than rowboats and canoes that are on the premises); personal property covered more specifically in whole or in part by other insurance, except to the extent that the loss exceeds this other insurance; and personal property in which other parties also have an insured interest and the named insured's interest in that property is covered by other insurance.

Property that is not covered unless specifically described in the declarations or added by endorsement includes vehicles designed for use on public thoroughfares; outdoor signs; outdoor swimming pools, fences, piers, wharves, and docks; beach or diving platforms; retaining walls not a part of insured buildings; and walks, roadways, and other paved surfaces.

If the contract contains a coinsurance clause, the following property is not covered unless the insured prefers to remove this exclusion through an endorsement: cost of excavations, grading, or filling; foundations of buildings, machinery, boilers, or engines below the undersurface of the lowest basement floor or, if there is no basement, below the surface of the ground; pilings which are underground or below the low water mark; or underground piers, pipes, flues, and drains. As explained in Chapter 17 the purpose of this exclusion is to reduce the amount of insurance required to avoid a *coinsurance penalty*. The excluded property is much less susceptible to damage than the rest of the building, but it would be a mistake to conclude that it is never damaged.

If the contract contains an 80 percent or higher coinsurance clause, the form adds some property that would not otherwise be covered. First, the insured may apply on each location up to 2 percent of the amount of insurance on personal property of the insured at that location to cover *personal property of others* in the care, custody, or control of the insured. This extension may make separate coverage of personal property of others unnecessary, but the maximum coverage at each location is limited to $2,000. Second, the named insured may apply up to 10 percent, but no more than $25,000, of the amount of insurance on buildings to cover for 30 days: (1) *new buildings being constructed on the premises* and intended for similar occupancy and (2) *buildings acquired at other locations* used for similar occupancies or warehouse purposes. The named insured may also apply up to 10 percent, but not more than $10,000, of the amount of insurance on personal property of the insured to cover for 30 days such *property newly acquired* by the named insured at *locations elsewhere* than at the described premises. Third, the named insured may apply up to 5 percent, but no more than $500, of the amount of insurance on personal property of the insured to cover *personal effects of the named insured, officers, partners, or employees.* No one individual can collect more than $100 per loss under this extension. No payment is made if the loss would be covered under other insurance except for this extension. Fourth, the named insured can apply up to 5 percent, but no more than $500, of the amount of insurance on personal property of the insured to cover the cost of research and other expense incurred to reproduce, replace, or *restore valuable papers and records*. This extension is important because otherwise the insurer is responsible only for the cost of blank materials plus the cost of transcribing or copying such records. Fifth, the insured may apply up to 5 percent, but not exceeding $1,000, of the sum of the amounts of insurance on the buildings and the personal property of the insured to cover *outdoor trees, shrubs, and plants* on the described premises against losses caused by fire, lightning, explosion, riot, civil commotion, or aircraft. The maximum payment on any one tree, shrub, or plant is $250.

Location   Most losses are covered only if they occur at the location or locations specified in the declarations section. Personal property is also covered if at the time of the loss it is in the open, including within vehicles, within 100 feet of the described premises.

If the contract contains an 80 percent or higher coinsurance clause, the insured may apply up to 2 percent of the sum of the insurance on the building and personal property of the insured items to cover owned property (other than merchandise and manufacturing stock) damaged off premises. The maximum coverage under this extension, however, cannot exceed $5,000. The property must be off premises because it was temporarily removed to be cleaned, repaired, reconstructed, or restored. The property is not covered if it is in transit or if it is located at any premises owned, leased, operated, or controlled by the named insured.

Other Conditions   Permission is granted (1) to make additions, alterations, and repairs and (2) for the property to be unoccupied in ways that are usual or incidental to the nature of the described occupancy.

The first permission removes a question that might otherwise arise under the increase in hazard provision in the standard policy. The second permission relaxes the unoccupancy limit in the standard policy, but not the vacancy limit.

A *protective-safeguards* clause obligates the insured to maintain, so far as it is within his or her control, the protective safeguards set forth in endorsements to the contract. Examples of such safeguards are automatic sprinklers and guards. Failure to maintain these safeguards suspends the insurance.

The cancellation provision is the same as the one in the standard fire policy, but it may be possible to increase the number of days before the cancellation becomes effective to 30–60 days or even longer.

Amount of Recovery   The property can be insured on a specific or a blanket basis. These two bases were explained in Chapter 17.

Several clauses deal with the amount of recovery. For example, the form specifically obligates the insurer to pay the cost of removing debris caused by a covered peril.

Tenant's improvements and betterments are valued at their actual cash value if these improvements are repaired or replaced at the expense of the named insured. If the improvements are not repaired or replaced, the tenant is paid a fraction of the original cost determined by dividing the unexpired term of the lease by the time between the date such improvements were made and the expiration date of the lease.

Coinsurance is not required, but the form contains a coinsurance clause that becomes effective if elected by the insured. We have already cited several additional benefits that are provided by this form only when the contract contains an 80 percent or higher coinsurance clause. To avoid the problem that increasing values during the policy period pose for the insured, it may be possible to secure an agreed-amount endorsement explained in Chapter 17. Also available is an inflation-guard endorsement that increases the amount of insurance by a specified percent each quarter.

A $100 deductible per occurrence applies separately to each building and personal property therein and to personal property in the open. The maximum deductible per occurrence is $1,000.

Other Forms and Endorsements

Optional Perils Endorsement An optional perils endorsement adds five perils to those already covered under the extended coverage endorsement and the vandalism and malicious mischief endorsements. The five additional perils are (1) breakage of glass that is part of the building, (2) falling objects such as a tree, (3) the weight of ice, snow, or sleet, (4) the accidental discharge or overflow of water or steam from within a plumbing, heating, or air conditioning system or domestic appliance (but only when the discharge or overflow results from the breaking or cracking of any pipes, parts, or fixtures forming a part of the system or appliance), and (5) collapse of the building or any part of it. Collapse does not include mere settling, cracking, shrinkage, bulging, or expansion of pavements, patios, foundations, walls, floors, roofs, or ceilings.

Sprinkler Leakage Endorsement A sprinkler leakage endorsement extends the fire insurance contract to protect the insured against loss caused when water is released from an automatic sprinkler system for reasons other than fire. The water or other agent may escape from any part of the system—the pipes, tanks, pumps, valves, or heads—and in any part of the building. The water may in fact come from a sprinkler belonging to someone else.

Special Building Form Instead of purchasing a general property form with some or all of the named perils endorsements described above, a business may elect to cover its buildings with a special building form that provides all risks coverage. All causes of loss are covered except those specifically excluded. Among the excluded perils are wear and tear; smog; smoke; vapor or gas from agricultural or industrial operations; mechanical breakdowns; settling, cracking, shrinkage, bulging, or expansion of pavements, foundations, walls, floors, roofs, or ceilings; animals, birds, vermin, termites, or other insects; earthquakes; landslides; flood; war; nuclear reactions or radiation; and the explosion of steam boilers owned by, leased by, or operated under the control of the insured.

The definition of the property covered is essentially the same as under the general property form. Three more liberal extensions of coverage are (1) on newly acquired property as *additional* insurance up to 25 percent of the building limit, but not exceeding $100,000, (2) on off-premises property as additional insurance up to 2 percent of the building limit, but not exceeding $5,000, and (3) on outdoor trees, shrubs, and plants as additional insurance up to $1,000, but not more than $250 per item.

On most losses the amount the insurer pays is determined in essentially the same way as under the general property form. For example, the coinsurance and deductible provisions are the same. However, if the replacement cost new is $1,000 or less, the insurer pays this amount.

Special Personal Property Form Instead of insuring some or all of its personal property under a general property form plus some named-perils endorsements, a business may purchase for that property a special personal property form. Like the special building form, the special personal property form provides all risks coverage.

The excluded perils are essentially the same plus mysterious disappearance. Theft losses can be excluded under an optional theft exclusion endorsement.

Personal property is defined essentially the same way as under the general property form but coverage for some property is limited to certain specified perils, special dollar limits, or both. For example, jewelry and watches are covered only against specified perils and only up to $2,500 per occurrence. Patterns, dies, molds, models, and forms are also covered only against specified perils and up to $2,500 per occurrence.

Extra expense losses caused by damage to either the building or the personal property therein are covered up to $1,000 per occurrence. Otherwise the amount the insurer must pay is determined essentially the same way as under the general property form.

Rent or Rental Value Form   A rent or rental value form extends the type of losses covered under the fire insurance contract to cover one type of net income loss that is very important to many businesses. Rent insurance protects a landlord or tenant against the loss of rent paid under a written or oral contract. Whether the landlord or the tenant needs this insurance depends upon whether the rent continues during the period the property is untenantable. Rental value insurance protects an owner-occupant against loss of the use value of the building. Rental value insurance can also be used to protect a tenant against the loss of use of the building less any contract rent that is discontinued.

Rent and rental value insurance can be written in many different ways. Contracts protecting landlords with multiple units may be written to cover the loss of probable rents on the entire property, or the coverage may be limited to the loss on those units that are rented at the time the premises are damaged.

Seasonal properties can be covered only with respect to those months during which they are normally rented. Some forms are written on a 60, 80, or 100 percent coinsurance basis, the value for coinsurance purposes being rentals for one year starting with the date of the damage; other forms contain no coinsurance provision but limit the recovery in one month to some fraction such as $\frac{1}{12}$ of the face amount. To illustrate, assume a year's rentals amount to $60,000 and a 60 percent coinsurance clause applies. If the insured carries $24,000 of rent insurance, the insurer will pay $24,000/.60 ($60,000) or $\frac{2}{3}$ of any rent loss subject to a maximum payment of $24,000. If the $\frac{1}{12}$ fraction applies, all losses are paid in full up to a monthly maximum of $\frac{1}{12}$ of $24,000 or $2,000.

If the rent fluctuates, usually because it is tied to some uncertain amount such as sales, a premium adjustment form can be used that provides a refund if the insurance carried exceeds the coinsurance percentage in the form times the actual average annual rental value.

Business Interruption Forms   Under a business interruption form, the insurer promises to pay the gross earnings that the firm could have made while the business is shut down because of damage caused by an insured peril less those expenses that do not continue. Gross earnings for a *nonmanufacturing* firm are in most cases net sales (gross sales less returns and allowances) less the cost of goods sold. Gross earnings for a *manufacturing* firm are the net sales value of production less the cost of raw materials and supplies used in converting these raw materials into finished stock. The distinction is important because the mercantile firm is protected against interruption to the *selling* process, whereas a manufacturing firm is protected against interruption to the *manufacturing* process. A manufacturing firm that had voluntarily ceased manufacturing in order to concentrate on selling finished goods in its warehouse would collect nothing under business interruption insurance if a fire damaged the manufacturing plant and warehouse, but the damage would have been repaired before the firm would have voluntarily resumed its manufacturing operations. To cover loss of profits on finished goods, a manufacturer can have added a *manufacturer's selling price endorsement,* which states that losses on finished goods will be settled at their selling price, not their actual cash value.

Because the loss of gross earnings less the noncontinuing expenses equals the net profit loss plus the continuing expenses, the loss that is covered can be computed either way. The reader should note that even a firm operating at a slight loss would suffer a business interruption loss if its operation would have enabled it to meet some of the continuing expenses.

The gross earnings form must contain a 50 percent, 60 percent, 70 percent, or 80 percent coinsurance clause. The value to which the coinsurance percentage is applied is the gross earnings expected except for the interruption during the one-year period following the commencement of the shutdown. Note that noncontinuing expenses are not deducted from this figure because these expenses would be difficult to estimate, especially at the time the contract is purchased. Since one factor affecting the amount of insurance to be purchased is the value to which the coinsurance percentage will be applied in case of a loss, the drafters of the form decided to ignore the difficult-to-estimate noncontinuing expenses in calculating the value. The insured will therefore have to purchase more insurance to avoid a coinsurance penalty, but this disadvantage is supposed to have been offset by lower premium rates.[2]

The method for determining the amount the insurer will pay can be summarized in the following formula:

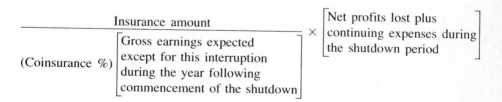

$$\frac{\text{Insurance amount}}{(\text{Coinsurance \%}) \begin{bmatrix} \text{Gross earnings expected} \\ \text{except for this interruption} \\ \text{during the year following} \\ \text{commencement of the shutdown} \end{bmatrix}} \times \begin{bmatrix} \text{Net profits lost plus} \\ \text{continuing expenses during} \\ \text{the shutdown period} \end{bmatrix}$$

To illustrate the application of this formula, assume that the following abbreviated financial statement summarizes the annual operations of a small manufacturing firm whose operations are not seasonal and have not changed over time:

---

[2] Note that in case of a year's shutdown, the insured will collect less than the value for coinsurance purposes unless there are no noncontinuing expenses. The insured can, however, continue to collect if the shutdown exceeds one year, until the proceeds are exhausted.

Net sales value of production	$800,000
Cost of raw materials	400,000
Payroll	200,000
Other expenses	150,000
Profits	50,000

Assume further that the firm is shut down for three months as a result of a fire and that the entire payroll plus one-half of the other expenses is continued. Under a 50 percent coinsurance gross earnings form with a $200,000 policy limit, the firm will collect the following amount:

$$\frac{\$200,000}{0.50\ (\$800,000\ -\ \$400,000)}\ [\tfrac{1}{4}(\$50,000)\ +\ \tfrac{1}{4}(\$200,000)\ +\ (\tfrac{1}{4})(\tfrac{1}{2})(\$150,000)]$$

$$=\frac{\$200,000}{0.50\ (\$400,000)}\ (\$81,250)$$

$$=\$81,250$$

If an insured who selects a 50 percent coinsurance clause, as in the above example, purchases insurance equal to 50 percent of the value for coinsurance purposes, the insured will be protected against total shutdowns for *at least* six months if his or her business is normally stable throughout the year. How much longer the insured will be protected depends upon how many of his or her expenses can be discontinued. If the business is seasonal and the shutdown occurs during the busy season, insurance equal to 50 percent of the value for coinsurance purposes might not provide protection for even a half-year. It is clear that the amount of insurance to be purchased depends upon the probable period of shutdown, the seasonal characteristics of the business, the expenses that can be discontinued if absolutely necessary, and the premium discounts for higher coinsurance percentages.

One other provision in the gross earnings form should be noted briefly. If the insured incurs extra expenses in order to resume operations at an earlier date than would otherwise be possible, the insurer will reimburse the insured for these expenses to the extent that these efforts actually reduce the business interruption loss.

If the business is almost certain that it will lay off some of its employees almost immediately after a shutdown, it can exclude a portion of its payroll from coverage under an *ordinary payroll exclusion endorsement.* "Ordinary payroll" is defined as the payroll for all employees of the insured except officers, executives, department managers, employees under contract, and other "important" employees. "Important" employees are those whom employers are likely to continue on the payroll for some time following a shutdown. The attraction of this endorsement is that ordinary payroll is subtracted from the annual gross earnings base to which the coinsurance percentage is applied. If ordinary payroll is a substantial expense item for the firm, this subtraction may reduce greatly the amount of insurance the business must buy to avoid a coinsurance penalty. However, the excluded payroll is not covered even if the insured elects with good reason to retain some of these employees. Furthermore, the minimum coinsurance percentage is 80 percent. A decision to use this endorsement depends upon the ratio of ordinary payroll to gross earnings, the insured's desire to decide later whether part of this payroll should be continued, the effect of different coinsurance percentages, and relative premium costs. Instead of excluding ordinary payroll completely, the business may, under an *ordinary payroll limited coverage endorsement*, cover ordinary payroll for a maximum of 90 consecutive days. This endorsement reduces the coinsurance base by the ordinary payroll for a year less 90 days.

An alternative, simpler approach to business interruption insurance is an *earnings form*. Like the gross earnings form, this form covers the loss of profits and continuing expenses during a business shutdown. The difference is that the form contains no coinsurance provision. Instead, for each 30 days the business is suspended, the insured recovers some fraction (one-third, one-fourth, or one-sixth, depending upon one's choice at the time one buys the insurance) of a specified total limit of liability.

Extra Expense Insurance Form   An extra expense insurance form protects the insured whose business would otherwise be interrupted because of damage to physical facilities against the extra expenses incurred in order to continue the business temporarily in some other way. These expenses might include the rental of temporary premises or equipment, payments to some other firm to service the insured's customers, or additional transportation expenses. One extra expense form covers the necessary extra expenses incurred up to the date on which normal operations could reasonably be expected to be resumed but in no case for more than one year. A second form, which is more popular because the premium rate is less, usually states the percentages payable for expenses incurred during the first month, during the first two months, etc. One set of acceptable limits is 40 percent during the first month, 70 percent during the first two months, 90 percent during the first three months, and 100 percent during the first four months. Another more expensive set of limits would be 40 percent during the first month, 80 percent during the first two months, and 100 percent during the first three months.

Other Important Endorsements   Three other important endorsements that may be included in a fire insurance contract are discussed in the following paragraphs.

Earthquakes are excluded under almost all risk contracts. Yet earthquake is a peril with severe consequences which occurs more often than most people believe. Some geographical areas of course have a much higher loss potential than others. *Earthquake insurance* is usually purchased as an endorsement to the standard fire policy which extends the covered perils to include earthquakes. Even though losses to foundations and excavations are excluded if caused by other perils, earthquake losses to this property is covered unless specifically deleted. This difference in treatment may cause a coinsurance problem because the amount of insurance required to avoid a coinsurance penalty would be higher for earthquake losses. Furthermore, coinsurance is mandatory, 80 percent being the minimum requirement.

Earthquake insurance is subject to a large deductible—at least 2 percent in most states, 5–10 percent in western states. The deductible may be as high as 40 percent. Because the deductible amounts can be substantial, some insurers sell contracts that cover the deductible amount subject themselves to a deductible of ½ percent or $1,000, whichever is larger.

Replacement cost insurance can be written as an endorsement to the fire insurance contract or as a separate cover. In either case it provides the insured with the difference between the actual cash value of the loss and the replacement cost without any deduction for depreciation. Originally, this insurance could be written only on building structures, but insurers are now willing to write replacement cost new insurance on contents as well. The discussion here is limited to insurance on buildings.

This coverage must be carefully underwritten because of the possible moral and morale hazards. Most, but not all, contracts contain a series of provisions designed to reduce these hazards. First, the insurance contains a 100 percent coinsurance clause applicable to the replacement cost new of the property. In other words, the insured must carry insurance equal to the cost of replacing the entire building structure if he or she wishes to avoid a coinsurance penalty. Second, the building must be actually repaired or replaced within a reasonable time after the loss. The new building can be a very different building, but the recovery is limited to the cost of repairing or replacing the insured structure. If repair or replacement is not completed within a reasonable time, the settlement is on an actual cash value basis. Third, the building must be rebuilt on the same site. This provision is relaxed more frequently than the others. Its purpose is to avoid tempting any insured to improve the location value of his building by causing the loss. If the building code has been changed to prohibit building the same structure on the same site, the risk manager should have this restriction removed. Replacement cost insurance is especially important when there is a partial loss because the insured will probably elect to make the necessary repairs. Not to do so would cause the insured to lose the rest of his or her investment in the building.

Demolition insurance should be considered when the insured has a building which, because of a city ordinance, will cost more to repair or replace than it would under ordinary circumstances. The fire insurance contract covering the direct loss would pay only the actual cash value of the damage. The owner would have to bear (1) the cost of demolishing the undamaged portion of the building, (2) the actual cash value of this undamaged portion, and (3) if he or she rebuilds, the additional cost, if any, of constructing a new building which would satisfy the ordinance. If only repairs are involved, the owner must bear the additional cost of repairs meeting the standards.

It is possible to purchase demolition insurance (a demolition clause plus an increased cost of reconstruction endorsement) which, if written in conjunction with replacement insurance, would cover all the losses mentioned in the preceding paragraph. Without the replacement cost insurance, the additional cost of a building meeting the standards is covered, but there would be some deduction for depreciation. The more common forms, however, are much more limited. For example, many forms cover only the situation when the building must be demolished and pay only the demolition costs and the actual cash value of the demolished section. They contribute nothing to the increased costs of reconstruction or repair.

Difference in Conditions Insurance

Difference in conditions insurance (DIC) is designed for businesses that wish to supplement their basic property insurance policies (say, a fire and extended coverage insurance contract) with a separate contract that will cover additional perils. DIC is not excess insurance; it covers losses not covered by the basic insurance. DIC can be customized to meet the needs of the insured. Typically, it provides all risks protection subject to certain exclusions that include fire and other perils covered under the basic insurance policies. A deductible ranging from $2,500 to $25,000, depending upon the size of the insured business, usually applies to all losses. If the policy includes coverage for flood and earthquake damage, such coverage is subject to a separate, much larger deductible. Property in transit and overseas property may be covered as well as the property covered under the basic policies. Chapter 31 will describe how DIC and umbrella liability insurance described on pages 372–373 are used in the management of foreign exposures. A major attraction of DIC is that the insured has more flexibility in establishing the policy limit because the contract does not usually contain a coinsurance clause. The policy may be written to cover business interruption and other net income losses as well as direct and indirect property losses.

THEFT INSURANCE

If a business has named-perils coverage on a building or its contents, it should seriously consider separate theft insurance as a way of protecting the business against this exposure. In addition, although theft is generally one of the perils covered under an all risks policy, the contract usually excludes or limits the amount of protection on certain types of property, such as money, that is highly susceptible to theft losses.

Theft insurance protects a business against losses by burglary, robbery, or some other form of theft by persons other than employees. Dishonesty insurance or fidelity bonds, to be discussed later, cover losses caused by dishonest acts of employees.

Theft insurance may be divided into two basic categories: (1) limited and (2) comprehensive or broad-form contracts. Although the boundary line between these two categories is not crystal clear, the distinction is nevertheless useful. We shall discuss some leading examples of each type.

Limited Contracts

The limited contracts protect the business against some particular kinds of theft. Examples are: (1) the mercantile open-stock burglary policy, (2) the safe burglary policy, (3) the mercantile robbery policy, and (4) the paymaster robbery policy. Some insureds do not seem to be aware of the limited nature of the protection under these contracts.

The *mercantile open-stock burglary* policy covers (1) burglary and (2) robbery of a watchperson. (Under certain circumstances, insurers will endorse this contract to cover all forms of theft.) *Burglary* is defined in the contract as the felonious abstraction of insured property from within the premises by a person making felonious entry therein by actual force and violence as evidenced by visible marks at the place of entry. A person who gains legal entry but forces his or her way out is not a burglar; neither is a person who enters through an open window. Robbery of a watchperson means the felonious taking of property by violence or threat of violence inflicted upon a private watchperson employed exclusively by the insured while the watchperson is on duty within the premises.

Excluded perils include war, vandalism (it is, of course, often difficult to distinguish between vandalism and attempted theft), fire, or infidelity of employees.

The property insured may be owned by the named insured or may be property in which he or she has some interest, including a liability interest. The insured can, however, elect to include the interest of other persons in property held by the insured in any capacity. The property covered is merchandise, furniture, and fixtures; money and securities are not covered. Damage to the premises is covered if the insured is the owner or is liable for the loss.

The covered premises include the interior of the portion of the building occupied by the insured. Show cases and show windows not opening directly into the interior are not covered unless they are within the building line.

The premises must not have been open for business when the loss occurred. Otherwise, the time limitations in the contract are the usual ones.

The coverage is suspended while any change occurs in the condition of the exposure to loss.

The policy is written on an actual cash value basis. The most distinctive feature is a special coinsurance clause which applies to merchandise other than jewelry or property held by the insured as a pledge or collateral. This coinsurance clause differs from the usual coinsurance clause in that the denominator (the coinsurance percentage times the value) in the fraction can never exceed a coinsurance limit that depends upon the insured's trade group.[3]

The *mercantile safe burglary* policy protects the insured against loss of property as a result of forcible entry into a safe or vault. Manipulation of the combination to the safe is not covered.

The *mercantile robbery* policy combines two separate policies: the *interior robbery* policy and the *outside robbery* policy. The interior robbery policy covers robbing of a messenger or custodian (not a watchperson, porter, or janitor under this interior section) within the premises, kidnapping a messenger or custodian while he or she is outside the premises and forcing the messenger to admit the robbers into the premises, and stealing objects from a show window after breaking the glass while the premises are open for business. Robbery implies violence or threat of violence or the taking of property after a custodian or messenger has been intentionally or accidentally killed or rendered unconscious.

The *messenger or outside robbery* policy provides similar robbery protection on property being conveyed by a messenger outside the premises. A messenger is any employee duly authorized by the insured to have custody of the property outside the premises.

[3] See footnote 4 in Chap. 17.

The *paymaster robbery form* protects the insured against loss of his or her payroll as a result of robbery on the premises or in the hands of a messenger. Other money and securities not intended for the payroll are covered up to 10 percent of the policy amount. If the robbery occurs while the employees are being paid, the employees who have been paid are also protected. The policy can be endorsed to provide all risks coverage. The principal attraction of the paymaster robbery form is that a firm whose money exposure is substantially greater during pay periods can protect these peak exposures more economically under this form because the rates recognize the temporary nature of the exposure.

Comprehensive or Broad-Form Contracts

Comprehensive contracts include all contracts that cover any form of theft not specifically excluded. The two contracts that best illustrate this group are: (1) the money and securities broad form and (2) the comprehensive destruction, disappearance, and dishonesty policy.

Money and Securities Broad Form   The money and securities broad form may be used to provide on-premises protection, off-premises protection, or both. It is designed primarily to cover losses to money and securities, but it also provides substantial theft protection on other property.

The on-premises section covers the destruction, disappearance, or wrongful abstraction of money and securities while the property is on the premises or within any recognized safe depository, from any cause that is not specifically excluded. In other words, the protection not only extends beyond burglary and robbery into theft but is all risks protection. It covers fire, windstorm, explosion, and numerous other perils in addition to any form of theft. The only excluded perils are war, infidelity losses by any employee or authorized representative (but this exclusion does not apply to an employee burglary or robbery), accounting errors, or the giving or surrendering of money or securities in any exchange or purchase. This broad coverage of money and securities is important because most property insurance contracts provide limited, if any, protection on this valuable property. Property other than money and securities is protected against safe burglary and robbery. In other words, the safe burglary and interior robbery policies become minor components of this comprehensive form.

The off-premises section also covers money and securities on an all risks basis. The property is protected while it is being conveyed by a messenger or any armored motor vehicle company or is within the home of any messenger. Property other than money and securities is covered against robbery only.

Comprehensive Destruction, Disappearance, and Dishonesty Policy   The comprehensive destruction, disappearance, and dishonesty policy, which is often called a 3-D policy, is a schedule policy that permits the insured to select one or more coverages. The five coverages contained in the basic contract are: (1) employee dishonesty coverage, (2) money and securities broad form—on-premises, (3) money and securities broad form—off-premises, (4) money orders and counterfeit paper currency coverage, and (5) depositors' forgery coverage.

Each of these coverages can be purchased as a separate contract, but in addition to the convenience of having many coverages under one contract, the 3-D contract forces the insured to make an active negative decision with respect to those coverages he or she decides not to buy.

The employee dishonesty coverage is either a commercial blanket or a blanket position bond, both of which will be explained shortly in the section under dishonesty insurance. The second and third coverages mentioned above are the two components of the money and securities broad form that have just been described. The fourth coverage covers loss due to the acceptance in good faith of illegal or counterfeit money orders, or United States or Canadian paper currency in exchange for merchandise, services, or money. The final coverage protects the insured against forgery losses on outgoing instruments. Outgoing instruments include checks, drafts, promissory notes, bills of exchange, or similar written promises, where the insured makes the promise or is supposed to have made the promise. The forgery may consist of an impersonation of a real payee, a fictitious payee, or some alteration in the amount of an otherwise valid instrument. This coverage protects the insured's bank as well as the insured.

Despite the comprehensive nature of the 3-D contract, an insured who purchases all five coverages will still find some important gaps in the theft protection. It is possible, however, to endorse the 3-D contract to plug most of these gaps. For example, the policy can be endorsed to provide mercantile open-stock burglary insurance (note that the money and securities broad form section does not provide this protection) or mercantile open-stock theft insurance and forgery insurance on incoming instruments. Paymaster coverage can also be added for the insured who wishes this more economical protection as a supplement or substitute for the money and securities coverage.

DISHONESTY INSURANCE

Dishonesty insurance is more frequently called *fidelity bonding*. [Unlike theft insurance, this form of insurance is almost never provided under all risks coverage on buildings or their contents.] Although some fidelity bonds closely resemble the surety bonds discussed in the next section, most fidelity bonds are more closely akin to insurance contracts. The distinctions between bonding and insurance and between surety bonds and fidelity bonds were examined in Chapter 12. Attention here is limited to the characteristics of some of the more important types of fidelity bonds.

Types of Dishonesty Insurance

Dishonesty insurance can be divided into three major classes: (1) bonds covering specific individuals, (2) bonds covering specific positions, and (3) blanket bonds.

Bonds Covering Specific Individuals Under an *individual* bond, a specific person is named. In order to collect under this bond, the employer must show that he or she has suffered a loss as a result of a dishonest act committed by this employee, either alone or in collusion with others.

A *name schedule* bond differs from an individual bond only in that it contains two or more names and that each of the principals is bonded for a separate amount.

Bonds Covering Specific Positions *Position bonds* cover a named position, regardless of the specific individuals occupying the position. Consequently, these bonds are more attractive than individual or name schedule bonds to firms with a considerable turnover. Each person occupying the position is covered up to the amount specified in the contract.

Position schedule bonds differ only in that two or more positions are included for separate amounts under the same contract.

Blanket Bonds Blanket bonds cover all regular employees of the insured. One of the major problems associated with individual and position bonds is deciding which individuals or positions should be bonded. Blanket bonding avoids this problem and also provides automatic coverage for new employees. Finally, if a fidelity loss occurs, the employer can collect even if he or she cannot identify the specific individual involved. Such specific identification is required under individual and position bonds. For these reasons, blanket bonds are the most popular form of fidelity bonds. A disadvantage of the blanket approach is that each employee is bonded for the same amount. Some businesses, therefore, purchase blanket insurance as primary insurance and individual or position insurance as excess insurance or vice versa.

The blanket bond may be a *primary commercial blanket bond* or *a blanket position bond*. The major difference between these two policies is the statement of the policy limits. The primary commercial bond limits the insurer's liability to a stated amount per loss; the blanket position bond limits the insurer's liability to a stated amount per person involved in the loss. The application of these limits is illustrated in the following table. In most businesses, fidelity losses involve only one employee, and for this reason primary commercial blanket policies are the more popular of the two blanket forms.

| | Insurance payment | |
Loss		$10,000 blanket position	$20,000 primary commercial blanket
One employee,	$24,000	$10,000	$20,000
Two employees,	24,000	20,000	20,000
Three employees,	24,000	24,000	20,000

Coverage Analysis

Except for the characteristics already noted, most fidelity bonds contain essentially the same kinds of provisions.

The *peril* covered is any fraudulent or dishonest act of an employee. It includes such acts as larceny, embezzlement, theft, forgery, misappropriation, wrongful abstraction, and willful misapplication. Inventory shortages must be conclusively demonstrated to have been caused by employee dishonesty before they are covered. Despite a common belief that fidelity bonds cover only the loss of money or securities, this insurance covers any type of *property*. There are no exclusions. The insured property may be owned by the insured, held by the insured in any capacity, or property for which he or she is liable. Thus the contract may protect *persons* other than the insured. Only direct *losses* are covered. A fidelity bond is a floater policy. The usual *territorial limits* are the United States, its possessions, or Canada. Other locations are covered if the employee is assigned there for a limited period.

The *time* when the loss must occur is described in several interesting provisions. The contract usually runs from noon on a specified date until it is canceled by either party. In other words, it is a continuous contract. It is true, however, that as soon as the employer becomes aware of any dishonest act committed by the employee while in his or her service or before, the coverage with respect to that employee stops.

Under most bonds, the loss must occur while the contract is in force. In addition, because fidelity losses are not usually discovered until some time after they occur but insurers cannot, for practical reasons, continue to be responsible indefinitely, these contracts state a *discovery period* following the cancellation of the contract during which the employer must report any loss. Note that the discovery period, which is commonly 6 to 24 months, does not start with the loss but with the cancellation of the contract. A continuous blanket bond may cover a loss incurred ten years ago as a result of an act by an employee who left the employer three years ago if the employer can prove his loss. *Discovery bonds* are available that pay for losses discovered during the bonding period, regardless of when they were incurred.

Because the discovery period begins to run after the contract is canceled, an employer might hesitate to replace an existing contract. Insurers answer this problem by including a *loss under prior bond* provision (or superseded suretyship rider), under which the insurer under the replacement contract agrees to be responsible for any losses which are not covered under the prior bond but which would have been covered except for the discovery-period limitation. The insurance with respect to any employee is not cumulative. For example, if an employee is bonded for $10,000, the insurer will pay only $10,000, even if the coverage is continuous and the employee takes $8,000 each October for five years.

BOILER AND MACHINERY INSURANCE

One of the major gaps in contracts covering explosion (e.g., the extended coverage endorsement) is protection against the bursting of steam boilers. This coverage is written separately because, as will become apparent shortly, boiler and machinery insurance has some unique characteristics.

Boiler and machinery insurance is not limited to steam boilers but also covers similar equipment subject to internal pressure such as air tanks, compressors, de-vulcanizers, furnaces, kettles, mangle rolls, refrigerating systems, and steampipe lines. Damage caused by accidents involving fly-wheels, electrical machinery, and turbines can also be included under this insurance. The boiler and machinery insurance contract identifies, through a series of schedule endorsements, each insured object and the accident against which that object is insured. For example, a broad form of the boiler schedule defines an accident as any sudden and accidental breakdown of the object or part thereof. A limited form defines an accident more narrowly as a sudden and accidental tearing asunder. Under this form bulging, burning, or cracking of a boiler would not be covered.

One of the unique features of boiler and machinery insurance is the emphasis upon loss control. Over one-third of the premium is used to pay for inspections by highly skilled engineering staffs. In fact, many insureds purchase this insurance primarily because of the inspection service for which the relatively few insurers writing this line of insurance have become famous. In states requiring inspections of boilers and similar equipment, the insurance inspection is generally considered more than adequate.

The contract is also unique in that, if the maximum liability of the insurer per accident is not exhausted in paying for property damage, the excess is available as liability insurance but only with respect to damage to property in the care, or custody, or control of the insured. More specifically, the policy covers, in the order in which they are named, the following losses up to the policy limit per accident: (1) damage to property of the insured, (2) expenses incurred for the reasonable extra cost of temporary repair or of expediting the repair of the damaged property, and (3) liability for damage to the property of others that is in the care, custody, or control of the insured.

Thus, if the policy limit is $50,000 per accident and the insured incurs $30,000 in property damage, $1,000 in expediting expenses and $20,000 liability for damage to the property of others in the care of the insured, the insurer must pay the property damage, the expediting expenses, and $19,000 of the property damage liability. In addition to making settlement or paying judgments under the liability sections, the insurer promises to defend the insured and pay *all* defense costs in addition to the other losses and irrespective of the policy limit. The direct property loss is covered on a replacement cost new basis unless the insured elects to purchase only actual cash value coverage.

The contract excludes property losses caused by fire, explosions outside the object, or flood, even if these perils are brought on by the specified accident. All property and liability losses caused by war, nuclear reaction, nuclear radiation, or nuclear contamination are excluded.

The contract can be endorsed to cover business interruption insurance and extra expense insurance that is similar to the coverages described earlier.

OCEAN MARINE INSURANCE

Contracts concerned primarily with water transportation are considered to be ocean marine insurance. For a considerable time ocean marine insurance was the only kind of modern insurance. Prior to the fourteenth century it was customary for money lenders to make *respondentia* loans under which they agreed that if the cargo failed to arrive at its destination, the loan was canceled and no repayment was necessary. Modern ocean marine insurance was born in the Mediterranean area when the twin functions of lending and insuring were separated and a separate insurance contract was issued. Until the seventeenth century or later, people were generally not insurance conscious because of the feudal system and the modest accumulations of most families. There was also a strong religious sentiment against thwarting the "will of God." Merchants, however, were risking substantial sums at sea, and they feared the perils of the sea. It took the London fire of 1666 to create a similar awareness of the fire peril and to inspire the formation of the first fire insurers.

In order to take advantage of an extensive body of court interpretations, and because of the rich tradition of marine insurance, cargo insurance contracts covering water transportation are often phrased in antiquated language (e.g., "Touching the Adventures and Perils which we, . . . , are contented to bear"). In addition, the contracts are often a hodgepodge of unrelated provisions. Consequently, these contracts are among the most difficult to analyze. On the other hand, they are notable for the broad protection they afford.

Events Covered

With respect to perils, the minimum coverage is fire and perils of the sea. Although "perils of the sea" are not defined, they are understood to include all perils arising out of water transportation, such as collisions with other vessels, grounding on a sandbar, and heavy weather. Fire and theft are perils *on* the sea, not *of* the sea. Other perils that may be added include theft, explosion, onshore risks, accidents involving machinery, and barratry (or roughly, embezzlement by the master or the crew). Sometimes the contract is written on an all risk basis.

The property covered is the cargo being shipped. Freight charges are usually included if the person shipping the cargo suffers the loss.

Cargo insurance contracts usually cover the named insured "for account of whom it may concern," the loss, if any, being payable to the insured or order. In other words, the contract is freely assignable to any person. Insurers grant this right because neither the named insured nor any assignee has any physical control over the exposed cargo.

Because the cargo is usually insured for the amount of the invoice including all charges therein, plus any prepaid, advanced, or guaranteed freight, the insurance covers loss of profits and freight charges, if any, in addition to direct losses. Although a delay clause excludes loss of markets or any other loss resulting from any delay for any reason, losses of this sort can be covered for an additional premium.

Ocean marine insurance contracts also contain some special terms applicable to losses. Losses may be divided, first, according to whether they affect only the insured or some other person. The first group may in turn be divided into total losses or particular average losses,[4] the last category including all partial losses to a particular interest. Losses that involve persons other than the insured are called "general average" losses.

---

[4] Since the term "average" means loss in marine insurance, it is sufficient to refer to these losses as particular averages.

In order to be considered a general average loss, (1) there must be a voluntary loss for the purpose of saving a joint venture, and (2) the voluntary act must be successful. For example, if a vessel, valued at $1 million and carrying two sets of cargo, cargo A valued at $200,000 and cargo B at $300,000, starts to sink because of heavy seas, the captain may decide to jettison half of cargo A in order to reach the destination. In such a case, the loss of $100,000 worth of cargo A is considered a general average loss. It is a rule of the sea, dating back to the days before Christ when the city of Rhodes in Greece was a commercial power, that general average losses are to be shared by all the interests who benefit from a general average loss on the basis of the value of their interests at the time the loss occurred. Since the value of all interests at the time of the loss totaled $1,500,000, the vessel owner must pay the owner of cargo A $\frac{2}{3} \times$ $100,000, or $66,667. The owner of cargo B must pay $\frac{3}{15} \times$ $100,000, or $20,000, and the owner of cargo A must bear the remainder of the loss, or $13,333. Marine insurers will pay these general average charges on behalf of their insureds.

The contract usually insures the cargo or the hull "at and from" ports or places within a destinated geographical area. The at-and-from wording means that the coverage is effective while the vessel is in port as well as at sea. Most policies also contain a warehouse-to-warehouse clause, which extends the coverage from the point of origin, which may be an inland location, to the final destination, which may also be an inland location.

Cargo policies written on a voyage basis cover that single voyage, but open policies usually cover all shipments made on and after a certain date. Either party may cancel an open policy by giving 30 days' written notice to the other; otherwise the insurance is continuous. If the policy is canceled, the coverage continues on shipments made prior to the cancellation date. Some open policies, however, are written for a specific period.

Amount of Recovery

Because cargoes can fluctuate greatly in value during an ocean voyage, it is customary to insure cargoes on a valued basis. If the cargo is totally destroyed, the insurer must pay the face value. The valuation in the contract, however, is expected to be realistic. Instead of specifying a stated number of dollars, the contract customarily states that the value shall be the amount of the invoice plus any prepaid, advanced, or guaranteed freight.

If the cargo is only partially damaged, the insured and the insurer must agree on the percentage of damage. If they cannot agree, the damaged cargo is to be sold for the account of the owner and the amount received compared with what would have been received had the cargo been in sound condition. In either case, the liability of the insurer is determined by applying the percentage of damage to the amount of insurance. For example, assume that a cargo insured for $4,000 could have been sold for $6,000 in sound condition but is worth only $4,500 in damaged condition. Since the damage is 25 percent, the insurer must pay 25 percent of $4,000 or $1,000. Note that if the amount of insurance is less than the value of the cargo in sound condition, the amount of the insurance payment is equal to the amount under a 100 percent coinsurance clause.

Because marine insurance contracts cover so many perils, they would be very expensive unless they excluded relatively small losses. Marine insurers recognized from the beginning that it was wiser to omit coverage on small losses than to narrow the scope of the perils clause. Small losses are omitted through one or more franchise or deductible clauses, the franchise principle being the most common.

If the insured has two or more contracts, the contracts apply to any loss in the order in which they were written.

INLAND MARINE INSURANCE

Inland marine cargo insurance covers shipments primarily by land or by air. Although the trucker, railroad, or airline may be a common carrier with the extensive liability described in Chapter 7 in the section "Bailee Liability Exposures," the shipper may still be interested in cargo insurance because (1) it is usually more convenient to collect from an insurer than a carrier, (2) a common carrier is not responsible for perils such as an act of God, an act of war, exercise of public authority, or inherent defects in the cargo, and (3) the carrier may have issued a released bill of lading.[5] Unless the insured makes only a few shipments each year, it is generally less expensive to buy cargo insurance than to increase the limits under the bill of lading.

No one cargo insurance contract exists. Instead, different insurers may issue different contracts, and a given insurer will tailor the contract to the insured's needs. A convenient way to classify the contracts is according to the type of transportation covered. One or more of the following modes of transportation may be covered— railroad, motortruck, or air. Incidental water transportation may or may not be included. Shipments by mail are covered under separate first-class mail, parcel post, or registered mail insurance. Special contracts have also been designed to handle shipments on the insured's own trucks. Another classification of these contracts would group them according to the perils covered. Most provide protection against a broad list of specified perils, but some, especially those covering air transportation of high-value items, are written on an all risk basis. Finally, some contracts cover one trip, while others cover all shipments during the term of the policy.

Inland marine transit policies covering shipments by mail are especially interesting because similar insurance is sold by the U.S. Postal Service, but for persons who make enough shipments to pay more than the minimum premiums for the private insurance, the cost of the private protection will be less. Furthermore, the private protection may be more convenient because it is not necessary for the insured to leave his or her premises to effect the coverage.

Inland Marine Insurance Floaters   Inland marine insurers also have written some floater policies that include a substantial transportation element. Four important types of business floaters are: (1) equipment floaters, (2) merchandise or stock floaters covering property in the hands of others, (3) installation floaters, and (4) bailee's customers' contracts covering property in the hands of the insured.

---

[5] See Chap. 7, fn. 15.

Equipment floaters cover movable property that is being used by the insured in his or her business, but they exclude merchandise on sale or consignment or in course of manufacture. Illustrations of equipment floaters that indicate the type of property covered are: (1) a contractor's equipment floater covering power shovels, air compressors, concrete mixers, pumps, boilers, bulldozers, caterpillar tractors, scaffolding, and the like, (2) a farm equipment floater, (3) an oil-well-drilling equipment floater, and (4) a physician's, surgeon's, and scientific-instrument floater.

For many reasons, a business may have placed its property in the hands of others, and this property is subject to transportation perils. *Processing risk contracts* protect an owner against loss to goods while they are en route to or from or in the hands of some other person for some type of processing. For example, a garment contractor's floater provides a clothing manufacturer with all risks protection on his or her property while it is being sent to, in the hands of, or being returned by contractors or subcontractors who insert shoulder pads, make buttonholes, embroider the material, or process the clothing in some other way. *Consignment floaters* cover property consigned to a factor or agent for various purposes. The consignment may be for exhibit, trial, auction, approval, distribution, or sale. These floaters, in addition to covering the property in transit, provide coverage at the consignee's premises.

Sales of air conditioning or heating apparatus or heavy machinery often involve installing the property or equipment sold, during which title to the property or responsibility for any losses usually remains in the hands of the seller. *Installation floaters* cover this exposure from the time the property leaves the seller's premises until the purchaser takes title.

Bailee liability insurance protects a bailee against liability for damage to property in his or her care, custody, or control. *Bailee's customers' insurance* enables the bailee to protect his or her customers' goods, regardless of the bailee's liability for the damage. Bailees may purchase this insurance in order to improve relationships with their customers. Although bailee's customers' insurance is not limited to inland marine insurance, it has been most fully developed by marine insurers. The most common purchasers of inland marine bailee's customers' insurance are laundries, dry cleaners, tailors, cold-storage companies, and furriers. Other processors and consignees may also be interested in this insurance, which protects the property from the time the bailee accepts the goods until they are returned to the customer.

SURETY BONDS

Since the essential characteristics of surety bonds and the ways in which they differ from insurance were analyzed in Chapters 11 and 12, the discussion will be limited here to the expressed obligations commonly guaranteed through surety bonds. Although any expressed obligation could be the subject of a surety bond and new types of surety bonds are constantly being written, the more common surety bonds can be grouped into the following classes: (1) contract bonds, (2) court bonds, and (3) license and permit bonds. Illustrations of the many other bonds available are *lost instrument* bonds, which protect the issuer of a lost instrument such as a stock or bond if it issues a replacement to the owner and some other party appears later with the original document and a valid claim against the issuer; *self-insurance* bonds, which a firm may have to post before it will be permitted to self-insure its workers' compensation obligation; and *financial responsibility* bonds, which a car owner may have to file in lieu of an automobile liability insurance policy if he or she wishes to retain the right to drive an automobile after an accident.

Contract Bonds

Under contract bonds, the surety guarantees the promise the principal has made to the obligee under some contract. Usually the contract covers construction, supply, or maintenance. Some of these bonds promise that the surety will carry out the contract if the principal fails to do so; others promise to pay damages.

Construction Contracts Construction contract bonds can in turn be divided into bid bonds and final or performance bonds. *Bid* bonds guarantee that if the bidder wins the award, he or she will sign the contract and post a performance bond. The *performance* bond guarantees that the contractor will complete the work in accordance with the agreement between the contractor and the owner. In addition, the surety usually guarantees that the contractor will pay all labor and material bills incurred, but the unpaid laborers and material suppliers have no right to proceed directly against the surety. Finally, the performance bond may guarantee that the obligee will not suffer any loss for some specified period through defects in the construction.

Court Bonds

Court bonds include all those bonds that may be filed in connection with judicial proceedings. They fall into two general classes: (1) litigation bonds, and (2) fiduciary bonds.

Litigation Bonds Litigation bonds may be required by the court whenever the plaintiff or the defendant asks the court to take some action on his or her behalf that may injure the other party to the suit. A few examples will illustrate the numerous bonds in this category. Perhaps the best-known surety bond is a *bail* bond, which stipulates a penalty to be paid if a defendant does not appear in court at the time of the trial. An *attachment* bond guarantees that if the plaintiff asks the court to attach certain property of the defendant to prevent him or her from disposing of that property to avoid paying the judgment, and the plaintiff loses the case, the plaintiff will pay the defendant any damages sustained as a result of the temporary attachment. A *release of attachment* bond posted by the defendant guarantees that the plaintiff will not lose from the release of such an attachment. An *appeal* bond guarantees that if an appeal to a higher court sustains the judgment of the lower court, the person making the appeal will pay the original judgment, interest on the judgment, and the court costs.

Fiduciary Bonds Fiduciary bonds guarantee that persons entrusted through court order with the management of property for the benefit of some other person will perform their duties honestly and capably. The principals under these bonds include the following fiduciaries: executors or administrators of estates, guardians of minors or the mentally incompetent, receivers or trustees of a bankrupt business, or assignees for the benefit of creditors.

License and Permit Bonds

License and permit bonds are often required by federal, state, or local law when a person applies for a license to engage in a particular occupation or business or for a permit to engage in a specific activity. These bonds can be divided into two major classes: (1) those that guarantee the licensing authority that the licensee will be responsible for losses to the government or to the public caused by violations of certain regulations or in some cases from the activity itself, and (2) those that guarantee the payment of certain taxes on products processed or sold.

Some of the bonds in the first group give injured third parties the right to proceed directly against the surety, while others protect only the public authority against damage to its own property or suits by private persons. Some of these bonds, which could be considered to constitute a third category, also provide for the forfeiture of the bond penalty if the licensee violates certain regulations even if no damage results.

SOME KEY CONCEPTS

Statutory fire policy   The policy, required by state statute or by administrative regulation, to which forms and possibly endorsements are attached to produce a fire insurance contract.

General property form   The form commonly attached to a statutory fire policy to provide fire insurance on buildings and contents.

Extended coverage endorsement   An endorsement that extends fire insurance to include additional perils such as windstorm, hail, and explosion. An *optional perils endorsement* adds more named perils.

Rent insurance   Insurance that protects the owner or the tenant against loss of the contract rent while the premises are rendered untenantable by fire or other covered perils.

Special building form   A form that extends fire insurance on the building to cover all perils not specifically excluded. A *special personal property form* does the same for personal property.

Difference in conditions insurance   Supplementary insurance that typically provides all risks coverage but excludes the perils covered under the insured's basic property insurance policies, such as fire and extended coverage insurance.

Replacement cost insurance   Insurance that obligates the insurer to pay the cost of repairs or replacement without any deduction for depreciation.

Business interruption insurance   Insurance that protects the insured against the loss of net profits that would have been earned and expenses that continue during a period of business interruption caused by a covered peril.

Extra expense insurance   Insurance that protects the insured against extra expenses incurred to keep operating following a loss that would otherwise have interrupted operations.

Theft insurance   Insurance that may be limited to certain types of stealing (such as burglary or robbery) or may cover any form of stealing not specifically excluded.

Fidelity bond   An insurance contract that protects an employer against dishonest acts of employees.

Contract bond   A surety bond under which the surety guarantees the performance of the principal under some contract.

Boiler and machinery insurance Protection for an insured against property and liability losses caused by a sudden and accidental breakdown of a boiler or some other scheduled machinery.

Cargo insurance An ocean or inland marine insurance contract that protects the insured against the loss of or damage to shipments.

Inland marine insurance floaters Inland marine insurance contracts that cover movable property that is subject to transportation risks as well as other perils.

REVIEW QUESTIONS

1 The standard fire policy is only part of a fire insurance contract. Explain.

2 What combination of forms and endorsements is a business most likely to purchase to protect its buildings and personal property against property losses?

3 Summarize the events covered and the amount the insurer would pay according to the standard fire policy.

4 How does the general property form alter the events covered and the amount the insurer would pay according to the standard fire policy?

5 List the perils covered under a general property form assuming the insured purchases the extended coverage endorsement, the vandalism and malicious mischief endorsement, the optional perils endorsement, and the sprinkler leakage endorsement.

6 How do the special building form and the special personal property form differ from the general property form?

7 Which of the following property losses would be covered under a general property form including an extended coverage endorsement issued to a department store occupying a rented building? Explain your answers.

  a Fire destroys some merchandise held for sale.

  b Fire destroys some cash belonging to the store.

  c A burglar steals some merchandise held for sale.

  d A windstorm damages some permanent improvements the store has made to the real estate.

  e Vandals cause some damage to desks and chairs owned by the store.

  f A truck, not owned by the insured, crashes into the front of the store.

  g A steam boiler explodes, causing damage to the boiler itself, the building, some furniture and equipment, and some merchandise.

  h A fire causes the store to cease operations for two months. As a result the store loses $30,000 in profits and continuing expenses.

  i An explosion damages some customers' goods being repaired at the store.

8 In question 7, which losses would be covered if the department store had a special building form and a special personal property form instead of a general property form?

9 Assume the following annual data for a department store with stable operations from month to month:

Net sales	$750,000
Cost of goods sold	350,000
Payroll	200,000
Other expenses	140,000
Profit	60,000

    a If the store has a gross earnings endorsement with a face amount of $100,000 and a 60 percent coinsurance clause, how much will the insurer pay if the store must cease operations for three months because of explosion damage? Assume that during these three months half of the payroll and other expenses continue.

    b How much insurance would the store need to recover this loss in full?

10 Explain briefly.

    a Rent and rental value insurance

    b Extra expense insurance

    c Demolition insurance

11 What provisions are usually included in replacement cost insurance endorsements in order to avoid the possible moral and morale hazards associated with this coverage?

12 a What is difference in conditions insurance?

    b Why might insureds find DIC insurance attractive?

13 Why might a business with basic property insurance protection still be interested in separate theft insurance?

14 Why are some theft insurance contracts considered to be limited theft contracts?

15 Describe the events covered and the amount the insurer would pay under a comprehensive destruction, disappearance and dishonesty policy?

16 Compare

    a A name schedule bond with a position schedule bond.

    b A primary commercial blanket bond with a blanket position bond.

17 Why is the discovery period an important feature of a fidelity bond?

18 Summarize the protection provided by boiler and machinery insurance.

19 "Ocean marine insurance contracts are all risks contracts." Do you agree with this statement? Why or why not?

20 A cargo insured for $10,000 is damaged by fire. In sound condition it would have sold for $8,000 at its destination. In damaged condition it sells for $2,000. How much will the insurer pay?

21 A vessel, valued at $1,500,000, is carrying three cargoes belonging to A, B, and C, each cargo valued at $500,000. In heavy weather the ship is in danger of sinking unless the load is lightened, and the captain orders half of A's cargo thrown overboard. As a result of this act the ship is able to proceed to its destination.

    a If none of the parties are insured, how will the loss be settled?

    b If all the parties are insured, how will the loss be settled?

    c If the jettison is not successful and the ship sinks to the bottom of the ocean, how will the loss be settled if all parties are insured?

22 A person making extensive shipments argues that she does not need to insure these shipments because the transportation carrier is responsible for any losses that might occur. How would you advise her?

23 How do inland marine insurance cargo policies differ from those issued by ocean marine insurance?

24 Describe briefly the types of business floaters issued by inland marine insurance.

25 A school district asks for bids on the construction of a new school. What types of bonds might be used in connection with this construction project? For each bond, identify the obligee, the principal, and the expressed obligation.

26 a Distinguish between litigation bonds and fiduciary bonds.

    b Give three illustrations of each type.

SUGGESTIONS FOR ADDITIONAL READING

Bickelhaupt, D. L.: General Insurance (11th ed., Homewood, Ill.: Richard D. Irwin, Inc., 1983), chaps. 17–21 and 25–27.

Fire, Casualty, and Surety Bulletins (Cincinnati: The National Underwriter Company, monthly).

Gordis, P., and E. A. Chlanda: *Property and Casualty Insurance* (Indianapolis: The Rough Notes Company, revised annually).

Huebner, S. S., K. Black, and R. Cline: *Property and Liability Insurance* (3d ed., Englewood Cliffs, N.J.: Prentice-Hall, Inc., 1982), chaps. 2–11, 17–23, 26, 29–31, and 36.

Kulp, C. A., and J. W. Hall: *Casualty Insurance* (4th ed., New York: The Ronald Press Company, 1968), chaps. 5, 6, 14, and 16.

Long, J. D., and D. W. Gregg, (eds.): *Property and Liability Insurance Handbook* (Homewood, Ill.: Richard D. Irwin, Inc., 1965), chaps. 4–10, 23, 26, 27, 32–34, 40, 41, 43, 48, and 50.

MacDonald, Donald L.: *Corporate Risk Control* (New York: The Ronald Press Company, 1966), chaps. 12, 13, 16 and 19.

Malecki, D. S., J. H. Donaldson, and R. C. Horn: *Commercial Liability Risk Management and Insurance, vols. I and II* (Malvern, Pa.: American Institute for Property and Liability Underwriters, 1978).

Riegel, R., J. Miller, and C. A. Williams, Jr.: *Insurance Principles and Practices: Property and Liability* (6th ed., Englewood Cliffs, N.J.: Prentice-Hall, Inc., 1976), chaps. 7–10, 12, 13, 16 and 20.

Rodda, W. H.: *Marine Insurance: Ocean and Inland* (3d ed., Englewood Cliffs, N.J.: Prentice-Hall, Inc., 1970).

————, J. S. Trieschmann, E. A. Wiening, and B. A. Hedges: *Commercial Property Risk Management and Insurance*, vols. I and II (2d ed., Malvern, Pa.: American Institute for Property and Liability Underwriters, 1983).

Winter, W. D., *Marine Insurance* (3d ed., New York: McGraw-Hill Book Company, 1952).

CHAPTER 19

LIABILITY INSURANCE AND PACKAGE CONTRACTS

LEARNING OBJECTIVES

After you have completed this chapter, you should be able to:

1 Summarize the major provisions of a comprehensive general liability insurance policy.

2 Explain some of the major coverages that can be added to a comprehensive general liability insurance policy through the broad form endorsement.

3 Describe some of the important differences between most general liability policies and those covering liability arising out of errors or omissions in the rendering of professional services.

4 Tell what automobile coverages are available for businesses.

5 Summarize the major provisions of the Business Auto Policy and the Personal Auto Policy.

6 Analyze the events covered and the amount of recovery under a workers' compensation insurance policy.

7 Describe briefly the purpose of umbrella liability insurance.

8 Define "package contract" and summarize briefly the leading example, the special multi-peril policy.

INTRODUCTION

The preceding chapter has been concerned with property insurance that protects the insured against direct and indirect property losses and net income losses. This chapter deals for the most part with insurance that protects the insured against legal responsibility for losses to the person or property of others. Liability insurance includes general liability insurance, professional liability insurance, automobile liability insurance, and workers' compensation insurance. The discussion of automobile liability insurance will also deal with automobile physical damage insurance, which typically is part of the same contract.

The remainder of the chapter describes briefly some package policies that combine basic property insurance and liability insurance and some miscellaneous property and liability insurance not previously discussed.

GENERAL LIABILITY INSURANCE

General liability insurance protects insureds against liability arising out of their premises or out of their operations on or off those premises. General liability insurance policies usually consist of a jacket that is common to all general liability insurance plus a coverage part that is peculiar to each type of general liability insurance. The jacket contains a general insuring agreement, describes some supplementary benefits such as defense services, defines certain terms, and lists a number of conditions such as inspections and audits, the insured's duties following a loss, and subrogation. The declarations section of the jacket identifies the insured and names the coverage parts that are included. Each coverage part describes the sources of liability covered by that part, the exclusions, the persons insured, and the limits of liability.

The major general liability coverage parts are: (1) owners', landlords' and tenants' liability, (2) manufacturers' and contractors' liability, (3) completed operations and products liability, (4) independent contractors' liability, (5) contractual liability, and (6) comprehensive general liability.[1]

Coverage parts can also be attached that will produce a combination automobile-general liability policy.

Each of these six parts is described briefly below. Because a business would be well advised in most cases to purchase the comprehensive general liability part, that part is analyzed in much more detail than the other parts.

Owners', Landlords', and Tenants' Liability Insurance

Owners', landlords', and tenants' liability insurance covers the ownership, maintenance, or use of the insured premises and all operations necessary or incidental thereto. However, the contract specifically excludes: (1) the types of losses that are covered under the completed operations and products liability part and (2) injury or damage arising out of structural alterations that involve changing the size of or moving buildings, new construction, or demolition operations.

[1] In 1985 the Insurance Services Office intends to introduce two new general liability insurance policies. Each of these two policies will provide in more readable fashion the coverage provided by the comprehensive general liability coverage part plus the broad form comprehensive general liability endorsement to be discussed later in this chapter. Like the present coverage part, one policy will be written on the usual "occurrence" basis. The other will be a "claims-made" policy similar to that introduced in professional liability insurance to be discussed later in this chapter.

O.L. & T. insurance has separate limits per occurrence for bodily injury payments and property damage payments.

Manufacturers' and Contractors' Liability Insurance

The M. & C. coverage part closely resembles O.L. & T. insurance except that it is designed for a different type of insured, whose premiums are determined on a different basis. Because contractors in particular may be engaged in many projects involving structural alterations, construction, and demolition, the exclusion of these sources of liability would greatly reduce the usefulness of this insurance. Consequently, this exclusion is replaced by one that excludes operations performed for the named insured by independent contractors except maintenance and repairs at premises owned by or rented to the named insured or minor structural alterations at such premises.

Completed Operations and Products Liability Insurance

A third coverage part provides insurance against liability arising out of products or completed operations. Product claims are covered if the damage occurs away from the premises and after the insured has relinquished possession to others. If the damage occurs on the premises, the claim is covered under the O.L. & T. or M. & C. parts. Similarly the O.L. & T. or M. & C. parts cover damage that occurs off the premises but while the product is still in the hands of a representative of the insured. Completed operations claims are subject to similar limitations. The damage must occur away from the premises and after the operation has been supposedly completed or abandoned. Specifically excluded is damage arising out of the existence of tools, uninstalled equipment, or abandoned or used materials. If these conditions are not met, the insured must turn to the O.L. & T. or M. & C. parts for protection.

Independent Contractors' Liability Insurance

A fourth part covers for O.L. & T. insureds the structural damage exclusion and for M. & C. insureds the independent contractors exclusion.

Contractual Liability Insurance

Liability under any contract except the "incidental" contracts to be discussed in connection with the comprehensive general liability part is excluded under the preceding coverage parts. A separate coverage part covers other designated contracts. Some insurers will cover all written contracts.

Comprehensive General Liability

The comprehensive general liability part covers all sources of liability that are not specifically excluded. In a declarations section the policy lists all the covered sources of liability known to exist at the effective date of the policy under four headings that correspond to the coverage parts described above except for contractual liability: (1) premises-operations, (2) independent contractors, (3) completed operations, and (4) products.

An advance premium is charged based on the known sources of liability. After the policy period has expired, the actual exposures during the year are determined and the premium adjusted accordingly.

The C.G.L. thus covers all present locations and operations plus any premises and locations acquired during the policy period. The O.L. & T. and M. & C. contracts provide automatic coverage for 30 days, but the insured must notify the insurer that he or she wants the protection continued after that time.

The C.G.L. may cover some perils that would not be covered if the insured purchased all the separate coverage parts, but this "unknown hazard" argument is almost impossible to support with examples.

The premium for the C.G.L. is based only on the actual exposures. For example, if the business does not develop any independent contractor liability exposure, the insurer does not charge for the coverage against this potential exposure.

C.G.L. coverage appeals to many insureds because it combines in a single part coverage that could otherwise be duplicated only by several coverage parts. This single part is easier to understand and to explain to others. On the negative side, the insured loses some flexibility. The completed operations-products liability coverage can be excluded by endorsement, but otherwise all other sources of liability that can be covered must be covered. Also the same limits per occurrence apply to all sources of liability. If the insured purchased instead separate coverage parts, he or she could select different policy limits for each part.

The jacket plus the C.G.L. part is analyzed below, using the format suggested in Chapters 16 and 17.

Events Covered   The *peril* covered is an occurrence for which the insured is legally responsible. An *occurrence* is defined as an accident, including continuous or repeated exposure to conditions, that results in bodily injury or property damage neither expected nor intended from the standpoint of the insured. Some courts argue that an event is not an accident unless it is sudden, but the inclusion in this definition of continuous or repeated exposure to conditions eliminates that possible limitation. The last part of the definition excludes those occurrences that are fortuitous from the viewpoint of the claimant but not for the insured.

The covered *sources of liability* are all sources not specifically excluded as indicated above. The contract covers all premises and operations known to exist when the contract becomes effective plus those that may be acquired during the policy period.

Several important sources of liability are specifically excluded. For example, liability assumed under any contract is not covered, unless the contract is an "incidental contract" such as a lease of premises or an easement agreement. However, this exclusion does not apply to a warranty of fitness or quality of the named insured's products or services.

The ownership, maintenance, operation, use, loading, or unloading of most automobiles, aircraft, and watercraft is excluded. Because courts do not agree on the meaning of "loading and unloading," it is often not clear whether an automobile liability insurer, say, or the general liability insurer is responsible. One way to avoid the delay and trouble experienced in resolving this issue is to purchase both forms of insurance from the same insurer. This exclusion does not apply to vehicles not subject to motor vehicle registration or designed for use principally off public roads.

Bodily injury to an employee of the insured arising out of employment is excluded. Workers' compensation or employers' liability insurance covers this exposure.

The policy covers bodily injuries or property damage arising out of defective products or work completed, but it does not cover: (1) the loss of use of tangible property not physically injured or destroyed resulting from (a) a delay or lack of performance by the insured under any agreement or (b) failure of the insured's products or work to meet the warranted level of performance, quality, fitness, or durability, (2) liability for replacing any defective product or work, or (3) the cost of withdrawing, inspecting, repairing, replacing, or loss of use due to known or suspected defects in the product or work.

An important property damage exclusion states that the insurer is not responsible for damage to (1) property owned by, occupied by, or rented to the insured, (2) property used by the insured, or (3) property in the care, custody, or control of the insured, or over which the insured is for any purpose exercising physical control. The third part of this exclusion does not apply to occurrences involving elevators. It is often difficult to determine in advance what property is technically in the insured's care, custody, or control. Because the insurance contract is a contract of adhesion, the courts will lean toward a liberal interpretation of this exclusion, but in doubtful situations the insured should obtain, where possible, an understanding with the insurer in advance of any loss.

Also excluded is liability under dram shop laws or other special statutes applying to firms manufacturing, distributing, selling, or serving alcoholic beverages, or owning or leasing premises used for such purposes. Insureds actively engaged in such activities, but not mere owners or lessors of premises, are also not covered if liability is imposed under the common law for selling, serving, or giving alcoholic beverages to a minor or to a person under the influence of alcohol or causing or contributing to the intoxication of any person.

An interesting exclusion concerns the discharge, dispersal, release, or escape of smoke, vapor, soot, fumes, acids, alkalis, toxic chemicals, liquids or gases, waste materials or other irritants, contaminants, or pollutants into or upon land, the atmosphere, or any body of water. Only sudden and accidental discharges, dispersals, releases, and escapes are covered. The purpose of this exclusion is to encourage the insured to protect the environment.

Two other exclusions remove liability for property damage to premises transferred to someone else and arising out of those premises, and liability arising out of demolition operations performed by or on behalf of the insured.

The *persons* protected under this part are the named insured, including the spouse if a sole proprietor, partners if a partnership, and if a corporation, an executive officer, director, or stockholder while acting in his or her capacity as a representative of the corporation. Also covered is any organization or person managing real estate for the named insured. Employees of the named insured, other than executive officers, are not protected by the policy unless the insured pays an extra premium for such protection.

Several kinds of *losses* are covered under the contract. First, the insurer promises to pay all sums that the insured becomes legally obligated to pay as a result of bodily injury or property damage. "Bodily injury" is defined as bodily injury, sickness, or disease sustained by any person. It does not include personal injuries such as libel, slander, false arrest, and invasion of privacy. "Property damage" is defined as injury to or destruction of tangible property. It does not include damage to intangible interests such as an infringement of patents or copyrights or unfair trade competition.

Chapter 7 indicated that punitive damages are being awarded in more and more cases. In some states insurers are not permitted to protect businesses against punitive damages because to do so would soften the punishment. In other states a punitive damage exclusion may or may not be present.

Second, the insurer will pay expenses incurred by the insured in order to provide necessary immediate medical and surgical relief at the scene of the accident. This relief includes such items as first aid and transportation to a hospital in an ambulance. The insurer pays these costs even if the insured is not liable, but if some other party is responsible, the insurer has the right through subrogation to collect from that party.

Third, the insurer promises to defend at its expense any suit against the insured coming within the scope of the policy even if the suit is groundless, false, or fraudulent. However, the insurer need not defend the insured in court if it decides that a negotiated settlement would be a better solution. If the case goes to court, the insurer promises to pay the premiums on release of attachment and appeal bonds. It will pay all costs levied against the insured and *all* interest accruing after the judgment has been entered until it has paid its share of that judgment. Finally, it promises to reimburse the insured for all reasonable expenses incurred at the insurer's request, including loss of wages not to exceed $25 per day to assist in investigating or defending the claim.

The bodily injury or damage must occur at *locations* within the following territory: the United States, its territories or possessions, or Canada; international waters or air space (but the injury or damage cannot occur in the course of transportation to or from any country other than Canada); and anywhere in the world if the injury or damage arises out of a product sold for use within the United States or Canada. The occurrence is excluded if it arises out of operations on or from premises owned by, rented to, or controlled by the named insured that have not been insured under the policy.

Amount of Recovery The insurer's responsibility for damages because of bodily injuries is limited to a stated amount per occurrence. Property damage claims are subject to a separate per-occurrence limit. All bodily injury or property damage arising out of continuous or repeated exposure to substantially the same general conditions is considered to arise out of one occurrence.

In addition to these two per-occurrence limits, the insurer places an aggregate limit on the insurer's total responsibility during the policy year for damages because of bodily injuries that would be covered under the completed operations and products liability coverage part. An aggregate limit also applies to property damage claims that would be covered under: (1) the completed operations and products liability coverage part, (2) the manufacturers' and contractors' liability coverage part, or (3) the independent contractors' liability coverage part. This aggregate limit on property damage claims applies separately to each of the three affected sources of liability.

The defense and other supplementary benefits are not subject to these policy limits.

Broad Form Comprehensive General Liability Endorsement   Two important limitations of the C.G.L. coverage part are that (1) contractual liability coverage is limited to liability assumed under "incidental contracts" and (2) personal injuries are not covered unless they involve bodily harm.

A broad form comprehensive general liability endorsement is available that liberalizes the C.G.L. coverage part in several ways, including removal of these two limitations. More specifically, this endorsement adds twelve coverages, subject to some exclusions not stated here. Six of these twelve additions are as follows:

1 The definition of "incidental contract" is extended to include any contract or agreement relating to conduct of the insured's business.

2 The insurer promises to pay damages arising out of personal injuries (meaning injuries arising out of false arrest, invasion of privacy, libel, or slander) or injuries arising out of advertising activities.

3 Under medical payments coverage, the insurer pays, regardless of fault, the medical expenses of persons (not the named insured or tenants) injured by a condition which, if liability exists, would be covered under the O.L. & T. or M. & C. coverage parts. This extension is health insurance, not liability insurance. Payments made under this coverage do not reduce the amounts payable under the liability coverage, but they may persuade the recipients not to make a claim under the liability section.

4 The insured is covered against liability arising out of the giving or serving of alcoholic beverages at functions that are incidental to the named insured's business.

5 Fire legal liability coverage protects the named insured against liability for property damage to structures or portions thereof rented to or leased to the named insured if such damage is caused by a fire.

6 Employees are added to the list of persons insured.

PROFESSIONAL LIABILITY INSURANCE

Professional liability is usually excluded by endorsement under the policies heretofore described, when the insured has a significant exposure to this source. To fill the gap, a wide variety of professional liability policies, sometimes called errors and omissions insurance, has been developed. Illustrative of these contracts are policies issued to druggists, hospitals, physicians, surgeons, dentists, lawyers, accountants, building managers, members of boards of directors, and insurance agents and brokers. Many of these coverages can be written as endorsements to other liability insurance contracts. In each case the insured agrees essentially to pay all sums that the insured becomes legally obligated to pay because of damages arising out of malpractice, error, or mistakes in rendering or failing to render the appropriate professional services. A detailed analysis of these contracts would reveal some significant differences that we will not consider in this text. It is important, however, to indicate some important differences between the typical professional liability insurance policy and most other general liability insurance policies.

1 Most professional liability policies limit the insurer's liability to a stated amount per claim and an aggregate amount during the policy period. More than one claim may be associated with injury to a single person. For example, a husband and his wife may both present claims because of injuries to the husband. No distinction is made between injuries to persons and injuries to property.

2 Except with respect to some product liability losses, professional liability policies exclude the kinds of losses that are covered under other general liability insurance contracts. A hospital or a druggist, for example, still has need for other types of general liability insurance.

3 Professional liability insurance has traditionally applied to claims arising out of services that were performed or should have been performed during the policy term, even if the accident, such as the taking of a drug, occurs later. The recent malpractice insurance crisis, noted in Chapter 7, has caused many leading insurers to limit their coverage to claims made within the policy period, regardless of when the service was performed. If the insured or the insurer cancels a "claims-made" policy, the insured usually can purchase "tail" coverage that extends, up to some specified limits, the period in which he or she can report claims for an injury that occurred prior to termination of the "claims-made" policy.

4 Under many professional liability insurance policies, the insurer does not have the right to settle a claim in the manner it deems most expedient. Because the insured's professional reputation and livelihood may be at stake, the insurer may not be permitted to negotiate a settlement with the plaintiff without the insured's consent.

AUTOMOBILE INSURANCE

Most automobile insurance contracts are schedule contracts that permit the insured to purchase both property and liability insurance under one policy. The contract can be divided, however, into two separate contracts—one providing insurance against physical damage to automobiles and the other protecting against potential liability arising out of the ownership, maintenance, or use of an automobile. Some automobile insurance contracts, notably those issued by insurers associated with automobile finance companies, cover only physical damage insurance.

Types of Contracts

Unlike the standard fire insurance policy, automobile insurance contracts are not prescribed by statute. Many insurers use the same contracts by voluntary agreement, but others, including the four largest writers of automobile insurance, have designed their own. They are so similar, however, that an analysis of the standard contracts will enable the reader to understand the most important provisions in most, if not all, automobile insurance contracts.[2]

Two standard automobile insurance contracts can be used by business risk managers. The first is the Business Auto Policy (BAP) designed for (1) corporations and partnerships insuring any type of automobile (for example, private passenger automobiles, trucks, or taxis), and (2) sole proprietors insuring any automobile other than a private passenger automobile. The second is the Personal Auto Policy (PAP) designed primarily for nonbusiness automobiles but which sole proprietors can purchase to insure private passenger automobiles used in their business. Both of these policies are written in more simplified and readable language than the standard contracts they replaced in the late 1970s.

The major provisions of these two policies are discussed below. We will also describe briefly two special types of automobile insurance for automobile garages and dealers.

Business Auto Policy

The business auto policy permits the insured to purchase five kinds of protection: (1) physical damage or property insurance, (2) liability insurance, (3) medical payments insurance, (4) uninsured motorists insurance, and (5) personal injury protection, required in those states with no-fault statutes.

Property Insurance Under the property insurance part of the BAP, the insured may choose the *perils* against which he or she wishes to be insured. The choices that are available are:

1 A list of specified perils that includes fire, explosion, theft, windstorm, hail, earthquake, flood, vandalism, and the sinking, burning, collision, or derailment of any conveyance transporting the automobile.

2 "Comprehensive" perils. This comprehensive insurance protects the insured against all risks or perils other than collision or overturn and the excluded perils discussed below. It is expressly agreed that for the purpose of determining the perils which this comprehensive insurance covers, losses caused by the following perils shall not be considered collision losses and are, therefore, covered: missiles, falling objects, and collision with birds or animals. Breakage of glass, however caused, is also not considered to be a collision loss excluded under this coverage.

The insured who elects comprehensive insurance need not purchase the specified perils coverage, because comprehensive insurance includes all the perils mentioned plus many more. It would, for example, cover paint damage caused by a road-tarring machine.

---

[2] Minor differences may be important in particular cases, and the analyst must look for these differences. The nonstandard contracts may be more liberal in some respects and less liberal in others.

3 Collision or overturn. Losses that would not be considered collision losses excluded under comprehensive coverage might also be considered collision losses under the collision coverage. Damage caused by a falling brick, for example, could be either a comprehensive loss or a collision loss. If the insured has only comprehensive insurance, he or she should claim a comprehensive loss; if the insured has only collision insurance, he or she should claim a collision loss. If the insured has both coverages, he or she can collect under either coverage but not both. Since collision insurance is almost always written with a deductible, while comprehensive insurance is usually written on a full coverage or smaller deductible basis, the insured should usually claim a comprehensive loss.

4 Disablement of a private passenger automobile from any cause resulting in towing costs and costs for labor performed at the place of disablement. This coverage would pay, for example, for towing costs incurred if an automobile cannot be moved under its own power because of deep snow. Because the maximum possible loss covered by this insurance is relatively small, this is not an important kind of insurance. Furthermore, it permits adverse selection against the insurer. The maximum payment per disablement is $25.

Excluded perils are tire blowouts and punctures, wear and tear, mechanical and electrical breakdown, and freezing, unless the damage results from some peril such as a theft or vandalism covered under the policy. Perils set in motion by these excluded perils, such as a collision resulting from a mechanical breakdown, are not excluded. Other excluded perils are war, the explosion of a nuclear weapon, and radioactive contamination.

The insured may also select what *property,* in this case what automobiles and their equipment, is to be insured. An automobile is defined as a land motor vehicle, trailer, or semitrailer designed for travel on public roads. Not considered to be automobiles are (1) such specialized equipment as bulldozers, power shovels, street sweepers, and cranes, and (2) vehicles designed for use principally off public roads. The choices are as follows:

1 Only owned automobiles. To purchase this coverage or the next two the insured must own five or more automobiles.

2 Only owned private passenger automobiles.

3 Only owned automobiles other than private passenger automobiles.

4 Only owned automobiles that are specifically described. This coverage is designed for insureds owning less than five automobiles.

5 Only automobiles that are leased, hired, rented, or borrowed. Not covered under this or any other coverage are automobiles that the insured leases, hires, rents, or borrows from any employee or any member of the employee's household.

Under the first three coverages, the policy automatically covers owned automobiles of the type specified that are acquired after the policy begins. Under the fourth coverage, newly acquired automobiles are covered only if two conditions are met. First, either the insurer must already cover all the insured's owned autos, or the new automobile must replace one that was previously insured. Second, the insured must tell the insurer within 30 days after the acquisition that the new automobile is to be insured.

Personal property carried in the automobile is not covered. Specifically excluded are (1) tape decks or other sound reproducing equipment not permanently installed in the automobile, (2) tapes, records, and other sound producing equipment, and (3) any sound receiving equipment such as a citizens' band radio or two-way mobile telephone, unless permanently installed in the dash or console opening normally used for installing a radio.

The *person* whose insurable interest is covered is the named insured.

The protection is limited to direct property *losses* with one exception—extra transportation costs incurred because of the theft of a private passenger automobile insured under either the specified perils or the comprehensive coverage. The contract states that the insurer will pay $10 a day for transportation expenses commencing 48 hours after the theft and ending when the automobile has been returned or the insurer pays for the loss. The maximum payment per theft is $300.

The *place* where each automobile will be principally garaged is stated in the declarations. The automobile is covered, however, so long as it is being used in the United States, its territories or possessions, Puerto Rico, or Canada. The notable omission is Mexico, where the driving conditions and repair facilities are considered significantly different. Some insurers will add Mexican coverage by endorsement, but insureds commonly purchase this insurance from a Mexican insurer at the border.

The contract, which usually has a *term* of one year, is effective at 12:01 A.M. standard time, at the named insured's address on the commencement date and terminates at the same hour on the expiration date. The contract usually contains a typical cancellation clause, but in some jurisdictions on all renewals, and 60 days after the effective date of a contract issued to a new insured, the insurer may cancel only for specified reasons. Most states with cancellation laws also require the insurer to give the insured written notice of their intent not to renew some time, such as 20 days, before the contract expires.

Several conditions affect the *amount of recovery*. Unless the policy is endorsed to provide coverage on a stated amount basis, the insurer promises to pay the smaller of these two amounts: (1) the actual cash value of the damaged or stolen property at the time of the loss, or (2) the cost of repairing or replacing the damaged or stolen property with another of like kind and quality.

Collision insurance may be and almost always is subject to a deductible. Because of the high frequency of small collision losses, a deductible greatly reduces the cost of collision insurance. Comprehensive insurance may also be subject to a deductible but the deductible is not applied to losses caused by fire or lightning. The most common type of deductible is the straight deductible under which the insurer deducts a stated amount such as $250 from each separate loss.

The named insured's BAP pays first if the loss involves a covered owned automobile that is also covered under other insurance. If the loss involves a covered non-owned automobile that is also covered under other insurance (for example, insurance purchased by the owner of a car rented by the named insured), the other insurance pays first. If, for some reason, more than one policy covers on the same basis, either primary or excess, the named insured's policy pays a pro rata share based on the ratio of its limit of liability to the total of the limits of liability under all the policies involved.

Liability Insurance Under the liability insurance part of the BAP the *peril* covered is an accident for which the insured is legally liable. Accident is defined to include but is not limited to continuous or repeated exposure to the same conditions resulting in bodily injury or property damage to the insured neither expected nor intended.

The *source of liability* covered is the ownership, maintenance, or use of a covered automobile. The insured can determine which automobiles he wishes to cover by selecting one or more of the following options:

1 Any automobile. This option includes the automobiles covered under options 2, 6, and 7 plus any others not specifically excluded.

2 Only owned automobiles.

3 Only owned private passenger automobiles.

4 Only owned automobiles other than private passenger automobiles.

5 Only owned automobiles than are specifically described.

6 Only automobiles that are leased, hired, rented, or borrowed. Not covered under this coverage are automobiles leased, hired, rented, or borrowed from any employee or any member of an employee's household.

7 Only automobiles owned by employees or members of their households but only when the automobile is used in the named insured's business or personal affairs.

Under all these options, trailers and semitrailers with a load capacity of 2,000 pounds or less are covered without an additional charge if they are designed primarily for travel on public roads. Mobile equipment, as defined earlier, is covered without an additional charge while being carried or towed by a covered automobile.

The BAP offers no protection against liability (1) assumed under any contract, (2) for the bodily injury, disease, or death of an employee (other than a domestic employee not entitled to workers' compensation benefits) of the insured arising out of or in the course of employment by the insured, (3) for damage to property owned or transported by the insured or in the insured's care, custody, or control, (4) for bodily injury or property damage resulting from the loading of property before it has been put in or on the covered automobile or from the unloading of property after it has been taken off or out of the covered automobile and (5) for bodily injury or property damage caused by the dumping, discharge, or escape of irritants, pollutants, or contaminants, unless the dumping, discharge, or escape is sudden and accidental. A mandatory endorsement excludes (6) liability for which the insured is covered under a nuclear energy liability insurance policy.

The named insured is an insured *person* for any covered automobile. With two exceptions, anyone else using a covered automobile owned, hired, or borrowed by the named insured is an insured person if they are using that automobile with the permission of the named insured. The two exceptions are (1) someone else using an automobile the named insured borrows from any employee or a member of an employee's household, and (2) someone else using a covered automobile while working in a business of selling, servicing, repairing, or parking automobiles. To illustrate, if a parking attendant damages another car while parking the named insured's car, the insurer will not defend the parking attendant or his or her employer. It will defend the named insured if the named insured is legally responsible. In addition to the named insured and persons driving with permission, anyone liable for the conduct of another insured is protected, but only to the extent of that liability. For example, a corporation may direct one of its employees to spend the day delivering packages for a local charity. All three persons are insured. The corporation is the named insured, the employee is a person driving the corporation's car with its permission, and the charity is a person responsible for the conduct of that employee. Not insured, however, is the owner or anyone else from whom the named insured hires or borrows a covered automobile unless that automobile is a trailer connected to a covered owned automobile.

Employees are not insured against liability for bodily injury to any fellow employee arising out of and in the course of his or her employment. This exclusion is necessary because although workers' compensation is the exclusive remedy of an injured employee against his or her employer, several states permit the injured employee to sue a negligent fellow employee.

The major *losses* covered are the court awards and settlements that insureds would otherwise have to pay. In addition, the insured will investigate any claims covered by the policy, defend the insured, and pay certain supplementary expenses. Punitive damages are specifically excluded.

The *locations* and *times* covered are the same as those under the property insurance part.

The *amount of recovery* is determined by several provisions. A single limit per accident applies to all court awards or settlements. Separate limits for bodily injury and property damage losses are available by endorsement.

Defense and investigation costs are not subject to this limit, but payment of this amount toward an award or a settlement ends the insurer's obligation to defend the suit. Bail bond costs related to the accident are covered up to $250. The insurer will also pay the insured up to $50 a day for earnings lost because the insured attends hearings or trials at the insurer's request. The insurer will also pay the premiums on appeal bonds and release of attachment bonds (see page 346) required in connection with the suit, costs taxed to the insured, interest accruing on an award from the time it is made until the time it is paid (but only on an amount up to the limit of liability), and reasonable expenses incurred by the insured at the insurer's request.

Deductibles are not common, but are available for firms with a fleet of cars.

If other insurance also covers the loss, the rules are the same as for property insurance with one exception. If a covered trailer is connected to another vehicle, the named insured's BAP is primary if the trailer is connected to an automobile owned by the named insured, excess if it is connected to a non-owned automobile. The excess liability coverage provided by the named insured's BAP is more significant than the excess property insurance because it increases the total protection more often and by larger amounts. To illustrate, if a rented car is driven by an employee on company business the total protection for the employee and the named insured is that car rental agency's limit of liability plus the named insured's limit of liability. If the car rental agency and the named insured both have the same property insurance coverages, there would be no loss in excess of the owner's limits. If the rental agency has property insurance on the vehicle, the only reason the named insured's policy might have to pay is that it includes a smaller deductible.

Medical Payments Insurance   Medical payments insurance, covering expenses for medical services, is a form of health insurance added by endorsement to the BAP. The legal liability of the insured for these expenses is not an issue. The insurer promises to pay all reasonable medical and funeral expenses incurred within three years following an accident that occurred while a person was entering, occupying, or leaving a covered automobile. The insured determines what is a covered automobile by selecting one or more of the following options:

Only owned automobiles
Only owned private passenger automobiles
Only owned automobiles other than private passenger automobiles
Only owned specifically described automobiles

If a covered automobile is out of service because of breakdown, repair, servicing, loss or destruction, another automobile used as a substitute is covered. Note that these other persons must be occupying a covered automobile—not an automobile hit by a covered automobile.

No coverage is provided for any insured occupying a vehicle located for use as a premises, for any employee of the named insured sustaining injury arising out of and in the course of that employment (except for domestic employees not covered under workers' compensation), for any insured while working in a business of selling, repairing, or parking automobiles, or any person using a vehicle without a reasonable belief that he or she is entitled to do so.

Medical expenses paid under this endorsement do not reduce the insurer's responsibility under liability insurance. Thus, if an insured is legally responsible for medical expenses incurred by a passenger, that passenger could collect twice from the insurer for the same medical expenses. The only other insurance affecting the insured person's recovery under this part is other automobile medical expense insurance. Where other medical expense insurance also covers the loss it is treated the same way as other liability insurance. For example, if the named insured is injured while occupying someone else's auto, the medical expense insurance on that auto is primary. The named insured's BAP is excess. If someone other than the insured is legally responsible for the loss, the insurer has no subrogation rights under medical payments insurance.

The policy limit under this part is a stated amount per injured person per accident. Because the usual occupants of covered automobiles are employees, this coverage is a much less frequent part of the BAP than of the PAP.

Uninsured Motorists Insurance   The problem of the uncompensated automobile accident victim was discussed at length in Chapter 8. In order to provide protection against uninsured motorists and against hit-and-run drivers, insurers have developed uninsured-motorists insurance, which can be added by endorsement to the BAP. Under this endorsement any person injured while occupying the insured automobile can submit a claim to the insurer issuing the endorsement, which will act as if it represented the negligent "uninsured" driver or hit-and-run driver. A vehicle is considered to be "uninsured" if it is insured for less than the limit of the insured motorists insurance.

It should be noted that the insured victim cannot collect under this coverage unless the uninsured motorist (or the hit-and-run driver) was negligent. On the other hand, it is not necessary for the insured to obtain a judgment before seeking or obtaining reimbursement from the insurer. Instead, the insured and the insurer must decide through negotiations whether the uninsured motorist was negligent. If they disagree, the matter is to be settled by arbitration in accordance with the rules of the American Arbitration Association. Although the insurer is forced under this section to assume a position counter to that of the insured, settling these claims has not been nearly so awkward as might be assumed, and relatively few cases have had to be arbitrated. If the insurer pays the insured, it possesses subrogation rights against the uninsured motorist. If the uninsured motorist is financially responsible even though he or she does not have insurance, the insurer will probably sue the uninsured motorist in order to recover the money it has paid out.

The automobiles that can be covered under this insurance are the same as those that can be covered under medical payments insurance with one addition. The named insured can limit the protection to those owned automobiles that are subject to a compulsory uninsured motorists law.

The policy limit is a single limit per accident. Any workers' compensation or compulsory temporary disability benefits are deducted from what would otherwise be paid under this endorsement before the application of the policy limits.

Personal Injury Protection In states that have passed no-fault laws (see Chapter 8), the BAP coverage on the named insured's owned automobiles must provide the no-fault medical expense and income or service replacement benefits specified in the statute. To illustrate, in Minnesota, a fairly liberal state, a personal injury protection endorsement obligates the insurer, in accordance with the Minnesota act, to provide certain no-fault benefits on behalf of "eligible insured persons." These eligible insured persons include (1) the named insured or any resident relative who is injured while occupying almost any motor vehicle or being struck while a pedestrian by such a vehicle, (2) any other person injured while occupying the insured motor vehicle or being struck while a pedestrian by that vehicle, or (3) any other person who is injured while occupying a motor vehicle (other than a public or livery conveyance) not owned by but operated by the named insured or a resident relative if the bodily injury results from the operation of the motor vehicle by the named insured or relative. Benefits are not paid to persons in the second or third categories if they are named insureds or relatives under another personal injury protection endorsement. The insurer promises to pay benefits for medical expenses, 85 percent of losses of income because of disability up to $200 per week, expenses incurred to replace essential services up to $15 per day, funeral expenses up to $1,250, and losses of income or services suffered by the survivors of deceased persons up to $200 per week. For each eligible injured person the maximum amount payable for the medical expenses is $20,000; the maximum payment for all other losses combined is $10,000. The coverage applies to accidents within the United States or Canada.

As explained in Chapter 8, all no-fault laws permit tort liability actions under certain conditions. Most bodily injuries, and in some states property damage, will, it is hoped, involve only the no-fault endorsements and the physical damage coverages. In more serious cases, however, the liability coverages are still needed.

Personal Auto Policy

As mentioned earlier, the personal auto policy is designed for family use but sole proprietors can also use the PAP to insure private passenger automobiles used in their business. Pickup, sedan delivery, or panel trucks can be insured *but not for business use*. The PAP includes (1) property insurance, (2) liability insurance, (3) medical payments insurance, and (4) uninsured motorists coverage. Personal injury protection or no-fault coverage is added where necessary by endorsement. The PAP will be more briefly summarized below than the BAP because of the many similarities between the two policies.

Property Insurance   The PAP covers all *perils* except those specifically excluded. Collision is excluded unless it is specifically covered. Glass breakage and collision losses caused by missiles, falling objects, contacts with birds or aimals, fire, theft, explosion, earthquake, windstorm, hail, water, flood, vandalism, riot, or civil commotion are not excluded even if collision is excluded. Otherwise, the excluded perils are similar to the BAP exclusions.

The *property* covered is principally the owned vehicles shown in the declarations including their equipment. These vehicles may be private passenger autos; small trucks—more specifically pickup, sedan delivery, or panel trucks; trailers designed to be pulled by a private passenger auto; and farm wagons or farm implements but only while towed by a private passenger auto or small truck. Any automobiles or trailers that are acquired by the named insured or spouse during the policy period are covered only if the named insurer or spouse requests coverage within thirty days after he or she becomes the owner.

Personal property carried is not covered. The BAP exclusions applying to sound reproducing and producing equipment are also part of the PAP.

The *persons* covered are the named insured and his or her spouse if a resident of the same household. If the named insured dies, his or her legal representative is covered.

The *losses* covered are the same as those under the BAP—the cost of repairing or replacing a covered automobile that is damaged or stolen plus the extra transportation cost incurred if the automobile is stolen.

The *locations* and *times* covered are the same as for the BAP except for a more liberal cancellation provision. Ten days notice by the insurer is required if cancellation is for nonpayment of premium or if the cancellation notice is mailed during the first 60 days the policy is in effect, provided the policy is not a renewal policy. Otherwise, 20 days notice is required, and the insurer agrees to cancel only for nonpayment of premium, or if the driver's license or motor vehicle registration of the named insured, the spouse, or any other driver who drives with the named insured or customarily uses the covered auto has been suspended or revoked during the policy period. The insurer also agrees that if it decides not to renew the policy it will mail a nonrenewal notice to the named insured at least 20 days before the end of the policy period.

The *amount of recovery* is determined for the most part in the same way as under the BAP. The principal difference is that since this PAP property insurance does not cover the use of any non-owned automobiles, the insurance is always primary insurance. If other insurance covers the same loss, the PAP pays the proportion of the loss that its limit of liability bears to the total of all applicable limits.

Liability Insurance   Under the liability insurance part of the PAP, the *peril* covered is an accident.

The *source of liability* covered is the ownership, maintenance, or use of the owned automobiles or trailers that can be covered under the property insurance part plus, for the named insured, spouse, and any "family members," most other automobiles and trailers. A family member is a person related to the named insured or spouse by blood, marriage, or adoption who is a resident of the named insured's household.

No person is protected against damage to property owned by, rented to, used by, being transported by, or in the use of that person with two exceptions. First, the exclusion does not apply to damage to a non-owned residence or private garage. Second, it does not apply to private passenger cars or trailers unless they are owned by or furnished for the regular use of the named insured, the spouse, or any other family member. Thus, if the named insured drives a friend's car occasionally, this liability insurance provides protection against damage to that car if the named insured is negligent.

Other exclusions cut out liability for injuries to employees in the course of employment (except for domestic employees not subject to workers' compensation); liability arising out of using the vehicle to carry persons or property for a fee (not share-the-expense car pools); liability for the ownership, maintenance, or use of a motorcycle or other vehicles with less than three wheels; and the liability of any person employed in the business or occupation of selling, repairing, servicing, storing, or parking of automobiles.

The *persons* covered other than the named insured, spouse, and any family member differ depending upon the automobile involved. For covered owned automobiles or trailers the other insured persons are (1) any person using the automobile or trailer except a thief (or anyone else who could not reasonably believe he or she was entitled to use the vehicle), and (2) any person or organization legally responsible for the use of the vehicle. For other automobiles, covered only if used by the named insured, spouse, or any family members, any other person legally responsible for this use of the automobile is also covered but not if this person owns or hires the automobile or trailer. This means that if the named insured rents a car on a trip to Hawaii, the named insured is covered but the car rental agency is not. (The car rental agency should have its own liability insurance policy covering both the agency and persons renting its cars.) The named insured and spouse are covered when they drive cars owned by or furnished for the regular use of some other family member but no other family member has this coverage; no one is covered if the car driven is owned by or furnished for the regular use of the named insured or spouse but not specifically declared. (BAP insureds who wish to extend such drive-other-cars coverage to specific individuals and their families can purchase endorsements naming these individuals. For example, a corporation may name a president-owner in such an endorsement.)

The *losses* covered are the same as those covered under the BAP—the payment of awards and settlements, investigation and defense costs, and supplementary expenses such as bail bond costs, and the earnings lost and reasonable expenses incurred by the insured at the request of the insurer to help defend the insured against the claim.

The *location* and *time* provisions are the same as for the property insurance.

The *amount of recovery* provisions are basically the same as under the BAP—a single liability limit per accident and a provision making the liability insurance excess when it covers an automobile not owned by the named insured or spouse.

Medical Payments Insurance The medical payments insurance provided under the PAP differs from the BAP coverage in two major respects. First, the named insured or any resident relative need not be in an insured automobile to collect benefits. They are covered if injured while getting in, getting out of, or occupying any automobile not excluded. They are also covered if, as a pedestrian, they are struck by an automobile. (Through an endorsement BAP insureds can extend such broad protection to specific individuals and their families.) Second, any amounts paid under this coverage either reduce or are reduced by any amounts paid or payable under the liability or uninsured motorists parts of the policy. In other words, the injured party cannot collect twice under this policy for the same medical expenses.

Uninsured Motorists Coverage The uninsured motorists coverage is also basically the same as its BAP counterpart except that the named insured or any resident relative need not be in a covered automobile to collect benefits.

Personal Injury Protection Personal injury protection or no-fault insurance coverage is added by endorsement and provides the same coverage as the equivalent coverage under the BAP.

Garage Liability Insurance

Designed for automobile dealers, repair shops, service stations, and the like, garage liability insurance combines automobile liability insurance with general liability insurance. The general liability insurance covers the premises-operations hazard and the completed operations-products hazard. The automobile liability insurance may be limited to automobiles not owned or hired, or it may cover all automobiles—owned, hired, customers', and others not specifically excluded.

Elevator liability insurance and garagekeepers' legal liability insurance can also be included. The latter coverage protects the insured against liability for damage to automobiles in his or her care or control if this damage is caused by certain specified perils.

Special Physical Damage Insurance for Automobile Dealers

Because automobile dealers have some unique exposures, some special physical damage insurance policies have been designed for them. One contract permits the dealer to purchase insurance against certain perils on new and used cars consigned to or owned by the dealer. Fire and the extended coverage perils are much more important threats to the dealer than to other automobile owners because of the stationary nature of much of the exposure.

When a customer buys an automobile on the installment plan, he or she is usually required to purchase physical damage insurance, including a loss-payable clause that protects the dealer in the same way that the standard mortgagee clause in the fire insurance contract protects the mortgagee. Sometimes, however, dealers protect themselves against failure of the purchaser to buy insurance through single interest insurance that covers only their own interests.

WORKERS' COMPENSATION INSURANCE

For many businesses, workers' compensation insurance claims more premium dollars than any other line of insurance. Although state funds write workers' compensation insurance in 19 jurisdictions, and many firms elect to self-insure their workers' compensation obligation because they have numerous exposure units, private insurers currently make over 60 percent of the workers' compensation payments (excluding special federal "black lung" benefits paid to coal miners and their survivors). All this private insurance is provided under a standard workers' compensation and employers' liability insurance policy, a revised, more readable version of which was introduced in early 1984 by the National Council on Compensation Insurance. The standardization is voluntary except in a few states and with respect to certain provisions that are often required under state law. This voluntary action reflects, in part, the fear that otherwise the states might respond with standard policies of their own. It also reflects the fact that once the basic promise to pay workers' compensation benefits has been made, it is extremely difficult, if not impossible, to design a competitive contract with additional benefits. If this last statement is not immediately clear to the reader, it should become more evident after reading the following contract analysis.

Events Covered

The standard workers' compensation and employers' liability policy is really two policies in one—workers' compensation insurance and employers' liability insurance. Consequently, in certain sections of this analysis we shall have to distinguish between the two coverages.

Perils and Sources of Liability Under the workers' compensation section, the policy covers accidental bodily injuries and diseases for which the insured may be legally responsible under the workers' compensation law, including any amendments made during the policy period. Under the employers' liability section, the peril is an accidental bodily injury or disease sustained by an employee, arising out of and in the course of his or her employment by the insured, that is not covered under the workers' compensation law but for which the insured is legally liable. For example, certain illnesses such as the common cold, which may lead to pneumonia, might not be considered occupational diseases even if the employer were responsible for the illness. Employers' liability insurance may also be helpful to a business that employs different types of workers, some of whom are not included under the workers' compensation law. Moreover, under certain special circumstances, an injured employee may sue and recover from some third party on the ground that the third party's negligence caused the accident. The third party may in turn be able to sue the employer, something which the employee could not do. Employers' liability insurance would provide the necessary protection unless, as is usually true, the third party's right to sue the employer arises out of a hold-harmless agreement with the employer. Under the employers' liability insurance the insurer also agrees to pay damages claimed (1) under the "dual capacity" theory explained in Chapter 8 against the employer in a capacity other than the employer, (2) by others for care of the worker and loss of his or her services, and (3) by the spouse, child, parent, brother, or sister for consequential injuries to them. Despite the importance of this employers' liability insurance, almost all claims under the standard policy are paid under the workers' compensation section.

The employers' liability section does not provide any coverage with respect to (1) any employee hired in violation of the law with the knowledge of any executive officer, (2) bodily injury intentionally caused or aggravated by the employer, or (3) the discharge of, coercion of, or discrimination against any employee in violation of law.

Persons The person insured under the contract is the employer. If he or she should die, his or her legal representatives are insured if the insurer receives written notice of the insured's death within 30 days after it occurs. Assignment of the policy without the insurer's consent is not binding on the insurer.

Although the employees are not insureds, they receive certain valuable rights under the workers' compensation section—not under the employers' liability section—which improve their status compared with that of the usual liability claimant. For example, the employee can proceed directly against the insurer, instead of indirectly through the employer. Furthermore, if the employee tells the employer about an injury and the employer fails to pass on the information to the insurer, the insurer must still pay the claim.

Losses The workers' compensation section protects the insured against his or her obligations under the workers' compensation law, but the employer must reimburse the insurer for any excess payments arising out of four events. These events are (1) the insured's serious and willful misconduct, (2) employment of any person in violation of law with the knowledge of any executive officer, (3) failure to comply with a health or safety law or regulation, or (4) the discharge of, coercion of, or discrimination against any employee in violation of the workers' compensation law.[3] The employers' liability policy does not cover punitive or exemplary damages added because any employee was hired in violation of the law.

Location   The workers' compensation section applies to the workers' compensation laws of each of the states listed in the contract by the insured. The workplaces of the insured are listed in the contract, but nonlisted workplaces are also included under both sections of the contract unless the insured has other workers' compensation insurance for these operations or is a qualified self-insurer.

The employers' liability section applies only to injuries sustained in the United States of America, its territories or possessions, or Canada, but this limitation does not apply to injuries to a citizen or resident of the United States or Canada who is temporarily outside these countries.

Time   The policy starts at 12:01 A.M. and usually runs for a term of one year. The cancellation provision is typical, except that it is to be amended to conform to any provisions in the state workers' compensation law. Many of these state laws require separate notification to state industrial commissions.

The contract covers accidental injuries occurring during the policy period. Diseases are covered if the last day on which the insured was exposed to this disease while working for the employer occurs during the policy period.

Amount of Recovery

There is no policy limit with respect to the workers' compensation section. The insurer must pay whatever the law provides, even if a large number of employees are involved.

The employers' liability promise, however, is limited to a specified amount per accident for bodily injury by accident. For bodily injury caused by disease, separate limits apply per employee and for all employees combined. The defense and other supplementary benefits are not subject to these limits.

State Fund Contracts

The workers' compensation insurance contracts provided by state funds are essentially the same as the standard private contracts except that there is often no employers' liability coverage. In addition, state funds provide no out-of-state coverage for multi-state employers.

---

[3] Note that this section applies only to payments in excess of those regularly provided under the workers' compensation law. As explained earlier, the employers' liability insurance provides no coverage with respect to most of these excess payments exclusions under the workers' compensation section.

Separate Employers' Liability Insurance

Employers' liability insurance is also occasionally written as a separate policy for employers not subject to the workers' compensation law. The protection is essentially the same as that provided under the employers' liability sections of the standard workers' compensation and employers' liability policy.

Excess Workers' Compensation Insurance

As we have noted earlier, many large firms prefer to self-insure their workers' compensation obligation. Some states, such as New York, require self-insurers to protect themselves against unusual losses through excess workers' compensation insurance. As was indicated in Chapter 8, most firms that retain workers' compensation loss purchase some form of excess insurance. This insurance usually assumes one of two forms: (1) specific excess insurance, and (2) stop-loss aggregate or aggregate excess insurance. Under the first form, the insurer agrees to pay losses in excess of a stated amount, such as $25,000 per accident. Under the second form, the insurer must pay total losses during the year in excess of some stated amount, such as 75 percent of the customary workers' compensation premium. This latter form is commonly sold as part of a package plan providing safety and claims services with respect to all losses. For example, one plan charges 25 percent of what would have been the premium for a standard policy in return for safety and claims service and aggregate excess insurance. The business retains the other 75 percent for paying claims and saves whatever is not needed for paying losses. Under both forms the insurer may limit its maximum liability to some stated number of dollars. The risk manager should realize that the firm is exposed to losses beyond this point.

UMBRELLA LIABILITY INSURANCE

"Umbrella" liability insurance, which is not standardized and varies greatly depending upon the insurer, provides two types of protection. First, umbrella insurance is excess insurance over the insured's traditional liability insurance policies of all sorts—general liability, automobile liability, aviation liability, workers' compensation, and others. Second, umbrella insurance covers sources of liability not covered under the insured's other liability policies, subject to a minimum deductible of some large amount such as $25,000 per occurrence. Illustrations might be contractual liability not covered under the primary insurance, non-owned aircraft liability insurance, and liability for invasion of privacy in an advertisement. The maximum limit of liability under the umbrella insurance is usually at least $1 million per occurrence and may range as high as $25 million or more per occurrence.

To obtain umbrella liability insurance, a business must have certain basic liability insurance protection. For example, the bodily injury liability limits must exceed some amount such as $600,000 per occurrence. The underlying general liability insurance contract must be a comprehensive general liability insurance policy. If this underlying contract does not protect the insured against product liability or liability for personal injuries arising out of false arrest, libel and slander, or invasion of privacy, the deductible with respect to these losses is raised to $100,000 or more per occurrence.

PACKAGE CONTRACTS

Instead of purchasing separate property insurance and liability on their premises and operations, many insureds—especially small and medium-sized businesses—prefer to purchase one of the package contracts developed by insurers starting in the 1960s. These package contracts, which combine property and liability insurance in one contract, are attractive mainly because:

1 The premium is frequently less than the premium for the separate coverages included in the package.

2 Many insureds find it much more convenient to deal with one contract and one insurer. Larger businesses often prefer to get the best combination of coverage, service, and cost for each type of insurance.

Special Multi-Peril Policy

The special multi-peril policy (SMP), a standard policy for which most businesses are eligible, will serve as an illustration of a package contract. The SMP has four sections. Section I can be written to provide either (1) fire and extended coverage plus vandalism insurance or (2) all risks coverage on the named insured's buildings and personal property. If fire and extended coverage plus vandalism insurance is provided, the contract can be endorsed to cover additional named perils. Business interruption insurance can be added by endorsement, regardless of the perils selected. Section II is basically comprehensive general liability insurance, except that newly acquired premises and operations are covered only for 30 days. Section III is a comprehensive destruction, disappearance, and dishonesty policy. Section IV is boiler and machinery insurance. Two important gaps are automobile insurance and workers' compensation insurance.[4]

Businessowners' Package Program

In 1975, a new businessowners' package program was developed as a standard policy alternative to the SMP program. This program, which is designed for small and medium-sized businesses, was a competitive response to some nonstandard package policies that were much simpler to explain, administer, and rate than the SMP program.

Like the SMP program, the new program includes both property (including net income) and liability insurance. Two forms are available. The *standard* form provides named-perils property coverage; all risks property coverage can be obtained under a *special* form. A limited number of optional coverages are available.

---

[4] The special multi-peril policy was described in much more detail in the fourth edition of this text.

Condominium Association Insurance

Apartment buildings, offices, shopping centers, and the like are often owned cooperatively under a condominium arrangement. Under a condominium individuals own units of space enclosed with collectively owned boundaries. The individuals own their units; they are also members of the condominium association that owns the undivided interest in the condominium properties. The condominium agreement defines this undivided interest. The definitions vary widely but common examples are the land; elevators; heat, light, and power facilities; entrances, exits, and hallways; and swimming pools. The interest also usually includes load-bearing walls and unfinished floors, ceilings, and perimeter walls, but not wall decorations, floor coverings, and interior partitions.

The condominium association can insure this undivided interest under an SMP policy with special condominium property insurance forms attached. One protects the association against the same perils as the basic property form; the other against all perils not specifically excluded. The property is defined to be consistent with the usual undivided-interest definition. Through an endorsement, however, the property definition can be modified to meet the definition used by the association being insured. The SMP policy is primary if it covers the same loss as insurance purchased by the owner of a condominium unit.[5]

Section II of the SMP policy provides liability insurance with each unit owner being included as an additional insured with respect to his or her own unit.

MISCELLANEOUS PROPERTY AND LIABILITY INSURANCE

Private and public insurers issue many kinds of insurance in addition to those described to this point. Some of these contracts are described briefly below:

Glass insurance covers damage to glass and to any lettering or ornamentation caused by breakage of the glass or by chemicals accidentally or maliciously applied. The only exclusions are fire, war, and nuclear reaction. Under most property insurance contracts the insurer rarely exercises its right to repair or replace the damaged property, but glass insurers compete primarily on the basis of their replacement service. Prompt replacement cuts indirect and net income losses, and insurers can take advantage of quantity discounts.

Credit insurance protects the insured business against abnormal losses on accounts receivable. Credit insurance differs from accounts receivable insurance, which covers abnormal bad debts losses suffered by an insured because records are damaged or destroyed by any peril not specifically excluded. Where credit insurance applies, the records are not destroyed but one or more debtors for some reason (e.g., bad luck, a recession, or poor management) fail to pay what they owe by the due date. Only firms such as manufacturers and wholesalers that sell to other businesses are eligible for this insurance.

---

[5] A special homeowner's form has been developed for owners of condominium apartments. See Chap. 32.

Export credit insurance protects exporters against credit risks (insolvency of the buyer) and political risks (inconvertibility of foreign currency to dollars and cancellation or restriction of export or import licenses) on sales to buyers in friendly foreign countries. Until recently the credit risk was underwritten by the Foreign Credit Insurance Association, an unincorporated association of over 55 stock insurers. The Export-Import Bank underwrote the political risks. The Export-Import Bank now underwrites both types of risks.

Valuable papers insurance provides all risks coverage on valuable papers and records such as plans and drawings, mailing lists, and financial records. This insurance covers the costs of research and other expenses incurred to restore the papers and records that were taken, damaged, or destroyed.

Title insurance reimburses the insured for any losses that may be incurred if his or her title to real estate proves to be defective. Title insurers search records in their own offices and other sources and protect the insured against existing defects that they fail to discover. Only one premium is paid at the commencement of the insurance, which continues until the insured's interest in the property ceases. Some states and counties operate a Torrens system, under which a hearing is held in order to discover defects. If no defects are discovered, the title is registered, and the owner is, except under certain circumstances, assured of a clear title. The registration fee includes a contribution to a fund that is used to indemnify persons who can prove later that they have some right that existed prior to the registration.

Aviation insurance, a rapidly growing field, includes a wide variety of contracts. Like automobile insurance, aviation insurance includes both property insurance on the planes and liability insurance.

Nuclear energy insurance also includes both property insurance and liability insurance. Nuclear energy property insurance protects the operator of a nuclear reactor against damage to the reactor itself and other property on the described premises as the result of a nuclear explosion or *any other peril not specifically excluded.* Because of the large values exposed to loss and the catastrophic possibilities, this insurance is underwritten only by a stock insurer pool and a mutual insurer pool. Individual insurers write radioactive contamination insurance for firms with nuclear hazards less than those faced by firms eligible for nuclear energy insurance. Nuclear energy liability insurance protects the insured and *any* other person who may be held liable for the loss (e.g., a negligent motorist who collides with the facility) against liability arising out of a nuclear incident.

The two pools mentioned above have gradually increased the limits of their liability coverage to $160 million per incident. Under the 1957 Price-Anderson Act, the maximum liability of each operator is limited to $560 million per incident.[6] The Nuclear Regulatory Commission promises to indemnify operators for losses up to this limit less the private protection required by law. This private protection includes the private pool insurance plus a retroactive assessment on the entire nuclear power industry. This assessment, which the commission makes only if the loss exceeds the

---

[6] Dan R. Anderson, "Limits on Liability: The Price-Anderson Act versus Other Laws," *The Journal of Risk and Insurance,* vol. XLV, no. 5 (December, 1978), pp. 651–674.

pool insurance, is $5 million per reactor which in 1983 would provide $410 million of additional private protection. Consequently the federal government's share of the liability exposure is currently zero. The 1979 incident at the Three Mile Island facility in Pennsylvania intensified interest in whether the $560 million limit under the Price-Anderson Act is adequate. An increase in the near future is considered highly probable.

Crop insurance is sold by private insurers and by the Federal Crop Insurance Corporation. Three major classes of private insurance exist: (1) crop-hail insurance, whose name signifies its function, (2) insurance on fruit and vegetable crops against frost and freezes, and (3) insurance covering hail, drought, excessive heat, flood, excessive moisture, and many other perils. The federal program covers all natural perils. Both the federal coverage and the broad private form are written only in selected areas.

Errors and omissions insurance protects mortgagees against their failure through an error or omission to obtain the insurance protection they normally require on the property that serves as security for the loan. This form of errors and omissions insurance is not the same as the professional liability insurance discussed earlier.

Electronic data processing insurance has become increasingly important with the widespread growing use of computers. Under this insurance all risks coverage is provided on a variety of EDP exposures including the computer hardware; tapes, discs, and cards on which information has been stored; and valuable papers and records including documentation materials or information that has not yet been stored on tapes, discs, or cards. The coverage on the tapes, discs, and cards and the valuable papers and records covers the cost of research and other expenses required to reproduce this information. Other expenses that can be insured include the inability to collect on accounts receivable if the records of accounts receivable are destroyed before or after storage; extra expenses incurred to hand process information until the computer is restored to normal, to rent substitute equipment, or to speed up repairs; and business interruption caused by damage or destruction of the EDP equipment.

Motortruck cargo legal liability insurance obligates the insurer to pay any loss to cargo for which the trucking concern, as a common carrier, is liable if the cause of the loss is one of a stated number of perils. As a common carrier, the trucker has the responsibility discussed in Chapter 7, and the Interstate Commerce Commission requires motor carriers engaged in interstate commerce to purchase this insurance unless they can demonstrate their ability to self-insure this obligation. Under the contract the insurer does not pay unless the carrier is legally responsible for the loss, but the carrier can be legally responsible without the insurer incurring any liability because the cause is not one of the specified perils. Covered perils are typically fire and lightning, windstorm, perils of the seas, lakes, and rivers, collisions, collapse of bridges, and flood. In order to satisfy the Interstate Commerce Commission, the contract must be endorsed to extend the insurer's liability to all perils, but the extension of liability is limited to $2,500 per truck and $5,000 per loss at any one time and place. If a loss involves a peril not covered under the basic policy but covered under the endorsement, the insurer can recover any payment it makes from the insured.

Fire legal liability insurance can be written either as a separate contract or as an endorsement to a general liability insurance contract. Under this insurance, the insurer agrees to pay all sums which the insured may be legally obligated to pay because of damage to property, real or personal, in his or her care, custody, or control, if the cause of the loss is fire or some other peril stated in the contract, such as explosion or smoke. Usually the insurer is liable only if the negligence of the insured or his agent is responsible for the loss, but some contracts cover liability assumed by the insured under a written agreement. Under some contracts, the insurer is responsible only for direct losses to the property; other contracts also cover liability for loss of use of the property.

Instead of purchasing fire legal liability insurance, the bailee may turn to other insurance solutions. For example, a tenant of real property may ask the landlord and the landlord's insurer: (1) to waive the subrogation clause under the landlord's policy with respect to the bailee or (2) to include the bailee under the policy as an additional insured. In either case, the insurer may be reluctant to relieve the tenant of any responsibility, and even if the insurer agrees, the loss may exceed the insurance, in which case the landlord may sue for the excess loss. Listing all the tenants in a large building as additional insureds would also be an inconvenient and complicated process.

Sprinkler leakage property insurance, which was discussed in Chapter 18, covers the insured's liability for damage to property in the insured's care, custody, or control. Separate *sprinkler leakage liability insurance,* on the other hand, protects the insured against legal responsibility for damage to the property of others caused by sprinkler leakage, so long as that property is not in the portion of a building occupied by the insured. For example, this insurance will protect the firm if it occupies the top floor of a building and if, through the negligence of one of its employees, an automatic sprinkler fuse is broken with resultant damage to the property of others on the lower floors or in other buildings. Liability assumed by the insured, however, is not covered unless this assumed liability has been specifically insured. This extension of coverage is important, for example, when a tenant under a lease assumes liability for such damage.

Water damage liability insurance bears the same relation to water damage property insurance that sprinkler leakage liability bears to sprinkler leakage property insurance.

Unusual coverages are illustrated by *all risks business interruption insurance, all risks worldwide blanket protection* covering direct and net income losses to both real and personal property anywhere in the world, and *cast insurance* protecting the insured against the failure of a performer to appear on a movie set, a theater stage, or a television program.

KEY CONCEPTS

Comprehensive general liability insurance Insurance that promises to defend the insured and pay claims for which the insured may be legally liable caused by accident and arising out of a source of liability not excluded under the contract.

Personal injury endorsement An endorsement that extends a liability insurance policy to cover personal injuries other than bodily injuries. Injuries arising from false arrest and invasion of privacy are two common examples.

Broad form comprehensive general liability endorsement An endorsement that adds twelve coverages to the comprehensive general liability insurance contract including personal injury liability, medical payments, and fire legal liability coverages.

Business auto policy   The standard auto policy designed for corporations and partnerships and for sole proprietors insuring vehicles other than private passenger automobiles.

Personal auto policy   The standard auto policy designed for families and for sole proprietors insuring private passenger automobiles.

Professional liability insurance   Insurance that protects professionals against liability for errors or mistakes in rendering or failing to render professional services.

Workers' compensation insurance   Insurance that protects the employer against its obligations under workers' compensation statutes.

Umbrella liability insurance   Insurance that provides excess protection against perils covered under basic liability contracts plus coverage, subject to a deductible, against some events not covered under the basic contracts.

Special multi-peril policy   A package policy designed for small and medium-sized businesses that includes property and liability insurance in one contract. Two notable exclusions are automobile insurance and workers' compensation insurance.

REVIEW QUESTIONS

1 Explain briefly each of the six major general liability coverage parts.
2 Why is the comprehensive general liability coverage part recommended for most insureds?
3 Summarize the events covered under a comprehensive general liability insurance policy.
4 Summarize the provisions in a comprehensive general liability insurance policy dealing with the amount of recovery.
5 In what ways does the broad form comprehensive general liability endorsement expand the coverage provided under the CGL policy?
6 Which of the following losses is covered under a CGL policy issued to a department store occupying a rental building (1) without a broad form endorsement and (2) with a broad form endorsement?
   a An employee trips a customer with an extension cord.
   b A customer is injured in a defective revolving door.
   c A customer slips on a greasy substance on an escalator.
   d Employees of a contractor hired to build an addition to the building drop a plank on a bystander's leg.
   e A customer who has bought a power mower is injured, while cutting grass, when the blade comes loose from the shaft.
   f A customer trying out a ladder in the store is injured when one of the steps breaks under the customer's weight.
   g A customer is embarrassed when falsely accused of shoplifting and arrested.
   h An employee is injured while riding in an elevator.
   i A fire caused by an employee damages some customers' property in the repair department.
   j An employee assaults a customer.
   k A bystander is injured while watching store employees unload a refrigerator at the home of a customer.
   l An employee accidentally sets fire to the building and causes extensive damage.
7 Does a claim under the CGL policy affect the coverage available for later occurrences during the policy period?
8 How does professional liability insurance differ from most other general liability insurance contracts?

9 Which of the standard automobile insurance contracts would be applicable in each of the following cases?

   a A sole proprietor insures a private passenger automobile for business and personal use.

   b A partnership insures two private passenger automobiles for business and personal use.

   c A corporation insures a 2-ton truck and two private passenger automobiles.

   d A corporation insures a panel-type truck with a load capacity of 1,200 pounds.

   e A sole proprietor insures a taxicab.

10 A firm purchases protection against the "comprehensive" perils and collision. A $250 deductible applies to collision losses. A cornice falls off a building and lands on the roof of the insured vehicle, causing $1,000 damage. How much will the insurer pay?

11 Which of the following losses is covered under the comprehensive coverage?

   a A cold snap damages the insured's car radiator.

   b A thief steals a $300 typewriter from the back seat of a salesperson's car.

   c An insured truck is swept away in a flood.

   d The insured's brakes fail, and the car collides with a brick wall.

   e The insured's car, which is being shipped by rail, is completely destroyed when the train is derailed.

12 a A private passenger car belonging to a sole proprietor is destroyed in a fire. Before the vehicle can be replaced, the firm must spend $40 a day for taxi fares for 20 days. If the car is insured against fire losses, will the insurer contribute to the cost of the taxi fares?

   b Would your answer be different if the car was stolen and was insured against theft? How?

   c What is the reason why insurers will pay one of these net income losses but not the other?

13 In what ways does the cancellation provision in the personal auto policy differ from the cancellation provision in the business auto policy?

14 Automobile physical damage insurance contracts contain no coinsurance clauses. Why?

15 a A sole proprietor has a private passenger car insured under a personal auto policy. An employee is instructed to drive a private passenger car belonging to a neighboring firm on company business. The borrowed car is damaged in a collision. Is the collision damage to the borrowed car covered under the sole proprietor's policy if the car is insured under the neighboring firm's policy? If it is uninsured?

   b Would your answer be different if the employee was the sole proprietor's son?

16 Mr. Jones, a sole proprietor, has a personal auto policy covering the family automobile. His son, Tom, owns an uninsured automobile. If Tom drives a friend's uninsured automobile and causes collision damage valued at $1,000, what is the obligation of Mr. Jones's insurer?

17 A corporation has a business auto policy. Which of the following losses are covered under the liability part of the policy assuming (1) only owned automobiles are covered? (2) any automobile is covered? Assume that negligence is involved in each case.

   a An employee driving a company car on company business injures a pedestrian.

   b An employee driving her own car on company business injures a pedestrian.

   c An employee driving a company car with the permission of his employer on an errand for the Red Cross injures a pedestrian.

   d A company car that was carrying some merchandise belonging to another firm collides with a telephone pole. The merchandise is destroyed.

   e Two employees are injured when the employee driving a company car tries to pass another car on a hill.

   f An attendant in a parking lot drives one of the corporation's private passenger cars into another car parked in the same lot.

   g A salesperson collides with another automobile while driving a hired automobile.

   h The corporation president has an accident while driving one of the private passenger cars on vacation in Mexico.

18 Explain the difference between the medical payments coverages in automobile liability insurance and general liability insurance with respect to coverage of the insured and his or her family.

19 The president of a corporation collides with a parked car when she takes her eyes off the road to stare into the window of a competitor. The damages are as follows:

President	Medical expenses	$ 500
	Pain and suffering	400
Guest in the firm's car	Medical expenses	3,000
	Loss of wages	2,000
	Pain and suffering	2,000
Occupant in the parked car	Medical expenses	20,000
	Loss of wages	10,000
	Pain and suffering	15,000
Parked car		2,000

The firm has a business automobile policy covering any automobile with the following limits:

Liability: $100,000 per accident
Medical payments: $1,000 per person
How much will the insurer pay
  a If the president is considered negligent?
  b If the president is not considered negligent?
  c If the president is considered negligent and at the time was driving her personal uninsured car?

20 a What social problem gave rise to uninsured-motorists coverage?
  b Must the uninsured motorist be financially irresponsible before the insured can collect under this coverage?
  c How are disputes handled between the insured and the insurer?

21 Mr. Jones, a sole proprietor, has a personal auto policy covering the family auto. What is the insurer's responsibility in each of the following cases? Assume the personal auto policy includes both liability and $1,000 medical payments coverage.
  a Tom Jones, the son, has an automobile of his own that is not insured. Tom has an accident while driving the family automobile. An injured pedestrian suffers a loss of $2,000, including $500 in medical expenses.
  b Mr. Jones has to miss work for two weeks while appearing in court and otherwise helping the insurer to defend a case in which Mr. Jones is the defendant.
  c A guest in the Jones's car is injured when Mr. Jones collides with another car at an intersection. Mr. Jones is negligent. The guest suffers a loss of $3,000 including $500 in medical expenses.
  d In question (c), assume that the other driver was negligent and that Mr. Jones also suffered a loss of $200 in medical expenses.
  e Mr. Jones is injured while a friend who was driving Mr. Jones's car collides with another automobile. The friend was negligent. Mr. Jones suffers a loss of $8,000, including $3,000 in medical expenses.

22 Many states now have automobile no-fault laws. How do these laws affect automobile insurance contracts?

23 The risk manager of a local garage cannot decide whether to buy a business auto policy or a garage liability policy. What are the major differences in the protection afforded by these two policies?

24 Why do automobile dealers need a special form of automobile physical damage insurance?

25 **a** In what sense is the standard workers' compensation insurance contract two policies in one?

   b Cite an example to illustrate why employers in your state might need the employers' liability protection in this contract.

26 An employer purchases workers' compensation insurance in late October. The following month the weekly benefits under the workers' compensation law are increased, effective June 1. What steps, if any, must the employer take as a result of the amendment to the state statute?

27 Compare the rights of the employee under the workers' compensation and employers' liability sections of the standard contract.

28 A sole proprietor purchases a standard workers' compensation and employers' liability insurance contract with an all states endorsement attached. Which of the following losses is covered?

   a An employee is injured while driving a company car on company business.

   b The sole proprietor is injured while inspecting a machine at her plant.

   c A clerical employee contracts pneumonia because the temperature in the office where he worked was too low.

   d A child below the legal working age is injured on the job. The sole proprietor knew about this violation of the law. In addition to the regular workers' compensation benefits, the employer is also responsible for some penalty payments.

   e An employee hired three months ago is disabled by silicosis. He was exposed to this disease during these three months and also during the 20 years he worked for his former employer.

29 A risk manager has decided that he wishes to self-insure his workers' compensation losses. He is concerned, however, about sizable losses arising out of a single accident or an unusually large number of accidents in any single year. How would you advise him?

30 **a** How does umbrella liability insurance supplement basic liability insurance?

   b Compare and contrast umbrella liability insurance and difference in conditions insurance as supplementary coverages.

31 Boiler and machinery insurance, glass insurance, credit insurance, and title insurance have service features that may make them attractive to some risk managers who are not impressed by the identification they afford. What are these service features?

32 The Carry Transport Company has a motortruck cargo legal liability policy. Theft losses are not covered under this policy. Is the insurer responsible for the following losses to cargo in the company's custody?

   a A truck carrying cargo is completely destroyed in a collision with another truck.

   b Thieves hijack a truck carrying cargo.

   c A flash flood completely destroyes a truck and its cargo.

   d A fire destroys completely four trucks in a terminal.

   e A fire destroys cargo that had been placed in a warehouse one week before, at which time the consignee was asked to pick it up.

33 List the exposures that can be insured under electronic data processing equipment insurance.

34 Describe briefly the major types of insurance included in the special multi-peril policy.

SUGGESTIONS FOR ADDITIONAL READING

Bickelhaupt, D. L.: *General Insurance* (11th ed., Homewood, Ill.: Richard D. Irwin, Inc., 1983) chaps. 23 and 25.

Fire, Casualty, and Surety Bulletins (Cincinnati: The National Underwriter Company, monthly).

Gordis, P., and E. A. Chlanda: *Property and Casualty Insurance* (Indianapolis: The Rough Notes Company, revised annually).

Huebner, S. S., K. Black, and R. Cline: *Property and Liability Insurance* (3d ed., Englewood Cliffs, N.J.: Prentice-Hall, Inc., 1982), chaps 12–16, 19, 24, 25, 27, 28, and 32–35.

Kulp, C. A., and J. W. Hall: *Casualty Insurance* (4th ed., New York: The Ronald Press Company, 1968), chaps. 9, 10, and 15.

Long, J. D., and D. W. Gregg, (eds.): *Property and Liability Insurance Handbook* (Homewood, Ill.: Richard D. Irwin, Inc., 1965), chaps. 17–19, 22–25, 36–38, 42, and 53–57.

MacDonald, Donald L.: *Corporate Risk Control* (New York: The Ronald Press Company, 1966), chaps. 12, 19, and 20.

Malecki, D. S., J. J. Donaldson, and R. C. Horn: *Commercial Liability Risk Management and Insurance, vols. I and II* (Malvern, Pa.: American Institute for Property and Liability Underwriters, 1978).

Riegel, R., J. Miller, and C. A. Williams, Jr.: *Insurance Principles and Practices: Property and Liability* (6th ed., Englewood Cliffs, N.J.: Prentice-Hall, Inc., 1976), chaps. 11–15 and 17–19.

Rodda, W. H.: *Marine Insurance: Ocean and Inland* (3d ed., Englewood Cliffs, N.J.: Prentice-Hall, Inc., 1970).

————, J. S. Trieschmann, E. A. Wiening, and B. A. Hedges: *Commercial Property Risk Management and Insurance,* vols. I and II (2d ed., Malvern, Pa.: American Institute for Property and Liability Underwriters, 1983).

Somers, H. M., and A. R. Somers: *Workmen's Compensation* (New York: John Wiley & Sons, Inc., 1954).

Special Multi-Peril Guide (Indianapolis: The Rough Notes Company, updated periodically).

Winter, W. D., *Marine Insurance* (3d ed., New York: McGraw-Hill Book Company, 1952).

CHAPTER 20

SOCIAL INSURANCE PROGRAMS

LEARNING OBJECTIVES

After you have completed this chapter, you should be able to:

1 Define social insurance and distinguish social insurance from social security and most private insurance.
2 Determine whether a person is eligible for retirement, death, or disability benefits under OASDI and calculate the benefit amounts.
3 Explain the eligibility requirements and benefits provided by the two parts of Medicare.
4 Describe how the four components of OASDHI are funded and comment on their actuarial soundness.
5 Present arguments for and against the use of state funds in workers' compensation programs.
6 Summarize the main features of temporary disability insurance legislation in the five states with such plans.
7 Describe the Rhode Island catastrophic medical expense plan.
8 Explain for a typical state who is eligible for unemployment insurance benefits and the amount and duration of the benefits provided.
9 Comment on the funding of state unemployment insurance benefits.

INTRODUCTION

This chapter is the first of six chapters dealing primarily with insurance programs or contracts that are important in personnel risk management. Chapter 9 described the principal personnel loss exposures of (1) the employees of a business, and (2) the business itself. Chapter 9 also described why a business would be interested in the employees' personnel loss exposures as well as its own. Although developing and administering a program that will help employees handle their loss exposures is often the total or partial responsibility of someone other than the risk manager, for example, the personnel department, this task is part of the total risk management function. The risk manager must (1) identify the potential loss exposures, (2) measure those exposures, (3) select the best tools, (4) implement the tools that are selected, and (5) monitor the results of the selection and the implementation.

These six chapters are concerned with risk finance tools and their uses in personnel risk management. This first chapter deals with social insurance programs, which provide the first layer of protection for most employees. Chapters 21 and 22 describe the major types of private employee benefit plans, which provide the second layer of protection. Individual life and health insurance contracts, which are more often purchased by families than by businesses, are described in Chapters 23 and 24. Families purchase these contracts as a third layer of protection to tailor their total program to meet their own needs and desires. Chapter 25 tells how a business can use these individual contracts (1) to handle its own personnel loss exposures, and (2) to supplement other employee-benefit programs or be the only employee benefit program in a certain area.

Because social insurance programs provide the first layer of protection in most family insurance programs, they are clearly an appropriate starting point for a discussion of employee personnel insurance benefits. A risk manager of a firm, of course, cannot turn to social insurance to handle the risks to the firm itself, but as noted in Chapter 9, the risk manager has reason to be interested in the losses facing the employees and the way they are handled. Five reasons why all managers, including the risk manager, should have a specific interest in social insurance as a risk management tool are the following:

1 In counseling individual employees, the risk manager must understand the important social insurance benefits to which each employee is entitled.

2 The existence of social insurance programs reduces the gap to be filled by employee benefit plans sponsored by private industry and by public and private charities.

3 Tax savings may depend upon the proper integration of a social insucance program with an employee benefit plan.

4 The cost of social insurance programs is almost always borne completely or in part by employers.

5 All private enterprises (and all citizens) should be concerned about the proper sphere of government action and the administration of government programs.

This chapter provides some background material on the nature and objective of social insurance in general and describes the leading specific programs.

WHAT IS SOCIAL INSURANCE?

For the purposes of this text, social insurance includes all insurance required by law for substantial numbers of the general population, administered or closely supervised by the government, and supported primarily by earmarked contributions, with a benefit structure that usually redistributes income to achieve some social objective, not private equity.[1] Several features of this definition are worthy of brief comment.

First, although all current social insurance programs deal with personnel risks, the concept may be extended in the future to property and liability risks. Indeed the national flood insurance and crime insurance programs described in Chapter 34 and some other public property or liability insurance programs already have some of the characteristics of social insurance. No-fault automobile insurance, being a close relative of workers' compensation, is probably the best example. Social insurance programs have emphasized personnel risks because all members of society may incur important economic losses occasioned by death, old age, poor health, or unemployment.

Second, the term is reserved for programs that apply to large segments of the general population and that are compulsory for most eligible persons. Plans established by the government solely for its present or former employees, such as the Civil Service Retirement System, are not considered social insurance. Federal government life insurance programs for veterans are omitted for the same reason and because they are voluntary.

Third, although some government agency is commonly the insurer, the level of direct supervision by the government may be limited to the settlement of contested cases or checking compliance with insurance requirements, most of the daily operations being conducted by private insurers.

Fourth, although the definition does not rule out some financial support from general government funds, most of the financing comes from contributions made specifically for this purpose. Although others may sometimes make these contributions, usually they are paid by employees or their employers.

Fifth, like all insurance, social insurance pools the risks associated with covered perils, such as death, poor health, and unemployment. In addition social insurance benefit structures usually stress "social adequacy" rather than "private equity." Instead of relating the benefits for any individual directly to the contributions made by that person or by others in his or her behalf, the system usually favors some groups whom it is considered socially desirable to help. For example, the program may favor persons with low prior wages or a large number of dependents. As will be demonstrated later, however, the United States has been reluctant to ignore completely private equity considerations.

Social insurance, therefore, need not be underwritten by a public insurer. Furthermore, not all public insurance is social insurance. With one possible exception (Supplementary Medical Insurance, because it is not compulsory) the discussion in this chapter is limited to social insurance programs.

Social Security, Social Insurance, and Public Assistance

Social insurance is part of a social security system. A *social security* system includes all government measures designed to protect its citizens against (1) perils such as

---

[1] This definition was developed by the Committee on Social Insurance Terminology of the American Risk and Insurance Association.

death, poor health, unemployment, and superannuation and (2) poverty and substandard wages, hours, or conditions of employment. A social security system includes loss-control measures (e.g., safety regulations, "full" employment measures, and public health activities) and transfers, of which social insurance is the principal example. The other major transfers included in the system are *public assistance* and *income supplements.*

The major distinction between social insurance and public assistance is that public assistance benefits are paid, in principle, only to those persons who can demonstrate their individual need, and then only to the extent of that need. Public assistance programs are usually financed out of general revenues. Social insurance benefits, on the other hand, do not require the demonstration of individual need and are usually related in some way, however crude, to contributions made by the beneficiary or made in his or her behalf. The two most important public assistance programs are (1) Aid to Families with Dependent Children, a federal-state program that provides cash benefits to certain needy families with children, and (2) Medicaid, which provides important medical services to certain needy persons in the following categories—the aged, the blind, the disabled, and families with dependent children.

Income supplements are closely related to public assistance. Payments are based on need, but need is determined not through a demonstration of individual needs but by the difference between some guaranteed minimum income and the family's actual income. For example, under the Federal Supplemental Security Income program, aged, blind, and disabled persons are guaranteed a specified monthly income. The SSI payment is the difference between this amount and other income excluding (1) the first $20 of OASDHI or other income, and (2) the first $65 of earned monthly income plus one-half of any excess. In 1984 the guaranteed income is about $314 for an individual maintaining his or her own household, and $472 for a couple. SSI differs from a pure income supplement plan in that the recipients must also not have other resources such as savings accounts in excess of a specified amount.

IS SOCIAL INSURANCE "INSURANCE"?

One question that has generated considerable heat for many years is whether social insurance is "insurance." Many observers believe that the answer is clearly "no" with respect to many social insurance programs. They point to the emphasis upon social adequacy, the absence of a legal contract, and the method of financing, which often defers many of the costs to future generations. They believe that the benefits are better described as transfer payments from one sector of the population to another. They believe that public acceptance of social insurance programs is often influenced by the "halo effect" of the insurance label and that unfair comparisons are often drawn between the relative performance and efficiency of social insurance and of private insurance.

The answer to the question depends upon how one defines insurance. If an insurance program must possess all the characteristics typical of private insurance, social insurance is clearly not insurance, as will be demonstrated below. On the other hand, social insurance is a device for pooling and sharing the risks of death, old age, unemployment, and poor health. Consequently it possesses the only necessary conditions for insurance specified in the definition given in Chapter 12.

Most private insurance, however, differs from social insurance in several important respects.

1 Each individual decides how much, if any, private insurance he or she wants to purchase. Employees, it is true, may have no choice under employee benefits plans, but the decision is made voluntarily by someone other than the insurer, e.g., their employer or union.

2 Benefits and premium rates are prescribed by a contract that cannot be changed except by mutual consent.

3 The benefits are related on an actuarial basis to the contributions paid; i.e., private equity is an important goal of private insurance pricing.

4 Numerous insurers compete with one another for business.

Social insurance programs are compulsory for most people; benefits and contribution rates are prescribed by law but are subject to change; social adequacy is usually stressed; and although numerous private insurers may be involved, the program is often administered by a single government insurer.

Certain characteristics of social insurance enable it to encompass some risks, such as unemployment, that private insurers have been reluctant to write. The compulsory feature avoids adverse selection; the flexibility in benefits and contribution rates plus the compulsory feature enables the program to be adapted to changing conditions.

REASONS FOR SOCIAL INSURANCE

The first social insurance program in the United States, workers' compensation, is about 75 years old, but it was not until the Social Security Act of 1935 that the United States adopted an extensive social insurance system. The reasons for the various social insurance programs are not the same, but certain basic changes in our economy explain the increasing interest in the general concept of social security.

In a predominantly agricultural community, families had relatively few needs, were largely self-sufficient, and were bound together by common interests. It was not too much of a burden for the family to maintain disabled, aged, widowed, orphaned, or unemployed family members. Because their needs were modest, they could perform some of the family household tasks, and there was usually ample space.

With increasing industrialization and urbanization, the picture changed. First, continued employment depended upon the ability of the employer to provide a job, and this ability, in turn, depended upon the functioning of a complex interdependent economy. Second, it created new occupational accidents and injuries, particularly around the turn of the century. Third, families became less self-sufficient. More and more household products and services were purchased from outsiders. An extra hand became less useful unless he or she added cash to the family budget. What is more important, the loss of the breadwinner's check became a financial catastrophe. Fourth, families became more widely separated geographically, and this separation, together with a divergence in interests among generations, tended to weaken family ties. Fifth, assisting an unfortunate family member became more burdensome because of smaller living quarters, increased obligations to children, and a desire to maintain or improve the standard of living of the immediate family.

Since it was no longer so easy to turn to relatives in time of need, more families (in the narrow sense) had to handle their risks themselves or turn to outsiders for assistance. Few families could accumulate enough assets in advance to meet the losses caused by death, poor health, unemployment, or superannuation. Private charities, churches, labor unions, fraternal organizations, and the like provided valuable but limited assistance. Private life insurance had been developing steadily since the Civil War, but by the time of the Great Depression of the 1930s, most of the population had very limited coverage at best. The insurance protection against poor health and old age was even less effective; unemployment insurance was limited to some trade-union plans and a few employer plans. Some persons could not afford private insurance protection; others were ineligible because of poor health; and still others did not appreciate their need for insurance. Government assistance during the nineteenth century and the early twentieth century took the form of poorhouses or "outdoor" relief for needy persons. The relief was either an outright grant in cash or services or was given in exchange for some services such as work on a public project. This meager assistance was usually provided by state or local governments.

By the close of the nineteenth century, the inability of individual families to provide a minimum "floor of protection" for themselves and the dissatisfaction with the stigma associated with accepting relief caused Germany to adopt a fairly complete social insurance system. Great Britain acted during the first two decades of the present century. Other countries followed the lead of these two nations. The United States, however, did not adopt a comprehensive program until 1935.

The United States was slower to act for several reasons. First, our population enjoyed a more favorable economic status. Second, our nation stressed the freedom and responsibility of the individual for his or her own future. Third, the life insurance industry, although limited by today's standards, was more fully developed. Fourth, it was not clear whether the states or the national government should take the lead in developing social insurance. Fifth, states varied in their need for, and attitude toward, social insurance programs. Sixth, states feared that some businesses would leave or not enter their state if their taxes were higher than those of other states. The Great Depression, however, shook our confidence in individual responsibility, made us more aware of the risks facing our population, and caused more people to turn to the federal government for assistance. Further industrialization and improved education also increased our social conscience. The Social Security Act of 1935 was a response to this important change in our attitudes, but, as will become apparent in the discussion of our social insurance system, the circumstances that retarded the development of any social insurance system influenced the nature of the programs adopted. Since 1935, the factors favoring an extensive social insurance system have become more important. Until recently, as the economy prospered, we revised our standards for social insurance upward because our concept of a minimum floor of protection changed, and our ability to bear the taxes involved improved. During the past few years, as concern about the costs and financial solvency of the system increased, benefits in some component programs have been reduced. Social insurance, however, still provides an extremely important part of the average family's total insurance protection.

Although the preceding paragraphs offer a sufficient explanation for the passage of the Social Security Act, other reasons must be cited for the adoption of other social insurance programs. Workers' compensation, for example, arose out of dissatisfaction with the employers' liability method of handling industrial injuries and diseases. The defects in the employers' liability system and the historical beginnings of workers' compensation have been outlined in Chapter 8 and need not be repeated here. The Medicare program, established in 1965, reflected dissatisfaction in many quarters with the efforts of private health insurers to provide medical expense coverage for the aged.

SOCIAL INSURANCE SYSTEM OF THE UNITED STATES

A summary view of the social insurance system of the United States will help the reader to view each individual program in its proper perspective. The major social insurance programs providing protection for large segments of the general public against each of the four personnel perils included under these programs are as follows:[2]

A Death
   1 Old-Age, Survivors, and Disability Insurance
   2 Federal and state workers' compensation legislation (occupational death only)
B Old age
   1 Old-Age, Survivors, and Disability Insurance
C Poor health
   1 Disability income benefits
      a Old-Age, Survivors, and Disability Insurance
      b Federal and state workers' compensation legislation (occupational illness only)
      c Temporary nonoccupational disability insurance legislation in Rhode Island, California, New Jersey, New York, and Hawaii
   2 Medical expense benefits
      a Medicare—Hospital Insurance and Supplementary Medical Insurance
      b Federal and state workers' compensation legislation (occupational illness only)
      c Medical expense insurance plans in Maine and Rhode Island
D Unemployment
   1 State unemployment insurance

The widespread effects of these programs, their relative importance, and their growth are indicated by the estimates in Table 20.1 of the cash benefit and medical expense payments under these programs in 1950, 1960, 1970, 1980, and 1982.

---

[2] The major omissions are the Railroad Retirement System, Railroad Temporary Disability Insurance, and Railroad Unemployment Insurance, which apply only to workers in one industry, and veterans' programs.

TABLE 20.1
CASH BENEFIT PAYMENTS AND MEDICAL EXPENSE PAYMENTS UNDER SELECTED
SOCIAL INSURANCE PROGRAMS (IN MILLIONS)

Type of benefit and program	1950	1960	1970	1980	1982
Cash benefits:					
OASDI	$ 961	$11,245	$31,863	$120,512	$155,834
State unemployment insurance	1,408	2,867	4,184	18,756	21,514
Federal and state workers' compensation	415	860	1,981	9,480	11,680
State temporary disability insurance	89	311	665	1,400	1,636
Medical expense payments:					
Hospital Insurance			5,124	23,073	35,632
Supplementary Medical Insurance			1,975	10,635	15,454
Federal and state workers' compensation	200	435	1,050	4,020	5,020

Source: Social Security Bulletins, monthly.

OLD-AGE, SURVIVORS, AND DISABILITY INSURANCE

Old-Age, Survivors, and Disability Insurance (OASDI), which technically consists of two programs—Old-Age and Survivors Insurance and Disability Insurance—is one of the three components of Old-Age, Survivors, Disability, and Health Insurance (OASDHI). The other two parts are Hospital Insurance and Supplementary Medical Insurance—popularly known as Medicare. OASDHI was established under the Social Security Act of 1935 and its amendments. This act, which was a landmark in social legislation, also introduced a federal-state program of unemployment compensation; federal-state programs of public assistance to the needy aged, blind, disabled, and dependent children; and federal-state programs creating and extending public health services, health and welfare services for children, and vocational rehabilitation services. Although these other programs are extremely important, OASDHI is much larger in scope and is often misleadingly termed "Social Security."

The OASDI sections of the Social Security Act have been amended frequently. Originally the system was designed primarily to provide retirement benefits, but OASDI today also provides death benefits (added in 1939) and disability benefits (added in 1954). Although the many details involved make a complete explanation of the system impossible, the major charactecistics of OASDI can be outlined. Because future changes in the legislation are likely, a more detailed discussion is impractical.[3] The description that follows is based upon provisions in effect in early 1984.

Eligibility Requirements

In order to receive benefits, a worker must have qualified by working in covered employment for a specified period of time. Over nine out of ten types of employment

---

[3] Following each change in the legislation, the Social Security Administration published a booklet entitled *Your Social Security,* which describes the major features of OASDI. The changes are also summarized in an issue of the *Social Security Bulletin.*

are covered on a compulsory basis. Student workers in institutions of learning, hospitals, college clubs, fraternities, or sororities are excluded. Railroad workers are protected by a separate federally operated Railroad Retirement System, but under some circumstances they may receive OASDI benefits in addition to or in lieu of the railroad retirement benefits. Ministers and members of religious orders and employees of state and local governments may be covered under the system under certain conditions. Self-employed persons, domestic workers, and farm laborers are covered on a compulsory basis if they earn at least some small specified amount.

To receive OASDI benefits, the worker must usually be "fully insured." To receive some death benefits, however, it is sufficient to be "currently insured." In order to explain the requirements of fully or currently insured status, we must define first "a quarter of coverage." In 1984 a worker received credit for one quarter of coverage for each $390 of annual earnings in covered employment. Each year the amount one must earn to receive credit for one quarter is increased to reflect changes in average national earnings. (Prior to 1978, a worker received credit for a quarter of coverage if he or she earned at least $50 in a calendar quarter. In 1978 a worker received credit for one quarter of coverage for each $250 of annual earnings. Since 1979 the $250 has been increased each year by the percentage increase in average national earnings.)

To be fully insured, a worker must have quarters of coverage equal to at least the number of years elapsing since 1950 or, if later, since the end of the year in which the worker was 21. However, the worker never needs more than 40 quarters of coverage and must have at least 6 quarters. For example, a worker aged 38 on January 7, 1985 will be fully insured in 1985 if he or she has at least 16 quarters of coverage.[4] To be currently insured, a worker must have at least 6 quarters of coverage among the last 13 quarters, including the current quarter.

To receive disability benefits a worker must, in addition to being fully insured, have at least 20 quarters of coverage in the 40 calendar quarters prior to his or her disability. Blind persons and workers disabled before age 31 can qualify with less than 20 quarters of coverage.

Benefits

Benefits are paid if the worker (1) retires, (2) dies, or (3) is totally disabled for a long period.

Retirement   The basic benefit is a monthly retirement income for life to a worker aged 65 or over. The worker may elect to retire as early as age 62, but the benefit is reduced. The retirement income is equal to the worker's primary insurance amount (PIA), which usually depends upon the worker's average indexed monthly earnings (AIME) during the period beginning with 1956 or the year in which he or she became 27, if later, and ending with the year before he or she becomes (or would have become) age 62, dies, or becomes disabled, whichever happens first. The earnings counted in computing this average are unlikely to be the worker's actual earnings over this period

---

[4] These quarters may have been earned prior to the year in which the worker became 22 or, if later, 1951.

for several reasons. First, the earnings each year are limited to the amount subject to an OASDI tax over the period. From 1951 to 1954, the maximum amount taxed was only $3,600; from 1955 to 1958, the maximum was $4,200; from 1959 to 1965, it was $4,800; from 1966 to 1967, $6,600; and from 1968 to 1971, $7,800. Since 1971, the maximum has increased each year—in 1972 it was $9,000; in 1973, $10,800; in 1974, $13,200; in 1975, $14,100; in 1976, $15,300; in 1977, $16,500; in 1978, $17,700; in 1979, $22,900; in 1980, $25,900; in 1981, $29,700; in 1982, $32,400; and in 1983, $35,700. In 1984 the wage base is $37,800. Each year the wage base is adjusted upward as average national earnings increase. Second, the earnings each year (limited to the wage base) are indexed or adjusted to reflect changes in average national earnings from that year to the second last year of the base period. To illustrate, if average national earnings had increased 50 percent over that time span, the worker's earnings that year will be increased 50 percent. The earnings during the last year of the base period are not adjusted. Third, the worker can substitute years before or after the base period for years within the period if he or she would benefit from the change.[5]

For workers who were age 62 prior to 1979 a method that is being phased out will be used to calculate the primary insurance amount. For workers aged 62 in 1984 or later a decoupled formula method will be used. For workers who reached age 62 during 1979–1983 inclusive, a transitional guarantee method is used that gives the worker the higher of two benefits—one determined using the decoupled formula method and the other using a modification of the old formula. Only the decoupled formula method will be discussed here.

Under this method the PIA formula used to calculate retirement benefits depends upon the year in which the worker was age 62. For example, for workers who reach age 62 in 1984 the PIA formula used if they retire at age 65 in 1987 will be as follows:

90 percent of the first $265 of the AIME plus
32 percent of the next $1,345 plus
15 percent of the excess

multiplied by a factor that represents the cumulative increases in the Consumer Price Index (CPI) from 1983 to 1986. For example, if this factor is 1.15 and the AIME is $1,000, the PIA will be $546. If the AIME is $2,000, the PIA will be $838. In December 1987 the benefit will be increased automatically to match the increase in the CPI from the third quarter of 1986 to the third quarter of 1987. Each December thereafter these workers will receive similar automatic adjustments for changes in the CPI.

The PIA increases, but not proportionately, with the AIME. The relationship favors persons with lower AIMEs. The benefit formula represents a compromise between the desire to provide socially adequate benefits for all workers and the wish to preserve some elements of private equity.

---

[5] This option will help workers who were not in covered employment during part of this period, whose earnings during part of the period were very low, or who earned the maximum amount each year but whose average monthly wage is reduced because of the small maximum amounts taxed in the early years. Earnings in the year in which the worker reaches age 62 or later years can be substituted for lower indexed earnings in earlier years and thus raise the average.

For workers retiring at age 65 with more than 10 "years of coverage" the program provides a special minimum PIA. For workers retiring in 1984 this special minimum PIA is $17.85 times the number of years of coverage in excess of 10 years but not more than 20 ($17.85) = $357. In December, 1984 the $17.85 will be increased, as it will be each December to reflect the increase in the Consumer Price Index noted above.

Each year the PIA formula changes. The 90, 32, and 15 percent factors remain the same, but the dollar amounts are adjusted to match increases in average national earnings. The CPI multiplication factor also is updated.

For workers who retire at age 62 in 1984 the PIA formula is the same as the one presented above except that no adjustment is made for CPI changes from 1983 to 1986. For workers retiring at age 62, dying, or becoming disabled in a given year, the PIA formula is the one designated for that year. For workers retiring at age 63 or later, the PIA formula is the one designated for the year in which they reached age 62 plus the CPI adjustments during intervening years.

Workers retiring at age 62, however, receive a pension that is less than the PIA formula amount. For each month the worker retires prior to age 65, the PIA is reduced ⅝ of 1 percent. Thus if he or she retires at age 62, the earliest age, the reduction is 20 percent. If the worker retires after age 65, the PIA is increased by ¼ of 1 percent for each month (3 percent a year) the retirement is delayed.

Under certain conditions, the spouse and children of retired workers are eligible for dependents' benefits. These benefits, which are expressed as a percentage of the PIA, are summarized in Table 20.2. The total monthly benefits paid to one family are limited to a specified maximum that is a function of the PIA.

The family of a retired worker, aged 65 or over, will lose in benefits one-half the amount that the worker earns after retirement in excess of a specified amount—$6,960 in 1984 and adjusted annually each year as average national earnings increase. However, no reduction in benefits is made if the worker is aged 70 or over. If other members of the family earn more than the threshold earnings amount, only their own benefits are reduced. However, for beneficiaries under age 65 the limit is less—$5,160 in 1984 and adjusted annually.

TABLE 20.2
OASDI DEPENDENTS' RETIREMENT BENEFITS

Type of benefit	Amount expressed as a percentage of the worker's primary insurance amount*
Monthly life income for spouse aged 62 or over	50, reduced by $25/36$ of 1% for each month benefit starts before 65th birthday
Monthly income for dependent children to age 18	50 for each child
Monthly income for spouse until youngest dependent child is aged 16	50

* If a worker's primary insurance amount is reduced because he or she retired before age 65, these percentages are applied to the unreduced amount.

Until 1984 OASDI benefits were not subject to federal income taxes. Now half of the OASDI benefit is taxable unless it is more than half of the amount by which the adjusted gross income (including for this purpose interest on tax-free municipal bonds) plus one half the OASDI benefit exceeds a specified base amount. For individuals this base amount is $25,000; for married couples filing joint returns the base amount is $32,000. If half the OASDI benefit is more than half of the excess amount, only half of this excess amount is taxable.

Death   The survivorship benefits that are payable in case the insured worker dies are presented in Table 20.3. The worker's PIA is computed using the formula that would be used if on the date the worker died he or she had instead applied for retirement benefits beginning at age 62 (without any percentage reduction for early retirement).

The family maximum discussed in connection with the retirement benefits also applies here, as does the earnings test. Two points that deserve special emphasis are (1) the magnitude of the survivorship benefits for a young person with a large family and (2) the gap that exists in the protection between the times when the youngest child attains age 18 and the surviving spouse reaches age 60.

Disability   The major disability benefits are a disability "freeze" and disability income payments. To receive these two benefits, the worker must be unable to engage in any substantially gainful activity, the disability must have lasted at least 5 months, and the condition must be expected to result in death or to continue for at least 12 calendar months.

The first benefit freezes the workers' earnings record as of the date of disability. In other words, the worker's insured status for retirement and survivor's benefits and the

TABLE 20.3
OASDI SURVIVORSHIP BENEFITS

Type of benefit	Amount expressed as a percentage of the worker's primary insurance amount*
Monthly life income for surviving spouse aged 60 or over	100, reduced by $19/40$ of 1% for each month benefit starts prior to spouse's 65th birthday
Monthly income for dependent children to age 18	75 for each child
Monthly income for surviving spouse until youngest dependent child is aged 16	75
Monthly life income for dependent parent aged 62 or over	75 for each parent; 82.5 if only one parent
Lump-sum payment to surviving spouse or to person who paid burial expenses	$255

   * Computed as if the insured were applying for retirement benefits at age 62 as of the date of death.

average monthly wage are determined by ignoring the time during which the worker was disabled.

The second benefit provides an income for the disabled worker, dependent children, and the worker's spouse (until the youngest dependent child is aged 16) beginning after the worker has completed 5 months of disability. The benefit amounts are usually determined in the same way as the retirement benefit amounts except that the maximum family benefit may be less and no adjustment is made for early retirement. The worker receives the PIA. The benefit for each child is 50 percent of this amount and the spouse's benefit another 50 percent. At age 65, the disability payments cease and the retirement payments begin.

Some Examples   Retirement, death, and disability benefits for some selected 1984 family situations are presented in Table 20.4. The examples serve as a review of the preceding discussion. No benefits are shown for workers retiring at age 65 because these workers, who reached age 62 in 1981, will have their PIA determined under the transitional guarantee method. Chapter 33 describes in more detail the OASDI benefits payable in one two-wage-earner family situation.

Future Changes Already Enacted   The Social Security amendments of 1983 introduced several benefit changes that will not become effective until 1985 or later. Some of the more important future changes are as follows:

TABLE 20.4
ILLUSTRATIVE 1984 MONTHLY CASH BENEFITS UNDER OLD-AGE, SURVIVORS, AND DISABILITY INSURANCE*

Family situation	Average indexed monthly earnings				
	$400	$800	$1,200	$1,600	$2,000
Primary insurance amount (1984 formula)	$283	$411	$539	$667	$729
Retirement:					
Worker, aged 62	226	329	431	534	583
Worker and spouse, both aged 62	332	483	633	784	856
Survivorship:					
Widow or widower, aged 65	283	411	539	667	729
Widow or widower, aged 60, no child	202	294	385	477	521
Widow or widower, under 60 and 1 child	424	616	808	1,000	1,094
Widow or widower, under 60 and 2 children	424	701	986	1,167	1,275
Disability:					
Worker	283	411	539	667	729
Worker and spouse with child	340	616	808	1,000	1,094
Maximum family benefit**	424	701	986	1,167	1,275

  * Rounded to nearest dollar.
  ** The maximum family benefit for the 1984 PIA formula is 150 percent of the first $342 of the PIA, 272 percent of the next $151, 134 percent of the next $150, and 175 percent of the PIA in excess of $643. A special maximum family benefit applies to disability benefits—the lesser of (1) 85 percent of the average indexed monthly earnings or, if greater, the PIA or (2) 150 percent of the primary insurance amount.

1 For persons reaching age 62 during 2000–2005 the retirement age at which full benefits will be paid will be increased by two months a year until it reaches age 66, at which age it will remain for persons reaching age 62 during 2006–2016. For those persons reaching age 62 during 2017–2022 the retirement age will again be increased two months a year until it reaches age 67, at which age it will remain for future retirees.

2 Early retirement will still be permitted as early as age 62 but when the normal retirement age rises above age 65 the percentage reduction for retirement that early will be larger.

3 Starting in 1990 the delayed retirement benefit will gradually increase until 2008 when the current 3 percent increase a year will become 8 percent.

4 Starting with the December 1984 benefit increase, if at the beginning of the year the balance in the OASDI Trust Funds is less than 15 percent (becoming 20 percent in 1989) of the expected disbursements that year, the annual automatic benefit adjustment will be the lower of (1) the increase in the Consumer Price Index or (2) the increase in average national earnings.

5 Beginning in 1990, the earnings test for beneficiaries aged 65 through 69 will be revised so that OASDI benefits will be decreased by $1 for each $3 earned above the specified dollar limits instead of each $2.

Taxes

Employees and their employers contribute equally to the cost of OASDI. A self-employed person pays about 40 percent more than an employee. The present scheduled tax rates for 1984 and later are shown in the table at the top of page 397.

The 1984 tax rate is applied to the first $37,800 of a worker's earnings. This taxable earnings base will increase in 1985 and in later years in the manner described earlier. These rates do not include the charges for Hospital Insurance that are presented in the next section.

During 1984 employees can offset 0.3 percentage points of their OASDI tax by a tax credit against their income tax. Self-employed persons also receive special tax credits or tax deductions on a continuing basis. These tax credits provide some indirect general revenue funding of OASDI.

Funding

Congress has expressed its intent to maintain OASDI on a self-supporting basis. The tax schedule is designed to achieve this result for at least the next 75 years, if many underlying assumptions regarding mortality, interest rates, total employment, and the like are satisfied.

The taxes deemed necessary to meet the administrative expenses and the costs of the retirement benefits, the death benefits, and some disability benefits such as the "freeze" are placed in the Old-Age and Survivors Insurance Trust Fund. The remainder are placed in the Disability Insurance Trust Fund. Most of the assets remaining after current expenditures are invested in interest-bearing government securities.

Calendar year	Employer, %	Employee, %	Self-employed, %
1984–1987	5.70	5.70	11.40
1988–1989	6.06	6.06	12.12
1990 on	6.20	6.20	14.40

The program is not "fully funded," a term described under "Actuarial Cost Method" in Chapter 22. If OASDI were to cease operations today, the money in the trust funds would not be enough to support continued benefits to those already receiving them and to return a "fair" amount to other contributors. In fact, if the program were to be terminated today, payments to persons already receiving benefits could not be continued for even one year. The present intent is to maintain the program on a pay-as-you-go basis with a small trust fund. So long as the system operates indefinitely, a "full reserve" is not required for the plan to meet its obligations on a self-supporting basis. In fact, it can be argued that a full reserve would be unwise for various reasons, one of which would be the excuse it would offer for unwarranted liberalization of benefits.

Issues   Only a sample of the many issues surrounding OASDI can be discussed here. These issues will be categorized according to whether they affect coverage, benefits, or financing.

Because most employments are now covered under OASDI, much less pressure exists than in the past for the inclusion of new occupations. The Social Security Act amendments of 1983 added newly hired federal civilian employees and the employees of nonprofit organizations. The only major group still not included on a compulsory basis is state and local government employees.

Several features of the benefit structure are highly controversial. First, the balance between social adequacy and private equity implicit in the present benefit structure is not acceptable to many. One proposal, not seriously considered at this time, is that all beneficiaries receive the same benefit, regardless of their past earnings records. At the other extreme, a few critics argue that benefits should be related proportionately to average monthly earnings. Between these two extremes there are numerous possible positions. The desired relationship between benefits and contributions depends, among other things, on one's preferred balance between public and private responsibility for protection above the minimum benefit level, one's concept of a fair redistribution of income, and one's degree of concern about possible adverse effects upon the private insurance business.

The 1979 Advisory Council recommended that the present primary insurance amount formula be replaced by a two-bracket formula:[6] 61 percent of the first $442 of average indexed monthly earnings, the $442 being adjusted annually to reflect

[6] Report of the 1979 Advisory Council on Social Security, Washington, D.C., December, 1979, pp. 7–8.

increases in average national earnings since 1979, plus 27 percent of any additional average indexed monthly earnings. Such a formula would produce a retirement benefit that would keep out of poverty a person who earns the federal minimum wage working full time for at least thirty years. Current and future workers should also be able to expect that the additional benefits generated by increased earnings would provide a reasonable return on the additional taxes these workers would contribute because of these higher earnings.

Second, the earnings test that causes beneficiaries earning more than a certain amount a year to lose benefits or to receive reduced benefits has been attacked on the ground that it forces some able aged persons out of the labor force or prevents them from obtaining benefits to which they are allegedly entitled because they have paid for them through contributions to the program. The test is also considered unfair because it considers only wages and salaries, not interest and dividends. Removing the test, however, would increase the cost of the program to meet what many consider to be a relatively unimportant need.

Third, although most of the differences in treatment of men and women have been removed, several additional changes have been proposed. For example, homemakers (usually women), it is often argued, should be permitted to pay OASDI taxes on the imputed value of their services. Another suggestion would give the homemaker credit for one-half the spouse's earnings, the other one-half being credited to the spouse. Each member of a two-wage-earner couple would receive credits based on one-half their combined earnings.

One important financing issue is whether contributions should be increased by raising the earnings base or the contribution rate. In deciding among these two alternatives a major consideration is the relative impact upon high- and low-paid workers. It is also argued that a high earnings base would permit the program to capture more contributions in periods of economic prosperity and to reduce contributions in periods of economic decline. The most controversial proposal is the use of general revenues to pay part of the cost of the system. Because of the windfall benefits provided many aged persons during the early years of the program and the emphasis upon socially adequate benefits for workers with low earnings or many dependents, the contributions paid by many young workers and their employers have reached the level at which they could be used to obtain superior benefits from private insurers, assuming no further liberalizations in the benefits. To correct this situation and to make possible some benefit increases and other liberalizations, it has been suggested that some specific fraction of the cost of the benefits be financed out of general revenues. The fundamental principle of contribution-related benefits would be retained and benefit liberalizations would require increased contributions. In opposition it has been argued that employer contributions are not made in behalf of their own employees but as their share of the cost of the entire program, that it is unfair to shift the burden of OASDI benefits to general revenues, that benefits will be unduly liberalized when the new funds are made available, and that the role of general revenues will be expanded beyond the proposed one-third. As indicated earlier, the 1983 amendments introduced some indirect general revenue financing.

Changing demographic and economic trends resulted in what was termed the Social Security financing crisis during the early seventies. The system faced a serious cash flow during the remainder of the decade and a predicted deficit on the average over the next 75 years. The Social Security amendments of 1983 raised taxes and lowered some benefits to deal with this problem.

HOSPITAL INSURANCE

Hospital Insurance is one of the two components of Medicare-Hospital Insurance, also known as Medicare Part A and Supplementary Medical Insurance, also known as Medicare Part B. Medicare was established under a 1965 amendment to the Social Security Act.

All employments covered under OASDI plus railroad employment are covered under the Hospital Insurance (HI) program. Benefits are paid to aged and disabled persons meeting certain requirements. OASDI and Railroad Retirement System beneficiaries, aged 65 or over, are eligible for HI benefits. Also eligible are those aged persons who would be receiving OASDI benefits except for the fact that their current earnings cause them to lose their benefits. As a transitional feature, benefits are also paid to most other persons aged 65 or over before 1968. Persons aged 65 after 1967 but before 1973 (1971 for women) must have some quarters of coverage but they need not be fully or currently insured. Aged persons who do not otherwise qualify can enroll voluntarily by paying the full cost of their coverage.

Disabled OASDI and Railroad Retirement System beneficiaries become eligible for these benefits after they have been entitled to disability benefits for at least 24 months. The OASDI beneficiaries include disabled workers, disabled widows or widowers, and disabled child beneficiaries. Fully or currently insured persons and their dependents with chronic kidney disease who need dialysis or transplants are also covered.

The program provides (1) hospital benefits, (2) skilled-nursing facility benefits, and (3) home health-services benefits. The hospital benefits include such items as room and board in a semiprivate room, general nursing service, operating room, laboratory tests and x-rays, drugs, dressings, and the services of interns and residents in training. The maximum duration is 90 days in a single "spell of illness," which begins on the first day that the person receives hospital or skilled-nursing facility services and ends when a person has not been in any hospital or skilled-nursing facility for 60 consecutive days. Each person also has a "lifetime reserve" of 60 additional benefit days, which can be used to supplement the 90 days provided for each spell of illness. Each time this reserve is used, the number of days remaining is reduced. The patient pays the first $356 of the costs associated with each spell of illness, and after the person has received 60 days of care in a hospital, he or she pays $89 a day for the next 30 days. A deductible of $178 per day applies to expenses incurred during each "reserve" day. The program provides for annual adjustment of these deductibles to reflect changes in hospital costs. For example, when HI started in 1966, the initial deductible applicable to each spell of illness was $40.

Similar services are covered in a skilled-nursing facility after the person has been in the hospital for at least three days and, although not well, no longer needs intensive hospital care. The maximum duration is 100 days in a spell of illness. A deductible of $44.50 a day (subject to future annual adjustments) applies after the first 20 days.

Home health services following hospitalization include such items as part-time visiting-nursing care and use of medical appliances but not full-time nursing care or drugs. No limit is placed on the number of home health visits.

The transitional benefits for aged persons not covered under OASDI are financed through general revenues, but most HI benefits are financed through a contribution rate levied on the OASDI maximum earnings base. The scheduled contribution rates are as follows:

Year	Employee, %	Employer, %	Self-employed, %
1984	1.30	1.30	2.60
1985	1.35	1.35	2.70
1986 on	1.45	1.45	2.90

These contributions are appropriated to a Hospital Insurance Trust Fund from which benefits and expenses are paid.

An unusual feature of this program is the involvement of private insurers in the administration of the program. Each hospital or other provider of services can deal directly with the federal government, but most have elected to receive their payments through a fiscal intermediary approved by the federal government—usually a Blue Cross association. These fiscal intermediaries are reimbursed for their reasonable costs of administration. The experience of these agencies in dealing with overutilization of services and excessive charges was partially responsible for involving them in the program. Hospitals and other agencies are themselves required to meet certain standards and to take steps to discourage overutilization of their services. Professional standards review organizations (PSRO), composed of practicing physicians in the local area, are responsible for a comprehensive, on-going review of the services provided under both parts of Medicare.

Until the Social Security amendments of 1983, hospitals and other providers of services were reimbursed on the basis of the "reasonable cost" of providing those services, not their charges, unless these charges were less. The 1983 benefits introduced a prospective payments plan that will over a three-year period phase in standard payment amounts for 467 categories of hospital treatment. Under this approach hospitals will have a strong incentive to provide these services for less than the standard payment amounts.

SUPPLEMENTARY MEDICAL INSURANCE

Unlike the other OASDHI programs, Supplementary Medical Insurance (SMI) is voluntary. Subject to certain exceptions, all aged persons are eligible to participate. However, in order to avoid adverse selection against the program, persons wishing to participate must elect coverage during specified enrollment periods. Also eligible are the OASDI and Railroad Retirement System disability beneficiaries and persons needing kidney transplantation or dialysis who qualify for hospital insurance.

The benefits include doctors' services, certain medical services and supplies, such as artificial limbs and ambulance services, and the home health services covered under HI, but the patient need not be hospitalized first to receive these services. Except for a special limit on the treatment of mental disorders, no limit is placed on the protection afforded. However, there is a deductible equal to the first $75 of expenses incurred in a calendar year plus 20 percent of the excess.

Participants pay a $14.60 monthly premium, which is more than matched by the federal government out of general revenues. These moneys are appropriated to a Supplementary Medical Insurance Trust Fund. Because these premiums are based upon short-range costs estimates, they are subject to annual changes. When the program started in July, 1966, the monthly premium was $3.

Like HI, SMI involves private agencies in its administration, commonly a commercial insurer. However, unlike HI, SMI provides two methods for paying doctors' bills. The doctor, like the hospitals under HI, may submit the claim directly to the fiscal agency, in which case he or she must accept the SMI payment as the total fee. The SMI payment is limited to the customary charge made by the physician for the services rendered and to the charges made by most physicians in the locality for such services. If the doctor refuses to submit his or her bill to the administering agency or the patient prefers this approach, the patient can submit an itemized bill, paid or unpaid, for reimbursement. If the doctor's charges exceed the SMI payment, the patient is responsible for the excess.

NATIONAL HEALTH INSURANCE PROPOSALS

Pressures have developed to cover persons other than the aged and disabled under these public medical expense programs, to add new types of benefits, and to tighten controls over the rapidly rising cost of services provided under the programs. Proposals have also been made to increase the number of days of hospital coverage, to eliminate or reduce the deductible amounts, to add prescription drug coverage, and to finance both HI and SMI completely with appropriations from general revenues. Many who oppose the financing of OASDI by general revenues support general revenue financing of Medicare because the benefit amounts are not a function of past earnings. On the other hand, proposals have also been made to apply a daily deductible to the first 60 days of HI hospital coverage and to increase and index the $75 SMI deductible. One proposal would apply the HI deductible per day to the first 60 days in exchange for unlimited hospital days thereafter with no deductible per day.

Until a few years ago most persons appeared to favor a national medical expense insurance program that would cover all citizens. However, opinions varied widely on what type of program was needed. For example, one program would use tax credits to finance the purchase of approved private policies. A second, called "catastrophic" medical expense insurance, would cover only those expenses that exceeded a certain threshold. A third would provide all citizens, through a government insurer, comprehensive medical expense insurance with no deductibles or maximum limitations. A fourth approach would require employers to provide and pay part of the cost of a minimum health expensure insurance program for employees and their dependents. Persons not covered under an employee benefit plan would be insured under separate programs financed in part by taxes. The rapidly rising cost of medical care and increasing concern about cost containment have at least temporarily reduced support for a national medical expense insurance program.

WORKERS' COMPENSATION

In this text, workers' compensation has been discussed in Chapter 8 in connection with property and liability risk management, because from the viewpoint of the firm, this legislation creates an absolute liability where formerly only negligence liability existed.

Methods of Insurance

In 44 of the 50 states, insurance of workers' compensation is provided by private insurers. In 13 of these states, insurance is also provided by state funds, i.e., insurers operated by the state, it being optional for a private employer to insure either with a private insurer or with the fund. In 8 of these 13 states, some or all public employers are required to insure with the fund. In 6 states, the state fund is the exclusive means of insurance, and in only 2 of these may the employer ''self-insure,'' an option that is available in all but one of the other 44 states. In order to self-insure, however, the employer must receive specific permission from the industrial commission or other administering agency. Such permission is usually conditioned upon proof of the employer's financial ability. In many states a deposit of some sort is required. Few employers elect to retain this obligation but, because they are generally large employers, they pay almost 20 percent of the claims (excluding special federal ''black lung'' benefits paid to coal miners and their survivors). Retention has also become more common in recent years.

State funds are a subject of much controversy, ranging from the broad question concerning whether such institutions should exist to the practical performance of individual funds. Proponents of the exclusive fund argue that the state should have full control of the administration of workers' compensation in order that the interest of the worker may be fully protected; that a single fund lowers the cost of workers' compensation insurance by eliminating expenses of competition; and that it is contrary to the spirit of workers' compensation to permit it to be made a subject of private profit. Against the exclusive fund are brought the arguments that it is contrary to the American principle of private enterprise; that it is subject to political influence in appointments and operation; that its economy is illusory because of hidden subsidies, the alleged general inefficiency of public administration, and limited loss control and loss adjustment services.

Proponents of competitive funds support them by arguing that employers who are required to insure should not be forced to patronize a private insurer; that employers who are unable to obtain insurance with private insurers should have access to a public source of coverage rather than be forced out of business; that the state fund provides a useful yardstick for measuring the effectiveness of insurance; and that it increases the effectiveness of price competition. Opponents argue, but less vehemently than in the case of exclusive funds, that even the competitive fund is contrary to the American way; that it is unnecessary, since private insurance is available and since, through assigned risk plans, they provide for insurance of the unwanted employer; and that private business operation is more efficient than public business operation.

Because the 19 state funds are a heterogeneous group, these arguments have varying validity and are asserted with different intensity depending upon the state involved.

TEMPORARY DISABILITY INSURANCE LEGISLATION

Five states have legislation that requires employers to pay cash benefits to employees who are temporarily disabled. The primary intent of this legislation is to cover nonoccupational illnesses. The five states, in the order in which they enacted this legislation, are Rhode Island (1942), California (1946), New Jersey (1948), New York (1949), and Hawaii (1969).

The details of the legislation in the five states are too complicated and too numerous to discuss at length. Some major features of this legislation, however, and some of the differences among the states are described below.

Relationship to Unemployment Insurance

California, New Jersey, and Rhode Island relate their temporary disability insurance programs to their unemployment insurance programs. The coverage, qualifications for benefits, and the benefits are similar to those in the unemployment insurance program, and the two programs are administered by the same public agency. This tie-in is natural because of the administrative savings made possible by such an integration and because of the desirability of continuing approximately the same payments to an unemployed person who becomes disabled and thus becomes ineligible for unemployment insurance benefits.[7] New York, on the other hand, considered nonoccupational disability to be more closely related to occupational disability. Consequently, New York's temporary disability insurance legislation is an amendment to that state's workers' compensation law. Hawaii created a new administrative division in its Division of Labor and Industrial Relations.

Coverage

All five states cover employers of one or more employees. Agricultural work, domestic employment, government service, employment for nonprofit organizations, self-employment, and work for interstate railroads are common exclusions.

---

[7] Several other states have amended their unemployment insurance laws to provide for the continuance of unemployment insurance payments to unemployed job seekers who become disabled.

Qualification for Benefits

Qualifications for benefits vary, but in general the claimants must be unable to perform their regular and customary work, they must have earned at least a certain amount or have worked at least a specified period of time prior to their disability, and they must demonstrate continued attachment to the labor force.

Benefits

The weekly benefit amounts depend upon the worker's wages in some previous period, within certain maximum and minimum amounts. In all states the worker must wait approximately one week before benefits begin, but in California the waiting period does not apply to hospitalized patients. In New Jersey the waiting period is compensable after benefits have been paid for three consecutive weeks. The maximum potential duration of benefits is a uniform 26 weeks in Hawaii and New York. In the other states, the maximum potential period is also 26 weeks, but the individual potential period depends upon the worker's earnings in some previous period.

California and New York have weekly dollar maximums. Hawaii, New Jersey, and Rhode Island express their maxima as a percentage of the state average weekly wage.

Only one state, Rhode Island, pays additional amounts for dependents ($3 per dependent child up to $12).

Other sources of income, such as workers' compensation, wages, private pensions, and OASDI benefits, usually reduce or terminate the benefits. No state permits a person to receive unemployment compensation and temporary disability insurance benefits at the same time.

In addition to cash benefits, until 1979 the California program provided hospital benefits of $12 per day for 20 days per spell of continuous disability. This feature of the California plan had special significance because it was the first state medical expense insurance plan.

Insuring Agency

In Rhode Island, all benefits are provided through a monopolistic state fund. In California and New Jersey, all employers are insured under a competitive state fund unless they apply for and secure approval of a privately insured plan or a self-insured plan. In California a private plan (insured or self-insured) must provide more liberal benefits than the state plan in at least one respect and be at least as liberal in all other respects. Private insurers are also prevented from selecting only those groups whose age, sex, and wage composition might create adverse selection against the state plan. New Jersey requires that a private plan be at least as liberal as the state plan in all respects. New York requires that the employer insure through a competitive state fund or a private insurer unless he or she obtains permission to self-insure this program. New York permits a private plan that provides temporary disability income benefits somewhat below the statutory benefits if it provides other types of benefits, such as medical expense benefits, to make up the difference. Private plans insure less than 10 percent of the covered employees in California, about 30 percent in New Jersey, and over 90 percent in New York. Hawaii requires employers to purchase insurance from private insurers unless they secure permission to self-insure. A special state fund pays benefits to unemployed workers. Like New York, Hawaii permits an employer to deviate from the statutory benefits if it provides a comparable package of total health insurance benefits.

Financing

Employees pay the entire cost of the state plan in Rhode Island and California. In the other states both employees and employers contribute; the employer's contributions vary depending upon the underwriting characteristics and loss experience of their employees.

Issues

The spread of private employee benefit plans providing incomes for workers who are temporarily disabled has diminished interest in these programs, but state legislatures still occasionally debate the advisability of this form of social insurance. Some persons would favor including a benefit of this sort under OASDI; some believe that OASDI should through a comprehensive temporary disability insurance program replace both compulsory temporary disability insurance and workers' compensation. Eligibility requirements and benefits levels are frequently debated, but the most critical issue in existing programs has been the place of private insurance. The questions are similar to those considered in the preceding section with regard to workers' compensation, but the problem of adverse selection has received much more attention.

STATE CATASTROPHIC MEDICAL EXPENSE INSURANCE PLANS

In 1973, Maine became the first state to enact a catastrophic medical expense insurance plan. Rhode Island was next in 1974, followed by Minnesota in 1976. In 1981 Minnesota's program stopped accepting new applications. Only the Rhode Island plan, which is the best known, will be described here.

The Rhode Island plan, financed from state general revenues, pays the annual medical expenses incurred by a family in excess of a specified out-of-pocket expenditure. For a family with no private health insurance this deductible is $5,000 or, if higher, 50 percent of family income (adjusted for family size). For a family with qualified private basic and major medical expense insurance the deductible is $500 or, if higher, 10 percent of family income. Separate deductibles apply to Medicare beneficiaries.

All private insurers must offer a qualified plan to all persons and employers in the state; the premiums are subject to strict regulation; insurers are permitted to form a reinsurance pool to spread the losses under qualified policies; and providers of services must be certified and charge rates in the public interest.

UNEMPLOYMENT INSURANCE

As we have stated earlier, the Social Security Act of 1935 introduced a system of grants to states that had unemployment insurance programs. Wisconsin and New York were the only states with programs at the time the act was passed, although a few other states had legislation that was not yet effective. This situation soon changed because of the nature of the federal legislation. By 1937, all states had unemployment insurance systems.

The Role of the Federal Government

The Social Security Act levied a 3 percent payroll tax on all employers of eight or more persons, but the legislation did not apply to certain types of employment, such as domestic service, agricultural work, casual labor, and work for most nonprofit organizations, and government employment. The employer could credit against this tax his or her contributions to an approved state program (including any reduction in these contributions as a result of experience rating), but the credit could not exceed 90 percent of the federal tax. For example, if the state tax was 2.7 percent, the effective federal tax was only 0.3 percent. If the state had no unemployment insurance program, the federal tax would be 3 percent. Essentially, the same rules apply today, except that as a result of several amendments, the tax is now levied on employers of one or more workers in each of 20 days in a year or who have a payroll of $1,500 in a calendar quarter. Agricultural workers and domestic servants are now covered subject to some special wage requirements. The federal tax still does not apply to nonprofit organizations or services for a state or local government, but the federal tax rate is not reduced by the state tax unless the state plan covers most employees in these two categories. The federal tax rate is 3.5 percent applied to the first $7,000 of an employee's wages. The maximum offset for contributions to an approved state program remains 2.7 percent. The present effective federal tax then is 0.8 percent. Effective January 1, 1985, the federal tax rate will be increased to 6.2 percent, the maximum offset credit to 5.4 percent. The federal tax rate will be reduced to 6.0 percent (an effective federal tax of 0.6 percent) when the federal account has repaid moneys it borrowed from the United States Treasury in the mid-1970s to pay temporary extended benefits in addition to the permanent program described below.

The incentive to establish a state unemployment insurance program was further strengthened by the fact that the federal government uses its tax income to defray the administrative costs of the state systems. The remainder is used to establish a fund from which states may, under certain conditions, obtain loans (interest free until 1982) and to pay its share of the extended benefits described below.

The federal government does not prescribe any eligibility requirements or benefit levels for approved plans, but it does require that benefits shall not be denied to any person who refuses employment that (1) is available because of a labor dispute, (2) requires or prohibits union membership, or (3) is subject to substandard conditions. Benefits must be paid through public employment offices. In periods when state insured unemployment rates exceed specified amounts (6 percent or 5 percent and at least 1.2 times the rate in the two preceding calendar years), states must increase the maximum number of weeks an unemployed worker will receive benefits by 50 percent. The maximum extension required is 13 weeks; the combined regular and extended benefit period, however, need not exceed 39 weeks. The federal government reimburses the states for one-half the cost of benefits in excess of 26 weeks (up to a maximum of 13 weeks) for benefits paid during an extended benefit period. A supplemental-benefit program, scheduled to expire at the end of 1984, extends the benefits an additional 8 to 14 weeks, depending upon the state unemployment rate. The federal government finances this program without any state contributions.

Another important requirement is that the state taxes be placed in an unemployment trust fund maintained by the federal government but in which a separate account is established for each state. Withdrawals from the fund are to be used almost exclusively for unemployment benefits to insureds. Under some conditions, some of the state moneys may be used to pay administrative expenses, but the bulk of these expenses are met by the federal grants.

States can experience-rate employers under plans meeting minimum federal standards.

State Programs

State unemployment insurance programs vary greatly with respect to coverage, qualifying requirements, benefit levels, and financing. Only a brief summary of the major provisions is presented here.[8]

Coverage   State plans must cover the employees subject to the federal tax plus those that must be covered for federal approval. In addition, many states reduce the 20-day or $1,500 payroll required. They may also cover additional types of employment.

Eligibility for Benefits   To be eligible for benefits, a worker must first demonstrate his or her attachment to the labor force. In most states this attachment is demonstrated by having earned certain minimum wages (usually some multiple such as $1\frac{1}{2}$ or $\frac{30}{26}$ times the high-quarter earnings) during a base period, which is generally the first four of the last five completed calendar quarters prior to the date a claim is filed. In addition, the worker must be unemployed (or working less than full time and earning less than some specified amount), must (except in a few states) be physically able to work, and must be available for work; i.e., must be willing and able to take any suitable employment. In many states the worker must in addition be actively seeking work. In all states he or she must register for work with the state employment service. The benefits may be postponed or reduced, if the worker leaves his or her job voluntarily without good cause, is fired because of misconduct, refuses suitable work, is idle because of a labor dispute, misrepresents the facts to receive benefits to which he or she is not entitled, or receives other forms of income such as wages in lieu of notice, dismissal payments, workers' compensation benefits, OASDI benefits, or a

---

[8] For more details, see U.S. Department of Labor, Bureau of Employment Security, *Comparison of State Unemployment Insurance Laws,* revised periodically.

pension. Benefits are postponed in many states for some of these causes instead of being canceled for the duration of the worker's unemployment on the theory that after the passage of the postponement period, the person's unemployment is not attributable to the reason for which he or she was disqualified. The most severe penalty is cancellation of the worker's wage credits during the base period, which might prevent the worker from collecting benefits from a second spell of unemployment because he or she would not be able to demonstrate attachment to the labor force.

Benefits Most states require that an unemployed person be unemployed for one week before benefits are payable. However, once a person has satisfied this waiting-period requirement, he or she need not satisfy it again with respect to future spells of unemployment during a "benefit year." A benefit year is usually the year beginning with the date the person files an unemployment claim.

About two-thirds of the states relate the worker's benefit during a benefit year to his or her earnings during that calendar quarter of the worker's base period in which he or she had the highest earnings. About one-third of these states multiply these high-quarter earnings by $\frac{1}{26}$, which would give a worker with 13 full weeks of employment about 50 percent of his or her average weekly wage as a benefit. About half the states basing benefits on high-quarter earnings use larger fractions to allow for some periods of unemployment during the base quarter. All but one of the remaining high-quarter-earnings states use a lower fraction for persons with high earnings than for those with low earnings. The remaining state pays half of the full-time average weekly wage in the high-earnings quarter. The other jurisdictions relate their benefit to the workers' earnings during the entire base period. Thirteen states pay additional weekly allowances for dependents.

The benefits developed by these formulas are subject to both minimum and maximum limits. More than two-thirds of the states have maximums ranging from 50 to 67 percent of the statewide average weekly wage.

Some jurisdictions pay benefits for a uniform period, usually 26 weeks, during a benefit year to all unemployed workers. The remainder limit the maximum duration in two ways. First, they specify some maximum period, usually 26 weeks. Second, if this would produce a shorter period, they either limit (1) the maximum dollar payout to some fraction, such as $\frac{1}{3}$ or a fraction that declines as the earnings increase, of the base-period wages, or (2) the maximum number of weeks to some fraction, such as $\frac{3}{4}$, of the number of weeks of employment in the base period. As required by federal law all jurisdictions provide for extended benefits, usually by 50 percent up to a maximum of 39 weeks when unemployment in the state reaches a specified level.

Some states impose special requirements on seasonal workers. For example, wage credits earned in seasonal employment may be counted only in connection with unemployment during the operating season.

Unemployment benefits are subject to federal income tax if the adjusted gross income plus the unemployment insurance benefit exceeds $18,000 for single persons and $24,000 for married persons filing a joint return. The amount taxed is the lesser of (1) the unemployment benefits paid or (2) half the excess of the adjusted gross income plus the employment benefits over the specified thresholds.

Financing In all but three states, employers pay the entire cost of the program. In some states the taxable wage base is higher than the $7,000 federal base. In a few cases this base is tied to the state average wage. Most states have a standard tax rate of 2.7 percent, but in all states the rates paid by employers depend upon their experience and the status of the state unemployment trust fund. When the state fund is in its most favorable condition, the minimum rates range among the states from 0 percent (11 states) to 1.2 percent. Under the least favorable state fund condition, maximum state rates range from 2.7 percent to 7.5 percent. Some states have substantial balances in the Unemployment Trust Fund; others have less than the maximum amount they have paid in a 12-month period. Over one-third of the states currently have a deficit account because of moneys they borrowed earlier from the fund. In states that run a deficit for two years in a row, the federal unemployment tax is higher than the 0.8 percent collected in other states.

Some Important Issues

Unemployment compensation plans have been subjected to much criticism in recent years. Some of the major issues are described briefly in the following paragraphs.

Since unemployment is in many respects a national problem, it is argued that one federal system should replace the heterogeneous state plans. A less radical suggestion is that state plans be required to meet certain federal standards. In opposition to these arguments, it is claimed that the state plans have performed satisfactorily and that federal intervention would ignore local conditions and needs and violate states' rights.

State plans have been criticized for basing eligibility on work during too distant a base period and for setting too high a requirement. The maximum weekly benefits are said to be too low, forcing too many workers to receive less than 50 percent of their lost wages. Basing maximum duration on wages earned during the base period has, it is alleged, resulted in inadequate benefits for many workers, particularly low-income workers. On the other hand, the plans may be too liberal with respect to part-time workers and similar groups who may obtain the benefits designed for low-income-full-time workers. The 50 percent goal itself has been questioned as being overly generous because it was established at a time when income tax rates were much lower.[9]

Because the program must be administered with discretion, the state administrations have been called too restrictive by some and too lax by others.

The financing of the plans has been a prime target for criticism. The financial status of the plans as a result of low tax rates and some recent recessions is a matter of universal concern. The logic behind a taxable wage base that is much lower than the OASDI wage base has been questioned. The merits of experience rating have been debated at length. Critics argue that (1) a single employer has little control over his or her unemployment rate, (2) some employers fire employees before they become eligible for benefits in order to cut their losses or deny claims of eligible employees, and (3) experience rating feeds inflation and deepens depressions by producing low

[9] Martin S. Feldstein, "Unemployment Insurance: Time for Reform,: *Harvard Business Review*, vol. LIII, no. 2 (March–April 1975), pp. 51–54.

rates during boom periods and high rates during recessions. Several technical questions have been raised concerning the application of experience rating. The principal pro arguments are that experience rating provides an incentive for employers to stabilize employment and penalizes employers who contribute to unemployment. Indeed it is sometimes argued that rates should be even lower for those employers with little unemployment and even higher for those with high unemployment.[10]

SOME KEY CONCEPTS

Social insurance   All insurance required by law for substantial numbers of the general population, administered or closely supervised by the government, and supported primarily by earmarked contributions, with a benefit structure that usually redistributes income to achieve some social objective, not private equity.

Social security system   All government measures designed to protect its citizens against (1) personnel risks and (2) poverty and substandard conditions. Social insurance is one part of a social security system.

Old Age, Survivors, Disability and Health Insurance (OASDHI)   The major social insurance program of the United States established by the Social Security Act of 1935 and greatly expanded since that time. The program has four components with separate trust funds—Old Age and Survivors Insurance, Disability Insurance, Hospital Insurance (Medicare Part A) and Supplementary Medical Insurance (Medicare Part B).

Earnings base under OASDHI   The maximum annual taxable earnings under OASDHI and the maximum annual earnings used in calculating OASDHI benefits.

Fully insured status   The status usually required to receive OASDHI benefits. To be fully insured a worker must have quarters of coverage equal to at least the number of quarters elapsing since 1950 or, if later, since the end of the year in which the worker was 21, subject to a minimum requirement of 6 quarters of coverage and a maximum requirement of 40. To earn quarters of coverage, a worker must have earned specified amounts in covered employment.

Primary Insurance Amount (PIA)   An amount calculated on the basis of the worker's average indexed monthly earnings (AIME) that increases as the AIME increases but not proportionately. The basic monthly retirement benefit for a person retiring at age 65 is the PIA. Other OASDI benefits are some multiple of the PIA.

Temporary disability insurance legislation   Laws in five states that require employers to establish income replacement plans for workers who are temporarily disabled.

State catastrophic medical expense plans   Medical expense plans in Maine and Rhode Island designed to pay a family's annual medical expenses in excess of a deductible, which is higher for families with higher incomes.

Base period   In most states the period during which earnings in covered employment determine eligibility for unemployment insurance and the amount of those benefits. Generally the first four of the last five completed calendar quarters prior to the date the claim is filed.

REVIEW QUESTIONS

1 a Is "social insurance" insurance?
  b If so, what distinguishes social insurance programs from other insurance programs?

[10] Ibid., pp. 59–60.

2 Distinguish among social security, social insurance, and public assistance.

3 a Discuss the impact of the industrial revolution and other economic and social changes upon the quest for security.

b Was the United States a leader in the development of social insurance programs? Why or why not?

4 Social insurance programs have often been criticized on the ground that they are not "actuarially fair."

a Explain this criticism.

b In what other ways do social insurance programs differ from private individual insurance?

5 What programs were established under the Social Security Act of 1935?

6 a How would you determine whether a person was fully insured under OASDI at the present time? currently insured?

b Why is the person's status important?

7 Construct examples to illustrate how OASDI benefits favor persons *(a)* with low incomes and *(b)* with many dependents.

8 One person worked continuously in OASDI-covered employment from 1951 to 1984 when he retired. Another person, who worked about half that time, also retired in 1984.

a Were both persons eligible for retirement benefits?

b How do their monthly checks compare?

9 In determining the OASDI retirement benefit for a person aged 65, why is it important to know the year when that person reached age 62?

10 A man aged 35 has a wife aged 35 and two children, aged 3 and 8. His average indexed monthly wage for OASDI is $2,000.

a If this man is currently insured, what benefits will his family receive if he dies today?

b If this man is fully insured, what benefits will his family receive if he dies today?

11 What types of disability are covered under OASDI?

12 Explain briefly the automatic adjustment features of OASDI.

13 Is OASDI "actuarially sound"?

14 Identify some of the leading current issues with respect to OASDI, and discuss the arguments presented in connection with each issue.

15 Compare Hospital Insurance and Supplementary Medical Insurance with respect to *(a)* eligibility requirements, *(b)* benefits, and *(c)* financing.

16 Nineteen states have state workers' compensation funds. Describe the two types of state funds that exist in these states.

17 a What is the relationship between temporary disability insurance and unemployment insurance?

b Compare the approaches in the five states with TDI programs with respect to (1) the determination of benefits, (2) the type of insurer, and (3) the financing.

c Since only five states have TDI programs, some persons argue that these programs are not very important. Do you agree?

18 What is the role of the federal government with respect to unemployment insurance?

19 Comment on each of the following criticisms of state unemployment insurance programs:

a The eligibility and benefit provisions favor secondary wage earners, such as part-time and seasonal workers.

b The maximum weekly benefits are too low.

c The system encourages strikes and quitting without good cause.

d The system does not protect the worker against long-term unemployment.

20 a How is unemployment insurance financed?

b Comment upon the desirability of experience rating unemployment insurance.

SUGGESTIONS FOR ADDITIONAL READING

Boskin, J. J. (ed.): *The Crisis in Social Security: Problems and Prospects* (San Francisco: Institute for Contemporary Studies, 1977).

Burns, E. M.: *Social Security in the United States* (New York: McGraw-Hill Book Company, 1962).

Haber, W., and M. G. Murray: *Unemployment Insurance in the American Economy* (Homewood, Ill.: Richard D. Irwin, Inc., 1966).

Munnell, Alicia H.: *The Future of Social Security* (Washington, D.C.: The Brookings Institution, 1977).

Myers, R. J.: *Social Security* (2d ed., Homewood, Ill.: Richard D. Irwin, Inc., 1981).

Pechman, J. A., H. J. Aaron, and M. K. Taussig: *Social Security: Perspectives for Reform* (Washington: The Brookings Institution, 1968).

Rejda, G. E.: *Social Insurance and Economic Security* (2d ed., Englewood Cliffs, N.J.: Prentice-Hall, Inc., 1984).

Report of the National Commission on Social Security Reform (Washington, D.C., January, 1983).

Report of the 1979 Advisory Council on Social Security (Washington, D.C., December, 1979).

Robertson, A. Haeworth: *The Coming Revolution in Social Security* (McLean, Va.: Security Press, 1981).

Social Security in America's Future, Final Report of the National Commission on Social Security (Washington, D.C., 1981).

Williams, C. A., Jr., J. G. Turnbull, and E. F. Cheit: *Economic and Social Security* (5th ed., New York: John Wiley & Sons, Inc., 1982).

CHAPTER 21

EMPLOYEE BENEFIT PLANS: I

LEARNING OBJECTIVES

After you have completed this chapter, you should be able to:

1 Compare group insurance, individual insurance, and noninsured employee-benefit plans.
2 Summarize the major features of group life insurance plans.
3 Distinguish between temporary disability insurance and long-term disability insurance as to waiting period, weekly benefit amount, and benefit duration.
4 Describe briefly commercial insurance, Blue Cross-Blue Shield, and independent medical expense insurance plans.
5 Compare service medical expense benefits and cash benefits.
6 List the alleged advantages and disadvantages of health maintenance organizations.
7 Explain experience rating, retroactive premium adjustments, minimum premium plans, and administrative service only agreements used by group life and health insurers.
8 Explain the tax advantages of a noncontributory group life insurance or medical expense insurance plan.
9 Describe the nature and purpose of supplementary unemployment compensation.

INTRODUCTION

Private employee benefit plans have become an important condition of employment for most employees. Through these plans, some employees secure protection that they

413

could not purchase at a reasonable price on their own. Most secure protection at a lower after-tax cost. Employers use these plans for a variety of reasons—for example, to attract and retain high-quality employees, to free employees from certain worries, to provide incentives for improved performance, to achieve certain tax savings, or to match the plans of competitors.

In designing an employee benefit program the risk manager must consider both (1) the needs and desires of employees, and (2) management objectives. Among the many decisions that must be made are (1) the division of the total compensation package between pay, employee benefits of the sort described in this text, and other employee benefits such as paid holidays and employee discounts on purchases of the firm's products, (2) the types of benefits to be provided, (3) who will be eligible for these benefits and how their benefits will be determined, (4) whether employees should be asked to pay part of the cost, and (5) whether the program should be insured and, if so, by whom and in what way.

This chapter is the first of two dealing with employee benefit plans, and the first of five describing life and health insurance contracts and their uses. Employee benefit plans have become an important condition of employment for most employees. A business should be vitally interested in these plans because of their impact on industrial relations and the sizable expenditures they require. After outlining the nature and scope of employee benefit plans, we shall examine the arrangements that are usually made to provide the most common types of benefits. Protection against death, disability, and unemployment is discussed in this chapter; pensions, property and liability insurance programs, prepaid legal expense plans, and cafeteria or flexible benefit plans will be described in Chapter 22.

NATURE AND SCOPE OF EMPLOYEE BENEFIT PLANS

Employee benefits can be defined broadly to include all compensation other than direct wages (for example, pensions, death benefits, sick pay, medical expense reimbursements, unemployment benefits, holiday pay, bonuses, company cars for personal use, and purchase discounts). Each year the Chamber of Commerce of the United States reports what employee benefits (defined this broadly) cost a sample of large firms as a percent of their payrolls the previous year. In recent years employee benefits have cost these employers about 37 percent of their payrolls.[1]

About two-thirds of this cost was associated with benefits that are related to personnel loss exposures and thus to risk management. Legally required payments for social insurance programs cost about 9 percent. Voluntary employee benefits payable in case of death, poor health, or retirement cost about 15 percent.

Unfortunately data are not available on the proportion of all wage and salary workers who are protected by each type of benefit.[2] A one-time survey by the

---

[1] *Employee Benefits*, (Washington, D.C.: Chamber of Commerce of the United States, annual).

[2] Until 1977 the *Social Security Bulletin* reported periodically on the proportion of wage and salary workers who were covered under private plans sponsored or initiated individually or jointly by employers and employees to provide benefits of the sort in which we are most interested. See the fourth edition of this text, pages 390–91.

President's Commission on Pension Policy revealed that in 1979 about 48 percent of all workers were covered under a pension plan, 56 percent of all workers age 25 or over.[3]

A 1982 survey by the United States Department of Labor tells what proportion of the persons who worked full-time that year for medium and large firms were covered by each major type of benefit.[4] The findings are presented below.

Type of benefit	Proportion covered
Death	96%
Disability	
Short-term disability	93
Formal sick leave	67
Temporary disability insurance	51
Long-term disability	43
Medical expenses	
Worker	97
Dependents	93
Dental expenses	68
Retirement	84

Workers for small firms are less likely to receive these benefits.

With the exception of some independent medical expense plans, described later in this chapter, the following description of employee benefit plans is restricted to plans covering employees of a single employer, partly to simplify the presentation and partly because about 75 to 90 percent of the covered employees, depending upon the benefit, belong to single-employer plans. The importance of the multi-employer plans, however, must be acknowledged. These plans cover the employees of two or more employers in an industry, in an area, or in an industry within an area. The two most important types are (1) plans covering employees of members of a trade association, and (2) plans covering members of a union who work for two or more employers. This second type of plan involves a welfare fund managed by trustees. Two major characteristics of these multi-employer welfare funds are (1) the continuation of coverage if an employee moves from one firm under the plan to another firm under the same plan, and (2) the nature of the financial support, typically an employer contribution based on the number of hours worked by covered employees.

Other groups of workers whose plans will not be discussed in the following sections are union members under union-controlled plans and members under a professional association plan.

Employee benefit plans always provide insurance protection from the viewpoint of

---

[3] *Coming of Age: Toward a National Retirement Income Policy* (Washington, D.C.: President's Commission on Pension Policy, February 26, 1981).

[4] *Employee Benefits in Medium and Large Firms,* 1982, Bulletin No. 2176 (Washington, D.C.: U.S. Department of Labor, Bureau of Labor Statistics, August, 1983).

the employee. Employees transfer their loss exposures to the plan which combines all of these exposures. The employer, however, can insure all, some, or none of these exposures. Many multi-employer plans retain part or all of their loss exposures, but each employer included in the plan can regard the plan itself as an insurer because the plan pools the exposures of many employers. Until recently the employer typically chose to insure all or most of the exposures to death, disability, medical expenses, and retirement under a group insurance plan. Paid sick leave plans, however, were always self-insured as were unemployment benefits that supplemented the government benefits. Most pension plans were insured, but because the largest employers tended not to insure at least part of their exposure under these plans, more employees have been covered for many years under self-insured pension plans than under insured plans. During the past decade larger employers have also elected to retain more of their exposures to death, disability, and medical expenses.

Before turning to the major types of employee benefit plans, because so much of this protection is provided through group insurance, we shall contrast the group method of underwriting insurance protection with individual underwriting.

GROUP UNDERWRITING CONTRASTED WITH INDIVIDUAL UNDERWRITING

Group underwriting differs from individual underwriting in several respects.

1 Group selection is substituted for individual selection. If the group is acceptable to the insurer, everyone in the group is eligible for the protection. As a result, the insurer covers some persons who could not obtain individual insurance at any price. In order to keep the proportion of such persons in each insured group at a minimum, certain underwriting safeguards have been adopted with respect to life and health insurance plans.

First, those types of groups are most acceptable *(a)* for which insurance is incidental to the major purpose of the group, *(b)* in which there is a constant flow of younger persons into the group while older and impaired lives are leaving it, and *(c)* for which some physical qualifications are required for joining. By these standards, a group of employees working for a single employer is most satisfactory. As insurers have gained more experience with group insurance and as competition increases, these standards have been relaxed. Today insurers write such groups as members of a professional association or a college alumni society.

Second, the number of insureds in the group must equal or exceed a certain minimum. This requirement decreases the chance that impaired lives will form an important part of the group and reduces the administrative costs per insured life. The most common size requirement is 10 lives, but in group health insurance there is often a lower minimum or even no minimum.

Third, if participation is voluntary, a certain percentage, usually 75 percent, of the employees is required to participate. Otherwise, the participating group might include an abnormally high percentage of impaired lives since those in poor health will almost certainly elect to participate. This requirement, however, has also been relaxed over time.

Fourth, the employees must meet certain eligibility requirements. For example, an employee must accept the coverage within a certain period after he or she becomes eligible. Otherwise the employee must prove individual insurability to join the group. Another eligibility requirement states that insured members must be active employees, not inactive members of the board of directors. Transitory workers are commonly excluded by a one-to-six month qualification period.

Fifth, the benefit amounts must be either the same for all participants or determined automatically on some basis such as salary, position, service, or some combination of these factors. Otherwise the impaired lives would probably select large amounts of life and health insurance while the healthy lives would select smaller amounts. It has become fairly common, however, to give the employee some choice, such as life insurance equal in amount to annual salary or to salary for two years.

Sixth, some maximum must be placed on the amount of life insurance and disability income protection on any single life. This maximum is generally related to the total amount of insurance in force on the group because one objective is to avoid a disproportionate amount of protection on any one life.

2 A master contract is issued to the employer as the policyholder. The employees, who are not technically parties to the contract, receive individual certificates as evidence of their protection.

3 Salaried employees of insurers who are specially trained in group insurance almost always assist the commissioned agent or broker originating the sale and handle the details associated with installation of the plan.

4 The employer assists the insurer in administering the plan. In some instances, the employer performs all the administration, even to the point of paying the claims.

5 The group contract may be designed within limits to meet the specific needs of the particular employee group. In this respect, group insurance has considerably more flexibility than does individual insurance.

6 Statutory standard provisions are less important than in individual insurance. Not all states have laws providing for standard provisions, and those that do have such laws do not, except for group life insurance, include more than a few provisions.[5]

7 Because the wholesale method of distributing the coverage permits reduced administrative costs and commissions, and because the employer performs some of the administrative tasks, the premium for group insurance is less than the premium for equivalent individual insurance. Furthermore, the experience of the particular group may be considered in determining the final cost of the group protection.

GROUP LIFE INSURANCE

Employee benefit plans providing death benefits usually take the form of group life insurance. This insurance is either some form of yearly renewable term insurance or nonterm insurance. Term insurance obligates the insurer to pay a specified amount if the person dies during the specified term. Nonterm insurance usually provides lifetime protection. It combines an increasing savings component with decreasing term insur-

---

[5] The group life standard provisions cover such matters as a grace period, incontestability, misstatement of age, and conversion rights. For conversion rights see below.

ance. The difference between term and nonterm insurance will be examined in considerable detail in Chapter 23. Because over 90 percent of the group life insurance in force is yearly renewable term insurance, we will discuss that type of protection in more detail than the other types.

Yearly Renewable Term Insurance

Group yearly renewable term insurance provides one-year term insurance that is automatically renewed each year the worker belongs to the plan. The amount is usually some multiple of the employee's earnings. Other approaches vary the benefit according to the employee's position or cover all employees for the same amount. The proceeds are payable in a lump sum or in installments.

If the employee withdraws from the group, he or she usually has the right, without proving insurability, to purchase within 31 days an individual nonterm insurance contract bearing a premium based upon his or her attained age. These individual contracts are explained in Chapter 23. During the 31-day decision period, the group insurance protection continues. This right to convert the group protection to individual protection is valuable if on the termination date the employee is uninsurable or would have to pay substandard rates for an individual contract. Otherwise the employee would be able to purchase this same insurance at the same price without the conversion right. If the employer or the insurer terminates the master contract, employees with several years of service (usually five) may convert at least part of their group protection, commonly up to $2,000.

Under this type of plan, the cost of insuring any single employee increases as he or she ages, but if the age composition of the group remains approximately the same,[6] the total premium rate for the group does not change greatly. If the plan is *contributory* (i.e., if the employee also contributes to the cost), the employee's contribution is typically $0.60 or less per month per $1,000 of insurance during his or her membership in the group. At the younger ages this contribution is usually more than enough to pay for the employee's personal protection. It may even be more than enough to pay the annual premiums on individual term insurance. In later years, however, the total cost will far exceed the employee's contribution. Some employees may, if the plan is voluntary, elect not to participate under the plan until the premium for individual protection exceeds the required contribution under the group plan, but they will have to prove insurability at that time. If they become uninsurable, they will have good reason to regret their earlier decision.

The initial premium rate depends primarily upon the age composition and the size of the group. The size is important because the expense loading does not increase proportionately with the amount of insurance in force. An additional charge is also levied for certain substandard industrial classifications. The final cost, however, depends also upon the dividends paid by participating insurers and the retrospective premium adjustments of nonparticipating insurers. The dividends and premium adjust-

---

[6] The age composition, not the average age, must remain about the same. To illustrate, the cost of insuring two persons aged 20 and 60 exceeds the cost of insuring two persons aged 40.

ments for large groups are roughly a return of the premiums not needed for (1) the claims and expenses of the particular group, and (2) some contribution to contingency reserves and to deficiencies in the premiums collected from some groups. As the size of the group decreases, the claim experience fluctuates over a wide range, and the insurer's experience on all groups combined is weighted more heavily in the formula. Some other pricing concepts that either supplement or replace these standard experience and retrospective rating adjustments will be described later in this chapter.

The employer's contribution toward the cost of a qualified group term insurance plan is a business expense for the firm. The employee can exclude from his or her taxable income that portion of the employer's contribution used to purchase the first $50,000 of protection. Beneficiaries do not have to pay any federal income tax on the proceeds.[7] This tax feature, plus the inclusion of noncontributory insurance benefits in union demands, has been largely responsible for the trend toward noncontributory plans. For example, for an employee in a 30 percent federal income tax bracket, an employee is as well off with a $70 annual contribution by the employer to a group life insurance plan as with a $100 salary increase, $30 of which must be paid to the tax collector and the remaining $70 contributed to the group plan.

In addition to this tax feature, other arguments in favor of a noncontributory plan are that (1) the employer has more freedom in designing, administering, and revising the plan, and (2) all eligible employees are covered, thus reducing (a) the problems with would-be beneficiaries where there is no coverage, and (b) the expenses of keeping records of contributions. On the other hand, a contributory plan (1) makes it possible to provide larger benefits, and (2) may increase the employees' interest in the plan. They may appreciate more what the employer is doing for them, and they may sometimes make valuable suggestions. Employee interest, of course, may also be developed in other ways, such as improved communications between labor and management. Many group term insurance plans include dependents as well as employees, but for a lesser amount.

Survivor Income Benefit Insurance

Survivor income benefit insurance differs from the usual form of yearly renewable term insurance in that generally (1) the death benefit is payable only if there is a qualified survivor such as a spouse or dependent child, (2) the benefit is a monthly income that is related to the deceased employee's earnings, and (3) the benefits stop if the survivor dies before the maximum number of payments have been made. To illustrate, one plan pays a surviving spouse 25 percent of the deceased's monthly earnings and each of the surviving children 15 percent, subject to a family maximum of 40 percent. The spouse receives his or her benefit to age 62 unless he or she dies or remarries earlier. Instead of basing the benefit on the deceased employee's earnings,

---

[7] If the worker irrevocably assigns the group protection to a beneficiary, the proceeds are also not counted in the worker's estate for estate tax purposes.

If the plan discriminates in favor of ''key employees'' (for example, officers or shareholders owning more than 5 percent of the firm), those key employees will not be able to exclude from their incomes the portion of the employer contribution used to purchase the first $50,000 of their protection.

some plans provide flat monthly benefits; others vary the benefit according to the employee's position. The family maximum benefits also vary. For example, some plans will pay a surviving spouse a lifetime income if he or she does not remarry. Some permit the employee to designate a beneficiary other than a spouse or children, but in this case the benefit is paid only for a specified period. Finally the insurer may pay a lump-sum benefit if the spouse remarries.

If the employee terminates employment, he or she can convert the commuted value of the survivor income benefit.

Until recently, survivor income benefit insurance was available only through pension plans.[8] However, the first group life insurance contract, written for Montgomery Ward in 1912, was based on similar principles, taking into account family conditions and salary status. The reader should also compare this approach with the survivorship benefits provided by Old-Age, Survivors, Disability, and Health Insurance, which were described in Chapter 20.

Nonterm Insurance

Group life insurance written on a nonterm basis assumes two forms: (1) group paid-up insurance (a two-part protection plan combining an increasing amount of paid-up lifetime protection with a decreasing amount of term insurance), and (2) group ordinary life insurance, which provides lifetime protection in exchange for level premium payments during the worker's participation in the program. Both forms differ from group term insurance in that an employee who withdraws from the group is entitled to some cash or insurance benefits without paying any more premiums. These benefits are especially attractive to employees retiring at advanced ages because of the sizable premiums they would have to pay for converted protection under group term insurance.

An increasing number of firms with group term insurance handle this conversion problem by continuing the term insurance in decreased amounts on retired employees. The cost to the firm is a sizable increase in the total premium without any contribution by the retiree. Many employers contribute moneys in advance of an employee's retirement to a retired lives reserve that can be used to pay part or all of the cost of the term insurance continued after retirement.

Self-Insured Death Benefits

Until recently formal death benefits were rarely self-insured by the employer. Most death benefits still are paid by insurers, but self-insurance has become more common. Only the largest employers are likely to accept this responsibility because of the wide fluctuations in mortality experience among smaller groups. Some large employers reason that their loss experience is better than insurers recognize in their pricing

---

[8] For a discussion of the relative advantages and disadvantages of providing preretirement death benefits from a pension plan, see Dan M. McGill, *Fundamentals of Private Pensions*, 5th ed. (Homewood, Ill.: Richard D. Irwin, Inc., 1984), chap. 8.

procedures. Consequently, they prefer to self-insure, but to avoid servicing problems, they have hired insurers to provide actuarial and financial advice and to administer claims payments. One attraction of self-insured plans is that some expenses such as premium taxes can be avoided.

Two disadvantages to employees of self-insured death benefits are (1) the possible loss of a tax benefit, and (2) the absence of conversion rights. Unless a Section 501(c) 9 trust (a voluntary employees' beneficiary association) is established as the funding vehicle, death benefits paid directly by the employer in excess of $5,000 are considered taxable income to the beneficiary. The granting of conversion rights would be a risk venture and force the employer to qualify legally as an insurer. The employer, however, may purchase conversion contracts from an insurer.

Death Benefits in Pension Plans

Pension plans, described in Chapter 22, commonly provide some death benefit if a worker dies prior to retirement. When the worker retires, he or she can select an option that will continue some benefits for a spouse following his or her death.

DISABILITY INCOME INSURANCE

Group health insurance plans provide (1) disability income protection, and (2) medical expense protection. Each type of protection will be discussed separately.

To save space, however, we shall first summarize briefly the tax situation with respect to both these coverages. Unless they are "unreasonable," employer contributions to health insurance plans are tax-deductible by the employer and nontaxable income for the employee. Furthermore, in determining taxable income an employee need not report any medical expense benefits actually received. A more complicated rule applies to disability benefits. Employer-financed-disability-income benefits are taxable income unless the worker is permanently and totally disabled as defined under Old-Age, Survivors, and Disability Insurance. Workers who are so disabled qualify for tax credits determined as follows: For an unmarried person the tax credit is 15 percent of $5,000 reduced by one-half of the adjusted gross income (including any tax-free benefits such as OASDI benefits) in excess of $7,500. For a married couple both of whom are disabled the two dollar amounts in the formula are $7,500 and $10,000, respectively; for a married person filing a separate return, $3,750 and $5,000. For all three categories, of course, the tax credit cannot exceed the disability income received. The tax rules regarding medical expense insurance thus provide a strong reason for favoring employer-pay-all plans. The tax reason is not nearly as strong for disability income benefits. The other arguments with respect to contributory and noncontributory arrangements are the same as those presented under "Group Life Insurance" earlier in this chapter.

Except for self-insured paid sick-leave plans, which are discussed later, group disability income insurance is usually underwritten by commercial insurers. This protection is provided through (1) temporary disability income insurance, (2) permanent disability income insurance, (3) dismemberment insurance, (4) disability provisions in group life plans, and (5) disability provisions in group pension plans. Dismemberment insurance that is written in conjunction with accidental death insurance provides for the payment of a lump sum if the insured suffers a loss of life or a scheduled dismemberment or loss of sight sustained solely as a result of accidental means within 90 days after the accident. The other protection types are important enough to be discussed separately.

Temporary Disability Income Insurance

Group temporary disability income insurance, often referred to as group accident and health insurance, provides a specified weekly benefit for a totally disabled person for a maximum duration of 13 or 26 weeks, or less commonly, 52 or 104 weeks. No distinction is made between disabilities caused by accident or sickness except that no benefits are usually payable for at least the first 7 days of sickness-incurred disability, whereas a shorter waiting period or none at all may apply to disabilities caused by accidents. The weekly benefit is usually two-thirds of weekly earnings, subject to some maximum weekly amount.

Occupational injuries and diseases are commonly excluded under the contract. Temporary disability income benefits, however, sometimes exceed the statutory workers' compensation payments. Consequently, some employers prefer to cover occupational injuries as well, but deduct workers' compensation payments from the group insurance benefit.

If an employee terminates employment, his or her insurance automatically terminates except that an employee who is absent on account of injury or sickness continues to be covered until premium payments are discontinued or, if earlier, until maximum benefits have been paid for any one disability.

The initial premium rate for a specified set of temporary disability benefits depends primarily upon the proportion of female lives and the size of the group. Females are much more susceptible to short-term disability and therefore increase the costs. Expenses do not increase proportionately with the weekly indemnity in force. If other group health insurance coverages are to be included in the plan, the expense loading is usually less than the sum of the expense loadings applicable to each component. Including life insurance in the package may also reduce the expense loading. Rates may be higher for certain substandard industries and when an abnormally large proportion of the group is in the upper age brackets. As in group life insurance, dividends and retroactive premium adjustments must be considered in determining the final costs of all forms of group health insurance.

Long-Term Disability Insurance

Starting in the 1960s long-term disability (LTD) insurance began to attract considerable interest and attention. Initially these plans were limited to the firm's higher-paid management employees. Many plans are still so limited, but most cover a broader class of employees.

LTD plans typically pay a totally disabled employee a monthly income for some long-term period after the completion of a waiting period. Payments are usually continued to age 65 but payments may be limited to five or ten years. The employee is often considered disabled the first two or five years if he or she cannot perform the duties of his or her own occupation. To receive benefits after the first two or five years, the worker must be unable to engage in any occupation for which he or she is reasonably fitted by education, training, or experience. Some insurers, however, use the "own occupation" standard for much longer periods; for example, to age sixty-five. Generally excluded causes of disability are limited to self-inflicted injuries, war, and injuries sustained by the insured while commiting a felony.

The waiting period is usually five or six months, which restricts benefit payments to seriously disabled workers and lessens the chance of overlaps with TDI or paid sick-leave plans. If the firm has no short-term disability plan, the waiting period may be only 60 or 90 days.

The monthly income payment is usually some percentage, such as 60 percent, of the worker's most recent base wage, subject to some maximum dollar amount. Benefits are usually reduced by any Old-Age, Survivor, Disability, and Health Insurance, workers' compensation, other public programs, or private pension benefits. For example, a plan may state that the benefit is 60 percent of the worker's prior earnings less the worker's OASDI benefit. Under a second plan the benefit may be 70 percent of the worker's prior earnings less the worker's and his or her dependents' OASDI benefits. A third example is 50 percent of the worker's prior earnings but no more than 70 percent of the prior earnings less the worker's and dependents' OASDI benefits.

Because the OASDI definition of total disability—inability to engage in any substantially gainful activity—tends to be more restrictive than LTD definitions, many disabled workers would receive LTD benefits without any OASDI offset.

Some LTD plans provide for periodic adjustments in the benefits being paid to disabled workers as price levels change. The adjustment is usually limited to 3 percent with the original benefit being the minimum benefit paid. A more common approach ignores the automatic cost of living increase in OASDI benefits in determining the OASDI offset to LTD benefits.

Another feature of some LTD plans is a pension accrual benefit that either continues contributions to the firm's pension plan on behalf of the disabled employee or supplements the employee's pension after he or she reaches retirement age.

The rates for LTD coverage depend primarily upon the age and sex composition of the group. Experience rating and retrospective rate adjustments also affect the rates.

Disability Provisions in Group Life Insurance Plans

Most group life insurance contracts being issued today waive future premiums for a totally and permanently disabled employee. Some provide for the payment of the face amount if the employee either dies or becomes totally and permanently disabled. A one-year waiver of premiums, called an "extended death benefit," also is found in some contracts.

Disability Provisions in Pension Plans

Pension plans, described in Chapter 22, have early retirement and withdrawal benefits that are available to totally and permanently disabled persons as well as to others, but the use of these options reduces or eliminates the retirement benefit. Sometimes early retirement is possible only if the employee is totally and permanently disabled. Another approach in such cases is to liberalize the vesting conditions described on pages 446–447. The most liberal benefits, found in few plans, provide for the waiver of future contributions toward the pension plan, the payment of a total and permanent disability income, or both.

Sick-Leave Plans

Sick-leave plans are underwritten exclusively by the employer. These plans usually continue the wages or salary of the disabled worker in full for a specified period, which may be graduated by length of service. Under most plans, sick leave is not cumulative. Many sick-leave plans supplement in some way an insured program providing benefits in case of temporary disability, e.g., by payments during the first two weeks, after which the insurance program takes over. Some workers collecting temporary disability insurance or workers' compensation benefits receive additional amounts under the sick-leave plan.

The sick-leave risk is retained because the loss can be predicted with a fair degree of accuracy, the loss severity is small, and employees, many claim, are less likely to feign illness if they are accountable to their employer. In addition, insurers are reluctant to provide benefits equal to the full wage. Sick-leave payments are usually made out of current operating income.

MEDICAL EXPENSE INSURANCE

Group medical expense insurance is underwritten by commercial insurers, by Blue Cross and Blue Shield associations, or by independent plans.

Commercial Insurance Plans

Group medical expense insurance plans underwritten by commercial insurers, usually the stock or mutual insurers described in Chapter 26, cover about half of the employees with this form of protection. Previous references to insurers in this book did not distinguish between commercial insurers and other private insurers because the commercial insurers so dominate most other lines of insurance.

The "commercial" label is not a satisfactory way to distinguish these insurers from other medical expense insurers, but this terminology is widely accepted and no better term has been suggested. This common practice will be followed here but it should be noted that if "commercial" implies aggressive solicitation of insureds, Blue Cross Blue Shield and some independent plans also try hard to expand their membership. If "commercial" implies a profit-seeking objective, mutual insurers, which are owned by their policyholders, should not be considered commercial insurers. Some independent plans, on the other hand, are profit-making ventures.

The medical expense plans underwritten by commercial insurers fall into three categories: (1) group hospital, surgical, medical, and dental insurance, (2) group major medical expense insurance, and (3) health maintenance organization (HMO) care.

Group Hospital, Surgical, Medical, and Dental Insurance   Group hospital, surgical, medical, and dental expense insurance policies provide basic protection against most illnesses as opposed to major medical expense insurance, which is designed to cover only financially serious illnesses. Such contracts typically include hospital, surgical, and medical expense insurance. Dental insurance, usually written under a separate contract, is becoming more common.

Group hospital insurance commonly pays daily room-and-board charges up to some specified dollar amount for hospital confinement up to some specified number of days such as 70 or 120. Some policies pay the daily room-and-board limit even if the insured pays less. Many, if not most, commercial insurers now also write insurance covering the cost of a semiprivate room, regardless of the actual charges. This third approach resembles the service benefits provided by Blue Cross associations.

Group hospital policies also cover other hospital expenses such as operating-room charges. Often these expenses are covered up to some multiple of the daily room-and-board limit, but many policies cover all these expenses. Others pay all these other expenses up to some multiple of the daily room-and-board allowance plus some fraction of the expenses in excess of this amount.

Posthospitalization nursing home services are included under an increasing number of plans.

Not covered under a typical plan are treatment in a government hospital unless charges are made for reasons other than the presence of insurance, workers' compensation injuries or diseases, self-inflicted injuries, or injuries caused by war. Alcoholism, drug addiction, and mental disorders are sometimes excluded but usually some limited coverage is provided. Some states require such coverage.

Group surgical expense insurance pays the cost of stated surgical operations up to limits stated in a schedule.

Group medical expense insurance covers doctors' nonsurgical care. This care may be covered no matter where it is provided or be limited to inhospital care.

Group dental insurance generally covers most types of diagnostic, preventive, and restorative dental care. The insurer typically agrees to pay 50 to 80 percent of the expenses in excess of some small deductible up to some maximum limit. The benefits for preventive care are usually more generous than those for restorative care. For example, the insurer may pay a larger percent of charges for preventive care.

Other group benefits such as vision care and prescription drugs have become more common in recent years.

Dependents, including the employee's spouse and children up to some age such as 19, or if attending school, 22, may be insured under each of these plans. These dependents usually receive the same benefits as the employee.

A common feature of these group coverages is a coordination-of-benefits provision under which (1) individuals covered under two or more group contracts (say, a working spouse) cannot receive combined benefits in excess of the expenses covered at least in part under any of the contracts involved, and (2) the order in which the insurers involved will pay benefits is established. For example, a plan covering a person as an employee will pay before a plan covering the same person as a dependent. To illustrate how this provision applies, assume that a woman is covered as an employee under one group contract and as a dependent under a second. She incurs $2,000 in hospital expenses and $1,000 in surgical fees. If it were the only contract, the first contract would pay $1,500 toward the hospital expenses and $800 toward the surgical fees. Because of the coordination-of-benefits provision the first policy pays $1,500 + $800 = $2,300. The second policy pays $3,000 − $2,300 = $700.

Under most plans, employees terminating their employment can replace their group coverage with an individual contract. The benefits under this individual contract are almost always more limited than the group coverage. Some states require insurers to provide such conversion rights. At least one state requires insurers to offer to continue the group coverage for a specific number of months or, if earlier, until the employee is reemployed.

The premiums charged initially for these benefits depend upon the size of the group and its sex, age, and geographical composition. Later, except when the group includes only a few employees, these initial premiums are adjusted to reflect the actual experience of the group. To add dependents the insurer may charge a single rate, regardless of the number; one rate for one dependent and another for two or more dependents; or one rate for a spouse, another for children only, and a third for both spouse and children.

Group Major Medical Expense Insurance   Group major medical expense insurance provides protection against financially catastrophic illnesses. This insurance usually supplements a group hospital, surgical, or medical expense plan, but sometimes, as comprehensive insurance, it combines basic and major medical expense protection.

Supplementary major medical expense insurance usually has the following characteristics:

1 All types of medical expenses are covered on a blanket basis. The plan does not distinguish between a dollar of surgical fees and a dollar of hospital charges.

2 Medical expenses are covered once they exceed a specified deductible within a stated period such as three months. Under a ''corridor'' deductible, the most common approach, the major medical expense insurance covers expenses in excess of the basic plan benefits plus some corridor amount, typically $100.

A separate deductible usually applies to each separate illness, but only one deductible is applied if two or more members of the same family are injured in a common accident. If no treatment is rendered or recommended for an illness for a specified period such as six months, that illness is assumed to have terminated and a new deductible is applied to the next expenses incurred.

Instead of applying to each illness the deductible sometimes applies to all expenses incurred by an individual or family within a specified time period with a new deductible applicable to each period.

3 In order to discourage overutilization of services by the insured and overcharging by the persons rendering the services, the insurer usually promises to pay only 75 to 80 percent of the charges in excess of the deductible. The 20 to 25 percent borne by the insured is called the "participation" (and sometimes the "coinsurance") percentage. Some plans pay 100 percent of the expenses but place internal limits on the hospital daily room-and-board charges, surgical fees, and certain other services. Under an increasing number of plans the insurer pays 75 to 80 percent of the expenses above the deductible up to some specified amount such as $5,000 and 100 percent in excess of that amount up to the maximum limit.

4 The maximum insurance payment is some large amount such as $500,000 or $1 million. A few plans provide unlimited benefits.

The maximum payment may apply to each illness or to each person over his or her lifetime. If a member of a plan with a lifetime limit receives benefits, he or she can usually have the maximum benefit restored to its original amount by proving insurability or by not receiving any benefits for more than a stated period.

5 Typical exclusions are workers' compensation cases, treatment in a government hospital for which no charge would ordinarily be made, self-inflicted or war-caused injuries, cosmetic or plastic surgery except to correct defects caused by an accidental injury, or ordinary vision care and dental care except that occasioned by accidental damage to natural teeth. Some plans provide dental insurance by removing the dental care exclusion.

Treatment for mental illness is almost always covered but is usually subject to some special restrictions. For example, the treatment may have to be rendered in a general hospital or may be subject to some lower policy limits. Drug addiction and alcoholism treatments are being covered in an increasing number of plans, usually on a restricted basis.

To illustrate how such a plan might work, assume a corridor deductible of the basic benefits plus $100, a 20 percent participation, and a $500,000 maximum. If the basic benefits are $39,900, the major medical insurer will pay as follows:

Total expenses	Major medical expense insurance payment
10,000	$0
50,000	.80 ($50,000 − $39,900 − $100) = $8,000
100,000	.80 ($100,000 − $39,900 − $100) = $48,000
500,000	.80 ($500,000 − $39,900 − $100) = $368,000
750,000	0.80 ($750,000 − $39,900 − $100) = $568,000 but $500,000 maximum.

Comprehensive major medical expense insurance, the less common form of major medical expense insurance, provides some basic protection and protection against major illnesses in one package. Comprehensive plans can be divided roughly into two categories. Under the first category the insurer pays 75 to 80 percent of the expenses in excess of some small deductible, say, $100, up to some high maximum dollar limit. Under the second category the insurer pays hospital and surgical expenses up to, say,

$1,000, without any deductible. The insurer pays 75 to 80 percent of (1) the hospital and surgical expenses in excess of $1,000, and (2) other medical expenses in excess of, say, a $100 deductible. Under many current plans the insurer's share rises to 100 percent on expenses in excess of a certain amount.

Health Maintenance Organization Care The newest development in commercial insurance plans is a concept developed by the independent plans to be described later. Under this approach the commercial insurer makes available a health maintenance organization (HMO) option under its group plan. An HMO provides comprehensive health care in return for a prenegotiated lump-sum or periodic payment for this care. Most HMOs are closed panel or prepaid group practice plans whose salaried physicians and other professionals provide the prescribed services. Some HMOs are associations of professionals with individual practices. The insurer may assume various roles in the development and operation of affiliated HMOs. For example, the insurer may provide financial support by acquiring an ownership interest, lending money, or agreeing to share in operating losses. It may also provide marketing services. Through its regular insurance offerings it may provide out-of-area emergency coverage or other protection not provided by the HMO.

Although the concept originated in 1929, in 1970 there were still only 25 HMOs in the United States. Organized medicine opposed or discouraged group practice plans and many states passed laws that made it impossible or extremely difficult to develop such plans. This opposition declined in the 1950s and 1960s, but most people were still unfamiliar with the concept and reluctant to abandon the fee-for-service solo-physician approach with which they were more familiar. Rapidly rising medical costs in the late 1960s caused many government officials to favor HMOs as a form of cost control. HMOs were encouraged under most national medical expense insurance proposals. By the close of 1982 about 269 such plans existed, of which many were affiliated with commercial insurers.

Some areas of the country have witnessed a much wider acceptance of HMOs than have others. The Health Maintenance Organization Act of 1973 stimulated their growth in two ways. First, the act authorized grants and loans to develop new public and nonprofit HMOs and expand old ones that meet certain requirements. For example, to be certified, the plan must provide certain basic health services. If it has provided comprehensive health services for at least five years or has an enrollment of at least 50,000, it must have annual open enrollment periods unless it developed a deficit in its most recent fiscal year. Finally, 48 months after qualification it must charge all individuals or families the same fees under a "community rating" system. Certified profit HMOs are eligible only for loan guarantees. Second, the federal law supersedes state laws that may impede the development of certified HMOs. Third, if there is a certified HMO in the area that has not closed its enrollment, employers of 25 or more persons must offer their employees the option of joining an HMO.[9]

---

[9] Because of the original comprehensive benefit, open enrollment, and community rating requirements imposed on certified HMOs, many were not expected to seek certification. The reason was that they might be placed at a severe cost disadvantage compared with other HMOs or more traditional plans. "HMOs: Are They the Answer to Your Medical Needs?" *Consumer Reports* (October, 1974), pp. 756–762, especially p. 760. Amendments in 1976 reduced the benefits that had to be offered and relaxed the open enrollment and community rating requirements to those described in the text.

Advantages alleged for HMOs include the following: (1) By joining an HMO, the subscriber obtains one-stop health care. He or she is assigned to a primary-care physician such as a general practitioner or pediatrician who refers the subscriber to specialists when necessary. Usually the HMO houses a team of doctors, nurses, laboratory technicians, and administrative staff in a single building. Treatment rooms for minor surgery may be provided or, in many cases, complete hospital facilities.[10] (2) HMOs require little or no paper work on the part of the patient other than the information normally required by health providers. (3) Because HMOs provide service benefits instead of cash benefits, their subscribers are protected against any increase in the cost of these services during the coverage period. (4) HMOs are efficient, cost-conscious operations. Because these organizations provide services for a fixed fee, they have an incentive not to render unnecessary services. The salaried physicians employed by the plan share this incentive, and these physicians, nurses, and other staff are subject to some control by HMO management. The comprehensiveness of the services rendered at a single location enables the plan to utilize its facilities, equipment, and staff in a most efficient manner. Finally, probably because HMO plans provide outpatient and preventive care, HMO subscribers have, according to many studies, lower hospital utilization rates and inpatient surgical procedure rates than members of other plans.

Critics argue that (1) HMOs may have an incentive to provide too few services, (2) subscribers must use the plan's doctors and facilities, which in some cases are quite limited in number or of low quality, (3) the medical care may be too impersonal, (4) some subscribers overutilize the plan services at the expense of others, and (5) many plans provide no out-of-area coverage. Supporters downplay the importance of these arguments.

Blue Cross and Blue Shield Plans

Medical expense plans underwritten by Blue Cross or Blue Shield associations cover almost as many employees as commercial group insurance plans.

Blue Cross Plans A Blue Cross association is a local nonprofit hospital care expense prepayment association[11] that belongs to a nationwide federation called the Blue Cross Association (now part of the Blue Cross and Blue Shield Association). Subject to some general membership standards, each Blue Cross association is essentially an independent operation and the exclusive agency within a given area. The associations were organized originally by the member hospitals in each area, but the public and the medical profession are also usually represented on each board of directors.

Some states have more than one Blue Cross plan. Many Blue Cross plans are part of a merged Blue Cross and Blue Shield organization. All Blue Cross and Blue Shield

[10] HMOs that do not own or contract hospital services usually arrange traditional hospital insurance for their subscribers. Out-of-area benefits are also provided in this fashion.

[11] The association is nonprofit because no dividends are paid to the controlling hospitals. Profits are supposed to be used to reduce rates or improve contracts in the future. The hospitals do benefit from the plans indirectly.

Plans are supposed to be merged corporations by 1985. The goal is also no more than one Blue Cross and Blue Shield corporation per state.

Each association contracts with its subscribers and with its member hospitals. Unlike commercial insurers Blue Cross associations issue a separate contract, not just a certificate to each member of an insured group. There is no one subscriber or member-hospital contract form. The contracts differ among the associations, and in addition, many associations offer more than one subscriber contract.

Despite such diversity, a summarization is useful. The most popular subscriber contract (and the ideal one from the viewpoint of the associations) provides for a stated period, such as 70, 180, or 365 days, full coverage of (1) room-and-board costs, usually on a semiprivate basis, and (2) charges for a long list of hospital extras if these services are provided by a member hospital in the plan area.

This contract is called a "service contract" because it provides the benefits prescribed, regardless of the actual dollar charges by the member hospital, and because the association pays the hospital directly. Commercial insurers generally reimburse the insured up to stated dollar limits for amounts the insured pays the hospital. As stated earlier, however, most commercial insurers also now write contracts that cover the services rendered regardless of the actual charges. The insured may also be able to assign his or her insurance benefits to the hospital. HMOs, like this Blue Cross plan, provide service benefits, but under the group practice approach the services must be provided by the HMO staff.

If a subscriber is hospitalized in a nonmember hospital, which is not common because over 90 percent of the hospital beds are in member hospitals, the plan usually provides a per diem amount that is commonly less liberal than the cash equivalent of the service benefits. Finally, if the subscriber is hospitalized in a member hospital in a different plan area, an Interplan Service Benefit Bank arrangement usually makes it possible for the member to receive the same benefit.

When a person moves into a new area, an Interplan Transfer Agreement enables that person to maintain continuous coverage.

Many plans cover care in a nursing home following hospitalization. They also cover outpatient x-ray and laboratory examinations and x-ray or radiation therapy. Otherwise outpatient care is usually limited to accident victims.

The most common and the most important variation from this typical contract covers room-and-board costs up to a specified daily allowance. Other common variations are dollar limitations on some of the hospital extras, small deductibles, and partial benefits for an additional specified period.

Common exclusions are workers' compensation cases, cases for which hospitalization is provided by law, and hospitalization primarily for diagnostic studies and rest cures. Although some plans provide full benefits for services rendered in a general hospital, only limited benefits are usually provided for nervous and mental diseases, alcoholism, and drug addiction. As noted earlier, some states require such coverage. Preexisting conditions are sometimes excluded entirely or during a waiting period of 6 to 24 months.

Dependents may be covered under the contract, the coverage for children usually commencing at birth and continuing to age 19, or, if the child is attending school, to age 22.

The contracts between the associations and the member hospitals are primarily concerned with the method of determining the payment for services rendered to subscribers. Although the payment may be (1) a straight per diem (based on average charges) for each day of care, or (2) all or part of the actual hospital bill, the usual procedure is to base the payment upon cost statements prepared by the hospital. Some plans have used average cost statements instead of individual cost statements in order to encourage efficient hospital administration. Costs are interpreted liberally to include obsolescence and depreciation, interest, and contingency allowances, but the Blue Cross association usually pays less than the charges to nonmembers. This differential has been justified on the ground that (1) billing costs are low, (2) there is no collection problem with Blue Cross subscribers, and (3) hospitals are encouraged to control costs. Because the payments to the hospitals under these contracts will no doubt be influenced by the financial condition of the association, the member hospitals are in fact, if not in name, the ultimate insurers. Under some plans, the hospitals specifically guarantee the benefits.

At least one BCBS plan now uses a different approach. Under its most popular contract it states that the subscriber will receive service benefits only if he or she is treated in a hospital that has agreed to accept a specified amount from the plan for that treatment. Otherwise the patient must pay the hospital the difference between the actual charges and the specified payment.

A coordination-of-benefits provision, described earlier in this chapter, is a common feature of Blue Cross plans. The association may also have subrogation rights.

Employees terminating their employment can convert their group protection to individual coverage. The individual coverage, however, tends to be somewhat more limited and relatively more costly.

The premium structure for Blue Cross plans includes one rate for subscribers and either one rate for dependents, regardless of the number, or two dependent rates—one for a spouse only and the other for a spouse and children. Although philosophically Blue Cross associations favor community rating—the same rates for all groups—competition with commercial insurers has forced most associations to consider the actual experience of groups in excess of a certain size.

Blue Cross associations, often joined by the local Blue Shield association, also underwrite supplementary major medical and comprehensive extended benefit plans. These plans may extend the basic contract to cover more days of hospitalization or pay 80 percent of the hospital charges, physicians' fees, and other expenses incurred in excess of some corridor deductible. Once the expenses exceed a specified amount Blue Cross's share may rise from 80 percent to 100 percent.

To a greater degree than commercial insurers, but much less than independent plans, Blue Cross associations, sometimes in cooperation with a Blue Shield association, have made available an HMO option under their group plans.

Blue Shield Plans   A Blue Shield association is a local nonprofit surgical and nonsurgical physician's care expense prepayment association that belongs to a nationwide federation called the Blue Shield Association (now part of the Blue Cross and Blue Shield Association). The locally autonomous Blue Shield associations were organized originally by local medical societies, but the boards of directors commonly include some nondoctors. As noted in the discussion of Blue Cross plans, all Blue Shield plans should be merged shortly with a Blue Cross plan and each state should have at most one Blue Cross and Blue Shield Association.

All Blue Shield contracts provide surgical benefits; most cover charges for inhospital nonsurgical physician's care; and some include benefits applying as well to home and office calls by a doctor. Under their "full service" contract the association pays all doctors their "usual, customary, and reasonable" charges. As long as the doctor charges the patient the same amount as others are charged for the same service and as long as the doctor's charge is not unreasonably high relative to the charges made by other doctors in the area for the same service, the plan will pay the entire charge. Participating physicians agree to accept the Blue Shield benefit as full payment for their services. Nonparticipating physicians who charge more than the Blue Shield payment may collect the full amount of their bill from the patient who will in turn collect the Blue Shield benefit directly from the association.

If the subscriber is treated by a participating physician in a different area, the full benefits are payable, and although no formal promise is made, the participating physician usually accepts the benefits as full payment for patients who would be entitled to service benefits at home.

Dependents may be covered under the same terms as under Blue Cross contracts.

The exclusions and limitations in Blue Shield contracts are similar to those in Blue Cross contracts.

The associations pay the participating physicians the allowances in the contracts, but the physicians would no doubt accept some modification of these payments if the Blue Shield association encountered financial difficulties. Most of the plans in fact are specifically underwritten by the participating physicians.

Like Blue Cross associations, Blue Shield plans grant terminating employees conversion rights.

The Blue Shield rate structure closely resembles that of Blue Cross associations.

Blue Shield associations, like Blue Cross associations and often in conjunction with them, have extended major medical expense insurance benefits to their subscribers. They have also cooperated with Blue Cross associations in their HMO projects.

Independent Plans

Independent plans include a wide variety of insurers not classified as commercial insurers, Blue Cross associations, or Blue Shield associations. Most of the persons covered under independent plans belong to industrial plans that serve defined groups of employees or union members. The most popular of these industrial plans are welfare funds covering members of a single union and jointly managed by employers and employee representatives.

Industrial plans covering the employees of a single employer are much less important. These plans are more properly regarded by the employer as retention instead of insurance, the employer's motive usually being a desire to avoid the expense loading of the insurer and to administer his or her own claims. In addition, many employers provide limited plant facilities, which consist usually of the services of an industrial nurse or first-aid attendant and of a full-time or part-time physician. The purpose of these facilities is generally to administer preliminary and other physical examinations, to render emergency treatment, and less commonly, to consult with the employees with respect to temporary minor illnesses. As a rule, the services and the facilities increase as the size of the firm increases.

The leading nonindustrial independent plans include plans sponsored by a community or a private group clinic. Community plans, which are open to most individuals or groups in the community, including employee groups, are usually sponsored by a local consumer organization and operated on a nonprofit basis. Private group-clinic plans are prepayment plans operating under the direction, control, and ownership of a group of doctors or dentists depending upon the services rendered. Dental society plans are nonprofit prepayment dental care plans resembling Blue Shield plans. Examples of large nonindustrial community plans are the Health Insurance Plan of Greater New York and the six Kaiser Foundation Health Plans. The Ross-Loos Medical Clinic on the West Coast is the largest private group clinic. The Delta Dental Plan of Minnesota illustrates the dental society approach.

The benefits provided under these plans vary greatly, but most of them provide fairly complete protection for their members against most types of medical expenses, including those for preventive care. Physical examinations and immunization shots, for example, are often included among the benefits. Over half of the persons covered under independent plans are covered under programs that provide at least one type of medical service through salaried physicians, nurses, and others or through contractual arrangements with community hospitals or clinics. These group-practice arrangements were the original HMOs and still dominate that field. Thus independent plans have exerted a much greater influence on current trends in medical expense insurance than their share of the enrollment would suggest.

Cost Containment

Because the cost of medical care has increased much more than the Consumer Price Index, risk managers, insurers, and the government have been investigating ways to contain these expenses. The government has considered reducing the tax incentives for the employer to provide medical expense insurance for employees. Tax-free comprehensive coverage, it is argued, removes or reduces the incentives their employees would otherwise have to control their individual costs. Risk managers have experimented with plans that encourage employees to elect plans with higher deductibles and share some or all of the resulting reductions in plan costs. As noted earlier, HMOs have became more popular in part because, it is believed, they are cost-effective operations. Other cost containment measures include wellness programs, hospital staff utilization review committees; broadening benefits to include outpatient care such as pre-admission testing, home care, and skilled nursing facility care; second opinion benefits or requirements; noncoverage of routine diagnostic tests or certain surgical procedures unless specifically ordered and justified by the attending physician; and preferred-provider plans. Under a preferred-provider plan patients typically receive better benefits if they go to a hospital or doctor with whom the plan has negotiated reduced payments for its members.

MINIMUM PREMIUM AND OTHER SPECIAL PRICING METHODS

For a variety of reasons, insurers have developed several rating methods applicable to group life, disability, and medical expense insurance plans that convert the plan into a quasi-retention program. These methods may either replace or supplement standard experience rating and retroactive premium adjustments.[12] Risk managers use these newer rating plans: (1) to lower administrative costs, (2) to reduce the opportunity cost of advance premium payments, and (3) to tighten claims administration. On the other hand, some of these plans require the business to assume more risks.

For example, under a minimum premium plan, the insurer becomes liable for claims only after the annual, monthly, or quarterly claims total more than, say, 90 percent of the premium normally charged for that period. The insurer may or may not administer the claims up to that threshold, but in either event, the claims are the responsibility of the employer and are paid out of the employer's funds. The premium charged is 10 percent of the normal premium which the insurer uses to pay expenses, absorb losses in excess of the threshold, and earn a profit. The advantage to the insured is that the state premium tax levied on premiums is less, the insured retains the use of substantial moneys until they are needed to pay claims, and the insured is motivated to and can become more deeply involved in claim administration. The business is still protected against losses in excess of the threshold.

A second approach is to create a claims stabilization reserve that is owned by the policyholder and is credited each year with the amount by which premiums paid that year exceed losses and an agreed expense and profit loading. If the premium is less than the losses and the expense loading, the claims stabilization reserve is reduced by the deficiency. The insurer pays interest on the balance in the claims stabilization reserve. This interest may be paid directly to the policyholder or credited to the reserve. If the balance exceeds a specified amount, the excess is returned to the policyholder as a dividend. The entire reserve is returned to the policyholder if either the insurer or the insured cancels the contract.

Because of the large reserves that must be established in many employee benefit plans, especially group long-term disability plans, to cover payments to be made in the future, many insureds now pay the policyholder interest on these reserves. Alternatively, the insurer may be responsible only for the claims paid each year and charge a premium based only on these paid claims. The employer takes the risks associated with future payments on events that have already occurred.

A final example is an Administrative Services Only agreement under which the insurer in effect is merely a servicing agent for a retention program.

SUPPLEMENTARY UNEMPLOYMENT COMPENSATION

Unemployment compensation pays only a fraction of the wage loss, subject to a maximum weekly benefit. (These social unemployment insurance benefits were described in Chapter 20.) During the 1950s several major unions negotiated private

---

[12] For some additional methods see J. S. Rosenbloom and G. V. Hallman, *Employee Benefit Planning* (Englewood Cliffs, N.J.: Prentice-Hall, Inc., 1981), pp. 393–399.

supplementary unemployment plans for their members. No major SUB plans have been adopted since 1956, but unions continue to express considerable interest in these benefits.

Supplementary unemployment compensation plans vary greatly in detail, but the purpose generally is to provide a combined weekly basic and supplementary unemployment compensation benefit equal to a specified percentage (e.g., 95 percent under the United Automobile Workers plan reduced by a flat dollar amount per week because of the elimination of work-related expenses) of the employee's take-home pay, excluding compensation for overtime. The duration of the benefits depends principally upon how long the employee has worked for the firm. The payments are generally made out of trust funds financed by fixed employer contributions per employee. The plans are administered jointly by the employer and the union.

A second approach to private unemployment compensation is dismissal compensation or severance pay plans. Payments are made under these plans for a permanent severing of the present employment relationship. The employee need not remain unemployed. The benefits usually depend upon the duration of employment and the wage or salary and are in most cases payable in a lump sum. Some plans, for example, provide one week's pay for each year of service. Employers usually meet these payments out of current income, but some create an advance fund for these benefits. Usually the employer is solely responsible for the active administration of the plan, but a union often reserves the right to protest the administrative decisions of the employer.

SOME KEY CONCEPTS

Employee benefit plan   A plan established by an employer (usually) to help employees deal with the financial effects of personnel losses on their families. The concept has been extended recently to include plans dealing with some family property and liability exposures.

Individual insurance   Insurance arranged to meet individual needs that is individually underwritten and individually priced.

Group insurance   Insurance covering the members of a group such as the employees of a single employer. The benefits are not tailor-made to the needs of each member. If the group is acceptable to the insurer, all members are covered.

Yearly renewable term insurance   The type of protection usually provided under group life insurance plans. The insurer promises to pay the face amount if the insured dies; each year the promise is renewed. The plan does not provide any cash values.

Long-term disability insurance   Insurance that typically pays a disabled person a specified amount beginning after a stated number of weeks or months have elapsed and continuing generally until age 65.

Service benefits   Benefits consisting of service by a hospital, doctor, or other medical facility that does not depend upon the dollar charges for those benefits. To be distinguished from cash benefits that provide specified dollar amounts to pay part or all of the charges actually incurred.

Major medical expense insurance   Insurance designed to cover financially catastrophic illnesses. Supplements separate basic medical expense insurance or is part of comprehensive insurance which combines basic and major medical expense insurance.

Health Maintenance Organization   An organization that for an annual fee provides medical service benefits, usually through its own facilities and professional staff.

REVIEW QUESTIONS

1 Compare the following benefits provided by employee benefit plans with respect to the proportion of wage and salary workers covered.

   a Death benefits

   b Short-term disability

   c Long-term disability benefits

   d Medical expense benefits

   e Dental expense benefits

   f Retirement benefits

2 Under group insurance, group selection is substituted for individual selection.

   a What is group selection? How does it work?

   b In what respects is group insurance more attractive than individual insurance? less attractive?

3 An employer is concerned about purchasing group yearly renewable term insurance because this employer fears that as each employee grows older, the premium will increase until finally it becomes prohibitive. How would you advise the employer?

4 Unions have pressed for noncontributory plans in recent years.

   a What is a noncontributory group life insurance plan?

   b What are the advantages and disadvantages of a noncontributory plan?

5 An employee, aged 45, who has worked for a firm for 20 years, resigns to take a job with a new firm in another state. The employee has been covered during the past 15 years under a $20,000 group life insurance plan. What rights does the employee possess if the group life insurance plan provided:

   a Term insurance

   b Nonterm insurance

6 How would you answer question 5 if the employee was retiring at age 65 instead of resigning?

7 Describe the benefits provided by survivor income benefit insurance.

8 Why are employee benefit plans providing death benefits seldom self-insured?

9 What tax benefits does the employee receive under employer-financed disability income and medical expense insurance plans?

10 Comment briefly upon the following characteristics of group temporary disability income insurance:

   a Duration of benefits

   b Waiting period

   c Weekly benefit amount

   d Conversion rights

11 Each of two firms employs the same number of employees and provides the same group life insurance and temporary disability insurance. One firm, however, pays a higher group life insurance premium and a lower group temporary disability insurance premium than the other. How would you explain these differences?

12 A worker earning $3,000 a month is totally disabled for one year. What benefit would the worker receive under a long-term disability insurance plan?

13 Compare sick-leave plans with temporary disability insurance plans with respect to:

   a The wages replaced

   b The duration of the benefit

   c Whether the benefit is insured

14 **a** Describe briefly the protection provided under group hospital, medical, surgical, and dental insurance.

b Why is this insurance often called first-dollar insurance?

15 a What purpose is served by a coordination-of-benefits provision?

b Assume a person is covered as an employee under one group contract and as a dependent under another. This person incurs $10,000 in hospital expenses and $4,000 in surgical fees. If it were the only contract, the first plan would pay $6,000 toward the hospital expenses and $2,000 toward the surgical fees. How much will each contract pay?

16 The Beta Corporation has a basic medical expense program to which it has added supplementary major medical insurance with a $100 corridor deductible, a 20 percent participation percentage, and a $500,000 maximum. If the basic benefits are $10,000 how much will the major medical expense insurer pay toward each of the following total expenses?

a $8,000

b $50,000

c $250,000

d $500,000

e $1,000,000

17 a What is a health maintenance organization?

b What advantages are claimed for HMOs?

c On what grounds have HMOs been criticized?

d What is the connection between commercial group insurance plans and HMOs?

18 Explain the relationship between Blue Cross and Blue Shield associations.

19 a Blue Cross benefits have been distinguished from those typically provided by commercial insurers on the ground that they provide prepaid service benefits rather than cash benefits. Explain.

b How do the service benefits of an HMO differ from those typically provided by Blue Cross?

20 Compare Blue Cross service benefits with those provided by Blue Shield plans.

21 Do Blue Cross associations pay hospitals the amounts they would charge noninsured patients? Explain.

22 Describe briefly the different types of independent plans.

23 How important are HMOs among independent plans? Explain.

24 Recent high unemployment rates have focused attention on the rights of terminated employees to continue their group medical expense protection. What are these rights?

25 Describe briefly the nature and purpose of

a Minimum premium plans

b Administrative Services Only agreements

c Claims stabilization reserves

26 Supplementary unemployment benefits have also received considerable publicity in recent years. What benefits do these plans provide?

SUGGESTIONS FOR ADDITIONAL READING

Contemporary Benefit Issues and Administration (Brookfield, Wis.: International Foundation of Employee Benefit Plans, 1979).

Gregg, D. W., and Lucas, V. B. (eds.): *Life and Health Insurance Handbook* (3d ed., Homewood, Ill.: Richard D. Irwin, Inc., 1973), Part V.

How Major Industrial Corporations View Employee Benefits Programs (New York: Market Research Department, *Fortune*, 1974).

Ilse, Louise W.: *Group Insurance and Employee Retirement Plans* (Englewood Cliffs, N.J.: Prentice-Hall, Inc., 1953).

Life, Health and Other Group Benefit Programs (Brookfield, Wis.: International Foundation of Employee Benefit Plans, 1978).

Mehr, R. I., and S. G. Gustavson: *Life Insurance: Theory and Practice,* (3d ed., Dallas: Business Publications, Inc., 1984), chaps. 13–15.

————, and B. A. Hedges: *Risk Management: Concepts and Applications* (Homewood, Ill.: Richard D. Irwin, Inc., 1984), chaps. 11, 12, 20, and 21.

Rosenbloom, J. S. (ed.): *The Handbook of Employee Benefits* (Homewood, Ill.: Dow Jones-Irwin, 1984).

————, and G. V. Hallman: *Employee Benefit Planning* (2d ed., Englewood Cliffs, N.J.: Prentice-Hall, Inc., 1984).

Spencer, B.: *Group Benefits in a Changing Society* (rev. ed., Chicago: Charles D. Spencer & Associates, Inc., 1981).

CHAPTER 22

EMPLOYEE BENEFIT PLANS: II

LEARNING OBJECTIVES

After you have completed this chapter, you should be able to:

1 Distinguish between pensions and profit-sharing plans.
2 Describe and illustrate a defined contribution plan and a defined benefit plan.
3 Tell how ERISA limits the eligibility requirements and maximum benefits that can be included in a pension plan.
4 Explain the leading annuity forms including the one required by ERISA.
5 List the minimum vesting schedules required by ERISA.
6 Describe the tax advantages of a noncontributory pension plan.
7 Explain the minimum pension funding rules and the plan termination insurance established by ERISA.
8 Describe briefly the four major types of insured pension plans and compare the flexibility of each of these four types with that of a self-insured plan.
9 Explain why thrift and savings plans have become more popular since Section 401 (k) plans were introduced.
10 Summarize the present status of group property and liability insurance.
11 Explain and illustrate variable, flexible, or cafeteria benefit plans.

INTRODUCTION

This chapter continues the discussion of employee benefit plans. Four types of benefits will be described: (1) pensions and deferred profit-sharing plans, (2) thrift and savings plans, (3) property and liability insurance, and (4) legal services. A new, increasingly important, approach to packaging employee benefits—variable, "cafeteria," or flexible benefit plans—will also be explained.

PENSIONS AND DEFERRED PROFIT-SHARING PLANS

Employers contribute more money toward pension and deferred profit-sharing plans than to any other type of employee benefit plan. Pension plans provide a retirement income, usually for life, the size of the benefit being generally determined by such factors as service and compensation. Profit-sharing plans, on the other hand, are established by an employer for the purpose of permitting employees to share in the business's profits. For example, the employer may contribute each year to the plan a certain percentage of gross profits, of net profits, or of net profits in excess of some specified amount. Many profit-sharing plans provide for the distribution of these contributions immediately or periodically. Deferred profit-sharing plans, however, generally provide for distribution of the funds credited to a particular employee only upon the occurrence of certain events such as retirement, disability, death, or termination of employment.[1]

As a retirement plan vehicle, deferred profit-sharing plans are at a disadvantage because (1) the profits and consequently the retirement income to be provided by the employer's contributions cannot be predicted with a high degree of certainty; (2) unless the trustee of the fund purchases annuities with the employer's contributions,[2] the plan cannot guarantee a lifetime income; and (3) if the plan is to qualify for certain tax advantages under the Internal Revenue Code, it is impossible to give adequate recognition to service rendered by older employees prior to the establishment of the profit-sharing plan. On the other hand, a profit-sharing plan has many relative advantages. For example, because employees share the firm's profits with the employer, they have a direct interest in the firm's profitability. Deferred profit-sharing plans also have more appeal for many employers than do pension plans because they fear that their long-term obligation under a pension plan may prove to be quite a burden, particularly in years when the firm is not earning large profits. Under deferred profit-sharing plans, their contributions are related to actual profits. Many firms supplement a pension plan with a deferred profit-sharing plan.

Although deferred profit-sharing plans are an important and growing employee benefit, most of the discussion that follows will be devoted to pensions which cover more workers than deferred profit-sharing plans and have certain advantages as a retirement plan vehicle.

In establishing or modifying a pension plan, the risk manager must make certain

---

[1] By year-end 1975, nearly 200,000 deferred profit-sharing plans and about 100,000 cash profit-sharing plans were operating in the United States. For an intensive study of the characteristics of these plans in 38 large businesses, see Bert L. Metzger, *Profit-Sharing in 38 Large Companies*, vols. I and II (Evanston, Ill: Profit-Sharing Research Foundation, 1975). By 1980 more than 14 million workers participated in deferred profit-sharing plans. See "Present Trends in Profit-Sharing Characteristics," *Employee Benefit Plan Review*, Thirty-Fourth Year, no. 9 (March, 1980), p. 14.

[2] The trustee could purchase an immediate annuity at the time the employee retires or deferred annuities during the employee's working career.

crucial decisions. He or she must consider the total impact of the decisions upon the firm's industrial relations, the costs involved, and the tax implications (to be discussed in the section "Source of Funds"). The major decisions to be made involve (1) the eligibility requirements, (2) the retirement benefits, (3) other types of benefits, (4) the source of funds, (5) the actuarial cost method, and (6) the funding agencies.[3] The Employee Retirement Income Security Act (ERISA) of 1974 places some important constraints on these decisions. This act applies to most pension plans except governmental plans, church plans, union plans that do not provide for employer contributions, and certain nonqualified plans including those maintained for a select group of management or highly compensated employees.

Eligibility Requirements

Although pension plans may be designed to cover all employees, normally some eligibility requirements are established. These requirements are commonly higher for pension plans than for other employee benefit plans. Four types of requirements are in common use either singly or in some combination: (1) Employees may be required to have worked for the employer some minimum period. The purpose here is to reduce the administrative costs associated with rapid turnover. (2) A minimum-age requirement may be established in order to reduce turnover costs. Persons above a maximum age may not be permitted to participate because of the high cost of providing them with an adequate pension. (3) Because the Old-Age, Survivors, Disability, and Health Insurance program of the federal government provides benefits based only upon annual earnings up to some specified dollar value, the plan may exclude employees whose earnings are less than that amount. (A more usual procedure today, however, is to include such employees but to pay them a relatively smaller pension.) (4) The type of employment may determine whether the employee is eligible. For example, the plan may be limited to full-time employees, salaried employees, union employees, or the employees of one particular plant.

Under ERISA the maximum service and age eligibility requirement is the later of one year of service or age 25. However, a plan that provides immediate full vesting may require three years of service. Under a plan that defines the benefit at retirement rather than the annual contributions (see pages 443–444) employees hired five years or less before their normal retirement date may be excluded from coverage.

In addition to meeting these coverage requirements, employees must satisfy certain other conditions in order to receive the different types of benefits. These conditions will be described in connection with their respective benefits.

Retirement Benefits

The principal benefit under a pension plan is a lifetime income for the employee after his or her retirement.

---

[3] This chapter concentrates on single-employer pension plans. For a recent discussion of multi-employer plans, see Daniel F. McGinn, *Joint Trust Pension Plans* (Homewood, Ill.: Richard D. Irwin, Inc., 1978).

Qualification Requirements In order to receive the full benefit produced by the benefit formula, an employee must usually have attained a normal retirement age. The plan may also impose a minimum service requirement. Age 65 is the normal retirement age in most plans, but many persons have suggested raising the age limit to 68 or 70 because of the increasing proportion of older persons in our population and their improved health and abilities.

Retirement at some age may be compulsory. If there is no compulsory retirement age, the business must decide which employees it will permit to continue beyond the normal retirement age. This can be a painful and difficult decision. Under a 1978 amendment to the Age Discrimination in Employment Act of 1967, workers cannot be compelled to retire because of age alone prior to age 70.

If a person does not retire at the normal retirement age, the prevailing practice has been to pay the same benefit upon actual retirement that the worker would have received at normal retirement age. The most liberal approach would count the extra service, recognize the wages earned during that service, and adjust the benefit actuarially to recognize the longer accumulation period and shorter payout period. In an internal bulletin, which is subject to change, the federal government has stated that it is not necessary under ADEA to give service credits, to recognize the additional wages earned, or to make actuarial adjustments. The bulletin also permits reductions in group life insurance for workers after a certain age, such as age 65, that can be cost-justified. In other words, the employer can reduce the protection so that the cost of protecting older workers is not less than if they had been younger. Long-term disability benefits can also be reduced to the extent that they are cost-justified. Either the monthly benefit or the duration can be reduced. Medical expense benefits can be reduced but only to the extent that the reduction is offset by Medicare. Because of a 1982 tax law, however, Medicare's payments must be secondary to payments by the employer's plan.

Early retirement is possible under most plans under certain conditions. If the employer's consent is necessary, attainment of age 55 is a common requirement. If the employer's consent is not necessary, a combination age and service requirement is usually found. Sometimes the worker must be totally and permanently disabled, in addition to meeting the other requirements. Early retirement pensions are generally much smaller than normal retirement pensions because fewer contributions have been made, the contributions have been accumulated at interest for a shorter period, and the payout period is much longer. Occasionally, however, a supplement is provided because the worker is totally disabled or because the early retirement is in the interest of the employer.

Benefit Formulas An ideal goal of pension planners is to provide for long-service employees, say those with 30 to 35 years of service, an initial pension that, including OASDI benefits, will enable the worker and his or her family to maintain essentially the same standard of living the first year of retirement as was provided by his or her average annual earnings during the last few years of employment. (Ideally this pension would also be indexed so that following retirement the pension would increase as the cost of living increased.) To satisfy this initial pension objective the pension need not equal those prior earnings. After a person retires, he or she no longer incurs any expenses associated with work. For several reasons taxes on the pension will be less than the taxes on prior earnings (for example, part or all of the OASDI benefit will not be taxed, OASDHI taxes stop, the pension will be less than the earnings, and persons aged 65 or over may be entitled to some special tax credits). Finally, he or she need no longer save for retirement. In a report for the President's Commission on Pension Policy, Preston Bassett estimated the annual pension that would enable a single person or a couple retiring in 1980 with selected pre-retirement earnings to maintain their pre-retirement standard of living, assuming no increases in the cost of living after retirement.[4] Four examples are presented below:

Preretirement earnings	Equivalent standard of living pension	
	Dollar amount	% of preretirement earnings*
Single Person:		
$10,000	$ 7,272	73
$50,000	25,675	51
Couple		
$10,000	7,786	78
$50,000	27,384	55

* Note that the percentage decreases as the prior earnings increase and that the percentage is higher for couples than for single persons.

The ideal goal, therefore, would be a private pension that, added to the OASDHI pension, would provide an income equal to, say, 50–80 percent of the worker's prior earnings. The percentage would vary inversely with the worker's income. As will be explained later, most private pension plans are integrated with OASDHI so that the private plan replacement rate is higher for the higher-paid workers, thus partly offsetting the higher OASDHI replacement rate for the lower-paid workers, as explained in Chapter 20.

Cost and other considerations, however, cause most plans to provide pensions that are smaller than the ideal amount. Furthermore, the benefit formulas are more complex. These formulas can be divided into two major categories: (1) defined contribution or money purchase formulas and (2) defined benefit formulas.

Under a *defined contribution* formula, the benefit is the amount that can be provided by annual contributions expressed as a percentage of the employee's pay. The cost to the employer is known, but the benefits are not. The formula also provides very limited benefits for newly covered older workers and may be more difficult to explain to the participants. The major attractions of this approach to employers are that the cost is fixed and the plan is relatively simple to administer. Both employers and employees benefit from the financial soundness of the operation. To use a term explained on page 397 and again later in this chapter, the plan is always fully funded. Nonprofit

---

[4] Preston C. Bassett, cited in *Coming of Age: Toward a National Retirement Income Policy* (Washington, D.C.: President's Commission on Pension Policy, Feb. 26, 1981), pp. 42–43.

organizations and public bodies tend to have defined contribution plans, but until recently other employers strongly preferred the defined benefit approach, except in connection with deferred profit-sharing plans. As will be explained shortly, however, although defined benefit plans are still much more common among large business employers, defined contribution plans have become relatively more important. In addition small employers often find this approach useful, especially in connection with the Keogh Plans and IRAs discussed in Chapter 25. ERISA limits the maximum annual contribution for any employee under this defined contribution approach to 25 percent of his or her compensation that year or, if less, a specified dollar amount ($30,000 until 1986 when it will be adjusted annually to match increases in the Consumer Price Index). The contributions subject to these limits include the employer's contributions and the smaller of (1) the employee's contributions in excess of 6 percent of salary or (2) one-half of his or her actual contributions.

Under a *defined benefit* formula, the benefits are specified and the contributions are the amount necessary to produce these benefits. Usually the benefit is (1) a specified percentage of the employee's earnings per year of service, (2) a flat dollar amount per year of service, (3) a flat percentage of the employee's earnings, or (4) a flat amount per month. For example, the benefit may be (1) 2 percent of average earnings per year of credited service, (2) $15 per month per year of service, (3) 50 percent of the employee's final earnings, or (4) $600 a month. Under some plans providing flat-percentage or flat-dollar benefits, the employee must have completed some minimum period of service to receive this benefit. For shorter service periods, the benefit is proportionately reduced.

Most defined benefit plans use a formula based upon the employee's length of service and average earnings. The average earnings may be based on the total compensation the employee received during his or her service under the plan, but more commonly it is the average salary during the last three or five years, called the "final average salary." Instead of basing the benefit on the final three or five years, the plan may use the three or five consecutive years of highest compensation. Most retirees, past and future, judge pension plans on the relation between the benefits and their final salaries, not their average career salaries, and final salaries may be substantially higher than career salaries because of promotions or inflation. On the other hand, the employer faces more financing uncertainties under a final pay plan. These uncertainties were intensified in some recent years when salaries increased much more rapidly than expected. For this reason, and because ERISA places more constraints on defined benefit plans than on defined contribution plans, some employers have replaced their defined benefit plan with a defined contribution plan.

ERISA limits the highest annual benefit provided by employer contributions under defined benefit formulas to the lesser of 100 percent of the employee's average compensation in the highest three consecutive years or, if less, a specified amount ($90,000 until 1986, when it will be adjusted annually to match increases in the Consumer Price Index).

Many pension plans are *integrated* with OASDI. For example, the benefit provided by the employer's contributions might be 50 percent of final earnings less 50 percent of the OASDI worker's benefit (not including any dependent's benefit) at the time of retirement. OASDI dependents' benefits and cost of living increase after retirement would not be considered in this calculation. Another approach would be a benefit equal to 30 percent of final earnings in excess of an "integration level" which, in principle, is the earnings subject to OASDI taxes. A closely related approach would be 50 percent of final earnings in excess of the integration level, plus 20 percent of final earnings up to that level. A final example is 0.5 percent per year of final salary up to the integration level, plus 1.5 percent per year of final salary in excess of the integration level. For the plan to qualify for the tax advantages described later in this chapter, the integration must be such that the combined pension and OASDI worker's benefit financed by the employer does not increase as a percent of the salary base as the salary increases. As explained in Chapter 20, OASDI benefits are a higher percent of lower average indexed monthly earnings. Consequently, a private pension plan can provide relatively higher benefits for higher paid persons and still qualify for favorable tax treatment. The limits are determined by a set of Internal Revenue Service regulations.

Annuity Forms Under ERISA, unless the employee elects otherwise, the plan must provide an income for the remainder of the employee's life with at least half of that amount being continued for a surviving spouse who was married to the employee for at least one year prior to the date the payments began. This "joint and survivorship annuity" provides a smaller monthly income for the employee than the normal "straight life annuity" option that would provide a monthly income only during the employee's lifetime. Under this latter alternative, if the employee has contributed to the cost of the pension, provision is made for the return in a single payment or in installments of the excess of the employee's contributions, with or without interest, over the benefits received prior to death.

Other common options, calling for actuarially equivalent benefits, include a life annuity with n years certain (a lifetime income with a guarantee that the payments will be continued for at least n years) and an annuity that provides a larger monthly income until OASDHI benefits become available.

Cost of Living Adjustments Since the post-World War II period the effects of inflation on pension benefits have been a matter of intense concern. Increases in the cost of living during the employee's working career and after his or her retirement can reduce drastically the purchasing power of a pension benefit. Basing the benefit upon the employee's final salary is the most common way to handle increases in the cost of living during his or her earnings career, but this approach does not solve the problem after retirement. A second solution is to allow the monthly benefit to rise and fall with the value of the investments in the pension fund, the changes in which are presumed to correspond roughly with changes in the cost of living. A third solution is ad hoc adjustments. This third solution is the most common approach to making cost of living adjustments for persons already retired. This approach is popular because the employer is not committed to any specific action. Some plans promise to adjust the pension after retirement according the changes in Consumer Price Index, but even though the annual increase is capped at 3 percent or less, this promise is too expensive to be a common approach.

As noted earlier, rapidly rising salaries during some recent years have increased greatly the cost of final pay plans to employers. Plans relating benefits to the performance of the plan's investment portfolio have varied in popularity over time according to the effectiveness of the investment portfolio as a hedge against inflation.

Past-Service Benefits   When a pension plan is installed, it is common practice to give present employees credit for their past service. Past-service credits, however, may be limited to a specified number of years or produce less of a pension than future service.

Other Types of Benefits

Three other types of benefits commonly found in pension plans are (1) death benefits, (2) disability benefits, and (3) withdrawal benefits.

Death Benefits   If the employee dies before retirement, the beneficiaries are entitled to a return of his or her contributions, with or without interest. In addition the plan may provide a lump sum benefit. Sometimes the plan provides a lifetime income, expressed as a percentage of the employee's pension, for widows or widowers of long-service, older employees. Survivor income plans, a newer concept (described in Chapter 21), provide the survivor or survivors of a deceased employee (not just long-term employees) with some percentage of the employee's monthly pay until the survivor dies, reaches a certain age, or marries (remarries if the survivor is the deceased's spouse).

Disability Benefits   Specific total and permanent disability benefits are found in most plans, but usually an employee must have completed several years of service to be eligible for this protection and must have been disabled for a minimum number of months. These benefits usually supplement early retirement or withdrawal benefits, but they may be completely independent of those benefits. Sometimes they waive any future contributions to the pension plan in behalf of the employee.

Withdrawal Benefits and Vesting Provisions   If an employee terminates the employment relationship, that employee is entitled to a return of his or her contributions with interest.[5] Often the employee may elect to receive these contributions as a lifetime income at retirement age. Whether he or she will retain any part of the benefits purchased by the employer's contributions will depend upon the vesting provisions.

ERISA requires that pension plans contain a vesting schedule at least as favorable to the employee as one of the following:

1 100 percent vesting after 10 years of service
2 25 percent vesting after 5 years of service increasing by 5 percent for each of the next 5 years and by 10 percent for each of the next 5 years. Under this schedule initially

---

[5] Under a defined contribution plan that bases the pension on the performance of some common stock portfolio the withdrawing employee may receive less than the amount of his or her contributions.

benefits will vest faster than under schedule 1 but 100 percent vesting will not be achieved until after 15 years of service.

3 50 percent vesting for employees with at least 5 years of service when age and service total 45 (for example, age 40 and 5 years of service, age 36 and 9 years of service, or age 43 and 5 years of service), increasing by 10 percent for each of the next 5 years. However, regardless of age, an employee must achieve 50 percent vesting after 10 years of service, increasing by 10 percent for each of the next 5 years. Consequently the age plus service calculation applies only in five combinations:

Age	Years of service
40 or older	5
39	6
38	7
37	8
36	9

Many plans contain vesting provisions that are more favorable to employees, the most liberal being full immediate vesting. Even these plans, however, usually require the employee to wait until retirement age to receive the vested benefits. During the congressional debates preceding the passage of ERISA some support developed for a portability requirement that would permit withdrawing employees to take their vested benefits with them to their new employers or to a special agency created for this purpose. This portability requirement was not included in the final legislation. However, the act did establish a Social Security Administration clearing house to keep track of benefits that are vested after termination of employment. It also permits employees whose employers consent to a transfer to do so under certain conditions without having to pay taxes on the transfer.

Under the Tax Equity and Fiscal Responsibility Act of 1982 Congress imposed two more stringent minimum vesting provisions on "top-heavy" plans.[6] A pension plan is top heavy if more than 60 percent of the sum of the account balances under a defined benefit plan belong to "key employees" (for example, officers and shareholders with more than a 5 percent interest). The two vesting schedules are (1) 100 percent after three years of service or (2) 20 percent after two years of service, increasing by 20 percent for each of the next four years.

Another requirement imposed by ERISA that is related to the vesting provisions establishes a minimum rate at which the employee must accrue benefits during his or her participation under the plan. The purpose of this requirement is to prohibit small accruals in the early years of participation that would reduce the value of the vesting provisions.

Accrued benefits under defined benefit plans must meet one of three tests:

---

[6] Top-heavy plans are also subject to special limits on includable compensation and must provide minimum benefits for non-key employees.

1 The cumulated accrued benefit must be at least 3 percent per year of final benefit payable to a participant who works from the earliest possible age to normal retirement age or, if earlier, to age 65.

2 Except for amendments the accrual rate for any later year cannot be more than 133 percent of the rate for the current year.

3 The accrued benefit must be a pro rata part of the benefit the participant will receive at normal retirement age.

Source of Funds

Pension plans, like group life and group health insurance plans, may be contributory or noncontributory. The arguments for each approach have been presented in the previous chapter. A noncontributory pension plan, however, may not enable the employee to avoid completely the tax on the employer's contributions; it *may* only reduce or defer that tax, as we shall explain in the next paragraph. This can still be an important advantage.[7]

If the pension plan, contributory or noncontributory, is qualified with the Internal Revenue Service, the employer may deduct contributions as a business expense; the employee need not report these contributions as income *at that time;* and the earnings on the pension funds are tax-exempt. When the employee retires, however, if the plan was noncontributory, he or she must report the periodic pension payments as taxable income. If the plan was contributory, the employee is entitled to a return of his or her contributions tax-free. If the worker would recover these contributions (plus any other "cost basis") in three years or less, the pension payments are not taxable until they exceed the worker's contributions. If the worker would not recover these contributions in three years, a portion of each payment, called the exclusion ratio, is not taxable. For example, if the worker receives a lifetime income without any benefits for survivors, the nontaxable portion is the employee's cost basis divided by the product of the annual pension payment times the employee's life expectancy according to IRS tables. For example, if the cost basis is $6,000, each monthly payment is $100, and the worker's life expectancy is 15 years, the nontaxable portion is $6,000 divided by 12($100) (15) = $18,000. Consequently, one-third of each $100 payment is not taxable; two-thirds is taxable. If the annuity form includes a survivorship benefit, the exclusion ratio is reduced. Because the taxable income may be less than the deductions and exemptions available after retirement, the worker may pay no tax. Usually, however, some of the pension income will be taxed, but at lower tax rates than would have been applied to the employer contributions during the employee's working career.

If the retiring employee receives a lump sum rather than a lifetime income, that portion of the lump sum attributable to pre-1974 service is taxed as a capital gain unless the employee elects the tax rule applicable to later service. The portion attributable to post-1973 service is taxed as ordinary income subject to some special 10-year averaging rules that lower the tax substantially.

---

[7] Even if the tax is merely deferred, the plan provides the employee with the use of the money in the meantime without an interest charge. In other words, he or she has an interest-free loan.

To qualify a plan, a firm must demonstrate, among other things, that the plan is a legally binding arrangement and does not discriminate in favor of officers, stockholders, supervisors, or high-salaried employees. The plan must also comply with ERISA. The risk manager must keep these requirements in mind as he or she makes each decision with respect to the pension plan. Mention has already been made of the OASDHI integration requirements.

Actuarial Cost Method

The manner in which the cost of the benefits is to be budgeted is called the "actuarial cost method." One possibility is a pay-as-you-go plan with no advance preparation. Most formal plans, however, have always been funded, in the sense that contributions to the pension fund in the early years exceed current disbursements. The excess amounts are invested, and the accumulated amounts plus the income from investments are available to pay part of the costs in the future. ERISA requires that all formal plans meet certain advance funding requirements. The failure of many corporate pension plans to meet their obligations was one of the principal arguments favoring the passage of ERISA.

Several methods of advance funding are conceptually possible and have been practiced in the past. Under one method, the annual contributions would be estimated to be sufficient to provide the full retirement benefit for employees retiring that year. No advance preparation would be made for the future retirement of active employees. Another procedure would be to contribute each year the "normal cost" of the plan according to some actuarial assumption plus the assumed interest on any "supplemental liability." For example, the normal cost might be the sum of the level annual contributions that would have been required to provide the specified pension benefits for each employee if level contributions had been made since each employee entered the service of the employer. Because such contributions would not have been made for the participants who were employed when the plan was installed, the fund would start off with a "debt." In more technical terms, there would be an initial supplemental liability.[8] The interest payments on this liability would prevent the debt from increasing. Under this method, the fund would usually be greater than under the first method, but the advance preparation would not be complete. Full funding could be accomplished if in addition the supplemental liability were liquidated over a period of time. Failure to do this, however, would not usually prevent the plan from meeting its promised payments *if* the plan continued to operate indefinitely.[9] Usually enough new contributions would be made to provide benefits for retired persons without exhausting the funds. But if the plan were terminated, the deficiency would become apparent. Long-term employees approaching retirement might receive only a small fraction or none of the pension they had expected. Although many more actuarial cost methods

---

[8] This liability is equal to the present value of the benefits that will be paid the current participants in the plan less the present value of the normal cost contributions in behalf of these participants. Alternatively, it may be viewed as the accumulated value of the past normal cost contributions that have not been made.

[9] Compare this statement with the one made under "Funding" in Chap. 20 with respect to OASDHI and with the one made in Chap. 27 with respect to private life insurers.

could be described, this discussion should be sufficient to indicate the principles involved and the variations possible.[10]

ERISA established some minimum funding rules. The normal cost of whatever actuarial method is adopted must be funded currently. These contributions cannot be deferred. In addition the initial supplemental liability must be paid off in equal installments over 30 years (40 years starting January 1, 1976, for plans in effect on January 1, 1974). In other words all plans must be fully funded by that time.[11]

Funding Agencies

The pension plan may be (1) self-insured or (2) insured. There are several types of insured plans, some of which arose as a direct response to competition from self-insured plans.

Self-Insured Plans   Under most self-insured plans, the employer transfers funds periodically to a trustee, commonly a bank or trust company. The trustee invests these funds and often performs certain administrative tasks such as sending out the pension checks. The trustee, however, assumes no risks, the mortality, investment, expense, turnover, and other risks being assumed by the employer. A consulting actuary, who advises the employer with respect to the funding arrangements, also assumes no risks.

As explained below, insured plans originally permitted much less flexibility in (1) designing benefit formulas, (2) budgeting costs over time, and (3) investing the pension moneys. In recent years, however, insured plans have changed their position substantially with respect to these matters. ERISA has also reduced the flexibility possible under both self-insured and insured plans with respect to budgeting costs over time (see above) and investments. The act established a prudent person rule for any person exercising discretionary authority or control in the management of a plan or rendering investment advice for a fee. Fiduciaries managing pension plan investments are specifically required to diversify these investments to reduce the chance of large losses unless they can show clearly that it would be prudent not to do so. Thus fiduciaries are less likely than in the past to invest the bulk of their pension assets in equities.

Despite the greater flexibility now possible under insured plans and the restrictive effects of ERISA, an employer may prefer a self-insured plan because it still affords greater flexibility. The employer may also reason that he or she can avoid commissions and premium taxes (in states where annuities are taxed), but the self-insured firm must pay the trustee and the consulting actuary and perform certain services itself. The primary disadvantage is the risk involved. The mortality risks alone are enough to

---

[10] Another method that is commonly used with insured plans is discussed in the section below, "Insured Plans."

[11] There are some exceptions. First, if the plan is amended, a new 30-year period applies to the funding of those amendments. If the actuarial assumptions as to death rates, investment return, turnover rates, and the like are changed, the resulting changes in the accrued liability must be amortized over 30 years. Finally, if actual experience differs from the actuarial assumptions, the experience gains or losses are to be amortized over 15 years.

restrict this approach to large employers, but, as noted above, there are also no guarantees from an outsider with respect to investment results or expenses of operation.

Insured Plans   Insured pension plans can be characterized as (1) group deferred annuity plans, (2) deposit administration plans, (3) separate account plans, or (4) individual policy pension trusts. Since each type presents different advantages and problems for the employer, we shall discuss each separately.

1 Until the mid-1960s, most of the insured group pension plans were *group deferred annuity plans,* which provide for the annual purchase of a number of single premium deferred annuities. These annuities, purchased by a lump-sum payment, obligate the insurer to pay the employee a lifetime income starting at retirement. Although much less popular today, these plans still cover many employees of smaller employers. The usual monthly retirement benefit for future service is a stated percentage of average earnings over the credited years of service times the number of years of service. This benefit is equal to the sum of the amounts obtained by multiplying the earnings each year by the specified percentage. For example, if the benefit is 2 percent of average earnings per credited year of service and an employee has five years of credited service, during which he or she earned $20,000, $22,000, $24,000, $26,000, and $28,000 respectively, the annual retirement benefit is 5(.02) ($24,000) = $2,400 or $400 + $440 + $480 + $520 + $560 = $2,400. Consequently, if the employer (alone or together with the employee) purchases each year a single premium deferred annuity providing at retirement age the specified percentage times the earnings during that year, he or she will have purchased by that retirement age the annuity contracts necessary to pay the specified retirement benefit. Furthermore, at the end of any year, the employer will have purchased the contracts necessary to pay the pension benefits earned to that date. The annual purchase of annuity contracts in these amounts is the usual procedure under a group deferred annuity plan.

Past-service liability is liquidated by purchasing over a specified period deferred annuities sufficient to provide past-service benefits. Many purchase patterns are possible, but under most plans annuity contracts are purchased first for those employees nearing retirement.

As compared with self-insured plans, group deferred annuity contracts offer both advantages and disadvantages. The primary advantage to the employer (and to the employee) is the actuarial soundness of the arrangement. A third party guarantees that the pension payments will be made for life, and if the plan were to be terminated during the early years, the pension benefits earned to date (with the possible exception of some past-service benefits) would be completely funded.[12] The employer can fulfill promises to employees without any sizable risk. The employer need not be concerned about survival rates in excess of those assumed in the annuity premiums, about lower interest earnings, or higher expenses. Some risk remains, however: (1) The purchase prices of the annuities are subject to change after an initial guarantee period, and (2) the

---

[12] ERISA requires that all pension plans be fully funded after 30 or 40 years, as described earlier.

purchase prices are established at a conservative level to permit the types of dividend and retroactive premium adjustments already noticed in connection with group insurance. Another advantage of this approach is that the employer transfers to the insurer most of the administrative worries (actuarial, financial, legal, loss-adjustment) associated with operating a pension plan.

The principal disadvantage is the relative inflexibility of the group deferred annuity plan with respect to benefit formulas, premium payments, and supporting investments. Although other benefit formulas can be used, the career average formula is the only formula other than a money purchase arrangement for which the group annuity has all the advantages cited above. In the past the funding discipline imposed by the group annuity plan also limited the freedom of the employer more than self-insured plans or other types of insured plans. ERISA has reduced the importance of this difference, but it still remains. Finally, the premiums charged by the insurer depend upon the return it obtains on its invested assets. It can invest these assets, however, only subject to certain legal restrictions. For example, only a small portion of a life insurer's general assets can usually be invested in equities, which at times have been more attractive investments than most alternatives. In addition to these disadvantages, the operating expenses of an insured plan may exceed the corresponding cost of a self-insured plan, largely because of state premium taxes.

2 *Deposit administration plans* are more flexible than group deferred annuity plans, but they also include fewer guarantees by the insurer. These plans now outnumber group deferred annuity plans and, including the separate account plans described below, cover most of the employees of large employers covered under insured pension plans. Under deposit administration plans, which are usually noncontributory, the employer's contributions or deposits are paid into a fund that accumulates at interest. The accumulations constitute an undivided fund; i.e., there are no accounts for individual employees. No annuity contracts are purchased until the employee retires or, in some cases, until his or her pension is vested. Employee contributions, if any, are usually segregated, and individual records are established. Sometimes annuities are purchased immediately with these contributions.

Deposit administration contracts can be used with any type of benefit formula because the necessary contracts can be purchased at the time of retirement. The funding arrangement can also be flexible because, except for the purchase of contracts on retiring employees, the employer has great freedom with respect to annual contributions, although probably not quite as much as he or she would have under a self-insured plan. The insurer or perhaps a consulting actuary usually recommends a range within which the contributions should fall, but the latitude within this range is great, and the employer may sometimes ignore the recommendation. The employer cannot, however, ignore the ERISA requirements noted earlier. The investment of the pension funds is subject to the restrictions on insurance investments already noted.

The third-party guarantee under deposit administration plans is not as complete as that under group deferred annuity plans. For this reason and because of the high minimum administrative costs involved, the deposit administration plan is usually reserved for larger firms. On the other hand, the deposit administration plan does contain some important guarantees by the insurer. The most important guarantee is the promise of a lifetime payment to the retired employees. The other guarantees are a minimum interest return and annuity rate schedule applicable to the moneys deposited in the undivided fund. Although these guarantees may change over time, they always apply with respect to the dollars received while they were in effect. The principal of the fund, of course, is not subject to any fluctuations. A closely related plan is an *immediate participation plan*. The major differences are that (1) no contracts are purchased when an employee retires, (2) the insurer does not maintain a contingency reserve, and (3) the employer participates immediately (instead of waiting for insurer dividends) in the total experience of the plan.

3 *Separate account plans* are the most recent addition to insured pension plans. Basically separate account plans are deposit administration plans, but the insurer places at least part of the employer's contributions in a separate account that is not commingled with the insurer's other assets and is not subject to the investment limitations placed on insurers. For example, a large portion of the account may be invested in equities. Although some employers are large enough for the insurer to establish a separate account for their individual pension plans, generally a separate account commingles the contributions of many employers. Thus separate accounts permit considerable flexibility with respect to the investment of pension funds, but the employer generally cannot dictate the particular investments to be made.

Separate accounts were made possible during the 1960s when most states adopted enabling legislation and the Securities and Exchange Commission approved such plans.

Separate account plans may be used to fund a plan that provides a retirement benefit which is adjusted according to changes in the cost of living or in the value of the separate account investment portfolio. Their more common use, however, is to fund plans that provide a defined fixed-dollar benefit. In this instance fluctuations in the investment portfolio's value and rate of return affect only the cost to the employer.

4 Under the individual policy plan, known as an *individual policy pension trust* (often shortened to *pension trust*), the employer and perhaps the employee transfer funds to a trustee who purchases individual level-premium insurance policies on the lives of the participating employees. The trustee owns the contracts subject to conditions outlined in the trust agreement.

Group pension plans cover far more employees than individual policy plans, but individual policy plans are much more numerous. Many insurers limit their group plans to employee groups including a minimum of 25 lives. For groups including 50 lives or less, the individual plan may be no more costly than the group plan.

The policies under a pension trust are usually retirement annuities or retirement income annuities. Retirement annuities, purchased by level annual premiums, provide a lifetime income at retirement. Retirement income contracts differ only in that they provide death benefits if the employee dies before retirement. For more details see Chapter 23. The initial contract for each employee is generally sufficient to provide his or her retirement benefit if the formula is unchanged and if the employee's present compensation is continued until retirement date. If the retirement benefit is increased or decreased because of changes in compensation or the benefit formula, new contracts are purchased or old ones reduced. This procedure can become awkward, especially since evidence of insurability may be required in connection with all retirement income contracts because of the death benefits.

Plan Termination Insurance

If a single employer, defined benefit pension plan is terminated and the assets are not sufficient to pay the *vested* benefits to employees, a government insurance program, established by ERISA, guarantees the employees that they will receive these vested benefits up to a specified maximum. This plan termination insurance is administered by the Pension Benefit Guaranty Corporation, a newly created agency in the Department of Labor. In 1975, the maximum insured monthly benefit was $750 at age 65 (but not in excess of the worker's average monthly income during the five highest-paid consecutive years of participation). If the benefit was paid before age 65, the $750 limit was adjusted downward. The $750 limit has been adjusted upward each year since 1975 as national earnings increase. The Pension Benefit Guaranty Corporation has the authority to insure benefits in excess of the $750 adjusted limit if it chooses to do so.

Voluntary terminations for good cause are covered by this government program as are terminations ordered by the Pension Benefit Guaranty Corporation. If the Corporation pays any pension benefits, the employer remains liable up to 30 percent of his or her net worth at the time of the termination.

The annual premium paid by the employer is $2.60 per participant. PBGC has indicated its desire to increase this rate substantially.

Multiemployer plans are subject to some special, more complex coverage and cost provisions.

Disclosure Requirements and Fiduciary Standards

ERISA increased substantially the amount of information that must be included in the annual pension plan report. For example, the report must describe investment transactions in considerable detail. The present value of accrued benefits must be reported, classified according to certain termination distribution categories required by the law. Any change in actuarial assumptions or cost methods must be justified.

Participants must be given simple summaries of the plan. They have the right to receive additional information concerning their own benefits.

Mention has already been made of the new responsibilities imposed upon fiduciaries making investment decisions. Other fiduciaries also come under a new federal prudent person rule, must be bonded, and are subject to civil actions, fines, and other penalties for their misdeeds.

THRIFT AND SAVINGS PLANS

Thrift and savings plans, henceforth called savings plans, have become much more popular in recent years. One reason is a special version known as 401(k) salary reduction agreement plans.

General Characteristics

Savings plans permit employees to accumulate funds for future purposes on a tax-deferred basis. Participation in the plan is optional and an employee usually may, subject to certain constraints, select the level of his or her participation. For example, the employee may be able to place 2, 4, or 6 percent of his or her salary in the plan. Employers typically promise to contribute some percent, such as 50 percent of the employee's contribution, up to some specified amount. Because taxes on the employer's contributions are deferred and higher paid employees are more likely to make higher percentage contributions, the Internal Revenue Service generally prohibits employers from matching employee contributions in excess of 6 percent. Employees may contribute more than 6 percent but total employee contributions are also limited (to 10 percent plus the lowest percentage any employee can place in the plan) because the investment income earned on these contributions is tax deferred.

The employer and employee contributions are paid to a trust fund which often consists of more than one investment vehicle (for example, a common stock fund and a bond fund), in which case the employee can elect how to allocate his or her contributions among these vehicles.

Benefits are distributed to employees or their beneficiaries if they retire, die, or are permanently and totally disabled. If they sever their employment prior to any of these events, their claim to employer contributions depends upon the vesting provisions in the plan. The ERISA minimum requirements apply, but the vesting provisions tend to be more generous to employees than those found in pension plans. Earlier withdrawals by active employees may also be permitted subject to some penalty or constraint. For example, such withdrawals may be limited to proven financial needs such as education costs or heavy medical expenses. Employees may also be permitted to borrow a certain portion of the vested share of their account.

401(k) Salary Reduction Agreement Plans

Under an Internal Revenue Service interpretation of Section 401(k) of the Internal Revenue Code, employees can elect to have their taxable salary reduced by the amount that they contribute to a savings plan. For the employer to be able to offer such a plan, the average percent of salary deferred by the higher-paid one-third of the employees cannot be too much higher than the average percent deferred by the lower-paid two-thirds. More specifically, if the lower two-thirds defer on the average some fraction between 0 and 2 percent, the top one-third can defer 2½ times that percent. If the lower two-thirds defer between 2 percent and 6 percent, the top one-third can defer that fraction plus 3 percent. If the lower two-thirds defer more than 6 percent, the top one-third can defer 1½ times that fraction. Many firms have installed such plans because of the tax advantage to employees.

GROUP PROPERTY AND LIABILITY INSURANCE

Until recently, employee benefit plans were limited almost exclusively to personnel risks. Many plans now provide employees some protection against their property and liability risks—typically, automobile insurance and homeowner's insurance. Personal catastrophe liability insurance is also available. For the employee these plans offer possibly lower rates, installment payment of premiums through periodic payroll deductions, more liberal underwriting, loss-control services, and possibly, through group pressure, more sympathetic treatment of claims.

The reasons why these programs were not introduced at a much earlier date fall into two major categories: First, until about 15 years ago little demand existed for this type of protection among employers or employees. Because employers are the source of the income payments interrupted by poor health, unemployment, death, or retirement, it was natural for them to think about and for employees to demand some employer-arranged protection against those risks. The link between the employment relationship and an employee's property and liability risks is much less direct. Furthermore, whereas all employees are exposed to serious losses associated with personnel risks, property and liability exposures can vary widely among employees. For example, not all employees own automobiles or dwellings. This disparity, which was much greater in the past than it is at present, would cause some employees to benefit much more than others from the introduction of property and liability insurance plans. The tax incentives that contributed greatly to the development of plans covering personnel risks were (and still are) lacking. Finally, employers could not get excited about a benefit that could cost them more money, might prove difficult to administer, and could cause employee dissatisfaction. They reasoned that because their employees would be deeply concerned about how their property and liability insurance claims were adjusted, they would have to spend considerable time selecting and monitoring the insurer. If the service proved unsatisfactory, the employee might blame the employer. Employees in turn were reluctant to leave present insurers whose service had been satisfactory. Many employees, insured by low-cost auto and homeowners's insurers, discovered that their own premium savings would be much less than the 20 or 25 percent claimed for the plans.

Second, until about the same time property and liability insurers did little to develop group property and liability insurance. Individual insurance provided a sufficient volume of sales to keep these insurers occupied, and group insurance posed legal, technical, and marketing problems that they were not prepared to handle. Almost all state insurance departments considered group plans, particularly the ''true'' group variety with group selection and uniform group rating, to be (1) unsafe, and (2) unfair to persons outside the group and to the better-quality insureds within the group. Group property and liability insurance poses more technical problems than does group life and health insurance, because property and liability insurance exposures vary more in quality among employees, underwriting experience of the group depends upon the behavior of persons who are not members of the group (e.g., dependents and friends driving the employee's car), and much more attention must be paid to post-sales servicing. Many insurers also feared that in a voluntary employee-paid arrangement many employees would for various reasons elect not to participate, thus causing underwriting problems and reducing the opportunity for cost savings. Finally, many property and liability insurance agents opposed the extension of group insurance[13]

---

[13] Many life and health insurance agents also opposed the development of group life and health insurance in its early years. They still favor dollar limits on the amount of protection that can be written on an individual life and on the types of groups that can be insured. They argue, with some support from more objective observers, that unlimited extension of the group concept is unsafe and deprives the individual of counseling and tailor-made protection.

because, unlike group life and health insurance, which often stimulates the sale of individual insurance, group property and liability insurance could provide almost all the property and liability protection required by the typical employee, thus lessening significantly the demand for individual insurance.

In the late sixties several events improved the prospects for the future development of group property and liability insurance for employees. First, union leaders looking for new fringe benefits for their members became interested in group property and liability insurance as an employer-provided benefit. Employer interest in group protection also increased. Second, several large insurers began to market aggressively this form of insurance. They believed that in this way they could increase significantly their share of the family insurance market; the method they used avoided some of the technical, legal, and marketing problems that had hindered earlier attempts; and some state regulatory officials and legislatures adopted a more favorable outlook toward the group concept. These trends have continued to the present time, and group property and liability insurance has become more common. The discussion that follows deals only with employee groups, but plans have also been developed for members of professional societies, credit unions, and other groups.

Most of the present programs are "mass merchandising" plans under which individual policies are sold to the employees of a business on a payroll-deduction basis. Employees usually pay the entire premium; the employer makes the necessary arrangements and deducts the premium from wages. Some of these plans include life insurance, health insurance, and mutual funds as well as property and liability insurance. Because of expense savings (e.g., lower commissions and the premium collection service provided by the employer) and the opportunity to render more effective loss-control services, initial rates (or rates less dividends) are less than for comparable individual insurance from the same insurers. However, the rate structure is the same as for individual insurance; i.e., each employee pays the same rate relative to that paid by other employees that he or she would pay if they all purchased individual insurance from the same insurer. Furthermore, although the standards are more liberal than for individual insurance, the insurer reserves the right to reject individual applications. Personal counseling is provided through a representative who often has an office on the employer's premises. Some insurers write this business through a single agency; others permit any of their agents to solicit the business. "Mass merchandising," therefore, is a hybrid of individual and group insurance.

"True" group property and liability insurance, like group life and health insurance, is characterized by group selection and a uniform average rate for all employees. Employers would normally be expected to pay part or all of the cost per employee. Because this concept represents a more revolutionary break with the past and introduces more technical and legal problems, it has developed more slowly than mass merchandising. However, as the legal barriers fall, as union interest increases, and as insurers market true group insurance more aggressively, many observers believe that the stage is being set for a rapid expansion in this area.

The future growth rate of group property and liability insurance will depend to a large extent upon (1) the insurers' ability to reduce premiums substantially through this device and to publicize the savings, (2) employer willingness to assume part or all of the premium cost and union pressures in this direction, (3) congressional enactment of tax incentives, (4) changes in the cost of more traditional benefits, and (5) the ability of insurers to package this protection with other employee benefits.

GROUP PREPAID LEGAL EXPENSE

In 1973, Congress amended the Taft-Hartley Act to allow prepaid legal services as an employer-shared benefit under collective bargaining. Prepaid legal expense plans have existed for decades, but it was not until recently that they attracted much interest. The congressional action increased the attention that legal services are receiving as an employee benefit.

In support of such plans it is argued that middle-class families use legal services less than they should because they are unfamiliar with these services and fear their cost. The poor, it is argued, are eligible for free legal aid, and the wealthy understand and can pay for these services.

Present plans differ as to whether they are underwritten by commercial insurers, whether they are open or closed plans, and what benefits they provide. Commercial insurers are relative newcomers to this field. Many plans are underwritten by bar associations, labor unions, consumer associations, credit unions, and similar groups.

Open plans permit the insured to select his or her own lawyer and, subject to certain dollar limits, pay that lawyer's fees. Closed plans provide without charge the services of a closed panel of lawyers.

The benefits vary greatly. Some plans cover only fortuitous events; others cover certain predictable expenses such as preparation of wills and estate planning. To illustrate, one policy issued by a commercial insurer to employee groups provides each insured family with six hours of general consultation and advice, one simple will, two legal documents, and services in connection with bankruptcy proceedings, simple probate, debt collection, real property foreclosures, and adoptions.

OTHER EMPLOYEE BENEFIT PLANS

Many other types of risk management-related employee benefit plans exist, some of which will be discussed in Chapter 25. Some other illustrations are employee stock ownership plans, preretirement counselling, financial counselling for key executives, and employee assistance programs. Employee assistance programs usually help employees with chemical dependency, family relationship, and financial problems. The program may provide only initial counselling and recommendations for further treatment or in addition provide that treatment.

FLEXIBLE, VARIABLE OR "CAFETERIA" BENEFITS

A relatively new concept in employee benefit planning is flexible, variable, or "cafeteria" benefits. This approach permits each employee within limits to design within some dollar cost constraint his or her own benefit package. For example, a young, married worker with dependents may choose substantial protection against death, disability, and medical expenses over a generous contribution to a pension plan. An older worker might make the opposite choice. A worker without dependents might favor more holidays over an increase in economic security benefits.

In favor of flexible benefits, it has been argued that, as a form of job enrichment, this approach increases the worker's autonomy, self-respect, and dedication to his or her job.[14] Through this device employees also better understand their benefits and appreciate them more. Finally, supporters claim, flexible benefits help employers control costs. For example, it is not necessary to protect all employees under a package of benefits designed to meet the unique needs of each special-interest group represented among the employees. Furthermore, employees become more cost-conscious, especially if the addition of new benefits or the rising cost of certain benefits does not increase the dollars they can spend on their individual combinations of benefits. Benefits that prove unpopular may be dropped, reducing administrative costs.

Costs, however, may increase. Permitting employees to design their own protection packages may increase administrative costs. An extensive continuing education program, which may also prove costly, should be part of a variable benefits plan if employees are to make intelligent choices. Certain economies of scale may also be lost if some benefits are selected by many fewer employees. Adverse selection against the plan may also occur if employees select benefits against losses for which they have reason to believe their probability of occurrence is higher than average. Some observers question whether most employees want to become as involved in decision making as a flexible benefits plan requires.

Until a few years ago flexible benefit plans were rare. Three developments that account for a recent upsurge in these plans were as follows. First the Revenue Act of 1978 made clear that a nondiscriminatory flexible benefit plan produces taxable income on employer contributions only if the contributions are used to purchase an immediately taxable benefit such as additional salary or paid holidays. Second, some regulations and court cases involving age and sex discrimination have raised the cost of more traditional plans. For example, pregnancy must now be treated the same as an illness. As a consequence, an employer may reason that it cannot afford to provide as liberal disability or medical expense benefits for all employees as it has in the past. Third, and perhaps most important, the IRS regulations implementing Section 401(k) have been interpreted to permit employees covered under a flexible benefit plan to reduce their taxable salaries, the reduction being used on a before-tax base to fund a variety of employee benefits.

The flexible benefit plan introduced by a large bank will act as an illustration.[15] A core of fixed benefits provides a minimum threshold of support in certain areas financed by the employer. This core includes a pension plan, a long-term disability plan, and a dental plan. A semiflexible set of benefits also provides an employer-financed minimum level of benefits, but in different areas, and the employees can

[14] William B. Werther, Jr., "A New Direction in Rethinking Fringe Benefits," *MSU Business Topics,* vol. XXII, no. 1 (Winter, 1974), pp. 35–40. For a description of one such plan see "American Can Expands Flexible Benefits Program," *Business Insurance,* December 11, 1978, pp. 33–34. TRW is generally credited as being the pioneer in this area.

[15] "Benefits Revolution Picks Up Steam As More Firms Combine Flexible Benefits With Salary Reduction," *Employee Benefit Plan Review* (May, 1983), pp. 10, 16.

choose higher limits if they so desire. This set includes such benefits as life insurance and medical expense insurance. A completely flexible set of benefits includes those needed by some, but not all, employees. Examples are dependent life insurance, dependent care reimbursements, and reimbursements for health care costs not covered under the semi-flexible medical expense insurance.

The bank's employees are provided with credits that they can use to "purchase" (1) higher limits of coverage under the semi-flexible set or (2) one or more of the benefits under the completely flexible set. If the employee does not use all these credits, he or she may receive some of them in cash. On the other hand, if the credits are not sufficient for the employee to obtain all the benefits he or she wishes, the employee may purchase the additional protection with pre-tax dollars through a salary reduction agreement.

SOME KEY CONCEPTS

Profit-sharing plan   A plan that permits employees to share in the employer's profits on a cash or a deferred basis.

Employee Retirement Income Security Act (ERISA)   A law passed in 1974 that placed some major constraints on the eligibility requirements, vesting provisions, funding, and other features of pension plans. Other employee benefit plans were also affected but to a much lesser extent.

Defined contribution plan   A pension plan that specifies the annual contribution made in behalf of the employee. The benefit is the amount that can be purchased at retirement with the accumulated contributions less expenses plus investment returns.

Defined benefit plan   A pension plan that specifies the employee's retirement benefit. The annual contributions are the amounts required to produce this benefit.

Vesting provision   The provision in a pension plan that determines the benefit purchased with employer contributions that will be received by an employee terminating his or her employment prior to retirement.

Actuarial cost method   The manner in which the cost of pension benefits is to be budgeted over time.

Thrift or savings plan   A savings plan established by the employer in which the employee normally determines the level of his or her participation and the employer matches part of the employee contribution. 401(k) versions have become very popular because of some important tax advantages.

Variable, flexible, or cafeteria benefit plan   An employee benefit plan that permits each employee subject to some constraints to design his or her own benefit package.

REVIEW QUESTIONS

1 How does a deferred profit-sharing plan differ from a pension plan?
2 a In designing a pension plan, the employer may elect to use one or more of four types of eligibility requirements. Describe each type briefly.
   b What constraints does the Employee Retirement Income Security Act place upon the employer's options?
3 The normal retirement age under a pension plan is 65.

   a Is age 65 also the usual compulsory retirement age?

   b What provisions are usually made for early retirement? deferred retirement?

4 a Distinguish between defined benefit and defined contribution formulas.

   b Which formula is more common?

5 An employee participated for 30 years under the ABC Manufacturing Corporation pension plan. His annual salary the first year he participated was $10,000. This salary increased $500 each year until he retired.

   a What would be his monthly pension if the ABC pension plan provides for each year of service 1½ percent of his average career salary? of his "final" (last five years) salary?

   b How does ERISA constrain the maximum pension benefit?

6 Under the normal straight life annuity form a pension plan would provide a retiring employee $1,000 per month for the rest of his or her life. What provision must be made if the employee wishes to provide some income for a surviving spouse?

7 Are pension plans inflation-proof? Explain.

8 a Explain the three vesting schedules required under ERISA.

   b Would you favor more liberal vesting provisions? Support your position.

9 How is the employer constrained from:

   a Establishing a benefit formula under which an employee would earn most of his or her benefits the final years of employment?

   b Establishing a benefit formula that would benefit primarily higher-paid executives?

10 Compare the tax advantages of a noncontributory pension plan with the tax advantages of a noncontributory group life insurance plan.

11 a Are most pension plans fully funded? Explain.

   b How does ERISA constrain the funding of pension plans?

   c Do you consider ERISA funding requirements to be too restrictive? Explain your position.

12 If a private pension plan is discontinued because of financial difficulties, how will ERISA affect:

   a The rights of employees?

   b The responsibility of the employer?

13 One of the major decisions in pension planning is whether to self-insure or to insure. What factors should be considered in making this decision?

14 Compare the four most popular types of insured pension plans with respect to flexibility in benefit formulas, flexibility in budgeting, responsibility of the insurer, and flexibility in investments.

15 ERISA introduced some new disclosure requirements and imposed some heavy responsibilities upon fiduciaries. Explain.

16 Thrift and savings plans have become more popular recently. Why?

17 a What property and liability insurance protection is now available under employee benefit plans?

   b What benefits are claimed for employees under these plans?

   c Why are such benefits much less common than personnel insurance protection?

18 a How does "mass merchandised" property and liability insurance differ from "true" group insurance?

   b What do you predict will be the future growth of "true" group insurance?

19 a Distinguish between open and closed prepaid legal expense plans.

   b What benefits are provided under such plans?

20 What benefits do employees receive under an employee assistance plan?

21 Do you favor the variable or cafeteria benefit approach? Explain your position.

22 Why do 401(k) Salary Reduction Agreements make flexible benefit plans more attractive?

SUGGESTIONS FOR ADDITIONAL READING

Allen, E. T., J. J. Melone, and J. S. Rosenbloom: *Pension Planning* (5th ed., Homewood, Ill.: Richard D. Irwin, Inc., 1984).

Coming of Age: Toward a National Retirement Income Policy (Washington, D.C.: President's Commission on Pension Policy, February 26, 1981).

Contemporary Benefit Issues and Administration (Brookfield, Wis.: International Foundation of Employer Benefit Plans, 1979).

Gregg, D. W., and V. B. Lucas (eds.): *Life and Health Insurance Handbook* (3d ed., Homewood, Ill.: Richard D. Irwin, Inc., 1973), chaps. 33–35 and 38–41.

How Major Industrial Corporations View Employee Benefits Programs (New York: Market Research Department, *Fortune* magazine, 1974).

Kimball, S., and H. Denenberg: *Mass Marketing of Property and Liability Insurance,* Department of Transportation Automobile Insurance and Compensation Study (Washington, D.C.: U.S. Government Printing Office, 1970).

McGill, Dan M.: *Fundamentals of Private Pensions* (5th ed., Homewood, Ill.: Richard D. Irwin, Inc., 1984).

McGinn, D. F.: *Joint Trust Pension Plans* (Homewood, Ill.: Richard D. Irwin, Inc., 1978).

Mehr, R. I., and S. G. Gustavson: *Life Insurance: Theory and Practice* (3d ed., Dallas: Business Publications, Inc., 1984), chaps. 16 and 17.

————, and B. A. Hedges: *Risk Management: Concepts and Applications* (Homewood, Ill.: Richard D. Irwin, Inc., 1974), chaps. 11, 12, 20, and 21.

Pension Facts (Washington, D.C.: American Council of Life Insurance, annual).

Pension Plan Guide (Chicago: Commerce Clearing House, Inc., multivolume looseleaf service).

Pension and Profit Sharing (Englewood Cliffs, N.J.: Prentice-Hall, Inc., multivolume looseleaf service).

Pfennigstorf, W., and S. L. Kimball (eds.): *Legal Service Plans: Approaches to Regulation* (Chicago: American Bar Foundation, 1977).

Rosenbloom, J. S.: *The Handbook of Employee Benefits* (Homewood, Ill.: Dow Jones-Irwin, 1984).

————, and G. V. Hallman: *Employee Benefit Planning* (2d ed., Englewood Cliffs, N.J.: Prentice-Hall, Inc., 1984).

Spencer's Retirement Plan Services (Chicago: Charles D. Spencer & Associates, Inc., multivolume looseleaf service).

CHAPTER 23

INDIVIDUAL LIFE
INSURANCE CONTRACTS

LEARNING OBJECTIVES

After you have completed this chapter, you should be able to:

1 Describe the branches of life insurance sold by commercial insurers.
2 Summarize the main features of each of the four basic types of life insurance contracts and the most important modifications and combinations.
3 List the factors that affect the cost of life insurance.
4 Explain how you would evaluate the relative advantages and disadvantages of straight life insurance and universal life insurance.
5 Describe briefly the option clauses included in a life insurance contract, especially the nonforfeiture options and the settlement options.
6 Compare the insurance sold by fraternals and mutual savings banks with that sold by commercial insurers.

INTRODUCTION

Life insurance has already been discussed in connection with employee benefit plans. This chapter deals with life insurance issued to individuals. Individual insurance is purchased primarily by families, but businesses buy considerable amounts for the purposes described in Chapter 25.

Life insurers issue many different types of individual contracts. This chapter describes the basic policy types and a few of their more important modifications and combinations. It also analyzes some major policy provisions, placing emphasis upon those that require the insured to make decisions.

BRANCHES OF LIFE INSURANCE

Life insurance can be classified according to whether it is underwritten by commercial insurers, fraternal insurers, or mutual savings banks. At the close of 1982, commercial insurers had issued over 97 percent of the private life insurance in force and practically all the annuities. Fraternal life insurance in force was about 2 percent of the total and mutual savings bank insurance less than 1 percent.[1] Because of the dominant role of commercial insurers, this chapter will be devoted almost exclusively to their contracts. Much of the discussion, however, is applicable to the contracts of fraternal insurers and mutual savings bank insurers, whose important special characteristics will be discussed at the close of this chapter.

Commercial insurance in turn falls into two major classes—individual insurance and group insurance. *Individual* insurance differs from group insurance in that the contract covers a person or a family as opposed to a group of persons. Each contract covering a person or family is separately sold, underwritten, and administered. Individual insurance can be subclassified as ordinary insurance or industrial insurance.

Ordinary insurance is generally sold in amounts of at least $1,000; the premiums are quoted on an annual basis but may be paid on a semiannual, quarterly, or monthly basis; and only the first premium is collected by the agent, the remainder of the payments being made directly to the insurer. As is demonstrated in Table 23.1, ordinary insurance is the most important branch of individual insurance. Unless otherwise specified, our discussion in this text will refer to this branch of insurance, although we shall describe other branches as well.

Industrial insurance is usually sold in amounts less than $1,000; the most common method of premium payment is weekly; and the premium is customarily collected at the home of the insured by a "debit agent." The face amount is usually adjusted to the size of the premium the insured wishes to pay. Industrial policies are very similar to ordinary policies, the principal differences being the absence of loan values, the prohibition of assignments, the requirement that the proceeds be paid in a lump sum, and the automatic inclusion of accidental death and dismemberment provisions. Although still a sizable proportion of the total insurance in force, industrial insurance has declined relatively in importance.

Group insurance, described in Chapter 21, covers a group of persons under one contract, the contract being sold, underwritten, and administered on a group basis. Group insurance is the most rapidly growing branch of insurance.

Credit life insurance is listed as a fourth branch of insurance in Table 23.1, but it is probably better described as a unique application of ordinary insurance or group insurance. The insurance in force devoted to this use has increased very markedly since 1945; group credit life insurance has increased more rapidly than individual insurance.

Credit life insurance policies are issued through (1) lending institutions, such as banks and credit unions, or (2) retailers, such as department stores and automobile dealers selling goods or services on a charge account or an installment basis. Under

---

[1] 1983 Life Insurance Fact Book (Washington, D.C.: American Council of Life Insurance, 1983), pp. 100–101.

TABLE 23.1
COMMERCIAL LIFE INSURANCE IN FORCE IN THE UNITED
STATES, 1920–1982 (IN BILLIONS)

Year	Ordinary	Industrial	Group	Credit	Total
1920	$ 32.0	$ 6.9	$ 1.6	$ *	$ 40.5
1925	52.9	12.3	4.2	*	69.5
1930	78.6	18.0	9.8	0.1	106.4
1935	70.7	17.5	10.2	0.1	98.5
1940	79.3	20.9	14.9	0.4	115.5
1945	101.6	27.7	22.2	0.4	151.8
1950	149.1	33.4	47.8	3.8	234.2
1955	216.8	39.7	101.3	14.5	372.3
1960	341.9	39.6	175.9	29.1	586.4
1965	499.6	39.8	308.1	53.0	900.6
1970	734.7	38.6	551.4	77.4	1,402.1
1975	1,083.4	39.4	904.7	112.0	2,139.6
1980	1,760.5	36.0	1,579.4	165.2	3,541.0
1982	2,216.4	32.8	2,066.4	161.1	4,476.7

* Less than 0.1
Source: 1983 Life Insurance Fact Book, (Washington, D.C.: American Council
of Life Insurance, 1983), p. 15.

group credit insurance, the creditor is the policyholder and often pays the premiums. Under individual insurance (which in this field is characterized by group underwriting), the debtor is the policyholder and almost always pays the premiums. The insurance in either case is on the life of the debtor, and if he or she dies, the insurer pays the unpaid balance of the debt to the creditor thus canceling the debt. Under some individual policies, the protection does not decrease over time, and the balance is paid to some other designated beneficiary. Several states have recently corrected important abuses in this field, such as unduly high commissions given by some insurers to creditors in connection with individual insurance and excessive premium rates for both individual and group insurance.

TYPES OF CONTRACTS

The basic types of life insurance contracts are (1) term insurance, (2) whole life insurance, (3) endowment insurance, and (4) annuities. Some important modifications and combinations are (1) modified life and graded premium contracts, (2) family policies, (3) family income policies, (4) family maintenance policies, (5) retirement income contracts, (6) preferred risk policies, (7) variable life insurance, (8) adjustable life insurance, (9) universal life insurance, (10) extralife or extraordinary life insurance, (11) joint life insurance, and (12) flexible premium variable life insurance. Guaranteed insurability and double indemnity riders, which are, strictly speaking, neither a modification nor a combination of the basic policy types, will also be discussed.

Basic Policy Types

Term Insurance   Term insurance protects the beneficiary if the insured dies within the term specified in the policy. If the insured lives to the end of the term, the policy expires. In other words, term life insurance resembles automobile insurance, fire insurance, and the like, which are always term insurance. Common types of term life insurance are 1-year term, 5-year term, 10-year term, 20-year term, and term to age 60 or 65. The term insurance is usually level over the policy period, but decreasing term insurance is also common.

Term insurance may be renewable, convertible, or both. If the policy is renewable, the insurer will renew the policy, regardless of the insurability of the insured, for the number of times specified in the contract—commonly to age 60 or 65. The premium paid upon renewal is the cost of a new policy issued to standard (as opposed to substandard) lives at the attained age. If the policy is convertible, the insured can convert the policy to nonterm insurance, either (1) as of the attained age, or (2) as of the date of issue of the term policy. In the latter case, the premium paid is the premium that the insured would have been charged if he or she had been covered under the nonterm contract from the beginning. In addition, the insured will be asked to make a lump-sum payment (which may be computed in various ways) to make up for the deficiency in premiums to the date of the conversion. These two rights are important because they make the term insurance more flexible.

Because of its nature, term insurance provides the maximum protection per premium dollar for a stated period of time. The relative protection provided by different types of contracts may be computed from Table 23.2, which presents the premium rates charged by one large nonparticipating insurer for some leading term insurance and nonterm insurance contracts. In order to avoid the complicating and nonguaranteed effect of dividends, the rates of a nonparticipating insurer were selected to illustrate the rates, although about 50 percent of the life insurance in force is participating.

One common use of term insurance is to meet a need for protection that expires at the end of a specified period. For example, term insurance may be purchased to complete the payments under a mortgage or to reimburse a business if its key engineer should die before an important project is completed. Young husbands or wives with high protection needs but little income may purchase renewable and convertible term insurance to protect their families in their early years. Others may purchase only renewable term insurance for the investment reasons cited in the next section.

Whole Life Insurance   Whole life insurance protects the beneficiary when the insured dies, since the contract can be continued in force as long as the insured lives. Whole life insurance contracts may be placed in two categories, depending upon the premium payment period: (1) straight life insurance, and (2) limited payment life insurance. Under straight life insurance,[2] the premiums are payable for the remainder of the insured's lifetime. Under limited payment life insurance, the premiums are

---

[2] Sometimes referred to as "continuous premium whole life insurance" or as "ordinary life insurance." The latter term is unfortunate because of the use of the term "ordinary" to denote a branch of insurance.

TABLE 23.2
BASE PREMIUM RATES* PER $1,000 INSURANCE CHARGED BY ONE LEADING NONPARTICIPATING INSURER FOR CONTRACTS ISSUED TO MALE NON-SMOKERS† WITH A FACE AMOUNT OF $100,000.

Age	Term 1-year‡	Term 10-year§	Straight life	Paid-up at 65	20-pay-ment life	Endowment at 65
20	$ 1.62	$ 1.68	$ 7.38	$ 8.08	$11.11	$ 9.14
25	1.65	1.70	8.85	9.75	12.67	10.83
30	1.69	1.86	10.35	12.24	14.52	13.10
35	1.72	2.21	12.78	15.59	17.80	17.80
40	2.15	3.32	16.42	20.48	22.24	24.83
45	3.44	5.82	21.45	27.90	27.90	35.62
50	5.91	9.72	27.99	42.29	34.52	54.29
55	9.45	15.19	35.82	67.78	41.93	90.78
60	15.30	18.83	47.00		51.00	
65	24.00		62.30		64.00	

* To obtain the premium, first calculate the base premium by multiplying the rate in the table by the amount of insurance in thousands. Next add to this base premium a policy fee of $30. To illustrate, the premium for a $100,000 straight life contract issued at age 35 is ($12.78 × 100) + $30 or $1,308. The result is a decreasing rate per $1,000 insurance as the amount of insurance increases.
† The base premium rates for women are less than those for men. For example, the base premium rates for a female nonsmoker aged 35 would be $11.55 for a straight life insurance contract, $14.19 for a paid-up-at-65 contract, $16.76 for a 20-payment life contract, and $17.20 for an endowment at 65 contract.
‡ Renewable to age 70 and convertible prior to age 65. Not issued after age 65.
§ Renewable to age 65 and convertible prior to age 60. Not issued after age 60.

payable for the remainder of the insured's lifetime or until the expiration of a specified period, if earlier. Some examples of limited payment contracts and the level premiums for some whole life contracts are presented in Table 23.2.

The level premium concept underlying these policies is extremely important, because (1) otherwise, permanent protection would be unavailable, since no insurer renews term insurance indefinitely, and (2) a savings or investment element is created, which may prove useful in emergencies or during retirement. To understand these two arguments, one must know how the level premium concept works. Assume that a person aged 35 wants $1,000 of permanent protection against death. Two contracts that would provide this protection are a straight life insurance contract and a one-year term policy renewable for life. In practice, this second contract is not issued by any insurer because the insurance would be too costly to be salable at the advanced ages, especially since only persons in poor health would be likely to continue the protection. Conceptually, however, this comparison is revealing.

One clear difference between the two approaches would be the premium-payment pattern. The yearly renewable term would be much cheaper in the early years, but in the late fifties or early sixties, depending upon the table of premium rates selected, the annual yearly renewable term premium would exceed the level premium for the straight life contract. Eventually, the total premiums paid for the term insurance would exceed the total premiums paid for the straight life contract, even if the loss of interest in the early years on the difference between the term premium and the straight life premium is acknowledged. Of course the persons who die in the early years will contribute much more in premiums if they purchase straight life insurance.

Because insureds with straight life contracts pay more than the cost of term protection in the early years, the insurer is able to use part of the premium in those years to establish a "savings account" or investment element.[3] This investment element is part of the face amount paid if the insured dies, and the cost of the "pure" insurance component, therefore, is actually less than the premium for a yearly renewable term contract of the same face amount as the straight life contract.

The investment element is credited with a guaranteed interest rate by the insurer and continues to grow throughout the policy period. During the early years of the contract, the growth is obvious, but as mortality rates increase, it takes place only because the interest on the savings account is more than adequate to make up for the deficiency in the level premium relative to the cost of the pure protection. With each increase in the investment element, the amount of pure protection decreases. Eventually, the fact that the amount of pure protection is decreasing more than offsets the increasing mortality rates, and as a result the cost of the pure protection decreases. Under the usual current mortality assumptions, a person aged 99 is assumed to die within the next year. Therefore the insurer must be prepared to deliver the face amount to the insured when he or she reaches age 100. At age 100 the investment element must equal the face amount, and the cost of the pure protection the last year is zero.[4]

Straight life insurance, therefore, may be viewed by the insured as a combination of decreasing term insurance (the pure-protection element) and an increasing investment element that equals the face amount at age 100.

The investment element is available to the insured at any time in the form of a cash value or some form of insurance. (The so-called nonforfeiture options are described later in this chapter in the section "Option Clauses.") In practice, the investment element will ordinarily be less, especially in the early years, than the preceding discussion would lead one to believe. The reason is that the insurer is permitted to give some recognition to its heavier expenses the first year (for example, the fee for a medical examination, the cost of preparing new policy records, and the agent's first-year commission, which is larger than the commission in succeeding years) before it diverts any of the premium into the investment element. Generally, therefore, there is

---

[3] The following discussion illustrates the principle involved. For a more rigorous discussion, see Davis W. Gregg and Vane B. Lucas (eds.), *Life and Health Insurance Handbook* (3d ed., Homewood, Ill.: Richard D. Irwin, Inc., 1973), pp. 69–70. Professor Robert Mehr has argued that this "economic" interpretation of straight life insurance may be misleading. He emphasizes that a straight life insurance policy is (1) a single contract, and (2) purchased under the installment plan. See R. I. Mehr, "The Concept of the Level-Premium Whole Life Insurance Policy—Reexamined," *Journal of Risk and Insurance,* vol. XLII, no. 3 (September, 1975), pp. 419–431. See also R. W. Cooper, "The Level Premium Concept: A Closer Look," *CLU Journal,* vol. XXX, no. 2 (April, 1976), pp. 24–32. For a thought-provoking argument that the savings and protection elements should be marketed by independent institutions, see William C. Scheel, "The Effects of Risk Reduction Inherent in Universal Life Insurance," *Journal of Risk and Insurance,* vol. XLVI, no. 2 (June, 1979), pp. 45–59 and vol. XLVI, no. 3 (September, 1979), pp. 451–482. See also the discussion of universal life insurace on pp. 479–480 of this text.

[4] Under policies issued prior to the late 1940s, the limiting age was assumed to be age 96 insteead of age 100.

no investment element the first year, the cash values usually becoming available during the second year.

Straight life insurance provides permanent insurance protection at the lowest cost. It may be used to leave a legacy to some person or organization, regardless of when the insured dies, or to pay probate costs and estate and inheritance taxes. It also permits an insured to accumulate some savings through life insurance. As will be explained in the section on nonforfeiture options, straight life insurance is a highly flexible contract.

Limited payment contracts also combine decreasing term insurance with an investment element, but the investment element is more important than in straight life insurance because of the higher limited payment premiums during the early years. The cash value patterns under the nonterm insurance contracts for which premium rates were presented in Table 23.2 are given in Table 23.3 for contracts issued at age 35. Figure 23.1 displays the same information in a different form. Figure 23.1 also shows the cash value patterns for two types of endowment insurance, another form of basic nonterm insurance which we will describe shortly. The reader's attention is directed particularly to (1) the absence of a cash value the first year under most contracts, (2) the cash values at age 100 under the whole life contracts, (3) the continued growth in the cash values under the limited payment contracts after the end of the premium-payment period, and (4) the comparison between the cash value patterns of the limited payment life contracts and the endowments.

Limited payment life insurance is attractive when an insured wishes to stop premiums after a specified period but wants the original face amount of protection to be continued for the rest of his or her life. For example, one may want to stop paying premiums at age 65, the normal retirement age, or 20 years from now, when one's peak earning period as an actor or an athlete has passed. Limited payment contracts are often used as gifts because the donor can complete the premium payments within a specified period. These contracts also appeal to persons who wish to devote a larger portion of their premiums to savings than is possible under straight life insurance. Most young married persons desiring a whole life policy who are considering a 20-payment

TABLE 23.3

CASH VALUES PER $1,000 INSURANCE PROVIDED BY ONE LEADING NONPARTICIPATING INSURER TO AN INSURED AGED 35

End of policy year	Straight life	Paid-up at 65	20-pay- ment life	Endowment at 65
1	—	—	—	—
2	—	—	—	—
3	$ 3	$ 5	$ 12	$ 13
5	24	30	45	47
10	85	101	136	138
15	156	185	249	253
20	256	297	387	398
Age 65	428	528	528	1,000
Age 100	1,000	1,000	1,000	

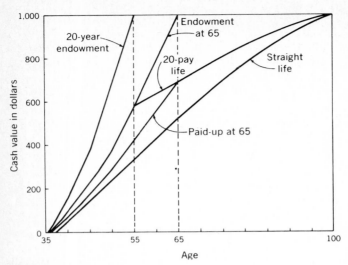

FIGURE 23.1
Cash values per $1,000 insurance provided under some representative contracts issued to an insured age 35.

life policy would be well advised to spend the same amount of premium to purchase a larger face amount of paid-up-at-65 or straight life insurance. Otherwise they are trading important additional protection for slightly higher cash values during the next 20 years[5] and the cessation of premium payments in 20 years when these payments should be much easier to meet than when the purchasers are young.[6]

Endowment Insurance   Endowment insurance protects the beneficiary if the insured dies within the endowment period, and in addition it provides for the payment of the face amount to the insured if he or she is living at the end of the endowment period. Endowment insurance may be regarded as a combination of term insurance for the endowment period and a pure endowment that would provide benefits only for those who survive. Endowment insurance, like all nonterm insurance contracts, may also be considered a combination of decreasing term insurance and an increasing investment element. The investment element, of course, is relatively more important for endowments than for whole life contracts. Two examples of endowment contracts are 20-year endowments and endowments at age 65. The relative importance of the investment elements in these contracts is shown in Figure 23.1.

Endowment insurance may be a useful way for some persons to accumulate a specified sum over a stated period of time whether they live or die. The objective may be

---

[5] The difference in cash values would be less than that shown in Figure 23.1 because the face amounts would be higher for the paid-up-at-65 or straight life insurance than for the 20-payment life policy.

[6] If unforeseen circumstances do make it desirable to terminate premium payments at that time, the nonforfeiture options described under "Option clauses" later in this chapter can be exercised to provide continuing protection under paid-up-at-65 or straight life insurance.

funds to finance a child's college education, to pay living expenses during retirement, or to retire a debt. Because a substantial portion of each annual premium is used to build up the investment element in the contract, the purchaser of an endowment should value savings much more than protection and should be convinced that insurance is a good investment. Endowment insurance has become much less important in recent years.

Life Insurance as an Investment Some observers believe that insureds would always be better off to "buy term and invest the difference" between the premiums for a nonterm policy and for a term policy. Their argument is basically that insureds can obtain more attractive yields and capital appreciation from most other investments. A few comments are in order here. First, although this advice to buy term and invest the difference may be sound for many persons, it is not a universal truth. Second, in making any evaluation of insurance as an investment, an insured should clearly understand its major advantages and disadvantages. The advantages are as follows:

1 Life insurance is a secure investment. Although losses may be suffered, they are very few. Even during the Great Depression, the industry achieved an enviable record.

2 Insureds are reluctant to skip premium payments or to make withdrawals from their savings accounts (although the liquidity of this asset is also a valuable feature in emergencies). Consequently, the savings plan is likely to be completed.

3 The insured does not have to be concerned with investment decisions or details.

4 The cash values in the contract guarantee the insured a minimum rate of return that tends to increase with the duration of the contract.

5 Actual interest returns commonly compare favorably with returns on other long-term, fixed-return investments of similar quality. Because a life insurance premium purchases a package of decreasing protection and increasing savings, the return on the savings element in a life insurance contract is a complicated concept. One widely used approach calculates the rate of return one would have to make on some alternative investment program to achieve the same results over a specified period at the same cost as the purchase of the nonterm insurance contract for which the rate of return is being sought. More specifically, assume that a person aged 35 is considering the purchase of a $1,000 straight life insurance contract for which the cash value at the close of the twentieth policy year is about $300. Instead of buying this policy he or she could buy decreasing term insurance and invest the difference between the premium for the straight life insurance and the premium for the decreasing term insurance in a savings account, mutual fund shares, or some other medium.[7] The face value of the decreasing

---

[7] Interest in buying term insurance and investing the difference has generated *minimum deposit plans* under which the insured purchases a straight life insurance policy and borrows the annual increase in cash value to pay part of the premium. If the insured dies, the beneficiary receives the face amount less the cash value or the decreasing term element in the policy. If the plan is arranged correctly, most of the interest on the amount borrowed is deductible for income tax purposes. Consequently this plan has proved attractive to many individuals in high income tax brackets. For more details on this approach and its advantages and disadvantages, see Garry M. Rollins, "Minimum Deposit Plans—Miracles or Mirages," *Journal of Risk and Insurance*, vol. XLVI, no. 2 (June, 1979), pp. 23–44. See also Joseph M. Belth, *Life Insurance: A Consumer's Handbook* (Bloomington: Indiana University Press, 1973), pp. 154–158.

term insurance must be such that, added to the increasing investment, it equals $1,000. In this way, if the insured dies prior to the expiration of the twentieth year, the beneficiary receives the same amount whether the insured purchases the straight life insurance or the separate term insurance-investment plan. The rate of return on the life insurance savings element is assumed to be the rate of return one would have to make on the separate investment fund for it to equal the $300 cash value at the close of the twentieth year.[8]

In 1979 Consumers Union applied this method to determine the rates of return on the savings components of 277 "cash value" policies (straight life or paid-up at some advanced age) sold by over 100 insurers.[9] In each case Consumers Union determined the cost of the alternative term insurance using "low-cost" term rates developed by the Society of Actuaries, a professional association of life insurance actuaries. Higher term rates would have produced higher yields; lower term rates would have produced lower yields.[10] For the median $100,000 policy issued to a male at age 35 by a participating insurer (an insurer that pays dividends to policyholders; see page 486) the annual yield over a 29-year period was 4.7 percent. The nine-year annual yield was only 1.2 percent, the 19-year annual yield 4.5 percent. For the median $100,000 policy issued to a male at age 35 by a nonparticipating insurer, the 29-year yield was 3.48 percent. The yields varied greatly among insurers; they also differed depending upon the issue age and the amount purchased. For example, for $100,000 participating life insurance policies issued at age 35, the annual yields over a 29-year period ranged among insurers from 8.07 percent to 2.24 percent. The best 29-year yields available from participating insurers ranged from 7.64 percent for a $100,000 policy issued at age 25, to 8.93 percent for a $25,000 policy issued at age 45.[11]

In evaluating these returns it is important to remember that these returns are substantially tax sheltered. No federal income taxes are payable on the investment return on the straight life insurance until the person cashes in the contract. Moreover, at that time only the excess of the cash value over the premiums paid (less dividends) is taxable. As a result most persons will pay less taxes than they otherwise would; some will pay no

---

[8] This method was developed by an insurance company actuary, Albert Linton. For some frequently quoted articles on this method, see M. A. Linton, "Life Insurance as an Investment," in David W. Gregg (ed.), *Life and Health Insurance Handbook* (2d ed., Homewood, Ill.: Richard D. Irwin, Inc., 1964), p. 242; J. M. Belth, "The Rate of Return on the Savings Element in Cash-Value Life Insurance," *Journal of Risk and Insurance,* vol. XXXV, no. 4 (December, 1968), p. 573; J. R. Ferrari, "Investment Life Insurance versus Term Insurance and Separate Investment," *Journal of Risk and Insurance,* vol. XXXV, no. 2 (June, 1968), pp. 181–198; Stuart Schwarzschild, "Rates of Return on the Investment Differentials between Life Insurance Policies," *Journal of Risk and Insurance,* vol. XXXV, no. 4 (December, 1968), pp. 583–595; W. C. Scheel, "The Rate of Return on the Savings Element in Cash-Value Life Insurance: Comment," *Journal of Risk and Insurance,* vol. XXXVIII, no. 4 (December, 1971), pp. 633–637, and Professor Belth's response, pp. 638–639; and R. C. Hutchins and C. E. Quenneville, "Rate of Return Versus Interest-Adjusted Cost," *Journal of Risk and Insurance,* vol. XLII, no. 1 (March, 1975), pp. 69–79.

[9] "Life Insurance: Part 2 of a Special Two-Part Report," *Consumer Reports,* vol. 45, no. 3 (March, 1980), pp. 163–188. See also Part 1 in *Consumer Reports,* vol. 45, no. 2 (February, 1980), pp. 79–106.

[10] For example, insureds who can obtain lower-cost association or group term insurance would not have to earn as much on the separate investment to accumulate a sum equal to the cash value.

[11] Similar returns were reported in a recent Federal Trade Commission staff report. See *Life Insurance Cost Disclosure,* Staff Report to the Federal Trade Commission by the Bureau of Consumer Protection of the Bureau of Economics, July, 1979, tables 11-7 and 11-8.

tax. If the insured's combined federal and state income tax bracket is 50 percent, a taxable investment would have to earn 12 percent to equal 6 percent tax free.

6 As we shall explain shortly, the cash value can be converted into an annuity without any additional expense loading and with perhaps some favorable tax consequences.

7 In case of death, the investment passes to the beneficiaries directly, thus avoiding the expense and delays of probate action.

On the other hand, for a given issue age, the return one would have to make under an alternative investment combined with separate term insurance in order to accumulate the same amount as the cash value under a nonterm insurance contract is less under contracts such as endowments, which place more emphasis upon the investment element than does straight life insurance.

The reader should also remember that the equivalent investment return is much less in the short run; at the end of one or two years it is commonly negative. A person who is saving to meet short-term needs would be well advised to invest in some other media, such as money market funds, bank savings accounts, savings and loan association deposits, or credit union shares.

A common objection to life insurance as an investment is that it provides no protection against long-period inflation. Like other fixed-dollar investments, such as corporate bonds and bank savings accounts, life insurance does not provide any opportunity for capital appreciation. Equities, on the other hand, permit capital gains and in the long run, the value of a diversified portfolio of common stocks has tended to rise when consumer prices rise, thus preserving real purchasing power.

Equities, however, may decline in value and the investor may suffer capital losses instead of making capital gains. Persons differ in their willingness and their desire to assume the risks associated with investments in equities. Furthermore, in some recent years common stocks have not fared as well as some other investments as a hedge against inflation. Because it is impossible to predict with much confidence the future state of the economy, the best approach for most persons is some blend of fixed-dollar investments and equities, the exact proportion depending upon one's personal assessment of the returns and risks associated with various proportions. Because life insurance has some advantages as a long-term fixed-dollar investment, risk managers may wish to use some nonterm life insurance purchased from a low-cost insurer as one of their fixed-dollar investments.

As indicated at the close of Chapter 26, many life insurers are now part of a financial services corporation that also markets such products as property and liability insurance, consumer loans, real estate, stocks and bonds, and mutual funds. The agent who represents such corporations may be able to provide products that meet the full range of investment needs and desires ranging from buying term insurance and investing the difference to purchasing life insurance with cash values.

Annuity Contracts Annuity contracts differ considerably from the life insurance contracts we have been discussing. Under an annuity, already explained in Chapter 22 in connection with pension plans, the insurer promises to pay the insured an income for a specified period. The specified period may be a definite number of years, in which case the contract is called an *annuity certain*. Most annuities sold as separate contracts, however, provide payments conditioned in some way upon the continued survival of the annuitant.

These *life-contingency contracts* assume many forms. A straight life annuity will provide payments as long as the insured lives. Even if the annuitant dies after having received only a few payments, the insurer has fulfilled its obligation. On the other hand, even if the annuitant lives to a very advanced age, the insurer must continue to make the payments. Under some annuity contracts involving life contingencies, a minimum number of payments is guaranteed. For example, under a life annuity contract with 10 years certain, the insurer promises to make payments for 10 years, regardless of whether the annuitant lives. After the 10 year period has passed, the insurer will continue the payments as long as the annuitant survives. Under an installment refund annuity, the guaranteed period is that necessary to refund the purchase price. For example, if the purchase price is $1,400 for a $10 monthly income, the insurer will make payments for 140 months and continue the payments thereafter until the annuitant dies. A cash refund annuity differs from an installment refund annuity in that the excess, if any, of the purchase price over the annuity payments made to the date of death is refunded in cash instead of in installments. Table 23.4 demonstrates the effect of the different refund features upon the purchase price for a given monthly income, on the assumption that the purchase price is payable in one lump sum and that the annuity payments begin one month after the purchase. The refund feature increases the cost of the annuity, especially if the refund is to be paid in cash instead of installments.

Like cash value life insurance, annuities can also be surrendered for their cash value instead of a lifetime income. Some persons in higher tax brackets who are not interested in the lifetime income feature of annuities purchase an annuity as a way to defer taxes on the interest earnings on the cash value accumulations until they surrender the contract for its lump sum value.

TABLE 23.4
PREMIUM RATES CHARGED BY ONE LEADING
NONPARTICIPATING INSURER FOR IMMEDIATE
ANNUITIES ISSUED TO MEN, PROVIDING $10
MONTHLY INCOME*

Age†	Straight life annuity	Installment refund annuity	Cash refund annuity
55	$1,256	$1,256	$1,308
65	1,080	1,129	1,159
75	867	941	990

* If the state imposes a premium tax on annuities, these basic rates must be multiplied by a tax factor. In North Carolina, for example, the tax factor is 1.025.

The rates for women are much higher. For example, for a woman age 65, the three rates are $1,211, $1,237, and $1,266.

† A pro rata allowance is made for each complete month elapsed since the insured's last birthday.

Annuities can also be classified according to other characteristics, all of which must be considered if an annuity contract is to be described completely. First, annuities can be classified as immediate or deferred, depending upon whether the benefits are payable immediately after the purchase of the contract, as in Table 23.4.[12] Second, annuities may be paid for by a single premium as in Table 23.4 or by annual premiums. Third, annuities may cover one life or joint lives. If two or more lives are covered, the payments may stop at the death of the first annuitant or at the death of the last annuitant. Payments of the first type are provided under joint life annuities, of the second type, under joint life and survivorship annuities.

The final classification to be considered is of relatively recent origin and depends upon whether the contract promises to deliver periodically (1) a fixed number of dollars or (2) a fixed number of units, the value of which will depend upon the market value of a portfolio of equity assets[13] or, less commonly, upon changes in the Consumer Price Index. Contracts of the first type are called *fixed* or *conventional* annuities; contracts of the second type are termed *variable* annuities.

Variable annuities were introduced for the first time in 1952 by the Teachers Insurance and Annuity Association (TIAA), an insurer that restricts its contracts primarily to college educators. TIAA established a running mate, the College Retirement Equities Fund (CREF), to underwrite these new contracts. In brief, the dollar amount to be provided under the contracts at the retirement date depends upon the performance of the CREF portfolio to that date. At retirement, the annuitant is guaranteed a certain number of annuity units per months for the remainder of his or her life (a refund feature may be included), the units being revalued once a year upon the basis of the performance of the CREF portfolio. The variable annuity was introduced because of the failure of the fixed annuity to produce (1) an initial retirement income reflecting changes in the cost of living during the premium-payment period, and (2) a constant purchasing power income during the retirement period. The variable annuity blends the characteristics of a mutual fund with those of an annuity. A variable annuity is superior to a mutual fund as a retirement vehicle because it provides a lifetime income. It is an inferior way to accumulate funds to meet short-term needs or to create an estate to be passed on to survivors.[14] Many life insurers sell both products.

TIAA-CREF studies revealed that over several selected periods in the past, equal annual contributions toward a fixed annuity and a variable annuity would have produced a retirement income satisfying (for practical purposes), over the long run, both of these criteria. The variable annuity alone produced payments that fluctuated more violently than the cost of living.

Although a few commercial insurers that specialize in variable annuities were formed during the 1950s, none of the major life insurers issued any contracts until

---

[12] Under most individual deferred annuity contracts, the insured is entitled to a refund of the premiums or a cash value, if higher, if he or she should die or surrender the contract prior to the maturity date.

[13] Currently variable annuities are usually associated with common stock investments, but the concept can be expanded to include other investment portfolios (for example, short-term money market investments) so long as the value of the unit varies depending upon the performance of the underlying investment portfolio.

[14] The two products are also taxed differently. Which system is more favorable to the consumer depends upon the circumstances.

1964, when a few insurers began to write group annuity contracts for selected groups. This belated and relatively limited activity on the part of major insurers can be attributed to legal obstacles, strong differences of opinion within and outside the industry concerning the desirability of marketing variable annuities to the general public,[15] technical problems such as the nature of the separate fund, and a natural hesitancy to enter a new field without extensive advance preparation.

Legal obstacles occurred first at the state level because state insurance laws had to be changed to permit the writing of group and individual variable annuities. After a few states had made the necessary changes, the Supreme Court of the United States ruled in 1959 that insurers specializing in variable annuities are subject to regulation by the Securities and Exchange Commission under the Investment Company Act of 1940. In April, 1964, after considerable legal sparring, the SEC announced its intent to approve group variable annuities for insured pension plans on a fairly liberal basis. Shortly thereafter many insurers became active in this field. SEC requirements for writing individual variable annuities have been more restrictive, but most leading insurers now sell this product. Sales of this product tend to rise and fall with the performance of the stock market.

Modifications and Combinations

In order to illustrate the ways in which the basic policy types can be modified and combined, several popular nonbasic insurance contracts are described very briefly below.

1 *Modified life and graded premium life* contracts are whole life contracts for which the premiums are not level over the premium-payment period. Under the modified life contract, the premium is lower than the level premium (but greater than the premium for term insurance) during the early years (generally the first three or five years), after which, in order to be actuarially equivalent, it increases to a higher amount than the level premium. Graded premium contracts resemble modified life contracts except that the premium increases gradually over the early years instead of remaining level over that period.

2 A *family* policy covers all members of the family under one contract. For example, one insurer issues a two-parent family policy that combines $5,000 of whole life insurance on the primary insured with $1,250 term insurance to age 65 on the spouse,[16] $1,000 term insurance to age 22 on the children, including children born after the inception of the contract, and $1,250 term insurance on the primary insured payable only if he or she dies after the spouse and before age 65. The term insurance is usually convertible at the time it expires. A family may purchase more than one unit. Not all family policies contain the same combination of coverages, but they are based on the same general principles.

---

[15] For example, opponents argued that policyholders would lose faith in life insurance if the monthly income drops, that life insurance agents were not qualified to sell a contract providing a variable income, and that supporting the variable annuity was equivalent to surrendering to inflation.

[16] Adjustments are made in the term insurance amount if the spouse is younger or older than the primary insured.

3 A *family income* policy combines whole life insurance with decreasing term insurance. The policy provides for *(a)* a monthly payment of 1 percent (or 2, 3, or 4 percent) of the face amount of the whole life policy from the date of death until the expiration of the family income period (usually 10, 15, or 20 years, beginning at the date of issue of the contract) and *(b)* the payment of the face amount at the end of the family income period or the date of death, whichever comes later. For example, a 2 percent $10,000 20-year family income policy issued at age 35 would make possible the following benefits.[17]

Date of death	Benefits
Policy issue date	$200 a month for 20 years, $10,000 at end of 20 years
Ten years later	$200 a month for 10 years, $10,000 at end of 10 years
Fifteen years later	$200 a month for 5 years, $10,000 at end of 5 years
Twenty or more years later	$10,000 payable immediately

The purpose of this contract is to provide a large sum of money if the insured should die while the family is young. The sum decreases as the children become older but never drops below the basic policy amount.

The $10,000 is, of course, provided by the whole life contract. The $200 a month comes from two sources: the interest on the $10,000 being held by the insurer and decreasing term insurance.[18] Generally the decreasing term insurance is provided by a rider attached to a new whole life insurance contract. The decreasing term insurance is usually convertible if the insured acts prior to five years, say, before the expiration date. The converted policy cannot exceed some portion, say, 80 percent, of the amount of the term insurance on the conversion date.

4 A *family maintenance* contract combines whole life insurance with *level* term insurance. The family maintenance contract differs from the family income contract only in that the payments are always made for the same number of years as the family maintenance period if death occurs during this period. For example, if the contract illustration used in the preceding paragraph had been a family maintenance contract, the payment, if death had occurred on the policy issue date, 10 years later, or 15 years later, would have been $200 a month for 20 years and $10,000 at the expiration of that time. If death occurred 20 or more years later, $10,000 would be payable immediately.

Some authorities prefer this contract to a family income contract because the family may continue to grow after the insurance is purchased. Even if the family does not grow, the level insurance may be required as a hedge against inflation.

5 A *retirement income* contract combines an annual premium deferred annuity contract with decreasing term insurance. Generally the contract provides a death benefit of $1,000 or the cash value, if greater, for each $10 of retirement income. In the

---

[17] Some contracts also provide for the immediate payment of a lump sum of $150 or $200 per $1,000 of whole life insurance.

[18] In this instance the term insurance decreases from about $37,000 to zero over the 20-year period.

early years of the contract, the cash value is much less than $1,000, and the term insurance provides most of the death benefit, but eventually the term insurance decreases to zero.

6 *Preferred risk* policies or *specials* are contracts (usually whole life contracts) sold at lower rates because of (1) higher underwriting standards or (2) minimum amount requirements.

7 The *guaranteed insurability* rider, when attached to a new life insurance policy, gives the insured the option to purchase at standard rates at certain specified ages additional amounts of insurance. The rider thus provides protection against uninsurability or insurability only at substandard rates and forces the insured to make definite decisions at the option dates. The following contract is illustrative: Attached to a base policy of $10,000 issued at age 20, this rider guarantees the right of the insured to buy $10,000 additional protection at (1) each of the following ages: 25, 28, 31, 34, 37, and 40, (2) on the insured's wedding date, and (3) at the birth of each child.

8 The eighth contract to be considered in this section is a life insurance contract with a *double indemnity* rider attached. The rider usually provides that if death *(a)* results directly and independently of all other causes from accidental bodily injuries evidenced by a visible contusion or wound on the exterior of the body (except in case of accidental drowning or internal injury revealed by an autopsy) and *(b)* occurs within 90 days after the injury was sustained, double the face amount of the contract is to be paid the insured. The rider then proceeds to exclude certain types of deaths that might otherwise be covered such as those resulting from suicide or from any medicine, drug, poison, chemical, gas, or fumes accidentally or otherwise taken, administered, absorbed, or inhaled. The coverage usually terminates at age 70 or earlier. Triple indemnity riders based on the same principles are also available.

The authors agree with many insurance authorities that the double indemnity rider should not be included in most insurance programs. The need for insurance proceeds is no larger in the case of a death caused by accidental means than by other means. Indeed the opposite may be true. The rider is most misused when it is purchased at the expense of protection against all causes of death.

9 *Variable life insurance* is a recent development in life insurance contracts. One approach permits the insured to purchase each year without proving insurability additional one-year term insurance that will preserve the purchasing power of the face amount of insurance. To illustrate, if the Consumer Price Index is 20 percent higher than when a $10,000 policy was purchased, the insured will be permitted to purchase a $2,000 one-year term policy. The annual term insurance offer terminates at age 65 or, if earlier, the first year the offer is not accepted. As mentioned in Chapter 12, one insurer adjusts the face amount of a variable life insurance policy as the Consumer Price Index rises. This approach is unusual because the insurer assumes the risk of price changes. A third approach is to adjust both the face amount and the cash value according to the performance of some separate investment account. Variable life insurance is a natural development following the maturation of the variable annuity concept.

10 *Adjustable life insurance*, sometimes known as "life cycle" insurance, permits the insured to change the face amount and the premium each year as his or her needs, capital accumulation objectives, and ability to pay the premium changes. To illustrate, using the plan issued by the insurer that introduced this insurance in 1971, the insured states the first year the amount of insurance and the annual premium desired. Depending upon the relationship between the face amount and the premium, the policy may provide only level-premium term insurance for five years, term insurance for a longer period, straight life insurance, or limited-payment life insurance with a payment period as short as five years. If the insured changes the premium, but not the face amount, the type of insurance changes. If the premium is increased (reduced) and the existing insurance was term insurance, the term is increased (reduced); if the premium increase is large enough, the term insurance is converted into straight life insurance or limited-payment life insurance. If the existing insurance was straight life or limited-payment life insurance, the premium-payment period is shortened (lengthened). If the premium reduction is large enough, the straight life or limited-payment life insurance is converted into term insurance. Instead of, or in combination with, changing the type of insurance, a premium increase (reduction) may be used to increase (reduce) the amount of insurance. Increases in the face amount are subject to evidence of insurability except that every three years the face amount can be increased without proving insurability by the percentage increase in the Consumer Price Index, subject to a maximum increase of 20 percent. A guaranteed insurability rider, for which there is an additional charge, would permit the insured to increase the face amount without proving insurability on specified option dates. The policy can also be extended for an extra premium to provide protection similar to the family policy described above.

11 *Universal life insurance,* which is offered as an alternative to whole life insurance, has attracted considerable attention and stimulated heated debates since its introduction in 1979. Universal life insurance is not standardized among insurers. Several versions of this insurance are available, but they usually share the characteristics listed below. Universal life insurance resembles whole life insurance in that it combines term insurance and savings (also called a cash value) in one contract.[19] The basic difference is that a universal life policy identifies explicitly (1) the amounts of these two components and (2) the rate of return on the savings or cash value portion. This rate of return is a guaranteed rate (3 or 4 percent) plus an additional rate that is tied generally to some short-term money market rate of return. The additional rate may be limited to savings in excess of $1,000.

The death benefit is usually determined in one of two ways. Under one plan the insured specifies the death benefit. As is true for adjustable life, each year, if the insured wishes, he or she can increase or decrease the amount of this death benefit, increases being subject usually to proof of insurability. In any given year, the amount of term insurance included in the universal life insurance contract is equal to the difference between that year's death benefit and that year's cash value. If this difference gets less than a certain amount, the insurer automatically increases the death benefit to bring the difference to an acceptable level.[20] Some portion of the cash value is deducted to pay for this increased term insurance.

Under the other plan the insured specifies the amount of the term insurance. In any

[19] One common package combines decreasing term insurance with a deferred annuity.
[20] Otherwise the policyholder might lose the tax advantages of life insurance noted on p. 472. A 1982 law tightened this requirement.

given year the death benefit is this specified insurance amount plus that year's cash value.

Another distinctive feature of universal life insurance is flexibility in the timing and amount of premium payments and withdrawals. As long as the cash value is sufficient to cover current mortality costs, the policyholder can reduce or skip premium payments. He or she can also withdraw some of the cash value with no interest charge. On the other hand, the policyholder can increase the number and amount of premium payments, thus increasing the cash value or savings component.

A third difference between universal life insurance and other cash value life insurance is the amount of information disclosed each year in a statement sent to the policyholder. This statement indicates the protection amount, the cash value, the interest rate being paid on the cash value, and the portions of the premium used to (1) pay for the term insurance, (2) increase the savings component, and (3) pay the insurer's acquisition and servicing fees. The insurer's fees are usually much higher the first year than they are later. Commission rates tend to be less than those associated with whole life insurance.

Whether universal life will provide higher long-run rates of return on the savings component than does whole life insurance depends to a large extent on how investments in short-term money market certificates (or other universal life investments) will compare with the long-run returns on the mix of investments that usually determine the rate of return on whole life insurance.

12 *Extralife, econoplan,* or *extraordinary life insurance.* Another recently developed alternative to traditional whole life insurance is typically called extralife, econoplan, extraordinary life, or some modification of these terms. Issued by mutual insurers, this insurance enables the insured to purchase a specified amount of life insurance for about two-thirds of the premium that would be paid for conventional whole life insurance. The face amount consists of two parts: (1) the amount of whole life insurance that the premium payment would normally purchase plus (2) some combination of paid-up insurance and one-year term insurance purchased with the amount of the premium the insurer would normally return as dividends on the whole life insurance. (For more information on policyholder dividends and the ways they can be used, see page 486 in this chapter.) Over time the paid-up additions grow until the one-year term insurance is no longer needed to bring the amount payable upon death to the face amount the insured purchased. Thereafter, the dividends can be paid in cash or placed under one of the dividend options to be explained later. Although the dividends are likely to be sufficient to generate the needed paid-up insurance and term insurance, they cannot be guaranteed.

13 *Joint life insurance.* Joint life insurance covers two or more lives under the same contract. The insurer pays the face amount when the first of the covered lives dies. Joint life insurance has become more popular as the number of two wage-earner families has increased.

14 *Flexible premium variable life insurance.* The final and newest modified policy is flexible premium variable life insurance. This modification combines variable life insurance with universal life insurance. Policyholders can raise or lower their premiums, skip premiums, or use a portion of the policy's cash value to pay premiums.

The death benefit and the cash value vary according to how the insurer's associated separate investment account performs.

MAJOR POLICY PROVISIONS

The major policy provisions may be divided into two groups: (1) the nonoption clauses, which do not require the insured or the beneficiary to make decisions, and (2) the option clauses, which require such decisions.

Nonoption Clauses

Some important nonoption clauses are the grace period clause, the suicide clause, and aviation and war clauses. All these clauses, like the entire contract, assignment, and incontestable clauses described in Chapter 15, are required or permitted statutory standard provisions clauses in most states.

The *grace period* clause establishes a period of one month or 31 days after the premium-due date during which the premium may be paid without penalty. Under most laws, the insurer could charge interest following the due date, but this is seldom, if ever, done. The *reinstatement* clause gives the insured the right to reinstate a policy after lapse for nonpayment of premiums if the policy has not been surrendered for cash and if the reinstatement is effected within a certain period after the lapse, usually five years. Overdue premiums must be paid with interest, and the person must present evidence of insurability.[21] The *misstatement of age* clause states that if the insured misstated his or her age, the amount payable is the amount the premium being paid would have purchased at the correct age at issue. The discovery of the misstatement is not limited by the incontestable clause. The clause may result in either an increase or a decrease in the face amount. The *suicide* clause excludes deaths by suicide, sane or insane, within one or two years from the date of issue. The reasoning is that persons do not plan suicide this far in advance and that the public interest is best served by making the proceeds available to the innocent beneficiaries where the policy has not been purchased with suicide in mind. *Aviation* clauses that limit the insurer's liability to the premiums paid plus interest if death occurs as a result of certain hazardous types of aviation (pilots of nonscheduled passenger flights, for example) are seldom used today, the preferred method of dealing with this extra hazard being by payment of an additional premium. *War* clauses, which limit the liability of the insurer if the death results from war or, in some cases, occurs while the insured is in service outside the home area, are generally used only when a war appears likely or already exists. After the war, the clauses are usually canceled.

---

[21] Two reasons why the insured may be interested in reinstating the policy instead of purchasing a new one are that (1) the heavy first-year expenses in a new contract can be avoided, and (2) older policies frequently have more liberal settlement options or some other attractive features. On the other hand, the cost of the old policy may have been so high (particularly if the policy is nonparticipating and life insurance costs in general have declined) that it may pay to switch policies.

Option Clauses

The option clauses deal with policy conversions, nonforfeiture options, loans, settlement options, and divided options.

Statutory standard provisions usually (1) prescribe the minimum nonforfeiture values and require a cash value option and at least one insurance option, (2) demand a loan provision and limit the maximum interest charge, and (3) make mandatory the annual payment of dividends if the insurer is financially able to do so. Otherwise, the statutes require only that the insurer present tables showing the amounts available under the various options. Consequently, considerable variation is possible among insurers with respect to these options.

Policy Conversions   The *policy change* clause permits the insured to convert the policy, without demonstrating evidence of insurability, to some other form requiring a higher premium. The conversion is retroactive, the insured usually making up the deficiency in the premiums already paid by a lump-sum payment equal to the difference in the reserves under the two plans. Conversion to a lower premium plan, if permitted at all, generally requires proof of insurability.

Nonforfeiture Options   As we have pointed out earlier in this chapter, nonterm insurance contracts combine decreasing term insurance with an increasing savings component.[22] This savings component, called the "nonforfeiture value," is available to the insured who wishes to surrender his or her policy. The cash values provided under several leading policies issued at age 35 were presented in Table 23.3.

Two other nonforfeiture options are also available. Both permit the insured to continue some insurance protection without paying any additional premiums. The *paid-up insurance* option permits the insured to exchange the cash value[23] at *net rates*[24] for a policy providing the same benefits as the surrendered contract but for a reduced amount. The *extended term insurance* option permits the insured to continue the face amount of insurance[25] in force as term insurance for as long a period as the cash value applied as a *net* single premium will provide.[26] However, if the original contract was an endowment contract and the cash value is sufficient to provide insurance for more than the remainder of the endowment period, the excess cash value is used to purchase a pure endowment payable to those insureds who survive to the end of the endowment period.

Specific illustrations of surrender value patterns for three popular types of policies issued at age 35 are presented in Table 23.5. If the insured does not pay a premium when it is due and does not select a nonforfeiture option within a specified period,

---

[22] Some term insurance contracts of long duration also provide for nonforfeiture values.

[23] More exactly, the cash value less any policy loans plus any dividend accumulations or cash values on dividend additions.

[24] No expense loading.

[25] More exactly, the face amount plus any dividend accumulations or additions less any policy indebtedness.

[26] More exactly, the cash value less any policy loans plus any dividend accumulations or cash values on dividend additions.

TABLE 23.5
NONFORFEITURE VALUES PROVIDED BY ONE LEADING NONPARTICIPATING INSURER TO AN INSURED AGE 35

End of policy year	Straight life				20-payment life				Paid-up at 65			
	Cash value	Paid-up insurance	Extended term insurance		Cash value	Paid-up insurance	Extended term insurance		Cash value	Paid-up insurance	Extended term insurance*	
			Years	Days			Years	Days			Years	Days
5	$ 24	$ 68	9	9	$ 45	$118	15	162	$ 30	$ 82	11	60
10	85	208	13	147	136	312	21	273	101	239	16	87
15	156	335	14	346	249	495	24	271	185	381	18	81
20	256	486	14	291	387	Fully paid			297	564	18	10
Age 65	428	621	12	237	528	Fully paid			528	766	15	310

such as three months, one of the insurance options, usually the extended term insurance option, becomes effectively automatically.

Loan provisions   The *loan provision* permits the insured to borrow an amount which, accumulated at interest, will not exceed the cash value[27] on the date to which premiums have been paid. Interest accrues on the loan from day to day, and the policy terminates when the total indebtedness exceeds the cash value. The loan may be repaid in whole or in part at any time. In case of death, the indebtedness is subtracted from the proceeds.

The interest rate is charged in part to offset earnings lost because the insurer loses the interest it would have made if it had invested the money elsewhere and, to be able to grant policy loans upon demand, the insurer must keep more of its assets in lower-yielding liquid investments than it otherwise would. The insurer also incurs some costs in administering the loan. On contracts issued until a few years ago the interest rate was 5 or 6 percent. On new contracts insurers can charge up to 8 percent. In some states insurers can charge a flexible rate based on Moody's index of yields on seasoned corporate bonds.

The *automatic premium loan provision*, which is not included by most insurers except upon request (and in this sense only is an option clause), provides that if the insured fails to pay any premium, the insured is assumed to have paid the premium by borrowing against the policy.

Settlement Options   The settlement options make it possible to have the death proceeds and usually the cash value payable in some manner other than a lump sum. The insured may at any time select options that the beneficiary must accept, or the insured may permit the beneficiary after his or her death to change the selection. If the insured does not make any selection, the beneficiary usually has this right.

Although other options may be available upon request, the four most common options applicable to death proceeds are the following:

1 *Interest* option. The insurer holds the proceeds for some specified period, a guaranteed rate of interest being payable to the primary beneficiary. The primary beneficiary may have the right of withdrawal in whole or in part. At the end of the specified period (for example, the death of the primary beneficiary), the proceeds are payable, perhaps according to some other option.

2 *Installment time* option. The proceeds are payable as a monthly income for a specified number of years. The monthly income is computed on the basis of a guaranteed interest rate on the unpaid balance.

3 *Installment amount* option. The proceeds are payable as a specified monthly income for such time as the proceeds will provide. The time is computed on the basis of a guaranteed interest rate on the unpaid balance.

4 *Life income* option. The proceeds are used as the purchase price for an annuity at net rates. The common annuity forms are the straight life annuity, an annuity with a specified number of years certain, a cash refund annuity, and an installment refund

---

[27] More exactly, the cash value plus dividend accumulations or the cash values of dividend accumulations.

TABLE 23.6
MONTHLY INSTALLMENTS PER $1,000 PROCEEDS PROVIDED BY ONE
LEADING NONPARTICIPATING INSURER UNDER THE INSTALLMENT
TIME AND LIFE INCOME SETTLEMENT OPTIONS

Installment time option		Monthly life income option			
		Age of payee		Years certain	
Number of years	Monthly installment	Male	Female	10	20
2	$42.77				
3	28.90				
4	21.97	45	50	$4.13	$4.00
5	17.81	50	55	4.51	4.29
10	9.51	55	60	4.98	4.59
15	6.76	60	65	5.56	4.90
20	5.39	65	70	6.26	5.18

annuity. The monthly payments are based on guaranteed interest and mortality rates. Some insurers offer a variable annuity settlement option.

The policy specifies the guaranteed interest rate applicable to option 1 and the monthly benefits possible under options 2 and 4. A portion of a table of monthly values under options 2 and 4 is reproduced as Table 23.6. Option 3 values are computed on the same assumptions as option 2 values, and a rough estimate of the time over which they will be paid is obtainable from the same table.[28] For example, under a $10,000 policy, $100 a month would be payable for over 9 years but less than 10 years. *In each case, the insurer may declare some excess interest each year that will increase the amount or the time of the monthly payments.* For example, although the installment time option amounts in Table 23.6 are calculated on the basis of a 2.75 percent interest return, this particular insurer is currently paying a considerably higher rate (7.5 percent) on the unpaid balance of the proceeds.

The insured may also elect to receive the cash value of the contract according to one of these options. In addition, the policy commonly permits the insured to purchase a joint and survivorship annuity at net rates. The insurer whose settlement option values were reproduced in Table 23.6 provides a guaranteed monthly income of $4.87 for a male aged 65 and a wife aged 60 per $1,000 of cash value applied under this option, two-thirds of this amount being continued for the lifetime of the survivor. For a husband and wife, both 65, the joint income would be $5.28. Currently this insurer is paying much higher amounts than these two guaranteed values.

Settlement options give the insured guaranteed interest and mortality rates, some tax advantages,[29] conversion rights at net cost, freedom from investment worries, and the

[28] In practice, however, a separate exact computation is made for the value selected.

[29] For example, only the interest portions of the payments are taxable, and the spouse of a deceased person may receive annually $1,000 in interest of this sort tax-free under all options other than the interest option.

ability to evaluate a lump-sum payment in terms of the income it replaces. If the insured wishes to have the proceeds managed by some third party but wants more flexibility than that provided by the settlement options, a lump-sum payment may be paid to a trustee under a trust agreement. The return on the trusteed proceeds, however, is not guaranteed; it may be greater or less than if the insurer had retained the proceeds.

Dividend Options   Participating policies provide dividends for policyholders when the premium charged exceeds the actual cost of the protection. Sizable dividends are probable under participating policies because the initial premiums include a substantial "cushioning" factor.

The usual dividend options in a participating contract permit the insured to receive annual dividends as (1) a cash payment, (2) a reduction in the next premium, (3) paid-up additional life insurance, the additional insurance being purchased by the application of the dividend as a single premium at net rates, (4) a deposit with the insurer accumulating at not less than a guaranteed rate of interest, or (5) one-year term insurance, the dividend being used as a single premium to purchase the term insurance at net rates. The amount of term insurance under this fifth option may be limited to the cash value under the contract, in which the case the remainder of the dividend is accumulated at interest for use in future years.

The dividends may be used to reduce the number of premiums by converting the policy to a paid-up contract with the same face amount when the cash value under the contract plus the cash value under dividend additions or the dividends accumulated at interest equal the cash value of a paid-up policy. The dividends may also be used to mature the policy as an endowment when these same values under the contract equal or exceed the face amount of the contract. Other options may also be permitted.

The paid-up additions option has the advantage of providing additional protection and, over a long period, will provide almost as much cash value as if the dividends were accumulated at interest.[30]

Flexibility Provided by Options   The four sets of options discussed in this section make the life insurance contract a highly flexible instrument. An example will serve to summarize the preceding discussion and to demonstrate this flexibility.

A person aged 35 purchases a $100,000 straight life insurance contract. At any age, the purchaser may elect to convert this contract to a limited payment contract or an endowment contract. He or she may choose to receive dividends according to one of the dividend options. At any age, the insured may elect to borrow on the policy or to surrender the contract and exercise the nonforfeiture options. For example, at age 65, the insured may decide to surrender the contract, have it continued as paid-up insurance of a reduced amount, or have the insurance continued in the same face amount for some limited period. If the insured elects a cash value, he or she may ask to have the proceeds paid out according to one of the settlement options, including a retirement income under an annuity. Finally, in case of death before surrender of the policy for cash, the death proceeds may also be placed under one of the settlement options.

[30] Since the interest on the accumulations is taxable annually while the interest on the cash value may never be taxed, the effective return may actually be greater.

SPECIAL CHARACTERISTICS OF FRATERNAL LIFE INSURANCE AND SAVINGS BANK LIFE INSURANCE

Although most of the discussion of types of contracts and major policy provisions applies to the contracts issued by fraternal societies and by mutual savings banks in three states, these insurers have some special characteristics, a few of which are noted below.

Fraternal Societies

Fraternal societies include in their membership persons sharing a common occupation, religion, nationality, race, or sex. The societies are characterized by a system of lodges and a representative form of government. Fraternals first started to sell life insurance to members after the Civil War. Although many fraternals continue to emphasize the social and benevolent activities for members (picnics, lodge meetings, homes for the aged, orphanages, and the like) for which they were originally formed, some fraternals now concentrate most of their attention on the sale of life insurance. Although the practices of the leading fraternals closely resemble those of commercial insurers, some fraternals issue policies that are not quite so liberal. Similarly, the leading fraternals run a financially sound operation, but the financial condition of some fraternals is inferior to that of most commercial insurers.[31] The contracts of *all* fraternals differ from those of commercial insurers in that the fraternal policy is an ''open'' contract. The fraternal policy is assessable, and the contract includes, in addition to the policyholder's certificate and application, the articles of association or incorporation, the constitution and the by-laws, and all amendments to these documents. Leading fraternals claim that they do not need the assessment right any more than do the commercial insurers, which do not possess the right. Consequently they look upon the assessment right as a safeguard, not a drawback for their insureds. The share of the market controlled by fraternals as a group is decreasing, but some of the leading fraternals, particularly those associated with religious groups, have been increasing their market share.

Mutual Savings Banks

Mutual savings banks in Connecticut, Massachusetts, and New York are authorized under certain conditions to issue to residents individual and group life insurance policies that are very similar to those sold by commercial insurers. The amounts, however, are limited. In New York, for example, a person cannot usually own more than $30,000 of individual savings bank life insurance. No agents are employed, the insurance being sold over the counter at the bank. For this and other reasons, the premiums compare very favorably with those of conventional insurers, regardless of the method used to compare the costs.[32] An interesting feature of this savings bank operation is the ''unification'' in each state of the mortality experience of the par-

---

[31] Initially, fraternals attempted to underwrite life insurance on a pure assessment basis and because of inadequate assessments encountered financial difficulties.

[32] See Chap. 27.

ticipating banks, which produces for each bank through a pooling operation the same ratio of actual to expected mortality.[33]

SOME KEY CONCEPTS

Ordinary insurance   Individual life insurance generally sold in amounts of at least $1,000. *Industrial insurance* is the other major class of individual life insurance.

Term insurance   Life insurance under which the insurer promises to pay the face amount if the insured dies during the specified term.

Whole life insurance   Life insurance under which the insurer promises to pay the face amount when the insured dies. Straight life insurance and limited payment life insurance are the two classes of whole life insurance.

Annuity   A form of insurance under which the insurer promises to pay the insured an income for a specified period or as long as the insured and perhaps a beneficiary lives.

Variable life insurance   Life insurance under which the face amount varies according to some index or the performance of some investment portfolio.

Adjustable life insurance   Life insurance under which the insured can change the face amount and the premium each year as his or her needs, capital accumulation objectives, and ability to pay the premium changes.

Universal life insurance   A life insurance package that identifies explicitly the amount of the term insurance and the savings component included in the package plus the rate of return on the savings portion. Each year the insured can increase (subject to proof of insurability) or decrease the death benefit and skip, reduce, or increase the premium.

Nonforfeiture options   Ways in which an insured can elect to claim the cash value of a nonterm life insurance contract if he or she decides to surrender the contract. The three most common options are cash, paid-up insurance, and extended term insurance.

Settlement options   Ways in which an insured or the beneficiary can elect to have the death proceeds or the cash nonforfeiture value distributed. The most common settlement options are an interest option, an installment time option, an installment amount option, and a life income option.

REVIEW QUESTIONS

1 Nine years ago a male nonsmoker insured, now aged 34, purchased a ten-year renewable and convertible term insurance contract from the insurer whose rates were presented in Table 23.2.

  a What annual premium does the insured pay for a $100,000 policy?

  b If the insured wishes to renew the term insurance policy next year, what annual premium will he pay?

  c If the insured wishes to convert the term insurance policy to a straight life insurance policy next year, what annual premium will he pay?

2 "A straight life insurance contract combines an increasing savings account with decreasing term insurance." Do you agree with this statement?

3 Construct a chart similar to Figure 23.1 for the following contracts issued to (1) a person aged 20 and (2) a person aged 45:

---

[33] A distinctive feature of the Connecticut central organization is that in 1963 it was authorized to serve savings banks in other states. However, no states other than the three discussed here have as yet authorized their banks to sell savings bank life insurance.

a Straight life insurance
b 10-payment life
c 20-payment life
d Paid-up at 65
e 20-payment endowment
f Endowment at 65

4 An executive in the firm argues that she sees no reason to purchase life insurance other than term insurance because (a) she is self-disciplined enough to save regularly and (b) she can earn a large return on a savings account. Is she correct? Why or why not?

5 Some people refer to annuities as an upside-down application of life insurance. What do they probably mean by this reference?

6 A person purchases an annual premium-deferred installment refund annuity. What benefits are provided under this contract?

7 a "Purchasing a conventional annuity with half of your premium and a variable annuity with the other half will provide a life income at retirement that will rise and fall with the cost of living." Is this statement correct?
b Are variable annuities generally available?
c Compare and contrast a variable annuity with a mutual fund.

8 Compare the benefits provided under the following contracts:
a A 20-year 1 percent $10,000 family income policy and a 20-year 1 percent $10,000 family maintenance policy
b $10,000 renewable and convertible term insurance and $5,000 straight life insurance with a guaranteed insurability rider

9 Smith has an adjustable life insurance policy which currently provides $50,000 of straight life insurance. How can he change the nature of his protection if he increases the premiums? If he decreases his premiums?

10 a How does a universal life insurance policy differ from straight life insurance?
b What are the advantages and disadvantages of universal life insurance relative to straight life insurance?

11 Ms. Brown purchased a $100,000 20-payment life insurance contract at age 35. She is now 50 and is unable to continue her premium payments. What options are available? Use Table 23.5 to calculate the benefit amount under each option.

12 Suppose that Ms. Brown (see question 11) had used the same premium to purchase a straight life insurance contract.
a How much insurance would she have been able to purchase? Assume that the rates in Table 23.2 apply.
b What could she do under this contract if at age 50 she was unable to continue her premium payments? Use Table 23.5 to calculate the benefit amount under each option.

13 An insured dies leaving a wife aged 60. If the insured had a $40,000 insurance policy, how much monthly income would his widow receive if all the proceeds were applied under each of the four most common settlement options? Assume that the insured's life insurance policy contains a table of settlement options similar to Table 23.6, that the time under the installment time option is 20 years, and that the monthly life income option is a life annuity with 20 years certain.

14 How much insurance would an insured aged 55 need to accomplish each of the following objectives if he died today?
a $400 a month to his widow for 10 years.
b $400 a month for the remainder of his widow's life, the income to be paid during the first 10 years, regardless of whether she lives or dies. His wife is also 55 years of age.

15 a Compare the additional paid-up insurance dividend option with the one-year term insurance dividend option.
  b How can the insured through dividends convert a straight life insurance contract into a limited payment life insurance contract?
16 Describe briefly:
  a The "open" contracts of fraternals
  b The role of mutual savings bank life insurance

SUGGESTIONS FOR ADDITIONAL READING

Gregg, Davis W., and Vane B. Lucas (eds.): *Life and Health Insurance Handbook* (3d ed., Homewood, Ill.: Richard D. Irwin, Inc., 1973), chaps. 5–9, 13–14, 17–19, 53–54, and 57–58.

Greider, J. E., M. L. Crawford, and W. T. Beadles: *Law and the Life Insurance Contract* (5th ed., Homewood, Ill.: Richard D. Irwin, Inc., 1984).

Huebner, S. S., and K. Black: *Life Insurance* (10th ed., Englewood Cliffs, N.J.: Prentice-Hall, Inc., 1982), chaps. 5–15.

McGill, D. M.: *Life Insurance* (rev. ed., Homewood, Ill.: Richard D. Irwin, Inc., 1967), chaps. 3–7, and 22–34.

Mehr, R. I., and S. G. Gustavson: *Life Insurance: Theory and Practice* (3d ed., Austin: Business Publications, Inc., 1984), chaps. 3–7 and 9–11.

CHAPTER 24

INDIVIDUAL HEALTH INSURANCE CONTRACTS

LEARNING OBJECTIVES

After you have read this chapter, you should be able to:

1 Summarize the major benefits provided by a typical disability income policy.
2 Explain the most important types of cancellation and renewal provisions found in disability income insurance contracts.
3 List the factors that affect the cost of disability income insurance.
4 Describe briefly the disability benefits that can be obtained through a rider on a life insurance contract.
5 Compare individual medical expense insurance benefits with those provided through employee benefit plans.

INTRODUCTION

Health insurance, like life insurance, is provided under both employee benefit plans and individual contracts. This chapter deals with individual health insurance. Families purchase most of this insurance, but businesses also purchase individual contracts for the reasons described in Chapter 25.

After describing the branches of health insurance and indicating the scope and growth of this line of insurance, this chapter will describe the basic individual policy types and some major provisions. Of the two types of health insurance, disability income insurance will be discussed in much more detail than medical expense insurance. Individual medical expense insurance contracts, though less liberal, tend to resemble more closely their group counterparts.

BRANCHES OF HEALTH INSURANCE

Table 24.1 shows the number of persons protected against loss of income and medical expenses under both employee benefit plans and individual insurance at the close of 1981. Employee benefit plans, through commercial group insurance and, to a lesser extent, paid sick-leave plans, account for about four-fifths of the persons with short-term disability income protection and about two-thirds of those with long-term protection. Commercial insurers write practically all the individual disability income insurance. Commercial insurers also protect over half the persons with medical expense insurance. Blue Cross, Blue Shield, and medical society plans are the second most popular types of insurers. Independent plans do not cover as many persons as the other two groups, but, as noted earlier, they are an important source of new ideas in health care. Over four-fifths of the persons covered under Blue Cross, Blue Shield, and independent plans belong to employee benefit plans. Consequently individual insurance accounts for only about one-fourth of the persons with hospital insurance and a much smaller fraction of the persons with other medical expense coverages.

TABLE 24.1
NUMBER OF PERSONS PROTECTED BY PRIVATE INSURANCE AGAINST DISABILITY INCOME LOSS AND MEDICAL EXPENSES, END OF 1981

Type of protection	Number insured, millions	
	Short-term	Long-term
Disability income loss:		
Commercial insurance:		
Group insurance	25.8	15.9
Individual insurance	10.5	5.8
Net total corrected for duplication	34.6	21.7
Formal paid sick leave*	23.0	
Other	2.7	
Net total	60.3	21.7

Medical expenses	Hospital expense	Surgical fees	Charges for physicians' care	Major medical expense	Dental expense
Commercial insurance:					
Group insurance	105.4	105.5	97.3	115.9	
Individual insurance	25.6	12.4	11.2	6.6	
Net total corrected for duplication	108.4	102.0	93.9	107.4	61.1
Blue Cross, Blue Shield, and medical society plans	85.8	71.8	68.1	48.4	12.5
Independent plans	40.3	44.8	43.3	33.7	35.5
Net total all insurers	188.3	176.9	163.9	157.7	86.3

* Net figures after adjustment for duplication of other coverage.
Source: Source Book of Health Insurance Data, 1982–83 (Washington, D.C.: Health Insurance Association of America, 1983), pp. 13–20.

Classification of Commercial Individual Insurance Contracts

Most individual health insurance corresponds to ordinary insurance in life insurance. These *ordinary* contracts will be described at length in the chapter.

Industrial policies are marketed on the same basis as industrial life insurance and bear essentially the same relationship to ordinary insurance that industrial life insurance bears to ordinary life insurance. *Special risk* policies are specially designed contracts providing substantial benefits, protection against unusual hazards, or both. For example, the contract might indemnify a motion-picture corporation if sickness prevents a movie actress from performing on schedule, or it might promise to provide a certain income if a person is disabled while in a war area or while engaged in some scientific experiment, such as a flight into space. *Limited* policies include a heterogeneous group of contracts that provide protection only against specified types of accidental injuries or diseases or that protect the insured only for a few days or weeks. Popular examples include the ticket accident policy sold in railway stations, the aviation ticket policy sold in connection with flights by the insured, automobile accident policies, and dread disease contracts, most of which protect the insured against medical expenses associated with a specified list of important diseases. Although these policies can be used to fill gaps in broader-gauged coverage or to increase coverage amounts when the chance of loss is temporarily increased, they may mislead insureds into believing they provide more complete protection. Because of the relatively (and increasingly) less important role of both industrial and limited policies and the restricted use of special policies, they will not be discussed further.[1]

Disability riders attached to life insurance policies are important enough to merit separate treatment with "ordinary" health insurance later.

Credit health insurance, like credit life insurance, is best described as a unique application of health insurance providing disability income protection. Lending institutions and merchants selling on a charge-account or an installment basis have used this insurance to protect themselves and the debtor against the debtor's failure to meet installment payments if he or she becomes disabled. Under this insurance, the insurer makes these payments during the debtor's disability, subject commonly to some maximum number of payments. As is true of credit life insurance, most of this insurance is written on a group basis.

DISABILITY INCOME CONTRACTS

Disability income contracts may in some instances also provide medical expense protection, but they are designed primarily to provide income coverage. Because of the many variations that exist in practice, disability income contracts are difficult to summarize. Most contracts, however, fall within the general framework described below.

---

[1] A type of group insurance that perhaps should be regarded as a type of limited insurance is blanket insurance. Like group insurance, it covers a group of persons under one contract, but unlike group insurance, it does not specify the individuals, whose identities are constantly changing. Like limited insurance, blanket insurance usually provides protection for the individuals only for short periods or against specified types of accidents and diseases. An example is blanket insurance providing death and dismemberment benefits for employees when their duties require them to travel by air. Such insurance can also be obtained on a group basis with the names of the employees specified.

Benefits

Disability income policies usually cover either accidental injuries alone or both accidental injuries and sickness combined. In the latter type of policy, it is common practice to issue a separate contract covering each of the two perils because of the differences in the protection afforded against them.

The *accident* policy or the accident portions of a combined policy generally provide protection against loss "resulting directly and independently *of all causes* from *accidental bodily injury* occurring while this policy is in force." Under this provision the result, but not the means, must be accidental. For example, an insured may strain his or her back while lifting a heavy object. The requirement that the loss result independently of all other causes is supposed to cut out claims where some preexisting impairment or sickness causes the accident and to reduce claims where the preexisting condition increases significantly the severity of the loss. In practice, the full loss is usually payable if the accident is the dominating cause even if it is not the sole cause.

Certain types of accidents are excluded, for example, losses caused by war, suicide and intentionally inflicted injuries, injuries while in military service during wartime, and injuries sustained while a crew member of an aircraft or a student pilot.

Most disability income policies are schedule policies permitting the insured to select the types of benefits he or she wishes to purchase. Sometimes, however, the contract provides only one or a few of the possible coverages; sometimes the contract is a package including all or most of the common coverages. The following discussion is directed toward the schedule policies.

The most important benefits included in the schedule are the total disability income and the partial disability income benefits. The total disability income provision provides a stated weekly or monthly benefit for a specified number of weeks or months (for example, 60 months) if the injury within a short period following the accident (commonly 100 days) completely prevents the insured from engaging in his or her regular occupation. Some insurers consider persons totally disabled up to age 65 or even for life if they cannot work at their own occupations. The requirement that the disability commence shortly after the accident eliminates the claims of doubtful origin that occur later, but it may also eliminate some legitimate claims. The payments will generally be continued after the expiration of the "own occupation" benefits either for life or for some stated number of years as long as the insured is prevented from engaging in any gainful occupation for which he or she is reasonably fitted by education, training, and experience. A common proviso is that in no case is a person to be considered totally disabled if he or she engages in any occupation for remuneration or profit. This provision is important if, say, a disabled surgeon is unable to continue his or her medical career but makes as much money as a used car salesperson.

The partial disability provision, which is often omitted, provides a specified weekly income (commonly two-fifths or half of the monthly total disability income benefit) for a specified number of months (for example, six months) if the injury within a short period following the accident or immediately following a period of total disability renders the insured able to perform one or more but not all the duties of his or her occupation.

The determination of total or partial disability depends upon the physical capacity of the insured, not the loss of wages. The fact that the insured's employer may continue his or her wages does not reduce the insurance benefit.

Many insurers now provide *residual* benefits if the insured returns to work but his or her income is reduced 20 percent or more because of the disability. The benefit is the total disability benefit times the percent by which the insured's income is reduced by the disability. An increasing number of insurers sell *immediate residual* policies that do not require a period of total disability prior to the payment of residual benefits. Under these policies the test of a person's eligibility for benefits is the effect of the disability on his or her earnings, not the physical condition.[2]

Another important disability benefit is provided by the dismemberment and loss-of-sight provision. A "capital sum" such as $10,000 or 208 times the total disability weekly indemnity, is payable for the loss of both hands, both feet, the sight of both eyes, one hand and one foot, or either hand or foot and the sight of one eye if the loss occurs within specified times (for example, 90 days or during a period of compensable total disability) following the accident. Lesser amounts are provided for other dismemberment and sight losses and a separate provision may provide similar benefits for various fractures and dislocations. The dismemberment benefits may be in addition to total disability income payments, or they may establish a minimum number of such payments.

The contracts also commonly contain an accidental death benefit, which is a limited kind of life insurance. Another provision doubles the amount payable under the benefits described to this point if the injuries result from *specified types* of accidents, such as those occurring while the insured is a passenger in or upon a public conveyance, except aircraft, or as a result of the collapse of the outer walls or the burning of a building if the insured is in the building at the time of its collapse or at the commencement of the fire. The comments made in the last chapter with respect to the double indemnity clause in life insurance could be repeated here, because the value of this clause is even more questionable than the double indemnity rider. Other "fringe" benefits may also be included.

The *sickness* portion of the policy generally provides protection against loss resulting from sickness first manifesting itself after the effective date of this policy. Preexisting sicknesses, in other words, are excluded.

The only disability income benefit under the sickness portion may be total disability income, but the residual and immediate residual benefits described earlier are becoming more common. If the insured is completely unable to engage in his or her regular occupation, the insurer will, usually after a waiting or so-called elimination period of one or two weeks, pay a specified weekly income for a stated period, say, two or five years. Longer-term benefits are available, but seldom beyond age 65. When the maximum duration of benefits is more than a short period such as two or five years, the test of disability is often changed after that period to inability to engage in any occupation

---

[2] An even newer concept is an *income replacement* policy. Two key features of this policy are that (1) the benefit is related to the loss of income, not the degree of disability, and (2) the elimination or waiting period described in this paragraph starts on the date a physician diagnoses the underlying injury or sickness. The benefit is, say, 80 percent of the prior income less the new net income subject to the specified maximum benefit.

for which the insured is fitted by education, training, and experience. As was true for accident benefits, however, some insurers continue the "own occupation" definition of total disability for longer periods.

The elimination period in sickness insurance contracts, which may be much longer than the one cited above (for example, six months), serves the same purpose as the deductible in property and liability insurance—to cut costs of unimportant losses and morale hazard. Accidental injury benefits may also be subject to an elimination period, but their use there is much less common.

If a disabled person recovers but later is disabled from the same cause, a question often arises as to (1) whether a new elimination period applies before benefits start, and (2) whether benefits already paid are subtracted from the maximum amount to be paid. Contracts usually handle this problem by stating that if the insured recovers for at least, say, six months, the second disability will be considered a new one.

Standard Provisions

The contract provisions discussed to this point are not covered under the 1950 Uniform Individual Accident and Sickness Policy Provisions Law mentioned in Chapter 15. Some of the 12 required uniform provisions (the entire contract clause and the time limit on the defense of misrepresentation) have already been described. Another important uniform provision prohibits the insurer from contesting a claim for loss commencing three years or later from the date of issue of the contract on the ground that the condition existed prior to that date unless the condition is specifically excluded in the contract. Other required provisions deal with reinstatement, a grace period, claims notices, claim forms, proofs of loss, claims payments, beneficiary changes, physical examinations and autopsies, and time limits on legal actions.

Common optional provisions deal with the adjustments to be made in the amounts paid because of changes in occupation during the policy term or misstatements of age in the application. An optional provision dealing with duplicate insurance states that the insurer will pay only that proportion of its benefit that the benefits provided by all policies of which the insurer had notice prior to the loss bear to the total of all benefits applicable to the loss. For example, an insurer providing a benefit of $400 a month would pay only two-thirds of that amount if the insured had another $200-a-month policy in force and failed to tell the insurer about this duplicate insurance. Other optional provisions deal with the deductibility of unpaid premiums from claim payments, the necessity of conforming to state statutes, and the exclusion of losses caused by the commission of a felony, an illegal occupation, or the illegal use of intoxicants and narcotics. The important optional standard provisions that give the insurer the right to cancel the contract are discussed next.

Cancellation and Renewal Provisions

An important consideration in purchasing disability income insurance is the right of the insured to continue the coverage at his or her option for many years, regardless of the insured's health. Formerly, many insurers included a cancellation provision in their contracts that permitted the insurer to cancel the contract at any time after a stated number of days' notice. This practice is rare today. Many contracts still give the insurer the right to refuse to renew the contract after the original term expires, but this right is often restricted to reasons specified in the contract. Over half the contracts written currently are more liberal noncancelable and guaranteed renewable policies. Noncancelable policies are renewable at the option of the insured to some advanced age such as 60 or 65. Guaranteed renewable contracts, which are less common in disability income insurance, differ from noncancelable policies in one important respect: The insurer reserves the right to change the table of premium rates applicable to outstanding policies in the same series but not with respect to a single insured. In other words, the insurer cannot raise the rate for a single insured merely because his or her attractiveness as an insured decreases unless it raises the rate for all insureds in the same class.

Some Special Features of Noncancelable and Guaranteed Renewable Policies

Disability income contracts that are noncancelable or guaranteed renewable may contain some provisions not found in contracts that are conditionally renewable or renewable at the option of the insurer. For example, a benefit usually found in long-term noncancelable and guaranteed renewable contracts but not other contracts is the waiver or premiums payable under the contract if the insured is totally disabled for more than a specified period of time.[3]

A provision permitted by law only in noncancelable or guaranteed renewable contracts is an average earnings clause. Under this clause, if the total monthly income benefits payable under all valid coverages (not including workers' compensation or employee benefit plans unless specified) exceed the greater of (1) the insured's monthly earnings at the time disability commenced, or (2) his or her average monthly earnings for the two preceding years, the insurer is liable only for that proportionate part of the benefits under the policy that the higher earnings figure bears to the total of the valid coverages. This clause, however, cannot reduce the benefits under all valid coverages below $200 or, if less, the total benefits under all such coverages. The portion of the premium paid during the past two years for the benefits not paid because of this provision is returned to the insured. To illustrate: Assume that an insured's gross monthly earnings at the date of the disability were $400, while average monthly earnings during the past two years were $300. If another contract provides benefits of $300, a contract with an average earnings clause and benefits of $200 a month would pay only 40 percent of $400, or $160. Such a clause is important in noncancelable and guaranteed renewable contracts because of the potential fluctuations in earnings over the long run.

In recent years insurers have added some interesting benefits to traditional noncancelable and guaranteed renewable insurance. One applies the family income concept developed by life insurers. The insurer promises to pay additional monthly income to a totally disabled insured for the remainder of a stated period that commences when the

[3] The waiver may be limited to the time during which monthly income benefits are payable.

policy is issued. Under a guaranteed insurability rider the insured can purchase certain additional monthly disability income protection at specified option ages without proving insurability. The insured may wish to increase the protection because his or her income increases, the cost of living rises, or he or she wishes more adequate protection. Some insurers will attach an inflation rider that will tie the benefits to the Consumer Price Index subject to some maximum percentage adjustment.

Premium Rates

The premium rates for disability income insurance depend upon the benefits offered, the cancellation and renewability provision, and the occupation, age, and sex of the insured. To illustrate, one insurer sells only to persons in relatively safe occupations a contract that is noncancelable to age 65 and guaranteed renewable thereafter to age 72. The policy provides total disability, residual disability, and waiver of premium benefits. The disability income benefits would be continued for 2 or 5 years or to age 65, depending upon the duration purchased by the insured. Possible elimination periods are 30, 60, 90, 180, 365 or 730 days. For a policy with a 30-day elimination period, the insurer charges males $20 plus the following rates per $100 monthly indemnity:

Age and sex	Maximum duration		
	2 years	5 years	Age 65
Age 30:			
Male	$24.60	$29.70	$38.90
Female	34.80	41.80	56.40
Age 50:			
Male	45.80	59.70	72.90
Female	54.50	76.90	95.00

Elimination periods longer than 30 days would reduce the rates substantially.

Some insurers now market modified premium plans under which the insured pays initially a lower premium than would otherwise be the case with one or two upward adjustments being made at later ages. Two other special arrangements provide cash values similar to those found in life insurance. Under one plan the insurer will pay the total premiums less any claim payments to an insured who surrenders his or her policy or to the beneficiaries of a deceased policyholder. Some of these policies mature at a specified date such as age 65. Under a second plan the insurer returns the premium paid during 10-year periods if there are no claims. If claims have occurred but are less than a stated percentage of the premiums, the insurer will return part of the premiums paid.

Riders on Life Insurance Policies

Two major disability benefits may be added to life insurance contracts: (1) a waiver of premium, and (2) a disability income. Both benefits are commonly provided by means of riders attached to life insurance contracts, but the waiver of premium benefits is often included in the life insurance contract itself. All life insurers issue waiver of premium insurance, although not on all types of contracts. Many insurers also offer a total disability income rider. The waiver of premium may be purchased without the disability income benefit, but the opposite is not possible.

The waiver of premium benefit provides that if the insured, as a result of either accidental bodily injury or disease, is totally and (presumably) permanently incapable of engaging in any occupation for wage or profit (interpreted by most courts to mean any occupation for which he or she is fitted), the insurer will waive the payment of premiums on the contract during the continuance of the disability. The disability must occur, however, prior to some advanced age such as 55 or 60 and must not have resulted from intentionally self-inflicted injury, war, or a violation of the law. Before the disability is presumed to be permanent, it must usually have lasted at least six months, but the waiver is retroactive. Blindness and double dismemberment, however, are considered immediately as having caused total and permanent disability.

The waiver of premium rider provides in effect a disability income benefit, but the insured has no freedom of choice with respect to the expenditure of the income. Instead, a very important expense, the policy premium, is paid in his or her behalf. The disability income rider, on the other hand, provides income that the insured may spend as he or she wishes.

This rider usually pays $10 a month per $1,000 to a totally and (presumably) permanently disabled person, as defined above in connection with the waiver of premium benefit.[4] The income is payable during the continuance of the disability until age 60 or 65, at which time the rider converts the life insurance contract into a matured endowment contract. Some riders provide only $5 a month while others pay $20 a month. In many cases the income is payable for life without any change in the life insurance contract. No payment is usually made, in any event, however, for the first five or six months of disability, the first payment being made at the end of the sixth or the seventh month.

The disability income rider is appealing because, on a guaranteed renewable basis[5] and for a relatively attractive price made possible by the packaging concept, the insurer promises to pay a disabled person an income to an advanced age or for life, regardless of whether the cause of the disability is accidental injury or sickness. The major drawback is the required relationship between the rider and a life insurance contract.

The premiums for life insurance waiver of premium and disability income riders are level over the premium-payment period of the life insurance contract or until the coverage under the rider ceases, whichever comes first. The rates for standard lives depend primarily upon the issue age and sex of the insured. Applicants rated substandard for reasons of occupation or health may be denied this coverage or charged a

---

[4] Average earnings clauses similar to those used in noncancelable and guaranteed renewable contracts are seldom found. The most interesting and apparently successful attempt to reduce the overinsurance problem is the practice of one insurer which, in addition to an average earnings clause that provides only enough income to bring the benefits from all contracts up to 75 percent of the former earned income, defines total disability as a reduction in earned income of at least 75 percent.

[5] However, the disability income benefit and the waiver of premium benefit are usually excluded from the operation of the incontestable clause.

higher premium rate. One nonparticipating insurer charges a male aged 35 $0.54 for a waiver of premium rider attached to $1,000 of straight life insurance and $4.20 for a rider providing waiver of premium and $10 a month disability income. The corresponding rates for females are about 50 percent higher.

MEDICAL EXPENSE CONTRACTS

Most individual medical expense insurance is written by commercial insurers. Medical expense insurance is sometimes included in the individual disability income contracts discussed above, but most insureds buy their medical expense insurance separately. There are two types of benefits: (1) basic and (2) major medical.

Illustrative of the *basic medical expense insurance* contracts is one providing the following benefits:

Hospital room-and-board coverage up to $100 per day for up to 120 days
Miscellaneous hospital expenses up to 20 times $100 for inpatient services, 10 times $100 for outpatient services
Surgical fees up to scheduled amounts, maximum amount $1,000
Inhospital visits by a physician up to $10 per day for up to 60 days of hospital confinement

Instead of paying actual expenses up to stated limits, many insurers also sell hospital "indemnity" policies. Under this approach the insurer pays a specified amount per day, week, or month of hospital confinement, regardless of the actual charges incurred.

In general, individual contracts tend to be less liberal than group plans with respect to the types of expenses to be covered and the maximum benefits. More conditions and diseases tend to be excluded or made subject to special restrictions.

Under individual *major medical expense insurance* contracts, the insurer usually promises to pay 75 to 80 percent of eligible expenses in excess of a stated deductible up to some specified maximum. Sometimes the insurer pays all the excess expenses but there are limits on hospital daily room-and-board charges, surgical fees, and other named services. The policy may permit upward adjustment in these limits at a later date. Some insurers pay 75 to 80 percent of the expenses up to a certain amount, 100 percent of the excess up to the stated maximum. Some individual major medical expense insurance contracts are purchased with sizable deductibles (say $15,000) to supplement group protection.

Most individual medical expense contracts are guaranteed renewable to some specified age such as 60 or 65. The right the insurer reserves under guaranteed renewable policies to change premiums for a policyholder class is especially important to an insurer of medical expenses, because these expenses are subject to inflationary pressures. The guaranteed renewability feature, however, does protect the insured in case his or her health deteriorates. This protection is not present in those policies that permit the insurer to cancel the contract during the policy term or to refuse renewal at the end of each term.

SOME KEY CONCEPTS

Disability income contract   A health insurance contract under which the insurer promises to pay income benefits to insureds who are disabled.

Noncancelable contract   A health insurance contract that is renewable at the same premium at the option of the insured to some advanced age such as 60 or 65.

Guaranteed renewable contract   A health insurance contract that is renewable at the option of the insured to some advanced age such as 60 or 65, but the insurer reserves the right to change the table of premium rates applicable to outstanding policies in the same series.

Residual disability benefit   A benefit included in many disability income policies that continues some income if an insured who was totally disabled returns to work but because of a continuing partial disability his or her income is less than it otherwise would be. Immediate residual policies do not require a prior period of total disability.

Waiver of premium provision   A provision included in many life insurance and health insurance contracts under which the insurer waives premium payments for totally and presumably permanently disabled insureds during the continuance of the disability.

Medical expense contract   A health insurance contract under which the insurer promises to provide medical services or reimburse the insured for medical expenses incurred.

REVIEW QUESTIONS

1 Compare the number of persons protected against disability income losses under individual insurance contracts with those protected under employee benefit plans. Make the same comparison with respect to medical expenses.

2 Compare the accident portion of a disability income contract with the sickness portion with respect to:
  a Types of benefits provided
  b Use of waiting periods
  c Duration of total disability benefits

3 Disability income contracts have been criticized on the ground that they provide benefits based on the extent of physical disability rather than on loss of earnings.
  a What is meant by this criticism?
  b Is the criticism justified?

4 Compare the partial disability benefits in an individual health insurance contract with the permanent partial disability benefits provided by workers' compensation.

5 Health insurers have been widely criticized in the past for denying claims on the ground that the condition causing the disability existed prior to the starting date of the contract. How does state law limit the insurer's right to deny such claims?

6 a Are most disability income contracts cancelable?
  b Compare noncancelable and guaranteed renewable contracts.
  c Is the guaranteed renewability feature rendered meaningless if the insurer reserves the right to change the premium rate?

7 Cite three special features of noncancelable and guaranteed renewable policies.

8 What factors affect the rates charged for individual disability income insurance?

9 What are the advantages and disadvantages associated with using riders on life insurance contracts to provide protection against disability income losses?

10 What is a hospital "indemnity" benefit?

11 In what sense do individual medical expense contracts tend to be more limited than group plans?

12 Are most individual medical expense contracts cancelable?

SUGGESTIONS FOR ADDITIONAL READING

Dickerson, O. D.: *Health Insurance* (3d ed., Homewood, Ill.: Richard D. Irwin, Inc., 1968), chaps. 5–16.

Gregg, D. W., and V. B. Lucas (eds.): *Life and Health Insurance Handbook* (3d ed., Homewood, Ill.: Richard D. Irwin, Inc., 1973), chaps. 20–24.

Huebner, S. S., and K. Black: *Life Insurance* (10th ed., Englewood Cliffs, N.J.: Prentice-Hall, Inc., 1982), chaps. 16–18.

Mehr, R. I., and S. G. Gustavson: *Life Insurance: Theory and Practice* (3d ed., Austin: Business Publications, Inc., 1984), chap. 12.

CHAPTER 25

BUSINESS USES OF INDIVIDUAL LIFE AND HEALTH INSURANCE

LEARNING OBJECTIVES

After you have completed this chapter, you should be able to:

1 Explain the purpose and features of key-person insurance.
2 List the advantages of a business purchase agreement for the heirs of a deceased owner and for the surviving owners.
3 Describe the major features of a business purchase agreement, including the use of insurance to fund the agreement.
4 Explain why and in what ways a business might use individual life and health insurance instead of group insurance to protect its employees against their potential personnel losses.
5 Tell a self-employed person what type of pension plan he or she can establish for his or her business.
6 Explain the popularity of Individual Retirement Accounts and the constraints placed on contributions to IRAs.

INTRODUCTION

The individual contracts discussed in the two preceding chapters have many business uses. A firm may use these policies (1) to protect itself or (2) to protect its employees on an individual instead of on a group basis. This chapter describes these business uses and the decisions they entail.

In connection with some of these applications, the firm will probably need the services of a team of four persons—a lawyer, an accountant, a trust officer, and an insurance agent.

503

INSURANCE FOR THE FIRM

The firm uses individual personnel insurance to protect itself against credit losses, key-person losses, and business-liquidation losses. Since credit life and health insurance was described in Chapters 23 and 24, the discussion here will be limited to key-person insurance and business purchase insurance.

Key-Person Insurance

Key-person insurance is insurance purchased by a firm to protect itself against financial losses caused by the death or disability of a key employee. These losses were described in Chapter 9. If the potential losses are serious, most firms will elect to purchase insurance because the uncertainty will be great and there will be no other way to transfer the risk. However, even after risk analysis has determined the amount of the potential loss and the duration of the exposure, and after the risk manager has decided that a private insurance contract will be used to protect the firm, there are still several decisions to be made. These involve the amount of insurance, the type of policy, and the disposition of the policy if the key employee resigns or retires.

The amount of insurance will depend upon the estimated losses, the cost of providing various degrees of protection, and the alternative uses for the premium dollars. Because protection is the purpose of key-person life insurance, the insurance policy should emphasize protection as opposed to investment. Term insurance (in some cases, decreasing term insurance) is in order if the protection need is of short duration, but the longer the duration, the stronger is the case that can be made for straight life insurance (with perhaps a decreasing term rider) because of its flexibility. A contract with some investment element may also be proper if the firm wants to meet protection and investment objectives with one contract. For example, the firm may want to protect itself against a key-employee replacement loss if the key person dies during his or her employment period, and if the key person survives to retire, it may want to provide him or her with an income out of the cash value during retirement. Another possibility is that the cash value would be used by the firm itself to cover the costs of replacing the retired key employee. A final consideration in selecting the contract is the physical condition of the key person, for the age and health of the person to be insured may limit the number of available contracts. An application for term insurance is more likely to be refused for these reasons than is an application for any other type of insurance.

If the key employee retires or resigns, the firm may continue the policy in force, surrender the policy for its cash value if any, sell the policy to the key employee, or, as noted above, use the policy to provide an income for the key person during retirement.

Because of the nature of the insurance, no question arises concerning the owner and beneficiary of the policy. The employer applies for the policy, pays the premiums, owns the policy, and is the beneficiary under the policy. The premiums are not a deductible expense for federal income tax purposes, but the proceeds are not subject to income tax.

Key-person health insurance may include any of the loss of income contracts discussed in Chapter 24.[1] The duration of the potential loss is a key consideration. Noncancelable and guaranteed renewable contracts pose a decision similar to life insurance if the key employee resigns or retires. The ownership, beneficiary, and tax considerations are identical with those mentioned in connection with life insurance.

Business Purchase Insurance

Business purchase insurance is insurance purchased in connection with a business purchase agreement. Under this agreement, the firm, the co-owners, or some employees have agreed to purchase some or all of the deceased or permanently disabled owner's business interest. In a case of temporary disability, an agreement is usually made to continue part of the disabled owner's salary. The purpose of the agreement and the insurance is to avoid the business discontinuation losses described in Chapter 9. The advantages of the agreement are thus the converse of the potential losses. For the heirs, the agreement provides:

1 A fair valuation of their interest (protection against harsh bargaining or a "freeze-out" by the survivors is assured)
2 A continuous market for their interest
3 A speedier and more orderly settlement of the insured's estate

For the surviving owners, the advantages are:

1 A fair purchase price for the interest of the deceased
2 A speedier and more orderly settlement of the deceased's or disabled person's interest
3 Protection against the inclusion of undesirable business partners
4 Protection against restrictions in credit following the death or disability of an owner
5 Protection against lowered employee morale following the death or disability

Finally, the firm benefits, even if the owners do not die or become disabled, for the following reasons:

1 The firm's credit standing is improved.
2 Employee morale is improved.

Although a business purchase agreement need not be funded with life insurance or health insurance, insurance is an ideal funding vehicle because it provides the funds at the exact moment and only if they are needed.

In preparing the agreement and purchasing the insurance, a risk manager must make decisions with respect to the purchase price, the type of insurance, the ownership of the insurance, the beneficiary under the insurance policy, and the disposition of any

---

[1] It may also include a business overhead expense insurance policy, discussed below.

ownership interest of the deceased or disabled owner in policies covering the other owners. We shall discuss each of these decisions. Because business purchase agreements covering disability are still relatively rare, most of the discussion will relate to the agreements covering death and retirement.

As in Chapter 9, unless otherwise noted, the discussion of business purchase agreements applies to all three forms of business organization—sole proprietorship, partnership, and close corporation.

Valuation   The valuation of a business interest is always difficult, and in business purchase agreements this difficulty is compounded by the fact that the value to be estimated is the value at some uncertain date in the future. Consequently, it is common practice not to set a fixed amount as the purchase price but to establish a formula for determining the value at the date of death or permanent disability. Sometimes a fixed amount is established with the understanding that this amount will be corrected periodically, but these revaluations are usually few and far between.

Despite the inaccuracies inherent in any of these valuation procedures, the value arrived at is more likely to be fair than one left to chance and possibly influenced greatly by the unequal bargaining positions of the heirs and the prospective purchasers. An additional advantage to the heirs of a definite business purchase agreement valuation is that this valuation will, with the proper precautions, be accepted by the tax authorities as the valuation for estate tax purposes. Otherwise the business interest may be valued at much more than it is worth for tax purposes.

Type of Insurance   Business purchase life insurance contracts, like key-employee life insurance contracts, should emphasize protection rather than investment. The case for term insurance is weaker, however, because the need for the protection is likely to be long term. Business purchase health insurance contracts should provide disability income until a relatively advanced age. Some insurers market business interest disability insurance that pays a substantial lump sum after the insured has been disabled for, say, two years. A nonterm life insurance policy with waiver of premium and disability income riders will often be useful because it provides benefits in case of death or disability.

Ownership of the Insurance   Ownership considerations vary, depending upon the type of business organization. The prospective purchaser of a sole proprietor's business interest is typically a key employee, and that employee usually owns the policy and pays the premium. In a partnership or a close corporation, two possibilities exist. The firm may own the policy and pay the premiums, or each owner may purchase insurance contracts covering associates. Factors affecting this decision include the number of policies involved, tax considerations, and whether creditors would have access to the proceeds.

Disability insurance policies may be arranged in the same way, but another common practice is to have each owner carry his or her own disability income insurance. If the owner becomes disabled for more than a specified period, the survivors agree to buy out his or her interest in installments through a series of promissory notes payable over a specified period.

Beneficiary   The beneficiary under the life insurance policies may be (1) the surviving purchasers, (2) the firm (not possible in a sole proprietorship), (3) the heirs of the deceased, (4) the estate of the deceased, or (5) a trustee. Although the surviving purchasers or the firm are legally bound under the purchase agreement to pay the purchase price to the heirs in exchange for the business interest, some delay and unpleasantness may occur if the purchasers or the firm are named as beneficiaries. The danger that all will not proceed according to plan is even greater when the heirs or the estate are named, because the heirs and the executor or administrator will then control both the proceeds and the interest.[2] If the agreement contains any loopholes, it may never be executed. The advantage of a trustee is that an unbiased intermediary is charged with the proper use of the insurance proceeds.

The beneficiary under the disability income contracts is the disabled sole proprietor or partner. In the case of a corporation, the disabled stockholder is the beneficiary if the stockholders buy the policy; otherwise, for tax reasons, the corporation is the beneficiary.

Disposition of Policies No Longer Needed   If the prospective employee purchaser of a sole proprietorship should resign, be discharged, or die, the purchase agreement is terminated. The sole proprietor should have the right to purchase the policy from the employee or his or her heirs, because the original purpose for the policy no longer exists. Although some tax problems may arise, the sole proprietor may in turn transfer this value to a prospective purchaser under a new agreement. The purchase price is usually the cash value or some similar price.

In a partnership or corporation, the same situation arises when the partners or stockholders are the owners of the policies, as opposed to the firm. The surviving associates should be able to purchase the policies on their own lives from the retiring or deceased owner or his or her legal representatives.

Excess Payments   The purchase price of the deceased's business interest may exceed the face amount of the life insurance or the payments under the disability insurance contract. For example, if the purchase price is to be determined by a formula, no one knows what the price will be at the time the insurance is purchased, and the amount purchased may turn out to be too small. Provision must be made in such a case for making the excess payments immediately or in installments secured by promissory notes and other safeguards.

An extreme example of an excess payment occurs when one or more of the owners are uninsurable and there are no existing policies that could profitably be transferred for value to fund the agreement.

---

[2] One reason for naming the heirs as beneficiaries is that they would then be in a position to select the most appropriate settlement options. Many insurers, however, now make it possible for them to select the options when a trustee is the direct beneficiary.

Business Overhead Insurance

Business overhead insurance is a special form of disability income insurance that pays up to a specified limit the office overhead expenses that necessarily continue for up to one or two years while a professional person or owner of a small business is disabled. The payments usually begin after a short elimination period. Overhead expenses include such items as rent, utility bills, employees' salaries, and depreciation. Not included are the insured's own compensation or compensation paid to someone else to perform the insured's duties during the disability.

The premium paid for business overhead insurance is a tax-deductible item. The benefits are taxable income but are offset by the actual expenses.

INSURANCE FOR EMPLOYEES

Key-person insurance and business purchase insurance are designed to protect the firm against key-person or business discontinuation losses. The other major business uses of individual insurance are to protect the employee. They fall into the following categories: (1) tax-free death benefit insurance, (2) disability salary continuation insurance, (3) split-dollar insurance, (4) deferred compensation insurance, (5) individual policy pension trusts, (6) wholesale insurance, and (7) franchise insurance. Most insurance protecting employees is group insurance, but individual insurance is also used extensively because (1) many firms are too small to qualify for group insurance; (2) the individual insurance plan may actually be no more costly for small groups than a group insurance plan; (3) the employer may wish to choose the employees to be protected on some basis (say, key employees) that would not be practicable or even permitted under group insurance; or (4) the employer may not wish to formalize the benefit. Each of the seven uses specified above will now be discussed separately.

Tax-Free Death Benefit Insurance

An employer may pay up to $5,000 directly to the dependents or estate of any deceased employee on either a contractual or voluntary selective basis without entailing any income tax liability for the dependents. Moreover, the payment is a tax-deductible item for the firm. Although the firm need not purchase insurance to fund these payments, such a practice is common because the uncertainty is great and the cost of transferring the risk to an insurer is relatively low. Although the premiums paid for the insurance are not tax-deductible, the proceeds are not taxable to the employer.

Disability Salary Continuation Insurance

Individual disability insurance may be used to provide an income for a disabled employee.[3] If the insurer sends the periodic checks directly to the employee, the firm may deduct the premiums as a business expense. If the insurer pays the firm, the

---

[3] For the tax treatment of sick pay see p. 421.

premiums are not deductible, but the insurance proceeds are not taxable income for the firm, and its payments to the disabled employee are a deductible expense.

If a plan provides for salary continuance in case of death or disability, a life insurance policy with a disability income rider can be very useful.

Split-Dollar Insurance

As was pointed out in Chapter 9, the protection needs of an insured tend to decline with age. Split-dollar insurance is a way of providing decreasing insurance for employees at an attractive price. A specified amount of insurance is purchased on the life of the employee, and the annual premium is split into two parts. Each year the employer pays a portion that is equal to the increase in the cash value during the policy year. The employee pays the difference—a decreasing amount that may disappear after a relatively short time.

The employer owns the policy and is the irrevocable beneficiary with respect to the cash value, which always equals or exceeds his or her contribution toward the policy. Thus the employer's only loss is the interest he or she might have earned on these contributions. The employee's beneficiary receives the difference between the face amount and the cash value.[4] The employee gains because he or she receives what is in effect an interest-free loan. The employee, however, may have to pay a federal income tax on part of the premium paid by the employer. The taxable income each year is (1) the cost of term insurance, according to the Internal Revenue Service, equal to the face amount less the cash value for that year less (2) the portion of that year's premium paid by the employee.

Deferred Compensation Plans

Deferred compensation plans provide for the payment of an annual income to a key employee after retirement, in exchange for a reduced salary during the earning career. The advantage to the employee of a deferred compensation agreement is not having to pay any income tax on the funding payments, whereas an equivalent increase in salary would be taxable. The employee will have to pay a tax on the retirement payments when they start, but presumably at that time his or her income tax bracket will be much lower. The firm cannot deduct the funding payment, but the retirement payments by the firm are deductible as a business expense.

Large firms may elect to fund deferred compensation plans by accumulations of cash or securities during the employee's earning career. Many of these plans, however, are funded by insurance. Insurance is particularly popular with small firms, regardless of the types of benefits, and with both large and small firms when death and disability benefits are also included in the agreement. As we have already noted earlier in this chapter, the same policy may serve as key-person insurance and as a funding vehicle for a deferred compensation plan. The type of life insurance to be used also depends

---

[4] If dividends are applied under the fifth dividend option to purchase term insurance equal to the cash value, the employee's beneficiary will receive the face amount of insurance.

upon the combination of benefits included in the agreement. The firm pays the insurance premiums and collects the proceeds. The proceeds do not constitute taxable income for the firm.

Certain precautions are usually taken for tax reasons. First, the plan often requires that the employee remain with the firm until retirement and that after retirement the employee be available as a consultant and not enter into any competing employment. In other words, the promise to pay retirement benefits is conditional, not absolute. Second, the plan is not technically secured by the fund or the insurance. The conditional features of the plan necessitate this proviso.[5]

Individual Policy Pension Trusts

Pension plans designed to provide benefits for large groups of employees were discussed in Chapter 22. Individual insurance policies can be used as the funding instrument for these pension plans. In fact, although group pension plans cover far more employees than individual policy plans, the individual policy plans are much more numerous. Many insurers limit their group plans to employee groups including at least 25 lives. For groups including 50 lives or less, the individual plan may be no more costly than the group plan.

Wholesale Insurance

Wholesale insurance is life insurance written on groups that are too small to qualify for group insurance. The employer arranges for the collection and payment of the premiums on a group basis, but individual contracts are issued and the insurability of each individual applicant is evaluated separately. Physical examinations, however, are usually waived. As in group insurance, the amount of the protection is determined automatically on the basis of salary, position, service, or some other factor. In short, wholesale insurance, like individual policy pension trusts, is a hybrid of group insurance and individual insurance. The contributions by the firm are tax-deductible as a business expense but do not constitute taxable income to the employee.

Franchise Insurance

Franchise insurance is the health insurance equivalent of wholesale insurance and is often referred to by that name.

---

[5] Another compensation method inspired by tax factors is the restricted stock option. Under this method, the firm gives certain employees the option to buy a stated number of shares of the firm's common stock at a specified price. The option must be exercised within an agreed time. If the price of the stock should rise within that time, the option becomes highly valuable. The employee may purchase life and health insurance in connection with this option for two reasons: First, if the employee exercises the option but may pay the purchase price in installments or with borrowed funds and then dies or becomes disabled, the insurance proceeds can be used to continue the installment payments or to pay back the loan. Second, if the employee dies or becomes disabled before he or she has elected to exercise this option, the insurance proceeds can be used to make the purchase.

RETIREMENT PLANS FOR THE SELF-EMPLOYED

Until the enactment of the Self-Employed Individuals Retirement Act of 1962, self-employed persons did not receive any tax incentives in connection with their personal retirement programs. Consequently many self-employed persons incorporated their businesses in order that as employees they might share the employee benefit plan tax advantages cited at several places in Chapters 21 and 22. Under the 1962 act, as amended, until 1984 self-employed persons were permitted to deduct for federal income tax purposes the annual amount they set aside for retirement but in no case more than 15 percent of their earned income or, if less, a specified amount ($15,000 in 1983). Starting in 1984, the maximum deductible contribution has become the ERISA limit which for defined contributions is 25 percent of earned income (25 percent of *net* earned income for the owner-employee, which is 20 percent of *gross* earned income) but not more than $90,000 (to be indexed starting in 1986).

In order to receive these tax benefits, the self-employed must qualify their retirement programs (called H.R. 10 or Keogh plans, after the act's sponsor) with the Internal Revenue Service. The principal methods of funding these plans are (1) individual annuity contracts issued to individual self-employed persons or group annuity contracts issued to members of a professional association, (2) transfer to a trustee who can invest the funds in almost any form of investment—typically common stocks, mutual funds, life insurance, or savings accounts, or (3) a special custodial account with a bank or a savings and loan association.

Until 1984, if the self-employed person had any full-time employees with at least three years of service, he or she had to contribute toward the employees' retirement at least the same percentage of their compensation as the percentage applied to his or her own earned income. The employees' benefits were fully and immediately vested. Starting in 1984 these mandatory coverage and vesting provisions have been replaced by the minimum ERISA coverage and vesting requirements presented in Chapter 22.

Because of the changes noted above, Keogh plans now closely resemble corporate pension plans. More Keogh plans, however, are likely to be subject to the special rules for "top-heavy" plans.

INDIVIDUAL RETIREMENT ACCOUNTS

Under ERISA originally only an employee not covered under a pension plan was permitted to establish an individual retirement account (IRA) that would enable the employee to accumulate a retirement fund with before-tax dollars. Neither the contributions to the fund nor their earnings on the investments in the fund were taxable until the worker's retirement. The maximum tax-deductible contribution was the lesser of $1,500 or 15 percent of the employee's compensation. If the worker had an unemployed spouse, the worker and spouse could contribute up to $1,750 by establishing two IRAs—one for the worker and one for the spouse. The contributions could be invested in insurance annuities or endowment contracts, mutual funds, special government bonds, or savings and loan associations, credit unions, or bank accounts. Employers sometimes arranged payroll deduction plans in which employees could participate voluntarily. Some small businesses with pension plans replaced these plans with IRAs and increased their workers' salaries by the amounts they had previously contributed to their pension plans.

Starting in 1982, the rules were liberalized substantially. Now workers covered under a pension plan are also permitted to establish an IRA. The maximum tax-deductible contribution is the lesser of $2,000 or 100 percent of the employee's compensation. If the worker has an unemployed spouse, the worker and spouse may contribute up to $2,250.[6]

SOME KEY CONCEPTS

Key-person insurance   Insurance purchased by a business on the life or health of a key person whose death or disability would cause a financial loss to the business.

Business purchase insurance   Insurance used to fund a business purchase agreement under which the firm, the coowners, or some employees have agreed to purchase some or all of a deceased or permanently disabled owner's business interest.

Deferred compensation plan   A plan under which an employee elects to receive an annual income from his or her employer after retirement in exchange for a reduced salary prior to retirement. To receive this postretirement income the employee must usually remain with the firm until retirement and not work for a competitor after retirement.

Split-dollar insurance   A nonterm life insurance arrangement under which the employer pays each year a portion of the premium that is equal to the increase in the cash value that year; the employee pays the remainder of the premium. If the employee dies, the employer receives that portion of the proceeds equal to the cash value; the employer's beneficiary receives the remainder of the proceeds.

Keogh plan   A retirement plan for a self-employed person and his or her employees that was once subject to very special rules but now more closely resembles corporate pension plans.

Individual Retirement Account   A special voluntary retirement arrangement for workers not covered under a pension plan where they work and available as an extra voluntary retirement arrangement for workers covered at work under a pension plan.

REVIEW QUESTIONS

1 The Ajax Manufacturing Corporation has a key engineer, aged 40, who has been largely responsible for the firm's outstanding success. He is considered replaceable within 10 years if he should die or become disabled, but in the meantime the profits of the firm would be reduced about $40,000 per year. Key-employee insurance seems advisable.

a How much insurance should the firm buy?

b What type insurance should be purchased?

---

[6] Under a Simplified Employee Pension plan, an employer can contribute larger tax-deductible amounts to a pension program utilizing individual IRAs. Originally these contributions were limited to those applicable to Keogh plans, but starting in 1984 these limits have also been raised to the regular corporate plan limits. However, the plan must still cover all eligible employees, the employer must not discriminate in favor of highly compensated employees, and the employees must have the right to withdraw at any time funds contributed to their IRAs.

    c What beneficiary designations should be made?

    d What are the tax implications of this insurance?

    e What should be the disposition of the insurance policies if the key employee retires or resigns?

2 Adams and Brown are equal partners in a small wholesaling firm. What would be the advantage of a business purchase agreement (a) to the heirs if either Adams or Brown should die? (b) to Adams or Brown if either died or became disabled?

3 An abbreviated balance sheet for the Adams-Brown partnership is presented below:

BALANCE SHEET FOR ADAMS-BROWN PARTNERSHIP

Cash		$ 10,000
Accounts receivable	$84,000	
Less reserve	4,000	80,000
Merchandise		200,000
Equipment		110,000
Real estate		80,000
Goodwill		20,000
		$500,000
Accounts payable		$160,000
Mortgage on real estate		40,000
Adams, capital		150,000
Brown, capital		150,000
		$500,000

The annual earnings have been averaging around $50,000. The average price-earnings ratio in the stock market for a business of this quality is about 10 times earnings. What should be the valuation in the business purchase agreement?

4 If Adams and Brown agree to fund the agreement through insurance:

    a Who should purchase the insurance? Why?

    b What type of insurance should be purchased?

    c Who should be the beneficiary under the insurance policies?

5 Would your answer to question 4 be different if Adams and Brown were stockholders in a close corporation instead of partners?

6 Carter is a sole proprietor.

    a Does she need a business purchase agreement?

    b If so, what would be the nature of the agreement and the insurance arrangements?

7 Since group insurance is less expensive than individual insurance, why should any firm consider the purchase of individual insurance to protect employees against their personnel losses?

8 Explain the tax features of:

    a Tax-free death benefit insurance

    b Disability salary continuation insurance

    c Deferred compensation plans

9 a What is split-dollar insurance?

    b How does the employee benefit from split-dollar insurance?

10 Compare wholesale insurance and franchise insurance with group insurance.

11 A self-employed dentist has two full-time employees. What type of pension plan can the dentist establish for herself and her two employees?

12 a Who can establish an individual retirement account?

b What dollar limitations are placed on IRAs?

SUGGESTIONS FOR ADDITIONAL READING

Dickerson, O.D.: *Health Insurance* (3d ed., Homewood, Ill.: Richard D. Irwin, Inc., 1968), chap. 21.

Gregg, D. W., and V. B. Lucas (eds.): *Life and Health Insurance Handbook* (3d ed., Homewood, Ill.: Richard D. Irwin, Inc., 1973), chaps. 42–48.

Huebner, S. S., and K. Black: *Life Insurance* (10th ed., Englewood Cliffs, N.J.: Prentice-Hall, Inc., 1982), chap. 3.

Mehr, R. I., and S. G. Gustavson: *Life Insurance: Theory and Practice* (3d ed., Austin: Business Publications, Inc., 1984), chap. 21.

White, E. H., and H. Chasman: *Business Insurance* (5th ed., Englewood Cliffs, N.J.: Prentice-Hall, Inc., 1980).

CHAPTER **26**

SELECTING
THE INSURER: I

LEARNING OBJECTIVES

After you completed this chapter, you should be able to:

1 List six ways in which insurers can be classified.
2 Distinguish a stock insurer from a mutual insurer, a Lloyds Association, and a reciprocal exchange.
3 Describe how insurers can be classified according to their pricing policies.
4 Explain the major marketing systems used by insurers.
5 Describe the operations of groups of insurers, cooperative underwriters' associations, and reinsurance associations.
6 Explain how and why many insurers have become members of a financial services combination or an integrated insurance operation.

INTRODUCTION

A risk manager must select an insurer or insurers to implement the insurance program. The risk manager will need to understand the different types of insurers and their principal characteristics, but should realize that the variations among the insurers of each type are more important than the variations among the average insurers of different types. This chapter discusses the types of insurers according to several methods of classification. It also describes the role of groups, reinsurance associations, and business combinations marketing both insurance and noninsurance products and services. Chapter 27 deals with the factors one should consider in choosing among particular insurers and the sources of information concerning these factors.

516

TYPES OF INSURERS

About 5,000 private insurers write insurance in the United States. They can be classified in various ways, of which the following are the more important: (1) by the type of insurance written, (2) by the legal form of business organization, (3) by domicile and admission status, (4) by pricing policy, (5) by marketing method, and (6) by the kinds of insureds serviced. Government insurers can also be classified under each of these categories, but these categories are much more meaningful in the private sector. Consequently, government insurers will be discussed only as a legal form of organization.

Types of Insurance Written

Insurers can be classified first according to the types of insurance they write. Two methods of classifying insurers are of interest here. By the first, insurers can be classified according to whether they are primarily or solely (1) originating, primary, or direct insurers, or (2) reinsurers. Primary or direct insurers emphasize sales to the general public; reinsurers insure those portions of the direct business that the direct insurers for one reason or another do not wish to retain. Reinsurance is discussed in Chapter 27.

By a second method of classification, insurers can be grouped according to whether they write personnel, property, or liability insurance, or some combination of these major divisions of insurance. Some insurers write only one of the many kinds of insurance under one of these major divisions (e.g., life insurance, fire insurance, or automobile insurance); others write practically all kinds of insurance under all three divisions (e.g., most kinds of property and liability insurance plus health insurance). Many insurers fall between these two extremes.

Legally insurers can be divided into two groups: (1) life insurers who can write life insurance and health insurance, and (2) nonlife insurers who can write any type of insurance other than life insurance.

Legal Form of Business Organization

Probably the best-known classification of insurers is according to the legal form of business organization. Three major classes exist—private proprietary insurers, private cooperative insurers, and governmental insurers—but each of these classes includes a variety of subclasses.

Proprietary Insurers Proprietary insurers are characterized by profit-seeking owners[1] who are responsible for the management of the firm and who bear the risks

---

[1] Because stock insurers, the leading proprietary insurers, are usually more easily organized under state laws than are mutual insurers, some persons interested in forming a mutual insurer organize instead a stock insurer and minimize the profit objective. Many are converted at a later date to a mutual. To organize a stock insurer, one must satisfy certain capital and surplus requirements. To organize a mutual, one must meet initial surplus requirements and in addition have applications for more than a stated number of persons on more than a stated number of separate exposures with aggregate premiums in excess of a certain amount. Some stock insurers are owned by a parent mutual as part of a group operation.

of the insurer. There are two types of proprietary insurers: (1) stock insurers, and (2) Lloyds Associations.

The *stock* insurer is a corporation whose owners are stockholders. The operations of a stock insurer closely resemble the operations of profit-seeking corporations in any line of endeavor. The stockholders elect the board of directors, who delegate management responsibilities to the officers of the insurer. Stockholders receive dividends declared by the board of directors and may sell their shares of stock to others at the market price. The dividends and the market value will depend to a large extent upon the success of the operations of the insurer. The corporation possesses a cushion against unfavorable years consisting of the capital and paid-in surplus subscribed by the stockholders and the additional surplus retained from gains during years of favorable operation. This cushion permits stock insurers to follow their customary practice of charging policyholders a definite premium (subject, in some instances, to a retrospective rating plan, discussed in Chapter 28).[2] The importance of the stock method of operation is evident from Table 26.1, which shows the proportion of each kind of insurance written by each of the major forms of business organization. It is clear that stock insurers predominate in property and liability insurance but write only about half the personnel insurance premiums.

Table 26.1 also indicates that stock insurers write practically all forms of property and liability insurance. Table 26.2 indicates the diversified interests of stock insurers in a different way. This table shows the distribution of the premium income of each type of insurer by kind of insurance.

Lloyds Associations derive their name from the resemblance between their operations and those of Lloyd's of London. *Lloyd's of London* (known as the corporation of Lloyd's since it was incorporated in 1871) is an association of individuals who underwrite insurance as individuals. The function of the association is merely to provide certain services, such as underwriting information, policy writing, loss adjustments, and office space; to screen carefully prospective members; and to prescribe certain regulations aimed at maintaining the financial solvency of members. The association was formed in 1769 by a group of underwriters who used to gather at Edward Lloyd's coffee house to transact their business.

Over 23,000 members underwrite insurance as individuals through Lloyd's of London. Until 1969, an underwriter had to be a citizen of the British Commonwealth. Most underwriters are engaged in other businesses (e.g., bankers, professional athletes, and members of Parliament) and limit their participation in this insurance operation to the furnishing of the necessary capital and the risk-bearing function. The insurance decisions are made by lead underwriters who have the authority to commit the underwriters who belong to his or her "syndicate." Over 450 syndicates have been formed ranging from a few members to thousands of members. Each underwriter may belong to more than one syndicate. Although the insurance is provided through

---

[2] In some lines, particularly in life insurance and workers' compensation insurance, stockholders' dividends are often limited in some way, and policyholders share in the profits. Sometimes policyholders are also given a vote in the management of the firm. In no cases, however, do policyholders share the losses except through a reduced dividend. Stock life insurers issuing participating insurance often issue nonparticipating insurance at lower guaranteed rates.

TABLE 26.1

PREMIUM INCOME OF UNITED STATES PRIVATE INSURERS, 1982

Property and liability insurers

Type of insurance	Premium income,* $ millions	Proportion (percent) written by			
		Stock insurers	Mutual insurers	Reciprocal exchanges	Lloyds Associations
Multiple-peril					
Homeowner's	$12,416	72.2	20.9	6.8	0.1
Commercial	7,009	84.8	13.9	1.1	0.2
Fire	3,154	79.2	17.3	3.4	0.1
Allied fire	1,683	73.6	21.6	4.7	0.1
Ocean marine	1,101	92.6	6.8	†	†
Inland marine	2,510	85.6	10.4	3.9	0.1
Theft	115	88.7	11.3	†	†
Fidelity	360	97.0	3.0	†	†
Surety	1,094	96.7	3.2	†	†
Glass	29	84.6	13.8	†	†
Credit	67	95.6	4.4	—	—
Boiler and machinery	293	93.3	6.6	†	†
Automobile					
Physical damage	18,005	56.2	32.6	11.1	†
Liability	26,226	57.7	32.2	10.1	†
Liability other than automobile	7,159	79.7	14.7	5.3	0.3
Workers' compensation	13,945	77.1	21.7	1.2	†
Other	4,496	85.4	14.4	0.6	‡
Total	$99,662	69.5	24.0	6.4	0.1

Life and health insurers

	Premium income, $ millions	Stock insurers	Mutual insurers	Blue Cross Blue Shield, and other health insurers
Life, including annuities§	$ 83,116	57	43	. . .
Disability income¶	7,806	100		. . .
Medical expense#	85,856		54	46
	176,778		78	22

* Net premiums written for property and liability insurers.

† Included under "other" insurance. Mutual premium volume under "other" insurance also includes $360 million written by the Factory Mutuals (see p. 534), which is not reported on a segregated basis. The inclusion of ocean marine, theft, and other lines under the "other" category for reciprocals and Lloyd's causes the percentages for "other" insurance to sum to more than 100 percent.

‡ Less than 0.1 percent.

§ The life insurance premium income of fraternals, assessment associations, and mutual savings banks is omitted. These insurers write under 3 percent of the life insurance in force.

¶ A very small fraction of the premium income of the independent plans (included in the table as other health insurers) is for disability income insurance.

Administrative Services Only (see Chap. 21) premiums have been credited to stock and mutual insurers.

Sources: Property and liability insurance data from *Best's Aggregates and Averages* (Oldwick, N.J.: Alfred M. Best Company, Inc., 1983), pp. 6, 171–175, 50B–53B, 64B–65B. Life insurance data from *1983 Life Insurance Fact Book* (Washington, D.C.: American Council of Life Insurance, 1983), pp. 18, 55. The share of the life insurance premiums paid to stock insurers was set equal to their share of the total life insurance in force. Health insurance data from *Source Book of Health Insurance Data, 1982–83* (Washington, D.C.: Health Insurance Association of America, 1983), pp. 26–27. The 1981 premium totals in this *Source Book* were adjusted upward by the 1981 to 1982 percentage increase in health insurance premiums reported for life insurers in the *1983 Life Insurance Fact Book*.

TABLE 26.2

PREMIUM INCOME OF EACH MAJOR TYPE OF UNITED STATES PRIVATE INSURER, 1982

Property and liability insurers

Type of insurance	Stock insurers		Mutual insurers		Reciprocal exchanges		All insurers	
	Premiums, $ millions	% of total	Premiums, $ millions	% of total	Premiums, $ millions	% of total	Premiums, $ millions	% of total
Multiple-peril								
Homeowner's	$ 8,970	13.0	$ 2,600	10.9	$ 844	13.1	$12,416	12.5
Commercial	5,944	8.6	974	4.1	79	1.2	7,009	7.0
Fire	2,498	3.6	545	2.3	107	1.7	3,154	3.2
Allied fire	1,238	1.8	363	1.5	79	1.2	1,683	1.7
Ocean marine	1,019	1.5	75	.3	†	†	1,101	1.1
Inland marine	2,149	3.1	260	1.1	99	1.5	2,510	2.5
Theft	102	.1	13	.1	†	†	115	.1
Fidelity	349	.5	10	‡	†	†	360	.4
Surety	1,058	1.5	35	.1	†	†	1,094	1.1
Glass	24	‡	4	‡	†	†	29	‡
Credit	65	.1	3	‡	—	—	67	.1
Boiler and machinery	273	.4	19	.1	†	†	293	.3
Automobile								
Physical damage	10,127	14.6	5,877	24.5	1,994	31.0	18,005	18.1
Liability	15,122	21.8	8,445	35.3	2,656	41.3	26,226	26.3
Liability other than automobile	5,707	8.2	1,052	4.4	377	5.9	7,159	7.2
Workers' compensation	10,754	15.5	3,020	12.6	171	2.7	13,945	14.0
Other	3,838	5.5	648	2.7	27	.4	4,496	4.5
Total	$69,238	100.0	$23,943	100.0	$6,433	100.0	$99,662	100.0

Life and health insurers

Type of insurance	Commercial insurers		Blue Cross, Blue Shield, and other health insurers		All insurers	
	Premiums, $ millions	% of total	Premiums, $ millions	% of total	Premiums, $ millions	% of total
Life, including annuities	$ 83,116	60.6	. . .	. . .	$ 83,116	47.0
Disability income	7,806	5.7	. . .	. . .	7,806	4.4
Medical expense	46,260	33.7	$39,597	100.0	85,857	48.6
Total	$137,182	100.0	$39,597	100.0	$176,779	100.0

* See Table 26.1 for other footnotes.
† Included under "Other" insurance.
‡ Less than 0.1 percent.
Sources: See Table 26.1

syndicates, a member is not legally responsible for the failure of other members of the syndicate or other syndicates to fulfill their promises. Syndicates or underwriters not participating in the particular contract are technically outsiders to the entire transaction.

At first glance, the financial guarantee behind a contract from Lloyd's of London may appear somewhat questionable because of the heavy reliance upon the financial conditions of the particular underwriters signing the contract. For several reasons, however, a Lloyd's contract is considered to be financially secure. The persons who wish to be underwriters are carefully screened with respect to their financial status and moral integrity; their liability is unlimited; their accounts are supervised by the association; they must deposit with the corporation a substantial amount of cash or approved securities or a satisfactory letter of credit as security behind the underwriter's promise; and the association maintains a central guarantee fund to which all members contribute, which can be used to pay any unsatisfied obligation. In addition, the reputation of Lloyd's of London is jealously guarded by the membership.[3]

Another possible defect is that because the insured has purchased a separate contract from each underwriter, technically he or she must proceed in case of a dispute against each underwriter. Lloyd's underwriters, however, agree in their contracts to accept the outcome of a suit against one member.

Lloyd's of London members possess almost unlimited freedom with respect to the types of insurance they may write and the rates they may charge. Members, in fact, differ with respect to these matters, although there is a tendency to follow the established leaders in certain fields. This extreme flexibility has led to some of the unusual contracts attributed to Lloyd's of London, but most of the insurance written is less spectacular. Half the insurance written is reinsurance (see Chapter 27); marine insurance is the major direct line. Because individuals are the insurers, only short-term life insurance contracts are written, and the volume of business is small. In order to place business with underwriting members, one must operate through a Lloyd's broker. This fact poses a problem for an insured in the United States because Lloyd's of London underwriters can be represented in the United States with respect to all lines of insurance only in the two states in which they are licensed—Illinois and Kentucky. However, in a number of states, Lloyd's and other nonadmitted insurers can be represented by a broker with respect to "surplus-line" insurance, i.e., insurance that is not available from duly licensed insurers in that state. In the other states, technically the buyer must contact a Lloyd's representative in Illinois, Kentucky, Canada, or London, but it is customary for a licensed agent to conduct the negotiations in the

---

[3] In 1979, however, Lloyd's suffered its most severe financial setback in more than a century. Several prominent members were threatened with personal bankruptcy and one syndicate sued Lloyd's itself claiming that the exchange was partly responsible for the staggering claims it suffered. The following examples illustrate why 1979 was a bad year. In 1979 insureds started to file substantial claims under the computer leasing policy described in Chapter 12. In July, a $45 million tanker sank carrying $40 million of naphthalene. RCA lost a satellite six days after it was launched, which resulted in a substantial claim. See "Bad Luck Forces Updating at Lloyd's of London," *Business Week,* Feb. 25, 1980, pp. 94–108.

Some scandals during the early eighties caused Parliament to pass in 1982 a new Lloyd's Act that made some important administrative and structural changes. The scandals involved misappropriation of premiums and placement of reinsurance in some dubious offshore companies. See Godfrey Hodgson, "Restoring the Lloyd's of London Mystique," *The New York Times Magazine,* Mar. 11, 1984, pp. 48–56, 125–130.

insured's name. Most American insurance with Lloyd's of London is insurance that is not readily available in the local market or reinsurance purchased by American insurers. Nevertheless about 60 percent of the premium volume developed by Lloyd's underwriters is purchased by insureds or insurers in the United States.

Although Lloyd's is licensed only in two states, the underwriters agree in the insurance contract to submit to and abide by the decisions of United States courts. Moreover, they have established an American trust fund for the specific protection of United States policyholders.[4]

Lloyds Associations in the United States pattern their operation after those of Lloyd's of London, but the United States Lloyds differs from the original Lloyd's in many significant ways. The number of underwriters is very small; their financial resources are meager compared with those of Lloyd's of London underwriters; their liability may be limited; an attorney-in-fact speaks for all the underwriters in the association; and the insurance operations are almost always restricted to one state (usually Texas). Only about 50 associations are currently in operation.[5] The insurance written by over half these associations is completely reinsured by some other insurer—usually a stock insurer. Table 26.1 indicates the relatively small role played by these associations, net of reinsurance, and the limited kinds of insurance they write.

In 1979, New York state authorized the formation of an Insurance Exchange patterned after Lloyd's of London. Unlike Lloyd's, however, syndicates, not individuals, are the members of the New York exchange. Instead of unlimited liability, a syndicate must back its promises with the required capital and surplus plus a $500,000 initial deposit guarantee fund. Most syndicate members are insurers, others are individuals. The reasons for forming the exchange were to increase the capacity of the United States insurance industry by attracting more capital, to make that industry more competitive by removing some regulatory constraints, and to capture some of the premiums now going to Lloyd's.[6] Florida and Illinois also authorized such exchanges shortly thereafter.

Cooperative Insurers Cooperative insurers are organized not for profit but for the benefit of the policyholders, who elect the management and bear the risks of the insurer. Three types of cooperative insurers will be discussed in this chapter: (1) advance premium mutual corporations, (2) assessment mutual associations or corpora-

---

[4] The underwriters have also made deposits in Illinois and Kentucky for the specific benefit of policyholders in those states.

[5] Several states (New York, for example) forbid the formation of new Lloyds Associations, but in most states such an association is formed with comparative ease. All that may be required is a certain minimum number of underwriters, each of whom can demonstrate a certain minimum net worth. In some states, however, certain minimum deposits are also required.

[6] The law that established the New York Insurance Exchange also created a Free Trade Zone that exempted certain types of insurance written by specially licensed insurers from that state's premium and policy form approval requirements. The law also exempted insurance on exposures outside the United States from the New York state premium tax. Insurers writing insurance through the Free Trade Zone thus can compete more effectively with alien insurers. (See Chapter 34 for more details on the premium and policy form approval requirements and state premium taxes.) The Free Trade Zone applies only to business coverages with annual premiums of $100,000 or more and to unusual or hard-to-place insurance such as oil spill insurance and liability insurance on amusement parks.

tions, and (3) reciprocal exchanges sometimes referred to as "interinsurance exchanges." Three other types of cooperative insurers, which closely resemble the advance premium mutual corporation but which possess some unique characteristics and which are usually regulated under a separate section of the state insurance laws, are fraternals, mutual savings bank insurers, and medical and dental expense associations such as Blue Cross, Blue Shield, and Delta Dental. These organizations have already been described elsewhere in this text, and the reader should review those discussions in connection with this section.

The *advance premium mutual* is a corporation owned by its policyholders. The corporation sets premium rates at a level that is expected to be at least sufficient to pay the expected losses and expenses and to add to its contingency reserves.[7] Policyholders receive the dividends, if any, declared by the board of directors, the dividends representing the amount by which the premium and other income exceeds the needs of the insurer. The surplus built up out of past operations serves as a cushion against years of poor experience.

The contracts issued by the advance premium mutual may be assessable or nonassessable. If assessable, the assessment may be unlimited or limited. In either case, however, the mutual never expects to exercise this right, though it may be forced to do so. Nonassessable policies can be issued by mutuals whose surplus position is strong enough to satisfy the state requirements on this score. Most advance premium insurance contracts are nonassessable.

Advance premium mutuals write about one-half the life insurance in force and almost one-quarter of the property and liability insurance.

Although some mutuals write all types of property and liability insurance, most mutuals engage in a much more limited operation. Table 26.1 indicates that advance premium mutuals, which are responsible for most of the mutual premium volume, are most important in the more common property and liability lines, such as workers' compensation and automobile insurance.

Assessment mutuals, though many in number, write a very small proportion to the total premium volume, most of which is paid for fire insurance on farm properties. Assessment mutuals play an even less important role in personnel insurance, but a few assessment health insurance associations are large insurers.

Assessment mutuals differ from advance premium mutuals in that they always have the right to assess their policyholders and the chance of an assessment is high. A "pure" assessment mutual would charge an initial premium large enough to cover the expenses that will be incurred even if no losses are experienced and would assess the policyholders to pay any extra costs arising in connection with losses. At the other and much more common extreme, the assessment mutual would collect an initial premium sufficient to pay expenses and typical losses. Assessments are levied whenever unusual losses occur, the assessment in some instances being limited in advance to some

---

[7] The first mutual insurer in the United States, the Philadelphia Contributionship for the Insurance of Houses from Loss by Fire, founded in 1752 by Benjamin Franklin and others, still operates. This insurer and a few others issue perpetual policies. The insured pays a very large initial premium the first year and nothing thereafter. The investment return on the premium is sufficient to pay the costs of the insurer and to return a dividend to the policyholder. The initial premium is returned when the insured drops the insurance.

specified amount. Some mutuals, legally termed "assessment mutuals," have never levied an assessment and could, in fact, be classified as advance premium mutuals.

Property assessment mutuals usually confine their operations to a county or counties and at most operate in a few states. Because of the limited scale of their operations, their experience may show wide fluctuations from one year to the next; some, however, are large enough to maintain a fairly stable experience. Most personnel insurance assessment mutuals are also small, but some have a large number of policyholders in widely scattered geographical areas and maintain legal reserves similar to those established by advance premium mutuals.

Reciprocal exchanges resemble advance premium mutuals, but in their purest form they differ from these mutuals in many ways. First, they are not corporations but unincorporated associations.[8] Second, the association is not technically the insurer. Instead, the association makes it possible for the policyholders to insure one another individually and not jointly. Each member of the reciprocal insures and is insured by every other member of the reciprocal. This reciprocal exchange of contracts is the essence of the arrangement. In order to simplify the administration of the agreement, each subscriber receives only one contract, which states that he or she is in effect exchanging contracts with other members of the association. The administration of the agreement is in the charge of an attorney-in-fact, who performs such duties as soliciting new members, rejecting undesirable applicants, paying losses, investing funds, and establishing premiums. Third, individual accounts are maintained for each member, the accounts of the association being the sum of the accounts of the members. The accounts are credited with the premiums and a share of the investment income and debited with a share of the expenses and losses. Deficiencies in the account are not expected, but if they occur, they can be repaired by an assessment, which may be limited. A surplus in the account may result in a dividend, and if any surplus remains in the account when the member terminates membership, it is returned to him or her.

In practice, however, so many modifications have been introduced that it is often difficult to distinguish a reciprocal exchange from an advance premium mutual. First, undivided surplus funds are commonly kept in addition to the individual surplus accounts, and in some instances the undivided surplus funds replace completely the individual accounts. Second, because assessments are seldom necessary, the distinction between individual liability and joint liability is almost never effective. In fact, if sufficient undivided surplus funds exist, states permit the issuance of nonassessable contracts.

About 65 reciprocals exist today. They write no life insurance and only about 6 percent of the property and liability insurance. Tables 26.1 and 26.2 show the limited number of lines in which they are active. Many reciprocals are associated with a trade association or an automobile association, but a few are multiple-line insurers seeking with considerable success insureds of all types in most states. One of the largest automobile insurers in the United States is a reciprocal exchange.

---

[8] A reciprocal is easier to form than a mutual. A minimum deposit may be required, but usually all that is needed is a minimum number of applications with aggregate premiums or exposure units in excess of a certain amount. If no minimum deposit is required, the only funds necessary are the advance premiums deposited by the subscribers.

A key factor in the success of a reciprocal exchange is the attorney-in-fact. The prospective subscriber should examine carefully the ability and reputation of the attorney-in-fact as well as the power of attorney that prescribes his or her authority and duties. In some cases, a policyholders' advisory committee may exist, and its effectiveness should be determined. This investigation is important because the attorney-in-fact, who has nothing to lose from the failure of the reciprocal other than a job,[9] may be tempted to increase the volume of business, regardless of its quality, because he or she is reimbursed on a commission basis. On the other hand, it should be emphasized that many excellent, progressive reciprocals can be found.

Government Insurers   The last form of business organization to be discussed is the government insurer. The principal government insurers are operated by the federal and state governments, but some are local government agencies. In most instances, the government plans are intended to be self-supporting, but in a few instances a direct subsidy exists. In all cases the governmental unit would probably supply funds in time of financial distress.

The *federal government* insurers include the largest insurance operation in the nation, the Old-Age, Survivors, Disability, and Health Insurance program under the Social Security Act. Other important federal government insurers include the Railroad Retirement Board (benefits under the Railroad Retirement System), the Veterans Administration (servicemen's life insurance and veterans' mortgage and property improvement loan insurance), the Postal Service (insurance on parcel post and registered mail shipments), the Federal Housing Administration (mortgage and property improvement loan insurance), the Federal Deposit Insurance Administration (insurance on bank deposits), the Federal Savings and Loan Insurance Corporation (insurance on savings and loan association shares), the National Credit Union Association (insurance on credit union shares and deposits), the Federal Crop Insurance Corporation (insurance on farmer's crops against natural hazards), the Nuclear Regulatory Commission (nuclear energy liability protection in excess of that available from private sources), the Maritime Administration (war risk marine insurance binders, which become effective during time of war after private insurance is canceled), the Export-Import Bank of Washington (protection on exports against insolvency of the purchaser and such political losses as inconvertibility of foreign currencies), the Overseas Private Investment Corporation (insurance on business properties abroad against expropriation or other political losses), the National Insurance Development Fund (direct crime insurance), the National Flood Insurance Fund (flood insurance), and the Securities Investor Protection Corporation (protection for investors in case of brokerage house insolvencies).

The two most important types of *state* funds are unemployment insurance funds in all states and workers' compensation insurance funds, which compete with private insurers in 13 states[10] and possess a monopoly in six states.[11] The variation among

---

[9] The retention of one's job may of course be a sufficient incentive. Future employment may also be affected.

[10] Arizona, California, Colorado, Idaho, Maryland, Michigan, Minnesota, Montana, New York, Oklahoma, Oregon, Pennsylvania, and Utah.

[11] Nevada, North Dakota, Ohio, Washington, West Virginia, and Wyoming.

these funds with respect to services rendered, acceptable classes of insureds, pricing policies, tax status, and other matters is too great to be detailed here. Another type of state fund associated with workers' compensation laws is the second-injury fund.[12]

Other state funds include temporary disability insurance funds in California, Hawaii, New Jersey, New York, and Rhode Island, a life insurance fund in Wisconsin, and funds operating within the Torrens title system in California, Massachusetts, North Carolina, and Ohio.[13]

Government underwriting of insurance on its own property and personnel insurance benefits for its employees is best classified as self-insurance or retention. Sometimes, however, a state fund underwrites insurance benefits for local government employees (say, teachers).

Some of these government insurers provide protection in direct competition with private insurers; but many are underwriting risks that private insurers have generally considered to be uninsurable. Table 12.3 permits some comparisons between the scope of some leading government insurance operations and private insurance.

Domicile and Admission Status

Private insurers are classified as domestic, foreign, or alien insurers, depending upon whether they are organized under the laws of the state to which the classification is applicable, of some other state, or outside the United States. All domestic insurers must be authorized by state insurance officials to conduct an insurance business. Foreign and alien insurers are considered to be admitted insurers if they have been licensed by the state insurance official. An unlicensed or nonadmitted insurer cannot be represented by agents within the state unless it is a surplus lines insurer operating under the state's surplus line law. Under these laws surplus lines' agents or brokers (described in the section below under "Marketing Methods") are permitted to place insurance with nonadmitted insurers meeting certain requirements if such insurance is not available from admitted insurers. Some insurers are admitted in one or more states and nonadmitted in others.

Pricing Policy

Differences in pricing policies of private insurers have become more marked in recent years, though the differences are more notable in property and liability insurance than in personnel insurance. Insurers can be classified according to whether they issue participating or nonparticipating contracts and according to whether they use independent or bureau rates.

Participating or Nonparticipating Insurers   Policyholders of participating insurers share in the experience of the insurer through dividends, assessments, or both. Policyholders of nonparticipating insurers pay a definite premium (subject in some

---

[12] See Chap. 8 for more information on second injury funds.
[13] County Torrens title funds are active in several states.

cases to retrospective rating). The same insurer may issue participating and nonparticipating insurance. Insurers issuing participating insurance include some capital stock insurers (mostly life insurers), most advance premium mutuals, all assessment associations, and most reciprocal exchanges. Nonparticipating insurers include most stock insurers (for at least part of their business), some advance premium mutuals, and some reciprocal exchanges.

Some participating insurers set their rates at a high level to permit the payment of large dividends, while others establish lower rates and expect to declare lower dividends. Some advance premium mutuals and reciprocal exchanges are classified as nonparticipating insurers because they issue nonassessable contracts, fix rates at the lowest feasible predictable level, and pay no dividends.

Independent or Bureau Insurers   The second classification according to pricing policy is not important in personnel insurance, where each insurer uses its own independent rate structure. In property and liability insurance, however, in most states an insurer may develop its own rates or, as a member or subscriber to a rating organization, called a ''rating bureau,'' it may use the rates developed by the bureau from pooled experience.[14] Many bureau members or subscribers modify the bureau rates in some respect, thus occupying a position midway between the independents and those insurers using the bureau rates.

Marketing Methods and Supervisory Systems

Private insurers may market their product in four different ways: (1) through independent agents, (2) through employees on a direct writing basis, (3) through exclusive agents, or (4) through brokers. Insurers may supervise their agents and sales representatives under (1) a general agency system, (2) a branch office system, or (3) a direct reporting system. A particular insurer may use two or more of these methods or supervisory systems. Furthermore, persons the text describes as sales representatives may call themselves agents, and persons the text would call agents may call themselves brokers.

Marketing Methods   *Independent agency insurers* market their product through agents who represent two or more insurers.[15] The agent is an independent businessperson who receives a commission as compensation for his or her services and who retains the right to renew the insurance contracts of his or her customers with a different insurer. The agency expiration list, which records the names and addresses of present policyholders and the dates their policies expire, belongs to the agent, and if the agent and the insurer agree to sever their relationship, the insurer cannot give any information in this list to a new agent. Independent agents may write their own policies and handle all financial transactions (billing, collecting, and extending credit) with their

---

[14] Rating bureaus are described more fully in Chap. 28.

[15] Office agents are sometimes also appointed by a few independent agency insurers. These agents are based in the home or branch office, receive more administrative assistance, and are paid lower commissions.

insureds. Increasingly, however, independent agency insurers are taking over the policy writing, billing, and collecting functions. In this way independent agency insurers have been able to reduce selling and servicing costs, including commissions, and to strengthen their relationships with their insureds.

Despite their independent status, independent agents have the authority to commit immediately the insurers they represent to insure most applicants. Moreover, all agents are considered legal agents of the insurer, who is bound by their actions and knowledge.

Independent agency insurers are almost always property and liability insurers. They include stock and mutual insurers as well as reciprocal exchanges and Lloyds Associations. In fact, most stock and most mutual property and liability insurers are agency insurers. They write about two-thirds of the total property and liability insurance premiums. Their share of the premiums paid by business insureds is more than two-thirds; by families close to one-half.

Direct writers sell insurance through commissioned or salaried (plus bonuses) employees, called "sales representatives," who represent only the insurer employing them. Generally, the insurer does more of the policy writing, billing, and collection work under this system than under the agency system. Sales representatives usually have the power to bind the insurer they represent and are legally that insurer's agents. Consequently their errors are attributed to the insurer.

All legal forms of business organization in property and liability insurance include some direct writers, but most direct writers are cooperative insurers, including most of the larger mutuals.

Insurance is sometimes marketed directly by advertisements inviting mail or other applications. Because few persons take the initiative to buy insurance, relatively little is sold solely through such advertising. On the other hand, more interest exists in such direct purchases now than in the past. Most of the insurance that is sold in this way is health insurance and mutual savings bank life insurance. Some insurers sell aviation accident insurance directly through vending machines.

Exclusive agency insurers occupy a position somewhere between independent agency insurers and direct writers. Like direct writers, these insurers require exclusive representation (at least for their regular business), regard the policyholders as their customers, and perform much of the administrative work in behalf of the agent. On the other hand, the agents are regarded as independent businesspersons and are always reimbursed on a commission basis. Typically, however, the renewal commission is much less than the commission on new business. Many authorities prefer to classify exclusive agency insurers as a modified version of the direct writers.

The leading examples of exclusive agency insurers are some leading mutual property and liability insurers and almost all life insurers, regardless of the form of business organization. In life insurance, however, the renewal commissions usually belong to an agent who has completed a certain period of service, even if he or she leaves the insurer.[16]

---

[16] Unlike property and liability insurance contracts, life insurance contracts, except for term insurance, do not have to be resold periodically. Also, the insured would usually suffer if the contract were surrendered and rewritten in another insurer just to maintain the relationship with the agent.

Insurers accepting brokerage business are the fourth and final category of insurers classified according to marketing methods. Unlike the insurers' producers discussed above, in principle *brokers* are independent businesspersons who do not represent any insurer. Brokers offer to analyze risks for their clients and to shop among insurers to obtain the optimum protection at the optimum price. For their services, brokers receive part or all of the producer's commission from the insurer or producer with whom they place the business. Some insurers accept and even encourage the direct placement of insurance with brokers, while others require the placement through one of their producers. Some insurers will not pay the broker any commission for business he or she places with them, and the broker may hesitate to suggest the use of their facilities.

Because brokers are not legal agents of the insurer, they cannot bind any insurer, and no insurer can be held responsible for brokers' mistakes. However, in several states statutes make the broker the agent of the insurer with respect to the acceptance of premium payments from the insured. In other states this practice is customary and in many instances has been supported by the courts.[17]

In practice, brokers do develop relationships with particular insurers and place most of their business with them. These relationships speed up and cut the cost of placing the insurance for the broker and often enable the broker to place business that would otherwise be impossible to insure.

Brokers may be one-person operations concentrating upon risk analysis and the purchase of insurance for families and small firms or they may be sizable operations providing, in addition, engineering, appraisal, actuarial, risk management, and other services and specializing in the accounts of large business firms. The latter are more common because (1) these clients are more likely to demand the services of a broker, and (2) since the broker often receives a lower commission rate than the insurer's producer, the broker usually prefers larger premium accounts. For the same reasons, brokers tend to concentrate their operations in large cities.

Brokers are most important in property and liability insurance where a few large firms account for a substantial share of the business property and liability insurance written; they rarely specialize in life insurance. On the other hand, property and liability insurance brokers also originate a considerable amount of personnel insurance, particularly group insurance and pensions. Independent agency property and liability insurers are much more likely to accept brokerage business than are direct writers and exclusive agency insurers.

Some states do not issue brokers' licenses. In those states brokerage concerns must represent the insurers with whom they do business. In these states the difference between the agency representing several insurers and the so-called broker is primarily a matter of philosophy. The broker is supposedly less hesitant to seek new insurer connections if the needs of his or her client require them. The term that has been used to describe brokers operating in this fashion is *broker-agents*.

Broker-agents are also common in states that do permit the licensing of brokers. Sometimes the broker is licensed as both an agent and a broker; sometimes he or she is licensed only as an agent and operates in accordance with the philosophy described in

---

[17] Edwin W. Patterson, *Essentials of Insurance Law* (New York: McGraw-Hill Book Company, 1957), p. 492.

the preceding paragraph. Finally, it is a common practice for agents to place business that their regular channels reject with some insurer they do not normally represent.

In most states, *surplus or excess line brokers or agents* may be licensed to obtain insurance from nonadmitted insurers. Under these statutes, the excess line broker or agent must demonstrate that the insurance sought is not available in the admitted market, pay the state premium tax, and post a bond guaranteeing that he or she will comply with the statute. Surplus line agents or brokers are sometimes also agents or brokers engaging in regular business, but more often they are specialists serving ordinary agents and brokers and sharing their commissions with them.

Risk managers can purchase coverage from nonadmitted insurers in three ways.[18] First, they may deal with a surplus lines agent or broker located in the same state as the exposure being insured. Most family and small business coverage is placed in this way. Second, the insurance may be purchased through a surplus lines agent or broker located in some other state. These agents or brokers tend to specialize in large, multi-state exposures and account for most of the non-admitted insurance in force. Finally, many large businesses prefer to deal directly with the nonadmitted insurer.

Although they are often confused with brokers or broker-agents, *risk management* or *insurance consultants* are independent businesspersons who offer advice about risk management insurance to their clients. Like brokers, they do not represent any insurers, but unlike brokers, they are paid by their clients on a fee basis and do not share in the commissions paid by insurers. Because their remuneration is not tied to the amount of insurance purchased by the client or to the particular insurer providing the protection, it can be argued that the suggestions of the consultant are more likely to be objective than those of agents, sales representatives, or brokers. On the other hand, the extra fee involved is a disadvantage, and their interest in the risk problems of the firm may not be a continuing one. Insurance consultants operate for the most part only in large cities, and their clients are usually firms or public bodies large enough to have complicated insurance problems but not large enough to have a full-time risk manager on their staff.

Independent agents and brokers often enter into special commission arrangements with the risk managers of large organizations. Instead of having the insurer pay its usual commissions, these risk managers may negotiate with the agent or broker either (1) a reasonable fee for the services rendered that does not depend upon the amount of insurance recommended, or (2) a lower commission than would otherwise be paid. Sometimes the agent or broker renders extra services for which a fee is negotiated in addition to a standard commission. Many agents and brokers oppose fees on principle because they believe that the commission system is a much fairer and less expensive approach that has worked well over the years. They believe that negotiated fees are highly subjective, that the number of hours spent on a client's business often does not measure the value of the services rendered, and that a fee system is more expensive to operate because of the record-keeping it entails (for example, expenses incurred while on the case). Nevertheless, the fee approach has become more popular.

[18] Samuel H. Weese, *Non-Admitted Insurance in the United States* (Homewood, Ill.: Richard D. Irwin, Inc., 1971), pp. 9–11.

Supervisory Systems Under the *general agency system of* supervising agents, the insurer appoints a general agent to represent it in a specified territory.[19] The general agent may sell insurance and in addition may appoint other agents to work under him or her. The general agent's compensation includes a commission on the business he or she personally produces, an overriding commission on the business produced by agents, and, in an increasing number of cases, a contribution toward expenses.

By definition, this system is not applicable to direct writers. The other two systems to be noticed are used by both agency insurers and direct writers.

In life insurance, a general agent usually represents only one insurer, and much of his or her activity centers around the recruiting, training, and supervision of agents. In property and liability insurance, where the system is much less common and is diminishing in importance, the general agent usually represents several insurers, and in addition to the production function, he or she is often authorized to underwrite some of the business written through the agency, provide engineering services, and settle most claims. In many cases, the general agent who provides extensive services of this nature produces no business personally and is termed a "managing general agent."[20]

The general agency system is most attractive to small insurers and large insurers entering new areas because (1) when the volume of business is small, the overhead cost is reduced, and (2) if an established general agency is used, the insurer gains the prestige of the agency plus a network of agents and their customers. Insurers, regardless of size, often prefer this agency system; they argue that because of the method of remuneration, the general agent has the maximum incentive to produce new business, service the present insureds, and run an efficient operation.

Negative aspects from the insurer's point of view are (1) the relatively high costs of operation when the volume of business is high, (2) the diverse, and sometimes inefficient, practices employed by general agents, (3) the pressures that general agents can exert through threats that they and their appointed agents will cease representing the insurer, and (4) the failure of most insureds to recognize the insurers with whom the general agency has placed the insurance.

There is a definite trend, however, toward reducing the independence of general agents, particularly in life insurance. Insurers now pay more of their expenses, exercise more supervision over their selection and training procedures, and perform more of their clerical chores. Consequently, the differences between the general agency system and the branch office system are diminishing.

Under the *branch office system,* the insurer establishes a branch of the home office, sometimes called a "service office" in the territory and places an employee, called a "branch manager," in charge of the office. The branch manager may sell insurance, but he or she is less likely to do so than a general agent. The branch manager appoints agents, but the contracts are between the agents and the insurer, not between the agents and the branch manager. The branch manager usually receives a salary plus a commis-

[19] Agents may also be involved under more than one system. For example, the authors know one local agent who has contracts with (1) a managing general agent, (2) two insurers through their branch offices, and (3) a few insurers operating under the direct reporting system.
[20] The distinction between a large local agency and a general agency that is not a managing general agency is often vague.

sion or bonus depending upon the extent and quality of business produced by the branch.

By definition, the branch office represents only one insurer or group. In property and liability insurance, the branch is usually authorized to perform most of the home office underwriting and claims functions.

The branch office method of operation is becoming more popular in all lines of insurance. Reasons for this preference include (1) the relatively low cost when the volume of business is great, (2) the degree of control that the home office has over the branch manager and his or her methods of operation, (3) the increasing importance of electronic data-processing equipment and its emphasis on uniformity, and (4) an increasing desire to acquaint insureds with the name of the insurer. On the other hand, the branch office method is an expensive system for the small insurer or, to a lesser extent, a large insurer entering a new territory, which must struggle with a low volume of business to create a market for itself. Moreover, some insurance executives argue that, despite the incentive arrangements for branch managers, the independent status of the general agent is the most effective incentive plan that can be devised.

Under the *direct reporting system,* the agents report directly to the home office of the insurer. The identifying characteristic of this system, then, is the absence of either a general agent or a branch office.

The principal appeal of this system is the absence of branch office and general agency costs. This appeal is greatest when the volume of business in the area is small and the problems simple, and when the insureds can be serviced by one or at most a few agents. The principal drawback is the absence of local supervision and assistance. Life insurers seldom use this system, but property and liability insurers employ it extensively, particularly in rural areas and small towns.

Special agents or field persons are salaried (or salaried plus bonus) representatives of insurers marketing their product under the nonexclusive agency system. A special agent serves as the liaison between the insurer and the agent or broker. His or her work includes the following: locating new agents and brokers for the insurer; persuading existing agents and brokers to place more business with the insurer; educating the agent or broker with respect to coverages, agency management, and sales techniques; assisting the agent or broker in actual sales presentations, particularly with respect to the more technical aspects; and in general creating a favorable image for the insurer.

In exclusive agency and direct writing insurers, representatives from the home or branch office provide similar services and in fact are also often referred to as "special agents."

Insureds Serviced

Insurers may finally be classified according to the types of insureds serviced. Some insurers seek all types of insureds, subject to certain underwriting restrictions (and these vary widely), whereas others limit rather severely the types of insureds they will underwrite. For example, a manufacturing firm may establish a captive insurer as part of its risk management program for reasons cited in Chapter 11 (possible tax savings and access to reinsurance markets), and this insurer may underwrite only the risks of the parent company. Some insurers are organized by finance companies to write property insurance on automobiles financed through dealers using the finance company services. Other insurers, usually cooperative insurers, limit their customers to the members of a trade association, an automobile association, an industry, a church, an occupation, or some other group.

GROUPS AND COOPERATIVE REINSURANCE AND UNDERWRITING ASSOCIATIONS

In addition to individual insurers, the insurance market includes important (1) groups, (2) underwriters' associations, and (3) reinsurance associations.

Groups

A group or fleet of insurers includes two or more insurers operating as a team under common ownership or management. Group operations are most important in property and liability insurance but are becoming more commonplace in life insurance. Groups commonly include insurers that can write all kinds of insurance.

Group operations were originally important for two reasons. First, at one time the property and liability insurance industry limited, through a voluntary agreement, the number of agencies per insurer. Nothing, however, prevented insurers from forming subsidiaries which could have their own agents. Agreements limiting the number of agents would be illegal today. Second, prior to multiple line legislation, as noted earlier, fire and marine insurers could not write casualty insurance and vice versa. Consequently, in order to write additional lines of insurance, fire and marine insurers commonly established casualty insurers and vice versa. Though these two reasons no longer exist, organizations that have operated for many years are not easily scrapped.

Some factors continue to favor group operations. First, an insurer can expand its scope more rapidly by obtaining the controlling interest in an existing firm than by extending its own operations. Second, to enter the life insurance field, a property and liability insurer must organize a new life insurer or acquire an old one. Similarly, to enter the property-liability insurance field, a life insurer must operate through a separate corporation. Each type of insurer has become increasingly interested in the other's market. Third, some insurers prefer to use two or more marketing systems, a different insurer being used for each system. For example, an insurer may form a subsidiary to market preferred automobile insurance for which the agent receives a lower commission. One large direct writer of insurance for families has formed a subsidiary that uses independent agents to sell property and liability insurance to businesses.

Underwriters' Associations

Especially in fire insurance, insurers often cooperate in the underwriting of some or all of the policies they issue. These cooperative underwriting organizations are generally associated with one or more of the following conditions: (1) a unique or particularly hazardous exposure, (2) very high policy limits, or (3) a need for highly specialized talent.[21] Some examples will illustrate the nature of these associations.

The Factory Mutual Insurance Companies includes four mutual insurers specializing in sprinklered properties of superior construction.[22] These associated insurers are noted for their engineering advice and services and their unique contract (for example, vandalism and structural collapse are always included, and there is no coinsurance clause). Typically, one of the four insurers writes a direct policy, and the other three members act as reinsurers, the percentage of risk reinsured by each insurer being indicated in a rider to the contract. The association provides appraisal, inspection engineering, loss-adjustment, and rate-making services for its members.

The stock insurers' equivalent (in many ways) of the Factory Mutuals is Industrial Risk Insurers, an organization including about 45 of the leading stock insurers and devoted to the underwriting of highly protected properties. IRI issues its policies directly, and its liability is uniformly apportioned among the member insurers. Unlike the Factory Mutuals, IRI operates through agents, and its member insurers write only a small portion of their business through IRI.

Property and liability insurance for the operators of atomic reactors are supplied by two associations—American Nuclear Insurers (a stock insurer pool) and the Mutual Atomic Energy Reinsurance Pool, which reinsures the exposure of six insurers operating as the Mutual Atomic Energy Liability Underwriters.

United States Aircraft Insurance Group handles the aviation insurance business of its stock members. The Improved Risk Mutuals organization serves its mutual members in about the same way as the IRI serves its stock members. Assigned risk pools or joint underwriting associations in some property and liability lines, such as automobile and workers' compensation insurance, insure applicants unable to procure insurance directly.

Numerous other associations could be cited, but these examples are sufficient to indicate their number and importance and the fact that they compete against one another as well as against nonmember insurers.

Reinsurance Associations

Insurers are also organized into associations to provide reinsurance facilities. Some reinsurance associations, such as the Excess and Casualty Reinsurance Association, an association of stock insurers, reinsure primarily nonmembers. Most associations, however, such as The Worker's Compensation Reinsurance Bureau and the Mutual Reinsurance Bureau, exist mainly to reinsure members. Reinsurance pools are much more common in property and liability insurance than in personnel insurance.

---

[21] G. F. Michelbacher, *Multiple-Line Insurance* (New York: McGraw-Hill Book Company, 1957), p. 294.

[22] A stock insurer owned by the four Factory Mutual insurers accepts good insureds who do not meet the association standards. It is also licensed to write liability insurance.

FINANCIAL SERVICES COMBINATIONS

Beginning in the late 1960s many insurers became for the first time part of some business combination marketing noninsurance products and services. In some instances stock insurers have been acquired by some corporation, including conglomerates, whose primary business is not insurance. In more instances, a holding company has been formed by the persons who own a stock insurer, the stock of the holding company has been exchanged for the stock of the insurer, and the holding company has then acquired or established subsidiaries in fields that insurers have been forbidden to enter. Both of these routes to diversification are closed to mutual insurers unless they first convert their mode of operation to that of a stock insurer, a change that is permitted under the laws of some states. In order to correct this competitive disadvantage of the mutuals and to discourage the use of holding companies, which pose some important regulatory problems, many states have relaxed laws limiting the proportion of their assets insurers can invest (1) in the aggregate in common stock, or (2) in the common stock of one corporation. Generally these new laws permit insurers to own a controlling interest in subsidiaries engaged in closely related or ancillary activities. Such activities include but are not limited to some other form of insurance, mutual fund investment management, mutual fund broker-dealerships, personal finance companies, banks, savings and loan associations, computer services, computer leasing, and real estate development. In short, insurers are permitted under this legislation to expand their operations to include a broad range of financial services and closely related services; they are not permitted to enter unrelated fields. The scope of holding companies is not limited in this way, but most holding companies formed by insurers have elected to concentrate on financial services. For this and other reasons, most stock insurers expanding into noninsurance areas have formed or become part of a parent holding company. Mutual insurers have become the parents of subsidiaries.[23]

Why have insurers sought product diversification through business combinations?

1 Life insurers decided in the sixties that in order to increase their share of the consumers' savings dollar they needed to market equity products, which they could not legally do directly, except for variable annuities. This consumer interest in equity products declined during the seventies, but has strengthened again recently.
2 Insurers for both selfish and unselfish reasons wished to improve their services to policyholders. They believe that "one-stop service" is more convenient for customers and improves the likelihood that they will receive unbiased advice (e.g., in choosing between mutual funds and cash value life insurance).
3 Insurers hoped to improve their profit picture in the following ways:
   a Synergism, or the concept that the whole may be greater than the sum of its parts. For example, the demand for one product may stimulate the demand for another, and certain overhead costs may not increase as rapidly as the business expands.

[23] In some instances, mutuals have become the parents of holding companies, which then acquire or form subsidiaries. Some mutuals have been converted into stock insurers in order to achieve more flexibility.

 b Entering new fields that are profitable even without the influence of synergism.
 c Reducing annual fluctuations in profits through diversification.
 d Securing more freedom in external financing. Although insurers may have the
  authority to borrow through bonds or debentures, they are reluctant to do so.
4 Insurers hoped by increasing the range of their operations to improve their ability to
 attract and retain high-quality personnel.

Few leading insurers at the present time are not part of some business combination
marketing noninsurance products and services. Many have developed integrated packages of insurance and other financial services.

At the beginning of this decade the deregulation of the banking industry, high
interest rates, high inflation, high income tax rates, new computer technology, and
increased consumer financial knowledge, interest, and sophistication caused renewed
interest in integrated financial services concerns.[24] Many persons believe that the
financial services industry is being converted from distinct and separate financial
institutions into more integrated institutions with a variety of new services. Under this
scenario most financial institutions will soon be able to provide the services formerly
provided by insurers, banks, mutual funds, and real estate or securities brokerage
firms. Some believe that the market will be dominated by a small number of such
integrated institutions operating worldwide except for small companies with a competitive edge in specialty markets. Others believe that the case for integrated services has
been oversold and that previous attempts have been disappointing. In their opinion
companies that are firmly established in a specialized area such as insurance will, if
they can adapt to change, compete successfully against fully integrated financial
service companies.

Another more recent development is a form of vertical integration by the insurance
business itself. Several insurers have recently purchased some major insurance brokerage concerns; some major brokers have in turn formed their own insurers. According to one consultant, brokers and direct-writing companies currently control nearly
two-thirds of the total insurance marketplace, a fact that has caused many independent
agency insurers to believe they must control at least part of their distribution system.[25]
As a result, some observers believe that in the future businesses will buy much more
insurance through brokers or agencies owned by insurers and from insurers owned by
brokers or agencies. This vertical integration has been justified as a more economical,
effective method of serving the ultimate consumer. On the other hand, some persons
have questioned whether independent agents and brokers who own insurers or are
owned by insurers can maintain their objectivity.[26] The insurers, agents, and brokers
involved say that they must maintain their objectivity to be successful.

---

[24] For more observations on this development see "Financial Services Skirmishing," *The National
Underwriter, Property and Casualty Insurance Edition*, Oct. 29, 1982, pp. 3, 41.

[25] See, for example, "Consultant Sees Changes Ahead in Distribution," *Business Insurance*, Oct. 18,
1982, pp. 3, 16.

[26] See, for example, "Do Mergers Threaten Brokers, Buyers?" *National Underwriter, Property and
Casualty Edition*, Oct. 15, 1982, p. 36.

SOME KEY CONCEPTS

Stock insurer   A proprietary insurer owned by stockholders who elect a board of directors.

Mutual insurer   A cooperative insurer owned by its policyholders.

Participating insurer   An insurer whose policyholders participate in the experience of the insurer through dividends, assessments, or both.

Independent agency insurer   An insurer that markets its services through independent agents who may represent many insurers.

Direct writer   An insurer that markets its services through its own employees.

Broker   A person or organization that "shops the market" in behalf of the prospective insured; unlike an agent, not legally an agent of the insured. Some brokers are broker-agents.

Risk management consultant   Independent persons who offer risk management advice to their clients. Unlike brokers or agents, they do not receive any commissions from insurers for business placed with those insurers.

Independent insurer   An insurer that sets its own prices. An independent insurer does not use the rates developed by a rating bureau.

Group of insurers   Two or more insurers operating as a team under common ownership or management.

REVIEW QUESTIONS

1 How can insurers be classified according to the types of insurance they write?

2 "Stock insurers, which are always nonparticipating, independent agency, proprietary insurers, write most of the premium volume in all branches of insurance."
   a In what respects is this statement false?
   b In what respects is this statement true?

3 Lloyd's of London is internationally renowned for its insurance activities, but technically Lloyd's is not an insurer. Explain this statement.

4 a Are Lloyds Associations United States branches of Lloyd's of London?
   b In what ways do Lloyds Associations differ from Lloyd's of London?

5 Some risk managers refuse to purchase insurance from mutual insurers because they believe that all mutual policies are assessable. Are they correct in their reasoning?

6 a In which lines of insurance do mutuals account for at least 30 percent of the premium volume?
   b In which lines of insurance is the mutuals' share less than 10 percent?

7 Compare the following types of insurers with respect to (1) the controlling group, (2) the liability of the "owners," i.e., whether it is joint and several or individual, and (3) ownership of the surplus.
   a Reciprocal exchange
   b Advance premium mutual
   c Lloyds Association
   d Capital stock insurer

8 The Buttonwood Mutual is legally a small township mutual operating in one state on the assessment basis.
   a Should an insured be surprised if the management collects an assessment each year?
   b Do all assessable mutuals levy assessments?

9 The Gray Company is considering the formation of a captive insurer. Which of the following legal forms would be easiest to establish? Why?

    a Capital stock insurer

    b Advance premium mutual insurer

    c Reciprocal exchange

10 a Which government insurers compete with private insurers?

    b Which government insurers provide insurance not available from private insurers?

11 An insurer domiciled in another state wishes to sell insurance in your state.

    a If this insurer is not licensed by your state insurance department, what terms would you use to describe its status in your state?

    b Why is this status important to insureds? to the insurer?

12 "All participating insurers are cooperative insurers, and all cooperative insurers are participating insurers." Comment on the truth or falsity of this statement.

13 a What is the function of rating bureaus?

    b Contrast the importance of rating bureaus in property and liability insurance with that of rating bureaus in personnel insurance.

14 a Distinguish among agency insurers, direct writers, and exclusive agency insurers.

    b Do parallel marketing systems exist in other businesses?

15 Does the fact that an insurance representative calls himself or herself an agent, a broker, or consultant mean that he or she is functionally what the term implies?

16 Compare a property and liability insurance agent, a property and liability insurance sales representative, a property and liability insurance exclusive agent, and a life insurance agent with respect to:

    a Binding authority

    b Commissions

    c Number of insurers represented

17 "One-stop selling" is an important trend in insurance as it is in other businesses.

    a What does "one-stop selling" mean in insurance?

    b What advantages and disadvantages does it offer?

18 Compare a broker, an agent, and a consultant with respect to:

    a Binding authority

    b Commissions

    c Legal responsibility of insurers for their actions

    d Number of insurers represented

19 In many states the law provides only for agents' licenses.

    a Are there any brokers in those states?

    b Do broker-agents exist in the other states? Why?

20 Special agents or field persons and group representatives play an important role in the marketing of insurance, regardless of the type of marketing structure. What is this role?

21 a The general agency system is most attractive to small insurers and to large insurers entering new areas. Why?

    b What are the other marketing systems, and what are their advantages and disadvantages from the insured's point of view?

22 a What is a group or fleet operation?

    b What factors favor group operations?

23 The Factory Mutuals and the Industrial Risk Insurers are two major underwriting associations.

    a In what ways do these two associations resemble one another?

    b In what ways do they differ?

24 Describe briefly the purpose of each of the following:

a Nuclear energy insurance pools
b Reinsurance pools
25 Why and how have insurers sought product diversification through business combinations?
26 Will all insurers soon become part of an integrated financial services institution? Explain.
27 A recent development is vertical integration by the insurance business itself. Explain.

SUGGESTIONS FOR ADDITIONAL READING

See suggestions for Chapter 27.

SELECTING
THE INSURER: II

LEARNING OBJECTIVES

After you have completed this chapter, you should be able to:

1 List the major factors affecting an insurer's financial strength.

2 Describe how asset and reserve valuations and reinsurance affect an insurer's financial strength.

3 Explain the National Association of Insurance Commissioners' Insurance Regulatory Information System.

4 List the factors to be considered in assessing the services provided by an insurer or a producer.

5 Explain the interest-adjusted cost method, its advantages, and its limitations.

6 Calculate and evaluate the expense ratio of a property and liability insurer.

7 Tell where you can get information needed to evaluate an insurer's financial strength, service, and cost.

8 List the advantages and disadvantages of competitive bidding applied to insurance buying.

INTRODUCTION

This chapter describes the factors that should be considered in choosing a particular insurer or a particular producer and cites some useful sources of information concerning each of these factors. The discussion is limited to private insurers because most (but not all) government insurers provide compulsory insurance. We turn first to the choice of an insurer.

CONSIDERATIONS THAT AFFECT THE CHOICE OF AN INSURER

In selecting a particular private insurer or underwriters' association, a risk manager must consider three factors—security, service, and cost. We discuss each of these factors in more detail below. *Because variations among the insurers of the same type are greater than the variations among the average insurers of different types, it is dangerous to select one insurer in preference to another simply because of its legal form of business organization, marketing system, or pricing policy.* Thinking in terms of stereotypes can be very misleading in this as in other areas of life.

Some risk managers will have a more limited choice of insurers than others because of such factors as their geographical location (for example, the number of operating insurers varies among states and localities), the nature of the firm's operations, its loss record, and the type of insurance sought (professional liability insurance, for example, is sold by relatively few insurers), and their size (small firms have less clout with insurers than large firms).

Security

Security refers to the financial ability of the insurer to fulfill its promise when the occasion demands. If the promise covers a long term, as is true in life insurance, the security of the promise is especially difficult to determine because many changes can occur over a lengthy period.

Security depends upon a number of variables, including the ratio of the policyholders' surplus (capital plus surplus, including voluntary contingency reserves) to the liabilities, the volume of business written, the nature and valuation of the assets, the nature and valuation of the liabilities, the profitability of past operations, the stability of the lines of insurance written, the pricing methods, the capability of the management, the underwriting policy, reinsurance facilities, and many others.

Some of these terms may be unfamiliar to the reader and the implications of others may not be clear. This ambiguity will most probably apply to the composition of the assets and liabilities of an insurer, the underwriting policy, reinsurance, past profitability, and pricing methods. Pricing methods have been mentioned in the preceding chapter and are developed in detail in Chapter 28, but a brief discussion of the other topics at this point will add to an understanding of insurer solvency.

In the annual statements insurers submit to state insurance departments, they are required to follow certain practices that are not in accordance with "generally accepted accounting principles." Because these practices are generally more conservative than GAAP, statutory accounting with some modifications is considered appropriate for regulators and policyholders interested mainly in insurer solvency. On the other hand, investors and insurance company managers need statements that are prepared in accordance with GAAP to understand the true condition of the insurer and to facilitate comparisons with other investment opportunities. All stock insurers and many mutual insurers now use GAAP in preparing their annual reports to stockholders and policyholders. This discussion assumes statutory accounting because this approach is used not only in insurers' annual statements to state insurance departments but also in the sources of information on insurer solvency listed on pages 560–562.

Policyholders' Surplus Ratio and Other Audit Ratios   One measure of an insurer's security is the ratio of its policyholders' surplus to its liabilities. The policyholders' surplus is the amount by which the difference between the assets and the liabilities can decline before the liabilities will equal or exceed the assets. No correct value exists for this ratio. It is useful, however, to study trends in this ratio for the insurer being analyzed and to compare this insurer's ratio with that of other insurers. In making such comparisons, however, the risk manager must recognize that (1) the accuracy of the policyholders' surplus ratio depends upon how accurately the insurer has evaluated its liabilities and assets, a subject to be discussed below, and (2) one insurer may require a larger ratio to be equally secure because it faces greater underwriting and investment risks. To illustrate, other things being equal, the policyholders' surplus ratio should be greater the smaller the volume of business written, because, on the basis of the law of large numbers, one would expect the experience on a small volume of business to fluctuate more widely. An insurer that invests heavily in common stocks should have a higher ratio than one that purchases mainly government bonds.

In its Insurance Regulatory Information System, designed to detect property and liability insurers that are having financial difficulties, the National Association of Insurance Commissioners uses 11 tests that it considers to be superior to the policyholders' surplus ratio.[1] The NAIC has also developed an Insurance Regulatory Information System for life and health insurers that contains 12 audit ratios, none of which is the policyholders' surplus ratio. Because these audit ratios employ terms and concepts yet to be described, further discussion is deferred until the end of this section on variables affecting financial security.

Liabilities   The principal liabilities of an insurer are claim or loss reserves and premium reserves required by state law. They comprise over 90 percent of the liabilities of both property and liability insurers and life insurers.

Loss or claim reserves must be established, because on any given date the insurer has some claims that have been reported but not paid and others that have not even been reported. Reported claims may not have had time to clear the normal channels; they may be doubtful claims; they may have presented unusual problems whose solution is time-consuming; or they may have been settled under an agreement to make payments to the insured or other claimant over a long period of time. Claims may not have been reported because the insured is slow in notifying the insurer or because an agent is tardy in

---

[1] *Using the NAIC Insurance Regulatory Information System: Property and Liability Edition 1981* (Milwaukee: National Association of Insurance Commissioners, 1982). *Using the NAIC Insurance Regulatory Information System: Life and Health and Fraternal Edition 1981* (Milwaukee: National Association of Insurance Commissioners, 1982).

transmitting the insured's notice. Some losses are not even discovered by the insured until sometime after they occur.

Insurers use a variety of methods to determine their claim reserves. A discussion of these methods is beyond the scope of this text, but it should be noted that subjective estimates of reserves on individual claims and several averaging techniques are in common use. An analysis of an insurer's annual statement to the state insurance department will reveal whether the insurer has been underestimating its claim reserves in the lines where they are most important.[2]

Property losses tend to be reported and settled promptly, but liability claims are often reported late, may take months and even years to settle, and may involve a promise to pay a claimant an income for life. Consequently, the claim reserves of an insurer specializing in property insurance will be relatively small, whereas the claim reserves of a liability insurer will be a major portion of its liabilities. The small claim reserves of a personnel insurer are associated primarily with its health insurance business, its matured annuities,[3] and the life insurance proceeds placed under settlement options.

The second statutory reserve is the *premium reserve*. Property and liability insurers must maintain an unearned premium reserve on each unexpired contract that is equal to the premium on the contract times the fraction of the policy period that has not expired. For example, the unearned premium reserve on December 31 necessitated by a $300 premium one-year contract written on July 1 is ½ ($300), or $150. If the term of the contract had been for three years instead of one year, the unearned premium reserve would have been ⅚ ($300), or $250. If the term had been six months, the unearned premium reserve would have been zero.

It is important to recognize the hidden equity in this reserve. The statutory pro rata requirement assumes that the insurer should recognize as a liability the amount it would have to pay its insureds if it were to cancel its outstanding contracts on the statement date. The insurer could, however, probably reinsure its entire business with another insurer for considerably less than the unearned premium reserve, because the reinsurer would recognize that most of the expenses other than claims expenses (commissions, underwriting expenses, policy-writing costs) associated with the business have already been paid.[4] For the same reason, if the insurer continues in business, it could probably meet its future obligations under outstanding contracts with a portion of the unearned premium reserve. As a result, financial analysts generally consider most of the expense portion of the unearned premium reserve (less the federal income tax liability on this amount) or, for many insurers, about 30 to 40 percent to be hidden surplus that should

---

[2] See Schedule P in the annual-statement blank, which shows how the insurer's estimates of incurred losses for a given year in the liability and workers' compensation lines have changed over time as (1) more of the claims that occurred that year have been reported, and (2) more reported claims have either been paid or closed without payment. One would expect these periodic estimates to be more stable for the larger, more mature insurers because they have a larger volume of experience on which to base their results.

[3] Reserves on matured annuities and proceeds placed under settlement options are in fact often considered part of the policy reserve (see later in this section) instead of claim reserves.

[4] Even if the contract were canceled, the agent would be expected to return a pro rata portion of his or her commission to the insurer. Hence, even under these circumstances the pro rata portion of the premiums exceeds the needs.

be added to the policyholders' surplus in evaluating the solvency of an insurer.[5] This correction is especially important for an insurer whose surplus appears to be decreasing because it is expanding its premium volume at a rapid pace, thus increasing its unearned premium reserve.

In the past, unearned premium reserves were very important liability items for insurers writing primarily fire and marine insurance because a large portion of the business was written for terms of three or five years. The introduction of installment-payment plans has reduced the importance of the premium reserve. Premium reserves are a less important item for liability insurers because the policy terms are generally short; much of the premium is payable on an audited basis, which means that it is earned when paid; and the claim reserve item is much larger.

The premium reserve for life insurers is called the "policy reserve." This reserve may be calculated according to the net level premium reserve method or by one of several "modified" reserve methods. The net level premium reserve, which is the most conservative measure, is the difference between the present value (based on certain interest and mortality assumptions) of the obligations assumed by the insurer under the outstanding contracts less the present value of the net premiums (premiums less the expense allowance included in the premium) still to be paid under those contracts.

To illustrate the net level reserve method, assume that 10 years ago an insurer issued $1,000 straight life insurance contracts to each of a group of males aged 35, assuming a 3 percent interest return and the 1958 Commissioners Standard Ordinary Mortality Table.[6] The lump-sum value of the insurer's obligation to each surviving policyholder under the outstanding contracts is about $459. This is the net price that a person aged 45 would have to pay for the same protection if he or she were to buy now into the group. The lump-sum value of the remaining premiums to be paid under these outstanding contracts is about $303 per contract. Thus the reserve per contract is about $156. At the issue date, the reserve was zero because the two present values were the same, namely, $359. Twenty years after the issue date, the reserve would be $573–$239, or $334. Because no one was expected to live beyond age 100 under the 1958 CSO table, the reserve 65 years after the issue date would be $1,000 − 0, or $1,000.

If the insurer were to cease issuing new contracts, the net premium income from the contracts in force plus a lump sum equal to this policy reserve would, if the mortality and interest assumptions were correct, enable the insurer to meet exactly its obligations as they came due.

Note that this concept is far more complicated than the unearned premium reserve. The complication is introduced because mortality rates increase over time, while the usual life insurance contract is a long-term obligation purchased by a level premium.[7]

---

[5] Other sources of redundancy are (1) the duplication of the reserve for premium taxes with the unearned premium reserve, and (2) the disallowance of certain uncollected premiums as assets while including the unearned portion of these premiums in the reserve.

[6] States prescribe the basis upon which minimum reserves are to be computed. See below and in Chap. 28.

[7] Unearned premium reserves are established for one-year term life insurance contracts.

The explanation of the reserve presented above is in prospective terms. An alternative explanation in retrospective terms may be easier to understand. Under the retrospective method, the reserve is that portion of the net premium plus assumed interest that remains after the insured's share of the assumed death claims has been paid. If the same mortality and interest assumptions are made, the reserve produced in this way is exactly the same as the one produced by the prospective method. Except for the treatment of expenses, this explanation of the reserve is the same as the explanation of the cash value presented in Chapter 23. It should be remembered, however, that the two concepts serve entirely different purposes. The reserve is a measure of how much the insurer should have on hand to meet its obligations in the future; if the mortality assumptions are overoptimistic, the correction that is needed is an increase or strengthening of the reserves. The cash value, on the other hand, results from the excess premiums paid by the insureds during the early years of their contracts; if the mortality assumptions underestimate the death rates, the insurer cannot reduce its contractual cash values, but it will wish that it could do so.

The net level premium reserve method is a conservative approach for essentially the same reason that the unearned premium reserve is redundant. The expense loading in the premiums is ignored in the computation, on the assumption that the expenses will be incurred as the expense loadings are received. Actually, the insurer will incur most of its expenses the first year, and if the full net level premium reserve is to be maintained, the insurer will have to reduce its surplus position. In future years, the expense allowances will exceed the expenses incurred, and the surplus withdrawn because of that contract will gradually be replaced. Unlike their treatment of property and liability insurance, however, state authorities have recognized this problem and permit insurers to use one of several modified reserve systems instead of the net level premium reserve method. A description of these systems is beyond the scope of this text,[8] but, in effect, they work on the assumption that the net premium is less than the actual net premium in the first year and greater in later years. The present value of the modified premiums must, however, equal the present value of the actual net premiums. As a result of the modification, the reserve at the end of the first year is less than the net level premium reserve, but it grows more rapidly after that date until at some point, which varies among the different methods, the modified reserve equals the net level premium reserve.[9] Insurers tend to be more conservative than the law requires in their application of these modifications.

Interest and mortality assumptions also affect the reserves. The lower the interest rate and in most cases the more rapid the increase in mortality rates with age, the higher the reserves. The usual assumptions are 3 or 4 percent interest and the 1980 Commissioners Standard Ordinary Table.

Health insurers establish unearned premium reserves for policies they can cancel or refuse to renew. The premium reserves on noncancelable and guaranteed renewable contracts are based upon the same principles as the policy reserves of life insurers.

---

[8] See any standard life insurance text.

[9] The modified reserves are thus closer to the actual cash values than is the net level premium reserve, but the legal minimum reserves do exceed the legal minimum cash values during the early years.

Other liability reserves in addition to claim reserves and premium reserves include reserves for taxes, reserves for dividends voted to policyholders and stockholders, reserves for dividend accumulations (life insurance only), and reserves for other expenses incurred but not paid. Since 1951, life insurers have also been required by state law to maintain a specified security valuation reserve to provide for possible future losses in the values of stocks and bonds. Contingency reserves or earmarked surpluses include such items as voluntary reserves for fluctuations in securities or loss experience.

Assets   Primarily because of the time lags that compel insurers to establish claim reserves and premium reserves, because of stockholder contributions to capital and surplus, and because of retained earnings, insurers have sizable assets. At the close of 1982, the assets of life insurers totaled almost $590 billion while property and liability insurers controlled assets of over $248 billion.

Both types of insurers keep most of these assets invested in order to cut the cost of the insurance to policyholders, increase dividends to stockholders, or accomplish both of these objectives. The importance of the investment return in property and liability insurance is emphasized by the fact that during 1982, while property and liability insurers reported an (unadjusted for the hidden profit in the increase in the unearned premium reserve[10]) underwriting loss of about $8.3 billion on premiums of $104 billion, they had a net investment gain of almost $18.4 billion. Net investment profit includes realized and unrealized capital gains. Net investment income (not including realized or unrealized capital gains and less investment expenses) was about $15.7 billion. During the same year, net investment income was responsible for about 27 percent of the total income of United States life insurers. The *portfolios* of property and liability insurers and life insurers differ, however because of basic differences in the insurance products they market.

Property and liability insurers issue for the most part short-term contracts; their benefits tend to vary with the price-level indexes; they are subject to catastrophe losses; and, unlike life insurers, they do not assume explicitly any rate of return in their pricing procedures. Consequently, in addition to the obvious requirement that investments should be of high quality and secure, the investment portfolio should provide liquidity and some opportunity for appreciation during periods of inflation. Although property and liability insurers do not assume explicitly any rate of investment return in setting their prices, they do consider investment income, at least implicitly, in determining the profit loading they include in their premiums.[11] A satisfactory yield on investments thus enables the insurer to compete more effectively in a price-conscious market; it also benefits the stockholders, if any. Stockholder dividends are in fact usually limited to part of the investment earnings, these earnings being much more stable than the underwriting profit.

An investigation of actual property-liability insurer investment portfolios will illustrate the application of these principles. On the average, over 58 percent of the assets

[10] See pp. 543–544.
[11] State regulations sometimes require them to do so.

are invested in bonds, government bonds (because of their liquidity) accounting for about 80 percent of this type of investment. Common stocks in well-known corporations with a ready market account for almost one-sixth of the assets. However, some significant differences are found among individual insurers. Some insurers consider the insurance business itself to be risky enough and place more of their money in government bonds. Most mutual insurers fall into this group. Other insurers invest more heavily in common stock. Some insurers are specialists in particular classes of securities such as municipal bonds.

Life insurers, on the other hand, issue long-term fixed-amount obligations, are seldom faced with a catastrophe, and use an assumed interest rate in their premium, reserve, and cash value computations. Hence in addition to security, their investment portfolios must emphasize stability and yield. Liquidity is of minor importance. A yield equal to at least the assumed rate of return over a long period is vital if the insurer is to continue its operations.

About 46 percent of the assets of life insurers is invested in bonds, but because of their relatively low rate of return, government bonds account for only about one-fifth of the bond total. The second most important type of investment is mortgages, which make up about 24 percent of the total assets. Both the bonds and the mortgages are usually long-term commitments. Stocks account for only about one-tenth of the assets, policy loans about 9 percent, and real estate only 4 percent. Because of more severe investment restrictions imposed by state laws and because of more general agreement on the best composition of the portfolio, the assets of one life insurer are more likely to resemble the assets of another than do the assets of property and liability insurers, but there are still some considerable variations, particularly with respect to the relative importance of bonds versus mortgages.

The *valuation* of the more important assets by all types of insurers is also important. Bonds that are amply secured and not in default as to interest or principal are carried at their amortized value. For bonds purchased at more than their par value, this means that their value decreases from the purchase price to the par value at the maturity date. The value increases when the bond is purchased at a discount. In either event the values are independent of market fluctuations, on the assumption that the insurer's cash flow will enable it to hold the bond to maturity. Mortgages, if properly secured, are set equal to the amount loaned. Stocks are valued according to "convention values" prepared by a committee of the National Association of Insurance Commissioners. For the most part, these are the market values on the preceding December 31. Certain assets, such as the home office building, are usually valued at nominal amounts.[12]

During the early 1980s when interest rates rose about 10 percent, the market value of insurers' bonds portfolios dropped substantially below their book value. Insurers also reevaluated and lessened their investments in long-term bonds. Some states have considered requiring insurers to report the market value of their bond portfolio in addition to its book value.

---

[12] During the Great Depression (1931–1934) and on several occasions between 1907 and 1922, the NAIC established values in excess of the market value on the ground that the market values were temporarily depressed below their real worth. Because a market value does not exist for some stocks, a special formula must be employed.

Underwriting The underwriting policy of the insurer determines the kinds of insurance it will write, the provisions it will use in its contracts, the pricing system it will apply, the persons it will insure, and the amounts of insurance it will issue to individual insureds or in particular areas. Initiation of policy decisions with respect to the kinds of insurance to be written is likely to come from top management, but the other policy decisions are likely to originate in the underwriting department of the insurer or in two or more departments including the underwriting department. Implementation of these policy decisions is usually the function of the underwriters.

The variety in the *kinds of insurance written* has already been noted, the range extending from the insurer writing only one kind of insurance, say, automobile insurance, to the insurer that writes all kinds of insurance except a few highly specialized lines. Because some lines of insurance are more profitable and stable than others and because several accounting ratios such as the ratio of losses incurred to premiums earned depend to a large extent upon the mix of business written, the types of insurance issued must be considered in evaluating the solvency of the firm.[13]

The *contract provisions* describe the product that the insurer is selling, and care must be taken not to expose the insurer to losses not anticipated in the price through contract provisions that are ambiguous or overgenerous or that enable the insured to wait until a loss is fairly certain before purchasing the contract. The contracts should encourage the insured to prevent losses and to minimize those that do occur. As we have noted on page 290, many property and liability insurance contracts are drafted by rating bureaus.

The *pricing system* to be used is extremely important and is related to the types of insureds to be covered.[14] Some insurers are very selective and operate with low average rates, while others are interested in all grades of insureds. Still others solicit only the less desirable kinds of insureds. The pricing systems of some insurers permit them to discriminate greatly among insureds, whereas others have only a few prices that they apply to broad classes of insureds. The prices in most instances are determined by the actuarial department of the insurer or by property and liability insurance rating bureaus, but the underwriters are usually consulted in connection with the actuarial decision, they apply the rating system to insureds or check the application of the rates by producers, and they actually make the rates in situations that are not covered by the rating system.[15]

Once the rating system has been established, the underwriting department must determine the policies that are to be followed in *selecting those persons they are willing to insure and on what terms.* Their objective is to select insureds consistent with their pricing system. Some selection is necessary because if the insurer were to accept every applicant, the persons who would be most likely to seek insurance would be those normally uninsurable at any price or else insurable but only at a higher price than is provided under the rating system. In addition, all insureds would seek the lowest price

---

[13] For a convincing demonstration of how some lines produce more stable loss experience than others, see J. D. Hammond and Ned Shilling, ''Some Relationships of Portfolio Theory to the Regulation of Insurer Solidity,'' *Journal of Risk and Insurance,* vol. XLV, no. 3 (September, 1978), pp. 377–400.

[14] Since pricing methods are described in Chap. 28, this discussion will be brief.

[15] For example, fire insurance on snow fences is usually priced in this way.

under the rating system. Selection against the insurer in this way is referred to as *adverse selection*. In practice, the insurer cannot avoid underpricing the insurance protection for some insureds, but in the interest of equity to its policyholders and its own continued solvency, it should seek to minimize this problem. On the other hand, it cannot be so selective that it insures only a small number of persons, because in that event its experience will be unstable.

The underwriting department accomplishes its objectives first through instructions to agents and through their cooperation. This approach is of particular importance to the insurer in property and liability insurance, where the producer normally has the authority to bind the insurer. The instructions vary greatly among insurers. The cooperation of the producer is essential because there are always persons in the acceptable class who are clearly not acceptable on the basis of information available only to the producer.

If the producer does not have binding authority with respect to the contract, the underwriting department has the opportunity to pass on the application before the insurance goes into effect. As a result of its investigation, the underwriting department may accept the application, reject it, or make an alternative offer. The alternative offer may take the form of an entirely different contract (e.g., a 20-year endowment contract for a 20-year term insurance contract), some modification in the contract provisions (e.g., an exclusion of disability claims arising out of some preexisting condition), or an increased premium.

If the producer has already bound the insurer with respect to the contract, the underwriter can at most cancel the contract in accordance with the policy provisions. The cancellation may be accompanied by an alternative offer. Because cancellation, however, is unpleasant for the insurer and the insured and is a source of poor public relations, the underwriter is more likely, except in extreme cases, to give advance notice of its intention not to renew the contract.

Underwriters rely upon several sources in their investigation. First, information is provided by the prospective insured and the producer. Second, sources of information are available in the offices of the underwriting department. For example, most life insurers belong to the Medical Information Bureau. These insurers must report to the bureau all applicants for insurance with an impairment named on an official list. This information is considered highly confidential, and impairments are reported in code. The bureau disseminates the information it receives to member insurers. Insurers also cooperate for the exchange of information concerning suspicious fires. Financial ratings of insureds can be checked in various reporting services. Fire exposures can be checked by consulting the inspection report completed for schedule-rating purposes. On renewal business, the underwriter can analyze past experience. Supplementary information may also have been provided or may be available in the claim department, the department that audits the insured's books for pricing purposes, or in the engineering or inspection department that has been providing loss-control services. In addition to the information provided by these two sources, the underwriter can also gather additional information on its own initiative. In personnel insurance, for example, a medical examiner's report may be required. In all lines of insurance, the insurer's own inspection department or, as is more likely, an independent agency may be asked to prepare a confidential report on the applicant. Personnel insurers make more extensive use of these reports than do property and liability insurers.

Reinsurance   In addition to selecting insureds whose quality is consistent with the insurer's pricing system, the underwriter must avoid exposing the insurer to excessive losses caused by any one event. Otherwise the uncertainty for the insurer is great, and its financial solvency may be jeopardized. Excessive losses can result because the protection issued to one insured is too great or because many insureds are affected by the same event.

The maximum loss the insurer believes it can safely retain varies with the size of the insurer, its financial condition, its management philosophy, the characteristics of the exposure under consideration (death of a person, fire damage to a frame building, or workers' compensation claims from a single accident), and other factors. Setting a high retention exposes the insurer to more risk; setting a low retention may deprive the insurer of some highly desirable business.

Underwriters can attack this problem in part by refusing to write insurance for amounts in excess of their retentions. They may, for example, refuse to write life insurance on an applicant in excess of $100,000, automobile bodily injury liability insurance policy limits in excess of $100,000 per accident, or fire insurance with respect to properties in a city block if the property is adjacent to one that is already insured or if the total insurance on properties in the block will exceed $500,000.

This approach will not, however, prevent catastrophe losses from occurring when a large number of small exposures covering a broad area are damaged by a single event such as a hurricane. It will also fail when the exposures are mobile and happen to be concentrated at the same spot when an accident occurs. For example, a ferry may sink, taking down with it 100 automobiles, most of which are insured by the same insurer. A third possibility is that the insurer may write several kinds of insurance and that the aggregate loss under the several different kinds of insurance in a single event may be substantial. Finally, although no single event may be troublesome, the losses for the year may be excessive.

It is not good business, moreover, to refuse to write insurance in excess of the retention amount. Imagine the displeasure of the applicant and particularly of the producer when the application is rejected or accepted in part! For these reasons and others to be noted later, insurers commonly insure that portion of their liability under their contracts in excess of their retention with one or more insurers. This process is called *reinsurance*, the originating insurer is the "ceding insurer" "primary insurer," or "direct insurer," and the accepting insurer is the "reinsurer." An alternative approach that is less often used is to issue a joint policy with one or more other insurers. Some examples of this latter practice were presented in Chapter 26.

Reinsurance may be arranged in many ways. At one extreme there is *facultative reinsurance*, which is arranged on a particular exposure after the problem has arisen. The advantages of this approach are the opportunities for tailor-made protection and for underwriting advice from the reinsurer. The disadvantages are the delay, the possible failure to obtain coverage, and the administrative expenses involved. At the other extreme is the *automatic treaty*, under which the ceding insurer agrees to pass on to the reinsurer all business included within the scope of the treaty, the reinsurer agrees to accept this business, and the terms—e.g., the premium rates and the method of sharing the insurance and the losses—of the agreement are set. The advantages and disadvantages are the counterparts of those cited for facultative reinsurance. An example of an arrangement between these two extremes is the facultative treaty, under which the terms are set but neither the ceding insurer nor the reinsurer is obligated to participate in the arrangement with respect to any particular business.

Most reinsurance is provided by professional reinsurers who specialize in reinsuring the portfolios of other insurers. However, the reinsurer may be another insurer whose major business interest also is dealing directly with the public. Some insurers of this type have very active reinsurance departments or subsidiaries that aggressively seek business from other insurers, but most are reinsurers only because many reinsurance agreements obligate the ceding insurer to reinsure some of the liability assumed by the reinsurer under its direct business. The third type of reinsurer is a pool that may or may not include the ceding insurer. These associations were discussed in Chapter 26.

Reinsurance arrangements may distribute the insurance and the losses in many different ways. Four of these distribution methods will be described for illustrative purposes:

1 Under a *quota-share* split, the insurance and the loss are shared according to some preagreed percentage. For example, if a $100,000 policy is written and the agreed split is 50-50, the reinsurer assumes one-half of the liability; the insurer and the reinsurer each pay one-half on any loss.

2 Under a *surplus-share* agreement, the reinsurer accepts that amount of the insurance in excess of a stated amount, and the loss is prorated according to the amount of insurance assumed. For example, if $100,000 is the stated amount, the reinsurer's liability under a $200,000 policy would be ($200,000 − $100,000)/$200,000 or ½ of any loss. Under a $100,000 contract the reinsurer would accept no liability. Under an $160,000 contract the reinsurer would pay ⅜ of any loss.

3 Under an *excess-loss* arrangement, the reinsurer agrees to pay that portion of the loss incurred under an individual contract in excess of some specified amount, such as $100,000.

4 *Catastrophe* reinsurance, like excess-loss reinsurance, requires the reinsurer to pay excess losses, but in this instance the losses are those incurred by the insurer as a result of a single event under all contracts covered under the agreement. For example, the reinsurer might be obligated to pay that portion in excess of $1 million of the losses incurred (less losses reinsured in other ways) as a result of a hurricane.

Variations are possible under all these methods. For example, the reinsurer may pay only 80 percent of the excess loss under the excess-loss method. In life insurance, the reinsurance agreement may apply only to the decreasing pure-protection portion of nonterm insurance policies and not to the savings or investment element. In all lines and under all arrangements, the reinsurer may limit the maximum amount for which it is responsible. For example, catastrophe reinsurance may be purchased in layers. Under the first layer, the reinsurer might pay 80 percent of the first $10 million of losses in excess of $500,000. Under the second layer, the reinsurer might pay 90 percent of the losses in excess of $1,500,000.

The effect of reinsurance on the ceding insurer's balance sheet differs depending upon the way the insurance and the losses are distributed. Under the excess-loss or catastrophe reinsurance arrangements the balance sheet is not affected. The ceding insurer pays a premium for the excess coverage but maintains responsibility for the complete unearned premium reserve. Quota-share or surplus-share arrangements, on the other hand, increase the ceding insurer's policyholders' surplus. The ceding insurer pays the reinsurer a percentage of the direct premium that corresponds to the percentage of the direct insurance that is reinsured. For example, under a 50-50 quota share arrangement the ceding insurer pays the reinsurer half of the direct premiums. The reinsurer, however, pays the ceding insurer a commission which is usually related to the expenses that insurer incurred in originating the business. The ceding insurer also transfers to the reinsurer responsibility for the unearned premium reserve on that portion of the premium it has transferred. The net effect of this transaction is that the ceding insurer will transfer approximately the hidden equity in its unearned premium reserve to its surplus. This transfer is permitted only if the reinsurer is an authorized reinsurer under state law. Some insurers, especially new and rapidly growing insurers, use quota-share or surplus-share arrangements for this very reason.

Other uses of reinsurance are to retire completely or in part (in an area or a line of business, for example) from the insurance business, to transfer insurance from one member of a fleet to another, and to obtain advice from an outsider (the reinsurer) with respect to a particular insured or a new line of business. The major contribution of reinsurance to insurer solvency, however, is the more widespread distribution of risk it makes possible.

Past Profitability For property and liability insurers, annual increases in retained earnings depend upon (1) underwriting profit, (2) net investment income (dividends, interest, and rents), (3) realized capital gains, (4) unrealized capital gains, (5) dividends to policyholders, (6) income taxes, and (7) dividends to stockholders. Statutory underwriting profit, which is the official measure required under state regulation, is determined by subtracting from the premiums earned the losses and expenses incurred. When an insurer's premium volume is increasing (decreasing), statutory underwriting profit understates (overstates) the "true" profit because it ignores the hidden profit in the increase in the unearned premium reserve discussed earlier in this chapter. In other words, the insurer has already paid many of the expenses, which, it is assumed in the unearned premium reserve calculation, will be incurred in the future. Consequently, many analysts add to (subtract from) the statutory profit some (commonly 30 to 40) percentage of the increase (decrease) in the unearned premium reserve less the additional (reduced) income taxes that this would create.

Another more commonly used adjusted measure of underwriting profit would add (1) the loss ratio (losses incurred divided by premiums earned) to (2) the expense ratio (expenses incurred divided by premiums written).[16] Premiums written exceed premiums earned when the premium volume is increasing because the insurer receives many premiums in a year that will be only partially earned that year. Because insurers incur most of their expenses in the first month a contract is in force, their expenses tend

---

[16] As explained on p. 560, the premiums earned and premiums written should be net of reinsurance.

to be more closely related to premiums written than to premiums earned. Hence it is considered more appropriate to use premiums written in calculating expense ratios. If the combined loss and expense ratio is less than 100 percent, the insurer's underwriting has been profitable. Otherwise, it has not.

Profit, of course, should be related to some base such as net worth, investment profit should be considered as well as underwriting profit, and the variation in annual profit rates as well as the average level should be considered in analyzing profitability. As explained in the next section, the NAIC now includes both underwriting and investment income in its overall operating ratio test of profitability. This ratio is the loss ratio plus the expense ratio minus the ratio of the net investment income to the premiums earned.

Unlike property and liability insurers, life insurers do not distinguish between their underwriting profit and their net investment profit. Their increases in retained earnings depend upon (1) their net gain from operations, (2) dividends to policyholders, (3) income taxes, (4) net realized and unrealized capital gains, and (5) dividends to stockholders. Net gain from operations is determined by subtracting from income (principally premiums and net investment income consisting of interest, dividends, and rents) benefit payments, increases in policy reserves, and operating expenses and taxes. The use of modified reserves, mentioned earlier, partially corrects for the disparity between the timing of expenses and the uniform expense loading in each annual premium.

NAIC Audit Ratios   Now that the concepts necessary to understand most of the audit ratios used by the NAIC in its Insurance Regulatory Information System have been introduced, we can continue the discussion of these ratios started in the beginning of this chapter. The 11 property and liability insurer ratios and the range that the NAIC considered "usual" or acceptable in 1983 were as shown below and on the next page.

Test	Usual range
Overall:	
1. Net premiums written to adjusted (for unearned premium reserve redundancy, for example) policyholders' surplus	300% or less
2. Change in premium writings to net premiums prior year	−33% to 33%
3. Surplus released through reinsurance to total adjusted surplus	25% or less
Profitability:	
4. Two-year overall operating ratio (loss ratio + expense ratio − investment income ratio)	100% or less
5. Net investment income to average invested assets	5% or more
6. Change in adjusted surplus to current-year adjusted surplus	−10% to 50%
Liquidity:	
7. Liabilities to liquid assets (mainly cash and invested assets)	105% or less
8. Agents' balances or uncollected premiums to surplus	40% or less
Reserve adequacy:	
9. Change in estimate made at end of preceding year (one-year hindsight) on how much it would cost to adjust losses outstanding as of that date to prior year's adjusted surplus	25% or less

10. Change in estimate made two years ago (two-year hindsight) on how much it would cost to adjust losses outstanding as of that date to prior year's adjusted surplus	25% or less
11. Estimated deficiency in current loss reserve to adjusted surplus	25% or less

To illustrate, for an insurer's ratio to fall in the usual range, its net premiums written should not exceed 3 times its adjusted policyholders' surplus; its two-year overall operating ratio should not exceed 100 percent, which permits some underwriting loss to be offset by net investment income; its net investment income should be at least 5 percent of its average invested assets; and the estimate the insurer made at the end of the preceding year on how much it would cost to adjust losses outstanding at that time should not have to be adjusted upward more than 25 percent of the prior year's surplus now that the insurer has more information about those losses. Limiting the premiums to surplus ratio to 300 percent means that unless an insurer increases its present surplus, its premium volume should not be more than three times the amount of its present surplus. In other words, the surplus amount, coupled with this audit ratio, limits the capacity of the insurer to write premiums.

If an insurer has four or more ratios outside the usual range, its annual statements and financial ratios are reviewed by experienced financial examiners to determine whether the deviations are acceptable.

Other audit ratios that have been suggested include agents' balances to total assets stocks at cost to stocks at market value, and bonds at cost to bonds at market value.[17]

The twelve ratios included in the NAIC Insurance Regulatory Information System for life and health insurers are as follows:

1 Change in capital and surplus
2 Net gain to total income
3 Commissions and other expenses to premiums
4 Investment yield
5 Nonadmitted assets to admitted assets
6 Real estate to capital and surplus
7 Investments in affiliates to capital and surplus
8 Surplus relief
9 Change in premiums
10 Change in product mix
11 Change in asset mix
12 Change in reserving ratio

Security Comparisons among Stock and Mutual Insurers   Now that we have explained the principal factors affecting solvency, we turn to a comparison of stock and mutual insurers with respect to some of the many variables affecting solvency. The reader is reminded that insurers can also be classified in other ways and that the

---

[17] See J. S. Trieschmann and G. C. Pinches, "A Multivariate Model for Predicting Financially Distressed P-L Insurers," *Journal of Risk and Insurance,* vol. XL, no. 4 (September, 1973), pp. 327–338.

TABLE 27.1
STOCK AND MUTUAL PROPERTY AND LIABILITY INSURER POLICYHOLDERS' SURPLUS RATIO, LOSS RATIOS, EXPENSE RATIOS, AND ADJUSTED UNDERWRITING PROFITS, 1960–1982

Year	Policyholders' surplus ratio		Loss ratio*		Expense ratio†		Adjusted under-writing profit‡	
	Stocks	Mutuals	Stocks	Mutuals	Stocks	Mutuals	Stocks	Mutuals
1960	71%	48%	63.6%	64.2%	34.8%	25.6%	1.6%	10.2%
1961	85	43	64.4	63.6	35.0	25.6	0.6	10.8
1962	76	54	64.5	66.7	34.5	25.7	1.0	7.6
1963	82	50	66.3	71.4	34.7	26.5	−1.0	2.1
1964	84	49	68.0	73.4	33.9	25.9	−1.9	0.7
1965	77	47	69.2	73.1	32.7	25.0	−1.9	1.9
1966	63	44	66.1	70.9	31.9	24.2	2.0	4.9
1967	66	44	67.2	72.7	31.7	24.5	1.1	2.7
1968	65	43	68.8	74.4	31.2	24.6	0.0	1.0
1969	50	37	70.3	76.5	30.3	24.1	−0.6	−0.6
1970	49	37	69.7	73.3	29.6	23.4	0.7	3.3
1971	54	42	66.7	69.1	29.1	23.1	4.2	7.8
1972	58	48	66.0	68.1	29.4	23.8	4.6	8.1
1973	48	46	68.6	71.2	29.6	24.3	1.8	4.5
1974	33	39	75.3	76.4	29.7	24.8	−5.0	−1.2
1975	36	40	78.8	80.2	28.7	24.2	−7.5	−4.4
1976	38	41	74.6	77.1	27.4	22.5	−2.0	0.4
1977	37	42	70.1	72.4	26.9	21.5	3.0	6.1
1978	38	43	69.0	72.9	27.6	21.7	3.4	5.4
1979	40	45	71.6	76.3	27.9	21.7	0.5	2.0
1980	44	48	73.9	77.0	28.5	22.1	−2.4	0.9
1981	40	50	75.5	79.8	29.4	23.1	−4.9	−2.9
1982	41	54	78.6	82.1	30.1	23.5	−8.7	−5.6

* Loss ratio = losses incurred/premiums earned
† Expense ratio = expenses incurred/premiums written
‡ Adjusted underwriting profit = 1 − loss ratio − expense ratio
Source: Best's Aggregates and Averages (Oldwick, N.J.: Alfred M. Best Company, Inc., annual).

variation among insurers in each class is greater than the variation among the class averages. Consequently we will limit this comparison of average stock and mutual insurers to a few statements:

First, stock and advance premium mutual *life* insurers are so similar in their methods of operation that one type is probably no more financially sound than the other.[18]

Second, according to Table 27.1, at the close of 1982 stock property and liability insurers reported a policyholders' surplus ratio (policyholders' surplus divided by total

[18] Mutual insurers who set their initial premiums very high in order to return a sizable dividend have a safety factor built into their premiums that is not available to stock nonparticipating insurers, but the chance that this cushion will be needed is extremely small. On the other hand, stock insurers have an additional cushion in their capital stock, but this too in most instances is relatively unimportant.

liabilities) of 0.41 while advance premium mutuals indicated a ratio of 0.54. The variation among individual insurers was great. Moreover, the ratios vary over time. The average stock ratio exceeded the average mutual ratio until 1974. The average mutual ratio has been higher since that year.

Mutual insurers report higher adjusted underwriting profits than stock insurers because many mutuals charge premiums close to or equal to those charged by many stock insurers and are able to return a dividend because of more selective underwriting or lower expense ratios. The important effect of investment income on profits has already been noted earlier in this chapter under "Assets." For a discussion of the total profitability of insurers, see Chapter 34, "Financial and Structural Problems of Insurers."

Neither type of insurer can claim to be clearly superior to the other in terms of its financial strength. On the other hand, individual insurers vary greatly with respect to financial strength.

Service

Service is an intangible factor and one that it is difficult to define. Service is generally considered to include (1) assistance in the recognition and evaluation of risks, (2) the provision of insurance contracts that meet the specific needs of the insured, (3) a "fair" attitude toward cancellations, (4) aid in loss control, (5) promptness and fairness in the settlement of claims, and (6) help in meeting legal requirements such as filing proof of insurance or claim reports with a state agency. It may also include the extension of short-term credit with respect to the premiums. The need and desire for these services differs among insureds, and the ability and willingness (as expressed through its underwriting policies) of insurers to service a particular insured also varies. In property and liability insurance, the insurer's ability and desire to service the insured depends upon such factors as the insured's industry, location, quality of exposure, complexity of operations, and desire for unusual coverages or limits. In personnel insurance, illustrative factors are occupation, location, state of health, economic status, family status, investment opportunities, and the amount and type of coverages sought.

Evaluation of insurers in terms of the service they render is even more difficult than their evaluation according to financial strength, because all the judgments must be qualitative. Again, however, certain statements about stock and mutual insurers are possible.

First, stock and mutual life insurers must be rated on a par with respect to service because of the similarity of their contracts, claims procedures, support of medical research and distribution of medical information, and loss-adjustment procedures.

Second, stock and mutual property and liability insurers both claim superiority with respect to loss control. Both have a record of substantial activity at the association and individual-insurer level, and quantitative evaluation of their relative merits is impossible. Only in workers' compensation is there any objective information with respect to promptness of claims handling, and this evidence indicates that neither type of insurer is superior to the other. With respect to assistance from the producer regarding risk analysis, design of the insurance program, and aid in presenting claims, it is generally agreed that the distinction between direct writing and agency insurers is more important than the difference between stock and mutual insurers. Both stock and advance premium mutual insurers usually operate through agents, but among the largest mutuals the direct writing system is more important. Other things being equal, the agency system is considered by many to result in superior service because of the independence of action, the smaller number of customers served, the greater emphasis upon continued service, and the attraction of higher-quality personnel. Other things are seldom equal however, and this generalization is subject to numerous exceptions. Even the generalization is by no means universally accepted. On one point, the stocks do have a clear superiority. Their insurance offerings are more varied, and they write practically all coverages. For confirmation of this point, see Table 26.2. Some evidence exists that they may be more liberal in their underwriting standards. This greater liberality may result in less stringent initial underwriting, fewer cancellations, or both.

Cost

The cost of the insurance protection is an obvious basic consideration. In our discussion *cost* refers to the initial premiums paid to the insurer less any returns because of dividends or rate adjustments. In this sense, cost is measurable, and its apparent objectivity is one reason why undue emphasis is often placed upon this factor. Cost is not always measurable in advance, however, thus complicating the decision. Furthermore, relative costs should always be balanced against relative services. Financial strength, of course, should never be compromised.

In personnel insurance, the distinction between stock and mutual insurers is not nearly so important as the distinction between participating and nonparticipating insurers. The dividends paid to stockholders do make a difference, but much more important are the differences in the mortality, investment, and expense experience.[19] Participating insurers charge more than nonparticipating insurers for the same coverage but return a dividend on the basis of their actual experience.[20] The dividends may or may not be sufficient to offset the additional premium. There is no inherent reason why the dividends should be more or less sufficient, but historically nonparticipating insurers have on the average and at most times proved to be too conservative in their estimates. Whether this conservatism will be true in the future is an open question. In short, the difference in costs under the two procedures cannot be determined in advance.[21] The choice is largely a matter of the insured's estimates regarding the future in relation to the nonparticipating insurer's estimates and any value the insured assigns to the possible uses of dividends.

[19] In 1982, stockholder dividends amounted to 3 percent of the premium income of stock life insurers. This analysis ignores profits that are not distributed to policyholders. It also ignores investment income, which in 1982 accounted for about 22 percent of the total income of stock life insurers.
[20] Additional expenses introduced by this procedure include extra commissions (if the commission rate is unchanged) and the costs of determining and distributing the dividends.
[21] Insureds who die during the early years of their contracts will almost always pay less under nonpar contracts because dividends under par contracts during these years are generally small.

Life insurers can be compared with respect to the premiums they charge in various ways. Until recently the most popular approach was to calculate the projected annual "net costs" of the policies issued by two or more insurers. This "traditional" net cost is computed as follows: First, add up the premiums for the period over which the net cost is to be determined. This period is usually 20 years. Second, subtract the projected dividends, if any, from the premiums. Third, subtract the cash value at the end of the period. Fourth, divide the result of the first three steps by the number of years in the period. To illustrate, if a nonparticipating straight life insurance policy requires an annual premium payment of $22 and provides a cash value of $335 at the end of 20 years, the 20-year annual net cost, according to this method, is

$$\frac{\$22\,(20) - 0 - \$335}{20} = \$5.25$$

A major criticism of this method is its failure to recognize the loss of possible investment returns on the premiums paid. The importance of this second factor is obvious when this method yields a negative cost for the insurance.

The favored method at present is the interest-adjusted method, which is superior to the traditional method in that it recognizes the time value of money. Though not without its critics,[22] this method has been endorsed by a life insurance industry committee and the National Association of Insurance Commissioners. Two indexes are calculated: an interest-adjusted surrender cost index and an interest-adjusted payments index. The surrender cost index, which assumes the contract is surrendered at the end of the period, is determined as follows: First, calculate the accumulated value of the premiums at the end of, say, 20 years on the assumption that these premiums are invested at, say, 5 percent interest. Second, deduct the accumulated value of the dividends paid over these 20 years. Third, deduct the cash value or special termination dividend paid at the end of 20 years. Fourth, divide the remainder by the accumulated value of $1 invested at the beginning of each year for 20 years.[23] The result is the amount the insured would have to invest each year at 5 percent to accumulate a sum equal to the premiums less dividends accumulated at 5 percent less the cash value at the end of 20 years. For example, using the same straight life insurance policy used to illustrate the net cost method, the 20-year interest-adjusted surrender cost index is

$$\frac{\$22(34.719) - 0 - \$335}{34.719} = \$12.35$$

The interest-adjusted payments index does not assume surrender of the contract.

[22] See, for example, William C. Scheel, "A Critique of the Interest-Adjusted Net Cost Index," *Journal of Risk and Insurance*, vol. XL, no. 2 (June, 1973), pp. 245–261. Professor Scheel proposes instead a Risk Premium Index. Professor Joseph Belth has proposed several alternatives, some of which are described in several articles in the *Journal of Risk and Insurance* and in J. M. Belth, *Life Insurance: A Consumer's Handbook* (Bloomington: Indiana University Press, 1973). See also William C. Scheel, "Yearly Prices of Protection and Rates of Return in a System of Life Insurance Cost Disclosure," *Journal of Risk and Insurance*, vol. XLIV, no. 1 (March, 1977), pp. 37–53.
[23] $1.05^{20} + 1.05^{19} + \ldots + 1.05 = 34.719$.

This index is calculated in the same way except that the cash value or special termination dividend is ignored. Using the example above, the index is

$$\frac{\$22(34.719) - 0}{34.719} = \$22$$

Both the traditional and the interest-adjusted methods have been criticized on various counts. First, the net cost and the interest-adjusted surrender cost index assume that the insured will live and surrender the policy at the end of a stated period. The insured may not live that long, though the probability of this occuring is low. Even though the insured lives, he or she may not wish to surrender the policy. To answer this objection, the present procedure is to calculate the interest-adjusted payments index as well as the interest-adjusted surrender cost index. Second, comparisons are usually made for 10 and 20 years. For other periods, the cost ranking of insurers may be different. Third, the interest assumption may change the ranking. Fourth, insurers are constantly changing their premiums, dividend scales, and cash values, causing cost rankings to change. Fifth, the company rankings vary depending upon the type of policy being studied. It is misleading, but common, to assume otherwise. Sixth, dividend projections are subject to considerable error. Seventh, the policies being compared may not be the same (for example, the settlement option guarantees may be more liberal in a contract with a higher interest-adjusted net cost).

Despite these difficulties, cost comparisons should be made. Both the interest-adjusted surrender cost index and the interest-adjusted payments index should be considered. Small differences in cost should be ignored, but the differences that exist in practice are large enough to make the comparison worthwhile.[24]

In property and liability insurance it is possible to make some definite statements regarding relative average costs. The average advance premium mutual insurer either charges lower initial premium rates than the average stock insurer or charges the same premiums and pays a dividend. The mutual contract may be assessable, in which case the cost may exceed the stock premium, but an assessment by an advance premium mutual is a rare event. Consequently, the average stock insurer charges more for a specific contract than does the average advance premium mutual. Some of the difference in cost may be attributable to more selective underwriting by the mutuals, but the major reason is the difference in acquisition costs, which in turn reflects the marketing system used rather than the legal form of organization. Table 27.1 provides some insight into the relative importance of these two factors, but the stock and mutual ratios are not strictly comparable because these two types of insurers charge different average premiums. Differences in service and financial strength, it has been shown, are difficult to evaluate. The difference in acquisition costs is decreasing, however. Moreover, the variation in costs among the insurers of each type is sizable.

---

[24] For example, in one comparison of $100,000 straight life contracts issued at age 35, the 20-year interest-adjusted surrender cost index ranged from $12 to $964 for participating insurers and from $415 to $945 for nonparticipating insurers. The premiums varied from $1,718 to $2,487 for participating insurers and from $1,162 to $1,909 for nonparticipating insurers. See "Life Insurance: Part 2 of a Special Two-Part Report: *Consumer Reports,* vol. 45, no. 3 (March, 1980), pp. 174, 180.

In comparing the expense ratios of individual insurers, particularly their acquisition expense ratios, three factors must be kept in mind. First, if the home or regional office of the insurer assumes more responsibility for policy writing, record keeping, and billing operations, the acquisition expense ratios will decline but general expenses will rise. The effect on the total expense ratios will depend upon the relative efficiency of the more centralized operation. Second, the ratio of commissions paid to premiums written is affected, in some cases drastically, by whether the commissions and premiums have been adjusted for reinsurance transactions. The major reason for this effect under quota-share and surplus-share arrangements is that the reinsurer pays the originating insurer a "commission" on the business reinsured. In the annual statement, this reinsurance commission received is deducted from the commissions paid agents. To illustrate, assume that an insurer pays its agents commissions equal to 30 percent of its $1,000,000 premiums written. Further assume that this insurer cedes $400,000 of these premiums to a reinsurer under a quota-share arrangement for which the reinsurer pays a 40 percent commission. The commission rate on premiums before reinsurance would be 30 percent. The commission rate after reinsurance would be ($300,000 − $160,000)/($1,000,000 − $400,000), or 23 percent. The 30 percent figure more accurately reflects the commission expenses of the insurer. Third, reinsurance also affects the other expense-ratio components, because it changes the premium base upon which they are calculated. The expense ratios presented in Table 27.1 for all stock insurers and all mutual insurers combined are affected only slightly by these considerations. The reason is that for all insurers combined the differences between premiums written and premiums net of reinsurance and between direct commissions and commissions net of reinsurance tend to be relatively small.

Assessment mutuals are low-cost operations; the expenses are generally held to a minimum, and the insureds have a more personal relationship to the insurer. The cost, however, is indefinite.

Sources of Information

Several sources are available to the insured who wishes information concerning an insurer's financial strength, service, and cost.[25]

Published sources provide the most detailed information. The sources to be noted are illustrative only and are not meant to be exhaustive. The annual reports that insurers must submit to the state insurance department provide extensive information on the financial affairs of the insurer and may be consulted by the public. Sometimes the insurance commissioner issues an annual report that condenses much of this information. Many insurers will send interested parties copies of their reports to stockholders. The reader is reminded that audited annual reports of stock insurers and, at their

---

[25] For an interesting survey of what factors affect the selection of an insurer or a producer in practice, see *Businessmen's Attitudes toward Commercial Insurance,* Sentry Insurance National Opinion Study conducted by Louis Harris and Associates and the Department of Insurance, The Wharton School, University of Pennsylvania, 1975, pp. 37 and 47. Among the many findings were the following: Price is not the primary determinant; availability of satisfactory coverage is most important. Coverage, payment on claims, and protection against rate escalation are the real keys.

option, of mutual insurers will be prepared in accordance with generally accepted accounting principles, not statutory accounting principles. Several insurance departments now issue Shoppers' Guides, which compare the premiums charged by insurers operating in the state for specified types of insurance (usually, homeowners' and automobile insurance) and exposures (for example, an unmarried male, aged 22, driving his own car eight miles to and from work). Reporting services, however, are the most frequently consulted sources. Some illustrations are presented below.

Best's Insurance Reports, Life-Health presents each year the background history of most life and health insurers, the lines they write, the states in which they operate, and detailed financial data.[26] Each insurer is assigned a financial size category depending upon the net worth and one of six policyholder ratings based on Best's opinion of the relative financial strength of that insurer. The six policyholder ratings are A + and A (Excellent), B + (Very Good), B (Good), C + (Fairly Good), and C (Fair). The rating is based on Best's assessment and weighting of five factors: (1) competent underwriting, (2) cost control and efficient management, (3) adequate reserves for undischarged liabilities of all types, (4) net resources adequate to absorb unusual shock, and (5) soundness of investments. Because of the large proportion of insurers receiving high grades, the major value of these ratings is that they tell the risk manager what insurers he or she should probably avoid. The ratings can also prove useful when a risk manager is approached by an insurer about which he or she knows little or nothing. If this insurer has a C grade, the risk manager should not consider it. On the other hand, the insurer may be graded A + , in which case the risk manager should investigate the insurer further. Comparative comments are also made on investment yields, expenses, mortality costs, lapses and surrenders, and net costs. *Best's Flitcraft Compend* indicates the principal policy provisions, the premium and dividend rates, and the settlement option values used by most life insurers.[27] Interest-adjusted cost data are also provided on both a payments and a surrender cost basis. *Best's Settlement Options* contains tables of settlement option values and, in addition, describes in detail the practices of most insurers with respect to settlement options.[28] *Who Writes What in Life and Health Insurance* lists the contracts and underwriting practices of the leading life and health insurers.[29] *Time Saver for Health Insurance* analyzes the policies and rates of most health insurers.[30]

In 1980 Consumer Reports published a two-part special report comparing costs for policies issued by the lowest-cost life insurers and by the highest-cost life insurers.[31] The report shows the annual premium, the interest-adjusted surrender cost index, and the interest-adjusted payments index for $25,000 and $100,000 term and straight life insurance contracts issued at ages 25, 35, and 45. In 1974 the Subcommittee on

[26] *Best's Insurance Reports, Life-Health* (Oldwick, N.J.: Alfred M. Best Co., Inc., annual).

[27] *Flitcraft Compend* (Oldwick, N.J.: Alfred M. Best Co., Inc., annual).

[28] *Best's Settlement Options* (Oldwick, N.J.: Alfred M. Best Co., Inc., annual).

[29] *Who Writes What in Life and Health Insurance* (Cincinnati: The National Underwriter Company, annual).

[30] *Time Saver for Health Insurance* (Cincinnati: The National Underwriter Company, annual).

[31] "Life Insurance: A Two-Part Special Report," *Consumer Reports,* vol. 45, nos. 2 and 3 (February and March, 1980), pp. 79–106 and 163–186.

Antitrust and Monopoly of the United States Senate (see Chapter 34) published a comprehensive study showing how the prices charged in 1973 by 195 life insurers compared according to eight different measurement methods including the interest-adjusted method.[32]

In property and liability insurance, *Best's Insurance Reports, Property-Casualty* occupies a position analogous to *Best's Insurance Reports, Life-Health* in life and health insurance.[33] *Who Writes What* is analogous to *Who Writes What in Life and Health Insurance.*[34] *Best's Aggregates and Averages* reports important financial data for leading insurers and the industry.[35] The *Fire, Casualty, and Surety Bulletins* provide up-to-date information on leading property and liability insurance coverages and important legal interpretations.[36]

In 1983 Standard & Poor's started to provide to insurers upon their request a rating of their financial ability to pay claims under their insurance contracts. The insurers can then make the rating public. Insurers are placed in one of eight categories, ranging from AAA to D, with a plus or minus sign sometimes being added. The rating depends upon seven factors: industry risk, insurer characteristics, underwriting performance, investment activities, earnings protection, leverage, and financial flexibility.

Other sources of information are contacts with individual insurers and agents who can supply specimen contracts and premium information; contacts with other insureds, especially those facing the same problems; meetings such as those sponsored by the Risk and Insurance Management Society; and the insured's personal experience.

Of the three factors to be considered in selecting an insurer, service is not only the most difficult factor to evaluate but also the one about which objective information is most scarce. Some state insurance departments report how promptly individual insurers pay workers' compensation claims; a few report the proportion of claims contested for each insurer. At least one department, New York, has ranked automobile insurers according to the number of complaints settled in favor of the insured relative to their automobile insurance premiums written. *The National Underwriter,* a leading insurance weekly, presents annually for a long list of automobile insurers the ratio of suits outstanding to premiums earned. In July, 1977, *Consumer Reports* rated the performance of 34 insurers writing about two-thirds of the automobile insurance in force as (1) much better than average service, (2) better than average service, (3) average service, (4) worse than average service, or (5) much worse than average service.[37] The ratings were based on how 168,000 consumers rated their insurers on how they handled claims, the quality of their nonclaim services, and the likelihood that they would cancel an existing policy or refuse to renew it. In 1973 and 1974 *Fortune* magazine's market research department published two surveys of the Top 500 and Second 500 industrial

[32] *The Life Insurance Industry,* Hearing before the Subcommittee on Anti-Trust and Monopoly of the Committee on the Judiciary, 93rd Congress, Second Session, 1974.

[33] *Best's Insurance Reports, Property-Casualty* (Oldwick, N.J.: Alfred M. Best Company, Inc., annual).

[34] *Who Writes What* (Cincinnati: The National Underwriter Company, annual).

[35] *Best's Aggregates and Averages* (Oldwick, N.J.: Alfred M. Best Company, Inc., annual).

[36] *Fire, Casualty, and Surety Bulletins* (Cincinnati: The National Underwriter Company, monthly).

[37] "Managing Your Auto Insurance Part 2: Which Companies Give the Best Service," *Consumer Reports* (July, 1977), pp. 375–384.

corporations that indicate the extent to which they placed business with several leading property and liability insurers and with employee benefit plan insurers. Opinions are also presented on the underwriting philosophy of the property and liability insurers and the quality of the service rendered by the employee benefit plan insurers.[38] Although useful, this published information is limited to selected lines, types of service, or times. The risk manager can consult his or her counterparts in other organizations, but the value of their opinions depends upon their objectivity, their experience, and the similarity of their risk problems to those of the manager making the investigation.

CONSIDERATIONS THAT INFLUENCE SELECTION OF A PRODUCER

In addition to choosing an insurer a risk manager must choose a producer (an agent, broker, or sales representative). In selecting an insurer, a risk manager must pay attention to financial strength, service, and cost. In selecting a producer, service and cost are the primary factors to be considered. However, it is important that the producer use insurers who are financially strong. In some cases the producer, but not the insurer, may be legally responsible for his or her errors or omissions. Furthermore, the producer's financial statements will shed light on the nature and stability of his or her operations.

The producer's ability to service the insured depends upon the producer's knowledge of the insurance business, understanding of the risk manager's special problems, and ability (in terms of time, interest, analytical skill, markets, and facilities) to help the risk manager to design and implement with minimum delay and cost an optimum protection program. The producer's task does not terminate, however, with the design and implementation of the original program. Insurance needs are constantly changing, and the program must be kept up to date. In addition, when losses occur, the producer can render valuable assistance. He or she may also provide or request additional services such as appraisals or loss-control advice.

As was true of insurers, *the variation among producers of a single type is more marked than the variation among types of producers.* From what was said earlier, however, property and liability insurance agents and brokers probably rate somewhat higher than exclusive agents and sales representatives with respect to service because of their independence of action and their ability to concentrate on fewer customers.

With respect to cost, exclusive agents and sales representatives generally receive less compensation than independent agents and brokers. Commissions paid to independent agents and brokers, however, are usually a smaller percent of larger premiums. The insured and the producer commonly negotiate the amount. As a result the larger the business the smaller the difference in marketing cost between independent agency insurers and direct writers tends to become. Risk managers who place a high value on service are more likely to turn to agents and brokers. This is evident from the fact that the exclusive agents and sales representatives have been most successful in the mass

---

[38] *How Major Industrial Corporations View Property/Liability Insurance* (New York: Market Research Department, *Fortune* magazine, 1973). *How Major Industrial Corporations View Employee Benefits Programs* (New York: Market Research Department, *Fortune* magazine, 1974).

market, where the service demands are at a minimum. In other words, business risk managers have been more prone to turn to agents and brokers than have family risk managers. As noted previously, however, independent agency insurers have been adopting certain practices of the direct writers and vice versa. Authorities differ on the relative roles each type of insurer will play in the business markets of the future.

Sources of Information

Obtaining information about prospective producers is much more difficult than investigating insurers. The service to be provided by the producer is the principal issue, and, as noted above, published sources cannot provide this information. Other risk managers may be able to provide useful evaluations of producers as well as of insurers, but the most satisfactory source of information is personal contact with the producer. The more informed the risk manager, the more fruitful this contact is likely to be.

One positive indication of a producer's ability is a Chartered Life Underwriter (CLU) or Chartered Property and Casualty Underwriter (CPCU) designation. To obtain one of these designations, a candidate must have passed a series of examinations covering such diverse fields as risk management, insurance, law, economics, social legislation, finance, taxation, law, accounting, and management. The examinations are prepared and graded and the designations awarded by the American College of Life Underwriters and the American Institute of Property and Liability Underwriters, respectively. A newer designation, Associate in Risk Management (ARM), is awarded by the Insurance Institute of America upon the completion of three intensive examinations on risk management. Another innovation is the Certified Employee Benefit Specialist designation awarded by the International Foundation of Employee Benefit Plans to persons who complete a 10-part program on employee benefit plans, social insurance, accounting, management, finance, and industrial relations.

Two exam-based designations for financial consultants or planners whose services extend beyond insurance to include such areas as investment advice and tax planning are ChFC, Chartered Financial Consultant, and CFP, Certified Financial Planner. The ChFC is awarded by the American College of Life Underwriters, the CFP by the College for Financial Planning. Although many highly competent producers do not have these designations and the designations do not necessarily indicate competence, the risk manager should be aware of the existence and meaning of CLU, CPCU, ARM, CEBS, ChFC, and CFA.

SELECTION PROCEDURES

Up to this point, the text has dealt with types of insurers and the factors to be considered in selecting particular insurers and producers. The discussion now turns to several different *procedures* that the risk manager may use in the selection process. The discussion is meant to be indicative rather than exhaustive. First, the risk manager may select a single producer or group of cooperating producers to control the entire program, or he or she may select different producers for the various parts of the total program. Second, in selecting insurers or producers the risk manager may use open competitive bidding, modified competitive bidding, or individual negotiations. In either case, the insured may select the producer and the insurer concurrently or select the producer first and then the insurer.

Controlling-Producer or Piecemeal Approach

Under the *controlling-producer arrangement,* one producer or two or more cooperating producers are charged with responsibility for the total program and with obtaining the necessary insurance protection from the insurers they represent. The controlling producer may be an agent, a broker, or less often a sales representative representing one insurer. Relationships with the controlling producer are expected to be close and to continue indefinitely. The major advantage of this system is centralized authority and responsibility, which should minimize the possibility of gaps and overlaps in the program, reduce the time and effort the risk manager must spend on insurance, and simplify loss adjustments. The principal disadvantage of this system is a *potentially* high premium.

Under the *piecemeal approach,* responsibility for the insurance portion of the risk management program is divided among several agencies, brokers, or sales representatives. The major advantage of this approach is that in each area the risk manager can seek out the producer offering the best combination of service and cost. The result may be better overall service, lower cost, or both. Two possible disadvantages are an uncoordinated program with gaps and overlaps and increased demands upon the risk manager.

Competitive Bidding or Negotiations

Under *open competitive bidding* the risk manager or a risk management consultant (also selected on the basis of service and cost) draws up a set of rigid specifications and invites competitive bids for all or separate parts of the program. The principal appeal of competitive bidding lies in the lower premium cost it produces and, if price is the only consideration, the relative simplicity and objectivity of the decisions involved.[39]

Objections to open competitive bidding are that price may be overemphasized; framing the specifications is a sizable, complex task; the specifications may be incomplete or incorrect; and bidders are not free to suggest alternative ideas that, in the long run, may produce less costly protection. If the process is repeated too frequently, the insurer or producer may not have the time or the inclination to develop a close working relationship with the business. An opposite viewpoint is that the service provided by the insurer and the agent is sharpened by this competitive threat.

These problems affect part-time risk managers more adversely than full-time risk managers. Employing a risk management consultant would eliminate some of these disadvantages for the part-time risk manager, but the consultant's fee would have to be added to the cost.

[39] The decision may not be simple, however. For example, should mutual dividends, which cannot be guaranteed, be ignored?

Under *modified competitive bidding,* the risk manager or risk manager consultant invites the bidders to suggest substantially different insurance coverage as long as they satisfy certain broad directives. Such a procedure would complicate the decision process and make it more subjective, but it is more flexible than open competitive bidding and stimulates qualified insurance personnel to do more thinking about the program.

Individual negotiations with insurers and producers is the most common procedure, particularly among small businesses that do not have the desire or the ability to frame specifications or broad directives. Sometimes the business contacts only one producer or insurer with respect to the total program or part of that program. The result may or may not be the optimum, considering the premium paid, the services rendered, and the implicit and explicit cost of a more thorough selection procedure.

The above discussion assumes that under either competitive bidding or individual negotiations the producer and the insurer are selected concurrently. For example, competitive bids may be submitted by Independent Agent A representing insurer 1, Independent Agent A representing Insurer 2, Independent Agent B representing Insurer 3, Broker C representing Insurer 4, and Direct Writer 5. The risk manager, perhaps with the aid of a risk management consultant, would select the best producer-insurer combination. Alternatively the firm might contact each of these four producers separately and select what appears to be the best combination after individual negotiations. During these individual negotiations the independent agents and the broker might propose alternative insurers, but the choice of the producer and the insurer would be made concurrently.

Recently, some large businesses and some governmental bodies have adopted a system under which they first select an agent or broker and in many cases even fix his or her fee or commission before investigating who will be the insurer. (By definition a sales representative cannot be chosen under this process because he or she represents only one insurer.) The agent or broker then seeks the optimum insurer, which sells the insurance either directly to the insured, net of commission, or sets its commission equal to the agreed-upon fee or commission. If the commission exceeds the amount the agent has agreed to accept, the excess amount may be used by the insured to purchase additional risk management services.

Sometimes two or more producers are selected tentatively, the final selection depending upon what type of insurance they are able to arrange. To avoid having two or more of these producers approach the same insurer, each is assigned authority only to negotiate with specified insurers.

In favor of this relatively new selection aproach it is argued that (1) negotiated fees or commissions tend to be less than commissions, (2) the producer's compensation is not tied to the amount of insurance recommended, (3) the producer may be asked to provide certain services that would otherwise have to be provided internally or by outsiders, and (4) insurers will more seriously negotiate coverage, service, and price with a single producer who has negotiating authority for the insured as the only agent of record. A major disadvantage is that many independent agency insurers may be reluctant to participate in such an arrangement, especially if it requires the sale of insurance net of commission, because it might harm their relationships with their agents under the traditional system. Many agents are also reluctant to participate because they are not accustomed to this way of doing business or because they oppose the approach on principle. Some reasons why some brokers and agents oppose fees replacing commissions have already been presented on page 530. Finally, special care may be required to avoid violation of certain states laws such as antirebating statutes which prohibit agents or brokers from sharing their commissions with insureds.

SOME KEY CONCEPTS

Policyholders' surplus ratio The difference between an insurer's assets and its liabilities divided by its liabilities. One measure of an insurer's financial strength.

Audit ratios Ratios derived from an insurer's financial statement that are useful in assessing its financial strength. Audit ratios are part of the Insurance Regulatory Information System.

Loss reserves Liability items in an insurer's balance sheet reflecting the fact that it has not yet paid claims made or to be made because of losses that have already occurred.

Adverse selection Selection against the insurer that would result if the insurer were to accept every applicant because the persons who would be most likely to seek insurance would be those for whom the insurer's premium would understate their loss potential.

Reinsurance Insurance purchased by an insurer to protect itself against losses on policies it has written that it does not wish to bear entirely itself.

Interest-adjusted cost indexes A surrender cost index and a payments index that are commonly used to compare the cost of life insurance among insurers.

Modified competitive bidding A process under which the risk manager invites producers and insurers to suggest insurance coverages that will best meet the needs of his or her firm subject to some broad directives and cost considerations.

REVIEW QUESTIONS

1 Security is generally considered to be the most important consideration in selecting an insurer.
   a What is meant by security?
   b What variables determine the security of an insurer?
2 The balance sheet for insurer A indicates unearned premium reserves equal to 10 percent of liabilities and loss reserves equal to 79 percent of liabilities.
   a What is the unearned premium reserve?
   b What is the loss reserve?
   c What types of insurance does this insurer probably write?
3 Financial analysts often subtract a fraction of the unearned premium reserve from the total liabilities and add it to the surplus to determine the policyholders' surplus ratio.
   a What is the policyholders' surplus ratio?
   b Why do financial analysts correct the unearned premium reserve?
   c Describe briefly the 11 NAIC property and liability audit ratios.
4 The redundancy in the unearned premium reserve has sometimes been blamed for "capacity" problems.
   a What is a capacity problem?
   b What is the relationship of this problem to the unearned premium reserve?
5 How do life insurers determine net level premium reserves?
6 To what extent is there a redundancy in the policy reserves of life insurers?

7 If a life insurer's interest return drops permanently to a lower level:
  a What action should it take with respect to its reserves?
  b What action can it take with respect to its cash values?
8 Life insurers control more than twice as many assets as property and liability insurers. Why?
9 a Compare the investment portfolio of the typical life insurer with the portfolio of the typical property and liability insurer.
  b Explain the major differences.
10 The balance sheet of an insurer indicates that its assets consist primarily of bonds, mortgages, and common stocks. How are each of these types of investments valued?
11 a What is meant by "underwriting policy"?
  b What are some of the more common variations in underwriting policy? How does each of these variations affect insurer solvency?
12 Insurer A reports an expense ratio of 0.30 while insurer B reports an expense ratio of 0.45. Does this mean that insurer A is the more efficient insurer?
13 Insurance underwriters can turn to several sources for information concerning the desirability of an applicant for insurance.
  a What are these sources?
  b How does the binding authority of the agent affect the underwriter's possible courses of action?
14 Reinsurance facilities affect the insurer's solvency and its ability to service its policyholders. How?
15 Distinguish between facultative reinsurance, facultative treaty reinsurance, and automatic treaty insurance.
16 An insurer wishes to enter into one of the following reinsurance arrangements:
  a A quota-share arrangement with the ceding insurer retaining 60 percent of any loss
  b A surplus-share arrangement, under which the ceding insurer will retain policy amounts up to $100,000
  c An excess-loss arrangement, under which the ceding insurer will retain all losses under $100,000
  How much will the reinsurer pay under each of these arrangements if the loss is
  (1) $40,000 under a $80,000 policy?
  (2) $40,000 under a $200,000 policy?
  (3) $200,000 under a $200,000 policy?
17 a How does catastrophe reinsurance differ from the arrangements cited in question 16?
  b What other functions are performed by the underwriting department in addition to selecting among applicants and avoiding undue concentrations of exposure?
18 a Which are safer operations on the average, stock insurers or mutuals?
  b Even if you could determine that one type of operation was safer on the average, how significant would this finding be in selecting a particular insurer?
19 Many insurers claim that they render superior service, but a survey of agents several years ago determined that few of them were able to define what *service* means. What are some of the ingredients of superior service?
20 A supporter of mutual insurers argues that mutuals render better service because the policyholders own the insurer. Comment on this claim.
21 a "The average mutual property and liability insurer charges lower rates than the average stock property and liability insurer." Is this statement correct?
  b "The average mutual life insurer charges lower rates than the average stock life insurer." Is this statement correct?
22 What sources can the risk manager consult to obtain information concerning an insurer's financial strength, service, and cost?

23 a Would you favor the use of competitive bidding in the selection of an insurer?
  b Would you favor selecting the producer before selecting the insurer?

A REVIEW CASE BASED ON CHAPTERS 26 AND 27

A risk manager considering the purchase of automobile insurance on a fleet of five private passenger cars has narrowed the choice to two insurers. Some facts about each of these two insurers are presented below. All balance sheet and income and expense data are in millions of dollars. Assume a "hidden surplus" equal to 30 percent of the unearned premium reserve.

Evaluate each of these insurers with respect to security, service, and cost. (In your answer include a calculation of the policyholders' surplus ratio and the ratio of commissions to premiums, both with and without reinsurance.) What additional information would you like to have? Where could you obtain similar information for evaluating other insurers?

	Stock insurer A		Mutual insurer B	
	Last year	Year before last	Last year	Year before last
1. Balance sheet				
Assets:				
Bonds	$ 450	$430	$42.0	$36.0
Stocks	450	420	2.0	2.0
Other	100	100	6.0	6.0
	$1,000	$950	$50.0	$44.0
Liabilities and net worth:				
Loss reserves	$ 500	$480	$22.0	$19.0
Unearned premiums	200	180	11.0	11.0
Other liabilities	40	40	2.0	2.0
Capital or guaranty fund	10	10	0.5	0.5
Net surplus	100	90	14.5	11.5
Voluntary reserves	150	150	. . .	. . .
	$1,000	$950	$50.0	$44.0
2. Statutory underwriting gain				
Premiums written:				
Direct	$620	$570	$31.0	$30.0
Reinsurance ceded	100	90	1.0	1.0
Net	$520	$480	$30.0	$29.0
Premiums earned:				
Premiums written	$520	$480	$30.0	$29.0
Unearned premium reserve increase	20	30	0.0	0.0
Net	$500	$450	$30.0	$29.0

	Stock insurer A		Mutual insurer B	
	Last year	Year before last	Last year	Year before last
Losses incurred:				
Direct	$360	$380	$20.0	$18.7
Reinsurance recoveries	60	65	0.5	0.4
Net	$300	$315	$19.5	$18.3
Expenses incurred:				
Commissions				
Direct	$100	$ 90	$3.1	$3.0
Reinsurance	20	16	0.4	0.4
Net	$ 80	$ 74	$2.7	$2.6
Other expenses	118	106	6.0	5.8
	$198	$180	$8.7	$8.4
Underwriting gain (loss)	$2	$(45)	$1.8	$2.3
3. Adjusted underwriting gain (loss)				
Loss ratio	0.60	0.70	0.65	0.63
Expense ratio	0.38	0.38	0.29	0.29
Combined loss and				
expense ratio	0.98	1.08	0.94	0.92
Underwriting gain (loss)	0.02	(0.08)	0.06	0.08
4. Investment profit				
Investment income	$40	$38	$2.4	$2.3
Realized gains (losses)	(5)	10	0.0	0.0
Unrealized gains (losses)	(10)	10	0.3	0.4
Investment expenses	2	2	0.1	0.1
Investment profit (loss)	$23	$56	$2.6	$2.6
5. Premium distribution	Nationwide, 40% automobile insurance		Midwest only, 80% automobile insurance	
6. Marketing method	Independent agency		Direct writer	
7. Pricing practice	Bureau prices		Own prices, 20% below bureau	
8. Servicing facilities	Safety inspections, claims adjustments in most areas by own staff		No safety inspections, claims adjustments in most areas by independent adjusters	
9. Best's rating	A		A	

SUGGESTIONS FOR ADDITIONAL READING

Basile, Andrew J.: *Reinsurance—A Practical Guide* (Oklahoma City: Interstate Service Corporation, 1978).

Best's Aggregates and Averages (Oldwick, N.J.: Alfred M. Best Company, Inc., annual).

Best's Insurance Reports, Property-Casualty (Oldwick, N.J.: Alfred M. Best Company, Inc., annual).

Best's Insurance Reports, Life-Health (Oldwick, N.J.: Alfred M. Best Company, Inc., annual).

Bickelhaupt, D., *General Insurance* (11th ed., Homewood, Ill.: Richard D. Irwin, Inc., 1983), chaps. 25, 26.

Businessmen's Attitudes Toward Commercial Insurance, Sentry Insurance National Opinion Study Conducted by Louis Harris and Associates and the Department of Insurance, The Wharton School, University of Pennsylvania.

Cummins, J. D. and S. N. Weisbart: *The Impact of Consumer Services on Independent Insurance Agency Performance* (Glenmont, N.Y.: IMA Education Research Foundation, 1977).

Denenberg, H. S., et al.: *Risk and Insurance* (2d ed., Englewood Cliffs, N.J.: Prentice-Hall, Inc., 1974), chaps. 12 and 28–30.

Gart, Alan: *The Insider's Guide to the Financial Services Revolution* (New York: McGraw-Hill Book Company, 1983).

Gerathewold, Klaus: *Reinsurance Principles and Practice,* Vols. I and II, Verlag Versicherungswirtschafte e. V. (Available in the United States from Englewood Cliffs, N.J.: Underwritings Printing and Publishing Co., 1980 and 1983.)

Greene, M. R., and J. S. Trieschmann: *Risk and Insurance* (6th ed., Cincinnati: South-Western Publishing Company, Incorporated, 1984), chaps. 5–7.

————, and O. N. Serbein, *Risk Management: Text and Cases* (2d ed., Reston, Va.: Reston Publishing Company, 1983), chap. 14.

Gregg, D. W., and V. B. Lucas (eds.): *Life and Health Insurance Handbook* (3d ed., Homewood, Ill.: Richard D. Irwin, Inc., 1973), chaps. 61–70.

Insurance Facts (New York: Insurance Information Institute, annual).

Kenney, Roger: *Fundamentals of Fire and Casualty Insurance Strength* (4th ed., Dedham, Mass.: The Kenney Insurance Studies, 1967).

Kulp, C. A., and J. W. Hall: *Casualty Insurance* (4th ed., New York: The Ronald Press Company, 1968), chaps. 17, 18, and 23.

Launie, J. J., J. F. Lee, and N. A. Baglini: *Principles of Property and Liability Underwriting* (2d ed., Malvern, Pa.: Insurance Institute of America, 1977).

Life Insurance Fact Book (Washington, D.C.: American Council of Life Insurance, annual).

Long, J. D., and D. W. Gregg, (eds.): *Property and Liability Insurance Handbook* (Homewood, Ill.: Richard D. Irwin, Inc., 1965), chaps. 58–71 and 74.

Mehr, Robert I.: *Fundamentals of Insurance* (Homewood, Ill.: Richard D. Irwin, Inc., 1983), chaps. 19–22.

————, and E. Cammack: *Principles of Insurance* (7th ed., Homewood, Ill.: Richard D. Irwin, Inc., 1980), chaps. 21–25.

————, and B. A. Hedges: *Risk Management in the Business Enterprise* (Homewood, Ill.: Richard D. Irwin, Inc., 1963), chaps. 16 and 19.

———— and ————: *Risk Management: Concepts and Applications* (Homewood, Ill.: Richard D. Irwin, Inc., 1974), chap. 17.

Michelbacher, G. F., and N. Roos: *Multiple-Line Insurers: Their Nature and Operation* (2d ed., New York: McGraw-Hill Book Company, 1970), chaps. 4, 5, and 8–12.

Mowbray, A. H., R. H. Blanchard, and C. A. Williams, Jr.: *Insurance* (6th ed., New York: McGraw-Hill Book Company, 1969), chaps. 24–26, 28–30, 32, and 33.

Peterson, Timothy M.: *Loss Reserving: Property/Casualty Insurance* (Chicago: Ernst and Whinney, 1981).

Rejda, George E.: *Principles of Insurance* (Glenview, Ill.: Scott, Foresman and Company, 1982), chaps. 25, 26.

Riegel, R., J. Miller, and C. A. Williams, Jr.: *Insurance Principles and Practices: Property and Liability* (6th ed., Englewood Cliffs, N.J.: Prentice-Hall, Inc., 1976), chaps. 4–6 and 22.

Strain, R. W. (ed.): *Life Insurance Accounting* (Santa Monica: The Merritt Company, 1977).

_____: *Property-Liability Insurance Accounting* (Santa Monica: The Merritt Company, 1974).

_____: *Reinsurance* (New York: The College of Insurance, 1980).

Troxel, T. E., and C. L. Breslin: *Property-Liability Insurance Accounting and Finance* (2d ed., Malvern, Pa.: American Institute for Property and Liability Underwriters, 1983).

Using the NAIC Insurance Regulatory Information System: Life and Health and Fraternal Insurance, (1981 ed., Milwaukee: National Association of Insurance Commissioners, 1982).

Using the NAIC Insurance Regulatory Information System: Property and Liability Insurance, (1981 ed., Milwaukee: National Association of Insurance Commissioners, 1982).

Webb, B. L., J. J. Launie, W. P. Rokes, and N. A. Baglini: *Insurance Company Operations,* Vol. I and II (2d ed., Malvern, Pa.: American Institute for Property and Liability Underwriters, 1981).

CHAPTER **28**

INSURANCE PRICING METHODS

LEARNING OBJECTIVES

After you have completed this chapter, you should be able to:

1 Describe how state statutes and business considerations affect an insurer's pricing objectives.
2 Explain briefly the ways in which class rating differs from individual rating.
3 Tell why insurers tend to restrict modification rating plans to the larger insureds.
4 Describe how schedule rating can be used by insurers to encourage loss control and to meet competitive pressures.
5 Compare experience rating with retrospective rating.
6 Explain the reasons why rating bureaus exist in property and liability insurance.
7 Tell how policyholder dividends affect insurance premiums.
8 Explain briefly the premium structures in fire insurance, automobile liability insurance, workers' compensation, and life insurance.

INTRODUCTION

We have already emphasized the importance of considering cost in the selection of an insurer. In order to evaluate properly the cost of the protection provided by a particular insurer, the risk manager must understand the principles and procedures of insurance pricing. Moreover, once the insurer has been selected, the risk manager can use this knowledge to obtain the lowest possible price for his or her firm. Finally, because in-

surance is a public interest business,[1] the risk manager, as a citizen, has a strong interest in insurance pricing.

This chapter is designed to provide an understanding of the objectives of insurance
pricing, the principal pricing methods, rating bureaus, and dividend-distribution formulas.[2] In addition, the price structures in some specific kinds of insurance are discussed in order to illustrate (1) the application of these general concepts, and (2) the
important differences that exist among lines of insurance because of variations in the
problems presented and in pricing philosophies.

PRICING OBJECTIVES

An insurer's pricing objectives are determined by law and by business considerations.
State law usually requires that most property and liability insurance rates be reasonable, adequate, and not unfairly discriminatory. (An insurance rate is the price per unit
of insurance or exposure. An insurance premium is the total price, which is usually
calculated by multiplying the rate times the number of units of insurance or exposure.
For example, the premium for a $10 million property insurance policy may be
$20,000, or 100,000 times a rate of $0.20 per $100 of insurance.) Life insurance rates
must be adequate and not unfairly discriminatory; it is assumed that because there are
no rating bureaus in life insurance, competition will prevent these rates from becoming
unreasonable. Health insurance rates are generally subject to the same standards as
those of life insurance. In addition, about one-third of the states have laws that prohibit
approval of a health insurance policy if the benefits provided therein are unreasonable
in relation to the premium charged.

Insurance rates for a given policy are reasonable if they are not, on the average, too
high. The profits of the insurer should not be excessive. Insurance rates for a given
policy are adequate if they are, on the average, high enough. They must be sufficient to
cover the expected losses and expenses of the insurer; otherwise the insurer may
become insolvent and the policyholders will suffer. Insurance rates are not unfairly
discriminatory if each insured pays his or her "fair" share of the cost. This is a vague
requirement, but it is generally (though not universally) considered to mean that rate
differences among insureds should, subject to practical limitations, reflect differences
in expected losses and expenses. If the expected losses and the expected expenses for
one individual are twice the sum of these items for a second person, the insurance
premium for the first insured should be twice that for the second. To achieve perfect
equity in this sense, however, is impossible because an insurer cannot determine accurately the expected loss for each insured and allocate precisely the portion of the
insurer's expenses that should be assigned to each insured.

These three objectives are also dictated by business considerations.[3] An insurer
whose rates are excessive for some or all of its customers will, if it is subject to

---

[1] *German Alliance Ins. Co. v. Lewis*, 233 U.S. 389 (1914).

[2] Insurance pricing has already been mentioned briefly in Chaps. 26 and 27. Illustrative premiums have
also been presented in connection with some of the coverages.

[3] The market is not so perfect as this discussion would lead one to believe, particularly with respect to the
relative prices charged by one insurer, but the general tendencies are present.

competition, not be attractive to knowledgeable clients in the overpriced categories. If some or all of its prices are unduly low, the result may be a large volume of business at inadequate prices.

Textbook discussions of insurance pricing, including ours, usually understate the important role competition plays in insurance pricing. For example, as this text is being revised, property and liability insurers are competing intensely on price for commercial business. Through the modification rating plans discussed below, large buyers usually benefit more from this competition than do small businesses.

Business considerations also suggest some other criteria. The pricing structure must be workable, understandable, impossible (or at least difficult) to manipulate to the insured's advantage, and relatively inexpensive to apply. If necessary, some accuracy must be sacrificed to attain these goals. The rates should be responsive to changes in the long run, but because of the adverse public relations and administrative costs associated with frequent rate changes, the rates should be stable in the short run. Finally, the rates should encourage loss-control activities. The insured should be able to recognize the effect that his or her own efforts will have on the general rate level, and on his or her own premium relative to that paid by other persons. Some authorities argue that society gains even if the incentive exceeds the reduction in the expected cost that is likely to result from the loss-control activities.

Public policy considerations may suggest the socialization of some risks on some basis other than private equity.[4] For example, in order to keep the price of automobile insurance within the reach of younger drivers, older drivers may be asked to pay more than their fair share of the total costs. This objective conflicts with the unfair discrimination standard noted earlier and requires special pricing arrangements. Also, some criteria that might be related to loss experience may not be socially acceptable. For example, a few states have prohibited the use of age, sex, and marital status in pricing automobile insurance.

PRINCIPAL PRICING METHODS

Insurance pricing methods can be divided into three major categories: (1) individual rating, (2) class or manual rating, and (3) modification rating, usually referred to as "merit rating."

Individual Rating

Under individual rating, each insured is charged a unique premium based largely upon the judgment of the person setting the rate, supplemented perhaps by whatever statistical data are available and by a knowledge of the premiums charged similar insureds. It takes into account all known factors affecting the exposure, including competition from other insurers. Under this method the person *applying* the rating method to the individual insured is also the rate *maker*.

---

[4] Spencer L. Kimball, "The Purpose of Insurance Regulation," *Minnesota Law Review*, vol. XLV (1961), pp. 512–514.

This method is not in common use in insurance today. Ocean marine insurance rates and, to a much lesser extent, inland marine insurance rates are set in this fashion. Individual rating is used in other lines of insurance only for unusual exposures that cannot be handled under the other two rating methods, and it is used in pricing reinsurance. Consequently, risk managers of large business firms are much more likely to encounter this method than are other risk managers. Some risk managers of giant firms that self-insure the more common exposures and seek outside protection only for the unusual may be concerned solely with individual rating.

Class Rating

Under class rating, insureds are classified according to a few important and easily identified characteristics, and the insureds in each class are charged the same rate. This method of rating is often referred to as "manual rating" because the class rates are printed in a manual that the producer can consult to determine the appropriate rate for the insured. Under this method, the person applying the rates to determine the premium is not the rate maker. Except for determining the correct class for the insured, the person applying the rates has no decisions to make and, at least in theory, the rate should be the same, no matter who applies the rate. Determining the correct class, however, often involves considerable judgment, and the risk manager should check to see that his or her firm has been placed in the most favorable class possible.

The typical insured is more likely to encounter this method than any other, since this procedure is used to set most individual life insurance and health insurance rates, family automobile insurance rates, homeowner's insurance rates on dwellings, general liability and workers' compensation rates for small businesses, and many others.

Besides simplifying and speeding up the application of the rates, class rating makes it possible to use statistical methods more extensively in making the rates. Class rating groups together similar insureds, and the exposure units in the class may be numerous enough to provide a useful indication of the loss experience to be expected in the future. The attention paid to the statistical indications varies greatly among lines and even among states within the same line. This diversity can be attributed to variations in the rating problems presented, the data available, the prevailing rating philosophies, and the statistical support required to satisfy the state regulators.

Two basic approaches to determining changes in class rates are (1) the loss-ratio approach, and (2) the pure-premium approach.[5] Under the *loss-ratio approach,* (used in fire insurance and marine insurance, for example) the actual loss ratio during some representative period in the past is compared with a permissible or expected loss ratio. The actual loss ratio is usually the ratio of the losses incurred to the premiums that

---

[5] For a more detailed discussion of the loss-ratio and pure-premium approaches see B. L. Webb, J. J. Launie, W. P. Rokes, and N. A. Baglini, *Insurance Company Operations* (Malvern, Pa.: American Institute for Property and Liability Underwriters, 1978), vol. II, pp. 36–41. See also C. A. Kulp and J. W. Hall, *Casualty Insurance* (4th ed., New York: The Ronald Press Company, 1968), pp. 796–804. Mathematically, the two methods are equivalent as long as the expenses are assumed to increase proportionately with the premiums. The pure-premium approach, however, presents the information in a different fashion and appears to stimulate a more careful analysis.

would have been earned if the current premium rates had been in effect during the experience period. The permissible loss ratio is the portion of the premium that the actuary allocates for losses. For example, if the expense allowance is 0.41 and the profit allowance 0.05, the permissible loss ratio is $1 - 0.41 - 0.05 = 0.54$. The indicated rate change is determined by the formula $\dfrac{(r - R)}{R}$ where r is the actual loss ratio and R is the permissible loss ratio. For example, if r is 0.27 and R is 0.54, the indicated rate change is a 50 percent decrease. If r is 0.65, the indication is a 20 percent increase. For many reasons, the actual process is more complicated. For example, the actual loss experience may be so limited in quantity that what happened during the experience period is largely a matter of chance. Consequently, other evidence must be given some weight in the pricing process. The losses may also have to be adjusted to reflect changes in such variables as construction costs, hospital charges, or the liberality of juries. These adjustments should update the loss experience to the present, and through trend factors, predict what the losses will be during the period to be rated. Finally, instead of assuming the same permissible loss ratio for all classes, the insurer may assume that the expense allowance should be a higher or lower percent of the premium for some classes.

Under the *pure-premium approach* (used, for example, in automobile insurance, worker's compensation insurance, and life insurance), changes in the average rate level for all classes combined are usually calculated using a loss-ratio formula of the type described above. Changes in the rate relativities (the rate for each class relative to the average rate) are determined by computing first for each class an indicated pure premium or the actual losses per unit of exposure, such as one car-year or $100 of payroll.[6] For example, the pure premium indicated by class experience for class A may be $200 per car-year. For class B, the only other class, the pure premium may be $400. If the $200 and $400 pure premiums would not produce the change in the average rate level for the two classes combined, which was calculated using the loss-ratio formula, they are adjusted upward or downward to produce that result. For example, both the $200 and $400 may have to be adjusted upward 5 percent to $210 and $420. The indicated pure premiums are then loaded for expenses and profit to arrive at the annual rate. For example, if the permissible loss ratio is 0.60, the indicated class premium rate for class A is $210/0.60 = $350.

The actual process is more complicated for the same reasons that, in practice, the loss-ratio method is more complex. For example, the actual losses during the experience period may have to be supplemented by other evidence and the losses may have to be adjusted for price level changes or other changes in the environment.

As explained in Chapter 27, unlike life insurers, property and liability insurers do not explicitly assume any rate of return on their investments in determining their premiums. However, they do consider investment income, at least implicitly, in establishing the profit loading included in their rates. This practice is more common today than in the past. Until a few years ago most insurers used a 2½ percent or 5 percent profit loading in their rates depending upon the type of insurance that was being rated. In

---

[6] The pure-premium is, therefore, a rate. This terminology is confusing but generally accepted.

their opinion the underwriting profits generated by these loadings plus the investment profits enabled them to earn a reasonable rate of return. Some state regulators who believed that insurers were not adequately recognizing investment income mandated lower profit loadings. In recent years high interest rates greatly increased insurers' investment profits and consumer and insurer awareness of these profits. Under a total return philosophy many insurers have reduced their underwriting profit loadings, thus increasing the permissible loss ratio.[7] The loadings vary by line depending upon the insurers' assessment of the reasonable rate of return on that line, the variation in the annual rates of return, and the investment return generated by the premiums written. Insurers differ on whether total return pricing is appropriate and how many insurers will adopt and maintain this philosophy.

Life insurance rating is a special case because of the long-term contracts, the increase in mortality rates with age over the contract term, the use of an assumed rate of return on the insurer's investments, and the quality of the statistical information available. Further discussion will be deferred to the sections on specific premium structures.

Modification Rating

Under modification or merit rating, the rate maker distinguishes among insureds in the same rating class on the basis of differences in expected losses or expenses per exposure unit. The variations may be expected because of differences in past experience, size of the exposure, or a detailed analysis of the quality of the exposure. Four principal modification rating methods will be discussed: (1) schedule rating, (2) experience rating, (3) retrospective rating, and (4) premium-discount plans.

With some exceptions these plans are reserved for larger firms. A small relative difference between the modified rate and the class rate becomes important only when the premium is large; the loss experience of a particular insured becomes credible only when the number of exposure units is large; the expenses associated with modification rating become reasonable only when they result in substantial dollar premium changes; and expense savings for the insurer become more noticeable as the premium increases.

Schedule Rating Under schedule rating, the modification is based upon a comparison between some specified characteristics of a standard insured and the corresponding characteristics of the insured who is being rated. The person applying the schedule adds a charge to the standard rate for each way in which the rated insured is worse than the standard and subtracts a credit for each way in which the rated insured is better. The characteristics considered in the schedules and the charges and the credits are sometimes very precisely stated, and two persons applying the same schedule will arrive at approximately the same result. Other schedules are so highly flexible—the characteristics are so vaguely defined and the credits and charges can fall anywhere

---

[7] In some cases the profit loading was negative. The investment profits alone were expected to exceed a reasonable return.

within a broad range (e.g., up to 55 percent)—that schedule rating approaches individual rating. Regardless of whether the schedule is flexible or inflexible, the persons constructing (not applying) the schedule are forced to rely almost entirely on their judgment in choosing the characteristics to be compared and in evaluating their importance.

One great advantage of schedule rating is that an analysis of the schedule will reveal those areas where the quality of the insured's exposure could be improved. As such, schedule rating is a boon to loss-control efforts because it enables the insured to estimate the insurance savings associated with a loss-control measure.

Detailed, inflexible schedule rating is less important today than it was previously because a detailed schedule is expensive to apply and because the less flexible schedules have placed too much emphasis upon tangible or physical factors. The most important application of detailed schedule rating is the pricing of fire insurance and some inland marine insurance for most business exposures. Highly flexible schedules are in common use in such lines as automobile liability, general liability insurance, and, more recently, workers' compensation.

Experience Rating   Under experience rating (sometimes called "prospective experience rating"), the modification is based upon the relative loss experience of the individual insured during some representative period in the past. Although the formulas used in practice assume a variety of forms, the following formula illustrates the basic principles:

$$\text{Experience modification} = \frac{A - E}{E} \times C$$

where A represents the actual losses of the individual insured during the experience period, E represents the expected losses if the insured had been the average insured in the class (expected losses = permissible loss ratio times the premium over the experience period at class rates), and C is the credibility factor, which in this case depends upon the relative credibility of the individual experience and the class experience.[8] A table of credibility factors contains credibility factors that increase with the quantity of the exposure of the insured during the experience period. In accordance with the law of large numbers, other things being equal, the experience of the insured becomes more reliable as a guide to the future the larger the number of exposure units. The credibility factor exceeds zero only for insureds eligible for experience rating. Judgment always plays an important role in the construction of this table, but in some lines statistical theory also enters the picture.

To illustrate the application of experience rating, if the expected losses for the insured over a three-year experience period were $20,000, the actual losses $14,000, and the credibility factor 40 percent, the experience modification is a 12 percent decrease calculated as follows:

[8] Note the similarity to the loss-ratio formula used to establish class rates.

$$\frac{\$14,000 - \$20,000}{\$20,000} \times .40$$

$$= \frac{-\$6,000}{\$20,000} \times .40$$

$$= -.30 \times .40$$

$$= -.12$$

If the manual premium to be paid during the next year had been $10,000, the premium after experience rating would be 0.88($10,000) = $8,800.

An important feature of experience rating that has not been recognized in the preceding discussion is the emphasis it places upon loss frequency as opposed to loss severity. Loss severity is considered to be largely a matter of chance, and various devices are used to limit the effect of a single loss upon the experience rate. Consequently, an experience-rated insured who suffers one $100,000 loss over the experience period will probably pay a much lower premium than another insured whose class premium would have been the same as that of the first insured but who suffered 20 losses of $5,000 each.

Experience rating, therefore, varies the premium according to the loss experience of the insured, but the effect of single losses is limited, and the credibility factor dampens the effect of both good and bad experience unless the insured's exposure during the experience period was very large and the plan provides for full credibility.

Experience rating affects relatively few insureds because of its eligibility requirements, but in the liability lines, including workers' compensation where it is most important, these insureds pay much and sometimes most of the premiums.

Retrospective Rating Under retrospective rating (sometimes called "retrospective experience rating"), the modification depends upon the insured's experience during the *policy* period and a premium discount for expense savings attributable to the size of the insured. Theoretically the retrospective premium equals the actual losses and expenses of the insured chargeable to the policy period plus a net insurance charge, but the premium is not permitted to exceed a specified maximum or fall below a specified minimum. The purpose of the net insurance charge is to make up the premium deficiency for the insurer that results because the excess premiums paid by those insureds charged the minimum premium are less than the premium deficiencies of those insureds paying the maximum premium.

The following formula or some slight variation is used in practice:

Retrospective premium = [basic premium
+ (losses)(loss-conversion factor)] × tax multiplier

subject to stated maximum and minimum premiums.

The basic premium includes the net insurance charge, which is based upon a statistical analysis of a frequency distribution of losses, and the expenses less taxes that do not vary directly with the losses. The basic premium does not increase proportionately with the size of the insured in recognition of the fact that the expenses of servicing an insured do not increase this rapidly. The loss-conversion factor adds to the losses the expenses that do vary with the losses. The tax multiplier loads the premium for taxes.

The effect of retrospective rating is demonstrated graphically in Figure 28.1. The insured's premium cannot be specified at the beginning of the policy period, but assuming that the extent of the insured's exposure can be estimated fairly closely, the premium will fall somewhere on the line in the diagram.

To illustrate how the retrospective premium is calculated, assume that except for retrospective rating the premium is $100,000. The basic premium is $23,600, the minimum premium $51,000, the maximum premium $131,500, the loss-conversion factor 1.125, and the tax multiplier 1.078. If the losses during the policy period are $40,000, under these assumptions the retrospective premium will be [$23,600 + ($40,000) (1.125)] × 1.078, or $73,951. Losses of $87,453 or more would cause the insured to pay the maximum premium.

Because the insurer cannot make a good estimate of the losses incurred until some time after the policy period has ended, the plan provides for provisional premiums with subsequent adjustments upward or downward depending upon how the experience develops. If the adjustment is upward, the business can be viewed as having in effect an open line of credit with the insurer until the adjustment is made. Because it may take several years after the policy period before the insured and the insurer can agree on what the still unpaid losses will cost, several adjustments may be necessary before the final retrospective premium is determined.

Retrospective rating is very responsive to fluctuations in the insured's experience. Insurers limit its use to very large firms whose fluctuations are likely to be small and who are financially able to absorb those fluctuations that occur. For the large firm with a superior experience record, retrospective rating is very attractive. It is even more attractive for the insured whose past experience is such that experience rating results in a debit or increase over the manual rate but who believes that its future experience will be excellent. Insurers will sometimes insist upon retrospective rating when they have reason to expect poorer experience than anticipated under experience rating.

The risk manager may be called upon to make some important decisions with respect to retrospective rating. These decisions will all be subject to the consent of the insurer. First, the plan is usually elective, and the insured must decide whether to stick with the experience-rated premium to which the firm is usually otherwise entitled to or

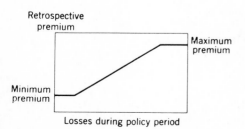

FIGURE 28.1
Retrospective premium as a function of the losses.

assume some risk. Second, if the plan is elected, the risk manager has to choose the applicable minimum premium and maximum premium factors and in some cases the loss-conversion factor. The considerations affecting these choices are too advanced for this text, but one example can be presented. The insured may reason that decreasing the maximum premium would reduce the chance of a sizable premium loss. This reasoning is correct insofar as the highest possible cost is concerned but as a result the net insurance charge and the basic premium would be increased. Consequently, the premiums over the most likely range of losses would be higher.

A modified form of retrospective rating, called paid loss retro, which is even closer to self-insurance, has recently been developed. The major difference is that, except for the basic premium times the tax multiplier which is paid at the beginning of the policy period, the insured pays the retrospective premium in yearly installments, each year's installment being the expenses and losses paid by the insurer that year because of accidents that occurred during the policy period. The reserves that the insurer establishes each year to cover future payments because of accidents that have already occurred are ignored in the premium calculation, but the insured does agree to pay the insurer in future years the amount it needs to pay to cover losses because of accidents that occurred during the policy period. The maximum premium still limits the maximum amount paid. The insured may prefer this approach because (1) the insured retains the use of the premium dollars longer, and (2) the premium paid never depends upon the insurer's *estimate* of future payments. The insurer will, in turn, add an extra charge to the premium because it loses some investment income. Chapter 30 describes one large corporation's paid-loss retro plan.

Size-Discount Plans Size-discount plans produce relatively lower class premiums, schedule premiums, or experience premiums for large-premium insureds on the ground that they will probably experience more favorable expense ratios, loss ratios, or both merely because they are large. The most important size-discount plans are those which recognize that not all the expenses of servicing an insured increase proportionately with the size of the premium. Size-discount plans usually provide a table of discounts that are applied to the premiums otherwise developed. For example, if the experience premium is $15,000, the amount in excess of $5,000 may be discounted 10 percent to produce a premium of $14,000.

RATING BUREAUS

In personnel insurance, the actuarial staff of each insurer establishes its price structure. In property and liability insurance, as was noted earlier, many or all insurers price some insurance policies in concert. The cooperating insurers are members of, or subscribers to, a rating bureau, which pools the experience of these insurers to establish insurance rates. Adherence to these rates may or may not be required.

Bureau operations have been defended on the ground that they produce more credible statistical data for rate making, they make available a group of highly qualified experts at minimum cost, and, to the extent that they require adherence to their rates, they reduce the possibility of cutthroat competition, unfair discrimination, and insolvency.

The disadvantages of unbridled competition are considered especially important in insurance because, if insurers become insolvent, they will be unable to fulfill their promises to their insureds. Such competition is possible in insurance because the price is based on an estimate, and the insurer may be unduly optimistic in its attempts to meet competition. The rates developed by rating bureaus are generally subject to close public supervision by the state insurance department. Because bureau rating reduces the number of rate structures to be reviewed, the department can spend more time on each structure. On the other hand, it has been argued that when rating bureaus seek adherence to their rates, they impede progress because all bureau decisions must be agreed upon by many insurers. In addition, a rigid rating bureau makes impossible or at least difficult price and coverage competition that would encourage new products and pricing methods and more efficient operations. It has also been argued that the threat of insolvency and unfair discrimination as a result of open competition has been greatly overemphasized.

With a few exceptions state laws provide for three types of bureau operations. The arrangements may differ by line in the same state or by state in the same line. Under the first or more inflexible arrangement, all insurers must belong to one rating bureau, and no insurer can deviate from the bureau rates. This arrangement is found most often in workers' compensation insurance. Under the second and most common arrangement, membership in a bureau is optional. Members or subscribers are free to deviate from the bureau rates, but the burden of the proof is on the deviators. Finally, under an "open competition" approach each insurer must determine its own rates. Rating bureaus or data service organizations can exist, but membership must be optional and the bureau can act only in an advisory capacity.

Starting in the late 1960s, about 20 states have adopted laws making the "open competition" system applicable to most property-liability insurance lines. Recently several states have extended their open competition laws to include workers' compensation insurance. In addition to these statutory changes, under the second system many insurers who were formerly bureau insurers now set their own rates. Furthermore, the national bureaus responsible for most lines other than workers' compensation no longer require adherence to their rates even though they legally could do so. Rating bureaus, therefore, play a less important role than they did previously, especially in enforcing adherence to a uniform set of rates, but they remain a significant part of insurance pricing.

DIVIDENDS

About one-fourth of the property and liability insurance in force and one-half of the personnel insurance in force is advance premium participating insurance, which provides for the payment of dividends to policyholders. Because insurance costs depend upon these dividends as well as the initial premiums, dividend practices should be considered part of insurance pricing.

The dividends paid by an insurer depend on its profitability. Insurers usually pay out less than they can afford in their most profitable years in order that they need not decrease the level in less profitable years.

The risk manager is interested not only in the general level of dividends but also in their distribution among insureds. Most property and liability insurers return the same percentage dividend, say, 10 percent, to all insureds purchasing a particular policy. Sometimes the dividends vary by classes or broad groups of classes, and in some instances, particularly in workers' compensation insurance, the dividend varies with the loss experience of the particular insured and the size of the insured's premium. Under this last practice, the large insured with good experience obtains the most substantial return. Less common practices vary the dividend according to either the loss experience or the premium size but not both.

Life insurance dividends come from more sources than property and liability insurance dividends and are apportioned according to a much more detailed formula. This discussion will be limited to individual life insurance because the relationship of group insurance dividends to the experience of the particular group has already been discussed in Chapter 21.

The three most important sources of dividends for a life insurer are (1) savings in mortality costs because the estimated death rates exceed the actual death rates, (2) savings in the allowances for expenses, and (3) an investment return in excess of that assumed in computing the premiums. Life insurers must also set aside some surplus in order to maintain a steady dividend policy and to establish contingency reserves. The divisible surplus, however, is a larger proportion of the total surplus than is the case for property and liability insurers and, as noted above, includes some excess investment return. These differences arise because investment return is relatively more important for life insurers, because an assumed investment return is part of the life insurance rate-making formula, and because a life insurer whose loss experience is relatively stable can operate more safely than can property and liability insurers with a low ratio of surplus to liabilities.[9]

In life insurance, the most common plan for distributing the divisible surplus among the insureds is the three-factor method. The essence of this method is that each insured receives a dividend from each of the three sources of dividends according to the contribution to that source of policies of the same type, issue age, and issue year. Younger persons, for whom the death rates are most likely to be overstated, receive the largest return on mortality savings. The same is true of insureds with policies having low cash values. Expense savings go mainly to those insureds paying large expense loadings and, if no size discount is applied to the initial premiums, may be much greater relatively for the larger contracts. Policyholders whose contracts have large cash values receive the largest dollar return from the excess investment return. There is a tendency for dividends to increase with the age of the contract because the cash value and the share in the excess investment return increase over time.[10]

---

[9] In fact, some states, such as New York, limit this ratio for mutual insurers to a certain percentage in order to avoid an unnecessary accumulation of surplus and to force payment of policyholder dividends.

[10] During periods of low investment earnings, however, the investment return may not be important enough to produce this effect and may even be negative.

SOME SPECIFIC PREMIUM STRUCTURES

The concepts discussed to this point will now be illustrated by a discussion of the pricing structures in some specific lines of insurance. The lines selected for illustrative purposes are fire insurance, automobile liability insurance, workers' compensation insurance, and life insurance. These lines have been chosen either because of their importance or because they provide good examples of the major approaches to insurance pricing. Only the more important aspects of insurance pricing in each of these lines and only the typical rating patterns can be considered. In some states and for some insurers, the pricing procedures may differ greatly from those discussed.

Fire Insurance

The principal fire insurance rating organization is the Insurance Services Office, which has regional and branch offices throughout the United States. Most insurers base their business insurance rates on the inspections and rates developed by the ISO. To duplicate the ISO effort in this respect would be expensive and inefficient. Insurers may, however, deviate from the ISO rates by a uniform percentage applied to all insureds or broad groupings of insureds. Such deviations reflect differences in overall experience.

Dwelling and homeowner's premium structures are often developed by individual insurers on the basis of their own experience. The process is less complicated and the insurer's own experience is credible.

The practices described here are those of the ISO.

Class Rates Almost all fire insurance rates can be divided into two basic types: (1) class or manual rates, and (2) schedule rates. Class rates are generally used to price such exposures as dwellings, private garages, small apartment houses, and small mercantile and manufacturing properties. The factors considered in classifying insureds are (1) the type of occupancy, (2) whether the property is a building or contents, (3) the grade of the community fire protection, (4) the construction (generally brick, frame, or fire-resistant), and (5) the amount of insurance purchased. Changes may also be added for substandard conditions. Coinsurance clauses and discounts are not applicable to most class-rate exposures.

Class rates are based in part upon statistical data gathered under either a Personal Lines Statistical Plan or a Commercial Risk Statistical Plan. To determine what changes, if any, should be made in existing rates, the usual practice is to determine, first, the rate change need for all rating classes combined, second, the rate change required for major industry groups, and third, the rate change for each rating class. The loss-ratio approach is applied to regional data as well as state data when the state experience has low credibility.

One important factor affecting fire insurance rates is the community's protection grade which is based upon an inspection of that community by the Insurance Services Office. The schedule used by the inspectors assigns up to 5,000 points to the community for deficiencies in the following factors, listed in order of importance: (1) water supply and distribution; (2) fire department equipment, personnel, and efficiency;

(3) fire safety controls such as building laws and laws on flammable or compressed gases; and (4) fire service communications such as alarm boxes and fire department telephone service. Additional points may be assigned for adverse climatic conditions, conditions not otherwise recognized, such as susceptibility to brush fires, and an excessive divergence between the water supply rating and the fire department rating because the effectiveness of the fire department depends upon the water supply and vice versa. Class 1 communities score 0 to 500 points, class 2 communities, 501 to 1,000 points, etc. Most cities with paid fire departments fall in classes 3 to 6. The risk manager may be able to reduce his or her fire rates and those of neighbors by convincing the community to take steps to improve its grade.

Schedule Rates   Schedule rates apply to most insureds who are not class-rated and are thus likely to be of more concern than class rates to risk managers of large business firms. ISO has developed a Commercial Fire Rating Schedule which is used in most states to determine the schedule rate. First, ISO makes a detailed inspection of the exposure's construction (e.g., thickness of walls, concealed spaces), occupancy (manufacturing, wholesale grocery), exposure (construction, occupancy, and distance from adjacent buildings), and protection (automatic sprinklers, guards). Using this information, the schedule rate is then determined by a rather complex procedure which (1) adds charges to the rate for ways in which the particular exposure is considered to be more expensive to insure than a standard exposure located in the same community, and (2) subtracts credits for ways in which the particular exposure is considered less expensive to insure. The features to be included in the schedule and the charges and credits are based not upon detailed past experience but upon some past experience, some controlled experimentation, and the combined judgment of the persons who drafted the schedule. One attraction of this form of schedule rating is that it gives the risk manager an incentive for loss control by providing the business with detailed information on the factors affecting its rate, and on the financial impact of making changes in the exposures itself.

The schedules used to rate large insureds and superior properties with approved automatic sprinklers (called highly protected properties) give the person applying the schedule much more leeway in determining the features to be considered and the charges or credits to be added to or subtracted from the rate.[11]

Under an expense modification plan, large insureds may, if the insurer agrees, have their schedule rate reduced to reflect (1) savings in acquisition costs or other expenses, and (2) favorable features, such as training of employees, not recognized in the more common schedules. The discount is most likely to be granted when there is competition for the insured's account.

A large firm that operates at two or more locations may be eligible for a multiple-location rating plan, which enables the insured to reduce the rate otherwise payable by (1) a premium size or quantity discount credit, (2) a credit based on the extent to which

---

[11] For a discussion of the schedule-rating plans applicable to substandard properties under FAIR plans, see Chap. 34.

the property values are dispersed, and (3) a modification for better than average experience.

Automobile Liability Insurance

Automobile liability insurance rating has many facets. First, independent insurers write more automobile insurance than do bureau insurers. Because of space considerations, however, and because the bureau rating procedures are fairly typical, we shall limit this discussion to the rating structures and methods of the one rating bureau active in this field. That rating bureau is the Insurance Services Office, mentioned earlier in connection with fire insurance rates.

Second, private passenger automobile rates depend upon different factors than do the rates for commercial cars (for example, trucks and delivery sedans) and public automobiles (for example, taxis and buses). Commercial and public automobile rates will be discussed only very briefly, because the same basic principles underlie these rates and rates for private passenger automobiles.

Class Rates   Most automobile liability insureds are class-rated. Private passenger car rates are determined as follows: First, for each car to be insured under the contract, a base premium is determined from the rating manual. The base premium depends only upon the policy limits desired and the territory in which the car will be principally garaged. Because smaller claims are much more likely than large claims, the base premium does not increase proportionally with the policy limit.

Second, a rating factor stated as a percentage of the base premium is calculated by adding together a primary rating factor and a secondary rating factor. The primary rating factor varies among insureds depending upon the use of the automobile (pleasure, but not driving to work; driving to or from work with a one-way mileage less than 15 miles; driving to and from work that is 15 miles or more away; business use; or farm use); the age and sex of those who customarily use the car; whether youthful operators are married; whether youthful operators own the car or are principal operators; whether youthful operators have completed an approved driver-training course; and whether youthful operators are good students. For youthful drivers there are only two use categories: (1) pleasure, but not driving to work and not farm use, and (2) all other. The primary rating factor divides insureds into 161 classes. For example, if the car is used only for pleasure driving and the only operator in the household is a female driver, aged 30 to 64, the primary classification rating factor is 0.90. If the car is used by this female operator to drive to work for a one-way distance of less than 15 miles, the factor is 1.15. Business use would increase the factor to 1.35. If a car used only for pleasure driving is owned by an uninsured male 17 years of age without driver training and with low grades, the factor is 3.50. A driver-training course and good grades would reduce this factor to 2.50. Other things being equal, the rates for youthful male owners decrease each year until they are 21, remain stable until age 25, at which time they would again decrease but still retain an extra charge until age 30, at which time they are no longer considered to be youthful owners.

The secondary rating factor depends upon whether more than one car is being insured, the type of car (standard performance, intermediate performance, high performance, or sports car), and the number of driving record points assessed against the insured under a safe-driver insurance rating plan. Under this plan the insured is assessed one point for each accident during the past three years causing bodily injuries or property damage exceeding $200 involving a car operated by the named insured or a resident relative. However, no point is assigned if the named insured can demonstrate that the accident occurred under certain circumstances—e.g., if the insured has secured a judgment against the other person or if the automobile was lawfully parked at the time of the accident. Up to three points may be assigned for various traffic convictions such as drunken driving. The factor is zero for a person insuring only one standard-performance car with no points. If the person were insuring two or more cars, the factor would be -0.15. For a person with four points insuring a single standard-performance car, the rating factor is 2.20.

The final step is to multiply the base premium by the sum of the primary and secondary classification rating factors.[12] For example, assume a base premium of $200 for a given territory and policy limits. A youthful male owner, aged 17, without driver training, with low grades, and with four points under the safe-driver plan would pay $200 (3.50 + 2.20) = $1,040 to insure one standard-performance car. A driver-training course, good grades, and no safe-driver plan points would reduce this premium to $200 (2.50 + 0.00) = $500.

As noted at the beginning of this chapter, the use of age, sex, and marital status in pricing automobile insurance has been seriously questioned in several states. Critics argue primarily that using these factors is not socially acceptable, that age and sex are not within the control of the insured, and that some wide variations exist in the quality of insureds in the same rating class. For example, although as a group unmarried 17-year-old male drivers owning their own cars cause many accidents, some members of this group are among the safest drivers on the road. A few states prohibit the use of these factors. Insurers respond that no other factors are as reliable as predictors of future experience, and that eliminating these factors will cause older drivers and others to pay more than they should. Alternative factors such as the number of years the operator has been licensed and the number of miles the car will be driven per year are being considered.

Rates for local and intermediate commercial vehicles such as trucks depend upon the territory where the vehicle is principally garaged, whether the vehicle is part of a fleet, the policy limits, the weight of the vehicle, the radius of operation, and the type of business. Long-distance (over 200 miles) vehicles are rated essentially the same way except that the process considers the two terminals included in the vehicle's operations that are farthest apart.

---

[12] If the number of youthful operators is less than the number of cars, the youthful-operator classification is applied only to cars equal to the number of youthful operators. The cars with the highest base premiums are assigned to the youthful-driver classification.

Public automobile rates vary according to the territory of principal garaging and the business classification—private livery, public livery, taxicabs, and buses classified by number of passengers.

The bureaus make extensive use of statistics in establishing both the general rate level and the rate relativities. In the private passenger rate-making procedure, the first step is to determine the statewide rate-level change by applying the loss-ratio method to statewide data. The second step is to develop the proposed rate-level changes by territory using the pure-premium approach. Finally, countrywide data are analyzed to determine whether any changes should be made in the rate relativities among classes in the same territory.

Modified Rates Modification rates assume many forms in automobile liability insurance. Important modification rating plans include a fleet-rating plan, an experience-rating plan with or without a schedule-rating supplement, and retrospective rating.

The automobile fleet plan provides discounts if five or more automobiles under one ownership are insured. It is assumed that some of the automobiles in a large fleet are always out of operation because of repairs, spares, or some other reason.

The experience-rating plan, which is fairly typical, is also available for fleets of automobiles. In most states the experience rate may be further modified according to a highly flexible schedule. The schedule provides for a maximum credit of 25 percent and a maximum debit of 20 percent based on very broad directives with respect to management, employee characteristics, condition of equipment, and safety organization. The experience and schedule rate may in turn be reduced if the expenses—usually commissions—incurred in producing the business are less than normal. This schedule and expense modification plan was the forerunner of the comparable plan for fire insurance described earlier.

The retrospective-rating plan is plan V described below in connection with workers' compensation insurance rates.

Workers' Compensation

Workers' compensation insurance may be underwritten by private insurers or by state funds. Only the rate structures of private insurers will be considered here. Although state-domiciled private bureaus (called "independent bureaus") or state-controlled bureaus make the rates in many states, the principal rating bureau is the National Council on Compensation Insurance, which makes the rates in about half of the states and serves in an advisory capacity in most of the others. The Council includes both stock and nonstock members and subscribers. Recently a few states have elected to extend their open competition laws to include workers' compensation insurance. In most states, however, independent insurers do not exist. Because all insurers in these states use the same initial rates, more workers' compensation insurance is written by both stock and mutuals on a dividend basis than in any other line of property and liability insurance.

Class Rates About 70 percent of the employers purchasing workers' compensation insurance are class-rated. Their payroll is divided into classes on the basis of the type of industry (piano manufacturing), the occupation of the employee (clerical office employee), or the industrial operation performed (manufacturing concrete at the job location by a contractor constructing bridges). Generally the entire payroll falls into one class determined by the industry except for clerical office employees, drivers, and certain other "standard exceptions." Because the payroll (to which the rate per $100 of payroll must be applied to determine the premium) can be estimated only at the beginning of the year, the insured pays a deposit premium, which is adjusted at the end of the policy period or on an interim basis.

In no property and liability insurance field do the rate makers pay more attention to statistical indications than in workers' compensation insurance. For each of the payroll classes, statistical information is available concerning the exposures in terms of $100 of payroll, and the losses are subdivided into three classes—serious disability losses, nonserious disability losses, and medical expenses.

The first step in revising workers' compensation class rates is to determine the statewide rate change by what is essentially a loss-ratio approach. The second step is to determine the rate relativities using pure premiums.

Modified Rates Modification rating plans are extremely important in workers' compensation insurance. These include an experience-rating plan, a premium-discount plan, several retrospective-rating plans, and in some states a flexible schedule rating plan. Experience rating and retrospective rating were first developed as workers' compensation insurance rating tools.

An insured whose annual premium at manual rates would average about $2,500 must be experience-rated. The detailed plan cannot be discussed here, but we should note that it is the most carefully and objectively designed experience-rating plan in insurance.

If the insured's annual premium exceeds $5,000, the premium is subject to a discount because of expense savings. The discounts are tabled and increase as the premium increases. Two sets of discounts are provided—stock discounts and nonstock discounts. Nonstock discounts are smaller because the insurers using these discounts prefer to pay dividends.

As an alternative to the premium-discount plan, an insured whose annual premium exceeds $5,000 may elect to be retrospectively rated under plan I, II, III, or IV. In practice, however, insurers usually limit retrospective rating to insureds paying annual premiums of at least $25,000. Some require a $100,000 or higher premium. Each of these plans specifies the set of maximum and minimum premiums corresponding to the standard premium—the premium that would be paid without the benefit of retrospective rating or premium discounts. Because of their importance, each of these plans will be described briefly.

Under plan I, the maximum premium is the standard premium, and the minimum premium exceeds the basic premium. At most, the insured loses his or her premium discount. Under plan II the maximum premium is greater than the standard premium, and the minimum premium is less than the plan I minimum. In other words, the possible fluctuation in the premium is much greater. The basic premium is considerably less. Plan III has the same maximum premium as plan II, but the minimum is much less since it is the basic premium times the tax multiplier. This plan produces a lower premium than plan II only when the experience is superior, because dropping the minimum premium increases the basic premium. Plan IV is characterized by a lower maximum premium than either plan II or plan III, but the minimum premium is lower than under plan I. It is suitable for insureds who find I too conservative and II or III too risky.

To illustrate these differences, assume that an insured has a $50,000 standard premium. In one state, the ratios of the basic, minimum, and maximum premiums to this standard premium would be as shown in the table below. For example, under plan II the base premium would be $12,350, the minimum premium $27,450, and the maximum premium $68,500.

Plan	Basic premium, percent	Minimum premium, percent	Maximum premium, percent
I	37.4	71.4	100.0
II	24.7	54.9	137.0
III	29.9	29.9 × tax multiplier	137.0
IV	29.8	60.2	118.5

Instead of electing plan I, II, III, or IV, an insured may elect plan V. Plan V has two distinctive characteristics. First, the insured may, subject to the consent of the insurer, select any reasonable set of minimum and maximum premiums. In other words, plans I, II, III, and IV are special cases of plan V. Second, plan V can be applied, separately or in some combination, to workers' compensation insurance, automobile liability insurance, general liability insurance, automobile physical damage insurance, burglary insurance, and glass insurance. Because plan V is so flexible, it has become much more popular among eligible insureds than plans I, II, III, or IV.

Life Insurance

In the property and liability insurance lines discussed, rating bureaus either establish the rates for much of the insurance written or have played an important role in developing the rating methods used in those lines. Consequently, particular attention has been focused upon bureau rating methods. In life insurance there are no rating bureaus; each insurer has a staff of actuaries to set its own prices or relies upon the services of consulting actuaries. Despite this independence of action, however, the same basic principles underlie the approach of all life insurers. Because the special characteristics of pricing group insurance and pension plans have already been noted briefly, this discussion will be limited to individual life insurance.

Class rates predominate in individual life insurance. For standard lives, the rates for a particular contract depend upon the age at issue, sex, and in most cases upon the face value of the contract. The class rates for substandard lives also depend upon the severity of their impairment or the dangers associated with their occupation.

Life insurance class rates can be and are established on a much more mathematically precise basis than is possible in the other lines of insurance. This statement is not meant to imply that life insurance rating is a completely objective, accurate process; as will be shown below, considerable judgment enters into the making of life insurance rates.[13]

The primary reasons why life insurance rating can be more precise than rating in other lines are that (1) because all losses are total and a fixed amount is paid in case of death (or survival under an annuity contract), the only loss information required is the probability of death at each age, and (2) the mortality rates at each age, although subject to long-term trends, are fairly stable in the short run. Furthermore, because all insurers classify standard lives in the same simple way, the experience of the principal insurers can be combined to provide highly credible experience, which may or may not be adopted by a particular insurer as a basis for its rates.

This combined experience or an insurer's individual experience forms the foundation for a mortality table that shows the mortality rates at each age. These mortality rates differ from the pure experience in that they have been (1) graded to eliminate irregular chance fluctuations, and (2) loaded to provide a margin of safety. On the assumption that some arbitrary number of persons, such as 1 million, is alive at the initial age in the table, the table shows, in addition to the mortality rates at each age, the number of deaths that will occur at that age out of the initial 1 million and the number who will survive to the next age.

The most recent mortality table based upon combined experience is the 1980 Commissioners Standard Ordinary Table, so-called (1) because in 1980 the National Association of Insurance Commissioners approved its use for minimum reserve valuations, and (2) because the table applies to ordinary insurance on standard lives. This table is reproduced as Table 28.1. Several other combined mortality tables are in current use, such as the 1971 Group Annuity Table and the 1961 Standard Industrial Table. The safety margins in the annuity tables must of course work in the opposite direction. Most participating insurers use one of these combined experience tables to establish their premiums. Nonparticipating insurers, in order to compete, modify these mortality rates according to their own experience or other, combined experience with no safety margins.

Life insurance rates, unlike property and liability insurance rates, depend upon an explicitly assumed interest return on the insurer's investments. The importance of this interest return will be evident in the example presented in the next paragraph. Participating insurers, because of their dividend policy, can be conservative in their interest assumptions, while nonparticipating insurers must be as realistic as possible.

To illustrate the uses of the mortality data and the assumed interest rate and the basic

---

[13] For a critical comment on the scientific accuracy of insurance rates, including life insurance rates, see A. H. Mowbray, R. H. Blanchard, and C. A. Williams, Jr., *Insurance* (6th ed., New York: McGraw-Hill Book Company, 1969), pp. 414–416. See also Dr. Irving Pfeffer's comments on the "fallacy of actuarial perfection" in *Insurance and Economic Theory* (Homewood, Ill.: Richard D. Irwin, Inc., 1956), pp. 5–6.

TABLE 28.1
1980 CSO MORTALITY TABLE

	Male			Female		
Age	Number living	Number dying	Probability of dying	Number living	Number dying	Probability of dying
0	1,000,000	4,180	.00418	1,000,000	2,890	.00289
1	995,820	1,066	.00107	997,110	867	.00087
2	994,754	985	.00099	996,243	807	.00081
3	993,770	974	.00098	995,436	787	.00079
4	992,796	943	.00095	994,649	766	.00077
5	991,853	893	.00090	993,883	755	.00076
6	990,960	852	.00086	993,128	725	.00073
7	990,108	792	.00080	992,403	715	.00072
8	989,316	752	.00076	991,688	694	.00070
9	988,564	732	.00074	990,994	684	.00069
10	987,832	721	.00073	990,310	673	.00068
11	987,111	760	.00077	989,637	683	.00069
12	986,351	838	.00085	988,954	712	.00072
13	985,513	976	.00099	988,242	741	.00075
14	984,537	1,132	.00115	987,501	790	.00080
15	983,405	1,308	.00133	986,711	839	.00085
16	982,097	1,483	.00151	985,872	887	.00090
17	980,614	1,638	.00167	984,985	936	.00095
18	978,976	1,743	.00178	984,049	964	.00098
19	977,237	1,819	.00186	983,085	1,003	.00102
20	975,416	1,853	.00190	982,082	1,031	.00105
21	973,563	1,860	.00191	981,051	1,050	.00107
22	971,703	1,836	.00189	980,001	1,068	.00109
23	969,867	1,804	.00186	979,933	1,087	.00111
24	968,063	1,762	.00182	977,846	1,114	.00114
25	966,301	1,710	.00177	976,732	1,133	.00116
26	964,591	1,669	.00173	975,599	1,161	.00119
27	962,922	1,647	.00171	974,438	1,189	.00122
28	961,275	1,634	.00170	973,249	1,226	.00126
29	959,641	1,641	.00171	972,023	1,264	.00130
30	958,000	1,657	.00173	970,759	1,311	.00135
31	956,343	1,702	.00178	969,448	1,357	.00140
32	954,640	1,747	.00183	968,091	1,404	.00145
33	952,893	1,820	.00191	966,687	1,450	.00150
34	951,073	1,902	.00200	965,237	1,525	.00158
35	949,171	2,003	.00211	963,712	1,590	.00165
36	947,168	2,121	.00224	962,122	1,693	.00176
37	945,047	2,268	.00240	960,429	1,815	.00189
38	942,779	2,432	.00258	958,614	1,956	.00204
39	940,346	2,623	.00279	956,658	2,124	.00222
40	937,723	2,832	.00302	954,534	2,310	.00242
41	934,891	3,076	.00329	952,224	2,514	.00264
42	931,815	3,127	.00356	949,710	2,725	.00287

TABLE 28.1 (*continued*)

	Male			Female		
Age	Number living	Number dying	Probability of dying	Number living	Number dying	Probability of dying
43	928,688	3,594	.00387	946,985	2,926	.00309
44	925,094	3,876	.00419	944,059	3,135	.00332
45	921,218	4,192	.00455	940,924	3,349	.00356
46	917,026	4,512	.00492	937,575	3,563	.00380
47	912,514	4,854	.00532	934,012	3,783	.00405
48	907,660	5,210	.00574	930,229	4,028	.00433
49	902,450	5,604	.00621	926,201	4,288	.00463
50	896,846	6,018	.00671	921,913	4,573	.00496
51	890,828	6,503	.00730	917,340	4,871	.00531
52	884,325	7,039	.00796	912,469	5,201	.00570
53	877,286	7,642	.00871	907,268	5,580	.00615
54	869,644	8,314	.00956	901,688	5,960	.00661
55	861,331	9,019	.01047	895,728	6,350	.00709
56	852,312	9,767	.01146	889,378	6,733	.00757
57	842,545	10,523	.01249	882,645	7,088	.00803
58	832,022	11,308	.01359	875,557	7,416	.00847
59	820,714	12,122	.01477	868,141	7,761	.00894
60	808,592	13,002	.01608	860,380	8,148	.00947
61	795,590	13,954	.01754	852,232	8,633	.01013
62	781,636	15,000	.01919	842,599	9,246	.01096
63	766,636	16,145	.02106	834,353	10,029	.01202
64	750,491	17,367	.02314	824,324	10,922	.01325
65	733,124	18,636	.02542	813,402	11,867	.01459
66	714,488	19,898	.02785	801,535	12,825	.01600
67	694,590	21,144	.03044	788,710	13,747	.01743
68	673,446	22,351	.03319	774,963	14,600	.01884
69	651,095	23,550	.03617	760,363	15,481	.02036
70	627,545	24,795	.03951	744,882	16,470	.02211
71	602,750	26,099	.04330	728,412	17,649	.02423
72	576,651	27,477	.04765	710,763	19,098	.02687
73	549,174	28,909	.05264	691,665	20,826	.03011
74	520,265	30,274	.05819	670,839	22,762	.03393
75	489,991	31,452	.06419	648,077	24,782	.03824
76	458,539	32,341	.07053	623,295	26,783	.04297
77	426,198	32,869	.07712	596,512	28,657	.04804
78	393,329	33,000	.08390	567,855	30,352	.05345
79	360,329	32,808	.09105	537,503	31,900	.05935
80	327,521	32,372	.09884	505,603	33,365	.06599
81	295,149	31,723	.10748	472,238	34,575	.07360
82	263,426	30,886	.11725	437,481	36,048	.08240
83	232,540	29,826	.12826	401,433	37,145	.09253
84	202,714	28,431	.14025	364,288	37,817	.10381
85	174,283	26,656	.15295	326,471	37,903	.11610
86	147,627	24,520	.16609	288,568	37,309	.12929
87	123,107	22,103	.17955	251,259	36,010	.14332

TABLE 28.1 (continued)

Age	Male			Female		
	Number living	Number dying	Probability of dying	Number living	Number dying	Probability of dying
88	101,004	19,521	.19891	215,249	34,048	.15818
89	81,483	16,891	.20729	181,201	31,518	.17394
90	64,592	14,325	.22177	149,683	28,552	.19075
91	50,267	11,912	.23698	121,131	25,301	.20887
92	38,355	9,721	.25345	95,830	21,927	.22881
93	28,634	7,792	.27211	73,903	18,587	.25151
94	20,842	6,167	.29590	55,316	15,450	.27931
95	14,675	4,842	.32996	39,866	12,651	.31732
96	9,833	3,781	.38455	27,215	10,226	.37574
97	6,052	2,906	.48020	16,989	8,069	.47497
98	3,145	2,069	.65798	8,920	5,850	.65585
99	1,076	1,076	1.00000	3,070	3,070	1.00000

principles of life insurance rate making, the following simplified example is presented. Assume that a male aged 35 wants to pay one lump sum for a $1,000 five-year term insurance contract. What is the appropriate lump sum on the assumption that the 1980 CSO mortality rates and a 4 percent interest return will be maintained and that expenses can be ignored? This lump sum is called the ''net single premium.'' For explanation purposes,[14] assume that this person is one of the 949,171 who have survived to age 35 according to Table 28.1 and that all these persons are interested in the same insurance.[15] According to Table 28.1, out of these 949,171 persons, 2,003 will die the first year, 2,121 the second, 2,268 the third, 2,432 the fourth, and 2,623 the fifth. The actuary assumes that these death claims will not be paid until the end of the year in which the death occurs. Because of this time lag and because of the assumed interest return, it is not necessary to collect $2,003,000 now to pay the death claims occurring the first year. The necessary fund is only $2,003,000/1.04, or $1,925,884[16] because this amount invested for one year at 4 percent will yield $2,003,000. The amount that must be collected now to meet the claims payable at the end of the second year is $2,121,000/(1.04)², or $1,961,077, because this amount invested for two years at 4 percent will yield $2,121,000. A similar procedure is followed for the other three years. The complete computation is shown in tabular form on the next page. The increasing importance of the interest assumption in the later contract years is obvious.

The net single premium is equal to this fund divided by the number of insureds. In this case, the net single premium is $10,137,931/949,171 = $10.68.

---

[14] Most actuaries prefer an explanation in terms of probabilities, but the approach used here is easier for the nontechnical reader to understand.

[15] The fact that the number of persons purchasing the insurance almost certainly will be different from 949,171 will not affect the answer so long as the mortality *rates* still apply.

[16] The reader who checks our arithmetic by dividing $2,003,000 by 1.04 will find that the necessary fund is $1,925,962. The $1,925,884 fund was obtained by multiplying $2,003,000 by .9615, the rounded value of 1/1.04. This rounding error does not affect the final premium.

(1) Contract year	(2) Death claims	(3) Present value of $1 payable at end of year, 4%	(4) Present value of death claims (2) × (3)
1	$2,003,000	$0.9615	$ 1,925,884
2	2,121,000	0.9246	1,961,077
3	2,268,000	0.8890	2,016,252
4	2,432,000	0.8548	2,078,874
5	2,623,000	0.8219	2,155,844
			Total $10,137,931

If the insureds pay for this contract with five annual premiums, the five annual premiums will have to be greater than a single premium payment at the beginning of the five years, because (1) not all insureds will live to pay the five annual premiums and (2) the insurer will not have the use of all the premiums for five years. The actuary first determines the lump-sum equivalent of a $1 annual premium over the next five years on the assumption that the premiums are paid at the beginning of the year. All 949,171 insureds will pay $1 on the issue date, but only 947,168 insureds will pay $1 one year later, and because of the loss of interest on this money, its present value is only $947,168/1.04, or $910,702. Similar computations are made for the other years and are summarized in the table following.

(1) Contract year	(2) Premium payors	(3) Present value of $1 payable at beginning of year, 4%	(4) Present value of $1 premium payments, (2) × (3)
1	949,171	$1.0000	$ 949,171
2	947,168	0.9615	910,702
3	945,047	0.9246	873,790
4	942,779	0.8890	838,131
5	940,346	0.8548	803,808
			Total $4,375,602

This present value of the $1 premium payments per policyholder is $4,375,602/949,171, or $4.61. The present value of $2 premium payments would be twice this value, $3 premium payments three times this value, etc. Consequently,

$$\begin{array}{c}\text{Desired}\\\text{annual}\\\text{premium}\end{array} \times \begin{array}{c}\text{present value of \$1}\\\text{premium payments}\end{array} = \begin{array}{c}\text{net}\\\text{single}\\\text{premium}\end{array}$$

or

$$\frac{\text{Desired annual}}{\text{premium}} = \frac{\text{net single premium}}{\text{present value of \$1}}$$
$$\text{premium payments}$$

$$= \frac{\$10.68}{\$4.61} = \$2.32$$

Although these principles have been stated in terms of a specific example, they are general in their application. For example, in order to determine the net annual premium for a straight life policy, the only difference would be that each table would be extended to include 65 contract years, i.e., to age 100, at which time it is assumed that all of the 949,171 insureds will have died.

The gross premium is the net premium loaded for expenses. Participating insurers usually add to the net premium a percentage of the premium plus (1) a constant per $1,000 of insurance, or (2) a constant per $1,000 of insurance and a constant per policy. As might be expected, nonparticipating insurers must be more precise in their initial premium computations.

SOME KEY CONCEPTS

Open rating   A type of rate regulation under which the regulator relies primarily upon competition to keep rates reasonable, adequate, and not unfairly discriminatory.

Rating bureau   An organization that develops rates based on the pooled experience of its members and subscribers. The rates may be only advisory, or members may be required to adhere to these rates.

Class rating   A rating method under which the rate depends upon a set of characteristics that define a class. For example, a fire resistant building with an approved roof used as a small office building in a community with excellent fire, water, and police facilities.

Schedule rating   A more refined version of class rating in which the rate depends upon a more detailed analysis of the exposure's characteristics. Schedules vary in the degree of flexibility they permit the person determining the rate.

Experience rating   A rating method under which the insured's rate depends at least in part on the insured's own prior loss experience.

Retrospective rating   A rating method under which the insured's premium depends upon the insured's own loss experience subject to minimum and maximum premium constraints.

REVIEW QUESTIONS

1 **a** Most state laws require that property and liability insurance rates be *reasonable, adequate,* and *not unfairly discriminatory*. What do these terms mean?
   b What are the legal requirements with respect to life insurance rates? Why do they differ from the requirements with respect to property and liability insurance rates?
2 **a** Distinguish between individual and class rates.
   b Cite some examples of each of these two types of rates.
   c What risk managers are most likely to be concerned about individual rates?
3 In the past insurance losses totalled $132 million. Premiums at current rates were $200

million. If insurers need 40 percent of their premiums to pay their expenses and earn a reasonable profit, should premium rates be increased or decreased? How much?

4 Explain the factors that complicate the loss-ratio approach to pricing.

5 a How can a risk manager make use of the results of schedule rating?

  b When does schedule rating approach individual rating?

6 a The class premium for a firm would have been $8,000, but the firm is eligible for experience rating. During the experience period, the firm had actual losses totaling $12,000. An average firm in its rating class would have suffered losses totaling $16,000. The credibility percentage for this firm is 30 percent. How much will the class premium be reduced as a result of experience rating?

  b How would you answer the above question if the actual losses were $20,000?

  c Does it make any difference under experience rating whether a firm has 5 losses of $20,000 each or 100 losses of $1,000 each? Explain.

7 a Compare retrospective rating with self-insurance.

  b Under what conditions might an insurer require retrospective rating?

8 How is the retrospective premium affected by:

  a Lowering the maximum premium and raising the minimum premium?

  b Raising both the maximum premium and the minimum premium?

9 Rating bureaus are less important in property and liability insurance than they were formerly.

  a Which of the three bureau systems do you prefer? Why?

  b What are the advantages of rating bureaus?

  c How important are rating bureaus in life and health insurance?

10 a Do property and liability insurers always pay all policyholders in the same rating class the same percentage dividend? If not, what do they do?

  b If a life insurer earns 1 percent more on its investments than it assumed in establishing its rates, which policyholders will receive the greater dividend return as a result—term insurance policyholders or straight life insurance policyholders? Which group would gain more from mortality savings? Why?

11 a What types of business firms are class-rated by fire insurers?

  b Are fire insurance class rates based on statistical analysis?

  c How can a class-rated business firm cut its rate?

12 Describe briefly the basic approach to schedule rating in fire insurance.

13 a What factors affect the automobile liability class rate that a sole proprietor will have to pay?

  b How do the policy limits affect the class rate?

14 Are the automobile liability insurance class rates paid by persons in a medium-sized city in your state based solely upon the automobile liability experience in that city? Explain your answer.

15 A large firm has a fleet of automobiles consisting of 40 private passenger automobiles and 15 trucks. What automobile liability insurance modification rating plans are applicable to this firm?

16 a What factors affect workers' compensation class premiums?

  b To what extent do the class rates paid by a firm in a particular industry depend upon the loss experience in that industry?

17 On what basis should a firm decide among workers' compensation retrospective-rating plans I, II, III, IV, and V?

18 Compute the net level annual premium for each of the following policies:

  a A three-year $1,000 term life insurance policy issued to a female at age 25

  b A three-year $1,000 endowment policy issued to a female at age 25

19 Compare life insurance, workers' compensation, and fire insurance rating with respect to:
 a Reliance upon statistical data
 b Recognition of investment return
20 Participating and nonparticipating life insurers differ somewhat in their approach to pricing. How and why?

SUGGESTIONS FOR ADDITIONAL READING

Fire Insurance Rate Making and Kindred Problems (New York: Casualty Actuarial Society, 1960).

Freifelder, L. R.: *A Decision Theoretic Approach to Insurance Ratemaking* (Homewood, Ill.: Richard D. Irwin, Inc., 1976).

Hartman, G. R.: *Ratemaking for Homeowners Insurance* (Homewood, Ill.: Richard D. Irwin, Inc., 1967).

Huebner, S. S., and Kenneth Black, Jr.: *Life Insurance* (10th ed., Englewood Cliffs, N.J.: Prentice-Hall, Inc., 1982), chaps. 19–23, 25, 27.

Jordan, C. W., Jr.: *Life Contingencies* (2d ed., Chicago: Society of Actuaries, 1967).

Kahn, P. M. (ed.): *Credibility: Theory and Applications* (New York: Academic Press, Inc., 1975).

Kallop, R. H.: "A Current Look at Workers' Compensation Ratemaking," *Proceedings of the Casualty Actuarial Society,* vol. LXII, nos. 117 and 118 (May, 1975, and November, 1975), pp. 62–133.

Kulp, C. A., and J. W. Hall: *Casualty Insurance* (4th ed., New York: The Ronald Press Company, 1968), chaps. 11 and 19–22.

McGill, D. M.: *Life Insurance* (rev. ed., Homewood, Ill.: Richard D. Irwin, Inc., 1967), chaps. 8–12.

Mehr, R. I., and S. G. Gustavson: *Life Insurance: Theory and Practice* (3d ed., Dallas: Business Publications, Inc., 1984), chaps. 23, 24.

Menge, W. O., and C. H. Fischer: *The Mathematics of Life Insurance* (2d ed., New York: The Macmillan Company, 1965).

Pfeffer, Irving, and D. R. Klock: *Perspectives on Insurance* (Englewood Cliffs, N.J.: Prentice-Hall, Inc., 1974), chaps. 22, 25, and 26.

Proceedings of the Casualty Actuarial Society (annual).

Seal, Hilary L.: *Stochastic Theory of A Risk Business* (New York: John Wiley & Sons, Inc., 1969).

Stephens, V. M., W. S. McIntyre, and J. P. Gibson: *Risk Financing: A Guide to Insurance Cash Flow* (Dallas: International Risk Management Institute, Inc.).

Transactions of the Society of Actuaries (periodic).

Webb, B. L., J. J. Launie, W. P. Rokes, and N. A. Baglini: *Insurance Company Operations* (2d ed., Malvern, Pa.: American Institute for Property and Liability Underwriters, 1981), vol. II, chaps. 8–10.

CHAPTER 29

PREPARATION FOR LOSS ADJUSTMENTS

LEARNING OBJECTIVES

After you have completed this chapter, you should be able to:

1 List the different types of loss adjusters an insured might encounter.
2 Summarize the responsibilities of the insured following a property loss.
3 Describe some special problems that may arise in property loss adjustments.
4 Summarize the responsibilities of the insured following a liability loss.
5 Describe some special problems that may arise in liability loss adjustments.
6 Summarize the responsibilities of the insured following a personnel loss.
7 Describe some special problems that may arise in personnel loss adjustments.

INTRODUCTION

In addition to analyzing risks faced by the firm and designing and implementing the best insurance program for it, the risk manager must know how to deal with insurers following a loss in order to assure a prompt and equitable adjustment of a claim. This chapter discusses, first, the different types of adjusters who may be involved in the negotiations, and second, several important loss-adjustment principles and procedures. The second topic is discussed separately for property insurance, liability insurance, and personnel insurance.

TYPES OF ADJUSTERS

Not all insurers employ the same types of adjusters to handle claims, and the same insurer may use different types of adjusters, depending upon the size or type of loss or the geographical location. The risk manager should be aware of the different types of adjusters because their mode of operation varies as well as their authority to adjust claims. One type represents insureds, not insurers, in the loss adjustment. The types to be discussed here are (1) agents or sales representatives, (2) salaried adjusters on the insurer's staff, (3) independent adjusters, and (4) public adjusters.

Agents and Sales Representatives

Small property insurance claims (e.g., losses of $200 or less) are often adjusted by the agent or, much less frequently, by the sales representative. Producers may also render valuable services for the insureds in connection with other losses.

Staff Adjusters

Most insurers writing a large volume of property and liability business in a particular area have a staff of salaried adjusters to service that area. These specialists are used except when the insurer has written only part of the insurance involved in a loss, in which case it is generally considered more efficient and economical to turn the claim over to an independent adjuster. The authority of these adjusters varies according to the insurer. Staff adjusters of some insurers are authorized to use their own judgment in settling almost every claim, while others must refer practically every case to the home or branch office. Still others possess final authority on claims up to some specified amount. The adjuster is more likely to possess final authority with respect to property claims than to liability claims.

Most life insurance claims are handled very promptly by the claims departments in the branch or home offices. Field adjusters, however, are employed extensively with respect to health insurance claims.

Independent Adjusters

Independent adjusters are persons or firms engaged in loss-adjustment work as independent persons or organizations. Many operate from only one office; some have many branches in more than one state. They service insurers on a fee basis. Sometimes they specialize in a particular line of insurance such as automobile insurance. Insurers often hire independent adjusters to handle claims in areas where they write little business, to supplement staff adjusters during peak claim periods, and to adjust claims requiring highly specialized skills. Many self-insurers hire independent adjusters to service their plans.

A special class of independent adjusters consists of two adjustment bureaus, each of which was formerly owned by a group of stock insurers who used their services on a regular basis. The General Adjustment Bureau, Inc., now a public corporation, has offices throughout the world. The Underwriters Adjusting Company, a subsidiary of a financial services holding company, operates nationally. These bureaus are most active in property insurance but also handle liability insurance claims. Insurers are most likely to seek their services if the insurance is shared with other insurers and in those areas where their volume of business does not justify the employment of a staff adjuster. Insurers also tend to turn to these bureaus when a disaster strikes and many adjusters must be sent into the disaster area to handle the numerous claims that develop.

Public Adjusters

Although insureds can represent themselves in loss adjustments, it is common practice in property insurance for an insured with a large loss to be represented by a public adjuster.[1] The public adjusters assist the insured in the preparation of the necessary records (to be discussed later) and in negotiations with the insurer's representative. Because of the public adjuster's familiarity with loss-adjustment principles and procedures, it is argued that in many cases he or she increases the insured's recovery. As his or her fee, the public adjuster commonly receives a stated percentage, say, 10 percent, of the amount paid by the insurer.[2]

PRINCIPLES AND PROCEDURES

Although loss-adjustment principles and procedures in property, liability, and personnel insurance have much in common, considerable variation exists among the most important problems in each branch. For this reason, the three branches will be discussed separately.

Property Insurance

Insurance contracts impose certain obligations upon the insured following a loss. Failure to meet these obligations may prevent the insured from recovering on what is otherwise a valid claim. In property insurance contracts, the insured is usually instructed to (1) notify the insurer, (2) protect the property from further damage, and (3) assist the insurer in its investigation of the loss.

Notice of Loss   The insured must usually notify the insurer or, in most instances, a duly authorized agent "immediately" or "as soon as practicable." The courts interpret both terms to mean as soon as is reasonably possible. Furthermore, notice to the agent is always sufficient. A few contracts require that the notice be given within a specified period following the loss.

The policy usually requires that the notice be given in writing. Actually, however, oral notice to the insurer is usually sufficient unless the insurer or its agent objects.

---

[1] Compensation claimants' attorneys play a similar role in liability insurance.
[2] Some public adjusters must unfortunately be classified as "ambulance chasers," but the merits of others are widely recognized—even by adjusters for the insurers.

Even if the insurer objects, the policy requirement is ineffective if the insurer then proceeds to adjust the claim. In spite of these liberal interpretations, however, the insured will be wise to give the notice in writing because he or she may need a copy as evidence in case the notice is questioned. Some policies, such as those covering theft losses, where prompt action may reduce substantially the amount of the loss, require telegraphic notice or some other special form of communication.

The insured may also be expected to notify someone other than the insurer. Under a theft insurance policy, for example, the insured must tell the police, as well as the insurer, about the loss.

Protection of Property from Further Damage   All property insurance contracts require the insured to protect the property from further damage. Failure to meet this requirement will release the insurer from any responsibility for further damage. Although not all policies specifically state that the insurer will reimburse the insured for any reasonable expenses incurred in protecting the property, such reimbursement is usually made. Only in marine insurance contracts, however, is this reimbursement in addition to the face value of the contract. In some contracts, such as business interruption insurance, the reimbursement is specifically limited to the reduction in the loss.

Ideally, the adjuster will arrive promptly on the scene and suggest the types of protective measures that should be adopted. The degree of supervision exercised by the loss adjuster over the insured's protective work depends upon the loss situation and the adjuster's evaluation of the insured. Sometimes the adjuster assumes the insured's responsibility completely. The insured should not hesitate, however, to take any action that appears reasonable and necessary before the arrival of the adjuster.

Examples of protective measures that have proved beneficial in some instances are the following: nailing of tar paper over holes in a roof, draining of plumbing in cold weather, separation of wet debris from woodwork, removal of contents from a building threatened by further damage, drying and greasing of wet machinery, prompt distribution of perishables to retailers or consumers or to cold-storage plants, separation and drying of wet merchandise, and coverage of exposed equipment with tarpaulins.

Assistance in the Investigation   The third duty of the insured following the loss is to assist the loss adjuster in the investigation. The adjuster must determine (1) whether the loss actually occurred, (2) whether it is covered under the contract, and (3) the extent of the loss. The burden of proof is upon the insured, and the better prepared he or she is to aid in these determinations, the more satisfactory and prompt the final loss adjustment is likely to be. If the adjuster has some doubt concerning whether the loss is covered, he or she may ask the insured to sign a nonwaiver agreement that states that the insurer is not admitting its liability by its investigation. Despite the nonwaiver agreement, however, the insurer may be held liable if it causes the insured undue expense or inconvenience. Sometimes in a doubtful situation the insurer does not request a nonwaiver agreement but sends the insured a reservation-of-rights letter in which it reserves the right to deny the claim later.

Usually it is a simple matter to determine whether the loss occurred, and the insured will have no difficulty in proving the case. In some instances, however, particularly with respect to theft and mysterious disappearance losses, the adjuster may have to rely heavily upon the reputation of the insured.

To determine whether the loss is covered, the adjuster must be thoroughly acquainted with the property insured, the circumstances surrounding the loss, and the insurance contract. He or she must know whether the contract was in force at the time of the loss and whether the contract covers the peril, the person(s), the property, the location, and the type of loss (direct or net income) involved in the claim. The contract may also specify some conditions not falling into any of these categories that, if they exist, suspend or terminate the coverage. The insurer can supply contract information, but the adjuster must rely upon the insured to provide information concerning the property and the circumstances of the loss. This the insured can do by exhibiting the remains of the property and the space it occupied and by offering testimony, fire department or police department records, plans and specifications, deeds, bills of sale, or other evidence.

The most difficult task in adjusting property losses is the valuation of the loss. For direct property losses, the usual basis of recovery is the actual cash value of the loss. As pointed out in Chapter 17, this measure is usually the cost of repair or replacement new less depreciation (including obsolescence) or the decrease in market value, but other measures are possible. Even after a measure has been agreed upon, disagreement may arise concerning such concepts as depreciation and market value. Replacement cost coverage, explained in Chapter 18, eliminates the depreciation measurement problem.

The insured and the adjuster may use one or more of several methods to establish the value of the property and the loss. For example, they may look at the property together and agree on the loss;[3] they may make or have made separate estimates and reconcile their differences; they may prepare specifications for repair or replacement and submit these to be bid upon; they may accept the valuation of a single expert; or they may accept the amounts shown in accounting records.[4]

Property insurance contracts generally require the insured to produce upon request at reasonable times and places all records pertinent to the valuation procedure. If the records have been destroyed or if they are otherwise unavailable, the insured does not usually lose his or her right to press the claim, but the insured's own best interests are served if he or she can provide records substantiating the claim because the adjustment process will then be speeded up and is more likely to be equitable. Under some contracts, the insured is required to keep records of the insured property that will enable the insurer to determine accurately the amount of the loss.

Net income losses are even more difficult to evaluate than direct property losses. The length of time required to restore premises to a tenantable condition, the net profit and continuing expenses that would have been covered by sales during the period a store must be out of operation, and the profits that a manufacturer would have made on the sale of some finished goods are examples of losses falling in this category. Often the losses must be estimated from sketchy accounting data.

---

[3] Most small- and moderate-sized losses are adjusted in this way. P. I. Thomas and P. B. Reed, *Adjustment of Property Losses* (4th ed., New York: McGraw-Hill Book Company, 1977), p. 9.

[4] Ibid., pp. 9–12. Thomas and Reed list 11 different methods.

The difficulties in measuring losses are compounded when the contract contains a coinsurance clause, because this clause may make necessary a valuation of the undamaged as well as of the damaged property. Except when the loss is small, the insurer is likely to require a detailed inventory of the damaged and undamaged property, and the insured is well-advised to keep adequate up-to-date records for this purpose. The fire insurance contract specifically charges the insured with the preparation of such inventory records after any loss, but this provision is seldom enforced with respect to the undamaged property unless there is a coinsurance clause.

Within some specified period following the loss, such as 30 or 90 days, the insured must file a sworn detailed proof of loss with the insurer. The proof-of-loss form describes the time and cause of the loss, the persons who have interests in the property, the amount of the claim, and other facets of the loss. The insurer usually furnishes a blank proof-of-loss form which the insured completes and signs. Most claims are adjusted swiftly and without difficulty, and in such cases the adjuster commonly completes the proof-of-loss form for the insured's signature after the adjustment has been completed. In situations where the insured's story may change over time or where a dispute has arisen, the adjuster may refuse to proceed with the adjustment until the insured has executed a proof of loss. Failure of the insurer to act within a reasonable time after the filing of a proof of loss may cause the insurer to lose its right to object to any features of the claim.

Several legal interpretations and statutes soften the impact of the proof-of-loss requirement upon the insured. Although contracts specify the number of days within which the proof of loss must be filed, several states by statute or by court interpretation have either made it unnecessary for insureds to comply with this time period or require the insurer to give additional notice of its intention to enforce this provision. The courts have also held that a material misstatement by the insured in the proof of loss shall not affect the insured's right of recovery unless the misstatement was intentional. The insurer or its representatives may be held to have waived the proof-of-loss requirement if they deny liability, if they promise to prepare the proof-of-loss statement for the insured, or if they begin to adjust the loss without notifying the insured that proof of loss will be required. The insured cannot be accused of failure to comply with the proof-of-loss provisions because of some defect that the insurer does not promptly point out. The insured can change the filed proof-of-loss form if he or she believes that the initial loss estimates were in error. Despite these favorable interpretations, the insured should make every attempt to comply with the policy provisions. The insured's case may be the exception that proves the rule.

Usually the insurer will pay the claim shortly after the insured files the proof of loss. Some contracts specify a time period within which the claim must be paid.

Special Problems   In some property-loss adjustments, problems arise that necessitate additional steps in the loss-adjustment procedure. For example, the procedure may be more lengthy and complex when there is (1) other insurance, (2) a third party who is responsible for the loss, or (3) some dispute over the valuation of the loss.

If two or more contracts cover the loss, it is usually clear from contract provisions how the loss is to be apportioned among the various insurers, but sometimes the situation is ambiguous. For example, there may be two contracts, each of which claims to provide excess insurance over any other insurance covering the loss. The courts usually resolve such situations in a way that is beneficial to the insured. In the case cited, they would probably require the insurers to share the loss on a pro rata basis. Most cases of this sort, however, are handled without going to court. Most insurers abide by Guiding Principles (1963), which prescribes certain rules to be followed in settling disputes because of overlapping coverages.

The second special problem to be discussed arises when the insured has a legal right to recover his or her loss from some third party. The third party may be responsible as a result of negligence, a contract, or a statute. Common law and the subrogation clause in the insurance contract provide that the insurer, upon payment of the loss, may take over the right of the insured to collect from the responsible third party to the extent of the insurance payment. The insured, therefore, must be careful after (and before) a loss not to prejudice this right of the insurer. The right is particularly important in transportation insurance because of common carrier liability and in automobile collision insurance because another party is often at fault.[5] In no event should the insured release the party responsible without the consent of the insurer simply because he or she is willing to pay the part of the loss that is not insured.

The insurer may seek to recover from the third party in the name of the insured or in its own name. If the loss exceeds the insurance payment, the insured may join in the suit, sue in his or her own name for the entire amount or his or her interest only, or rely on the insurer to sue for the entire loss. The ways in which the insured and the insurer may share such recoveries were discussed in Chapter 17 under "Subrogation."

The third special problem occurs when the insured and the adjuster cannot reach an agreement concerning the valuation of the property or the loss. In such an event, two contract provisions are pertinent. Under the first, either the insurer or the insured has the right to demand in writing that the differences be resolved by an appraisal. Each party names an appraiser to represent the party, and the appraisers then select a competent and disinterested umpire. If the appraisers cannot agree on an umpire, provision is made for selection by the courts. The appraisers then value each property item and the loss to that item. Only their differences are submitted to the umpire. In the absence of fraud, collusion, or mutual mistake, an award signed by any two of the three persons is binding. The insured must pay his or her representative's fee plus one-half of the bill of the umpire and other appraisal charges.

The insured must submit to the demand of the insurer for an appraisal, but in most instances,[6] if the insurer refuses to submit to a similar demand of the insured, the insured's only remedy is to sue.

The second provision that becomes pertinent in a valuation dispute gives the insurer

---

[5] Automobile collision subrogation claims often involve two insurers. Under a nationwide inter-company arbitration agreement, most insurers have agreed to submit to local arbitration committees all automobile physical damage subrogation claims below a stated amount. Almost all claims are settled merely on the basis of claim files.

[6] There are exceptions. For example, under the Minnesota statutory fire policy, if either party fails to select an appraiser within 20 days after the demand is made, a presiding judge of the district court of the county where the loss occurs may appoint an appraiser for the party that fails to appoint one itself.

the right instead of paying the loss in cash to buy all or any part of the property at the agreed or appraised value or to repair, rebuild, or replace the property. Although this provision gives the insurer an out if it disagrees with either the insured's or the appraiser's estimate of the loss, in most property lines the insurer seldom exercises this option because of the difficulties involved in disposing of property or in repairing, rebuilding, or replacing to the insured's satisfaction.

These options are used, however, in settling personal property claims when the insurer can better dispose of the property than can the insured. For example, some merchandise damaged by smoke can often be reclaimed and sold by salvors employed by the insurer more advantageously than they could be sold by the insured. In other instances, the insured conducts the sale under the supervision of the insurer.

Replacement in kind instead of a cash payment is the usual rule when the insurer can replace the property more promptly or more economically than can the insured. Two illustrations of losses of this type are glass losses and jewelry losses.

Liability Insurance

Liability insurance claims present some responsibilities and problems for the insured that differ from those associated with property insurance claims. Whereas property insurance claims are termed "first-party" claims because the insured has suffered the loss, liability losses are called "third-party" claims because the insured is legally obligated to pay some injured third party. The discussion in this section will emphasize the special characteristics of liability insurance claims. Workers' compensation and medical payments claims, which are more closely akin to health insurance claims, are covered in the next section.

Special Interest of Business Risk Managers Business risk managers are much more interested in the outcome of a liability claim than are family risk managers. Family risk managers, to be sure, are extremely concerned about escaping any possible loss to themselves, but they commonly have little direct interest in the manner in which the claim is handled unless they know the injured party. Business risk managers, on the other hand, do have a direct interest because every claimant is a potential customer or because the integrity of their business is at stake. A lengthy publicized trial alleging some defect in the firm's product, for example, can do the firm immeasurable harm. Furthermore, because of experience and retrospective rating, the firm is interested in minimizing losses that have occurred and in gathering important loss-control data for the future. The same observation with respect to experience and retrospective rating could have been made with respect to property losses.

Common Principles and Procedures Whenever an accident occurs, the insured should notify the insurer as soon as possible. The observations made earlier with respect to notices of property losses also apply here, but three differences should be noted. First, the insured should notify the insurer concerning any accident that might result in a claim from a third party. The notice must contain any reasonably obtainable information concerning the time, place, and circumstances of the accident and the names and addresses of injured persons and witnesses. The insured should not with-hold the notice until the injured party presents a claim. Even if the injured party maintains that he or she was not injured, the insured should notify the insurer. Second, the courts will interpret the notice requirement in liability insurance contracts more strictly, because prompt investigation of the circumstances surrounding the accident is essential to protect the insurer's interest. The major problem in investigating liability claims is that of gathering the facts and interpreting them in the light of the law, the judge, the jury, and the plaintiff's attorney. Witnesses and evidence can quickly disap-pear, or witnesses can change their stories, and with the passage of time, minor injuries can assume major proportions in the mind of the claimant. Third, in addition to the no-tice-of-accident requirement, the contract demands that insureds forward *immediately* to the insurers every notice of a claim or suit, summons, or other process delivered to insureds or their representatives.

During the adjustment process, the insured must cooperate with the insurer. The insurer provides the lawyers and is responsible for, and in charge of, the defense of the claim, but if the insurer requests the insured to do so, the insured must attend hearings and trials and assist in the general conduct of the suit by such means as securing and giving evidence, obtaining witnesses, and effecting settlements if the insurer believes that this process offers the best solution.[7] For this assistance the insurer reimburses the insured for all reasonable expenses incurred at the insurer's request, including usually actual loss of earnings not to exceed a specified amount per day.

The insured must be careful both at the time of the accident and after it not to make voluntarily any payment, assume any obligation, or incur any expense other than the cost of essential immediate medical treatment of others. Paying these medical expenses is not regarded as an admission of liability but the mark of a decent person and a wise precautionary measure because it may substantially reduce the ultimate loss. The other acts, however, can prejudice the insurer's ability to defend the claim.

The insured need not submit a proof of loss in connection with liability losses. Such proof is unnecessary because the amount of the loss is fixed either by the judgment awarded by the courts or in an out-of-court settlement between the insurer and the claimant.

Special Problems   Special problems sometimes arise in connection with liability insurance claims. They may occur when (1) some third party is primarily responsible for the loss, (2) the suit or the judgment is in excess of the policy limits, or (3) the insured and the insurer cannot resolve their differences without resorting to a suit.

If some third party is primarily responsible for the accident for which the insurer pays a judgment in behalf of the insured, the insurer takes over any right the insured may have to sue the third party. This right may arise, for example, under a hold-harm-less agreement or because some other party, such as an agent, is primarily responsible.

---

[7] Under some professional liability contracts, the insurer cannot settle the claim out of court without the consent of the insured. Under most liability contracts, however, the insurer has the right to effect a settlement if that appears to be the most economical solution. Most claims are in fact settled in this fashion. Business risk managers, however, often attempt to influence the settlement of product liability claims. See above.

Although insurers seldom exercise this right with respect to liability losses, the insured must be careful to preserve whatever right exists.

Often the injured party will sue for an amount far in excess of the policy limits. In such a case, the insurer is expected to notify the insured immediately in order that he or she may participate in the defense if desired because he or she also faces a potential loss.

A related problem arises when the claimant agrees to settle for an amount within the policy limits but threatens to sue for a much larger amount. If the insurer refuses and the claimant sues for and is awarded an amount in excess of the policy limits, the insurer is responsible for this excess only if a court decides that the adjuster was negligent or did not act in good faith in behalf of the insured.

Liability insurance contracts do not specify any interval during which the insured must commence suit against the insurer in case of a disagreement, but they do assert that no one has a right of action against the insurer (1) unless the insured has complied with all the policy provisions and (2) until the insured's liability has been established either by a judgment awarded by a court or by a written agreement among the insured, the insurer, and the claimant. These conditions affect both insureds and claimants. If the insurer claims that the insured has violated the contract, the insured must defend himself or herself in court against the claimant before he or she can sue the insurer. The claimant has no rights under the contract if the contract is void with respect to the insured. Except in a few states with direct-action statutes that supersede these policy provisions, the claimant can never proceed directly against the insurer until the insured's liability has been established by the courts.

Personnel Insurance

Personnel insurance losses may be caused by death or the attainment of a specified age or by an accidental injury or sickness. Losses of the first type are much easier to adjust than are those of the second type.

Death   When an insured dies, a life insurance contract instructs the beneficiary to submit written proof of loss to the insurer. Because it is easy to verify whether death has occurred, because there are few, if any, exclusions in the contract, because the incontestable clause eliminates after a few years the possibility of a defense of misrepresentation, and because the amount to be paid is stipulated in the policy, almost all claims will be paid within 24 hours after the insurer receives the proof of loss.

The three most troublesome areas in the adjustment of life claims are vague beneficiary designations, disappearance cases, and double indemnity claims. Beneficiaries are sometimes designated in terms that are broad enough to include several persons, e.g., "my wife," or are changed immediately preceding death in a manner that is not strictly correct. Insurers handle these problems by paying the proceeds into court under what is called an "interpleader action" and letting the court make the decision. Disappearance cases are relatively rare but happen enough to pose a problem. At common law a person is presumed to be dead seven years after he or she mysteriously disappears, and if the contract is still in effect at the expiration of that period, the insurer must pay the claim.

Double indemnity causes problems because of its restrictive insuring clause and the suicide exclusion.

Group life insurance claims are handled in essentially the same way as individual life insurance claims, but the proof of loss is usually transmitted to the insurer through the employer. Some large firms are even authorized to pay their own claims.

Attainment of a Specified Age   Annuity contracts involving life contingencies require that the insured post proof that he or she has attained that age. The insured may also be asked to present evidence that he or she is living on the due date of each annuity payment that is contingent upon his or her continued survival.

Group pension plans may require in addition certification that the employee has retired. If the pension plan is self-insured by the employer and if the trustee is to mail the checks, the employer must provide the trustee with the necessary information.

Poor Health   The procedure to be followed in adjusting health insurance claims is discussed at length in the mandatory standard provisions in the health insurance contract. The insured (or beneficiary, if a death benefit is involved) is to notify the insurer or its authorized agent in writing within 20 days after the occurrence or commencement of any loss or as soon thereafter as is reasonably possible. The insurer must furnish the insured proof-of-loss forms within 15 days after the insured notifies the insurer. If the insurer fails to meet this deadline, the insured can satisfy the proof-of-loss requirement by submitting written proof describing the occurrence and the character and extent of the loss. If the claim is for an income benefit, the insured must return the proof-of-loss form or the substitute written proof within 90 days after the termination of the period for which the insurer is liable. If the claim is for other benefits, such as medical expense reimbursements, the proof must be submitted within 90 days after the loss, e.g., when the hospital bill is paid. These 90-day limits are waived if it is not reasonably possible to give proof within such time. In that event, proof must be submitted as soon as possible, but unless the insured lacks the legal capacity to submit proof of loss, the deadline is one year from the time proof is otherwise required.

The insurer promises to pay losses other than income losses immediately after it receives due written proof of the loss. There is a trend toward the use of forms under which the insurer pays directly the hospitals, doctors, and others, but the insured can always request that he or she receive the payment. Claims for income losses will, subject to due written proof of loss, be paid at the expiration of each four weeks during the benefit period. If the disability lasts many months, this four-week payment schedule can be very advantageous for the insured.

The standard provisions also give the insurer the right, at its own expense, to examine the insured at reasonable times and places and to perform an autopsy in case of death. The right of examination is exercised only in troublesome cases. The autopsy right is seldom used.

Finally, the standard provisions state that suits against the insurer must be commenced no earlier than 60 days after the insured has furnished the insurer written proof of loss and no later than three years after the date the proof was supposed to be furnished.

The discussion to this point has been concerned with individual health insurance issued by commercial insurers. Under group insurance contracts, the employee usually obtains the proof-of-loss form from the employer. After the forms are completed by the employee and the doctor or the hospital, the employee sends them to the insurer. If the insurer approves the claim, the insurer sends the employee a check. Alternatively, under many plans, the employee can assign the benefits to the doctor or to the hospital, who collects directly from the insurer and bills the employee for any difference. Under some plans the employee returns the forms to the employer, who forwards them to the insurer. If the claim is approved, the insurer sends the payment to the employee through the employer or directly to the vendors of the medical care. Sometimes the employer has the authority to approve all claims up to a certain size and to draw drafts on the insurer with respect to the approved claims.

The Blue Cross or Blue Shield procedure is similar if the insured goes to a nonmember hospital or a nonparticipating physician. Otherwise, the procedure is simpler. The insured presents a subscriber's identification card or his or her contract to the doctor or hospital, which in turn completes the necessary claim forms and sends them to the appropriate medical expense association. The hospital or doctor bills the insured for the excess of the total bill over the medical-association payment. Because health maintenance organizations are the actual providers of all or most of the medical care provided under their contracts, the insured is simply not billed for covered services.

Medical payments losses under liability insurance contracts are not subject to the standard provisions under individual health insurance, but the liability contracts do provide for prompt notice to the insurer, written proof of loss, examinations by physicians selected by the insurer and authorization for the insurer to obtain pertinent medical reports, permission for the insurer to pay directly the person or organization providing the medical services, and suits against the insurer.

Workers' compensation and automobile no-fault claims resemble health insurance claims in some respects and liability claims in others. For example, workers' compensation claims are like health insurance claims in that (1) if the circumstances surrounding the injury or disease satisfy certain criteria (established in this instance by the workers' compensation law of the state), the claim is to be paid; (2) the insurer is directly and primarily responsible to the injured party; (3) the insurer may be sued directly by the injured party; and (4) the principal adjustment problems are the same as those to be discussed shortly for health insurance. On the other hand, they resemble liability insurance claims in that (1) the contract contains both a notice-of-injury provision and a notice-of-claim or suit provision; (2) the insured must assist and cooperate with the insurer in the handling of the claim; (3) failure of the insured to meet his or her obligations under the contract may give the insurer the right to recover from the insured the amounts paid to the injured party; and (4) the insurer possesses subrogation rights. All claims must be filed with the state workers' compensation board, and disagreements between the injured employee and the employer are handled first by a hearing before the board.

The key problem in adjusting claims involving accidental injuries and sickness is the subjectivity of many elements included in the claim. The insured may or may not be ill, the illness may or may not be disabling, the medical treatment may or may not be necessary, and the hospital and doctor bills may or may not be reasonable. An insured who was legitimately disabled for a time may be guilty of malingering, perhaps because of the insurance payments, or may truly not have recovered. The above statements are not meant to imply that the situation is hopeless for the insurer; relatively standard patterns can be expected with most illnesses. The insured, however, should appreciate the importance of an untarnished reputation and a cooperative attitude in securing a favorable hearing on his or her claim.

A FAIR SETTLEMENT

The objective of the loss adjustment is a fair and prompt settlement of the claim. Insureds should realize that it is as wrong for an insurer to overpay its claims as to underpay them. Overpayments will usually be reflected in increased insurance costs or in a weakened financial condition of the insurer.

Small losses that, strictly speaking, are not covered under the contract are paid by some insurers as nuisance claims. The loss in goodwill and the expenses of an extensive investigation are considered more costly than the claim itself. Other equally reputable insurers argue that this practice leads to a misunderstanding of the insurance coverage and can prove very costly if all insureds submit such claims.

Many insureds are disappointed by loss adjustments because they have not read their contracts. A loss the insured thought was covered under the contract is either excluded or not specifically included, or the contract limits the amount recovered to less than expected. These disappointments are best averted at the time the risk management program is designed and not at the time of the loss adjustment.

Other insureds will be disappointed because of honest disagreements concerning the circumstances of the losses and the interpretations of the contracts. If an insured is convinced that he or she is correct after continued discussions with the insurer and if this conviction is confirmed by some informed, objective third party, the insured should contact the state insurance department. If the department agrees with the insured, it may be able to force the insurer to act more favorably by moral suasion or by a threat to cancel its license to operate in the state. The insured may also resort to the legal remedies provided under the contract.

Still other insureds, whose ethics are normally unquestionable, tend to exaggerate their claims either (1) because they consider it smart and socially acceptable to collect excess amounts from the impersonal insurers (which, they point out, have been collecting much more in premiums from insureds than they have paid in losses), or (2) because they consider it necessary to ask for too much initially in order to receive fair settlements. The first attitude would be disastrous if it were adopted by everyone, and yet it is true that society does to a certain degree condone such procedures. The second attitude is unnecessary so far as most (but unfortunately not all) adjusters are concerned.

Some risk managers whose firms are experience-rated or retrospectively rated have accused insurance adjusters of loose and indifferent handling of claims because they have no incentive to keep costs down. Some insurers, on the other hand, point out that they are sometimes pressured to pay product liability and workers' compensation claims that they would have preferred to fight. Neither practice is in the long run in the best interest of the insurer or of the risk manager.

Often the insured is dissatisfied, not with the final settlement, but with the treatment received at the hands of the adjuster and the work he or she was asked to do. Some adjusters—but not most—are discourteous and overdemanding. In defense of some of the actions of adjusters, it should be noted that they deal with some insureds who are misinformed, uncooperative, or dishonest, even to the point of purposely causing the loss to make a profit on the insurance.[8] If the insured can erase at an early date any doubt the adjuster may have concerning the insured's motivations, the stage should be set for a more amicable and fair adjustment. If the insured and the insurer cannot reach an agreement, the courts will also look with more favor on the insured who has played the game openly, fairly, and intelligently.

SOME KEY CONCEPTS

Staff adjusters Loss adjusters who are salaried employees of the insurers they represent.
Independent adjuster A loss adjuster who, like an independent agent, sells his or her services to two or more insurers.
Public adjuster A loss adjuster who for a fee will represent the insured in settling a loss.
Proof of loss A form that must be submitted by the insured, except in connection with liability losses, providing information on the nature and extent of the loss and the claim being made.
Guiding Principles A set of rules adopted by most insurers to settle disputes involving overlapping property insurance coverages.

REVIEW QUESTIONS

1 With what types of loss adjusters may a risk manager have to deal? How do they differ?
2 When should a risk manager turn to a public adjuster for assistance in preparing a claim?
3 What is the insured obligated to do under a property insurance contract following a loss?
4 What is the most difficult problem encountered in adjusting property losses? How is the problem handled?
5 Why are the Guiding Principles important to risk managers?
6 A firm has a $40,000 fire insurance contract covering a $100,000 building. Because of the negligence of an employee of a neighboring firm, a fire starts that spreads to the insured's property causing a $60,000 loss.
   a How will the insured and the insurer handle this loss?
   b If, as a result of a suit, the insured and the insurer recover $50,000 from the neighboring firm, how will they share this $50,000?
7 If the insured and an insurer cannot agree upon the amount of property loss, what can they do?
8 Why are business risk managers especially interested in the settlement of liability claims?
9 Under the liability insurance contract, what is the insured obligated to do after an accident?
10 A firm has a bodily injury liability insurance contract with a limit of $50,000 per accident. An injured person offers to settle a claim for $30,000 but threatens to sue for $80,000 if this

---

[8] For example, see "Insurance Companies, Cheated for Centuries, Are Still Being Taken," *The Wall Street Journal* (Dec. 23, 1974), p. 1.

offer is refused. The insurer prefers to refuse the offer. What is the situation if the injured party sues and wins?

11 One firm has a liability claim against another firm that the risk manager of the first firm knows is insured by a particular insurer. The vice-president of the risk manager's firm suggests that the firm sue the insurer in court. What will probably be the risk manager's reply?

12 "Life insurance claims adjusting is trouble-free." Comment upon this statement.

13 Many of the mandatory standard provisions in a health insurance contract deal with the obligations of the insured and the insurer following a loss. What are these obligations?

14 a In what respects do workers' compensation loss adjustments resemble health insurance loss adjustments?

   b In what respects do workers' compensation loss adjustments resemble liability insurance loss adjustments?

15 How do the claims adjustment procedures vary among commercial medical expense insurers, Blue Cross and Blue Shield associations, and HMOs?

16 What in your opinion is a "fair" settlement of a claim?

17 Why is a firm that is experience-rated or retrospectively rated directly concerned about its insurer's claims practices?

SUGGESTIONS FOR ADDITIONAL READINGS

Donaldson, J. H.: *Casualty Claims Adjustment* (4th ed., Homewood, Ill.: Richard D. Irwin, Inc., 1984).

Johns, Corydon T.: *An Introduction to Liability Claims Adjusting* (3d ed., Cincinnati: National Underwriter Company, 1982).

Thomas, P. I.: *How to Estimate Building Losses and Construction Costs* (4th ed., Englewood Cliffs, N.J.: Prentice-Hall, Inc., 1983).

————, and P. B. Reed: *Adjustment of Property Losses* (4th ed., New York: McGraw-Hill Book Company, 1977).

Webb, B. L., J. J. Launie, W. P. Rokes, and N. A. Baglini: *Insurance Company Operations* (2d ed., Malvern, Pa.: American Institute for Property and Liability Underwriters, 1981), vol. II, chaps. 12–14.

CHAPTER 30

BUSINESS RISK MANAGEMENT— TWO ILLUSTRATIVE CASES: THE ABC CORPORATION AND ONE LARGE CORPORATION'S INSURANCE PROGRAM

LEARNING OBJECTIVES

After you have completed this chapter, you should be able to apply with more confidence the risk management concepts presented earlier in this text to hypothetical and real life business risk management problems.

INTRODUCTION

Most of this review chapter on business risk management applies many of the concepts presented in Chapters 3 to 29 to the risk management problems of a hypothetical medium-size firm. The reader should realize, however, that (1) a complete analysis would require much more space than is available in this chapter. Furthermore, (2) loss control should receive much more attention than it will receive in this case study, (3) the cost of the insurance relative to the benefits provided is also a much more important consideration, and (4) many equally appropriate or better solutions could have been suggested. In addition, in order to focus attention on the major concepts, the circumstances have been deliberately oversimplified. On the other hand, an illustrative case is the best way to review and integrate risk management concepts, and the authors believe that this case, despite its limitations, will serve that purpose.[1]

The second part of the chapter will present a brief summary of the property and liability insurance program of a larger real-life corporation with more diversified exposures.

---

[1] For other cases that illustrate the concepts presented in this text, see the suggestions for additional reading at the end of this chapter.

THE ABC CORPORATION

The business whose risk management problems are to be analyzed is the ABC Corporation, a small concern manufacturing automobile parts. Adams, the president, owns 60 percent of the stock: Brown, the vice-president, owns 20 percent; and Carlson, the secretary-treasurer, owns the remaining 20 percent.

The firm, which is located in the Midwest, owns one brick building, which houses all the manufacturing operations and the executive offices. This building, which was built 12 years ago at a cost of $360,000 plus the land, has three stories and a basement and provides 50,000 square feet of working space. The building has no automatic sprinklers. An appraisal firm has estimated that it would cost $600,000 to rebuild the building new today but that because of depreciation the actual cash value of the building is $480,000. A railroad siding is adjacent to the east side of the building, for which the firm has assumed liability under a fairly typical sidetrack agreement. A parking lot for 100 cars is located on the west side of the building. The remainder of the two acres owned by the firm is landscaped with trees, shrubs, and a lawn. The building is 200 feet from the street.

The firm also rents a brick building across the street as a warehouse for finished goods and as a garage for a fleet of five private passenger cars and 10 delivery trucks. The actual cash value of the warehouse is $240,000. Each private passenger car and truck could be replaced in the used-car market for $6,000 and $14,000, respectively. Equivalent new private passenger cars and trucks would each cost $10,000 and $20,000, respectively. The rent under a lease that has five years to run is $1,200 a month, but the firm estimates that the value of equivalent premises would be $2,400 at today's rentals.

The firms sells its products only to wholesalers and manufacturers. Sales have remained fairly stable over the years and do not fluctuate seasonally. These sales create a sizable dollar volume of accounts receivable. About 80 percent of the sales are made to customers within a radius of 50 miles; deliveries are usually made by employees driving the firm's own vehicles. The deliveries to other areas are made by motortruck or rail common carriers. No shipments are made outside the United States.

The machinery in the factory would cost $240,000 to replace with new machinery, but its value in its depreciated condition is only $192,000. The furniture would cost $50,000 to replace new, but because of depreciation its actual cash value is only $25,000. Raw materials, goods in process, and finished goods are valued as shown in the balance sheet.

The firm has some valuable papers including some specifications for its machinery, but the cost to reproduce these papers is estimated at less than $10,000.

The firm has 60 employees, about 30 of whom are involved in the manufacturing process. The others are the officers, the office force, warehouse employees, and salespersons. One of the employees is a key engineer, aged 40, whose ingenuity has been largely responsible for the success of the firm. Salespersons drive company cars in their work. The annual payroll is $1,200,000; payments by check are made biweekly. Because of a labor shortage in its locality, the firm would prefer to continue its employees on the payroll during a shutdown of two months or less. Otherwise, it would consider dropping about one-half of the employees, for whom the annual payroll amounts to $420,000.

The firm has been slow to modernize its bookkeeping and secretarial operations, but it expects to purchase electronic data processing equipment within the next year.

TABLE 30.1
ABC CORPORATION BALANCE SHEET, DECEMBER 31, 1984

Assets			
Current assets:			
Cash		$ 20,000	
Accounts receivable	$230,000		
Reserve for doubtful accounts	20,000	210,000	
Inventories			
Finished goods	120,000		
Goods in process	100,000		
Raw materials	40,000	260,000	
Supplies on hand			
Factory and shipping supplies	6,000		
Stationery and supplies	4,000	10,000	$ 500,000
Plant and equipment:			
Building	$360,000		
Reserve for depreciation ($10,000/year)	120,000	$240,000	
Machinery and equipment	120,000		
Reserve for depreciation ($10,000/year)	20,000	100,000	
Furniture and fixtures	40,000		
Reserve for depreciation ($4,000/year)	20,000	20,000	
Motor vehicles	200,000		
Reserve for depreciation ($20,000/year)	80,000	120,000	
Goodwill		20,000	500,000
Total assets			$1,000,000
Liabilities			
Current liabilities:			
Accounts payable		$200,000	
Mortgage on building		140,000	$ 340,000
Stockholders' equity			
Capital stock		$240,000	
Retained earnings		420,000	660,000
Total liabilities and equity			$1,000,000

The most recent balance sheet and income statements are presented as Tables 30.1 and 30.2.

Risk Analysis

On the basis of the financial statements and other information regarding the firm's operations, the risk manager should, as a first step, list in some orderly fashion the potential losses to which the firm is subject and provide some measures by which they may be evaluated. No attempt will be made here to perform a complete risk analysis, but the approach will be indicated by recognizing most of the potential losses faced by the firm and by listing for each kind of loss the maximum possible loss in dollars. The maximum loss is assumed to be a total loss unless otherwise indicated. The possible causes of loss or perils and the probabilities of the various losses are not stated. The analysis, which relates to this particular firm the loss exposures discussed in Chapters 5 to 9, is outlined in Table 30.3. The table is sufficiently self-contained not to require any further discussion, but the reader is reminded that the balance sheet values are used only when they are not in conflict with the values in the text and that the insured can incur several types of loss at the same time or during the same year. For example, one fire could cause the corporation to lose its main building and all its contents, suspend operations for six months, and pay employees substantial workers' compensation benefits. The firm could sustain at least one major fire and one major windstorm loss the same year.

What losses are important to the firm? Some important considerations are (1) the cash on hand ($20,000), (2) the ability of the firm to meet its current debt; i.e., its net working capital (cash + accounts receivable + inventories and supplies − accounts payable, or $20,000 + $210,000 + $270,000, the $500,000 of current assets, less $200,000, or $300,000), (3) net "quick" assets (cash + accounts receivable − accounts payable, or $20,000 + $210,000 − $200,000, or $30,000), (4) the net worth ($660,000), (5) the net profit ($100,000), and (6) the annual cash flow (net profit +

TABLE 30.2
ABC CORPORATION: INCOME STATEMENT FOR THE 12
MONTHS ENDED DECEMBER 31, 1984*

Sales	$2,750,000
Less returns and allowances	150,000
Net sales	2,600,000
Less cost of raw stock used in production	560,000
Gross earnings	2,040,000
Less payroll	1,200,000
Less other expenses	700,000
Net operating profit	140,000
Less provision for income taxes	40,000
Net profit	$ 100,000

* The information in the usual profit and loss statement has been rearranged in order to simplify the presentation.

TABLE 30.3
ABC CORPORATION: RISK ANALYSIS

Type of loss	Maximum possible loss	
	Actual cash value	Replacement cost new
Property losses:		
Main building	$480,000	$600,000
Raw materials	40,000	40,000
Goods in process	100,000	$100,000
Finished goods		
In main plant or warehouse	60,000	60,000
In transit	60,000	60,000
Machinery	192,000	240,000
Furniture and fixtures	25,000	50,000
Supplies	10,000	10,00u
Motor vehicles		
Private passenger cars	30,000	50,000
Trucks	140,000	200,000
Cash	20,000	20,000
Debris removal costs	20,000	20,000
Reproduction of valuable papers	10,000	10,000
Net income losses:		
Loss of net profits and continuing expenses during shutdown of manufacturing operations	Assuming 6 months as a maximum possible shutdown period, half of gross earnings ($2,040,000) less noncontinuing expenses, estimated at $400,000	
Loss of customers after resumption following shutdown	Difficult to estimate, but assumed to be small	
Leasehold interest	$1,200 a month for remainder of 5 years starting as of date of loss	
Inability to collect on accounts receivable	$210,000	

* If the ABC Corporation had on its premises patterns or dies belonging to its customers, an important bailee liability exposure would exist.

† If the corporation had assumed responsibility under the lease on the warehouse for negligent acts of the landlord or under sales agreements for negligent acts of its customers, two more important contractual liability exposures would exist.

depreciation expense, or $100,000 + $44,000, or $144,000). The importance of each of these amounts depends upon the risk management objectives described in Chapter 1. For example, if mere survival is the objective, the firm cannot afford to lose an amount close to or equal to its net worth of $660,000. Indeed, loss of an amount equal to its net working capital of $300,000 might so impair its liquidity as to force the firm to close its doors. If the objective is to limit fluctuations in annual earnings to 10 percent a year, a loss exceeding .10 ($100,000) or $10,000 would be serious but not catastrophic.

TABLE 30.3 (continued)

	Maximum possible loss	
Type of loss	**Actual cash value**	**Replacement cost new**
Liability losses:		
Liability for damage to warehouse and garage*	$240,000 plus $2,400 a month rent for 8 months maximum replacement time	
Premises—operations		
Main building		
Warehouse and garage		
Operations on and off premises	Unlimited	
Contract†		
Sidetrack agreement		
Product (auto parts)		
Independent contractors		
Fiduciary (Employee Retirement Income Security Act)	Difficult to estimate but substantial	
Automobiles		
Owned vehicles		
Borrowed or hired vehicles	Unlimited; subject in some states to automobile no-fault statutes	
Employee autos used on company business		
Employer	Benefits specified in workers' compensation statutes	
Personnel losses:		
To employees:		
Losses of earning power and unexpected expenses caused by	Difficult to estimate, but firm is only partly responsible, and needs are usually dictated by agreement with the union	
Death		
Poor health		
Old age		
Unemployment		
To the firm:		
Loss of profits or replacement costs resulting from death or long-term disability of the key engineer	Half of annual profits, or $50,000 for 3 years until replacement can be obtained and trained	
Liquidation losses if a stockholder dies or becomes disabled for a long period	Difficult to estimate, but could be forced to sell assets at one-half of their book value	

Selection of Tools

Once the risk manager has defined the problem and the firm's objectives, he or she must decide which tool or combination of the basic tools—avoidance, loss control, combination or separation, transfer, and retention—to use to handle the risks involved. Although it would be possible to use statistical decision theory to make this selection in the manner described in Chapters 13 and 14, enough has probably already been said about this approach, given the present state of the art. Instead, the insurance method described in the first part of Chapter 13 will be the primary method used. First, the insurance contracts that seem to meet best the problems of this firm will be divided into three groups in order of decreasing priority—essential, desirable, and available—according to the criteria outlined in Chapter 13. Each contract will then be considered separately in order to determine whether some other tool would offer a more satisfactory approach to the problem.

Initial Listing of Insurance Coverages The initial listing of *essential* insurance contracts includes the coverages that either are required by some outside party or protect the insured against losses that would threaten the continued existence of the firm. Although a special multi-peril policy may be the best way for the business to obtain several of these coverages, separate contracts will be used in this initial listing to permit a more detailed analysis of the relative importance of various types of insurance. The *essential* coverages include the following:

1 *Workers' compensation insurance.* This insurance is required by law. Even if this were not the case, workers' compensation insurance should be essential insurance because of the potential severity of job-related injuries and diseases.

2 *Group life, group health, and pension benefits.* These benefits are required under a contract with a union representing the factory employees. It will be assumed that the firm recognizes that it must protect the other employees in a similar fashion or it will lose them. Some features of the ABC Corporation employee benefit plan are described at the close of this chapter.

3 *Fire and extended coverage insurance* equal to the actual cash value of the building owned by the firm and the contents of that building and the rented building. The mortgagee requires this insurance on the main building. The potential losses to the other items are sizable enough to threaten the continued existence of the firm. In order to reduce the rate but allow some margin for an increase in value, the insurance on the building would be written on a 80 or 90 percent coinsurance basis. Because the total contents value is fairly stable, a reporting form is not necessary, but a blanket policy covering the contents at both the owned and rented locations would be highly desirable because the proportion of the finished goods at each location fluctuates markedly. It may be possible, however, to reduce the premium by placing separate amounts of insurance on the machinery, the inventory, and the furniture and fixtures.

4 *Earthquake insurance and flood insurance.* The reason for including these coverages is the high severity of the losses that might be caused by these perils.

5 *Business interruption insurance,* which will pay losses arising out of damage to the owned property arising out of fire or extended coverage perils. The gross earnings form with a 50 percent coinsurance clause and no payroll endorsements would be desirable because of the estimated maximum shutdown and the nature of the payroll. The amount of insurance should be 0.50 (gross earnings shown in Table 30.2), or 0.50 ($2,040,000) = $1,020,000 plus some safety margin in case the gross earnings increase.

6 *Boiler and machinery insurance.* On the assumption that a boiler explosion would not affect more than one-quarter of the values at the main location and no other premises, a policy limit of $400,000 should be sufficient to take care of the most important direct property losses. The policy should be endorsed to cover business interruption losses of the same amount as the other business interruption insurance.

7 *Primary commercial blanket bond* as part of a comprehensive destruction, disappearance, and dishonesty policy. The proper limit for this fidelity bond is difficult to determine but a formula suggested by the Surety Association of America is often used as a guide: Under this formula the first step is to calculate a dishonesty exposure index as follows: (1) 5 percent of the inventories plus (2) 20 percent of the other current assets plus (3) 10 percent of net sales.[2] For the ABC Corporation this index is 0.05 ($260,000) + 0.20 ($240,000) + 0.10 ($2,750,000), or $336,000. The second step is to obtain the recommended limit from a table prepared by the association. For an exposure index of $336,000, the recommended limit is between $75,000 and $100,000. Given the nature of the inventory, a much higher loss is possible.

8 *Comprehensive general liability insurance.* Liability losses have an unlimited potential. The comprehensive form was selected because the firm has several of the common sources of liability and may develop the others. As Chapter 19 indicated, the CGL policy provides automatic coverage for new sources of liability the firm may develop during the policy period, but the premium is based only on the exposures actually developed. The policy should cover personal injury liability, not just bodily injury liability. Recent court awards in the state in which the firm is located indicate that the personal injury liability limits should be at least $2 million per occurrence and the property damage limits at least $400,000 per accident.

9 *Fiduciary liability insurance* to cover the employer's fiduciary obligations under the Employee Retirement Income Security Act. Although this insurance is not required by ERISA, the potential loss to those directors and officers involved as fiduciaries could be extremely large. ERISA does require that, subject to certain exceptions, all persons who handle plan assets be covered under a *fiduciary bond.*

10 *Business auto liability insurance.* Liability losses again have an unlimited potential. The BAP should cover the ownership, maintenance, or use of any auto. Owned car, hired car, and nonownership liability exposures already exist. The policy limits should be the same as those for the CGL policy.

11 *Insurance to fund a buy-and-sell agreement* that is to operate if one of the owners dies. The corporation is to own the policies. The insurance on Adams is to be 60 percent of the present agreed valuation, the insurance on Brown, 20 percent, and the insurance on Carlson, 20 percent. The valuation at the date of death is to be determined by a trustee, the difference between the final valuation and the present agreed valuation to be paid directly by the survivors in installments over a period of 10 years. The present agreed valuation is $1,000,000, which exceeds the book value because the owners agree that the book value understates the asset values, including goodwill.

The *desirable* coverages are designed to handle those losses that would cause the

---

[2] Peter A. Zimmerman, "Proper Limits for Fidelity Bonds," AMA Insurance Series no. 114 (New York: American Management Association, 1957), pp. 49–55. Also see *How Much Dishonesty Insurance?* (New York: The Surety Association of America, 1956). In a May 14, 1979 letter to one of the authors, a Surety Association representative stated that the formula is still appropriate.

firm serious economic distress but would probably not force the owners to cease operations. The following contracts fall in this category:

1 *Vandalism insurance,* added by endorsement to the fire insurance policy on the owned building, its contents, and the contents of the rented building. Vandalism is unfortunately a frequent peril. Its consequences can be very great, but it has a smaller potential than, for example, windstorm or explosion.

2 *Accounts receivable insurance* in an amount sufficient to satisfy the minimum coinsurance requirements. The importance of this insurance depends upon whether the firm has a few accounts that it is likely to collect or many accounts that would be extremely difficult to collect. This firm is assumed to face the possibility that enough accounts would be affected to cause a serious loss.

3 *Automobile comprehensive and collision insurance* equal to the actual cash value of the owned motor vehicles. A loss to any single vehicle, especially the private passenger cars, is likely to be small, but several vehicles may be involved in the same accident or in accidents in a single year.[3]

4 *Cargo insurance,* covering shipments in the insured's own trucks or while in the hands of a common carrier. The limits depend upon the maximum value shipped in each vehicle.

5 Three of the five coverages included in the comprehensive destruction, disappearance, and dishonesty policy—*money and securities coverage on and off premises* and *depositor's forgery coverage* plus endorsements to cover *payroll robbery* and *mercantile open-stock burglary.* The fidelity bond that can be part of this policy has already been listed as an essential coverage. The money and securities coverage limit should be set at the level at which these assets are commonly kept on the premises, the payroll coverage being designed to handle the periodic payroll exposure. If this limit is low, the money and securities coverage should be shifted to the available category. The depositor's forgery coverage is also difficult to classify; it would depend upon such factors as the nature of the check-signing authority, the maximum check amount written, and the frequency with which bank statements are checked. The mercantile open-stock coverage should equal the coinsurance limit to avoid a coinsurance penalty, but excess losses are very unlikely.

6 *Replacement cost insurance* on the owned building, written as an endorsement to the fire insurance contract and converting that contract from an actual cash value basis to a replacement cost new basis. Some analysts would consider this insurance to be essential insurance because the loss that is covered would be accompanied by other losses with high potential such as the actual cash value of the building and contents and possible interruption of operations. Replacement cost insurance is placed in the serious category here because the risk manager may not want to place the same emphasis on the difference between the replacement cost new and the actual cash value of the loss as on the actual cash value itself.

7 *Leasehold interest insurance* to protect against the loss of $1,200 per month for the remainder of the 5-year lease. In real life, few insureds purchase this form of

---

[3] If the fleet is financed through a bank or other lending agency, physical damage insurance may be required, making this coverage essential.

insurance. This firm, however, faces a larger loss than is typical relative to the size of its operations. Each month that passes without a fire, however, reduces the possible loss.

8 *Fire legal liability insurance,* with a limit of $260,000 per accident because this approximates the value of the rented building plus the landlord's rent loss.

9 *Insurance to fund a buy-and-sell agreement,* which is to operate if one of the owners is totally and permanently disabled. The need for this agreement is deemed to be a little less critical than if one of the owners dies, but this division, like many other features of this analysis, is debatable.

10 *Life insurance on the key engineer,* with a total and permanent disability rider attached. The policy amount should be at least $100,000.

The *available* coverages include all those coverages that might be of some value to the business but that do not fall in the first two categories. Usually they deal with losses that are likely to be small or are highly predictable. This list could be very extensive; some illustrative items are the following:

1 Glass insurance
2 Water damage insurance
3 Extra expense insurance
4 Valuable papers insurance
5 Credit insurance
6 Depositor's forgery coverage on incoming instruments
7 Water damage liability insurance

Revised List   Once the risk manager has listed the potential losses, the second step in the analysis is to determine which of these losses could be better handled through some noninsurance method. Avoidance will not be considered in this analysis. Abandonment, it is assumed, is not possible, and the other, more common form of avoidance is applicable only with respect to risks that have not yet been assumed, not those that already exist.[4] Combination can also be ignored because it is assumed that no mergers are contemplated and that the size of the firm is fairly stable. This leaves, then, for consideration loss control, noninsurance transfers, and retention.

With respect to the *essential* coverages, some opportunities may exist for loss control. It is extremely doubtful that these efforts can reduce the severity of the insured losses to such an extent that the classification of the insurance as essential will be changed, but safety measures may reduce significantly the insurance premium or the cost of retaining the losses. Although no more will be said about loss control here, the possibility of reducing expected losses or their variability through this tool should always be carefully considered.

Opportunities to transfer any of the insured losses in this essential category through some noninsurance device appear to be lacking, but this possibility should also be explored.

---

[4] Disposing of property exposed to loss is a definite possibility, but according to the definitions in this text, this disposal is an example of transfer, not of avoidance.

The classification of these coverages as essential implies that it would not be wise for the corporation to retain the types of losses included under these contracts except under certain circumstances:

First, the policy limits may be less than the maximum possible loss because higher limits either are not available or their cost seems excessive to the corporation. In ABC's case unlimited liability insurance is assumed not to be available.

Second, despite the severity of the potential loss, the premium, using the worry method described in Chapter 13, may be much larger than the insured is willing to pay. For example, because of ABC's location a flood or an earthquake is unlikely, but the insurance premium may not reflect adequately this extremely low probability. We will assume here that ABC elects for this reason to retain its flood and earthquake exposures.

Third, some of the essential coverages may fall in this category solely because they are required by some other party, even though the potential losses are small or predictable. Perhaps this requirement can be relaxed.

Finally, the firm should consider seriously the possibility of using deductibles to retain small losses. More specifically, deductibles might be used advantageously with respect to the general liability insurance, the automobile liability insurance, the fire and extended coverage insurance, and the boiler and machinery insurance. Because the firm does not have enough exposure units to predict its losses within a narrow range, the deductible amount should be small, say, under $1,000. The exact amount will depend upon an analysis of the premiums, the willingness of the management to bear some risk, and the question of whether the deductible applies to each loss or to total losses during the year.

Noninsurance methods have more widespread application with respect to the *desirable* coverages. One specific illustration of a loss control measure that ABC should consider is the creation and storage at some other location of a duplicate set of accounts receivable records. We will assume that the firm decides to reduce the probability of an accounts receivable loss in this way and that, as a result, it does not consider accounts receivable insurance to be attractive at the price the insurer wishes to charge. Otherwise the observations made in the discussion of essential coverages with respect to loss-control activities are also applicable here. At least one noninsurance transfer device might be applicable. As we noted earlier, the firm could ask the owner of the warehouse and garage to excuse the firm under the lease from any responsibility for damage to the building as a result of fire or other specified perils. It may be reluctant to do so, however, because the landlord may take this opportunity to change the terms of what is now a favorable lease. Another possibility is to ask the landlord to have the firm named in the landlord's insurance contract on the building, but it will be assumed that the landlord's insurer is unwilling to do this. Retention is a possibility with respect to all the losses included under these desirable contracts, but the losses are serious enough to suggest insurance unless the (1) premiums are unreasonably high or (2) the risk management objective is mere survival and the firm is not inclined to worry about losses that do not threaten its survival. The firm is, of course, retaining losses in excess of the suggested policy limits. Self-insurance is not possible because the number of units is small, but the risk manager should consider small deductibles under the vandalism insurance and the dishonesty insurance. The automobile collision insurance should definitely be subject to some deductible, such as $1,000 per vehicle, because of the substantial premium savings. A smaller deductible should apply to the automobile comprehensive insurance because a fire, a windstorm, or some other peril can severely damage simultaneously several vehicles stored in the garage. Deductibles are not readily available under the other forms of property and liability insurance, but they should also be investigated. The disability income insurance on the owners should contain a waiting period of at least one month. Instead of purchasing replacement cost insurance the firm may prefer to finance the difference between the replacement cost new of the building and its actual cash value with long-term debt.

The case for insurance is least strong with respect to the *available* coverages. It will be assumed that this firm's loss-control activities can be effective enough in some of these areas to make retention attractive because the resulting maximum loss would be very small. This assumption will be made with respect to losses that would otherwise be covered under water damage insurance, water damage liability insurance, credit insurance, and depositor's forgery insurance. Because the losses that would be covered under the valuable papers insurance are unlikely to exceed $10,000, retention is feasible and desirable. Since the chance that the firm will incur any extra expenses in order to continue operating is small, this loss can be retained, but it should be recognized that the firm by this decision is retaining any loss of customers following a business interruption.[5] Glass insurance, on the other hand, is to be purchased because the price is reasonable and the firm values highly the replacement service.

Any losses for which insurance is not usually available, such as strike losses or war losses, must of course be retained, although it may be possible to reduce the expected losses through loss-control measures or some noninsurance transfers.

The Risk Management Program   The result of this analysis is the following combination of tools:

A Loss-control measures—probably the installation of automatic sprinklers, careful housekeeping, accounting controls, the duplication and separate storage of accounts receivable records, night guards, safety inspections of vehicles, annual physical examinations for the owners and key employees, and many other activities whose benefits at least offset their costs
B Retention
   1 Losses in excess of the limits of the insurance purchased
   2 Losses excluded under the insurance purchased
   3 Losses up to the deductible amounts under the automobile physical damage insurance plus any other deductibles selected by the risk manager
   4 Earthquake losses
   5 Flood losses
   6 Water damage losses

---

[5] This protection can be included under business interruption insurance, but it will be assumed here that this potential loss is retained.

7 Sprinkler leakage losses (unless the insurance is purchased following a decision to install sprinklers)

8 Cost of replacing valuable papers other than merely copying them from a preserved source

9 Forgery losses on incoming instruments

10 Theft of property other than money and securities that is not classified as either robbery or burglary

11 War losses

12 Loss of profits and continuing expenses during a shutdown of manufacturing operations as a result of a strike or any peril other than fire, the extended coverage perils, or accidents involving boilers and machinery

13 Loss of customers following resumption of business after a shutdown

14 Credit losses including those arising out of the destruction or disappearance of accounts receivable records

C Noninsurance transfers

  1 None

D Insurance

  1 First priority

    a Workers' compensation

    b Group life insurance, group health insurance, and a pension plan

    c Fire and extended coverage insurance on owned building and contents in both buildings

    d Business interruption insurance against fire and extended coverage perils

    e Primary commercial blanket fidelity bond

    f Boiler and machinery insurance, including business interruption insurance

    g Comprehensive general liability insurance

    h Fiduciary liability insurance and fiduciary bonds

    i Business automobile liability insurance covering any autos

    j Life insurance on owners in connection with a buy-and-sell agreement

  2 Second priority

    a Vandalism insurance

    b Automobile comprehensive and collision insurance

    c Transportation insurance

    d Comprehensive destruction, disappearance, and dishonesty policy, coverages other than a fidelity bond

    e Replacement cost insurance

    f Leasehold insurance

    g Fire legal liability insurance

    h Disability insurance to fund a buy-and-sell agreement

    i Life and disability insurance on key engineer

  3 Third priority

    a Glass insurance

Much of the property and liability insurance in this list can be obtained under the SMP policy. Without endorsements that contract will provide the fire and extended coverage insurance, $1,000 of extra expense insurance, replacement cost insurance if repair costs do not exceed $1,000, and broad general liability insurance. Through Sections III and IV the insured can obtain the equivalent of a comprehensive destruction, disappearance, and dishonesty policy and boiler and machinery insurance. Through endorsements the insured can add vandalism insurance, business interruption insurance, mercantile open-stock burglary insurance, replacement cost insurance, glass insurance, and comprehensive general liability insurance.

If the firm carries out its plan to install electronic data processing equipment, it should investigate the desirability of electronic data processing insurance.

The risk manager must also decide which insurer or insurers should underwrite the insurance sections of the program and how it should be placed. The considerations involved have been outlined earlier. If this firm has had very good loss experience, the risk manager would be well advised to make extensive use of experience- and retrospective-rating plans. The risk manager should also check on the firm's schedule rates to determine whether the insurer's evaluation of the firm's exposure is correct. The advance preparation that will be helpful if a loss does occur has been suggested earlier.

Employee Benefit Plan

The ABC Corporation employee benefit plan provides benefits when an employee dies, is injured or gets sick, or retires. The union is currently negotiating with the ABC Corporation on the addition of dental care benefits. In the future it intends to request as additional employee benefits automobile insurance, homeowner's insurance, and pre-paid legal expense benefits. It may instead investigate the feasibility and desirability of a flexible benefits plan. Some features of the current employee benefit plan are the following:

Death Benefits   All employees who have worked for the ABC Corporation for at least 3 months are covered under a survivor income benefit insurance plan. This plan pays the surviving spouse of a deceased worker 25 percent of the deceased's monthly earnings. If at least one child survives the benefit is increased to 40 percent. The spouse's benefit is paid until age 62, death, or remarriage, whichever comes first. The children's benefit continues as long as there is at least one child who is under age 19 and unmarried. Originally employees paid part of the cost of this program, but a few years ago the union argued that for tax reasons the employer should pay the entire cost.

Disability Income Benefits   After 3 months ABC employees are also covered under a noncontributory group temporary disability insurance program. If totally disabled, an employee will receive two-thirds of his or her weekly wages, but no more than $300, for up to 26 weeks. The benefits start immediately if the employee is injured in an accident, after 7 days if he or she becomes sick. Management employees are also covered under a contributory long-term disability insurance program. Under this LTD plan, after 6 months of total disability a covered employee will receive a monthly income equal to 60 percent of his or her most recent wage but not to exceed $2,000. This benefit will be reduced by amounts the worker receives from workers' compensation or Old-Age, Survivors, and Disability Insurance.

Medical Expense Benefits ABC employees and their families are eligible immediately for medical expense protection. The employer pays for the employee's insurance; the employee for dependents' insurance. The employee can choose between (1) a health maintenance organization plan and (2) a group hospital-medical-surgical insurance plan plus a supplementary major medical expense insurance plan with a $100 corridor deductible and a $500,000 maximum benefit.

Pensions Employees are covered under an insured pension plan when they reach age 25 or complete one year of service, whichever comes first. The benefit for production workers is $15 per month per year of service; for other workers 1½ percent of the worker's average annual pay during his or her final 5 years times the number of years of service. Under both plans no employer-purchased benefits are vested during the first 10 years, after which time these benefits are 100 percent vested. The union intends to seek a more liberal vesting provision within the next two or three years.

The normal retirement age is 65. Employees can retire as early as age 55 at an actuarially reduced benefit. Employees who continue to work after age 65 do not increase their monthly pension except to the extent that their continued employment increases their final pay.

ABC's personnel office administers the program, which is a noncontributory, fully funded, insured deposit administration plan. The union would prefer joint administration.

Until the Employee Retirement Income Security Act was passed in 1974, the ABC plan was much less liberal. Employees were not covered, regardless of age, until they had worked for ABC for 5 years. No benefits were vested until the employee had participated under the plan for 20 years. The plan was also not fully funded. The plan assets were also more heavily invested in common stocks than is currently true.

A Reminder

It is important at the conclusion of this analysis to repeat what was said at the beginning of this discussion concerning the nature, purpose, and limitations of the analysis. The analysis is not perfect nor complete, and alternative solutions may be better than the one suggested.[6] On the other hand, the case does review and integrate many of the concepts described earlier and illustrates how these concepts can be applied to actual situations.

A SECOND ILLUSTRATIVE CASE: ONE LARGE CORPORATION'S INSURANCE PROGRAM

The ABC Corporation was a hypothetical medium-sized corporation with modest retention possibilities and a fairly standard insurance program. This second case treats more briefly the insurance component of the risk management program of a larger real

[6] For example, one alternative solution might include the special building form and special personal property form described on pp. 329–330.

TABLE 30.4
XYZ CORPORATION SUMMARY BALANCE SHEETS (IN MILLIONS)

	19x4	19x3	19x2	19x1	19x0
Assets					
Current assets	$ 681	$ 625	$507	$378	$377
Property, plant, equipment	486	429	366	349	304
Other assets	116	85	74	66	60
Total assets	$1,283	$1,139	$947	$793	$741
Liabilities					
Current liabilities	$ 457	$ 408	$313	$247	$262
Long-term debt	298	267	228	244	217
Deferred taxes and other deferrals	71	57	48	36	25
Total liabilities	$ 826	$ 732	$589	$527	$504
Stockholders' equity	$ 457	$ 407	$358	$266	$237

life corporation which makes more extensive use of retention. To conceal the identity of the corporation the facts have been altered slightly.

The XYZ Corporation is a large, diversified multinational company. In addition to manufacturing a wide variety of products, XYZ operates numerous retail outlets. At present, 19x5, XYZ has 44,300 employees, 1,530 vehicles, and 152 barges.

Summary balance sheets and income statements for 19x0–19x4 are presented in Table 30.4 and Table 30.5.

A summary of XYZ's 19x5 insurance program is presented in Table 30.6. Particularly noteworthy are the following:

1 The high cost of workers' compensation insurance as measured by the standard premium, even with a $500,000 per occurrence deductible. The steps taken to reduce

TABLE 30.5
XYZ CORPORATION SUMMARY OF EARNINGS (IN MILLIONS EXCEPT PER SHARE AMOUNTS)

	19x4	19x3	19x2	19x1	19x0
Revenues	$1,724	$1,538	$1,484	$1,362	$1,136
Costs and expenses	1,582	1,414	1,377	1,280	1,073
Earnings before taxes on income	$ 142	$ 124	$ 107	$ 82	$ 63
Taxes on income	71	61	54	40	31
Earnings from continuing businesses	$ 71	$ 63	$ 53	$ 42	$ 32
After-tax earnings loss from discontinued businesses	1	—	(8)	(2)	2
Net earnings	$ 72	$ 63	$ 45	$ 40	$ 34
Average number of shares outstanding	17.5	17.4	16.4	15.4	15.4
Net earnings per share	$ 4.14	$ 3.59	$ 2.77	$ 2.58	$ 2.20

TABLE 30.6
SUMMARY OF XYZ CORPORATION'S EARLY 19x5 INSURANCE PROGRAM

Policy	Limit	Deductible	Premium
Workers' compensation	Unlimited except for $100,000 per occurrence on employers' liability coverage	$500,000 per occurrence on workers' compensation claims	$7,500,000*
General liability			
Bodily injury	$500,000 per occurrence, aggregate	$300,000 per occurrence on product liability only	555,000*
Property damage	$500,000 per occurrence, aggregate		
Automobile liability	$1 million per occurrence		310,000*
Umbrella liability	$50 million per occurrence		365,000
Property	About $20 million purchased in five different layers from nine insurers		
Highly protected property		$250,000 per occurrence	355,000 net
Other property		$250,000 per occurrence	701,000
Aircraft hull and liability			35,000
Directors and officers liability			40,000
Fidelity bond		$100,000 per occurrence	50,000
Ocean marine		$50,000 per occurrrence	500,000
Travel accident			16,000

* Standard premiums (premiums XYZ would have paid under experience rating before the application of premium discounts). As explained below, the actual premium paid is expected to be much less.

this cost and that of the general liability and automobile liability insurance will be explained below.

2 The presence of an umbrella liability insurance policy which provides excess coverage over the basic general liability and automobile liability insurance contracts.

3 The absence of automobile physical damage insurance. This exposure is completely retained.

4 The purchase of property insurance in five layers of protection as follows:
Layer 1, 2 insurers, $750,000 in excess of a $250,000 retention
Layer 2, 3 insurers, $1,750,000 in excess of $1,000,000
Layer 3, 1 insurer, $5,000,000 in excess of $2,750,000

Layer 4, 2 insurers, $4,400,000 in excess of $7,750,000
Layer 5, 1 insurer, $8,000,000 in excess of $12,150,000
5 The division of property insurance into insurance on highly protected property and other property.
6 The sizable premium paid for ocean marine insurance.

Each retail outlet is valued at about $250,000. Because the property insurance has a $250,000 per occurrence deductible, the complete destruction of a retail outlet by a fire would cost XYZ $250,000. The complete destruction of two or more such outlets by a tornado would also cost XYZ $250,000, the other $250,000 being covered by insurance. A $200,000 loss to one retail outlet in January followed by a $150,000 loss to a second retail outlet in August would cost XYZ $350,000 because the $250,000 deductible is applied separately to each occurrence.

XYZ has a "paid loss-retro" plan with the insurer that writes its workers' compensation, general liability, and automobile liability insurance; this plan greatly reduces the expected cost of this insurance below the standard premiums noted earlier. Under this plan the maximum premium is 150 percent of the standard premium subject to the plan. The premium subject to the plan is the sum of the standard premiums for the three coverages included under the plan, $8,365,000, less $40,000 paid for excess insurance not covered under the plan. The minimum premium is 50 percent and the basic premium 10 percent. The loss conversion factor is 1.162. A key feature of the plan is that XYZ pays the insurer immediately only the basic premium—this year $832,500 plus the $40,000 premium for the excess insurance. At the end of this policy year and each successive year XYZ is obligated to pay the insurer only the amount the insurer pays out that year in losses and loss adjustment expenses because of accidents charged to that policy year. XYZ assumes that it can earn 15 percent on the money it invests in its operations instead of paying all of the premium in advance. Consequently, unless the retrospective premium either exceeds the maximum premium or is less than the minimum premium, an unlikely event, the net present cost of the insurance for this policy year is the present value of the after-tax cost of (1) the excess insurance premium, (2) the basic premium, (3) the paid losses, (4) the paid loss-adjustment expenses, and (5) a special interest charge levied by the insurer because it does not collect premiums in advance of its loss and loss-adjustment expense payouts.

To compare this cost with the $8,365,000 standard premium requires certain assumptions about total losses and loss-adjustment expenses and their distribution over time. One illustration, believed to be the most plausible, assumes that accidents during the policy period would cause the insurer to pay out over the next nine years losses and loss-adjustment expenses totalling almost $8 million. Almost one-quarter of this amount would be paid during the first year, 21 percent during the second year, and 11 percent during the third year. The remainder would be spread over the next six years with only 1 percent being paid during the ninth year. At 15 percent interest, the present value of these expenditures would be only about $5.4 million. The insurer's interest charge is about $250,000 payable six years later; the present cost of this charge, assuming a 15 percent discount factor, is about $116,000. Under this assumption, therefore, the present value of all five before-tax-costs—excess insurance, base premium, paid losses, paid loss-adjustment expenses, and the special interest charge—

would be about $6.4 million. Because of some very important tax arrangements, which are too complicated to detail here, tax savings would reduce these costs even further.

REVIEW QUESTIONS

1 Criticize the risk management program developed for the ABC Corporation in this chapter.

2 Prepare an alternative risk management program for the ABC Corporation, and compare it with the program suggested in this chapter.

3 One aspect of the suggested risk management program for the ABC Corporation that was left somewhat indefinite was the use of deductibles in the property insurance contracts. How would you advise the ABC Corporation on this point?

4 In what ways did the Employee Retirement Income Security Act increase the cost of the ABC Corporation pension plan?

5 Prepare a risk management program for some firm in which you are interested.

6 Evaluate the XYZ Corporation insurance program and suggest how it might be improved.

SUGGESTIONS FOR ADDITIONAL READING

Greene, Mark R., and Oscar N. Serbein: *Risk Management: Text and Cases* (2d ed., Reston, Va.: Reston Publishing Company, 1983).

Howard, W. M.: *Cases on Risk Management* (New York: McGraw-Hill Book Company, 1967).

Malecki, Donald S., James H. Donaldson, and Ronald C. Horn: *Commercial Liability Risk Management and Insurance,* vol. II (Malvern, Pa.: American Institute for Property and Liability Underwriters, 1978), chaps. 14 and 15.

Mehr, R. I., and B. A. Hedges: *Risk Management in the Business Enterprise* (Homewood, Ill.: Richard D. Irwin, Inc., 1963), part VI.

Rodda, W. H., J. S. Trieschmann, E. A. Wiening, and B. A. Hedges: *Commercial Property Risk Management and Insurance* (2d ed., Malvern, Pa.: American Institute for Property and Liability Underwriters, 1983), chaps. 1, 2, and 16.

Rosenbloom, J. S.: *A Case Study in Risk Management* (Englewood Cliffs, N.J.: Prentice-Hall, Inc., 1972).

G. International Risk Management

CHAPTER 31

FOREIGN LOSS EXPOSURES AND THEIR TREATMENT

LEARNING OBJECTIVES

After you have completed this chapter, you should be able to:

1 Explain the factors influencing the degree of centralization of international risk management.

2 Describe how foreign loss exposures may differ from those in the United States.

3 Distinguish between admitted and nonadmitted insurance, and describe the advantages and disadvantages of each type.

4 Tell what insurance is available against political risks and foreign exchange risks.

5 List the special advantages of captive insurers in international risk management.

6 Describe why the employee benefits provided by a multinational corporation are likely to vary among employees at different locations.

INTRODUCTION

Up to this point, this text has dealt almost exclusively with loss exposures located in the United States, and their treatment. Increasingly, United States businesses and other organizations have loss exposures in other countries as well as at home. Some companies have a limited number of foreign operations; others are multinational corporations with a widespread network of international affiliates. Managing the international loss exposures of these firms requires basically the same skills and knowledge as managing United States loss exposures, but some additional problems require special handling and abilities. This brief chapter introduces the reader to some of these special problems. The topics to be considered are (1) organization for international risk management, (2) differences in loss exposures, (3) admitted versus nonadmitted insurance, (4) insurance against political risks and foreign exchange risks, (5) the use of retention, especially captive insurers, and (6) international employee benefits management.[1]

ORGANIZATION FOR INTERNATIONAL RISK MANAGEMENT

The existence of foreign exposures may significantly affect how a business organizes its risk management division and its administrative policies and practices. The key issue is the degree to which the United States risk manager has the authority and responsibility to manage loss exposures abroad.

By 1980, according to the Risk and Insurance Management Society survey cited in Chapter 2, 60 percent of the respondents with significant operations outside the United States described their international risk management as centralized.[2] Furthermore, over one-third expected more centralization by 1985; only 10 percent expected less centralization. In Dr. Norman Baglini's study of global risk management, based on a 1980 survey of 142 United States international corporations, 84 percent of the respondents considered their company's risk and insurance management program to be centralized.[3]

The degree of centralization, however, may be less than these percentages suggest. For example, only 14 percent of Dr. Baglini's respondents reported that their risk management programs were basically the same in foreign affiliates as in the United States.[4] About 41 percent differed in how they finance losses at home and abroad; about 16 percent paid less attention abroad to loss control. The remaining 30 percent said that the decision-making authority of the risk manager was stronger with respect to United States operations than to foreign operations. The respondents expected these differences to decrease in the future.

Centralization, however, is not always the best approach. Indeed, complete centralization is unlikely for a variety of reasons. Factors that influence the degree of centralization are:[5]

1 Whether the corporate parent has a worldwide staff for other functions, has a separate international division, or treats affiliates as autonomous profit centers

---

[1] For a more extensive discussion of international risk management, see Norman A. Baglini, *Risk Management in International Corporations* (New York: Risk Studies Foundation, 1976), Donald L. MacDonald, *Risk Control in the Overseas Operation of American Corporations,* Michigan International Business Studies, no. 15 (Ann Arbor: Division of Research, Graduate School of Business Administration, The University of Michigan, 1979), and Norman A. Baglini, *Global Risk Management* (New York: Risk Management Society Publishing, Inc., 1983). The authors have relied heavily on these studies, especially on Dr. Baglini's 1983 study, in preparing this chapter.

[2] *The Present Status and Future Role of Risk Management: A Survey of U.S. Risk Managers,* conducted by The Risk and Insurance Management Society, Inc., and *Time* magazine, April, 1981, p. 11.

[3] Baglini, *Global Risk Management,* p. 22.

[4] Ibid., pp. 5–8, 98–99.

[5] Baglini, *Risk Management in International Corporations,* pp. 48, 63–65.

2 The degree to which the parent has operating control over affiliates, which depends in part upon whether the parent has a controlling interest in each affiliate

3 The extent to which the legal, economic, political, and social environments vary among the host countries and the United States

4 The quality of the United States risk management department and its ability to provide high quality services to foreign affiliates

5 The quality of corporate staff specialists in related areas such as loss control, financial analysis, and taxes

6 Whether there are economies of scale in purchasing insurance and other risk management services

7 The potential for an integrated system to avoid gaps or overlaps

8 The extent to which the parent and affiliates exchange experience statistics and other data

To illustrate, a business is more likely to have a corporate worldwide risk strategy and a centralized risk management function if (1) it is a multinational corporation with a worldwide staff for other functions, (2) the parent has operating control of its affiliates, (3) the host countries have fairly similar legal, economic, political, and social environments, which do not differ dramatically from that of the United States, (4) the parent's risk management department is highly qualified to manage the loss exposures of the affiliates, (5) the parent has strong staff specialists in loss control, financial analysis, and taxes, (6) there are economies of scale in purchasing risk management services, (7) an integrated system would contribute greatly to the avoidance of gaps and overlaps, and (8) the parent and the affiliates exchange experience statistics and other data.

The parent may apply its worldwide risk management strategy in different ways to each affiliate. For example, the parent's risk manager may have complete responsibility and authority over a wholly owned Canadian affiliate. He or she may have little to say about the risk management affairs of a joint venture in Thailand.

POLICY STATEMENTS

One indication of the degree of centralization of the risk management function would be a risk management policy statement that applies to worldwide operations. In 1980 Dr. Baglini found that only about 61 percent of his respondents had *any* risk management policy statements. On the other hand, among those who did have such statements, about 70 percent applied their statements to both domestic and foreign operations. About 22 percent had separate statements for domestic and foreign operations. The remaining 8 percent had statements applicable to domestic operations.[6]

AREAS OF RESPONSIBILITY

Another measure of the degree of centralization of the risk management function is the degree of responsibility of the United States risk manager for various risk management

---

[6] Baglini, *Global Risk Management*, pp. 25, 26.

activities of foreign affiliates. Among the 1980 RIMS survey respondents with international exposures, almost 90 percent reported that the domestic risk management staff provided or coordinated advice on settling large losses.[7] About 69 percent said that their foreign subsidiaries participated in consolidated worldwide insurance programs for major coverages. About 55 percent expected corporate control over international insurance purchasing to increase by 1985; only 3 percent anticipated a decrease. However, only 52 percent of the United States risk managers provided or coordinated loss control services. On the basis of a 1974 survey, Baglini had concluded that international loss control was a much less common area of responsibility because (1) domestic loss control is also less likely to be an area of responsibility for the risk manager, (2) it is more difficult to administer loss control programs from abroad, and (3) foreign countries have up to the present placed less emphasis on loss control.[8]

In this earlier study Dr. Baglini also found that United States risk managers seldom had full responsibility for employee benefit plans in foreign affiliates. One reason is that the parent's personnel department may have full or shared responsibility for this risk management function. A second reason is that, in many countries, the nation's social security program is all or most of the employee benefit package for most employees. Finally, the diversity in employee benefit programs among nations may favor local management.

DIFFERENCES IN LOSS EXPOSURES

Foreign exposures, like domestic exposures, can be divided into (1) property—direct, indirect, and net income, (2) liability, and (3) personnel exposures, but the frequency and severity of these losses can vary greatly among nations. There are also two additional sources of loss: (1) political risks and (2) foreign exchange risks.

Difference in Frequency and Severity

Most losses are caused by essentially the same perils as domestic losses: (1) natural perils, (2) social perils, and (3) economic perils. Fires, windstorms, floods, earthquakes, sickness, theft, riots, vandalism, negligent acts, and personal failures or economic recessions that affect the ability of a business to pay its creditors are a few of the many perils with which international risk managers will have had experience at home.

The probability distribution of the potential losses from each peril may be considerably different for each affiliate.[9] Take, for example, the fire peril. The affiliates may be housed in many different structures or engaged in the manufacture or distribution of quite different products. The structures may differ because of variations in the building materials and skilled labor available, building codes, the climate, and building customs and traditions. The personal property may vary as to ignitibility, combustibility, and

---

[7] *The Present Status and Future Role of Risk Management*, p. 11. About 82 percent had at least one type of program consolidating domestic and foreign exposures such as consolidated insurance or a captive insurer.

[8] Baglini, *Risk Management in International Corporations*.

[9] For a detailed analysis of trends abroad in the peril of fire, theft, and legal liability, see MacDonald, op. cit., chaps. 3, 4, and 5.

damageability. The probability distributions may also be influenced by differences in the arson hazard and in the quality of the fire protection provided by the community and by the affiliate itself.

Some regions of the world are much more subject to floods, earthquakes, and epidemics than the United States; others are less subject to such perils. The same is true of violent crimes, vandalism, riots, business failures, recessions, and most other perils. The kidnapping of employees for political reasons is a much more common peril in some foreign countries than in the United States. Social, legal, political, and economic differences are the reasons for this variation.

In most countries liability losses are less frequent and less serious than in the United States. Earnings lost by disability or death tend to be lower as do the quality and cost of medical care. Social and legal factors commonly reduce the likelihood of the injured party bringing a suit, the probability of the claimant winning the suit, and the size of the award or settlement. Recently, however, this difference has been considerably narrowed in certain areas such as Western Europe.

Personnel losses may be more or less frequent. The probability of being killed or injured in a riot or in an occupational accident may be higher or lower; so may the likelihood that the worker may live to claim a pension. If wages are lower, death, disability, and pension benefits may be less per recipient.

Inflation is a much more serious problem in many foreign countries than in the United States. To the extent that inflation affects the frequency and severity of losses, the risk manager's job is further complicated.

Political Risks

In addition to the usual perils, the international risk manager must be concerned with potential losses to foreign exposures caused by acts of the host government or other political forces in the host country.[10] Expropriation or confiscation of property is the most common and most serious exposure. A frequently cited example is the takeover a few years ago by the Iranian government of many foreign-owned private businesses. Other examples are the imposition of trade barriers, the cancellation of import or export licenses, terrorism, kidnapping, breach of contract, and some foreign exchange actions that are described in the next section.

Risk managers must be aware of political risks. They may be asked to help decide how to evaluate the loss potential and whether to avoid or otherwise deal with the exposures. Generally, however, the risk manager is only one of many officers concerned about this problem. The extent to which insurance can be used to protect the firm against this peril is described later.

Foreign Exchange Risks

The second special peril to be considered in international risk management is the foreign exchange risk. The potential loss is that the value of the assets in the host

---

[10] The action may be taken by the home country. For example, when the United States decided not to participate in the 1980 Olympic Games to protest the Russian invasion of Afghanistan, NBC, which would have televised the events, suffered a substantial loss, which fortunately for the network was insured.

country may decrease if the value of the local currency falls relative to the United States dollar.[11] This decline may be caused by (1) an official devaluation, in which case the peril may be considered a political risk, or (2) market forces such as an actual or expected balance of payments deficit.

To illustrate foreign exchange losses, assume that over a period of time the local currency drops 20 percent relative to the United States dollar. This means that the parent's assets in that country would be worth 20 percent less in United States dollars than if the exchange rate had not changed.

Foreign exchange exposures are speculative loss exposures, not pure loss exposures. Instead of decreasing relative to the United States dollar, the local currency may increase its relative value, causing the assets to be worth more than previously.

Risk managers are not usually responsible for dealing with losses or gains caused by fluctuations in exchange rates. However, in some cases to be described later in this chapter, he or she may be able to obtain insurance against foreign exchange losses. In addition, the risk manager will take these fluctuations into account in determining the severity of potential losses and the arrangements that are made to deal with these losses. For example, the dollar value of property, liability, and personnel losses will rise or fall as the local currency rises or falls relative to the dollar. If insurance has been purchased with policy limits stated in dollars, these limits must be adjusted to reflect changes in the potential losses caused by changes in the exchange rates. The exchange rate problem is complicated by the fact that, although there have been many dramatic one-step changes, the change is usually gradual, with many small changes accumulating over time.

Some countries prohibit exchanging local currency for other currencies except under special circumstances. Like official devaluations of the local currency, this foreign exchange problem can be considered a political risk. To illustrate how strict exchange controls can affect the risk manager, assume that fire destroys some equipment in a country that prohibits exchange of its currency for United States dollars. Assume further that an insurer domiciled in the host country is obligated to pay the loss in local currency but that the equipment can be replaced only in the United States. In this situation the parent will have to secure the dollars necessary to replace the equipment from some source other than the insurance proceeds.

METHODS OF RISK IDENTIFICATION

According to Dr. Baglini, in identifying foreign loss exposures risk managers are more likely to rely upon external sources of information than upon internal sources.[12] Over 60 percent of his respondents used as one of their methods of risk identification surveys conducted by insurers, insurance brokers, or insurance consultants. About 56 percent used inspections by the corporate risk manager or the local risk manager, the local risk manager apparently being the only inspector in many of these cases. Dr. Baglini

---

[11] A less common concern is a decrease in the value of the United States dollar relative to the currency in some other country. For example, if equipment used in the United States must be obtained from some other country, an increase in the relative value of that country's currency would increase the cost of replacing damaged equipment.

[12] Baglini, *Global Risk Management,* pp. 10–11.

attributes this heavy reliance on external sources and local personnel to the differences in foreign loss exposures, the relatively small amount invested in some countries, and the autonomy granted many foreign affiliates.

ADMITTED VERSUS NONADMITTED INSURANCE

The insurance management portion of international risk management is complicated by the fact that a decision must be made whether to use admitted or nonadmitted insurance. Admitted insurance contracts conform with the laws and regulations of the host country. The contract is written in the language of the host country and reflects that country's business customs and practices. Premiums and losses are usually paid in local currency, the premiums being tax deductible for the local affiliate. Nonadmitted insurance is not approved by the local regulators. Usually this insurance, written by United States or British insurers, is written in English and reflects United States customs and practices.[13]

For what reasons might a risk manager prefer nonadmitted insurance?

1 Simplicity and understandability.
2 Often considerably broader coverage.
3 In some cases, substantially lower rates for the same coverage.
4 Premiums and losses payable in dollars. Dollar payments are especially useful in countries with strict exchange controls.
5 Enforceable in United States courts.
6 Possible centralization on a global basis.

On the other hand, in some countries nonadmitted insurance is illegal, and businesses that use it may be subjected to rather severe penalties. A second disadvantage is that in countries that do not permit nonadmitted insurance, the premium paid for the nonadmitted insurance is not tax deductible for the affiliate. Third, proceeds paid in dollars may in some countries be subject to the host country's full corporate income tax. Fourth, in those countries that prohibit nonadmitted insurance, the nonadmitted insurer cannot service claims. Consequently, the affiliate must arrange for local claims adjustment services.

Admitted insurance also has several advantages and disadvantages. The more important advantages are as follows:

1 Compliance with local government laws and regulations.
2 Premiums paid in local currency, which provides a use for local currency in countries with strict currency exchange regulation.
3 Losses payable in local currency. This provides a hedge against changes in exchange rates unless the loss involves property to be replaced outside the host country.
4 Premiums tax deductible for the local affiliate.

---

[13] Baglini, *Risk Management in International Corporations,* pp. 79–101. See also MacDonald, op. cit., chaps. 7 and 8.

5 Loss settlements generally less complex if the loss involves only property and persons in the host country.

6 Insurance costs automatically allocated among affiliates because each affiliate pays its own premium.

7 Goodwill with local business interests.

The major disadvantage is that the risk manager may not know what the admitted insurance provides. He or she may not know the language. Translating the policy into English may be only a partial solution because the language may still be unclear and so much depends upon local customs and practices. The coverage under admitted insurance also tends to be less broad, with many unexpected limitations or requirements. If the insurance management program consisted entirely of admitted insurance, the variations in coverage among the various affiliates would be great.

Instead of providing insurance on a completely nonadmitted or admitted basis, most international businesses use a combination approach. Some possible combinations are the following:

1 Admitted insurance only for those coverages that are compulsory in the host countries plus nonadmitted Difference in Conditions and umbrella liability coverage to make the perils covered coincide with United States coverage. Because DIC excludes the perils covered under the basic admitted coverages, worldwide excess property insurance may also be purchased to increase the amount of protection against these perils.

2 Same as 1 except that admitted insurance is used for the broadest available coverage subject to cost comparisons.

3 Local admitted insurance which is reinsured completely by the business's captive insurer. More will be said about this practice below.

4 Admitted insurance plus nonadmitted Difference in Conditions and umbrella liability insurance, both the admitted and the nonadmitted insurance being written by an international insurer or insurer group.

Over 60 percent of Dr. Baglini's respondents placed at least part of their insurance through a United States international insurance broker or agent. Almost half used foreign brokers to place some of their insurance. Some combination of local and United States brokers or agents has become more popular in recent years.

INSURANCE AGAINST POLITICAL RISKS AND FOREIGN EXCHANGE RISKS

Insurance is not generally available against political risks and foreign exchange risks, but there are some notable exceptions.

First, as indicated in Chapters 19 and 26, United States exporters can purchase export credit insurance. This insurance covers the failure of the foreign buyer to pay for the exports at the agreed price in dollars for (1) private reasons—e.g., insolvency or dishonesty, or (2) political reasons beyond the control of either the buyer or the seller. The political risks component of this coverage protects the exporter against losses caused by government actions such as confiscation, delays in exchange transfers, prohibitions against converting the foreign currency into dollars, cancellation or restriction of export or import licenses, and war, including revolutions against the government. Although this insurance is marketed by the private Foreign Credit Insurance Association, it is underwritten by a government agency, the Export-Import Bank. Until late 1983 the Export-Import Bank insured only the political risk component; FCIA insured the bad debt portion. Severe losses, however, caused FCIA to ask to be relieved of this underwriting responsibility.

Second, as mentioned in Chapter 26, a United States government agency, the Overseas Private Investment Corporation (OPIC), will insure new investments in designated developing countries against political risks. The covered perils include expropriation, nationalization, war, revolution, and inconvertibility of the investment and the income it produces into dollars. From 1974 to 1978, a pool of private insurers, the Overseas Investment Insurance Group (OIIG), wrote some political risk insurance in partnership with OPIC. OIIG provided basic coverage; OPIC wrote excess insurance. Since that time, OIIG has been replaced by the Overseas Investment Reinsurance Group (OIRG), a consortium of private United States and foreign insurers which writes only reinsurance.

Third, at least six private insurers (Lloyd's and five United States insurers) supply political risk insurance in competition with OPIC and, more importantly, on exposures not serviced by OPIC.[14]

To the authors' knowledge,[15] insurance is generally not available against short-run foreign exchange losses caused by market forces, but financial managers—not usually risk managers—try to handle such losses in various ways. For example, a firm may sell some equipment to a customer in a country whose currency, it is found, may decline relative to the United States dollar by the payment date. To hedge against this loss, the firm may buy a contract in the futures market under which it promises to deliver to a third party on the payment date a specific amount of the foreign currency at the present exchange rate for dollars. The amount is the price of the equipment. Although the process may not work as smoothly in practice as in theory, the business should have some protection against movements in the exchange rate. If the foreign currency does decline in relative value, the firm will lose on the sale of the equipment, but gain on the futures contract. If, instead, the foreign currency increases in relative value, the firm will gain on the equipment sale, lose on the futures contract. Financial managers also try to maximize holding of currency they expect to increase in relative value and to maximize debts in currency they expect to decline. Of course, their expectations may not be fulfilled.

Long-run foreign exchange losses caused by market forces must generally be handled in the same way but a few European countries have developed exchange risk

---

[14] For a comprehensive analysis of political risks and political risk insurance, see MacDonald, op. cit., pp. 171–179.

[15] The authors, however, do not claim to know all the types of insurance that are available throughout the world. MacDonald, op. cit., p. 182, reports an unusual provision in one DIC policy which protects the insured against devaluation of the local currency during the settling of a claim to be paid in that currency for fire damage.

guarantee programs designed to protect sellers or lenders located in those countries from long-term (normally two years) exchange losses subject to a deductible equal to 2 or 3 percent of the loss.[16]

RETENTION AND DEDUCTIBLES

As reported in Chapter 11 for domestic risk management, many of the risk managers in the 1980 RIMS survey used complete retention or retention through deductibles to handle international exposures. Their use internationally, however, was less common than their use domestically.[17] About 21 percent completely retained at least one kind of property exposure; 43 percent had deductibles in their property insurance programs. About 15 percent completely retained at least one kind of liability exposure; 25 percent had deductibles in their liability insurance programs. All of these percentages were expected to increase in the future. About 61 percent of Dr. Baglini's respondents reported that they retained some of their exposures to fire losses.[18] The percentage retaining riot exposures was 53 percent, flood exposures 70 percent, and earthquake exposures 72 percent. About 22 percent retained part of their premises-operations liability exposures; about 30 percent retained some of their product liability exposures.

CAPTIVE INSURERS

Among the respondents in the 1980 RIMS survey, 12 percent reported international property captive insurers; 8 percent had international captive liability insurers.[19] International captives, therefore, are about as common as domestic captives as a way to handle property exposures but less common as a way to handle liability exposures. For both exposures, their use was expected to increase. Among Dr. Baglini's respondents 46 percent owned or participated in a captive insurer.[20]

Captive insurers can serve more purposes in international risk management than in domestic risk management. The advantages and disadvantages of a captive insurer presented in Chapter 11 still apply, but there are these additional advantages.[21]

1 In some countries, insurers do not or cannot legally use modification plans as highly refined as those described in Chapter 28. Consequently, retention becomes more attractive to a risk manager who believes that the loss and expense allowance in the premium greatly exceeds the affiliate's expected losses and expenses. Such a situation may simply lead to retention without a captive insurer, but for an increasing number of international firms retention means a captive insurer.

2 In countries prohibiting nonadmitted insurance, a captive insurer may be able to reinsure a locally admitted insurer. The business may benefit because (1) the locally

---

[16] See the discussion of foreign exchange losses in chap. 18 of Mark R. Greene and Oscar N. Serbein, *Risk Management: Text and Cases* (2d ed., Reston, Va.: Reston Publishing Co., Inc.).

[17] *The Present Status and Future Role of Risk Management*, pp. 30–31.

[18] Baglini, *Global Risk Management*, p. 33.

[19] *The Present Status and Future Role of Risk Management.*

[20] Baglini, *Global Risk Management*, p. 41.

[21] Ibid., pp. 42–47.

admitted insurer may be willing to write broader protection than would otherwise be the case, or (2) this arrangement permits the business to retain a large portion of the exposure while giving the appearance of being locally insured.

3 Because exposures are scattered throughout the world, servicing these exposures under a retention program may be facilitated through a captive insurer which can have a core of traveling loss-control and loss-adjustment specialists.

4 A captive insurer can serve as a vehicle to move money through international markets. Two examples will illustrate this point. First, because reinsurance premiums are often not subject to strict exchange controls where they exist, the use of a captive to reinsure a local insurer permits the captive to receive the reinsurance premiums in dollars, or in some currency that can be readily converted into dollars. Second, the captive can lend money to profitable affiliates in countries with high income taxes, thus reducing those affiliates' profits and taxes. If the captive is domiciled in a country such as Bermuda with little or no income tax, the high interest payments on the loan are subject to little or no foreign income tax.

5 With a captive as an alternative, the business may be able to negotiate better terms with local insurers.

To a larger extent, probably, than is true of purely domestic captives, captives operating internationally are emerging as profit centers interested in insuring the exposures of outsiders.

INTERNATIONAL EMPLOYEE BENEFITS MANAGEMENT

Up to this point this chapter has been concerned almost exclusively with the management of foreign property and liability loss exposures. The development of multinational companies has also been accompanied by increased emphasis on the international management of employee benefits.[22]

As noted earlier, employee benefit practices vary widely among nations. Multinational companies seek a reasonable balance between centralized control and this diversity in local practices. Centralized control, which tends to produce more newly uniform benefits, is important if the firm wishes to (1) treat its employees in all locations essentially the same, (2) transfer employees from one location to another without causing their benefits to change substantially, and (3) have more control over their worldwide benefit costs. On the other hand, social insurance programs, tax laws, and employee benefit practices vary widely among nations.[23] For example, countries differ greatly in the extent to which their citizens still depend upon their families for support in times of adversity or old age. In some countries employees customarily spend their entire working career with one company; in other countries rapid turnover is common. At some locations the social insurance benefits are more generous than in the United States; at other locations the social insurance benefits are much less generous. Private

---

[22] For a concise, comprehensive discussion of international employee benefits management, see Sven K. Grasshoff, "International Benefits Management," chap. XIII in H. Wayne Snider (ed.), *Employee Benefit Management* (New York: The Risk and Insurance Management Society, Inc., 1980).

[23] For specific examples see ibid., pp. 204–206.

pension plans differ according to whether it is customary to provide a lump-sum retirement benefit, how soon pension benefits are vested, whether employers can claim a tax deduction for reserves they establish on their own books for future benefits, how closely they are regulated by the government, and what opportunities exist for investing funds set aside. Local managers also differ in the degree to which they wish to participate in local employee benefit decisions. For both personnel administration and cost control reasons, the trend is toward more centralization of international employee benefits management. United States-type benefits are also becoming more frequent abroad.[24]

THE FUTURE

International risk management will become more common and more important in the future. This chapter has been written from the vantage point of a United States parent, but most of what has been said also applies to multinationals headquartered in other countries. The status of risk management abroad has increased considerably in recent years and this trend is expected to continue. As the concept spreads, more foreign businesses will establish risk management divisions to handle the pure risks associated with their domestic operations. It may also become easier for international businesses, United States-based and others, to convince affiliates of the need for a coordinated risk management strategy.

SOME KEY CONCEPTS

International risk management The management of the domestic and foreign loss exposures of a business with international operations. Businesses vary in the degree to which they centralize the management of these risks.

Political risks Potential losses to foreign loss exposures caused usually by the host government or other political forces in the host country. Illustrations are confiscation of property, cancellation of import licenses, and kidnapping.

Foreign exchange risks Potential losses to foreign loss exposures arising usually out of declines in the value of the foreign currency relative to domestic currency. Foreign exchange risks are speculative risks, not pure risks, because the exchange rates may change in a favorable direction.

Admitted insurance Insurance that conforms with the laws and regulations of the host country. Nonadmitted insurance is not approved by the local regulators.

REVIEW QUESTIONS

1 a Is the risk management of international exposures a centralized or decentralized function?
  b Is there a trend to centralization or decentralization?
2 What factors influence the degree of centralization?
3 Among the many exposures of a foreign affiliate a risk manager identifies the following potential losses:

[24] Ibid., p. 217.

Physical damage caused by fire

Physical damage caused by windstorm

Liability suit arising out of a defective product

Bodily injury to an employee arising out of an industrial accident

For each of these losses explain why the probability distribution used for domestic losses of the same kind may not be appropriate.

4 Describe (a) political risks, and (b) foreign exchange risks.

5 a How does admitted insurance differ from nonadmitted insurance?

b Why might a risk manager prefer to use a nonadmitted insurer to insure foreign exposures?

c Why might a risk manager prefer to use an admitted insurer to insure foreign exposures?

d How might a risk manager combine the use of nonadmitted and admitted insurance?

6 What insurance is available to protect a business against (a) political risks? (b) foreign exchange risks?

7 Why do captive insurers play a more prominent role in international risk management than in domestic risk management?

8 Do multinational corporations provide the same employee benefits at all their locations? Explain.

SUGGESTIONS FOR ADDITIONAL READING

Baglini, Norman A.: *Global Risk Management* (New York: Risk Management Society Publishing, Inc., 1983).

————: *Risk Management in International Corporations* (New York: Risk Studies Foundation, 1976). See also the extensive bibliography provided in this book.

Bickelhaupt, David L., and Ran Bar-Niv: *International Insurance* (New York: Insurance Information Institute, 1983).

Crowe, Robert M. (ed.): *Insurance in the World's Economies* (Philadelphia: Corporation for the Philadelphia World Insurance Congress, 1982).

Greene, M. R., and O. N. Serbein: *Risk Management: Text and Cases* (2d ed., Reston, Va.: Reston Publishing Company, Inc., 1983), chap. 18.

MacDonald, Donald L.: *Risk Control in the Overseas Operation of American Corporations*, Michigan International Business Studies, no. 15 (Ann Arbor: Division of Research, Graduate School of Business Administration, The University of Michigan, 1979).

Snider, H. Wayne (ed.): *Employee Benefits Management* (New York: The Risk and Insurance Management Society, Inc., 1980), chap. 13.

The Present Status and Future Role of Risk Management: A Survey of U.S. Risk Managers, conducted by The Risk and Insurance Management Society, Inc., and *Time* magazine, April, 1981.

THREE

FAMILY RISK MANAGEMENT

Each family must manage its own risks. Consequently, every person has some interest in family risk management. Because risk management is of necessity a part-time concern for family managers, it is fortunate that family exposures are much less complex and extensive than business exposures.

The first chapter in Part 3 deals with property and liability risk management; the second, with personnel risk management. Much relevant material from preceding chapters is incorporated by reference.

CHAPTER 32

FAMILY PROPERTY AND LIABILITY RISK MANAGEMENT

LEARNING OBJECTIVES

After you have covered this chapter, you should be able to:

1 Analyze the property and liability loss exposures of a family.
2 Tell how a family might use noninsurance tools to handle some of these exposures.
3 Summarize the events covered and the amount the insurer promises to pay in case of a loss under Homeowner's Form 3.
4 Show how Homeowner's Form 1, Form 2, Form 4, and Form 5 differ from Form 3.
5 Explain briefly the farmowner's-ranchowner's package program.
6 Tell condominium-unit owners what homeowner's form has been designed for them.
7 Explain why a family might need personal umbrella catastrophe liability insurance.
8 Design a risk management program for an hypothetical or real-life family.

INTRODUCTION

This first chapter on family risk management deals with the nature and importance of property and liability risks and how they might be handled by noninsurance and insurance tools.

RISK ANALYSIS

A family, like a firm, must first recognize and measure its exposures to potential loss. The techniques and principles that can be employed have already been discussed in Chapters 3 and 4 and need not be repeated here. It is true, of course, that families do not maintain financial statements, but records are usually available or can be constructed that give a fairly accurate picture of the family's property and activities. When matched against a logically classified comprehensive list of all the property and liability risks that may be faced by any family, this picture can be converted into a portrayal of the circumstances of a particular family. The remainder of this section is devoted to the development of that logical classification of risks.

The basic risk classification is the same as that developed in Chapters 5 through 8. Potential property losses include (1) direct losses, (2) indirect losses, and (3) net income losses. The potential liability losses are those associated with torts or, to a much lesser extent, breach of contract.

A family's real and personal property is exposed to direct loss. The real property, if any, is typically a dwelling; the personal property includes such items as household goods, clothing, and the family automobile. A complete inventory of this property would indicate its present and probable location (commonly the permanent residence, a summer cottage, or property in the hands of some bailee) and the nature of the family's interest (usually sole owner, part owner, or mortgagee). According to one measure the maximum possible loss is the cost of replacing the property new less physical depreciation and economic obsolescence. Replacement cost new, however, is becoming a more popular measure of losses to dwellings and to a lesser extent of losses to personal property other than vehicles.

Although the family may suffer from the loss of use of personal property as well as of real property, the most important net income losses involve damage to real property, because most items of personal property can be replaced much more quickly. The most common net income loss is additional living expenses (for example, extra costs for housing, food, transportation, laundry) incurred by the family during the period when they cannot live in their home or apartment.

Families seldom have to worry about losses arising under workers' compensation statutes, because these laws apply to domestic service in only a few states.[1] Other tort actions, however, are very important and are frequently underestimated as a source of liability losses. The magnitude of liability losses in the form of judgments, defense and court costs, and indirect expenditures of time, energy, and money has already been emphasized in Chapter 7. The fundamental legal principles associated with tort actions and no-fault statutes have been discussed in that chapter and Chapter 8. Only the sources of these tort actions for a family are discussed here.

The ownership, maintenance, or use of an automobile is the best-known source of liability, the awareness of this danger being stimulated by financial responsibility laws, no-fault automobile insurance laws, and the extensive publicity accorded to automobile accidents and suits. Less often appreciated are potential losses arising out of the

---

[1] In most states, however, families may voluntarily choose to bring their domestic servants under the workers' compensation law.

ownership, maintenance, or use of other types of property, such as dwellings; the responsibility assumed under leases and other contracts; possible contingent liability arising out of the operations of independent contractors such as plumbers and painters, and the exposure through personal activities of various sorts, such as entertaining guests, engaging in sports, or merely walking down the street.

USE OF NONINSURANCE TOOLS

Noninsurance tools can prove very useful in dealing with these risks. Families should consider particularly two risk control techniques—risk avoidance and loss control; and two risk financing methods—transfer and retention.

Avoidance

A family may be wise to forgo certain activities or the ownership of certain property if the risks involved are great relative to the advantages. For example, the ownership of a car by a college student may not be worth the risks involved. A young family may postpone a move to more luxurious quarters for the same and other reasons. Avoidance, however, is much less useful than the other tools.

Loss Control

Efforts to reduce the chance that the loss will occur or the severity of losses that do occur should always be tried when economically feasible. Safe driving habits, good housekeeping, and urging one's community to improve the quality of its fire-fighting facilities illustrate this approach. Except in automobile insurance, where owners are now commonly rated in part on the basis of their own experience, insurance premiums do not vary with the experience of the individual family as they do in the case of large firms, but the family does benefit substantially with respect to the losses they retain. In addition, if every family in the same rate class were to become more safety-conscious, the class rate could eventually be reduced.

Transfer

A family may transfer a property or activity to someone else. Although the motive for the transfer is generally something other than transfer of the associated pure risks, the transfer of these risks is an important by-product. Examples would be the sale of a car or the transfer of driving responsibilities to someone outside the family.[2]

Risks may be transferred without transferring the property or the activity. Tenants are likely to find this device very useful in their dealing with landlords. For example, the landlord may be made responsible for any damage to the property by certain specified perils, and it may be agreed that the rent is to cease if the property becomes

---

[2] In the latter situation, the family may not escape completely the risks involved. For example, the car driven may be owned by the family in a state with a statute making the owner liable.

untenantable. Generally speaking, however, transfer devices of this sort, other than insurance, are seldom available for families.[3]

Retention

Active or planned retention is an extremely useful way to handle many potential *property* losses. Some of these losses cannot be avoided, prevented, or transferred at any price and therefore must be retained. War damage is an example of this sort. Another illustration is the loss of use of most types of personal property even though direct losses to this property may be insurable.

As we have explained in Chapter 11, retention is a particularly useful tool when potential losses that are transferable are so small that the family can handle them with relative ease out of current income or by withdrawals from savings accounts. Small automobile physical damage losses, small dwelling losses, and other small property losses fall in this category. The point at which these losses cease to be small depends upon the economic status and personality of the family, but most families should consider seriously the retention of some small losses. A small potential loss will typically cause the family little or no worry. If transferred to, say, an insurer, the expense incurred in adjusting these losses will be relatively high.

Retention is also attractive when the risk is small. The family can predict fairly well what will happen, and prepare for these losses in its budgeting. Most, if not all, the family losses falling in this group—mysterious disappearance of fountain pens and pencils, tears in clothing, and misplaced tools—are also small losses, and the argument for retention of these losses is thus strengthened.

Retention is much less applicable to liability losses because they tend to be large and infrequent. Every family must be prepared, however, to bear some liability risk itself, since insurers, who usually offer the only transfer device, place limits on their maximum responsibility.

Taxes affect family retention decisions differently than they influence business decisions. Families cannot deduct property and liability insurance premiums from their taxable income. Property losses can be deducted but only to the extent that they exceed 1 percent of the family's adjusted gross income.[4] Liability losses can be deducted only if they were incurred in connection with business or professional pursuits.

USE OF INSURANCE

Although noninsurance tools, particularly loss control and retention, are extremely important, all families are likely to turn to insurance for at least some protection, and most families will make extensive use of this tool. The contracts most likely to be used are (1) some homeowner's contract, and (2) the personal auto policy, or some

---

[3] Families may move in with friends and relatives after a property loss, but unless the move had been anticipated prior to the loss, the change of domicile is a transfer of an actual loss, not risk.

[4] Until 1982, property losses could be deducted to the extent that they exceeded $100.

independent version of these two contracts. Families may also be interested in personal catastrophe liability insurance and fidelity and surety bonds.

In 1978, families spent over 11 percent of their personal income for various forms of private insurance and public insurance.[5] Of this amount homeowner's contracts or some related form of protection cost 0.45 percent. Automobile insurance cost 1.43 percent. Other major expenditures were life insurance (1.91 percent), health insurance (3.22 percent), pension plans (0.94 percent), and OASDI (3.12 percent). These expenditures do not include employer contributions under employee benefit plans.

Homeowner's Insurance Program

The homeowner's insurance program consists of package policies combining most of the property and liability insurance that a family needs into one contract. Prior to the development of the homeowner's program in 1950, families interested in broad protection had to purchase several different contracts to approximate their coverage under a homeowner's contract. Although these separate contracts and others are still available, most homeowners and tenants are eligible for and purchase homeowner's contracts.[6]

The reasons why homeowner's contracts have become so popular are that (1) they provide at least as broad coverage as the separate contracts, (2) they avoid gaps between and overlaps among separate coverages, (3) purchasing and renewing one contract is more convenient and more efficient than arranging several contracts, and (4) the premium is considerably less than the sum of the premiums for equivalent separate coverages. The cost is less because (1) it is less expensive to sell and service a package contract, (2) the "quality" of insureds purchasing homeowner's contracts tends to be better, particularly with respect to certain perils, such as theft, against which only the loss-prone seem to insure under separate contracts, and (3) some features of the homeowner's contracts cause insureds to purchase higher amounts of insurance relative to the values exposed to loss. Higher insurance-to-value ratios mean lower rates per $100 of insurance for the reasons specified in Chapter 17's discussion of coinsurance.

Starting in 1975, the original homeowner's program was gradually replaced by a more readable version called *Homeowners 76*. This revised program also made some small changes in the coverage. There are still, however, five basic forms: Form 1 (titled the "Basic Form"), Form 2 (the Broad Form), Form 3 (the Special Form), Form 4 (the Contents Broad Form), and Form 5 (the Comprehensive Form). Owner occupants of a one- or two-family dwelling used exclusively for private residential purposes (including incidental office occupancy) and containing no more than two boarders per family are eligible for Forms 1, 2, 3, and 5. Owner occupants of other dwellings and tenants are eligible for Form 4 only. Form 3, the most popular form, is analyzed in

---

[5] R. W. Vinson and R. J. O'Donnell, *A Study of Personal Security Expenditures* (New York: Insurance Information Institute, 1979).

[6] The market for the older contracts is limited primarily to persons with low-valued dwellings, persons with undesirable exposures, and persons who do not occupy the dwellings but rent them to others.

detail below. The discussion of the other forms will be limited to the major ways in which they differ from Form 3. The discussion ignores further, less basic changes introduced in 1982 in some states.[7]

Form 5 usually costs about 40 percent more than Form 2, Form 3 only slightly more. Form 1 costs about 15 percent less. The premium for a given form depends upon the community protection class and the amount of insurance placed on the dwelling. The premium increases less than proportionally as the dwelling insurance amount increases.

Form 3   Form 3, like the other four, is divided into Section 1 dealing with property insurance and Section II dealing with liability insurance. The insured must buy both sections.

Section 1 protects the insured's dwelling and other structures, such as a detached garage, against all *perils* not specifically excluded. Excluded perils include earth movements (except fire, explosion, theft, or glass breakage resulting from the movement); flood; war; nuclear incidents (except fire resulting from the incident); wear and tear, mechanical breakdown, rust, mold, wet or dry rot, contamination, inherent vice, latent defects or marring; birds, vermin, rodents, insects or domestic animals; and continuous or repeated seepage of water or steam over a period of time from within a plumbing, heating, or air conditioning system or from within a household appliance. Pavements, patios, foundations, walls, floors, roofs, or ceilings are not covered against settling, cracking, shrinkage, bulging, or expansion. Freezing of a plumbing, heating, or air conditioning system or of a household appliance is not covered while the dwelling is vacant or unoccupied unless the insured has used reasonable care to maintain heat in the building and drain the system or appliance. A fence, pavement, patio, swimming pool, foundation, retaining wall, or dock is never covered against loss by freezing, thawing, or the pressure or weight of water or ice. Vandalism and breakage of glass, however caused, are excluded if the dwelling has been vacant for more than 30 consecutive days prior to the loss.

Personal property, on the other hand, is protected only against a long list of specified perils: fire; lightning; windstorm; hail; explosion; riot; civil commotion; aircraft; vehicles; smoke; vandalism; theft; falling objects (including trees); weight of ice, snow, or sleet; collapse of all or part of a building; glass breakage to residence; sudden and accidental tearing asunder, cracking, burning, or bulging of a steam or hot water heating system, an air conditioning system, or a water heater; accidental discharge, or overflow of water or steam from within a plumbing, heating or air conditioning system, or from domestic appliances; freezing of these systems or appliances; and sudden and accidental injury from artificially generated electric current. Like the dwelling, the personal property is not covered against earth movements,

[7] For example, internal limits were raised from $100 on money to $200; from $500 on accounts, deeds, manuscripts, and the like to $1,000; and from $500 for loss by theft of jewelry, watches, and fur items to $1,000. On the other hand, the 1982 version excludes physical damage to all motorized vehicles including those not licensed for road use. The new version also eliminates from coverage owned watercraft with inboard motor power of less than 50 horsepower. The base deductible is increased from $100 to $250 and the base liability limit from $25,000 to $100,000.

flood, war, and nuclear incidents. Coverage against each of the specified perils is further limited by the way in which the peril is defined, or by specific exclusions. For example, damage by windstorm or falling objects is not covered unless the roof or an exterior wall has been damaged first. Smoke from agricultural smudging or industrial operations is excluded. Theft includes attempted theft and loss of property from a known location where it is likely that the property has been stolen. Theft need not be proved but a loss of property is not presumed to be a theft. Theft committed by an insured is not covered. If the premises are not occupied, losses caused by freezing of a plumbing, heating, or air conditioning system or a domestic appliance are not covered unless the insured has used reasonable care to maintain heat in the building, shut off the water supply, and drain these systems or appliances. Accidental discharge or overflow of water or steam from within a plumbing, air conditioning, or heating system or from within a domestic appliance is not covered if the loss is caused by freezing.

The *property* covered is (1) the dwelling, (2) other structures such as a detached garage but not including property used for business purposes or property (other than a private garage) rented or held for rental to someone other than a resident tenant, (3) trees, shrubs, plants, and lawns, but this property is not protected against damage caused by certain of the specified perils such as windstorm, hail, or vehicles owned or operated by an occupant of the premises, and (4) personal property. The dwelling item includes materials and supplies located on or adjacent to the premises intended for use in construction, alteration, or repair of the dwelling. All personal property that one would normally associate with a dwelling is covered except a few items that are specifically excluded. For example, all motorized vehicles (other than those used for the service of the premises and not licensed for road use), such as automobiles and snowmobiles, are excluded. No coverage is provided for business property or for animals, including birds and fish. Also excluded is any sound producing or receiving equipment operated by power from the electrical system of a motor vehicle or any tape, record, or other medium for use with this equipment while this property is in or upon a motor vehicle.

Persons whose property is insured include the named insured and, if they are residents of the same household, the spouse, relatives of either, and any other person under 21 in the care of the named insured, the spouse, or a resident relative. In addition, if the named insured or spouse dies, his or her legal representative is insured. If an insured uses personal property owned by others such as a friend or neighbor, that property is covered. At the request of the named insured or spouse, the insurer will also cover the personal property of others, even if it is not being used by an insured, while the property is on that part of the residence premises occupied by an insured. Furthermore, at the request of the named insured or spouse, the insurer will cover the personal property of any guest or residence employee while the property is in *any* residence occupied by an insured; for example, a hotel room.

The policy covers some direct, indirect, and net income *losses*. In addition to paying the cost of replacing or repairing damaged or stolen property, the policy covers the "necessary" increase in living expenses of all sorts incurred by the named insured or spouse while his or her dwelling is being repaired or replaced. Also covered are debris removal costs, the named insured's liability for fire department charges levied because of a fire on the insured's premises or exposing property, and the loss of fair rental value on that part of the premises rented to others or held for rental if that part is uninhabitable.

The protection extends to *locations* anywhere in the world, subject to a few exceptions. For example, personal property contained in an apartment regularly rented or held for rental to others by an insured is not covered. Several exceptions apply to theft losses. Theft from an unattended unlocked automobile away from the premises is not covered unless it is a public conveyance or unless the insured parks his or her car in a public garage or parking lot and leaves the keys with an attendant. Also not covered away from the premises is theft from an unattended private watercraft unless it is from a securely locked compartment. Theft of watercraft or trailers away from the premises is also excluded.

The *term* of the contract is usually three years with the premium being paid in annual or more frequent installments. If the premium is paid in installments, the premium can be adjusted each year. The cancellation provision is more liberal than usual. If the insured does not pay the premium, the insurer may always cancel after 10 days' notice. If the policy is a new one which has been in effect for less than 60 days, the insurer can cancel for any reason after 10 days' notice. If the policy is either a renewal policy or a new policy which has been in effect for 60 days or more, the insurer can cancel only after 30 days notice, and only for one of two reasons: (1) a material representation of fact by the insured in his or her application, or (2) a substantial change in the exposure since the policy was issued. However, if the term of the policy is more than one year, the insurer can cancel as of the policy anniversary date for any reason after 30 days' notice. Similarly, if the insurer intends not to renew the policy, it need not give a reason but it must give the insured 30 days' notice.

If the policy covers a loss, several provisions affect the *amount* an insured can collect. The policy limits prescribe the maximum amount the insured can recover. Once the insured selects the amount of property insurance to be placed on the dwelling, the minimum amount of insurance to be placed on each of the other property insurance items is fixed as a percentage of the dwelling insurance, as follows:

Other structures	10% but may be increased[8]
Personal property	50% but may be increased or reduced to 40%
Additional living expense	20%

For example, if the insured selects $100,000 insurance on the dwelling, these other insurance amounts are $10,000, $50,000, and $20,000.

Personal property that is usually located at any insured's residence other than that specified in the declarations is covered only up to $1,000 or, if greater, up to 10

---

[8] The contracts issued by many insurers state that if there are no other structures, the insurance on the dwelling is increased by this 10 percent but not for the purpose of satisfying the replacement cost requirements to be described shortly.

percent of the personal property limit, $5,000 in the above example. This special limit, however, does not apply to newly acquired premises until 30 days after the named insured or spouse begins to move the property there.

Smaller internal limits per loss apply to certain types of property; money ($100); accounts, deeds, manuscripts and the like ($500); theft of watches, jewelry, and fur items ($500); theft of silverware, goldware, or pewterware ($1,000); grave markers ($500); guns ($1,000); watercraft ($500); trailers ($500); and trees, shrubs, plants, and lawns (5 percent of the dwelling limit but no more than $250 per tree, shrub, or plant). Fire department charges are covered up to $250.

A replacement cost provision states that under certain conditions the insured can recover more than the actual cash value of any loss to building items (not personal property). The insurer promises to pay (1) the actual cash value of the loss or (2) if higher, the amount obtained from the following calculation:

$$\frac{\text{Amount of insurance on building}}{80\% \text{ of replacement cost new of building}} \times \frac{\text{Replacement cost new}}{\text{of damaged portion}}$$

Consequently, if the insured maintains insurance equal to at least 80 percent of the replacement cost new of the total structure (less the cost of excavations; underground flues, pipes, wiring, and drains; and foundations), all the building losses will be paid on a replacement cost new basis up to the face value of the contract. For example, assume that a dwelling with an actual cash value of $100,000 would cost $120,000 to replace new today. To repair some fire damage to the dwelling would cost $20,000, but because of depreciation the actual cash value of the damage, let us assume, is only $16,000. If the policy limit on the dwelling is at least 0.80 ($120,000), the insurer would pay $20,000. If the policy limit were some smaller amount, say, $90,000, the insurer would pay the higher of two amounts: (1) $16,000, the actual cash value, or (2) the value derived below:

$$\frac{\$90,000}{0.80 \ (\$120,000)} \times \$20,000 = \$18,750$$

If the cost to repair the damage without any deduction for depreciation is more than either $1,000 or 5 percent of the insurance on the building item, the insurer will pay only the actual cash value until the damage is actually repaired or the property replaced.[9]

The contract contains a $100 deductible per occurrence applicable to all perils. The deductible does not apply to additional living expense claims or to fire department service charges.

Section II includes three separate and independent coverages: (1) liability insurance, (2) medical payments to others, and (3) insurance against physical damage to the

[9] For a nominal fee many insurers will issue a replacement-value guarantee under which the insurer agrees to rebuild your home even if the replacement cost new exceeds the amount of insurance you purchase on the dwelling. To obtain this benefit, however, you must insure your dwelling for the amount the insurer tells you it is worth at the time you purchase the insurance.

property of others. The *peril* under the *liability insurance* is an occurrence for which the insured is legally liable.

The liability may arise out of any *source* not specifically excluded. All premises on which the named insured or spouse maintains a residence are covered under this contract, provided that they are so declared in the insured's application. So are other premises and private approaches thereto used in connection with the residence. Business or rental property (not including occasional rental of the insured's residence and some other specified rentals of the residence or garage) and farms are not covered. Other covered premises are individual or family cemetery plots or burial vaults, non-owned premises such as a summer cottage in which an insured is temporarily residing, and vacant land, other than farm land, owned by or rented to an insured, including land on which a one- or two-family dwelling is being constructed for the insured.

Because business or professional pursuits are specifically excluded, the policy covers only personal activities. An important personal activity that is excluded is the ownership, maintenance, use, loading, or unloading of motor vehicles owned or operated by, or rented or loaned to, any insured. However, recreational motor vehicles (such as snowmobiles) are covered while on the premises. So are motor vehicles not subject to registration because they are used exclusively on the premises (such as power lawn mowers and snowplows) or are kept in dead storage on the premises. Furthermore, motorized golf carts are covered while they are being used off-premises for golfing purposes.

Another important exclusion applies to watercraft owned by or rented to an insured if it has inboard motor power of more than 50 horsepower, or is a sailboat 26 feet or more in length. Watercraft powered by owned outboard motors with more than 25 combined horsepower are also excluded unless the motors were acquired after the policy was issued. All aircraft are excluded.

Other important exclusions eliminate injury or damage expected or intended by the insured, liability assumed by the insured under any agreement that is not in writing, and damage to property used by, rented to, or in the care of the insured. However, the insurer does agree to pay any sums that the insured shall become legally obligated to pay as damages if the damage is caused by fire, explosion, or smoke. Employers' liability claims are not excluded, but the insured must declare the number of residence employees if the number is two or more. The form does not cover workers' compensation claims.

The *persons* insured under the contract are the named insured and, if they are residents of the household, his or her spouse, the relatives of either, and any other person under 21 in the care of an insured.

The *losses* covered under the contract fall into the following categories: First, the insurer promises to pay all sums that the insured becomes legally obligated to pay as a result of bodily injury or property damage. Protection against both bodily injury and property damage claims is included under one insuring agreement. Second, the insurer will pay expenses incurred by the insured in order to provide first aid at the scene of the accident. Third, the insurer promises to defend the insured and pay the types of costs described in Chapter 16, including the insured's loss of earnings up to $50 per day while attending hearings and trials.

There are no *location* limitations not already noted. The *time* provisions are those already noted for the property coverage.

The *medical payments to others coverage* obligates the insurer to pay the medical expenses and funeral expenses incurred by others within three years from the date of an accident. This coverage is health insurance, not liability insurance. The insured need not be at fault. It is sufficient that the accident occur (1) while the injured party is on the premises, as previously defined, with the permission of an insured, or (2) while the injured party is elsewhere if the injury (a) arises out of the premises, (b) is caused by the activities of an insured, (c) is caused by a residence employee while engaged in employment by an insured, or (d) is caused by an animal owned by or in the care of any insured. The insurer does not cover injuries to the named insured or spouse or to any person, other than a residence employee, regularly residing on the premises. Residence employees are not covered if the accident occurs off the premises unless the injury arises out of employment by any insured. No person will receive any benefits under this coverage, however, if they are eligible for workers' compensation or compulsory temporary disability insurance benefits. Receipt of a medical payments benefit does *not* reduce the amount a person may recover from suing the insured under the liability coverage.

The *damage to property of others coverage* is the property damage equivalent of the medical payments coverage. The insurer agrees to pay for damage to or destruction of the property of others caused by an insured. The liability of the insured is not an issue. Excluded are losses arising out of the ownership, maintenance, or use of motor vehicles, aircraft, or watercraft; loss to property owned by or rented to any insured, any resident of the named insured's household, or any tenant of the insured; or losses caused intentionally by an insured age 13 or over. Note that these exclusions do not eliminate damage to non-owned or nonrented property in the care, custody, or control of an insured. However, if coverage is provided under Section 1, as it may be, that section is responsible for the loss.

The insurer promises to pay all liability claims up to a single limit per occurrence, the minimum possible limit being $25,000. The supplementary payments—defense and settlement costs and the like—are paid in addition to the single liability limit. The medical payments coverage has a minimum limit of $500 per person per occurrence. The limit under the section covering physical damage to property is always $250 per occurrence.

Form 1   Form 1 differs from Form 3 primarily in two respects. First, both the dwelling and the personal property are protected against a list of specified perils. Furthermore, this list is shorter than the list applicable to personal property under Form 3, and some of the perils that are covered under both forms are more narrowly defined in Form 1. Form 1 covers only fire, lightning, windstorm, hail, riot, civil commotion, explosion, aircraft damage, vehicle damage, smoke, vandalism, residence glass breakage (up to $50 per occurrence), and theft. Explosions of steam boilers, however, are excluded. Vehicle damage is not covered if the vehicle is driven by an occupant of the premises. Smoke damage is limited to that resulting from the faulty operation of a heating or cooking unit in the described premises. Theft includes attempted theft, but the form does not mention loss of property from a known place under circumstances when it is likely that the property has been stolen. Second, the additional living expense insurance limit is 10 percent, not 20 percent, of the dwelling limit.

Form 2   The principal difference between Form 2 and Form 3 is that both the dwelling and the personal property are protected against the perils listed under the Form 3 personal property coverage. Until recently, Form 2 was the most popular homeowner's policy.

Form 4   Form 4 is used to provide protection for a tenant or for a homeowner who is not eligible for the other forms. This form is the same as Form 2 except that no coverage is provided on the dwelling or other structures. The insured selects the amount of personal property insurance, subject to a minimum requirement. Additional living expenses are covered up to 20 percent of this limit. In addition, if the named insured has any interest in improvements, alterations, or additions made to that portion of the premises used exclusively by the named insured, the limit on this improvements and betterments coverage is 10 percent of the personal property insurance limit.

Form 5   Form 5, which is the most liberal of the homeowner's forms, differs from Form 3 in that the property insurance is all risks with respect to both the dwelling and the personal property.

Endorsements   Endorsements may be attached to the contract to limit, modify, or expand the coverage. For example, one endorsement *increases the deductible* to $250 or $500. Another permits the insured to *schedule certain items of personal property,* such as a fur coat, a diamond ring, or a musical instrument. This additional coverage is important because of the internal limits noted earlier on jewelry, watches, and furs; silverware, goldware, and pewterware; and some other types of property. Each scheduled item is protected on an all risks basis up to the amount specified in the schedule. If an insured has a *business office on the principal residence* that is incidental to the occupancy of the premises as a dwelling, the insured can through an endorsement extend the definition of ''personal property'' to include the office furnishings and equipment and to include the liability exposure (other than professional liability) associated with this occupancy. A fourth example extends theft protection under Forms 2, 3, and 4 to *property in unattended watercraft, motor vehicles, or trailers.* Form 5 already provides this coverage. A fifth example enables the insured to recover the *replacement cost new value of personal property.* A final example is termed an *inflation guard endorsement.* This endorsement increases the Section 1 coverage limits at a rate of 1 percent per quarter for the first 10 quarters of a 3-year term and 2 percent at the end of the eleventh quarter—a total of 12 percent.

Homeowner's Actual Cash Value Insurance   A few years ago, insurers developed a Form 8 which is a modified Form 1 designed for insureds with dwellings whose replacement cost new is much greater than their actual cash value, thus making it unlikely that the replacement cost is a valid measure of the loss to the insured. The principal modification is the omission of the replacement cost provision, all losses being adjusted on an actual cash value basis. The policy is also more limited in some other ways. Theft coverage for off-premises losses, for example, is limited to $1,000 or, if greater, 10 percent of the personal property insurance limit.

Condominium-Unit-Owner's Insurance   Homeowner's Form 6 meets the needs of apartment-condominium-unit owners. Condominium arrangements and the SMP approach to insuring the undivided interest in the condominium properties were described in Chapter 19.

Form 6 covers the same perils as tenants' Form 4. Condominium-unit owners, however, are not tenants, and Form 6 and its endorsements reflect this difference. Form 6 differs from Form 4 in that (1) the additional living expense limit is 40 percent, not 20 percent, of the personal property limit, and (2) alterations and additions, the unit owner's interest in the building, are adjusted on a replacement cost basis and limited to $1,000. This alterations insurance is excess over any recovery by the association under its insurance. An important multi-purpose endorsement increases the limit on these alterations and converts the named-perils coverage to all risks. This endorsement can also be used to permit unlimited rentals to others, to cover actual loss of rents under the additional living expense coverage, and to insure appurtenant private structures on the premises solely owned by the insured. Loss-assessment insurance can also be provided through this endorsement that will reimburse the insured for his or her share of an assessment levied by the condominium association to cover an uninsured property or liability loss to the association.

Farmowner's-Ranchowner's Program

A farmowner's-ranchowner's program provides package protection similar to the homeowner's program for owners of farms and ranches. Because a farm or a ranch is both a home and a business, the farmowner's-ranchowner's program differs from the homeowner's program in several ways.

Owner occupants, owner nonoccupants, and tenants may be insured under this program. Owner nonoccupants, however, are not eligible unless either the owner or a management contractor manages the operation.

The program includes eight coverages as follows:

A. Farm dwelling

B. Unscheduled personal property (household)

C. Additional living expense

} Owners:
Like homeowner's Forms 1 or 2
Tenants:
Like homeowner's Form 4

D. Scheduled farm personal property

E. Unscheduled farm personal property

} Protection against fire and lightning, the extended coverage perils, vandalism and malicious mischief, electrocution of livestock, overturn, and theft

| F. Farm barns and other buildings | Protection against fire and lightning, the extended coverage perils, and vandalism and mischief |
| G. Personal liability ⎫
H. Medical payments ⎭ | Similar to the homeowner's liability and medical expense protection |

Farm- or ranchowner occupants need not purchase the entire package. For example, Coverages D, E, and F are optional. Other private structures are not automatically covered; they must be scheduled on the policy. Like the homeowner's policies, the farmowner's-ranchowner's form can be endorsed in many ways.

Automobile Insurance

The other property and liability insurance contract that will be purchased by most families is the personal auto policy or its equivalent nonstandard contract. The PAP has already been discussed in detail in Chapter 19.

Personal Umbrella Catastrophe Liability Insurance

Many insurers issue a personal umbrella catastrophe liability insurance policy. One such policy provides $1 million or more excess liability insurance over a $100,000 comprehensive personal liability insurance policy (or Section II of a homeowner's contract) and a $300,000 automobile liability insurance policy. Where applicable, the policy also provides excess insurance over primary aircraft liability insurance, watercraft liability insurance, and employers' liability insurance. In addition, this policy covers many losses not covered by these primary policies, but the insurer is responsible only for that portion of any such loss in excess of some deductible.

Examples of losses covered under this policy that are not covered under the primary insurance are personal injury claims based on false arrest, wrongful eviction or malicious prosecution, liability for automobile accidents occurring outside the United States and Canada, liability for losses to property (other than aircraft or watercraft) rented to, occupied or used by, or in the care, custody, or control of the insured, and liability of others assumed under any contract, whether it be oral or written.

Fidelity and Surety Bonds

The basic characteristics of fidelity and surety bonds and the major differences between bonding and insurance have already been described in Chapters 11 and 12. All that is necessary here is a brief discussion of the bonds that are important in family risk management.

A family will not ordinarily have any occasion to be an obligee under a fidelity bond. Some families will protect themselves in this manner against losses caused by dishonest domestic servants. Surety bonds are also not likely to play an important role in the risk management plans of most families, but in particular cases they can prove extremely important. Among the more commonly used surety bonds, all of which have been described on pages 345 to 347, are the following: probate bonds, such as the executor's bond, administrator's bond, or guardian's bond; court bonds, such as bail bonds, appeal bonds, attachment or release of attachment bonds; and bonds for lost instruments. Under some of these bonds, the family member will be the principal. For example, he or she may be the executor of a relative's estate. In other cases, the family member will be the obligee. For example, a moving and storage concern may furnish a bond to guarantee its safe handling of the family's property.

AN ILLUSTRATIVE CASE

The principles and practices that have been discussed will now be applied to a particular case. The reader is warned not to expect a single solution to the problems presented. He or she should also realize that as the family situation changes over time, the risk management program may have to be revised. Finally, the reader should recognize that so many considerations are involved in designing a risk management program that it is impossible to deal with more than the major dimensions in this short case.

Risk Analysis

The first step in developing a risk management program is, as has already been stated, the recognition and evaluation of the risks facing the family. Assume circumstances as follows: Mary and John Smith, both age 35, have one child, aged 8. Mary works for a small office supply firm which pays her an after-tax annual salary of $27,000. Her prospects for advancement in the firm are bright. Mary has some valuable noncontributory employee benefits at work. She is covered under a $20,000 group life insurance program, a comprehensive major medical expense plan with a $100 deductible and a $500,000 maximum limit, a dental expense plan, and a pension plan that at age 65 will pay Mary $12,000 a year for the rest for her life. If John is alive when Mary retires and Mary selects a joint and two-thirds survivorship option, the annual pension income while both are alive will be $11,400. The pension plan provides no preretirement death benefits or disability benefits other than protection of her retirement benefits in case she is permanently and totally disabled. The group life insurance, medical expense insurance, and dental expense insurance terminate upon Mary's retirement. All of these employee benefits are paid in addition to OASDI benefits.

John works for a medium-size manufacturing firm which also pays him an after-tax annual salary of $27,000. His employer provides the following noncontributory employee benefit plans: a group life insurance plan with a face amount equal to one year's salary, a long-term disability plan that would pay 65 percent of the lost wages, a comprehensive major medical expense plan with a $100 deductible and a $250,000 maximum limit, a dental expense plan, and a pension plan that at age 65 will pay John $12,000 a year for the rest of his life. If Mary is alive when John retires and John selects a joint and two-thirds survivorship option, the annual pension income will be initially $11,400. The pension plan provides a $10,000 preretirement death benefit but no disability benefit other than protection of his retirement benefits in case he is permanently and totally disabled. Upon John's retirement the group life insurance is continued for half the preretirement amount, but the medical expense insurance, dental expense insurance, and long-term disability insurance are terminated. All of John's employee benefits are paid in addition to OASDI benefits except the long-term disability insurance from which John's OASDI worker's disability income benefits are subtracted.

The Smiths have a home, valued at $120,000 including the land. They built the home five years ago. The unpaid balance on the mortgage, which has 20 more years to run, is $70,000. The home, when furnished, would probably rent for about $1,200 per month and, if built new today, would cost about $150,000. The land, the cost of excavations, foundations, and the like are valued at $40,000.

The Smiths also have two cars, one valued at $10,000 with a replacement cost new of $12,000 and the other valued at $4,000 with a replacement cost new of $10,000; typical furniture, clothing, and the like[10] valued at $54,000 with a replacement cost new of $70,000; savings, checking, and money market accounts totalling $15,000; two individual retirement accounts each worth $4,500; and in a safe deposit box, some common stocks and mutual fund certificates with a current market value of $40,000.[11]

The Smiths are an active family with strong interests in sports. They participate in many social and civic activities. They often lend their cars to friends or organizations, and they in turn drive cars belonging to others. John, in addition, frequently drives a company car on business trips.

Each summer the Smiths rent a cabin in the northern part of the state for two weeks. They drive to the cabin in their car, to which they attach a rented utility trailer containing about $6,000 in furniture, clothing, and the like, for which the replacement cost new is $8,000.

The Smith family circumstances have been deliberately oversimplified, but it is still necessary to sort out and arrange the loss exposures in some systematic fashion. Using the basic risk classification developed earlier in the text, we have the picture shown on the next page.

All these losses are possible, but the chance of losing the savings and checking accounts and securities is slight. The other property losses can be caused by a very large number of perils, some of which are fairly common (for example, fire or an automobile collision), while the chance of others (for example, flood and earthquake in most areas) is very slight. The perils also differ according to whether they usually cause large or small losses.

Families seldom suffer contingent liability losses because of the operations of independent contractors, but many families experience the other liability losses, and their consequences may be very severe.

---

[10] A detailed listing of this property is omitted here to save space and to simplify the discussion.

[11] The reader will probably notice the absence of any reference to life insurance or to life insurance cash values. This omission is intentional because the same illustration is used in the next chapter to develop a life and health risk management program, and the omission of any existing insurance simplifies that discussion immeasurably.

Type of loss	Maximum possible loss	
	Actual cash value	Replacement cost new
Property losses:		
Direct losses:		
Dwelling	$120,000 including the land, cost of excavations, etc.	$150,000
Furniture, clothing, etc.		
On premises	$ 54,000	$ 70,000
Off premises	6,000	8,000
Savings, checking, and money market accounts	15,000	15,000
Individual retirement accounts	9,000	9,000
Securities	40,000	40,000
Cash	500	500
Automobiles	10,000 and 4,000	12,000 and 10,000
Debris removal	5,000	
Net income losses:		
Additional living expenses	2,500 per month for 9 months	
Liability losses:		
Owned premises		
Owned automobile	Almost unlimited in potential except for liability with respect to cabin and subject in some states to automobile no-fault statutes	
Business activities		
Personal activities		
Contractual liability under lease		
Contingent liability for operations of independent contractors		

Use of Noninsurance Tools

In designing their risk management program, the Smiths can use several noninsurance tools. Avoidance of risk may be a consideration if they have an opportunity to acquire new property or to engage in some new activity, but this technique will probably seldom be employed.

The Smiths should, of course, take all economically feasible steps to reduce the frequency and the severity of the losses. Some specific examples of possible methods were cited at the beginning of this chapter.

The principal opportunity for the Smiths to employ the transfer device is with respect to the rented cabin, but it will be assumed here that the landlord will rent to the Smiths only if they assume responsibility for losses resulting from their own negligence.

Retention will play a very important role. Some causes of loss to real property such as rust, insect damage, and war cannot be handled in any other way. The same is true of some causes of loss to personal property, and liability losses in excess of the limited amounts that can be transferred to an insurer or some other transferee. The Smiths should, in addition, retain as many small losses as possible. The exact amount depends upon the personality of the Smiths and the transfer costs in each instance,[12] but the Smiths should be able to bear losses up to $500 per occurrence without too much inconvenience.

Use of Insurance Tools

The Smiths should make extensive use of the insurance device in their planning. Several alternative insurance programs are possible. One program, which in one company and one area would cost the Smiths annually about $1,000, would be the following:

1. Homeowner's Form 3 ($100 deductible)		2. Personal auto policy—both cars	
$100,000	Dwelling	Actual	Comprehensive,
10,000	Other structures	cash	collision
50,000	Personal property	value	($100 deductible)
20,000	Additional living expense	$200,000	Liability
200,000	Liability	4,000	Medical payments
1,000	Medical payments	100,000	Uninsured motorists
250	Physical damage to property of others	No-fault endorsement	

This program would provide fairly complete property and liability insurance protection for the Smiths at a reasonable cost. It covers most of the types of losses and perils to which the Smiths are exposed and includes deductibles that reduce the cost with no significant loss in protection. Because the dwelling limit exceeds 80 percent of the replacement cost new of the dwelling less the land value and less exclusions such as the cost of excavations [80 percent of ($150,000 − $40,000)] the policy covers building losses on a cost of replacement new basis. However, the program does not cover all property perils, liability as a result of business pursuits may be retained, and covered property and liability losses may exceed the specified limits. Furthermore, the program still covers many small losses that the Smiths might be well advised to retain.

It is, of course, possible to tinker with this program in countless ways. For example, the dwelling limit could be cut to $88,000 without losing the replacement cost feature if the dwelling value is stable. It is doubtful that the loss will exceed this amount, but it could, and the dwelling will likely increase in value. The limits applicable to the other

---

[12] A "bargain," for example, cannot be ignored, but bargains are rare with respect to small-loss coverage.

property items would also be decreased. Finally, although this point is not effective here, the dwelling coverage cannot be cut below the protection required by the mortgagee. The inflation-guard endorsement noted under "Endorsements" at the end of the discussion of the homeowner's insurance forms would be useful if property values are expected to increase fairly rapidly. The Smiths might also want replacement cost insurance on the personal property covered under their homeowner's insurance.

Another possible change is an increase in the liability limits under both the personal liability and automobile liability components. Considering the loss potential and the small increase in premium for higher limits, this change would be a wise move. In fact, even if it is necessary to decrease some of the property insurance limits to obtain the extra liability protection, this premium conversion deserves serious consideration. The premium could be reduced by making more extensive use of deductibles. For example, the automobile comprehensive coverage could, like the collision coverage, be made subject to a $100 deductible. The family might also consider a $500 deductible for both these coverages and the homeowner's contract.[13] Personal catastrophe liability insurance should also be considered as a way of increasing the liability limits and expanding the covered sources of liability.

Professional pursuits may result in extensive liability claims. The Smiths should check on whether they are covered under their employers' general liability insurance policies. If not, they should investigate whether individual coverage is available at a reasonable price.

Form 3 could be replaced by Form 5 or Form 2. Form 5, which would protect the personal property as well as the dwelling against all perils not excluded, would in this case increase the premium by over $120. Form 2, which would reduce both the dwelling and the personal property protection to named-perils coverage, would reduce the premium by only about $20.

SOME KEY CONCEPTS

Additional living expenses   The extra expenses incurred by a family for housing, food, transportation, and other living costs when they cannot live in their home or apartment because a fire or other peril has made it untenantable until it has been repaired.

Homeowner's Form 3   The most popular homeowner's contract. Form 3 provides all-risks property coverage on the dwelling, named-perils property coverage on the contents, additional living expense insurance, and liability insurance. Form 3 does not include automobile insurance.

Homeowner's Form 5   The most comprehensive homeowner's contract. Form 5 resembles Form 3 except that it provides all-risks property insurance on both the dwelling and the contents.

Homeowner's Form 4   The homeowner's form designed for tenants. Form 4 resembles Form 2 except that it does not provide any property insurance on a dwelling.

---

[13] Remember, however, that only losses per accident exceeding 1 percent of adjusted gross income are deductible from taxable income. Some authorities would argue against any automobile physical damage protection, particularly collision insurance, after the car is a few years old. Accordingly the Smiths might want to discontinue collision insurance on the older car valued at $4,000.

Condominium-unit-owner's insurance   A homeowner's form designed for apartment–condominium-unit owners. This Form 8 resembles Form 4 except for some changes reflecting the fact that condominium-unit owners are not tenants.

Personal umbrella catastrophe liability insurance   A liability insurance policy that typically provides excess insurance over the insured's primary personal liability and automobile liability insurance plus protection against many losses not covered by the insured's primary liability policies in excess of some deductible.

REVIEW QUESTIONS

1 **a** Outline the potential direct property losses a typical family faces.

 b Outline the potential net income losses a typical family faces.

2 Outline the potential liability losses a typical family faces.

3 One person observed that a family should never retain any losses that it can transfer at a reasonable price because a family cannot predict its losses with much confidence.

 a Evaluate this observation with respect to property losses.

 b Evaluate this observation with respect to liability losses.

4 **a** Which of the homeowner's contracts is the most popular?

 b Analyze this contract with respect to coverage and the amount of recovery.

5 **a** Which of the homeowner's contracts provides the broadest coverage? How does it compare with Form 3?

 b Which of the homeowner's contracts provides the most restricted coverage? How does it compare with Form 3?

6 Can tenants purchase a homeowner's contract? Explain your answer.

7 Explain why the premium for a homeowner's contract may be less than the sum of the premiums for separate contracts covering fire, the extended coverage perils, theft, and liability for activities other than automobile liability.

8 A family has a dwelling valued at $80,000 (replacement cost new $100,000) and contents valued at $40,000. This property is insured under a homeowner's Form 3 with $80,000 insurance on the dwelling, a $200,000 liability limit, and a $2,000 per person medical payments limit. How much will the insurer contribute toward each of the following losses? Why? Assume that each of the property losses is stated in actual cash value terms. Replacement costs would be 25 percent higher. Assume a $100 deductible clause.

 a A windstorm destroys a detached garage valued at $6,000.

 b Fire causes $30,000 damage to the dwelling and $8,000 damage to the contents. The family must live elsewhere for four months while repairs are being made. Their monthly living expenses during these four months are $3,000 a month. The family's normal monthly living expenses are $1,400 a month.

 c Vandals cause $1,000 damage to the interior of the premises.

 d Some furniture, valued at $2,000 and stored in a warehouse, is completely destroyed in a warehouse fire.

 e Smoke from a fireplace in the living room causes $1,600 damage to wallpaper.

 f An automobile, valued at $5,000, is completely destroyed in a fire at a garage where it had been left for servicing.

9 Assuming the exposures and coverage specified in question 8, which of the following losses is covered at least in part?

 a A fire in the dwelling damages a camera that the husband borrowed from a friend.

 b A fire in the dwelling damages clothing belonging to an overnight guest.

 c A leak in a hot-water tank causes damage to contents stored in the basement.

d Paint being sprayed on a neighbor's dwelling is accidentally sprayed on the insured's dwelling.

e A thief steals cash from the premises.

f A thief steals some clothing from an unlocked car parked in front of a hotel.

g A thief steals a fur coat from a hotel room in West Germany.

h A ring mysteriously disappears.

i A burglar breaks into a laundry and takes some clothing belonging to the insured.

j A thief breaks into the insured's home and takes a fur coat belonging to an overnight guest.

10 Assuming the exposures and coverage specified in question 8, how much will the insurer contribute toward each of the following losses? Assume that the insured was negligent unless otherwise stated.

a The husband injures a companion while hunting. The companion suffers a loss of $16,000, including $2,000 in medical expenses. The husband is not legally liable.

b The situation is the same as that described in *a* except that the husband is legally liable.

c The wife injures a pedestrian with the family automobile. The pedestrian's loss is $13,000, including $3,000 in medical expenses.

d A domestic employee falls off a defective chair, suffering a loss of $4,000, including $500 in medical expenses.

e A son, aged 4, deliberately throws a rock through a neighbor's window, valued at $100. The parents are not legally responsible for their son's action.

f The husband, who is a teacher, injures a student in a physical education class. The student sustains a loss of $100 in medical expenses.

g The insured's young daughter falls down a stairway in the home. Her loss is $1,000 including $500 in medical expenses.

h The family dog bites a guest, causing a loss of $150, including $100 in medical expenses.

i While driving into his garage, the husband strikes a neighbor's child, causing a loss of $80 in medical expenses.

j Four dinner guests become violently ill as a result of certain impurities in the food. Each guest suffers a loss of $20,000 including $10,000 in medical expenses.

11 What additional protection would a family have if they purchased a personal umbrella catastrophe liability policy as well as a homeowners' Form 3 and a personal auto policy?

12 Name three surety bonds that a family might purchase.

13 In what ways would you change the program suggested for the Smith family? Why?

14 Prepare a property and liability insurance program for your own family.

SUGGESTIONS FOR ADDITIONAL READING

Fire, Casualty, and Surety Bulletins: Personal Lines Section (Cincinnati: The National Underwriter Company, monthly).

Golonka, Nancy: *How to Protect What's Yours* (Washington, D.C.: Aeropolis Books Ltd. and the Insurance Information Institute, 1983).

Guiane, G. E.: *Homeowners Guide* (Indianapolis: The Rough Notes Company, Inc., revised periodically).

Wood, G. L., C. C. Lilly, III, D. L. Malecki, and J. S. Rosenbloom: *Personal Risk Management and Insurance* (2d ed., Malvern, Pa.: American Institute for Property and Liability Underwriters, 1980).

See chapters on family insurance in the books suggested for Chapters 12, 18, and 19.

CHAPTER 33

FAMILY PERSONNEL
RISK MANAGEMENT

LEARNING OBJECTIVES

After you have completed this chapter, you should be able to:

1 Distinguish among programming, estate planning, and financial planning.

2 Explain briefly the federal estate tax and the importance of the marital deduction.

3 Describe briefly how a family can reduce the federal estate tax through gifts prior to the parents' deaths.

4 Tell how trusts might be used to reduce federal income and estate taxes.

5 Explain what personnel loss exposures might rationally be retained.

6 Display in a chart the income and cash needs of a hypothetical or real-life family in case a family member dies, is disabled, or retires.

7 Design a personnel risk management program for the family whose needs you displayed under objective 6.

INTRODUCTION

In addition to managing its property and liability risks, a family must make important decisions with respect to personnel risks associated with death, accidental injury, sickness, unemployment, and old age. This chapter deals with the recognition and measurement of these exposures, the selection of the optimum tools of risk management, and the implementation of those tools. The chapter concludes with an illustrative case.

Since much of the material required for this presentation has already been discussed in previous chapters dealing with business personnel risk management, it will be incorporated in this chapter by cross reference.

NATURE AND IMPORTANCE OF PERSONNEL RISKS

The nature, severity, and frequency of losses faced by families as a result of the five personnel perils mentioned above have already been analyzed in detail in Chapter 9. The reader is urged to review that analysis before continuing with the rest of this chapter.

The analysis of these personnel risks and the selection and implementation of the tools best suited to meet the needs and desires of a particular family are usually called *programming,* if the principal potential loss is a loss of earning power. If unexpected expenses (primarily taxes) following death and the disposition of business interests or other investments are also very important, the process is usually called *estate planning.* The two terms are often used interchangeably, the difference between them being only a matter of degree. Programming and estate planning are in turn a part of *total financial planning.* Financial planning includes, in addition to programming and estate planning, such activities as general tax management and investing with the objective of improving, not just protecting, the family's standard of living.

In programming illustrations, a graphic portrayal of the income that the family needs and desires in case of the death, disability, or superannuation of one of its members (generally, an employed husband, an employed wife, or both) is extremely useful.[1] In addition to stating the needs clearly and precisely, the chart enables the family to view its total problems at a glance. As stated in Chapter 9, following the death or disability of an employed husband or wife, the family will need some help in meeting extra expenses. It will also need (1) for a short period, a readjustment income close to the actual loss, (2) after the readjustment period until the children, if any, are self-sufficient, a reduced but still substantial income, and (3) after the children are on their own, a further reduced but adequate lifetime income for the surviving spouse or the disabled worker and spouse. If the employed husband or wife does not die prior to retirement, the family will need a replacement income following his or her retirement.

One approach that has proved useful is for one chart to show the monthly income to be replaced if the employed husband or wife were to die immediately. The horizontal axis or the time axis shows the ages of the spouse and the children at frequent critical periods (for example, when the youngest child reaches age 18). A second chart shows the amount that would be needed (1) if the employed person were to be disabled immediately and (2) because disability needs terminate at retirement, after the expected retirement age. In this instance, the horizontal axis shows in addition the age of the employed husband or wife. For examples of these two charts and their uses, assuming the person is an employed wife with an employed husband, see Figures 33.1 and 33.2, which will be described more completely in the chapter's illustrative case.

---

[1] Except for an occasional reference, unemployment is omitted from consideration in this chapter because the major tools other than retention used to handle this risk (loss-control measures by employers, social insurance, and supplementary unemployment benefits) involve no decision making by the family.

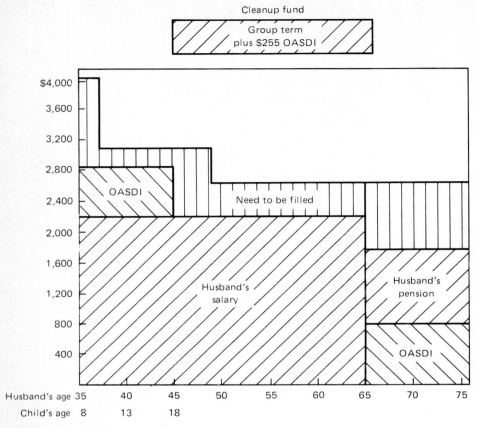

FIGURE 33.1
Smith family needs in case wife dies, and protection they now have. Death is assumed to occur immediately.

If death or disability strikes at some later date, the desired monthly income pattern will probably change. These changes over time are most commonly either ignored, noted on the static chart, or otherwise recognized by nongraphic means, but to give a dynamic picture, a series of charts can be prepared with different starting dates.

Figures 33.1 and 33.2 ignore the effect of inflation. Even if the breadwinner were to die immediately, inflation might increase the amounts required in future years to provide the purchasing power specified in the charts. For example, when the spouse is aged 45, if prices rise 50 percent in the next ten years, the monthly need will rise from $3,150 to $4,725. Similarly, the disability and retirement needs may be higher because of inflation.

Boxed areas above or below the chart can be used to describe the need for cleanup funds, mortgage funds (although, as assumed in Figures 33.1 and 33.2, this item may be built into the monthly income needs), and a medical expense fund. Cleanup costs include funeral expenses, probate costs, and estate taxes.

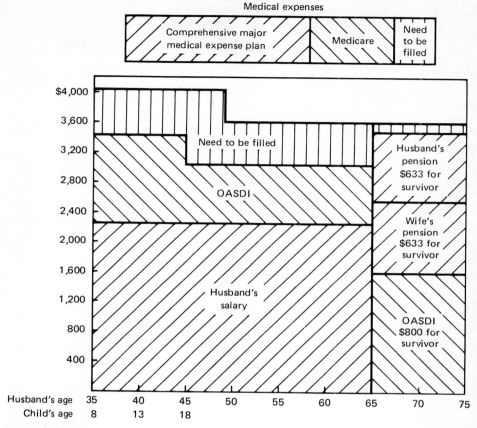

FIGURE 33.2
Smith family disability income, medical expense, and retirement needs, and protection they now have. Disability is assumed to start immediately.

USE OF NONINSURANCE TOOLS

All families utilize some noninsurance tools in dealing with personnel risks. As in the case of business firms, however, these noninsurance tools are almost always (1) loss control or (2) retention.

Loss Control

Loss-control methods can be illustrated first by various health and safety practices and by education and training designed to keep each member of the family in good health and productive in an economic sense. Families differ markedly in the extent to which they practice these methods and their effectiveness, but more efforts along these lines would probably yield sizable dividends for most families. On the other hand, it is clearly impossible to rely completely upon loss control.

A second, entirely different type of loss control uses a will, gifts, and trusts to reduce the impact of estate taxes upon death. In estate planning, the proper application of these tools is an essential part of the procedure. Their proper use demands an extensive knowledge of legal instruments and taxes, but a few major principles can be presented here.[2] Only the federal estate tax will be discussed, but state inheritance and estate taxes can also cause substantial estate shrinkages.

Perhaps the most important estate tax consideration is the marital deduction, which reduces the taxable estate by the amount left to a surviving spouse. The surviving spouse need not be given the property outright; it is sufficient (but not necessary because of a provision in the Economic Recovery Tax Act of 1981 that authorized "qualified terminable interest property") for the spouse to have the power to appoint who will receive the property upon his or her death. To illustrate the effect of the marital deduction, the following examples show for selected adjusted gross estates the taxable estate and the estate tax, assuming all, one-half, or none of the person's estate is left to his or her spouse. The adjusted gross estate is the gross estate less all debts and expenses including probate costs, burial expenses, and the medical expenses unpaid at the date of death. The taxable estate is the adjusted gross estate less the amount left to the spouse. How the estate tax is calculated will be explained shortly.

| Adjusted estate | Amount left | | Taxable estate | Estate tax |
	To spouse	To children		
$ 400,000	$ 400,000	0	0	0
400,000	200,000	$ 200,000	$ 200,000	0
400,000	0	400,000	400,000	$ 25,500
800,000	800,000	0	0	0
800,000	400,000	400,000	400,000	25,500
800,000	0	800,000	800,000	171,500
1,200,000	1,200,000	0	0	0
1,200,000	600,000	600,000	600,000	196,500
1,200,000	0	1,200,000	1,200,000	331,500
1,600,000	1,600,000	0	0	0
1,600,000	800,000	800,000	800,000	171,500
1,600,000	0	1,600,000	1,600,000	504,500

The effect of the marital deduction on the estate tax is even greater than its effect upon the taxable estate for two reasons. First, estate tax rates are highly progressive, rising from 18 percent on the first $10,000 to 55 percent on the amount over $3 million. Second, for persons dying in 1984 the calculated tax is reduced by a tax credit of $96,300, which means that no tax is payable on estates valued at about $325,000 or

---

[2] The principles described in this discussion are also important in arranging the insurance part of the plan. For example, the proper designation of beneficiaries is extremely important. Life insurance policies are also useful as gifts in trust or as direct gifts.

less. This tax credit is scheduled to increase each year until in 1987 it is $192,800, which means that no tax will be payable on estate valued at $600,000 or less.

Taking full advantage of the marital deduction, however, may not be the best decision. For example, assume that a husband dies leaving all of an $800,000 adjusted estate to his wife, who already has independent assets valued at $400,000. Upon the husband's death the taxable estate and the estate tax are both zero. When the wife dies, her taxable estate will be $1,200,000[3] and her estate tax $331,500. If the husband had instead left $300,000 of his $800,000 adjusted estate directly to their children, the tax on his estate would still be zero. The wife's taxable estate would be reduced to $900,000 and the estate tax to $210,500. If the husband had left all of his estate directly to their children, his taxable estate would also have been $800,000 and the estate tax $171,500. The wife's taxable estate would be $400,000 and the estate tax $25,500. In this case, therefore, this last disposition would yield the smallest combined tax. This example illustrates the necessity for carefully considering all the circumstances involved.

Gifts prior to death can also be used to reduce the estate tax. Gifts are subject to an annual gift tax paid by the donor but only the amounts paid in excess of $10,000 to a single donee. Thus no gift tax would be incurred if a father or mother gave each of five children $10,000 a year. The annual exclusion is doubled to $20,000 per donee if one spouse receives the consent of the other to claim their combined exclusion. Gifts from one spouse to another are not subject to any dollar limit. In other words, an unlimited marital deduction applies to gifts between spouses. Other gifts that exceed the annual exclusion are subject on accumulative basis to gift tax rates that are the same as the estate tax rates. The tax credit of $96,300 also applies, which means that taxable gifts must accumulate to over $325,000 before the donor will incur any gift tax. By 1987 this tax credit will be $192,800.

Prior to the Tax Reform Act of 1976, gifts reduced combined gift and estate taxes more than they do currently because (1) gift tax rates were lower than estate tax rates, and (2) taxable gifts were ignored in calculating estate taxes, thus lowering the estate tax bracket. The tax rates are now the same, and the gift and estate taxes are unified. When the person dies, the estate tax is first calculated on the assumption that the taxable estate is the sum of the taxable gifts and the "true" taxable estate. The estate tax then is reduced by the amount of any gift tax paid. The result is that the "true" taxable estate is subject to the same higher tax brackets that would have applied if the taxable estate had been this "true" taxable estate plus the taxable gifts. Also, only one $96,300 ($192,800 in 1987) tax credit is applied to the combined gift and estate taxes. To illustrate, if the taxable gifts accumulate to $400,000 and the "true" taxable estate is $400,000, the gift taxes would have accumulated to $25,500 ($121,800 less the tax credit of $96,300). The estate tax would be $171,500, the tax on a $800,000 estate, less the $25,500 already paid in gift taxes.

In addition to making certain that a person's estate will be distributed according to

---

[3] The sum of $1,200,000 ignores changes in the values of the assets constituting the estate, the wife's withdrawals for living expenses, and the probate costs at the time of her death.

his or her wishes, a will can direct the estate into the most favorable tax channels.[4] If no will exists, the estate is distributed according to state law. Serious adverse tax consequences may result.

Trusts are useful in connection with both estate taxes and income taxes as well as in many other ways. Under a trust a donor transfers property to a trustee who manages and distributes the property in accordance with the terms of the trust agreement for the benefit of a third person, the trust beneficiary. Trusts can be divided into two major classes: (1) living trusts (*inter vivos* trusts), which operate during the donor's lifetime, and (2) testamentary trusts, which become effective at the donor's death. The latter could involve the proceeds of life insurance policies. The study of trusts is too highly specialized to be attempted in any detail in this text,[5] but the following example will illustrate their use: Through a trust arrangement, a mother could transfer property to her child but have a trustee administer and distribute the property on the child's behalf. The property could include a life insurance policy on the mother's life. Such a transfer would constitute a gift, but it would be taxable only if the annual contribution exceeded $10,000 a year. Income taxes on the investment return on the assets in the trust would be lowered if the trust's or the child's income tax bracket were less than the mother's. Finally, when the mother dies, probate costs would be less because these assets would not be part of her estate. Of course, these advantages would have to be balanced against the legal charges, trustee fees, and other costs associated with establishing a trust.

Retention

Retention is the second frequently used noninsurance tool. In three situations the use of this tool appears rational. First, insurance is about the only satisfactory method by which a family can transfer personnel losses to an outsider,[6] and complete insurance protection is almost always impossible to obtain because of underwriting restrictions, the cost involved, or both. In other words, in this situation a family has no choice. Recognition of this fact, however, together with some advance financial and psychological preparation, should make it easier to bear the losses when they do occur.

To illustrate this use of retention, contrast the amount of protection that a family should have against the death or disability of a breadwinner according to the needs approach described in Chapter 9 with the human life value loss. The family retains the difference between the values derived under these two approaches. If the dependents know about the lower "minimum needs" value before the death or disability of the breadwinner, they should be better able to adjust to the lower standard of living that almost inevitably follows.

[4] Tax laws and consequently the most favorable tax channels often change over time. For this reason and because it is much more important that the deceased's objectives should be satisfied, tax considerations should not be overemphasized.

[5] For a text describing trusts in a nontechnical manner, see Gilbert T. Stephenson and Norman A. Wiggins, *Estates and Trusts* (5th ed., New York: Appleton-Century-Crofts, Inc., 1973). For a one-chapter discussion of the subject, see V. N. Woolfolk, "Trusts and Their Uses," in D. W. Gregg and V. B. Lucas (eds.), *Life and Health Insurance Handbook* (3d ed., Homewood, Ill.: Richard D. Irwin, Inc., 1973), chap. 56.

[6] Families sometimes transfer these risks to relatives or the public (through public-assistance plans), but this is seldom a satisfactory way of handling the loss.

Second, although this decision must depend in part upon the income status and personality of the individual family unit, most families would be well advised to consider retaining such potential losses as (1) small medical expenses and (2) short-term income losses.

A third situation in which retention may be rational applies only to preparation for retirement. The advantages and disadvantages of insurance as an investment have already been discussed in Chapter 23. As stated there, because of the advantages risk managers may wish to use low-cost nonterm life insurance and annuities as one of their fixed-dollar investments. Families, however, should also use other types of investments, such as savings accounts, credit union shares or deposits, money market funds, municipal bonds, and common stocks to prepare for their retirement. Some may have such attractive alternative investment opportunities and the self-discipline necessary to carry out their investment plans that they may not care to use any insurance in their preparation for retirement. Some may prefer to rely heavily upon other investments prior to retirement, at which date they will transfer some of the risk by using part of the accumulated funds to purchase an annuity. The proper balance is an individual family decision, but it must be made with knowledge and appreciation of the advantages of *all* forms of investments.

USES OF INSURANCE

Families make more extensive use of insurance to handle their personnel risk problems than do business firms for several reasons. First, many employee benefit plans that create retained risks for the employer constitute insurance protection for the employee. For example, a pension plan that is self-insured by the employer provides insurance protection for the employee, the employer being the insurer. Likewise, supplemental unemployment benefits are insurance benefits for the employee even though they are self-insured by the employer. Second, a family is less able to retain risks because of its more limited exposure and less flexible financial position.

The average family has three layers of insurance protection: (1) social insurance (usually OASDHI), (2) an employee benefit plan, and (3) individual insurance. The protection afforded by OASDHI was explained in Chapter 20; the other two layers were discussed in Chapters 21 through 25.

To determine how much individual insurance and which combination of policies are best in the particular instance, the risk manager should follow these steps:

1 From the needs determined in the risk analysis, subtract the amounts already provided by programs that involve little or no decision making by the insured; e.g., OASDHI benefits and lump-sum payments under group life insurance programs.

2 From the needs that remain, subtract the benefits already provided by other programs (generally individual life insurance contracts) that do involve some decision—usually the choice of the proper settlement option.[7] In choosing these options,

---

[7] Sometimes a change in existing contracts is in order, but generally speaking, a prima facie case exists for maintaining existing contracts. The primary argument against surrendering old contracts in order to purchase new ones or to use the funds in some other manner is the high initial expense in personnel insurance policies and the use of a large part of the premium dollar in the early years to pay for this expense. An argument in favor of replacement is that if the contract is nonparticipating, interest rates on current contracts may be much more attractive.

two important principles should be kept in mind. First, the higher the mortality rates used to compute the periodic payments the stronger the case for choosing a life annuity. Second, contracts with high guaranteed interest rates should be used to provide periodic payments over many years through life annuities or installment options of long duration. Conversely, contracts with options based upon relatively low interest rates should be used to fill the short-term needs.

3 From the needs that are not met by existing insurance protection, determine what amount the insured wishes to retain. These losses will supposedly be met out of assets already accumulated (stocks, bonds, savings accounts, and the like) or to be accumulated in the future.

4 The needs that remain after the completion of the first three steps must be met through insurance, and the problem is to select some combination of insurance policies that will meet those needs.

The death proceeds needed at any age and the cash value accumulations required at retirement age can be determined with the aid of settlement options. For example, assume that the need is (1) $600 a month for 20 years if the insured dies prior to age 65, there being no lump-sum needs, and (2) a life income of $690 a month for the insured (a male) after he reaches age 65, with payments certain for 10 years. Using the table of settlement options reproduced in part as Table 23.6, one can calculate the required death proceeds as 600/5.39 × $1,000, or about $111,000, and the cash value accumulations as 690/6.26 × $1,000, or also about $111,000.

These two amounts, plus the family's views on budgeting the premiums, suggest the types of life insurance and annuities to be purchased. To illustrate, suppose the desired death proceeds are to be $111,000 in case of death at any time prior to age 65, but the amount of retirement income to be provided through insurance is zero. If the insured wishes to budget premiums uniformly over his or her earning career, the appropriate contract is a term-to-65 contract. If the same circumstances prevailed but $111,000 was also to be accumulated at retirement age, as is true in the case illustrated, an endowment at 65 would be the most suitable contract. The selection is not usually this simple, a combination of insurance policies usually being required to meet the stated needs. For example, if the desired death proceeds are $111,000 and the retirement accumulations at age 65 $60,000, one possible combination (but probably not the best) would be a $60,000 endowment-at-65 and a $51,000 term-to-65 contract. If a straight life contract produced a cash value at age 65 of $500 per $1,000, another combination would be a $102,000 straight life insurance contract and a $9,000 endowment at age 65. Because of quantity discounts it may be almost as cheap (or even cheaper) to purchase one contract that does more than the insured requires rather than purchase an exact fit.

After the cost of the combination selected has been computed, it is highly possible that the members of the family will wish to reconsider the losses they have agreed to retain, in which case a new combination of insurance policies must be selected.

The need for disability income and medical expense contracts is met by selecting those contracts that (1) provide disability income payments at the desired times and in the desired amounts and (2) pay the prescribed medical expenses. Because health insurance contracts are less flexible than life insurance contracts, one will rarely be able to find a contract that meets the needs exactly. For example, it is not always possible to find a disability income contract that will provide an income to *any* specified age. Consequently, some revision of the potential losses to be retained is almost always a necessary part of this insurance decision. This decision will be described more fully in the illustrative case that follows, but two general remarks are in order here. First, the risk manager should remember that life insurance contracts can be endorsed to provide attractive disability income benefits. Second, noncancelable and guaranteed renewable contracts should be given very serious consideration because of the certain protection they provide to advanced ages.

The graphic presentation suggested in the risk analysis section can also be used to advantage in selecting the tools of risk management. Different shadings or colors are used to represent OASDHI, employee benefit plan protection, existing individual insurance, and the remaining needs, if any. This graphic presentation simplifies and emphasizes the required changes in the total personnel insurance program. The graphic approach is illustrated in the case that follows.

Beginning in the late sixties insurers have made increasing use of computers to perform the necessary calculations and to prepare tabular and graphic presentations for insureds.

AN ILLUSTRATIVE CASE

The case to be presented is oversimplified in order to emphasize the principles involved instead of the details. The reader should also remember that (1) several solutions might be suggested to the personnel risk problems posed by this family and that (2) a change in the circumstances of the family might make the suggested solution inappropriate. For the latter reason, any program should be subjected to some periodic review.

Risk Analysis

Mary and John Smith, both age 35, have one child, aged 8. Mary works for a small office supply firm which pays her an after-tax annual salary of $27,000. Her prospects for advancement in the firm are bright. Mary has some valuable noncontributory employee benefits at work. She is covered under a $20,000 group life insurance program, a comprehensive major medical expense plan with a $100 deductible and a $500,000 maximum limit, a dental expense plan, and a pension plan that at age 65 will pay Mary $12,000 a year for the rest of her life. If John is alive when Mary retires and Mary selects a joint and two-thirds survivorship option, the annual pension income while both are alive will be $11,400. The pension plan provides no preretirement death benefits or disability benefits other than protection of her retirement benefits in case she is permanently and totally disabled. The group life insurance, medical expense insurance, and dental expense insurance terminate upon Mary's retirement. All of these employee benefits are paid in addition to OASDI benefits.

John works for a medium-size manufacturing firm which also pays him an after-tax annual salary of $27,000. His employer provides the following noncontributory employee benefit plans: a group life insurance plan with a face amount equal to one year's salary, a long-term disability plan that would pay 65 percent of the lost wages, a comprehensive major medical expense plan with a $100 deductible and a $250,000 maximum limit, a dental expense plan, and a pension plan that at age 65 will pay John $12,000 a year for the rest of his life. If Mary is alive when John retires and John selects a joint and two-thirds survivorship option, the annual pension income will be initially $11,400. The pension plan provides a $10,000 preretirement death benefit but no disability benefit other than protection of his retirement benefits in case he is permanently and totally disabled. Upon John's retirement the group life insurance is continued for half the preretirement amount, but the medical expense insurance, dental expense insurance, and long-term disability insurance are terminated. All of John's employee benefits are paid in addition to OASDI benefits except the long-term disability insurance from which John's OASDI worker's disability income benefits are subtracted.

The Smiths have a home, valued at $120,000 including the land. They built the home five years ago. The unpaid balance on the mortgage, which has 20 more years to run, is $70,000. The home, when furnished, would probably rent for about $1,200 per month and, if built new today, would cost about $150,000. The land, the cost of excavations, foundations, and the like are valued at $40,000.

The Smiths also have two cars, one valued at $10,000 with a replacement cost new of $12,000 and the other valued at $4,000 with a replacement cost new of $10,000; typical furniture, clothing, and the like[8] valued at $54,000 with a replacement cost new of $70,000; savings, checking, and money market accounts totalling $15,000, two individual retirement accounts each worth $4,500; and in a safe deposit box, some common stocks and mutual fund certificates with a current market value of $40,000.[9]

The Smiths are an active family with strong interests in sports. They participate in many social and civic activities. They often lend their cars to friends or organizations, and they in turn drive cars belonging to others. John, in addition, frequently drives a company car on business trips.

Each summer the Smiths rent a cabin in the northern part of the state for two weeks. They drive to the cabin in their car, to which they attach a rented utility trailer containing about $6,000 in furniture, clothing, and the like, for which the replacement cost new is $8,000.

If Mary or John should die, the surviving spouse will lose the present value of the deceased's future after-tax earnings less her or his maintenance cost. Assume Mary dies. Even if her salary would not have increased over time (an unlikely event in this case), the present value at age 35 of her future earnings, assuming a maintenance cost of $12,000 and an after-tax interest return of 5 percent, is about $230,000. The extra expenses would include such items as funeral expenses, probate costs, and federal

---

[8] A detailed listing of this property is omitted here to save space and to simplify the discussion.

[9] The reader will probably notice the absence of any reference to life insurance or to life insurance cash values. This omission is intentional because the same illustration is to be used in the next chapter to develop a life and health risk management program, and the omission of any existing insurance simplifies that discussion immeasurably.

estate taxes. For present purposes, our estimate of these extra expenses will be $20,000.

If Mary or John should be totally and permanently disabled, the economic loss to the family would be even greater because the maintenance cost could not be deducted. For example, under the assumptions noted above for Mary, the economic loss would be about $415,000. Temporary disability would shorten the period of lost earnings. Medical expenses, of course, could be substantial, even for a short-term illness.

If Mary and John both live to age 65 and retire, they will need sufficient income to cover their expenses for the rest of their lives. If only Mary or John survives to age 65, that person will need enough money to pay her or his expenses.

If the child dies or becomes disabled, the Smiths would lose the money they "invested" in the child. If the child is disabled, the Smiths may also have to support the child for years after which the child would normally have become independent. The child's medical expenses could be a serious problem even if the child does not die or become disabled.

As noted in Chapter 9, the "needs" approach to determining the income needs in case of death, disability, or retirement is more realistic. The Smiths agree that they need to replace lost income only if Mary or John dies, is disabled, or retires. The same is true of unexpected expenses associated with death. With respect to medical expenses, however, the potential losses caused by the entire family are to be recognized. Implicitly, therefore, the Smiths have elected to retain the risks associated with the child's death or disability other than the child's medical expenses.

The Smiths also agree to retain some of the losses associated with Mary's or John's possible death, disability, or retirement. Mary and John recognize that if these events occur, the survivor's standard of living will be reduced somewhat.

Specifically, Mary and John estimate that if either dies, the family would need 90 percent of their current joint after-tax income to continue during a two-year readjustment period; 70 percent thereafter, until the child graduates from college at age 22; and 60 percent for the remainder of the surviving spouse's life. These percentages are based on the assumption that the surviving spouse will continue to work and that mortgage payments of $700 a month will continue for 20 years.

If either Mary or John is disabled, they estimate they will need 90 percent of their current joint after-tax income until their child completes college, and 80 percent from that point until retirement.

After retirement, Mary and John want a retirement income equal to 80 percent of their current joint after-tax salaries with 50 percent of these salaries being continued for the surviving spouse.

To simplify the presentation, from this point on we will consider only the needs of the surviving husband and child if Mary dies, is disabled, or retires. Under all three outcomes, we will further assume that John continues to work until age 65, at which time he retires. A final simplifying assumption (that is incorrect in this case) is that all the OASDI and pension benefits provide after-tax income.

The income needs and desires of the Smith family if Mary dies, is disabled, or retires are presented in the first column of Table 33.1. These needs, together with the cash needs for a cleanup fund in case of death and medical expenses, are more clearly

TABLE 33.1
SMITH FAMILY INCOME NEEDS, PRESENT PROTECTION, AND NEEDS NOT COVERED
ASSUMING MARY DIES, IS DISABLED, OR RETIRES

John's age	Monthly need	Present protection	Remainder
Mary dies:			
35 through 36	$4,050	$600—OASDI $2,250—John's earnings	$1,200
37 through 44	$3,150	$600—OASDI $2,250—John's earnings	$300
45 through 48	$3,150	$2,250—John's earnings	$900
49 through 64	$2,700	$2,250—John's earnings	$450
65 on	$2,700	$800—OASDI $1,000—John's pension	$900
Mary is disabled:			
35 through 44	$4,050	$1,200—OASDI* $2,250—John's earnings	$600
45 through 48	$4,050	$800—OASDI $2,250—John's earnings	$1,000
49 through 64	$3,600	$800—OASDI $2,250—John's earnings	$550
Mary and John retire:			
65 until first person dies	$3,600	$1,600—two OASDI pensions $950—Mary's pension $950—John's pension	$100
After first person dies	$2,250	$800—OASDI pension $1,267—survivor's pensions	$183

* Actual OASDHI benefits would depend upon Mary's past taxable earnings and the benefit formulas described in Chap. 20. In order to qualify for OASDHI disability income payments, Mary's disability must be expected either to result in death or to last at least 12 months. Furthermore, a 5-month waiting period must elapse before any benefits will be paid.

and dramatically stated in Figures 33.1 and 33.2. In Table 33.1 and the two figures the death and disability needs are expressed on the assumption that Mary dies or is disabled immediately. If she dies or is disabled later, certain needs such as the dependency period income will change. These changes can be illustrated graphically by charts based on other assumed death or disability ages or notations on the static charts.

All of these needs statements ignore the likelihood that Mary's salary would probably have increased over time and that the cost of living would probably also increase. The needs statements can be adjusted to reflect these increases. To do so would unduly complicate this introductory presentation, but in real life cases these increases cannot be ignored. Otherwise the family is retaining the risk of inflation except for sources such as OASDI benefits which are inflation-adjusted. Another point that will not be considered in this analysis, but should be in real life, is that just as the needs are stated on an after-tax basis, so should the replacement income from OASDI, private pensions, and other sources.

Recommended Tools and Their Implementation

Now that the problem has been defined, the next step is to determine the extent to which it has already been solved. The following facts are pertinent. Smith is entitled to the OASDHI benefits shown in Table 33.1. The OASDHI benefit structure was explained in Chapter 20. The benefits assumed here are hypothetical. Mary's primary insurance amount is assumed to be $800 as is John's. Until age 18, the child would receive 75 percent of Mary's PIA if Mary dies, 50 percent if she is disabled. John would receive no spouse's death or disability benefit because his earnings are too high. Neither Mary nor John would receive a spouse's retirement benefit because their own PIAs are higher.

John's earnings would be an important source of continued income if Mary dies or is disabled. After John reaches age 65, his earnings would stop, but his OASDI retirement benefit and his private pension would replace a good share of his earnings. If Mary and John retire, they both are entitled to OASDI retirement benefits and private pensions.

Mary also has a $20,000 group life insurance policy which, together with the OASDI $255 lump-sum benefit, would provide enough money for a cleanup fund. Mary is also covered at work under an excellent medical and dental expense insurance program.

Mary and John have decided that, except for their individual retirement accounts, their other noninsurance assets would be used (1) to meet those losses that the family has already agreed to retain because in its planning it elected to ignore some types of losses (e.g., the child's death or disability) and (2) to provide some supplementary benefits in connection with those needs that have been recognized (e.g., retirement income in excess of the amounts indicated in the table). In other words, the remaining needs shown in Table 33.1 are to be met through insurance.

Several insurance programs are possible, but a specific program will be developed for illustrative purposes. The desired death protection and retirement needs will be considered first. The death protection needs may be reorganized and summarized as follows:

1 $450 a month for John beginning at age 65
2 $450 a month for John beginning at age 45
3 $450 a month for 4 years beginning 10 years from now
4 $900 a month for 2 years

Need 1 should be filled first because the proceeds used to meet this need can be placed under the interest option until the income is required, thus reducing the earlier income needs. If the appropriate settlement option values are those in Table 23.6, the insurance proceeds that must be applied at age 65 to provide John with $450 a month are 450/6.26 × $1,000, or approximately $72,000. If this amount is placed on a 3 percent interest option until it is needed at age 65, it will yield 72 × $2.47, or about $178 a month until that time. Thus need 2 is reduced to about $272 a month, need 3 to $272 a month, and need 4 to $722 a month.

The proceeds required to satisfy needs 2 and 3 can also be used to provide some of the income required under need 1 because these proceeds would not be required until 10 years from now when John would be age 45. If the appropriate settlement option values are again those in Table 23.6, the proceeds required to satisfy need 2 would be 272/4.13 × $1,000, or about $66,000. The proceeds required to satisfy need 3 would be 272/21.97 × $1,000, or about $12,000. These two proceeds, which total $78,000 and would not be required for 10 years, would under the interest option yield in the meantime 78 × $2.47, or about $193 monthly. Need 4, therefore, is further reduced to $529 a month. According to the Table 23.6 settlement option table, the proceeds required to provide $529 a month for two years would be 529/42.77 × $1,000, or over $12,000.

According to this analysis, if Mary dies immediately, the insurance amount required to meet the remaining needs would be $72,000 + $66,000 + $12,000 + $12,000, or $162,000.

As already noted, because of inflation, if the Smiths want to maintain the desired standard of living for John and the child, they may need life insurance on Mary's life with a face amount higher than $162,000. On the other hand, if prices would not increase, the $162,000 face amount is probably higher than the Smiths' needs. For example, as stated in Chapter 23, the settlement option values in Table 23.6 are minimum guaranteed amounts. Actual payments per $1,000 of insurance are likely to be higher. Furthermore, if Mary died at, say, age 45 instead of age 35, the needs would be less. Consequently, the face amount should decrease over time.

According to Table 33.1, the Smiths have already met most of their retirement needs through OASDHI and their employers' pension plans. However, because the private pension income is taxable and the OASDI benefit may be taxable, the remaining need will be greater than the table indicates. On the other hand, the Smiths intend to continue depositing $4,000 annually in their individual retirement accounts until they reach age 65. The after-tax income from these IRAs, added to the after-tax OASDI and private pension benefits, should at least equal the stated retirement need.

To summarize, to protect John and the child in case Mary dies, the Smiths need in addition to their present protection a $162,000 life insurance contract. Because the Smiths have already adequately prepared for their retirement, they need not purchase any annuities or life insurance with a cash value. They should purchase a $162,000 term-to-age-65 insurance contract.

This analysis assumes that the Smiths need no life insurance after age 65. The Smiths, however, may want some whole life insurance through which they can create an estate to be transferred upon their death to their child. Furthermore, a cleanup fund may be needed regardless of when death occurs. Finally, depending upon the return on alternative investments, life insurance may be an attractive savings medium.

The premium for this much protection may be more than the Smiths are willing and able to pay. If this is true, the objectives must be revised downward. The least important needs must be identified and treated. For many families, the two needs likely to be reduced first are those for a life income for the spouse (because there may be time to adjust to the changed situation by then) and for retirement income. In this example, we will assume that no downward revision is necessary. However, the disability portion of the program should also be analyzed before any final decision is made.

When placed under the appropriate settlement options,[10] this new life insurance plus the existing protection will produce the income pattern stated in the objectives. The options may be selected by the insured or left to the discretion of the beneficiary, depending upon the wishes of the insured. Finally, the contracts should be checked carefully with respect to such details as the method of naming beneficiaries.

The discussion now turns to disability income and medical expense needs. The disability needs must be rewritten in a slightly different fashion from the way they appear in Table 33.1 because, unlike life insurance proceeds, disability income benefits cannot be deferred under an interest option. The suggested revision is as follows:

1 $700 a month beginning two weeks after the disability commences and terminating when the husband is aged 65. (This $700 provides $100 more than is required before the disabled husband reaches age 45, $300 less during ages 45 through 48, and $50 more from age 49 through 64. Securing the necessary contracts is simplified by this change.)

2 $1,200 a month beginning two weeks after the disability commences and terminating five months later. This need arises because of the five-month waiting period under OASDHI.

As was demonstrated in Chapter 24, disability income contracts are not completely flexible with respect to the maximum duration of benefits payable. Noncancelable contracts, however, are available that would take care of the first need because the required duration is to age 65. The second need can be satisfied approximately with a contract providing benefits for up to 26 weeks. One way to reduce the costs of these policies would be to increase the waiting period. Another approach to the first need would be to attach a disability income rider to part of the life insurance to be purchased. This approach is worthy of consideration because of the expense savings associated with the use of riders.

The life insurance and the disability income contracts, as well as any medical expense contracts that might be needed, should be endorsed, whenever possible, to provide for waiver of future premiums in case of total and permanent disability.

No individual medical expense insurance is required except possibly to cover expenses that exceed the $500,000 limit on the employer-provided comprehensive medical expense insurance. This need is lessened by the fact that, we will assume, Mary and the child are also covered under John's employer's contract, subject to a coordination-of-benefits provision.

Although Mary and John work for employers with strong employee benefit plans, as improvements they might suggest higher life insurance limits, a long-term disability insurance plan for Mary, a comprehensive medical expense insurance limit of $1 million or more, some postretirement death and medical expense benefits, and a cafeteria or flexible benefits plan.

In closing, we should note once again that the solution to a programming problem is

---

[10] Insurers vary with respect to the flexibility of their settlement options. For example, some permit options to be changed at any time, while others do not.

not unique. The suggested solution, however, indicates the type of reasoning that should be employed in order to select the proper tools to meet the stated needs.

SOME KEY CONCEPTS

Programming   The analysis of a family's personnel loss exposures and the selection and implementation of the tools best suited to meet that family's needs and desires, assuming the principal potential loss by far is a loss of earning power.

Estate planning   The analysis of a family's personnel loss exposures and the selection and implementation of the tools best suited to meet that family's needs when estate and inheritance taxes and the disposition of business interests or other investments are important concerns.

Financial planning   Estate planning plus tax planning, investment counseling, and other measures designed to improve a family's standard of living, not just to protect it in case a personnel loss occurs.

Marital deduction   A deduction that reduces the federal taxable estate by the amount of the estate left to a surviving spouse.

Trust   An arrangement under which a donor transfers property to a trustee who manages and distributes the property in accordance with the terms of a trust agreement for the benefit of a trust beneficiary.

REVIEW QUESTIONS

1 Illustrate how you would portray graphically the financial needs of a family consisting of an employed husband, aged 30, a wife the same age who is a homemaker, and a daughter, aged 3, in case the husband dies, is disabled, or retires.

2 a A family consists of a husband aged 45, a wife aged 40, and two sons aged 21 and 18. The husband is the sole owner of assets totaling $900,000. The other members of the family control very few assets. The husband and wife have agreed that all the assets except a $100,000 life insurance policy are to pass directly to the children upon his death. Comment on this arrangement.

  b Would your comments on the above situation be different if the wife also controlled assets valued at $900,000?

  c How could this family make use of gifts to reduce its estate tax?

3 a Distinguish between an *inter vivos* and a testamentary trust.

  b What advantages are afforded by trust arrangements?

4 Under what conditions is retention a rational approach to family personnel risk management?

5 Outline the steps you would follow to determine the additional personnel insurance required by a family.

6 Would you recommend that a contract issued when the assumed mortality rates were high be applied under a five-year fixed-period option?

7 a Prepare an alternative risk management program for the Smith family in case Mary dies, is disabled, or retires.

  b In what ways is your program superior to the one in the text? Inferior?

8 Prepare a risk management program for the Smith family in case John is the person who dies, is disabled, or retires.

9 How would Figures 33.1 and 33.2 be changed

  a if prices were assumed to rise 4 percent each year?

b if 10 years elapse and new charts must be drawn?
c if at the same time Mary dies John is permanently and totally disabled?

SUGGESTIONS FOR ADDITIONAL READING

Belth, Joseph M.: *Life Insurance: A Consumer's Handbook* (Bloomington: Indiana University Press, 1973).

Dickerson, O. D.: *Health Insurance* (3d ed., Homewood, Ill.: Richard D. Irwin, Inc., 1968), chap. 21.

Fundamentals of Federal Income, Estate and Gift Taxes (Indianapolis: The Research and Review Service of America, revised periodically).

Greene, M. R., and R. R. Dince: *Personal Financial Management* (Cincinnati: South-Western Publishing Co., 1983).

Gregg, D. W., and V. B. Lucas (eds.): *Life and Health Insurance Handbook* (3d ed., Homewood, Ill.: Richard D. Irwin, Inc., 1973), chaps. 52–60.

Hallman, G. V., and J. S. Rosenbloom: *Personal Financial Planning* (3d ed., New York: McGraw-Hill Book Company, 1983).

Huebner, S. S., and K. Black: *Life Insurance* (10th ed., New York: Prentice-Hall, Inc., 1983), chaps. 2 and 4.

Mehr, R. I., and S. G. Gustavson: *Life Insurance: Theory and Practice* (3d ed., Austin: Business Publications, Inc., 1984), chaps. 19 and 20.

Stephenson, G. T., and N. A. Wiggins: *Estates and Trusts* (5th ed., New York: Appleton-Century-Crofts, Inc., 1973).

Wolff, Thomas J.: *Capital Need Analysis—Basic Sales Manual* (Vernon, Conn.: Vernon Publishing Services, Inc., 1977).

Wood, G. L., C. C. Lilly, III, D. S. Malecki, and J. S. Rosenbloom: *Personal Risk Management Insurance* (2d ed., Malvern, Pa.: American Institute for Property and Liability Underwriters, 1980).

PART **FOUR**

RISK MANAGEMENT, INSURANCE, AND PUBLIC POLICY

As responsible citizens, risk managers should be intensely concerned with public policy in the performance of their risk management function. Public programs or legislation that relate directly to risk management have already been noted at many points throughout the text. For example, OASDHI, the nation's leading social insurance program, was described in Chapter 20. Workers' compensation and automobile no-fault legislation were discussed in Chapter 8. The effects of ERISA on private pension plans were an important part of Chapter 22. Other examples are OSHA, the Consumer Product Safety Act, the Internal Revenue Code, the Price-Anderson Act, and prohibitions against considering the age, sex, or marital status of the operator in pricing automobile insurance.

The one chapter in this fourth and final part of the text is concerned exclusively with one important part of public policy—government regulation of the insurance business. In *German Alliance Co. v. Lewis*, 233 U.S. 389 (1914), the Supreme Court declared insurance to be a business "affected with a public interest." Special attention is paid to the impact of the "age of consumerism" and programs in which the government and private insurers have joined forces to increase the availability of certain types of insurance.

CHAPTER **34**

GOVERNMENT REGULATION OF INSURANCE

LEARNING OBJECTIVES

After you have completed this chapter, you should be able to:

1 Describe briefly the purposes of insurance regulation.
2 Explain why competition alone is not an adequate regulator of insurance.
3 List the general statutory powers and duties of state insurance commissioners.
4 Describe the steps taken by state insurance commissioners to preserve insurer solvency.
5 Explain and evaluate the two major approaches to rate regulation.
6 Tell what steps states have taken to improve the availability of insurance.
7 Describe the programs Congress has established to meet the special availability problems involving properties in urban core areas, flood insurance on real property, and crime insurance.
8 Explain the relationship between investment income and the profit loading in property and liability insurance rates.
9 Describe briefly insurer guaranty funds.
10 Tell why state insurance commissioners are concerned about insurers being part of a holding company.
11 Present arguments for and against state regulation of insurance.
12 Trace the legal development of the role of the federal government in the regulation of insurance.

INTRODUCTION

The insurance business is a business ''affected with a public interest'' and thus subject to much closer regulation than most industries. This chapter discusses the purposes of insurance regulation, why competition is an inadequate regulator, the development and structure of state regulation, some current regulatory concerns, and the issue of state versus federal regulation.

THE PURPOSES OF REGULATION

Until the sixties the major objectives of insurance regulation were (1) preserving the financial solvency of insurers, (2) regulating rates to avoid excessiveness, inadequacy, or unfair discrimination in pricing, and (3) controlling trade practices to encourage fair competition and marketing. During that decade these objectives were restated to emphasize consumer needs and the services that should be rendered by private insurers. To illustrate, in 1968, Richard E. Stewart, then New York State Superintendent of Insurance, suggested that the purpose of insurance regulation should be to help insurance consumers "get the most for their money."[1] Within this broad purpose Superintendent Stewart identified three specific objectives:

1 Insurance must be made available to all who want and need it.

2 The insurance product should be of high quality and reliability. To illustrate, contract provisions should be clear and fair; arbitrary cancellations should be prohibited; and consumers should be protected against insurer insolvencies.

3 Insurance prices should be as low as possible, not subject to large and sudden changes, and fair as among policyholders. They should also increase, rather than decrease, the likelihood that the first two objectives will be achieved.

Some would impose an additional criterion on insurance rates, namely that they be "affordable" or related to the consumer's ability to pay. Because of this criterion, some of the programs described later are subsidized by the government. Also insurers may not be permitted to use as many rating classes as they would like, thus increasing the likelihood that insureds of different quality are placed in the same class. The higher-quality insureds in each class thus subsidize the lower-quality insureds in the same class who are thus better able to afford the coverage. Because "affordable" rates may not be "fair" in the private equity sense, regulators must determine the relative weight assigned to each objective.

COMPETITION AS A REGULATOR

According to classical economic theory, in a perfectly competitive world consumer satisfaction would be maximized without any government regulation. No business would make any excess profits; all businesses would operate at peak efficiency; prices would be the lowest possible; and insurers would not practice unfair price discrimination. Perfect competition is an economic model that does not now exist and may never

---

[1] Richard E. Stewart, "Ritual and Reality in Insurance Regulation," in S. L. Kimball and H.S. Denenberg (eds.), *Insurance, Government, and Social Policy* (Homewood, Ill.: Richard D. Irwin, Inc., 1969), p. 25. For another classic article on the objectives of insurer regulation see Spencer L. Kimball, "The Regulation of Insurance," reproduced on pp. 3–16 of the same book.

have existed. This model requires among other things (1) a large number of buyers and sellers, none of whom can influence the price for a given product, (2) identical products, (3) perfect information, and (4) perfect freedom of entry and exit.

In the real world imperfections abound in all industries, including the insurance business. Usually we find (1) a limited number of buyers and sellers who can influence the price, (2) real or perceived product differences, (3) imperfect information on the part of both the buyer and the seller, and (4) restrictions, legal or practical, on entry and exit to an industry.

A more attainable but still desirable state is "workable" competition. Workable competition exists when the following conditions, among others, are met: (1) A sufficient number of buyers and sellers exist to provide genuine alternative sources of supply and demand. (2) Closely related products are readily available. (3) Information, though incomplete, is available, and no actions are taken to withhold this information from any group of suppliers or sellers. (4) No artificial barriers to entry or exit exist. The existence of workable competition in an industry is tested by measuring (1) its performance, (2) its structure, and (3) its conduct. When the public through its representatives determines that workable competition does not exist or is threatened in a given industry, it turns to some form of government regulation. The greater the departure from workable competition, the tighter the regulation. This regulation commonly takes one or more of the following forms: (1) maintaining competition (antitrust laws), (2) setting the plane of competition (truth-in-lending laws), (3) replacing competition with regulation (utility commissions), and (4) substituting public for private enterprises (the U.S. Postal Service).

The insurance business is clearly not perfectly competitive. Whether it is characterized by workable competition is a subject of intense debate. Most observers recognize, however, that the degree of competition varies among lines of insurance and the markets serviced, for example, the geographical area or age group.[2]

Four characteristics of the insurance business have made it a special target for regulation:

1 Elimination of the marginal firm under a competitive environment is contrary to the basic purpose of the insurance institution, namely, to guarantee performance of future contingent financial obligations. Financial solvency is the foundation of public confidence in the private insurance mechanism and historically has been the primary objective of regulation.

2 The consumer is unable to evaluate the insurer's promises of future performance as well as he or she can evaluate tangible goods and services.

3 Complete freedom of entry of new insurance firms is not desirable because of the fiduciary nature of the policyholder-insurer relationship and the resulting opportunities for fraud and financial speculation by unregulated promoters.

---

[2] J. S. Hanson, R. E. Dineen, and M. B. Johnson, *Monitoring Competition: A Means of Regulating the Property and Liability Insurance Business,* vol. 1 (Milwaukee: National Association of Insurance Commissioners, 1974), pp. 248–390. See also Paul L. Jaskow, "Cartels, Competition and Regulation in the Property-Liability Insurance Industry," *Bell Journal of Economics,* vol. IV, no. 3 (Autumn, 1973), pp. 375–427.

4 Intensive unregulated competition in marketing insurance may produce unfair loss-adjusting practices, misleading policy language, and monopolization, all of which are recognized to be against the public interest.

Considerations such as these plus some actual abuses around the turn of the century (excessive profits, unfair discrimination, and insolvencies allegedly caused by destructive competition) caused the United States Supreme Court in 1914 to declare that insurance is a business "affected with a public interest."[3]

As will be evident in later sections, all four forms of regulation have been applied to insurance. The approaches vary among states, lines of insurance, and the activity that is being regulated. The basic theory has been to protect and preserve competition as the prime regulator of insurance activities and at the same time to superimpose boundary lines on marketing, investment, and pricing activities.

As noted, regulators are now being asked to play a more active role in helping insureds "get the most for their money" and in achieving certain social objectives. As will be illustrated later in this chapter, in some instances government and the insurance industry have cooperated in insurance ventures designed to achieve basic social objectives that otherwise private insurers would probably not have initiated.

THE STRUCTURE AND FUNCTIONS OF STATE REGULATION

The earliest insurers established in the United States received their charters from state governments or were incorporated under state statutes, as were other business institutions. Early regulations pertaining specifically to insurance dealt with the licensing of agents and insurers, contract provisions, and investments. The two primary objectives of regulation during this early period were raising tax revenues and assuring financial solvency.

Development of Commission Regulation

In 1851, New Hampshire appointed a three-man commission to examine insurers annually. In 1852, Massachusetts established a Board of Insurance Commissioners, composed of a secretary, treasurer, and auditor and charged with general enforcement of the insurance laws. Several other states created similar boards around the same time. By these acts, the modern system of state supervision came into existence. It was not until 1859, however, that New York became the first state to appoint a single insurance commissioner.

The most famous of the early insurance commissioners was Elizur Wright, who served as a member of a two-man board in Massachusetts from 1858 to 1867. As a professor of mathematics, Wright had become interested in the mathematics of level premium life insurance, the development of reserves, and nonforfeiture laws. In 1858, Wright secured passage by the Massachusetts legislature of a bill that required life insurers to maintain reserves that made it mathematically certain that money would be available to pay the benefits promised. As commissioner of insurance, he also secured

[3] *German Alliance Insurance Co. v. Lewis,* 233 U.S. 389 (1914).

passage of a nonforfeiture law and developed methods of reporting and accounting that became the blueprint for the sound development of private life insurance.

In 1866, a bill was introduced in Congress that would have established federal regulation of insurance but no action was taken. Three years later came the first of several decisions of the United States Supreme Court holding that issuing a policy of insurance was not a "transaction in Commerce," that "these contracts are not articles of Commerce," and that, therefore, Congress had no authority to regulate insurance as interstate commerce.[4] These decisions stimulated state legislatures to establish permanent administrative agencies to supervise insurance company activities. By 1871, practically all the states had some supervision and control of insurers through established commissions.

With the evolvement of many separate state insurance commissions and their crazy quilt of insurance regulations, it became apparent that some form of national association was needed to eliminate many of the inconsistencies in state regulations. The New York superintendent of insurance requested a meeting of all state insurance regulators. At this first meeting in 1871 the National Association of Insurance Commissioners was formed. Since that time the NAIC has continued to meet, at first annually and later semiannually, to discuss technical and legal problems relating to the development of uniform legislation and administrative solutions to the major problems confronting insurance regulators. All states now contribute to the work and the budget of the NAIC and have participated actively in its long list of legislative and administrative solutions. Several of the important accomplishments of this rather loosely knit organization are:

1 Creation of the valuation committee to establish uniformity in market values of stocks and bonds held by insurance companies
2 Development of the annual statement forms that serve as a basis for insurance company reports to state insurance departments
3 Development of administrative procedures for integrating supervisory activities
4 Drafting of uniform legislation

In 1944, the United States Supreme Court decided that insurance was subject to regulation by the federal government. As will be explained in some detail starting on page 714, however, Congress has so far left the regulation of insurance primarily to the states.

Functional Organization of State Commissions

In every state, and in the District of Columbia as well, one or more officials are specifically charged with administering the state insurance laws. By far the most common designation given to these officials is *insurance commissioner*. The prevailing administrative organization of the insurance department is that of a single head with one or more subordinates. The most common method of selecting the insurance commissioner is by executive appointment, but other personnel in the department are usually selected under civil service.

[4] *Paul v. Virginia*, 8 Wall. 168 (1869).

General Statutory Powers and Duties

The state insurance commissioner's duties typically consist of such activities as licensing insurers and agents, auditing detailed financial statements submitted annually by insurers, examining insurers periodically with respect to their financial strength and their market conduct, acting on consumer complaints, regulating rates, approving policy language and structure, and managing the conservation or liquidation of insurers with financial difficulties. We will examine in more detail the measures taken to preserve insurer solvency, regulate rates, and improve the supply of insurance.

Preservation of Insurer Solvency

One major objective of state regulation historically has been the preservation of the financial integrity of insurers. In accomplishing this objective, insurance departments have directed much of their activity toward periodic examination of insurers' financial affairs. Most insurance departments examine insurers at least once every three years. In the interim between examination dates, insurers are required to file detailed annual reports concerning all their financial activities. The Insurance Regulatory Information System used to analyze these reports was described in Chapter 27. In addition, the insurance commissioner may at any time choose to conduct special investigations or examinations or to request special information.

As a practical matter, most insurance departments are not adequately staffed to examine the affairs of all insurers, both domestic and foreign, that are doing business within their borders. Therefore, insurance departments feel the greatest responsibility toward careful examination of domestic insurers. In addition, they participate with other insurance departments in what is referred to as a convention or zone examination, which enlists examiners from several states for checking the affairs of insurers doing business beyond the borders of the state in which the insurer's office is located. Most states, following an NAIC recommendation, conduct two different examinations: a financial condition examination and a market conduct exam.

Insurance departments also enforce state laws concerning investment activities of insurers. State statutes, for example, describe certain types of securities that may be purchased and place restrictions on the distribution within the portfolio. Difficulties may arise in this connection when insurers do business in states with differing investment statutes. Fortunately, the states have followed the principle of recognizing the power that another state has over a corporation to the extent that it does not offend public policy of the recognizing state. Following this rule, an insurer seeking to become licensed in a state other than its home state may be admitted, even though its investments only substantially comply with the general state statutes governing those investments. On the other hand, the applying insurer must comply absolutely with its own state's investment statutes.

With respect to other matters, such as the kind of business that can be written and commission or expense limitations, the statute may demand that the insurer conduct its operations within and outside the state in accordance with the standards established for domestic insurers. The reasoning here is that the ability of the insurer to fulfill its obligations to policyholders within the state depends upon its total operations.

Later in this chapter we will discuss insurer guaranty funds, which protect insureds when the above measures fail to prevent an insolvency.

Rate Regulation

Insurance commissioners also have authority over the pricing of insurance. More than half the states still have a model property and liability insurance rating law, developed by the NAIC in the late forties, which has five important features:

1 All rates must be reasonable, adequate, and not unfairly discriminatory, but these standards are not defined.

2 Rates and rating plans must be filed. The commissioner can request supporting information.

3 The filed rates cannot be used until a specified waiting period, which may be extended by the commissioner, has expired or until the rates have been specifically approved. In practice the waiting period has sometimes been extended for many months. Because of this provision this rating law is known today as a *prior approval law*.

4 Rates that are permitted to go into effect may be subsequently disapproved.

5 Insurers may belong to or subscribe to the services of a rating bureau. Members may agree to adhere to the rates filed by the bureau.

The major alleged advantage of this approach is that it permits a reasonable blend of direct regulation and competition. The insurance commissioner is informed and can prevent a rate from becoming effective that in his or her opinion does not satisfy the standards. On the other hand, permitting the insurer to use the rate after a specified waiting period is supposed to protect the filer from unreasonable delays by the commissioner. Rating bureaus can exist as a stabilizing force but deviations and independent filings are possible.

Opponents argue that this approach does not permit insurers to respond rapidly enough to market pressures and changing loss experience. Even when the administration of the law is highly satisfactory, waiting for a decision causes some delays. What is worse, however, is that because the commissioner must approve or disapprove each filing, he or she is subjected to political pressures, particularly with respect to rate increases. Consequently requests for rate increases are often denied, delayed, or reduced. In administering the law, it is alleged, insurance department personnel are sometimes unduly arbitrary and demanding. Rate making necessarily involves some judgmental decisions, and some regulators impose their own judgments on insurers. The results in many states are inadequate rates, an inadequate supply of insurance, and few innovations. Opponents also argue that insurance department resources required to administer a law of this sort would be more profitably devoted to the regulation of other matters such as insurer solvency.

Alternative approaches to rate regulation include both more restrictive and less restrictive regulation than the model law approach. The most common type of more restrictive regulation requires all insurers to belong to a single rating bureau whose rates must be approved by the insurance commissioner before they can be used. Under some of these laws, however, individual insurers may be permitted to make a case for using rates other than those developed by the bureau. The most restrictive regulation requires all insurers to use rates promulgated by state authorities. Supporters of these laws believe that they produce more accurate rates, promote rate stability, and best protect the public interest. Opponents deplore the interference with what they consider the prerogatives of private management and the inability of insureds to benefit from the lower costs of efficient insurers. They also reiterate their objections to the model law.

A few states have less restrictive laws which, like the model law, permit insurers to agree to adhere to the rates developed by rating bureaus, but permit insurers to file and use their rates immediately, these rates being subject only to subsequent disapprovals.

About 20 states have *open-competition laws* that for most lines of insurance prohibit agreements among insurers to adhere to the same rates. In these states rating organizations, renamed data service organizations, are permitted to issue only advisory rates. In some of these states insurers need not file their rates; instead the state insurance department relies upon consumer complaints and periodic examinations of insurers. In the others the rates must be filed either at the time they go into effect or within a short time thereafter. Supporters argue that in states with these laws delays are eliminated, political pressures are reduced, more responsive rates result in a more adequate supply of insurance and encourage product innovations, and insurance departments can concentrate their attention on more important matters. Opponents fear that this type of regulation may be too lax and that if price competition is "either insufficient or irresponsible," the public interest is better served by closer supervision.

In December, 1968, following an extensive investigation, the National Association of Insurance Commissioners recommended that "where appropriate, reliance be placed upon fair and open competition to produce and maintain reasonable and competitive prices for insurance coverages wherever such competition exists.[5] Specifically, in states where greater reliance on competition seems appropriate, the NAIC recommended that new legislation either (1) "authorize the commissioner to suspend the prior approval requirement for any lines, subdivision, or class of insurance where conditions warrant such action," or (2) repeal the prior approval requirement (except for certain lines deserving special consideration). In this latter instance, however, the commissioner should be authorized "to reimpose prior approval for any line, subdivision, or class of insurance in which he finds that competition is insufficient or irresponsible."

During the late sixties and early seventies many states replaced more restrictive legislation with open-competition laws, but the number of states with open competition laws has remained about the same since that time. Inflation and compulsory no-fault automobile insurance have increased public support for more restrictive regulation; regulators in model-law states who prefer to place more reliance on competition have discovered that they can accomplish this objective through administrative actions not requiring a change in the law. As noted in Chapter 28, even in model-law states that permit rating bureaus to require adherence to their rates the national rating bureau

[5] "Report of Rates and Rating Organizations Subcommittee (F1)," *Proceedings of the National Association of Insurance Commissioners, 1969*, vol. 1.

responsible for most lines other than workers' compensation no longer requires adherence to its rates.

Despite the slowing down in the movement toward open-competition laws three important federal government reports in the late seventies favored greater reliance on competition as a regulator of insurance rates.[6] In December, 1980, following an intensive two-year investigation, the NAIC adopted a Property and Liability Model Alternative Competitive Pricing and Appropriate Support Systems Act. This model act did not replace the earlier NAIC model laws, but, for those states that prefer the open-competition approach, this proposal presents the NAIC position on what an open-competition act should be. The act goes further than most current open-competition laws because it limits the role of rating or data service organizations to providing advice only on the loss allowances in the rates. Each insurer must add its own allowance for expenses and profit to whatever it decides the loss allowance should be. An insurer cannot use any new family insurance rates until 15 days after they are filed. An insurer does not even have to file its business insurance rates. However, if the commissioner determines that the competition for some business insurance market is not effective, he or she can order insurers to file any rates proposed for that market and not to use those rates until 30 days later. The state insurance commissioner must also monitor the degree of competition in the various markets and improve the information available to consumers. Only one or two states have adopted this approach.

One of the most controversial features of the 1980 Act, now modified, was that, except for a two-year deferral, it treated workers' compensation insurance the same as most other property and liability insurance lines. The earlier model laws and existing open-competition laws treated workers' compensation differently. In all states workers' compensation insurance was subject to model-law or even more restrictive regulation. In many states all insurers were required to adhere to the rates developed by a rating bureau and approved by the commissioner. One frequently cited reason for this special treatment was that because workers' compensation insurance is social insurance, it should be subject to more careful scrutiny. More than ordinary emphasis, it was argued, should be placed on insurer solvency, rates that encourage loss control, and the prevention of unfair discrimination. For these reasons all insurers should be required to report their experience under a uniform statistical plan from which the bureau could develop more accurate rates. In 1982, in response to some criticism of the 1980 model act relative to workers' compensation insurance, the NAIC adopted a separate model workers' compensation open-competition act which still prohibits data service organizations from issuing more than advisory loss allowances. All insurers, however, are required to report their loss experience under a uniform statistical plan approved by the state insurance commissioner. About eight states now have workers' compensation open-competition laws, but half of these states permit the data service organization to issue advisory rates, not just advisory loss allowances.

To stimulate price competition in automobile and homeowners' insurance, several insurance departments have issued shoppers' guides. These guides offer tips on buying

---

[6] See items 13, 14, and 15 in the list of federal actions on pp. 717–718.

insurance and usually show the premiums that insureds with specified characteristics would pay each insurer operating in the state for these two kinds of insurance.

Rate regulation in life insurance takes a form substantially different from that described for the property and liability business. All states except Alaska have set maximum rates that may be charged for credit life insurance, generally $.75 or less per $100 of the initial loan amount. Outside of these and other minor exceptions, life insurers are legally allowed to charge any rate that they feel would be proper and adequate as long as they do not discriminate unfairly among insureds. However, they must establish sufficient reserves in their balance sheet, based upon the underlying assumptions of mortality, interest, and expense. State nonforfeiture laws prescribe the mortality tables and maximum-interest-rate assumptions for policy reserve computations. Therefore, any rating plan in life insurance that does not develop a sufficient quantity of assets to enable the insurer to satisfy these minimum reserves would be inadequate. Competition is expected to prevent excessive rates. To encourage competition, states generally require that insurers tell prospective policyholders the interest-adjusted costs of their contracts.

SOME CURRENT PROBLEMS IN REGULATION

Two current problem areas illustrate the difficulties faced by both the regulators and the regulated: (1) problems in supplying insurance to all who need it and (2) financial and structural problems of insurers.

Problems in the Supply of Insurance

Considerable evidence exists that the private insurance mechanism is unable to serve all consumer insurance needs. Poorer-quality exposures usually are eliminated in the selection process by restrictive underwriting rules or, if accepted, are priced at levels that few insureds can reasonably pay. This process has been described by its critics as "skimming the cream of the business" and as adverse to the public interest.

The central issue is: To what extent should the better, preferred classes of business be assessed higher premiums to help pay the claims or subsidize the rate structure for the marginal or residual risks within an overall competitive environment? Sound economic decisions by insurers dictate the elimination of unprofitable classes of business by either an unwillingness to write them in the first place, cancellation during the policy term, nonrenewal upon expiration, or setting very high rates—a procedure that makes the business profitable for the insurer but prices it out of reach of those consumers.

If some consumers are unable to secure insurance, they may not be the only ones who are disadvantaged. For example, if the defendant in a negligence action is not insured because he or she was unable to secure liability insurance, the plaintiff may be hurt as well as the defendant. A business that fails because of an uninsured property loss may impose a burden upon society as a whole.

State legislatures have responded to the new emphasis on making insurance more readily available in a number of ways. The restrictions placed on the cancellation and renewal of property and automobile insurance policies have already been noted in Chapters 17, 18, and 19. The open competition rating laws described above are supposed to increase the supply of insurance by giving insurers greater pricing flexibility.

To provide insurance for those consumers who cannot purchase automobile and workers' compensation insurance through voluntary channels, many states have required insurers operating in the state to set up some facility for accepting most, if not all, applicants. The four approaches used in automobile insurance will serve as an example of what can be done. The first two approaches are called *automobile insurance plans*.[7] Under the first, the most popular approach until recently, each insurer doing business in the state is assigned its proportionate share of the applicants according to the ratio of its premium volume to the total state premium volume. Under the second, a few insurers service an underwriting pool reinsured by all automobile insurers in the state. Under the most liberal automobile insurance plans, all applicants with a valid driver's license are eligible for coverage that includes liability limits exceeding financial responsibility requirements and physical damage insurance. Coverage may, however, be limited to liability insurance in an amount that will satisfy financial responsibility requirements. The rates exceed those charged by insurers in the voluntary market except by those specializing in substandard applicants. In 1972 Maryland established a state fund to insure drivers unable to obtain insurance in the voluntary market. The fund is supported by premiums, a tax on insurers, and a charge added to drivers' license fees.

Even the most liberal automobile insurance plans and the Maryland plan have been criticized for (1) the higher-than-normal rates they charge and (2) the stigma attached to the special attention paid to insureds under the plan. Consequently some states have established reinsurance facilities to which insurers can transfer the risk on insureds they prefer not to insure. The insured pays the same premium as other insureds in the same rating class and is unaware of the transfer to the facility. All insurers in the state share the experience of the underwriting pool. Under this approach some special arrangements must be made to prevent insurers from making excessive use of the reinsurance facility.

The medical malpractice insurance crisis, noted in Chapters 7 and 8, caused about 20 state legislatures to establish medical malpractice liability joint underwriting associations composed of all insurers writing liability insurance in the state.

Special problems exist in providing insurance on properties in urban core areas, flood insurance on real property, and theft insurance. In all three instances, Congress has enacted legislation designed to improve the supply of insurance. This legislation is described below.

Urban Property Insurance Program In the light of the large number of urban riots that occurred in the summer of 1967, President Johnson appointed a committee referred to as the President's National Advisory Panel on Insurance in Riot Affected

[7] For a description and evaluation of these approaches see J. Finley Lee and Associates, *Servicing the Shared Automobile Insurance Market* (New York: National Industry Committee on Automobile Insurance Plans, 1977).

Areas (also known as the Hughes Committee). This committee concluded that the property owners in urban core areas were having difficulty obtaining insurance in the private market.[8] The committee recommended the development of a state and national civil disorder insurance program requiring the meshing of both federal and state governments and the insurance industry. Some states already had voluntary urban area programs in effect. The Hughes Committee recommended extension and improvement of these plans, which they termed FAIR (Fair Access to Insurance Requirements) plans, and the formation of a federal reinsurance corporation to protect insurers against catastrophe losses.

Following up on the Hughes Committee report, Congress enacted on August 1, 1968, the Urban Property Protection and Reinsurance Act (Title XI of Public Law 90–448). Under this law the Federal Insurance Administration, an agency that was originally part of the U.S. Department of Housing and Urban Development but is now part of the Federal Emergency Management Agency, administered until late 1983 a National Insurance Development Fund, which reinsured private insurers against catastrophic losses from civil disorders. Insurers, however, could not purchase reinsurance on properties located in a given state unless the state (1) required all property insurers in the state to belong to an approved FAIR plan and (2) agreed to reimburse the fund for certain payments. Congress terminated the federal reinsurance program in late 1983 because of lack of interest among insurers, but the FAIR plans continue to operate.

In 1983 about 31 states plus the District of Columbia had FAIR plans. All FAIR plans cover both residential and commercial property in "urban areas," but most include only direct property losses caused by fire, the extended coverage perils, or vandalism. FAIR plans are not permitted to deny any applicant insurance merely because of environmental hazards such as a high crime rate, riot potential, or physical hazards other than those in immediately adjacent properties. Not every applicant, however, need be insured. All applicants are entitled to an inspection on the basis of which the building structure and its occupancy and the condition of adjacent property are evaluated. Based on this report the plan can (1) insure the property, (2) refuse to insure the property until certain changes are made, or (3) deny insurance for specific reasons not including environmental hazards.

State insurance commissioners have usually also required insurers to ignore environmental hazards in their pricing.[9] Because these losses must then be distributed more generally, the result is the socialization or broad pooling of certain hazards associated with urban core property.

Most FAIR plans are administered by a few servicing insurers representing a joint reinsurance association. Through this association all property insurers in the state share the FAIR plan business in proportion to their total writings. In some states insurers

[8] *Meeting the Insurance Crisis of Our Cities: A Report by the President's National Advisory Panel on Insurance in Riot-Affected Areas* (Washington, D.C.: U.S. Government Printing Office, 1968).
[9] Many states, however, originally permitted a special riot and civil disorder charge, averaging about 3 percent, on all properties insured in the state, to enable insurers to recoup some of their expected losses on urban core property. These special charges were gradually rescinded as the threat of more serious riots passed.

have established direct underwriting pools with their own staff to service FAIR plan business.

National Flood Insurance Program   The risk associated with flood losses to real property lacks many of the characteristics of an ideally insurable risk outlined in Chapter 12. Many persons are exposed to this loss, but a large proportion of these persons may suffer loss from a single event. Because most people with a serious interest in flood insurance have a high loss potential, the premium that would have to be quoted by a private insurer would be so large relative to the property value insured that the insurance would not be economically feasible. Consequently, private insurers have been reluctant to write flood insurance on real property except in rare cases. Flood insurance on personal property is readily available because this property is usually mobile.

Flood disasters, however, have created hardships for the persons directly affected and for society. In 1956, following some serious flood losses in the northeastern United States in 1954, Congress enacted a flood insurance program to be financed and administered by the federal government with some participation by private insurers. Because Congress later became unhappy about certain portions of the law, it never appropriated any funds for the program.

Congress, however, continued its interest in some type of national flood insurance program and, following extensive research and debate, passed the National Flood Insurance Act of 1968. Because so few properties were insured in the early years of the program, a fact that was dramatized by the June, 1972, floods in Wilkes Barre, Pennsylvania, and Rapid City, South Dakota, some major amendments were added in 1973.[10]

Under this act the Federal Emergency Management Agency (until 1979 the Secretary of Housing and Urban Development), through the Federal Insurance Administration, administers a National Flood Insurance Program that enables interested persons to purchase flood insurance on real and personal property located in communities that have adopted satisfactory land-control and land-use measures. Without this land-use restriction it was feared that the program would provide too much incentive for some people to build or to continue living or operating in areas that are highly susceptible to flood damage. Originally, to participate, a community that agreed to satisfy the land-use restrictions had to wait until the FIA determined actuarial rates for that community. Because determining these rates is a lengthy procedure, in 1969 an Emergency Program was introduced under which a limited amount of protection at subsidized rates was made available immediately to all communities who wanted to participate and had met all the requirements except for the FIA actuarial studies. The task of making these

[10] For a critique of the reasons for lack of coverage, see Dan R. Anderson, "The National Flood Insurance Program: Problems and Potential," *Journal of Risk and Insurance,* vol. XLI, no. 4 (December, 1974), pp. 579–599. For a more recent evaluation of the flood insurance program, see F. B. Power and E. W. Shows, "A Status Report on the National Flood Insurance Program—Mid-1978," *Journal of Risk and Insurance,* vol. XLVI, no. 2 (June, 1979), pp. 61–76.

studies is so great that they are continuing. Some communities, of course, do not wish to meet the land-use restrictions required to participate.

Two important provisions encourage community participation. First, in communities with one or more special flood hazard areas (areas having a 1 percent or higher annual chance of flooding) that do not participate in the flood insurance program, prospective borrowers cannot secure any financial assistance on any acquisition or construction in those areas from federal agencies (including FHA and VA loans). Federally regulated financial institutions can make such loans, but they must tell the purchaser what losses might be caused by floods and that federal flood insurance and disaster relief is not available. Second, in participating communities where such insurance is available, no federal officer or agency or federally regulated financial institution can approve any financial assistance for acquiring or constructing property in special flood hazard areas unless the property is insured against flood damage.

Protection up to certain specified limits is available (except on new construction in special flood hazard areas) at "chargeable" rates that are less than half of the estimated losses and expenses. The subsidized limits are as follows:

	Structure	Contents
Single-family residential	$ 35,000	$ 10,000
All other residential	100,000	10,000
All nonresidential	100,000	100,000

Higher amounts of insurance can be purchased at actuarial rates in communities for which these actuarial rates have been established.

The flood insurance policy covers losses from (1) the overflow of inland or tidal water, (2) the unusual and rapid accumulation or runoff of surface waters, (3) mudslides caused by accumulations of water, and (4) erosion losses caused by abnormal water losses. The policy does not cover water damage that results principally from causes on the insured's own property. Coinsurance is not required, but applicants are urged to insure to value. Separate deductibles of $500 apply to the building and contents items. Optional higher deductibles that will reduce the premium are available.

Until 1978, the insurer was the National Flood Insurers Association, a pool created by about 100 private insurers. The National Flood Insurance Fund paid the pool the difference between the chargeable premiums and the premiums required on a nonsubsidized basis. It also reinsured the private pool against annual losses in excess of 125 percent of the annual premiums. In 1978, following a dispute with the private pool, HUD (now replaced by FEMA) took over the insuring function. Private agents, however, still serve as marketing representatives. A private business provides administrative services.

In 1983 under a Write Your Own program private insurers were authorized to provide federal flood insurance as a rider to their homeowners' contract or a separate contract. The government subsidizes participating insurers whose losses and expenses exceed their premiums and investment income.

Federal Crime Insurance Program   The Housing and Urban Development Act of 1968, which created the federal riot reinsurance program, directed the Federal Insurance Administration to prepare a report on the availability of theft insurance at "affordable" rates and how it might be improved. According to the statute, an affordable rate is one that would permit the purchase of this insurance by a reasonably prudent person in the same circumstances. The FIA concluded that to make insurance available at such rates some form of subsidization would be required. In Title XII of the Housing and Urban Development Act of 1970, which was Congress's response to that report, the FIA was directed first to determine those states where crime insurance was unavailable at an "affordable" price. The approach actually used by the FIA to set affordable rates for businesses, for example, was to work out a rating formula by which a *medium-sized* business with about $100,000 in *gross receipts* located in an *average* crime area would pay a rate sufficient to bring in the same total premium dollars nationally as the rates being used by private insurers for these businesses. Using this base premium, a rate structure was then developed that, as explained below, varied rates among businesses according to their type, their gross receipts, and their location in a low, average, or high crime area.

According to the FIA a critical availability problem exists in slightly more than half the states, making property owners in those states available for federal crime insurance. Property owners in those states can obtain an application for this insurance from any insurance agent or broker in the state or from a national servicing company. The servicing company is selected by FIA using a competitive bidding procedure.

The *residential* insurance policy is a combination burglary and robbery policy. The maximum face amount is $10,000. All claims are subject to a deductible of $100, or 5 percent of the loss, whichever is greater.

For a residential property to be eligible for federal crime insurance, its exterior doors, other than sliding doors, must be equipped with either a "dead" bolt or a self-locking deadlatch. All sliding doors and windows opening onto stairways, porches, platforms, or other similar areas must also be equipped with some type of locking device. On the other hand, no person is to be denied insurance or to be canceled because of the frequency or amount of his or her losses. This practice is consistent with the philosophy underlying the act, which states that no one who has taken reasonable steps to protect his or her own premises should be penalized if despite these steps his or her experience is unfavorable. Rates for residential crime insurance vary with the amount of coverage and whether the property is located in one of the lowest crime areas, an average crime area, or one of the highest crime areas.

Commercial applicants can purchase robbery insurance only, burglary insurance only, or a package burglary and robbery policy. The maximum amount is $15,000 per occurrence. Except for nonprofit or public properties, the deductible is 5 percent of the loss or, if greater, an amount that varies from $250 for a business with gross receipts under $300,000 to $500 if the gross receipts are $500,000 or over. For nonprofit or public properties the deductible is $250 or, if greater, 5 percent of the loss.

To be eligible for burglary insurance, a commercial property must have its door-ways and accessible openings adequately protected during nonbusiness hours. The exact requirements, which are more extensive than those imposed on residences, vary according to the type of business.

Rates vary according to (1) the amount of coverage desired, (2) whether the policy covers burglary only, robbery only, or both these perils, (3) the type of business, (4) its gross receipts from the previous year, and (5) whether the business is located in a low crime area, an average crime area, or a high crime area.

The crime insurance premiums are credited to the National Insurance Development Fund established in connection with the federal riot insurance program. Losses and expenses incurred in connection with the program are paid out of this fund. If the losses and expenses exceed the premiums, Congress has authorized appropriations to reimburse the fund. The FIA, however, believes that the program should be self-supporting in the long run.

Profitability, Solvency, and Structural Issues

Three financial and structural issues that have received considerable attention in recent years are (1) insurer profitability, (2) insurer solvency, and (3) the operation of insurers as part of a holding company also engaged in other operations.

Insurer Profitability The profits of property and liability insurers have been investigated extensively because of (1) the statutory criterion of reasonableness established for insurance rates, and (2) the need for insurers to be competitive in capital markets to maintain or increase their capacity to meet the rising demands for insurance services. A rate structure is reasonable under rate regulatory laws if it produces a "reasonable" profit for the insurer. Two questions have arisen in determining whether an insurer's profit is reasonable. (1) Does the profit include both underwriting profit and investment profit? (2) How does one define a *reasonable* profit? The profit insurers' need to attract an adequate capital base depends upon such factors as the profitability of competing uses of capital, the annual variation in profits of insurers compared with the variation in the profits of other industries, and investor expectations and preferences.

Under a 1921 profit formula approved by the National Association of Insurance Commissioners, the profit loading to be included in property and liability insurance rates was set at 5 percent of the premium on the assumption that all investment profit was extra profit for the insurer. This 5 percent factor was and continues to be the profit loading used in most lines of insurance in most states. The propriety of the 5 percent figure and the failure to consider investment profit explicitly were questioned from time to time, but not until the sixties was this formula seriously challenged. Insurance premiums were rising rapidly and some regulators questioned whether one of the reasons was excessive insurer profits from both underwriting and investments which would suggest a reduction in the 5 percent loading factor. In response, most insurers argued initially that (1) the investment activities of an insurer were separate from its underwriting activities, and that only the owners should benefit or lose from the investment activity, (2) that policyholders have no legal title to the assets that produce the investment income, (3) that the investment profit on assets that might possibly be attributed to policyholder payments would be small, and (4) that the 5 percent loading was set at a level that would produce a reasonable overall rate of return for insurers. Critics of the industry view argued (1) that at the minimum, policyholders should be credited with the investment income on assets equal to that portion of the unearned premium reserve (about 60–70 percent) that is not "hidden" surplus, (2) that statutory profit reports understate the true underwriting profits of an insurer because they ignore prepaid expenses, (3) that policyholders should also be credited with investment income on loss reserves, and (4) that the current 5 percent profit loading plus investment profits produces higher than reasonable rates of return for the owners.

This debate generated several studies of the profitability of property and liability insurers.[11] The initial major study, conducted for the American Insurance Association by the Arthur D. Little Company, Inc., indicated that the *total* rate of return (including realized and unrealized capital gains as well as investment income and underwriting profits) on *invested capital* had lagged behind that earned by other industries with comparable risks.[12] According to the second Little report, from 1955 to 1967 the rate of return on *net worth* was 7.0 percent, compared with 11.8 percent for companies included in Standard and Poor's COMPUSTAT annual industrial tape. The findings were questioned by many critics but the Little studies were a major breakthrough in the recognition of total profits.

If insurer profits were too low during 1955–1967, as the Little report contended, the rates insurers were permitted to charge during that period may have been too low. The ability of insurers to attract sufficient capital was also threatened. Some observers argued, however, that if the profit rates of insurers were too low, the two most important reasons were (1) inefficiencies in their operations, and (2) premium writings that were too low relative to their net worth.

The National Association of Insurance Commissioners released in 1972 its first annual report on profitability. Currently, six different after-tax rates of return are reported using generally accepted accounting principles (GAAP): (1) underwriting income as a percent of sales, (2) insurance operating income—underwriting income plus the portion of the investment income attributable to reserves for unearned premiums and unpaid losses—as a percent of sales, (3) overall operating income—underwriting income plus all investment income—as a percent of mean net worth, (4) total return—overall operating income plus realized and unrealized capital gains or losses—as a percent of mean net worth, (5) overall operating income as a percent of mean assets, and (6) total return as a percent of mean assets.

[11] For a comprehensive study, see *Measurement of Profitability and Treatment of Investment Income in Property and Liability Insurance* (Milwaukee: National Association of Insurance Commissioners, June, 1970).

[12] Arthur D. Little Company, Inc., Report to American Insurance Association, *Prices and Profits in the Property and Liability Insurance Industry* (November, 1967). A later report to the National Association of Independent Insurers is entitled *Rates of Return in the Property and Liability Insurance Industry: 1955–1967* (June, 1969). For a sample critical review, see J. D. Hammond, and N. Shilling, "The Little Report on Prices and Profits in the Property and Liability Insurance Industry," *Journal of Risk and Insurance*, vol. XXXVI, no. 1 (March, 1969), pp. 129–145.

The most recent NAIC report available at this writing presents the following rates of return:

Year	Return on sales		Return on net worth		Return on assets	
	Underwriting income	Insurance operating income	Overall operating income	Total return	Overall operating income	Total return
1971	n.a.	5.2%	14.3%	20.8%	3.9%	5.6%
1972	n.a.	5.4	14.5	23.0	4.3	6.8
1973	n.a.	3.7	11.4	−0.9	3.2	−0.3
1974	n.a.	0.0	5.6	−21.7	1.4	−5.4
1975	−5.8%	−1.8	1.8	14.5	0.4	3.4
1976	−1.6	2.5	10.5	18.9	2.5	4.4
1977	1.3	5.5	17.8	16.2	4.2	3.8
1978	1.3	5.9	18.0	18.9	4.4	4.6
1979	−0.5	5.0	15.3	19.6	3.9	5.0
1980	−1.7	4.4	12.7	18.2	3.5	4.9
1981	−3.4	3.7	11.7	8.9	3.1	2.4
1977–81	−0.8	4.8	14.5	15.9	3.7	4.1

During this period, insurers had a premium to net worth ratio of about 2 to 1, a higher ratio than had previously been the case.

The report also compares (1) the overall operating income rate of return on net worth with similar rates of return reported for other industries by *Fortune* magazine and *Forbes* magazine, and (2) the overall operating income rate of return on assets with similar rates of return for other industries reported by *Forbes* magazine. For example, the comparison with *Fortune's* rate of return on net worth report is as follows:

Year	NAIC property-liability insurers	*Fortune* magazine: industry means				
		Diversified financial	Banks	Utilities	Transportation	Industrial
1971	14.3%	12.0%	12.1%	9.5%		9.8%
1972	14.5	11.9	11.9	9.7	3.8%	10.9
1973	11.4	11.2	12.5	10.0	4.7	13.7
1974	5.6	7.5	12.8	9.8	6.5	14.1
1975	1.8	8.9	12.1	9.9	3.7	11.4
1976	10.5	12.1	11.5	10.6	8.8	13.5
1977	17.8	16.7	11.6	11.1	10.1	13.3
1978	18.0	17.3	12.9	11.3	13.3	14.2
1979	15.3	17.5	14.1	12.0	13.2	16.1
1980	12.7	14.0	13.4	11.7	11.3	15.0
1981	11.7	11.4	13.0	12.7	13.3	14.3
1972–81	12.6	12.9	12.6	10.9	8.9	13.7
1977–81	14.5	15.4	13.0	11.8	12.2	14.6

Fortune's ''diversified financial'' group is composed largely of companies engaged mainly in property and liability insurance with or without life insurance and other financial services. The comparison shows that during 1971–1981 property and liability insurers earned about the same average rate of return as did banks, utilities, and industrial firms, but that these profits were more unstable over time.

The NAIC also calculates profitability measures by line and by state. Only two rates of return are calculated for each state: (1) underwriting income as a percent of premiums earned, and (2) insurance operating income as a percent of premiums earned.

As a result of these studies, some states have reduced the 5 percent profit loading. For example, one state moved progressively from no crediting of investment income against the 5 percent to crediting investment income on the unearned premium reserves, then crediting investment income on the loss reserves, and finally including capital gains as well as investment income. The profit loading dropped from 5 percent to 3.1 percent. A few states have established ''reasonable'' overall rates of return that recognize investment profits and set profit loadings consistent with those target returns. For example, in a highly controversial decision, using the Capital Asset Pricing Model,[13] a popular tool of modern financial theorists, former Commissioner Stone of Massachusetts determined that a reasonable after-tax rate of return on net worth for automobile liability insurance written in Massachusetts in 1978 would be about 20 percent. However, by investing assets corresponding to the owner's equity, the unearned premium reserve, and the loss reserves associated with automobile liability insurance, the average insurer would, he estimated, earn more than 20 percent in investment profits alone. Consequently, he set the profit loading at *minus* 5.5 percent. In Minnesota former Commissioner Markman determined in 1981 that the reasonable rate of return for writing workers' compensation insurance in that state was 18 percent. Because investment profit alone would exceed 18 percent, he ordered a profit loading of *minus* 10 percent. Finally, in 1982, because automobile liability insurance premiums produce more investment income than automobile physical damage insurance premiums, Florida Insurance Commissioner Gunther required insurers to include a smaller profit loading in their automobile liability insurance premiums.

A few states have enacted excess profits statutes that require property and liability insurers earning excess profits during a specified period from both underwriting and investments to return the excess to their policyholders. Only Florida and New York, however, have implemented their statutes.

Insurer Insolvency　The second major financial problem is potential insolvencies, which can occur even in highly profitable years for the industry. When an insurer becomes insolvent, not only do its investors lose their capital, but claims are not paid and unused premiums are not returned to policyholders. Public confidence in the

---

[13] Two articles describing the use of this model in rate regulation are Raymond D. Hill, ''Profit Regulation in Property-Liability Insurance,'' *The Bell Journal of Economics*, vol. X, no. 1 (Spring, 1979), pp. 172–191, and William B. Fairley, ''Investment Income and Profit Margins in Property-Liability Insurance: Theory and Empirical Results,'' *The Bell Journal of Economics*, vol. X, no. 1 (Spring, 1979), pp. 192–210.

For a discussion of the relationship between CAPM and risk management, see Chap. 13.

particular insurer is thereby destroyed and, in turn, the confidence placed in the whole private insurance institution is threatened. Fortunately few insurers become insolvent, but it happens often enough to be a matter of deep concern.

Various plans have been proposed or enacted to meet this problem. All states have created guarantee funds that can be used to meet the losses of claimants and creditors of insolvent property and liability insurers. Most of these insolvency funds are financed through postloss assessments on all insurers in the state. Some states have established similar life insurance insolvency funds. These funds have already made payments to many insureds who would otherwise have been hurt financially. On the other hand, some observers have questioned whether (1) these funds force well-managed insurers to pay costs generated by careless insurers, and (2) regulators have relaxed their supervision of marginal insurers because the consequences to insureds of an insolvency have been reduced. The introduction of the Insurance Regulatory Information System and recent reviews of the examination system are contrary indications.

Holding Companies   The final problem to be discussed in this section is that many insurers have formed holding companies and have shifted a large part of their capital to these companies for investment outside the insurance industry. This drain of existing capital capacity has the effect of indirectly reducing future insuring capacity, a matter that has greatly disturbed insurance regulators. Such transfers also reduce the capital available to cushion unfavorable underwriting or investment experience. Also, large conglomerates have acquired some insurers in order to employ some of those insurers' assets in their noninsurance activities. In a 1968 *Report of the Special Committee on Insurance Holding Companies*, The New York State Insurance Department expressed grave concern about insurers being controlled by noninsurance industry groups, pointing to the need for new legislation to regulate such events.

In the long run, many observers have predicted, the insurance industry will inevitably integrate with other financial institutions and be a part of what is referred to as "one-stop financial service institutions." The merging of banks, investment companies, and insurers would offer the consumer complete financial services under one roof. Credit services, coupled with investment and insurance services, would give the consumer a total integrated financial counseling service meeting the consumer's credit, savings and investment, and protection needs in a more efficient manner. As noted in Chapter 26, however, although many leading insurers are already part of a financial services combination, others have elected to continue specializing in insurance.

STATE VERSUS FEDERAL REGULATION

As noted earlier, states are currently primarily responsible for the regulation of insurers, but the federal government has gradually taken a more active role. From the time the case *Paul v. Virginia*, 8 Wall 168 (1869) was decided[14] until 1944, insurance was subject to *exclusive* state jurisdiction.

Some advantages of state regulation claimed by its supporters then and now are these:

[14] See p. 697.

1 State regulation has created a regulatory environment that has assured a financially strong, solvent, and vital insurance industry. In other words it works.

2 Insurance contracts are purchased to meet local exposures and risks. Local supervision is adaptable to local needs and concerns.

3 State supervision encourages innovations and experimentation. In several instances where uniformity is desirable, the NAIC has served as a forum for developing model legislation and procedures.

4 Federal supervision of insurance, if poorly administered, would affect adversely the entire private insurance business. Spotty or inept insurance supervision in a limited number of states does not seriously impair the activities of insurers and the needs of insurance consumers in the other states where supervision is proper and fair.

It would be incorrect, however, to assume that state regulation was not challenged during the years from 1869 to 1944. The inadequacy of state regulation served as the basis for legislation that was proposed in Congress in 1868, 1905, 1906, 1914, 1915, and 1933. In each of these years sponsors of legislation contended that state insurance regulation was inadequate and that the federal government should exercise control.[15] However, not until the Temporary National Economic Committee conducted its investigations in 1939 and 1940 was a detailed critique of state insurance regulation prepared.[16]

The Southeastern Underwriters Association Decision

The criticisms developed by the TNEC culminated in an important case involving an action against the Southeastern Underwriters Association alleging that 200 stock fire insurers had violated the Sherman Antitrust Act. Not only did the insurers involved sell over 90 percent of the fire insurance in the six states in which they operated, but by continued agreement and concert of action they were able to fix premium rates and agents' commissions and often used boycotts and coercion to force the purchase of a particular insurer's insurance. The following coercive devices were scored in the indictment:

1 Failure to provide reinsurance for noncomplying insurers

2 Withdrawal of agents' licenses where there was representation of competing insurers

3 Threatening consumers doing business with non-SEUA insurers with boycotts when they attempted to satisfy their other insurance needs

4 Policing by the rating bureaus and local boards of insurance agents of the activities of their members and imposing boycotts and intimidations in attempting to carry out their program

Litigation first developed on the issue of the jurisdiction of the federal government over insurance and was raised on demurrer by the insurers. The demurrer was sustained

---

[15] See the *Congressional Record*, vol. 40, p. 748.

[16] *Temporary National Economic Committee Reports, Final Report and Recommendations*, 77th Congress, Document 77 (Washington, D.C.: U.S. Government Printing Office, 1940).

in the lower courts but reversed by the United States Supreme Court in a 4-to-3 decision. The opinion of the Court, written by Justice Black, distinguished this case from those starting with *Paul v. Virginia* on the basis that the earlier cases involved the validity of state statutes, and that this was the first case squarely presenting the question of whether the commerce clause grants Congress power to regulate insurance when conducted across state lines. The Court determined that the federal government could regulate insurance either as interstate commerce or as a matter that affects interstate commerce and pointed out that the practices attacked under the indictment violated the Sherman Antitrust Act. The trial on the facts never took place since the indictment was dismissed by agreement between the parties after the decision on jurisdiction.

The Consequences of the SEUA Decision

The SEUA decision established federal jurisdiction over the activities of insurance conducted across state lines. This does not mean, however, that state regulation was entirely precluded, since some insurer practices and activities may be predominantly intrastate in character and thus subject to only state regulation. It follows then that as a consequence of this important case, the courts essentially established a dual system of regulation, with the state commissioners enforcing state law with respect to intrastate commerce and with respect to interstate commerce to the extent that the federal government will allow.

The most important federal statutes that might be involved in any interstate regulation of insurance are:

1 *The Sherman Act.* The Sherman Act is designed essentially to prevent restraints to free competition in business transactions. In particular this act would apply to all cooperative insurance activities. For example, the act would make illegal certain agreements or concerted actions with reference to the making of rates and the apportionment of risks under reinsurance pools. Agreements that relate to the appointment of agents and commission levels would also be subject to question.

2 *The Clayton Act.* Section 14 of the Clayton Act prohibits contracts "where the effects of such activities substantially lessen competition or tend to create a monopoly." The Clayton Act would prohibit in the insurance field certain stock acquisitions, interlocking directorates, unfair price discrimination, and brokerage agreements that may substantially lessen competition.

3 *Robinson-Patman Act.* Section (*a*) of the Robinson-Patman Act prohibits unlawful price discrimination between different purchasers of commodities of like kind and quality that tends to create a monopoly.

4 *Federal Trade Commission Act.* The Federal Trade Commission Act gives the FTC the power to investigate within reason and to restrain unfair trade practices.

Enactment of the McCarran-Ferguson Act
(Public Law 15, 15 U.S.C.A. 1012)

As a result of the Southeastern Underwriters case, Congress was petitioned by the insurance business and the state insurance departments to enact clarifying legislation that would establish the jurisdiction of the states over insurance. In attempting to draw the dividing line between the areas of jurisdiction of the federal and state governments, Congress sought to establish by Public Law 15 (technically Public Law 79:15 because it was Public Law 15 enacted by the 79th Congress) the preeminence of state insurance laws. In order to cover any gaps that may exist in inadequate state legislation, however, the act further suggested that "the Sherman Act, the Clayton Act, and the Federal Trade Commission Act would be applicable to the business of insurance to the extent that such business is not regulated by state law" except that agreements to boycott, coerce, or intimidate remain subject to the Sherman Act. The purpose of this provision essentially was to place responsibility on the states to set their regulatory houses in order and to dispel the threat of federal intervention unless state legislation proved inadequate.

Action by the States since 1944

The NAIC conducted many meetings and hearings to help determine the course of action to be followed by the states as a result of Public Law 15. Primary emphasis was placed on developing model property and liability insurance rating laws that could be adopted by the states and comply with the congressional intent behind Public Law 15. Because of the federal pressure implied by Public Law 15, most state legislatures acted rapidly by enacting in substance the model rating laws proposed by the NAIC and described briefly earlier in this chapter. These laws recognized the desirability of competition in rates as well as the necessity of cooperative rate making. At the same time, the laws sought to avoid the charge of inadequate regulation under the Sherman Act and the other antitrust laws by requiring rate approval or disapproval by the state commissioners.[17]

In accordance with and in some cases prior to the mandate given to the states under Public Law 15 to enact legislation that would adequately regulate insurance, most states passed what is referred to as the *Unfair Trade Practices Act for Insurance*. The purpose of this statute is "to prohibit and define unfair methods of competition and unfair and deceptive acts or practices in the business of insurance." The other states, while not enacting the model bill, have laws that have the same effect in regulating insurance advertising and trade practices.

Under these laws, unfair methods of competition are defined as follows:

1 Misrepresentation and false advertising in policy contracts
2 False information in advertising generally
3 Defamation of persons engaged in insurance
4 Boycott, coercion, and intimidation
5 Filing of false financial statements
6 Paying or receiving rebates
7 Unfair rate discrimination

Because of the difficulties in enforcing insurance regulations against out-of-state

[17] Some states, notably California, did not require rate filings. Instead they adopted a more competitive law. As noted earlier, today about 20 states have open-competition laws.

unlicensed insurers, the National Conference of Commissioners on Uniform State Laws developed a model *Unauthorized Insurers Process Act,* which attempts to give jurisdiction over foreign insurance companies operating within a given state. Section 5 provides that:

> . . . issuance or delivery of a policy of insurance by an unauthorized and unlicensed insurer to a citizen or resident of the adopting state shall be deemed to constitute designation of that state's insurance official as the attorney in fact upon whom legal process may be served.

The specific practice that this legislation attempts to control is a mail-order insurer operating in unlicensed areas.

During the late 1960s, the NAIC considerably strengthened the research capability of its central office staff and has since issued some high-quality reports on various aspects of regulation. Also, as noted earlier in the discussion of rate regulation, the NAIC has in recent years increased its interest and activities in stimulating competition among insurers, an approach that has been favored by the federal government in several reports noted in the next section.

Action by the Federal Government since 1944

The enactment of Public Law 15, which established the preeminence of state regulation, does not mean that the federal government has been sitting on its hands. On the contrary, certain activities on the part of the federal government have threatened the whole structure of continued state regulation.

Among these activities are the following, listed in roughly chronological order:

1 Hearings of the Subcommittee on Study of Monopoly Power (81st Congress, 1949), which investigated the possible existence of economic concentration and monopoly practices in insurance, particularly life insurance, which might indicate the need for federal intervention. No specific legislative proposal resulted from the hearings.

2 Regulation by the Federal Trade Commission of fraud committed in mail-order insurance.

3 Hearings before a subcommittee of the Committee on Interstate and Foreign Commerce on the fraudulent misclassification of insured purchasers of financed automobiles by some insurers, the "packing" of the finance instrument with excessive insurance charges, and the failure to refund premiums on canceled or lapsed policies.

4 Numerous prosecutions of health insurers by the Federal Trade Commission with respect to alleged deceptive advertising. This activity of the FTC was the first major test of the statement in Public Law 15 that certain federal acts were applicable to insurance "to the extent that such business is not regulated by state law."

5 Antitrust prosecutions in cases of boycott, coercion, and intimidation.[18]

6 Regulation of variable annuities and other equity-type contracts offered by life

---

[18] The two leading cases are *United States v. The Insurance Board of Cleveland,* 144 F. Supp. 684 (Ohio, 1956), and *United States v. New Orleans Insurance Exchange,* Civil No. 42–92, Eastern District, La., 1957.

insurers, which were held by the Supreme Court as *not* constituting "the business of insurance" (as described by the McCarran Act) and therefore not exempt from the Securities and Exchange Act of 1933 and the Investment Company Act of 1940. This decision established jurisdiction of the Securities and Exchange Commission over these types of investments. See: *Securities and Exchange Commission v. Variable Annuity Life Insurance Company of America,* 359 U.S. 65 (1959).

7 Special studies on automobile insurance conducted by the Interstate Commerce Committee of the United States House of Representatives and by the Department of Transportation. The DOT studies, parts of which are reported in Chapter 8, examined in great detail (1) the economic consequences of automobile accidents and the performance of present reparation systems, (2) the causes of automobile accidents, and (3) the structural trends and operational activities of automobile insurers in serving the needs of the consumer. Congress considered for several years a federal no-fault bill that would set minimum standards for state laws.

8 Enactment in 1974 of the Employee Retirement Income Security Act described in Chapter 22.

9 Proposed legislation that would have established minimum standards for state workers' compensation laws.

10 Investigations of the insurance industry by the Subcommittee on Antitrust and Monopoly of the United States Senate as part of a continuing probe of the substance and quality of state supervision of insurance. Subjects investigated or under investigation include: aviation and ocean marine insurance, critique of state supervision, rate regulation, alien insurers, insolvencies of insurers, high risk and substandard automobile insurers, insurance availability to problem risks, the life insurance industry with special emphasis on cost comparisons, and the use of age, sex, marital status, and territories in pricing automobile insurance.

11 Creation of the federal riot reinsurance, flood insurance, and crime insurance programs already described in this chapter.

12 Three reports on the insurance industry by the Federal Trade Commission staff. The first, completed in 1979, recommended that physicians' organizations not be permitted to control Blue Shield plans. The second, also released in 1979, described the possible rates of return on the savings element in a life insurance contract and urged more complete cost disclosure requirements. The third, which was financed by the FTC, was a study of the economics of insurance discrimination published privately in 1980, not by the FTC. The reason was that Congress decided in 1980 to limit FTC insurance studies to those requested by Congressional committees. In 1983 the House Committee on Energy and Commerce directed the FTC to study the advantages of the different types of life insurance policies and the adequacy of consumer information provided by life insurers.

13 A Justice Department report, completed under the Ford Administration, advocating a dual system of regulation.[19] Under this system insurers, at their option, could obtain either a federal or a state charter. Insurers who chose a federal charter would be exempt from state regulation on some but not all aspects of their operations.

---

[19] *The Pricing and Marketing of Insurance* (Washington, D.C.: U.S. Department of Justice, 1977).

For example, rates, reserves, and investments would be subject to federal standards, but contract provisions would continue to be regulated by the state. The bill would also have established a Federal Insurance Guaranty Fund to supplement the state guaranty funds described earlier.

14 A 1979 report by President Carter's National Commission for Review of the Antitrust Laws which recommended repeal of P.L.15. This Commission investigated several industries with antitrust immunities, not just insurance. Five options were considered for the insurance industry: (1) dual federal-state charters, (2) outright repeal of P.L.15, (3) a more narrow exemption for joint industry activities, (4) a policy statement favoring open competition over more restrictive rate regulation and a more limited and rigorous interpretation of the present exemption, or (5) the status quo. In its final report,[20] adopted in January, 1979, the Commission recommended that:

> **a** The current broad antitrust immunity granted by P.L.15 be repealed. In its place Congress should enact legislation affirming the lawfulness of a limited number of essential collective activities.
>
> **b** States should place maximum reliance on competition in pursuing their regulatory objectives.
>
> **c** Relevant Congressional Committees or a special commission established by the President should study further the economic regulation of insurance with special emphasis on equity and discrimination, availability and affordability, and the appropriate role of federal legislation.

15 A 1979 report by the General Accounting Office that questioned the effectiveness of state regulation of insurance, especially in regulating the financial and trade practices of insurers, automobile insurance policies, and insurance availability.[21]

16 Passage in 1981 of the Risk Retention Act described in Chapter 11.

17 Inclusion in the Tax Equity and Fiscal Responsibility Act of 1982 of several important provisions affecting private pension plans.

18 An early 1983 request by the Chairman of the Commerce, Transportation, and Tourism Subcommitee for a wide-ranging study of the insurance industry by the General Accounting Office.

19 A landmark U.S. Supreme Court decision that prohibits employers from using sex as a factor in determining monthly pension amounts. *See Norris v. Arizona Governing Committee,* No. 82-52 in the Supreme Court of the United States, October Term,1982.

20 A proposed Fair Trade Practices Act that would have prohibited the use of sex as a rating factor in all types of insurance. This proposal was debated intensely both before and after the Norris decision noted above.

21 A proposed Financial Services Competitive Equity Act that would have permitted banks, through holding company structures, to engage in almost all financial service activities, including insurance marketing and ownership of an insurer.

---

[20] "Final Report of Carter Antitrust Commission," *The National Underwriter,* Feb. 2,1979, pp. 2 and 30–33; Feb. 9, 1979, pp. 2 and 42–44.

[21] *Issues and Needed Improvements in State Regulation of the Insurance Business,* Comptroller General's Report to the Congress (Washington, D.C.: U.S. General Accounting Office, 1979).

Conclusions

Regulation of the private insurance industry appears to be in a state of flux, with the areas of federal and state activity rapidly changing. The trend of expanding federal activities indicates a narrowing of state jurisdiction and a reformation of the present system of regulation. The need for clarification of the boundary lines between federal and state jurisdiction, and the overlapping of jurisdiction and interest as regards the activities of this business point to increased conflict and litigation in the future.

The role of private insurance in the economy is an important one. The challenge that confronts government is the working out of a system of regulation—through effective legislation and effective enforcement—to adequately protect the public interest and to preserve the many benefits of private insurance.

SOME KEY CONCEPTS

State insurance commissioner   The state official charged with administering the state insurance laws.

Paul v. Virginia   The 1869 case in which the United States Supreme Court held that Congress had no authority to regulate insurance as interstate commerce.

Southeastern Underwriters Association decision   The 1944 decision in which the United States Supreme Court held that Congress could regulate insurance either as interstate commerce or as a matter that affects interstate commerce.

Prior approval law   A rate regulatory law that permits insurers to agree to adhere to rates developed by a rating bureau but requires that the state insurance commissioner approve the rates filed by an insurer before they can be used.

Open-competition law   A rate regulatory law that forbids agreements among insurers to adhere to rates developed by a rating bureau but permits insurers to use the rates they file with the commissioner either before or on the filing date.

Automobile insurance plan   A plan that provides private automobile insurance for those consumers who cannot obtain this insurance through normal channels.

FAIR plan   A plan that provides insurance on property in urban core areas that cannot be insured through normal channels but meets reasonable underwriting standards except possibly for environmental hazards.

Chargeable rates   The subsidized rates charged for National Flood Insurance up to the subsidized limits.

1921 profit formula   The formula that established the profit loading still included in most property and liability insurance rates.

Insurer guarantee funds   A state fund, usually supported by postloss assessments, that pays the losses sustained by insureds and creditors when an insurer becomes insolvent.

Public Law 15   A 1945 Act in which Congress declared that the Sherman Act, the Clayton Act, and the Federal Trade Commission Act would not apply to insurance to the extent that this business was regulated by state law.

REVIEW QUESTIONS

1 "Permitting insurance practices to be determined under conditions approximating perfect competition is neither desirable nor possible." Comment on the truth or falsity of this statement.

2 What are the objectives of current insurance regulation? How have these objectives been influenced by the "age of consumerism"?

3 a What was the nature of insurance regulation prior to the appointment of state insurance commissioners?

b Trace the development of state insurance commissions.

c Explain the role of the National Association of Insurance Commissioners.

4 The state insurance department has extensive regulatory authority over the solvency of insurers. Indicate the scope of this authority with specific examples.

5 Another important objective of insurance regulation is the prevention of unfair trade practices. Indicate the scope of this authority with specific examples.

6 a An insurer wishes to raise its automobile liability insurance rates 10 percent. In most states, what procedure must it follow?

b Can this insurer join with other insurers to establish a common price? Explain your answer.

7 a What competition is possible under the model rating laws?

b Some states have laws that restrict competition more than the model rating law, while others have less restrictive laws. What is the probable nature of these laws?

c Which method of rate regulation would you prefer?

8 a How have states restricted the cancellation rights of automobile insurers?

b Contrast an automobile insurance plan with an automobile reinsurance facility.

9 a How do FAIR plans improve the supply of insurance in urban core areas?

b How do FAIR plans socialize the risk of environmental hazards?

10 a Do purchasers of flood insurance pay the actuarial cost of their protection? Explain.

b In what ways does the flood insurance program encourage loss control?

c How is flood insurance marketed?

11 a Is federal crime insurance available in all states?

b What role do private insurers play in the program?

12 Should investment profits be considered in regulating insurance rates? Explain.

13 What information does the NAIC publish on the profitability of insurers?

14 a What are some implications of possible inadequate rates of return for property and liability insurers?

b Do you favor state insolvency funds? Explain your answer.

15 Prior to 1944 the states had the exclusive right to regulate insurance. What was the legal basis for this authority?

16 a What was the nature of the federal complaint against the Southeastern Underwriters Association that gave rise to a history-making decision by the United States Supreme Court?

b What ruling did the Court make, and how did it reach this decision?

17 In the absence of any qualifying federal legislation, what would be the impact upon insurance of:

a The Sherman Act?

b The Clayton Act?

c The Robinson-Patman Act?

d The Federal Trade Commission Act?

18 According to Public Law 15, what is the dividing line between state and federal jurisdiction over insurance?

19 What actions have been taken by the federal government since 1944?

20 Would you favor state or federal regulation of insurance? Why?

SUGGESTIONS FOR ADDITIONAL READING

Bickelhaupt, David L.: *General Insurance* (11th ed., Homewood, Ill.: Richard D. Irwin, Inc., 1983), chap. 24.

Federal Register, issues containing directives of the Federal Insurance Administration.

Fire, Casualty, and Surety Bulletins (Cincinnati: The National Underwriter Company, monthly), sections on Federal Insurance Administration programs.

Hanson, J. S., R. E. Dineen, and M. B. Johnson: *Monitoring Competition: A Means of Regulating the Property and Liability Business,* vols. 1 and 2 (Milwaukee: National Association of Insurance Commissioners, May, 1974).

Kimball, S. L.: *Insurance and Public Policy* (Madison: University of Wisconsin Press, 1960).

———, and H. S. Denenberg: *Insurance, Government, and Social Policy* (Homewood, Ill.: Richard D. Irwin, Inc., 1969).

Long, John D. (ed.): *Issues in Insurance*, vols. I and II (Malvern, Pa.: American Institute for Property and Liability Underwriters, 1978).

Meeting the Insurance Crisis of Our Cities: A Report by the President's National Advisory Panel on Insurance in Riot-Affected Areas (Washington, D.C.: U.S. Government Printing Office, 1968).

Patterson, E. W.: *The Insurance Commissioner in the United States* (Cambridge, Mass.: Harvard University Press, 1927).

Proceedings of the National Association of Insurance Commissioners (semiannually).

Reports of the Subcommittee on Antitrust and Monopoly, U.S. Senate, on various aspects of the insurance industry (Washington, D.C.: U.S. Government Printing Office, periodically since the late fifties).

Weisbart, S. N.: *Extraterritorial Regulation of Life Insurance* (Homewood, Ill.: Richard D. Irwin, Inc., 1975).

APPENDIX **A**

ASSETS-EXPOSURES ANALYSIS

Assets

A. Physical Assets

  1. Real property
    (a) Buildings

(1) Under construction	(6) Garages and hangers
(2) Owned or leased	(7) Dwellings and farms
(3) Manufacturing	(8) Tanks, towers, and stacks
(4) Offices	(9) Wharfs and docks
(5) Warehouses	(10) Pipes and wires (aboveground)

    (b) Underground property

(1) Cables and wires	(4) Mines and shafts
(2) Tanks	(5) Wells, groundwater
(3) Shelters, caves, and tunnels	(6) Piping and pipelines

    (c) Land
      (1) Improved
      (2) Unimproved
  2. Personal property (on and off premises and in transit)
    (a) Equipment and machinery
      (1) Machines and tools
      (2) Dies, jigs, molds, castings
      (3) Boilers and pressure vessels
        a. Fired vessels—steam and hot water boilers
        b. Unfired vessels
      (4) Mechanical electrical equipment—transformers, generators, motors, fans, pumps, compressors

---

Assets

---

2. Personal property (on and off premises and in transit) *(continued)*
      (5) Engines—diesel, gasoline, steam
      (6) Meters and gauges
      (7) Turbines—steam, gas, water
      (8) Conveyors and lifts, trams, elevators
  (b) Furniture and fixtures
  (c) Electronic data processing equipment
  (d) Improvements and betterments
  (e) Stock—supplies, raw materials, goods in process, finished goods
  (f) Fine arts—antiques, paintings, jewelry, libraries
  (g) Safety equipment—instruments, apparel, alarms, installations
  (h) Valuable papers

(1) Blueprints	(6) Tapes, cards, disks, programs
(2) Formulas	(7) Own securities—negotiable and nonnegotiable
(3) Accounts receivable	(8) Other corporate securities
(4) Patents and copyrights	(9) Cash (indicate currency)
(5) Titles and deeds	

3. Miscellaneous property
  (a) Vehicles (including contents)
      (1) Commercial
      (2) Private passenger
      (3) Contractor's equipment (licensed)
      (4) Warehouse equipment
  (b) Aircraft
      (1) Missiles and satellites
      (2) Lighter-than-air
      (3) Aircraft—jet, piston, fixed-wing, rotary wing
  (c) Animals
  (d) Antennas
  (e) Crops, gardens, lawns
  (f) Fences
  (g) Firearms
  (h) Nuclear and radioactive property—isotopes, tracers, reactors, cyclotrons, accelerators, betatrons
  (i) Promotional displays—signs, models, plates, handbills, exhibits
  (j) Recreational facilities—parks, gyms, lakes, cafeterias
  (k) Watercraft (including contents)—boats, yachts, barges, ships, submersibles, buoys, drilling rigs

B. Intangible Assets
(Assets not necessarily shown on balance sheet or earnings statement)

1. External assets
  (a) Markets
  (b) Resource availability
      (1) Supplies
      (2) Transportation
      (3) Employees (full-time and temporary)
      (4) Public utilities
      (5) Public protection
  (c) Communications—telephone, teletype, television, radio, newspaper
  (d) Locational—climate, political, economic and social stability, currency convertibility

---

Assets

B. Intangible Assets *(continued)*
  (e) Counsel and specialists—legal, architecture, accounting, insurance, real estate, general management, marketing, advertising, PR, banking
 2. Internal assets
  (a) Research and development
  (b) Goodwill and reputation
  (c) Financial
      (1) Credit cards
      (2) Credit lines (rec'd)
      (3) Insurance
      (4) Customer credit
      (5) Employee benefits program
      (6) Royalties and rents
      (7) Leasehold interest
      (8) Ownership of stock
      (9) Company foundations (nonprofit)
      (10) Tax loss carry-forward
  (d) Personnel (employees and executives)
      (1) Education and training
      (2) Experience
      (3) "Key" employees
  (e) Rights
      (1) Mineral and oil rights—aboveground, underground, and offshore
      (2) Air rights
      (3) Patents and copyrights
      (4) Royalty agreements
      (5) Distribution agreements
      (6) Manufacturing rights

Exposures to loss

A. Direct Exposures
 1. Generally uncontrollable and unpredictable
  (a) Electrical disturbance—lightning, burnout, sunspots, power surge, demagnetization of tapes
  (b) Falling objects—aircraft, meteors, missiles, trees
  (c) Land movement—earthquake, volcano, landslide, avalanche
  (d) Sound and shock waves—sonic boom, vibration, water hammer
  (e) Subsidence—collapse, settlement, erosion
  (f) War, insurrection, rebellion, armed revolt, sabotage
  (g) Water damage—flood, rising waters, flash flood, mudslide, tidal waves (tsunami), geyser, groundwater, sprinkler leakage, sewer backup
  (h) Weight of ice, snow
  (i) Windstorm—typhoon, hurricane, cyclone, tornado, hailstorm, rain, dust, seche, sandstorm
 2. Generally controllable or predictable
  (a) Breakage of glass or other fragile items
  (b) Breakdown—malfunction of part, lubricant, etc.
  (c) Collision, on and off premises—watercraft, aircraft, vehicles
  (d) Contamination—liquid, solid, gaseous, radioactive, pollution
  (e) Corrosion—wear, tear, abuse, poor maintenance
  (f) Employee negligence
  (g) Explosion and implosion
  (h) Failure of environmental control—temperature, humidity, pressure
  (i) Fauna—animals, rodents, insects, pests
  (j) Fire

Exposures to loss

---

2. Generally controllable or predictable *(continued)*

    (k) Installation and construction hazards—dropping, etc.

    (l) International destruction—jettison, backfiring, etc.

    (m) Perils of sea-pirates, rovers, barratry, etc.

    (n) Physical change—shrinkage, evaporation, color, mildew, expansion, contraction

    (o) Rupture or puncture of tank or vessel

    (p) Smoke damage, smudge

    (q) Spillage, leakage, paint spray

    (r) Structural defects, crane or elevator fall

    (s) Transportation—overturn, collision

    (t) Unintentional error—employee, computer, counsel

    (u) Vegetation

    (v) Vandalism, malicious mischief, defacing of property

    (w) Riots, civil disorders, strikes, boycotts, curfews

3. Primarily financial in nature

    (a) Employee dishonesty—forgery, embezzlement, larceny

    (b) Expropriation—nationalization, seizure, exercise of eminent domain, confiscation

    (c) Fraud, forgery, theft, burglary, robbery

    (d) Invalidity of deed, title, patent, copyright

    (e) Inventory shortage—mysterious disappearance, lost or mislaid property

    (f) Obsolescence

B. Indirect or Consequential Exposures

1. All direct exposures as they affect:

    (a) Suppliers

    (b) Customers

    (c) Utilities

    (d) Transportation—personnel and property

    (e) Employees

2. Extra expense—rentals, communication, product, etc.

3. Concentration of assets

4. Change in style, taste, desire

5. Bankruptcy—employee, executive, supplier, customer, counselor

6. Disruption of education system—racial, political, economic

7. Economic fluctuation—inflation, recession, depression

8. Epidemic, disease, plague

9. Increased replacement cost, depreciation

10. Invasion of copyright, patent

11. Loss of integral part of set, pair, group

12. Loss of rights resulting from records destruction

13. Managerial error in:

    (a) Pricing, marketing   (f) Political predictions

    (b) Distribution   (g) Investments

    (c) Production   (h) Dividend declaration

    (d) Expansion   (i) Tax filing

    (e) Economic predictions

14. Recall of product

15. Spoilage

Exposures to loss

C. Third-Party Liabilities (compensatory and punitive damages)
   1. Aviation liability
      (a) Owned and leased aircraft
      (b) Nonowned—officers and employees licensed
      (c) Grounding and sistership liability
   2. Athletic—sponsorship of teams, recreational facilities, etc.
   3. Advertiser's and publisher's liability
      (a) As agents
      (b) Libel, slander, defamation of character
      (c) Media use—radio, TV, newspaper, samples, exhibits
   4. Automobile liability
      (a) Operation of vehicles—owned and nonowned
      (b) Loading and unloading
      (c) Dangerous contents—flammables, explosives
   5. Contractual liability
      (a) Purchase agreements
      (b) Sales agreements
      (c) Lease agreements—real or personal property
      (d) Performance or service
      (e) Loans, mortgages, notes
      (f) Hold-harmless clauses
      (g) Surety agreements
   6. Directors' and officers' liability
   7. Easements
      (a) In gross
      (b) Appurtenant
      (c) Positive or negative under common law
      (d) Rights of access to light, water, drainage, support
   8. Employer's liability
      (a) Workers' Compensation or similar laws
      (b) Federal Employees Liability Act
      (c) Common law
      (d) U.S. Longshoremen and Harbor Workers Act
      (e) Jones Act
      (f) Defense Bases Act
      (g) Outer Continental Shelf Act
      (h) Unemployment compensation
      (i) Discrimination in employment
   9. Fiduciary and fringe benefits plans liability
      (a) Pensions, trusts, profit-sharing plans, investments
      (b) Insured—life, accident, health, etc.
      (c) Credit unions
  10. Malpractice liability—errors and omissions
      (a) Medical—doctors, nurses, specialists
      (b) Lawyers
      (c) Engineers
      (d) Trustees of pension plans
      (e) Patent infringement

Exposures to loss

C. Third-Party Liabilities (compensatory & punitive damages) *(continued)*

   11. Ordinary negligence
- (a) Of employees
- (b) Of agents
- (c) Of invited or uninvited guests
- (d) Of contractor or subcontractor
- (e) Failure to provide safety equipment, warnings, etc.
- (f) Inadequate enforcement of regulations
- (g) Improper preparation of food

   12. Nonownership liability
- (a) Leased real or personal property
- (b) Bailee's liability
- (c) Employee's use of vehicle, aircraft, watercraft

   13. Owner's liability
- (a) Attractive nuisance
- (b) Invited guests
- (c) Trespassers (false arrest)
- (d) Rights of others—riparian, mineral, light, air, view, lateral support, easements, part walls, licenses, drainage, eminent domain

   14. Product liability (each product sold, distributed, made)
- (a) Implied warranty
- (b) Express warranty
    - (1) By agents—sales, advertising, or general
    - (2) By employees
    - (3) Of merchantability
    - (4) Of suitability or fitness for use
    - (5) Of title
    - (6) By sample

   15. Protective liability
- (a) Industrial contractors hired
- (b) Construction or demolition

   16. Railroad liability
- (a) Sidetrack agreements
- (b) Right of way
- (c) Grade crossings

   17. Director's and officer's liability (stockholder derivative suits)

   18. Watercraft liability
- (a) Ownership, leased, operation
- (b) Types—boats, yachts, ships, submersibles, rigs, platforms

---

APPENDIX B

TWO ADDITIONAL THEORETICAL PROBABILITY DISTRIBUTIONS OF THE NUMBER OF OCCURRENCES PER YEAR

If the risk manager must use a theoretical probability distribution to estimate the probability distribution of the number of occurrences per year, Chapter 4 suggests the Poisson distribution as a reasonable approximation in many cases. This appendix describes two other approximations—the binomial and normal distributions. The binomial distribution, which was not discussed in Chapter 4, provides a better estimate in certain cases than the Poisson distribution. The normal distribution is seldom a better approximation, but if it is reasonably close, it permits the risk manager to extract some additional information with relative ease.

THE BINOMIAL DISTRIBUTION

If (1) a firm has n units (cars, warehouses, persons) independently exposed to loss, (2) each unit can experience at most one occurrence during the year (or other budget period), and (3) the probability that any particular unit will suffer an occurrence during the year is p, according to the binomial distribution the probability that the firm will suffer r occurrences during the year is

$$\frac{n!}{r! \, (n - r)!} p^r (1 - p)^{n - r}$$

The term $p^r (1 - p)^{n - r}$ is the probability that r particular units will suffer an occurrence while the other $n - r$ units do not experience an occurrence (see the discussion of compound probabilities in Chapter 4). The term $n!/[r!(n-r)!]$ is the number of ways in which the r units that are to experience an occurrence can be selected from the n units. For example, for the fleet of five cars used as an illustration throughout Chapter 4, the probability that cars 1 and 2 will suffer an occurrence but not cars 3, 4, and 5 is $p^2(1 - p)^3$. The fleet can experience exactly two occurrences in $5!/[2!(5 - 2)!]$ or ten ways: Cars 1 and 2, 1 and 3, 1 and 4, 1 and 5, 2 and 3, 2 and 4,

2 and 5, 3 and 4, 3 and 5, 4 and 5. Consequently the probability that the fleet will experience exactly two occurrences is $10p^2(1 - p)^3$.

If $p = \frac{1}{10}$, the probability distribution for the fleet of five cars is as follows:

Number of occurrences	Probability	
0	$\frac{5!}{0!5!}(\frac{1}{10})^0(\frac{9}{10})^5 =$	.59049
1	$\frac{5!}{1!4!}(\frac{1}{10})^1(\frac{9}{10})^4 =$	.32805
2	$\frac{5!}{2!3!}(\frac{1}{10})^2(\frac{9}{10})^3 =$	.07290
3	$\frac{5!}{3!2!}(\frac{1}{10})^3(\frac{9}{10})^2 =$	.00810
4	$\frac{5!}{4!1!}(\frac{1}{10})^4(\frac{9}{10})^1 =$	.00045
5	$\frac{5!}{5!0!}(\frac{1}{10})^5(\frac{9}{10})^0 =$	.00001
		1.00000

The probability of at least one occurrence is $1 - .59049$, or about .41. The probability that there will be more than one occurrence is $1 - .59049 - .32805$, or .08.

The expected value in the long run and the standard deviation can be calculated in the usual fashion, but there is an easier way. Statisticians have demonstrated that the expected value of a binomial distribution is n times p, while the standard deviation is $\sqrt{np(1 - p)}$. Therefore, for the fleet of five cars the expected number of occurrences is $5 \times \frac{1}{10}$ or .5. Thus, on the average the business will suffer one occurrence every two years. The standard deviation is $\sqrt{5 \times \frac{1}{10} \times \frac{9}{10}}$, or $\sqrt{45/100} = .67$. The risk relative to the mean is .67/.5, or 1.34. The risk relative to the maximum exposure is .67/5, or .134.

In Chapter 4, the Poisson distribution was also assumed to have a mean of .5. Note, however, that the probabilities of r occurrences and the standard deviation are not the same for the two distributions. Unlike the binomial distribution, the Poisson distribution assumes that each unit can suffer more than one occurrence per year. Given the same mean, the greater the value of p under the binomial distribution, the greater the difference between the two distributions will become.

In practice, although it is very helpful to know that the probability distribution of the number of occurrences may be described by the binomial distribution, one must still estimate p. Two risk managers faced with exactly the same situation may form different estimates. For example, one manager may estimate that the probability of an occurrence is .15, while the other estimates it as .05. The "true" unknown value may be .10. It should be clear that an error in the estimate of p affects the validity of the entire probability distribution. Even crude distributions, however, are better than no information at all if their limitations are duly recognized. Values of p can be estimated by a careful analysis of the firm's historical experience and by using supplementary information in the manner described in Chapter 4.

It is instructive to analyze the formula for risk according to the binomial distribution in more detail. According to the formula relating risk to the maximum exposure [risk $= \frac{\sqrt{np(1 - p)}}{n} = \sqrt{p(1 - p)/n}$], risk is zero when the chance of loss is zero or 1. This result is consistent with the definitions of chance of loss and risk. Further, risk is at its maximum when the chance of loss is .50. This result, which has intuitive appeal, says that a person has the most doubt concerning the outcome when there are two outcomes—a loss or no loss—and the odds are 50:50. However, if risk is defined as the standard deviation relative to the mean, i.e. $\sqrt{np(1-p)}\big/np = \sqrt{(1-p)}\big/np$, risk approaches its maximum value as p approaches zero. This relationship exists because the expected value approaches zero faster than the standard deviation. When p is close to zero, an extremely small standard deviation may still be a large percentage of the expected value.

For both risk measures, the risk decreases as the number of exposure units increases, but the decrease is not proportional to the increase in the number of units. This finding is consistent with the statements in Chapter 4 concerning the effect of increasing n. For example, as the number of exposure units increases from n_1 to n_2, other things remaining equal, risk defined relative to n decreases from $\sqrt{p(1-p)}\big/n_1$ to $\sqrt{p(1-p)}\big/n_2$. In other words, the risk associated with n_1 exposure units relative to the risk associated with n_2 exposure units is

$$\frac{\sqrt{p(1-p)/n_1}}{\sqrt{p(1-p)/n_2}} = \sqrt{n_2/n_1}$$

If $n_1 = 4$ and $n_2 = 16$, $\sqrt{n_2/n_1} = 2$. This result may be checked by computing the risk of each of the two values and comparing the results. Thus risk decreases as the number of exposure units increases, but only in relation to the square root of the relative increase. An increase of n from 100 to 10,000, therefore, is more effective in reducing risk than an increase from 10,000 to 100,000, although the absolute increase in the number of exposure units is much greater in the second case. Moreover, since the existing risk with 100 exposure units is much greater than the existing risk with 10,000 units, the absolute decrease in risk in the second case is much smaller. In other words, risk decreases with each unit increase in the number of exposure units, other things being equal. Each unit increase, however, cuts the risk less than the preceding unit increase. Risk defined relative to the mean behaves in the same fashion.

The binomial distribution is appropriate, regardless of the value of n, if each unit can suffer at most one occurrence per year. The Poisson distribution is better if each unit could suffer many occurrences per year. If each unit can experience at most one occurrence per year, the probability of that occurrence is less than $1/10$, and there are more than 50 units, the Poisson distribution closely resembles the binomial distribution and may be more convenient to use.

THE NORMAL DISTRIBUTION

As stated above, the binomial distribution is appropriate for all values of n if each unit can suffer at most one occurrence per year. However, if the firm has at least 25 units and p is more than $1/10$, the normal distribution, described in Chapter 4, is a close approximation to the binomial distribution. When this is true, it is customary to assume a normal distribution, because it is much easier to use. For example, as was indicated in Chapter 4, with a table of areas under the normal curve it is a relatively simple matter to determine the probability that the number of occurrences will fall within a certain range of values. To illustrate: If a firm has 100 units independently exposed to loss for which the probability of an occurrence with respect to any single unit is $1/10$, the expected number of occurrences is $100 \times 1/10$, or 10. The standard deviation of the number of occurrences is

$$\sqrt{np(1-p)} = \sqrt{100 \times 1/10 \times 9/10} = 3$$

Consequently, the probability is 95.45 percent[1] that the number of occurrences will be no less than $10 - 2(3)$, or 4, and no more than $10 + 2(3)$, or 16. The probability is approximately 2.3 percent that the number of occurrences will exceed 16.[2]

[1] Because the number of occurrences can only assume integral values, the probability that the number of occurrences will fall between 4 and 16 is greater than 95.45 percent. The correct probability is the chance that the number of occurrences will fall between 3.5 and 16.5, which is a range of plus or minus 6.5/3, or 2.2 standard deviations. This probability is 97.22 percent. This correction becomes less important as the number of exposure units increases.

[2] With the correction noted in footnote 1, the probability is 1.4 percent.

APPENDIX **C**

NUMBER OF EXPOSURE UNITS REQUIRED TO PREDICT THE NUMBER OF OCCURRENCES IN THE FUTURE WITH A SPECIFIED DEGREE OF ACCURACY

An important risk management problem is the determination of the number of exposure units the risk manager must have under observation in order for the probability to be a certain amount, say, 95.45 percent, that the actual number of occurrences during the forecast period will fall within some range around the expected number. For example, assume that the chance of an occurrence is $1/10$. What number of exposure units must the risk manager possess for the probability to be 95.45 percent that the actual number of occurrences will fall within the range whose boundaries are the expected number of occurrences plus or minus 10 percent? From what was said in the last paragraph of Appendix B, if the normal distribution describes the probability distribution of the number of occurrences, the problem can be restated as follows: 10 percent of the expected number of occurrences must equal 2 standard deviations. The solution then is as follows:

$$0.10 \, (np) = 2\sqrt{np \, (1 \, - \, p)}$$
$$0.10 \, (n \, \times \, 1/10) = 2\sqrt{n \, \times \, 1/10 \, \times \, 9/10}$$
$$n/100 = 2\sqrt{9n/100}$$

After squaring both sides,

$$(n/100)^2 = 4(9n/100)$$
$$n = 3{,}600$$

If the desired probability is only 68.27 percent instead of 95.45 percent, the problem can be restated as follows: 10 percent of the expected number of occurrences must equal 1 standard deviation. To achieve this degree of accuracy the number of exposure units required is 900.

733

If the desired probability is 95.45 percent that the actual number of occurrences will fall in the range defined as the expected number of occurrences plus or minus 5 percent, the solution is as follows:

$$0.05\ (np) = 2\sqrt{np\ (1\ -\ p)}$$
$$0.05\ (n\ \times\ \tfrac{1}{10}) = 2\sqrt{n\ \times\ \tfrac{1}{10}\ \times\ \tfrac{9}{10}}$$
$$n/_{200} = 2\sqrt{9n/_{100}}$$
$$(n/_{200})^2 = 4(9n/_{100})$$
$$n = 14{,}400$$

HOW TO CONSTRUCT A PROBABILITY DISTRIBUTION OF TOTAL DOLLAR LOSSES PER YEAR, GIVEN DISTRIBUTIONS FOR THE NUMBER OF OCCURRENCES PER YEAR AND THE DOLLAR LOSSES PER OCCURRENCE

The text indicates in Chapter 4 that, in most cases, it is impossible to determine reasonable approximations to the probability distribution of the total dollar losses per year from past experience, or by assuming a theoretical probability distribution. In many such cases, however, it is possible to determine acceptable approximations for the probability distributions for the number of occurrences and for the dollar losses per occurrence. Fortunately, given these two distributions, one can derive the probability distribution of the total dollar losses per year.

To illustrate, assume the following two distributions of the number of occurrences and the dollar losses per occurrence:

Number of occurrences	Probability	Dollar losses per occurrence	Probability
0	.80	$ 500	.90
1	.15	1,000	.10
2	.05		

If there is one occurrence, it may be either $500 or $1,000. The probability that an occurrence will cost $500 if it does occur is .90. Consequently the probability that there will be one occurrence and that it will cost $500 is $(.15)(.90) = .135$. The probability of one occurrence costing $1,000 is $(.15)(.10) = .015$.

If there are two occurrences, three combinations are possible: (1) two $500 losses with a probability (.0405) equal to the probability (.05) of two occurrences times the probability

(.90) (.90) that the two dollar losses will each be \$500, (2) two \$1,000 losses with a probability (.0005) equal to the probability (.05) of two occurrences times the probability (.10) (.10) that the two dollar losses will each be \$1,000, and (3) one \$500 loss and one \$1,000 loss with a probability (.009) equal to the probability (.05) of two occurrences times the probability [(.90) (.10) + (.10) (.90)] that either the first loss will be \$500 and the second \$1,000 or vice versa.

The only other possible outcome is no occurrence, for which the probability is .80. Consequently, the probability distribution of the total dollar losses per year is as follows:

Total dollar losses per year	Probability	
\$ 0	.8000	
500 (One \$500 loss)	.1350	
1,000 (One \$1,000 loss or two \$500 losses)	.0150	} .0555
	.0405	
1,500 (One \$500 loss and one \$1,000 loss)	.0090	
2,000 (Two \$1,000 losses)	.0005	
	1.0000	

If the probability distribution of either the number of occurrences or the dollar losses per occurrence contained more possible outcomes, the calculation would, of course, be much more cumbersome. Computer programs are available which will perform these calculations; or a Monte Carlo simulation approach may be used.[1]

---

[1] For a more extended discussion of this subject, see J. David Cummins and Leonard R. Freifelder, "Statistical Analysis in Risk Management: Analytical Tabulation and Simulation Methods," part V of a monthly series in *Risk Management*, vol. XXVI, no. 1 (January, 1979), pp. 26–37.

THE EXPECTED UTILITY APPROACH TO SELECTING RISK MANAGEMENT TECHNIQUES

A common approach to making decisions under uncertainty is the expected utility approach. This approach can be used to select the proper risk management techniques. The objective is to select the technique that will minimize the expected loss in utility. The expected loss in utility associated with a given decision is calculated in the same way as the expected dollar loss except that a utility index number is substituted for each of the dollar losses associated with that decision. The utility concept used in this method reflects the decision maker's risk attitudes as well as the changes in his or her satisfaction with certain increases or decreases in wealth. In the words of one authority, this utility reflects "an indecomposable mixture of attitude toward risk, profit, and loss in a particular kind of situation."[1]

A person's attitude toward risk is in fact the major determinant of the shape of his or her utility function. If the function is graphed, as in Figure E.1, with the potential dollar loss along the horizontal axis and the loss of utility along the vertical axis, a concave-upward curve indicates that the person is a risk averter; i.e., willing to pay something more than the expected dollar loss to avoid the risk. For example, for the person with the concave-upward curve in Figure E.1 (a risk averter), if the probability is .5 that there will be a $20,000 loss and .5 that there will be no loss, the expected dollar loss is $10,000. The expected utility loss is calculated as follows:

> .5 (loss of utility for $0 loss) + .5 (loss of utility for $20,000 loss)
> = .5(0) + .5(.63)
> = .315

This loss of utility corresponds to a dollar loss of $13,333. Thus, according to this model, the

---

[1] Robert Schlaifer, *Probability and Statistics for Business Decisions* (New York: McGraw-Hill Book Company, 1959), p. 42.

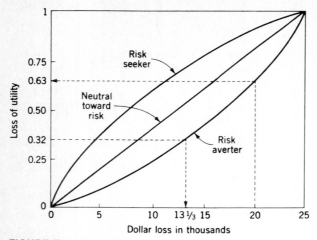

FIGURE E.1
Hypothetical utility functions.

person's uncertain position is equivalent to a certain dollar loss of $13,333. Consequently, this person should be willing to incur any certain dollar loss equal to or less than $13,333 in order to eliminate his or her uncertainty. In other words this person should be willing to pay up to $3,333 in excess of the expected dollar loss to transfer the risk to some other party. A person with a linear utility function (a person who is neutral toward risk) should be willing to pay the expected dollar loss to eliminate the uncertainty, but no more; a person with a concave-downward function (a risk seeker) should prefer to retain the uncertainty unless the transfer cost is less than the equivalent certain value, which will be some value less than the expected dollar loss. Actual utility functions may be more complex than the three shown here with both concave-upward and concave-downward sections.

To apply this method using the "reference contract" approach, one would proceed as follows:[2]

1 Derive the person's (dis)utility function in the following way:
    a Assign a (dis)[3]utility index of 1 to the worst loss that can happen, regardless of the decision.
    b Assign a utility index of zero to the best thing that can happen, namely no loss, regardless of the decision.
    c Ask the person the maximum amount he or she is willing to pay to be relieved of a .5 probability that the worst thing will happen, the only alternate outcome being no loss. Because this certain payment has the same utility index as the expected value of the uncertain position, its utility index is .5 (utility of the worst loss) + .5 (utility of no loss) = .5(1) + .5(0) = .5.

---

[2] Instead of keeping $p = .5$ and reducing the potential loss, as in the example below, one can hold the potential loss constant and change p. For example, the utility index of $35,000 would be .25 if this is the maximum amount the person is willing to pay to avoid a .25 probability that he or she will lose $100,000, the worst possible loss. For an extensive discussion of the reference-contract approach, see Robert Schlaifer, *Analysis of Decisions under Uncertainty*, vol. 1 (New York: McGraw-Hill Book Company, 1967).

[3] In order to conserve space, (dis) will be dropped in the remainder of this discussion, but the reader should remember that the utility index being derived is actually a loss of utility index.

d Ask the person the maximum amount he or she is willing to pay to be relieved of a .5 probability that the amount answered in step c will be lost, the only alternate outcome being no loss. This value has a utility index of .5(.5) + .5(0) = .25.

e Ask the person the maximum amount he or she is willing to be relieved of a .5 probability that the amount answered in step d will be lost, the only alternate outcome being no loss. This value has an index of .5(.25) + .5(0) = .125.

f Continue this procedure until the person has provided enough points to describe his or her utility function. Generally the last amount mentioned should be close to the lowest premium amount or dollar loss.

g Chart the points.

2 For each decision under investigation list the possible dollar losses and associated probabilities.

3 Using the chart developed in step 1, convert the possible dollar losses for each decision into utility index values.

4 Calculate the expected loss of utility.

5 Select that decision for which the expected loss of utility is the smallest.

APPLICATION

To illustrate how this method works, assume that the risk manager has a building for which the maximum insurable after-tax loss is $100,000. There are no noninsurable losses. The risk manager must choose between (1) retention, (2) partial insurance covering losses up to half the value of the building for which the after-tax premium is $640, and (3) complete insurance for which the after-tax premium is $710. The possible decisions, the possible building losses, and the total dollar loss to the firm associated with each possible decision-building loss combination can be summarized in the following matrix form:

	Building after-tax loss					
Amount	$ 0	$500	$1,000	$10,000	$50,000	$100,000
Probability	.800	.100	.080	.017	.002	.001
Decision:						
No insurance	$ 0	$500	$1,000	$10,000	$50,000	$100,000
Partial insurance	640	640	640	640	640	50,640
Complete insurance	710	710	710	710	710	710

Applied to these facts the expected utility method produces the following results:

1 Utility function derivation:

a Let the utility index for a $100,000 loss be 1.

b Let the utility index for a $0 loss be zero.

c Ask the person the maximum amount he or she is willing to pay to avoid a .5 probability that a $100,000 loss will occur. Assume an answer of $60,000. The utility index for $60,000 is thus .5.

d Ask the person the maximum amount he or she is willing to pay to avoid a .5 probability that a $60,000 loss will occur. Assume an answer of $35,000. The utility index for $35,000 is thus .25.

e Ask the person the maximum amount he or she is willing to pay to avoid a .5 probability that a $35,000 loss will occur. Assume an answer of $20,000. The utility index for $20,000 is thus .125.

f Assume that continuing this process produces the following results:

(1) Potential loss	(2) Probability	(3) Maximum transfer fee	(4) Utility index of maximum transfer fee
$100,000	.5	$60,000	.5
60,000	.5	35,000	.25
35,000	.5	20,000	.125
20,000	.5	11,000	.0625
11,000	.5	6,000	.0312
6,000	.5	3,500	.0156
3,500	.5	2,000	.0078
2,000	.5	1,100	.0039
1,100	.5	600	.0020
600	.5	350	.0010

g The utility function derived from columns (3) and (4) is shown in Figure E.2.

2, 3, 4 For each decision, list the possible dollar losses. Using the above utility function, convert each of these dollar losses into utility index values (graphically, by using a mathematical formula that describes the curve, or by linear interpolation between two values for which index values were derived—linear interpolation is used in this example). For example, the utility index for $500 is the utility index for $350 plus $^{15}/_{25}$ of the difference between the index for $350 and $600 or .0010 plus $^{15}/_{25}$ (.0020 − .0010) = .0016. Finally, calculate the expected loss of utility for each possible decision. For the decision to buy no insurance:

FIGURE E.2
Sample problem utility function.

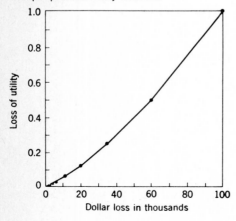

Potential dollar loss	Potential utility index	Probability	Expected utility loss	Expected dollar loss
$ 0	.0000	.800	.00000	$ 0
500	.0016	.100	.00016	50
1,000	.0035	.080	.00028	80
10,000	.0563	.017	.00957	170
50,000	.4000	.002	.00080	100
100,000	1.0000	.001	.00100	100
			.01181	$500

For the decision to buy partial insurance:

Potential dollar loss	Potential utility index	Probability	Expected utility loss	Expected dollar loss
$640	.0022	.999	.00220	$640
$640 + (100,000 − $50,000)	.4064	.001	.00041	51
			.00261	$691

For the decision to buy complete insurance:

Potential dollar loss	Potential utility index	Probability	Expected utility loss	Expected dollar loss
$710	.0024	1.0	.00240	$710

5 Select that decision for which the expected loss of utility is the smallest. In this case, according to this criterion, complete insurance is the best decision. Note that this is not the decision that produces the lowest expected dollar loss. According to that criterion, the individual should buy no insurance. This is not surprising, because an insurer must add an expense and profit loading to its estimate of the insured expected losses. In this example the expected utility model recognizes that the insured may be willing to pay some amount in addition to the insurer's expected loss estimate for three reasons:

a The risk manager may estimate the insured expected losses to be higher than the insurer's estimate.

b The risk manager's dissatisfaction with various dollar losses may increase more rapidly than the dollar losses; i.e., the dissatisfaction associated with a $100,000 loss may be more than ten times as great as the dissatisfaction associated with a $10,000 loss.

c The risk manager may worry about the risk associated with a retained exposure and be willing to pay something to be rid of this worry.

Like the worry method, the expected utility approach would also reflect any differential effect of taxes, noninsurable accidental losses if any are present, and any value the risk manager assigns to the loss control and other services provided by the insurer.

Because utility functions cannot be developed with great accuracy, a risk manager should not rely too heavily upon this approach when the differences in the expected utility loss are small. He or she may also wish to determine whether small changes in the utility values produce different decisions—this can be done by fitting several curves to the points given and making the necessary calculations for each curve.[4]

This model is not limited to insurance-retention decisions. Loss-control and noninsurance transfers can be included as possible decisions with their attendant costs and effects upon losses. Finally, decisions to use a combination of tools, such as loss control and retention or loss control and insurance, can be considered.

[4] In a recent experiment a group of insurance agents and risk managers found the expected utility method a less satisfactory method for determining how much insurance to purchase than the worry method and one other approach. A major reason for this dissatisfaction with the utility approach was that the utility method so often suggested no insurance when such a decision was not consistent with their instinct or the decision suggested by the other two methods. See John Neter and C. A. Williams Jr., "Acceptability of Three Normative Methods in Insurance Decision Making," *Journal of Risk and Insurance*, vol. XXXVIII, no. 3 (September, 1971), pp. 385–408, and "Performance of the Expected Utility Method and Two Other Normative Methods in Insurance Decision Making," *Decision Sciences*, vol. IV, no. 4 (October, 1973), pp. 517–532.

See also Paul J. H. Schoemaker, *Experiments on Decisions under Risk: The Expected Utility Hypothesis* (Boston: Kluwer-Nijhoff Publishing, 1980).

INDEX OF AUTHORS AND SOURCES

Pension Plan Guide, 462
Perlet, H. F., 293
Personal Injury Valuation Handbooks, 109, 132
Peterson, Daniel C., 180, 184, 196
Peterson, Timothy M., 571
Pfaffle, A. E., 46, 55, 56, 59, 728
Pfeffer, Irving, 23, 232, 592, 599
Pfenningstorf, W., 462
Pinches, G. C., 554
Power, F. B., 252, 253, 705
Practical Risk Management, 38
Present Status and Future Role of Risk Management, 30, 210, 637, 639, 645, 648
Price, Daniel N., 140
Prices and Profits in the Property and Liability Insurance Industry, 709
Pricing and Marketing of Insurance, The, 717
Pritchett, S. T., 22, 232
Proceedings of the Casualty Actuarial Society, 599
Proceedings of the National Association of Insurance Commissioners, 700, 721
Prosser, W. L., 109, 132
Proust, Z. A., 195
Prouty, Richard, 55, 56, 59

Quenneville, C. E., 472

Rates of Return in the Property and Liability Insurance Industry: 1955–1967, 709
Reed, P. B., 82, 92, 102, 604, 614
Rejda, G. E., 232, 412, 572
Rennie, Robert, 55
Report of the National Commission on Social Security Reform, 412
Report of the 1979 Advisory Council on Social Security, 397, 412
Reports of the Subcommittee on Antitrust and Monopoly, U.S. Senate, on Various Aspects of the Insurance Industry, 721
Restatement of Torts, 118, 128
Riegel, Robert, 232, 350, 382, 572
Rimco Risk Report, 38
Risk and Insurance Manager Position, The: A Study of Responsibilities and Compensation, 30, 43
Risk Management Manual, 38
Risk Management Reports, 38
Robertson, R. A., 412
Rodda, W. H., 92, 102, 350, 382, 634
Rokes, W. P., 572, 576, 599, 614
Rollins, Garry M., 471
Roos, Nestor, 571
Rosenbloom, J. S., 434, 438, 462, 634, 671, 689
Rowe, William O., 259
Ruppel, R. J., 191
Rutgers Law Review, 152

Schall, L. D., 18, 43, 265, 266
Scheel, William C., 468, 472, 558
Schlaifer, Robert, 259, 737, 738
Schlesinger, Harris, 274
Schoemaker, Paul J. H., 11, 13, 23, 742
Schwarzschild, Stuart, 472
Seal, Hilary L., 599
Self-Insurance: A Risk Management Alternative, 206, 213
Serbein, O. N., 22, 33, 43, 58, 79, 196, 212, 223, 258, 571, 634, 645, 648
Shannon, Mike, 206
Shilling, Ned, 548, 709
Shows, E. W., 705
Simonds, R. H., 190, 196
Siver, Edward W., 97
Smith, C. W. Jr., 252, 253, 254
Smith, Michael L., 92, 274, 320

Snider, H. Wayne, 213, 223, 646, 647, 648
Social Security in America's Future, 412
Social Security Bulletin, 229, 390, 414
Somers, A. R., 179, 382
Somers, H. M., 179, 382
Source Book of Health Insurance Data, 229, 492, 519, 520
Spaid, Orieon M., 223
Special Multi-Peril Guide, 382
Spencer, B., 438
Spencer's Retirement Plan Services, 462
Spilka, S. E., 228
Stanton, William J., 43
State No-Fault Automobile Insurance Experience, 1971–77, 152, 155
Stephens, V. M., 213, 259, 599
Stephenson, Gilbert T., 678, 689
Stewart, Richard E., 694
Strain, R. W., 572
Swandener, P., 22

Taussig, M. K., 412
Tax Information on Disasters, Casualty Losses, and Theft, 205
Temporary National Economic Committee Reports, 713
Thomas, P. I., 82, 92, 102, 604, 614
Time Saver for Health Insurance, 561
Transactions of the Society of Actuaries, 599
Trieschmann, J. S., 92, 102, 206, 232, 258, 306, 320, 350, 382, 554, 571, 634
Troxel, T. E., 572
Turnbull, J. G., 172, 412

Uniform Crime Reports, 91
U.S. News and World Report, 123

Vance, W. R., 293
Vaughan, E. J., 232
Vinson, R. W., 655
Vital Statistics of the United States, 162, 163, 166, 172

Waldo, D. R., 164
Wall Street Journal, 159, 613
Warren, David, 205
Wasserman, William, 79
Waterson, G. E., 152, 155
Webb, Bernard L., 572, 576, 599, 614
Weese, Samuel H., 530
Weisbart, S. N., 571, 721
Werther, William B., Jr., 459
White, E. H., 172, 514
Whitmore, G. A., 79
Who Writes What, 562
Who Writes What in Life and Health Insurance, 561
Widiss, A. I., 152, 155
Wiening, E. A., 92, 102, 350, 382, 634
Wiggins, Norman A., 678, 689
Willett, Allan H., 12, 23, 232
Williams, C. A., Jr., 12, 15, 23, 41, 43, 79, 172, 196, 232, 259, 306, 320, 350, 382, 412, 571, 592, 742
Williams, N. A., 213, 232
Winter, W. D., 350, 382
Wolff, Thomas J., 689
Wood, G. L., 671, 689
Woolfolk, V. N., 678
Workers' Compensation: Is There a Better Way? 155
Wright, P. B., 205
Wyatt, J. W., 43
Wyatt, M. B., 43

Young, W. F., Jr., 293
Your Social Security, 390

Zimmerman, Peter A., 623

SUBJECT INDEX

Absolute liability, 121, 123
  [*See also* Automobile compensation (no-fault) plans
    and proposals; Workers' compensation]
Accidental injury (*see* Poor health)
Accounts receivable insurance, 95–96, 376
Actual cash value, 90
Additional living expenses, 652
  insurance against, 657–658
Adhesion, contact of, 281
Adjustable life insurance, 478–479
Adjusters:
  agents and sales representatives, 601
  bureaus, 601–602
  independent, 601–602
  public, 602
  staff, 601
Adjustment bureaus, 601–602
Adjustment of losses (*see* Loss adjustments)
Administrative Services Only, 434
Agency, law of, 115, 142–143
Agency insurers, 527–528, 530
Agents, 527–528, 530
  (*See also* Producers)
Aid to Families with Dependent Children, 386
All risks contract, 298
American Arbitration Association, 365
American Bar Association, 127
American College of Life Underwriters, 564
American Institute of Property and Liability
    Underwriters, 564
American Insurance Association, 183
  no-fault plan of, 150, 151
American Management Association, 37, 46, 723–728
American Mutual Insurance Alliance plan, 150, 151
American National Standards Institute, 187
American Nuclear Insurers, 534
American Risk and Insurance Association, 385
American Society of Insurance Management, 37
Animals, liability of those who keep, 117
Annuities, 473–476
  (*See also* Pensions)
Aponte, J. B., 150
Appraisals, 41, 606–607
Arthur D. Little Company, Inc., 709
Assault and battery, 110
Assets, insurer:
  importance of investment return, 546
  life insurers, 547
  property and liability insurers, 546–547
  valuation of, 547
Assets-exposure analysis, 723–728
Assigned risk pools, 534, 703
Associate in Risk Management (ARM), 564
Assumption of risk, 113, 134–135
Attorney-in-fact, 522, 523–524
Attractive nuisance doctrine, 119
Audit ratios, NAIC, 542, 553–554
Automobile accident data, 144–145
Automobile compensation (no-fault) plans and propos-
    als, 147–153
  American Insurance Association no-fault proposal,
    150
  American Mutual Insurance Alliance–National Asso-
    ciation of Independent Insurers proposals, 150
  Columbia proposal, 149
  criticisms of tort liability system, 147–149
  debate issues, 151

Automobile compensation (no-fault) plans and
    proposals (*Cont.*):
  federal no-fault proposals, 150
  Keeton-O'Connell basic protection proposal,
    149–150
  National Conference of Commissioners on Uni-
    form State Laws, 150
  Puerto Rico social-protection plan, 150
  state laws, 151–153
  summary of key features, 150–151
Automobile insurance:
  for business, 358–369
    business auto policy, 359–366
    garage liability policy, 368–369
    no-fault endorsements, 365–366, 368
    personal automobile policy, 366–368
    special coverage for automobile dealers, 369
    types of contracts, 358–359
  for families, 664
  (*See also specific policies*)
Automobile insurance plans, 703
Automobile liability insurance pricing, 587–589
  class rates, 587–589
  experience- and schedule-rating plan, 589
  fleet-rating plan, 589
  rating bureaus, 587
  retrospective rating, 589
Aviation insurance, 375
Avoidance:
  use by business, 175–177
  use by families, 653

Back-dated liability insurance, 228
Bailee liability exposures, 124–127
Bailee liability insurance, 326, 327, 345, 357, 376–
    377
Bailees' customers' insurance, 345
  overlapping coverage, 606
Basic property insurance, 322–335
Basic protection plan, Keeton-O'Connell, 149–
    150
Beneficiary designation, 302, 484, 486, 507,
    509, 609
Binding power, 282, 528–530
Binomial distribution, 729–731
Blanket bonds, 312
Blanket coverage, 300
Blue Cross plans, 429–431
Blue Shield plans, 431–432
Boiler and machinery insurance, 340–341
Bonding, distinction between insurance and,
    215–216
Bonds (*see* Dishonesty insurance; Surety bonds)
Branch-office system, 531–532
Breach of warranty, 121–122, 284–285
Brokers, 529–530
  (*See also* Producers)
Bureau insurers, 527
  (*See also* Rating bureaus)
Bureau of Labor Statistics, 141
Burglary insurance (*see* Theft insurance)
Business auto policy, 359–366
  liability insurance, 362–364
  medical payments insurance, 364
  personal injury protection, 365–366
  property insurance, 359–361
  uninsured motorists insurance, 364–365

746